STUDIES IN THE ROMAN AND MEDIEVAL ARCHAEOLOGY OF EXETER

STUDIES IN THE ROMAN AND MEDIEVAL ARCHAEOLOGY OF EXETER

Edited by

STEPHEN RIPPON AND NEIL HOLBROOK

with contributions from

JOHN ALLAN, KAMAL BADRESHANY, PAUL BIDWELL, HUGO BLAKE,
ANDREW BROWN, DAVID DUNGWORTH, CARLOTTA GARDNER, NICKY GARLAND,
DAVID GOULD, ALEJANDRA GUTIÉRREZ, JONATHAN HART, NEIL HOLBROOK,
MICHAEL HUGHES, ROBERT KENYON, MANDY KINGDOM, MALENE LAURITSEN,
SARA MACHIN, SAM MOORHEAD, ANDREW PYE, STEPHEN RIPPON,
RUTH SHAFFREY, ROGER TAYLOR, CATHY TYERS AND PETER WARRY

EAPIT

Exeter:
A Place in Time

EXETER: A PLACE IN TIME 2/EXETER ARCHAEOLOGICAL REPORT 8

OXBOW | books
Oxford & Philadelphia

Published in the United Kingdom in 2021 by
OXBOW BOOKS
The Old Music Hall, 106–108 Cowley Road, Oxford, OX4 1JE

and in the United States by
OXBOW BOOKS
1950 Lawrence Road, Havertown, PA 19083

Hardcover Edition: 978-1-78925-619-2
Digital Edition: 978-1-78925-622-2 (epub)

A CIP record for this book is available from the British Library

Library of Congress Control Number: 2020952179

Printed in the United Kingdom by Short Run Press

Typeset by Versatile PreMedia Service (P) Ltd.

For a complete list of Oxbow titles, please contact:

UNITED KINGDOM
Oxbow Books
Telephone (01865) 241249
Email: oxbow@oxbowbooks.com
www.oxbowbooks.com

UNITED STATES OF AMERICA
Oxbow Books
Telephone (610) 853-9131, Fax (610) 853-9146
Email: queries@casemateacademic.com
www.casemateacademic.com/oxbow

Oxbow Books is part of the Casemate Group

This monograph was published with the aid of a grant from Historic England.

Historic England

Title page image: The Common Seal of Exeter. Made *c.* 1200 and still used in the early 20th century, this large silver seal matrix is the earliest example of a civic seal surviving in Britain. The inscription reads '+SIGILLUM CIVITATIS EXONIE' – the seal of the city of Exeter. The reverse records the maker named Luke and the donor, the wealthy Exeter citizen William Prudum.

Front cover: The Princesshay excavations in 2006 looking south-west towards the cathedral (© Gary Young, Exeter Archaeology)

Back cover: Exeter Museums Archaeological Field Unit Finds Officer Graham Langman examining the Roman pottery from the Coombe Street excavations.

Contents

List of Figures

List of Tables

Online material can be found at https://doi.org/10.24378/exe.1983

List of Appendices

Online material can be found at https://doi.org/10.24378/exe.1983

List of Abbreviations

AML	Ancient Monuments Laboratory
AMTL	ante-mortem tooth loss
BSE	back scattered electron images
CC	Cathedral Close
CG	Cathedral Green
CMB	Chamber Map Book, 1765–60
CPR	crude prevalence rate
CRB	City Rent Book
D&C	Dean and Chapter
DDD	degenerative disc disease
DEI	Devon and Exeter Institution
DISH	diffuse idiopathic skeletal hyperostosis
DRO	Devon Record Office (now known as the Devon Heritage Centre)
EA	Exeter Archaeology
EAACR	Exeter Archaeology Advisory Committee Report
EAAP	Exeter Archaeology Archive project
EAPIT	Exeter: A Place in Time project
EBWA	Exe Bridge Wardens' Account
ECC	Exeter City Council
ECLA	Exeter Cathedral and Library Archive
ED	Exeter Deeds
EMAFU	Exeter Museums Archaeological Field Unit
EOL	extra applied outer layer of clay
ERA	Exeter Receivers' Accounts
EUAD	Exeter Urban Archaeology Database
FH	Friernhay Street
GS	Goldsmith Street
HER	Historic Environment Record (maintained by Exeter City Council)
H/FL	hearth/furnace lining
HS	High Street
ICP–AES	Inductively Coupled Plasma Atomic Emission Spectroscopy
ICP–MS	Inductively Coupled Plasma Mass Spectroscopy
ICPS	Inductively Coupled Plasma Spectrometry
LEH	linear enamel hypoplasia
MAU	minimal number of animal units
MCR	Mayor's Court Rolls
MNI	minimum number of individuals
MY	Mermaid Yard
NAA	Neutron Activation Analysis
OA	osteoarthritis
PAS	Portable Antiquities Scheme
PCA	principal components analysis
PNB	periosteal new bone formation
ppm	parts per million
pXRF	portable X-ray Fluorescence
RAMM	Royal Albert Memorial Museum
RCD	Schmorl's nodes and rotator cuff disease
REE	Rare Earth Elements
RIB	Roman Inscriptions of Britain
RS	Rack Street
SEM-EDS	Scanning Electron Microscopy-Energy Dispersive X-Ray Spectroscopy
SJC	St John's Cartulary
SNS	seronegative spondyloarthropathies
SS	South Street
TNA	The National Archives
TPR	true prevalence rates
TS	Trichay Street
VC	Vicars Choral
XRF	X-ray Fluorescence

List of Contributors

John Allan is the Consultant Archaeologist of Exeter Cathedral, Archaeological Adviser to Glastonbury Abbey, President of the Devonshire Association, a past President of the Devon Archaeological Society, and former Joint Editor of the journal *Post-Medieval Archaeology*. For twenty years (1984–2004) he was Curator of Antiquities of Exeter City Museums. He has published about 180 papers on different aspects of the medieval and later archaeology of South-West England including ceramics, church architecture, numismatics, domestic buildings and cultural links to Brittany.

Kamal Badreshany is a Research Associate at Durham University who specialises in the scientific analysis of archaeological materials. He is head of the Durham Archaeomaterials Research Center (DARC; www.darclab.com), an analytical research facility based in the Department of Archaeology at Durham University. His research focuses on understanding the social and economic changes that accompanied the development of early urban landscapes in the ancient Levant. Recent publications include *The Development of Integrated Regional Economies in the Ancient Levant* (2019) and the *Economic Organisation of the Phoenician Homeland* (2019). He is co-director of excavations at the site of Tell Koubba, in Lebanon.

Paul Bidwell retired as Head of Archaeology and a Senior Manager of Tyne and Wear Archives and Museums in 2013, after excavating and publishing widely on the archaeology of Hadrian's Wall. He also led the development of the archaeological parks at the Roman forts of South Shields and Wallsend. He was appointed OBE in 2012. Until 1980 he worked for Exeter Museums Archaeological Field Unit, supervising and publishing the excavations on the fortress baths and the basilica and forum. He also wrote a general account of Roman Exeter and, together with Neil Holbrook, a comprehensive survey of Roman pottery from the fortress and town.

Hugo Blake was Reader in Medieval Archaeology in the University of London and is now a Research Associate in the Department of History at Royal Holloway. He specialises in Italian ceramics of the last millennium and recently edited a volume on *Italy and Britain between Mediterranean and Atlantic worlds: Leghorn – 'an English port'*. He was an editor of *Post-Medieval Archaeology* and is a past President of the Medieval Pottery Research Group.

Andrew Brown is Assistant National Finds Advisor for Iron Age and Roman Coinage at the British Museum's Portable Antiquities Scheme. He holds a PhD in archaeology from the University of Bristol and was the Suffolk Finds Liaison Officer (PAS) for eight years. He has written on the archaeology of Britain, Turkey, and the Mediterranean, notably 'Anatolia' in *A Companion to Greeks Across the Ancient World* (in press, 2020), and *50 Finds of Roman Coinage* (in press, 2020), and compiles the Iron Age and Roman coinage for the British Numismatic Journal's annual *Coin Register*.

David Dungworth is a freelance archaeologist specialising in the scientific study of glass and metal production. He worked for many years for English Heritage (and then Historic England) and helped produce numerous guidance documents and research reports. He organised the highly successful *Accidental and Experimental Archaeometallurgy* conference (2010) and co-edited the associated publication (2015). He has also carried out extensive and intensive research into medieval and later glass manufacture in England recently published as *Glassworking in England from the 14th to the 20th Century* (2019).

Carlotta Gardner is the William's Fellow in Ceramic Petrology at the Fitch Laboratory, British School at Athens. She recently completed her PhD at the Institute of Archaeology, University College London on *Metalworking Crucibles in Roman Britain* and specialises in the scientific analysis of archaeological materials.

Nicky Garland is a Research Associate at the Department of Archaeology, Durham University. He is currently working on the Leverhulme Trust funded project 'Monumentality and Landscape: Linear Earthworks in Britain' and has previously worked on research projects at Newcastle University, University of Leicester and Cotswold Archaeology. His recent publications include, among others, an article on 'The origins of British oppida' (2020) and contributions to volumes entitled *Iron Age and Roman Coin Hoards in Britain* (2020) and *Hadrian's Wall 2009–2019: A Summary of Excavation and Research prepared for The Fourteenth Pilgrimage of Hadrian's Wall, 20–28 July 2019* (2019).

David Gould was the Research Associate on the AHRC-funded *Exeter: A Place in Time* Project at the University of Exeter. His PhD, funded by the Universities of Exeter and Bristol, investigated the landscapes and history of medieval and post-medieval rabbit warrens across South-West England, and journal articles on this work have been published in *Landscape History*, *Landscapes* and *Cornish Archaeology*. He has also published an investigation of a Cold War weapons-testing facility in *Landscapes*.

Alejandra Gutiérrez is a ceramics and finds specialist interested in the study of material culture from the Middle Ages and Early Modern periods, especially pottery from Spain and Portugal. Her interest lies particularly in the movement of goods, trade and exchange along the Atlantic seaboard. She is a Research Fellow in the Department of Archaeology, Durham University (UK).

Jonathan Hart is a Senior Publications Officer at Cotswold Archaeology. He has worked extensively in fieldwork and contributed to numerous publications and outreach projects. In addition to journal papers, he is one of the main authors of several monographs including *Origins, Development and Abandonment of an Iron Age Village (DIRFT Volume 2)* (2015), *Living Near the Edge: Archaeological Investigations in the Western Cotswolds Along the Route of the Wormington to Sapperton Gas Pipeline, 2006–2010* (2016), and *Cannington Bypass, Somerset: Excavations in 2014. Middle Bronze Age Enclosure at Rodway and Roman Villa at Sandy Lane* (2018).

Neil Holbrook is Chief Executive of Cotswold Archaeology. He worked for the Exeter Museums Archaeological Field Unit between 1986 and 1989 and is the co-author with Paul Bidwell of *Roman Finds from Exeter* (1991). He was the co-director of the Roman Rural Settlement Project with Michael Fulford and joint series editor of the three monographs in the *New Visions of the Countryside of Roman Britain* series (2016–18). He also co-edited a volume examining the contribution of developer-led archaeology to our understanding of Roman towns in Britain (2015). Neil was president of the Bristol and Gloucestershire Archaeological Society for 2017–18.

Michael Hughes was a Principal Scientific Officer at the British Museum, Department of Conservation and Scientific Research, and Senior Lecturer in Forensic Science and Bioscience at the University of East London. At the Museum he applied analytical chemistry to items in the collections, including metals, glass and principally ceramics. His research has focussed on tin-glazed pottery made in Europe, and most recently on medieval and post-medieval wares found on sites in south-western and southern England and Scotland. He co-authored with Clive Orton the book *Pottery in Archaeology* (2nd edition) and has contributed chapters in monographs, excavation reports, and to journals in archaeology and archaeological science.

Robert Kenyon is an independent scholar. Extensive excavations in the City of London by Museum of London Archaeology (MOLA) at the Bloomberg London site, in 2010–14, produced an enormous quantity of Roman artefacts including a significantly large number of bronze coins of Claudius I (AD 41–54). His classification and analysis of those coin-finds will be available in a forthcoming MOLA monograph on finds from the site

Mandy Kingdom is an Honorary Research Fellow at the University of Exeter, having recently completed her doctoral studies there. She works part-time in commercial archaeology as a finds and environmental supervisor and is currently carrying out analysis on a large post-medieval skeletal collection. She also works part-time as a freelance human osteologist, having analysed and written specialist reports on cremations and inhumations from different time periods. Her PhD thesis *The Past People of Exeter: Health and Status in the Middle Ages* will hopefully be published as a BAR monograph in the near future.

Malene Lauritsen is a Lecturer in Archaeology at the University of Exeter. She recently completed her PhD *Exeter from Fort to City* on the faunal remains of Exeter under the supervision of Alan Outram and Stephen Rippon at the University of Exeter. Notable publications include 'Celebrating Easter, Christmas and their associated alien fauna' in *World Archaeology* 50(2) for 2018.

Sara Machin is a Visiting Research Fellow at the University of Reading and a Senior Specialist with Headland Archaeology (UK). She completed her PhD, *Constructing Calleva*, in 2018 on the ceramic building material from the Roman town of Silchester. Using multiple analytical techniques, including petrographic analysis, she characterised the production and consumption of material over the 400-year life of the town demonstrating changes in supply over time. She has contributed to the excavation and publication of the Imperial tilery and pottery production centre at Little London (*The Emperor Nero's Tilery and Pottery Works:* Fulford *et al.* forthcoming).

Sam Moorhead is National Finds Advisor for Iron Age and Roman Coinage at the British Museum's Portable Antiquities Scheme. He has written extensively on Roman coinage and ancient history, notably *The Frome Hoard* (2010), *AD 410 The Year that Shook Rome* (2010), *The Romans who Shaped Britain* (2012), *31 BC, Antony, Cleopatra and the Fall of Egypt* (2012), and *A History of Roman Coinage in Britain* (2013) for which he was awarded the Royal Numismatic Society Lhotka Prize. He is an Honorary Lecturer at the Institute of Archaeology (UCL) and in 2019 was awarded the Royal Numismatic Society Medal.

Andrew Pye was the Archaeology Officer for Exeter City Council from 1995 to 2020, and latterly also the Conservation Officer. In these roles he instigated and oversaw development related archaeological work in the city, managed regeneration and enhancement schemes such as Cricklepit Mill and the restoration and reinstallation of 17th-century panelling at North Street, administered and encouraged the publication of Exeter Archaeology projects after their closure, and mobilised city council support for EAPIT. Publications include several papers and chapters on fortifications and industrial sites in the South-West, and *The Historic Defences of Plymouth* (1996).

Stephen Rippon is Professor of Landscape Archaeology at the University of Exeter. He has recently completed excavating at the Iron Age, Roman and early medieval settlement at Dainton Elms Cross, in Ipplepen (Devon), and has published a series of studies of regional variation in landscape character covering the Roman and medieval periods including *Beyond the Medieval Village* (2008), *Making Sense of an Historic Landscape* (2012), *The Fields of Britannia* (2015) and *Kingdom, Civitas and County* (2018). He is current President of the Society for Medieval Archaeology, and a past President of the Medieval Settlement Research Group and Somerset Archaeological and Natural History Society.

Ruth Shaffrey is a Project Officer (Publications) at Oxford Archaeology South. She recently edited a book on prehistoric stone tools called *Written in Stone* (2017) but mainly writes about Roman and Iron Age rotary querns. She investigates what the querns are made from, for example published in 'A possible source for Iron Age rotary querns in the Upper Greensand Potterne Rock of the Devizes Area' (2019); quern morphology, for example in *Grinding and Milling* (2006); and the organisation of grain processing, about which she has published a series of papers including 'Grain processing in and around Roman Cirencester' (2018).

Roger Taylor undertook his doctoral research on the geology of Brittany, and then worked at the University of Keele before spending most of his career as a field geologist for the south-western regional office of the British Geological Survey. Working mainly in Devon and Cornwall, he built up detailed knowledge of the region's geology. Since retirement, he has collaborated with the area's archaeologists in many projects, and has published more than 100 contributions to academic papers arising from this work, especially on prehistoric, medieval and post-medieval ceramics, some found on sites as distant as Newfoundland and Maine. He has also been consultant petrologist for the Royal Albert Memorial Museum in Exeter and the geologist of the South-West Implement Petrology Group.

Cathy Tyers has been a dendrochronologist since 1984. She oversees all dendrochronological analysis and research projects commissioned by Historic England and, as part of her role in the development of national standards, she is involved in the technological advancement of scientific dating techniques (*e.g.* ^{14}C wiggle-matching of short tree-ring sequences from post-medieval buildings in England). Her research interests include the importation of oak and conifer timbers during the last millennium, medieval farmhouses in South-West England, and past landscapes and woodland management.

Peter Warry is an independent researcher in Roman brick and tile. His primary interests are in typology, use, economics and logistics rather than traditional fabric analysis. Published works include *Tegulae: Manufacture, Typology and Use in Roman Britain* (2006), 'Legionary tile production in Britain' (2010), 'The Silchester tile industry' (2012), *Ceramic Building Material from Nine Archaeological Excavations in the City of Gloucester* (2015) and 'Production, distribution, use and curation: a study of stamped tile from Gloucestershire' (2018). He is a Fellow of the Society of Antiquaries.

Preface and Acknowledgements

Background to the *Exeter: A Place in Time* project is given in the Preface to EAPIT Volume 1 (*Roman and Medieval Exeter and their Hinterlands*, edited by Stephen Rippon and Neil Holbrook), where there is a general set of acknowledgements. The project would not have been possible without the generous financial support of the Arts and Humanities Research Council (award reference AH/N001931/1) and Historic England (project 6902), and help-in-kind from Historic England (through the contributions of David Dungworth and Cathy Tyers, Chapters 10 and 11 below), Exeter City Council (most notably through its Principal Project Manager (Heritage) Andrew Pye), and the Royal Albert Memorial Museum (most notably through the help of its Assistant Curator Tom Cadbury). The Historic England elements of the project were managed by Karen Walker of Cotswold Archaeology, and we are grateful for the assistance and support of Kath Buxton, Rebecca Garrett and Michael Russell of Historic England. Neil Holbrook and Karen Walker thank Tom Cadbury of the Royal Albert Memorial Museum for facilitating access to the archives and Andrew Pye of Exeter City Council for access to its Historic Environment Record GIS. The stratigraphic analysis of the excavations at Trichay Street, 196–7 High Street and Rack Street (Chapters 5, 7 and 8 below) was undertaken by Nicky Garland, while that for Goldsmith Street Area III was prepared by Jonathan Hart (Chapter 6 below). The illustrations in EAPIT 2 Chapters 5–8 were produced by Lesley Davidson, Charlotte Patman and Aleks Osinska. We are particularly grateful to John Allan who significantly enhanced and improved the text relating to the medieval periods of these four sites. His first-hand personal knowledge of these sites has proved invaluable and has avoided some fundamental mis-interpretations of the medieval evidence. Paul Bidwell kindly commented in detail on the text of the Roman periods to telling effect. Authors of the remaining chapters provide their acknowledgements at the end of the individual chapters.

Summary

This is the second of two volumes that report on the *Exeter: A Place in Time* project (EAPIT) which explored how the Roman fortress/town and medieval city of Exeter developed over time within its regional context. This was achieved through the writing up of key unpublished excavations; analysis of the faunal assemblages; research into various categories of material culture; and the writing of a synthesis describing the evolution of Exeter over the Roman and medieval periods. That synthesis is presented in the first of the two books to be published (*Roman and Medieval Exeter and their Hinterlands*), with this volume containing a series of specialist contributions.

Chapter 1 is a brief introduction to the project (with greater detail appearing in Chapter 1 of *Roman and Medieval Exeter and their Hinterlands*). Chapter 2 contains short summaries of all the significant excavations within Exeter, while Chapter 3 presents a discussion of the Roman legionary fortress plan by Paul Bidwell, and gazetteers of the evidence for Roman streets and buildings. In Chapter 4 John Allan discusses the documentary evidence for St Pancras parish that was the location for three of the major excavations that EAPIT has written up and which are presented in Chapters 5–7 (Trichay Street, Goldsmith Street Site III, and 196–7 High Street). These three sites revealed some of the most complete sequences in Exeter, including buildings within the Roman legionary fortress, the civilian town, and the Late Saxon and later medieval city. Chapter 8 reports on a fourth excavation – Rack Street – that included sections across the defences of the fortress and Early Roman town. In Chapter 9 Malene Lauritsen reports on a series of important animal bone assemblages that had not previously been examined, while in Chapter 10 David Dungworth and Carlotta Gardner use modern scientific techniques to study the archaeometallurgical debris. In Chapter 11 Cathy Tyers reviews the dendrochronological evidence from archaeological structures within Exeter and what this tells us about timber supply. In Chapter 12 Paul Bidwell discusses the pottery supply to Roman Exeter and includes specialist reports on EAPIT's scientific analysis of key fabrics whose sources were not previously known. Chapter 13 reports on the analysis of Roman ceramic tile from Exeter and across Devon by Sara Machin and Peter Warry, while in Chapter 14 Ruth Shaffrey presents a review of the evidence for quern stone manufacture and distribution across Devon. In Chapter 15 Robert Kenyon shows how the analysis of Claudian bronze copies supports the suggested foundation date for the legionary fortress of *c.* AD 55, while in Chapter 16 Andrew Brown and Sam Moorhead compare the patterns of coin loss in Exeter with its South-Western hinterland and selected other Romano-British cites. In Chapters 17 and 18 John Allan, Alejandra Gutierrez and Hugo Blake discuss Exeter's medieval pottery supply, including specialist reports on EAPIT's programme of scientific analysis of various fabrics whose provenance was not previously known. Finally, in Chapter 19 Mandy Kingdom reports on 463 human burials from four excavated medieval cemeteries.

Résumé

Ceci est le second de deux volumes qui constituent le compte rendu des traveaux de Exeter: *Exeter un lieu en son Temps*. Le projet EAPIT a exploré comment la forteresse/ville romaine et la cité médiévale d'Exeter s'est développée dans son contexte régional. Ce but a pu être atteint en rédigeant le rapport des fouilles clés non encore publiées; des analyses d'assemblages de faune; des recherches dans diverses catégories de culture matérielle; et la rédaction d'une synthèse décrivant l'évolution d'Exeter à travers les périodes romaine et médiévale. Cette synthèse est présentée dans le premier des deux livres inédits qui doivent être publiés (*Exeter Romaine et Médiévale et son Arrière Pays*), avec ce volume contenant une série de contributions de spécialistes.

Le chapitre 1 est une brève introduction du projet (avec plus de détails apparaissant dans le chapitre 1 de *Exeter Romaine et Médiévale et son Arrière Pays*). Le chapitre 2 contient de courts résumés de toutes les fouilles importantes dans Exeter, tandis que le chapitre 3 présente une discussion du plan de la forteresse de la légion romaine de Paul Bidwell et un index des témoignages de rues, et bâtiments romains. Dans le chapitre 4 John Allan discute les témoignages documentaires de la paroisse de Saint Pancras qui fut le site de trois fouilles majeures que EAPIT a transcrites et qui sont présentées dans les chapitres 5-7 (Trichay Street, Goldsmith Street site III et 196-7 High Street). Ces trois sites ont révélé quelques unes des plus complètes séquences dans Exeter y compris des batiments à l'intérieur du fort de la légion romaine, la ville civile et de la fin de la période saxonne et la partie tardive de la cité médiévale. Le chapitre 8 rend compte d'une quatrième fouille Rack Street qui comprenait des sections à travers les défences de la forteresse et la ville du début de la période romaine. Dans le chapitre 9 Malene Lauritsen rend compte d'une série d'assemblages d'animaux qui n'avaient jamais été examinés auparavant, tandis que dans le chapitre 10 David Dungworth et Carlotta Gardner utilisent des techniques scientifiques modernes pour étudier les débris archéométallurgiques. Dans le chapitre 11 Cathy Tyers révise les témoignages dendrochronologiques des structures archéologiques dans Exeter et ce que cela nous apprend sur l'approvisionnement en bois de construction. Au chapitre 12 Paul Bidwell discute l'approvisionnement en poterie de l'Exeter romaine et comprend des rapports spécialisés sur l'analyse scientifique de EAPIT de matériaux clés dont les origines jusqu'alors n'étaient pas connues. Le chapitre 13 rend compte de l'analyse des tuiles de céramique romaines d'Exeter et d'á travers le Devon de Sara Machin et Peter Warry, tandis que dans le chapitre 14 Ruth Shaffrey présente une révision des témoignages de fabrication et de distribution des pierres de moulins á bras à travers le Devon. Dans le chapitre 15 Robert Kenyon montre comment l'analyse de copies de bronzes claudiens oeuvre en faveur de la date proposée pour la construction du fort de la légion romaine en 55 ap. J.-C., tandis que dans le chapitre 16 Andrew Brown et Sam Moorhead comparent les distributions de pièces de monnaie perdues à Exeter avec celles de son arrière pays du sud-ouest et d'autres cités romano-britanniques choisies. Dans les chapitres 17 et 18 John Allan discute l'approvisionnement en poterie d'Exeter y compris les rapports spécialistes de EAPIT sur le programme d'analyse scientifique des divers matériaux retrouvés dont on ne connait pas encore la provernance. Finalement, au chapitre 19 Mandy Kingdom rend compte de 463 inhumations humaines provenant des fouilles de quatre cimetières médiévaux.

Zusammenfassung

Dies ist der zweite von zwei Bänden zu den Ergebnissen des Projekts *Exeter: A Place in Time* (EAPIT), in dem die diachrone Entwicklung des römischen Lagers/Stadt und der mittelalterlichen Stadt Exeter innerhalb ihres regionalen Umfelds untersucht wurde. Zu diesem Zweck wurden wichtige, bislang unveröffentlichte Ausgrabungen aufgearbeitet; die Tierknochenfunde analysiert; verschiedene Kategorien der materiellen Kultur bearbeitet; und in einer Zusammenschau die Entwicklung der Stadt Exeter im Verlauf der Römischen Kaiserzeit und des Mittelalters beschrieben. Diese Synthese wurde im ersten der zwei Bände (*Roman and Medieval Exeter and their Hinterlands*) veröffentlicht, während sich der vorliegende Band einer Reihe von Fachbeiträgen widmet.

Kapitel 1 bietet eine kurze Einführung in das Projekt (dies wird in Kapitel 1 von *Roman and Medieval Exeter and their Hinterlands* ausführlicher behandelt). Kapitel 2 enthält kurze Zusammenfassungen aller wichtigen Ausgrabungen in Exeter. In Kapitel 3 legt Paul Bidwell eine Erörterung zum Grundriss des römischen Legionslagers sowie Fundlisten zu den römischen Straßen und Gebäuden vor. In Kapitel 4 diskutiert John Allan die Urkundenlage für das Kirchspiel St. Pancras, in dem drei der umfangreichen, im Rahmen von EAPIT aufgearbeiteten Ausgrabungen stattfanden, die in den Kapiteln 5–7 vorgelegt werden (Trichay Street, Goldsmith Street Site II und 196–7 High Street). Auf diesen drei Fundplätzen fanden sich einige der vollständigsten Befundabfolgen Exeters, u. a. von Gebäuden innerhalb des römischen Legionslagers, der Zivilsiedlung sowie der spät-angelsächsischen und mittelalterlichen Stadt. In Kapitel 8 wird von einer vierten Ausgrabung – in der Rack Street – berichtet, in der u. a. Profilschnitte durch die Verteidigungsanlagen des Lagers und die frührömische Stadt angelegt wurden. In Kapitel 9 referiert Malene Lauritsen über eine Reihe wichtiger, bislang unberücksichtigter Tierknochenkomplexe, und David Dungworth und Carlotta Gardner informieren in Kapitel 10 über die mit modernen wissenschaftlichen Methoden untersuchten archäometallurgischen Reste. In Kapitel 11 bietet Cathy Tyers einen Überblick über die an archäologischen Strukturen in Exeter gewonnenen dendrochronologischen Ergebnisse und die damit verbundenen Aussagemöglichkeiten zur Holzversorgung. In Kapitel 12 bespricht Paul Bidwell die Keramikversorgung Exeters unter Berücksichtigung von Fachbeiträgen zu EAPITs wissenschaftlichen Analysen wichtiger Warenarten, deren Herkunft bislang unbekannt war. Kapitel 13 handelt von den Analysen römischer Keramikfliesen aus Exeter und Devon, die von Sara Machin und Peter Warry durchgeführt wurden, und in Kapitel 14 legt Ruth Shaffrey eine Übersicht der Belege für die Mahlsteinherstellung und ihre Verbreitung in Devon vor. In Kapitel 15 zeigt Robert Kenyon wie die Analyse claudischer Bronzemünzkopien zur Unterstützung des vermuteten Gründungsdatums des Legionslagers um 55 n. Chr. herangezogenen werden kann, und in Kapitel 16 vergleichen Andrew Brown und Sam Moorhead die Muster der Münzverluste in Exeter mit seinem südwestlichen Hinterland sowie weiteren ausgewählten romano-britischen Städten. In den Kapiteln 17 und 18 erörtert John Allan Exeters mittelalterliche Keramikversorgung unter Einschluss von Fachberichten über das EAPIT-Programm zur wissenschaftlichen Analyse einiger der gefundenen Warenarten, deren Herkunft bislang unbekannt war. Zum Abschluss legt Mandy Kingdom in Kapitel 19 die Ergebnisse ihrer Untersuchungen von 463 menschlichen Bestattungen aus vier ausgegrabenen mittelalterlichen Friedhöfen vor.

Übersetzung: Jörn Schuster
(ARCHÆOLOGICALsmallFINDS)

1

Introduction: Studies in the Roman and Medieval Archaeology of Exeter

Stephen Rippon and Neil Holbrook

This is the second volume derived from the *Exeter: A Place in Time* project (EAPIT), an introduction to which can be found in EAPIT Volume 1 – *Roman and Medieval Exeter and their Hinterlands*. Whereas EAPIT 1 presented a discussion of the development of Exeter and its hinterland from the Roman through to the medieval period, this volume contains a series of more detailed contributions that provide some of the underpinning data used in Volume 1. This includes stratigraphic reports on four of the most important previously unpublished excavations – at Trichay Street, Goldsmith Street Site III, 196–7 High Street and Rack Street – that between them revealed for the first time parts of the Roman legionary fortress that underlies Exeter, as well as long sequences of occupation that tell the story of how Exeter subsequently developed as a Roman *civitas* capital, Late Saxon *burh*, and later medieval city. These descriptions of the stratigraphic sequence are not accompanied by the traditional specialist reports as the relevant assemblages were published in a series of three 'Exeter Archaeological Reports' (EAR) covering *The Animal Bones From Exeter 1971–1975* (EAR 2: Maltby 1979), the *Medieval and Post-Medieval Finds from Exeter 1971–1980* (EAR 3: Allan 1984a), and the *Roman Finds from Exeter* (EAR 4: Holbrook and Bidwell 1991). Microfiche in Holbrook and Bidwell (1991) and Allan (1984a) also contain lists of the dating evidence from Trichay Street, Goldsmith Street Site III, 196–7 High Street, and Rack Street as well as other sites excavated between 1971 and 1979 (the inventory of pottery from Roman sites excavated between 1980 and 1990 is now available on the EAPIT webpage (http://humanities.exeter.ac.uk/archaeology/research/projects/place_in_time/resources/inventory/).

In addition to the pottery, Exeter Archaeological Reports 3 and 4 included specialist reports on nearly the full range of artefacts types, although some were relatively brief (*e.g.* the Roman ceramic building material) or not covered (*e.g.* Roman querns). EAPIT therefore provided the opportunity to fill in some of the gaps such as Malene Lauritsen's analysis of the faunal assemblages that had not previously been examined (Chapter 9), Ruth Shaffrey's study of the Roman querns and millstones (Chapter 14), and Mandy Kingdom's analysis of the human remains from a series of medieval cemeteries (Chapter 19). We were also able to apply modern scientific and other analytical techniques to the finds now stored at the Royal Albert Memorial Museum (RAMM) which included David Dungworth and Carlotta Gardner's re-analysis of the archaeometallurgical debris (Chapter 10), Cathy Tyers' reassessment of the dendrochronlogical evidence (Chapter 11), and Sara Machin and Peter Warry's analyses of the Roman ceramic building material (Chapter 13). Robert Kenyon has reassessed the significance of Claudian bronze coins from Exeter (Chapter 15), while Andrew Brown and Sam Moorhead have reassessed the Roman coinage from Exeter in the light of data collected by the Portable Antiquities Scheme (https://finds.org.uk/) for South-West England as a whole (Chapter 16).

A particular focus of EAPIT was Exeter's ceramic assemblages and the evidence that they provide for its economy. Chapters 12, 17 and 18 therefore report on a series of scientific analyses that have established for the first time the sources of the clays used to make some of the important ceramic wares found in Exeter, and review how our understanding of its Roman and medieval trade has changed in recent decades. A theme that is common to most of these chapters is that rather than being simply specialist reports on the finds from an excavation, they have tried to explore what those artefact types tell us about landscape and society in Roman and medieval Exeter and its wider hinterland.

The structure of this volume is as follows. **Chapter 2** provides short summaries of all of the significant excavations within Exeter and its immediate hinterland, expanding and updating the online site list produced by the Exeter Archaeology Archive Project (https://doi.org/10.5284/1035173). **Chapter 3** presents three more detailed sets of data: a detailed discussion of the Roman legionary fortress plan by Paul Bidwell, and gazetteers of the evidence for Roman military and civilian streets and buildings. In **Chapter 4** John Allan provides a study of the documentary evidence for St Pancras parish that was the location for three of the major excavations that EAPIT has written up (see below). Exeter has exceptionally rich medieval archives, and although in the past it has been doubted whether it is possible to locate the documented tenements precisely on the ground, this is what Allan has now been able to achieve for an important block of central Exeter where some of its wealthiest citizens lived. **Chapters 5 to 7** then present the results of the three excavations in this central part of Exeter, at Trichay Street, Goldsmith Street Site III and 196–7 High Street. These three sites revealed some of the most complete sequences in Exeter, including buildings within the Roman legionary fortress, the civilian town, and the Late Saxon and later medieval city. In **Chapter 8**, the results from a fourth excavation – Rack Street – are then presented that included sections across the defences of the fortress and Early Roman town.

There follows a set of papers that describe the results of multi-period analyses of three categories of material. In **Chapter 9** Malene Lauritsen summarises the results of her PhD that studied a series of important Roman and medieval animal bone assemblages that had not previously been examined and which provide some of the data used by Mark Maltby in his overviews of Exeter's faunal material in EAPIT 1 Chapters 5–8). Of particular significance is the recognition of significant variations in meat consumption across different parts of Exeter in the medieval period, and the importance of marrow fat in past diets during all periods. **Chapter 10**, by David Dungworth and Carlotta Gardner, uses modern scientific techniques to study the archaeometallurgical debris from Roman and medieval Exeter which testifies to the significance of the South-West's mineral resources. Back in the 1970s Exeter saw some of the earliest applications of tree-ring dating in the South-West, and in **Chapter 11** Cathy Tyers reviews this dendrochronological evidence from archaeological structures within Exeter, and explores what it tells us about the supply of timber (that was primarily from local sources).

The next group of chapters explore Roman material culture in Exeter and its hinterland. In **Chapter 12** Paul Bidwell provides an overview of the pottery supply to Roman Exeter in its military and civilian phases. The chapter includes reports on various strands of EAPIT's scientific analysis of key fabrics found in Exeter whose source was not previously known, identifying clay sources immediately east of Exeter in the Ludwell Valley (South-Western Grey Ware storage jars), on the western side of the Blackdown Hills (South-Western Black-Burnished Ware 1), and in the Teign Valley in South Devon (the so-called 'Fortress Wares'). **Chapter 13** reports on the analysis of Roman ceramic tile from Exeter and across Devon by Sara Machin and Peter Warry, showing how production close to Exeter was gradually replaced by a series of kilns across its wider hinterland. In **Chapter 14** Ruth Shaffrey presents a review of the evidence for quernstone manufacture and distribution, showing how – with the exception of the Roman military period, when querns were imported from mainland Europe – only local sources of stone appear to have been exploited by Dumnonian communities. Two papers then explore the Roman coins from Exeter and the South-West more generally. In **Chapter 15** Robert Kenyon shows how the analysis of Claudian bronze copies supports the suggested foundation date for the legionary fortress at Exeter of *c.* AD 55, while in **Chapter 16** Andrew Brown and Sam Moorhead then take the story forward by comparing the patterns of coin loss in Exeter with its South-Western hinterland and selected other Romano-British cites. This shows that while Exeter saw similar patterns of coin loss compared to other towns, the South-West Peninsula was not as heavily monetised as other parts of lowland Roman Britain.

The final three papers explore aspects of Exeter's medieval archaeology. **Chapters 17 and 18** report on EAPIT's programme of scientific analyses of various ceramic fabrics found in Exeter and whose provenance was not previously known. Chapter 17 focusses on Exeter's pottery supply from local and north European sources, while Chapter 18 covers southern Europe. Finally, **Chapter 19** presents a summary of Mandy Kingdom's thesis on 463 human burials from four excavated medieval cemeteries: the Late Saxon minster and Cathedral Close, the Dominican friary (Black Friars), Franciscan friary (Grey Friars), and the extra-mural St Katherine's Priory in Polsloe. This reveals that the majority of Exeter's medieval population had adequate to good nutrition, health and longevity, and that life expectancy improved over time.

Throughout this volume excavations in and around Exeter are referred to by their EAPIT Site Number as listed in Chapter 2 (that also includes location maps).

The Royal Albert Memorial Museum and Art Gallery, Exeter City Council, holds the copyright for all images given as ©RAMM.

Note on nomenclature: Exeter's gates and quarters

The axes of Exeter – based upon the major roads that run between its four gates – run NE to SW and NW to SE (Fig. 1.1). An historical anomaly is, however, that the

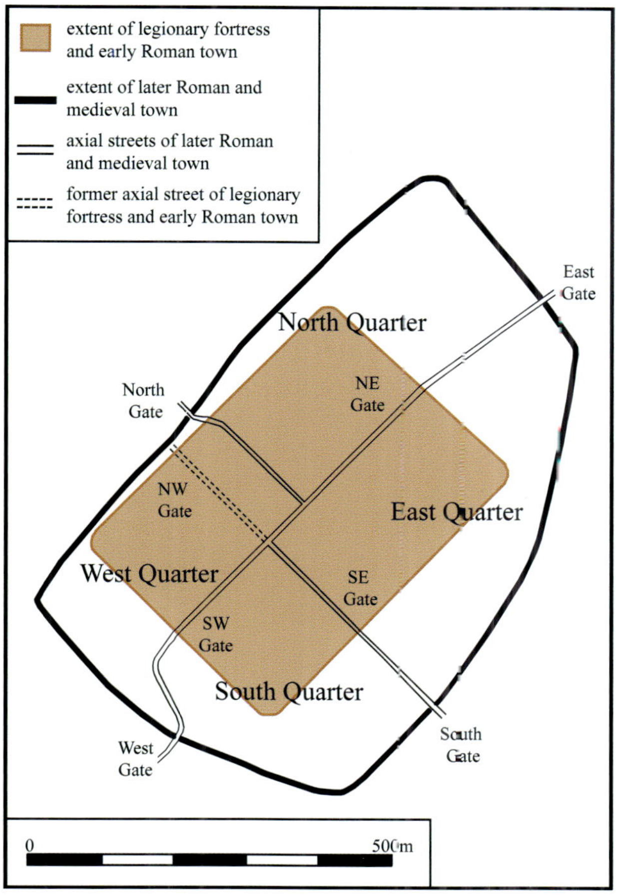

Fig. 1.1 The nomenclature used for the different phases of Exeter's gates and its quarters (drawn by David Gould)

medieval gates were – and still are – called North, East, South and West (and so – for example – the gate on the SE side of the city was and is called the South Gate as opposed to the South-East Gate, *e.g. Hooker's Chronicle* for the years 1308 and 1328, and *Hooker's Antique Description*, 52, 55, 59). To complicate matters further, when the Roman legionary fortress was discovered its gates were named according to their correct orientation which means that the North-West Gate of the Roman fortress and early town is just 40 m from what in the medieval period was called the North Gate. As all the existing literature on Exeter uses this different terminology it is retained here. Figure 1.1 also shows the four 'quarters' that Exeter is divided into.

Accessing unpublished reports

The two EAPIT volumes make extensive use of unpublished material. The primary excavation archives (written records, plans, black and white negatives and colour slides) and artefacts from excavations undertaken by the Exeter Museums Archaeological Field unit (EMAFU) – later renamed Exeter Archaeology – have been deposited with the Royal Albert Memorial Museum (RAMM) with the exception of the Princesshay (Site 156) and St Loye's College sites for which the RAMM has the artefacts and related records while the rest of the archives are digitised and have been deposited with the Archaeology Data Service (ADS).

Archives relating to the EMAFU's documentary and standing buildings research have been deposited with the Devon Heritage Centre with the exception of:

- archives relating to the cathedral and the houses of Cathedral Close that are held at the Exeter Cathedral Library and Archive.
- the Bowhill (Site 91) archive which is held at the Historic England Archive in Swindon.

The Exeter Archaeology database, including its digital image collection and digital records of projects, is held by Exeter City Council's Historic Environment Record.

Some pre-1990 archives have been digitised as part of the 'Exeter Archaeology Archive Project' that is available through the ADS (https://doi.org/10.5284/1035173). These include typescript reports prepared for the Exeter Archaeology Advisory Committee (that contain interim reports on many excavations and sometimes include a plan), a set of typescript reports on the Roman military phase in each of the excavations where it was uncovered, a set of reports on the fabric of the city wall, and a Site List of each of the major excavations carried out by the EMAFU between 1970 and 1990. Subsequent post-1990 archives have been generated by development-led archaeology, and have been undertaken by a number of different archaeological contractors including AC Archaeology and Cotswold Archaeology, as well as Exeter Archaeology prior to its closure. Their archives are variously deposited in the RAMM, ADS or are held by the contractor prior to deposition. Online summaries exist in OASIS, and summary reports and HER entries are held at the City and County HERs. Several excavations undertaken in the 2000s and later have been published or are shortly to appear, usually in the *Proceedings of the Devon Archaeological Society*, as a condition of planning permission.

The EAPIT webpage includes three further archive reports (http://humanities.exeter.ac.uk/archaeology/research/projects/place_in_time/):

- *Market Street/Smythen Street Roman Pottery Report* (Site 115).
- *Inventory of Roman Pottery from Sites Excavated in Exeter 1980–1990.* This complements the inventory for earlier excavations that was published on microfiche in Holbrook and Bidwell's (1991) *Roman Finds from Exeter*.

- *A Guide to the Archives of Archaeological Projects Carried out in Exeter, 1970–90* (Leverett *et al.* 2011).

Two of the Exeter Archaeological Reports series are now out-of-print and those volumes have now been digitised and are also available through the EAPIT webpage (http://humanities.exeter.ac.uk/archaeology/research/projects/place_in_time/resources/reports/):

- Volume 2: Mark Maltby's *Faunal Studies on Urban Sites: the Animal Bones from Exeter, 1971–1975* (1979, University of Sheffield, Department of Prehistory and Archeology).
- Volume 3: John Allan's *Medieval and Post-Medieval Finds from Exeter, 1971–1980* (1984, Exeter City Council and the University of Exeter).

2

Summaries of the Excavations within the City of Exeter 1812–2019

David Gould, Andrew Pye and Stephen Rippon

Introduction

The central area covered by this gazetteer falls within the Exeter City Historic Environment Record (HER). Originally compiled in the late 1990s, this established a numbering sequence for archaeological excavations undertaken within and around Exeter. Most of the excavations after 1970 were conducted by Exeter Museums Archaeological Field Unit (EMAFU) that was later renamed Exeter Archaeology (EA) and then ceased to operate in March 2012. In the run-up to their closure, English Heritage commissioned them to produce a guide to the archives of their projects carried out in Exeter between 1970 and 1990 (Leverett *et al.* 2011), and these represent the sites numbered 37–99 below and in the Exeter Archaeology Archive Project (EAAP) online resource: (https://archaeologydataservice.ac.uk/archives/view/exeter_parent_2015/site_list.cfm).

The summaries in this chapter are primarily drawn from City HER entries, Exeter Archaeology Advisory Committee Reports, summary site reports, and publications. Sites numbered 1–36 pre-date the work of the EMAFU, and some further early excavations were subsequently numbered by the City HER outside of this sequence: for example, the excavation undertaken in 1939 at the Bishop's Palace Garden was assigned the number 175 by the City HER. Post-1990 archaeological excavations have also been assigned numbers by the City HER, although as their numbering sequence also includes watching briefs and building surveys the numbering of the excavations and evaluations, whilst generally in chronological sequence, is not continuous. As a result, and for reasons of simplicity, a decision was made that EAPIT would adopt a simple continuous numbering sequence for the post 1990 excavations, starting at 101 and as the post-1990 gazetteer entries therefore diverge from the City HER numbering the latter are also given for each entry.

Each of the site summaries below gives the following information:

- Site name
- Date of excavation
- Location within Exeter and its immediate hinterland (*e.g.* the Roman insula number)
- EAAP/EAPIT site number
- City HER number
- References (in addition to those in the EAAP and City HER) including:
  - o Exeter Archaeology Advisory Committee Reports (EAACR), that are available online (https://archaeologydataservice.ac.uk/archives/view/exeter_parent_2015/downloads.cfm)
  - o Fox 1952a: *Roman Exeter (Isca Dumnoniorum): Excavations in the War-Damaged Areas 1945–1947*
  - o other published reports
  - o summary site reports (available in the City HER)
  - o annual summaries published in *Britannia* and *Medieval Archaeology*

Abbreviations and sources

EA: Exeter Archaeology
EAACR: Exeter Archaeology Advisory Committee Report
EAAP: Exeter Archaeology Archive Project (https://archaeologydataservice.ac.uk/archives/view/exeter_parent_2015/index.cfm)
EAPIT: Exeter: A Place in Time project
EMAFU: Exeter Museums Archaeological Field Unit
HER: Historic Environment Record (maintained by Exeter City Council)
RAMM: Royal Albert Memorial Museum

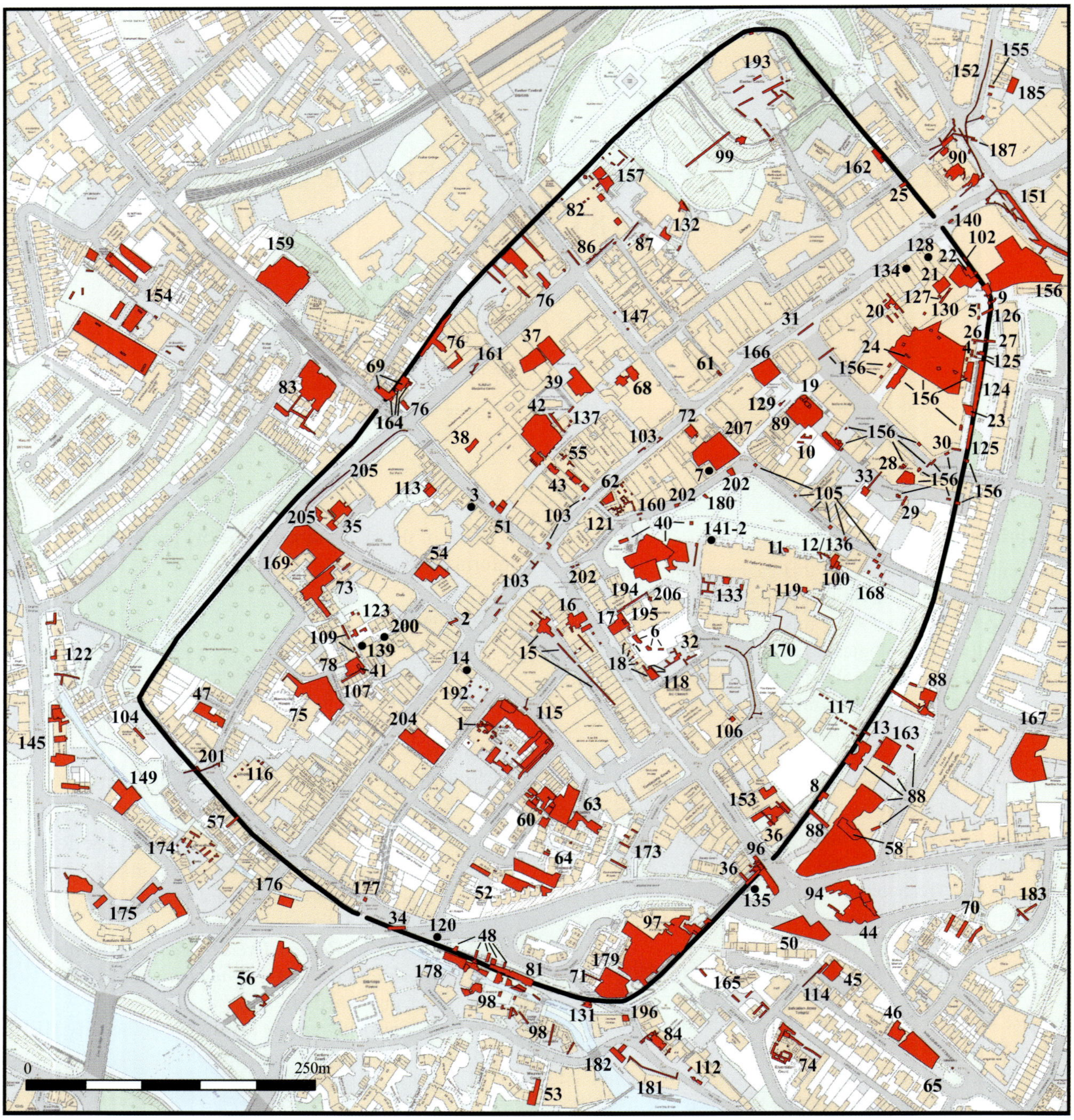

Fig. 2.1 Excavations within the historic core of Exeter (drawn by David Gould)

Smythen Street

- 1931
- Location: *insula* XI/XII
- EAPIT Site number: 1
- City HER number: 1
- Additional references: Montgomerie-Neilson and Montague 1931, 124–8; Fox 1952a, 100; Bidwell 1980, 73

Roman town: the remains of a later 2nd or early 3rd-century AD building were excavated. A room measuring 4.2 m by 3.2 m with walls standing to a height of 1.2 m was thought to have been equipped with a hypocaust. Nearby, a further short length of wall could not be directly associated with the others and may have formed part of a separate structure. ***Medieval***: some Saxo-Norman pottery was recovered; its context is unclear.

Mary Arches Street, Golden Ball Inn

- 1931
- Location: *insula* VII

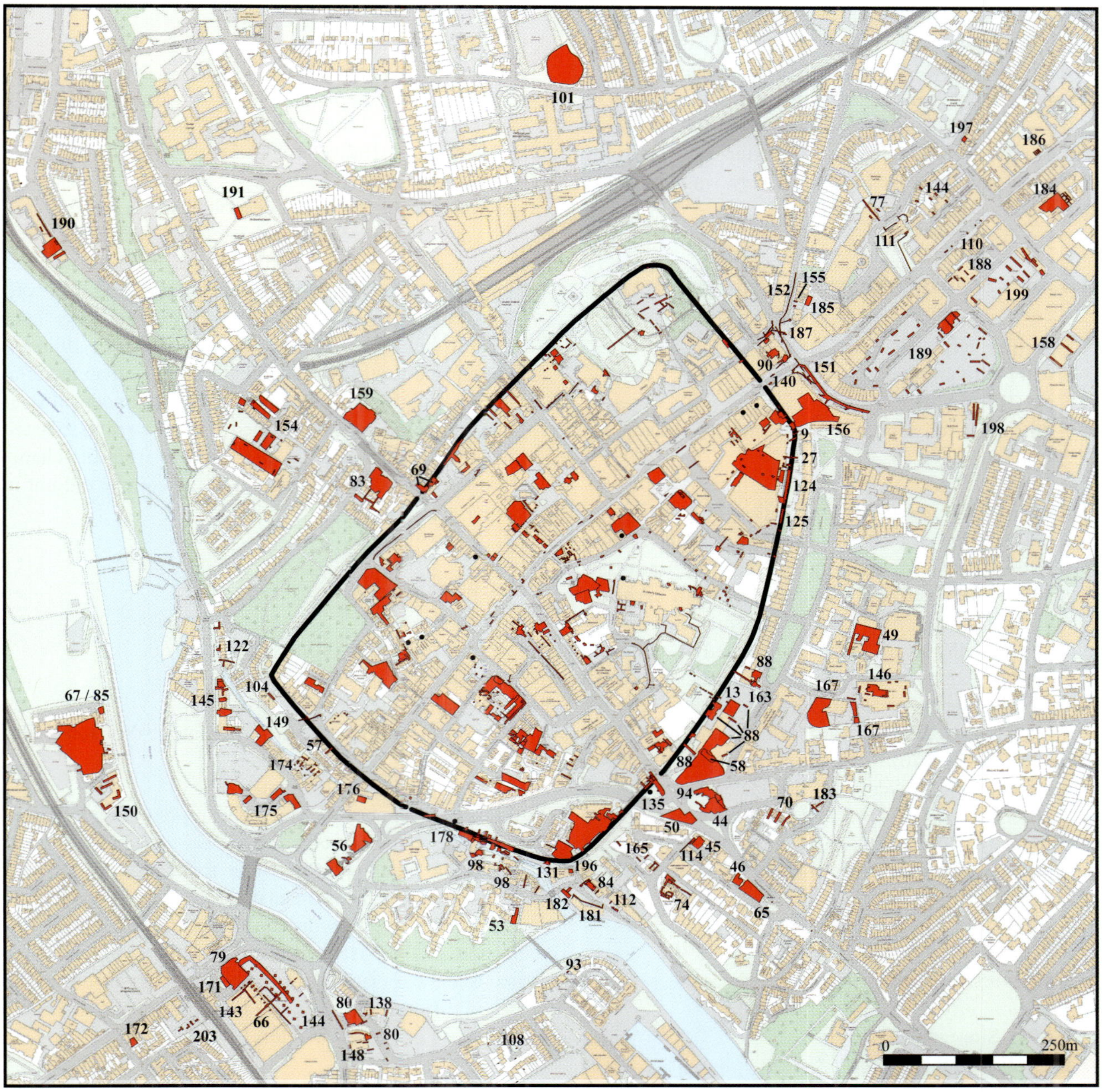

Fig. 2.2 Excavations within the immediate hinterland of Exeter (drawn by David Gould)

- EAPIT Site number: 2
- City HER number: 2
- Additional references: Montgomerie-Neilson and Montague 1931, 128–30; Fox 1952a, 100; Bidwell 1980, 72

Roman town: a 2nd or 3rd-century AD Roman wall *c.* 0.9 m wide was recorded running *c.* SW–NE following the demolition of the Golden Ball public house, along with the partially demolished walls of a 4th-century AD house, some of which were still extant above ground. ***Medieval***: much Saxo-Norman and some later medieval pottery was recovered. Some was believed to come from the robbing of Roman features. ***Post-medieval***: a well, probably associated with the Golden Ball, was also found.

North Street Gaumont Cinema

- 1931
- Location: *insula* III
- EAPIT Site number: 3
- City HER number: 3
- Additional references: Montgomerie-Neilson and Montague 1931, 130–1; Fox 1952a, 100; Bidwell 1980, 69

Roman town: walls and a well were recorded, and although no plan was drawn at the time the archaeological features were reported to lie 'near where the NE frontage of the cinema now stands'. The varying recorded depth of natural deposits across the site (2.4 m to 6.7 m) may be indicative of extensive quarrying. ***Medieval***: some Saxo-Norman pottery was recovered; its context is unclear.

St John's School Orchard

- 1932
- Location: city wall and defences
- EAPIT Site number: 4
- City HER number: 4
- Additional references: Montgomerie-Neilson and Montague 1934, 77–81

Roman/?early medieval: excavation of the city wall revealed a clean surface 0.9 m below pavement level, consisting of an extremely tough core of undressed blocks of pitched volcanic trap rubble. A shaft excavated against the inner face of the wall demonstrated that practically all the facing stones had been removed. A trench was dug into the footings of the wall and exposed its foundation that included a spread of cement mortar at the base (a further excavation of this area of the city wall was undertaken three years later: see Site 126). Another shaft was opened *c*. 16.4 m from the wall, and a layer of rubbish including much burnt tile, carbonised wood, and sherds of Roman pottery was found directly under a 17th/18th-century midden. Intrusive material in this Roman layer included sherds of medieval jars.

St John's School (Bedford Garage) Kiln

- 1935; 1955
- Location: city defences
- EAPIT Site number: 5
- City HER number: 5
- Additional references: Chapter 17 below; Exeter Excavation Committee 1935, 188; Fox and Dunning 1957, 43–7; Allan 1984a, 27–30

Late Saxon: a Late Saxon pottery kiln, thought to have functioned in the 10th and 11th centuries, was partially excavated and was subsequently preserved under the floor of Bedford Garage. Large quantities of pottery wasters (mainly plain unglazed jars) were recovered. The find demonstrates the production of high-quality wheel-thrown pottery in Exeter in the Late Saxon period. The kiln was re-excavated by Aileen Fox in 1955.

Old Deanery Garden (EAPIT 1, Figs 6.3, 6.5)

- 1932
- Location: *insula* XVII
- EAPIT Site number: 6
- City HER number: 6
- Additional references: Montgomerie-Neilson 1934, 55–7; Montgomerie-Neilson and Montague 1934, 72–8; Bidwell 1979, 21

Roman town: floor tiles described as 4th and 5th-century AD were recorded relatively close to the surface, and an open-air pool associated with the public baths was located *c*. 2 m below ground level. ***Late Saxon***: a wall 1 ft (0.3 m) high was described by the excavators as 'later shewn to belong to the early-medieval phase', although the evidence for this is not given; reused Roman material was found in the wall. ***Medieval***: many fragments of Beer stone mouldings were recorded – they were associated by the excavators with an altar reredos from the chapel of the College of Vicars, although the college did not in fact have a chapel.

16 Cathedral Yard

- 1932
- Location: *insula* XIV
- EAPIT Site number: 7
- City HER number: 7
- Additional references: Montgomerie-Neilson 1934, 61–2

Roman: deposits interpreted as representing a Roman street level were located *c*. 2.6 m below the modern street level. ***Later medieval***: parts of the foundations of a medieval building which contained moulded arch voussoirs, said to be *in situ,* were recorded. ***Post-medieval***: a well was recorded in the basement of the building, thought at the time to be associated with the wine cellars of the Royal Clarence Hotel, but probably of earlier date. No known plan exists of this excavation.

Palace Gate Convent Garden

- 1932; 1999
- Location: city wall
- EAPIT site number: 8
- City HER number: 8; 15065
- Additional references: Montgomerie-Neilson 1934, 63–5

Roman/Later medieval: excavations on either side of the city wall revealed evidence of both Roman and medieval fabric, and evidence of a medieval tower projecting from the front face of the wall. Part of the berm between wall and ditch, and a feature interpreted as an extra-mural road or track of Norman date, were also recovered, along with traces of a possible Roman road surface.

St John's School (St John's Bastion)

- 1933
- Location: city wall
- EAPIT: 9
- City HER number: 9
- Additional references: Montgomerie-Neilson 1934, 60, 78–81

Roman: trenches at the rear of the city wall uncovered a layer of Roman tile, possibly associated with a nearby tilery. ***Later medieval***: a trench exposed the outer face of the eastern angle tower of the city wall, revealing a double-chamfered plinth.

5 Cathedral Close (Annuellars' College)

- 1933
- Location: *insulae* XIX and XXIII
- EAPIT Site number: 10
- City HER number: 10
- Additional references: Montgomerie-Neilsen 1934, 62–3, 81–3; Fox 1952a, 103

Roman fortress: a section of the *via sagularis* was observed, although originally interpreted as the floor of a stable block. ***Roman town***: floor levels were recorded *c.* 2.4 m below the surface, dated by a coin and pottery of Claudian date. The floor surface, *c.* 0.5 m thick, was recorded as having a 'clean cut marge' (margin?), implying either a later intrusion through the feature or an edge possibly associated with a contemporary structure. ***Saxo-Norman***: sherds of Saxo-Norman pottery were recovered. ***Later medieval***: the remains of three later medieval boundary walls associated with the Annuellars' College were also found, with the fragmentary remains of a cobbled surface and a well.

Cathedral, St Andrew's Chapel

- 1936
- Location: *insula* XIX
- EAPIT Site number: 11
- City HER number: 11
- Additional references: Radford and Morris 1936, 225–8; Fox 1952a, 102; Bidwell 1980, 73

The excavation was located immediately outside the chapel and revealed disturbed deposits that had already been partially excavated and contained no reliably sealed layers *in situ*. ***Roman***: the remains of an apsidal room with a hypocaust below were recorded. ***Later medieval***: the foundation walls of St Andrew's Chapel were shown to be contemporary with the superstructure of the Cathedral at this point (*i.e.* late 13th century); the presence of a putative crypt below the chapel was disproved. A further block of masonry excavated to the SW of the main Roman structure was thought to be part of a separate medieval building.

Cathedral, outside of Speke Chapel

- 1936
- Location: *insula* XXXIX
- EAPIT Site number: 12
- City HER number: 12
- Additional references: Radford and Morris 1936, 226, 228–31; Fox 1952a, 102–3; Bidwell 1980, 24, 76

Roman fortress: a stretch of street – that can now be interpreted as the Roman military *via sagularis* – was exposed, demonstrating that it was at least 4 m wide. ***Roman fortress or Roman town***: a stretch of Early Roman wall about 0.65 m wide running SW–NE was recorded straddling the fortress defensive rampart and sealed by Roman deposits that were in turn cut through by the walls of a Late Roman town house; this stretch of wall was also recorded in the 1991 Cathedral Close excavation (Site 100). The wall might possibly represent part of a stone interval tower, and, although no other masonry elements have as yet been recorded on the fortress defences, it is possible that a scheme to upgrade the earth and timber structures was started towards the end of the military occupation, or early in the life of the Roman town, and was then abandoned (see EAPIT 1, Chapter 6). ***Roman town***: three later Roman walls were found running parallel to each other on a *c.* SW–NE alignment; that to the NW was built directly above a street level which had probably remained in use until the end of the 2nd century AD. Near this site, a tessellated pavement was found in 1843, measuring *c.* 7 m from NE to SW and was *c.* 2.4 m wide (Site 136). The pavement and walls probably belonged to the same building.

11–13 Trinity Street

- 1936
- Location: city wall and defences
- EAPIT Site number: 13
- City HER number: 13
- Additional references: Radford and Morris 1936, 238–40

Later medieval: trenches excavated immediately in front of the city wall uncovered its foundation trench extending *c.* 0.5 m forward of the visible face of the wall and filled with rammed gravel. The inner edge of a medieval defensive ditch was found *c.* 3 m from the front face of the wall, the intermediate space constituting the berm.

93–94 Fore Street

- 1938
- Location: *insula* XI/XII
- EAPIT Site number: 14
- City HER number: 14
- Additional references: Ransom Pickard 1938, 83; Fox 1952a, 100–1; Bidwell 1980, 73

Roman (or later?): an unpublished account of observations made by Col. Ransom Pickard is lodged in the RAMM; it was originally accompanied by plans and photographs which have subsequently been lost. It was claimed by the excavator that several Roman walls were found, although they had been underpinned and reused in medieval times. This hypothesis was challenged in an unpublished note of 1938 (possibly by C.A. Ralegh Radford) on the grounds that Pickard's interpretation was founded on a belief that volcanic trap rock, from which the walls were built, was not used for domestic buildings in medieval Exeter, which is untrue. However, R.G. Goodchild (in Fox 1952a), who must have seen the plans and photographs, considered that one wall, 9.2 m long and 0.6 m wide, was certainly Roman.

South Street (Fox 1952a Area I)

- 1945–6
- Location: *insulae* XIII and XVII
- EAPIT Site number: 15
- City HER number: 15
- Additional references: Fox 1952a, 31–42; Bidwell 1979, 21; Dunning and Fox 1951

Roman fortress: the fragmentary remains of two timber buildings and a length of Roman street were excavated (EAPIT 1, Fig. 1.3). The buildings can now be interpreted as part of the *latera praetorii* on the SW side of the *via principalis* of the fortress. The building to the NW of the street is likely to have formed a part of the *principia* of the fortress. The plan of the building on the other side of the street, probably part of the *praetorium*, was more complete, one room measuring *c.* 11 m × 7 m. The metalled street between them had a central drainage channel. ***Roman town***: the sites of these buildings were sealed by the gravel metalling of the later market place located to the SW of the forum. Two later parallel walls were also found, interpreted as part of a narrow portico in front of the SW range of the forum with an unenclosed metalled area behind. ***Later medieval***: an important group of 12th-century pottery including complete vessels and imports from Normandy was recovered from a pit.

South Street (Fox 1952a Area II)

- 1945–6
- Location: *insula* XIII
- EAPIT Site number: 16
- City HER number: 16
- Additional references: Fox 1952a, 31–42; Bidwell 1979, 21

Late Saxon: excavations were conducted on the site of St George's church, which had been demolished in 1843. The W and N walls of the nave were revealed, standing more than 3 m high; the quoins and W doorway displayed long-and-short work, indicating a Late Saxon date. The foundations of part of the S nave wall, a S porticus and a small chancel were found in excavation. The nave was 17 feet (5.2 m) wide and the entire church at least *c.* 48 feet (14.6 m) long. ***Later medieval***: a S aisle and SW tower were added in the later Middle Ages.

11–12 South Street (Fox 1952a Area III)

- 1946
- Location: *insula* XVII
- EAPIT Site number: 17
- City HER number: 17
- Additional references: Fox 1952a, 42–44; Bidwell 1979, 122, fig 22; Bidwell 1980, 52–3

Roman town: walls of two stone-built buildings were found, flanking the street to the SW of the basilica and forum. Two phases of construction were observed, although the buildings did not appear to have been extensively replanned. They were furnished with a portico which would have faced onto the street. The first room behind this portico would have measured *c.* 7.3 m by 7.6 m. Further traces of these buildings were seen in Site 195. The buildings may have formed part of the town's public baths.

20–21 South Street (Fox 1952a Area IV)

- 1946
- Location: *insula* XVII
- EAPIT Site number: 18
- City HER number: 18
- Additional references: Fox 1952a, 42–5; Bidwell 1979, 21, 122

Roman town: the demolition of 20–21 South Street exposed Roman strata at the base of the Deanery Garden wall. The remains consisted of an *opus signinum* floor with occupation deposits below and a robbed wall foundation, which was traced for 5.3 m towards South Street (at which point it was truncated by later cellars). Parallel to this wall and 6 m to the N were the remains of another Roman wall foundation, probably part of the same structure. The building was interpreted as dating to *c.* AD 200. Most traces of earlier deposits had been removed when the building was constructed. The building formed part of the town's public baths and date from the period when the baths were rebuilt and extended.

Catherine Street, Annuellars' College (Fox 1952a Area V)

- 1945–7
- Location: *insulae* XIV, XIX and XXII/XXIII/XXIV/XXVII/XXVIII/XXIX
- EAPIT Site number: 19
- City HER number: 19
- Additional references: Fox 1952a, 46–9; Bidwell 1980, 73–4; Holbrook *et al.* 1989

Roman town: excavation of an area beneath the courtyard and refectory of the medieval St Catherine's Almshouses revealed evidence of a Roman town house, consisting of the fragmentary remains of walls and small patches of mosaic floors. The site was further investigated in 1987–8 (Site 89).

Bamfylde House (Fox 1952a Area VI)

- 1945–7
- Location: *insula* XXII/XXIII/XXIV/XXVII/XXVIII/XXIX
- EAPIT Site number: 20
- City HER number: 20
- Additional references: Fox 1952a, 49–50; Bidwell 1980, 74

Roman town: excavations were carried out within the remains of the bombed 16th-century Bamfylde House Two Roman pits contained 1st and 2nd-century AD pottery, and the fragmentary wall foundations of two later Roman buildings were also recorded. ***Later medieval***: a 13th/14th-century pit and contemporary hearth were recorded in addition to the ground plan of the recently destroyed building.

St John's Hospital/Bluecoat School (Fox 1952a Area VII) (EAPIT 1, Fig. 7.14)

- 1945–7
- Location: *insula* XL
- EAPIT Site number: 21
- City HER number: 21
- Additional references: Fox 1952a, 50–1; Bidwell 1980, 74

Roman fortress: the earliest deposits were represented by a 1st-century AD clay floor containing a coin of Claudius I, the first time that evidence for pre-Flavian occupation had been excavated outside the fortress, and perhaps evidence for extra-mural civilian settlement. ***Roman town***: later Roman occupation was represented by a 2nd-century AD pit. ***Later medieval/post-medieval***: evidence included the remains of paths and trackways as well as substantial wall foundations and demolition deposits, associated with the Hospital of St John, which formerly stood on this site. The area was subsequently occupied by the Bluecoat School and Free Grammar School from which wall foundations and debris were also uncovered.

Former General Post Office (Fox 1952a Area VIII)

- 1945–7
- Location: city wall and defences
- EAPIT Site number: 22
- City HER number: 22
- Additional references: Fox 1952a, 55–7

Roman town: a trench against the back of the city wall was located behind the former General Post Office. The truncated remains of the Roman rampart constructed behind the wall and a section of the wall foundation itself were examined. The site was further investigated in Area F of the later Princesshay excavations (Site 156).

Post Office Street (Fox 1952a Area IX)

- 1950
- Location: city wall and defences
- EAPIT Site number: 23
- City HER number: 23
- Additional references: Fox 1952a, 57–9

Roman town: the external face of a section of the city wall was examined and found to contain at least 12 courses of Roman masonry above the level of a plinth, which had been underpinned with locally quarried red breccia blocks. Internally, the wall had been cut back and refaced with brick and stone above ground level, leaving a width of *c.* 2.20 m of Roman fabric. A layer of brown loam *c.* 0.60 m thick containing 1st and earlier 2nd-century AD pottery overlay the natural subsoil. Evidence for the earthen rampart having existed before the masonry city wall was constructed was also found; it was estimated to have been *c.* 1.50 m high. The city wall foundation was *c.* 3.3 m wide. The rampart, heightened by 0.5 m when the wall was built, was relatively well preserved, with a rough stone revetment *c.* 6.35 m to the rear of the front wall face.

9 Bedford Circus (Fox 1952a Trench 12)

- 1945–7
- Location: *insula* XXVIII/XXIX
- EAPIT Site number: 24
- City HER number: 24
- Additional references: Fox 1952a, 45–6

Later medieval: a trench contained debris from the building of Bedford Circus overlying a thick layer of black soil containing late medieval pottery. The site of this trench would subsequently fall within Area B/C of the later Princesshay excavations (Site 156).

Rougemont (Fox 1952a Trench 13)

- 1945–7
- Location: city defences
- EAPIT Site number: 25
- City HER number: 25
- Additional references: Fox 1952a, 52–3

Late prehistoric/Roman: the remains of a small oven lay in a hollow in natural deposits lying beneath the bank behind the city wall. Fox reported that it looked like Iron Age ovens from Maiden Castle but that it contained Roman pottery.

St John's School Garden (Fox 1952a Trench 14)

- 1945–7
- Location: city wall and defences
- EAPIT Site number: 26
- City HER number: 26
- Additional references: Fox 1952a, 53–5

Roman fortresss/town: a section across the foundations of the city wall by Southernhay revealed the rampart to its rear and defensive ditch to the front. Overlying a pre-Roman turf-line beneath the rampart was a thick layer of red clay, full of broken roof tiles (many of them wasters), pockets of charcoal and lumps of burnt clay. Pre-Flavian pottery was associated with the tilery waste.

39 Southernhay West (Fox 1952a Trench 15)

- 1945–7
- Location: city defences
- EAPIT Site number: 27
- City HER number: 27
- Additional references: Fox 1952a, 53–5

Later medieval: the trench sectioned the upper part of the defensive ditch in front of the city wall, the lowest layers in which contained late medieval pottery. The ditch was finally infilled in 1784.

17 Bedford Circus/Chapel Street (Fox 1952a Trench 16)

- 1945–7
- Location: *insula* XXII/XXIII/XXIV/XXVII/XXVIII/XXIX
- EAPIT Site number: 28
- City HER number: 28
- Additional references: Fox 1952a, 45, 51

Later medieval: due to disturbance during the construction of Bedford Circus, very few archaeological deposits remained and only a few medieval sherds were recovered.

Chapel Street, Abbot's Lodge (Fox 1952a Trench 17)

- 1945–7
- Location: *insula* XXII/XXIII/XXIV/XXVII/XXVIII/XXIX
- EAPIT Site number: 29
- City HER number: 29
- Additional references: Fox 1952a, 51–2

Roman fortress: a 0.20 m thick Roman military street, overlying the pre-Roman ground surface, was made of clean yellow gravel and bounded to the NNE by a drain; excluding the drain the street was at least 3 m wide. ***Roman town***: during the Early Roman civil period, a bed of trap 'spalls' (rubble) was put down which infilled the drain, while yellow gravel completed the remaking of the street which now extended about 3 m further to the NNE; it was exposed for a width of 6 m but was probably at least 7.5 m wide overall. The final resurfacing consisted of a mixture of trap and gravel. A possible Roman wall foundation in volcanic stone was recorded at the NNE end of the trench. ***Later medieval***: the Roman street was sealed by a medieval soil. A Second World War bomb crater at the SSW end of the trench prevented any further excavation in this direction.

14 Bedford Circus (Fox 1952a Area IX)

- 1950
- Location: *insula* XXII/XXIII/XXIV/XXVII/XXVIII/XXIX and city defences
- EAPIT Site number: 30
- City HER number: 30
- Additional references: Fox 1952a, 57–9; Bidwell 1980, 60

Roman town: a trench was excavated through the 30 feet (9.1 m) wide rampart at the rear of the city wall. The upper 8 feet [2.4 m] of deposits consisted of tipped soil associated with the building of Bedford Circus, meaning only the upper layers of the bank could be investigated.

High Street, Underground Passages

- 1950
- Location: *insula* XXII/XXIII/XXIV/XXVII/XXVIII/XXIX
- EAPIT Site number: 31
- City HER number: 31

- Additional references: Fox 1951b, 172–8; Stoyle 2014, 81–2

Later medieval: an isolated length of the city aqueduct passage was examined prior to post-War redevelopment. The method of construction was found to differ from that of sections examined in the 1931 survey of the city's underground passages. No dating evidence for the passage was found, but it is now believed to date from the early 16th century. During the same investigation, the passage below Catherine Street was also excavated (see Site 130).

2–8 Bear Street

- 1953
- Location: *insulae* XVII and XVIII
- EAPIT Site number: 32
- City HER number: 32
- Additional references: Fox 1953, 30–41; 1954, 274–8; Bidwell 1979, 21, 78

Roman fortress: a metalled street surface was found. ***Roman town***: the street continued in use in the Roman town and was flanked on the west side by a drain or conduit, which had been constructed from volcanic trap and apparently covered over with a roof of inverted roof tiles; it had silted up by the 3rd century AD. This may have been draining large quantities of water from the public baths on higher ground to the north.

Chapel Street (rear of 10 Cathedral Close)

- 1955
- Location: *insula* XXII/XXIII/XXIV/XXVII/XXVIII/XXIX
- EAPIT Site number: 33
- City HER number: 33
- Additional references: Fox 1956, 219–20; Greenfield 1964, 339–79; Bidwell 1979, 78–80; 1980, 67, 74

Roman town: a trench exposed Roman layers at a depth of 9–12 feet (2.7–3.6 m) below ground level. They probably represented the upper layers infilling the outer ditch of the legionary fortress, which was then unknown. They were overlain by part of a later Roman stone building with a mortar floor, superimposed hearths and a slate roof, and by later Roman pits. ***Later medieval***: a sequence of medieval deposits was excavated. The earliest contained Late Saxon pottery (but not recognised as such at the time); the later medieval levels included a building with a mortar floor, an open hearth and stone bases, interpreted as the footings for free-standing posts. John Hurst's report on the pottery (in Greenfield 1964, 357–76) represented a major advance in the medieval and later ceramics of South-West England.

West Street

- 1961–2
- Location: city defences
- EAPIT Site number: 34
- City HER number: 34
- Additional references: Fox 1963, 83

Roman town: excavation for a deep shaft to the sewers underneath the Inner Bypass at West Street exposed in section part of the town's defensive rampart behind the city wall. It was composed of light sandy soil standing to a height of *c*. 1.8 m above the natural red Permian clay.

10–18 Bartholomew Street East

- 1959
- Location: intra-mural
- EAPIT Site number: 35
- City HER number: 35
- Additional references: Fox 1961, 61–80; 1966, 49; Bidwell 1980, 24; Holbrook and Fox 1987, 23–57

Roman fortress: excavations revealed a series of Roman timber buildings subsequently recognised as having been located within the *intervallum* (the space between the back of the rampart and the *via sagularis*) on the NW side of the legionary fortress. The earliest buildings were associated with ironworking and may well have been relatively insubstantial structures. These industrial features and their associated structures were built and used before the construction of the *via sagularis*. One of the structures fell out of use after the construction of the street, while the other continued to be used until superseded by two successive ovens and finally by a row of small timber buildings of post trench construction. Demolition material showed that they had possessed plastered daub walls and tile roofs. The timber buildings would have abutted the rear face of the rampart and were destroyed by fire, possibly as part of the demolition of the fortress. ***Roman town***: the *via sagularis* was resurfaced during the earlier part of the Roman civil period but went out of use when the city wall was constructed. The robbed remains of a wall cutting the *via sagularis* may be associated with the rear of a building probably constructed during the second half of the 3rd century AD which fronted onto this new street. ***Later medieval***: post-Roman material was limited to two features interpreted as marking a tenement boundary. Also see Site 205.

South Gate (EAPIT 1, Fig. 6.11)

- 1964–5
- Location: intra-mural and city wall
- EAPIT Site number: 36
- City HER number: 36

- Additional references: Barber 1965, 88–109; 1967, 314–24; Fox 1968, 1–20; Bidwell 1980, 47–8; Henderson 1988, 91–119; 2001

Roman fortress/town: traces of a road probably leading from the legionary fortress to the port at Topsham were recorded. This road was relatively thinly metalled, *c.* 6 m wide, and exhibited a slight camber. The road was resurfaced with gravel on at least three occasions before the late 2nd century AD, reaching a thickness at the crown of 0.45 m. On the SW side of the road a substantial V-shaped ditch had been infilled during the Roman military period. This ditch was the first clear indication of a Roman military presence in Exeter and was interpreted as a defensive ditch of a fort, although it is now thought more likely to have bounded a compound outside the fortress. A small furnace and a small hearth both date to the mid 2nd century AD. Post-dating the filling of the ditch and located to the SW of the road, was a thick rubbish layer containing much charcoal and burnt clay and which covered both the ditch and the road. The furnace and the hearth both contained burnt bone and analysis of these bones showed that they contained small traces of lead which was interpreted as consistent with cupellation. These remains suggest open-air metalworking next to the road. ***Later Roman town***: the earliest phase of the later city defences, consisting of a revetted earthen rampart with ditches in front of it, was sectioned and found to terminate immediately SW of the earlier metalled road. The earliest defences were interpreted as having been replaced within a few years of AD 200 by a 3 m-thick stone wall standing *c.* 5 m high. The front of the primary rampart was cut back to accommodate the new wall and the cut material was piled up to form a correspondingly higher bank and walkway at the rear. Observation of the city wall footings on the NE side of South Street suggested that the overall width of the Roman gate cannot have exceeded 16.9 m. The adjacent area of the Roman town's defences was further investigated in 1988–94 (Site 96), while the site of the two northern trenches was further investigated in 2005 at Site 153.

Goldsmith Street I–II

- 1971
- Location: *insula* IV/V, cohort block C
- EAPIT Site number: 37
- City HER number: 37
- Additional references: Collis 1972; Hassall *et al.* 1972, 344; *Current Archaeology* 1973, 105; Wilson *et al.* 1973, 313; Bidwell 1980, 54; Henderson 1988, 91–119; Henderson *et al.* 1993a

Roman fortress: work in advance of the Guildhall Shopping Centre revealed traces of 1st-century AD timber buildings and cobbled surfaces associated with barracks of the legionary fortress. ***Roman town***: after the demolition of the military buildings, a clayey brown soil formed over the site from the 2nd century AD, perhaps the product of cultivation, with the site remaining unoccupied until the 4th century AD apart from a gully, a rough stone wall, and a few pits dug for clay. ***Late Saxon and Norman***: an important series of Late Saxon and Norman pits was excavated. ***Later medieval***: garden soils and pits of the 13th and 14th centuries were cut by mid 16th-century garden trenches.

North Street (EAPIT 1, Figs 1.6 and 8.15)

- 1971
- Location: *insula* IV/V
- EAPIT Site number: 38
- City HER number: 38
- Additional references: EAACR 1971; 1972; Salvatore 1993b; Thorp 2012

Roman fortress: the only confirmed Roman military feature was a pit containing material dating solely to the Claudio/Neronian period which was probably backfilled during the Roman military period or during the demolition of the fortress. ***Later medieval***: several medieval pits and gullies were recorded. A comprehensive survey of 38 North Street was also undertaken prior to demolition.

Goldsmith Street III (EAPIT 1, Fig. 6.14)

- 1971–2
- Location: *insula* IV/V, cohort block C
- EAPIT number: 39
- City HER number: 39
- Additional references: Chapter 6 below; Collis 1972; *Current Archaeology* 1973, 105; Hassall *et al.* 1972, 344; Wilson *et al.* 1973, 313; Bidwell 1980, 36, 54, 71–2; Henderson 1988, 91–119; 1991a; Henderson *et al.* 1993b

Roman fortress: further work in advance of the Guildhall Shopping Centre revealed parts of two barrack blocks within the legionary fortress. They were built back-to-back and separated by a 1 m-wide passageway and had been rebuilt on at least one occasion. ***Roman town***: the earliest Roman civilian activity was a series of late 1st-century AD dumped deposits, followed by the digging of pits and ditches which suggest a period of low-intensity use prior to the construction of the first civilian structures in the 2nd century AD. These timber buildings were repaired on several occasions, and at least one of them was probably a house. It is unclear how long these buildings remained in use, but by the 3rd century AD they were demolished and their building plots used for the construction of two stone (or stone-founded) buildings. One was a house of some quality with underfloor heating and tessellated flooring. These buildings underwent repair and modification before their final abandonment. ***Late Saxon and Norman***: a dense scatter of 10th to 12th-century pits was found throughout the site. Some rich groups of faunal remains and pottery were recovered; the deeper pits also contained waterlogged organic materials including timbers which yielded dendrochronological samples. ***Later medieval***: the sequence of pits continued in the 13th and early 14th centuries but in about the mid 14th century the practice of digging open pits in back gardens ceased. The most notable late medieval features were two large stone-lined pits, finally infilled in the early 16th century, which may have had an industrial function.

Cathedral Close (St Mary Major, War Memorial, Cathedral Yard and Cathedral Green) (EAPIT 1, Front Cover, Figs 1.5, 5.1, 5.4, 5.7, 5.8, 5.9, 6.3, 6.4, 6.13, 7.2, 7.3, 7.7 and 7.8)

- 1971–6
- Location: *insulae* XIII, XIV, XVIII and XIX, cohort block D
- EAPIT Site number: 40
- City HER number: 40
- Additional references: Chapter 19 below (for medieval cemetery); EAACR 1971; 1972; 1976; Hassall *et al.* 1972, 344; Webster and Cherry 1972, 148; *Current Archaeology* 1973, 102–10; Griffiths 1974, 169; Frere 1977, 415; Bidwell 1979, 115–20; 1980, 55, 73; 2002, 12–15; Henderson and Bidwell 1982; 145–75; Allan *et al.* 1984; Blaylock 1996; Henderson 1999

This record covers excavations in Cathedral Close at St Mary Major (1971), six excavations at the War Memorial (1971–3), Cathedral Yard (1975) and Cathedral Green (1976) that have been fully published (Bidwell 1979). ***Roman fortress***: the St Mary Major excavation revealed remains of the legionary bath-house. The discovery of a dolphin antefix, the same as that produced by the *legio II Augusta* at Caerleon, provides good evidence linking the Roman military remains at Exeter to the Second Augustan Legion. Further details of the legionary bath-house were uncovered during the Cathedral Yard/Green excavations. ***Roman town***: parts of the legionary bath-house were demolished and were incorporated into a civil basilica. Its identification allowed for a greater understanding of the walls and metalled surfaces found at Sites 15–18, which were subsequently recognised as lying on the SW side of the basilica and forum. Outside the basilica lay an open market place, while a section of early civil street surface separating the basilica from the adjacent *insula* was recorded. A late civil stone house and associated mosaic was recorded. ***Early medieval/Saxo-Norman***: the Roman levels lay below an area used for three successive cemeteries, the earliest probably in use at some date between the 5th and 7th centuries with its graves aligned NW–SE on the same alignment as the Roman town (see EAPIT 1, Chapter 7). It was succeeded by a cemetery in use from the 9th century to perhaps the early 12th, with graves on two different alignments, one of them orientated on the axis of a church with an apsidal E end which became the parish church of St Mary Major (see Chapter 19 below). The relatively large size of this early church (at least 34.2 m long), its reduction in size in the early 12th century and its location near the later Norman cathedral strongly suggest that this was the Late Saxon minster. ***Later medieval:*** parts of the chancel and west tower of the medieval St Mary Major church were uncovered and it is likely that much of the Saxon minster nave was retained in the later church when other parts of the minster were demolished. St Mary Major church was itself almost entirely destroyed in 1865–7 when it was remodelled.

St Nicholas Priory (EAPIT 1, Figs 8.6 and 8.7)

- 1971
- Location: *insula* VI
- EAPIT Site number: 41
- City HER number: 41
- Additional references: EAACR 1971; Webster and Cherry 1972, 173; Allan 1999a; 2019; Orme 2015a

Later medieval: excavation on the site of the church of St Nicholas Priory revealed three parallel E–W robber-trenches, with a further wall-trench at right angles to them. They probably represent the line of the 11th-century nave and the addition of aisles in the 14th and 16th centuries. An important assemblage of early 16th-century pottery was recovered from the robber trenches.

Trichay Street (EAPIT 1, Fig. 1.4)

- 1972–4
- Location: *insula* IV/V, cohort block C
- EAPIT Site number: 42
- City HER number: 42
- Additional references: Chapter 5 below; *Current Archaeology* 1973, 105; Wilson 1973, 313; Griffiths 1974, 170; Wilson *et al.* 1974, 452; Bidwell 1980, 34, 53–4 and 69; Allan *et al.* 1984; Henderson *et al.* 1993b; Quinnell 2017

Late prehistoric: further work in advance of the Guildhall Shopping Centre revealed three ring ditches which preceded Roman military structures, and although probably associated with settlement activity, are not closely dated. ***Roman fortress***: two phases of Roman military occupation were identified associated with the legionary fortress. The earlier phase saw the construction of a barrack block and a further building which may have housed a senior officer, while the later phase included modifications to form a barrack block composed of a detached centurion's residence and *contubernia*, and the construction of a workshop (*fabrica*) of probable courtyard plan. ***Roman town***: the earliest Roman civilian activity was represented by several wells, followed by a waterpipe trench forming part of a new aqueduct leading into the town from the north. This was succeeded by several timber buildings which were subsequently destroyed by fire and the amalgamation of *insula* IV and V which led to the formation of two building plots by the late 2nd to mid 3rd century AD. Several timber buildings were constructed within these two plots, followed in the mid 3rd to early 4th century AD by a stone house. A probable stockyard was created in the mid to late 4th century AD. ***Early medieval***: a layer of dark loam accumulated above the latest Roman deposits which indicates that there was some form of activity, if only cultivation or the dumping of organic waste, before occupation recommenced in the 10th century. ***Late Saxon***: the excavation examined three large tenements and a small part of a fourth property. The earliest Saxo-Norman features (10th/11th century) comprised wells, cesspits and refuse pits. ***Later medieval***: an early 13th-century limekiln, with two large lime-slaking pits nearby, was also recorded. This industrial activity was replaced by domestic occupation in the early 13th century. A concentration of rubbish pits and cesspits in the northern part of the site was still evident in the late 13th and early 14th centuries. The most notable features which date to *c.* 1350–1550 were two large stone-lined pits, abutting each other on either side of a tenement boundary: they may have had covering structures, although no traces have survived.

196–197 High Street (EAPIT 1, Fig. 7.9)

- 1972–3
- Location: *insula* IX
- EAPIT Site number: 43
- City HER number: 43
- Additional references: Chapter 7 below; EAACR 1974; 1975; Griffiths 1974; 169; Wilson *et al.* 1975, 276; Goodburn 1976, 358; Bidwell 1980, 54, 73; Allan 1984a, 41–5; Bedford and Salvatore 1993d

Roman fortress: further work in advance of the Guildhall Shopping Centre – where it fronts onto the High Street – revealed that during the Roman military period the site was occupied by one or more granaries, while a post-trench and small area of metalling might be associated with a loading bay set back *c.* 6 m from the edge of a fortress street. No evidence for the demolition of the granaries was found. ***Roman town***: the earliest post-military deposits comprised a small wooden structure and several boundary ditches, followed in the Hadrianic or Antonine period by the construction of a timber-framed building sat upon stone foundations. The demolition of this structure was followed by the construction of a new building which was destroyed by fire. In the final phase of Roman occupation, probably dating to after the mid 3rd century AD, a possible wooden structure was flanked to the SE by a stone building which contained at least one tessellated floor. ***Saxo-Norman/later medieval***: a layer of dark loam accumulated over the latest Roman deposits before the earliest Saxo-Norman occupation. The earliest features were a series of intercutting pits which may have lain behind a house on the High Street dating to the 10th/early 11th century. In the 11th century a timber building was constructed with accompanying cess-pits that was replaced in the late 11th/early 12th century by another building represented by partially robbed stone foundations which may have supported a timber superstructure. By the mid 12th century this building had been demolished (or possibly burnt down) and the area became an open space containing a possible fence line, two pits, and a well. In the late 12th century the area was covered by a soil deposit, succeeded by a sequence of hearths and pits. Late medieval stratified deposits survived only in one area where the sequence could be linked to the construction of a late medieval hall house whose fabric survived in both extant tenement walls flanking the site. Beside the tenement boundary with 196 High Street, a sunken strip of ground was likely to have been a side passage running towards the rear of the property. Elsewhere on the site, a pit containing the remains of a pair of casks was found beneath a cellar floor: the bottoms of the barrels were filled with white lime suggesting their use in leather-making. The pits were infilled in the early 16th century.

Valiant Soldier

- 1973–4
- Location: extra-mural
- EAPIT Site number: 44
- City HER number: 44
- Additional references: EAACR 1974; Wilson *et al.* 1975, 276; Bidwell 1979, 9; 1980, 41, figs 24 and 25; Allan 1984a; Holbrook and Bidwell 1991, microfiche; Bedford *et al.* 1994; Salvatore 2001; forthcoming; Quinnell 2017

Prehistoric: a possible pre-Roman feature was observed, perhaps part of a small structural ring ditch. Although no datable finds were recorded, it is possibly of the local later Iron Age tradition. ***Roman fortress***: the excavations on this extra-mural site, to the E of the South Gate, revealed remains of at least three Roman timber buildings arranged around a courtyard. These structures were thought to comprise part of a suite of buildings located within a compound to the SE of the legionary fortress. This area of military occupation was further investigated in 1988–9 at the Acorn Roundabout (Site 94). Two cremation burials represent the only known burials from Exeter's fortress period; a third cremation may also be military in date or belong to the early civil period. ***Roman town***: the area appears to have been given over to agriculture, and was divided into a series of small plots defined by gullies. A well, trackway, and six inhumation burials were also recorded. ***Late Saxon***: one Late Saxon pit indicates occupation from the 10th century. ***Later medieval***: four large 13th-century pits were the principal signs of occupation during the high medieval period. A small early 16th-century kiln producing ridge tiles, floor tiles and pottery was recorded.

Friars Gate (EAPIT 1, Fig. 8.6)

- 1973–4
- Location: extra-mural
- EAPIT Site number: 45
- City HER number: 45
- Additional references: EAACR 1973; Webster and Cherry 1974, 122, 188; Wilson *et al.* 1974, 452; Loe 1998a; Orme 2016

Roman town: occupation on this extra-mural site, SE of the South Gate, was represented by three Late Roman wells and by various pits. ***Later medieval***: the site fell within the precinct of the second Franciscan friary, to which the friars moved *c.* 1300. The robbed remains of a transept or chapel on the north side of the friary church were found. Six stone-lined graves containing high-status burials were excavated within it, and the bedding of its late medieval tiled floor was recorded. A large sand quarry preceding the church was found below part of the site. Further remains of the friary church and burials were recorded at Site 114. ***Post-medieval***: a substantial 18th-century sawpit was excavated.

Friars Walk

- 1973
- Location: extra-mural
- EAPIT Site number: 46
- City HER number: 46
- Additional references: Bedford and Salvatore 1994b

Roman fortress: excavations to the east of Site 45 revealed four pits and a well possibly of Roman military date. ***Later medieval***: a pit containing late 12th-century pottery was also found, indicating the spread of extra-mural settlement down Holloway Street.

Bartholomew Street West

- 1974
- Location: *insula* XXX/XXXI
- EAPIT Site number: 47
- City HER number: 47
- Additional references: EAACR 1974; Goodburn 1976, 360; Holbrook and Bidwell 1991, 19 m 285–6; Allan 1984a, 44, 56

Roman town: a kiln producing flagons and mortaria, including three stamps of VITANVS, was the earliest feature recorded dating to the period following the departure of the *legio II Augusta*. In the late 2nd century AD the site was terraced to accommodate a timber building, while domestic occupation had ceased by the late 3rd century AD when a large ditch was dug across the site. ***Later medieval***: a pit containing a group of late 12th-century pottery was found. Stone drains, replacing a stone-lined well, dated to the late 13th century may have related to the intra-mural Franciscan friary.

Cricklepit Street

- 1974
- Location: city wall
- EAPIT Site number: 48
- City HER number: 48
- Additional references: Griffiths 1974, 169; Goodburn 1976, 360; Bidwell 1980, 60–1; Simpson 1993

Following the collapse of a 40 m length of the city wall, five trenches were excavated in order to check the stability of the wall which revealed five main periods of activity. ***Roman fortress (extra-mural)***: a few indeterminate features dating to *c.* AD 60–75 were found. ***Roman town***: much material was dumped in the area during the late 1st or early 2nd century AD. Pottery from a low broad bank of dumped clay and soil, interpreted as representing the first rampart, indicates a late 2nd-century AD date. ***Later medieval***: the city wall, previously thought to be the original Roman structure, was shown to have been rebuilt completely in the late medieval period; late medieval floor-tiles were recovered from its foundation trench. A further section of the city wall in this area was investigated in 1987–9 (Site 81).

Southernhay Gardens

- 1974
- Location: extra-mural
- EAPIT Site number: 49
- City HER number: 49
- Additional references: Wilson *et al.* 1975, 276; Bidwell 1979, 11; Salvatore 1994a

Roman fortress/town: this extra-mural site *c.* 140 m E of the city wall revealed an Early Roman timber building and well, although it is unclear whether they represent military or civilian occupation. The site was unoccupied in the medieval period.

Holloway Street (EAPIT 1, Fig. 8.6)

- 1974
- Location: extra-mural
- EAPIT Site number: 50
- City HER number: 50
- Additional references: Chapter 19 below; EAACR 1974; Goodburn 1976, 360; Bidwell 1979, 9–10; Earwood and Salvatore 1994; Loe 1998c; Allan *et al.* 2016; Orme 2016; Salvatore forthcoming

Roman fortress: evidence of an extra-mural military compound was recorded at this site *c.* 60 m SE of the South Gate; it was divided into two distinct and stratigraphically isolated areas separated by a substantial ditch that formed part of Exeter's Civil War defences. A timber building was recorded within a fenced compound enclosure while two further buildings were recorded outside of the area delineated by the fencing. ***Roman town***: in the early 2nd century AD the site was occupied by a series of ditches dividing it into rectangular plots, while Late Roman burials were also recorded. ***Later medieval***: 21 burials within the lay cemetery of the Franciscan friary were recorded; they included men, women and children. ***Post-medieval:*** a defensive ditch of the Civil War cut through the medieval cemetery.

45–46 North Street

- 1973–4
- Location: *insula* VIII
- EAPIT Site number: 51
- City HER number: 51
- Additional references: Griffiths 1974, 170; Goodburn 1976, 358; Bidwell 1980, 69; Salvatore 1993b

Roman fortress: two timber buildings of post-trench construction were recorded, along with a small section of street that was resurfaced at least twice during the military period and which remained in use during the civil period. Further sections of this street have been recorded at Sites 42 and 54. A second street was found at right-angles to the first street; it had a width of *c.* 6 m and its edge was marked by an unusually deep post-trench of a military building. This stretch had also been resurfaced on several occasions.

Rack Street

- 1974–5 (and see Site 64 for the 1977–8 excavations)
- Location: *insulae* XV/XVA/XVI/XXXIV and XXXIII
- EAPIT Site number: 52
- City HER number: 52
- Additional references: Chapter 8 below; Goodburn 1976, 358; Bidwell 1980, 73–5; Bedford and Salvatore 1992c

Roman fortress: excavations revealed the southern corner of the defensive circuit of the legionary fortress, represented by its ditch; later disturbances had removed all traces of the fortress rampart. ***Roman town***: the earliest post-military activity was represented by the replacement of the fortress ditch by a larger ditch, as well as some small-scale extra-mural occupation. In the late 3rd/early 4th century AD, a timber building was constructed alongside a new street built over the line of the backfilled defensive ditch (a further timber building was recorded at Site 64); both buildings were destroyed by fire and were replaced by stone structures that were in turn demolished by the end of the 4th century AD. ***Early medieval***: following the demolition of the latest Roman buildings, the site appears to have remained unoccupied as a layer of dark loam accumulated above their demolition layers. ***Saxo-Norman***: by the 11th/12th centuries, trenches were being dug to extract stone from the Roman buildings. The earliest Saxo-Norman domestic occupation was represented by two probable wells, testifying to a sparse level of occupation in this peripheral part of the city. ***Later medieval***: parts of a building fronting onto the street were uncovered, to the rear of which were early 13th-century refuse pits. This building was replaced in the mid to late 13th century by a new building, with a further structure to the NW. These buildings had fallen out of use by the mid 14th century when their terraced footprints were infilled. Later medieval occupation was represented by a single building which dated to the early to mid 14th century. Scatters of quite substantial postholes in the back gardens probably represent several phases of activity associated with cloth-drying racks recorded in the documentary evidence hereabouts from the early 15th century.

Shilhay

- 1975
- Location: extra-mural
- EAPIT Site number: 53
- City HER number: 53
- Additional references: EAACR 1975; 1976; Allan 1984a

Post-medieval: excavations revealed debris from a clay pipe kiln of *c.* 1700 and parts of a late 18th-century barge quay.

Mary Arches Street

- 1975
- Location: *insulae* II and VII
- EAPIT Site number: 54
- City HER number: 54
- Additional references: Goodburn 1976, 360; Bidwell 1980, 53–4 and 69–72; Bedford and Salvatore 1992g

Roman fortress: three distinct phases of timber building construction all probably of the Roman military period were recognised. They seemed to represent two buildings separated by a street, perhaps officers' houses. ***Roman town***: the military buildings were succeeded by Roman civil buildings of timber and then stone.

198 High Street

- 1975
- Location: *insula* IX
- EAPIT Site number: 55
- City HER number: 55
- Additional references: EAACR 1976; Goodburn 1976, 358; Bedford and Salvatore 1993e

Roman fortress: the remains of a water-pipe trench was recorded along with some stake holes. ***Roman town***: a building of timber construction was subsequently built on the site, although this was replaced by a masonry building in *c.* AD 200. ***Later medieval***: by *c.* 1450, a building with a front cellar and side passage occupied the site, while a hall house was built *c.* 1500 and replaced *c.* 1575 by a three-storey house on the frontage of mixed construction, with stone side walls and timber front and back walls.

Exe Bridge (EAPIT 1, Fig. 8.10)

- 1975–9
- Location: extra-mural
- EAPIT Site number: 56
- City HER number: 56
- Additional references: EAACR 1975; 1976; Henderson 1981, 119–22; Brown 1991; 2019

Late Saxon: the latest deposit of the old river bed below the construction levels of the later medieval Exe Bridge preserved evidence of infilled channels and had an almost level compacted pebble and cobble surface; iron nails and horseshoe fragments recovered from this deposit indicate that a ford crossed the Exe before the bridge's construction. A copy of a mid 9th-century Frisian coin suggests a Late Saxon date for this ford. A timber excavated from the foundation levels of St Edmund's church may have been reused from a Late Saxon timber footbridge; tree-ring analysis show that it was felled in the late 10th century. ***Later medieval***: nine arches survived from the bridge built *c.* 1200 (which originally contained 17–18 arches), with St Edmund's church above the 2nd and 3rd river arches from the Exeter end forming part of the original construction. A small part of St Mary's chantry chapel, built opposite St Edmund's within a few decades of the bridge's construction, was also uncovered. On the mudbank to the west of Frog Street that formed after the bridge's construction, timber buildings were erected from the early 13th century and were later replaced by stone buildings. This area of waterfront occupation expanded during the later medieval period as progressively more land was reclaimed. Evidence of horn-working and/or tanning as well as metalworking were recovered from 13th and 14th-century deposits.

Beedles Terrace

- 1976
- Location: city wall and defences
- EAPIT Site number: 57
- City HER number: 57
- Additional references: EAACR 1976; Frere *et al.* 1977, 415; Bedford and Salvatore 1992b, Appendix 1

Roman: a 1st-century AD quarry pit was recorded outside the fortress/early town. ***Later medieval***: a bank of rubble set against the city wall was removed in three places, showing that the wall had been cut back and refaced during the medieval period. A feature that may have served as a small defensive ditch was also recorded.

Magdalen Terrace

- 1976 (for 1986–8 excavations see Site 88)
- Location: extra-mural, city defences
- EAPIT Site number: 58
- City HER number: 58
- Additional references: EAACR 1976; Frere *et al.* 1977, 415; Henderson 2001

Roman town: of the two defensive ditches outside the Roman town wall the earliest yielded a Hadrianic coin while the second contained 2nd-century AD samian. ***Saxo-Norman***: a third ditch contained late 12th-century pottery.

Polsloe Priory (St Katherine's Priory) (EAPIT 1, Fig. 8.6)

- 1976–9; 1991; 2009
- Location: extra-mural (outside area mapped in Fig. 2.1 and Fig. 2.2)
- EAPIT number: 59
- City HER number: not applicable (outside City HER area)
- Additional references: EAACR 1977; 1980; Webster and Cherry 1979, 250–1; Blaylock 1991d; Loe 1998b; Farnell 2009; Orme 2015b; Allan 2019

Later medieval: Polsloe Priory lies *c.* 2 km E of Exeter. The earliest buildings were a temporary chapel preceding the construction of the church nave, and timber buildings on the site of the cloister and kitchen. The plan of the church remained unchanged until its demolition after the Dissolution, although its internal arrangements were altered periodically. A small area of the cemetery was also excavated along with the South, East, and West Ranges and the Cloister. The West Range was retained after the Dissolution; all other buildings were thoroughly robbed. The excavation produced one of the most comprehensive plans of a monastic complex in the South-West. In 2009 a plot of land immediately to the east was excavated and the footprint of a medieval building was recorded, although none of its original fabric remained. Ceramic material from the backfill of the robbed walls dated from the 13th/14th century, with some tiles being wasters indicating the presence of a nearby kiln. The building has tentatively been identified as a watermill.

Preston Street

- 1976–7
- Location: *insula* XV/XVA, cohort block J
- EAPIT Site number: 60
- City HER number: 60
- Additional references: EAACR 1977; Bedford and Salvatore 1992e

Roman fortress: the fragmentary post-trenches of two timber buildings represented barrack blocks within the *praetentura* in the SE corner of the legionary fortress. Two pits, one Claudio-Neronian and the other Flavian, were located in a position that would potentially place them in the space between the back walls of a pair of barracks (assuming that a full cohort-block had occupied the area). Nearby excavations at Mermaid Yard (Site 63) shed further light on this part of the legionary fortress. ***Norman:*** a few 11th/12th-century pits were excavated. ***Later medieval***: the remains of a medieval street were recorded directly in line with the modern Rack Street.

228 High Street

- 1975
- Location: *insula* X/XXI/XXVI
- EAPIT Site number: 61
- City HER number: 61
- Additional references: Goodburn 1976, 360; Bidwell 1980, 23, 73; Bedford and Salvatore 1993b

Roman fortress: the remains of at least one phase of a large military timber building were noted together with a well-laid metalled surface. ***Roman town***: further building activity was recorded on the site after the large military timber building had been demolished although it is unclear whether this activity belongs in the Roman military or civil phase. A large post-trench building on the Roman alignment was erected in the late military or early civilian phase.

High Street, NatWest Bank

- 1977
- Location: *insulae* IX, X, XIII and XIV
- EAPIT Site number: 62
- City HER number: 62
- Additional references: Goodburn 1978, 459; Bidwell 1979, 24, 60, 120–1; 1980, 55, 73

Roman fortress: excavations in the cellars of the NatWest Bank demonstrated that stratigraphy had been completely removed down to Roman levels. From the Roman military period evidence of a water-pipe trench with two branches leading off it was located, probably representing the water supply to the legionary bathhouse. ***Roman town***: the base of a deep roadside ditch and the N corner of the basilica and forum were also located.

Mermaid Yard

- 1977–8
- Location: *insula* XV/XVA/XVI/XXXIV
- EAPIT Site number: 63
- City HER number: 63
- Additional references: Frere *et al.* 1977, 415; EAACR 1978; Goodburn 1979, 324; Bidwell 1980, 23, 46–7, 76; Bedford and Salvatore 1992f; Blaylock 1996

Roman fortress: excavations immediately E of Preston Street (Site 60) revealed a ditch which helped to establish the line of the legionary fortress's SE defences. Part of the rampart was also observed along with fragmentary remains of a timber building flanking the *via sagularis* (allowing for the position of the rampart relative to the *via sagularis* to be established for the first time). ***Roman town***: the defences were not demolished when the legionary fortress was abandoned, but instead remained in use until the late 2nd century AD. The remains of two successive buildings were found, the first was made of timber and constructed *c.* AD 275, the second was constructed in stone and had a coin of AD 346–50 in its demolition debris. ***Later medieval***: the site clearly lay close to the main medieval bell foundry in Exeter, evidenced by dumps of waste mould material.

Rack Street

- 1977–8
- Location: *insula* XV/XVA/XVI/XXXIV
- EAPIT Site number: 64
- City HER number: 64
- Additional references: Chapter 8 below; EAACR 1978, Goodburn 1978, 459; Bidwell 1980, 23, 46–7, 74–5

Roman fortress: excavations revealed the southern corner of the defensive circuit of the legionary fortress, represented by the ditch. A drainage ditch may have defined an extra-mural enclosure contemporary with the fortress and which had been infilled by the end of the military period. A roadside ditch flanked the *intervallum* street inside the line of the defensive rampart, although later disturbances had removed all traces of the fortress's rampart. ***Roman town***: the earliest post-military activity involved the replacement of the fortress ditch. In the late 3rd/early 4th century AD a timber building was constructed alongside a new street built over the line of the backfilled defensive ditches (another had been recorded at Site 52); both buildings were destroyed by fire and replaced by two (possibly three) stone structures which were demolished by the end of 4th century AD. ***Early medieval***: following the demolition of the latest Roman buildings, the site appears to have remained unoccupied and a layer of dark loam accumulated above the demolished buildings. ***Saxo-Norman***: by the 11th/12th centuries, trenches were being dug to extract stone from the long-abandoned Roman buildings. The earliest Saxo-Norman domestic occupation was a foundation slot and associated posthole, which together with the two wells discovered at Site 52 testify to a sparse level of occupation in this peripheral part of the city. ***Later medieval***: a building was identified on the edge of the excavation area and extended beyond it. Although only fragmentary evidence survived in this part of the site, it appears that the building was constructed within terraces cut into the underlying ground surface and that it, along with buildings recorded at Site 52, had fallen out of use by the mid 14th century. In the light of documentary evidence, the pits and postholes at the rear of the tenement probably represent cloth-drying racks.

Holloway Street

- 1978
- Location: extra-mural
- EAPIT Site number: 65
- City HER number: 65
- Additional references: EAACR 1978; Goodburn 1979, 326

Roman: excavations immediately east of Friar's Walk (Site 46) revealed a number of Roman pits and wells, suggesting the site was occupied during the Roman military period and also the 4th century AD. ***Later medieval***: several late 13th-century rubbish pits were excavated, presumably indicating some medieval development along Holloway Street after the foundation of the nearby extra-mural Franciscan friary in the early 13th century.

Albany Road

- 1978
- Location: extra-mural
- EAPIT Site number: 66
- City HER number: 66
- Additional references: EAACR 1984; Blaylock 1996; 2000

Later medieval/post-medieval: excavations south of the river Exe revealed the 16th/17th-century bronze bell and cauldron foundry run by the Birdall family, along with the remains of a medieval building and a prehistoric or Roman river channel. Also see sites 79, 143 and 171.

Flowerpot Lane

- 1978
- Location: extra-mural
- EAPIT Site number: 67
- City HER number: 67

No details of this site are listed in the EAACRs, while the HER reports that no archive can be found and the EAAP only has a list of small finds. The work on this site has since been superseded by large-scale excavations in 1986 (Site 85).

Queen Street, 22 Goldsmith Street and 211–219 High Street

- 1978
- Location: *insula* X/XXI/XXVI, cohort blocks A and C
- EAPIT Site number: 68
- City HER number: 68; 966
- Additional references: EAACR 1978; 1979; Goodburn 1979, 324; Bidwell 1980, 54–5, 73; Grew *et al.* 1980, 389; Bedford and Salvatore 1993c; Henderson 1999

A series of works in advance of the Marks and Spencer development was primarily focussed on 22 Goldsmith Street with a watching brief at 211–219 High Street but the site was called Queen Street to avoid confusion with Goldsmith Street III. ***Roman fortress/town***: metalled street surfaces and post-trenches of timber buildings dating to the Roman military and early civil periods were recorded as well as a late 2nd-century AD stone-lined well. The well contained waterlogged deposits that included a wooden bowl, barrel staves, leather, rush matting and a wooden comb. ***Saxo-Norman***: a series of 11th and 12th-century pits was excavated. They contained good samples of faunal remains and pottery. ***Later medieval***: large rectangular 13th-century pit and a well contained jugs and cooking pots dating to *c.* 1300. The rear of the site was a garden in the later medieval period, cut by early 16th-century gardening trenches.

North Gate

- 1978
- Location: city defences
- EAPIT Site number: 69
- City HER number: 69

- Additional references: Goodburn 1978, 459; 1979, 324–6; EAACR Report 1979; Salvatore 1993a; Blaylock 1995; Exeter Archaeology 2005

Late prehistoric: a buried ground surface below the later Roman defences yielded an Iron Age coin of Durotrigian type. ***Roman fortress***: deposits of possible Early Roman military date were discovered along with a gully that may have drained the legionary fortress ditch. ***Roman town***: the town walls and rampart banks were encountered. ***Later medieval:*** sections of the medieval town wall and a stone-capped drain extended along its face, cutting into the Roman military ditch. This area saw further investigation in 2010 (Site 164).

Good Shepherd Hospital

- 1979
- Location: extra-mural
- EAPIT Site number: 70
- City HER number: 70
- Additional references: EAACR 1979; Grew *et al.* 1980, 389

Roman: Although all Roman deposits had been removed by terracing in the 16th century, the presence of a few human bones in the topsoil suggests that there may have been an inhumation cemetery here. ***Post-medieval***: a pit and ditch infilled *c.* 1610–30 were also found.

Lower Coombe Street

- 1979
- Location: *insula* XXXIII/XXXV/XXXVI
- EAPIT Site number: 71
- City HER number: 71
- Additional references: Grew *et al.* 1980, 389; EAACR 1981

Roman: foundation trenches were dug along the NW side of the Combe Valley behind the city wall, and while no buildings were located the excavation revealed deposits that provided further information about the depth and form of the Coombe Valley in the Early Roman period.

41–42 High Street (Fig. 2.3)

- 1980
- Location: *insula* XIV
- EAPIT Site number: 72
- City HER number: 72

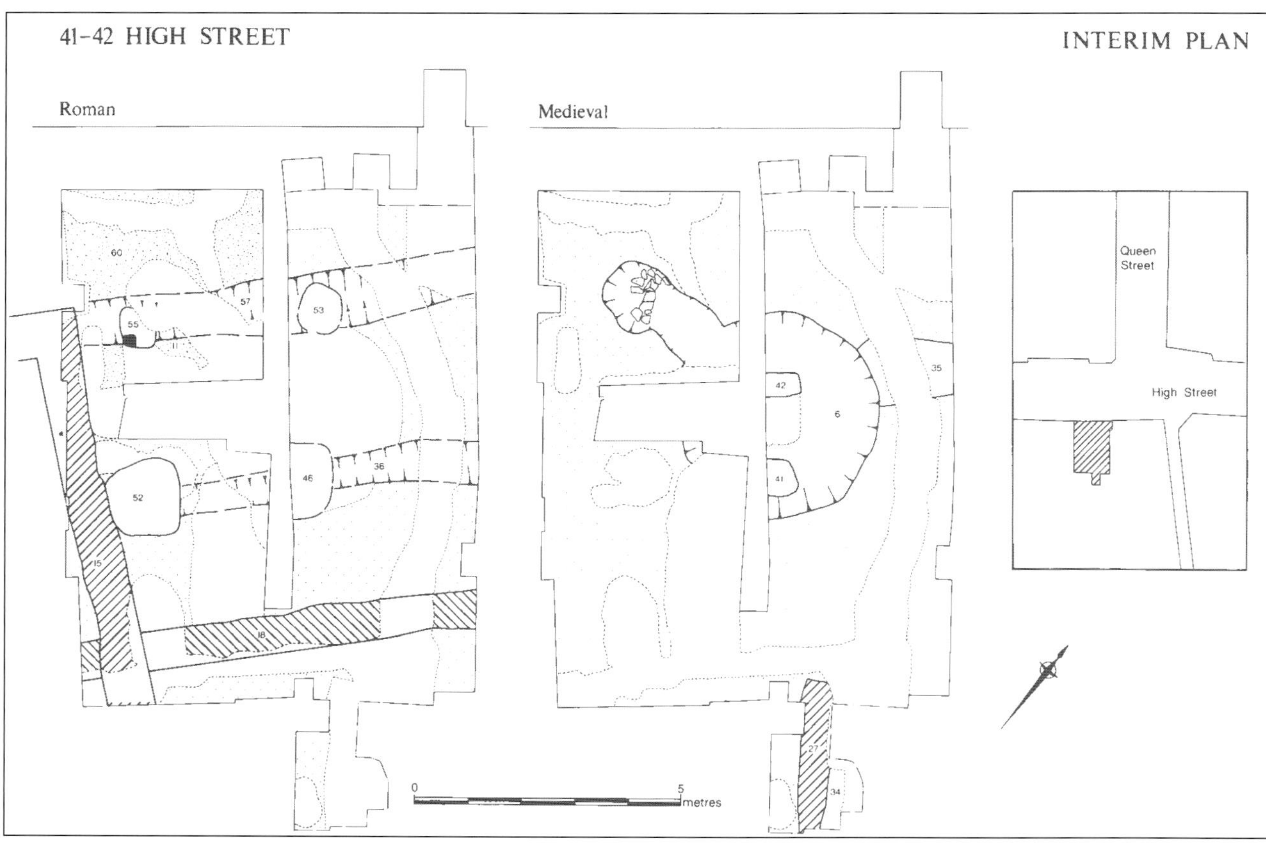

Fig. 2.3 Plan of the Roman and medieval features at 41–42 High Street (EAACR 1980)

- Additional references: EAACR 1980; Grew *et al.* 1981, 358; Youngs and Clark 1981, 207; Bedford and Salvatore 1993a

Roman fortress: the SE side of the *via decumana* was located along with a stone-built wall which was originally interpreted as having supported the aqueduct supplying the legionary bath-house (although this wall may represent a post-military building). ***Roman town***: several pits and a wall from the Roman civil period probably mark the line of a street, although no trace of the street itself was found. ***Later medieval***: a probable 13th-century limekiln (Fig. 2.3) appears to have been a short-lived venture located on an otherwise vacant plot. A medieval stone-lined industrial pit was also found.

Bartholomew Street East (EAPIT 1, Fig. 5.6)

- 1980–1
- Location: *insula* I, cohort block G
- EAPIT Site number: 73
- City HER number: 73
- Additional references: EAACR 1980; 1981; Grew *et al.* 1981, 358; Youngs and Clark 1981, 207; Bidwell 1980, 53; Salvatore and Simpson 1992

Roman fortress: five buildings within the *praetentura* of the legionary fortress were identified, three of which were clearly barracks, while the other two remained unidentified. Internal partitions within the barracks appear to have been removed while the buildings were still in use. Traces of a street and a post-trench, presumably indicating the remains of another Roman military building, were also recorded. ***Roman town***: this building was succeeded by a timber structure of the Early Roman civil period and then a stone building of the later civil period that was destroyed by fire; stakeholes were found cut into the fire debris overlying the Roman street level. Resurfacing of the military street was recorded. ***Later medieval***: the Roman levels were overlain by post-Roman dark soil, cut through by 12th and 13th-century rubbish pits, suggesting the area was occupied by domestic tenements. One particular pit, probably pre-dating *c.* 1300, contained a mould used to cast a bronze cauldron, providing the first evidence for a medieval bronze foundry in this part of Exeter. During the later medieval period, the site was occupied by gardens and kitchens of St Nicholas Priory and the remains of a large 14th-century timber building was recorded; it was replaced by a masonry building belonging to the Priory.

Lucky Lane/Colleton Crescent/Friars Gate (EAPIT 1, Fig. 8.6)

- 1980–1
- Location: extra-mural
- EAPIT Site number: 74
- City HER number: 74
- Additional references: EAACR 1980; 1981; Grew *et al.* 1981, 351; Youngs and Clark 1981, 187–8; 1982, 177, 180; Bedford and Salvatore 1994a; Orme 2016

Roman fortress: four Roman pits probably date to the military period. ***Later medieval***: the bulk of the features related to the remains of buildings associated with the 13th-century Franciscan Friary, principally the church and an attached chapel. Nearly all of the Friary's walls had been robbed of their stone at the Dissolution although the foundation trenches revealed the dimensions of the buildings. Some of the local medieval bricks found in demolition layers associated with the Dissolution are the oldest known in Exeter.

Friernhay Street (Figs 2.4, 3.6 and 3.11)

- 1981
- Location: *insulae* I, VI, cohort block H
- EAPIT Site number: 75
- City HER number: 75
- Additional references: EAACR 1979; 1981; 1984; Cherry 1982, 218–20; Rankov *et al.* 1982, 382–3; Youngs and Clark 1982, 180; Straker *et al.* 1984; Henderson 1988; 1999; Bedford and Salvatore 1992b

Roman fortress: a 55 m stretch of the fortress's SW defences was investigated where evidence of two defensive ditches (the outer of early civilian date), the rampart, and two wooden interval towers was recorded. The rampart was constructed of compacted clays, probably excavated during the digging of the first defensive ditch and was *c.* 4.6 m wide at its base and supported by a corduroy of timber strapping. Two interval towers were located *c.* 30 m apart with the most complete (that at the NW) being about 3 m². Two timber *intervallum* buildings were recorded fronting on to the fortress's main perimeter street (*via sagularis*) and which were later demolished and replaced by a series of ovens. The *via sagularis* was resurfaced at least once during the military period and remained in use into the early town; it was flanked by a water pipe along its SW perimeter. A post-trench represented the end *contubernium* of a barrack lying adjacent to the fortress's *via praetoria*. A V-shaped ditch at right angles to the outer defensive ditch represents part of an annexe on the SW exterior of the fortress (see also Figs 3.6 and 3.11). ***Roman town***: in contrast to the military period, remains of the Roman civil phase were found to be sparse although the *via sagularis* was resurfaced, forming part of the early town's street grid. A timber framed house of the early town was also recorded. In the later town, the former *via sagularis* went out of use and was replaced by a new street *c.* 30 m to the SW and a masonry building was constructed across the old street, while a stone boundary wall cut across the former defences of the fortress

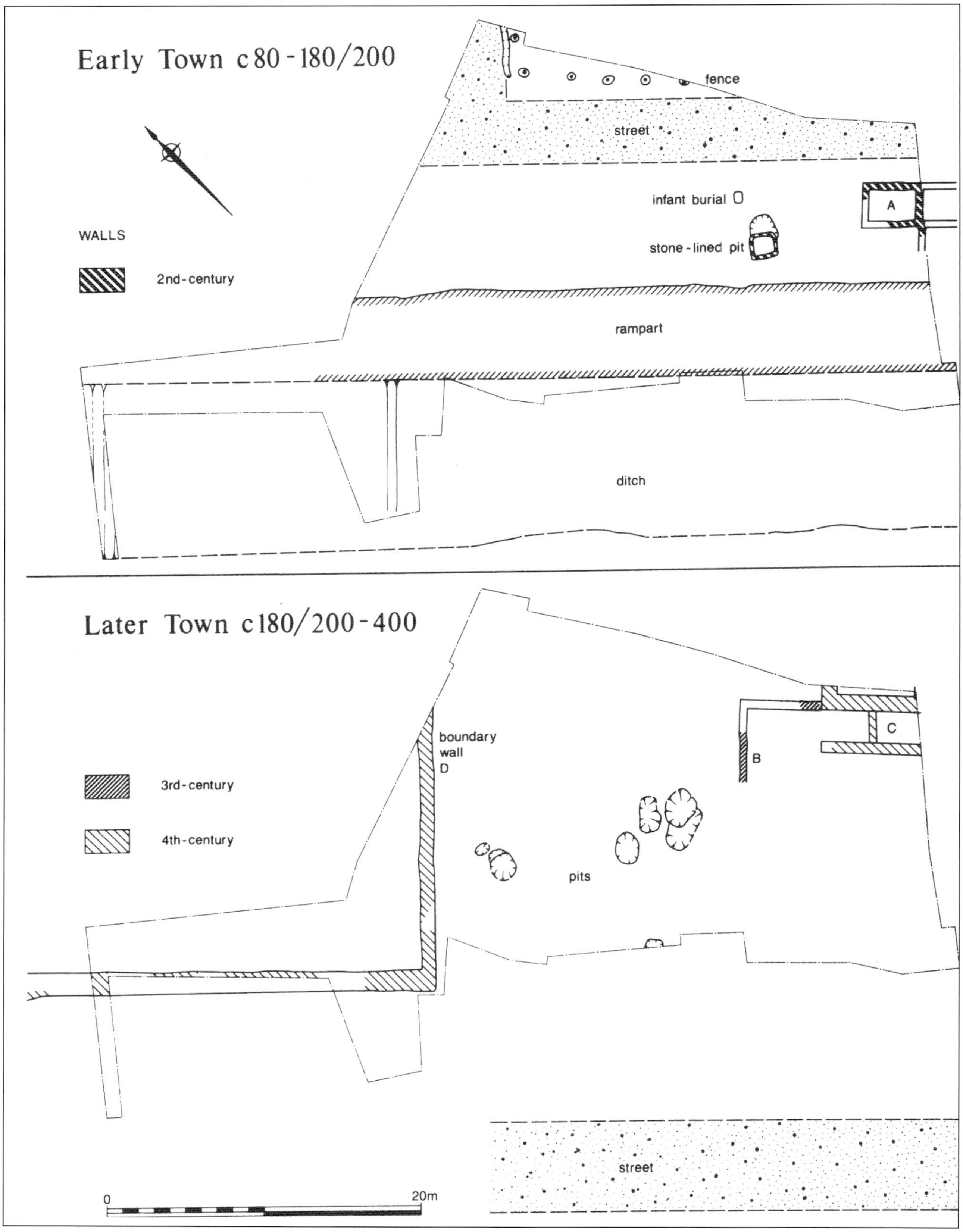

Fig. 2.4 Plan of Roman civil features at Friernhay Street (EAACR 1981)

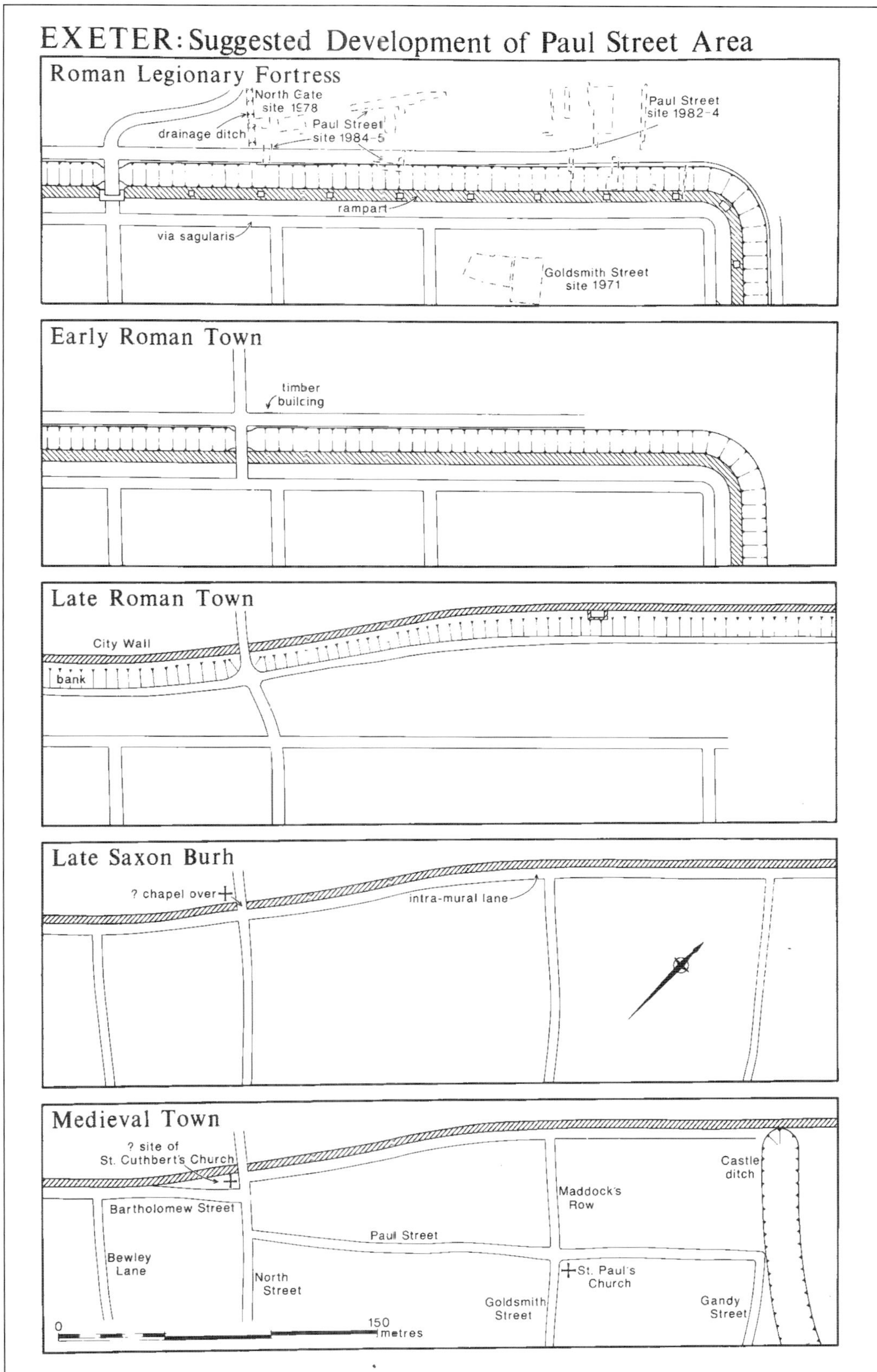

Fig. 2.5 Development of the Paul Street site (EAACR 1984)

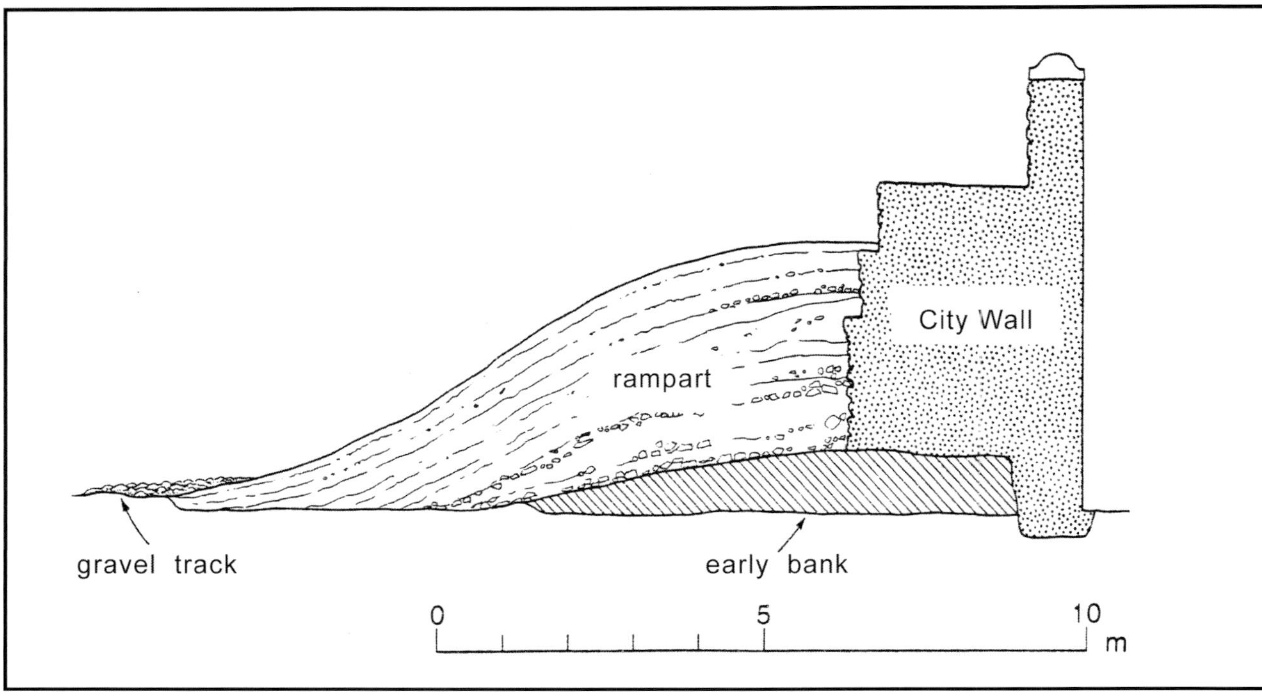

Fig. 2.6 Section through Paul Street's town defences (EAACR 1984)

and early town (Fig. 2.4). ***Later medieval***: by the 12th century, Friernhay Street had developed as a hollow way and eventually became infilled with dumps of loam and layers of metalling in the 14th and 15th centuries. The street frontage was probably not built up until the 14th century when a building with a terraced gravel floor and cob walls was erected. The site seems to have lain vacant for at least part of the 15th century, before a three-room house was built *c.* 1500.

Paul Street (Figs 2.5 and 2.6; and see EAPIT 1, Figs 6.10 and 8.29)

- 1981–5
- Location: *insula* IV/V, city defences and intra-mural
- EAPIT Site number: 76
- City HER number: 76
- Additional references: EAACR 1982; 1983; 1984; 1985; 1987; Egan 1983, 199; Frere *et al.* 1983, 320–3; Henderson 1983; 1984, 1–13; 1985b, 24–9; Youngs *et al.* 1984, 216; Frere *et al.* 1985, 303–5; Bedford and Salvatore 1993g; Blaylock 1995; 1996, 72–82; 2015, 271–308

Roman fortress: several stretches of the fortress's NW defences were recorded for the first time indicating that the fortress (and early town) were *c.* 1.6 ha larger than previously thought (Figs 2.5 and 2.6). ***Roman town***: evidence of a stone interval tower abutting the Late Roman town wall was recorded, along with a 2nd/3rd-century AD intra-mural street running parallel to the old fortress ditch: it is unclear whether this street ran around the entire circuit, although it was subsequently seen at Site 164. A timber building and timber bridge perhaps representing a temporary aqueduct were dated to the Early Roman town. ***Early medieval/ Saxo-Norman***: a probable early medieval boundary ditch was located running at right angles to Paul Street, while a layer of post-Roman dark soil was also recorded, sealed by a substantial layer of clay. ***Later medieval***: the medieval pits included a well lined with two superimposed casks whose heads had been removed, the lower one in an excellent state of preservation. ***Post-medieval***: a major assemblage of early 16th-century vessel glass was recovered, possibly representing the stock of a glass-seller. A bell foundry of *c.* 1625–1720, together with its workshops, furnace and casting pits, was recorded; the associated house on the street frontage lay outside the area of excavation.

King William Street

- 1983
- Location: extra-mural
- EAPIT Site number: 77
- City HER number: 77
- Additional references: EAACR 1984; Youngs *et al.* 1984, 215–16; Nenk *et al.* 1992, 209–11; Stoyle 2014

Later medieval: in 1931, authors of an archaeological survey of Exeter's underground passages had suggested that the line of Exeter's pre-14th-century aqueduct had tapped St Sidwell's Well and entered the city near the corner of Well Street and York Street. The King William Street excavation was therefore undertaken to investigate this putative Norman aqueduct. A deep trench *c.* 1.1 m wide and 3.25 m deep, with a clay-lined bottom, represented the medieval aqueduct predicted in 1931 but the pipe had been robbed.

St Nicholas Priory (EAPIT 1, Fig. 8.7)

- 1983–4
- Location: *insula* VI, cohort block H
- EAPIT Site number: 78
- City HER number: 78
- Additional references: EAACR 1984; Allan and Henderson 1984, 14–18; Youngs *et al.* 1984, 216; Bedford and Salvatore 1992a; Allan 1999a; 2019

Roman fortress: the wall-trenches of a pair of barracks within the legionary fortress were recorded. The discovery of these barracks represented a major advance in the understanding of the plan of the fortress and for the first time indicated that it could have easily accommodated a full legion (traces of these barracks were subsequently recorded at Site 107). ***Roman town***: two phases of timber buildings were constructed over the military demolition layer. One had been burnt. ***Early medieval***: the Roman layers were overlain by post-Roman dark soils. ***Later medieval***: parts of the W end of the priory church of St Nicholas, including the earliest west front, were revealed, along with the ground plan of a massive 14th-century western tower. Robbing of these walls took place at the time of the Dissolution.

Albany Road

- 1984
- Location: extra-mural
- EAPIT Site number: 79
- City HER number: 79
- Additional references: EAACR 1984; Henderson 1984, 28–36; Egan 1985, 182–3; Youngs *et al.* 1986, 129; Blaylock 1996; 2000; 2015, 271–308

Post-medieval: excavations S of the Exe Bridge revealed extensive evidence for bronze casting in the late 16th and early 17th century (the 17th-century bell-foundry at Paul Street (Site 76) was the direct successor of the Albany Road foundry). The immediate area was further investigated at Site 171.

Alphington Street/Shooting Marsh Stile

- 1984
- Location: extra-mural
- EAPIT Site number: 80
- City HER number: 80
- Additional references: EAACR 1985; Egan 1985, 188–9; Henderson 1985a, 1–18; Levitan 1985; Youngs *et al.* 1986, 128

Roman: the earliest levels on this site on the southern banks of the Exe consisted of coarse river gravels containing fragments of Roman tile. A scarp along the NE side of the site may represent the furthest point reached by the main river channel when it shifted back towards the St Thomas side, probably in a single catastrophic event during a major flood during the Saxo-Norman period. ***Saxo-Norman***: by the mid-11th century, a mill leat crossed the site on a line roughly parallel with Alphington Street. A small strip of marsh within the northern corner of the site was probably reclaimed with spoil derived from the excavation of the leat. ***Later medieval***: by the 12th or 13th century a hollow roadway crossed this area which was eventually filled in with layers of gravel metalling in the 14th and 15th centuries. A building situated between the leat and the road, with one wall forming a revetment to the leat, was interpreted as a mill.

Cricklepit Street

- 1987–9
- Location: city wall
- EAPIT Site number: 81
- City HER number: 81
- Additional references: EAACR 1987; 1989; Youngs *et al.* 1988, 239; Frere *et al.* 1990a, 350; Simpson 1993

Roman town: excavations in an area adjacent to Site 48 revealed a footing of the Roman town wall *c.* 3–3.5 m outside the line of the present city wall. ***?Roman town/later medieval***: *c.* 9 m of wall face was exposed standing to a height of almost 2 m, although its function and date was unclear; it may represent the Roman town wall as originally built, which collapsed and was rebuilt *c.* 1400, or it may represent buttressing or reinforcement of a medieval area at the foot of the wall at some time after its construction.

Bradninch Place

- 1985
- Location: city wall and defences
- EAPIT Site number: 82
- City HER number: 82
- Additional references: EAACR 1986

Roman town: a small excavation next to the city wall exposed the wall face and 'herring bone' core. Rampart material was also recorded.

Exe Street

- 1985–6
- Location: extra-mural
- EAPIT Site number: 83
- City HER number: 83
- Additional references: EAACR 1986; Simpson 1987, 58–66; Youngs *et al.* 1987, 121; Egan 1988, 202–4; Frere *et al.* 1988, 474

Roman: excavation outside the Roman fortress and town on the main road leading to the North Gate revealed numerous ditches, quarry pits, a late 2nd-century AD timber building, and two 1st-century AD cremations and a 2nd or 3rd-century AD inhumation. ***Early medieval/ later medieval***: it has been suggested that the area outside the North Gate may have served as a market place in the early medieval and/or Norman period as the road appears to have been relatively wide. By the 13th century it had become built up with houses, and some late 13th/early 14th-century pottery was recovered, although the earliest foundations uncovered dated from the 16th century.

The Quay House

- 1985–6
- Location: extra-mural
- EAPIT Site number: 84
- City HER number: 84
- Additional references: DAS Newsletter 1986, 11–12; EAACR 1986; Egan 1986, 356–60; 1988, 204–6; Henderson *et al.* 1987, 1–19; Henderson 1990; 1991b; Bedford 1995

Post-medieval: a sequence of successive quays and warehouse foundations spanning a period of at least 500 years was recorded, the earliest being the Elizabethan quay built in 1564–7.

Flowerpot Lane

- 1986–7
- Location: extra-mural
- EAPIT Site number: 85
- City HER number: 85
- Additional references: EAACR 1986; 1987; Henderson 1987, 53–4; Frere *et al.* 1988, 474; Ponsford 1992, 115–6; Stoyle 1995

Later prehistoric/Roman: a curving length of ditch, presumably later prehistoric in date, was succeeded by two phases of straight ditches flanking a trackway leading towards the river. One ditch produced sherds of late 1st or early 2nd-century AD pottery. ***Later medieval***: the earliest medieval features are 12th–13th century ditches, believed to be parts of a small rectangular ditched enclosure of the estate known as the Prebend of Hayes that was created in the late 11th or early 12th century to support one of four prebendaries attached to St. Mary's Chapel in Exeter Castle. A house is documented on the site of Hayes Barton from the later 13th century. Three or four phases of boundary ditches were observed dating to the 13th–15th centuries, and a number of postholes are likely to represent hedge lines. In the late 15th century, a large non-domestic building, believed to have been a barn, occupied the eastern corner of a yard bounded by cob walls. ***Post-medieval***: in the early 16th century, the ground level over the whole site was raised up to 0.5 m by means of an extensive spread of dumped alluvium, much of it dug from a series of ditches forming a moat. The earliest structure within this enclosure was a rectangular cob building which became the hall of Hayes Barton. The site was destroyed in the Civil War. It had previously been investigated in 1978 (Site 67).

Upper Paul Street

- 1986
- Location: *insula* IV/V/XX/XXV
- EAPIT Site number: 86
- City HER number: 86
- Additional references: EAACR 1986; Frere *et al.* 1987, 343; Henderson and Holbrook 1987, 5; Bedford and Salvatore 1993f

Roman fortress: the truncated top of the NW corner of the ditch of the legionary fortress was exposed immediately below the modern street. This enabled the size of the fortress to be estimated at 16.6 ha. ***Later Roman town:*** A wall of a later Roman stone house was also seen below the modern street level.

Castle Ditch and Bradninch Place

- 1986
- Location: *insula* IV/V/XX/XXV
- EAPIT Site number: 87
- City HER number: 87
- Additional references: EAACR 1986; Weddell 1987a, 52; Youngs *et al.* 1987, 120–1

Norman/later medieval: the position and depth of the ditch of the outer ward of Exeter Castle were established in two boreholes. It was 4.1 m below the modern ground surface, which was thought to be roughly equivalent to the early medieval ground level at the outer lip of the ditch. The ditch was recorded as having partially silted up and then backfilled with clay from a single source, probably the castle's rampart. Pottery from this infill dates from the 12th and 13th centuries. The ditch and rampart were also observed at Site 157.

Magdalen Street

- 1986–8
- Location: city defences and extra-mural
- EAPIT Site number: 88
- City HER number: 88
- Additional references: EAACR 1986; 1987; 1988; 1989; Frere *et al.* 1988, 473; Egan 1990, 161–3; Stoyle 1995

Excavations provided a comprehensive picture of the sequence of defensive features outside the city wall from the later Roman period to the Civil War. ***Roman fortress***: the Roman military buildings located in 1973–4 and 1978 at the top of Holloway Street (Sites 50 and 65) did not extend as far as this site, and instead the only Early Roman feature was a well. ***Roman town***: traces of the town's defensive ditches (previously identified in Site 58) were revealed. ***Saxo-Norman***: a *c.* 200 m long stretch of Saxo-Norman defensive ditch was recorded (it was seen subsequently in Sites 90 and 163). Pottery from the upper fill of this ditch suggests that it was filled in during the late 12th century. ***Later medieval***: houses were built over the line of the ditch next to the Magdalen Street frontage from the early 13th century. A sizeable V-shaped ditch was recorded, which cut through the remains of medieval houses and which contained early 15th-century pottery. It may have been a defensive feature at the time of the French raids at the beginning of the 15th century, or it may simply have been a large drainage ditch. Whatever the case, the presence of this ditch probably implies a period in the 15th century when the Magdalen Street and South Street frontages were not built up. A broad, shallow hollow way was also recorded. ***Post-medieval***: the hollow way was cut through by the ditch of a Civil War 'flanking' battery, probably installed early in 1643 to protect the approach to the South Gate. The ditch was 9 m wide and at least 2.3 m deep. Both features were buried by spoil from the large Civil War trenches dug later in 1643.

St Catherine's Almshouses (EAPIT 1, Figs 6.14, 6.15 and 8.9)

- 1987–8
- Location: *insulae* XXII and XXIII
- EAPIT Site number: 89
- City HER number: 89
- Additional references: EAACR 1987; 1989; Frere *et al.* 1988, 473; 1989, 313–4; Holbrook *et al.* 1989, 43–52; 1990; Henderson 1991a, 73–83; Parker and Collings 2002, 75–205

Roman fortress: the earliest phase of activity was the rampart, a ditch, and a timber interval tower on the eastern side of the Roman legionary fortress. ***Roman town***: the early civilian ditch remained open until the later 2nd century AD and was probably infilled when the enlarged town's earthen defences were constructed *c.* AD 160–80. While the outer ditch was still open, a new street was laid out immediately outside it and this was resurfaced on a number of occasions. The street remained in service after the filling of the ditch, which was directly overlain by a substantial timber building that was modified and rebuilt on at least one occasion before becoming derelict, when the whole site was covered with dumps of domestic refuse. The date of this street, first seen in 1945 (Site 19), is not clear: it may have been an extra-mural street of the fortress or the early town. A large Late Roman stone town house was constructed on the site and is known to have had at least two ranges. A 3 m length of corridor mosaic was uncovered, the most impressive recorded in Exeter, and along with Lady Fox's discovery of two mosaics in the same building in 1945–7 (Site 19), and the presence of decorated wall plaster found in demolition layers, clearly indicate the wealth of this Late Roman building (EAPIT 1, Fig. 6.15). ***Late Saxon/Norman:*** the earliest medieval activity is represented by the robber trenches of the Roman wall foundations, which contained 11th and 12th-century pottery. ***Later medieval***: in the 13th or early 14th century a large hall-house was erected on the tenement to the west of the almshouses, with some of its walls still standing to a considerable height. Prior to this excavation, it had been assumed that these walls were constructed in the 16th century when the Annuellars' College was established, but it is now clear that the college was created by the conversion of earlier buildings. The best-preserved structure within the almshouses complex is the chapel, a rectangular two-storey structure which survives to roof level as a shell and appears to date entirely to the 15th century (EAPIT 1, Fig. 8.9).

ABC Cinema

- 1987–8
- Location: extra-mural and city defences
- EAPIT Site number: 90
- City HER number: 90
- Additional references: EAACR 1987; 1988; Egan 1989, 29–32; Stoyle, 1995; Quinnell 2017

Late prehistoric: a fragment of a prehistoric structure was recorded, perhaps part of an Iron Age ring gulley. ***Roman***: 'one or two Roman features were located' but the earliest substantial remains date from the medieval period. ***Saxo-Norman***: the large ditch first discovered at Magdalen Street (Site 88) was encountered here in a position which demonstrated that Longbrook Street probably existed in the Late Saxon period, though the straightness of the street may suggest that it could be Roman in origin. It was further encountered at Site 163. ***Later medieval***: the site is crossed by the medieval Underground Passages and further progress was made in elucidating their history. ***Post-medieval***: several Civil War trenches of the type previously encountered outside the South Gate were found.

Bowhill House, Dunsford Hill

- 1987–93
- Location: extra-mural (outside area mapped in Fig. 2.2)
- EAPIT Site number: 91
- City HER number: not applicable (outside City HER area)
- Additional references: EAACR 1988; 1989; 1990; 1992; 1994; 1995; 1996; Blaylock 1991a; 1991b; 2004; Blaylock and Norton 1991; Hall and Blaylock 1991; 1994; Nenk *el al* 1991, 141; 254–5; Ponsford 1993, 214; Stead *et al.* 1994

Later medieval: a detailed survey of Bowhill House and several excavations were undertaken in order to understand its structural history in advance of its restoration by English Heritage and have been fully published (Blaylock 2004).

Guy's Allotments

- 1988; 1996
- Location: extra-mural (outside area mapped in Fig. 2.2)
- EAPIT Site number: 92
- City HER number: 92
- Additional references: EAACR 1989; 1996; Reed and Sage 1996

A small trial excavation on a disused allotment near the western edge of the floodplain of St Thomas revealed a sequence of alluvial deposits, including waterlogged plant remains. Trenching and augering in 1996 located an early river channel running through the site.

Haven Banks

- 1988
- Location: extra-mural
- EAPIT Site number: 93
- City HER number: 93
- Additional references: EAACR 1989

Post-medieval: A large artificial river channel associated with the construction of a new wharf at Exeter Quay in 1698–1701 was found.

Acorn Roundabout

- 1988–9
- Location: extra-mural
- EAPIT Site number: 94
- City HER number: 94
- Additional references: EAACR 1989; Frere *et al.* 1989, 314; Stoyle 1995; Bedford 1998; Salvatore 2001, 127; forthcoming

Prehistoric: three small sherds of Bronze Age pottery were found. ***Roman fortress***: features of probable Roman military date included a series of large circular pits, a group of postholes which may indicate a rectangular structure, the corner of another building and its associated fence line. These features lay to the north of an extra-mural military compound and were separated from it by the road leading to the fortress's south-east gate. ***Saxo-Norman***: a pit (tentatively interpreted as an oven), two ditches, and a group of stake and postholes, possibly relating to a structure, were dated to between the 10th–11th and 13th centuries. ***Later medieval***: a large number of rubbish and cesspits were dug including at what was probably the rear of a tenement fronting onto Magdalen Street: by the 16th or 17th century this area formed part of a Magdalen Street property. ***Post-medieval***: Civil War defences in this area consisted of two ditches running parallel with each other in a zigzagging pattern in front of the South Gate. After the Civil War the defensive ditches were infilled and a number of buildings constructed.

St Loyes Chapel

- 1988–90
- Location: extra-mural (outside area mapped in Fig. 2.2)
- EAPIT Site number: 95
- City HER number: not applicable (outside City HER area)
- Additional references: EAACR 1989; 1991; Nenk *et al.* 1991, 35

Later medieval: the 13th or early 14th-century St Loyes Chapel, *c.* 2.5 km E of Exeter in the Ludwell Valley, was found to overlie alluvial and colluvial valley-bottom deposits of considerable depth which probably derived from preceding medieval cultivation upslope. The chapel was examined in September 1990 prior to structural repairs and repointing, while the trial excavations in 1988 had located the position of its missing north-western wall.

South Gate (EAPIT 1, Figs 6.11 and 6.12)

- 1988–89
- Location: city wall and defences
- EAPIT Site number: 96
- City HER number: 96
- Additional references: Frere *et al.* 1990a, 348–50; EAACR 1994; Burnham *et al.* 1994, 286; Henderson 2001

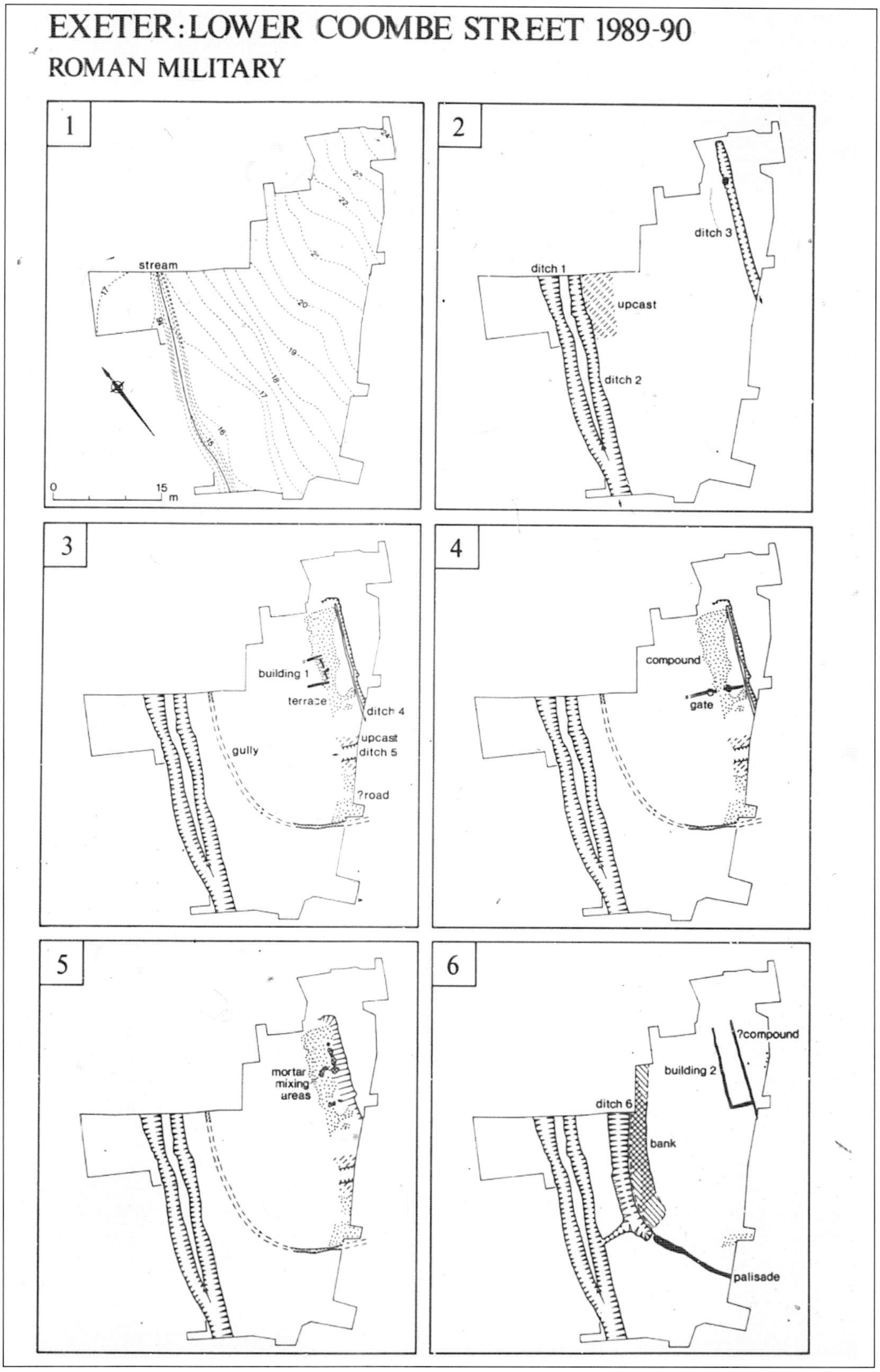

Fig. 2.7 The development of the Lower Coombe Street site during the Roman military period (Stead and Hall, fig. 6)

Roman fortress: the earliest feature was the Roman road leading towards Topsham from the SE gate of the legionary fortress. ***Roman town***: excavations allowed for a greater understanding of the development of the city wall and defences which had previously been investigated in this area during 1964–5 (Site 36). The earlier road was resurfaced on at least three occasions before the late 2nd AD century. During the late 2nd century AD, a defensive earth bank, presumably associated with an external ditch, was thrown up on the line of the later Roman town wall; where well-preserved, the bank was up to 12 m wide at its base, though its height barely exceeded 1.5 m. A timber gate was constructed across the Topsham road and probably consisted of a pair of towers; this was replaced by a stone gate in the late 2nd or early 3rd century AD. ***Early medieval/Saxo-Norman***: the Roman stone gate was replaced by another stone gate during the Late Saxon or Norman period, while a *c.* 5 m wide intra-mural trackway was constructed on top of the Roman defensive bank probably in the late 9th century. ***Later medieval***: a late medieval barbican is recorded, although its precise date of construction is unclear.

Lower Coombe Street (Fig. 2.7)

- 1989–90
- Location: *insula* XXXIII/XXXV/XXXVI, city defences
- EAPIT Site number: 97
- City HER number: 97
- Additional references: EAACR 1990; 1991; Frere *et al.* 1990a, 350; Frere 1991, 281–3; Stead and Hall 1991; Henderson 2001; Salvatore forthcoming

Roman fortress: this site lay 110 m SE of the Roman legionary fortress, but inside the southern corner of the later Roman/medieval city wall. The earliest remains formed part of a large Roman military compound occupied at the same time as the legionary fortress, with the SW corner of the compound likely to have been located at Lower Coombe Street (Fig. 2.7). However, its boundary features do not conform to the usual Roman military enclosures of similar date in Britain, *i.e.* a continuous ditch, or ditches, fronting a rampart; rather, the compound enclosure seen here was bounded by several different types of enclosure features, not all of which are contemporary. ***Roman town***: fragments of four timber buildings were found sealed beneath the later town's defensive rampart. No finds were recovered, though they post-date the military remains as their foundations cut through a layer of loam that sealed the earlier military enclosure. ***Saxo-Norman/later medieval***: a colluvial deposit up to 1 m deep contained considerable amounts of 10th/11th-century pottery and appears to have been cultivated as ridge and furrow. Two pits provided the only hint of habitation in this area in the 11th/12th century. ***Post-medieval***: one of the Coombe Street tenements was the site of a brickworks in the late 17th century.

Cricklepit Mill

- 1989
- Location: extra-mural
- EAPIT Site number: 98
- City HER number: 98
- Additional references: EAACR 1989; Henderson 1996; Parker 1996; Henderson and Collings 1997

Later medieval: two infilled back channels of the River Exe flowed to the N and S of a narrow, low-lying alluvial 'island' known as Millhay which is first documented in the 14th century. ***Post-medieval***: detailed surveys were undertaken of Cricklepit Mill's standing buildings, which were probably constructed in 1689 on the site of a mill first documented in the late 12th century, and the Dryhouse (a cloth-drying shed) erected in 1731. The mill's leat channels and derelict wheel were also partially recorded.

Castle Gardens

- 1990
- Location: *insula* IV/V/XX/XXV
- EAPIT Site number: 99
- City HER number: 99
- Additional references: EAACR 1990; Blaylock 1991c; Nenk *et al.* 1991, 141

Norman: trial trenches and fabric recording were undertaken at the S corner of the Inner Ward of Exeter Castle. A trench on the inside face of the wall revealed Norman footings and the top of the bank, providing the first opportunity to examine the relationship between the two. The wall may have been as wide as 3 m and was built of 'trap' stone rubble in a brown sandy mortar which is typical of Norman buildings in the city. The primary defences were probably completed around the 1070s and were then strengthened by the addition of a stone curtain wall. Much of the fabric of the standing wall in this area dates from the 19th century or later. The Eastern Angle Tower was also excavated which comprised a semicircular drum with shallow pilaster buttress made of volcanic stone ashlar and occasional white sandstone blocks. The tower is likely to date from the late 12th or 13th century.

Cathedral School

- 1991
- Location: *insula* XXXIX
- EAPIT Site number: 100
- City HER number: 100
- Additional references: EAACR 1992

Roman fortress: The front of the legionary fortress rampart was located in two places, enabling the line of the Early Roman defences to be precisely plotted in this area. The foundation pit for a timber corner-post belonging to an interval tower was also recorded. ***Roman town***: at the front of the rampart were a series of rubbish layers infilling the early civilian ditch. These were similar in appearance to corresponding deposits, dating from the period *c*. AD 160–180, recorded at other sites around the circuit of the defences. A short length of SW–NE wall, predating these rubbish layers, was interpreted as a revetment to the rampart and was traced for 1.8 m before turning NW and cutting at right angles across the rampart and has been interpreted as an interval tower. This possible tower overlaid the fill of the fortress ditch. Walls of a Late Roman house were traceable over much of the area (first seen at Site 12), and at one point a long narrow flue and stoking pit belonging to some form of Late Roman furnace (perhaps a corn-drying kiln) was located. ***Early medieval***: a boundary ditch – said to be early medieval and running on an alignment apparently intermediate between those of the Cathedral and The Close – cut through the Roman features. ***Later medieval***: this boundary feature was overlain by the late medieval rear range of 15 The Close, formerly the Cathedral Chancellor's house.

Danes Castle (EAPIT 1, Fig. 7.12)

- 1992–3
- Location: extra-mural
- EAPIT Site number: 101
- City HER number: 102
- Additional references: Higham and Henderson 2011

Early medieval/Late Saxon: underneath the remains of the castle was a field with remains of ridge and furrow, with a boundary ditch on the same orientation. ***Norman***: the remains of 'Danes Castle' were found preserved beneath a 19th-century reservoir and have been fully published (Higham and Henderson 2011). The circular ditch was *c*. 54 m wide in diameter, while the circular space enclosed by the rampart measured *c*. 16 m in diameter and was devoid of any trace of buildings or occupation debris. The rampart, which was of a simple dump construction formed from upcast derived from the excavation of the ditch, would probably have stood at least 4 m high. On the SW side of the castle, the ditch was interrupted by an unexcavated causeway *c*. 4 m wide which gave access to the site of an unfinished gate tower, set centrally within the body of the rampart. The completed tower would have been *c*. 4 m square, with the corners defined by timber posts set in large postholes. Excavation revealed, however, that only three of these postpits were ever dug, and no traces of post-pipes were found within them, suggesting that the castle was unfinished. It is thought that the castle was constructed during the Anarchy, when King Stephen besieged Baldwin de Redvers, the Earl of Devon, in Rougemont Castle, which lies *c*. 240 m to the S, for three months in 1136. Although there are no known references to Stephen constructing a castle, it seems likely that Danes Castle was built at that time as a temporary fortification (EAPIT, 1 Fig. 7.12).

City Wall, Princesshay

- 1992
- Location: city wall
- EAPIT Site number: 102
- City HER number: 103
- Additional references: EAACR 1992

Roman town: excavations for the insertion of water tanks serving the Princesshay fountain revealed the front of the Roman town wall at a level below the plinth.

Fore Street/High Street British Gas

- 1980: 1994
- Location: *insulae* VII, VIII, IX and X/XXI/XXVI
- EAPIT Site number: 103
- City HER number: 108; 128
- Additional references: EAACR 1981; Burnham *et al.* 1995, 367

Roman town: during a 1980 watching brief, five street layers were recorded belonging to a lane running parallel to the SE side of *insula* VIII *c*. 5 m from the street next to the basilica and forum. The area between the lane and the street was occupied by timber buildings during the 2nd century AD, with the plot perhaps representing an area occupied by a row of shops fronting onto one of the town's principal streets. Several trenches were subsequently dug between 188–212 High Street in 1994. A trench outside 188 High Street revealed a series of layers likely to be associated with successive phases of timber buildings. These were overlain by the remains of a substantial stone building, probably constructed in the 3rd century AD. The remains included an *opus signinum* floor and may be representative of two buildings separated by a passage or possibly a covered corridor which opened onto the street to the SE. A trench outside 211/212 High Street (Marks and Spencer) revealed a complex series of archaeological deposits, including evidence of a substantial 3rd-century AD Roman town house which was in turn located over deposits indicative of several phases of earlier Roman timber buildings. Heavily disturbed probably 3rd-century AD walling was also observed in a trench outside 207 High Street. A further trench at the top of Fore Street revealed Roman levels, including metalling of several Late Roman street surfaces, as well as mortar mixing pits and the possible remains of either Roman civil timber buildings or military deposits. ***Late Saxon/Norman***: evidence of a possible Late Saxon or Norman street or lane was recorded, overlying a deposit of post-Roman dark soil.

Paradise Place

- 1994
- Location: extra-mural
- EAPIT Site number: 104
- City HER number: 110
- Additional references: Burnham *et al.* 1994; EAACR 1994; Ponsford and Jackson 1995

Roman fortress: a mid 1st-century AD ditch which defined the SW side of a military compound lying between the legionary fortress and the Exe floodplain was recorded. ***Post-medieval***: a large Civil War ditch was traced running from the city wall to the floodplain; it was probably dug in 1645.

Cathedral Close

- 1994
- Location: *insulae* XIV, XIX and XXXIX, cohort block B
- EAPIT Site number: 105
- City HER number: 113
- Additional references: Bedford and Hall 1994; Nenk *et al.* 1995, 195; Burnham *et al.* 1995, 365

Roman fortress: A series of small pits were dug *c.* 3 m below the modern street level. The post trenches of two barrack blocks within the legionary fortress were uncovered in one pit. They were infilled with military-period material, probably associated with their demolition. ***Roman town***: the military deposits were sealed by later Roman deposits, including a clay floor and although no associated structures were found, a mid 2nd-century AD well was excavated. ***Early medieval***: the Roman layers were sealed by post-Roman dark soil averaging 0.49 m deep. A roadside ditch and associated metalled street surface were recorded on the same alignment as the modern street. ***Late Saxon?***: a single inhumation cut the dark soil layer; upon excavation it was thought to be Late Saxon in date, but it may have been later medieval. ***Later medieval***: some 12th or 13th-century street surfaces were recorded but medieval deposits had largely been truncated by later activities.

5–7 Palace Gate

- 1994
- Location: *insula* XXXVII
- EAPIT Site number: 106
- City HER number: 118
- Additional references: Burnham *et al.* 1995, 367

Roman: a small excavation revealed Early Roman rubbish layers over a fine pre-Roman colluvial deposit which had accumulated in the upper part of the Coombe Valley on the NE side of Palace Gate. ***?Post medieval***: wall stubs associated with earlier builds within the cellar were also recorded, along with a well.

Friernhay Street/Knapmans Yard/The Mint

- 1994
- Location: *insula* VI, cohort block H
- EAPIT Site number: 107
- City HER number: 119
- Additional references: Hall and Sage 1994; EAACR 1995; Allan 2019

Roman fortress: further traces of the post-trenches of three members in a group of six legionary barracks were recorded (also seen at Site 78). ***Roman town***: overlying the military levels was a light-brown clay soil *c.* 0.25 m thick containing Roman pottery and which was assumed to date from the late 1st and earlier 2nd centuries AD. ***?Early medieval/later medieval***: deposits of humic loam and silt overlay the later Roman deposits but preceded the late medieval church aisle; they may have accumulated over this long period. ***Norman and medieval***: these deposits were cut by trenches marking the robbing of the walls of the late medieval aisle added to the S of the priory nave. No burials were encountered.

Haven Road, Knapps site

- 1994
- Location: extra-mural
- EAPIT Site number: 108
- City HER number: 120
- Additional references: Hall 1994

Excavations revealed traces of a broad palaeochannel (separated from the modern course of the Exe by a shingle bank) which probably represented the main course of the river at some period after the Roman period but prior to the 16th century. Following a shift in the course of the main river channel to the NW, silty deposits accumulated in the old channel, with the earliest likely to be early medieval or later medieval, and the latest dating to the 18th century.

St Nicholas Priory (EAPIT 1, Fig. 8.7)

- 1992
- Location: *insula* VI, cohort block H
- EAPIT Site number: 109
- City HER number: 123
- Additional references: EAACR 1993; Nenk *et al.* 1993; Burnham *et al.* 1994; Allan 1999a; 2019

A trench was dug in Mint Lane outside the N wall of the priory's W range. ***Roman town***: a street aligned NE–SW was flanked by a wall foundation that may be the continuation of a boundary wall discovered at Friernhay Street in 1981 (Site 75). ***Norman***: footings of the late 11th/12th-century N wall of the W range of the priory (also investigated at Sites 41 and 78) were recorded in elevation over the whole length of the building; those of the contemporary N range were recorded in section where they were cut by the trench. At the S end a broad wall footing proved to be that of the N wall of the priory church, while a further wall to the S was the eastward continuation of the footings of a massive 14th-century tower seen in excavations to the west in 1983 (Site 78). All previous plans of the priory had taken the southern limit of the standing W range as the line of the N wall of the church, but this evidence changed this by moving the N wall of the church 2 m further N, confirming that some fabric of the W end of the standing W range is actually part of the church.

161–179 Sidwell Street

- 1991
- Location: extra-mural
- EAPIT Site number: 110
- City HER number: 133
- Additional references: EAACR 1991

Roman fortress/?Roman town: a compacted gravel road surface was recorded in a series of small test trenches over a length of 55 m. It is thought to be the main Roman road leading NE from the East Gate.

St Sidwell's Churchyard

- 1991
- Location: extra-mural
- EAPIT Site number: 111
- City HER number: 134
- Additional references: Knight 1991

Post-medieval: evidence for a spring was found close to St Sidwell's church. Several other springs are known in this area; they were tapped by the city's Roman and medieval aqueducts.

Exeter Quay

- 1988–9
- Location: extra-mural
- EAPIT Site number: 112
- City HER number: 150
- Additional references: Hall 1995

Post-medieval: A quay wall, thought to represent a slip associated with the dock constructed in 1680 and infilled in 1701 (see also Site 84).

18–19 North Street

- 1991; 1999; 2006
- Location: *insula* III
- EAPIT Site number: 113
- City HER number: 159; 15061
- Additional references: EAACR 1992; Parker 1999; Parker *et al.* 2013

Roman fortress: a post-trench of a timber building was recorded, overlain by a layer related to the demolition of the fortress buildings. ***Roman town***: a gravelled surface and a pit contained much burnt material and 2nd-century AD pottery. ***Early medieval***: the Roman deposits were sealed by a layer of dark soil. A single truncated Late Saxon pit was recorded, which appears to have originally been a rectangular feature revetted with two parallel rows of sharpened vertical oak stakes. ***Post-medieval***: a detached kitchen block at the rear of No. 18 connected to the main building by a timber-framed two-storeyed gallery (destroyed by bombing in 1942) was also excavated.

Friars Walk Sewer

- 1979
- Location: extra-mural
- EAPIT Site number: 114
- City HER number: 167
- Additional references: Allan *et al.* 2016

Later medieval: walls and robber trenches of the early 14th-century Franciscan friary were found (also investigated at Sites 45, 50, 65 and 74); a number of burials which appear to have been inside the friary were also recorded.

Market Street/Smythen Street

- 1995; 1998; 2001–2; 2012–14
- Location: *insulae* XI/XII, XV/XVA/XVI/XXXIV, cohort blocks I and J
- EAPIT Site number: 115
- City HER number: 168; 811; 15113
- Additional references: Hall *et al.* 1995; Burnham *et al.* 1996, 435; 2000,424; Gaimster *et al.* 1998, 238–40; Keppie *et al.* 1999, 367; Stead 1999; 2002; Burnham *et al.* 2002; Thomson *et al.* 2014

A series of excavations and watching briefs was undertaken adjacent to the 1931 Smythen Street site (Site 1). ***Roman fortress***: two early military ditches dug immediately prior to the construction of the legionary fortress were recorded, as well as a stretch of fortress street and post-trenches of three *contubernia* within the NE ends of two back-to-back barracks. ***Roman town***: a late 1st-century AD street (resurfaced in the 2nd century), and the mortar floor surfaces of a very substantial Late Roman building were recorded. The area was then covered by a cultivation soil that in turn was sealed by two Late Roman stone buildings: one was at least 38 m long, while to its NW, a second, parallel building range contained a room furnished with a pillar-based hypocaust. A short secondary block, comprising a hypocausted room flanked by a corridor, formed a link between the two ranges. A third building was identified by robber trenches. ***Early medieval***: Roman deposits were overlain by a 1.1 m layer of dark brown loam, representing early medieval dark soils. ***Later medieval***: 58 pits and robber trenches with associated pottery dating from the 11th/12th to the 14th/15th centuries were recorded. They included one pit with an important group of late 13th or early 14th-century pottery including near-complete Saintonge jugs. Walls representing at least two late medieval buildings displaying several constructional phases were also recorded.

51 Bartholomew Street West

- 1995
- Location: *insula* XXX/XXXI
- EAPIT Site number: 116
- City HER number: 158
- Additional references: Bedford and Hall 1995; EAACR 1995

Roman town: a quarry pit was sealed beneath two later Roman metalled surfaces positioned within a terrace and probably associated with the fragmentary remains of two later Roman walls. These walls were robbed sometime after the late 3rd/early 4th century AD, and the robber trench was cut by a pit also containing late 3rd/early 4th-century AD pottery. ***Early medieval/Late Saxon***: post-Roman dark soil covered the whole area, which was cut by a Late Saxon boundary ditch running NE–SW at right angles to Bartholomew Street. ***Later medieval***: several 12th and 13th-century pits were recorded. ***Post-medieval***: there was also a sequence of post-medieval buildings from the 17th to 19th centuries.

Bishop's Palace Garden

- 1939
- Location: *insula* XXXVIII and city wall
- EAPIT Site number: 117
- City HER number: 172
- Additional references: Morris *et al.* 1946

Roman town: a series of trenches behind the city wall provided evidence of the form of the rampart in this area. The excavation was not finished due to the outbreak of the Second World War.

Deanery South Street

- 1950
- Location: *insula* XVII
- EAPIT Site number: 118
- City HER number: 174
- Additional references: Bidwell 1980, 21, 122

Roman fortress: recording was undertaken after the collapse of the Deanery garden wall and its subsequent rebuilding which revealed in section the remains of a substantial Roman building probably associated with the nearby finds relating to the Roman bath-house found during the 1930s and 40s (Sites 6 and 18). Several gullies or pits cut into the natural gravels could, with hindsight, be dated to the Roman legionary fortress.

Bishop's Garden Palace Well Spring

- 1951–2
- Location: *insula* XXXIX
- EAPIT Site number: 119
- City HER number: 175
- Additional references: Fox 1952b; 1956; Allan *et al.* 1984; Brown 2005

Roman/later medieval: Sir Cyril Fox excavated beside the S wall of the cathedral choir, revealing what he believed to be the site of an ancient well spring with its associated structures. Several phases of development were observed. He thought the earliest was possibly Roman, and subsequent masonry of Saxon and Norman date. The sequence was re-examined and recorded in detail by Stewart Brown in 2005. The earliest masonry is now interpreted as part of a Norman stone building forming part of the Bishop's Palace. The second phase is part of the 13th-century Bishop's Palace; all subsequent phases represent a series of stages in the building of the eastern limb of the cathedral.

Western Way/West Street

- 1962
- Location: city wall and defences
- EAPIT Site number: 120
- City HER number: 177
- Additional references: Fox 1963

Roman town: excavation for a deep shaft to the sewers under Western Way exposed the rampart behind the city wall in section; it was 6 ft (1.8 m) high resting on 6–8 in (*c.* 17 cm) of soil. Observation in front of the wall failed to locate any evidence of a ditch.

2 Broadgate (Tinleys)

- 1994–5
- Location: *insula* XIII
- EAPIT Site number: 121
- City HER number: 192
- Additional references: EAACR 1996, 1–2; Burnham *et al.* 1996, 435; Bedford 1997

Roman fortress: a small patch of metalled surface dating to the Roman military period had been cut by a later wall that is likely to represent part of the *apodyterium* of the legionary bath-house. A second wall probably defined the front of the *apodyterium*, immediately behind a colonnade which fronted onto the via *decumana* of the fortress (but see now Bidwell's discussion in Chapter 3.1 below). A doorway or gap in the bath-house wall was also recorded. ***Roman town***: the surviving foundations of the wall adjacent to the bath-house probably represent parts of the basilica and forum which succeeded the bath-house. ***Later medieval***: a rubbish pit contained badly fractured human bones. Medieval walls represented the back wall of a building fronting onto the High Street, next to Broadgate. A further wall foundation, originally thought to represent the chapel of SS Simon and Jude which stood somewhere in this area *c.* 1200, is now believed to be later in date.

18 Bonhay Road

- 1996
- Location: extra-mural
- EAPIT Site number: 122
- City HER number: 196
- Additional references: EAACR 1997, 2–3

Post-medieval: evaluation next to Higher Leat revealed an 18th-century tanning pit lined with a barrel, the leat wall, and a row of early 18th-century cottages or workhouses.

21 The Mint

- 1998
- Location: *insula* XVI
- EAPIT Site number: 123
- City HER number: 305
- Additional references: EAACR 1996; Allan 1999a; 2019; Keppie *et al.* 1999, 367; Bradley *et al.* 1999, 239

Roman: Roman deposits were recorded in the sides of robber trenches of medieval walls forming the cloister of St Nicholas Priory (EAPIT 1, Fig. 8.7). ***Later medieval***: two phases of wall foundations of the E, N, and W claustral walks of St Nicholas Priory were recorded. The earlier phase probably dated to the mid/late 12th century, while the latter probably dated to the 15th century. A wall of a 15th-century *lavabo*, or trough for washing, forming an adjunct to the W walk, was also located.

Blackfriars Conduit

- 1950; 1954
- Location: city wall
- EAPIT Site number: 124
- City HER number: 315
- Additional references: Juddery and Stoyle 1995; Stoyle 2014

Later medieval: a small vaulted chamber lined with volcanic stone was discovered by workmen beneath the city wall in 1954. It had been built to house the pipe bringing the Black Friars' water supply into their precinct.

St John's School Trenches 2 & 3

- 1933
- Location: city wall
- EAPIT Site number: 125
- City HER number: 316
- Additional References: Radford and Morris 1935, 184–7

Roman town?: excavations of an area of city wall that had been investigated the previous year (Site 4) showed that the top of the foundations consisted of a slurry of mortar laid on a course of masonry. Above this, the core was laid in horizontal courses of obliquely-pitched stones, each brought to a level surface by a slurry of mortar which left frequent voids between the stones. At the original surface level, the outer face of the wall was marked by a slight projecting plinth beneath which the original wall was underpinned. ***Later medieval***: a large inclined buttress of late medieval or later date was built against the outer face of the wall.

St John's School Trench 1

- 1935
- Location: city wall
- EAPIT Site number: 126
- City HER number: 317
- Additional references: Radford and Morris 1935, 184–7

Roman town: a section of the city wall was recorded during the construction of Bedford Garage. A bank had been constructed over the natural ground surface, in which a foundation trench for the city wall had been dug that was filled with a rough foundation comprising unmortared rubble; the remainder of the trench was filled with rammed red marl mixed with stones. ***Post-medieval***: no remains of the original wall were preserved above the foundations, while in comparatively modern times the core of the wall had been quarried, the void being filled with small stones and builders' rubbish which yielded fragments of pottery of the late 18th or early 19th century.

St John's School Trench 4

- 1935
- Location: *insula* XL
- EAPIT Site number: 127
- City HER number: 318
- Additional references: Radford and Morris 1935, 184–7; Steinmetzer *et al.* forthcoming

Roman: a few fragments of Roman pottery and tiles, medieval pottery, and some charcoal were found. The presence of tile in this area was later recognised as representing a Roman tilery which was further investigated by the Princesshay investigations (Site 156). ***Later medieval***: the only find in the trench filling was a small fragment of green glazed medieval pottery at the level of the top of the passage.

St John's School Trial Trenches

- 1935
- Location: *insula* XL
- EAPIT Site number: 128
- City HER number: 319/950
- Additional references: Montague 1935, 188

Roman town: two short trenches across the northern end of St. John's playground revealed a large rounded cobbled stone that was interpreted as probable Roman street material on account of its similarity to Roman street material found at Site 7 and because a Roman street was expected here; no other archaeological features were found.

Catherine Street

- 1950
- Location: *insula* XXII
- EAPIT Site number: 129
- City HER number: 320
- Additional references: Fox 1951a, 40–41; Holbrook *et al.* 1990

Roman town: two rooms within a range of the later Roman town house found at Sites 19 and 89 were seen during a watching brief.

Princesshay/Catherine Street Conduit

- 1950
- Location: *insula* XL
- EAPIT Site number: 130
- City HER number: 321
- Additional references: Fox 1951b, 172–8; Stoyle 2014

Later medieval: the underground passage was encountered in a trench excavated for the main sewer laid along the line of Princesshay. The sections show that the conduit had been built in an open trench dug for over 3.3 m into the natural, with the conduit itself standing 1.2 m above the floor of the trench on a filling of clay and dark soil. The trench contained a quantity of rubbish including three sherds of green-glazed medieval pottery for which an early 14th-century date was proposed. During the same investigation, a length of conduit at High Street was also excavated (Site 31).

Cricklepit Street

- 1986–7
- Location: city wall
- EAPIT Site number: 131
- City HER number: 406
- Additional references: EAACR 1987; 1989; Simpson 1993

Post medieval: excavation confirmed that no Roman or medieval gate existed at this corner of the city wall. The stream flowing down the side of Coombe Street in the medieval period was found to pass through a gully several metres deep at the base of the wall. When the Watergate was built in 1565 a pavement of large Heavitree stone blocks was laid to receive the water from a chute projecting from the wall, and the blocks formed a paved ford or watersplash across Cricklepit Street. The Watergate was demolished in 1815 and the stream diverted into a sewer under the road.

Exeter and Devon Arts Centre (EDAC) Redevelopment

- 1998
- Location: *insula* IV/V/XX/XXV
- EAPIT Site number: 132
- City HER number: 813
- Additional references: Bradley *et al.* 1999, 238

Saxo-Norman: several Late Saxon boundary ditches were recorded, as well as the rampart of the outer bailey of the Norman Castle. ***Later medieval***: a few stakeholes and pits belonged to the later medieval period.

Cathedral Cloisters

- 1998
- Location: *insulae* XVIII and XIX, cohort block D
- EAPIT Site number: 133
- City HER number: 842
- Additional references: Stead and Parker 1998

Roman fortress: post-trenches of a timber building within the legionary fortress were recorded together with a gully which had been cut by an Early Roman pit. ***Roman town***: later Roman deposits were severely truncated by 17th-century cellars, although a 3rd or 4th-century AD stone wall was recorded: ***Later medieval***: substantial remains of the W cloister walk's foundations and walls were uncovered although the floor itself was truncated by the same 17th-century cellars. Three stone-lined burials were also found, representing internments made within the west cloister walk. ***Post-medieval***: the remains of two houses built on the site of the demolished west walk in the 1650s were exposed beneath 19th-century demolition rubble.

Berni's Restaurant, High Street

- 1935
- Location: *insula* XL
- EAPIT Site number: 134
- City HER number: 908
- Additional references: Montague 1935, 188–9

Roman: workmen discovered a Roman midden containing a large quantity of broken pottery, dating from the start of the Roman occupation in Exeter up to the Antonine period. ***Later medieval***: two cooking pots were also recovered, dating to around the 12th or 13th century.

James Street

- 1962
- Location: city wall and defences
- EAPIT Site number: 135
- City HER number: 959
- Additional references: Wright 1962; Blaylock 1995

Roman town: during the work on the new bypass, just south of the South Gate, the opportunity was taken to expose the Roman town wall. Excavations revealed that it had been added to an existing rampart *c*. AD 200. ***Later medieval***: the wall had been underpinned with Heavitree stone in the late medieval period and the ditch enlarged to over 6 ft (1.8 m) deep. The city council subsequently consolidated the masonry and a section of the wall now stands beside the new road.

Vicinity of the Speke Chapel, Exeter Cathedral

- 1843
- Location: *insula* XXXIX?
- EAPIT Site number: 136
- City HER number: 968
- Associated references: Fox 1952a, 102–3

Roman town: outside the Speke Chapel, at a depth of *c*. 1.2 m, a tessellated pavement was found in 1843, measuring *c*. 7 m by *c*. 2.4 m. An excavation on the site in 1936 (Site 12) failed to find this pavement, although other Roman features were recorded. The exact site of this site is therefore unknown.

Waterbeer Street (Police Station, at angle of Pancras Lane) (EAPIT 1, Fig. 6.16)

- 1887
- Location: *insula* IV/V, cohort C
- EAPIT Site number: 137
- City HER number: 969
- Additional references: Chapter 5 below; Fox 1952a, 99–100; Bidwell 1980, 71–2

Roman town: during the construction of the Police Station in Waterbeer Street in 1887, three sections of mosaic pavement were discovered that probably correspond to one reported by the antiquarian William Stukeley in Pancras Lane in 1723

Shooting Marsh Stile

- 1999
- Location: extra-mural
- EAPIT Site number: 138
- City HER number: 973
- Additional references: Exeter Archaeology 1998

Roman/Later medieval: a sequence of historic river gravels was seen. ***Post-medieval***: three probable 18th-century tanners' lime pits were found as well as a contemporary structure containing brick-burning debris.

St Nicholas Priory

- 1842
- Location: *insula* VII
- EAPIT Site number: 139
- City HER number: 978
- Additional references: N/A

Later medieval: a manuscript bequeathed to Exeter City Library from the collection of memoranda relating to the Courtenay family records the discovery of a lead coffin at St Nicholas Priory. The coffin was believed to contain the remains of Mawle the widow of Sir Hugh Courtenay whose will was dated 20 August 1464.

East Gate

- 1953
- Location: extra-mural
- EAPIT Site number: 140
- City HER number: 997
- Additional references: N/A

Later medieval: Lady Aileen Fox made an observation of the footings of the eastern drum tower of the medieval East Gate. The observation was not published, but a plan and notes were made.

Excavations in St Edmund's Chapel, Exeter Cathedral

- 1896
- Location: *insula* XIX
- EAPIT Site number: 141
- City HER number: 4528
- Additional references: McAleer 1991

Later medieval: many reused 12th-century architectural fragments were found in the foundations of the chapel. Most are lost but some are still held by the cathedral. The chapel was further investigated in 1936–7 (Site 142)

St Edmund's Chapel, Exeter Cathedral

- 1936–7
- Location: *insula* XIX
- EAPIT Site number: 142
- City HER number: 4537
- Additional references: McAleer 1984, pl. 1; Erskine *et al.* 1988, 85

Later medieval: during alterations to St Edmund's chapel to make it into a memorial chapel for the Devonshire Regiment, footings of its west wall were exposed. The chapel was previously excavated in 1896 (Site 141).

Cowick Street

- 1999–2000
- Location: extra-mural
- EAPIT Site number: 143
- City HER number: 15003
- Additional references: Blaylock 2000

Post-medieval: previous investigations on Albany Road in 1978 and 1984 (Sites 66 and 79) had exposed remains of the 16th/early 17th-century Birdall family bronze foundry. In 1999–2000 the area to the rear of the foundry was investigated including several clay quarry pits which had been backfilled with pieces of mould that had been broken after casting in order to remove the vessels. Post-foundry activity consisted of a number of 18th/19th-century pits and horticultural features.

Acland Road

- 2000
- Location: extra-mural
- EAPIT Site number: 144
- City HER number: 15085
- Additional references: Reed and Collings 2000

No archaeological features were recorded due to modern disturbances.

Bonhay Road

- 2000; 2001
- Location: extra-mural
- EAPIT Site number: 145
- City HER number: 15090; 15103
- Additional references: Mayes and Hardy 2004

Later medieval/post-medieval: excavations were undertaken on and near the site of Bonhay Mill, located near the junction of the Higher and Lower Leats. A possible weir comprising a timber beam, a large number of upright stakes, and a large quantity of unworked stone blocks were recorded. The channel in which the weir was built was then backfilled, and truncated by two phases of timber-revetted leat. Timbers from the weir structure and the two phases of leat were sampled for dendrochronological analysis, although only one timber, from the weir, produced a felling date of after 1596 (since the timber had no sapwood).

Southernhay East Car Park

- 2001; 2002–3
- Location: extra-mural
- EAPIT Site number: 146
- City HER number: 15098; 15205
- Additional references: Bedford 2001; Stead 2004; Quinnell 2017

Prehistoric: parts of a Middle Iron Age ring gully roundhouse and field system were excavated, producing a large assemblage of 'South-Western Decorated' pottery dating to the 2nd century BC. ***Roman***: deposits of potential Roman date were found but not further investigated due to their depth.

Queen Street

- 2001–2
- Location: *insula* IV/V, cohort block A
- EAPIT Site number: 147
- City HER number: 15106
- Additional references: Stead 2002

Roman fortress: in one of a number of trenches excavated during the Exeter gas main replacement scheme, Trench 9 revealed a post-trench and although its true nature is uncertain its depth (0.40 m) and profile are consistent with barrack post-trenches excavated elsewhere in the legionary fortress. The location of its NW edge is also consistent with a post-trench or *conturbernium* division within a barrack block. A steep-sided feature in Trench 11 was in a position corresponding to that of the veranda of a barrack, although it was considerably larger than a standard postpit and as such its identification relative to the legionary fortress remains inconclusive.

Northcott Warehouse

- 2001–2
- Location: extra-mural

- EAPIT Site number: 148
- City HER number: 15147
- Additional references: Stead and Dyer 2003

Later medieval: a leat, previously recorded at Site 80, was recorded.

Tudor Street

- 2003
- Location: extra-mural
- EAPIT Site number: 149
- City HER number: 15155
- Additional references: Passmore *et al.* 2009

Later medieval: several phases of repair to the Higher Leat were recorded, the earliest dating to 1380–1470. ***Post-medieval***: the excavation documented the progressively denser concentration of buildings, including a possible fulling mill and dyehouses, in an area heavily involved in the cloth industry following its initial development in the early 17th century.

Victoria Nurseries

- 2003
- Location: extra-mural
- EAPIT Site number: 150
- City HER number: 15198
- Additional references: Dyer 2003

Later medieval: a metalled trackway was observed, although the only dating evidence was a scrap of medieval or post-medieval pottery in the overlying silt layer. However, the trackway was succeeded by three ditches which contained roof slate and tile from the 14th or 15th centuries. The trackway and ditches follow the line of a boundary depicted on a map of 1790.

Paris Street/High Street

- 2003–4
- Location: extra-mural
- EAPIT Site number: 151
- City HER number: 15250; 15251
- Additional references: none

Roman town: two lengths of a V-shaped ditch containing Roman pottery were recorded during a watching brief. The ditch was interpreted as a boundary feature. ***Post-medieval***: a section of a probable Civil War defensive ditch was recorded.

Longbrook Street

- 2004
- Location: extra-mural
- EAPIT Site number: 152
- City HER number: 15278
- Additional references: Dyer and Allan 2004

Later medieval: the robbed pipe-trench of one of Exeter's medieval conduits was recorded during a watching brief. ***Post-medieval***: a 14 m length of the conduit of 1805–33 was also recorded.

George's Meeting House, South Street

- 2004
- Location: intra-mural
- EAPIT Site number: 153
- City HER number: 15289
- Additional references: Pearce and Parker 2005

Roman: soil horizons of this period had survived only as isolated patches. ***Later medieval***: a large number of pits were recorded, one of which may have been built to support a tanning tank, while most were probably for domestic rubbish. ***Post-medieval***: 11 burials associated with George's Meeting House, a former Unitarian (originally Presbyterian) site of worship from 1760–1983, were recorded. Two trenches to the SE of this site had been previously excavated (Site 36).

Mount Dinham, Dinham Road

- 2005; 2007–9
- Location: extra-mural
- EAPIT Site number: 154
- City HER number: 15304
- Additional references: Leverett and Valentin 2005; Passmore 2013; Holbrook 2015; Passmore forthcoming

Roman fortress: many features dating to the military period were recorded. The principal structure was a large building comprising an aisled hall, surrounded by small rooms and corridors, and a courtyard. This was constructed in the post-trench technique associated with Roman military buildings. Its plan is indicative of a large domestic building, and is provisionally interpreted as a *praetorium*, although the exact function is unknown (see EAPIT 1, Chapter 5). ***Roman town***: after the military building went out of use a 1st-century AD cremation burial was placed next to two of its walls (other Roman burials were recorded nearby at Sites 83 and 159). Later Roman features, of 2nd and 3rd-century AD date, were also found, but no associated buildings were located other than a mausoleum. Other pits, postholes and gullies of probable mid to late 2nd-century AD date suggest settlement and perhaps agricultural activities outside the Roman town. Ditches interpreted as an enclosure of Roman date were also located. ***Later medieval***: a layer of medieval soil covered the Roman deposits, indicating agricultural and/or horticultural use at this time. ***Post-medieval***: several boundary ditches and gullies were excavated, along with postholes possibly associated with post-medieval cloth drying. Tenter racks are shown here on Tozer's map of 1792 for example.

30–32 Longbrook Street

- 1994; 2015
- Location: extra-mural
- EAPIT Site number: 155
- City HER number: no HER number allocated yet
- Additional references: Collings and Matthews 1994; Smith 2014

Later medieval/post-medieval: remains of the late medieval and post-medieval frontage were identified. Other potential archaeological remains had been removed by modern disturbance.

Princesshay (EAPIT 1, Figs 6.14, 8.3 and 8.6C; this volume, front cover)

- 1991; 1997–2006
- Location: *insulae* XXII/XXIII/XXIV/XXVII/XXVIII/XXIX, XL city wall and defences, and extra-mural
- EAPIT Site number: 156
- City HER number: 136; 803; 15221
- Additional references: EAACR 1991; Bradley *et al.* 1999, 238–40; Keppie *et al.* 1999, 366–7; Burnham *et al.* 2000, 424; Burnham *et al.* 2007, 295–6; Pearce 2007; Quinnell 2017; Steinmetzer, Orme and Allan forthcoming; Steinmetzer, Stead, Pearce, Bidwell and Allan forthcoming

Numerous phases of investigations have been undertaken in the Princesshay area ranging from watching briefs, a series of 32 test pits, and several open area excavations. The large-scale excavations lay outside the legionary fortress but largely within the Late Roman/medieval city walls; several of the smaller investigations did, however, lie within the legionary fortress. ***Late prehistoric***: part of a small Iron Age roundhouse was excavated as well as an arc of ten large postpits, one of which was radiocarbon dated to the Late Iron Age. ***Roman fortress***: parts of the defensive ditches and interval towers of a military enclosure dated *c.* AD 50–75 were examined, while part of the defensive ditch of the fortress itself was seen in a trench along Chapel Street. ***Roman town***: Early Roman civil occupation was represented by a series of enclosures and extra-mural roads, with extensive evidence for tile production. Evidence of a group of substantial but heavily robbed town houses of the 3rd and 4th centuries AD was recorded in the main excavation area; they were extended and remodelled before their abandonment in the late 4th century AD (EAPIT 1, Fig. 6.14). Evidence of a further building was seen in a trial trench on Bedford Street where a slab of *opus signinum* was regarded as being *in situ* and probably represents later Roman building. Evidence of the Late Roman town's defences were also recorded. A continuation of the extra-mural road seen at Site 29 was also recorded in a trial trench on Chapel Street, while traces of the town's rampart were seen in several trial trenches. ***Saxo-Norman***: a hollow way running SW–NE contained three phases of metalling, the latest sealed by dark soil containing 11th/12th-century pottery; its position suggests it was part of the Late Saxon street layout. A large number of cess- and rubbish pits were also recorded. ***Later medieval***: most of the areas lay within the precinct of the city's Dominican friary, with the largest excavated area within its garden. This revealed evidence for the preceding urban occupation of the area and the largest collection of late medieval pottery in Exeter was recovered from a well. In other areas of the Princesshay excavations, parts of the nave and north nave aisle of the friary church were recorded. A linear feature may be the construction trench for the 1259 Bishop Bronscombe's aqueduct. Five inhumations recorded in a trial trench were probably related to the friary's cemetery. ***Post-medieval***: the principal Princesshay site was occupied by the mansion of the Earls (later Dukes) of Bedford from the Reformation until its demolition in 1773; there are strong grounds for believing that the core of the mansion consisted of the domestic ranges of the monastery. Bedford House was demolished for the construction of Bedford Circus in the 1770s, which was itself destroyed in the Exeter Blitz of 1942. Defensive ditches from the Civil War sieges of the city were also recorded outside the city walls to the NE.

Royal Albert Memorial Museum/Bradninch Place

- 1994; 2003; 2008–9; 2011
- Location: intra-mural and city defences
- EAPIT Site number: 157
- City HER number: 114; 15145
- Additional references: Bedford and Hall 1994; Nenk *et al.* 1995, 195; Burnham *et al.* 1995, 365; Exeter Archaeology 2003; Steinmetzer 2011; Passmore and Rainbird 2014

Roman town/Norman: several phases of archaeological excavation and recording revealed elements of the rampart of the Roman civil town and of the ditch and rampart of the outer bailey of the Norman Castle. The latter were found to cut two Roman quarry pits dating to the 3rd century AD; Roman quarrying in the immediate vicinity of Rougemont (an outcrop of volcanic basalt and trap) had previously been found in 2006 at Site 193.

Carnegie House

- 2008
- Location: extra-mural
- EAPIT Site number: 158
- City HER number: 15609
- Additional references: none

No archaeological features were recorded.

28–29 Lower North Street

- 2011
- Location: extra-mural
- EAPIT Site number: 159
- City HER number: 15659
- Additional references: none

Roman town: a posthole and two graves were recorded (although no bone survived). A further Roman burial had been recorded nearby at Site 154.

Cathedral Yard

- 2012–14
- Location: *insula* XIII
- EAPIT Site number: 160
- City HER number: no HER number allocated yet
- Additional references: Thomson *et al.* 2014

Later medieval/post-medieval: one of the series of watching briefs undertaken as part of gas main replacement works across central Exeter revealed several wall foundations and burial deposits N of the modern cemetery boundary, indicating the original graveyard was more extensive prior to the encroachment of properties along the N boundary of Cathedral Close in the late 16th and 17th centuries.

Paul Street

- 2012–14
- Location: *insula* IV/V
- EAPIT Site number: 161
- City HER number: no HER number allocated yet
- Additional references: Thomson *et al.* 2014

Roman fortress: one of the series of watching briefs undertaken as part of gas main replacement works across central Exeter recorded a large posthole and although no datable artefacts were recovered its size suggest a Roman military date. Its function is unclear: while possibly related to a tower of some sort, its spacing relative to the known examples of Exeter's interval towers is incorrect.

Timepiece Nightclub, Little Castle Street

- 2006–7
- Location: city wall and defences
- EAPIT Site number: 162
- City HER number: no HER number allocated yet
- Additional references: Passmore and Coles 2011

Roman town: the clay rampart to the rear of the Roman town wall was recorded. ***Post-medieval***: five graves from when the site was used as a Castle Street Congregational Chapel in the late 18th and 19th centuries were recorded.

Southgate Hotel, Southernhay

- 2009
- Location: extra-mural and city defences
- EAPIT Site number: 163
- City HER number: no HER number allocated yet
- Additional references: Pearce 2009

Roman/Saxo-Norman/later medieval/post-medieval: elements of the Roman, Saxo-Norman, later medieval, and Civil War defensive ditches were exposed just N of the South Gate. Burials from the former Trinity Burial Ground, which occupied the site between the late 17th and early 19th centuries, were recorded.

North Gate Court

- 2010
- Location: intra-mural and city wall and defences
- EAPIT Site number: 164
- City HER number: no HER number allocated yet
- Additional references: Farnell 2010a; Chapman *et al.* 2011, 384

Roman town: excavation immediately S of the work undertaken along Paul Street in 1981–85 (Site 76) revealed a continuation of the Roman road that had previously been recorded immediately outside the early civilian defensive ditch at Site 76. Elements of the later Roman town defences were recorded, including an exposure of the foundations of the city wall towards the front of the site nearest to Lower North Street where the wall fabric has been left in-situ to an unknown depth. The city wall and rampart had previously been recorded here in 1978 (Site 69).

Friar's Green

- 2011
- Location: extra-mural and city defences
- EAPIT Site number: 165
- City HER number: no HER number allocated yet
- Additional references: Passmore and Parker 2012

Post-medieval: a historic building appraisal and trial trench excavations were carried out at Magnolia House and Acacia House, Friar's Green. The site lies within a 1st-century AD Roman military compound outside of the South Gate identified at Sites 50, 96 and 97 and a Franciscan friary established *c.* 1300. Seven trenches were dug and no traces of the Roman or medieval periods were found, although post-medieval demolition and levelling deposits were encountered dating to between the late 16th and early 17th centuries.

St Stephen's Church

- 2011–12
- Location: *insula* XXII
- EAPIT Site number: 166
- City HER number: no HER number allocated yet
- Additional references: Stewart Brown Associates 2012

Saxo-Norman: excavation uncovered part of an early Norman crypt and a small fragment of its Saxon predecessor. ***Later medieval***: recording of the standing structure showed that the church was extended eastward in the early 14th century with the addition of a chancel built above an archway spanning a narrow street. The church acquired aisles and a west tower in the later medieval period. ***Post-medieval***: the church underwent major rebuilding in 1660–65, and extensive internal rearrangement and re-roofing in 1826.

Dean Clarke House, Southernhay

- 2013
- Location: extra-mural
- EAPIT Site number: 167
- City HER number: no HER number allocated yet
- Additional references: Rainbird 2014

Roman: four Romano-British pits containing 1st to 4th-century AD pottery were found, while a series of postholes did not form any coherent pattern. ***Post-medieval***: walls associated with the Dean Clarke House Hospital and a small building probably associated with Wynard's Almshouses, built by William Wynard in 1435, were also recorded.

Exeter Cathedral School

- 2004; 2013
- Location: *insula* XXXIX
- EAPIT Site number: 168
- City HER number: no HER number allocated yet
- Additional references: Dyer and Allan 2004; Rainbird 2013; 2015

Later medieval/post-medieval: small-scale excavation and examination of upstanding fabric showed that the boundary of this property incorporates the remains of a late medieval gatehouse; the wall itself appears to be part of the enclosure of the 13th-century Bishop's Palace.

23–27 Mary Arches Street and Quintana Gate, Bartholomew Street West (EAPIT 1, Fig. 6.14)

- 2017
- Location: *insula* I, cohort block G and intra-mural
- EAPIT Site number: 169
- City HER number: no HER number allocated yet
- Additional references: Farnell 2018

Roman fortress: the site – immediately N and W of the excavations at Bartholomew Street East (Site 73) – was located towards the W corner of the legionary fortress. Excavated remains included the fortress ditch and rampart, street, and internal timber buildings. ***Roman town***: in the later Roman town the plot was occupied by two stone structures including a large town house and a building with a hypocaust and a tessellated floor. ***?Late Saxon***: activity was limited, although a ditch that crossed the site and a small slag pit furnace base may be of this date. ***Later medieval***: in the medieval period the site fell within the grounds of St Nicholas' Priory. It appears to have remained undeveloped open ground or gardens although a number of pits were dug together with a large industrial feature whose function is currently unknown.

Cathedral Green/Palace Gate/Bishops Palace (Gas Main Replacement)

- 2012–14
- Location: city wall and defences
- EAPIT Site number: 170
- City HER number: no HER number allocated yet
- Additional references: Thomson *et al.* 2014

A series of watching briefs were undertaken as part of gas main replacement works at several sites in the city centre, with the largest located near Cathedral Green. ***Roman fortress***: evidence of the legionary fortress rampart was seen. ***Roman town***: walls and contemporary metalled surfaces, together with several silty clay deposits containing mid to late 2nd-century AD pottery and fragments of tile, point to later Roman buried soils and/or occupation deposits. ***Early medieval/Saxo-Norman***: 'dark earth' deposits were seen in three trenches, and disarticulated human bones in Kalendarhay were radiocarbon dated to between the 8th and 12th centuries (EAPIT 1, Fig. 7.8). ***Saxo-Norman***: a metalled surface was seen overlying the 'dark earth' in one trench. ***Later medieval***: burials found in Cathedral Yard were radiocarbon dated to between the 15th and early 17th centuries.

Exe Bridges Retail Park, Cowick Street

- 2011

- Location: extra-mural
- EAPIT Site number: 171
- City HER number: no HER number allocated yet
- Additional references: Blaylock 1996; 2000; 2015; Sims and Kerr-Peterson 2012

Later medieval: a section of leat was exposed, probably dating from the late 15th/early 16th century. ***Post-medieval***: features of a 16th/17th-century bronze foundry were recorded (the site was adjacent to the earlier investigations at Site 79).

31 Cowick Street

- 2016
- Location: extra-mural
- EAPIT Site number: 172
- City HER number: no HER number allocated yet
- Additional references: Hughes 2016

Later medieval: a watching brief recorded a buried soil layer containing decorated medieval floor tile and ridge tile. The presence of large numbers of wasters suggests a production site was located nearby during the 14th century, possibly linked with the supply of tiles to high status religious buildings in Exeter.

Western Way

- 2011
- Location: *insula* XXXIII/XXXV/XXXVI
- EAPIT Site number: 173
- City HER number: no HER number allocated yet
- Additional references: Passmore 2011b

No archaeological features were recorded.

Eagle Yard, Tudor Street

- 2014
- Location: extra-mural
- EAPIT Site number: 174
- City HER number: no HER number allocated yet
- Additional references: Rainbird *et al.* 2014; Rainbird and Govier 2017

Post-medieval: documentary sources indicate the site was first built upon during the 17th century in association with the local cloth industry, although no buildings associated with this were recorded during the investigation.

Renslade House, Tudor Street

- 2017–19
- Location: extra-mural
- EAPIT Site number: 175
- City HER number: no HER number allocated yet
- Additional references: Hughes 2019

Later medieval: 13th-century animal bones suggest that tanning, horn-working and fulling were carried on the site. ***Post-medieval***: from the 16th to the 17th centuries, the presence of casting waste marked the increasing importance of metalworking. A blacksmith's workshop and foundries, the largest of which – the Bonhay and Eagle Foundry – occupied part of the site from the 19th century until its partial demolition in the late 20th century.

Frog Street (former Radmore and Tucker site)

- 2018
- Location: extra-mural
- EAPIT Site number: 176
- City HER number: no HER number allocated yet
- Additional references: Clutterbuck 2019

Post-medieval: industrial activity in the form of furnaces and ancillary buildings were recorded, and although the specific industrial activity was not determined, documentary sources emphasise the significance of cloth-dyeing in this area.

West Street

- 2015
- Location: extra-mural
- EAPIT Site number: 177
- City HER number: no HER number allocated yet
- Additional references: Thomon *et al.* 2014

Later medieval/post-medieval: in one of a number of trenches excavated during the Exeter gas main replacement scheme, a structure built of volcanic trap rubble and bonded with red clay was seen. It may represent the remains of the city's West Gate.

Cricklepit Mill

- 2002; 2006
- Location: extra-mural
- EAPIT Site number: 178
- City HER number: no HER number allocated yet
- Additional references: Steinmetzer 2007

Post-medieval: excavation on the site of a new extension to Cricklepit Mill revealed the remains of three buildings depicted on sketches from 1825 as well as the remains of a cobbled surface that pre-dated the Civil War.

Quay Hill

- 2008; 2019

- Location: *insula* XXXIII/XXXV/XXXVI
- EAPIT Site number: 179
- City HER number: no HER number allocated yet
- Additional references: Rainbird and Valentin 2016

An excavation in 2008 was abandoned after the collapse of a retaining wall rendered the site unsafe. Further excavation and recording was commenced in 2019. ***Roman fortress***: a ditch contained pottery from the fortress period. Other linear features containing Roman pottery were also noted before work was abandoned.

Cathedral Close

- 2010
- Location: *insula* XIV
- EAPIT Site number: 180
- City HER number: no HER number allocated yet
- Additional references: Allan 2010

Roman town: five successive floor levels representing Roman civil buildings were identified. ***Later medieval***: four burials and disarticulated bone from the medieval cathedral cemetery were also exposed.

The Quay Antiques Centre

- 2014
- Location: extra-mural
- EAPIT Site number: 181
- City HER number: no HER number allocated yet
- Additional references: Smith 2014

Post-medieval: excavation within a sewer trench revealed a small bonded stone revetment wall, probably related to the remodelling of the quay in the late 17th century.

Exeter Quay Flood Defences

- 2014
- Location: extra-mural
- EAPIT Site number: 182
- City HER number: no HER number allocated yet
- Additional references: Wessex Archaeology 2015

Post-medieval: cobbled surface layers of the former quay were revealed in two evaluation trenches.

Bull Meadow Road, former Eye Hospital

- 2010
- Location: extra-mural
- EAPIT Site number: 183
- City HER number: no HER number allocated yet
- Additional references: Gent *et al.* 2011

Later medieval: a single posthole containing a sherd of 14th-century pottery was recorded. ***Post-medieval***: 17th/18th-century garden planting trenches and a dump or levelling layer were encountered. A short length of wall and 19th-century surfaces were also recorded, although their function is not known as contemporary mapping shows this area as open ground.

Verney Street

- 2011; 2016
- Location: extra-mural
- EAPIT Site number: 184
- City HER number: no HER number allocated yet
- Additional references: Pink 2011; Steinmetzer 2016

Roman town: several pits and ditches were recorded, including part of a curvilinear enclosure. One ditch may have an Iron Age date, although this dating rests on its relationship with the Roman ditches rather than from artefactual evidence. ***Later medieval***: a ditch running parallel to Sidwell Street as well as a large sub-circular pit were recorded. ***Post-medieval***: most features recorded on the site were post-medieval postholes and possible 17th or 18th-century rubbish pits.

1–11 Sidwell Street (John Lewis), rear of

- 2011
- Location: extra-mural
- EAPIT Site number: 185
- City HER number: no HER number allocated yet
- Additional references: Kerr-Peterson and Passmore 2012

Saxo-Norman: the earliest dated feature was an oval pit, which contained a sherd of Saxo-Norman pottery. Several other ditches and pits may be of a similar date. ***Later medieval***: a 14th or 15th-century boundary wall was recorded.

69–73 Sidwell Street

- 2012
- Location: extra-mural
- EAPIT Site number: 186
- City HER number: no HER number allocated yet
- Additional references: Passmore and Stead 2012

19th-century building activity on the site had removed any early archaeology.

Underground Passages

- 2012

- Location: extra-mural
- EAPIT Site number: 187
- City HER number: no HER number allocated yet
- Additional references: Hughes 2012

Later medieval: a trench was excavated with the aim of locating and exposing the tops of the Underground Passages (consisting of two separate conduits – the City Passage and the Cathedral Passage) that supplied water to medieval Exeter. Only a short undisturbed length of the construction cut of the Cathedral Passage was found due to later truncation, although a small section of vertical breccia masonry may have formed part of the side wall of the passage.

1 Cheeke Street

- 2017
- Location: extra-mural
- EAPIT Site number: 188
- City HER number: no HER number allocated yet
- Additional references: Rainbird 2017

No archaeological features were recorded as the site had been levelled during post-Second World War redevelopment.

St Sidwell's Point

- 2010; 2018
- Location: extra-mural
- EAPIT Site number: 189
- City HER number: no HER number allocated yet
- Additional references: Farnell and Salvatore 2010; Clarke 2018; Orellana 2019

Evidence of a previously unknown Early Roman fortification was found, represented by two parallel NWSE orientated ditches, the profile of one of which corresponded closely to the Punic typology commonly used during the Roman period for military defensive ditches. Pottery recovered also dated to the mid 1st–2nd century AD. Deposits of clay that had slumped into the ditch indicate the existence of a rampart. The ditches probably represent the remains of a fort, or fortlet or some sort of defended military compound. The two ditches were truncated by a later Roman civil boundary.

Brunel Close

- 2007
- Location: extra-mural
- EAPIT Site number: 190
- City HER number: no HER number allocated yet
- Additional references: Exeter Archaeology 2007

No pre-modern archaeological features were recorded.

St David's Church

- 2017
- Location: extra-mural
- EAPIT Site number: 191
- City HER number: no HER number allocated yet
- Additional references: Chapman *et al.* 2017; Steinmetzer forthcoming

Roman fortress: a small excavation within the western end of the present church recorded a large quantity of tile and possible tile kiln waste, indicating the location of a tile manufacturing site in the period *c.* AD 70–80. After the abandonment of the tile manufacturing, there was no evidence of subsequent occupation or activity on the site and the land reverted to agricultural use until the early 19th century.

95–96 Fore Street, rear of

- 2017
- Location: *insula* XI/XII
- EAPIT Site number: 192
- City HER number: no HER number allocated yet
- Additional references: Farnell and Passmore 2017

Archaeological deposits were recorded in six geotechnical pits, including several walls, although they were not securely dated.

Exeter Castle

- 2006
- Location: *insula* IV/V/XX/XXV
- EAPIT Site number: 193
- City HER number: no HER number allocated yet
- Additional references: Jenkins 1806; Phear 1892; Blaylock and Higham. forthcoming

Roman town: tile, red-painted wall plaster, tesserae, window glass and mortar fragments of a substantial but unlocated building were found, possibly a later town house. Evidence of earlier quarrying was also found, representing the first time Roman quarrying had been recorded in the immediate vicinity of Rougemont. ***Early medieval***: eight inhumations orientated ENE–SWS were recorded (18 graves were also recorded during building work in the 1890s and further burials had been found in 1774 building works, although they were not recognised as pre-Norman until this investigation). Some of the inhumations were charcoal burials and their presence suggests the presence of a pre-Norman chapel here, although no documentary or other archaeological evidence for one has been found. ***Norman***: evidence of the Norman rampart, together with its subsequent heightening, was noted. ***Later medieval***: walls of 12th/13th-century buildings including a chapel and gatehouse were recorded. ***Post-medieval***: buildings including the Devon Assize Hall Sessions House, as well as later landscaping activities including the demolition of the later medieval buildings, were recorded.

Kalendarhay

- 2018
- Location: Kalendarhay
- EAPIT Site number: 194
- City HER number: no HER number allocated yet
- Additional references: Allan 2018

Early medieval/Saxo-Norman: 63 fragments of disarticulated human bones were recovered. Three were submitted for radiocarbon dating and considered together they are likely to represent burials spanning the Late Saxon to the Norman periods with the burial deposit dating from the 8th to 12th centuries (EAPIT 1, Fig. 7.8).

Exeter Cathedral School (Kalendar Hall)

- 2013
- Location: *insula* XIII
- EAPIT Site number: 195
- City HER number: no HER number allocated yet
- Additional references: Simpson *et al.* 2014

Roman town: walls of two buildings belonging to the public baths previously recorded at Site 17 were found. ***Later medieval/post-medieval***: the retaining wall preserves fragments of a building of the late 14th-century college and evidence of many subsequent changes.

Custom House

- 2007
- Location: extra-mural
- EAPIT Site number: 196
- City HER number: no HER number allocated yet
- Additional references: Steinmetzer 2008

Post-medieval: the remains of a cobbled surface and Heavitree stone foundations pre-dating the Custom House were recorded in excavations within the building.

Well Street

- 2014
- Location: extra-mural
- EAPIT Site number: 197
- City HER number: no HER number allocated yet
- Additional references: Tizzard *et al.* 2017

Later medieval: an octagonal structure of Heavitree stone is thought to represent the late medieval phase of the holy well of St Sidwell. The structure was substantial enough to have supported a roof and was surrounded by a cobbled surface with a drainage channel. It was succeeded by a later 19th-century well adjoining it.

Honiton Inn, Paris Street

- 2018
- Location: extra-mural
- EAPIT Site number: 198
- City HER number: no HER number allocated yet
- Additional references: Beaverstock and Socha-Paszkiewicz 2018

No deposits earlier than the second half of the 19th century were recorded, other than some late 17th/18th-century waste from clay pipe manufacture that the excavators thought was redeposited.

Belgrave Road

- 2019
- Location: extra-mural
- EAPIT Site number: 199
- City HER number: N/A
- Additional references: Austin and Evans 2019; Clarke 2019

Two phases of trenching were carried out on this site, and no archaeological deposits were recorded.

The Mint

- 1812; 1837
- Location: *insula* VI
- EAPIT Site number: 200
- City HER number: no HER number allocated yet
- Additional references: Bidwell 1980, 72

Roman town: in 1812 a tessellated pavement was found in digging the foundations of the new Roman Catholic chapel in the Mint. In 1837 labourers laying gas-pipes in the Mint (presumably the alley itself) found a Roman foundation with a coin of Faustina II embedded in it.

Bartholomew Street West

- 2012–14
- Location: city wall and defences
- EAPIT Site number: 201
- City HER number: no HER number allocated yet
- Additional references: Thomson *et al.* 2014

Later medieval: one of the series of watching briefs undertaken as part of gas main replacement works across central Exeter revealed a NW–SE orientated wall foundation probably representing surviving courses of the medieval city wall.

Cathedral Yard

- 2006
- Location: *insulae* XIII and XIV
- EAPIT Site number: 202
- City HER number: no HER number allocated yet
- Additional references: Goodwin 2007

Roman fortress: six compact layers of silty clay were interpreted by the excavators as possibly representing street surfaces and associated makeup/levelling layers Its position suggests it was the street that ran SW of the legionary bath-house, although their makeup of silty-clay seems unlikely for Roman street surfaces. ***Roman town:*** a compact lime-mortar floor was tentatively identified as the surface of an aisle around the forum. An area of metalled surface may possibly be a Roman street surface, as suggested by the form and quality of its construction and the appearance of the underlying deposits while a Roman tile was also recovered. A wheel rut does not correspond to any known Roman road alignment. ***?Roman town/early medieval:*** a substantial robbed-out wall was recorded and the fairly clean fills of its construction cut were devoid of post-Roman material, suggesting it was either a later Roman or early medieval wall. One possible function for this structure is as part of the early minster precinct. ***Saxo-Norman/later medieval:*** several graves were excavated in four pits around Cathedral Yard. One grave contained bones that were radiocarbon dated to 1010–1160, while bones from another grave were radiocarbon dated to 1410–1630 (EAPIT 1, Fig. 7.8).

St Thomas Court

- 2017–18
- Location: extra-mural
- EAPIT Site number: 203
- City HER number: no HER number allocated yet
- Additional references: Litchenstein and Hughes 2020

Post-medieval: pits, ditches, buried soils and demolition layers of the post-medieval period were recorded as well as the remains of a probable late 19th/early 20th-century cellar.

City Arcade

- 2019
- Location: *insula* XI/XII
- EAPIT Site number: 204
- City HER number: no HER number allocated yet
- Additional references: Andrew Pye pers. comm.

Roman fortress: post-trenches relating to the legionary fortress's barrack blocks were recorded. ***Roman town***: a large circular pit with cross-shaped flues or trenches at its base, containing lime and charcoal deposits, may be a limekiln. Several probable rubbish pits were also found and the foundations of stone walls may represent Roman structural remains. ***Post-medieval***: numerous large rubbish pits were recorded dating to around 1700.

Mama Stones

- 2019
- Location: intra-mural
- EAPIT Site number: 205
- City HER number: no HER number allocated yet
- Additional references: Andrew Pye pers. comm.

Roman fortress: although most of the site had been heavily truncated by later building activities, remains of the legionary fortress's defensive ditch was seen as well as the base of the associated rampart. ***Saxo-Norman/later medieval***: the fortress ditch was cut by a medieval rubbish pit and a partially exposed trench containing a stone structure, although its function could not be established. Pottery recovered from the construction backfill dated from AD 950–1350.

The Deanery

- 2005–6
- Location: *insula* XVIII
- EAPIT Site number: 206
- City HER number: no HER number allocated yet
- Additional references: Goodwin and Gent 2007

Roman town: material possibly associated with the demolition of the Roman bath-house was encountered, above which was a layer of Roman soil. ***Saxo-Norman***: five incomplete burials were recorded, one radiocarbon dated to 1030–1220 cal AD (EAPIT 1, Fig. 7.8). The presence of these burials was unexpected as the college of the Vicars Choral extended along Kalendarhay to the north, forming the boundary to the cemetery of St Mary Major church and the Cathedral, suggesting that these burials predate these buildings and likely follow the establishment of the Late Saxon minster in *c.* 930. Although only one bone was radiocarbon dated, the alignment of these burials suggest they represent two phases of the Late Saxon minster cemetery, with two burials being possibly earlier, dating to the 7th–10th century. ***Later medieval***: the remains of the college of the Vicars Choral may be represented by a wall, probably part of a cell that opened to a small yard.

Royal Clarence Hotel

- 2016–19
- Location: *insula* XIV
- EAPIT Site number: 207
- City HER number: no HER number allocated yet
- Additional references: Andrew Pye pers. comm.

Roman town: following a fire on the site, archaeological monitoring and test pits recorded three pits, one containing a waterlogged deposit, and a posthole along with Roman pottery, glass and ceramic building material. ***Later medieval***: medieval pottery was also recovered.

3

Roman Exeter: The Fortress Plan, and Gazetteers of Evidence for the Street Plans and Stone Buildings

Paul Bidwell and David Gould

This chapter contains three sections all relating to the Roman fortress and town at Exeter. The first is a detailed description of the fortress plan by Paul Bidwell, the second a gazetteer of the evidence for the Roman streets in Exeter, and the third a gazetteer of the evidence for the Roman civilian buildings, updating the 'Gazetteers of Buildings' in Paul Bidwell's (1980, 53–55, 69–79) *Roman Exeter: Fortress and Town*. The Site Numbers referred to are those in Chapter 2 above.

Section 3.1: The plan and buildings of the legionary fortress at Exeter
by Paul Bidwell

Introduction

The history and setting of the fortress have been discussed in the first volume of these studies, together with its place in the evolution of fortress plans (EAPIT 1, Chapter 5). The opportunity is taken here to summarise the evidence for the Exeter plan. Its reconstruction has partly depended on Henderson's model for the blueprint which the original Roman surveyors seem to have followed (Fig. 3.1). This new study makes some additions and modifications, but none directly contradicts the underlying scheme which Henderson deduced.

The first attempt to reconstruct the plan of the fortress drew on the results of excavations in the 1970s (Bidwell 1979, fig. 2; repeated in Bidwell 1980, fig. 7, with the addition of buildings found at Queen Street in 1978 (Site 68)). Excavations in 1982 and 1986 (Sites 76 and 86) showed that the fortress had extended farther to the north-east and faced south-west, overlooking the river crossing, rather than in the opposite direction as Bidwell had suggested. Parts of barracks found near the western corner of the fortress at Bartholomew Street East in 1980–1 (Site 73) and at St Nicholas Priory in 1983–4 (Site 78) allowed Henderson to propose an overall reconstruction of its plan (1988, 94–5, fig. 5.3). He noted that the plots for the buildings had been laid out using multiples of the *pes monetalis*, and in a subsequent paper he explored the metrology of the fortress in great detail (Fig. 3.1; 1991, fig. 13.1, with minor amendments to the 1988 plan). In 1992–4 levels of the military period across all the unpublished sites in the fortress and its surroundings were described and illustrated in a series of detailed reports written mainly by Bedford and Salvatore but with some contributions by Earwood, Henderson and Simpson; they were intended to serve as the basis for a comprehensive account of the fortress which was never written. The reports included lists of pottery and coins; other categories of finds from sites excavated in 1971–9 had been published in Holbrook and Bidwell (1991), but later finds, apart from the pottery and coins, were not considered.

Detailed accounts of sites excavated in the two decades after the establishment of the Exeter Museums Archaeological Field Unit in 1971 were made widely available through the Archaeology Data Service as part of the Exeter Archaeology Archive Project (2015). Subsequent reports, published and unpublished, are referred to in the bibliography. Finally, Allan (2005, figs on p. 11 and back cover) reproduced Henderson's plan of the fortress with some updating as well as another plan showing what had actually been found in relation to the modern street system.

For basic information about most of the fortresses cited in this chapter, together with plans and bibliographies, see Bishop 2012; references to later or more detailed accounts are given where necessary. Figure 3.2 illustrates the Latin terminology for the various parts of the fortress.

The plan as reconstructed by Henderson

The dimensions of the fortress measured from the inner lip of the ditch are about 349 m by 476 m giving it an area

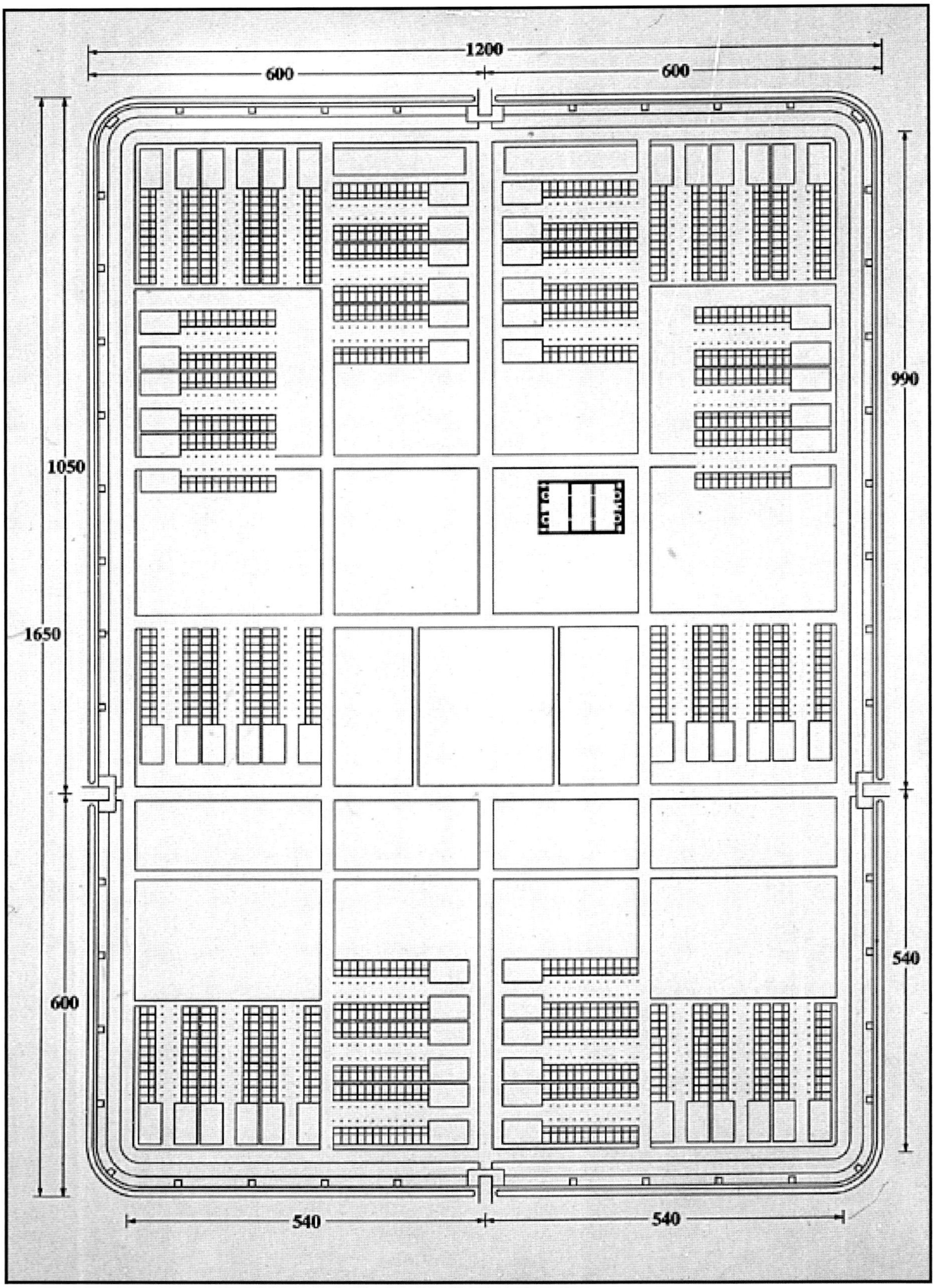

Fig. 3.1 Henderson's schematic reconstruction of the fortress plan based on 'standard plan units mɜasured in multiples of a quarter of an actus' *(Henderson 1991a, 73). The value used for the* pes monetalis *(pM) was 0.2959 m; an* actus *is 120* pedes *(after Henderson 1991a, fig. 13.5)*

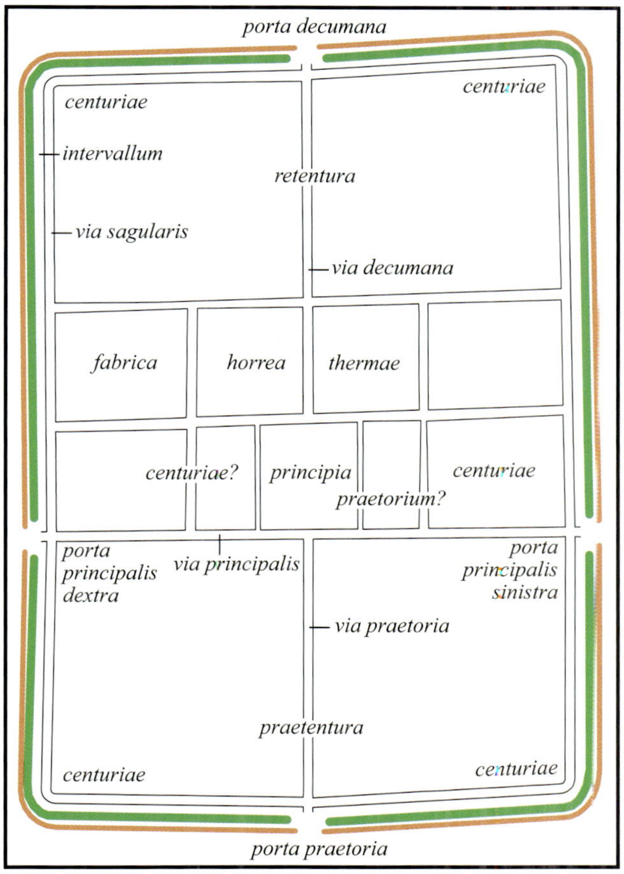

Fig. 3.2 Latin terminology for the different parts of the fortress. The areas flanking the principia *are the* latera praetorii *(drawn by David Gould)*

of 16.6 ha. The ditch and rampart have been seen on all four sides of the fortress (Table 3.1); its overall footprint is not in doubt, but there are minor irregularities in its outline (Fig. 3.3). Two interval towers spaced *c.* 30.0 m apart, the completely exposed example having a width of *c.* 3.0 m, were seen at Friernhay Street in 1981 (Figs 3.6 and 3.11; Site 75). Henderson deduced that the intended spacing between the towers was 99 *pedes monetales* and that the width intended for the towers was 11 *pedes monetales*. According to his reconstruction the entire circuit would have had 44 interval towers. The validity of his hypothesis was demonstrated by the discovery in its predicted position of another example at Catherine Street, on the side of the fortress opposite Friernhay Street (Site 89; Henderson 1991a, 73–5, figs 13.1 and 13.7–11). Additional confirmation came from the positions of towers found behind the Cathedral School in 1992 (Site 100) and at the Quintana Gate site in 2017 (Site 169).

Fixed points in the internal layout are provided by the *viae praetoria* and *decumana* which would have occupied a line bisecting the fortress from north-east to south-west. The south-east side of the *via decumana* was excavated at 41–42 High Street in 1980 (Site 72). The *via praetoria* has never been seen, and neither has the *via principalis*, the

Table 3.1 Excavations on the intervallum, rampart and inner ditch. The list begins at the northern corner and proceeds clockwise. Observations of the outer ditch, dug early in the civilian period, are also noted. EAAP = Exeter Archaeology Archive Project (2015)

Site no.	Location	Description	Publication
86	NE side: Upper Paul Street	Inner ditch	EAAP
89	NE side: St Catherine's Almshouses	Rampart, interval tower, inner ditch	EAAP
156	Princesshay	Inner ditch	Steinmetzer, Stead, Pearce, Bidwell and Allan forthcoming
33	NE side: Chapel Street	1955 excavation across line of defences but only top of outer ditch seen	Greenfield 1964
100	SE side: Cathedral School	Rampart and interval tower. Possible stone refacing; if so probably early town	EAAP
None	SE side: Bishop's Palace	Rampart	Thomson *et al.* 2014
63	SE side: Mermaid Yard	Part of rampart, inner and outer ditches	EAAP
52/ 64	SE/SW sides: Rack Street	Inner and outer ditches	Chapter 8, this volume
75	SW side: Friernhay Street	Complete transect including two interval towers	EAAP
169	NW side: Quintana Gate/ Mary Arches Street	Complete transect including interval tower	Farnell 2018
35	NW side: 10-18 Bartholomew Street East	*Via sagularis* and *intervallum* buildings	Holbrook and Fox 1987
76	NW side: Paul Street	Inner and outer ditches	EAAP

third of the major streets within the fortress; also still to be excavated are the four gates of the fortress. The general position of the *latera praetorii*, the row of building plots facing the *via principalis* with the *principia* at its centre, was evident by 1979 when the fortress was thought to have faced north-east. Now that it is known that the fortress faced in the opposite direction, towards the river, the *via principalis* would have been on the south-west side of the *latera praetorii*. Henderson's model for the metrology of the fortress defences indicated the positions of the gates at the ends of this street, their width of 66 *pedes monetales* interrupting the regular spacing of the interval towers (Henderson 1991a, fig. 13.8). Corroboration of this aspect of the model came subsequently from Henderson's demonstration that the first two of the six surfaces of the road at the site of the later South Gate of the Roman town could reasonably be assumed to have been of the fortress period (Site 96; Henderson 2001, 53–5, figs 1–4). At this point the road, which ran south-east to St Loye's and Topsham, was on the same line as that indicated for the *via principalis* by the metrology of the defences.

Knowledge of the fortress buildings within the framework determined by the major streets depends mainly on five large excavations in its north-western half, which were at Goldsmith Street and Trichay Street (Chapters 5–6 in this volume) and at Bartholomew Street East, Friernhay Street and St Nicholas Priory (Sites 73, 75 and 78). In the other half of the fortress, the baths have been partly excavated (Bidwell 1979), but the areas explored at Market Street in 1995–2002, though large, were badly damaged in places or did not always require full excavation is advance of development (Site 115; Stead 2002, with references to earlier work not included in Exeter Archaeology Archive Project 2015). Also of great importance have been the numerous minor excavations and watching briefs which began in 1945 during the clearance of War-damaged areas and are still continuing (see Chapter 2 above).

The cohort blocks: their locations and details of the barracks

In fortresses, the barracks (*centuriae*) were usually arranged in blocks of six, consisting of three facing pairs (maniples), each block accommodating one of the ten cohorts of the legion. Henderson assumed that as at Inchtuthil the cohort blocks were arranged symmetrically to either side of the central axis of the fortress, with the exception of the two blocks in the *latera praetoria*. The structural evidence is set out below. For convenience the cohort blocks in Henderson's model are designated A–J, the sequence running across the width of the fortress, starting in the northern corner and ending in the southern corner (Fig. 3.3). The barracks in each cohort block are numbered from 1–6, from north-west to south-east, or in the case of cohort blocks C–D and H–I, from north-east to south-west. The existence of two of the cohort blocks postulated by Henderson is very doubtful; they are not designated by letters and numbers, and their supposed structural remains are discussed in the next section.

As reconstructed by Henderson (1991, fig. 13.3), all the barracks were 60.4 m in length overall, each with 12 *contubernia* with a veranda at their front and a centurion's house 17.8 m in length. From the details now available it is clear that there were minor variations in the size and plans of the barracks.

Cohort block A (Fig. 3.4): two fragments of the rear (south-east) wall of A6 were seen at Queen Street in 1978 (Site 68). It extended *c.* 4.00 m further south-west than the limits of the cohort block as reconstructed by Henderson, who omitted the south-eastern fragment from his plan and showed a street running from north-west to south-east across its position (1991, fig. 13.1). He perhaps regarded the post-trench as a surveying error, but a similar departure from his overall scheme occurs at the north-east ends of G1–2 and J5 (see below). It is difficult to avoid the conclusion that the barracks in cohort blocks A, G and J were longer than those in C, the difference perhaps explained by the provision of an extra *contubernium* in each barrack.

Cohort block B: in 1994 a short length of what appeared to be the rear (south-east) wall of B6 was recorded during sewer repairs in the Cathedral Close (Site 105). It was found after the final version of Henderson's reconstructed plan was published but was in its predicted position.

Cohort block C: for J2–3 (Goldsmith Street I–III, Sites 37 and 39), see EAPIT2, Chapter 6, and for J5–6 (Trichay Street, Site 42), EAPIT2, Chapter 5.

Cohort block D: short lengths of post-trenches fitting the positions suggested by Henderson for D5–6 were seen in 1998 during an evaluation in the Cathedral Cloisters (Site 133).

Cohort block E: the barracks were probably those of the First Cohort, the size of which is uncertain (see below). If it was larger in numbers than the other cohorts, the entire area between the *via sagularis* and the *principia* might have been required for its accommodation. The only relevant observations were made when cellar walls were stripped out at the junction of Waterbeer Street and North Street in 1973–4 (Site 51). A street was seen which presumably marked the north-eastern limit of the cohort block; it ran at right angles to another street running from north-east to south-west. Timber buildings were seen on both sides of the junction to the south-west. The south-eastern building was represented by post-trenches which with a depth of 1.20 m were much more substantial than those of the barracks elsewhere in the fortress.

Cohort block F: nothing is known about this cohort block other than the line of the street that defined its north-east side, which was excavated at 2–8 Bear Street in 1953 (Site 32); it was a continuation of the street bounding the north-east side of cohort block E.

Cohort block G: fragments of G2–4 were excavated at Bartholomew Street East in 1980–1, together with a building of uncertain function to their north-east (Site 73). Henderson restored their plan in conformity with his standard barrack length (see below), but the detailed report can be taken to suggest that barrack G2 had originally extended further north-east (Fig. 3.5). This seems to be confirmed by the Quintana Gate/Mary Arches Street excavations in 2017 (Site 169) which located what appears to have been the eastern corner of G1 and two veranda

Fig. 3.3 Revised plan of the fortress. The numbers in red are those of the sites in the 'Gazetteer of Observations of the Streets Associated with the Fortress and Early Town' in Section 3.2 of this chapter. Wall lines found in excavations in 2019 approximately in the area of barracks I5 – 6 are not shown. Scale 1:2500 (drawn by David Gould)

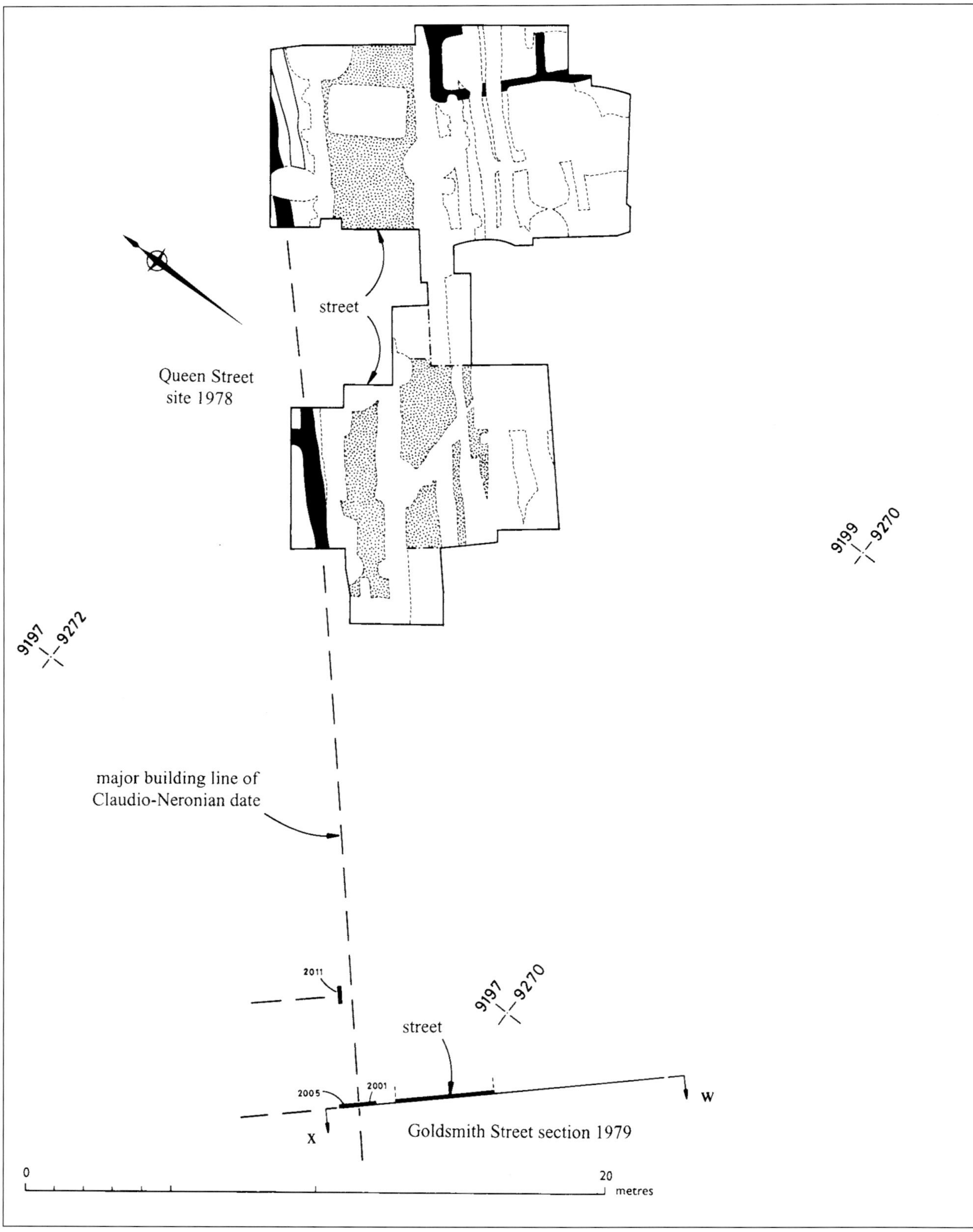

Fig. 3.4 Queen Street and Goldsmith Street (Site 68) 1978–9. The street ran along the south-east side of cohort block A. The post-trench running through the main areas represented the back wall of barrack A6 with part of an internal partition wall to the north-west. The post-trench seen in section to the south-west (labelled 2001) will have been for the back wall of the south-eastern 'immunes *barrack', and a possible partition wall (2011) was seen to the north-east. The post-trenches south-east of the street were thought to have been part of another cohort block, the existence of which now seems unlikely. This plan of Site 68 (Bedford and Salvatore 1993c) was republished to include the features to the south-east which were only seen in section as an appendix (Appendix 1, fig. app. 1.2) in the report on Goldsmith Street I–III (Sites 37/39). Scale 1:200*

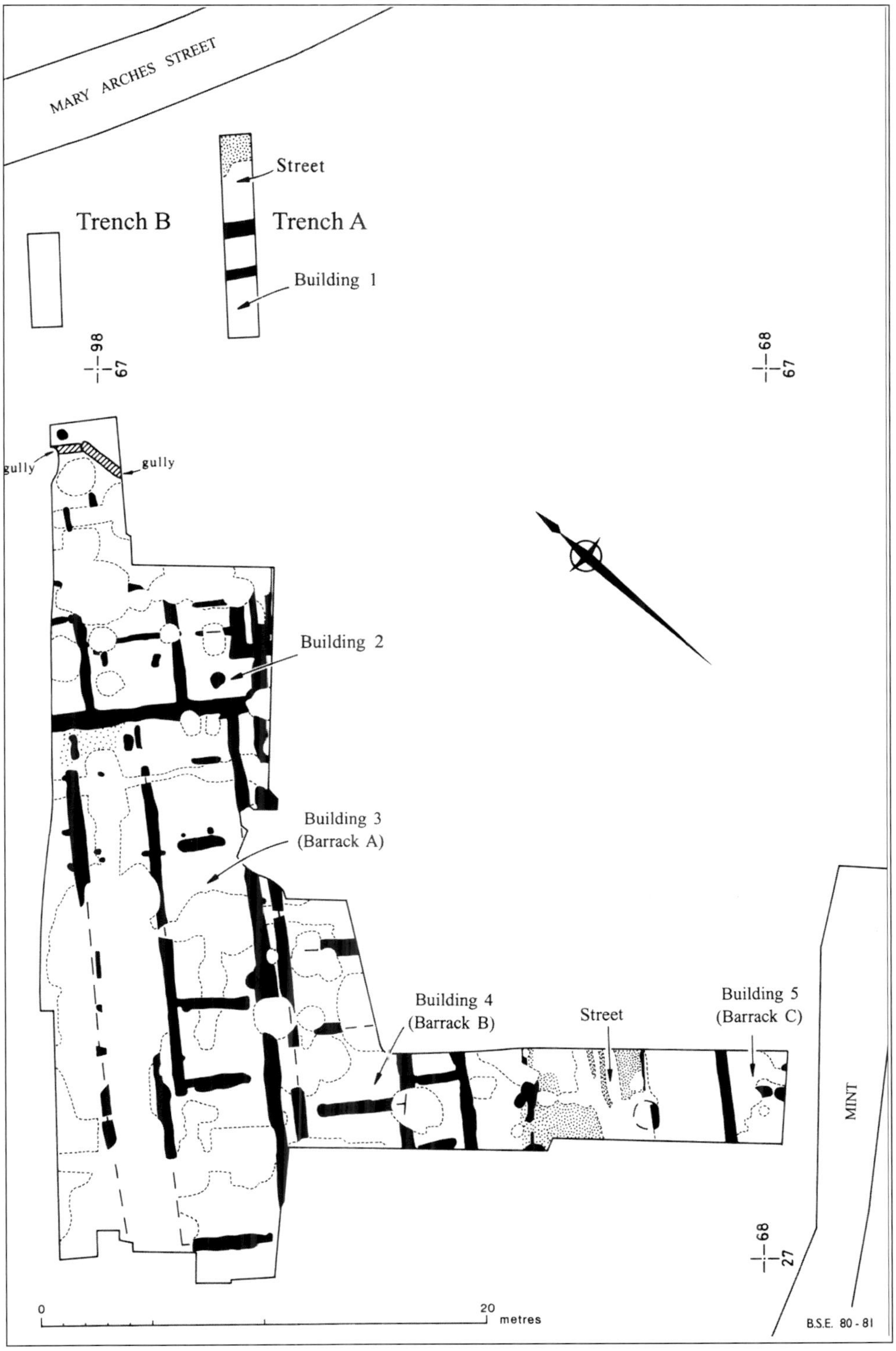

Fig. 3.5 Excavations at Bartholomew Street East in 1980–1 (Site 73). Buildings 3–5/Barracks A–C are barracks G2–4. More of Building 2, originally thought to have been a stable block, was seen in 2017 in the Quintana Gate/Mary Arches Street excavation (Site 169) which also uncovered part of barrack G1. Scale 1:250 (after Salvatore and Simpson 1992, fig. 3)

posts, extending *c*. 4.0 m north-east of the end of the barrack as reconstructed by Henderson.

Cohort block H: fragments of H4–5 were excavated at St Nicholas Priory in 1983–4 (Site 78) and at Friernhay Street/Knapmans Yard Mint in 1994 (Site 107). The 1994 trench also contacted the north-east wall of H6, and its south-west wall was seen at Friernhay Street in 1981 (Fig. 3.6; Site 75).

Cohort block I: the front (north-east) wall of I2 was recorded at Smythen Street/Market Street in 1998 (Site 115).

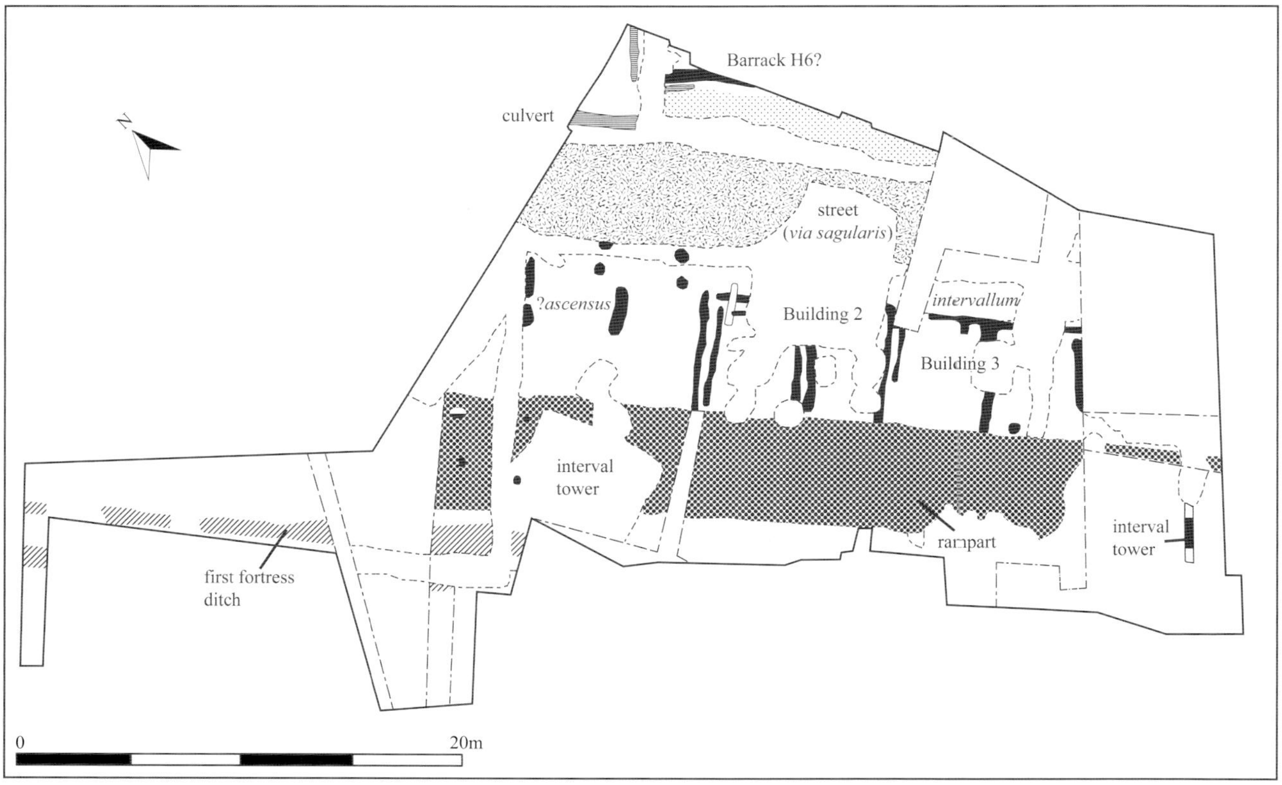

Fig. 3.6 Excavations at Friernhay Street in 1981, showing the earliest military features (Site 75). Scale 1:250 (Bedford and Salvatore 1992b, fig. 2; redrawn by David Gould)

Excavations in 2019 on the south-east side of Fore Street apparently revealed further barracks in this cohort block, presumably I5–6, but details are not yet available.

Cohort block J: the front wall of J1 and the adjacent rear walls of J2 and J3, together with a front wall and partition between two front rooms of J2 and part of a partition between two rear rooms of J3, were recorded at Preston Street in 1998 (Site 115). At earlier excavations in Preston Street (1976–7, Site 60), a post-trench in the position postulated as that of the veranda of J5 in Henderson's reconstruction extended at least 3.00 m beyond the suggested north-eastern limits of the cohort block. Elsewhere in the fortress, the supports of the verandas are represented by postpits rather than continuous post-trenches, and it is possible that the barracks of this cohort had small blocks for the accommodation of the under-officers at their ends (cf. Davison 1989, 33–5). In the same excavation, the wall dividing the front and rear rooms of J5 was seen, as well as the party wall between two of the rear rooms (Fig. 3.7). In 1977 at Mermaid Yard, a site immediately south-east of the earlier excavations, the rear wall of J6 was recorded (Site 63).

Overall, the arrangement of the cohort blocks in the north-western half of the fortress is clear, excluding the barracks of the first cohort. The extent of blocks C, G and H has been determined; only a small fragment of block A has been seen (the back wall of A6), but barracks almost invariably occupied the corners of fortresses. In the other half of the fortress, the remains of block J, though very fragmentary, correspond to the layout of block G. Scarcely anything that might have represented block I had been seen before 2019, but if there were four cohorts in the *praetentura*, the position suggested by Henderson was the only space available for it; the recent excavations in Fore Street seem to confirm the existence of this block. There are only the scantiest traces of blocks B and D, but enough to suggest an arrangement that mirrored that of blocks A and C.

In the more extensive excavations, most of the barracks displayed one or in some parts two periods of alterations or rebuildings which unfortunately were not associated with any dating evidence (summarised in Table 3.2). It would be rash to try and associate them with a particular stage in the history of the fortress, for example the reduction in its occupation in *c*. AD 75.

Two supposed cohort blocks flanking the via decumana*?*

A legion required ten cohort blocks to accommodate its full complement, but Henderson added two more to his reconstructed plan (Fig. 3.1). His main justification was that the positions of blocks A–D in the north-western half of the fortress would have left space for two blocks flanking the *via decumana*, so that the entire arrangement of

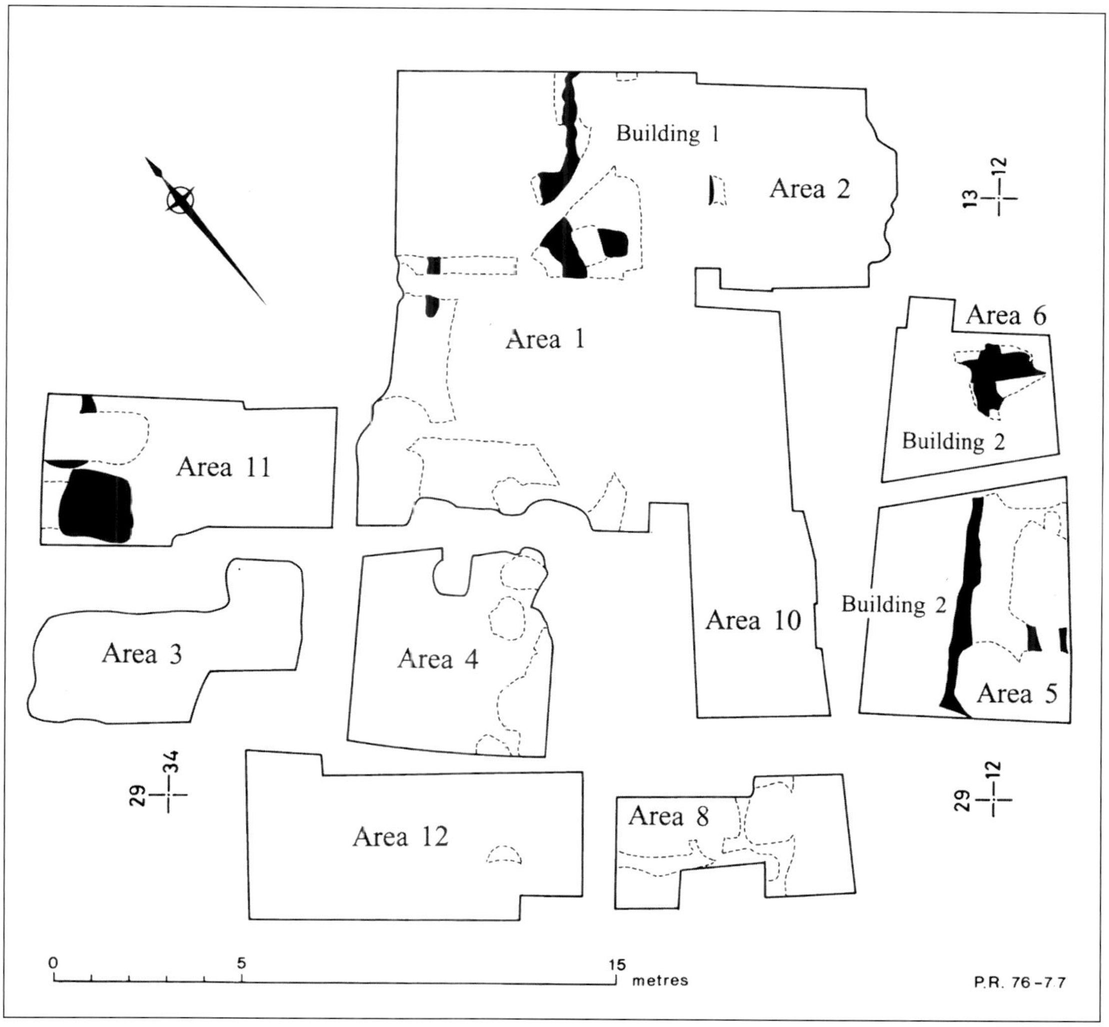

Fig. 3.7 Excavations at Preston Street in 1976–7 (Site 60). Building 1 is part of barrack J5 and Building 2 part of barrack J6. The features in Area 11 are pits, one possibly associated with the demolition of the barracks, the other perhaps earlier. The fragmentary survival is typical of the poor preservation in much of the southern quadrant of the fortress. Scale 1:250 (Bedford and Salvatore 1992e, fig. 2)

Table 3.2 Rebuildings of the barracks

Site	*No.*	*Part*	*Rebuilds*	*Comments*
37/39	C2	centurion's qtr	1	2nd rebuild probably same date as that of C3 and C6 *contubernia*
37/39	C2	*contubernia*	2	
37/39	C3	centurion's qtr	1	
37/39	C3	*contubernia*	2	2nd rebuild probably same date as those of C2 and C6
42	C6	*contubernia*	2	2nd rebuild probably same date as those of C2 and C6
39	–	*contubernia*	1	'*immunes*' barrack
73	G2	*contubernia*	1	
73	G3	*contubernia*	2	
78	H5	*contubernia*	1	internal partitions

barracks in the *retentura* would have mirrored that in the *praetentura*. Comparison with the plans of other fortresses does not entirely support to Henderson's reconstruction: there were usually four cohort blocks in the equivalent position, but there are exceptions. At Leon in Spain and at Neuss in Lower Germany there were large courtyard buildings, probably storehouses, in this position.

Whether these two cohort blocks had existed is open to doubt. Very little is known about the plots flanking the *via decumana*. Remains to the south-east of cohort block A have been recorded only on the other side of the street running along the side of Barrack A6 (Fig. 3.4). At Queen Street there were two phases of construction (1978, Site 68). Two post-trenches 4.10 m apart seemed to represent the side walls of a building, the front of which lay under the south-east side of a street (not shown on Fig. 3.4). A feature, possibly a post-trench, was also found under this street in a section recorded in 1979 16.5 m south-east of the Queen Street site (Site 68; Appendix 1, Fig. App. 1.1, context 2024, in report on Sites 37/39). This period of activity was succeeded by the construction of the street and another building immediately to the north-east of the earlier example on the main site; only the western corner of this later building, where there was a room with an internal area of *c*. 3.00 m by 2.00 m, fell within the limits of the excavation. The room was originally identified as the rear room of a *contubernium* (Fig. 3.3), and then, after revision of the conjectural plan of the cohort block, as the front room in a barrack facing in the opposite direction (Henderson 1991a, fig. 13.1). This hypothetical barrack would not have fitted into the regular spacing of a cohort block extending as far north-east as the *via sagularis* and mirroring the position of cohort block H (as shown in Henderson 1988, fig. 5.3). In the later reconstruction (Fig. 3.1), the building is taken to represent the third barrack to the south-west in a cohort block which was set back *c*. 12.0 m from the north-eastern *via sagularis*, allowing space for a building represented by post-trenches recorded at 228 High Street in 1975 (Site 61). A post-trench parallel to the *via sagularis* and much larger than those of the barracks was tentatively identified as the side wall of a granary. The remains, only seen in sections revealed when the walls of post-medieval cellars were removed, also included three parallel post-trenches spaced *c*. 1.0 m. They ran across at least part of the *via sagularis* and were tentatively identified as some sort of buttressing of the supposed granary to the south-west. Such an arrangement has yet to be recorded at other timber granaries, and it seems simpler to accept these post-trenches as settings for the supports of a raised floor in a granary which was built across the *via sagularis*. A building in this position would have belonged either to a late stage in the occupation of the fortress or even have had some sort of official function in the early town (see 'Other buildings in the fortress', below).

In addition, according to the later reconstruction, at the southern corner of the site of the supposed cohort block there should have been another barrack facing that to the north-east, but metalling continued for at least 2.0 m across the line that its end wall should have occupied, and no post-trenches were preserved in a contemporary surface that extended a further 2.0 m to the south-east (Site 68). Although it is possible that the planning of these supposed barracks could have been more irregular than elsewhere in the fortress, their existence still depends solely on a single room from which an entire cohort block has been projected.

The second of these supposed cohort blocks lay to the south-east of the *via decumana*. Two post-trenches apparently of the fortress period were seen in the Cathedral Close in 1994, but their positions do not fit Henderson's reconstruction (Site 105).

The presence of two successive buildings with different plans at Queen Street shows that the construction sequence in the area south-east of cohort block A differed from that on the site of the neighbouring barracks, and indeed at most if not all of the other barracks excavated elsewhere in the fortress. The only structure of any substance possibly preceding a barrack was a post-trench at Trichay Street, though it might have been part of an earlier barrack, the remainder of which was removed by a later rebuilding (Site 42; see below, Chapter 5). Other examples of two periods of buildings with different plans were represented by two substantial post-trenches meeting at a right angle north-east of cohort block G at Bartholomew Street East (Site 73) under the so-called stables (see below) and an earlier building (Building 4) on the site of the *fabrica* (Site 42: see below, Chapter 5). The absence of any definite earlier activities on the sites of the barracks indicates that they were amongst the first buildings in the fortress to have been built, and that temporary occupation was allowed in other parts of the fortress on sites perhaps intended for other types of buildings. The primacy of the barracks is also evident in the construction programme at Inchtuthil, along with some other essential buildings such as the granaries.

Cavalry barracks

Henderson (1988, 103–5) argued at some length that cohort blocks G and J accommodated two quingenary *alae*, each consisting of 480 cavalrymen. Their presence thus accounted for the apparent need for two additional blocks in the fortress. Henderson followed the then current thinking which envisaged separate buildings for the men and their mounts and interpreted a building north-east of cohort block G as a set of stables (Fig. 3.5, Building 2). Only a few years later, it began to be recognised that barracks which combined stables with quarters for the men were used to house cavalry. Sommer (1995) listed a number of barracks where there was clear evidence, in the form of roughly rectangular pits to collect urine, that the front parts were stables, with the rear rooms serving as living quarters for the men. Subsequent discoveries, particularly the complete excavation of series of examples at South Shields and Wallsend (Hodgson 2003; Hodgson and Bidwell 2004), confirmed Sommer's prediction that stable barracks would prove to be the standard form of cavalry accommodation. The absence in the barracks of cohort block G of pits to collect urine is enough to show that they were not built to accommodate cavalry.

In the fortress at Neuss (*Novaesium*), in north-western Germany, Claudio-Neronian buildings that can now be identified as stable barracks were in an area that seems to have accommodated an auxiliary unit (Koenen 1904, 143–5, Tafn IV and XV; von Petrikovits 1975, 56–7; Hodgson 2003, 73). At other fortresses, including Caerleon (Zienkiewicz 1993, 81–2), there are much less certain indications of auxiliary cavalry. There is no evidence at Exeter for this sort of accommodation. Moreover, a defended enclosure north-east of the fortress at Princesshay could have accommodated a cavalry unit (EAPIT 1, Chapter 5).

Part of a legion's regular strength included a small contingent of cavalry, the *equites legionis*. Josephus gave their number as 120 in the 1st century AD, and buildings that might have accommodated them have been variously identified (von Petrikovits 1975, 50–4; Pitts and St Joseph 1985, 169–70, 181–2; Manning and Scott 1989, 119–20). None has the urine pits typical of cavalry accommodation, and where the *equites legionis* were located in fortresses is still an unsolved problem.

'Immunes *barracks*'

Immediately south-east of cohort block C there seems to have been an additional pair of barracks. Their plot was defined by streets to their south-west and south-east, and by the cohort blocks to the north-west and north-east. Parts of five *contubernia* in the north-west barrack were seen in Area III at Goldsmith Street in 1971–2 (Site 39, Fig. 3.8; see below, Chapter 6, Fig. 6.1). Their post-trenches were larger than those in the adjoining cohort block, and the front rooms were smaller, but overall the floor areas of these barracks in their second phase were similar to the others at Exeter, contrary to Davison's (1989, 45) discussion of them. Post-trenches along the side of the street defining the south-east side of the plot were recorded in a section exposed in 1979, 16.5 m south-west of the Queen Street site (Site 68). They seem to have represented the back wall of a second barrack together with the side walls of a *contubernium*. Finally, at Pancras Lane, part of the larger Trichay Street excavations in 1972–3, the south-west end of the plot was explored in two narrow trenches (Site 42; see below, Chapter 5, Fig. 5.7). Henderson interpreted the remains as those of two adjoining 'centurial or officers' quarters' of unequal width, and they certainly did not represent a continuation of the *contubernia* to the north-east.

Henderson thought that these barracks were possibly for *immunes*, soldiers whose special skills excused them from routine duties, in this specific instance because they were craftsmen (*fabri*) working in the nearby *fabrica* (Henderson 1988, 103). As Salvatore and Steinmetzer (2018, 797) have noted, the small size of the rooms at the front of the north-western barrack, compared to their equivalents in the cohort barracks, might mean that they were used not for storing arms but were for the craft tools and other equipment of the *fabri*.

The previous Exeter reports have not noted the resemblances between the placing of these barracks in the fortress plan and the arrangements at Inchtuthil, where a 'barrack-like' building in the *latera praetorii* lay immediately south of the *fabrica* (Pitts and St Joseph 1985, 161–2, figs 43 and 79). At Exeter the *fabrica* was sited almost immediately south-west of the barracks, separated from them only by a small building which Henderson identified as perhaps the house of 'the officer in charge of the workshops' (Henderson 1988, 103). It is even possible that the Exeter barracks took the same form as those at Inchtuthil, with only one set of what in a normal barrack would have been the centurion's quarters. If the south-west end of the street between the barracks was not closed off, contrary to Henderson's reconstruction, there would have been more immediate access to the *fabrica*.

Whether the *immunes* were separated from their centuries is a question which has been much discussed (von Petrikovits 1975, 43–50; Baatz 1977; Pitts and St Joseph 1985, 170–1). The similarities between the siting of the *fabricae* and of barracks not associated with cohort blocks at Exeter and Inchtuthil strengthens the case for special accommodation of the *fabri*.

Barracks of the first cohort

From the Flavian period onwards, the barracks of the first cohort in new fortresses were usually placed on the dextral side of the *latera praetorii*. Nijmegen, in the Netherlands, is an exception, but the position of the first cohort on the dextral side of the *praetentura* can be explained by the proportions, width to length, of the fortress (Driessen 2009). The relative width of the fortress at Exeter is even smaller than that of Nijmegen (EAPIT 1, Chapter 5), and not enough is known of the equivalent area at Exeter to rule it out as the location for the barracks of the first cohort. However, the question depends partly on the size of the first cohort, the strength of which was substantially increased in or possibly before the Flavian period. Its accommodation at Inchtuthil, a fortress built in *c.* AD 82–86/7 and then abandoned, consisted of ten barracks rather than the six required by each of the other cohorts: a strength of 800 rather than 480 men is thus indicated for the first cohort. This extra provision is not quite as large as Hyginus specified in *de munitione castrorum*, describing the plan of a marching camp 'as the first cohort is of double strength, it will have a double assignment of space' (Miller and DeVoto 1994, 68; the translation is Frere's (1980, 51)). Frere argued that Hyginus's essay was of late 1st-century AD date and cited indications that at other fortresses of this period extra space had been allowed for the first cohort. Keppie (1984, 176) considered it possible that its augmented size might have continued from practice in the Republic. In the 2nd century AD the size of the cohort was reduced to that of the others.

The evidence from Claudio-Neronian fortresses is equivocal. At Claudian Colchester there seem to have been six barracks on the dextral side of the *latera praetorii*; at late Neronian Gloucester there were also barracks 100.0 m in length in the same relative position, but their exceptional size suggested that the strength of centuries had been augmented (Davison 1989, 56). Henderson's placing of the first cohort in the plan of

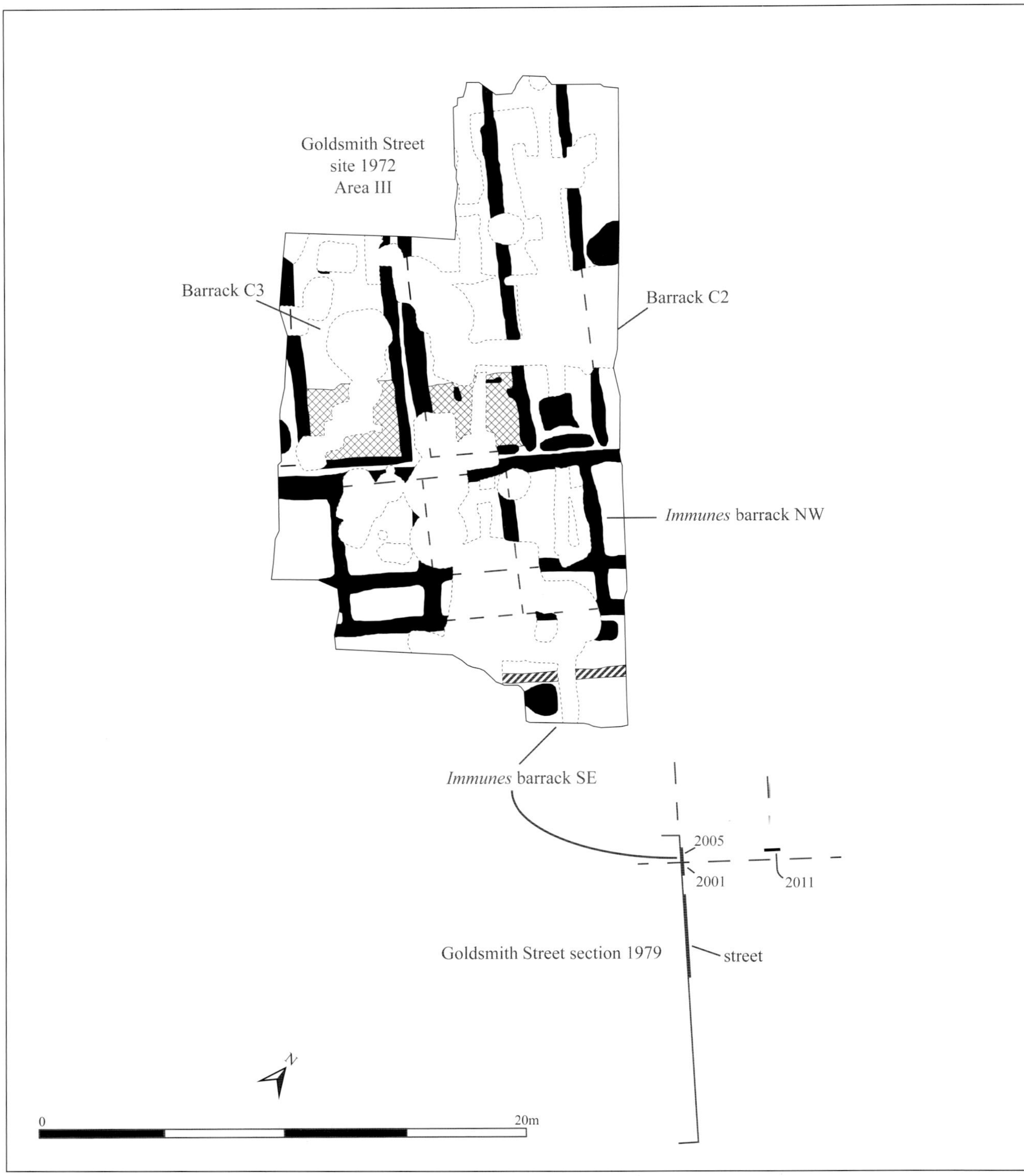

Fig. 3.8 The probable immunes barracks south-east of cohort block C at Goldsmith Street Area III and Queen Street (Sites 39 and 68). Scale 1:250 (redrawn by David Gould)

the Exeter fortress follows a common pattern, but other possibilities cannot be excluded. At Usk the dextral side of the *latera praetorii* was mainly occupied by *fabricae* (Manning and Scott 1989, 168–9, figs 71–2), and, as noted above, at Nijmegen the first cohort was accommodated in the *praetentura*.

The size and position of the barracks and the internal plan of the fortress

The complete dimensions of a barrack at Exeter have yet to be recorded, but reasonable estimates have been made for a number of examples. Lengths of *c.* 62.0 m were proposed for those of cohort block C by Bidwell (1980,

35, tab. 1). A more precise measurement was given by Henderson (1988, 102–3; 1991, 80–3, figs 13.3–4, 13.6, 13.12): allowing for a space of 2.0 m between the ends of the barracks and the north-western *via sagularis*, their length would have been 204 *pedes monetales* (60.4 m), giving them proportions width to length of 1:6. Space 2.0 m wide between the cohort blocks and the *via sagularis* was established by the positions of the back walls of barracks H1 and J6 and was assumed to have been repeated elsewhere.

It must be accepted that the dimensions of barracks elsewhere in the fortress differed from those in cohort block C. Barracks A6, G2, J6 and, it seems, G1 were between 2.5 m and 4.0 m longer than in Henderson's reconstruction. The dimensions of cohort blocks E–F and H–I, as estimated by Henderson, were mainly determined by the existence of *tabernae* and porticos lining the *viae praetoria* and *principalis*; the existence of at least some of these structures is doubtful (see below), and the barracks might have extended into areas which they were thought to have occupied. Variations in the lengths of barracks in other fortresses have been described by Davison (1989, 23–4).

The barracks at Exeter were thus up to 64.0 m in length, and it is conceivable that those in cohort blocks E–F and H–I were even longer. They were nevertheless much smaller than barracks in other legionary fortresses, which is accounted for not only by the small size of Exeter but also by its constricted width (Henderson 1988, 95; EAPIT 1, Chapter 5). The second factor is also the reason why cohort blocks H and I are placed with their centurions' quarters next to the *via praetoria* rather than the *via sagularis* which was the usual arrangement for barracks other than those in the *latera praetorii*. At Exeter there was not enough room to place four cohort blocks with the same orientation across the width of the fortress.

These apparent variations in the size of barracks, even the perhaps larger ones in cohort blocks E and F, could all be contained within the plots delimited by Henderson's design dimensions for the streets of the fortress (Fig. 3.1).

Accommodation for the tribunes and other senior officers

The legion had six tribunes and a *praefectus castrorum*, each with their own residences. These buildings took the form of large courtyard houses, usually with additional wings for domestic and administrative activities, which occupied plots along the *via principalis* on the side opposite the *principia* (Pitts and St Joseph 1985, 136–41). The only relevant excavation at Exeter was at Mary Arches Street in 1975 (Site 54) where a street ran between two buildings which might well have been senior officers' houses. Henderson in his reconstruction of the fortress plan allowed ten plots for these houses, which is more than necessary. Other buildings might also have been placed on this side of the *via principalis*, as at Usk where there were three granaries next to the *porta principalis dextra*.

The *praetorium* is discussed in the next section.

Other buildings in the fortress

It can be estimated that about 58% of the fortress interior was occupied by living accommodation, a figure calculated on the basis of the cohort blocks as reconstructed in this survey, adding the *praetorium* (see below) and seven houses for the senior officers. Rather more space was allocated to accommodation in three other fortresses analysed by von Petrikovits (1975, 116): 67.5% at Neuss in Germany, 76.3% at Inchtuthil (though several other building types were missing) and 79.5% at *Carnuntum* in Austria. The difference between Neuss and Exeter is not very large, and if the auxiliary barracks at Neuss, not paralleled in other fortresses, are excluded, the areas are similar. Since von Petrikovits' study was published, much has been added to the plan of Chester, and, though the function of some of the buildings is uncertain, only a little more than half of the interior seems to have been occupied by accommodation (Mason 2012, ill. 20b).

The areas at Exeter which were occupied by other building types thus seem to have been proportionate to those at some other fortresses. A few have been identified, but it is impossible to reconstruct the full complement. The *fabrica* south-west of cohort block C is referred to in this volume (see below, Chapter 5), but it was perhaps only one of several workshops with a variety of plans: von Petrikovits (1975, Tafn 3 and 6) identified two at Caerleon and four at Neuss, some tentatively, with further examples in the *intervallum* at both fortresses. Likewise, granaries were probably sited in several parts of the fortress; sites close to the gates were favoured, and at Exeter only a position next to the south-west gate, occupied by cohort blocks H and I, can be excluded. Large store buildings of courtyard type, presumably for consumables other than cereals, are also found in a number of fortresses (von Petrikovits 1975, Bilder 20–1). Finally, a variety of further building types occur in some fortresses, the functions of which remain uncertain; suggested identifications include market buildings (*macella*), guild buildings for privileged groups (*scholae*), prisons and religious buildings.

Details of buildings other than barracks that have been identified at Exeter are as follows:

The baths: see EAPIT 1, Chapter 5.

The hospital (valetudinarium): bathing was often a medical treatment, and the fortress hospital was usually next to the baths. At Exeter the hospital could have been sited immediately north-east or south-east of the baths. The former is more likely: to the south-east of the baths the ground begins to slope downwards; the level ground to the north-east would be more suitable for the hospital, which would have been a large courtyard building.

The granaries (horrea): in 1972–3, at 196–7 High Street (Site 43: see below, Chapter 7) a grid of postholes spaced *c*. 1.5 m apart represented the supports for the raised floor of one or more granaries. Both the spacing and the size of the individual postholes, usually 0.3–0.4 m deep and up to 0.15 m in diameter, were very similar to those of some of the granaries at Usk (Manning 1981, fig. 69). For another possible granary of a different type and later date, seen at 228 High Street in 1975 (Site 61), see above.

The headquarters (principia) *and legate's residence* (praetorium): these buildings were always adjacent, with the *principia* sited at the intersection of the *viae principalis* and *praetoria*. The *praetorium* was usually sited immediately behind the *principia*, both buildings occupying a plot of the same width, but at Exeter the position of the baths precludes this possibility if due allowance is made for the space taken up by the *palaestra*. There was probably space for the *praetorium* immediately south-east of the *principia*; the first cohort might have occupied the entire area to the north-east. If this was the case, Fox's House 2, excavated at South Street in 1945–6 (Site 15; Fox 1952a, 7–10, 33–6, fig. 3, pls XIV and XVII) would have been part of the *praetorium*. The excavated area included a range of rooms 9.8 m in width with a probable veranda to the south-east (Fig. 3.9). Immediately behind this feature was a room of considerable size, 5.7 m wide and at least 11.3 m in length; it had a clean, sanded floor in the centre of which was a rectangular hearth made of thick tiles and stone fragments (Fox 1952a, pl. IIIB; a *tegula* is visible). Dividing this room from a street to the north-west was a lobby or passage 2.35 m wide, probably with an entry from the street. On the south-west side of the large room, a door communicated with another room described as a kitchen. On the opposite side of the street, which was 2.75–3.05 m wide with a central drain, was a substantial wall represented by post holes 0.8 m deep spaced 0.9 m apart on average (Fox 1952a, 36–7). The wall was interrupted by an entry which was opposite the probable door opening into the lobby or passage of House 2.

A feature which distinguishes these buildings from others in the fortress is their construction with posts driven directly into the ground rather than set in trenches. The depth of the postholes in Fox's House 2 is uncertain, but their diameters were smaller than those of the other building. Tiles were found in the filling of the drain in the centre of the road and in occupation layers in House 2 (Fox 1952a, 8, 33), indicating that one or both of the buildings had tiled roofs, which elsewhere in the fortress only occurred at the baths. The occupation in House 2 seems to have been mainly domestic, but from both buildings there were fragments of crucibles. They were originally thought to have been used in preparing materials for enamelling (Fox 1952a, 64), but some have now been shown to have traces of leaded bronze while others were used in the refining or assaying of silver (Chapter 10 in this volume).

The width of House 2 (9.8 m) is similar to those of the centurial quarters in the Exeter barracks, but the latter were without verandas. Most of its width was occupied by a single large room which was at least 11.3 m in length which would have taken up more than half the overall length of centurial quarters of the dimensions known at Exeter. The rooms in centurial quarters were usually arranged around a central corridor (Hoffmann 1995, 128–9). The plan of House 2 combined with its exceptional construction make it most unlikely to have been part of a barrack. Instead, it might have been part of one range of a courtyard house, a standard plan for *praetoria* and the houses of tribunes. The other building (House 1), with its deeply-founded posts, was presumably one of the ranges surrounding the courtyard which formed the most extensive element of the *principia*. The overall dimensions of the whole complex, which would also have included a basilica and a rear range with a shrine (*aedes*) at its centre flanked by offices, can be estimated as *c*. 60–64 m by 64 m, perhaps larger than its equivalent at Usk, which would have had a maximum depth of 55.0 m, though there is no indication of its width (Manning and Scott 1989, 167, fig. 71).

Intervallum *buildings*: small buildings were found in the *intervallum* on the north-west side of the fortress at 10–18 Bartholomew Street East in 1959 (Site 35; Holbrook and Fox 1987) and further buildings to their south-west in 2017 at Quintana Gate/Mary Arches Street (Site 169). Similar buildings and large ovens excavated in 1981 at Friernhay Street on the south-west side of the fortress (Fig. 3.11; Site 75) are discussed elsewhere (EAPIT 1, Chapter 5, section on the dating of the fortress occupation).

Tabernae *and porticos lining the via decumana?*

In 1980 excavations below the floor of the basement in 41–42 High Street encountered a sequence of activities thought to have been of the fortress period (Site 72; Fig. 3.10). The earliest features were a street, the via *decumana* of the fortress, which was bordered by a drainage ditch; the ditch had been filled and replaced to the south-east alongside the widened and resurfaced street. Then two pairs of postpits were dug, those to the south-east, which cut the second ditch, measuring up to 1.24 m across and 1.30 m in depth. They were much larger than those 2.50 m to the north-west, the better-preserved of which was 0.70 m across and 0.40 m deep. The postpits were at first regarded as probably of the early civil period, and one contained a sherd from a samian bowl (Dr. 29) of late Flavian date. Henderson (1988, 97) later saw them as part of a portico at the side of the *via decumana*, a common feature of the principal streets in

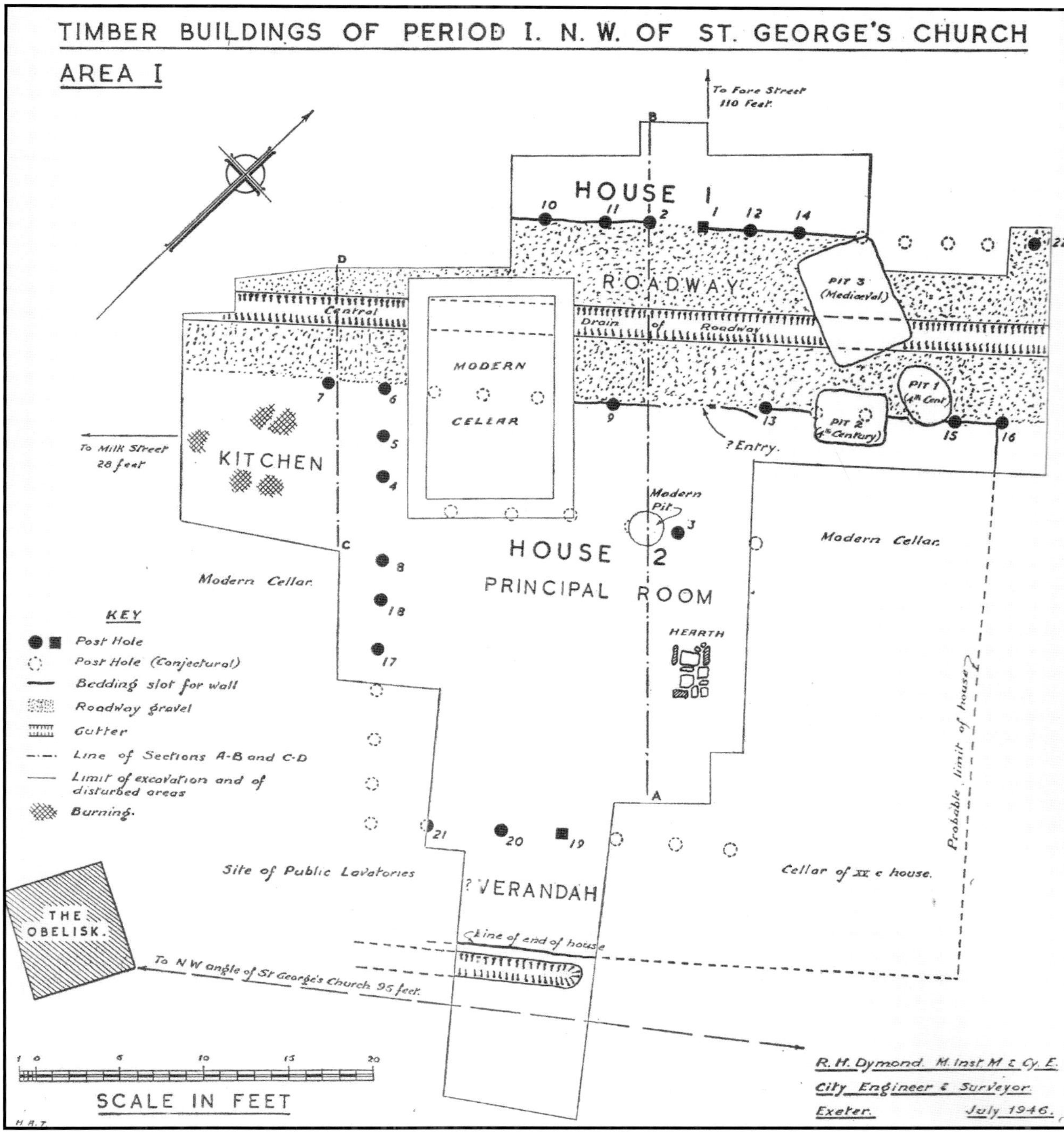

Fig. 3.9 Buildings excavated south-west of South Street in 1945–6 (Site 15). Found long before the fortress was discovered and regarded as part of a civilian settlement of Claudian origin, House 2 can now be identified as part of the praetorium *and House 1 as an element of the* principia. *The* via principalis *lies* c. *4.0 m to the south-west of the excavations (Fox 1952a, pl. XIV)*

fortresses, and then suggested that the space south-east of the portico might have been occupied by rooms roughly 2.00 m deep built against the 'aqueduct wall' (see below). These rooms, according to Henderson, would have been *tabernae*, open-ended structures behind porticos, the use of which is uncertain. They are prominent in the plan of the fortress at Inchtuthil, but as at other fortresses are very much larger (on average 8.23 m deep and 5.49 m at Inchtuthil: Pitts and St Joseph 1985, 179) than the space at Exeter would allow. Because they would have had to be improbably small and there is no structural evidence for their existence, Henderson's restoration of *tabernae* along the *via decumana* cannot be accepted.

That leaves for consideration the postpits Henderson took to represent a portico. In another, earlier excavation at Broadgate in 1977 (Site 62), four postpits in two rows were found on the north-west side of the *via decumana* (Bidwell 1979, 120, fig. 35), and Henderson suggested that

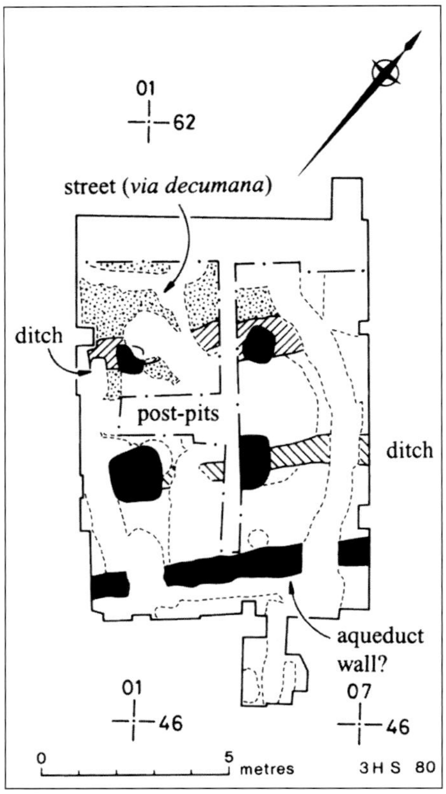

Fig. 3.10 Features at 41–42 High Street, 1980 (Site 72) Scale 1:200 (Bedford and Salvatore 1993a, fig. 2)

both sides of the street were thus lined with porticos. In Bidwell's report the postpits were associated with the early civil period, because they represented the fourth stage in a sequence of activity: first came two water pipes probably laid almost at the end of the fortress period, then a ditch was dug along the side of the street, which was then cut by a large pit (Bidwell 1979, 60, fig. 14), in turn cut by one of the postpits. Henderson did not state his reasons for rejecting this sequence. The excavation, in the security vaults of a disused bank, was very difficult, but most of the features were intercutting, and their relationships seemed clear enough.

At Usk there were porticos lining the *via principalis* which were not associated with *tabernae*; instead they ran along the fronts of open-ended compounds and, at one point, of a senior officer's house (Manning and Scott 1989, 114–20, figs 37–40). The roofs of the portico were supported by two rows of large posts set in pits, all of which were of roughly the same size and arranged so that each post was directly opposite its pair in the other row. At the two sites bordering the *via decumana* at Exeter, the pits were of different sizes, those in the rows closer to the street being much smaller, and they were not placed opposite the larger pits in the other rows.

Doubts about the date of the postpits at the Broadgate site extend to 41–42 High Street. The original interpretation of the Broadgate features as part of a timber building of the early civil period still seems valid and also applies to the postpits at 41–42 High Street. The smaller postpits alongside the street can be interpreted as supports for verandas, the larger examples set farther back forming the front walls of buildings of substantial size.

It is nevertheless possible that there were porticos along at least parts of the *viae principalis* and *praetoria*. The building that was probably the *praetorium* (Fox's House 2: Fig. 3.9) was traced to within *c*. 4.00 m of the estimated line of the *via principalis*. The end room, Fox's 'kitchen', was connected to the larger room to the north-east by a door and was certainly not part of an independent building. Even if its south-western limit lay just beyond the excavated area, there would have been room for a portico but not for *tabernae*.

Water supply

The fortress baths required a large volume of water for their daily operation, perhaps something in the order of 32,000 litres (Bidwell 1979, 41). Such quantities could only have been supplied by an aqueduct, a short length of which, it has been argued, was found under the basement of 41–42 High Street in 1980 (Site 72; first identified in Henderson 1984, fig. 14; Henderson 1988, 100–1, fig. 5.3). Its remains consisted of a foundation of trap rubble *c*. 0.70 m in width south-east of the postpits described in the preceding section. The wall above would have been no wider than 0.60 m if, as was usual, it was offset from the edges of the foundations. Lengths of solid walls supporting a channel or leat (*substructiones*) are used fairly commonly in the courses of aqueducts (Hodge 1992, 129, fig. 80), but they are much wider than the wall at Exeter. Hodge also considered that if the level of an aqueduct had to be higher than 1.50–2.00 m, it would have been carried by an arched structure rather than a solid wall. Henderson (1988, 101) estimated that his wall would have been *c*. 6.00 m high when it reached the fortress baths, presumably because of the fall of the ground to the south-west. There seems to be no reason why the wall in the High Street basement should not have belonged to a building fronting onto the street of the civil period between *Insulae X* and *XIV*, which had been the *via decumana* of the fortress (for another wall of the civil period in the basement, see the Exeter Archaeology Archive Project 2015, Committee Report, 27 June 1980, fig. 2).

A more likely source for the water supplied to the fortress was the aqueduct known to have supplied the early town. The launder which carried it over the ditch of the north-western defences near their northern corner is dated to AD 100/101, and a pipe line has been traced across the Goldsmith and Trichay Street sites (see below, Chapters 5–6). A plausible but hypothetical course for the aqueduct between the town and springs 0.9 km to the north-east at Well Street has been plotted by Henderson (1988, fig. 5.14). This extra-mural part of the aqueduct could have been constructed in the fortress period, its excavated elements in the town representing alterations to the route of the system early in the civil period.

Series of wooden water pipes have been found in the fortress: they were joined with iron collars and laid on wooden sleepers in flat-bottomed trenches *c.* 0.80 m wide. One problem in understanding the distribution systems which they represented is that some were used to supply fresh water, while others were for waste water. In the service areas south-east of the bath-house, it is uncertain which purpose the pipes served, but later pipes in the street to the south-east were connected to drains associated with the basilica and forum which replaced the baths (Bidwell 1979, 35–7, 77, figs 7, 12 and 19). The pipeline which was traced along the side of the *fabrica* (Site 42) turned south-east to run beside the granaries down to the *via decumana* (Bidwell 1979, 60, fig. 14); the pipe was clearly running to or from the baths, and because of the distance it traversed can scarcely have been for waste water. Another wooden water pipe was found in the *via sagularis* at Friernhay Street (Site 75; Fig. 3.11).

Conclusions

The analysis set out above relies on a combination of area excavations and many more fragmentary observations. Taken together, they have produced the most extensively explored plan of any Claudio-Neronian fortress in the Roman world (EAPIT 1, Chapter 5). Much of this was made possible by the efforts of the late Christopher Henderson and his colleagues who seized, and indeed sometimes ruthlessly engineered, any opportunity to record the Roman archaeology of Exeter. Another achievement was the deduction of the surveying principles on which the fortress plan was based, making sense of even the smallest discoveries. Nevertheless, the Exeter plan is far from complete, and after many years when little came to light, the recent excavations at Quintana Gate (Site 169) and Fore Street (Site 204) should add important details when they are fully published.

Section 3.2: Gazetteer of observations of the streets associated with the fortress and early town *by David Gould*

The following gazetteer lists all known elements of Exeter's Early Roman street system that have been revealed through excavation. The gazetteer combines evidence from the legionary fortress as well as the early civil town because, with a small number of exceptions, the fortress street system was maintained in the early civil town before an expansion of the street grid occurred from the later 2nd century AD once the new defensive circuit had been constructed (EAPIT 1, Chapter 6). It should

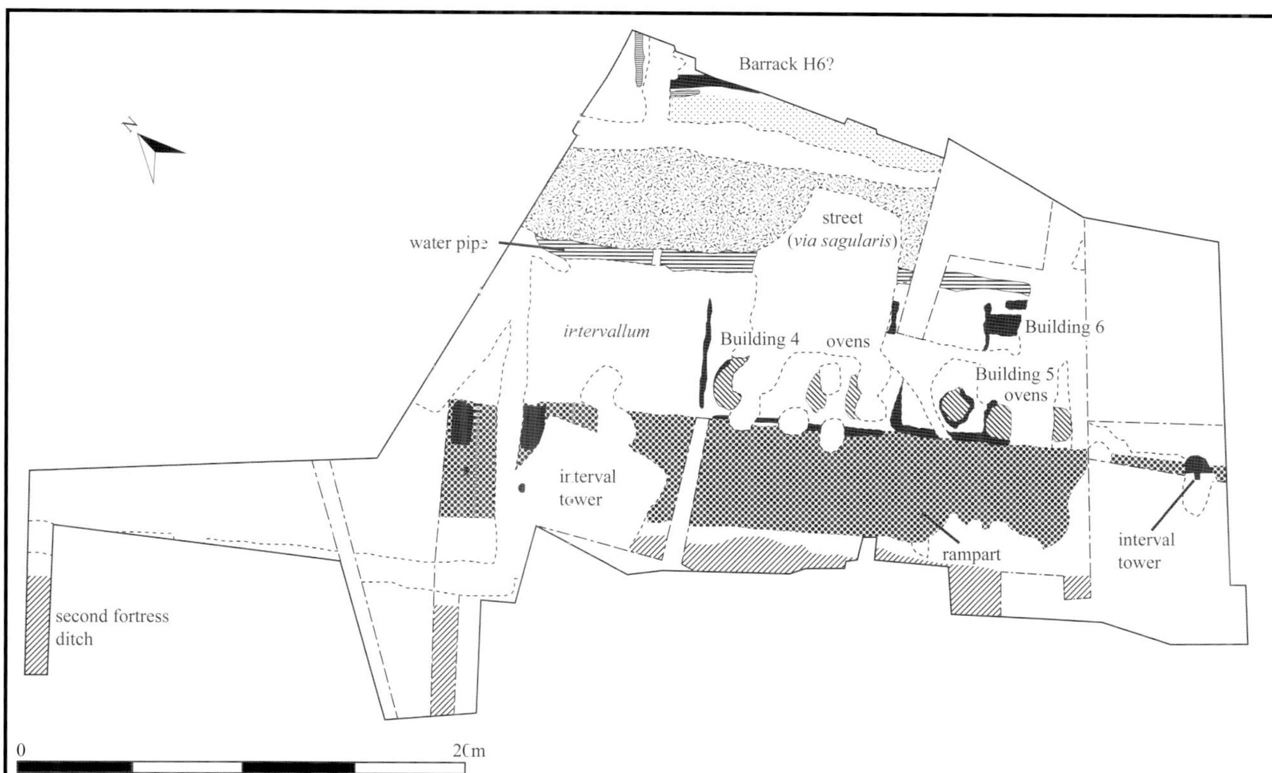

Fig. 3.11 Excavations at Friernhay Street in 1981 (Site 75), latest military features. Barrack H6 is labelled as Building 1 Scale 1:250 (Bedford and Salvatore 1992b, fig. 3; redrawn by David Gould)

be noted that the military streets were not in every case followed exactly in the early town. The *via decumana* of the fortress (Street D) was seemingly replaced by a new street *c*. 3 m further to the north-west to judge from the evidence adjacent to the forum (DCi). Presumably this was to create a wider plot for the forum.

Figure 3.13 depicts the street layout of Roman Exeter and the organisation of its *insulae* during the early civil period with the areas of excavated streets highlighted. Each major street has been assigned a letter (A, B, C, etc.) and where evidence has been found along those streets for contemporary Roman metalling then these have been assigned identifiers (A1, A2, B1, etc.). These excavated sections have then been given the suffix of -i in order to differentiate them from street sections that date to the late civil period; these late civil streets have been given the suffix -ii and are detailed in Section 3.3 of this chapter. It is necessary to assign these suffixes because in some cases these streets do not demonstrate continuity of use, as excavations have in some instances produced evidence of early civil street surfaces but no evidence of later Roman metalling. Streets and alleyways that were in use during the military period (Fig. 3.12), such as inter barrack block streets, but were not retained in the early town's street grid, have been assigned the letter X.

Each gazetteer entry below gives the following information:

- Street number
- Site name corresponding to the name of the excavation that produced evidence of the street as listed in Chapter 2 in this volume
- Excavation gazetteer number corresponding to the site numbers listed in Chapter 2 in this volume
- City HER monument number where the excavated street remains have been recorded by the City HER
- Location within Exeter (*i.e.* its *insula* number or whether it was extra-mural)
- The principal references recording details of the excavated street sections; the abbreviation EAACR refers to the Exeter Archaeology Advisory Committee Reports

Street Number: A1i

- Site Name: St Catherine's Almshouses
- Excavation gazetteer number: 89
- City HER monument number: 10089
- Location: extra-mural
- References: EAACR 1987; Frere 1988, 473

A section of metalled road surface outside, and parallel to, the NE line of the defences of the fortress and early town. The road, probably leading to the NE gate of the Early Roman town, was resurfaced on several occasions. Originally thought to date to the period of military occupation, the reassignment of the outer ditch to the early town suggests a civilian context. The street was obliterated in the late 3rd or early 4th century AD when a stone house was constructed above its line.

Street Number: A2i

- Site Name: Princesshay
- Excavation gazetteer number: 156
- City HER monument number: no HER number assigned
- Location: extra-mural
- References: Steinmetzer, Stead, Pearce, Bidwell and Allan forthcoming

The street was recorded as being over 2.5 m wide at this point.

Street Number: A3i

- Site Name: Chapel Street Abbot's Lodge (Fox 1952 Trench 17)
- Excavation gazetteer number: 29
- City HER monument number: 10011
- Location: extra-mural
- References: Fox 1952a, 51–2

A section of extra-mural road was at least 3 m wide although its full width was not seen during excavation. The road was resurfaced on at least three occasions and was equipped with a central drain.

Street Number: A4i

- Site Name: Paul Street; North Gate Court
- Excavation gazetteer number: 76; 164
- City HER monument number: 10093
- Location: extra-mural
- References: EAACR 1985; Henderson, 1985b, 24–25; Bedford and Salvatore 1993g, 1, fig. 3; Farnell 2010a, 3, fig. 3

Several sections of the extra-mural road running around the ditch of the early town were recorded in a number of trenches along Paul Street. It had a distinctive composition, metalled with pebbles and volcanic chippings in a clay bedding and had been resurfaced on several occasions. Although most of the evidence for the road's upper levels had largely been destroyed by post-Roman disturbance, in one area (Trench 16) it was established that the road continued in use until the late 2nd century AD. The road was recorded as being just over 4 m wide at the SW limit of the excavation but was around 15 m wide at the NE end of the site. It was hypothesised that the road may have widened here because it curved away from the fortress's defences to meet a street at right angles or that instead it may have split in two, with one section running around the defences and another leading off towards the NW. Subsequent discoveries of metalling at Site 164 have however challenged the notion that the road was narrower at the SW.

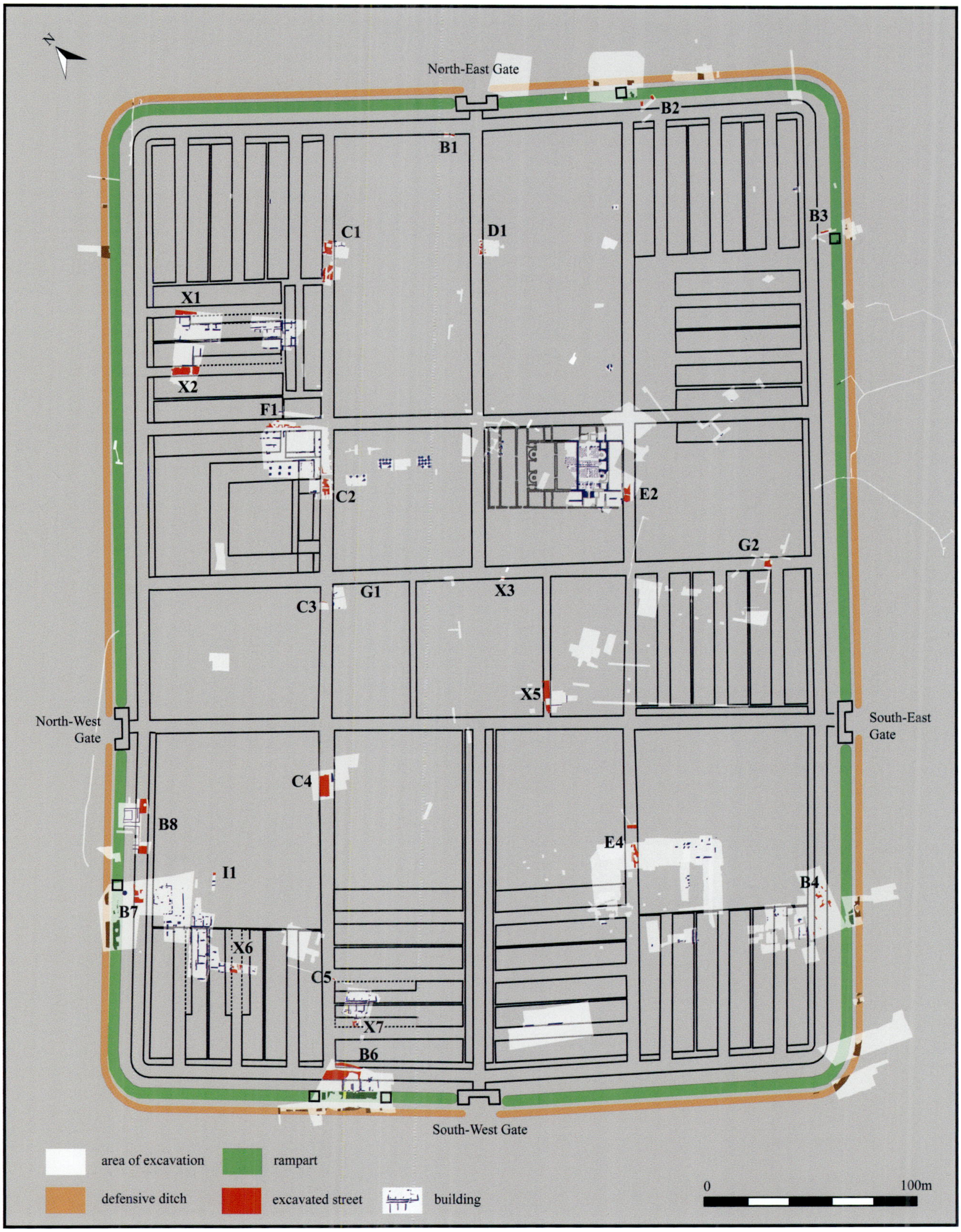

Fig. 3.12 Roman Exeter during the military period showing the areas where physical evidence of its street plan have been excavated (drawn by David Gould)

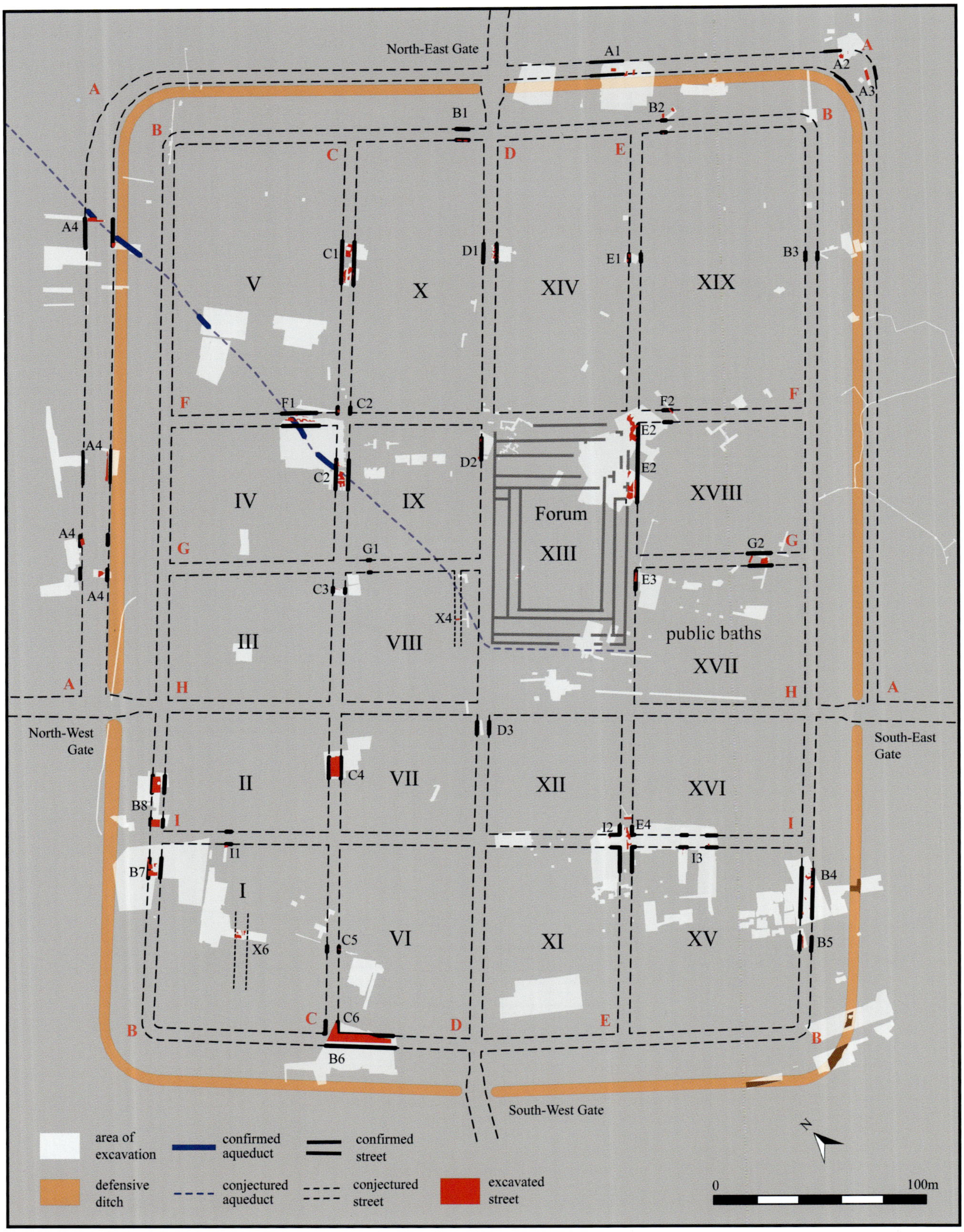

Fig. 3.13 Roman Exeter during the early civil period showing the areas where physical evidence of its street plan have been excavated (drawn by David Gould)

*Street Number: B1i (***via sagularis***)*

- Site Name: 228 High Street
- Excavation gazetteer number: 161
- City HER monument number: no HER number assigned
- Location: extra-mural
- References: Bidwell 1980, 23; Bedford and Salvatore 1993b, 1–2

Two sections of metalling were observed. Initially interpreted as part of a road or trackway running around the outer perimeter of the fortress, subsequent discoveries have shown that it probably represents part of the *via sagularis*, the perimeter street inside the rampart (Fig. 3.2).

*Street Number: B2i (***via sagularis***)*

- Site Name: 5 Cathedral Close (Annuellars' College)
- Excavation gazetteer number: 10
- City HER monument number: 10012
- Location: extra-mural
- References: Montgomerie-Neilson 1934, 62–3; Fox 1952a, 103

The observation in 1933 of rammed river gravels bonded with clay approximately 2.4 m below ground level was interpreted as the floor of a stable block. It is now recognised as part of the *via sagularis*. It is not known whether the north-east section of the *via sagularis* was retained in the early town.

*Street Number: B3i (***via sagularis***)*

- Site Name: Cathedral, outside Speke Chapel
- Excavation gazetteer number: 12
- City HER monument number: no HER number assigned
- Location: *insula* XIX
- References: Radford and Morris 1936, 229–31; Bidwell 1980, 24

A section of the *via sagularis* at least 4 m wide was recorded by Radford although only an approximate description of its location was given. It was resurfaced on at least three occasions and probably remained in use until the end of the 2nd century AD.

*Street Number: B4i (***via sagularis***)*

- Site Name: Mermaid Yard
- Excavation gazetteer number: 63
- City HER monument number: 10012
- Location: *insula* XV
- References: Goodburn 1979, 324; Bedford and Salvatore 1992f, 1, fig. 2

A section of the *via sagularis* was recorded here and may have continued in use the early civil period as it was resurfaced at least four times. Its full width was established at *c.* 6 m and it contained a central ditch which had also been recut at least once.

*Street Number: B5i (***via sagularis***)*

- Site Name: Rack Street
- Excavation gazetteer number: 64
- City HER monument number: 10012
- Location: *insula* XV
- References: Chapter 8 this volume; Bidwell 1980, 24; Bedford and Salvatore 1992d, 2, fig. 2

Traces of the ditch that ran alongside the *via sagularis* were recorded over a length of 9 m, with the street here being 5.5–6 m wide; later activity had removed all traces of the *via sagularis* itself.

*Street Number: B6i (***via sagularis***)*

- Site Name: Friernhay Street
- Excavation gazetteer number: 75
- City HER monument number: 10116
- Location: *insula* VI
- References: Bedford and Salvatore 1992b, 1–3, figs 2–3

The *via sagularis* was *c.* 4.8 m wide. It remained in use during the early civil period, although its width was reduced to *c.* 2.5 m. The first civil resurface was made up of demolition material which included much masonry rubble, probably from the fortress baths.

*Street Number: B7i (***via sagularis***)*

- Site Name: 23–27 Mary Arches Street and Quintana Gate, Bartholomew Street West
- Excavation gazetteer number: 169
- City HER monument number: no HER number assigned
- Location: *insula* I
- References: Farnell 2018, 4–5, figs 2–3

The full width of the military *via sagularis* was exposed, showing it to have been 4 m wide. It was resurfaced and widened early in the civil period, although it was encroached upon during the 2nd century AD when several large probable cesspits were dug through it. Further encroachments included a ditch that cut across the width of the street and extended through the surviving rampart to intersect with the partially infilled fortress ditch. This ditch indicates that this section of the *via sagularis* probably went out of use whilst the early civil ditch remained extant, presumably before construction of the later town defences.

*Street Number: B8i (***via sagularis***)*

- Site Name: 10–18 Bartholomew Street East
- Excavation gazetteer number: 35
- City HER monument number: 10155
- Location: *insula* II

- References: Fox 1961; Bidwell 1980, 24; Holbrook and Fox 1987, 28–9, 35–7

The military *via sagularis* remained in use during the civil period, when an episode of slight resurfacing occurred. Two sections of this street were recorded over a distance of 25 m and it was found to have been at least 4 m wide. Despite evidence of resurfacings, the street showed little sign of prolonged use and it had gone out of use before the late 2nd century AD when a layer of rubbish had accumulated above it.

Street Number: C1i/ii

- Site Name: Queen Street
- Excavation gazetteer number: 68
- City HER monument number: 10140; 10179
- Location: *insulae* V and X
- References: Goodburn 1979, 324; Bedford and Salvatore 1993c, 1–2, fig. 2

A metalled length of the fortress's right lateral street *c.* 17.5 m long was found to have been resurfaced several times, with at least two resurfacing episodes during the military period. Its maximum width is likely to have been *c.* 5.5 m, considerably wider than the 3.5 m wide stretch of street at C4i. The section of street here remained in use throughout the civil period.

Street Number: C2i/ii

- Site Name: Trichay Street
- Excavation gazetteer number: 42
- City HER monument number: 10036; 10141; 10179
- Location: *insulae* V and X, and IV and IX
- References: Chapter 5 in this volume; Henderson *et al.* 1993b, 5, fig. 3

Two further sections of the successor to the former right lateral street that had been laid down in the military period continued in use during the early civil period. The larger section had originally been laid down outside the fortress's *fabrica* and during the civil period separated *insulae* IV and IX. Immediately to the NE, a short section recorded in another trench would have separated *insulae* V and X; this section was found to have remained in use into the late civil period although similar evidence was not found for the longer section to its SW.

Street Number: C3i/ii

- Site Name: 45–46 North Street
- Excavation gazetteer number: 51
- City HER monument number: 10036; 10179
- Location: *insulae* III and VIII
- References: Salvatore 1993b, 1–2, fig. 2

A section of the right lateral street was resurfaced at least twice during the military period and remained in use during the civil period. Its full width was not seen but allowing for side ditches it cannot have exceeded more than 5 m as it was flanked by two buildings 5.8 m apart.

Street Number: C4i

- Site Name: Mary Arches Street
- Excavation gazetteer number: 54
- City HER monument number: 10036
- Location: *insulae* II and VII
- References: Bedford and Salvatore 1992g, 2, 11

A military street *c.* 3.5 m wide had been resurfaced at least once and in its earliest form appears to have been provided with a central drainage gully. It remained in use during the early civil period.

Street Number: C5i/ii

- Site Name: St Nicholas Priory
- Excavation gazetteer number: 109
- City HER monument number: 10179
- Location: *insulae* I and VI
- References: EAACR 1993

A section of street metalling was recorded.

Street Number: C6i

- Site Name: Friernhay Street
- Excavation gazetteer number: 75
- City HER monument number: 10116
- Location: *insulae* I and VI
- References: Bedford and Salvatore 1992b, 1–3, figs 2–3

The successor to the military-period street received four resurfacings during its lifetime although it was abandoned and covered over in the mid to late 2nd century AD.

Street Number: D1i (via decumana)

- Site Name: 41–42 High Street
- Excavation gazetteer number: 72
- City HER monument number: 10072
- Location: *insulae* X and XIV
- References: Bedford and Salvatore 1993a, 1, fig. 2

A section of the fortress's *via decumana* had been resurfaced and widened at least once and was flanked by a drainage ditch; the original ditch had been infilled during the street's widening and a second ditch was subsequently dug *c.* 3.5 m further to the SE of the original ditch, with evidence indicating that the road had been widened by at least 2 m along its SE edge although possibly more if the second ditch was immediately adjacent to the street's edge.

Street Number: D2i (via decumana)

- Site Name: High Street, NatWest Bank
- Excavation gazetteer number: 62

- City HER monument number: 10137
- Location: *insulae* XIII and IX
- References: Bidwell 1979, 120

A street-side ditch traced over a distance of 12 m was cut through a layer of metalling which probably represented the NW side of a street. The width of this street could have been no greater than 6.8 m, the distance between the ditch and the NW boundary wall of the basilica and forum. At some time, probably early in the civil period, the street's width was reduced by at least 1.8 m as it had been cut through by a large pit on its NW side, and after this had been filled in, by a four-post wooden structure.

*Street Number: D3i/ii (***via praetoria***)*

- Site Name: Fore Street/High Street British Gas
- Excavation gazetteer number: 103
- City HER monument number: no HER number assigned
- Location: *insulae* VII and XII
- References: EAACR 1994, 8; Burnham *et al.* 1995, 367

Civil street metalling was reported in Trench 6 of the 1994 High Street excavations.

Street Number: E1i

- Site Name: Cathedral Yard
- Excavation gazetteer number: 202
- City HER monument number: no HER number assigned
- Location: *insulae* XIV and XIX
- References: Goodwin 2007, 7, 9

An area of metalled surface may possibly be a Roman street surface, as suggested by the form and quality of its construction and the appearance of the underlying deposits, although a SW–NE depression interpreted as a wheel rut does not match the alignment of Street E. The identification of this metalled surface as a Roman street is therefore tentative.

Street Number: E2i/ii

- Site Name: Cathedral Close (Cathedral Green and St Mary Major)
- Excavation gazetteer number: 40
- City HER monument number: 10026; 10118; 10217
- Location: *insulae* XIII and XVIII
- References: EAACR 1976; Bidwell 1979, 26, 62, 77, 89–90, 95, 97, 101, 103, 108

The left lateral street of the fortress bounded the bathhouse to the NW; it may have been resurfaced at least once during the military period. The street continued in use during the civil period. The street was constructed before the fortress's baths, with a width of 4 m, before being extended to over 7.6 m when the baths were built, although it was subsequently reduced to a width of 5.2 m.

Street Number: E3i/ii

- Site Name: 11–12 South Street
- Excavation gazetteer number: 17
- City HER monument number: 10118; 10217
- Location: *insulae* XIII and XVII
- References: Fox 1952a, pl. XVI

A section of the street separating the basilica and forum from the *insulae* to its SE was recorded here.

Street Number: E4i/ii

- Site Name: Market Street/Smythen Street
- Excavation gazetteer number: 115
- City HER monument number: 15113; 10217
- Location: *insulae* XII and XVI
- References: Stead 1999, fig. 7; 2002, 7–9; Thomson *et al.* 2014; 35

A section of street was traced for 11 m during excavations in 2001–2 while a further small section was seen to the NW in a 2012–14 watching brief. The street was originally laid out during the fortress period and remained in use throughout the civil period, with four distinct resurfacing episodes recorded, the upper two dating from the civil period. It survived to a width of 3.5 m, although its full width could not be determined as it had been disturbed on both sides by later Roman buildings although in its later form, it would been at least 6 m wide. It was equipped with a central drain.

Street Number: F1i/ii

- Site Name: Trichay Street
- Excavation gazetteer number: 42
- City HER monument number: 10141
- Location: *insulae* IV and V
- References: Chapter 5 in this volume; Henderson *et al.* 1993b, 5, fig. 3

A section of street was originally laid out in the military period where it lay between two barrack blocks C5 and C6. The street was abandoned in the Hadrianic-early Antonne period and built over.

Street Number: F2i/ii

- Site Name: Cathedral Close (Cathedral Green)
- Excavation gazetteer number: 40
- City HER monument number: 10223; 10225
- Location: *insulae* XVIII and XIX
- References: Frere 1977, 415; Bidwell 1979, fig. 33, 118

A section of street was recorded here.

Street Number: G1i

- Site Name: 45–46 North Street
- Excavation gazetteer number: 51
- City HER monument number: no HER number assigned
- Location: *insulae* IX and VIII
- References: Salvatore 1993b, 2, fig. 2

The street had been resurfaced several times, at least twice during the military period and remained in use into the civil period.

Street Number: G2i/ii

- Site Name: 2–8 Bear Street
- Excavation gazetteer number: 32
- City HER monument number: 10122; 10172
- Location: *insulae* XVII and XVIII
- References: Fox 1953, 31–4; Bidwell 1979, 21, 78

This fortress street remained in use during the civil period. It was resurfaced with gravel after its level had been raised by a dump of clay and gravel during the late 1st/early 2nd century AD. Its width is unknown due to later disturbances, but it was more than 2.4 m wide and perhaps more likely to have been 3.7–4 m wide. A 37.5 cm wide stone-lined drain flanked the SW side of the street and was almost certainly one of the principal outfalls from the nearby public baths.

Street Number: I1i

- Site Name: Bartholomew Street East
- Excavation gazetteer number: 73
- City HER monument number: 10081
- Location: *insulae* I and II
- References: EAACR 1980; Salvatore and Simpson 1992, 2, fig. 3

A series of patchy street surfaces consisting of three successive layers of gravels represents part of a fortress period street, or perhaps more likely an alleyway, which continued in use throughout the civil period.

Street Number: I2i

- Site Name: Market Street/Smythen Street
- Excavation gazetteer number: 115
- City HER monument number: 10158
- Location: *insulae* XI and XII
- References: Hall *et al.* 1995, 9

Two layers of a metalled surface associated with the terminus of a wall slot of a timber building were recorded. The second surface was truncated by a pit which was subsequently sealed below a possible third surface.

Street Number: I3i

- Site Name: Market Street/Smythen Street
- Excavation gazetteer number: 115
- City HER monument number: 10157
- Location: *insulae* XV and XVI
- References: Hall *et al.* 1995, 7; Stead 1999, 4

The fragmentary remains of a well-metalled street. It had been built within a wide and shallow trench, because of which it does not seem to have been raised significantly higher than the surrounding ground level. It survived to a width of 4.5 m, although it is likely to have been wider as its NE edge had been destroyed by later activity. A further small area of compacted metalled surface was recorded in the 2001–2 excavations to the SE. It represents part of a late 1st-century AD street and was resurfaced with cobbles in the 2nd century.

Street Number: X1i

- Site Name: Goldsmith Street Area I
- Excavation gazetteer number: 37
- City HER monument number: 10023
- Location: Barrack C, 1–2
- References: Henderson *et al.* 1993a, 5, fig. 3

A section of metalled street between two centurial barrack blocks of the legionary fortress was excavated. It was not retained after the military period.

Street Number: X2i

- Site Name: Goldsmith Street Area II
- Excavation gazetteer number: 37
- City HER monument number: 10024
- Location: Barrack C, 3–4
- References: Henderson *et al.* 1993a, 5, fig. 3

A section of metalled street between two centurial barrack blocks of the legionary fortress was excavated. It was not retained after the military period.

Street Number: X3i

- Site Name: Cathedral Yard
- Excavation gazetteer number: 202
- City HER monument number: N/A
- Location: *insula* XIII
- References: Goodwin 2007, 4

Six compact layers of silty clay were interpreted by the excavators as possible street surfaces and dated to the Roman period. If correct, its location between the *principia* and baths suggests a military date, although these layers could instead be associated with levelling for the NW range of the forum.

Street Number: X4i

- Site Name: Fore Street/High Street British Gas
- Excavation gazetteer number: 103
- City HER monument number: 10155
- Location: *insula* VIII
- References: EAACR 1981

Five street layers were recorded belonging to a lane running parallel to the SE side of *insula* VIII about 5 m from the street next to the basilica and forum. The area between the lane and the street was occupied by timber buildings during the 2nd century AD, with the plot perhaps representing an area occupied by a row of shops fronting onto one of the town's principal streets.

Street Number: X5i

- Site Name: South Street
- Excavation gazetteer number: 15
- City HER monument number: 10008
- Location: *insula* XIII
- References: Fox 1952a, 32–33; Bidwell 1979, 78–81

A section of a fortress street *c.* 3 m wide was traced for approximately 15.5 m. It had been furnished with a central drain, which may have been covered with planks when the street was in use. It is thought that the street flanked the fortress's *principia*, positioned on its NW side, while other buildings in the *latera praetoria* lay to its SW side. During the civil period, this area was covered with an area of metalling representing the town's marketplace to the SE of the basilica and forum.

Street Number: X6i

- Site Name: Bartholomew Street East
- Excavation gazetteer number: 73
- City HER monument number: 10080
- Location: Barrack G, 3–4
- References: EAACR 1981; Grew *et al.* 1981, 358; Salvatore and Simpson 1992, 2–5

A section of street separating a pair of barracks of the legionary fortress was *c.* 5 m wide. Its surface consisted of patchy stony areas that may have formed through use and there was no clearly laid street surface. The street overlaid features interpreted as belonging to the primary construction of the barracks, suggesting that its surface layers became spread over the infilled post-trenches of the barracks' veranda whilst respecting the posts that once stood there. The street remained in use during the early civil period, bisecting *insula* I.

Street Number: X7i

- Site Name: St Nicholas Priory
- Excavation gazetteer number: 78
- City HER monument number: 10095
- Location: *insula* VI
- References: Bedford and Salvatore 1992a, 7

A section of street separating a pair of barracks of the legionary fortress. The metalling was lighter in the metre or so closest to the wall of the immediately adjacent barrack, underneath the area that would have been covered by its veranda, and heavier in the area forward of the veranda post, where it formed part of the street proper. It fell out of use after the military period.

Section 3.3: Gazetteer of observations of the streets associated with the expanded later town *by David Gould*

The following gazetteer lists all known new additions to Exeter's Late Roman street system that have been revealed through excavation; sections of the late street system that were in existence during the early civil period are listed above and have not been repeated here. Figure 3.14 depicts the street layout of Roman Exeter during the late civil period and the organisation of its *insulae* with the areas of excavated streets highlighted.

Streets A and B of the early civil period fell out of use during the late civil period and so are not represented here. These sections of excavated street have then been given the suffix of -ii in the following gazetteer in order to differentiate them from sections of excavated streets that date to the early civil period.

Roman Exeter was orientated towards the south-west with the result that Fig. 3.14, with north at the top of the page, has *insula* I positioned towards its bottom left. However, due to the growth of Exeter's street grid during the late civil period, several new *insulae* were created outside the early town's *insulae*. This has resulted in a system where, when depicted spatially, the numbering of Exeter's late civil *insulae* do not follow an orderly pattern; for example, *insula* XXX/XXXI is located immediately to the south of *insula* I. The numbering sequence of Exeter's late civil buildings follows this convention and are ordered according to the *insula* in which they were located. The numbering system of Exeter's late civil *insulae* was first devised by Bidwell in 1980 (*Roman Exeter: Fortress and Town*) although subsequent investigations have furthered our understanding of the late town's street grid, with the result that several of Bidwell's proposed *insulae* have been combined; for example, the south-westerly *insula* is here labelled as XXX/XXXI because no evidence has been found of Bidwell's proposed street that separated his *insulae* XXX and XXXI.

Street Number: D4ii

- Site Name: St John's School Trial Trenches
- Excavation gazetteer number: 128
- City HER monument number: no HER number assigned
- Location: *insulae* XL and X/XXI/XXVI
- References: Montague 1935a, 188

Two short trenches across the N end of St John's playground revealed traces of a probable Roman street. The exact locations of these trial trenches are unknown, however, other than that they were in the N end of St John's School's playground and that the original report states the

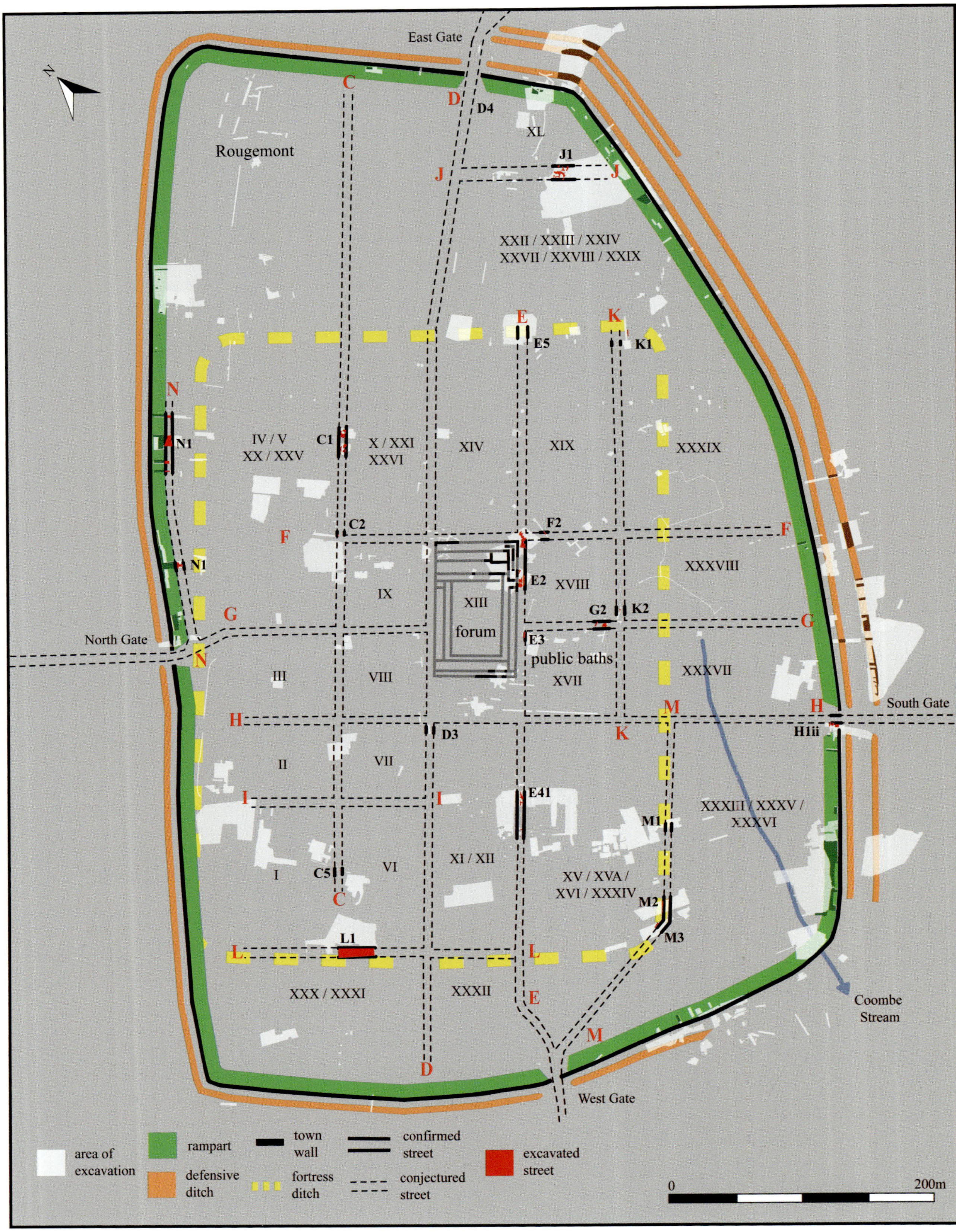

Fig. 3.14 Roman Exeter during the late civil period showing the areas where physical evidence of its street plan have been excavated (drawn by David Gould)

trenches were dug in an attempt to find the *Decumanus Maximus* between the end of Catherine Street and the Decuman Gate. If dated to the late town, this street is likely therefore to represent a section of Street D leading towards the East Gate, although it could also represent the earlier extra-mural road leading from the East Gate towards modern St Sidwell's.

Street Number: E5ii

- Site Name: St Catherine's Almshouses
- Excavation gazetteer number: 89
- City HER monument number: no HER number assigned
- Location: *insulae* XIV and XIX
- References: EAACR 1987; Frere 1988, 473

Street E was extended across the levelled defences of the early town but appeared to terminate at its intersection with early civil Street A.

Street number: H1ii

- Site Name: South Gate
- Excavation gazetteer number: 96
- City HER monument number: 10018
- Location: *insulae* XXXIII/XXXV/XXXVI and XXXVII
- References: Henderson 2001, 57–8

A military and early civilian extra-mural road overlain by later Roman street leading to the South Gate. Its full width has not been established but it was probably *c.* 9 m wide.

Street Number: J1ii

- Site Name: Princesshay
- Excavation gazetteer number: 156
- City HER monument number: no HER number assigned
- Location: *insulae* XXII/XXIII/XXIV/XXVII/XXVIII/XXIX and XL
- References: Steinmetzer, Stead, Pearce, Bidwell and Allan forthcoming

Following the construction of the new town defences in the late 2nd century AD, the ditches of an early civil extra-mural enclosure were infilled and a new street was laid over them in the mid–late 3rd century AD (Road III), replacing a mid–late 2nd-century AD street that had been constructed slightly to the SW (Road II). It was up to 10 m wide and was composed of trap rubble with chippings of the same material, possibly by-products linked to the construction of the town wall. In places where the street overlay the earlier enclosure ditches, it had slumped into their upper fills which required two main phases of infilling and resurfacing along with various minor episodes of localised patching and repair. Despite its substantial nature and evidence of maintenance and repair, the street did not survive past the late 3rd century AD as an extensive range of buildings was constructed across it.

Street Number: K1ii

- Site Name: 10 Cathedral Close
- Excavation gazetteer number: 33
- City HER monument number: no HER number assigned
- Location: *insulae* XXIV and XXIX
- References: Greenfield 1964, 342; Bidwell 1979, 78; 1980, 67

A 2nd/3rd-century AD building was excavated in 1955; the exterior levels of this period were described by Greenfield (1964, 342) as consisting of 'a single layer of broken trap rock, apparently laid on the subsoil'. Bidwell (1980, 67) interprets this as a street surface with a gully at its SE side.

Street Number: K2ii

- Site Name: 2–8 Bear Street
- Excavation gazetteer number: 32
- City HER monument number: 10173
- Location: *insulae* XVIII and XXXVIII
- References: Fox 1953, 33

A section of street was excavated at a right angle to Street G2ii. It likely replaced former Street B which had now been abandoned.

Street Number: L1ii

- Site Name: Friernhay Street
- Excavation gazetteer number: 75
- City HER monument number: no HER number assigned
- Location: *insulae* VI/VII and XXX/XXXI
- References: EAACR 1981; Rankov *et al.* 1982, 382

Both of the earlier streets at Friernhay Street (B6i and C6i) went out of use by the end of the 2nd century AD, with the former *via sagularis* replaced by a new street laid out 25 m to its SW.

Street Number: M1ii

- Site Name: Mermaid Yard
- Excavation gazetteer number: 63
- City HER monument number: no HER number assigned
- Location: *insulae* XV/XVA/XVI/XXXIV and XXXIII/XXXV/XXXVI
- References: EAACR 1978

The former defensive ditch of the early town was overlaid by a new street by the late 3rd century AD.

Street Number: M2ii

- Site Name: Rack Street
- Excavation gazetteer number: 64
- City HER monument number: 10187
- Location: *insulae* XV/XVA/XVI/XXXIV and XXXIII/XXXV/XXXVI
- References: Chapter 8 in this volume; EAACR 1978

A new street 6 m wide was laid outside the line of the backfilled town ditch in the late 3rd–early 4th century AD. Evidence was found of its surface being patched and re-made on several occasions as well as areas of crude localised resurfacings, suggesting that the street was maintained for a lengthy period.

Street Number: M3ii

- Site Name: Rack Street
- Excavation gazetteer number: 52
- City HER monument number: 10187
- Location: *insulae* XV/XVA/XVI/XXXIV and XXXIII/XXXV/XXXVI
- References: Chapter 8 in this volume; EAACR 1978

A further section of the street found at the 1977–8 Rack Street excavation (M2ii) had also been observed at the earlier 1974–5 Rack Street excavation. The street was on a slightly different alignment to M2ii, however, turning W towards the town's West Gate.

Street Number: N1ii

- Site Name: Paul Street
- Excavation gazetteer number: 76
- City HER monument number: 10264
- Location: intra-mural
- References: EAACR 1984; Henderson 1985b, 27–28

A substantial strip of gravel dating to the 3rd century AD was recorded in several trenches along Paul Street immediately to the rear of the rampart of the town defences and seems to have served as an intra-mural street, although in one trench it was composed of sandstone beach cobbles and roofing slates. It is unclear whether this street ran the whole course of the town walls. The street probably fell out of use in the middle of the 3rd century AD.

Section 3.4: Gazetteer of buildings associated with the early town
by David Gould

The following gazetteer lists all known buildings within early civil Roman Exeter with the exception of the forum/basilica and the public baths, both of which were discussed in depth in Bidwell 1979. Figure 3.15 depicts the street layout of Roman Exeter and the organisation of *insulae* during the early civil period with the locations of recorded buildings plotted. Each building has been assigned a number followed by the suffix -i in order to differentiate them from buildings of the late civil town, which have been given the suffix -ii and which are detailed in Section 3.5 of this chapter. In some instances, a single building number will refer to several construction phases on the same site and do not necessarily therefore refer to a single building but rather a succession of different buildings; because it is not possible to depict different construction phases on Fig. 3.15 it has been necessary to combine such examples under single entries. Where dating evidence is lacking, observations of timber buildings within the bounds of the early town have been ascribed to this period, although it is known that timber construction continued in Exeter throughout the Roman period.

Roman Exeter was orientated towards the south west with the result that on Fig. 3.15, with north at the top of the page, *insula* I is positioned at its bottom left. The numbering sequence of Exeter's Roman buildings follows this convention and are ordered according to the *insula* in which they were located with Building 1i therefore also being located at the bottom left of Fig. 3.15 rather than at its top left.

Each gazetteer entries below gives the following information:

- Building number
- Site name corresponding to the name of the excavation that produced evidence of the building as listed in Chapter 2 in this volume
- Excavation gazetteer number corresponding to the site numbers listed in Chapter 2 in this volume
- City HER monument number where the excavated building has been recorded by the City HER
- Location within Exeter (*i.e.* its *insula* number)
- The principal references recording details of the excavated buildings

Building Number: 1i

- Site Number: Bartholomew Street East
- Excavation gazetteer number: 73
- City HER monument number: no HER number assigned
- Location: *insula* I
- References: EAACR 1981

After the demolition of the fortress, a building represented by a clay floor covered by a thin trampled occupation layer was recorded. It appears to have been constructed of timber though no evidence of its walls was found, and it is possible that this floor was in fact the earliest layer associated with a later stone building (see 2ii).

Building number: 2i

- Site name: Mary Arches Street
- Excavation gazetteer number: 54
- City HER monument number: no HER number assigned

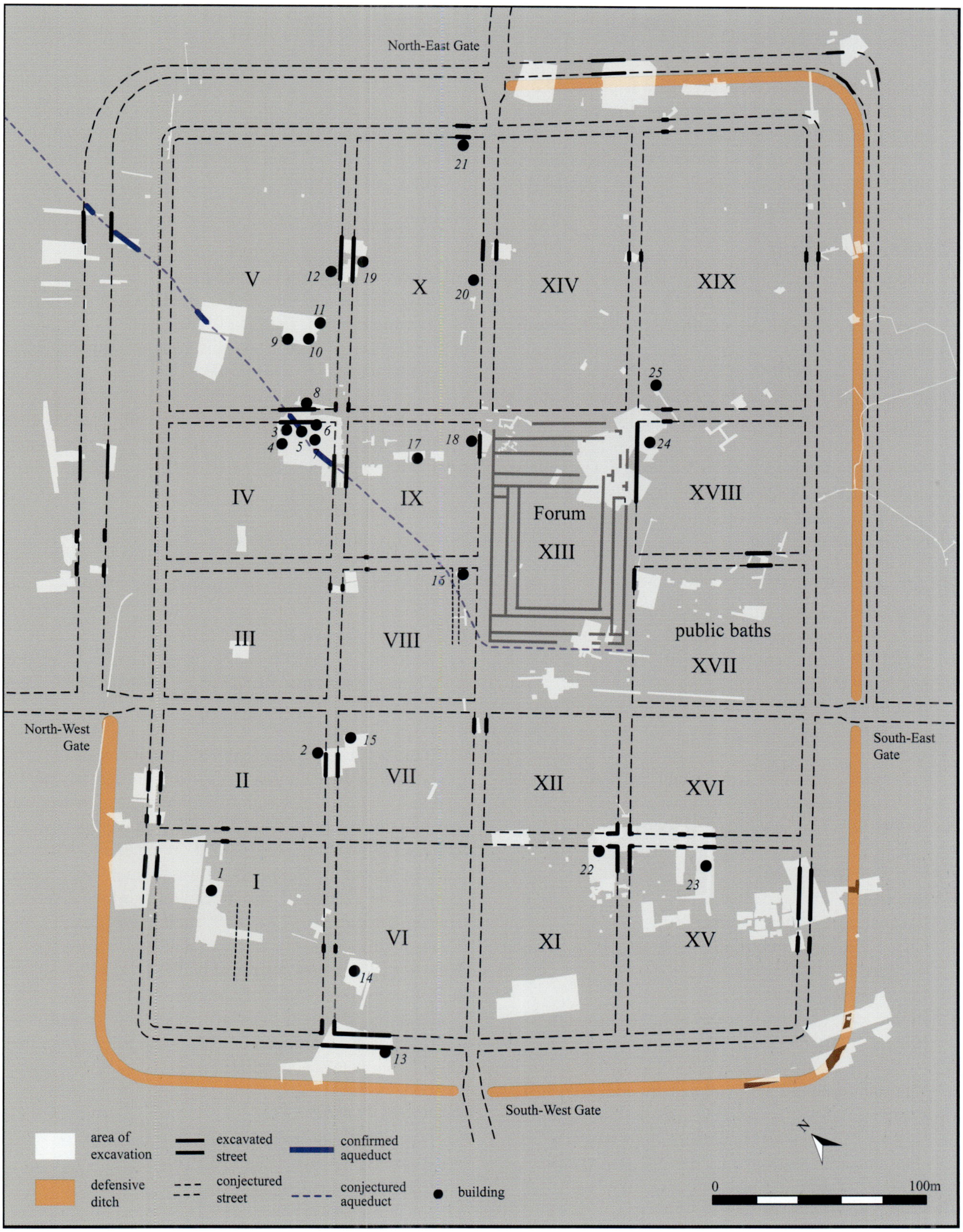

Fig. 3.15 Roman Exeter during the early civil period showing the areas where physical evidence of its buildings have been excavated (drawn by David Gould)

- Location: *insula* II
- References: Bidwell 1980, 53, 69 (*Insula* I: (1))

A masonry building (Building 6ii) was preceded by at least four successive timber buildings, the earliest contemporary with a street surface on the SE side of *insula* II (Street C4i), which overlay fortress buildings (and thus the street may have been wider in the civil period than it had been in the military period).

Building number: 3i

- Site name: Trichay Street
- Excavation gazetteer number: 42
- City HER monument number: no HER number assigned
- Location: *insula* IV
- References: EAPIT 1, Fig. 6.14; Chapter 5 in this volume, structure RC4; Bidwell 1980, 53 (*Insula* IV: (1))

A timber building 13 m by 6.5 m with a white plaster external rendering. It was destroyed by fire *c.* AD 120–60 and part of the site was subsequently occupied by another timber building (Building 4i).

Building number 4i

- Site name: Trichay Street
- Excavation gazetteer number: 42
- City HER monument number: 10232
- Location: *insula* V
- References: Chapter 5 in this volume, building not numbered

A possible structure, represented by nine postholes and two associated postpits, was recorded on the site of the former Building 3i, which had been destroyed by fire.

Building number: 5i

- Site name: Trichay Street
- Excavation gazetteer number: 42
- City HER monument number: no HER number assigned
- Location: *insula* IV
- References: Chapter 5 in this volume, structure RC3; Bidwell 1980, 53 (*Insula* IV: (1))

A timber building was defined by two trenches at right-angles and would have been more than 5.8 m long and at least 5 m wide and furnished with a thin clay floor. The building was destroyed by fire *c.* AD 120–60.

Building number: 6i

- Site name: Trichay Street
- Excavation gazetteer number: 42
- City HER monument number: no HER number assigned
- Location: *insula* IV
- References: Chapter 5 in this volume, structure RC2; Bidwell 1980, 53 (*Insula* IV: (1))

A timber building represented by two trenches that defined a structure 2.5 m wide; its length is unknown but cannot have exceeded 8.5 m as it presumably stopped short of a well recorded during the excavation. It was destroyed by fire *c.* AD 120–60.

Building number: 7i

- Site name: Trichay Street
- Excavation gazetteer number: 42
- City HER monument number: no HER number assigned
- Location: *insula* IV
- References: Chapter 5 in this volume, structure RC1; Bidwell 1980, 53 (*Insula* IV: (1))

A timber building consisting of three sill-beam trenches defining three sides of a building 2.3 m wide and more than 6 m long. It was destroyed by fire *c.* AD 120–60.

Building number 8i

- Site name: Trichay Street
- Excavation gazetteer number: 42
- City HER monument number: no HER number assigned
- Location: *insula* V
- References: EAPIT 1, Fig. 6.14; Chapter 5 in this volume, structures RC5–7, 8–9; Bidwell 1980, 53–4 (*Insula* V: (1))

A timber building was found to have undergone several phases of construction/reconstruction during the late 1st and 2nd centuries, although since the excavation area was cut by numerous medieval pits, the plan of this building is very fragmentary and its function uncertain. After the earliest timber building (RC5) was demolished, it was covered by a dump of yellow clay over which a second timber structure (RC6) was constructed before itself being dismantled and a third timber building constructed (RC7). This third phase was destroyed by fire *c.* AD 120–60 and a further two sequential buildings (RC8–9) were then constructed, although the later phase may instead have represented structural additions to the fourth phase rather than a completely new build.

Building number: 9i

- Site name: Goldsmith Street III
- Excavation gazetteer number: 39
- City HER monument number: 10125
- Location: *insula* V
- References: Chapter 6 in this volume, structure RC3; Bidwell 1980, 54 (*Insula* V: (2))

A timber building is considered to be a separate structure from Building 10i, although conceivably they could have formed a single building. Building 9i was at least 14 m long by at least 5 m wide and contained at least four rooms, one with an *opus signinum* floor. The external walls were of either sill-beam or post-in-trench construction. All the timber buildings recorded at Goldsmith Street appear to have been deliberately demolished although exactly when has not been established.

Building number: 10i

- Site name: Goldsmith Street III
- Excavation gazetteer number: 39
- City HER monument number: 10125
- Location: *insula* V
- References: Chapter 6 in this volume, structure RC1; Bidwell 1980, 54 (*Insula* V: (2))

A timber building of beam-slot construction survived in only a very partial state, and this may in fact be part of the same structure as Building 9i rather than a separate building.

Building number: 11i

- Site name: Goldsmith Street III
- Excavation gazetteer number: 39
- City HER monument number: 10124
- Location: *insula* V
- References: Chapter 6 in this volume, structure RC2; Bidwell 1980, 54 (*Insula* V: (2))

A timber building, of which only its E corner survived formed from 0.7 m wide stone footings.

Building number: 12i

- Site name: Queen Street, 22 Goldsmith Street and 211–219 High Street
- Excavation gazetteer number: 68
- City HER monument number: no HER number assigned
- Location: *insula* V
- References: Goodburn 1979, 324; Bidwell 1980, 54 (*Insula* V: (4))

Traces of a late 1st-century AD timber building at the side of an early civil street (Street C1i) were recorded immediately above the fortress levels in a trench at 22 Goldsmith Street; it was demolished before the Antonine period.

Building number: 13i

- Site name: Friernhay Street
- Excavation gazetteer number: 75
- City HER monument number: 10143
- Location: intervallum SW of *insula* VI
- References: EAACR 1981; Rankov *et al.* 1982, 382–3

The remains of a timber building behind the rampart of the former legionary fortress, of which only a partial plan was recovered, contained a room which measured *c.* 4 m by at least 3 m. The building had mortar and concrete floors and appears to have been in use throughout much of the 2nd century AD. Nearby, and probably associated with the building, was a mid 2nd-century stone-lined pit which produced two complete bronze *paterae*.

Building number: 14i

- Site name: St Nicholas Priory
- Excavation gazetteer number: 78
- City HER monument number: no HER number assigned
- Location: *insula* VI
- References: Allan 2019

At least two phases of Roman timber buildings were recorded overlying a post-military demolition layer of the former legionary fortress. The earliest building phase had an earth floor, which was succeeded by a clay floor in which were two postholes. No firm dating evidence was recovered, but their stratigraphic position and the dating of similar timber structures elsewhere in Exeter suggests that they probably date to the late 1st or early 2nd century AD.

Building number 15i

- Site name: Mary Arches Street
- Excavation gazetteer number: 54
- City HER monument number: no HER number assigned
- Location: *insula* VII
- References: Bidwell 1980, 54 (*Insula* VII: (1))

A timber building was erected shortly after the street was constructed in *c.* AD 80. It was destroyed by fire and at least three successive timber buildings were erected on its site before the construction of a masonry building in the later Roman period (Building 20ii).

Building number: 16i

- Site name: Fore Street/High Street British Gas
- Excavation gazetteer number: 103
- City HER monument number: no HER number assigned
- Location: *insula* VIII
- References: EAACR 1981, 8–9

A trench at Fore Street revealed a sequence of clay floors interleaved with layers of loam and deposits of burnt daub representing the remains of a series of timber buildings. Their location on a narrow plot between a lane and one of the town's principal streets next to the basilica and forum suggests they may have represented a row of shops.

Building number: 17i

- Site name: 196–197 High Street
- Excavation gazetteer number: 43
- City HER monument number: 10126

- Location: *insula* IX;
- References: Chapter 7 in this volume, structures RC1–2; Bidwell 1980, 54 (*Insula* IX: (1))

A timber building (RC1), its full dimensions are unknown. At some point in the late 2nd or 3rd century AD the building was demolished and a new structure (RC2) was erected and was defined by two parallel stone wall foundations. This building was destroyed by fire sometime between the late 2nd and early 3rd century AD. Ten post-holes cut into a clay levelling deposit might denote another timber structure datable to after the mid 3rd century AD.

Building number 18i

- Site name: High Street, NatWest Bank
- Excavation gazetteer number: 62
- City HER monument number: 10138
- Location: *insula* IX
- References: Bidwell 1979, 120–1; 1980, 55 (*Insula* IX: (2))

Four postpits formed part of a building which had encroached on Street D2i; traces of a timber building, possibly part of the same structure, were seen nearby in a section exposed by the collapse of a cellar wall.

Building number: 19i

- Site name: Queen Street, Goldsmith Street and 211–219 High Street
- Excavation gazetteer number: 68
- City HER monument number: 10141
- Location: *insula* X
- References: Bidwell 1980, 55 (*Insula* X: (1)); Bedford and Salvatore 1993c, 19–21

Part of a substantially constructed building was found immediately above the fortress levels. Its frontage onto Street C1i was at least 17.5 m long, and it appeared to have been divided into a series of rooms *c*. 2.4 m wide and at least 4.5 m long. It was cut by the post-trenches of another timber building which was demolished in the first half of the 2nd century AD. The site then remained free of buildings until the later 3rd century AD.

Building number: 20i

- Site name: Queen Street, Goldsmith Street and 211–219 High Street
- Excavation gazetteer number: 68
- City HER monument number: no HER number assigned
- Location: *insula* X
- References: EAACR 1979, 5; Bidwell 1980, 55 (*Insula* X: (3))

Floor levels associated with timber buildings were noted in the course of building work at 211–219 High Street

Building number: 21i

- Site name: 228 High Street
- Excavation gazetteer number: 61
- City HER monument number: no HER number assigned
- Location: *insula* X
- References: Bedford and Salvatore 1993b, 1–3

What appears to be a military-style timber granary was constructed over the NE *via sagularis* indicating that it dates to the civil period when the interior of the fortress had been reorganised. Possibly this indicates a continuing area under military control immediately inside the NE gate of the town.

Building number 22i

- Site name: Market Street/Smythen Street
- Excavation gazetteer number: 115
- City HER monument number: 11527
- Location: *insula* XI
- References: Stead 2007, 7

A linear feature 3 m long and 0.5 m wide was interpreted as a post-trench of a timber building; an irregular trench seen along part of the centre line of this feature contained a mixture of burnt clay and charcoal that was interpreted as backfill following the burning and removal of timbers from the post-trench. Although reminiscent of a military post-trench, the presence of a large quantity of pottery within the burnt fill, some datable to the late 2nd century AD, combined with the fact that it cut through what appeared to be a spread of levelling material, rather than simply subsoil, suggests that the post-trench represents a building of the Early Roman town.

Building number 23i

- Site name: Market Street/Smythen Street
- Excavation gazetteer number: 115
- City HER monument number: 11528
- Location: *insula* XV
- References: Stead 2007, 8

Evidence of a possible timber building 6.4 m wide consisted of a series of apparently associated post-trenches. Thirty-three sherds of pottery were recovered from these trenches, broadly datable to the late 2nd century AD suggesting a construction date of the same period, although it is possible that this fill was in some way related to the disuse of the structure rather than its construction.

Building number: 24i

- Site name: Cathedral Close (St Mary Major)
- Excavation gazetteer number: 40
- City HER monument number: no HER number assigned
- Location: *insula* XVIII
- References: Bidwell 1979, 64, 115; 1980, 55 (*Insula* XVIII: (1))

A timber building with a frontage 8.2 m long was erected on the NW side of this *insula* when the legionary baths were reduced in size *c*. AD 75; it was demolished when the basilica and forum were erected in *c*. AD 90. Floor levels associated with later timber buildings were also found; one was destroyed by fire in the late 2nd/early 3rd century AD.

Building number 25i

- Site name: Cathedral Close (Cathedral Green)
- Excavation gazetteer number: 40
- City HER monument number: no HER number assigned
- Location: *insula* XIX
- References: Bidwell 1979, 118; 1980, 55 (*Insula* XIX: (1))

Three successive timber buildings. An extraction-pit for a post of the third phase indicates the methodical demolition of this structure, after which its site was covered by a thin spread of clay and loam.

Section 3.5: Gazetteer of buildings associated with the later town
by David Gould

The following gazetteer lists all known buildings of Roman Exeter's late civil period. Figure 3.16 depicts the street layout of Roman Exeter and the organisation of its *insulae* during the late civil period with the locations of recorded buildings plotted. During the late civil period at Exeter, a number of stone-built town houses were constructed, several of which were evidently wealthy structures equipped with mosaics; sites where *in situ* mosaics have been found have been depicted separately to distinguish them from buildings without mosaics and a distinction has also been made between mosaics, which have decorative motifs picked out in *tesserae* of different colours, and monochrome tessellated pavements. Each building has been assigned a number followed by the suffix -ii in order to differentiate them from buildings of the early civil town listed in Section 3.4. In some instances, a single building number will refer to several construction phases on the same site and do not necessarily therefore refer to a single building but rather a succession of different buildings; because it is not possible to depict different construction phases on Fig. 3.16 it has been necessary to combine such examples under single entries.

Where dating evidence is lacking, observations of masonry walls (or more usually the robber trenches of these walls) within the bounds of the early town have been ascribed to the later civil period. The earliest known date of a masonry domestic structure in Exeter is the later 2nd-century AD Building 33ii.

Building number: 1ii

- Site name: Friernhay Street
- Excavation gazetteer number: 75
- City HER monument number: 10200
- Location: *insula* VI
- References: EAACR 1981; Rankov *et al.* 1982, 382–3

A substantial 4th-century AD stone boundary wall cut across the truncated former fortress rampart before turning NW along the line of the former first fortress ditch. It was traced for 18 m to the NE and 26 m to the SW. The same wall may have been encountered at St Nicholas Priory (Site 109); it may have defined a *temenos* associated with a temple.

Building number: 2ii

- Site name: Bartholomew Street East
- Excavation gazetteer number: 73
- City HER monument number: 10196
- Location: *insula* I
- References: EAACR 1981

A stone building 4.2 m wide had a mortar floor; its front wall line was represented by a rough stone footing composed of large irregularly set blocks of volcanic rubble. The building was destroyed by fire, with the destruction layers containing daub, tile, plaster and stone.

Building number: 3ii

- Site name: 23–27 Mary Arches Street and Quintana Gate, Bartholomew Street West
- Excavation gazetteer number: 169
- City HER monument number: no HER number assigned
- Location: *insula* I
- References: EAPIT 1, Fig. 6.14; Farnell 2018, 6 (structure 4)

A stone building apparently of a single construction phase, although its frontage lay beyond the limit of the excavation. Several sections of upstanding masonry walls survived as well as floor surfaces of angular trap stone cobbles topped with gravels, crushed tile and *opus signinum*.

Building number: 4ii

- Site name: 23–27 Mary Arches Street and Quintana Gate, Bartholomew Street West
- Excavation gazetteer number: 169
- City HER monument number: no HER number assigned
- Location: *insula* I
- References: EAPIT 1, Fig. 6.14; Farnell 2018, 6 (structure 5)

Two phases of stone building, the earlier phase being fragmentary and preserved only where a stone footing

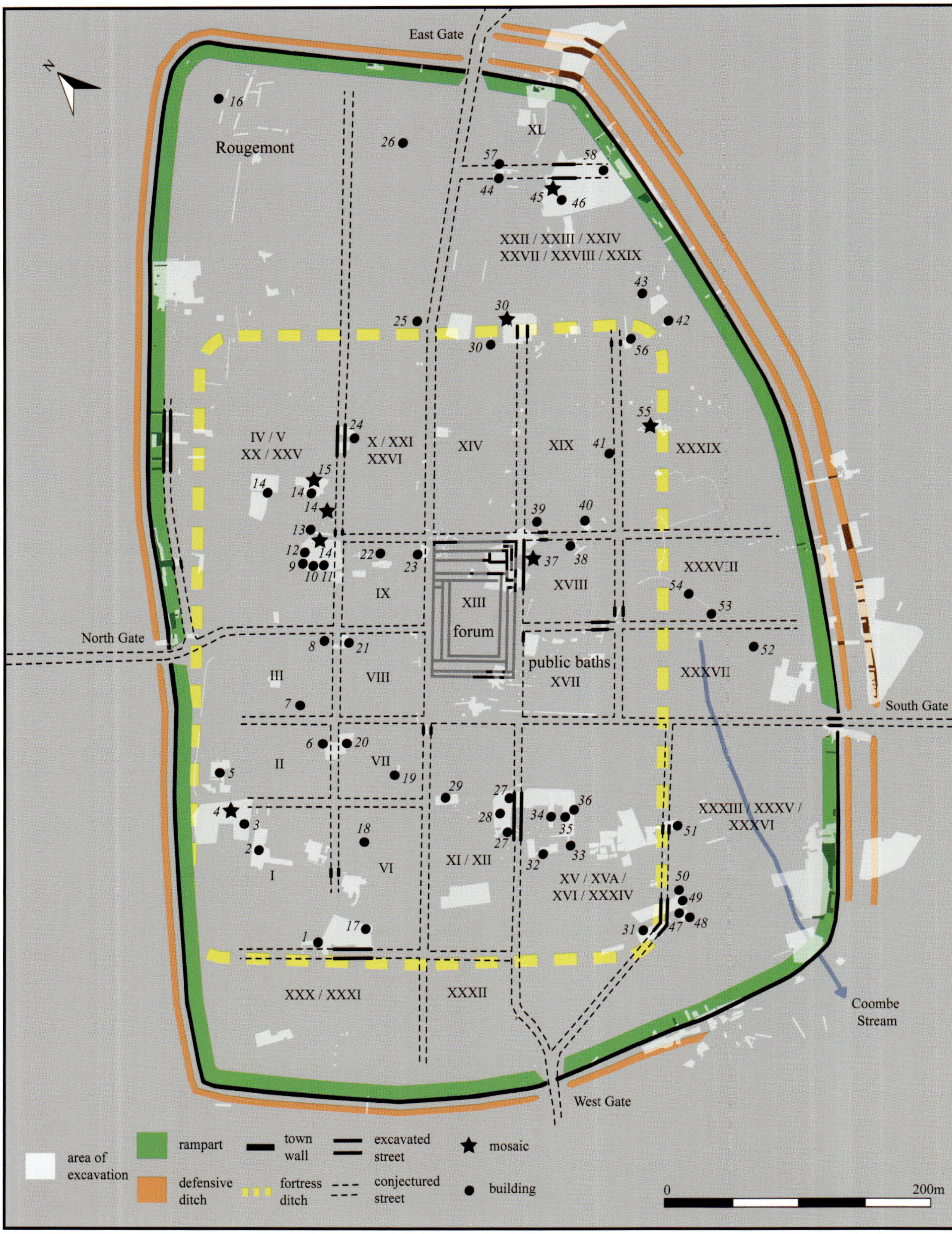

Fig. 3.16 Roman Exeter during the late civil period showing the areas where physical evidence of its buildings have been excavated (drawn by David Gould)

had subsided into an earlier well. Painted wall plaster was observed. The second phase comprised three rooms, one of which contained a probable hypocaust floor and traces of Purbeck marble, perhaps associated with this floor. Another room was constructed over the remains of the former *via sagularis,* and its demolition layer contained numerous *tesserae* including fragments adhered together by mortar.

Building number: 5ii

- Site name: 10–18 Bartholomew Street East
- Excavation gazetteer number: 35
- City HER monument number: no HER number assigned
- Location: *insula* II
- References: Fox and Holbrook 1987, 37

The robbed remains of a wall that cut the former *via sagularis* may be associated with the rear of a building that was probably constructed during the second half of the 3rd century AD.

Building number: 6ii

- Site name: Mary Arches Street
- Excavation gazetteer number: 54
- City HER monument number: no HER number assigned
- Location: *insula* II
- References: Bidwell 1980, 69 (*Insula* II: (1))

The corner of a masonry building was recorded during building work. A corridor or veranda at the side of the street was *c.* 1.5 m wide and at least 10 m long; behind it parts of two rooms were revealed, one measuring 7 m by at least 4 m. The building's walls cut through the remains of a series of successive timber buildings (Building 2i).

Building number: 7ii

- Site name: North Street Gaumont Cinema
- Excavation gazetteer number: 3
- City HER monument number: no HER number assigned
- Location: *insula* III
- References: Montgomerie-Neilson and Montague 1931, 130–1; Bidwell 1980, 69 (*Insula* III: (1))

Roman walls and a well were observed in the course of building work but no plan was recovered.

Building number: 8ii

- Site name: 45–46 North Street
- Excavation gazetteer number: 51
- City HER monument number: no HER number assigned
- Location: *insula* III
- References: Bidwell 1980, 69 (*Insula* III: (2))

A wall was seen at the eastern corner of this *insula*.

Building number: 9ii

- Site name: Trichay Street
- Excavation gazetteer number: 42
- City HER monument number: 10177
- Location: *insula* IV/V/XX/XXV
- References: Chapter 5 in this volume (structure RC12); Bidwell 1980, 68–70 (*Insula* IV/V: (1))

A building constructed in the mid 2nd/early 3rd century AD that would have been more than 5.2 m long and 4.1 m wide, possibly constructed of timber with a wattle and daub walls. It was floored with cobbles and may therefore have been a barn or storehouse rather than a house and was demolished in the mid 3rd/early 4th century AD.

Building number: 10ii

- Site name: Trichay Street
- Excavation gazetteer number: 42
- City HER monument number: 10177
- Location: *insula* IV/V/XX/XXV
- References: Chapter 5 in this volume (structure RC15); Bidwell 1980, 68–70 (*Insula* IV/V: (1))

A building was built over the footprint of demolished buildings 9ii and 11ii in the mid to late 4th century AD. Although its construction style is uncertain, the narrow width of its foundations suggests that it had a timber rather than stone superstructure.

Building number: 11ii

- Site name: Trichay Street
- Excavation gazetteer number: 42
- City HER monument number: 10177
- Location: *insula* IV/V
- References: EAPIT 1, Fig. 6.14; Chapter 5 in this volume (structure RC11); Bidwell 1980, 68–70 (*Insula* IV/V: (1))

A building constructed in the mid 2nd/early 3rd century AD was *c.* 7 m long and *c.* 5.6 m wide. It probably had a timber superstructure, while there was evidence of clay daub partition walls and an *opus signinum* floor in one room, with later structural additions including a hypocaust. It was demolished in the mid 3rd/early 4th century AD.

Building number: 12ii

- Site name: Trichay Street
- Excavation gazetteer number: 42
- City HER monument number: 10177
- Location: *insula* IV/V/XX/XXV
- References: Chapter 5 in this volume (structure RC14); Bidwell 1980, 68–70 (*Insula* IV/V: (1))

A small mid/late 4th-century AD timber structure was revealed by six very shallow postholes forming a broad circle 5 m in diameter; it was perhaps a small animal pen or the base for a hayrick.

Building number: 13ii

- Site name: Trichay Street
- Excavation gazetteer number: 42
- City HER monument number: 10177
- Location: *insula* IV/V
- References: Chapter 5 in this volume (structure RC10); Bidwell 1980, 68–70 (*Insula* IV/V: (1))

A mid 2nd/early 3rd-century AD timber building 4 m wide and more than 6 m long.

Building number: 14ii

- Site name: Trichay Street; Goldsmith Street I-II; Goldsmith Street III; Waterbeer Street (Police Station)
- Excavation gazetteer number: 42; 37; 39; 137
- City HER monument number: 10177; 10178
- Location: *insula* IV/V/XX/XXV
- References: see EAPIT 1, Fig. 6.14; Chapters 5 (structure RC13) and 6 (structure RC5) in this volume; Fox 1952a, 99–100; Bidwell 1980, 71–72 (*Insula* IV/V: (1) and (2)); Cosh and Neal 2005, no. 157.1

In the late 3rd century AD at the earliest, and indeed perhaps more likely not until the mid 4th century AD, a large stone-built house was constructed measuring more than *c.* 30 m long and *c.* 15 m wide, although it extended beyond the limits of the Trichay Street excavation area (Site 42). Fragments of mosaic pavement had been recorded in the vicinity prior to the excavation (at Site 137) and they may possibly have belonged to this building, while excavations at Goldsmith Street (Sites 37 and 39) may have revealed the NE and NW perimeter walls of the same building. If they do belong to the same building, then it would have been of courtyard plan *c.* 45 m by 60 m with the mosaics in the south-eastern range.

Building number: 15ii

- Site name: Goldsmith Street III
- Excavation gazetteer number: 39
- City HER monument number: no HER number assigned
- Location: *insula* IV/V/XX/XXV
- References: EAPIT 1, Fig. 6.14; Chapter 6 in this volume (structure RC4); Bidwell 1980, 71–2 (*Insula* IV/V: (2))

A building equipped with underfloor heating and tessellated and *opus signinum* floors suggests the presence of a town house. Although its full extent lay beyond the limits of the excavation, a corridor, or perhaps a portico, and five rooms were recorded.

Building number: 16ii

- Site name: Exeter Castle
- Excavation gazetteer number: 193
- City HER monument number: no HER number assigned
- Location: *insula* IV/V/XX/XXV
- References: Blaylock forthcoming

Pieces of Roman tile, red-painted wall plaster, *tesserae*, window glass and mortar from a substantial but unlocated building. Given its location within the later town walls, it probably represents an otherwise unknown building of the late civil period unless it was an extra-mural building of the early town.

Building number: 17ii

- Site name: Friernhay Street
- Excavation gazetteer number: 75
- City HER monument number: 10199
- Location: *insula* VI
- References: EAACR 1981; Rankov *et al.* 1982, 382

A stone building was built in the late 3rd or early 4th century AD extending over the line of the former *via sagularis* and its early civil successor (Street B6i).

Building number 18ii

- Site Name: The Mint
- Excavation gazetteer number: 200
- City HER monument number: no HER number assigned
- Location: *insula* VI
- References: Fox 1952a, 100; Bidwell 1980, 72 (*Insula* VI: (1))

In 1812 a tessellated pavement was found in digging the foundations of the new chapel in the Mint, while in 1837 labourers laying gas pipes found a Roman foundation with a coin of Faustina II embedded in it.

Building number: 19ii

- Site name: Mary Arches Street, Golden Ball Inn
- Excavation gazetteer number: 2
- City HER monument number: 10161
- Location: *insula* VII
- References: Montgomerie-Neilson and Montague 1931, 128–30; Fox 1952a, 100; Bidwell 1980, 72 (*Insula* VII: (2))

A 2nd/3rd-century AD wall approximately 0.9 m wide was recorded running on an approximately SW–NE alignment, along with the partially demolished walls of a 4th-century AD house, some of which were still extant above ground.

Building number: 20ii

- Site name: Mary Arches Street
- Excavation gazetteer number: 54

- City HER monument number: no HER number assigned
- Location: *insula* VII
- References: Bidwell 1980, 72 (*Insula* VII: (1))

A wall was traced along the side of the street on the NW side of the *insula*. It was directly opposite Building 6ii in *insula* II, with which its construction was contemporary.

Building number: 21ii

- Site name: 45–46 North Street
- Excavation gazetteer number: 51
- City HER monument number: 10182
- Location: *insula* VIII
- References: Goodburn 1976, 358; Bidwell 1980, 72 (*Insula* VIII: (1))

The corner of a masonry building was found at the junction of the streets on the NW and NE sides of the *insula*. Evidence of stone buildings was also found in a smaller trench in Waterbeer Street beside Street G1i.

Building number: 22ii

- Site name: 196–197 High Street
- Excavation gazetteer number: 43
- City HER monument number: 10180
- Location: *insula* IX
- References: Chapter 7 in this volume (structure RC3); Bidwell 1980, 73 (*Insula* IX: (1)); Cosh and Neal 2005, no. 157.2

The W corner of building was seen for a length of over 6 m and a width 3 m although it extended beyond the excavation area. It contained a tessellated floor, while fragments of tessellated pavement had also been reported along the frontage of 196–197 High Street in 1777 and 1874. The locations of these finds, if they are related to the same structure, suggests this building would have been more than 15 m long and may have encroached on the line of the street bordering the basilica and forum. The building was constructed after the mid 3rd century AD.

Building number: 23ii

- Site name: High Street, NatWest Bank
- Excavation gazetteer number: 62
- City HER monument number: no HER number assigned
- Location: *insula* IX
- References: Bidwell 1979, 121; 1980, 73 (*Insula* IX: (2))

A wall was revealed in section and it may have formed part of the same building as Building 22ii. Demolition deposits contained yellow-painted wall plaster.

Building number: 24ii

- Site name: Queen Street, 22 Goldsmith Street and 211–219 High Street
- Excavation gazetteer number: 68
- City HER monument number: no HER number assigned
- Location: *insula* X/XXI/XXVI
- References: Fox 1952a, 99; Goodburn 1979, 324; Bidwell 1980, 73 (*Insula* X: (1))

At the 22 Goldsmith Street, a masonry building was constructed after *c.* AD 250 in association with a builders' yard where evidence of mortar-mixing, preparation of *tesserae* and the working of Purbeck marble, sandstone and roof-slates was found. In 1843 and 1845, just to the NE of this site, part of a hypocaust, foundations and 'the remains of Roman zigzag or herring-bone pebble pavements' were found and which may be associated with this building.

Building number: 25ii

- Site name: 228 High Street
- Excavation gazetteer number: 61
- City HER monument number: no HER number assigned
- Location: *insula* X/XXI/XXVI
- References: Bidwell 1980, 73 (*Insula* XXI: (1))

When the cellar-walls of 228 High Street were removed in 1975, a Roman wall *c.* 60 cm wide was exposed; it was associated with several floor levels and appears to have been partly rebuilt.

Building number: 26ii

- Site name: Abbot of Newenham's town house, High Street
- Excavation gazetteer number: N/A
- City HER monument number: no HER number assigned
- Location: *insula* X/XXI/XXVI
- References: Shortt 1840, 55; Bidwell 1980, 74 (*Insula* XXVI: (1))

Shortt noted 'solid foundation of Roman masonry, of the usual materials, near which were found, at nine feet deep, a coin of Domitian' at the old town house of the Abbot of Newenham on High Street.

Building number: 27ii

- Site name: Smythen Street; Market Street/Smythen Street
- Excavation gazetteer number: 1; 115
- City HER monument number: 10126
- Location: *insula* XI/XII
- References: Montgomerie-Neilson and Montague 1931, 124–8; Fox 1952a, 100; Bidwell 1980, 73 (*Insula* XI: (1)); Hall *et al.* 1995, 9; Stead 2002, 10–12

In 1931 a room measuring 4.2 m by 3.2 m with walls still standing to a height of 1.2 m was excavated and was thought to have been equipped with a hypocaust. Further traces of this building, including a mortar floor surface and mortared walls, were recorded in 1995 and again in 2001–2002 when four parallel walls and traces of both *opus signinum* and mortar floor surfaces were found. The building would have been very extensive and was essentially rectangular in plan, consisting of a corridor flanked by a single range of rooms to the SE and a double range of rooms to the NW. A building was found in the NE corner of *insula* XI and the SE corner of *insula* XII indicating that the former Street I2i had fallen out of use in the late town as it had been built over by this building. Pottery recovered from the floor levels suggests a construction date of the mid to late 2nd century AD or later.

Building number: 28ii

- Site name: Market Street/Smythen Street
- Excavation gazetteer number: 115
- City HER monument number: 11530
- Location: *insula* XI/XII
- References: Stead 2002, 10

The poorly preserved remains of a stone building were recorded consisting of a 3.6 m length of wall aligned on the adjacent street (Street I2i), suggesting the street was still in use when the building was constructed. The walls were of volcanic trap rubble bonded with a hard lime mortar, while a mortar floor was also recorded. Its original layout remains unclear due to later disturbances and because its full extent lay beyond the excavation limits. The excavators interpreted this building as being earlier than the adjacent Building 27ii.

Building number: 29ii

- Site name: 93–94 Fore Street
- Excavation gazetteer number: 14
- City HER monument number: no HER number assigned
- Location: *insula* XI/XII
- References: Ransom Pickard 1938, 83; Fox 1952a, 100–1; Bidwell 1980, 73 (*Insula* XII: (1))

An unpublished account of observations made by Col. Ransom Pickard records that several Roman walls of volcanic trap rock were found here, although their true nature is unclear.

Building number: 30ii

- Site name: Catherine Street, Annuellar's College; St Catherine's Almshouses; Catherine Street
- Excavation gazetteer number: 19; 89; 129
- City HER monument number: 10169
- Location: *insulae* XIV and XXII
- References: EAPIT 1, Figs 6.14 and 6.15; Fox 1951a, 40–41; 1952a, 46–9; Bidwell 1980, 73–4 (*Insula* XXII: (1)); Holbrook *et al.* 1989, 43–52; Cosh and Neal 2005, no. 157.5–6, 8

In 1943 traces of mosaic were recorded following the destruction of buildings during the Blitz and in 1945–7 the remains of a late town house, consisting of fragmentary remains of walls and further small patches of tessellated floors, were excavated. Further elements of this building were uncovered in 1950 and 1987–8, with the latter excavation revealing a 3 m long corridor mosaic, the most impressive recorded in Exeter. The house was probably built in the late 3rd or early 4th century AD and abandoned by the third quarter of the 4th century at the latest.

Building number: 31ii

- Site name: Rack Street
- Excavation gazetteer number: 52
- City HER monument number: 10186
- Location: *insula* XV/XVA/XVI/XXXIV
- References: Chapter 8 in this volume (structure RC3); Bidwell 1980, 73 (*Insula* XVA: (1))

A mid 4th-century AD stone building was defined by three robber trenches. It was 12.3 m wide and over 5.2 m long. No internal features or floors survived.

Building number 32ii

- Site name: Market Street/Smythen Street
- Excavation gazetteer number: 115
- City HER monument number: 10241
- Location: *insula* XV/XVA/XVI/XXXIV
- References: Stead 1999, fig. 7

The report for the 1998 Market Street excavation records four sections of walls in its figure 7 'Later Roman features within the Smythen Street/Market Street sites'. The building was reconstructed as a NW–SE orientated building of three rooms, although it is not mentioned in the text of the report itself.

Building number 33ii

- Site name: Market Street/Smythen Street
- Excavation gazetteer number: 115
- City HER monument number: 10243
- Location: *insula* XV/XVA/XVI/XXXIV
- References: Hall *et al.* 1995, 7

The truncated remains of what the excavators describe as 'the corner of a construction trench', perhaps indicating a robber trench for a stone wall, were observed aligned NE–SW, parallel to the modern Preston Street.

Building number 34ii

- Site name: Market Street/Smythen Street

- Excavation gazetteer number: 115
- City HER monument number: no HER number assigned
- Location: *insula* XV/XVA
- References: Stead 1999, 5

The remains of a masonry wall foundation 0.35 m wide and made of volcanic trap fragments. No facework or associated surface features survived, however, and given its narrow width it is possible that it represents a property boundary rather than a building.

Building number: 35ii

- Site Name: Market Street/Smythen Street
- Excavation gazetteer number: 115
- City HER monument number: 11531
- Location: *insula* XV/XVA/XVI/XXXIV
- References: Stead 2002, 12–13

A building was identified by several associated robber trenches, although their attribution to the Roman period is tentative and based largely on the evidence of their finds as no architectural features survived; robbed out mortar did suggest the former presence of a mortar-bonded wall, however. The most extensive robber trench was aligned NE-SW and was traceable for 21 m.

Building number: 36ii

- Site Name: Market Street/Smythen Street
- Excavation gazetteer number: 115
- City HER monument number: 10242
- Location: *insula* XV/XVA/XVI/XXXIV
- References: Hall *et al.* 1995, 7; Stead 2002, fig. 7

The truncated remains of two intersecting construction trenches forming a corner were seen. The 1995 excavators (Hall *et al.*) assigned the trenches to the later Roman period, although Stead (2002) later expressed some doubt: although depicted in his report's figure of Late Roman features, these trenches were marked as 'phase uncertain' and it is perhaps noteworthy that their alignment of N–S and E–W differs from the other Late Roman buildings recorded at Site 115.

Building number: 37ii

- Site name: Cathedral Close (St Mary Major and Cathedral Green)
- Excavation gazetteer number: 40
- City HER monument number: 10255
- Location: *insula* XVIII
- References: Frere 1977, 415; Bidwell 1979, 115–8; 1980, 73 (*Insula* XVIII: (1)); Cosh and Neal 2005, no. 157.4

In the 1971 St Mary Major excavation a wall-foundation in a trench 1.2 m wide was observed; it is possible that a continuation of it was seen at the 1976 Cathedral Green excavation where the remains of two successive masonry buildings were excavated. The first phase survived only as fragmentary walls and their robber trenches but was thought to consist of an L-shaped range of at least five rooms and probably dated to the late 2nd century AD. Before *c.* AD 250 it was substantially rebuilt, although the NE range of the earlier building may well have been retained. One room contained a badly damaged mosaic.

Building number: 38ii

- Site name: Cathedral Cloisters
- Excavation gazetteer number: 133
- City HER monument number: 10208
- Location: *insula* XVIII
- References: Stead and Parker 1998, 3

A short length of wall foundation was recorded of probable 3rd or 4th-century AD date. It was 0.8 m wide, running NW–SE and consisted of clay-bonded volcanic trap rubble.

Building number: 39ii

- Site name: Cathedral Close (Cathedral Green)
- Excavation gazetteer number: 40
- City HER monument number: no HER number assigned
- Location: *insula* XIX
- References: Bidwell 1979, 118; 1980, 73 (*Insula* XIX: (1))

Two successive mortar floors on pitched rubble foundations, their full extents not established. The date of these floors is not clear, and they could be post-Roman: a few metres to the W a mortared floor on a pitched rubble bedding was associated with the 11th-century cathedral, although the uppermost layer encountered here was a deposit of dark humic soil which is also similar in character to the post-Roman 'dark earth' which covered later Roman levels elsewhere in Exeter.

Building number: 40ii

- Site name: Cathedral Cloisters
- Excavation gazetteer number: 133
- City HER monument number: no HER number assigned
- Location: *insula* XIX
- References: Stead and Parker 1998, 8

A small section of the foundation of a clay-bonded volcanic trap wall. Although it had been cut through by the masonry of the Norman cathedral, no other dating evidence was found and it cannot be related to any other feature recorded in the excavation trench. It might therefore feasibly be Late Saxon/Early Norman as opposed to Late Roman.

Building number: 41ii

- Site name: Cathedral, St Andrew's Chapel
- Excavation gazetteer number: 11
- City HER monument number: 10164
- Location: *insula* XIX
- References: Radford and Morris 1936, 227–8; Fox 1952a, 102; Bidwell 1980, 73 (*Insula* XIX: (1))

A small heated room with an internal apse floored with a thick layer of *opus signinum* with a quarter-round moulding. Beneath the floor was a system of radiating flues connecting with a hypocaust largely destroyed by the walls of the Norman cathedral.

Building number: 42ii

- Site name: Chapel Street Abbot's Lodge (Fox 1952 Trench 17)
- Excavation gazetteer number: 29
- City HER monument number: no HER number assigned
- Location: *insula* XXII/XXIII/XXIV/XXVII/XXVIII/XXIX
- References: Fox 1952a, 51–2; Bidwell 1980, 74 (*Insula* XXIV: (2))

Large pieces of bedded trap were seen and interpreted as the foundations of a building.

Building number: 43ii

- Site name: Princesshay
- Excavation gazetteer number: 156
- City HER monument number: no HER number assigned
- Location: *insula* XXII/XXIII/XXIV/XXVII/XXVIII/XXIX
- References: City HER event number 803.32

A slab of *opus signinum* was observed at a trial trench at Bedford Street; it was regarded as being *in situ* and probably represents the floor of a Late Roman building.

Building number: 44ii

- Site name: 28 Catherine Street (Fox 1952 Area VI)
- Excavation gazetteer number: 20
- City HER monument number: 10170
- Location: *insula* XXII/XXIII/XXIV/XXVII/XXVIII/XXIX
- References: Fox 1952a, 49–50; Bidwell 1980, 74 (*Insula* XXVII: (1))

Two short lengths of wall foundations, described as being made of trap and measuring 0.58 m by 0.79 m were recorded here. Although Bidwell (1980, 74) records these remains as one building, Fox (1952a, 50) wrote that they were on two slightly different alignments 'as though they belonged to two different buildings'. Both buildings overlay the late Street J indicating that it was constructed after that street had fallen out of use.

Building number: 45ii

- Site name: Princesshay
- Excavation gazetteer number: 156
- City HER monument number: no HER number assigned
- Location: *insula* XXII/XXIII/XXIV/XXVII/XXVIII/XXIX
- References: EAPIT 1, Fig. 6.14; Steinmetzer, Stead, Pearce, Bidwell and Allan forthcoming (building 1)

A building consisting of a range over 30 m long, with rooms attached to the NW, which extended beyond the excavated area. At least two of its rooms were equipped with hypocausts, while another room had a curved wall suggesting that it was either an apsidal room, perhaps part of a bath-house. The building likely had a mosaic: 500 loose *tesserae* were recovered, although (less likely) they may have come from Building 47ii. The building overlay former Street J indicating it was constructed after that street had gone out of use. The building was occupied between the late 3rd century AD and *c.* AD 370.

Building number: 46ii

- Site name: Princesshay
- Excavation gazetteer number: 156
- City HER monument number: no HER number assigned
- Location: *insula* XXII/XXIII/XXIV/XXVII/XXVIII/XXIX
- References: Steinmetzer, Stead, Pearce, Bidwell and Allan forthcoming

A lime mortar floor with a smooth upper surface; the surviving portion bisected by a row of stake-holes which probably represent a wall-line of a late 3rd-century AD timber building which was not orientated on the street grid. No trace of enclosing walls was found around the floor, suggesting that they had sat on the ground surface and thus left no trace.

Building number: 47ii

- Site name: Rack Street
- Excavation gazetteer number: 64
- City HER monument number: 10184
- Location: *insula* XXXIII/XXXV/XXXVI
- References: Chapter 8 in this volume (structures RC1 and RC2); Bidwell 1980, 74–6 (*Insula* XXXIII: (1))

A late 3rd/early 4th-century AD timber-framed building consisting of a row of five substantial postpits and a roughly parallel row of six postholes. At some point the building was burnt down and was succeeded by another timber-framed building that consisted of a series of post-trenches defining a building over *c.* 14 m long and *c.* 12 m wide. It had also been destroyed by fire by the mid 4th century AD and was succeeded by buildings 48 and 49ii.

Building number: 48ii

- Site name: Rack Street
- Excavation gazetteer number: 64
- City HER monument number: 10185
- Location: *insula* XXXIII/XXXV/XXXVI
- References: Chapter 8 in this volume (structure RC4); Bidwell 1980, 74 (*Insula* XXXIII: (1))

A stone building, represented by lines of robber trenches and various floor surfaces. Its dimensions are uncertain although it may have been *c.* 12.25 m long and 8 m wide.

Building number: 49ii

- Site name: Rack Street
- Excavation gazetteer number: 64
- City HER monument number: 10184
- Location: *insula* XXXIII/XXXV/XXXVI
- References: Chapter 8 in this volume (structure RC5); Bidwell 1980, 74–6 (*Insula* XXXIII: (1))

A stone building 12 m long by 8 m wide contained four substantial ovens; each displayed evidence of intense burning although it cannot be demonstrated that they were all in use contemporaneously.

Building number: 50ii

- Site name: Rack Street
- Excavation gazetteer number: 64
- City HER monument number: no HER number assigned
- Location: *insula* XXXIII/XXXV/XXXVI
- References: Chapter 8 in this volume (structure RC6); Bidwell 1980, 74–6 (*Insula* XXXIII: (1))

A 2.2 m wide cobbled alleyway separated this structure from Building 49ii to its SW, although the only evidence for it was a single robber trench, 0.9 m wide.

Building number: 51ii

- Site name: Mermaid Yard
- Excavation gazetteer number: 63
- City HER monument number: 10193
- Location: *insula* XXXIII/XXXV/XXXVI
- References: EAACR 1977; Bidwell 1980, 76 (*Insula* XXXIII: (2))

The remains of two successive buildings were found on the frontage of Street M. The first building was of timber construction and probably dates from *c.* AD 275 when the street was laid out. Its successor was constructed in stone and appeared to consist of a range of at least three small rooms. A coin of AD 346–50 was found in the debris resulting from the demolition or decay above the floor levels of the building.

Building number: 52ii

- Site name: Palace Gate Convent Garden
- Excavation gazetteer number: 8
- City HER monument number: 15065
- Location: *insula* XXXVII
- References: none

A watching brief in the courtyard fronting Palace Gate noted the exposure of some possible Roman masonry below the SE wall of the S range of the Palace Gate Convent. Further details are not recorded, although the City HER records the masonry as belonging to the late civil period.

Building number: 53ii

- Site name: Cathedral Green/Palace Gate/Bishops Palace
- Excavation gazetteer number: 170
- City HER monument number: no HER number assigned
- Location: *insula* XXXVIII
- References: Thomson *et al.* 2014, 11

At a watching brief in Palace Gate a probable Roman wall footing was revealed in section only and comprised volcanic trap rubble bonded with light yellow white lime mortar. It appeared to be orientated broadly E–W.

Building number: 54ii

- Site name: Cathedral Green/Palace Gate/Bishops Palace
- Excavation gazetteer number: 170
- City HER monument number: no HER number assigned
- Location: *insula* XXXVIII
- References: Thomson *et al.* 2014, 11

A Roman wall foundation, orientated N–S, was seen at a watching brief in Palace Gate. It comprised one layer of red sandstone blocks bound by a grey gritty mortar, possibly representing the corner of a structure.

Building number: 55ii

- Site name: Cathedral, outside of Speke Chapel; Cathedral School; Vicinity of St Peter's Cathedral Church
- Excavation gazetteer number: 12; 100; 136
- City HER monument number: 10165; 10166; 10266
- Location: *insula* XXXIX
- References: Radford and Morris 1936, 226, 228–31; Fox 1952a, 102–3; Bidwell 1980, 76 (*Insula* XXXIX: (1)); EAACR 1992; Cosh and Neal 2005, no. 157.9

In 1936, three Roman walls were found running parallel to each other from SW to NE. A tessellated pavement had been found nearby in 1843, measuring *c.* 7 m by *c.* 2.4 m and probably belonged to the same building. Further traces of this building were excavated in 1991 when a long narrow flue and stoking pit belonging to some form of furnace, perhaps a corn-drying kiln, was located.

Building number: 56ii

- Site name: 10 Cathedral Close
- Excavation gazetteer number: 33
- City HER monument number: 10174
- Location: *insula* XXXIX
- References: Fox 1956, 212–21; Greenfield 1964, 339–751; Bidwell 1980, 74 (*Insula* XXIV: (1))

Part of a building was excavated which was probably laid out in the late 2nd century AD. The corner of a single room 5.2 m by 4.5 m was explored; its interior was occupied by drains and hearths. Very little material was associated with its construction. It appeared to have been demolished at the beginning of the 4th century AD.

Building 57ii

- Site name: 28 Catherine Street (Fox 1952 Area VI)
- Excavation gazetteer number: 20
- City HER monument number: 10170
- Location: *insula* XL
- References: Fox 1952a, 49–50; Bidwell 1980, 74

One of the two lengths of wall recorded by Fox who felt that it represented a separate structure from Building 44ii located immediately to the SE.

Building number: 58ii

- Site name: Princesshay
- Excavation gazetteer number: 156
- City HER monument number: no HER number assigned
- Location: *insula* XXII/XXIII/XXIV/XXVII/XXVIII/XXIX/XL
- References: EAPIT 1, Fig. 6.14; Steinmetzer, Stead, Pearce, Bidwell and Allan forthcoming (building 2)

Immediately to the E of Building 45ii was another stone structure. It consisted of a rectangular main block 12.5 m by 10 m, with a wall dividing it into two rows of rooms. Patches of floor survived, and debris indicates that the building had a slate roof and at least three schemes of painted wall-plaster; impressions in the backs of some plaster fragments indicate that they came from a room with a hypocaust although whether they represent spread from Building 45ii is unknown. The building overlay former Street J indicating that it was constructed after the street had gone out of use. The building dates from the late 3rd century AD onwards.

4

Medieval Documentary Evidence Relating to the High Street, Trichay Street and Goldsmith Street Excavations

John Allan

Introduction

The excavations in High Street, Trichay Street and Goldsmith Street examined parts of two adjacent blocks of properties within the walled city (Fig. 4.1). Those at 196–8 High Street investigated part of a strip of narrow burgage plots fronting onto the centre of High Street, backing onto Waterbeer Street, and facing the principal entry into Cathedral Close at Broadgate. Situated at the heart of the commercial life of the city, these were among the most valuable of its tenements, occupied by leading citizens including several mayors. They are therefore especially well documented. The Trichay Street and Goldsmith Street excavations sampled the roughly square block further from the centre, defined until the 1970s by Waterbeer Street, Goldsmith Street, Paul Street and North Street. This area was more mixed in character and generally of rather lower status but also included some valuable properties.

The core of the area examined, including the sites of the excavations at 196 High Street and Trichay Street (Chapters 5 and 7 below), consisted of the parish of St Pancras. This was (and is) one of the smallest of the city's parishes, merely 1.7 acres (0.69 ha) in extent (Hoskins 1957, 123).[1] At the end of the period considered in this study, 35 men and two widows were listed there in the Military Survey of 1522, which recorded male servants as well as householders; just 18 individuals paid the Subsidy of 1544 (Rowe 1977, 9–10, 53–4).

Sources and methodology

Written sources

The records of the city of Exeter have been described as 'the best surviving series of civic documents for any provincial city in medieval Britain' (Kowaleski 2019, 1). The city's remarkably rich collections of medieval deeds include more than a hundred documents which can be related specifically to this area, and these form the principal body of documentation used in this study. Most of them include descriptions of the bounds of properties which allow their general locations to be established – for example the block of burgage plots between High Street and Waterbeer Street – but only a few, such as those on a street corner or beside a church, can readily be related to an individual tenement without reference to other information. A key in establishing their locations has been the use of much later documentation generated by institutions which held lands continuously from the later Middle Ages into the recent past. Their more recent records commonly contain more specific information which allows them to be fixed on a modern map (although even this task is not always simple in the period before house numbers came into general use); the rents and succession of leaseholders can then be followed backwards through earlier documents. The survival of outstanding runs of some classes of document at Exeter, such as city rentals and the records of the rents of Dean and Chapter properties, allow the histories of some individual tenements to be followed over many centuries. The pursuit of the rents, which were often distinctive sums, has been a key in following the ownership and possession of properties.

Several generations of historians have transcribed these documents. Much work was done in the 1920s and 1930s, notably by E. Lega-Weekes and R.C. Easterling, followed by M.M. Rowe in the 1960s and 1970s. In the 1980s and 1990s, in an effort to achieve a comprehensive listing of Exeter's medieval deeds, P.R. Staniforth and J.J. Crocker (then Juddery) of Exeter Archaeology undertook further transcriptions, building up a corpus of almost 4000 transactions recorded in these documents, which they presented in four 'grey literature' reports (Staniforth and Juddery

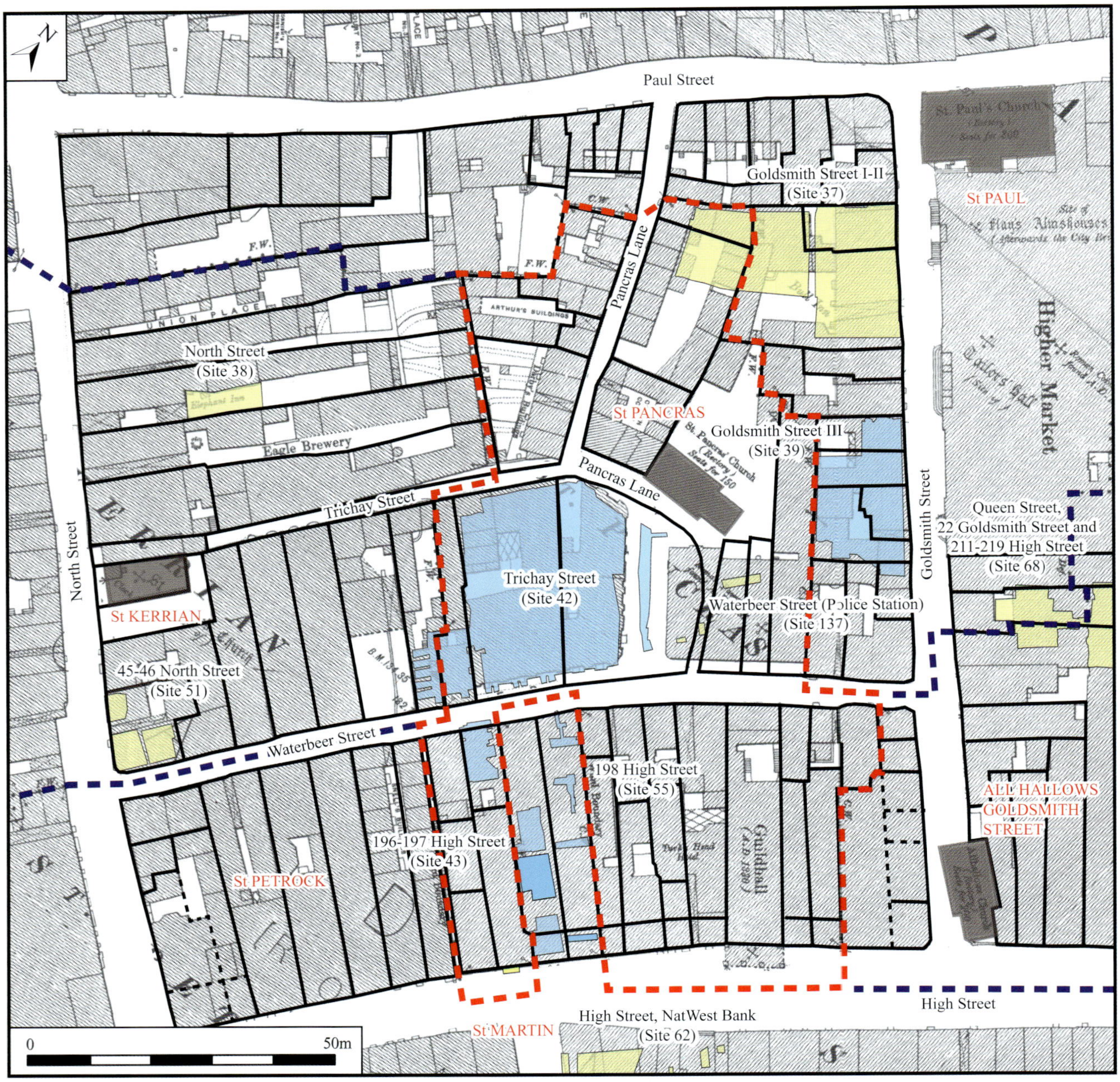

Fig. 4.1 Extract from the Ordnance Survey 1:500 map of 1876 showing the excavations at 196–8 High Street, Trichay Street and Goldsmith Street Area 3 (blue), other excavations (yellow), parish churches (grey), the boundaries of St Pancras parish (broken red lines) and other parishes (broken purple lines), with property bounds marked on the 1910 Valuation maps (bold lines). The notional north used in all Exeter documents is at the top of the page (OS 1:500 Sheet Devon LXXX.6.1, courtesy of the Devon and Exeter Institution; drawn by David Gould)

1991a–d), numbering them in a single sequence. In the present study I have used these as published sources, and (with the exception of a range of late 15th, 16th-century and later sources) have not usually consulted the original documents. Deeds listed by Staniforth and Juddery are cited first by their archive source and second by their sequence number, prefaced S&J. I have also used their transcriptions of the wills of medieval Exeter, and of other documents, now held in the Exeter Archaeology archive at the Devon Heritage Centre, with some material held online by Exeter City Council.

Maps

Since the use of mapping has been fundamental to this study, the sequence of maps showing this area will be described before the documentation is discussed. The earliest pictorial records are the view of Hooker and Hogenburg, which was based on field drawing undertaken in 1583 (Fig. 4.2A shows the engraved version published by Braun and Hogenburg in 1618), and Robert Sherwood's map of the city of *c.* 1630 (Fig. 4.2B: Rowe and Ravenhill 2002, 180, item 5/3/14). Hogenburg shows continuous buildings on all the main streets in these blocks

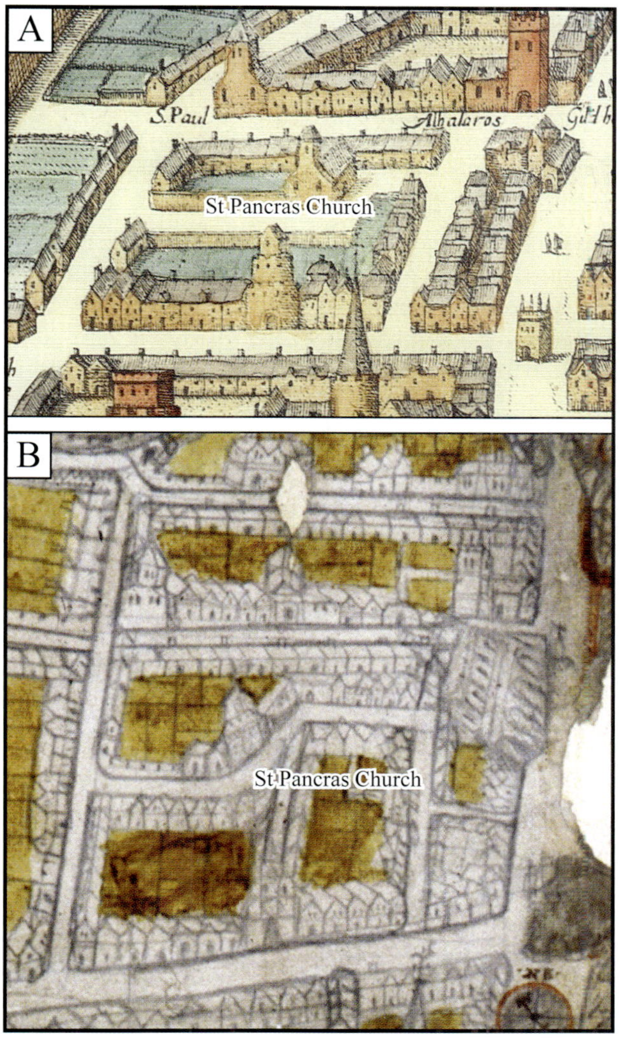

Fig. 4.2 The area as shown in (A) Braun and Hogenburg's engraving published in 1618 (© RAMM); (B) the Sherwood map of the city of c. 1630 (© Exeter City Council, courtesy of the Devon Heritage Centre). Both maps are orientated with High Street to the right, Paul Street to the left and North Street at the foot

but only garden walls along the lanes around St Pancras church; Sherwood shows a more crowded picture, with housing along most of the back lanes. As we shall see, documentary evidence indicates that there were houses along Pancras Lane and beside St Pancras church by the late 13th and early 14th centuries.

The next valuable record is the Map Book of the Chamber, which gives detailed plans of the properties belonging to the city, and also marks in outline those properties on which it charged high (or chief) rents. In fact they had little land in this part Exeter, but this source has proved crucial in reconstructing the histories of several tenements (Fig. 4.3).

The first detailed plan of properties within the city walls was Coldridge's map of 1819, superseded later in the 19th century by the highly accurate Ordnance Survey 1:500 map of Exeter of 1876 (Fig. 4.4A–B). The earliest

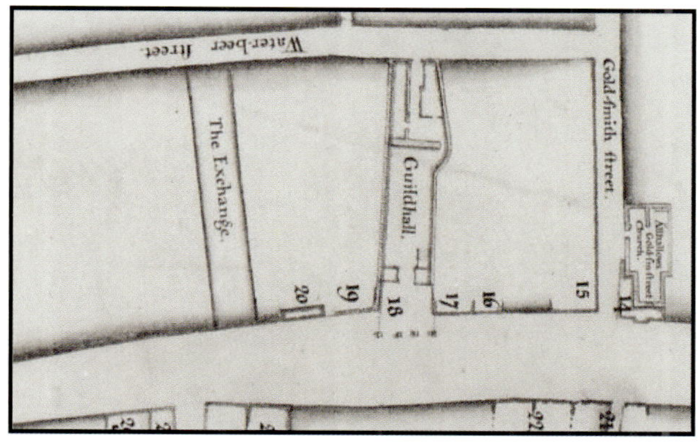

Fig. 4.3 Extract from Map 13 of the Map Book of the Chamber of 1756–60 (© Exeter City Council, courtesy of the Devon Heritage Centre). The accompanying text reads:

No. in the map	*No. in the Rental*	*Name of the lessee, and description of the premises*
In the Parish of Allhallows Goldsmith Street		
15	Do … 2 Maudlin … 22	John Tuckfield Esq. – Two Chief Rents, payable to the Mayor, Bailiffs and Commonalty out of these Lands, viz. 2s to St Mary Magdalen's Hospital, and 4s a Year to the General Account.
In the Parish of Saint Pancras		
16	Maudlin … 23	The Heirs of the late Robert Dodge, a Chief Rent of 10s a Year, payable to the M.B. and C. for this Tenement, being the 3 Tons Inn.
17	G.A. [General Account] St Pancras 1	Richard Densham, Esq. a Chief Rent of 5s 4d a Year, payable out of this Tenement, adjoyning to the East end of the Guildhall.
18	Do … 2	John Starr, a Cellar under the West side of the Arcade of the Guildhall, the Way, and Stairs to which goes through the Shop next adjoyning to the Guildhall, on that side.
19	Do … 3	The Heirs of Cheeseman, pay a Rent of 2d a Year, for resting the Beams of this Tenement in the West Wall of the Guildhall.
20	Do … 4	Richard Hart, part of a Shop, situate near the Guildhall and Bounded on the North and East with lands of the Dean and Chapter; on the West with lands of Sir William Courtenay Bart.; and on the South with Forestreet containing in length or front towards the said Street 21 feet, and in breadth 6 feet, and in height from the floor upwards 9 feet.

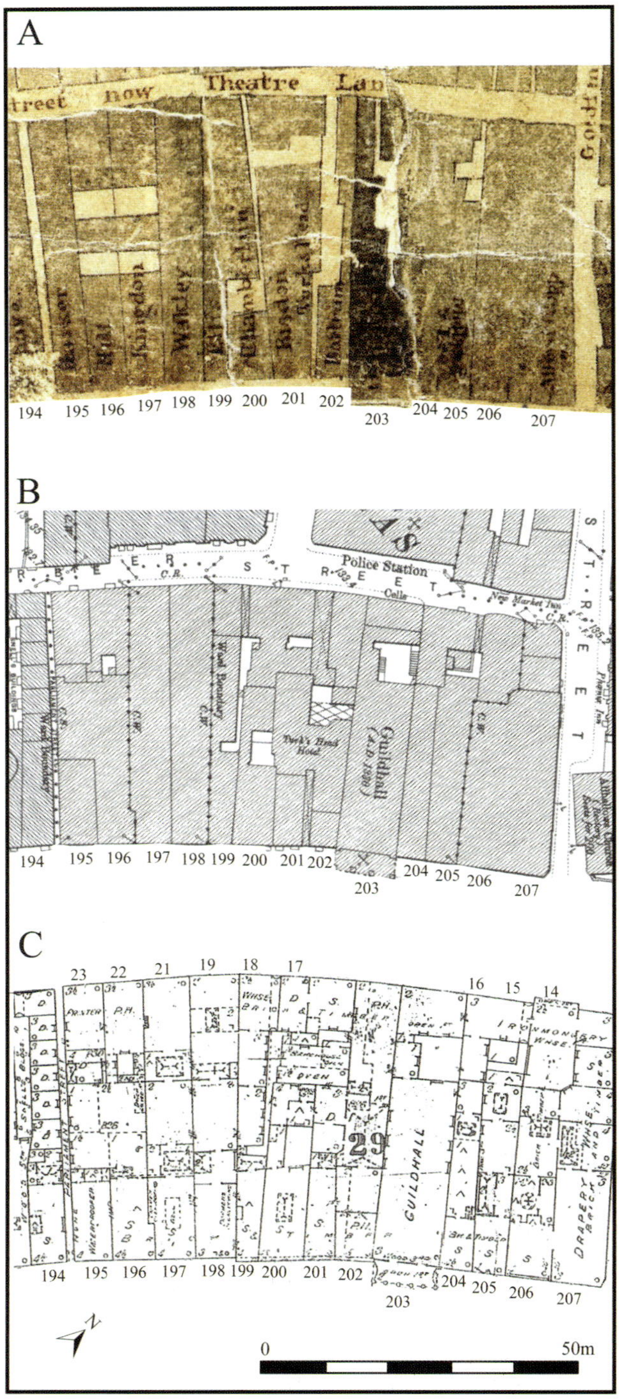

Fig. 4.4 Extracts from (A) Coldridge's map of Exeter of 1819 (© Exeter City Council, courtesy of the Devon Heritage Centre); (B) Ordnance Survey 1:500 map of 1876 (Devon sheet LXXX.6.17, Courtesy of the Devon and Exeter Institution); (C) the Goad insurance map of 1888 showing 194–207 High Street (courtesy of the Devon Heritage Centre)

surviving map of land ownership is the City Valuation of 1910 (copies at the Devon and Exeter Institution). Figure 4.1 shows the 1876 map with the property boundaries of 1910 superimposed, and with the parish boundaries highlighted. It also shows the earlier pattern of tenements in the central part of Waterbeer Street, recorded on Coldridge's map of 1819 (Fig. 4.4A) but cleared for the new Police Station before 1876.

Documentary evidence relating to 196–8 High Street and neighbouring tenements

The pattern of landowners, leaseholders and occupiers in the block of High Street properties around the Guildhall can be reconstructed more fully than has so far been achieved for late medieval Exeter, partly because properties owned by the Dean and Chapter and Vicars Choral of Exeter Cathedral, or paying rents to the City of Exeter, offer fixed points to which the deeds of adjacent plots can be related.

In order to interpret the evidence relating to the tenements in which excavation and building recording have taken place, it is necessary to examine all the deeds from St Pancras parish, then piece together the records of the block of 13 adjacent holdings on High Street (Nos 195–207), along with those of the Waterbeer Street properties at their backs, whose deeds are inter-related. Two tenements in this block (Nos 197–8) form an intruding portion of St Martin's parish, and two beside Goldsmith Street (Nos 206–7) fall in the neighbouring parish of Allhallows Goldsmith Street; the remainder are in St Pancras parish.

The relationships between the various documents are complex, and interpretation made more difficult by the fact that directions were switched in a few deeds (obvious in cases where High Street is in the north and Waterbeer Street in the south, much less so when east and west are confused). A more widespread problem has been that the modern calendars of these deeds have sometimes added mistaken identifications of parishes, to the confusion of the modern researcher. Nevertheless, the documentation is so rich that a substantial part of the centre of the city can be reconstructed.

The earliest pictorial record of the frontages is that by John White Abbott of 1797 (Fig. 4.5A); by that time only one property (No. 207) retained an unaltered medieval frontage. One of a number of 19th-century views is shown in Fig. 4.5B. The present appearance of the High Street frontages is shown in a photogrammetric survey undertaken for this study by Bill Harvey Associates (Fig. 4.6).

Landowners and rents

The Military Survey of 1522 provides the fullest evidence for the pattern of land ownership in this part of the city at the close of the Middle Ages (Rowe 1977). After listing those who lived in the parish, it records those who held lands in St Pancras but lived outside. The latter group consisted of nine religious institutions and eight lay individuals. They were listed with the value of their income, which is demonstrably the value of their annual rents.

Fig. 4.5 (A) John White Abbott's 'The High Street, Exeter, in 1797' (© RAMM); (B) mid 19th-century view of the same (© Devon Heritage Centre)

Fig. 4.6 Photogrammetric survey of the frontages of 195–203 High Street (© Bill Harvey Associates)

Since the rents commonly remained unchanged for centuries, even when property owners changed, as at the Reformation, most of the income of religious houses recorded in the survey can be matched to rents recorded in medieval and later sources. Figure 4.7 and Table 4.1 show the proposed locations of the lands of these institutions; the detailed evidence for their identification will be spelled out below.

Religious institutions owned six of the parish's eight valuable burgage plots on the High Street frontage in their entirety, and five of its 12 known High Street shops, with a combined income of £14 14s 0d (Fig. 4.7; Table 4.1). The total income of the eight lay owners living outside the parish was £9 17s 8d. Their holdings have proved more elusive, but since most of the High Street properties were owned by religious institutions the secular holdings must have been in the other parts of the parish.

Tenement histories

Rather than start in strict geographical order with No. 195 at the western end, we will begin at No. 196, since its rich documentation is a key to reconstructing the western part of the group.

196 High Street (St Pancras parish; cellar on Waterbeer Street excavated 1973 (Chapter 7 below); now entry to Guildhall Shopping Centre)

A fine series of Dean and Chapter leases relates to a High Street property on which tenants from Richard Prowse in 1562 to John Hill in 1813 and 1831 paid the yearly rent of £2 6s 8d (D&C 6006/13/2–6007/24/3; for the date of Prowse's lease see VC 21957). Coldridge's map of 1819 (Fig. 4.4A) records 'Hill' at 196 High Street, which therefore appears to be the property in question – a supposition supported by the final rental of Dean and Chapter lands of 1862 (ECLA CC71/77402, St Pancras, property T24, still leased by John Hill) and by further evidence outlined below. The tenement was one of the pair at the western corner of St Pancras parish, almost facing Broadgate.

Richard Prowse, the first man named in the series, was a merchant tailor and a major figure in the life of Elizabethan Exeter. He had taken the lease rather earlier,

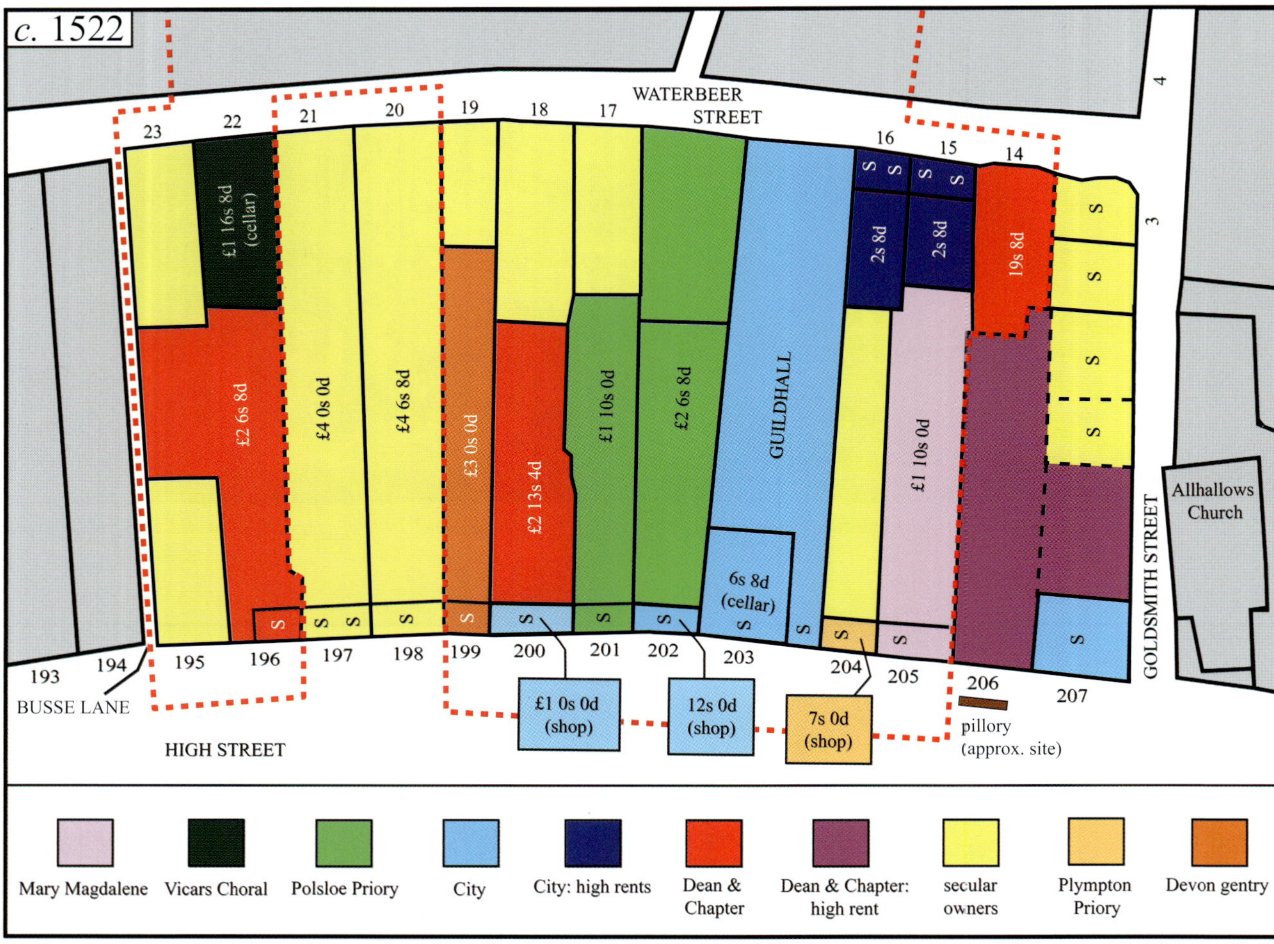

Fig. 4.7 Reconstruction of the ownership of the High Street properties of St Pancras parish c. *1522, with their ancient rents. The positions of shops recorded in the entire period 1350–1520 are marked 'S' (drawn by David Gould)*

paying the rent of £2 6s 8d to the Dean and Chapter in 1550, when he was made a free shopholder, sanctioned to make 'all manner of garments for men' (ECA Tailors' Act Book 1 f.15b, quoted in Osborne 2016, 605, biog. 60). From at least 1564 he also rented from the Vicars Choral of the cathedral their 'messuages and tenements near the Broadgate where Richard Prouze, taylor, dwells' (ECA CRB, 186a–b, f32). This was the cellar below the property of the Dean and Chapter, with the holding at the back of the tenement in Waterbeer Street, described below. By 1577 Prowse was one of the two highest taxpayers in St Pancras parish, and by far the highest in 1586; in the latter year only about 20 people in the city paid more than him (Rowe 1977, 62, 67). He subsequently became Bailiff, Receiver, Sheriff, Mayor (in 1578 and 1589) and Member of Parliament (in 1584: Osborne 2016, 771). His family retained the property into the early 17th century; in 1603 it was described as 'one tenement and one shoppe in the high street granted to Richard Prowse draper wherein John Prowse now dwelleth … £2 6s 8d' (D&C 3918).

The same tenement is mentioned in a second group of documents in the Dean and Chapter archives which relate to the prominent Exeter widow and benefactor Elizabeth Flay (Fig. 4.8). Flay is known to have lived in the parish of St Pancras, since it was there that she paid the poll tax of 1660; she was one of the two highest taxpayers in the parish, paying £4 (Hoskins 1957, 41). In the same year she leased from the Dean and Chapter 'one shop, four chambers over the shop whereof two of them are no biger then a standing bedstead will stand in them, one little narrow kitching over two payre of stares, one loft over the same' (D&C 4573/2/7a). Flay had paid the rent on this property before the Civil War (D&C 3920 dated 1640: Mrs fflay … £2 6s 8d); its identity with the one leased by Richard Prowse is stated in the renewal of her lease of 1662 (D&C 4573/2/7b; D&C 3559, 356–7).

Some later documents relating to this property provide information about its subsequent structural history and give further details of its layout. In 1702 it was stated that 'this tenement is a fair brick house, and lately built… Note that the cellar, entry passage and house behind the shop belcng to the Custos and College of Vicars' (D&C 4573/1/9). From 1702 until 1734 the Dean and Chapter leased it to Mary Crosse, widow, but

Table 4.1 Institutional landowners in St Pancras parish in 1522, with proposed identifications of the properties represented by their valuations (Rowe 1977, 12)

Landowner	*Income listed in survey*	*Proposed source*
Dean and Chapter	£5	Rents of 196 and 200 High Street @ £2 6s 8d & £2 13s 4d = £5 (for reasons which are unclear, this excludes any income from 14 Waterbeer Street, which was in the ownership of the Dean and Chapter by 1522)
Polsloe Priory	£3 16s 8d	Rents of 201 and 202 High Street @ £2 6s 8d and £1 10s = £3 16s 8d
Vicars Choral	£1 13s 4d	Rent of cellar @ 196 High Street with rooms behind, £1 6s 8d, increased to £1 16s 8d by the 1660s
Wynard's Almshouses	£1 11s 8d	Rent, 10 Waterbeer Street, later £1 12s
Mayor, Bailiffs and Commonalty	£1	Rent of shop on frontage of 200 High Street @ £1. Excludes the cellar below Guildhall and shop at 202 High Street
St Nicholas Priory	16s	Rent from 9 Waterbeer Street
Mary Magdalene Hospital	10s	Rent of 205 High Street @ 10s
Plympton Priory	7s	The 7s rent from the two shops at 204 High Street, given to St Mary Marsh
Feoffees of John Baron	6s 8d	Rent from 195 High Street

it was occupied by John Peryam, mercer; it was then described as consisting of 'shop and entry 37 feet by 13 feet in breadth (11.2 × 4 m)…[with] rooms above in four storeys…'. On a frontage which measured about 20 feet, the 13-foot width would allow a side passage to the cellar behind. The flat brick front shown in John White Abbott's painting 1797 and in 19th-century drawings (Figs 4.5A–B) was probably the one built at the start of the 18th century; the property next door (No. 195) is also a house of this period (Passmore 2011).

The cellar of the Vicars Choral below the Chapter's property

When Elizabeth Flay acquired the leasehold of the house in 1660, she also surrendered the lease of a cellar and other buildings in this tenement, also formerly held by Richard Prowse but in the separate ownership of the Custos and

Fig. 4.8 Portrait of Elizabeth Flay, who lived at 196 High Street in the period 1640–62 (Guildhall Collection, © RAMM)

College of the Vicars Choral. The lease states that the cellar lay below the property discussed above; the holding is described as follows:

> [One] entry there together with the street from the Channel lying before the said sellar extending from the High Street on the fore part to Water Beer street on the hinder part & also certain houses, buildings, yards & courtlaidges there between tenements of the Dean & Chapter on the south, Waterbeer Street on the north, a little narrow lane & the lands of the late dissolved hospital of St John Baptist on the west & a tenement sometime of John Blackaller on the east (VC 21957).

Flay's surrender of the lease in 1668 gives a further description:

> 1 sellar under the shop of Dean & Chapter in parish of St Pancras now in the possession of Edward Foxwell, mercer, & also 1 lying before the said sellar extending from the High Street on the fore part to the Waterbere Street in the back part & also all the houses, buildings, yards, & courtlages there between the tenement of the Dean & Chapter on the south, Waterbeer street on the north & a little narrow lane & the land of the late dissolved hospital of St John Baptist on the west & the tenement of John Blackaller wherein Johane Tuckfeild, widow, somtim dwelt on the east (VC 21958).

The history of this property in the century before the Reformation is richly documented; a sequence of about a dozen deeds spanning this period and relating to the holding survives in the papers of the Vicars Choral. They show that John Shaplegh, a member of Exeter's civic elite (Kowaleski 1995, 170), acquired the cellar by 1435. He leased it to the merchant John Baron, but when Baron died four years later Shaplegh acquired the interest of the Mary Magdalene Hospital in the curtilage and cellar behind the shop, and left the property in trust for the benefit of the Vicars Choral. In 1435 it was described as a message and curtilage, with two walls of stone and lime, in Waterbeer Street, and a cellar, with door and entry belonging to the message fronting onto High Street and extending back to Waterbeer Street (VC 3152). The subsequent documents record at length the trustees, the leaseholders of the adjacent properties, and sometimes other information; those which give information about the neighbouring tenements are listed in Table 4.2.

Further documents in the archives of the Vicars Choral and the Mary Magdalene leper hospital inform us about the history of the property before it was bequeathed to the vicars in the 1430s. The 'messuage

Table 4.2 Descent of John Shaplegh's tenement in St Pancras parish and adjacent properties, 1435–1509. The documents relate to the holding of the Vicars Choral, except those described in Dean and Chapter documents, which relate to the Chapter's holding on the street frontage

Date	*West boundary (195 High Street)*	*Shaplegh (196 High Street)*	*East boundary (197 High Street)*	*Document*
1435	John Baron, Thos [Cook]	Lease by John Shaplegh to John Baron merchant (two of three parts), the other Cokeworthy, total rent 17s [Note 1 below]	William Cremyll	VC 3152
1439	John Kirton, *Busshelane*	Hospital of St Mary Magdalen to John Shaplegh and John Cokeworthy [Note 2 below]	William Upton	VC 3171
1439	John Kirton, *Busshelane*	John Baron, John Smert [Note 3 below]	William Upton	MCR 18–19 Hen VI, m.16; S&J 3322
[1453]			[Upton to John Bobyche]	
1462	†Jn Baron and †T. Cook; N. Manlegh	Ex'ors to Henry Webber [Dean of the cathedral] *et al.* To be held by heirs of John Kelnelegh	John Bobyche	VC 3218, 3391
1464	†Jn Baron and †Thos Cook [Note 4 below]	Ex'ors of J. Shaplegh to Harry Webber *et al.* To be held by heirs of John Kelnelegh	John Bobyche	VC 3391
1467	Late of Jn Baron & †Thos Cook [Note 5 below]	As above, rent 26s 8d	John Bobyche	VC 3102
1467	Recently of John Baron	John Champernowne *et al.* release to John Strete, clerk [Note 6 below]	John Bibythe sometime of William Upton	D&C 157
1470	Recently of John Baron	Roger Keys [Precentor] to Henry Webber [Dean] and Chapter [Note 7 below]	John Bobysth sometime of William Upton	D&C 159; D&C 455
1472		Roger Keys to Nicholas Lavole[Note 8 below]		D&C 160
1473	John Baron and Thos Coke	John Kelly to Vicars Choral [Note 9 below]	John Bobyche	VC 21956
1509	Where Thomas Bond recently lived	John and Joan Redryse (heiress of Nicholas Lavole) release to the Dean and Chapter [Note 10 below]	Where John Scose now lives	D&C 162

Notes:

1. Messuage and cellar, Waterbeer St to N, the tenement of John Baron and John Smert and High St to S
2. And the tenement which Nicholas Manlegh inhabits
3. And the tenement which Nicholas Manlegh inhabits
4. And the tenement formerly inhabited by Nicholas Manlegh
5. 'Shop with two solars built above it on the N side of High Street opposite Broadgate', the annual rent £2 3s 4d, the tenement of John Kelly to the N, 'which shop and solars he had recently along with the said John Strete by grant of John Floyer and Nicholas Lavole.'
6. A shop and two solars above, annual rent £2 3s 4d
7. A shop and two solars above, annual rent £2 3s 4d
8. A tenement with a curtilege and cellar
9. In which John Levers now lives, in which John Smert once lived

with a cellar at its front... once belonging to John Gist the elder' had passed in 1409 from John Talbot to the cleric Richard Gabryell (VC 3139, S&J 3890). A rental of the leper hospital of 1419 records that John Smert and Denise Gabriel had previously paid the hospital a rent of £1 4s 0d 'for all that tenement, lately John Gist's, opposite Broadgate', and this rent was then paid by John Shaplegh, John Cokeworthy and Thomas Gybbes (ED/MAG/100 m25). In 1420 William Gybbes of Fenton granted it to his son Thomas, and to John Cokeworthy and John Shaplegh (VC 3111, S&J 3891), leading on to the sequence of transactions tabulated above. The 1409 document describes the property as 'a tenement (once John Gist senior's) on the north of High Street opposite Broadgate'; in 1420 it was called 'a messuage with a cellar at its front where John Gist and his wife Isabel lately lived in High Street opposite Broad Gate'.

John Gist

John Gist I, the first of three generations of men with that name, was a wealthy draper, highly active in civic affairs over a long period (1343–80) and six times mayor of Exeter in the years 1356–72 (Rowe and Cochlin 1964, 4). An entry in the Mayor's Court Roll of 1344 records his purchase of a messuage from Thomas of Kingston and his wife Joan, described as lying between High Street and Waterbeer Street, with the tenements of Walter Godwine and Laurence Frogwille to the west and Thomas Forbour's tenement to the east (MCR 17–18 Edw III, m30, S&J 0991). We shall see that No. 195 was a divided tenement with Frogwille at the rear, and shall meet a later Forbour at No. 197 to the east.

Following Gist's death in 1381, his estate was divided among members of the family. He left his second wife Agnes the following:

1. His tenement in which he lived, with a kitchen annexed to the same, with all the appurtenances, bounded to the east by the tenement of John Bridlegh, by the small lane called *Busselane* to the west, and by High Street to the south.
2. His tenement with the appurtenances granted by Gervase Byestwode, bounded to the east by the tenement in which he [Gist] lived, the said kitchen on the west, part the foresaid lane [Busse Lane] on the south and Waterbeer Street to the north.
3. A shop with a solar with the small lane called *Busselane* to the east, the tenement of Philip Lovecok to the west and north, and High Street to the south (MCR 4–5 Rich II, m25d).

The records of 1409 and 1420 described above indicate that John Gist lived at 196 High Street; this was therefore the first of the items in the will, passed to his son John in 1381. The will records that the annexed kitchen of the first property formed a boundary of the second. This is intelligible when it is appreciated that the central portion of the tenement strip of No. 195 had already become part of No. 196 – an arrangement which seems to have obtained at least by the 1330s, when Emma Barbour's tenement at 196 High Street was described as lying to the north and east of its neighbour – both behind it and beside it (see below).

Shortly afterwards, the part of the property which had belonged to Isabel Gist passed in 1381 to her son, John Gist II, sometimes known as 'the elder', and other members of the family. It was then described as follows:

> [1.1.] A hall with inner appurtenances and a cellar at the rear where his parents once lived in High Street opposite Broad Gate, with a 16s 2d rent from the chief hall and cellar at the rear.
> [1.2.] A shop above the said cellar with two solars above it at the rear of John Gist senior's tenement opposite Broad Gate (rent 3s 6d) (D&C 558, S&J 4033, 4034).

It will be evident that the tenement was already divided into two properties: one with its cellar, later owned by the Vicars Choral, and the other above it, which later became Dean and Chapter property. The second of the holdings listed in Gist's will, which lay to the west of No. 196 and was bounded by Waterbeer Street and Busse Lane, is identifiable as No. 23 Waterbeer Street. The third item in Gist's will was a shop with a solar on the High Street frontage on the western side of Busse Lane (= 194 High Street). Under the terms of the will, this passed to the merchant and hosteller Ralph Swan and his heirs (cf. MCR 3–4 Hen V, m4d; 4–5 Rich II, m25v). Swan was not among the rich elite, paying only 12d in the murage grant of 1377 (Kowaleski 1995, 391); the smaller size of his holding reflects his lower status.

Busse Lane

The Busse Lane mentioned in relation to all three of Gist's properties in High Street therefore lay to the west of the house where the Gists lived (Fig. 4.7); the same relationship between that property and the lane is described in two documents of 1439 listed in Table 4.2; it lay to the west of Shaplegh's cellar. In Elizabeth Flay's surrender of the lease of the same cellar from the Vicars Choral in 1668 it was called the 'little narrow lane' to the west (VC 21958).

The presence of an intervening property between the Gists' home and Busse Lane is evident from the description of the second property in the will of 1381, which lay between their dwelling house and the lane. This second holding is also recorded in a document of 1345 (No. 195 below, Godwine to Walrond). Again, the descriptions of Busse Lane as the western boundary of Gist's property may be presumed to reflect the arrangement of Gist's kitchen intruding into the central portion of the tenement strip of No. 195, and thus having a boundary with the lane.

It follows that Busse Lane is Parliament Street, which forms the parish boundary and was therefore a feature of the city by the early 13th century. This identification does not, however, explain how a part of Busse Lane could form the southern bound of a property on Waterbeer Street; the lane may have returned at the back of the shop on the High Street frontage of No. 195.

Busse Lane presumably took its name from a member of the Busse family, among whom were Walter Busse, who witnessed a deed in the city in the period 1171–89 (ED/M/7, S&J 0824), Robert Busse, goldsmith, who rented a property in High Street in 1262 next to a holding of Nicholas Soliman, goldsmith (D&C 48, S&J 0165; see also D&C 208, S&J 0172), and Richard Busse, clerk, who was granted yearly rent of a house in *c.* 1235–43 (D&C 1; D&C 752). Other Exeter citizens named Busse – probably members of the family – included William, who witnessed a deed of *c.* 1220 (VC 3376) and Reineri and Laurence, who were commemorated in the early 14th-century obit list of the Guild of Kalendar Brethren (Lepine and Orme 2003, 269). A further goldsmith named John Busse held a tenement in High Street in 1302, and two shops with two solars above, also in High Street, in 1310. Busse Lane will not refer to him, however, since he post-dates the first record of the name (ED/M/191; D&C 71). The possibility that in the 12th and 13th centuries this area was associated with goldsmiths may be noted.

One deed shows that Busse Lane was sometimes referred to in a cruder manner. In his will of 1324 Stephen of London left two properties, both described as lying beside the lane called *Bosslane* or *Gropecountelane* (MCR 17–18 Edw II, m31, S&J 4284). We shall see that they were probably the tenements which became 195 High Street and 23 Waterbeer Street (below).

No. 196 in the late 13th and early 14th centuries: Benedict and Stephen of London

An *inspeximus* of 1357 (D&C 103; S&J 3862) throws some light on the history of the tenement before the time of John Gist. It describes an agreement between Gist and his neighbour John Spicer following their examination of a grant of 1267, made by Benedict of London to John de Coleton, of an easement (right of way) relating to the wall which separated their two properties. We shall see that Spicer was at 195 High Street, and further evidence described below shows that John de Coleton preceded him there; thus Benedict of London was at 196 High Street in the 1260s, and this may be presumed to have been one of the two properties beside Busse Lane, mentioned in Stephen of London's will of 1324 (above).

195 High Street (St Pancras parish; front part at the time of writing in 2019 Greggs)

Front block in the late 13th century: Benedict of London

The boundary wall between Benedict of London's property and his neighbour's was 43 feet (13.07 m) long. This distance is very close to the length of the masonry recorded between the High Street frontage and the rear face of the cellar wall of No. 195 (Passmore 2011, fig. 2, basement *c.* 13.1 m from the frontage, including the northern wall thickness). It seems likely that this is the location of the documented stretch of wall, although the standing cellar walls are probably of later date. This implies that the division of the tenement strip of 195 High Street, whose central portion formed part of the property of the adjacent 196 High Street in the 19th and early 20th centuries, already obtained in the mid 13th century.

Front part in the late 13th and early 14th century: John and Joan de Coleton, Stephen of London, Henry de Tricote, Peter Soth and Martin le Keu

The information in the *inspeximus* of 1357 allows us to propose the location of a tenement mentioned in the will of Peter Soth, which dates from 1327 (ED/M/276; full transcription in Lepine and Orme 2003, 159–62). He left to Martin le Keu of Bridford a 12s rent from a tenement in High Street which formerly belonged to Joan de Coleton; the will states that Soth had acquired it from Henry de Tricote (active 1293–1307, died before 1312) who in turn had recovered it in the city court from Stephen of London. Alongside this, Soth also bequeathed to le Keu a 3s 4d rent from a tenement in Waterbeer Street which had likewise been recovered from Stephen of London; this was formerly of Roger Russel (active 1286–96) and had been acquired by Soth from Jordan de Brittestowe, a cleric. The possibility that the High Street property was John de Coleton's holding at 195 High Street, mentioned in 1267 (above), is strongly supported by the record of its neighbours in 1327: *la Smale Lane* and Stephen of London's tenement (cf. Benedict of London and Busse Lane in 1267). The Waterbeer Street property may have been No. 23, at the back of the same burgage plot.

Front part of No. 195 in the 1330s and 1340s: Chardstock, Godwine and Walrond

In 1332 a tenement on the north side of High Street, with Busse Lane to the west and Emma Barbour's tenement to the north and east, was granted by Henry of Chardstock and his wife Joan to Walter and Emma Godwine; in recognition, Walter and Emma gave Henry and Joan a gold brooch (MCR 5–6 Edw III, m48d; ED/M/305, S&J 0437, wrongly calendared as St Martin's parish). The lease of the same property was granted by Walter and

Emma Godwine in 1345 to John and Margery Walrond; it was then described as a messuage on the north side of High Street bounded to the north by the tenement of John Gist draper [the intruding kitchen block], with Gist's tenement to the east [196 High Street] and Busse Lane the western boundary (MCR 19–20 Edw III, m3, S&J 0880).

Front part of No. 195 in the late 14th century: Thomas Chaloner, John Spicer and John Rede

John Spicer took possession of the part of the tenement strip which fronted onto High Street ('a messuage in High Street between John Gist's tenement and *Busselane*') from Thomas Chaloner in 1356 (MCR 30–1 Edw III, mm5, 19); his inspection of a grant relating to the boundary with John Gist in the following year has been described above.

Spicer was another major figure in mid 14th-century Exeter; he was mayor of the city on five occasions in the period 1353–61 including the plague years 1359–60 (Rowe and Cochlin 1964, 5). Upon his death in 1361 he left instructions that 'his tenement next to *la Smalelane* in the parish of St Pancras', bounded to the north and east by lands of John Gist, should be sold to pay his debts (MCR 35–6 Edw III, mm4v, 8v). We learn from his will that Spicer was not living there at the time of his death; it was the tenement 'in which Walter Spyryng lately lived.' In 1369 Spicer's executors sold the lease to John Rede of Moreton, adding that John Gist's neighbouring tenement was opposite Broad Gate (*Fysschefoldyete*). There were several John Redes in Exeter at this time; one was a leading city merchant, paying 10s in the 1377 murage grant (Kowaleski 1995, 390), the third-highest figure in the city, exceeding even that paid by John Gist.

The 15th century

The 15th-century people in possession of this property are listed in Table 4.2 above: William Cremyll (before 1435), John Kirton (1439), then John Baron/John Baron and Thomas Cook (1435–before 1462), followed in the 1470s by John Kelly. Kirton, a merchant with legal training, was a significant figure in civic affairs, rising rapidly to the offices of Steward and Receiver and serving as a member of the Council until his death in 1461 (Kleineke 2013, lxxxiii). Baron, another merchant, was also active in city affairs, serving as a city steward in the 1420s (ED/M/715). All his documented properties were in this group of High Street tenements, including a share in the shop next door and a messuage further to the east, identified here as 199 High Street (below). I have not seen evidence showing which of these houses he lived in, but like Gist he evidently regarded himself as a parishioner of St Pancras; he left a substantial endowment to maintain a light in St Pancras church, recorded in the Military Survey of 1522 (Rowe 1977, 10). John Kelly was another leading citizen, three times mayor of the city between 1458 and 1478 (Rowe and Cochlin 1964, 7–8). He seems not to have lived at No. 196, however, since he served in 1473–4 as a churchwarden of the wealthy adjacent parish of St Petrock, where an earlier John Kelly (his father?) had been a churchwarden in the 1430s (Dymond 1882, 11, 28).

Central part of the 195 High Street burgage plot (part of 196 High Street: now H. Samuel)

We have seen that the subdivision of the burgage plot of 195 High Street, with the kitchen of 196 High Street lying behind the tenement at the frontage, and with the separate property on Waterbeer Street to the rear, is evident from John Gist's will (above). The documents quoted above show that the arrangement obtained already in the 1330s, when Emma Barbour possessed the central portion of the burgage plot. This provides an explanation of a detail in the *inspeximus* quoted above: following their examination, Gist and Spicer agreed to share responsibility for another wall to the north of Spicer's tenement, standing between Gist's house and Spicer's next to Busse Lane. This was presumably the wall separating Gist's kitchen from Spicer's holding on the High Street frontage (D&C 103, S&J 3862). This central section of the burgage plot remained part of 196 High Street into the 20th century.

Rear of 195 High Street: 23 Waterbeer Street (now H. Samuel)

In John Gist's will of 1381 (above), Philip Lovecok, the prominent Exeter citizen of the early 14th century, was named as the former owner of the rear tenement, and of the property to the west [No. 194]. He had been mayor on no fewer than ten occasions between 1315 and 1331 (Rowe and Cochlin 1964, 4–5; Gray 2005, 23–6); among the many deeds and wills which refer to Lovecok, I have not seen any record of which of his properties he actually lived in.

The same holding may be recognised as the second of the two properties between Busse Lane and Thomas Forbour's tenement [197 High Street], left by Stephen of London in 1324. In addition to the holding which extended the full length of the burgage plot from High Street to Waterbeer Street [196 High Street], he left a tenement on the Waterbeer Street frontage, backing onto the kitchen of Emma, wife of Thomas le Barbour (MCR 17–18 Edw II, m31, S&J 4284). This is identifiable as 23 Waterbeer Street.

The tenement in Waterbeer Street which Laurence Frogwill left in his will of 1349 to Robert of Clyve and Gervase Byestewode can also be identified as the same property, with John Gist to the east and William of Doune's former holding to the west (MCR 22–3 Edw III, m34v; Doune was a taxpayer in the 1332 lay subsidy: Erskine 1969, 110). John Gist subsequently bought the freehold from Byestewode; his family retained it until at least 1405 (see above). The probable explanation of the separate listing of Nicholas Manlegh after Baron and Cook (Table 4.2) is that he occupied the rear part of the property on Waterbeer Street (Table 4.2, n. 6).

194 High Street (?)(St Petrock's parish; now Patisserie Valerie)

Elizabeth Flay's surrender of the cellar of the Vicars Choral at 196 High Street in 1660 stated that the property was bounded on the west by the lands of the late dissolved hospital of St John the Baptist, and this phrase is repeated in 1668 and in later deeds (VC 21957, 21958). The hospital, however, was not recorded among the landholders in St Pancras parish in 1522 (Rowe 1977, 10); it seems unlikely, therefore that it was the owner of 195 High Street, which falls within the parish. Since a portion of No. 196 extended westward to touch the parish boundary on Busse Lane, it seems more probable that the 17th-century documents refer to the neighbouring plot on the western side of the lane, which lay in St Petrock's parish; in 1522 the hospital held property in St Petrock's with an annual rent of 13s 4d (Rowe 1977, 19). This holding is not readily recognisable in the early 15th-century rental of hospital lands (ECA Book 53A), so may perhaps have been passed to the hospital at a later date.

197 High Street (St Martin's parish: excavated site, now Jigsaw)

In 1319 Thomas Forbour acquired the lease of a tenement in High Street from Henry atte Lane (*de Venella*) excepting two selds [shops] on the frontage; his neighbours were William of Chagford to the east and Stephen of London to the west (VC 3027, 3038). Three years later, atte Lane also granted Forbour the two selds in High Street at the front of this holding; they were described as 'opposite Broadgate (*la Vyshfoldeyete)* between the porches of William of Chagford's tenement and Thomas' tenement (VC 3037, S&J 0987). The evidence that Stephen of London held 196 High Street has been described above, suggesting that the Forbour property was 197 High Street. The holding was later described as the eastern neighbour of the messuage on High Street acquired by John Gist in 1344 (MCR 17–18 Edw III, m30, S&J 0991), confirming this identification.

Forbour was another prominent figure in the merchant community of Exeter: a freeman since 1311 who became a major property holder, active in city government from the 1320s and mayor on three occasions in the years 1341–7 (Rowe and Cochlin 1964, 5; Rowe and Jackson 1973, 22). He died in 1349, perhaps a victim of the Black Death. In his will he passed to his daughter Joan 'his tenement and its appurtenances in High Street opposite Broad Gate … in which Isabel atte Bothele now lives', together with a property across the street at Broadgate (MCR 22–3 Edw III, m20v).

By 1356 the tenement had passed from Thomas Forbour to his son Henry, who sold the lease to John Benet of Hampton, cordwainer [shoemaker]; it was then described as 'where John now lives opposite Broad Gate (*la Fysshfoldesyete*), lying between Waterbeer Street and High Street, bounded on the east by Richard Oliver's tenement where William Roke lives, and on the west by the tenement of John Gist and his wife Isabel (VC 3039, S&J 0988). The rent was £4.

In 1363 John and Joan Bridlegh acquired the property from Henry Forbour; it was then described as the tenement opposite Broadgate 'where they live', running from High Street to Waterbeer Street, with John Gist to the west and John Aisshe to the east (VC 3040, 3077 – both wrongly calendared as being in St Pancras parish). In July 1405 a tenement described in the same way, with Gist to the west and Aisshe to the east, was granted by Maurice Garland of Teignmouth to William Frye and the mercer William Oke (MCR 6 Hen IV, m42: S&J 3875, also wrongly calendared as St Pancras parish).

I cannot readily reconcile this transaction with evidence that in the autumn of 1405 the tenement was held by the Gist family, unless the latter was a very temporary measure. In September 1405 Thomas Wandry and Henry Mayowe bought from Thomas Gist (son of John Gist II) the lease of a messuage on the north side of High Street 'joined to the stone wall of Thomas Gist's tenement' (D&C 125: S&J 3552). The identification of this holding as No. 197 (abutting the Gist home at 196 High Street: Table 4.2 above) is supported by two pieces of information. First, a deed of 1430 relating to William Cremyll's holding between Waterbeer Street and High Street and lying in St Martin's parish [thus either 197 or 198 High Street; for its identification as No. 197 see Table 4.2] is described as 'once Thomas Wandry's' (MCR 10–11 Henry VI, m4; S&J 3268; see below). Second, the will of Henry Mayowe of 1412 shows that he was a parishioner of St Martin's [thus also at either 197 or 198 High Street (MCR 13 Hen IV, m37v)]. He left to his wife Elizabeth the reversion of the tenement in High Street opposite Broadgate in which Desiderata, the widow of Thomas Wandry, then lived. After their deaths it was to be sold, the money to be used to celebrate a mass annually in the church of St Martin for the souls of Thomas Wandry and Henry Mayowe, with their wives and benefactors, 'as long as the said money lasts' (MCR 13 Hen IV, m37v). On this occasion the question of drainage arose once more: Wandry was given permission to set a gutter of wood and lead on the stone boundary wall running from Gist's tenement in the north as far as High Street in the south.

Fifteenth-century leaseholders

The sequence of 15th-century leaseholders of No. 197 can be reconstructed from the evidence listed in Table 4.2: William Cremyll before 1435 (VC 3152), then William Upton (1439–53), John and Denise Bobyche (1453–77) and Alan Sares (1477+). These were prominent members of the city. William Upton became a member of the Chamber in the 1430s and rose to be mayor in 1440 (Wilkinson 1931, 81–3; Rowe and Cochlin 1964, 7–8; Rowe and Jackson 1973, 4; Kleineke 2013, lxxxiii). He held property elsewhere in the city including a house in

North Street, but when he gave evidence in a dispute between Nicholas Radford and Thomas Tremayne in 1439, he described himself as an apothecary of St Martin's parish (Kleineke 2013, lxxxiii); this seems, therefore to have been his home. Bobyche, a freeman from 1445, was a member of the Chamber in 1450–5 (Wilkinson 1931, 83–9; Rowe and Jackson 1973, 50). Alan Sares was one of the city's principal property owners after his inheritance of much of the Wilford estate (see Sares/Farringdon entries in Waterbeer Street, described below).

Kelly v Sares, the disputed boundary between 196 and 197 High Street and rebuilding of No. 196 in the 1470s

In 1475 a dispute arose between the neighbours John Kelly and Alan Sares; it was no doubt because the Vicars Choral were part-owners of one of their properties that a document recording the judgment resolving the controversy was retained in the vicars' archive (VC 3170; see also 3211). The case concerned a 56 ft (17 m)-long wall of lime and stone 'towards Waterbeer Street' between the tenement formerly of Denise Bobyche, the widow of John [No. 197], and the neighbouring holding, formerly of John Shaplegh and now of John Kelly [No. 196]. It was determined that, although the boundary wall belonged to Sares, the gutter on it should be used by both parties, and should be repaired at their common cost; rainwater from Bobyche's house, then falling into the curtilage of Shaplegh's tenement, was to be diverted by Sares. However, when John Kelly erected a new building on the Shaplegh curtilage, Kelly was to be responsible for the dispersal of rainwater. The arbitrators ruled that any windows made in the new party wall built by Sares must be no lower than the existing openings, 14 feet (4.3 m) above ground.

The early 16th century: Blackaller and Tuckfield

Two documents (VC 21957, 21958) add information about the 16th-century owners and occupants of the property; the first states that this was 'a tenement sometime of John Blackaller', the second that it was 'the tenement of John Blackaller wherein Johane Tuckfield dwelt.' Joan Tuckfield (*c.* 1506–73), widow of Alderman John Tuckfield, was one of the most prominent of Exeter's 16th-century citizens and benefactors (Crocker 2016, 1, xviii, xxxiv; 2, 413–19); she is commemorated in a memorable portrait which formerly hung in Exeter Guildhall (Fig. 4.9). Her husband was one of the two wealthiest men in St Martin's parish in 1544, assessed at £100. This figure was exceeded by seven people, six of them in the neighbouring parish of St Petrock (Rowe 1977, 45–59). Following her husband's death, Joan was listed as one of the four wealthiest members of the parish in 1557/8 (Rowe 1977, 51, 57). This is striking evidence for the high status of the property in the early 16th century.

Fig. 4.9 Portrait of Joan Tuckfield, who lived at 197 High Street in the period 1544–57 (Guildhall Collection, © RAMM)

198 High Street (St Martin's parish; building recorded, some excavation; now Ann Summers)

The evidence that William of Chagford was at 198 High Street in 1319 has been described above (see 197 High Street); deeds of 1333 and 1349 record that he lived there with his wife Joan (MCR 22–3 Edw. III, m49; 6–7 Edw. III, m31v). In 1338 he granted to Katherine Strode (?his daughter) and her husband Thomas the lease of a tenement opposite Broad Gate, extending from High Street to Waterbeer Street; in recognition, the Strodes gave William a gold ring (MCR 11–12 Edw III, m7d; 20–1 Edw III, m14; S&J 0869). The Strodes sold the lease in 1346 to Robert Noble (mayor in 1348); three years later it passed to Richard Oliver of Kingston (MCR 20–1 Edw III, m14; 22–3 Edw III, m49; S&J 0870). The two documents record the neighbouring tenements as those of Thomas Forbour and formerly of Margaret Baker, but they contradict one another, with Baker to the east in the first and to the west in the second. We have encountered Forbour to the west at No. 197; thus the first document appears to be correct, and No. 198 the property described (east of Forbour). Oliver evidently did not live there; a deed of 1356 relating to the neighbouring property to the west described it as 'Richard Oliver's tenement where William Roke lives' (VC 3039).

We have seen that in 1363 John Aisshe was the eastern neighbour of John Bridlegh, and thus at 198 High Street;[2] he was also the western neighbour of Sampson in 1375 (below). He was described as a vintner and a merchant, and appeared in the murage grant of 1377, although paying only 12d – much less than his neighbours (Kowaleski 1995, 378). A document of 1382 indicates that there was a shop in separate ownership at the front of the property; the eastern neighbour of John Bridlegh's shop was then a shop belonging to Sir Richard Stapeldon (MCR 5–6 Rich. II, m35; S&J 3873).

In 1430 John Styping *alias* Hosier, a draper, granted to John Shaplegh a 13s 4d rent from a tenement and shop with solars above on the north side of High Street and in St Martin's parish [thus either 197 or 198 High Street: Fig. 4.1]. They lay between Waterbeer Street and High Street, with the tenement of Alice Cook (the widow of John Cook, draper) to the east and that once of Thomas Wandry, now William Cremyll and his wife Joan, to the west (MCR 10–11 Henry VI, m4; S&J 3268). We have seen that Wandry and Cremyll were at 197 High Street (Table 4.2 above), and will see below that Cook was the western neighbour of the leaseholder of at No. 199. I am not clear how Styping's holding fitted into this picture; the rent is much lower than that for the full tenements of 198 High Street (£4 6s 8d) or No. 199 (probably £3), so it seems likely that he held a portion of one or other property. Styping died two years later, leaving the messuage to his wife Constance, with instruction that she should sell it for the benefit of herself, their son, and John's soul. By that time the tenement to the west [197 High Street] was 'lately of Henry Mayow' (MCR 10–11 Hen VI, m47d).

Two further medieval deeds can be associated with 198 High Street. In 1450 William Hoigge granted to William Tuke a messuage between High Street and Waterbeer Street, with William Upton to the west (at No. 197 in Table 4.2) and John Baron to the east (at No. 199: see deed of 1477 below) (MCR 28–9 Hen VI, m38; S&J 3269). A final accord of 1453 records the price as £40 (MCR 32–3 Hen VI, m2).

In 1552 Walter Staplehill acquired from John Young of London the property in St Martin's parish 'in which he [Staplehill] dwelt'; it lay between the tenement occupied by Joan Tuckfield [No. 197 – above] and that of Sir William Courtenay [No. 199 – below], identifiable therefore as No. 198, with the yearly rent of £4 6s 8d (ECA Misc Roll 22, m6). In 1557/8 he was one of St Martin's four richest parishioners (Rowe 1977, 57). Staplehill too was a leading member of the urban elite, holding the posts of Bailiff, Sheriff, Receiver and Mayor in successive years in the period 1550–6 (Osborne 2016, 773). Despite his allegiance to the Catholic cause, John Hooker, the city's Protestant historian, left a sympathetic portrait of him, commending his diligence and his friendly and loving bearing to his Protestant fellows 'in those tyrannical days when fire and faggot carried the sway' (Gray 2005, 97).

Finally, a generation later, various details of the tenement were recorded in a dispute heard in Chancery in 1579–87, after it had passed to Gilbert Staplehill. The elements of the property mentioned were the shop; the buttery adjoining the shop; the hall, also adjoining the shop; the gallery over the entry adjoining the hall; the chambers, rooms and stairs over the shop and buttery; the cellar under the shop, and a back room or woodhouse beside Waterbeer Street in the northern part of the tenement, with the chambers, rooms and stairs over the same (TNA C3/211/46, Howell v Staplehill). The document makes it clear that the entire tenement strip from High Street to Waterbeer Street remained a single property in the late 16th century, as it was in the 19th and early 20th centuries.

199 High Street (St Pancras parish; now Whittard)

The history of this tenement can be traced from the mid 14th century, when it was leased by Margaret Baker (above, 198 High Street). Documentation relating to No. 200 High Street shows that it passed to Thomas Gerveys, followed by John Gerveys (before 1359; see below). Since Thomas was a famous Exeter citizen, serving as mayor on two occasions in the years 1333–8 and active in city life in the period 1326–48 (Rowe and Cochlin 1964, 5; witness to deeds of 1326–48: S&J *passim*), the tenement was remembered as his former holding long after his death in 1349.

A generation later, in 1375, the messuage in which Richard Bozoun bought a third share from Thomas Sampson fits this description; it extended between High Street and Waterbeer Street and lay to the east of John Aisshe and west of Roger Blouere's tenement (MCR 48–9 Edw III, m29, S&J 3872). Bozoun was later mayor of Exeter; Sampson was another major property holder.

In his will of 1421, John Talbot left to the mayor and citizens of the city of Exeter his shop with appurtenances in High Street, in the parish of St Pancras, between the shop of the Dean and Chapter which John Grene lately held to the east and the shop of John Cook, draper, to the west (MCR 9 Hen V/1 Hen VI, m13). The bequest was conditional upon the mayor and citizens constructing, within seven years of his death, a conduit to carry water into the city 'in common commodity and easement of all the commonalty of the city'. He instructed that after 99 years the shop should be sold; the proceeds were to be put to the conduit and water supply. The Dean and Chapter had two properties in the part of High Street which fell within St Pancras parish: Nos 196 and 200. Talbot's property to the west would therefore have been either No. 195 or 199. We have met the draper John Cook as the eastern neighbour of John Styping; thus Talbot's shop was probably at 199 High Street. This is confirmed by later evidence, described below.

Talbot's donation allows the history of the shop to be followed for much of the 15th century. The 8s rent 'for a shop in the High Street… late of John Talbot… which that John gave for the maintenance of the new common conduit for leading water into the said city, for a certain term of years' was paid in 1429–40 by Isabella Medeway, then William Hoygge (1449–81) (CRA; this may also have been the property granted to Hoygge in 1449 by Mayor and Commonalty, although the rent stated there was different – 6s (ED/M/794, S&J 3155)).

Naturally, the rent for the shop was appreciably lower than that for a full house plot, and the history of the property behind it in the late 15th century is different, being dominated by the figure of John Baron, who is recorded here in the documentation of adjacent tenements in 1441, 1453 and 1477 (above and below); we have discussed him at 195–6 High Street and will hear more of him at Trichay Street.

By the early 16th century the property had been acquired by the Courtenay family. An agreement of 1517 mentions the Courtenay holding, with land (?a separate tenement) on the Waterbeer Street frontage (MCR 8–9 Hen VIII, m51d; see below). A lease of 198 High Street dated 1552 named Sir William Courtenay as the landowner to the east, with Henry Harrys the occupier (below). Harrys' goods were valued at £50 in the subsidy of 1544, placing him in about 30th place among Exeter people by wealth (Rowe 1977, 53). He served as city Bailiff in 1551 (Osborne 2016, 768) and was the only churchwarden of the parish when its church goods were assessed in the following year (Cresswell 1916, 66: 'so poor and small a parish'). The holding presumably accounted for some or all of the £3 rent received by Sir William Courtenay from St Pancras parish, recorded in the Military Survey of 1522 (Rowe 1977, 10).

The sequence of post-medieval leases for 200 High Street, described below, also records the succession of neighbours at No. 199. In 1820 it was remembered that these were 'lands then or late belonging to Vic [Viscount] William Courtenay, formerly occupied by Benjamin Beard and John Blackmore, later in the possession of Susannah Kelly and Robert Sanders joiner, since of Nicholas Medland' (D&C 6010/26).

Rear of 199 High Street: 19 Waterbeer Street (St Pancras parish; now Shaul's Bakery)

In 1340 John Langedene transferred to William Danny a half-mark (£6s 8d) rent of a tenement held by Thomas Gerveys in Waterbeer Street (MCR 13–14 Edw III, m44). Gerveys then leased 199 High Street; the property may have been the rear portion of his burgage plot. If so, 19 Waterbeer Street had already become a separate holding by 1340.

200 High Street (St Pancras parish; Dean and Chapter property, now Shoezone)

Among the Dean and Chapter archives is a long sequence of leases of a burgage plot (often described as two tenements) in St Pancras parish lying between High Street and Waterbeer Street. It was leased at the ancient rent of £2 13s 4d to Roger Mase in 1574 and 1586, Robert Treling in 1615, John Vigures in 1631, John Robins in 1660, Benjamin Robins (1696–1714), John Fisher in 1732, John Grant in 1734 and Samuel Weymouth (1771–91), Richard Hart (1797–1818) and John Chamberlain in 1820 (D&C 6009/1/29B–6010/26). Chamberlain is recorded on Coldridge's map of 1819 at 200 High Street, and Hart is shown there on a slightly earlier illustration (reproduced in Ponsford 1978, fig. 45, opp. p. 145), which is therefore identifiable as the Chapter's property. Further leases to Henry Ellis in 1840–60 (ECA 48/12/1/26–30) and the rental of Dean and Chapter lands of 1862 (ECLA CC71/77402) confirm this identification; Ellis' silversmith's shop at 200 High Street is shown in at least two 19th-century illustrations (Fig. 4.5B; Ponsford 1978, figs 45, 50, opp. pp. 145, 161). In the bundle of leases to Ellis is a small plan drawn by John Tothill in 1767, showing that the two tenements occupied a single burgage plot measuring 21 feet wide and *c.* 84 feet long (6.4 × 26 m) (Fig. 4.10B). These dimensions correspond closely to those shown for 200 High Street in the Goad plan of the 1880s and the 1910 Valuation (Fig. 4.4B–C). They also correspond to those of the present shop on the site.

The origin of the Dean and Chapter's ownership can be traced to the mid 14th century. Since its eastern neighbour was owned by Polsloe Priory (see below), 200 High Street can be identified as the messuage in St Pancras parish inherited by the brothers John and William Caperoun in 1351 from their mother Denise and their aunt Cecily (D&C 101), and granted in 1359 by William Caperoun and his fellow chaplain Henry Pike to the Dean and Chapter of the cathedral (D&C 104; S&J 3866); Orme (1980, 54) lists W. Caperoun as an annuellar in 1356–61. The grant describes the property as extending from High Street to Waterbeer Street and lying between the tenement of the prioress and nuns of Polsloe [No. 201] and what had been John Gerveys' property [No. 199] (D&C 104; S&J 3866). It must have been sub-divided after 1359; in the post-medieval period the ancient rent of £2 13s 4d, which continued until 1862 (ECLA CC71/77402), related to the main part of the property fronting onto High Street.

A brief late 15th-century description survives. In 1477 the Dean and Chapter let 'a shop and two solars above plus the appurtenances to the north … opposite Broadgate' to John Slugg, mercer, and Juliana his wife, with an annual rent of £2 13s 4d (D&C 6009/1/14). Since the Dean and Chapter owned the property and the value of the rent corresponds with that for 200 High Street described above, the same property is indicated. Slugg was a prominent citizen; he became a freeman in 1465 (Rowe and Jackson 1973, 55), was described in the lease as a mercer, and rose to be a bailiff in the years 1482–94 and a member of the city's Council of Twenty-Four in 1495–9 (Dymond 1882, 32; Wilkinson 1931, 90–4). He probably did not

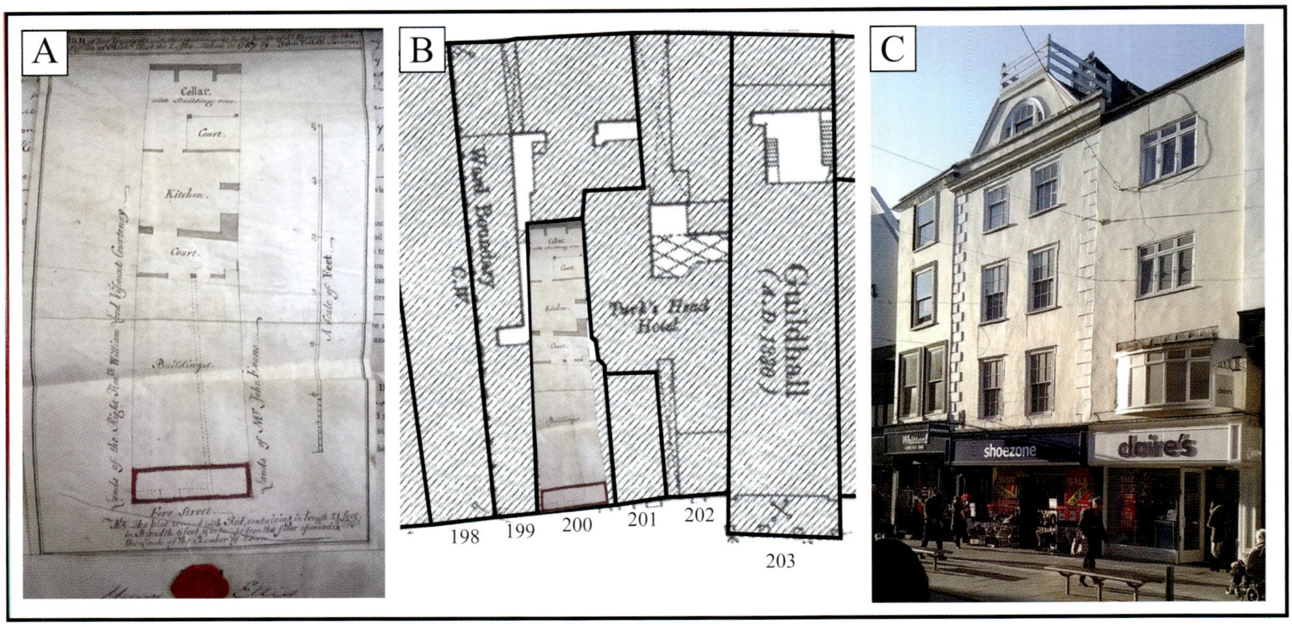

Fig. 4.10 (A) Plan of 200 High Street, drawn by the surveyor John Tothill in 1767, showing the Dean and Chapter's two tenements, with (the small red box at the front) the small shop on the High Street frontage in the separate ownership of the City Chamber (ECA 48/12/1/27, © Exeter City Council). (B) Its position in the OS map of 1876 (Devon sheet LXXX.6.17, courtesy of the Devon and Exeter Institution). (C) The frontage today, rising above its neighbours (© John Allan)

live here; a decade later he appears to have lived in St Petrock's parish, where he served as a churchwarden in 1484–5 (Dymond 1882, 32). In Henry VII's taxation of 1489 he paid 7s 4d for Thomas Style, who was presumably a sub-tenant, but quite a wealthy one; this was about the tenth-highest amount recorded in the Exeter returns, for which however the record is imperfect (Rowe 1977, 2).

200 High Street: former shop on the street frontage (St Pancras parish; City Chamber property, now Shoezone)

In 1360, the year following his donation of 200 High Street to the Dean and Chapter, William Caperoun acquired from John de Halberton the lease of a shop on High Street, described as being 20 feet long and 6½ feet wide (6.1 × 2 m) and 'under the said William's solar near the said William's shop, where William Forbour lives, on the west' (MCR 25–6 Edw III, m42, S&J 3554). This too formed part of 200 High Street; it did not pass to the Dean and Chapter but to the City, as is evident from an 18th-century plan of the tenement, drawn by the cathedral surveyor John Tothill, which marks in red a narrow strip on the street frontage in the separate ownership of the city (Fig. 4.10A); he records its dimensions as 21 × 6 feet × 9 feet high (6.4 × 1.8 × 2.7 m). The plot is also shown on the Map Book of the Chamber of the 1750s, where the same dimensions are recorded (Fig. 4.3, item 20). A property with the same dimensions (certainly the same) was leased by the city to the goldsmith William Cotton at 20s in 1556 (ED/M/1117). It is evident that the separate ownership of the shop on the frontage, recorded in the 18th century, originated before the mid 14th century.

One earlier deed may relate to this property. In 1337 the cordwainer Henry Potel granted two shops to Nicholas de Halberton (ED/M/330: S&J 0198). One was at 202 High Street (below); the other was nearby, its western neighbour being Thomas Gerveys' shop (199 High Street?), with John of Tavistock's shop to the east, and thus possibly part of the Halbertons' property at 200 High Street. However, I have not seen any other evidence that John of Tavistock held property on the western side of Guildhall; his tenement on its eastern side at 204 High Street, also with Henry Potel a neighbour, is described below.

Rear of 200–201 High Street: 17 Waterbeer Street (St Pancras parish, now Rachael's Rose)

In the 19th and early 20th centuries, rather than being three separate tenements corresponding to the properties on the High Street frontage, the rear parts of 199–201 High Street formed a single holding, subsequently numbered 17–19 Waterbeer Street (Fig. 4.11). Although the amalgamation of No. 19 with the other two appears to have been a later development, Nos 17 and 18 were evidently separate tenements from the High Street properties from at least the late 14th century, and were sometimes leased as a pair.

In addition to their donation of 200 High Street, Caperoun and Pike also gave to the Dean and Chapter in 1359 a 12d rent from the messuage on the south side of Waterbeer Street. It was then held by Richard and Eleanor Giffard and described as being 'almost opposite the lane

Fig. 4.11 Late medieval housing at 17–19 Waterbeer Street, now Rachael's Rose and Shaul's Bakery, showing the growth of separate houses and shops on this rear frontage (© John Allan)

leading to St Pancras church', lying between the tenements of Richard Broun, shearman, and a second tenement held by Richard Giffard (D&C 104, 105, S&J 3866). Since the same document states that Caperoun and Pike then held the entire burgage plot from High Street to Waterbeer Street, this was probably 18 Waterbeer Street – the rear of their main holding at 200 High Street. Already, then, by the 1350s three separate tenements had become established on the Waterbeer Street frontage, roughly opposite St Pancras Lane and thus to the west of the Guildhall; two were leased together. All were probably in the block 16–19 Waterbeer Street; we have seen that the two burgage plots to the west of them at 197–8 High Street did not have separate tenements on Waterbeer Street.

A further late 14th-century deed appears to relate to these properties. In 1372 William Beauso, taverner, granted to Robert Taverner and his wife Sarah a vacant plot next to the tenement where Raymond Goos lived (D&C 557, S&J 4032). Since Goos' eastern neighbour was the Guildhall, this was probably the ground to the west (17 Waterbeer Street). Taverner was a cook (Kowaleski 1995, 393). Similarly, a saddler named Thomas Cosyn is mentioned as a neighbour of John Batyn's house in 1439 (Kleineke 2013, 11–12, described in more detail below), and since the Guildhall was Batyn's eastern neighbour, Cosyn was probably to the west. He is otherwise unknown.

201 High Street (formerly belonging to Polsloe Priory; now Claire's; Prezzo to the rear)

The Dean and Chapter's lease of the two tenements at 200 High Street to Richard Hart in 1807 (described above) records that the tenement to the east [201 High Street] formerly belonged to Polsloe Priory (D&C 6010/26), and this information is repeated in the leases to Henry Ellis in 1830 and 1840 (ECLA 48/12/1/26, 27). The identification of this plot as the priory's land is supported by documents describing the property further to the east [No. 202] as lying between the Guildhall [No. 203] to the east and the tenement or shop of the prioress of Polsloe (*Polslo*) [No. 201] to the west (fine of 1381: MCR 5–6 Rich II, m40; MCR 8–9 Hen VIII, m51d). The priory's ownership evidently preceded the year 1287 (see 202 High Street below).

In 1349 Nicholas de Halberton left to his son John two shops and one solar in High Street, one of which consisted of a shop and solar lying between the Guildhall to the east [No. 203] and the shop of the prioress of Polsloe [No. 201] to the west – thus No. 202 (MCR 22–3 Edw III, m15d; ED/M/499; S&J 4050). The lease of No. 201

was subsequently bought by William Sleghe of Kenton, whose executors sold it to John Talbot in 1384, when it was described as 'a shop in High Street between the shops of John Cordiner on the east and Thomas Gerveys on the west (ED/M/499, S&J 4051–2; see also MCR 5–6 Rich II, m40). Talbot had recently bought the lease of No. 202 (see below).

In his will of 1410 Thomas Poleworthy, a baker, left to his wife the property in High Street where he lived. It was described as being between the tenement lately of William Corby and now of John Batyn to the east [202 High Street], and that lately of Walter Skinner to the west, with the tenement sometime of Robert Noble to the north (MCR 11 Hen IV, m.37) – therefore 201 High Street. This information helps fix the property of Robert Noble (= part of 17 Waterbeer Street).

202 High Street (formerly possession of Polsloe Priory; recently The Turk's Head, now Prezzo)

At the time of his death Martin Durling, who had been mayor of the city in 1270–2 (Rowe and Cochlin 1964, 5), held a tenement in High Street between those of the Prioress of Polsloe (*Polslo*) and the Guildhall, thus No. 202; it had formerly belonged to Bartholomew Put. In 1287 Bishop Quinel, executor of Durling's estate, granted it to two cathedral canons, William Bissiman and Roger le Rus (D&C 208, S&J 0172).

In 1316 William Gatepath left the same property ('his tenement in High Street on the west side of the Guildhall in which Matthew Skinner (*Pelliparius*) lives') to his son Henry (MCR 10–11 Edw II, m10v). From the Gatepaths it descended to the Spicers. Before 1361 the tenement, stretching from High Street to Waterbeer Street, and lying between the Guildhall and the tenement of the prioress of Polsloe, was acquired by John and Katherine Spicer. Under the terms of John's will of that year it was to be sold, and the profits distributed for the benefit of the souls of John Spicer and Katherine Gatepath (MCR 35–6 Edw. III, m4v).

The shop on the street frontage, with a solar above, was evidently leased separately for much of the 14th century. In 1337 Henry Potel, a successful cordwainer with property in several parts of the city, granted to Nicholas de Halberton a shop with a solar above in High Street, bounded on the west by the shop of the prioress of Polsloe [201 High Street], with the shop of the Mayor and Commonalty to the east [at the front of the Guildhall at 203 High Street: see Lloyd Parry 1936, 4–5] (ED/M/330: S&J 0198). The same property ('a shop and solar in High Street with the Guildhall to the east and the shop of the prioress of Polsloe to the west' [No. 201]) was bought in 1381 by John Talbot and John Philip of Youngcott from John and Joan Chudleigh (MCR 5–6 Rich II, m40, S&J 3776). Along with No. 201 and other holdings, it became the subject of a complex court case involving the families Chudleigh, Talbot, Halberton *alias* Trote and Youngcott (ED/M/499–500).

Before 1517, this tenement became a possession of Polsloe Priory, as is evident from a document of that year relating to the property to its rear (below, Simon and Breckenoll) and from documentation relating to the Dissolution and the history of the tenement later in the 16th century. Joyce Youings has shown that in 1543 Thomas Carew of Bickleigh began negotiations to acquire the small properties of Polsloe Priory in Exeter, which then remained crown lands (Youings 1952, 133–4). In 1545 these holdings were listed and valued, then granted to John Haydon and Thomas Gibbes, who may have been acting for Carew. The rents include 46s 8d for one tenement held by Richard Lymbury and an unrecorded sum from John *Jonys* for another such holding (Youings 1955, 57). As Collings has noted (Collings n.d.), these two men crop up in the list of taxpayers in St Pancras parish in 1544, Lymbury being assessed the third-highest in the parish, paying on £40 in goods, Jones being rated at the lower value of £8 in goods (Rowe 1977, 53–4). Jones was a capper [maker of caps] (Tapley Soper 1924/5, 118–19); Lymbury's higher standing is reflected in the fact that he took custody of some of the parish silver in the Prayer Book Rebellion of 1549. A pyx, a pax and a chalice were stolen when they were in his charge; when the inventories of church plate were compiled three years later, leading Exeter citizens swore to his honesty (Cresswell 1916, 67).

Lymbury and Jones were recorded once more when in 1555 the City Chamber sold some monastic properties which it had recently acquired. Among the lands 'lately belonging to the priory of Polsloo' was a tenement held by Lymbury and Jones. Lymbury's annual rent of 46s 8d was repeated, this time with 30s from John Jones (ECA Book 184b, discussed in Youings 1952, 136–7). The total value of the priory's rents in St Pancras in 1522 had been £3 16s 8d (Table 4.1); thus these two holdings accounted for the entire income of Polsloe Priory in the parish.

John Jones' possession confirms that No. 202 was the second of the Polsloe tenements recorded in the parish in 1522 (Table 4.1). This is evident from a deed of 1569 relating to William Cotton's former tenement to the north (described below; transcript in Tapley-Soper 1924–5) in which Jones' lands are described as lying to the east, south and west. When in 1572 Nos 201–2 were bought from Henry Jones by Edward Hert, they were described as two tenements with two shops and one kitchen, with solars built above, lying between the Guildhall and the lands of the Dean and Chapter, valued at £80 (ED/M/111A).

Waterbeer Street property at the rear of 202 High Street (recently the Turk's Head, now Prezzo)

In 1289 John of Butelesgate built a house 'behind the Guildhall'; the City Chamber gave consent on condition that an annual rent of 1d be paid to them (ED/M/157, S&J 0349). The precise position of the house was not stated in the deed which recorded the grant, but this has been established by Lloyd Parry (1936, 3) and Tony Collings (n.d.), who have shown that for well over 650 years the annual payment continued to be made, either by the owner or leaseholder of the property on the Waterbeer Street frontage on the western side of the Guildhall, the sums paid being entered in the City Receivers' accounts. Some of these later entries also explain the reason for the charge; the rental of 1700 states that the 'heirs of Sir Thos Hele do enjoy by grant of the City of 25 July 1289 liberty and power of fixing of their Timber of their bldg of their Tenement adjoining the Guildhall in the W pt thereof so as no damage comes to the City thereby by the yrly Rent of 1d' (CRA 1699–1700). The penny was received from John Martin in 1669–70 'for the rent of placing a beam of his tenement adjacent to the Guildhall aforesaid in the walls of said Guildhall' (CRA 1669–70); it was raised to 2d later in the 17th century, and was still paid at that sum by the Turk's Head, then at 202 High Street, as late as the 1930s (Lloyd Parry 1936, 3).

The records of this annual 1d rent in the Exeter City Receiver's accounts allow us to trace the leaseholders of the property in the late Middle Ages. In 1377–90 the payment was received from Raymond Goos for the tenement 'in which … Goos now lives next to the Guildhall'; the roll of 1377 states that the property was 'late of Roger atte Wille', a tucker who served as a city Steward in the 1350s and 1360s (D&C 101, S&J 3861). Since the owners and occupiers of the front part of 202 High Street were different (described above), it appears that Goos held the Waterbeer Street tenement separately from the tenements on the High Street frontage. He died in 1394; his will tells us that he left the property to his wife, that after her death it was to pass to his daughter Joan, wife of Richard Peuterer, and that Richard Whytelegh had granted it to him (MCR 17–18 Rich II, m28d). Goos was a significant figure: a merchant, one of the top 20 taxpayers in the city in 1377, and a man active in its administration (Kowaleski 1995, 384). His residence on Waterbeer Street illustrates the fact that some people of high status lived there.

The property was then leased by John Batyn, whose family paid the annual 1d rent for more than a century (1399–1517: CRA). There were at least three people with this name in Exeter in the early 15th century: a tucker, a saddler and a butcher, and they are not easily distinguished (Kleineke 2013, xlii). One was a major figure in city life who served four times as mayor of the city in the period 1416–24 (Rowe and Cochlin 1964, 7); he was presumably the John Batyn who held tenements in several city parishes (although of course more than one of the three John Batyns may have done so). Another (a different one?) was Alderman of the Western Quarter and Porter of the West Gate in the 1440s (Kleineke 2013, xlii); he may have been the parishioner in St Olave's in 1408 (DD 23129).

A remarkably vivid picture of the John Batyn who lived in Waterbeer Street is preserved among the colourful depositions recorded in the legal dispute of 1439 between Nicholas Radford and Thomas Tremayne, recently published by Kleineke (2013). Batyn described an occasion when, 'beyng in his shop in Waterbere street [he] sawe Nicholas Radeford come furth by his shop out of Northgate Strete and passyng out of Pauel Strete [now Goldsmith Street; see below] toward Seynt Paule chirche'. Radford, dressed with 'a russet cloke cast ouer his hede', was accompanied by William Tremayne, who asked Batyn's neighbour, the saddler Thomas Cosyn, whether his saddle was ready. Cosyn called Tremayne 'a goosehead' (Kleineke 2013, 11–12). From this source we learn that John Batyn and his son William were both tuckers, and that John's house in Waterbeer Street in St Pancras parish had a shop at its front, as did the house of his neighbour Thomas Cosyn.

By the end of the period when the Batyns held the property in Waterbeer Street, they were certainly renting it out; Tony Collings has noted that Stephen Clowe was the occupier in 1489–1510, and Batyn paid 3s for him in the taxation of 1489 (Collings n.d.; Rowe 1977, 2).

In 1517 John Simon and John Breckenoll [Briconer] bought the lease of this property from the heirs of William Batyn; it was then described as being bounded to the north by Waterbeer Street and the tenement of William Courtenay Esquire, with the prioress of Polsloe, the Dean and Chapter and William Courtenay to the west [199–201 High Street], a tenement of Polsloe Priory to the south [201 High Street?] and a tenement of the prioress and convent of Polsloe and the Guildhall to the east [202 and 203 High Street] (MCR 8–9 Hen VIII m51d). I have taken the reference to Polsloe Priory's holdings to the south and east as a key piece of evidence that No. 202 had become a possession of the priory by that time, accounting for the second of the two tenements of the prioress 'near the Guildhall on the west side', recorded in 1541/2 (quoted in Lega-Weekes 1934, 198).

By 1520 the 1d rent was being paid by the goldsmith William Cotton, whose association with the property continued for more than 30 years. In 1520 the occupier was William Tothill, followed in 1530 Hugh Warde, but by 1549–50 the holding had become 'that tenement in which … William Cotton now lives' (CRA 1549–50, m2). The association of the property with goldsmiths continued into the late 16th century; in 1567 the goldsmith William Pinfold held 'the tenement next to the Guildhall in the parish of St Pancras' (CRA E10-F5, quoted in Osborne 2016, 596); the city Receiver's account of 1569–70 records that he paid the 1d head rent on the property in that year.

Pinfold's unruly personal life caused him to stand trial in the Mayor's Court for a number of offences over a 12-year period (1561–73), providing a little information about the property. In 1561 he was accused of operating a tippling house selling wine and beer without licence, of being a receiver of suspicious persons, and of threatening one of the city stewards. For the last offence he was imprisoned in the pit below the Guildhall, but four months later the ruling against him was reversed and his accuser imprisoned in his place. In 1564 and 1573 he faced charges of fornication and adultery; in the later case he was accused of fathering the child of his servant 'in his lyvinge chamber whiles his wife was to morninge prayer' (Osborne 2016, 594–6, Biography 57).

203 High Street: Guildhall

Shops in front of the Guildhall

Lloyd Parry (1936, 5–6) has described the shops and temporary stalls in front of the Guildhall. At the time of the first surviving Receiver's account of 1305–6 there were already two shops 'beside the Guildhall in the western part' on which they charged an annual rent of 24s. A series of rents recorded in the city Receivers' accounts for 'two shops in the fore part of the Guildhall' was paid from 1377/8 by John and Isabel White at 10s (ED/M/519; CRA 1377/8), and from 1388 by the draper John Bonde of Moreton at 12s (ED/M/519; for Bonde's occupation see SJC, f75, city rental 1392–3, which records his rent of a shop beside the Guildhall), then at 16s by William Edmund (1399–1440) and Geoffery Turpyn (1449–60 × 1470: CRA 1399–1470). In 1480–1 this was described as 'a shop in the west part of the Guildhall ... which the clerk of the city and the assistant to the mace *(ad clavam)* now occupy to the use of the city' (RAB 1480–1). I have followed Lloyd Parry in placing these in front of the Guildhall, although they may have been adjacent, in front of 202 High Street, and this might fit better the facts that Isabel White lived there (CRA 1377/8), and that the 16s rent included a cellar which communicated with No. 202 (see below).

By the 1470s there were also two shops on the eastern side, let in most years for 2s 8d. They seem to have been cleared away when the new fore building was constructed on the Guildhall frontage in 1483–5; thereafter the only lettings in front of the hall were of stalls, especially during fairs and public holidays.

Cellar under the fore part of the Guildhall

Under the rooms at the front part of the Guildhall is an ancient stone-lined cellar, with a moulded stone doorway leading into the adjoining space below 202 High Street (plan in Blaylock 1990, 147). It was evidently associated with the shops on the western side of the frontage and continued in use after the changes to the frontage of the 1480s. Tony Collings (n.d.) has shown that for a long period (1636–1832) this cellar, rented from the city at 16s (cf. the 16s rent on the shops above), was used by the occupiers of 202 High Street. The Map Book of the Chamber of 1756–60 described it as 'a Cellar under the West side of the Arcade of the Guildhall, the Way, and Stairs to which goes through the Shop next adjoyning to the Guildhall, on that side' (Fig. 4.3, entry 19). As Collings has pointed out, the description of No. 202 as a 'tenement with a cellar' in Katherine Spicer's will (above) may show that this arrangement obtained from the mid 14th century.

204 High Street (now Fone Customize)

In 1328 Denise, widow of the Exeter cordwainer John de Tavistock, who was a son of Walter Caperoun, bequeathed a shop with its adjacent curtilage to the Exeter tanner Walter of Lydford. It was bounded on the west by the Guildhall – thus 204 High Street – with the tenement of Henry Potel to the east (MCR 1–2 Edw III, m21v).

In 1359 John and Agnes Spicer bought from Richard and Joan Whithorn the lease of two shops on High Street with an adjoining plot of land on the eastern side of the Guildhall, with the Guildhall garden *(herbarium)* to the north and John Spicer's tenement on their eastern side (MCR 32–3 Edw III, m46, S&J 3905). The two shops stood above a single cellar, and formed the frontage of a single burgage plot, as later descriptions show (1393 and 1417 descriptions; 'shops' to the west of 205 High Street in 1421, cited below).

Before 1393 this holding had passed to Richard Goldsmith (see below, 206 High Street). In that year he bequeathed two shops with two solars above them and two chambers near the solars at the rear of the messuage [204 High Street and 15–16 Waterbeer Street] (D&C 559, S&J 3869), with a separate bequest to his servant. When their lease was sold by John Scut to the Exeter weaver William May in 1417, three components of the holding were described. First, there were the two shops on the High Street frontage, with a cellar below and two solars above, and with an adjoining curtilage. They formed the eastern neighbour of the Guildhall, whose curtilage extended to form their northern boundary [203 and part of 204 High Street]. Second, there was a stable on the Waterbeer Street frontage, built above the common wall of the Mayor and Commonalty; this too lay to the east of the Guildhall, again with John Scut's land to the west [16 Waterbeer Street]. Third, the holding included two further shops with two solars above them in Waterbeer Street, also lying to the east of the Guildhall, with Scut's tenement to the south and that of John Salter, saddler, to the east [= 14 Waterbeer Street] (MCR 4–5 Hen V, m14, S&J 3310). The identification of the position of the properties is helped by clear evidence that John Salter's house became 14 Waterbeer Street (below). The positions of these properties are shown in Fig. 4.12B.

Within four years of his acquisition, May donated the two shops at 204 High Street to the priory of St Mary Marsh, a minor house of Augustinian canons in Marsh Barton (for which see Orme 2014, 128–30). According to a copy of the priory rental of 1421, William May, weaver, donated to the priory a yearly rent of 7s from two shops in High Street on the east side of the Guildhall; the description corresponds with earlier records of a pair of shops on the frontage (above). The priory was a dependent cell of Plympton Priory (Orme 2014, 128–30), and this surely explains the 7s valuation of the priory's income in St Pancras parish, recorded in the Military Survey of 1522 (Rowe 1977, 10).

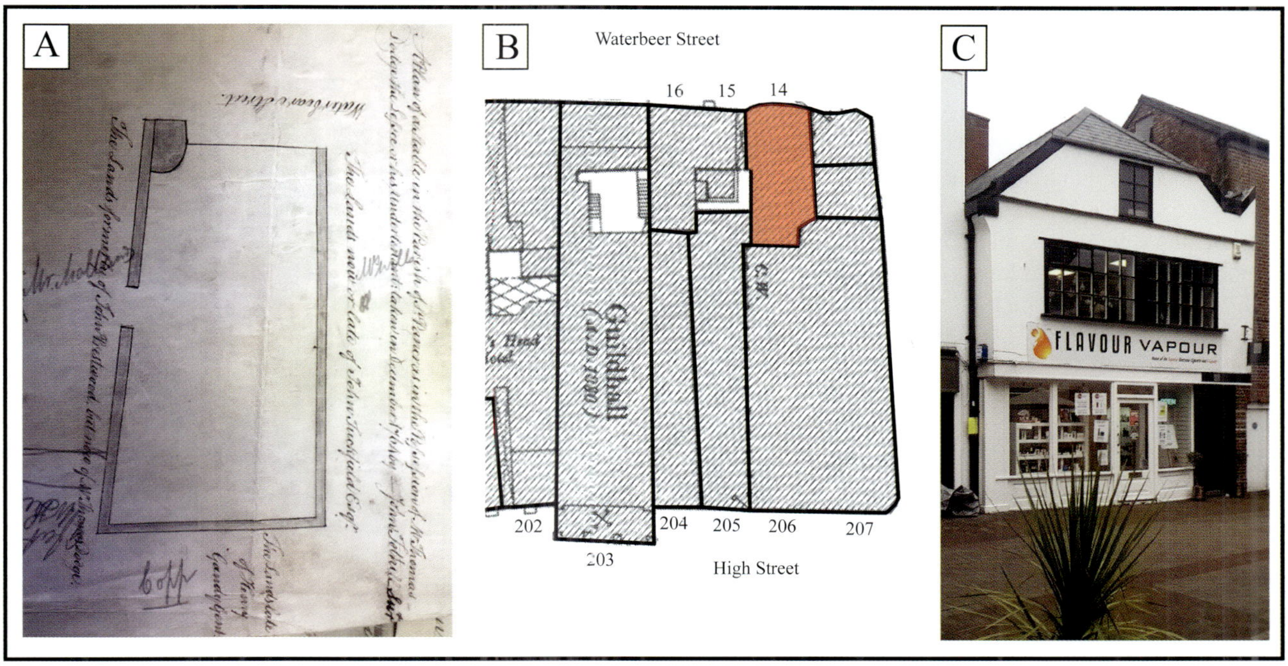

Fig. 4.12 (A) 'A plan of a Stable in the Parish of St Pancras in the Possession of Mr Thomas Dodge the Lessee or his undertenant, taken in December 1764 by John Tothill Surveyor', prepared for the Dean and Chapter, identified as 14 Waterbeer Street (© Exeter Cathedral Library and Archive). (B) The location of the property on the 1876 OS 1:500 map of Exeter (Devon sheet LXXX.6.17; courtesy of the Devon and Exeter Institution). (C) Its modern appearance (© John Allan)

Four years later, in 1426, the remainder of the first portion of the holding was sold by William May to Ellis Glechon, alias Barber/Barbour (MCR 4–5 Hen VI, m25, S&J 3321; see 15–16 Waterbeer Street below). In 1442 William May's widow, Agnes, sold the lease on all his remaining property to John Kirton (described above, 195 High Street). The fine describes the property to the north as belonging to Briconer and that to the east as the tenements of John Salter and the late William Prince (MCR 21–2 Hen VI, m2, S&J 3323). A few years later, in 1447, Walter Mirifild was in possession, as a deed relating to Prince's tenement to the east records (below: MCR 25–6 Hen VI, m40).

205 High Street (vacant at the time of writing in 2017)

The mid 18th-century Map Book of the Chamber records that the city then received an annual rent of 10s from 205 High Street, which was then the Three Tuns Inn (Fig. 4.3, property 16). The word 'Maudlin' in the map's accompanying text explains the origin of the rent: at the Dissolution the city had acquired this from the dissolved leper hospital of St Mary Magdalene outside South Gate. The Military Survey of 1522 records the rent from the hospital's property in St Pancras parish at 10s – clearly the same (Rowe 1977, 10). This rent (which had been 20s before 1379: see below) can be traced from the late 13th century, and provides a means of identifying a number of deeds relating to this property which allow its tenurial history to be traced from that time.

In 1288 Edward le Verour [glazier] granted to Stephen of London a tenement on the north side of High Street with a 20s rent payable to St Mary Magdalen leper hospital (ED/M/152 & 153; S&J 0173). Edward was the first known Exeter glazier; he had become a Freeman in 1284 (Rowe and Jackson 1973). Although it is unknown whether he was the occupier as well as the leaseholder, the deed raises the possibility that 205 High Street was the site of his workshop. His western neighbour was William Capero[u]n, cordwainer, with the tenement of Robert Bosse [or Busse] to the east and that of Roger Haueke to the north. In 1302 Stephen of London granted the property to William le Keu, cordwainer (ED/M/191 & 192: S&J 0177). By that time the neighbouring tenement to the west had become 'what was William Capero[u]n's', with John Busse, goldsmith to the west and with Roger Haueke once more to the north. The deed of 1302 is endorsed 'next to the pillory'. Like the stocks depicted under the Guildhall portico in a vignette in Rocque's map of 1744 (Blaylock 1990, 157), the pillory was one of the instruments of the city's justice displayed outside the Guildhall (Lloyd Parry 1936, 57), and evidently on its eastern side (see also 206 High Street below). This reference is consistent with the conclusion that 205 High Street is the property in question.

We have seen (above) that the widow of a son of Walter Caperoun, also a cordwainer, was at 204 High Street in 1328. The record of the tenement of Henry Potel to the east of 204 High Street in 1328 has been mentioned above.

In 1379 William Ingram, prior of the Mary Magdalene leper hospital outside South Gate, reduced the rent due from Richard Tykerigge and his wife Denise for a tenement on High Street from 20s to 10s. The deed states that Tykerigge had built houses there to the Magdalene's advantage, and this no doubt explains the reduction in rent (ED/MAG/66 S&J 3865). The document also provides valuable information about the surrounding properties. On the northern bound was a vacant plot next to Waterbeer Street, once of Thomas and Isolda Saddler [15–16 Waterbeer Street – see below], with Richard Goldsmith to the east [206 High Street] and the shops of Richard Tykerigge to the west [204 High Street] (ED/MAG/66 S&J 3865). A second deed of the same year records the Tykerigges' acquisition of the lease of a plot with the same bounds, with a house built on it (surely the same property), from Thomas Pye, bowyer, and his wife Philippa (MCR 3–4 Rich II, m13, S&J 3560).

15–16 Waterbeer Street (now House of Harris)

The history of the tenement to the rear of 204–5 High Street is closely bound up with the High Street properties, with some individuals (Scut, May, Barber, etc.) in possession of both. In 1377–8, the first year for which full accounts of its rentals survive, the city received a rent of 2s 8d from Richard Tykerigge for a vacant plot of land behind the garden (*herbarium)* of the Guildhall, which lay on the Guildhall's east side, behind the High Street frontage (Lloyd Parry 1936, 5–6). This rent can be followed in the receiver's accounts for the following century. In 1389–90 John and Denise Scut were being charged 2s 8d 'for a certain tenement new edified behind the garden of the Guildhall'; by the start of the 15th century they were paying this rent for 'a tenement new built next the Guildhall'. By 1420 they were charged simply for 'a tenement next the Guildhall' (CRA 1389–1420). In 1429–30 William May paid the same 2s 8d rent, but for the first time 'two shops on the east side of the Guildhall' are mentioned in the city receiver's account. In the 1430s Elias Barber (the Ellis Glechon, barber, above) likewise paid 2s 8d for the two shops in the same position. By 1442 May had died and his widow Agnes sold the lease on the entire holding to John Kirton. The fine describes the property to the north as belonging to Briconer and that to the east as the tenement of John Salter and the late William Prince (MCR 21–2 Hen VI, m2, S&J 3323). A few years later, in 1447, Walter Mirifild was in possession, as a deed relating to Prince's tenement to the east records (below: MCR 25–6 Hen VI, m40). From the 1440s two separate payments of 2s 8d start to appear in the receiver's accounts: one by Barber for two shops on the east side of the Guildhall and a second from John Kirton for two shops 'in the back part of the Guildhall which William May, weaver, late held'; this new pattern continues into the 1460s. By 1470 Kirton was dead; his heirs paid for his two shops. Barber too disappeared from the accounts; his shops were 'now of William Pyre'. In 1474 John Choun left to his wife the tenement 'in which he was living beside the Guildhall' (MCR 13–14 Edw IV, m34d; Lepine and Orme 2003, 57); in 1490–1 the city rented two shops and their appurtenances on the east side of the Guildhall, 'late of John Chown, sometime of William Pery and now of John Sayer', once more for 2s 8d, and the same sum was paid by John Grantham in 1499–1500 (CRA 6–7 Hen VII, m1; 15–16 Hen VII m2].

At some stage in the first decade of the 16th century the rents from these two pairs of shops were evidently amalgamated; from 1509 into the 18th century, the city receivers' accounts record the collection of an annual head rent of 5s 4d from a tenement, described variously as being on the north or the east side of the Guildhall. The frontage of 15–16 Waterbeer Street is shown in the Chamber Map Book, where the 5s 4d charge is repeated, making clear the location of these properties. From 1509 to 1550 this amount was charged to the heirs of John Sayer (or Shere); from at least 1519–30 Richard Chubbe was the tenant, but he does not appear in the military survey of 1522 and was evidently not the occupant. Robert Dyrham lived there in 1529–30 and John Treby in 1539–40; the latter was taxed on goods valued at £6 in 1544 (Rowe 1977, 54). In 1549–50 the city also received 5s 4d from the heir of John Shere for the rent of 'that tenement next the Guildhall … whereof that William Cotton is tenant' (although living on the west side of Guildhall). Two years later Cotton bought the lease from Shere ('John Sayer gent') for £36 (MCR 6 Edw VI, m10). William Hunt lived there in 1557–89, paying £8 in goods in 1557–8 and £6 in goods in 1577 – the fourth-highest figure in the parish (Rowe 1977, 58, 62).

206 High Street (Allhallows Goldsmith Street, now Millets)

A series of deeds in the Dean and Chapter archives records a sequence of transactions relating to this property at the end of the 14th century. In 1393, alongside his bequest of 204–5 High Street and 14–15 Waterbeer Street described above, Richard Goldsmith made a separate bequest to the Exeter goldsmith John Russel, his former servant [apprentice?] (D&C 559, S&J 3869). The bounds recorded in the deed allow this property to be located: to the east was the tenement of Richard Scmaister and William Gerveys [207 High Street], and to the west Richard Tykerigge's tenement [205 High Street] (D&C 559, S&J 3869).

Russel did not enjoy his inheritance for long, dying in 1397. We learn more about the holding from his will. He left his tenement in which he lived in High Street *'in aurifabria'* to his uncle John Blount and John Gysery; it lay between the holding late of Richard Tykerigge on the west [15–16 Waterbeer Street] and a vacant plot of the Mayor and Commonalty to the east [207 High Street]. Russell also left to Blount and Gysery the 16d annual rent from the shop and solar built above it in the back part of the tenement, 'which Simon Sprit is bound to pay' [14 Waterbeer Street] (MCR 20–1 Rich II m54d).

In 1405 John Roos and his wife Isabel leased the entire holding between Waterbeer Street and High Street, bounded by John Prince's tenement to the east [207 High Street] and John Scut's to the west [205 High Street] (MCR 6 Henry IV, m35, S&J 3874). In Roos' will of 1410 he left instructions to sell the messuage granted to him by Richard Olyver, Richard Skynner and John Holand, clerk (MCR 11 Hen. IV, m52v). Since this was the only property mentioned, both in his will and in the surviving Exeter deeds, he presumably lived there. John Hosier, a draper, acquired the lease in 1413. In 1414 it passed to John Briconer senior; at this date the London goldsmith William Prince and John Scut retained the neighbouring properties (MCR 6 Hen IV, m35; 1–2 Hen V, mm4, 42, S&J 3874, 3876–7). Briconer held the property for more than 20 years; in 1442 it was acquired by William Prince (MCR 4–5 Hen VI, m25; 21–2 Hen VI, m2, S&J 3321, 3323).

According to entries in the Mayor's Court Rolls of 1442, 1445 and 1447, a High Street tenement then occupied by William Prince lay between a property of the Mayor and Commonalty [207 High Street] and the tenement of William Somaister's heirs [the adjacent plot on Goldsmith Street] to the east, and Walter Mirfield to the west, with John Salter to the north (MCR 25–6 Hen VI, m40; S&J 3308; 28–9 Hen VI, m18; DC 273). These neighbours show that the holding was 206 High Street.

Among the archives of the Dean and Chapter is a 15th-century listing of charters made in their favour relating to properties in Exeter (D&C 571). Moore (n.d.) suggested it belonged to the reign of Henry VII, but it mentions John Salter the saddler as still living (he died in 1445/6: D&C 3625, f126), placing the portion of the document (Item 2) which mentions him before that date. It records the gift by William *Wulrond* [Walrond] of the 20s rent of a tenement in High Street to the east of the *collistrigii* [pillory – see 205 High Street above]. The rent given by Walrond therefore relates to one of the four properties on the eastern side of Guildhall, now 204–7 High Street, and probably not No. 204 (which would more obviously be described as 'next to the Guildhall') or No. 207 (which could have been described as being on the corner of Goldsmith Street). The document states that the tenement had been held by Richard Goldsmith and later John Goldsmith [John Russell, *alias* Goldsmith], more recently William *Pryne* [Prince], now John Salter, saddler,[3] and that James *Barbur* [Barber/Barbour] recently held it. The tenement was evidently held by three individuals, William Prince paying 11s 8d, John Salter 5s and Barber 3s 4d. The associations of Russell, Prince and Salter with 206 High Street have been described above, indicating that this was probably the property in question. Confirmation that this was indeed the case, and that the rent continued to be paid into the 19th century, may be found in the rental of Dean and Chapter property drawn up in 1862, prior to the transfer of their properties to the Ecclesiastical Commissioners (ECLA CC71/77402). This states that a yearly high rent of 15s 4d was then paid by Robert Howell on a tenement by the Guildhall; a later annotation adds '206 High Street'. The difference between the 20s rent of the 15th century and the 15s 4d rent of 1862 may reflect the separation of the rear of the property, donated separately by Salter upon his death (see below), although there remains a 4d discrepancy between the two figures.

Rear of 206 High Street: 14 Waterbeer Street (now Flavour Vapour)

Among the documents relating to Dean and Chapter properties in St Pancras parish is a fine sequence of 40-year leases of a tenement in Waterbeer Street, the yearly rent being 19s 8d (ECLA 6008/1/4–6010/35/30; CC 37/75671–6; see also ECLA 64/7/1). In 1603 it was leased to the lay vicar Hugh Geare, then Agnes Crymes (1629), Peter Risdon and his successors (1629–98), the druggist George Stoneing (1709–18), the innholder Robert Dodge and his descendants (1718–1810) and the ironmonger John Molland (1810–40+). The rental of Dean and Chapter properties of 1862 records Elizabeth Molland as the last of the line (ECLA CC 71/77402). In his unpublished notes on the parish, Tony Collings has shown that Molland's shop was at 14 Waterbeer Street, where he was succeeded by Munk, another ironmonger (Collings n.d.). This is therefore the tenement owned by the Dean and Chapter a point confirmed by a small plan drawn by the cathedral surveyor John Tothill in 1764 (Fig. 4.12A) preserved in a bundle of miscellaneous papers relating to St Pancras parish (with D&C 37/75671). It records the dimensions of the property – 38 × 18 feet (11.6 × 5.5 m); the modern shop on the site measures internally 11.6 × 5.5 m across the frontage (including the side passage), and the name 'Molland' is written in pencil in a later hand on one margin of the plan. June Risdon's will of 1663 (ECA 64/7/1) and Tothill's plan both described the holding as a stable, a description still used in 1820 although it had long been a shop. The plan also records former early modern owners of neighbouring properties: John Tuckfield to the east, John Prestwood to the west, and Henry Gandy to the south.

The origin of the Dean and Chapter's ownership of this holding is evident in a deed of 1445 which recorded John Salter's grant of a property in Waterbeer Street; its neighbours were a tenement of William Prince to the south, one lately of William Prince to the east, and one lately belonging to Richard Tykerigge to the west (D&C 273–6; S&J 3325). These relationships fit with the known neighbours of 14 Waterbeer Street (above).

The fact that the Dean and Chapter came to own this plot no doubt explains the survival in their archive of a series of documents relating to this property prior to their acquisition. It had formed part of the block of tenements acquired by Richard Goldsmith, and of the part which Goldsmith left to John Russell, described above. In 1395 Russell sold the lease of the shop in Waterbeer Street with the solar above it to the saddler Simon Spritte and his wife Millicent. The accompanying deed records further details of their holding: the entrance to Russell's kitchen formed the southern bound, with John Scut's tenement to the west (D&C 271, S&J 3867). Russell's will tells us that the Sprittes paid the same annual rent of 16d for their shop and the solar above it, and that they lay at the back part of his High Street tenement (MCR 20–1 Rich II m54d). Three years later, in 1398, the Sprittes also acquired the lease of the kitchen with its solar above, with the adjoining entrance on Waterbeer Street; Russell's executors reserved a gutter or conduit under the tenement to take water towards the street from their vacant lot in front of their deep cellar. The south bound then became the tenement at the rear of the kitchen, with William Gerveys' tenement to the east. At that stage Russell's executors retained his shop to the west [15 Waterbeer Street] (D&C 272; S&J 3868). In the same year (1398) the Sprittes (?unwisely) granted William Prince, the new leaseholder of 206 High Street, permission to build a wooden chimney (*caminum*) next to the wall of [which backed onto?] their kitchen (D&C 560; S&J 3870). The subsequent descent of the holding, through Roos, Hosier and Briconer to Salter, is outlined above.

207 High Street (Allhallows Goldsmith Street; now White Stuff)

No. 207 High Street occupies the corner of Goldsmith Street and High Street. We learn of a vacant plot owned by the Mayor and Commonalty on the eastern side of 206 High Street in the will of the Exeter goldsmith John Russell of 1397 (MCR 20–1 Rich II m54d). The property was still vacant in 1456, when the Mayor, Bailiffs and Commonalty of the city rented 'a toft or vacant plot of land in the parish of All Hallows' at 6s per year to the Exeter writer John Harry or Harrys. This was clearly 207 High Street, since it was bounded by Goldsmith Street to the east and High Street on the south, with the tenement of John Germyn on the west and the one lately of Adam and William Somaister on the north. Within three years, Harry was required to build a shop on High Street with a solar or solars above; the structure was to be substantially built and the work undertaken at his own expense. If he did not carry out the building works in the time required, the premises could be repossessed (ED/M/814). He seems not to have built the house by 1459–60, since the Receiver's account of that year records his payment of the 6s rent 'for a parcel of land next the tenement of John Germyn in the High Street'. A decade later, however, the rent was paid by Harrys for 'a parcel of land next the tenement late of John Germyn, on which are built two houses'. He must have lived into the 1480s, since he paid the same sum a decade later, but by 1499 the rent was paid by John Colshyll, whose family retained it at least until 1570. The city Receiver's accounts also record those who lived in the property in the early 16th century: Peter Johnson, 'cordyner' [cordwainer] in 1499–1500, followed by John Goose in 1509–40. The City Chamber still claimed a chief rent on this property in the mid 18th century (Fig. 4.3, item 15). A note in the rental which accompanies the Chamber Map Book (ECA 59) adds: '13.15: Isaac in his Survey Book fol. 15 says that the rent to the general account payable out of this tenement was 6s a year (whereas in the present rental but 4s a year is charged to Mr Tuckfield) and that was by grant to John Harry dated 36 Henry 6 1457 and in fol. 46 the rent to the Maudlin is 2s a year.' This was surely the pair of timber-framed houses on the corner of High Street and Goldsmith Street, shown in John White Abbott's view of 1797 (Fig. 4.13).

Fig. 4.13 Extract from John White Abbott's view of High Street in 1797, showing the late medieval timber-framed building at 207 High Street, here identified as the pair of houses built by John Harrys in the 1460s (© RAMM)

The Somaister property to the north of the corner, in Goldsmith Street, has previously been mentioned (see 206 High Street). The rental of St Mary Magdalene's leper hospital of 1419 records that William Somaister then paid them a 2s rent for a tenement in Goldsmith Street (*in aurifabria*) opposite Allhallows church (DHC ED/MAG/100 m25): this was evidently this one, since in 1447 the heirs of William Somaister were in possession of a holding lying to the east of William Prince's tenement [at 206 High Street: see above] and south of his shops on Goldsmith Street (see below).

Four shops on the west side (part now F. Hinds, 3 Goldsmith Street)

In 1447, a few years before John Harry took on the vacant plot on the street corner, the London goldsmith William Prince sold the leases of four shops with a deep cellar under them in Goldsmith Street to four men: John Bluet, Hugh Germyn, John More and John Page junior. Hugh Germyn was a wealthy draper who rose to be Mayor of Exeter on no fewer than ten occasions between 1443 and 1475 (Kleineke 2013, lviii). This seems not to have been his house, however: in 1439 he was living in the parish of Allhallows Goldsmith Street, but on the High Street (Kleineke 2013, 9).

Their shops occupied the Goldsmith Street frontage, extending from the corner of Waterbeer Street, which is recorded as their northern boundary, with William Somaister's heirs to the south [on Goldsmith Street] and the tenement of the saddler John Salter to the west [14 Waterbeer Street]) (MCR 25–6 Hen VI, m40, S&J 3308). The cellar was evidently a notable feature of these properties; the observation of 1447 that it was 'deep' was repeated in 1609, when it was called 'one great celler under the said messuages' (DHC Z1/19/1/25). The two small shops still surviving at the junction of Goldsmith Street and Waterbeer Street, each roughly square in plan (3–4 Goldsmith Street, now amalgamated to form F. Hinds, 3 Goldsmith Street), occupy more recent buildings above ground but retain their ancient stone-lined cellars, and thus, it may be suggested, the surviving half of this row of shops. These were therefore examples of row housing in which the house occupied the entire tenement plot.

Figures 4.14–22 summarise the proposed reconstruction of leaseholders and occupiers in these tenements outlined above.

Documentary and pictorial evidence relating to Goldsmith Street Area III and its setting

Introduction

The excavated area of Goldsmith Street area III (Site 39) examined four tenements in a row of 12 properties along the western side of Goldsmith Street. They formed part of the extensive parish of St Paul's, which not only included all the tenements in Paul Street but also portions of Bartholomew Street, North Street and Gandy Street, as well as the larger part of Goldsmith Street (Figs 4.1 and 4.23).

Prior to their demolition in the 1960s, the buildings on this side of Goldsmith Street consisted of a mix of 18th and 19th-century three and four-storeyed shops with smaller and earlier buildings (Fig. 4.23B–E). A.W. Everett, the local investigator of historic buildings, observed them as they underwent demolition, noting that some were appreciably older than their frontages; he thought they were probably of the 16th or 17th centuries (pers. comm. to the writer *c.* 1978; there appears to be no more detailed record).

The excavation took place on the site of 8–10 Goldsmith Street, tenements on which stood buildings of three and four storeys with late 18th or 19th-century fronts (Fig. 4.23B–E).[4] A row of three older houses (5–7 Goldsmith Street) had recently been demolished close to the excavated site. No detailed record of these buildings is known, but photographs show that they were two-storeyed, with their roof lines parallel to the street (Fig. 4.23B); they stood on very restricted tenement plots about 7 m deep. Small houses of this simple type were numerous in early modern Exeter (cf. *e.g.* Matthews *et al.* 2011, 176–7; Parker and Allan 2015, 42–9, 56–63), and are indeed shown both on the Hogenburg and Sherwood views (Figs 4.2A–B).

Earlier pictorial sources

Goldsmith Street seems hardly ever to have attracted the topographical artist, the only valuable early drawing of the street being that of Arthur Glennie showing the northern end of the street and St Paul's church *c.* 1827, distant from the excavated site (Parker and Allan 2015, 53, fig. 4.14).

Documentary evidence

The street name

According to the editors of *The Place-Names of Devon,* the name Goldsmith Street is first recorded in its Latin form (*in vico Aurifabrorum*) in documents of 1291 and 1301 (Gover *et al.* 1931, 22), but they found no records of the name in English before 1606. Examples in English are, however, recorded in 1450 and 1456 (as *Goldesmyth street* and *Goldsmythstrete)* (MCR 28–9 Hen VI, m18; ED/M/814).

Many of the city's goldsmiths had premises in High Street; for example, six of the nine men of this profession whose locations were noted in the writer's word search of medieval Exeter deeds were there. There are, however, various records of goldsmiths in this parish, some of them in Goldsmith Street. In 1231–2 Isabel, the widow of Alexander Goldsmith (*Aurifaber)*, granted to St John's Hospital a tenement described as extending from Hugh de Langeden's house as far as Allhallows church in length, and in width from Paul Street as far as the land of her son

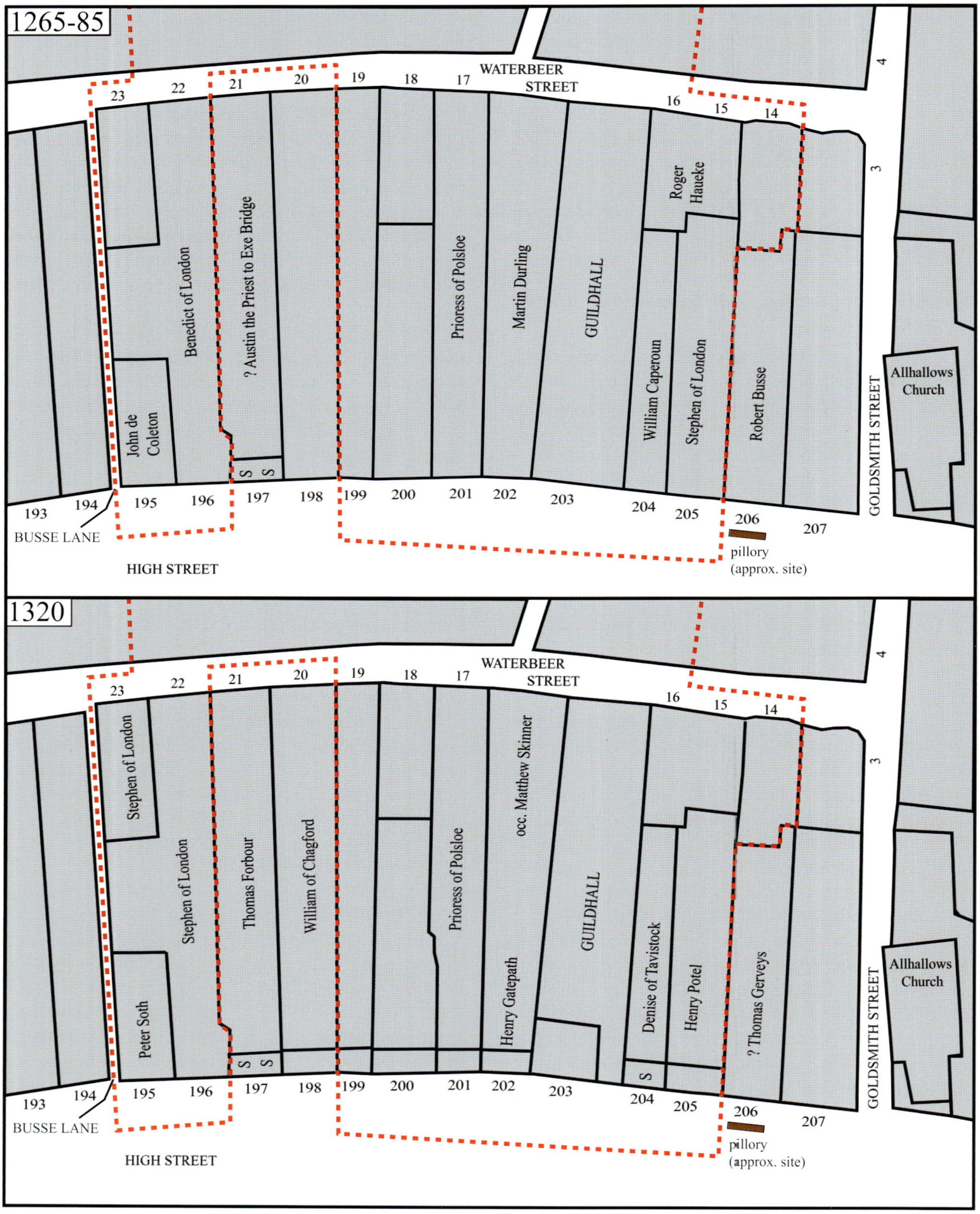

Fig. 4.14 Reconstructions of those in possession of 194–207 High Street c. *1265–85 and* c. *1320 (drawn by David Gould)*

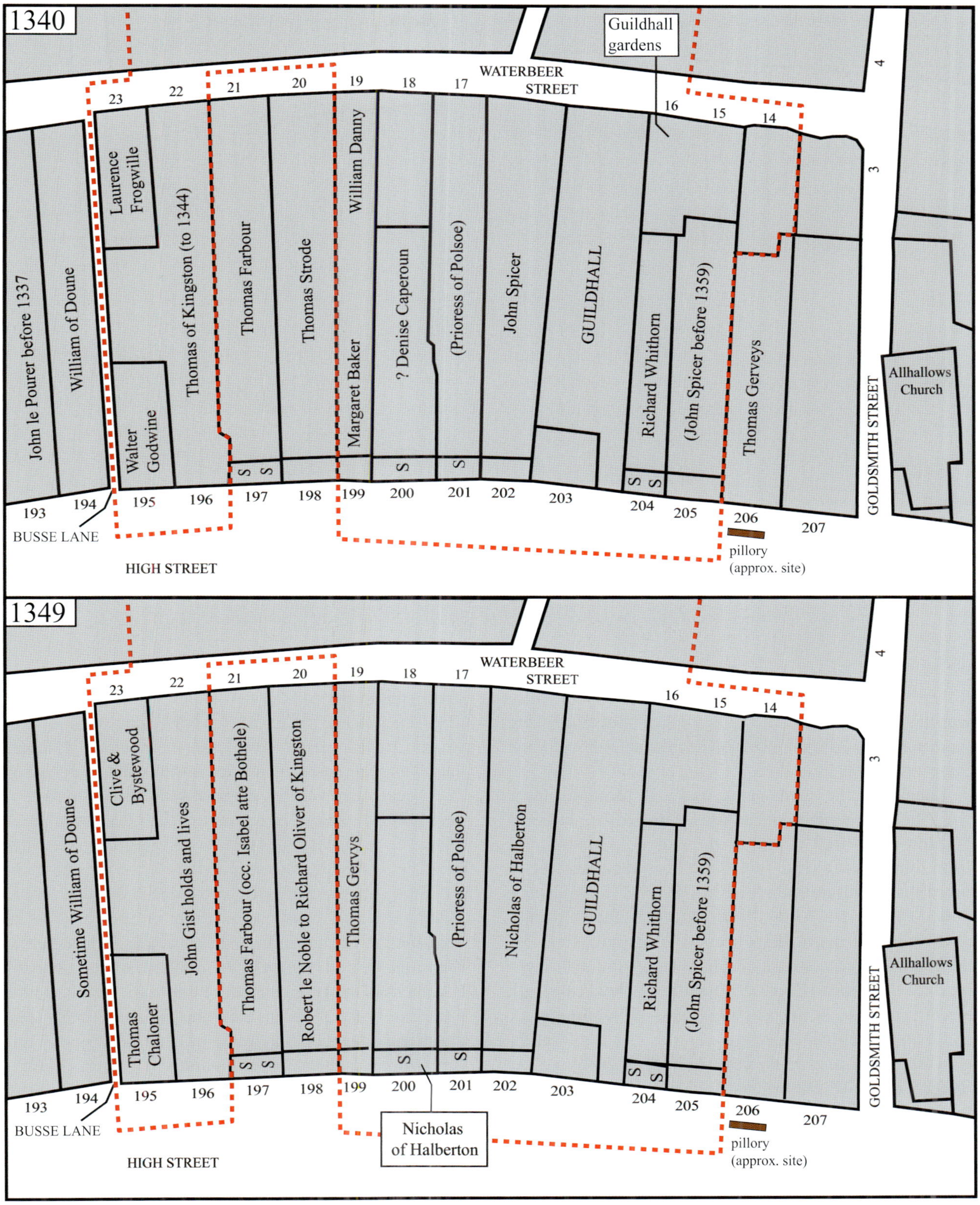

Fig. 4.15 Reconstructions of those in possession of 194–207 High Street c. *1340 and in 1349 (drawn by David Gould)*

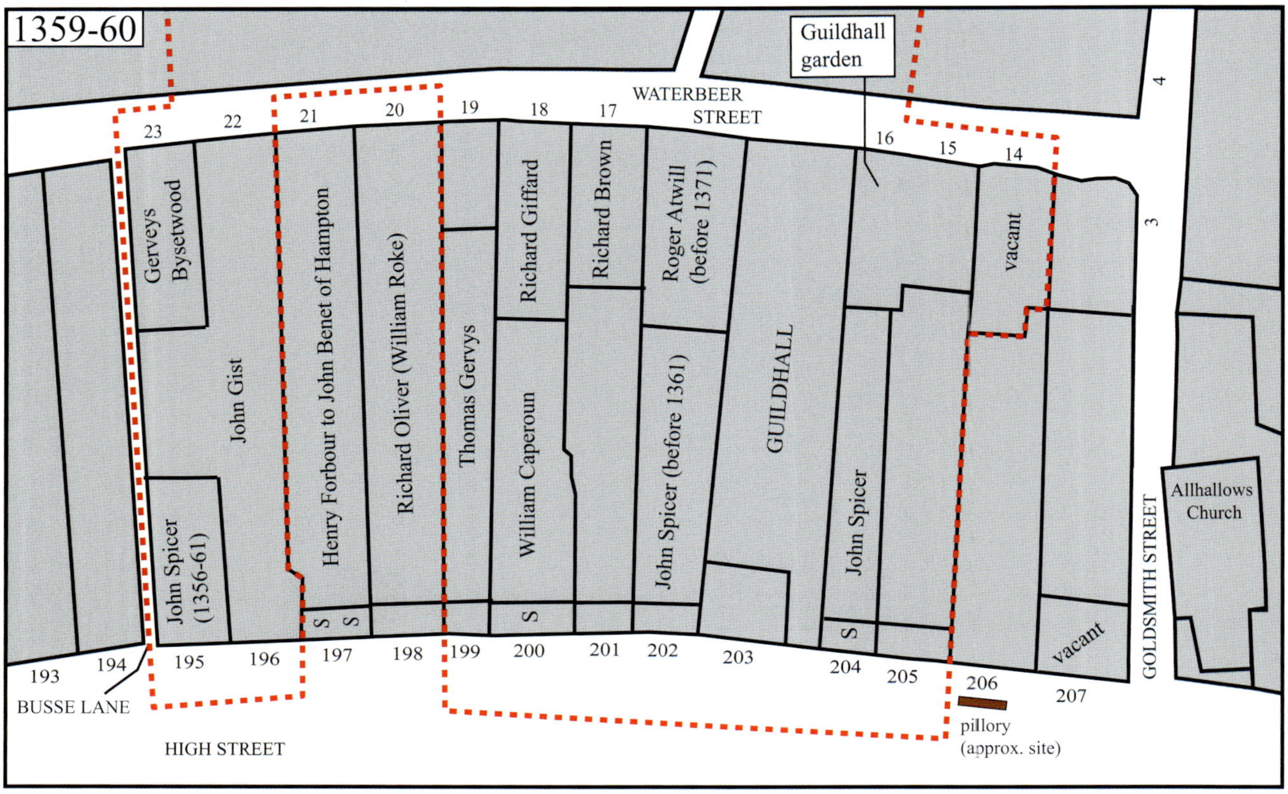

Fig. 4.16 Reconstructions of those in possession of 194–207 High Street c. *1359–60 (drawn by David Gould)*

Robert (CRA Book 53a, f30d, S&J 4079). This property was therefore on the eastern side of the street, and (since there was only a tiny house between the church and High Street) north of the church.

Long after the street name was first recorded, there were further goldsmiths in these properties. In 1343 Matilda Proute left to Isabel Horn the 12d annual rent from four selds in High Street 'between the tenement of John Busse and the church of All Hallows in Goldsmith Street' (MCR 16–17 Edw III, m52d). Thus the goldsmith John Busse seems to have been at 208 High Street. At the end of the 14th century Richard Goldsmith, who was indeed a goldsmith (D&C 559, S&J 3869), held two High Street properties beside Guildhall (Nos 204–5) (above), and John Russell, his successor who was also a goldsmith, held the rear portion of the same holding at 14 Waterbeer Street. The early 15th-century goldsmith Thomas Thorpe lived in Allhallows parish (Kleineke 2013, 33). There was therefore a long tradition of goldsmiths' premises in this central section of the High Street that mainly lay on the street frontage, but with one or two in neighbouring properties in Goldsmith Street and Waterbeer Street.

Goldsmith Street or Paul Street?

At an early stage in gathering documentation which might relate to the Goldsmith Street excavations, the writer was puzzled by the complete lack of deeds referring to tenements in Goldsmith Street, apart from those at the High Street end, in the parish of Allhallows. The document of 1231–2 describing a messuage as lying both 'in Goldsmith Street' (*in vico aurifabrorum*) and 'between All Hallows church and the lane which leads towards the church of St Paul', quoted above, first suggested the possibility that in the Middle Ages the larger portion of Goldsmith Street which falls within St Paul's parish was sometimes (?usually) called Paul Street by reference to the church at its northern end. This usage is confirmed by the documentation for the Tailors' Hall, a former city property on the east side of Goldsmith Street, not far from the church, and shown on the Map Book of the Chamber of the 1750s. A long sequence of 2s rents from this property can be traced back to the 1390s in the Exe Bridge Wardens' accounts. Those of 1390–1510 consistently describe it as being in Paul Street; in the following decades this changes to Goldsmith Street (EBW).

About 50 deeds dating before 1450 survive for Paul Street; by contrast only two from the same period have been found which mention properties in Goldsmith Street, and one of those as a secondary holding in a deed relating to a tenement on High Street. The change in name would explain this, and also explain the survival of medieval deeds for properties lying to the east or west of Paul Street, at right-angles to those in modern Paul Street which lie to the north or south of the street. It might also explain some otherwise puzzling property descriptions, such as that in 1312 for a tenement beside Walter la Chawe's, extending from Paul Street (*Poulestret*) as far as St Kerrian's Lane

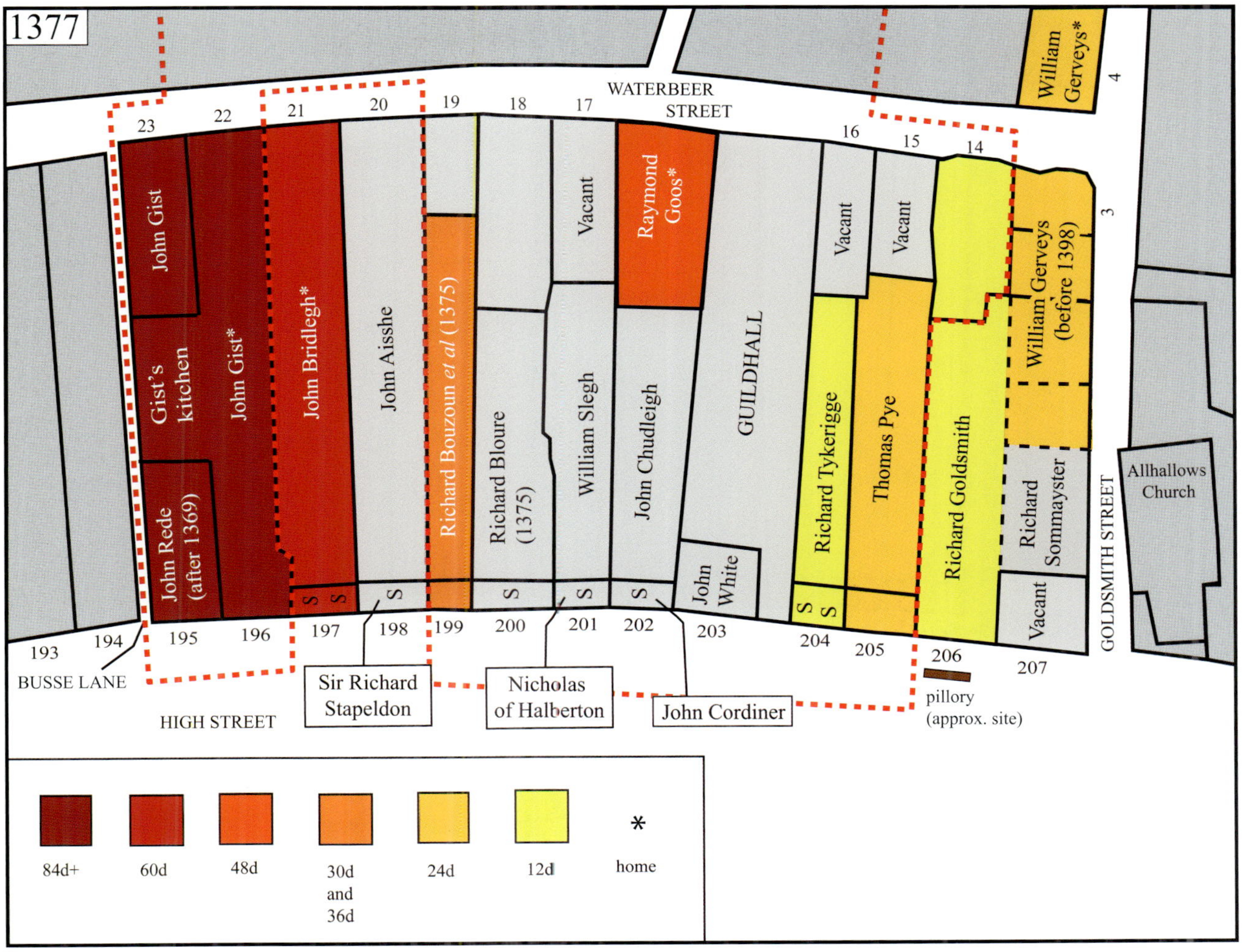

Fig. 4.17 Reconstructions of those in possession of 194–207 High Street in 1377 with their payments in the Murage Tax of that year (drawn by David Gould)

[Trichay Street] (MCR 5–6 Edw II, m17), or that of the William Gerveys on the corner of Waterbeer Street and Paul Street, described below.

Properties in Goldsmith Street in the parish of St Paul

The survival of documents

With a single exception, described below, I have not been able to identify any deeds relating to this block of houses on the western side of Goldsmith Street. This may in part be because I have not identified any cathedral properties, city rents or landmarks which might have helped the recognition of tenements in this block, and it is possible that deeds which describe tenements in Paul Street whose locations I have not established relate to these holdings. It is also possible that the lower values of houses here resulted in the creation of fewer deeds.

4 Goldsmith Street

If it is accepted that the northern part of Goldsmith Street was known in the later Middle Ages as Paul Street, a will referring to a plot close to (perhaps adjoining) the excavated area may be identified. In 1400 William Gerveys left the tenement in Paul Street in which he lived, with its appurtenances, to his wife Beatrice. It was a corner property, with Waterbeer Street to the south and Paul Street to the east, and was bounded on the north by the tenement sometime of William Lespek [Speke], with one 'which Raymond Goos lately held' to the west [MCR 1 Hen. IV, m. 22v; S&J 3233W]. The site became 4 Waterbeer Street (Fig. 4.23A; the small adjacent holdings may perhaps have been subdivisions of this). William was a member of the urban elite, a major office holder, and a man with other lands in the city centre; he was described by Kowaleski (1995, 383) as a rentier. He is a figure of surprisingly high status in this context.

5 or 6 Goldsmith Street?

Prior to 1400 the property to the north of the Waterbeer Street corner – presumably therefore 5 or 6 Goldsmith Street and thus the southern fringe of the excavation – had belonged to William Lespek (see above).

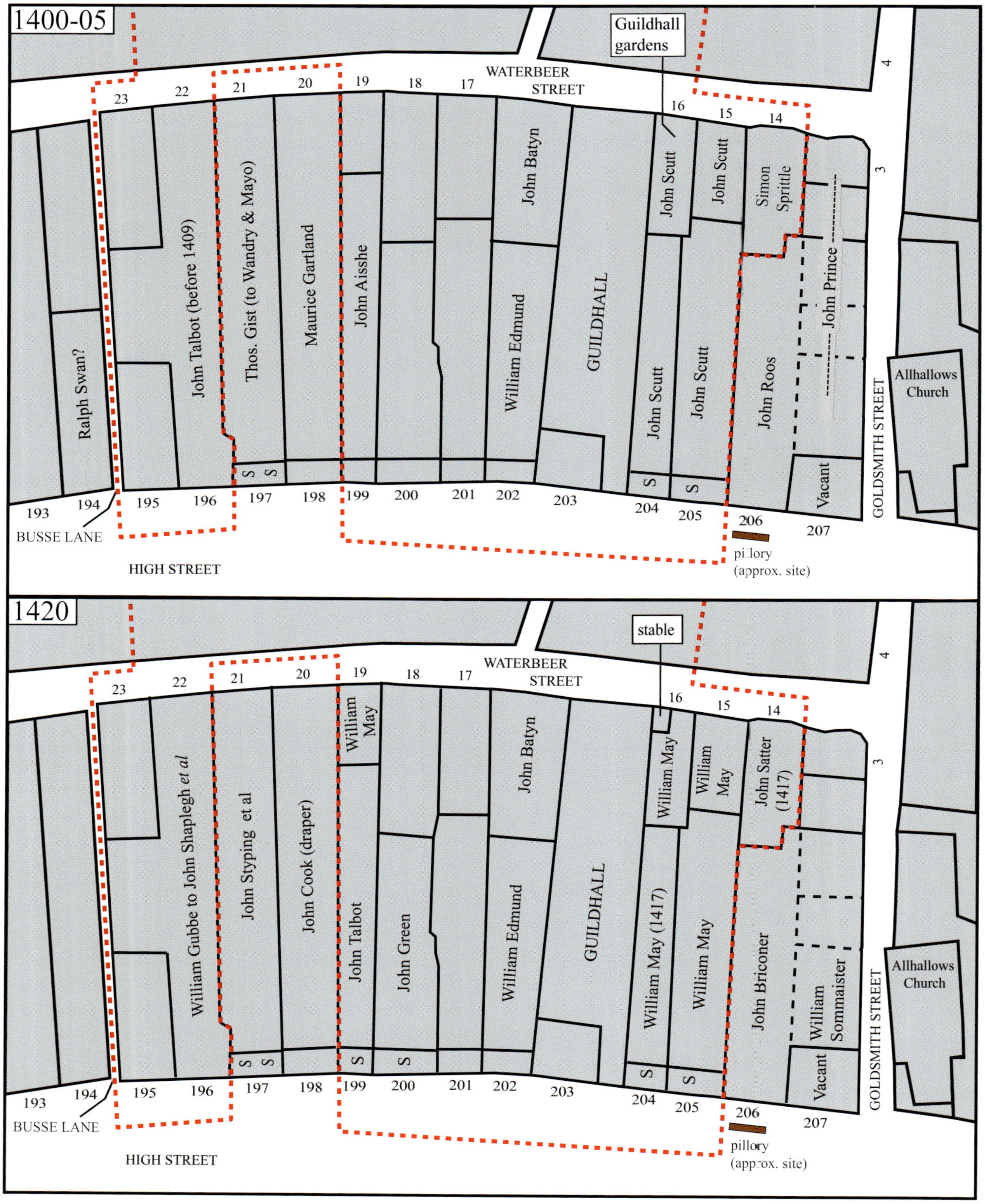

Fig. 4.18 Reconstructions of those in possession of 194–207 High Street in 1400–5 and c. *1420 (drawn by David Gould)*

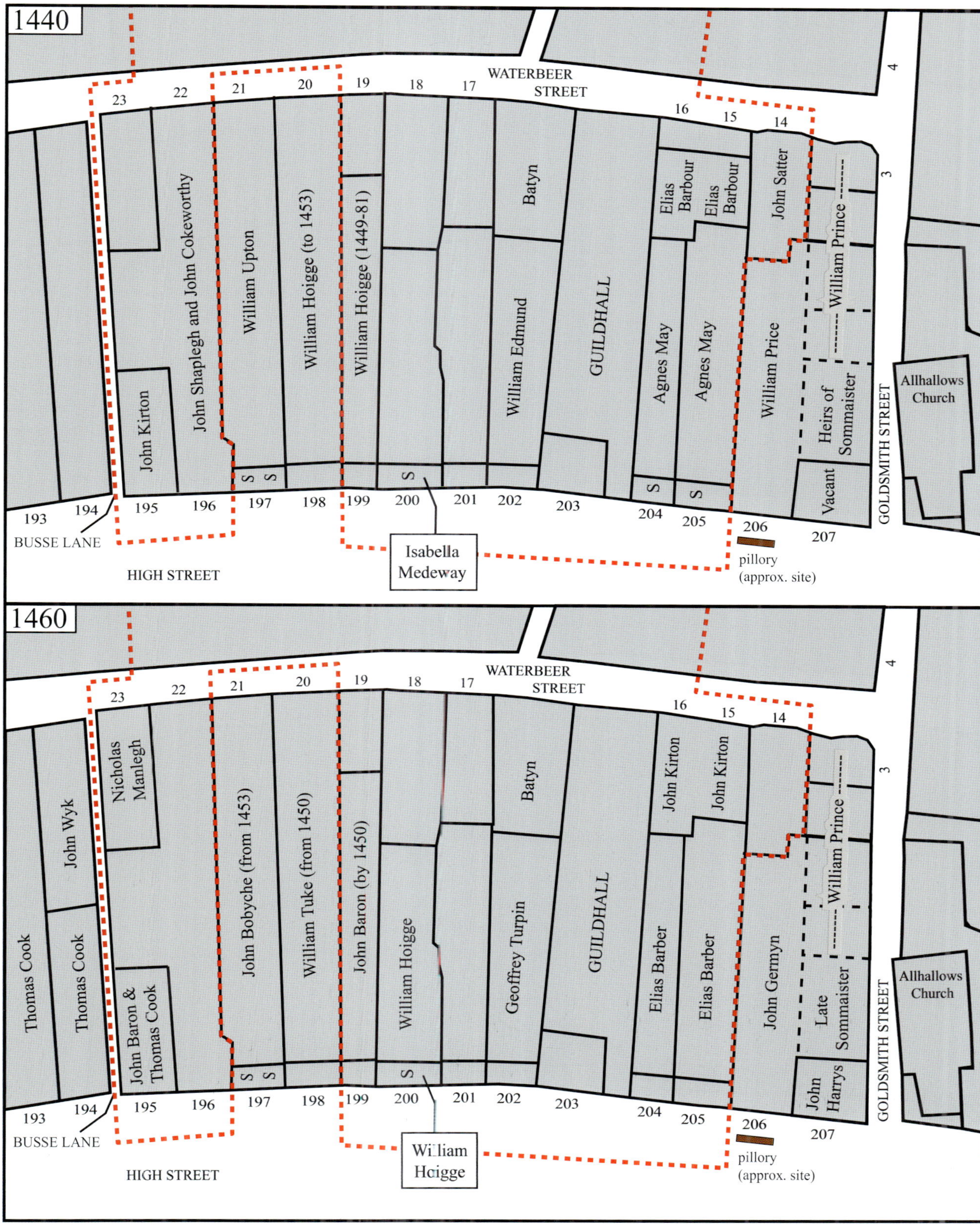

Fig. 4.19 Reconstructions of those in possession of 194–207 High Street in 1440 and 1460 (drawn by David Gould)

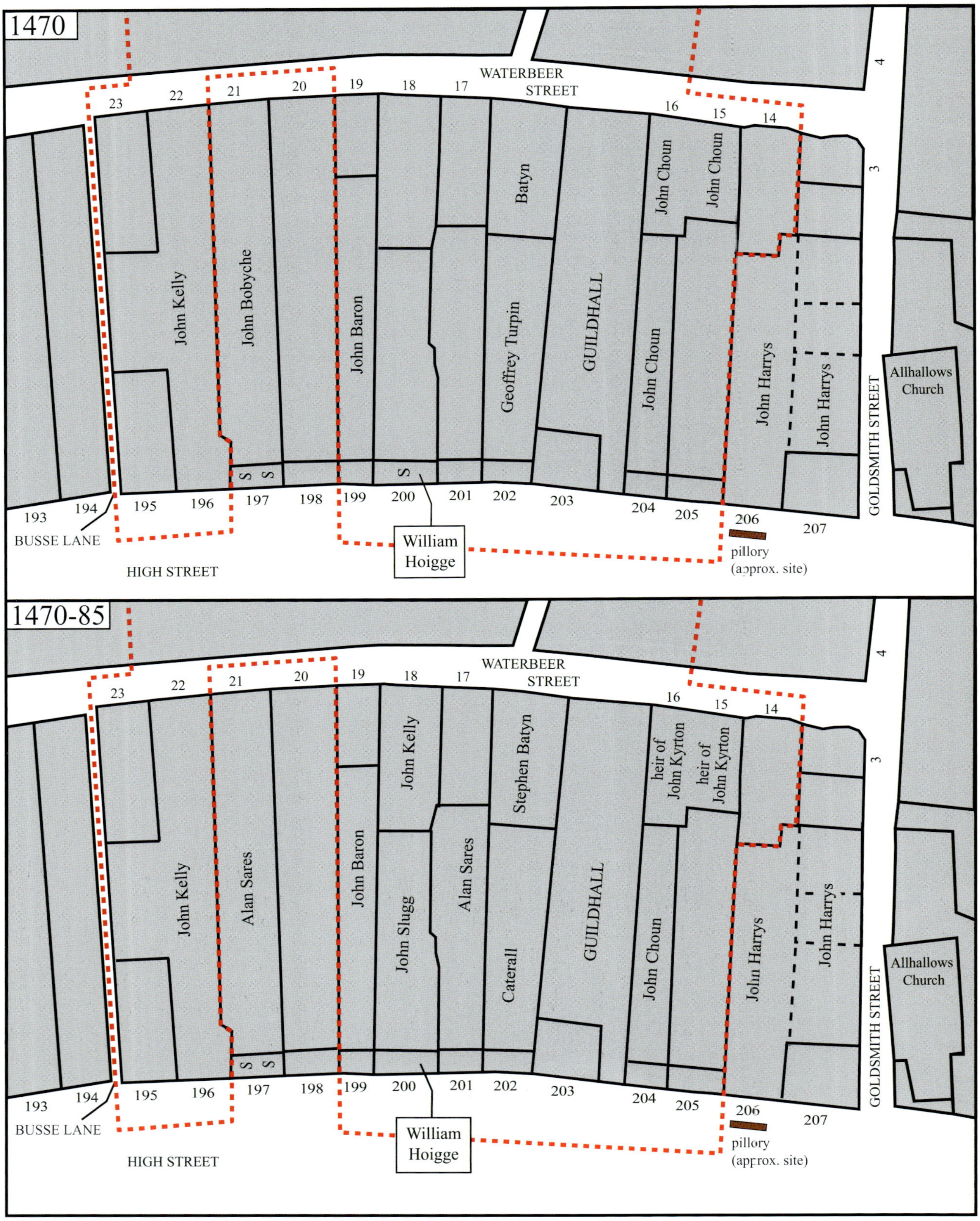

Fig. 4.20 Reconstructions of those in possession of 194–207 High Street c. *1470 and in 1475–80 (drawn by David Gould)*

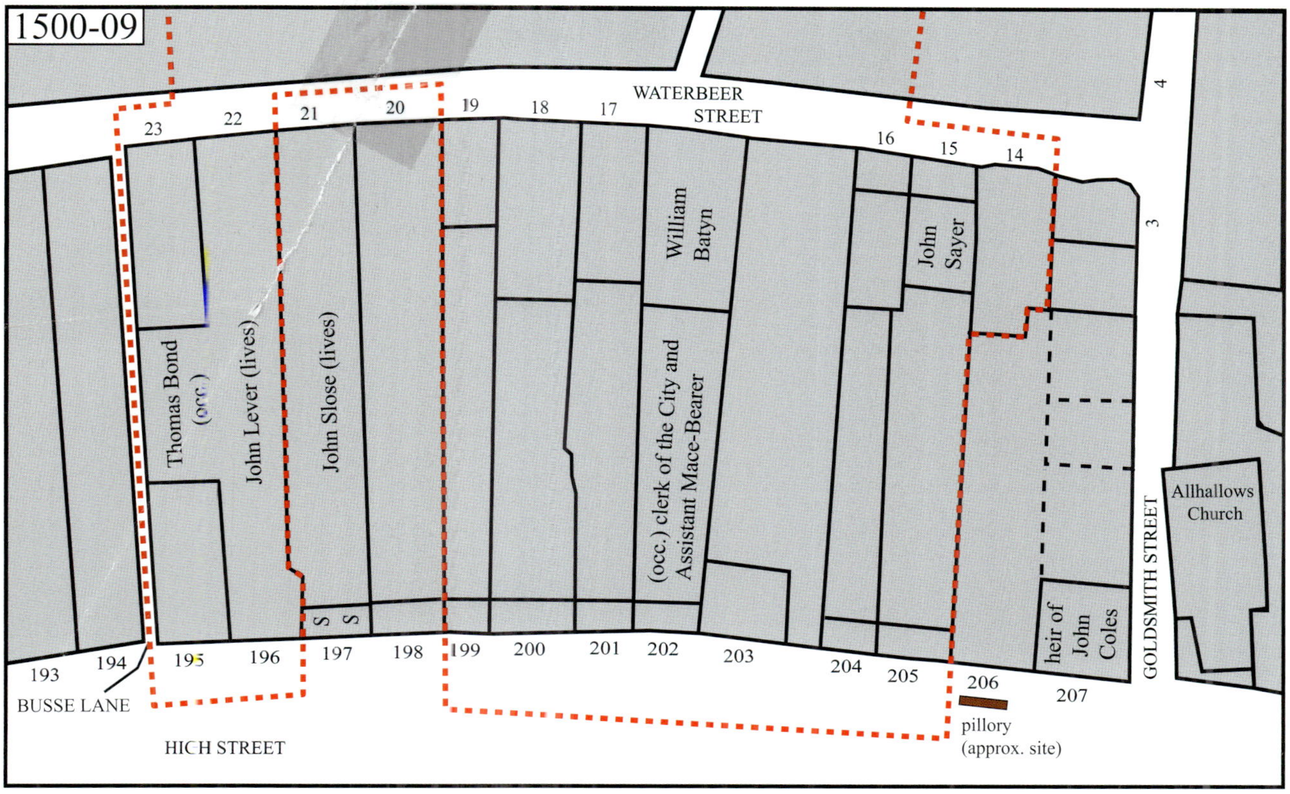

Fig. 4.21 Reconstruction of those in possession of 194–207 High Street in 1500–09 (drawn by David Gould)

Documentary evidence relating to the site of the Trichay Street excavation and its neighbours

As in High Street, reconstruction of the medieval owners and occupants of the excavated site entails consideration of a block of adjacent properties, in this case those on the north side of Waterbeer Street between North Street and Pancras Lane. Figure 4.24 shows the street in the 20th century, when large industrial buildings occupied some of the tenements; Fig. 4.25 shows the historic mapping relating to this block. Coldridge's map of 1819 (Fig. 4.25A) shows the area when early 19th-century road widening was in progress in North Street but before the major changes around Pancras Lane in the late 19th century. Figure 4.25B shows the OS 1:500 map with property boundaries added from the 1910 Valuation, and with three earlier detailed plans relating to individual tenements pasted into their positions.

In 1910 the block contained eleven historic properties: eight in St Kerrian's parish, two in St Pancras and one (latterly 7–8 Waterbeer Street) which straddled the boundary between the two parishes. The presence of a parish boundary in the middle of this property shows that it was an amalgamation of two earlier tenements. The street numbers used here are taken from the Goad map of 1888 as updated in 1921, which shows some changes from 1910. One other 19th-century change may be noted here: in 1910 4–5 Waterbeer Street were occupied by the large iron foundry of Garton and King. Comparison with the Coldridge map (Fig. 4.25A) strongly suggests that this was formed by amalgamating two older tenements.

The streets and the boundaries of the site

Both the Coldridge map and that of 1876 show that the excavated site was unusual among the old properties in the parish in containing two broad tenements [9–10 Waterbeer Street), with one narrow property [8 Waterbeer Street] along the western edge. They fronted onto Waterbeer Street, with the lane described by Coldridge as 'anciently Trickhay Street' to the north, and with St Pancras Lane to the east and north-east. The western side of the excavation approximated to the parish boundary dividing St Pancras parish from St Kerrian's. All these boundaries were of ancient origin, except the western one with Pancras Lane, which was greatly altered in the 19th century (Fig. 4.25A–B).

Waterbeer Street is first documented in 1253 (ED/M/75, S&J 0381) but was very probably of much more ancient origin, being an element of the late Saxon *burh*. Although the name Trichay Street is not found in medieval documents, the lane itself evidently existed by 1242–3, when a property in North Street, later John Trote's house, was described as lying between the King's Highway [North Street] and Geoffrey and Richard Stranga's land, and between the Strangas' house and St Kerrian's Lane

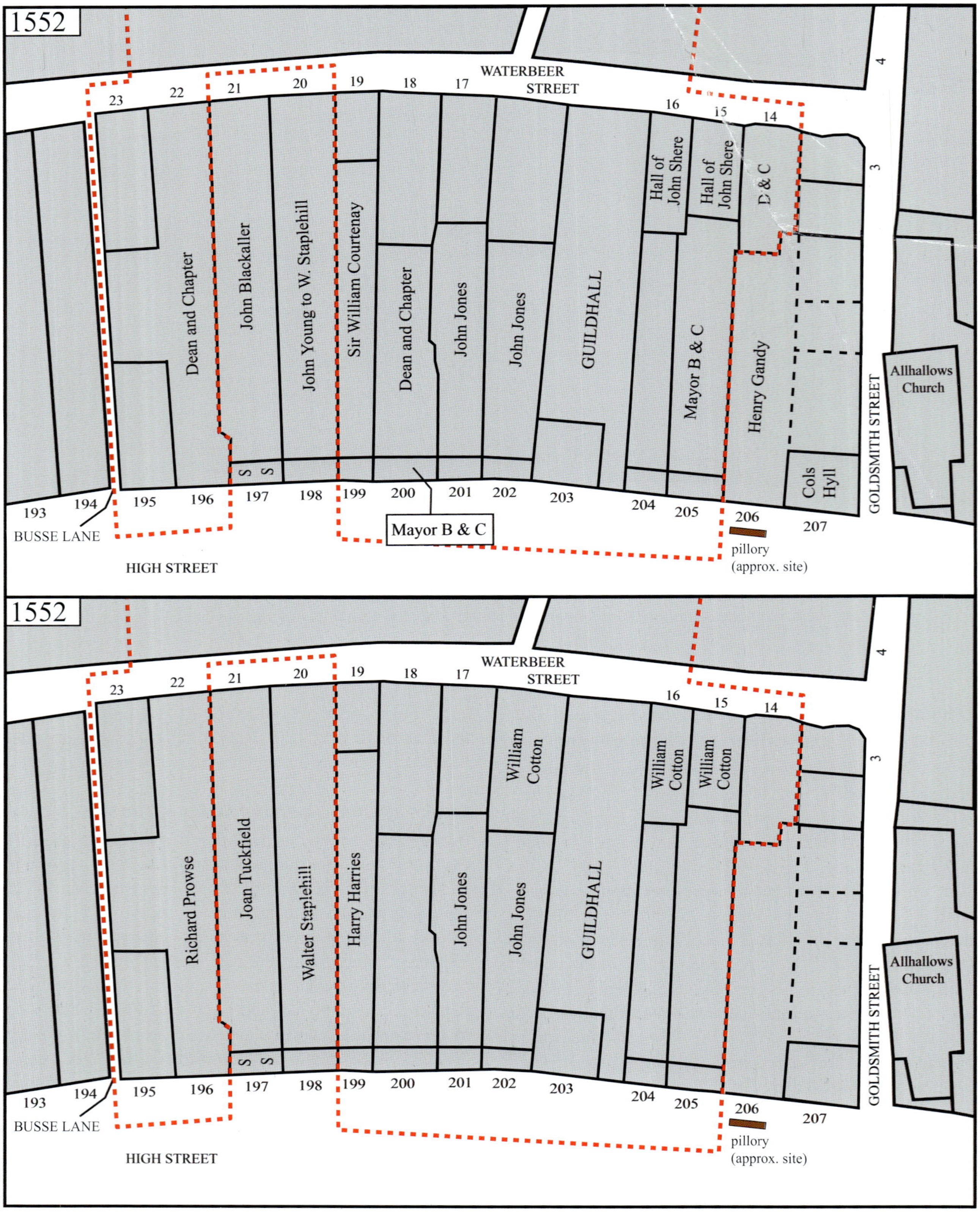

Fig. 4.22 Reconstructions of (a) owners and (b) occupiers of 194–207 High Street in 1552 drawn by David Gould)

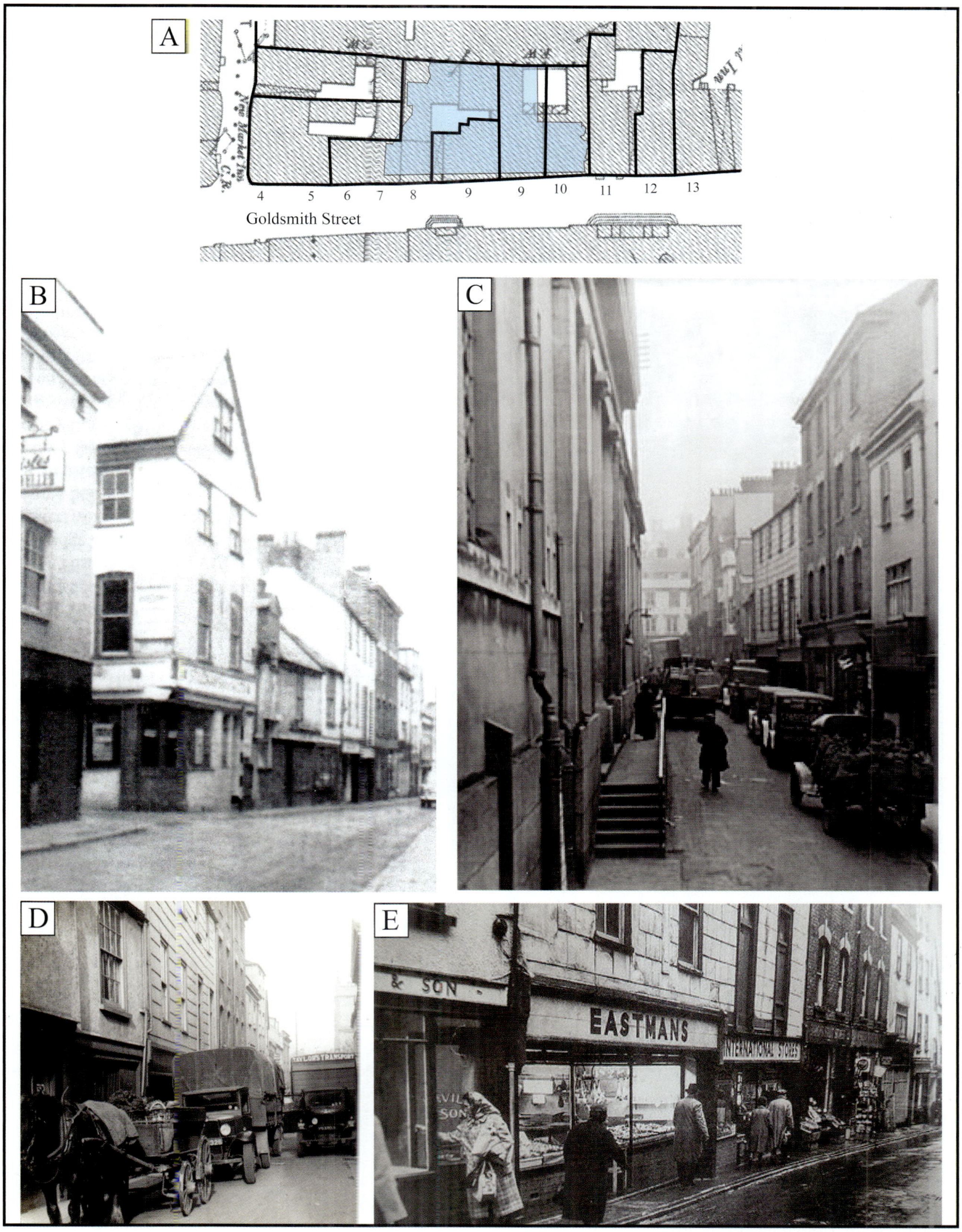

Fig. 4.23 The excavated properties in Goldsmith Street and their neighbours. (A) The excavated area (blue) with property boundaries of 1910 and late 20th-century house numbers. (B) View of c. 1960 with the gabled No. 4 at the corner of Waterbeer Street in the foreground, the earlier row Nos 5–7 beyond, and the excavated Nos 8–10 rising above them. (C) View towards High Street with No. 11 to the extreme right; (D) with Nos 5–6 to the left. (E) Photo dated 1963 with Eastman's at No. 8; the dark brick building beyond formed Nos 9–10 ((A) © Exeter City Council; (C–E) courtesy of the websites 'Demolition Exeter' and 'Exeter Memories')

Fig. 4.24 (A–C) Waterbeer Street in the 20th century: (A) with the frontage of the excavated site in the foreground and the turreted Police Station beyond; (B) in the 1930s or 1940s (?), with the Police Station to the right and the excavated building beyond; (C) in the ?late 1960s, after the demolition of the Police Station. (D) Pancras Lane looking north (courtesy of the websites 'Demolition Exeter' and 'Exeter Memories')

(*venella S Kerani*) (ED/M/51, S&J 0353). The lane was surely Trichay Street, which runs along the north side of the church. In 1317 a messuage fronting onto Waterbeer Street was described as being bounded by 'the lane behind from St Kerrian's church to St Pancras' (DRO Misc. Roll 2, entry 18: S&J 0392, cf. Fig. 4.25B–C) and a document of 1507 mentions 'a certain path leading from the church of St Pancras towards the church of St Kerrian' (MCR 23–4 Hen VII, m4d).

The sole instance of the name Trichay Street noted among the Exeter deeds occurs in a sale of 1580 relating to a garden with appurtenances, bounded by Trichay Street on its north side. The location of the garden, however, is a mystery. It lay between the land of the late King Edward

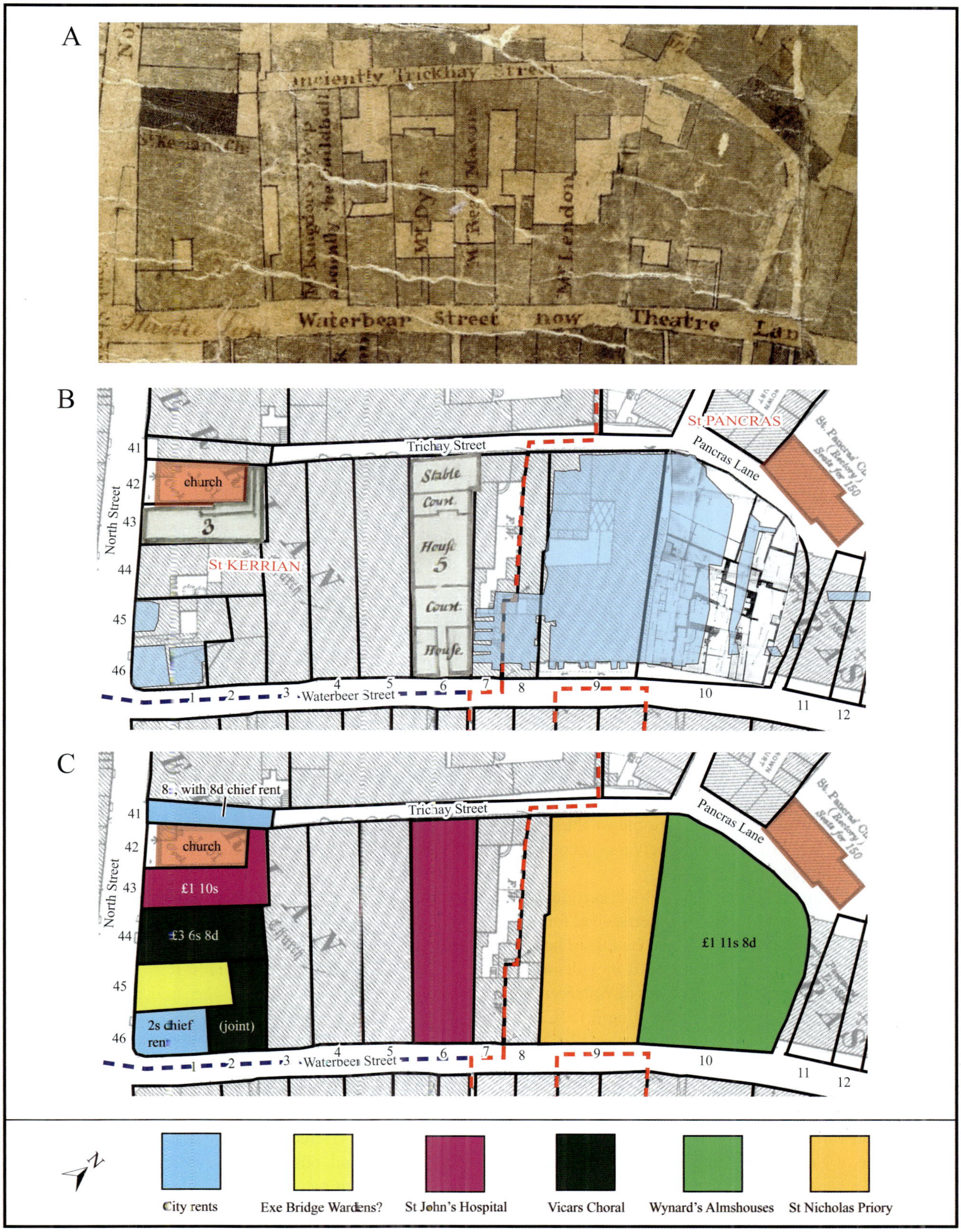

Fig. 4.25 The block of properties between Waterbeer Street and Trichay Street. (A) Extract from Coldridge's map of Exeter of 1819 (© Devon Heritage Centre). (B) Extract of the OS First Edition 1:500 map of 1876 with the boundary of St Pancras parish in red, the detailed plans of city properties from the Chamber Map Book of 1756–60 in pale green (courtesy of the Devon and Exeter Institution) and excavated areas in pale blue. (C) Landowners and rents in 1522 (drawn by David Gould)

VI [?dissolved monastic or hospital land] on the south, land of Nicholas Martyn and of the heirs of Stephen Vilvaine on the west, and the land belonging to parish of St Paul to the east.

(St) Pancras Lane too is documented from the 13th century; it is mentioned in 1285 (as *vico Sci Pancras*: Gover *et al.* 1931, 23), and in 1287 when a 4d rent of Walter la Chauve's former tenement in Pancras Street (*in vico S Pancratis*) was recorded (D&C 208; S&J 0590).

Finally, the parish boundary on the western side of the excavated site may be presumed to have been in existence by 1222, when the parishes of Exeter were demarcated (Orme 2014, 28).

The medieval property owners

In building a picture of the late medieval owners, leaseholders and occupiers in this block of tenements, the documents of two institutions are of central importance: those of the city and the Vicars Choral (Fig. 4.25C). The other prolific source of medieval city deeds – the Dean and Chapter of the cathedral – did not own any of these tenements.

City properties and rents

The city properties shown in the Map Book of the Chamber of the City are a good place to start (CMB Map 14; Fig. 4.25B). The book shows that in the mid 18th century the city owned two tenements in this block (43 North Street and 6 Waterbeer Street, leased respectively by Sarah Tucker and Charles Martyn) and collected chief rents from two others: one of 8d from 41 North Street (the house built over the end of Trichay Street), charged to the Wardens of St Kerrian's parish, the other of 2s on 46 North Street (the 'Tenement at the North Corner of Waterbeer lane'). Some of these rents can be traced back in the City Receivers' accounts of the previous 400 years.

The text of the Chamber Map Book provides the important information that its two properties had formerly been lands of St John's Hospital. The schedule of hospital properties in the St John Cartulary of 1401 includes a tenement 'once Fok's, now Margery Golde's in Waterberstrete 6s 2d' but I have not succeeded in locating it (SJC, 63).

The properties of the Vicars Choral

The Vicars Choral came to own land here in 1488, when Thomasia/Thomasine, the widow of Alan Sares, donated two properties in perpetuity to the vicars: a tenement on the east side of North Street, and a cellar (*selarium*) with a solar (*solarium*) above on the north side of Waterbeer Street (VC 3394; Fig. 4.25C). Their donation was presumably the reason that the Sares appeared in later years among those commemorated by the vicars (Lepine and Orme 2003, 323, 334). These tenements were owned by the vicars until 1547, when they were taken by the Crown, but they were restored by Queen Elizabeth in 1585 (VC 3328). They remained the vicars' property in the early modern period, being leased to the Mayne family at the yearly rent of £3 6s 8d in the period 1666–1761 (CC 21782–90).

Alongside the properties, the Vicars Choral evidently received from Thomasine Sares a fine collection of earlier deeds relating to them, since these also survive in the vicars' archives. They provide valuable information about the locations of the holdings, and record the sequence of leaseholders and neighbours over the previous 130 years. They state that the two properties abutted: the North Street holding formed the northern boundary of the one in Waterbeer Street, and both abutted a property of the Wilford family to the east. This information allows their positions to be proposed: 44 North Street and 2 Waterbeer Street are the only properties which had this relationship in 1910, with 3 North Street their neighbour to the east. The antiquity of this arrangement, with a parcel of the Waterbeer Street holding extending northward to touch the one in North Street, is demonstrated by later deeds which confirm the identification of the North Street plot, describing it as lying to the south of a property of the Mayor, Bailiffs and Commonalty (43 North Street: see above).

The tenement of St Nicholas Priory

The Military Survey of 1522 records that St Nicholas Priory owned land in St Pancras parish with an income valued at 16s, an appreciably lower sum than those from most of the High Street tenements (Rowe 1977, 10). The same property is recognisable among the parcels of the former possessions of St Nicholas Priory bought by William Hurst in 1549: one in the parish of St Pancras which he received via William Symonde at 16s (William Symonds, king's servant, 'gentleman': Youings 1955, 88–9 – probably the William Symons who paid on £20 of goods in St Pancras parish in the Subsidy of 1524/5: Rowe 1977, 38). Most of Hurst's property passed after his death to his son-in-law Richard Martyn, whose descendants retained the former Hurst estate into the 18th century. In the St Pancras Church Rate of 1612 Thomas Martyn was named among the five people 'such as have gardens & stables in ye parish', paying 2s (DHC Fursdon vol. 3, 74).

The probable identity of this tenement has been established in an unpublished study of the post-medieval documentation of 9 Waterbeer Street, undertaken by Tony Collings (DHC Exeter Archaeology archive, project 7249). He found a deed of 1806, certainly relating to this property, which mentions that it was formerly owned by William Clifford Martyn of Oxton, the last male heir of the Martyn family, who inherited Oxton from William Hurst (DHC D7/148/!a, 1b MacCaffrey 1978, 225). This appears therefore to have been the former possession of St Nicholas Priory acquired by Hurst, and passed subsequently to the Martyns.

The tenements at the western end of the block

Figure 4.26 shows an extract from the Hedgeland model – an evocative but unreliable depiction of these properties as they are said to have appeared in the mid 18th century.

41 North Street (now part of Wilko)

Nicholas Orme has described the circumstances which brought this property into being: in 1350 Sir Robert Tcly, the rector of St Kerrian's, was granted permission by the Mayor and Commonalty of Exeter to erect a house on the north side of St Kerrian's, presumably as his residence (Orme 2014, 123). The grant adds further details: the tenement sometime of Roger Layz, tailor, lay to the east, and the one 'sometime of Master John Whiteby, clerk' to the north (ED/M/388). Since the property was built over a former street, the city charged a small chief rent, and this can be followed in the city Receivers' accounts from that date. In 1351/2 it was the '6d new rent for a certain lane next the church of St Kerrian'; in 1399–1400 'all that plot in North Street used as a lane in that city from ancient times' (ED/M/388; ERA). The entry for 1399–1400 records 'a gate in a certain lane next to the church of St Kerrian'. The city retained the right to enter the property by a key in time of war or whenever the need or use of the city demanded it (Orme 2014, 123).

This 6d rent was paid by the rector of St Kerrian's throughout the later Middle Ages. Between 1377/8 and 1398/90 this was for 'the tenement of John Lusquyt, rector of the church of St Kerrian'... 'for a certain lane (*venella*) within his tenement'. Throughout the 15th century the sum was paid by a series of unnamed parish rectors. The account of 1500 adds an interesting detail: '6d from the rector of St Keram for having a certain entrance and a tenement situated near the church of St Keram, where the Mayor and his brethren are accustomed to begin their number for supervising the walls of the city and their defence'. The rent had risen to 8d by 1520 (CRA 1519/20 m.2: '8d from the rector of St Kieram for that tenement and entrance to it situated next the church of St Kieram'), and that sum was paid by the wardens of St Kerrian's into the 19th century (*e.g.* in 1798/9: ECA Book 159, Sundry parishes).

From the early 16th century the city Receivers' accounts also record an 8s rent from a property in St Kerrian's parish, described as 'that tenement and entrance to it next the foresaid church' (CRA 1529/30). The reference to an entrance sounds like the descriptions of No. 41 above. The first occasion on which this payment has been noted was in 1529/30, when it was paid by David Blake. The account for 1549/50 records the same 8s rent for 'the entrance next the church of St Keriam which David Blake late held, with 2s newly won rent of that tenement' (E1549/50 m30). The Receivers' accounts of the 1550s and 1560s provide further information which confirms that the property in question was indeed No. 41. In 1559/60 the city received the new 10s rent from 'a tenement and garden in the north part of the church of St Keriam' which John Dyer held (CRA 1559/60). In other years the holding was described as 'a tenement and kitchen'. It continued to provide a charitable income into the early 19th century (RCC 1909, 188–9).

Fig. 4.26 41–6 North Street as depicted in the Hedgeland model of c. 1820, with St Kerrian's church left of centre and Trichay Street at the extreme left. Although very unreliable in detail, the model offers a unique record of these houses (© RAMM)

42 North Street was St Kerrian's church

43 North Street (now part of Wilko)

One of the earliest Exeter deeds appears to relate to 43 North Street, the property south of the church. In 1163 Bishop Bartholomew endowed the Mary Magdalene Leper Hospital outside South Gate with a number of properties. One was described as 'land next to St Kerrian's chapel whence Algar [illegible] must pay 10s 1d' (ED/MAG/100, f18). Since the land to the north of the chapel was then a street, it was presumably the tenement to the south which was indicated. Similarly, this can be identified as the site of the 'shop in North Street with a solar above, lying between St Kerrian's church and Lord William de Chambernoun's tenement, at the front of Sarah and Nicholas' tenement towards the street', which was granted in 1284/5 by Sarah, the widow of William Utreseyne, and her son Nicholas, to Ellis de Yvelcestre and his wife Gonotta, the rent being a rose (ED/M/141). The wording suggests that there were two holdings here: a shop on the frontage and a property behind. The same arrangement is evident in a document of 1422, described below.

There follows an entry of extraordinary interest, allowing this property to be identified as the premises of Walter le Verrour/the Glazier, the celebrated craftsman who undertook the installation (and presumably the making) of the glass of the cathedral presbytery, including the great east window, in 1304, and who went on to install windows in the choir in 1310 (Brooks and Evans 1988). Master Walter has the distinction of being the first known English glazier whose work can be recognised (Marks 1987, 532). In his will of 30 January 1318 he desired that his tenement in the city of Exeter should be sold, and should pass to his executors for the payment of his debts (MCR 11–12 Edw. II. m17d). A quitclaim of two days later records that Richard de Pedrisfeld, his heir, released to William Boyvile, administrator of the goods of the late Walter de Peterisfeld called le Verour [the Glazier], his claim on the tenement in North Street (*Northestrete*) next to St Kerrian's church, once the said Walter's (ED/M/236, S&J 0372). Since the land on the north side of the church was a street before 1350 (above), it was presumably the one to the south of the church which Master Walter occupied. Since some of this site escaped the wholesale removal of archaeological deposits from the Guildhall Shopping Centre in 1974, it is even possible that archaeological evidence for the glazier's workshop survives below the standing modern building.

The Chamber Map Book shows this property as an L-shaped holding extending behind the chancel of St Kerrian's church [the rear of 42 North Street]; it was then occupied entirely by buildings, excepting a narrow passage round the chancel (Fig. 4.25B). The accompanying commentary gives its dimensions: 62 ft (18.9 m) from the street to the back, and 18 ft (5.5 m) across the frontage. Although the measurements are not a perfect fit, the antiquity of these boundaries seems to be indicated in a deed of 1351 which states that Robert Noble held the plot of land on the south side of St Kerrian's church measuring 66 × 20 ft, and another on the eastern side of the chancel measuring 10½ × 21 ft (ED/M/393). Noble had acquired the small plot east of the chancel from John de Hembury and the main part of the property from John de Sotton (ED/M/393).

The 66 ft-long tenement reappears in a deed of 1372 in which John Wayfeer of Glastonbury (*Glastingbury*) granted to Sir John Lusquyt, the rector of St Kerrian's, a property on the south side of St Kerrian's church which Wayfeer had by grant of Sir Robert Toly, the former rector. The deed also mentions John Whyker's tenement to the south and Thomas and Helewis Webbers' to the east (ED/M/442, S&J 3710).

We get a much clearer sense of the layout of this burgage plot in the early 15th century. In 1403 Thomas Lusquyst, the heir of John Lusquyt, the late parson of St Kerrian's, granted the main part of this property to Richard Crese, the rent being a red rose for seven years, then 10s a year for the grantor's life (cf. the 10s 1d of 1163; ED/M/576, ED/M/579, S&J 3274–5; see also MCR 3–4 Rich. II, m16. S&J 3722; VC 3081, S&J 3700). When this same tenement ('on the south side of St Kerrian's church') was acquired from Crese in 1422 by Thomas Hertyscote of Gittisham, it was described as consisting of 'a hall, a cellar with a solar above, a kitchen, a pantry with a chamber behind it, a vacant lot, a wall, a door with entry to the hall (being 5½ ft wide) and two doors in the same entry.' The west bound was not North Street but Crese's shop with solars at its rear (MCR 1–2 Henry VI, m10, S&J 3258). In other words, the main part of the holding lay behind a shop with solars which formed a separate property on the street frontage. This was presumably the 'shop and solars above the shop in North Street' granted in 1413 by Crese to John Batyn and John Forde (ED/M/618, S&J 3727).

Orme (2014, 121) has shown that from the late 12th century the church of St Kerrian belonged to the cathedral, and this connection is evident in the leaseholders of 43 North Street. In 1453 it was 'the tenement of John Burnebury, clerk', the Treasurer of the cathedral (VC 3166; S&J 3853; for Burnebury see Lepine and Orme 2003, 323, the location confirmed by the presence of the tenement lately of John Exebrigge to the south [44 North Street –see below] and Robert Wylford's garden to the east [3 Waterbeer Street –see below]).

We have seen that David Blake held the property north of St Kerrian's in the early 16th century. He also held 43 North Street, as is evident from the deed of 1413 relating to the shop and solars on the street frontage, described above, which is endorsed in a later hand 'lately David Blake'. We can perhaps take the 16th-century history of this tenement further with evidence from the city Receivers' accounts. In the 1550s they recorded for the first time a 30s rent from 'a tenement in North Street which the Mayor and Bailiffs of the said city late purchased from John Crudge, in which Peter Lake now lives and which he holds by indenture'. This sum corresponds to the £1 10s rent paid in later years on No. 43, recorded both in ECA Book 202 (which dates from *c.* 1755) and in Mannington's Survey (dated 1698: ECA Book 193, f149: I am grateful to Tony Collings for these references). By 1569/70 this rent was paid by Richard Newman (CRA 1569/70, m4). If it does relate to the same holding, No. 43 became one of the many properties bought by William Crugge in the early 16th century and passed to his family after his death in 1520 (described below).

44 North Street (now part of Wilko)

The fine sequence of early deeds relating to this property, and its donation to the Vicars Choral in 1488, have been described above. In 1351 this was the tenement once Ralph de Thornbyry's (ED/M/393). In 1367 John Giffard, chaplain, passed his share of a tenement in North Street to Sir Robert Toly, the rector of St Kerrian's whom we have met at 41 and 43 North Street. This was not 43 North

Street but the neighbouring property to the south; the deed mentioned Toly's own holding as its northern neighbour, and the grant included an acre of land outside the city at Velwell (*Felewille*) near Taddiford which was associated with 44 North Street in a number of late medieval deeds. In the following year Toly and John Dunscombe quit-claimed both the North Street property and the land at Velwell to Roger Plenta. In 1372 the North Street holding was described as 'John Whyker's tenement' (ED/M/442, S&J 3710). Five years later, it passed briefly to a group of prominent Exeter citizens including Martin Battishill, John Nymet and Raymond Goos before being acquired by Margaret Courtenay, Countess of Devon, and Henry Burton in 1379 (MCR 3–4 Rich. II, m16; S&J 3722). In 1407, the executors of Beatrice Westecote, the widow of Henry Westecote, sold the property to John Exebrigge and his wife Sarah; subsequently, in 1433, it passed to John and Joan Wise and Thomas Cook (VC 3108, 3386, 3098, 3158, 3162, 3174; summary in HMC VC, 15).

In 1440 both 44 North Street and 2 Waterbeer Street were acquired by John Polyng from Robert Caunte of Collumpton, the rent being 13s 4d; he held them until 1453, when they were acquired by Simon Broun/Brown, who sold to William Ellyot in 1466, from whom Alan and Thomasine Sares bought them in 1478, when the property was described as 'late of John Bolyng' (VC 3172, 3212, 3213, 3228, 3394). Sares' purchase of the two tenements consolidated his holding of a block of adjoining properties [with 1–3 Waterbeer Street, described below]. The subsequent donation to the Vicars Choral has been described above.

In this sequence of transactions we rarely learn of the occupier; an exception was John Crosse, saddler, who held and inhabited the tenement in 1449 (VC 3184; S&J 3701, identification confirmed by the neighbours: John Burneby to the north, William Cremyll to the south and Robert Wilford to the east). Crosse had been a witness in the case of Radford and Tremayne of 1439, where he described himself as a saddler of St Kerrian's parish; he had held the keys of Radford's houses in North Street and Corry Lane [Gandy Street], and could therefore account for Radford's movements (Kleineke 2013, 34).

45 North Street (now part of Wilko)

Deeds of 1367, 1368, 1377 and 1407, described above, all state that the tenement to the south of No. 44 had been another property of Robert Noble; the last records that by 1407 it had come into the ownership of Robert Wilford. It is likely that the property was often held with No. 46. This was evidently the case in 1440, 1449 and 1453, when William Cremyll was in possession of both this tenement and 46 North Street/1 Waterbeer Street, since he appears in deeds both as the southern neighbour of 44 North Street and as the western neighbour of 2 Waterbeer Street (VC 3166, VC 3184; see above; see also below). Further instances suggesting joint ownership are described in relation to 46 North Street (below). In 1910, when the property boundaries of central Exeter were first mapped, 45 and 46 North Street [the latter also known as 1 Waterbeer Street] were one property.

The rent of the Exe Bridge wardens

From 1407/8 until 1673/4 the Wardens of Exe Bridge received an annual 16d rent from a garden, described as being 'in North Street between the said street on the west and Waterbeer Street on the south' (*e.g.* Juddery 1990c, 51); the rolls after 1556 show that this was in St Kerrian's parish. In 1407/8 the rent was paid by William Wilford, and described as 'late of John Peauter'. As we shall see, there were five Wilford/Farringdon tenements near the corner of North Street and Waterbeer Street by the end of the 15th century. No. 44 North Street/2 Waterbeer Street was acquired by the Wilfords only in the late 15th century, and 3 Waterbeer Street would presumably have been described as lying in Waterbeer Street. The rent therefore seems to have come from the corner properties – either 45 or 46 North Street, with a garden which may have been either 1 or 2 Waterbeer Street. It is shown in Fig. 4.25C at 45 North Street, since 46 North Street clearly had no garden; an alternative might be that the house was 46 North Street, with the garden at No. 45.

The rent can be followed through the 16th and 17th centuries. In 1519/20 it was paid by the heirs of John Farringdon, and in 1529/30 by John Wadham, who still held it in 1567. By then, Wadham's rent was 35 years in arrears; he owed the wardens £2 8s (Juddery 1990a–c, *passim*). It was paid subsequently by the heirs of Wadham, William Hurst and Blewett (*e.g.* EBW 1638/9, 1643/4).

46 North Street/1 Waterbeer Street (now part of Wilko)

No. 46 was the tiny holding (*c.* 5 × 5.5 m in the Chamber Map Book), readily identifiable in some medieval deeds from its position on the street corner. In 1336 Oliver de Champernoun bought from William Danney and his wife Catherine a tenement whose west bound was North Street and south bound Waterbeer Street, and which was therefore this corner property. The deed records that Ralph de Thornb[yr]y's tenement lay to the north [44 North Street] and Thomas Gerveys' to the east [2 Waterbeer Street] (MCR 9–10 Edw. III, m36; S&J 0388); the fact that Thornbyry's holding was named as its neighbour shows that 45 North Street was then accounted either with No. 46 to the south or with No. 44 to the north.

The documents associated with the Vicars Choral, described above, tell us that the property to the west of 2 Waterbeer Street [1 Waterbeer Street/46 North Street] belonged in 1453 to William Cremyll, but by 1479 this too had come into the ownership of the wealthy Robert Wilford; in 1488 it was 'late of the said Robert' (VC 3394).

We learn more about this tenement from the will of Robert Wilford's daughter Elizabeth Farringdon, which is dated 1516 (MCR 8–9 Hen VIII, m36). It shows that she had inherited three tenements in Waterbeer Street from her father. She passed two to her daughters. The first – clearly this property – stood at the junction of North Street and Waterbeer Street and was called 'Our Lady at the Corner' – perhaps because it incorporated a niche holding a figure of the Virgin Mary.

The 2s chief rent levied by the city on this property in the 1750s has been mentioned. This can be traced back to the early 16th century, but I have not found it in earlier records. The city Receiver's account for 1519/20 states that nothing was raised from the tenement ('in North Street in the corner of the road there') from the executors of the most recent lessee, Peter William, 'because it is held by service … in the day of the election, done annually, now of the Prior of the Hospital of St John the Baptist'. The account of 1499/1500 records: 'from Peter William for that tenement situated in North Street which he holds from the Mayor and Bailiffs for doing service … in the day of the election of a new Mayor'. William was presumably the occupier, the owner being Elizabeth Farringdon.

2 Waterbeer Street (now part of Wilko)

The history of this tenement before 1488 has been described above (see 44 North Street). This was presumably the second of the two adjacent holdings in Waterbeer Street which Elizabeth Farringdon passed to her daughters in 1516 (above), in which a capper named William Tucker lived.

3 Waterbeer Street

The deeds relating to 43 and 44 North Street and 2 Waterbeer Street also record the owners of the property which formed the rear boundary of these three tenements, which lay to the east. In 1351 and 1352 it was held by Robert Noble (ED/M/393; MCR 5–6 Rich II, m35; S&J 3706, 3873), who had acquired it from John de Henbury. By at least the start of the 15th century it belonged to the Wilford family (ED/M/576), who held the property for the following century. It was owned by Robert Wilford in 1440 and 1453, and inherited by Alan Sares, Robert's son-in-law, by 1479, descending subsequently to the Farringdons.

4–8 Waterbeer Street

It has proved more difficult to piece together tenement histories for the burgage plots in the centre of this block, but for the period 1351–82 the abuttals recorded in a good collection of deeds and wills allow the sequence of those in possession of the properties on the north side of Waterbeer Street to be reconstructed, as follows:

1. The documentation which establishes that Robert Noble's house was at 3 Waterbeer Street (described above) also states that Walter Whithorn held the next property to the east (MCR 5–6 Rich II, m35, S&J 3873). This was therefore No. 4 Waterbeer Street, or Nos 4 and 5 if held jointly. When it passed to John Bridlegh in 1382 it was described as a messuage bounded to the south by Waterbeer Street and by Pancras Lane (*Prancardyslane*) to the north, with John Gist's vacant lot to the east (MCR 5–6 Rich. II, m. 35; S&J 3873; I take the *Prancardyslane* to refer to Trichay Street, cf 'the lane from North Street to St Pancras church' in ED/M/393).
2. John Spicer's will of 1361 records a property separating Whithorn's tenement to the west from John Gist's to the east. It was 'situated on the north part of … Waterbeer Street, opposite the lane called la *Smalelane'* [Busse Lane/Parliament Street, the only such lane recorded on the south side of Waterbeer Street]. Walter Spyryng had lived there, and John Gist's plot to the east of Spicer was then vacant (MCR 35–6 Edw III, m4v, 8v). Figure 4.27B shows the site of Nos 5–6 were undivided in the 14th century; this reconstruction has the merit of placing Spicer opposite the Little Lane [Busse Lane, now Parliament Street].
3. In his will of 1381 (described in relation to 196 High Street, above) John Gist left to his second wife Agnes 'all his garden with a house situated in the same' lying between Waterbeer Street and Trichay Street, with the tenement sometime of Walter Whithorn to the west (MCR 4–5 Rich II m25d). Figure 4.27B shows the suggested position.
4. The same document states that Stephen Dynneclyve's tenement lay to the east of Gist.

In the suggested layout of these properties shown in Fig. 4.27B, the identifications of lands close to North Street are secure but scope for mistakes increases as we move eastward, since it is possible that the medieval properties were divided or amalgamated subsequently. In this reconstruction the holding of Dynneclyve was the western part of the excavated area; a small part of Gist's house and garden was also excavated, although no physical evidence of late 14th-century date was found there.

The early 16th century: Ralph Bokerland; William Crugge; Charles Farringdon

In 1507 William Crugge paid £10 in silver to Ralph Bokelond and his wife Joan (daughter and heiress of William Cremyll) for a tenement, garden and appurtenances on the north side of Waterbeer Street, with 'a certain path leading from the church of St Pancras towards the church of St Kerrian' [Trichay Street] to the north (MCR 23–4 Hen. VII, m4d). Crugge was the richest Exeter merchant of his generation, and mayor in 1505, 1515 and 1518; he died in 1520 (Rowe and Cochlin 1964). John Hooker's brief portrait describes his

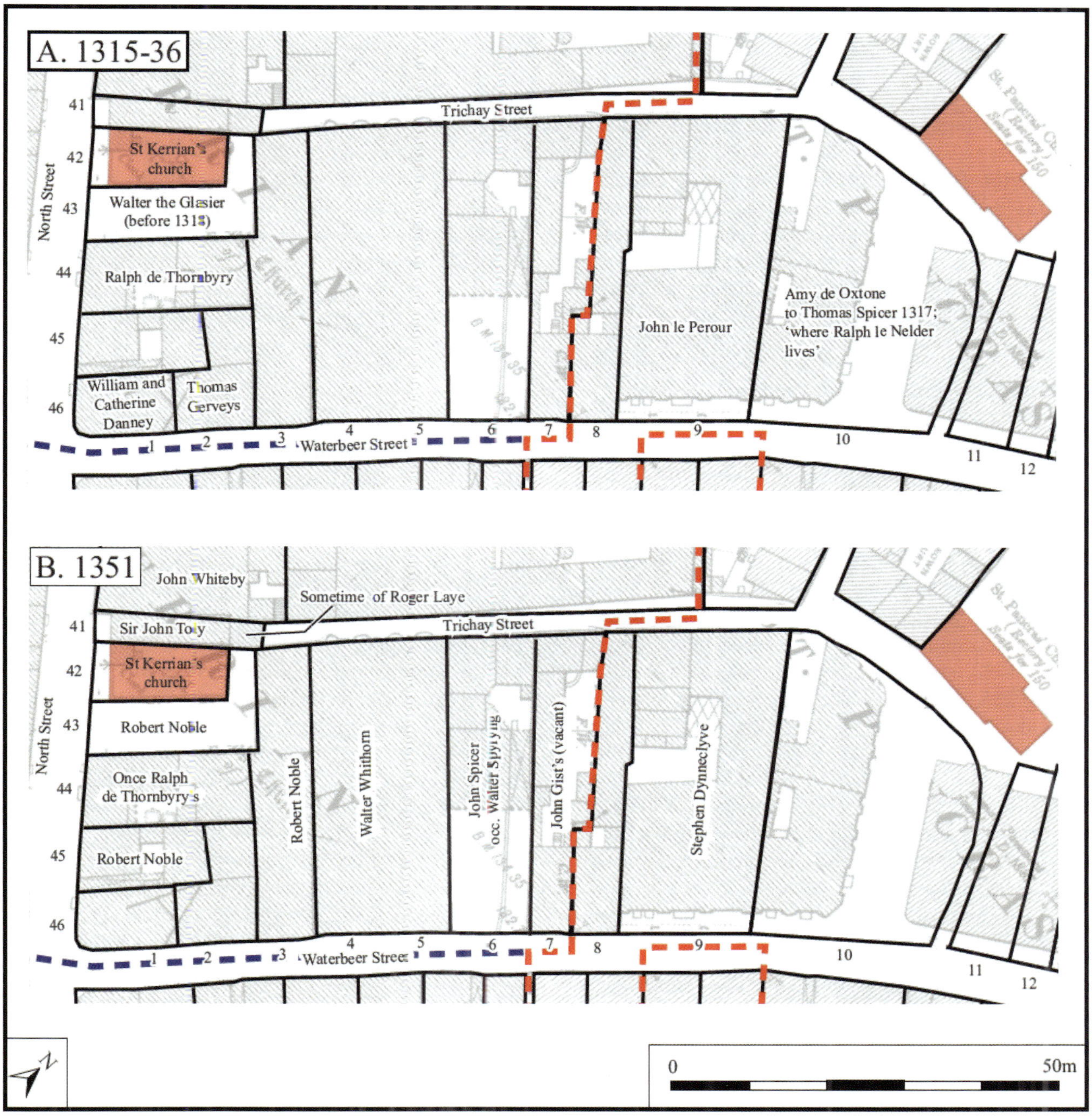

Fig. 4.27 Suggested reconstructions of those in possession of properties in Waterbeer Street and Trichay Street: (A) in 1315–36; (B) in 1351–82 (drawn by David Gould)

rise from humble beginnings as a tanner, and mentions that he was a 'great purchaser of lands' (Gray 2005, 75). The document describes him as a 'Tynnemchaunt' [tin merchant], and adds that the tenement of John Beare of Huntsham lay to the east and that of John Farringdon to the west.

Where was the tenement bought by Crugge? In the early 20th century there were eight properties on the north side of Waterbeer Street with Trichay Street to their north (Fig. 4.25, Nos 3–10). Two – probably three – can be excluded from the list of possible identifications, as they were owned by religious institutions (Nos 6 and 10, and probably No. 9: see above), and No. 3 was a Farringdon property. This leaves one of Nos 4–5 and 7–8 as the probable site. In the Military Survey of 1522, two years after Crugge's death, his widow and son were taxed for large sums in the parish St Kerrian but not for property in St Pancras (Rowe 1977, 9–12). Nos 4–5 and 7 were in St Kerrian's, and this seems to restrict the search to these three properties. On the other hand, in 1522 Crugge's neighbours, John Beare and Charles Farringdon, appeared among those taxed on property in St Pancras parish but not St Kerrian's (Rowe 1977, 9–12). I have not, therefore, been able to establish precisely which tenement Crugge bought.

Charles Farringdon's property in St Pancras parish was perhaps the third holding in Waterbeer Street mentioned in the will of his mother Elizabeth which she left to her son Charles (cf. 1–2 Waterbeer Street above). It is described there as 'that tenement or stable with a garden adjacent and the appurtenances which John Sooce senior now holds'. In 1522, however, Scoose [sometimes Scose/Scoos/Scosse] paid 16s 8d in tax in St Kerrian's and nothing in St Pancras (Rowe 1977, 11–12).

The eastern tenements in the block

The excavated area in the early 14th century: Amy de Oxton, Thomas Spicer and Ralph le Nelder

In 1317 Amy de Oxtone, widow, a member of a prominent city family, granted to Thomas Spicer the 2s 5d rent of a tenement in Waterbeer Street which lay between '*la Smale Lane*' on the east and John le Perour's tenement on the west and north. A note, added to the dorse in a later hand, states that this was next to Pancras Lane (ED/M/235, S&J 0382). The document therefore relates to land on the west side of the lane: the large D-shaped holding forming the eastern part of the excavated area, which became 10 Waterbeer Street. As we learn from the will of Walter Austyn of 1323, Spicer did not live there; the document states that this was 'where Ralph le Nelder lives', and Austyn's heirs were to receive the property if Spicer died without an heir (MCR 17–18 Edw II, m9; there is a minor discrepancy with the rent quoted above, recorded in 1323 as 2s 6d).

The excavated area in the early 15th century: William Wynard

Among 'those which have lands within the parish but live outside', listed in the Military Survey of 1522, were 'the heirs of Wynard to the use of the almshouse', who paid £1 11s 8d. The almshouse, which still stands outside South Gate, had been founded in 1436 by William Wynard, Recorder of the city, who had donated his lands to endow his foundation (Rowe 1977, 10; ED/WA/2). As Orme and Webster (1995, 244) put it, most of the almshouse's endowments 'escaped the Reformation', and are thus sometimes traceable in much later documentation. The rentals of the Wynard's Almshouse Estate survive only from 1838 and *c.* 1850, but they allow the property taxed in 1522 to be identified. Their sole holding in St Pancras parish was a house in Waterbeer Street where Miss Williams paid the freehold rent of £1 12s 0d; her family had held this land since the early 18th century (DHC 58/9 Box 9 (6, 9); 66/2/13/3a–b; there is a minor discrepancy between the £1 11s 8d payment of 1522 and the £1 12s 0d rent of later years.) This was the property listed by the Charity Commissioners in 1909 as comprising 'several dwellinghouses in the parish of St Pancras' with an annual rent of £2 (RCC 1909, 261). A plan of 1849 (D7/154/3: inserted into Fig. 4.25B) shows that it was the eastern part of the excavated site, which became No. 10 Waterbeer Street; there were then at least four houses on the plot. Thus Wynard may be presumed to have been the owner of the eastern half of the site in the early 15th century.

A summary of the leaseholders and occupiers in the best-documented years is shown in Fig. 4.28.

Documentation relating to the remaining parts of St Pancras parish

Documentary evidence gives some impression of the extent to which the areas of the parish which lay further from the centre of the city, surrounding the excavated site on the north side of Waterbeer Street and in Pancras Lane, were built up in the Middle Ages. By the mid and late 13th century burgage plots occupied parts at least of Pancras Lane (then regularly called St Pancras Street). In 1287 Martin Durling, the former mayor of the city, granted the 4d rent from what had been Walter la Chauve's tenement in Pancras Street to the Dean and Chapter towards the cathedral's building fund (D&C 208; S&J 0590). In 1302 Walter Pauncefoot granted forever to Master John Wele and Master Walter de Stapeldon (later to become bishop) the rent of a pair of white gloves from a tenement in Pancras Street (*in vico S Pancratii*), described as lying between the tenement of Thomas de la Porche to the east and that of Robert Deneys to the west (D&C 543; S&J 0593).

Some later medieval deeds give more specific details about the location of properties on this lane. In 1375 John Hanoyle and his wife Isabel bought the lease of a messuage and garden in Pancras Street (*vicus S Pancratii*), bounded on the south by Waterbeer Street, on the north by the chancel of St Pancras church and what had been Margaret de Kelly's garden, on the west by the lane from Waterbeer Street to St Pancras church and on the east by what was Thomas de Whiteslegh's tenement, now William Gerveys' garden (MCR 48–9 Edw III, m37; S&J 3880). These tenements can therefore be identified as 11 and 12 Waterbeer Street. The fact that Whiteslegh's former tenement was then described as a garden may indicate that it was abandoned after the Black Death.

The location of one further tenement beside Pancras Lane can be identified specifically: in 1451 John and Felice Kirton paid the large fine of £40 to Richard Kelly for a messuage with a garden adjacent to the west end of St Pancras church (MCR 29–30 Hen VI, m52d). The site indicated is shown as Fig. 4.28A; the high sum paid suggests a substantial holding, perhaps much larger than the area marked there.

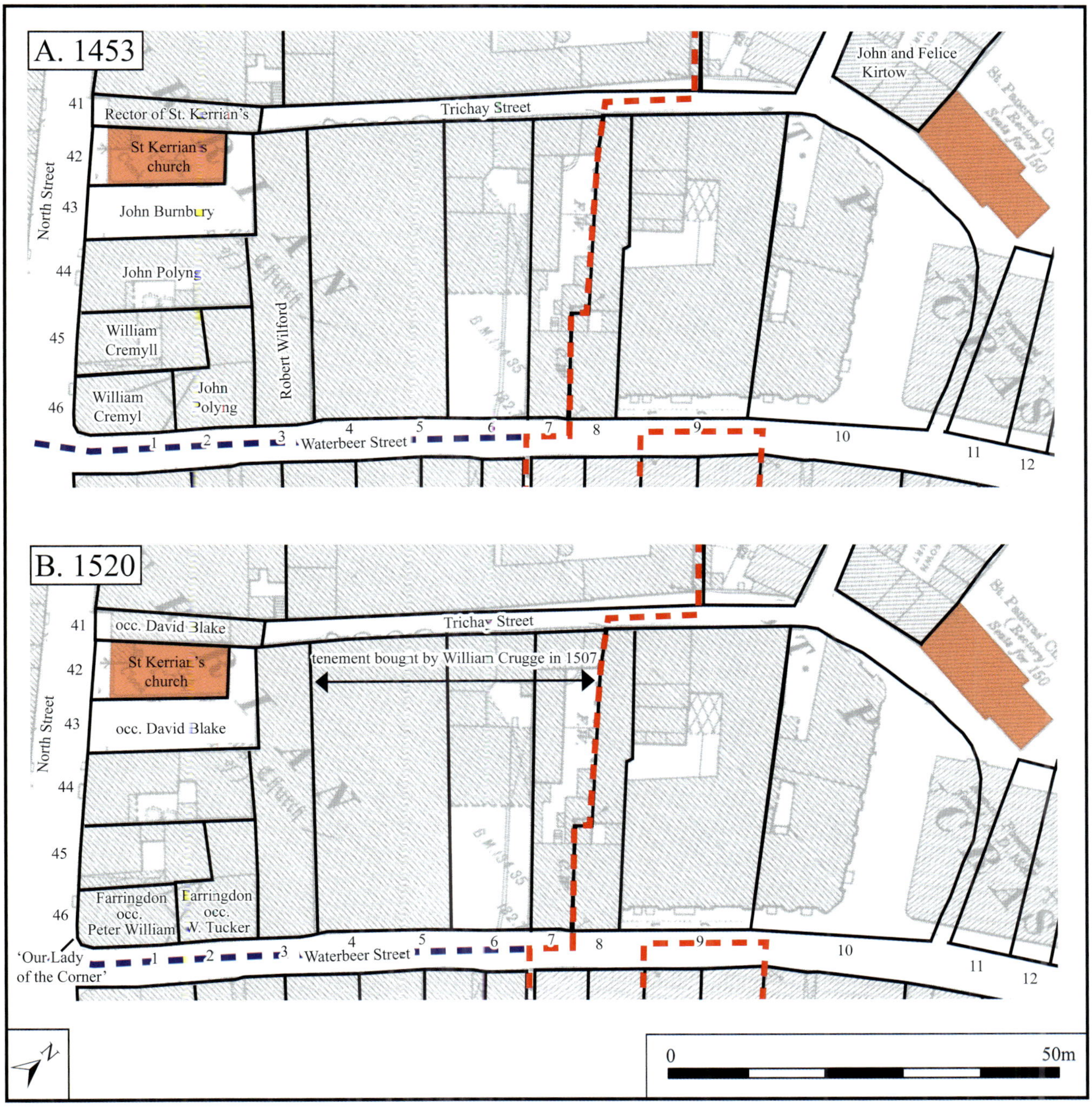

Fig. 4.28 Suggested reconstructions of those in possession of properties in Waterbeer Street and Trichay Street: (A) in 1453; (B) in 1520 (drawn by David Gould)

Acknowledgements

My great debt to the enormous amount of work in transcribing medieval Exeter documents, carried out by my former colleagues in Exeter Archaeology, Paul Staniforth and Jannine Crocker (formerly Juddery), has been described in the Introduction to this section. I am also most grateful to Professor Maryanne Kowaleski for carefully reading and commenting in detail on a draft of this chapter, sharing her unrivalled knowledge of the medieval documentation of Exeter, and making a number of valuable suggestions, greatly to the improvement of the text. My former colleague Tony Collings generously shared his deep knowledge of the post-medieval sources relating to Exeter's properties, gave me access to his transcripts of post-medieval surveys and other documentation, and lent me some of his accumulated files of site plans which I have found invaluable. Dr Todd Gray kindly drew my attention to the Staplehill documents in The National Archives and provided me with photographs of them. I am also grateful to Bill and Hamish Harvey for providing the photogrammetric survey of the High Street house fronts.

Finally, David Gould prepared the successive versions of the Figures with great efficiency and skill.

Notes

1 His figures were apparently taken from the 1877 Book of Reference to the Exeter Plan.

2 Prof. Kowaleski informs me that the Vicars Choral collectors' accounts record John Aisshe living in Richard Oliver's tenement in High Street in 1361, and that on 21 June 1382 he sued John Bridlegh for a broken agreement, but did not pursue the case (PCR).

3 Professor Kowaleski informs me that, although a saddler, John Salter was one of the three highest ratepayers in the city in 1446.

4 The numbering used from at least the 1880s. Following post-war renumbering, they are shown on the OS maps of 1962 and 1968 as Nos 7–9.

5

Excavations at Trichay Street and Pancras Lane, 1972–3

Nicky Garland, John Allan and Neil Holbrook

with a contribution by David Gould

Introduction

Between June and December 1972 a large area excavation was undertaken on a plot of land alongside Trichay Street, followed in March and April 1973 by a narrow trench dug below the surface of Pancras Lane centred at SX 9191 9266 (site code TS; Site 42 (see Chapter 2 above); Fig. 5.1). The site was defined by the street frontages of Waterbeer Street, Pancras Lane and the former Trichay Street. The excavations were undertaken in advance of redevelopment for the Guildhall Shopping Centre, which altered the street pattern in this area, effectively removing Trichay Street and Pancras Lane, and destroyed all archaeological deposits over an area of *c.* 1.7 ha of the Roman and medieval city (Fig. 5.1; Collis 1972 provides the background to the excavation). The site was selected for excavation as the proposals for the shopping centre entailed the complete removal of archaeological deposits from this site. A Roman mosaic had been recorded just 10 m to the north-east of the Pancras Lane trench in the 18th and 19th centuries (Goodchild 1952, 99–100). Immediately prior to the excavation, the site was occupied by a surface car park and was thus unencumbered by standing structures (Fig. 5.24, photo). The excavations were directed by Christopher Henderson, and Michael Griffiths was then the Director of the Archaeological Field Unit. Site supervisors included Stewart Brown, Mary Dale and John Salvatore.

This chapter offers first a summary of the archaeological evidence for the prehistoric and Roman military periods, based on a detailed archive report of this evidence prepared in 1993 (Henderson *et al.* 1993b). It then examines in detail the evidence for occupation of the site from the beginning of the Roman civil period (*c.* AD 75/80) to the mid 16th century. Simplified plans of the structural sequence are presented in Figs 5.2–5.4. Only limited analysis of the post-military stratigraphy had been undertaken prior to the start of this project. Brief annual summaries of the Roman evidence were published (Wilson *et al.* 1973, 313; 1974, 452), and the site figured in two city-wide Roman-period syntheses (Bidwell 1980, 53–4, 69–72; Henderson 1988, 110–18). The detailed report on the prehistoric and Roman military deposits, along with a context register and stratigraphic matrix for the Roman civil period onwards, is available at https://doi.org/10.5284/1035179. The site archive, containing detailed notes and a draft text by Christopher Henderson, provided a partial stratigraphic narrative of the Roman evidence. That account has informed much of the site interpretation presented in this chapter.

In the phase plans features are shown in bold colours, while layers are shown as lighter shades. A number of features discussed below are not illustrated (n.i.), as field drawings were not located in the archive. In this and the following three chapters references to previous volumes in the Exeter Archaeological Reports are, for the purposes of conciseness, abbreviated as follows: EAR1 = Bidwell 1979; EAR 2 = Maltby 1979; EAR 3 = Allan 1984; EAR 4 = Holbrook and Bidwell 1991. The relevant dating evidence is presented for each period after the stratigraphic narrative. This is drawn from the archive listings prepared by a variety of individuals in the 1970s and 80s. For the Roman period the coins were identified by Norman Shiel, the samian ware by Geoffrey Dannell, and the coarse pottery by Paul Bidwell. The principal dating evidence for all significant Roman contexts at sites excavated between 1971–9, along with simplified matrices, was presented in EAR4, MF1, 23–88 and these have been used as the basis for the assessments of the

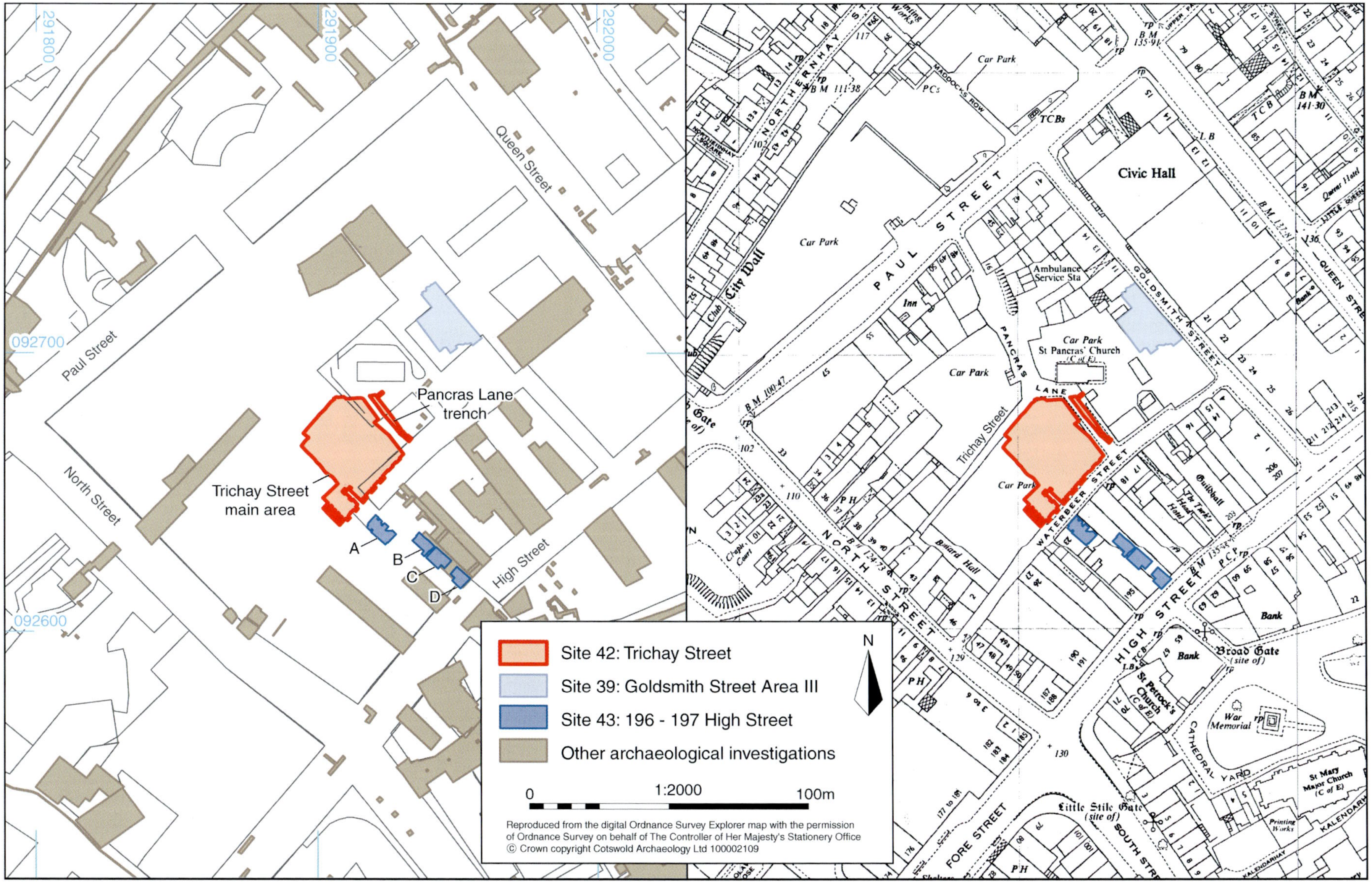

Fig. 5.1 Location of the Trichay Street, Goldsmith Street Area III and 196–7 High Street excavation areas. Left: the site is shown in relation to the present plan of the Guildhall Shopping Centre. Right: in relation to the 1954–68 Ordnance Survey map

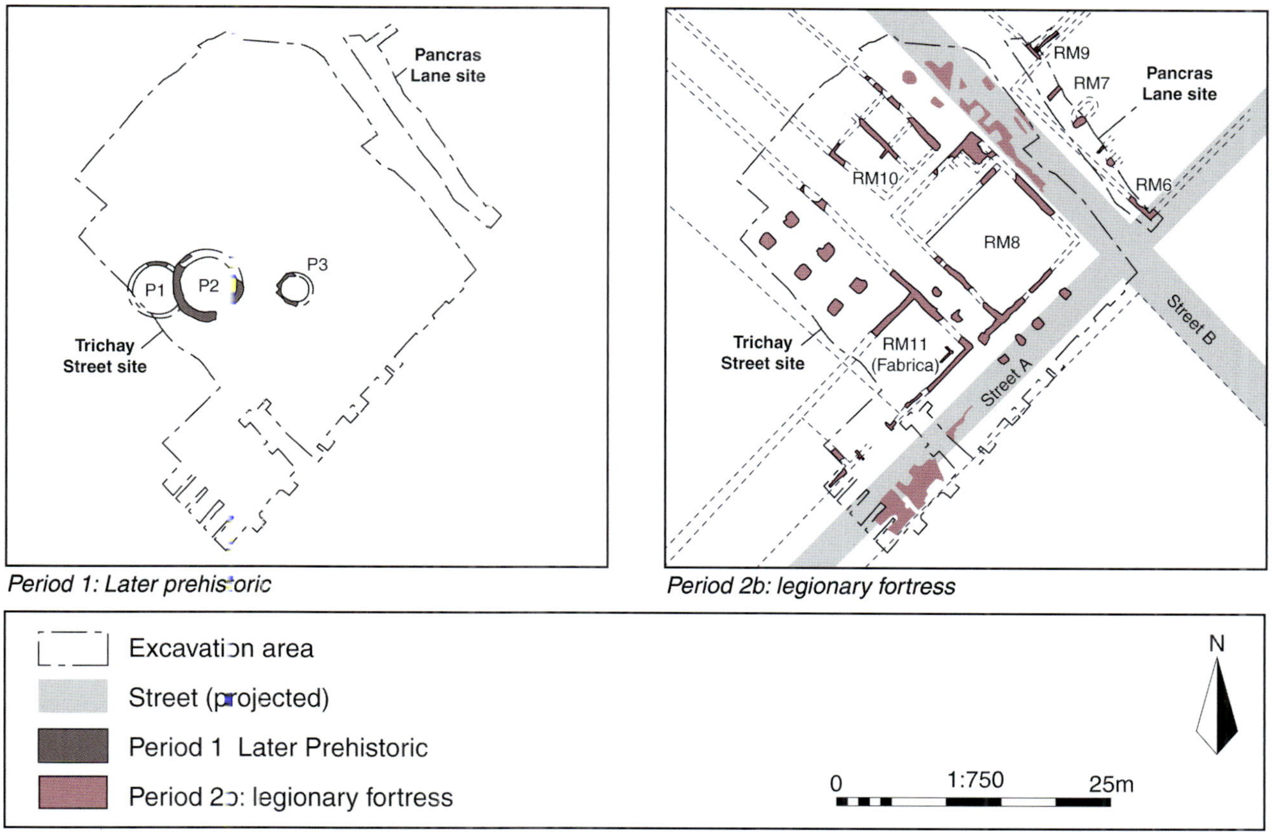

Fig. 5.2 Schematic phase plan showing the development of the site during the later prehistoric and Roman military periods (Periods 1 to 2)

dating evidence. References to coarse ware pottery forms are those presented in EAR4. The medieval pottery was identified by John Allan and the medieval dating evidence sections are derived from context listings prepared by him in the 1970s. No fresh examination of any of the pottery has occurred as part of this project. Where notable finds are mentioned in the site narratives reference is given to their publication in EAR3 or 4 where the objects are fully described and illustrated. The evidence for the four sites described in Chapters 5–8 is presented in the broad chronological periods adopted by the EAPIT project, with site by site period sub-divisions based upon the stratigraphic sequence represented.

The system of numbering adopted for the buildings described in this report in many cases differs from any previous numbering systems used in the site notes and interim accounts. The buildings have the letter prefixes P (prehistoric), RM (Roman military), RC (Roman civil) and Me (medieval). Table 5.1 provides a concordance of the numbering used in this report for Roman streets and buildings with that adopted in the city-wide gazetteers presented in Chapter 3.

It is important at the outset to record that the Trichay Street site was badly damaged by later disturbances. The cellars of a large Victorian warehouse had removed all but the deepest deposits along the Waterbeer Street frontage, and further damage had been caused both by post-medieval walls and service trenches, and by site clearance in the 1960s. Intensive medieval pit digging had removed more than half the remaining Roman deposits, leaving separate discrete upstands of stratification between later disturbances (Figs 5.6 and 5.19). Hardly any structural evidence remained from the medieval and later houses which occupied the site, and in no case was it possible to retrieve the full plan of a Roman building. The fragmented nature of the surviving stratigraphy is a major limiting factor in the interpretation of the site. Nevertheless, skilled excavation did succeed in relating the surviving detached blocks of stratification, and the combination of Roman military building plans, a succession of Roman civil buildings, and Late Saxon and medieval pits rich in artefacts and ecofacts, contributed significantly to understanding of the city.

The geology of this and the neighbouring Guildhall sites reported in the following two chapters is a weathered Permian clay – yellow on the surface, orange below, shading into rich purple at a depth of 2 m or more. This provided impermeable conditions with excellent preservation of organic remains, but also posed challenges to the excavators, particularly in winter.

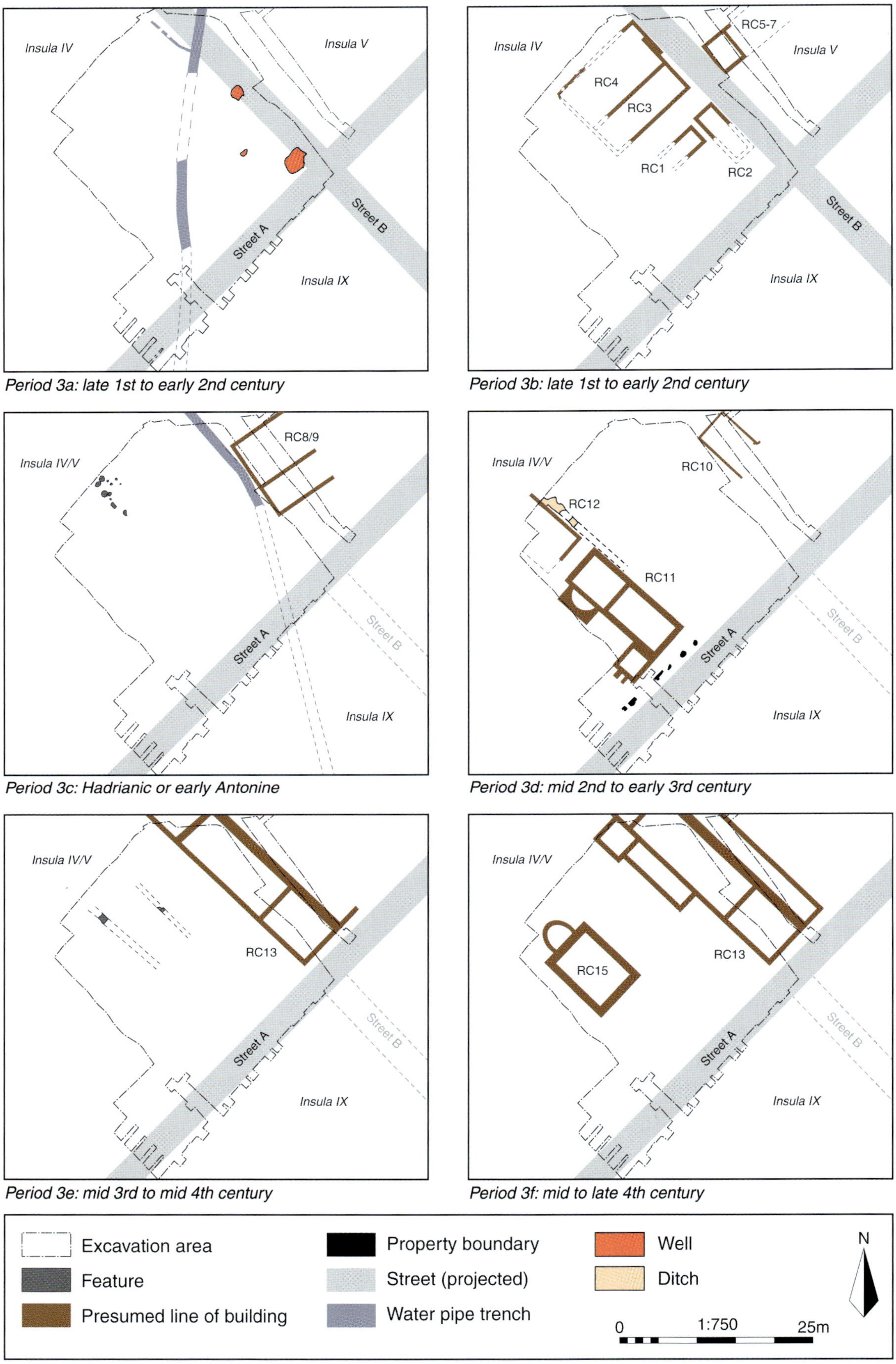

Fig. 5.3 Schematic phase plan showing the development of the site during the Roman civil period (Periods 3a to 3f)

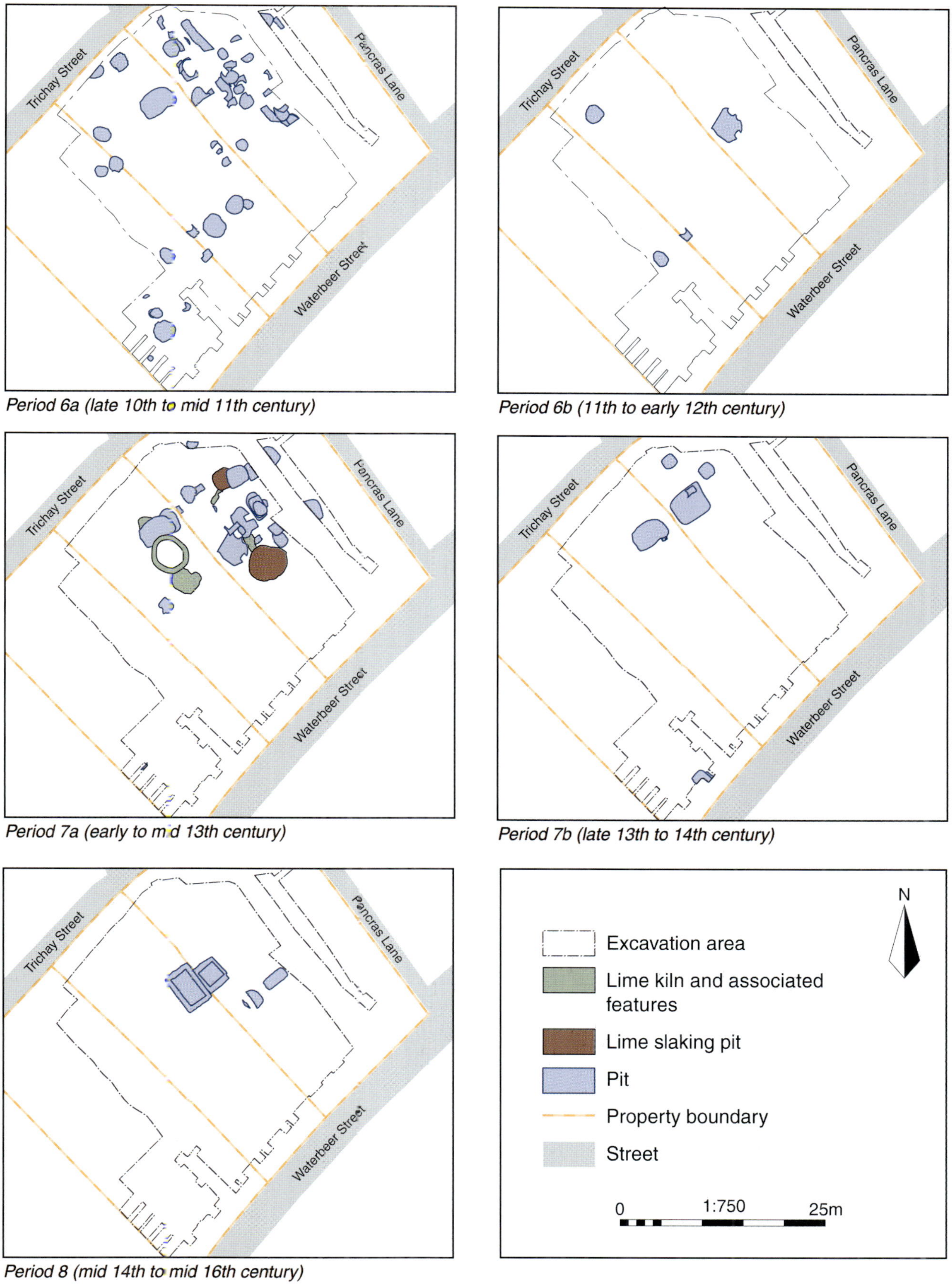

Fig. 5.4 Schematic phase plan showing the development of the site during the medieval periods (Periods 6a to 8)

Table 5.1 Concordance of the numbering of Roman streets and buildings used in this chapter with those used in the city-wide gazetteers in Chapter 3

This report	*Gazetteers (Chapter 3)*
Street A	Town Street C
Street B	Town Street F
RM10	Barrack C6
RM11	*fabrica*
RC1	7i
RC2	6i
RC3	5i
RC4	3i
RC5	8i
RC6	8i
RC7	8i
RC8	8i
RC9	8i
RC10	13ii
RC11	11ii
RC12	9ii
RC13	14ii
RC14	12ii
RC15	10ii

Period 1: Later prehistoric settlement?

Later prehistoric occupation is represented by three ring ditches which preceded the Roman military structures (P1–3). They defined three buildings of varying diameters, cut into the underlying natural clay (Fig. 5.5). Later Prehistoric Building 1 (P1) measured *c.* 4 m in diameter and seems to predate P2, the largest of the three structures *c.* 6 m in diameter. Alternatively Quinnell (2017, 15) suggests that P1 may have been an adjunct or annexe to P2. P3 was *c.* 3 m in diameter (Fig. 5.2). No postholes or stakeholes were identified within the post-trenches of these buildings or within them, but P3 enclosed a spread of soil containing charcoal and burnt bone which may represent its floor (Henderson *et al.* 1993b, 1–2). These features appear to be too small and have fills inappropriate for Bronze Age ring ditches and are more likely to have been structures. The sole dating evidence was a single sherd of a Roman military flagon recovered from the lowest fill of the ring ditch defining P2, which may or may not be intrusive. Quinnell (2017) suggests that P1–3 might have been houses of people working on the construction of the legionary fortress and we can note that 1st-century AD roundhouses are known from London (Hingley 2018, 40, 65–6). While

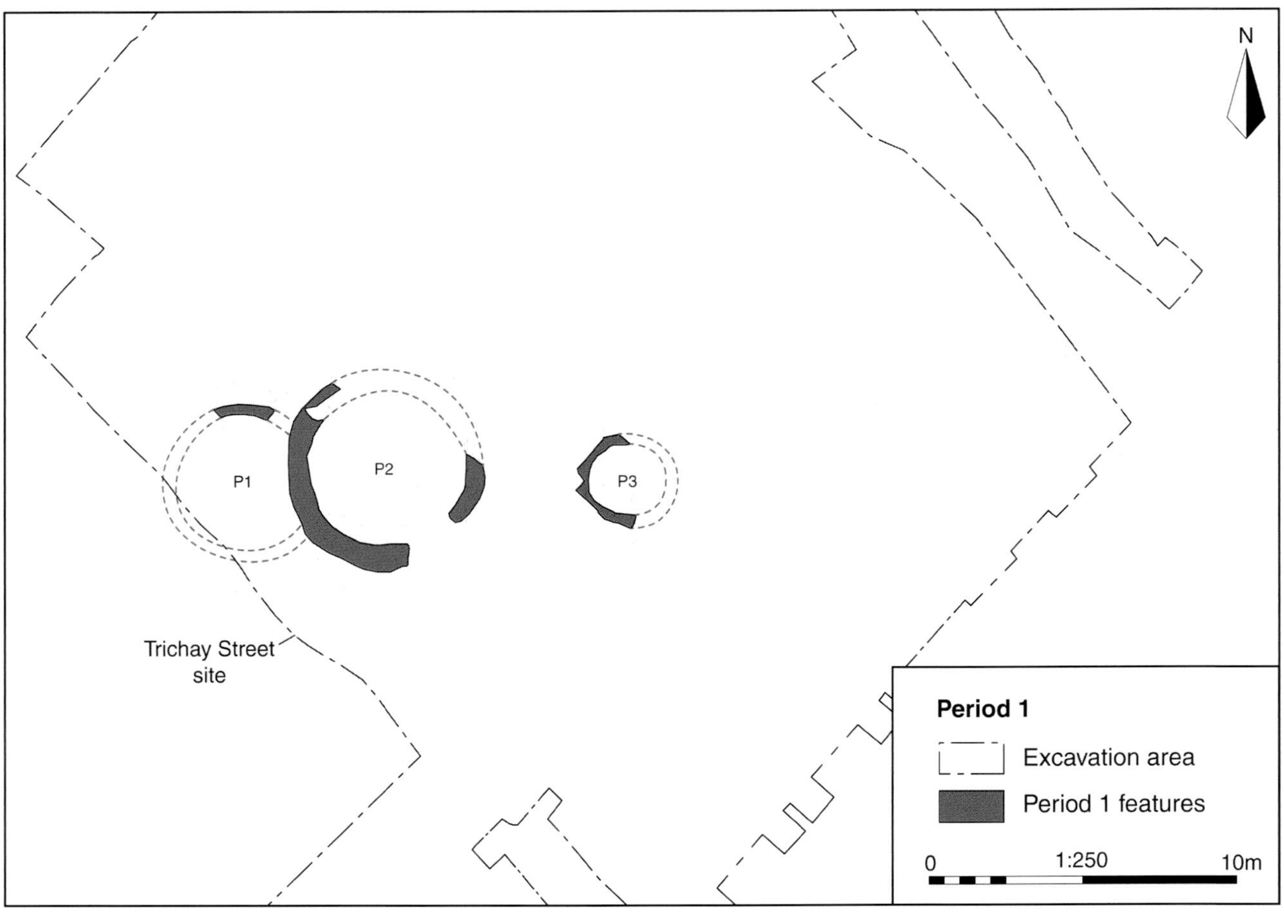

Fig. 5.5 Plan of Period 1 (later prehistoric) structures

Fig. 5.6 The aisled hall of the military fabrica *(Period 2b, RM11) looking south-east, with later prehistoric buildings P1 and P2 in the background. The photograph illustrates the damage sustained to the Roman structures from medieval and later activities. The bases of a number of circular and rectangular medieval pits are apparent. 2 m scale (© RAMM)*

this interpretation is possible, the houses could alternatively significantly predate the Roman conquest – with the single sherd being intrusive – and instead be part of the low intensity Iron Age occupation of the future site of Exeter evidenced by a scatter of features and finds in other parts of the city (Quinnell 2017).

Period 2: The Roman legionary fortress (*c.* AD 50/55–75/80)

The excavation site lay on the right (*i.e.* south-west facing) side of the *retentura* of the legionary fortress (see Chapter 3.1). It occupied a large plot defined by metalled streets, those on the south-east and north-east sides being revealed in the excavation (Figs 5.2 and 5.7, Streets A and B).

Two distinct phases of Roman military occupation were identified (Henderson *et al.* 1993b). The earlier phase (Period 2a) saw the construction of two military buildings (RM4 and 5), a barrack block (RM10; = Chapter 3.1, barrack C6) and a further building (RM8) which may have housed a senior officer. The later phase of activity (Period 2b) included modification to RM8 and 10, which then formed a barrack block composed of a detached officer's residence (RM8) and *contuburnia* (RM10), and the construction of a workshop (*fabrica*) (RM11). The *fabrica* was probably of courtyard plan, although only part of one aisled hall lay within the excavation area, along with a fragment of another room in the very south-west corner of the site (Bidwell 1980, 31–5; Fig. 5.7). That room was separated from the range containing the aisled hall by a *c.* 6 m wide entranceway containing slots for door jambs. The entry was probably covered, as it had a clay floor rather than metalling.

Evidence for smithing and the presence of copper-alloy offcuts from this building indicate that this part of the *fabrica* was used to repair legionary armour (Henderson *et al.* 1993b, 3; EAR4, figs 108–9, nos. 1–24). In the later phase, three further timber buildings were laid out at Pancras Lane (RM6, 7 and 9). Only limited evidence was recovered, but their position in the fortress plan suggests that they were barracks which were not part of a cohort block, but perhaps instead accommodation for *immunes*. A system of gullies and culverts served to drain the areas between the military buildings, and late in the period of military occupation water pipes laid in trenches were introduced to supply clean water to various parts of the fortress. The military buildings were overlaid by thick dumps of mixed clays and loams, doubtless derived from the demolition of the clay walls of the timber-framed buildings. The absence of such deposits overlying Streets A and B suggests that they continued in use following the foundation of the Roman town.

Period 3: The Roman town

Introduction

The Early Roman town was established within the defences of the former legionary fortress. Most of the fortress streets were retained and these served to form the *insulae* of the new town (Chapter 3.2). Street A as defined in this report equates with Street C of the overall town plan as defined in Chapter 3.2; Street B equates with town Street F. The Trichay Street site lay within *insula* IV and Pancras Lane *insula* V. The earliest post-military activity at Trichay Street was represented by several wells (Period 3a), followed by a water-pipe trench forming part of an aqueduct leading into the town from the north (Frere *et al.* 1983, 322–3; Henderson 1988, 113–15).

This feature was succeeded by several timber buildings (Period 3b) in *insulae* IV and V. The destruction of these buildings by fire and the amalgamation of *insulae* IV and V through the removal of Street B (Period 3c) led to the division of this area into two building plots by the late 2nd to mid 3rd century AD. Several timber buildings were constructed within these two plots (Period 3d), followed in the mid 3rd to early 4th century AD by a stone house (Period 3e). Subsequent alteration of buildings in these plots saw the creation of a probable stockyard in the mid to late 4th century AD (Period 3f). By the 5th century AD, this part of the Roman town appears to have been abandoned (Period 3g).

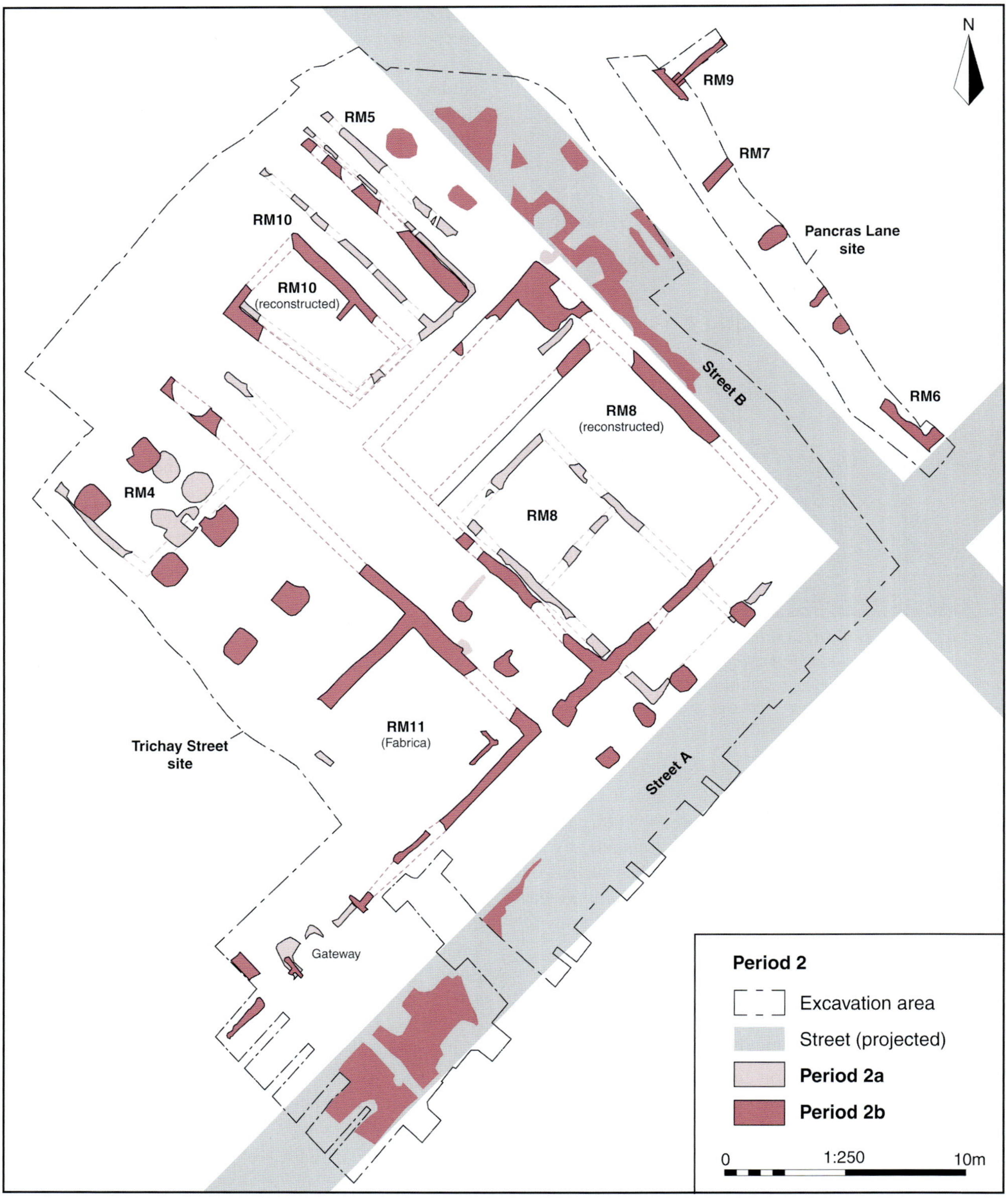

Fig. 5.7 Plan of Period 2: Roman military buildings within the legionary fortress

Period 3a: The earliest civilian activity (late 1st to early 2nd century AD)

Only small areas of Streets A and B survived above the legionary levels. In the Trichay Street excavation, almost all the later surfaces of Street A had been destroyed by cellars, but a small column of stratification survived in the Pancras Lane trench, and its continuation to the north-east was well preserved at Queen Street (Bidwell 1980, 47–9). It was clear that the street continued in use into the Late Roman town, being resurfaced at intervals into the 3rd and 4th centuries. It appears that both streets were retained from the legionary fortress. There was no evidence for side ditches alongside them.

Three wells were dug, two of them (3 and 348) beside the edge of Street B which was retained from the fortress (Fig. 5.8). The largest (3) measured approximately 3.1 m in diameter, more than 3.6 m deep and was probably timber-lined. It was dug close to the corner of Streets A and B, a location that was never developed for buildings in the fortress period (it was just outside the corner of the military *fabrica*). The backfill of the well produced a highly unusual artefact assemblage including a Purbeck marble torso of an eagle, 23 samian vessels, several complete or near-complete pottery vessels, a ceramic lamp, a

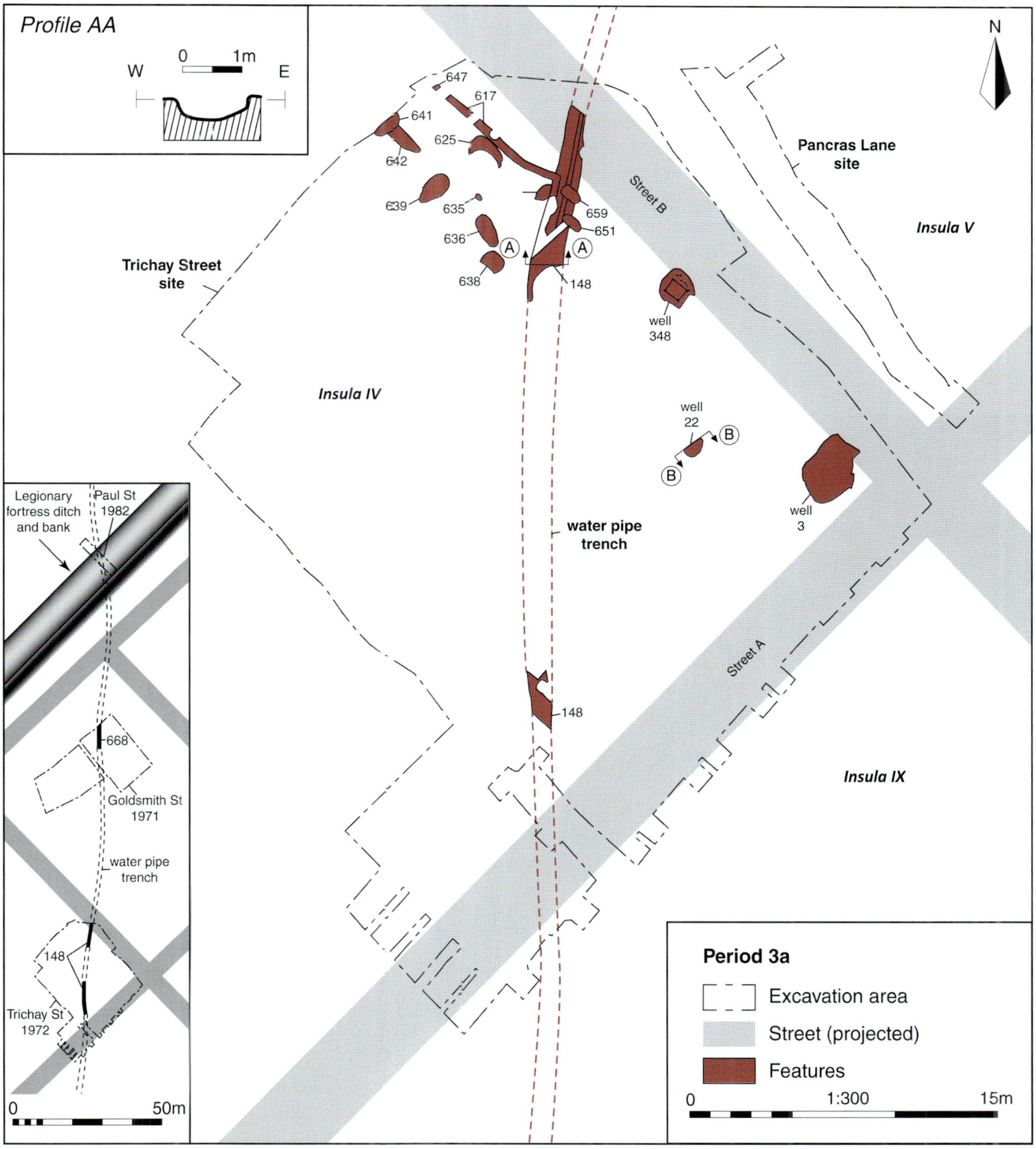

Fig. 5.8 Plan of Period 3a (late 1st to early 2nd century AD) activity, with inset profile of the aqueduct channel and its postulated course (after Henderson 1988, fig. 5.14)

bone hilt guard from a sword, an incomplete bone latch key and an iron spearhead (the finds are listed in detail in the dating evidence section below), as well as an animal bone assemblage of 105 NISP (number of identified specimens). The unusual character of the assemblage and its position within a body of water suggest that it was a votive closure deposit, placed once the well had fallen out of use. The date and context of the well are worthy of some consideration. Samian from the lowest three layers is not necessarily later than the military period, and the samian bowls that date after *c*. AD 80 came from the upper fills. It is possible therefore that the well originated in the fortress period, but was perhaps dug very late in the period of military occupation after barrack RMB8 had been demolished, and even perhaps after the aqueduct that supplied the bath-house had ceased to function. Certainly it is necessary to explain how the eagle fragment came to be placed in the well. If, as J. Toynbee suggested, it came from a major sculptural group representing Jupiter, the only plausible context for it would be in the *aedes* of the *principia* where it would have been the focus of the official rites of the legion (EAR1, 130–2). Such an important piece would hardly be broken up, leaving fragments scattered around for a decade or so. It seems much more likely that the fragments would be distributed in appropriate places, watery or otherwise, when the *principia* was demolished. Indeed it is possible that the upper fills might have been deposited at a slightly later date after the primary fills had compacted, in which case the lower fills might date to the time when the fortress was finally abandoned, and the upper fills to a decade or so later.

Well 348 was located 10 m to the north-west of well 3. It was 3 m deep, square in plan and timber-lined using riven oak boards secured to uprights at the edge of the well cut (Fig. 5.9). A third well (22), located to the west of well 3, was 1.05 m in diameter and appears to have had no timber lining (Fig. 5.10). The position of well 348 in between a number of Period 3b timber buildings that fronted onto Street B could suggest that it continued in use until the end of the 1st century AD (Fig. 5.11) when a new aqueduct was established (Henderson 1988, 115). This aqueduct fed a wooden water pipe laid within a trench (148) which traversed the excavation site on a broadly north/south alignment. The trench was 1.1–1.5 m wide, 0.35 m deep, had a broadly concave profile, and was traced over a length of *c*. 30 m. The upcast from

Fig. 5.9 Period 3a timber-lined well 348 looking north-west. 2 m scale (© RAMM)

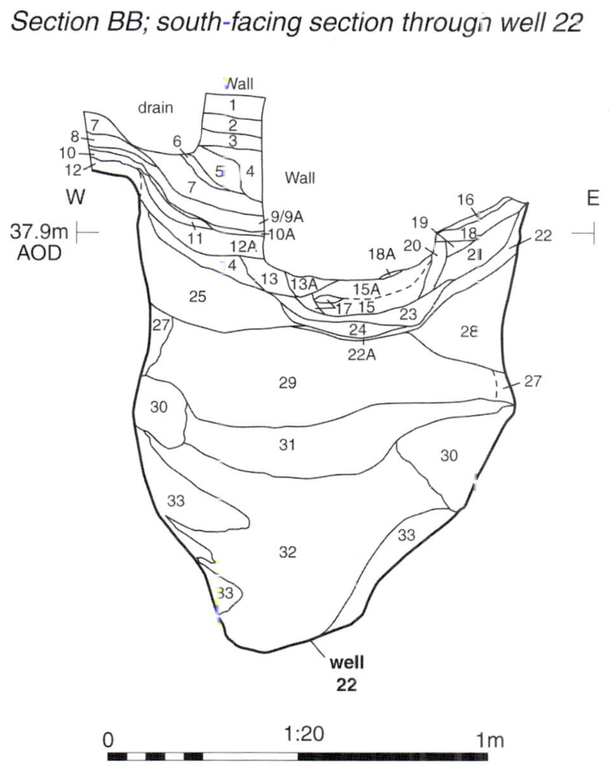

Fig. 5.10 Section BB, south-facing section across well 22 (scale 1:20)

the excavation of the trench (111, n.i.), found beside it, yielded a burnt bone knife handle (EAR4, fig. 122, no. 3) and other finds. The profile of the trench and the presence of a dumped deposit beside it (rather than backfilled into the cut) suggested to Henderson (pers. comm.) that in its initial stages this feature was an open leat, and this interpretation seemed to be supported by the fine silt which filled the trench bottom (Henderson 1988, 115; Fig. 5.8, profile AA). Part of a heavily corroded iron pipe collar was uncovered in the centre of the trench, suggesting that a wooden pipe was subsequently laid in the leat and the cut infilled. The width of the trench suggests that the pipe was laid on wooden sleepers laid at intervals across the width of the trench, as was shown at the fortress baths where the trenches were *c.* 0.8 m wide and the pipes encased in waterproof clay. The clay packing served both to protect the pipe from external damage and the effects of internal pressure (EAR1, 35–6). Only a single iron collar was found as the water pipe and other junction collars had later been robbed out. A branch from the main pipe trench (617) ran north-west to south-east for *c.* 8 m; it may have fed a structure such as a tank or fountain beyond the limits of the excavation area.

In the northern part of the site, the water pipe trench was dug through the military-period metalling of Street B, continuing beyond the limit of excavation. Further north, a feature of broadly similar date and appearance, and on the same alignment (GS 668), was excavated in Goldsmith Street Area I/II. This in turn aligned with two parallel rows of wooden posts found still further to the north in the partially infilled outer defensive ditch when excavations were conducted at Paul Street in 1982–5. The posts were interpreted as the remains of a small wooden bridge supporting a launder carrying an aqueduct into the Early Roman town (Henderson 1988, 113–15). Four of the bridge timbers at Paul Street were dated by dendrochronology and shown to have been felled in the winter of AD 100/101 (Hillam 1984a; Henderson 1988, 115); the digging of the leat at Trichay Street is interpreted as part of the same episode (EAPIT1, Chapter 6).

At the southern edge of the site, the cellars beside Waterbeer Street had removed all evidence of the trench where it crossed the line of Street A. Similarly, the cellar on the opposite side of Waterbeer Street at 196–7 High Street, which was on the projected course of the aqueduct, had removed all deposits of this date on the south-eastern side of the street (Chapter 7).

In the northern part of the site, ten pits were dug to the west of the water pipe trench. They were broadly sub-circular in shape and measured *c.* 0.3–1.8 m in diameter and 0.1–0.2 m deep. Their function is unknown; perhaps small-scale clay extraction? No dating evidence was recovered from their fills but they were all overlain by layer 577 (n.i.), a dump of mixed brown clays, *c.* 0.2 m deep, that also overlay the backfilled water pipe trench (148), but preceded the construction of the timber buildings of Period 3b. It was rich in artefacts including pottery, two coins, a ceramic lamp (EAR4, fig. 21, no. 8), glass fragments (including EAR4, fig. 94, no. 24) and a penannular brooch (EAR4, fig. 03, no. 35). This deposit does not appear to have overlain the three wells, and so it is possible that 348 and 22 were retained in use.

Dating evidence

- Well 3. Given the unusual, and potentially votive nature of the finds assemblage from this well, the finds are listed in detail here. The total weight of pottery from the well was 7.465 kg (minimum number of vessels = 84), including 23 samian vessels as follows:
  - Samian (all SG): Ritt. 1 (x 1), Claudian; Dr. 15/17 (x 1), pre-Flavian; Dr. 18 (x 6), x 1 Claudian, x 2 pre-Flavian, x 1 stamp 82, AD 65–90, x 1 Nero-Vespasian, x 1 1st century AD; Dr. 24/5 (x 1) Claudian; Dr. 29 (x 7), x 1 Claudian, x 1 AD 65–80 (EAR4, fig. 13, no. 49), x 1 probably pre-Flavian, x 1 pre-Flavian, x 1 AD 50–65 (EAR4, fig. 13, no. 51), x 1 AD 65–80 (EAR4, fig. 13, no. 50), x 1 AD 70–85; Dr. 37 (x 7), x 1 AD 70–85 (EAR4, fig. 13, no. 48), x 1 AD 75–90 (EAR4, fig. 13, no. 46), x 2 Flavian, x 1 AD 75–90 (EAR4, fig. 13. No. 47), x 2 AD 80–100.
  - The well also contained some near-complete coarse ware vessels, including a cooking pot (EAR4, fig. 38,

no. 20.1c) and carinated bowl (EAR4, fig. 64, no. 28.1). Coarse ware vessels include a South-Western BB1 flat-rimmed bowl type 52.1 and an Exeter Micaceous Grey Ware bowl (EAR4, fig. 64, type 28.1). Other finds comprised a fragment of a ceramic lamp (EAR4, 76); the Purbeck marble torso of an eagle (EAR1, 130–32; Henig 1993, 83–4, pl. 61, no. 3); an iron spearhead (EAR4, fig. 120, no. 2); a bone hilt-guard from a sword (EAR4, fig. 122, no. 1) and an incomplete bone latch key (EAR4, fig. 124, no. 24).

- Well 22. Samian: Dr. 18, Flavian?
- Well 348. Samian: Dr. 37, Flavian.
- Dump 111. Samian: Dr. 37, AD 85–100. Coarse wares: mostly residual from the military period.
- Robbed water pipe trench 148. Samian: Dr. 30, Hadrianic-Antonine.
- Dump 577 overlying pits. Coin 4, Augustus (copy), AD 43–50; coin 36, Claudius (copy), AD 43–64; Samian: pre-Flavian (x4), stamp 96, AD 45–60; Ceramic lamp *c.* AD 40–80 (EAR4, fig. 21, no. 8). Coarse wares: some contamination with later material.

The Period 3a features date to the late 1st or earlier 2nd century AD. While the large pottery group from Well 3 indicates a final infilling in the late 1st century AD, the water pipe trench is presumed to date to AD 100/101, the dendrochronological date from the timber bridge over the outer defensive ditch at Paul Street. This section of the water supply system was short-lived, however, and the wooden pipe and its iron collars were robbed in the Hadrianic or early Antonine period to judge from the pottery from the backfill of trench 148, and the dating evidence for the subsequent timber buildings RC3 and 4 which were constructed over its course.

Period 3b: Early Roman buildings RC1–7 (late 1st to early 2nd century AD)

Four modest timber buildings were constructed along the two sides of Street B in the late 1st or early 2nd century AD (Fig. 5.11). Two of them (RC3–4) overlay the line of the water pipe trench; the other two (RC1–2) were laid out to the south-east. All overlay the refuse layer 577. A further timber building lay on the north-eastern side of the street, which underwent three phases of construction/reconstruction within this period (RC5, 6, 7). Since the entire area was cut by many medieval pits, the plans of all these buildings are very fragmentary and their functions uncertain.

Building RC1

RC1 consisted of three trenches (523; 524; 580) defining three sides of a building 2.3 m wide and more than 6 m long. The trenches were narrow (0.3 m wide) and shallow (*c.* 0.1 m deep), with flat bottoms; their construction technique was completely different from the deep post-trenches of the military buildings. The excavators considered that they had held sill beams resting in the base of the trenches, which may have supported wattle and daub walls, possibly set between timber uprights. This interpretation is supported by the presence of large quantities of daub in fire debris following the destruction of this structure (Period 3c). A posthole (519), probably forming a structural support, lay on the north-western edge of trench 523. An internal floor surface consisting of a pale brown sandy clay (522) was laid between the trenches and extended to the south-east. This suggests that trench 580 may have been an internal wall and that the building extended to the south-east, although not by any great distance if it stopped short of Period 3a well 22.

Building RC2

Building RC2 lay immediately to the north-east of RC1. This too was heavily disturbed; its fragmentary remains consisted of two trenches (532; 534) representing its south-west and north-east walls, defining a structure 2.5 m wide with its long axis parallel to the frontage of Street B. Its length is unknown but cannot have exceeded 8.5 m, as it presumably stopped short of well 3. The wall-trenches were 0.2–0.35 m wide and 0.2 m deep, with U-shaped profiles, and were described in the site notes as beam slots (shallow trenches in which horizontal timbers would have been laid to support timber-framed walling). Slot 532 was backfilled with daub, suggesting that the walls were clad with this material, as suggested for RC1. The building had a thin layer of yellow clay floor (533). A single posthole (520) may have represented an internal structural feature. A small grey ware beaker (576; EAR4, fig. 63, type 5.1) – which contained a single 1st-century AD coin and an enamelled copper-alloy military strap end (EAR4, fig. 111, no. 48) – was buried underneath the floor. This pot was presumably a foundation deposit; no associated human remains were recovered. A thin gravel surface (535) was laid to the north-east and north-west of the building. A narrow alleyway between RC1 and RC2, 0.9 m wide, was surfaced with compacted gravel (531). Three 1st-century AD coins were recovered from the surface of the gravel (EAR4, coin nos. 25, 59, 62).

Buildings RC3 and 4

RC3 and RC4 lay to the north-west of RC2 and were laid end-on to the frontage of Street B. RC3 was defined by two trenches at right angles (589; 591), both *c.* 0.3 m wide, 0.15 m deep and flat-bottomed. They probably held horizontal timber beams onto which vertical posts were fastened. The building was more than 5.8 m long and at least 5 m wide; it had a thin clay floor (588, n.i.). It is unlikely that the building was much wider than this, as well 348 lay just beyond its eastern corner in an open area between RC2 and RC3.

RC4 was defined by a single flat-bottomed trench or beam slot 0.32 m wide, 0.16 m deep (509), with a posthole (624). Again the slot likely held a horizontal beam in

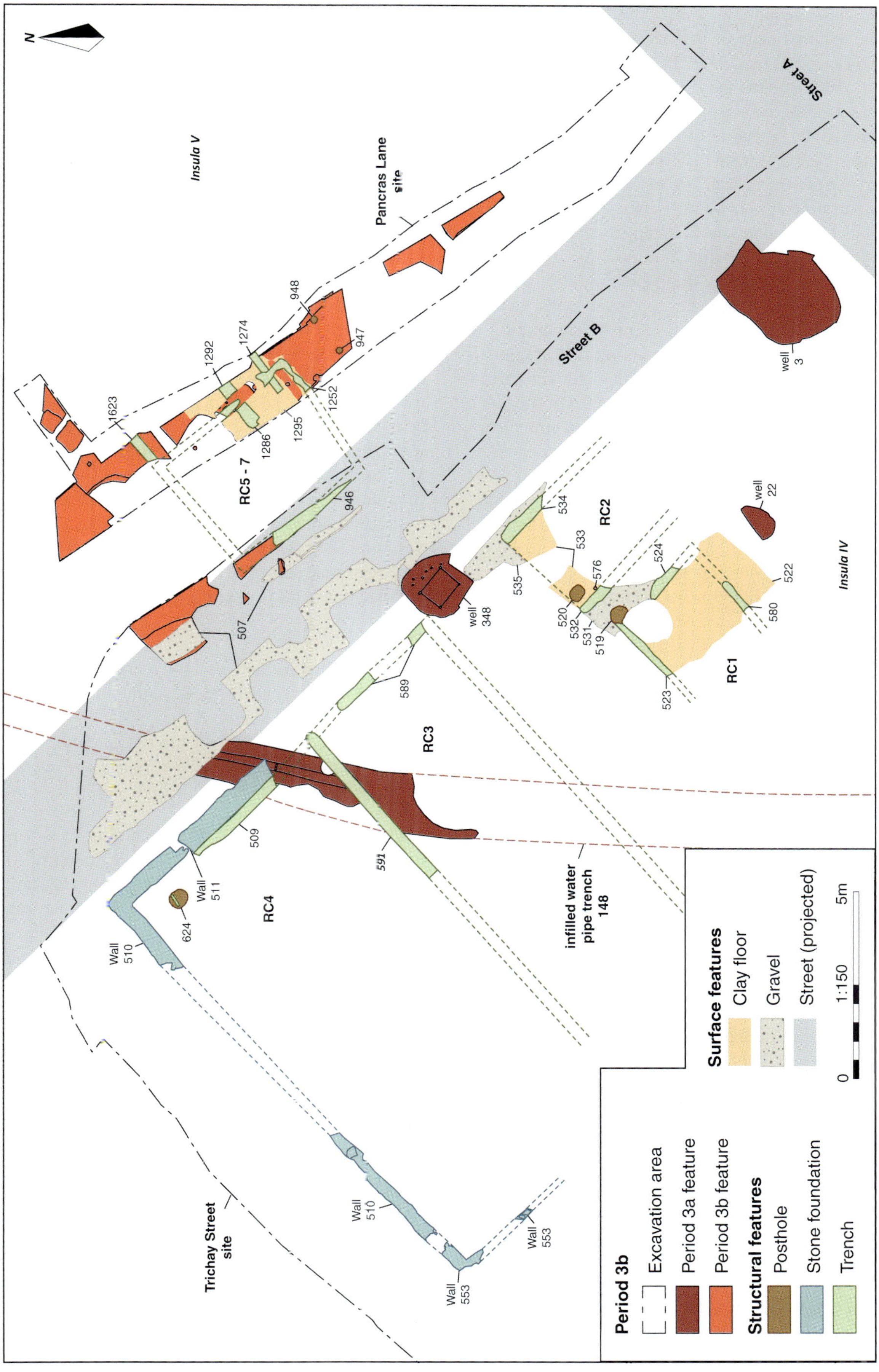

Fig. 5.11 Plan of Period 3b (late 1st to early 2nd century AD) buildings RC1–7

a similar construction style to RC3. White plaster, noted along the external edge of the trench, may represent the remains of external rendering. The posthole was 0.5 m in diameter and contained stone packing, which may show that it was used as a roof support. A compact gravel surface (507) flanked the frontages of RC3 and RC4 and overlay the military-period surface of Street B (578); it may have been part of a general resurfacing, perhaps after the removal of the water pipe in trench (148) at the end of Period 3a.

A small wall foundation (511) ran alongside the gravel surface (507) for 2.2 m before turning to the south-west. Although surviving only as fragmentary sections, due to later disturbance, the foundation appears to have extended to the south-west for a further 15 m before turning to the south-east (510; 553). The surviving wall fragments defined a structure 13 m long and 6.5 m wide. The narrow dry-stone foundation of volcanic trap was 0.5 m wide, and possibly formed the base for a timber-framed structure. A thin layer of white wall-plaster (552, n.i.) was present to the north-west of the wall and probably originated from its north-western (external) face. This plaster seems to have been an external render, as there is no indication that wall 510 was an internal partition, and was deposited during the demolition of RC4 in Period 3c. Wall foundation 511 lay parallel to post-trench 509 of RC4 but it was set 0.25 m to the north-east. Although medieval pits had removed the stratigraphic relationship between slot 509 and foundation 511, it is possible that the wall represents part of a later building, constructed to replace RC4. No evidence for the south-east wall was found.

Buildings RC5–7

Excavations at Pancras Lane, to the north-east of Street B, revealed small parts of three successive timber buildings. The earliest (RC5) was marked by a short length of trench (1292), 0.4 m wide, 0.08 m deep, in which a timber beam would have been laid. A thin layer of yellow clay daub (1291, n.i.), possibly some manner of wall finish, was noted against its south-eastern edge. Trench 1292 was abutted on both sides by a thin yellow clay floor (1295), indicating that it was an internal partition within RC5. Two other structural features were recorded: a stakehole (1294, n.i.), 0.2 m in diameter, and a postpit (1300, n.i.), 0.5 m in diameter. This building quickly fell out of use and was demolished.

A dump of yellow clay (1289), 0.08 m deep, overlay the demolished remains of RC5 and provided a base for the second phase of building (RC6). RC6 consisted of a trench (1274) and the foundation of a small partition wall (1286), laid parallel to one another about 2 m apart. The trench, 0.4 m wide and 0.15 m deep, is interpreted as a beam slot for a horizontal timber resting on the ground. The partition wall, 0.35 m wide, consisted of a layer of tile which may have formed the seating for upright posts. The difference between these construction techniques may indicate that the building's external and internal partition walls were built in different stages. A gravel floor surface (1273) and six stakeholes (1279–84, n.i.), each 0.05 m in diameter and forming no discernible pattern, were uncovered within the room bounded by the walls. A line of postholes (1275–8, n.i.) to the south-west of the structure, each *c.* 0.1 m in diameter and 0.35 m deep, may have marked a property boundary between RC6 and the street.

There was no evidence for the demolition of RC6, suggesting that it had been dismantled prior to the construction of the final phase of building (RC7). This was defined by a trench (946) marking the south-western wall, an L-shaped trench (1252) forming the eastern corner, and a trench (1623) defining the north-western wall. The trenches were 0.15 m wide and 0.1 m deep, and 1252 contained a number of postholes (*e.g.* 1250, 1251, n.i.), which indicate post-in-trench construction. These features defined a rectangular structure at least 6 m long and 4.5 m wide; the position of trench 1623 suggests that the building may have extended to the north-east. The interior was covered with a clay floor (945, n.i.) which was punctuated by a number of stakeholes and postholes. Two further postholes (947, 948), 0.15 m in diameter and 0.25 m deep, may represent part of a fence line along one side of the building, marking an external passage leading to Street B.

Dating evidence

- Gravel surface between RC1 and 2, 531. Coin 25, Claudius (copy), AD 43–64; coin 59, Nero, AD 64–8; coin 62, Nero, AD 64–8.
- Foundation deposit within RC2, 576. Complete Micaceous Grey Ware beaker type 5.1. Pot contained coin 34, Claudius (copy), AD 43–64.

There is little useful dating evidence from this period. RC1 and 2 could date from the late 1st century AD and thus be contemporary with the Period 3a wells. Buildings RC3 and 4 overlay the line of the water pipe trench. If it is assumed that private buildings would not have been permitted to be built above the line of a crucial piece of civic infrastructure, it follows that the water pipe would have been out of use before RC3 and 4 were constructed. In that case the two buildings are provided with a *terminus post quem* by the samian bowl of Hadrianic or Antonine date recovered from the backfilling of the water pipe trench after the pipe itself had been removed. The dating evidence for the Period 3c destruction of these timber buildings suggests that this event occurred in the Hadrianic or early Antonine period, so RC3 and 4 seem likely to have been relatively short-lived structures.

Period 3c: Destruction by fire and construction of buildings RC8 and 9 (Hadrianic or early Antonine)

In the Hadrianic or early Antonine period (*c.* AD 120–60) RC1–7 were destroyed by fire, marked by a thick layer of burnt daub and charcoal overlying the remains of these structures (*e.g.* 515, 939, n.i.) and Street B (930/932). A copper-alloy harness fitting (EAR4, fig. 112, no. 65) and a ceramic tazza (EAR4, fig. 75. no. 30) were among the finds recovered from the burnt deposits. The presence of this destruction deposit over the line of Street B indicates that the fire led to the abandonment of the street and consequently the amalgamation of *insulae* IV and V. Henceforth this new *insula* will be termed *insula* IV/V.

Buildings RC8 and 9

Following the fire, two sequential buildings were constructed on the Pancras Lane site over RC7 (Fig. 5.12). The first one (RC8) was defined by two trenches (935, 1604), each 0.4 m wide and 0.15 m deep, forming the south-western and north-western walls of a building more than 5.5 m long and 4.5 m wide. These trenches probably held horizontal timber beams. A hearth (907) was found in the building, suggesting domestic use. A water pipe trench (933) was dug immediately to the south-west of the building. The trench was 1.3 m wide and 0.47 m deep and had a broadly concave profile. The trench cut through the fire debris (930) and the surface of Street B. No traces of a wooden pipe or iron collars were uncovered during the excavation of the trench, however the excavators interpreted it as a water pipe trench due to its similar size and profile to the Period 2a water pipe trench 148. Once again, the width of the trench would be commensurate with the pipe laid on transverse sleepers placed at intervals. Although occupation deposits (903, n.i.) were uncovered within RC8, there was no evidence for demolition debris suggesting either that the building may have been carefully dismantled or that the later structure formed an addition to the earlier building.

Building RC9 consisted of two clay-filled foundation trenches (793, 928) laid at right angles. Trench 928, 0.38 m wide and 0.08 m deep, cut the backfilled water pipe trench 933. Trench 793 was 0.2 m wide, filled with a brown gritty clay and cut the earlier floor (792) of RC8. It is probable that both trenches supported the bases of wattle and daub walls that could have been structural additions to RC8, extending the building to the north-west and dividing it into several rooms. A hearth (773, n.i.) and several clay floors (792, 926) were present within the structure. A deposit of fragmented wall-plaster, 0.02 m thick, was associated with the demolition of RC9.

Another possible structure, represented by nine postholes and two associated postpits, was found 11 m to the west of RC8/9. No discernible pattern was observed but three postpits (557; 558; 675) to the north-west of the main group may indicate that the building required large structural supports, perhaps to support a heavy roof.

Dating evidence

- Burnt deposit over RC 3 and 4, 504. Samian: Dr. 37, AD 90–115; Dr. 33, mid 2nd century AD; Dr. 18/31 (x2) Hadrianic.
- Burnt deposit over RC 1 and 2, 515. Central France mortarium (Type TC10, Fabric FC7), *c.* AD 50–85 (EAR 4, fig. 79).
- Burnt deposit over road surface, 930. Samian: Dr. 36, Hadrianic.
- Water pipe trench 933. Samian: Dr. 67, Antonine; Dr. 37, *c.* AD 100–20 (EAR4, fig. 14, no. 63).

The evidence from Periods 3b and 3c suggests that the fire occurred in the Hadrianic or early Antonine period. The South-Western BB1 flat-rimmed dishes type 76 and 83.1 from deposit 504 support the 2nd-century AD dating provided by the samian.

Period 3d: Construction of buildings RC10–12 (mid 2nd to early 3rd century AD)

By the mid to late 2nd century AD, if not indeed in Period 3c, the site had been divided into two building plots separated by boundary ditch 571 in the south-west part of the Trichay Street site. In the north-eastern plot RC10 was built over the demolished remains of RC9, while two timber buildings (RC11–12) were erected in the south-western plot (Fig. 5.13).

Building RC10

On the Pancras Lane site, RC10 was constructed over several successive clay layers (924; 925), laid as levelling deposits over demolished building RC9. It consisted of two parallel trenches (758; 780/785) defining a structure 4 m wide and more than 6 m long. The trenches were each 0.3–0.4 m wide and 0.18–0.22 m deep. The burnt remains of a timber were recovered from trench 758, demonstrating that a horizontal beam was placed within each trench; vertical posts would no doubt have risen from it. A single posthole with packing stones (781), 0.4 m in diameter, may have been a roof support or internal fixture. Within the building there was a layer of brown gritty clay occupation debris (788), 0.12 m deep, and an external cobbled surface (759/923) to the south-west of it. Given the fragmentary preservation of this structure the features are not illustrated.

Building RC11

RC11 was constructed on shallow stone foundations (454; 455; 458), that defined three sides a building in excess of *c.* 7 m long and *c.* 5.6 m wide (Fig 5.13). The foundations were each 0.6 m wide and 0.4 m deep and consisted of trap-stone rubble bonded with clay and mortar. The full extent of these foundations did not survive, as the stone had been robbed from large parts of the wall-trench. It is probable that they supported a timber superstructure. A clay daub partition wall (457), 0.39 m wide, separated two rooms. Room 1 was floored with brick mortar (*opus signinum*) (459) laid on a rubble base. Room 2 had been almost entirely destroyed by later activities. A well (803) to the north-east of the

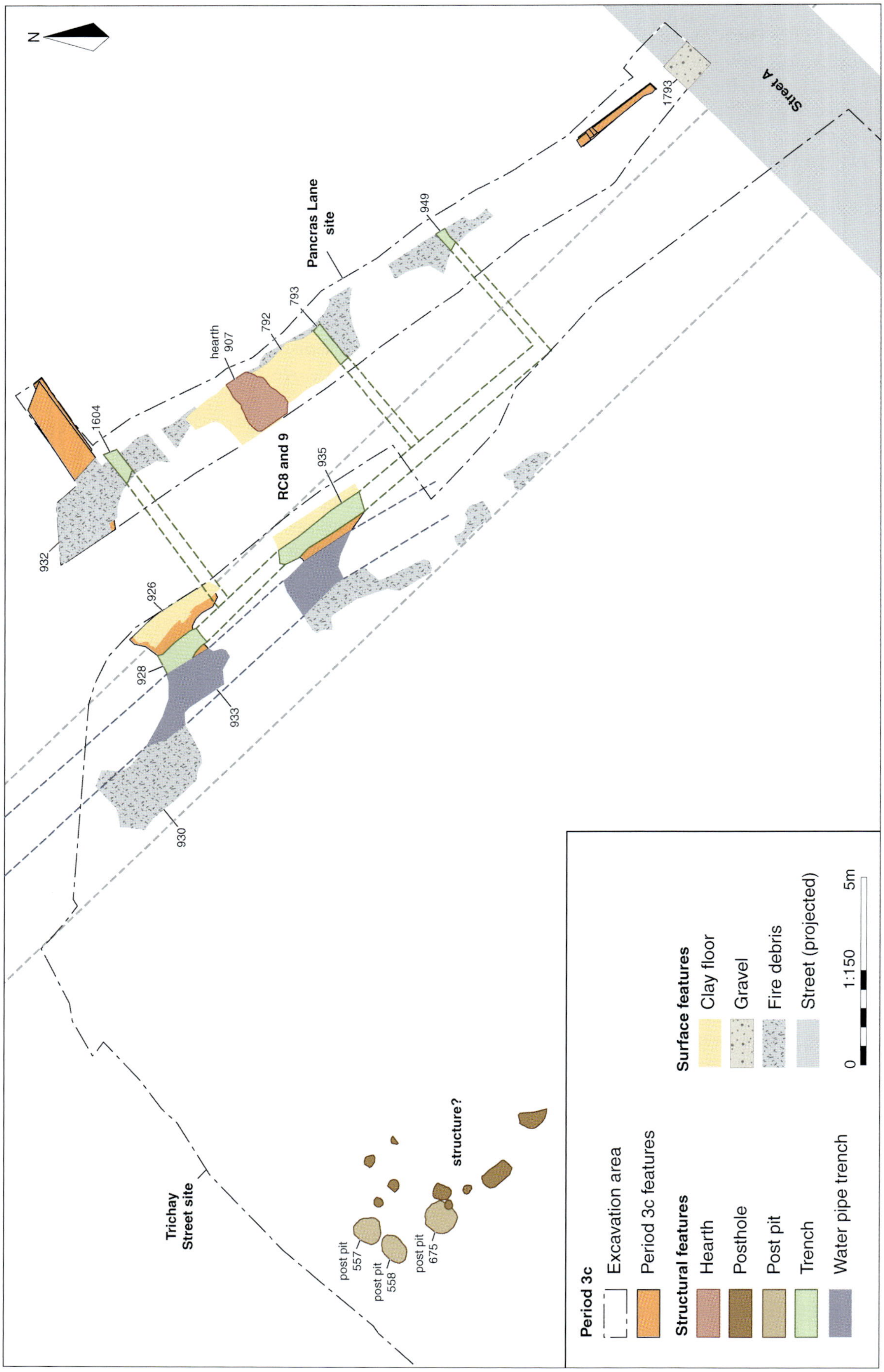

Fig. 5.12 Plan of Period 3c (Hadrianic or early Antonine) buildings RC8–9 and possible structure

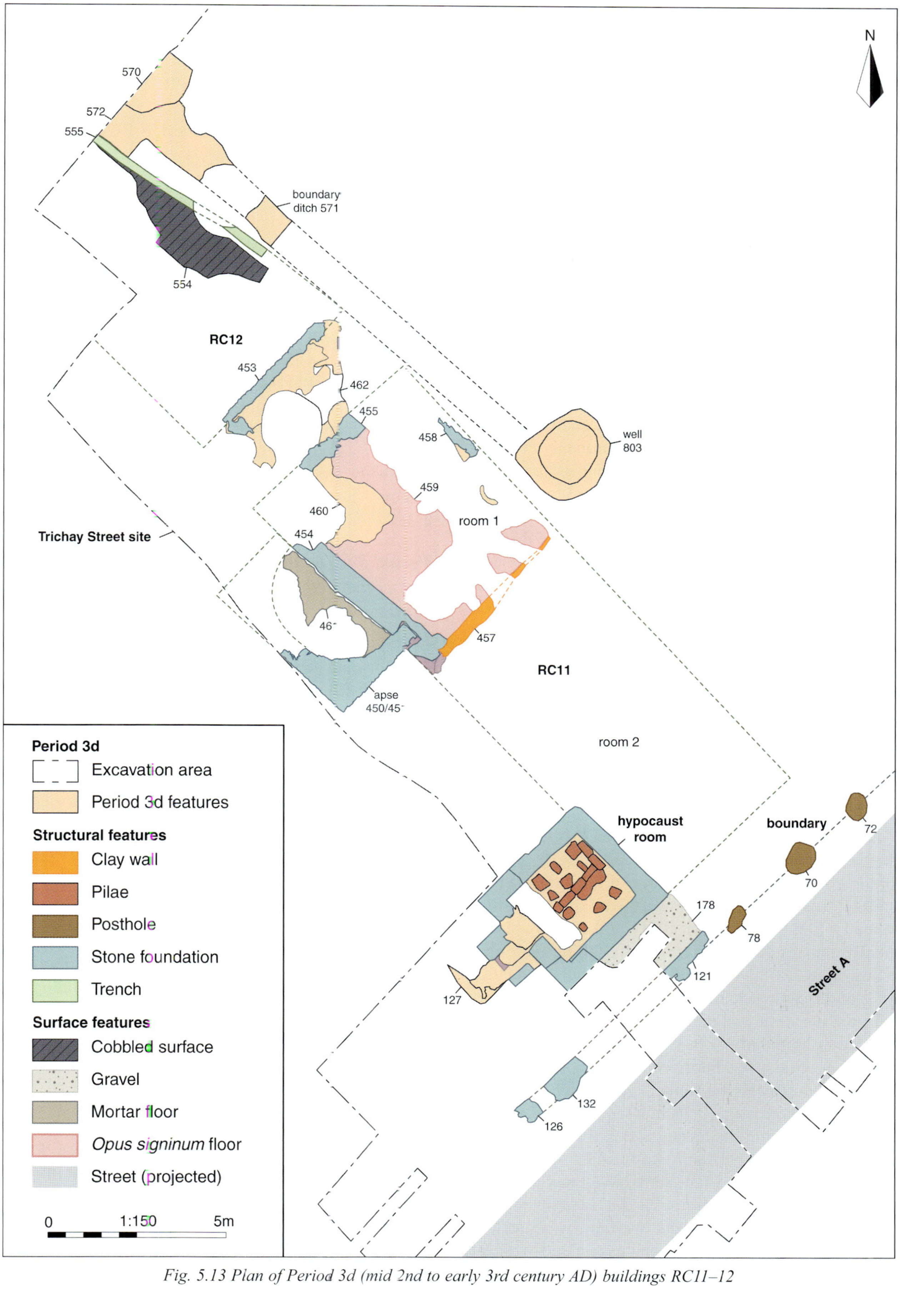

Fig. 5.13 Plan of Period 3d (mid 2nd to early 3rd century AD) buildings RC11–12

building was 1.7 m in diameter and more than 2 m deep. It may have been timber lined, given the presence of wood fragments recovered from its fills. The well was positioned along the line of boundary ditch 571 but the stratigraphic relationship between these features had been removed.

Several structural additions were subsequently made to RC11. A masonry apse (450; 451) measuring more than 2.5 m long and 2.3 m wide was added to the south-western side of Room 1; the apse foundation was cut into the foundation of the rear wall of the building. The apse had a mortar floor (461) 0.1 m thick. The apse probably represents an embellishment of RC11 by the addition of reception room (cf. Perring 2002, 35). Another room *c.* 4 m square, furnished with a hypocaust and with an associated drain (127), was also added to the south-western side of Room 2. An external stoke-hole was present on the south-western side. Ceramic tiles formed the bases of nine *pilae* in the room, with a continuous line of tiles down the centre of the room probably covering a stone-lined drain (127) which led out of the south-west side of the room and perhaps served to drain the hypocaust basement. A compound wall (121; 126; 132) and a post-built fence (70; 72; 78) lay a short distance to the south-east of RC11, providing a boundary separating the building from the frontage of Street A. The area between the hypocaust room and this boundary was surfaced with a layer of gravel (178).

Building RC12

RC12 lay 2.3 m to the north-west of RC11 and shared the same alignment. The building was flanked by boundary ditch 571 to the north-east, but one of its walls and trench 555 cut across the return of the ditch (572), which was also partly sealed by an internal surface. This indicates that this section of ditch had fallen out of use prior to the construction of RC12. It is possible that the north-west/south-east portion of the ditch (571) continued in use to define the edge of the building plot, unless it was an earlier (Period 3c) land division which defined a plot within which RC11 and 12 were subsequently constructed, the ditch finally falling out of use at this point. RC12 was defined by a wall foundation (453) and trench (555), representing the south-eastern and north-eastern walls, indicating a building more than 5.2 m long and 4.1 m wide. Wall foundation 453 was 0.4 m wide and comprised of mortar-bonded trap fragments, onto which a timber frame may have been placed. Trench 555 was 0.25 m wide and 0.16 m deep and contained burnt daub, suggesting that it held a sill beam for a wattle and daub wall. RC12 was floored with cobbles (554) and thus may have been a barn or storehouse rather than a house. An exterior surface between RC11 and RC12 was overlain by a patch of mortar (462) that may have been associated with the construction of these buildings.

Dating evidence

- Boundary ditch 571. Samian: Dr. 33, late 1st to 2nd century AD.
- Occupation layer 788 within RC10. Samian: Dr. 33, Antonine.
- Posthole 189 of fence bordering RC11. Coin 104, Commodus, AD 183–4, very worn.
- Cobble layer 923 outside RC10. Samian: Dr. 33, Antonine.
- Levelling deposit 924. Samian: Dr. 33, Antonine; South-East Dorset BB1 flat-grooved rim bowl type 43.
- Levelling deposit 925. Samian: Dr. 37, Antonine.

There is no useful evidence for the construction date of RC11 and 12. If the coin of Commodus from one of the postholes of the fence bordering RC11 is associated with the construction of the fence (perhaps it was a deliberate placement?) that then provides a strict *terminus post quem* of AD 183 for the boundary, although given the very worn state of this coin deposition before the 3rd century AD is unlikely. Construction within the mid 2nd to early 3rd century AD is indicated, with occupation continuing until at least the mid 3rd, if not well into the 4th, century AD.

Period 3e: Demolition of Buildings RC11 and 12, and construction of RC13 (mid 3rd to mid 4th century AD)

Demolition of RC11–12

At some date between the mid 3rd and early 4th century AD the buildings in the south-western plot were demolished, leaving layers of clay, mortar and plaster (*e.g.* 128; 440, n.i.) across the interior of RC11 and 12. A new ditch (539) re-established the property boundary formerly represented by ditch 571. Ditch 539 was dug *c.* 2 m to the north-east of the line of the original boundary and was not infilled until the late 4th century AD (Fig 5.14). Two postholes (559, 560) suggested the presence of a post-built fence line marking the edge of the building plot.

Building RC13

In the late 3rd century AD at earliest, and indeed perhaps not until the mid 4th century AD, a large stone-built house was constructed in the north-western building plot, flanking Street A (Fig. 5.14). Only fragmentary sections of its substantial stone foundations survived; other lengths had been robbed or destroyed in the medieval period. A reconstruction of the building suggests that it consisted of at least six rooms and was more than *c.* 30 m long and *c.* 15 m wide, and extended beyond the limits of the excavation area to the north-east and north-west. Several phases of construction were apparent. The first one consisted of a row of rooms, of which Rooms 1–3 lay within the excavation area. The wall foundations (253; 752) were 0.8–1.2 m wide and constructed of clay-bonded trap fragments. A course of large stone slabs, bonded

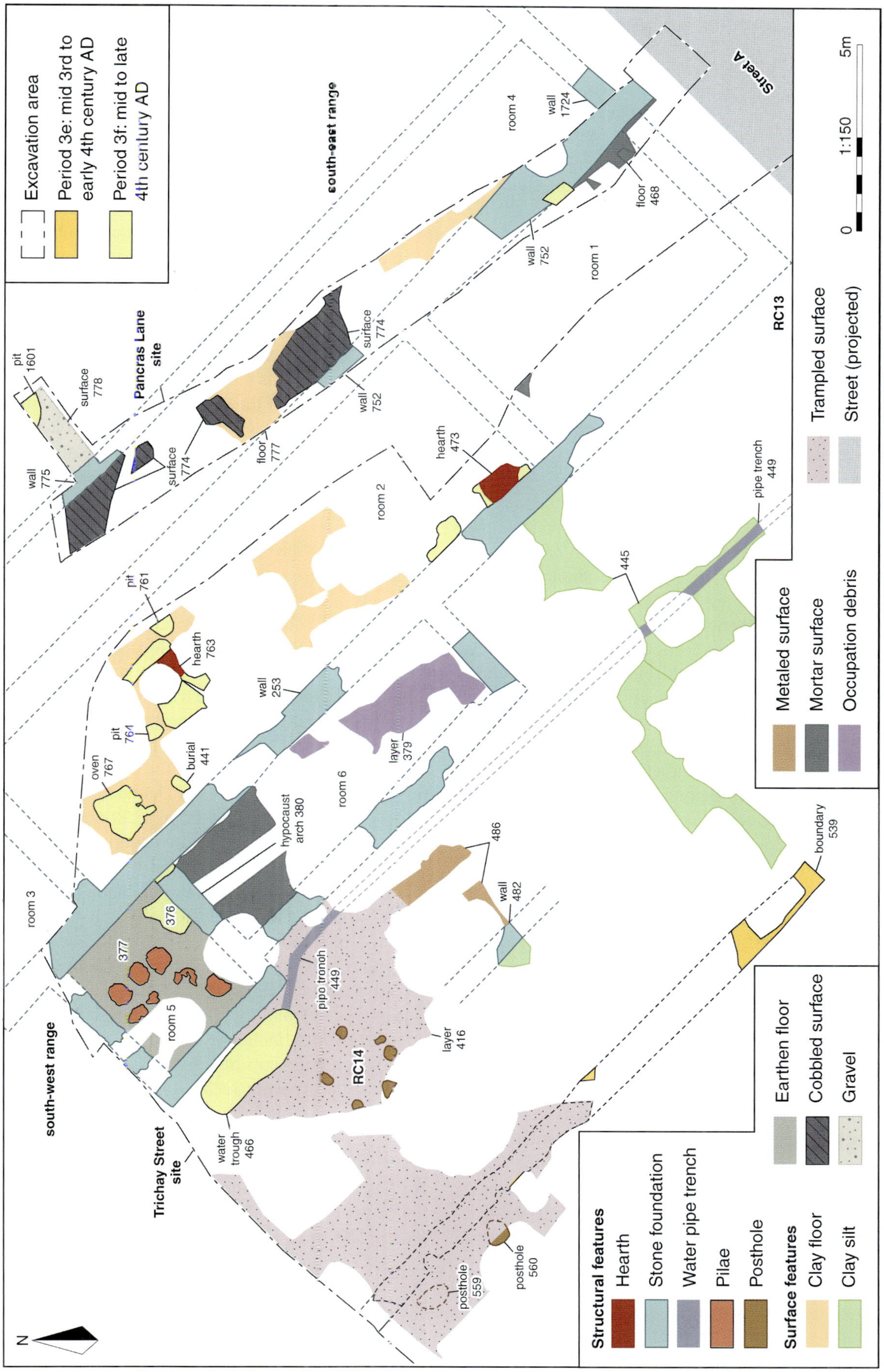

Fig. 5.14 Plan of Period 3e (mid 3rd to late 4th century AD) buildings RC13–14 and Period 3f yard

with white mortar, survived in the wall defining Room 1. The width and depth of the foundations indicates a stone superstructure rather than merely stone cill walls, possibly of more than one storey. Although much of the surviving evidence had been removed by later activities, a thin patch of mortar flooring (468) survived in Room 1. In Room 2 a child burial (441) had been placed beneath the floor. Although the bones have not been subjected to osteological examination, its 0.6 m length suggests it was probably a neonate and therefore reflects a wider tradition of these burials being placed in the service areas of town houses and villas as foundation deposits (Scott 1991). Room 2 was floored with a thin layer of clay, into which were cut an oven (767), two hearths (473; 763) and two small pits (761; 764). Remnants of occupation debris (*e.g.* 472, n.i.) were found on the floor. No surviving features or floor surfaces were present in Room 3, most of which lay to the north-west of the excavated area. To the north-east of the building, a layer of mortared river cobbles formed an external surface (774).

A possible second phase of construction saw the addition of a veranda or corridor, approximately 2.3 m wide, to the north-eastern face of the building (Room 4). A narrow wall foundation (775) *c.* 0.6 m wide and of a similar style of construction to that defining Rooms 1–3, was constructed parallel to the pre-existing north-eastern wall of the building (752). There is no evidence for the relationship between wall 775 and the remainder of the building, but following its construction, the external surface of river cobbles in this area (774) was overlaid by a thin (0.05 m thick) sandy clay floor (777). The south-eastern end of the corridor was defined by wall 1724. The construction of the wall and the laying of the floor surface suggest that this area was repurposed as an internal rather than external part of the building. Wall 752 projected south-eastwards beyond the point where it was abutted by 1724; either this latter section of walling was demolished when the corridor was constructed, or else there was another small room (porch?) occupying the space between the south-east end of the corridor and the street frontage. There was an external gravel surface (778) and a possible refuse pit (1601) to the north-east of wall 775.

Four fragments of mosaic pavement have been recorded in the past adjacent to Pancras Lane (Goodchild 1952, 99–100; Fig. 5.17). William Stukeley documented 'a great Roman pavement of little white square stones' in the 18th century and in 1887 two fragments of a probable white tessellated pavement were uncovered on either side of Pancras Lane, possibly representing part of the same pavement. A further fragment of a patterned geometric corridor mosaic was uncovered north-east of Pancras Lane in 1887 (EAPIT 1, Chapter 6, Fig. 6.16; Cosh and Neal 2005, mosaic 157.1). Bidwell (1980, 69) argued that the position of these fragments of mosaic a short distance to the north-east of the excavation area suggests that they formed floors within a different range of the same building. Excavations at Goldsmith Street may have revealed the north-eastern and north-western perimeter walls of the same building, which would thus have been of courtyard plan with the mosaics in the south-eastern range.

At some point during the life of RC13, perhaps at the same time as the addition of the front corridor, two rooms (5 and 6), 3.8 long by 3.3 m wide and 9.5 m long by 3.7 m wide respectively, were added to the rear of the south-west range. The walls were 0.65 m wide, founded on several layers of unmortared rubble footings, and survived as several courses of volcanic trap bonded by a hard gravel-rich white mortar. The masonry was laid in a herringbone fashion, in contrast to the regular horizontal courses found in the walls of Rooms 1–3. The similarity in the construction techniques of Rooms 5 and 6 suggests that they belong to a single phase of construction. The butt end of the south-east wall of Room 5 was separated from the robber trench of the primary wall 253 of Room 2 by a tapering baulk of fill which demonstrates that Room 5 was a structural addition. The walls of 5 and 6 also truncated layers that had accumulated against the south-west wall of Rooms 2 and 3 after their construction.

Room 5 was equipped with a hypocaust and parts of seven *pilae* survived *in situ*. The *pilae* were 0.65 m wide at the base, tapering to 0.4 m wide at the top, and survived to a height of 0.8 m. They were constructed of mortared river cobbles and were laid on an earthen floor (377) (Fig. 5.15). Room 6 was long and narrow and lay to the south-east of Room 5. The remains of a hypocaust arch, 0.6 m wide, pierced the wall dividing the two rooms. A post-medieval wall had truncated part of this arch, but the gap in the wall indicates that heat passed between the rooms (although no evidence for a hypocaust survived in Room 6). A layer of mixed charcoal and brown earth (376) overlay the earthen floor in Room 5 around the arch and presumably represents material associated with the general firing of the hypocaust. This would suggest that the stoke-hole lay in Room 6, although no evidence for it survived there. Indeed, as Room 6 possessed a mortar floor surface (380), it is conceivable that the hypocaust was an addition and that Room 6 originally served a different function. The mortar floor in Room 6 was overlaid by multiple layers of fine grey silty material up to 0.1 m thick, including a band of fine wood ash (379), from which fragments of a Purbeck marble bowl (EAR4. fig. 133, no. 4) were recovered. Fragments of slate in these deposits indicate the nature of the roofing of RC13.

Associated structure/boundary wall?

A small fragment of stone walling (482), 1.1 m long and 0.6 m wide, lay parallel and 3.5 m to the south-west of RC13. The wall was of similar construction to those of Rooms 5 and 6. A metalled surface (486) was laid in the area between wall 483 and RC13. This yielded an iron T-clamp, probably used to fix box tiles to a wall (EAR4, fig. 121, no. 16). Wall 482 perhaps defined the boundary of the land plot containing the house.

Fig. 5.15 General view of the heavily robbed remains of the Late Roman town house RC13 during the course of excavation, looking south-east. The extent of later disturbance is apparent. Room 5, with surviving remnants of hypocaust pilae, *lies in the foreground. 2 m scales (© RAMM)*

Dating evidence

Demolition of RC11

- Demolition layer 128. South-East Dorset BB1 cooking-pot with obtuse-angled lattice decoration (no earlier than *c.* AD 220).

Primary Construction of RC13

- Wall 253, from near the top of wall. Coin 335, *Constantinopolis* (copy), AD 330–40, very worn.

RC13 Secondary Construction

- Corridor wall 1724. Coin 108, Julia Domna, AD 196–211, well circulated.
- Earthen floor 337 in Room 5. Coin 175, Tetricus I, AD 270–3; Oxfordshire Ware bowl with flange with white paint.

Occupation

- Occupation debris 472 in Room 2. Coin 291, Constantine I, AD 330–5, very worn; coin 338, Constantine I, AD 335–7, very worn.
- Occupation debris 389 in Room 5. *Céraminque à l'éponge,* Raimbault (1973) form VI.

External Features

- Boundary ditch 539. New Forest beaker; North African amphora; South-East Dorset BB1 flanged bowl (type 45).
- Metalled surface 486. Coin 288, Constantius II, AD 324–30, virtually uncirculated.

The crucial piece of dating evidence is provided by the coin of AD 330–40 recovered from wall 253. The coin is recorded as coming from near the top of the wall, and hence some doubt must attach to its provenance. Construction of RC13 in the 4th, rather than the mid 3rd, century AD gains some support from two Constantinian coins found in an occupation deposit within Room 2, while the piece of Oxfordshire Ware from the floor of Room 5 probably dates no earlier than the start of the 4th century AD (when the ware first seems to have reached the Exeter region; EAR4, 81).

Period 3f: Construction of a yard and Buildings RC14 and 15 (mid to late 4th century AD)

In the mid to late 4th century AD the area to the south-west of RC13 appears to have been converted into use as a stockyard (Fig 5.14). A narrow trench (449), 0.18 m wide and 0.2 m deep, was traced on a north-west/south-east alignment for *c.* 18 m across this area before terminating in an unlined cut (466) dug into the underlying clay layers. The cut had sloping sides and was 3.3 m long, 0.6 m wide and 0.4 m deep. The excavator interpreted this as the trench for a water pipe which fed a water trough. The trench would have just been wide enough to accommodate a narrow wooden pipe (less likely a lead one), but it must have been subsequently robbed to salvage the iron pipe collars which were not present in the trench upon excavation. A layer of stony clay silt (445), 0.2 m deep, accumulated over the southern end of the backfilled water pipe trench. A metalled surface (465, n.i.), covering an area approximately 6 × 9 m, was laid in the area to the west of RC13. It was 0.2 m thick and consisted of river cobbles and limestone fragments overlaid by a 500 mm-thick layer of river gravel. A line of cobbles (464, n.i.) may represent a curb. The gravel sealed an earlier metalled surface (486) and the northern part of the backfilled water pipe trench. Surface 465 was in turn covered by a layer of fine, homogeneous, silty brown soil (416), 0.2 m deep, which contained oyster shell, cattle and sheep bones (some with evidence for butchery), mortar and fragments of roofing slate. Other finds from this layer included a number of coins of 3rd and 4th-century AD date, glass beads (EAR4, fig. 96, nos. 72–3), a copper-alloy finger ring (EAR4, fig. 114, no. 86), a fragment of a shale bracelet (EAR4, fig. 126, no. 17) and a bone pin (EAR4, fig. 123, no. 17). This layer may represent trampled midden material deposited in the yard area, perhaps supplemented by mud clinging to the hooves of animals and an accumulation of their dung. Around the trough some larger stones had been packed into the mud, perhaps to consolidate the area and prevent slippage of the mud into the trough. The lower fill of the trough was very similar to the surrounding mud and contained a considerable number of stones like those in the surrounding consolidation. It was not fully engulfed by the mud, however, so could have continued to function whilst the deposit accumulated in the yard. The presence of roofing slate and mortar in the deposit suggests that RC13 was at least partly in decay during the period that it accumulated. The trampled mud overlay the Period 3e boundary ditch (539) between the yard and the plot to the south-west, but the boundary was renewed by the construction of a post-built fence (see below). The size of the yard area, as denoted by the extent of surface 465, suggests that only a restricted number of animals could have been kept in this area.

Building 14 (RC14)

A small possible timber structure (RC14) was constructed in the yard area to the south-west of RC13. Six very shallow postholes or post-settings cut trampled layer 416, which accumulated over the gravel surface of the yard. The postholes therefore represent a later addition. The posts were each 0.2–0.45 m in diameter and 0.15 m deep and formed a broadly circular structure measuring 5 m in diameter. This structure was perhaps a small animal pen associated with the use of the yard, or conceivably the base for a hayrick. Each of the backfilled postholes was covered by Period 3g demolition material (410, n.i.) derived from RC13.

Building 15 (RC15)

RC15 was constructed in the south-western building plot over the footprint of demolished Period 3d buildings RC11 and 12 (Figs 5.16–5.17). A levelling deposit of charcoal-flecked clay (431) was placed over the demolished buildings in preparation for the construction of RC15. The building was defined by three partially robbed stone foundations (422; 488/494; 545). The foundation trenches were between 0.5–0.9 m wide and 0.2–0.3 m deep, filled by up to two courses of dry-bonded trap fragments. The construction style of this building is uncertain, but the narrow width of the foundations suggests that they supported a timber rather than stone superstructure. On the north-west side of the building there was the fragmentary remains of a projecting structure formed from a beam or post-trench (443) and three postholes (489; 543; 544). The slot abutted the north-western wall of the main building and may therefore be a later structural addition, perhaps just a small lean-to. There were four postholes (490; 491; 493; 497) within RC15, with 493 and 497 possibly forming the south-east wall of the building. Two postholes (480; 481) represent a north-west/south-east aligned post-built boundary fence that defined the south-western edge of the building plot. Two postholes (540; 541) on the north-eastern edge of the building may represent a parallel fence line.

Dating evidence

- *Yard*
- Surface 465. Coin 138, Claudius II, AD 268–70, very worn; Oxfordshire Colour-Coated Ware mortarium, probably 4th century AD.
- Trample 416. Coin 386, Valens, AD 363–7, very worn; coin 355, Constantius II, AD 337–41, well circulated; coin 347, Constantius II, AD 337–41 well circulated; coin 344, Constantine I, AD 335–7, virtually uncirculated; coin 315, *Constantinopolis*, AD 330–5, very worn; coin 296, Constantine II, AD 330–5, well circulated; coin 273, Allectus, AD 295–6; coin 263, illegible radiate, AD 270–90; coin 244, Tetricus II, AD 270–90; coin 215, Tetricus I, 270–90; coin 212, Tetricus I, AD 270–90; coin 196, illegible, AD 260–80; coin 184, Tetricus II, AD 270–3; coin 171, Tetricus I, AD 270–3; coin 157, Victorinus, AD 268–70; coin 140, Claudius II, AD 268–70. North African amphora.
- Clay silt 445. Coin 353, Constans, AD 337–41, very worn; coin 361, Constans, AD 341–6, very worn; New Forest Red-Slipped Ware; New Forest globular beaker or flagon.

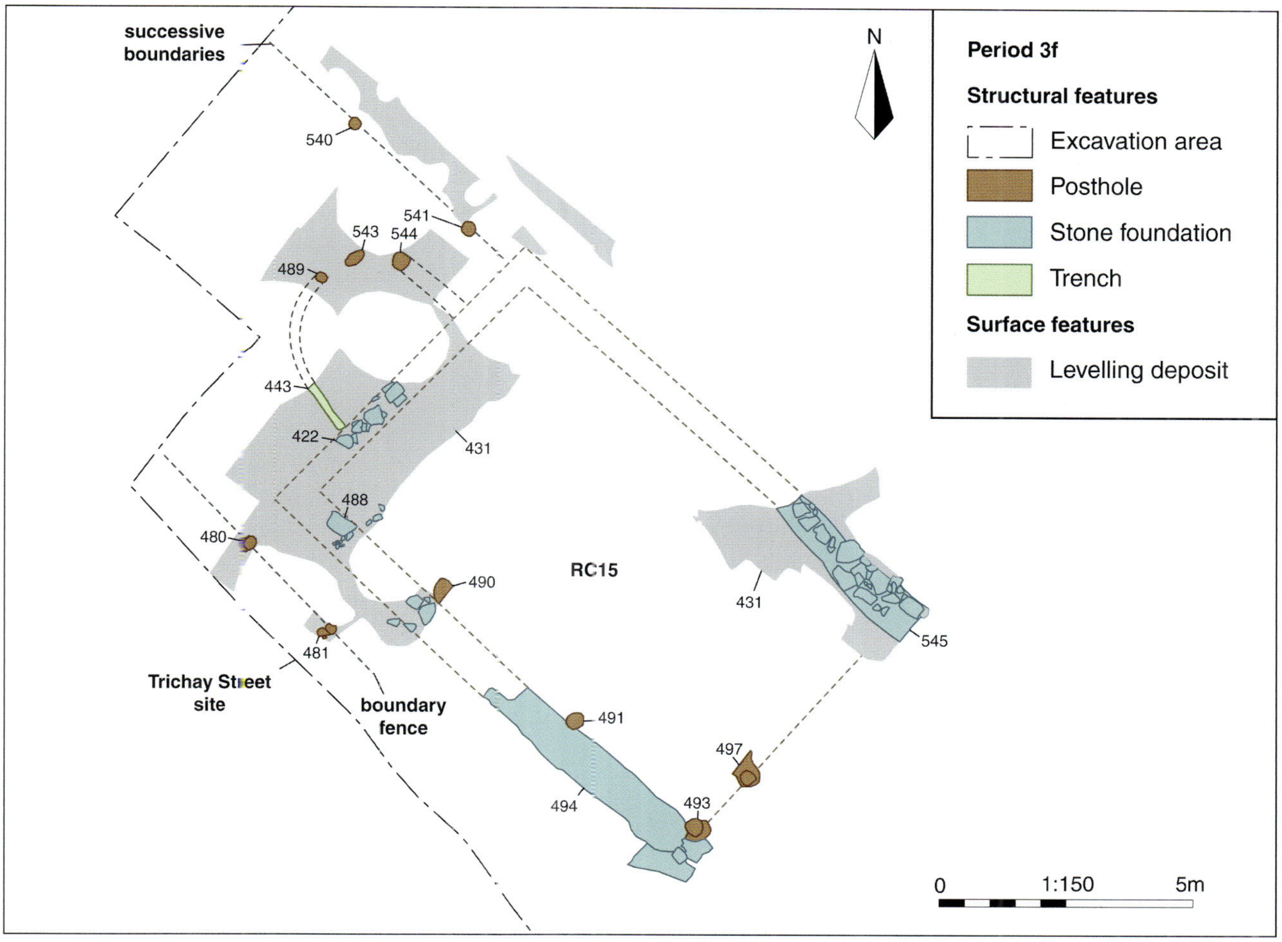

Fig. 5.16 Plan of Period 3f (mid to late 4th century AD) building RC15

- Water trough infill 466. Coin 294, Constantine II, AD 330–5, very worn.
- Boundary ditch 539. New Forest beaker; North African amphora; South-East Dorset BB1 flanged bowl (type 45).

Construction of RC14

- Posthole 407. Coin 217, Tetricus I, AD 270–90, little wear.
- Posthole 413. North African amphora.

Construction of RC15

- Levelling layer 431. South-East Dorset BB1 conical flanged bowl (type 45).

Secondary construction

- Posthole 544. South-East Dorset BB1 conical flanged bowl.

Period 3g: Demolition of buildings 13–15 (late 4th to 5th century AD)

The final phase of Roman occupation is represented by the demolition of RC13–15. Demolition deposits survived in Rooms 5 and 6 of the south-west wing of RC13. They varied from 0.15–0.65 m deep and consisted of layers of plaster, mortar and other debris including fragmented box tiles, South Devon roofing slates (EAR4, 282, fig. 137, nos. 1–3, 6) and a fragment of probable iron cylindrical pipe (EAR4, fig. 121, no. 23). A single pit (384, n.i.) was excavated against the exterior wall of Room 5, which appears to have been dug through these demolition deposits. The pit contained a quantity of cattle and sheep bones (200 NISP in all). On top of the demolition debris in Room 6 there was a deposit of oyster shells (364, n.i.), testimony to continued activity in this area after the demolition of this part of the building.

Dating evidence

- Demolition debris 362 within Room 5. Coin 352, Constans, AD 337–41, well circulated; Coin 341, Constantine II, AD 335–7, well circulated; Chocolate colour-coated ware; North African amphora.
- Demolition debris 368 within Room 5. Coin 336, *Constantinopolis* (copy), AD 330–40, very worn.
- Demolition debris 378 within Room 6. North African amphora.

- Pit 384. Coin 331, *Constantinopolis*, AD 335–7, well circulated.
- Demolition material 410 overlying backfilled posthole 411 of RC14. Coin 381, Valens, AD 364–7, well circulated.

Aspects of the Roman civil sequence *by Neil Holbrook*

Chronological development

To judge from the latest pottery recovered from the upper fills of well 3, which is datable to the period *c.* AD 80–100, civilian reoccupation of the former fortress site had begun by the end of the 1st century AD. The well had been dug near the corner formed by the intersection of Streets A and B, and it is conceivable that it was constructed during the period of military occupation; its final infilling, however, clearly relates to the period after the departure of the legion. Two other wells (22; 348) are also likely to date to the early decades of the town, although few finds were recovered from their backfills. It seems unlikely that the wells existed in isolation from nearby structures, and conceivably RC1 and 2 were built around the same time, although the buildings continued in use into the Hadrianic period at least. There is little evidence for buildings fronting on to Street A at this time. While the frontage had been heavily disturbed by later activity, and thus evidence would have not been preserved here, the rear parts of timber buildings extending to the north-west, back from the frontage, might have been expected to survive had they existed. The scatter of small pits in the northern part of the site further suggests that this part of the *insula* may have been open ground at this time. The timber buildings on the opposite side of Street B might also have originated in the late 1st century AD given that three successive phases of timber structures pre-dated destruction in the Hadrianic/early Antonine fire (*c.* AD 120–60). Well 3 does not outwardly appear to have been associated with any contemporary nearby buildings, a curious situation. Perhaps these were of sill-beam construction which has left no trace? The dating evidence from well 3 is consistent with it being backfilled before the introduction of piped water into the *insula* evidenced by trench 148. Wells 22 and 348 could have been dug a little later than 3 and thus have been associated with the Period 3b buildings RC3 and 4 constructed after the water pipe had been removed (the dating evidence is too imprecise for certainty). Perhaps there was only ever limited private access to the piped water supply?

It is reasonable, although not certain, that aqueduct trench 148 found in this excavation can be associated with the timber bridge dated by dendrochronology to AD 100/101 discovered at Paul Street in 1982 (Henderson 1988, 113–15). The only relevant dating evidence from this site was a samian bowl datable to *c.* AD 80–100 from the upcast derived from the digging of the trench. Henderson believed that trench 148 was an open leat in its initial form which was then replaced with a wooden pipe laid within the same cut. Further work is required to confirm this hypothesis, but on topographical grounds it is possible. To function effectively an open leat would have needed an extremely shallow gradient, and this is possible in Exeter as the natural ground surface only falls by 0.5 m at most between Paul Street and High Street. At Dorchester the aqueduct descended on an average gradient of 1:1,750 to deliver around 60 litres of water per second (Putnam 2007, 65). The sinuous course adopted by the water pipe is unusual. It was standard Roman engineering practice for water pipes to follow the alignment of the street grid (either laid along the side of a street, or directly underneath it). Branch pipes drawing off from the main supplied individual properties along the frontages. Hodge (1992, 320–2) notes no examples of water pipes diverging from the street grid to cross *insulae* on an oblique course, although a very late Roman water pipe at *Verulamium* might be another instance of this (Frere 1983, 226; 2011). At Exeter the course adopted by the water pipe demonstrates that the *insula* was largely undeveloped at the start of the 2nd century AD, its sinuous course perhaps designed to avoid the few buildings that had been constructed by this date. If correct, it indicates that this part of the *insula* was under-developed for a quarter of a century after the abandonment of the fortress, and indeed that it had not been laid out as formal building plots which had passed into private ownership. Rather than being part of the principal water supply associated with the wooden bridge over the outer fortress ditch at Paul Street, it would be more explicable if the pipe trench found at Trichay Street was in fact a branch line that fed off a main along one of the streets to feed a specific building or fountain. The water pipe must have been comparatively short-lived, as the pipe was robbed and its former line overlain by buildings RC3 and 4 which burnt down in the Hadrianic/early Antonine fire. It would be curious if a crucial piece of public infrastructure fell out of use so quickly, unless it did not work particularly well. If the water pipe was merely a branch line, however, its disuse and building over poses much less of a problem.

The backfill of the robbed pipe trench yielded a samian bowl of Hadrianic or Antonine date, so RC3 and 4 were not built before *c.* AD 120 at earliest. The addition of RC3 and 4 would have created quite a developed frontage to Street B in this part of the *insula*. The frontage of Street A was seemingly not developed at this time, however, a situation that persisted in later periods as well. Little survived of the fabric of Street A; perhaps it was not a principal thoroughfare hereabouts, although excavations further to the north-east at Queen Street revealed a metalled street and developed frontages (Bidwell 1980, 54). There was little surviving evidence for activities in the back lands behind the buildings in the central part of the *insula*. As the area seems not to have been used for pit digging, as evidence of this would probably have survived, it was presumably open ground.

The buildings on both sides of Street B succumbed to destruction by fire in the Hadrianic/early Antonine period. There is little to determine whether this was an accidental event or else a deliberate action to clear away redundant structures prior to an episode of replanning (a dangerous and risky undertaking of course unless the fire was very carefully controlled). If accidental it is curious that so few artefacts associated with the occupation of the buildings were recovered in the excavation, unless the ruins were heavily raked over once the fire abated. Following the fire, the Period 3c replanning represents quite a radical departure from the earlier layout with Street B being abandoned. The removal of a street to amalgamate two *insulae* is hard to parallel in Roman Britain. No evidence can be deduced from greenfield sites such as Caistor-by-Norwich, Silchester and Wroxeter where geophysical survey and aerial photographic transcription provide us with a good appreciation of urban form. In these places no evidence has been found for stone buildings overlying the lines of streets to indicate that the thoroughfare had been abandoned within the Roman period. Epigraphic evidence from outside of Britain shows that encroachment onto streets was forbidden in some town charters (Frere 1972, 13, n. 1; Crawford 1996, no. 25), and by analogy it is reasonable to assume that keeping streets clear of obstructions in Exeter would also have been the responsibility of the civic authorities. The abandonment of Street B must therefore have been an officially sanctioned action, which is interesting as it was associated with the subsequent development of at least part of the enlarged *insula* for private housing, whereas the few other examples of the suppression of streets in Britain took place prior to the construction of public buildings. In London, for instance, the streets surrounding the first forum were abandoned when the much larger second forum was constructed in the early 2nd century AD (Marsden 1987), while at Cirencester a metalled lane (rather than an inter-*insulae* street) was swept away for the construction of a public building (most likely a temple) in *c*. AD 150–70 (Holbrook 1998, 127–9).

The removal of the street separating *insulae* IV and V at Exeter was therefore an unusual event. How might it be explained? First it would seem to support the notion that the Early Roman town was not intensively developed. The street frontages would have been the prime locations, and if there had been pressure on space a street would hardly have been removed. Larger *insulae* did, however, create bigger spaces behind the frontages which might have been better suited to activities such as the rearing of stock or horticulture. The subsequent history of this newly amalgamated *insula* is also instructive. By the start of the 3rd century AD at least the space was occupied by two distinct building plots separated by an open space. This spatial layout could suggest that the land was in single ownership, so perhaps one individual acquired land plots in adjoining *insulae* and then sought to amalgamate the holdings through the suppression of the intervening street? The date of the fire and abandonment of Street B is suggested as *c*. AD 120–60, although there is only a small quantity of relevant dating evidence. It is conceivable that this event could have occurred a little later than is currently suggested by the dating evidence and have been associated with the replanning of Exeter consequent upon the expansion of the town and construction of the new earthwork defences *c*. AD 160–80. As part of this process elements of the street grid would have been extended into the newly enclosed area, although seemingly on a piecemeal basis over several decades as a street at Rack Street was not constructed until the late 3rd century AD (Chapter 8 below). The expansion of the defended area might therefore provide a context for some individuals to consolidate their holdings in the core of the town. Indeed the fire might conceivably have covered a more extensive area than just the Trichay Street site, as evidence for the destruction of timber buildings by fire has also been found at some other sites in central Exeter, although attempts to determine if this might have been a single event are hampered by the imprecise nature of the available dating evidence. At Goldsmith Street Area III some demolition debris from building RC3 had clearly been burnt (Chapter 6 below), and at 196–7 High Street building RC2 was covered by a layer of ash and burnt daub before it was rebuilt to the same plan (Chapter 7 below). A building south-east of the forum also burnt down (EAR1, 115–16). At Goldsmith Street the fire has a *terminus post quem* of *c*. AD 150; at High Street it is only broadly Hadrianic/Antonine, and at the Cathedral Close there is an Antonine *terminus post quem*. A more widespread fire around about the time that the town was equipped with a new, more extensive, circuit of urban defences is a possibility therefore.

Following the fire, redevelopment was concentrated in two areas (termed the north-east and south-west plots), presumably with an open area between them. In the north-east plot a timber building RC8 was constructed above the demolished remains of RC7, with a water pipe to its south-west. The pipe was laid along the edge of the now abandoned Street B and was thus aligned with the street grid, a more normal arrangement and one in contrast with the sinuous course adopted by the original water pipe. RC8 was replaced by RC9, and that in turn by RC10: little can be deduced of the plan or even orientation of these buildings and there is limited dating evidence for this phase of activity. Successive buildings RC8 and 9 were associated with Antonine samian, and so may date to the second half of the 2nd century AD. The last building in this sequence cannot date before the late 2nd century AD at earliest, and occupation quite likely continued into the 3rd century AD. The south-west plot was occupied by two buildings (RC11 and 12). The plan of RC11 indicates that it was designed to face to the north-west and thus front onto the open area. It was deliberately separated from the frontage of Street A by a boundary wall and substantial fence. RC11 displays a greater level of architectural pretension than previous structures, with a masonry apse, brick mortar (*opus signinum*) floor and a small stone-built room with a hypocaust. The adjacent building RC12 had a cobbled floor and probably had an agricultural or storage function rather than a residential one. There is little useful dating evidence for RC11 and 12. A coin of AD 183–4 came from one of the postholes of the fence separating RC11 from Street A; if it is associated with the construction of the fence (perhaps as a foundation deposit?) then it provides a *terminus post quem*, and makes it likely that occupation of RC11 continued into the 3rd century AD. The only useful dating evidence for the demolition of RC11 is a piece of South-East Dorset BB1 with obtuse-angled lattice decoration which dates this event to after *c*. AD 220. The nature of 3rd-century AD occupation on the site is uncertain. Conceivably RC11 and 12 could have continued in use for much of that century, or alternatively have fallen out of use as early as its second quarter. If the latter, this would indicate that that there were no structures on the site for a good number of decades before the stone house RC13 was built, although once again some uncertainty attaches to when that event took place.

In determining the date of RC13 much rests on the evidential value that can be placed on a coin of AD 330–40 recovered from the top of one of its walls. If this coin is considered to be firmly stratified, and thus to date the construction of the house, then this event would not have occurred until the middle decades of the 4th century AD. The field record that it came from the 'top of the wall' does cast doubt upon the provenance of the coin, however. Perhaps the coin was recovered during cleaning of the wall and so might have been introduced to the location during stone robbing activities in the medieval period? If we disregard this coin then the house could date as early as the mid 3rd century AD. We might note, however, the lack of evidence for resurfacing and reconstruction within the structure. If the house did date to the mid-late 3rd century AD, more evidence of such activities might be expected if occupation continued for well over a century. The lack of superimposed floor levels might be more consistent with construction in the 4th century AD therefore and this gains some support from two Constantinian coins recovered from an occupation deposit in Room 2. The mosaic pavement found in 1887, which presumably comes from another wing of the building (Fig. 5.17: CN157.1), cannot be closely dated on stylistic grounds, and Cosh and Neal date it as just '?4th century' (Cosh and Neal 2005, 157.1). The date of construction of RC13 can therefore be only broadly assigned to the period from the mid 3rd to the mid 4th century AD. There is no useful dating evidence for RC15 to the south-west of RC13, although the two structures were at least partly contemporary as they defined a small yard area. A trample deposit which formed on this external yard surface produced 16 coins, including one very worn issue of AD 363–7 and five others of the House of Constantine. These coins show that the deposit continued to collect material well into the second half of the 4th century AD, if not later, and the presence of fragments of roofing slate and mortar suggest that at least part of RC13 was derelict by this time. There is no useful dating evidence for the date at which RC13 was demolished, although the dark earth which accumulated above the ruins of the house has produced some of the latest Roman artefacts recovered from Exeter (a coin of AD 387–8 and a South-East Dorset BB1 squat cooking-pot type 21.20), alongside some clearly intrusive high medieval pottery (see Period 5).

Building techniques and architecture

The earlier Roman timber buildings display a variety of constructional techniques, although the levels of preservation were not as good as those encountered in some other towns (London and Colchester in particular) where greater detail of the precise methods utilised has been retrieved. Where building trenches were encountered, typically around 0.3 m wide with flat bases, it is likely that they held horizontal timber beams into which vertical posts were fastened. This therefore differentiates the manner of construction of these civilian buildings from the earlier military structures which were predominately formed from vertical posts set at intervals within construction trenches. One of the internal walls of RC5 preserved *in situ* the daub rendering applied the face of the wall (the wall itself was presumably formed from either wattle panels set between timber uprights, or else mud-and-stud infill utilising air dried bricks: Perring 2002, 94–5). Other building techniques used in the structures included post-in-trench construction in RC7 and mass walling: the walls of RC2 were defined by daub footings and some manner of earth-walled superstructure is presumably indicated (Perring 2002, 98–106). Some use was also made of dry-stone foundations. Both RC4 and RC15 had stone footings which probably formed the foundation for a timber base plate or else a mass-walled superstructure. Daub was the predominant material used in the superstructure of the buildings to judge from the quantities of burnt daub spread over the site after the fire in the Hadrianic or early Antonine period. Some of the walls were plastered and white-washed, with evidence for plaster deriving from demolition deposits associated with RC4, where it formed an external render, and RC9. Where floors survived they were often of beaten clay. Little can usefully be said concerning the design of these timber buildings as in no case does a complete ground plan survive. To judge from the fragmentary evidence, they were predominately simple strip buildings which probably combined both residential and commercial functions.

A greater level of architectural pretension is demonstrated by RC11, whose walls were constructed on shallow

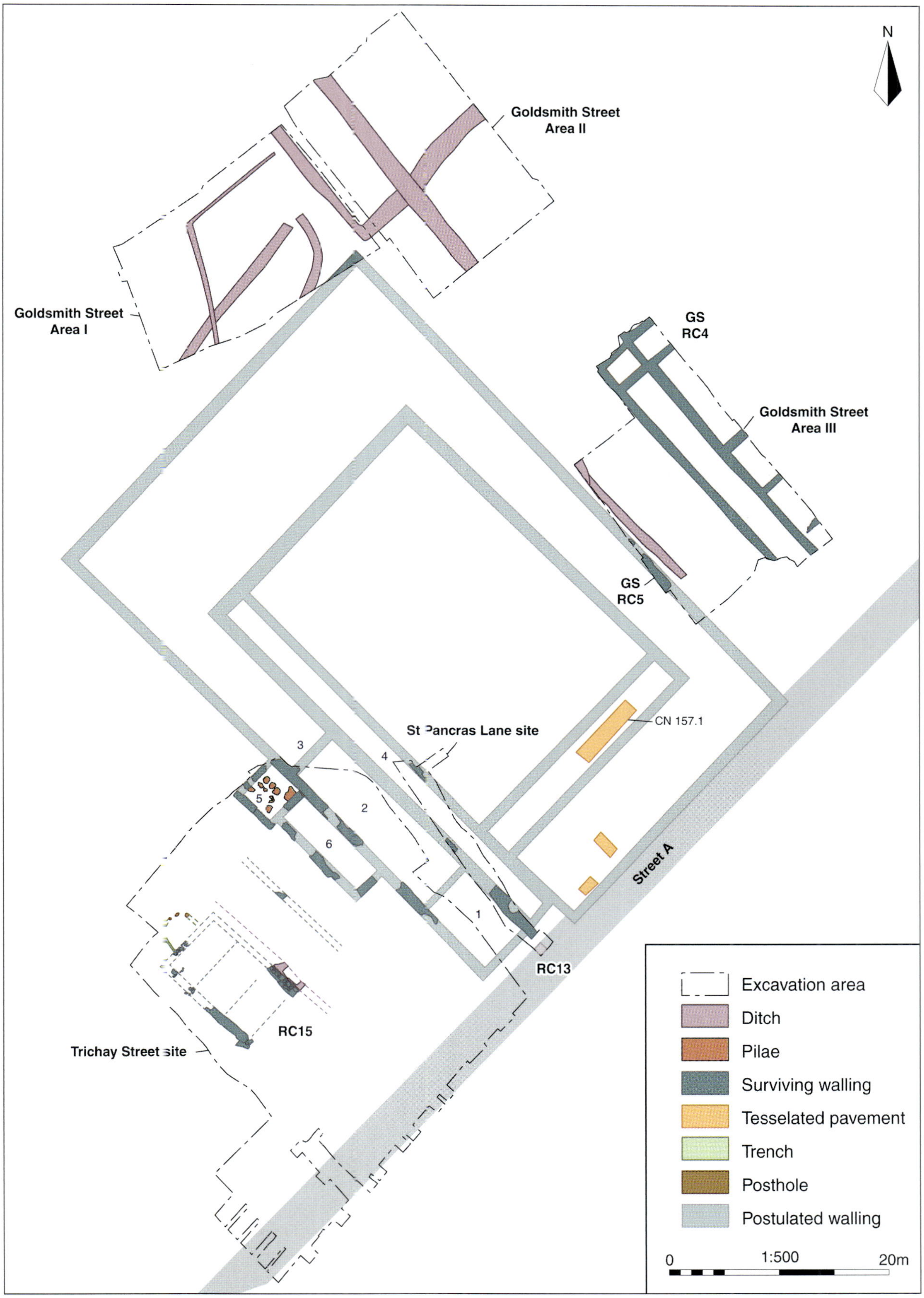

Fig. 5.17 Postulated extent of Period 3e Late Roman town house RC13. CN refers to the catalogue reference for the mosaic in Cosh and Neal 2005

stone foundations which must have supported a timber or mass-walled superstructure. At least one of the internal walls was made of clay. The building was screened from the frontage of Street A by a boundary wall and a substantial fence, and rather than facing the street it would have been approached from the north-east across the open area that lay between it and the buildings in the north-east plot. Room 1 was floored with brick mortar and is likely to have been a reception or dining room, with an apse to the rear (the apse seems to be a later addition). At the opposite end of the building a small masonry room equipped with a hypocaust was added to the rear of the building. Apses were not uncommon features of Romano-British houses from a relatively early date. A clay-walled house in Gutter Lane, London, built in the early 2nd century AD, had an apse furnished with a mosaic (Frere *et al.* 1989, 305; Neal and Cosh 2009, 370.49), and this architectural embellishment is seen more clearly in strip buildings which were aligned end-on to the street frontage at No. 1 Poultry. In timber building 65 the rearmost room (*i.e.* that furthest from the street) had an apse embellished with a mosaic, as was presumably also the case with the apsidal mosaic found nearby in a masonry house in 1869 (Hill and Rowsome 2011; Neal and Cosh 2009, mosaics 370.80, 370.88). Other simple masonry buildings with apses include examples from Caerwent (Bldg. 24N (first phase): Ashby *et al.* 1911) and Silchester (*insula* XXIIb.5: Creighton with Fry 2016, 62–6). In both these examples the apse formed a focal point at the end of the long axis of the house, and presumably served to embellish a rear reception or dining room. In RC11, however, Room 1 would have been entered directly from the open area in front of the building, or perhaps from a portico of which no trace has survived.

Small rooms equipped with pillared hypocausts such as that in RC11 were a component of a number of other Romano-British buildings, not all of them masonry structures. A clay and timber public building in Southwark possessed a small hypocaust room, 2.5 m square, itself walled in clay, and similar masonry chambers were added later when the building had been rebuilt in stone (Cowan 1992). Hypocaust rooms were also added to the rear of masonry strip buildings at No. 1 Poultry in London (Hill and Rowsome 2011). The function of these small chambers equipped with pillared, rather than channelled, hypocausts was presumably to serve as warm rooms for winter use. Black (1985) has discussed the function of such rooms in masonry houses and suggested that they may have served as a source of indirect heat for adjacent major rooms. That cannot have been the case with RC11, however, as the hypocaust was almost entirely detached from the adjacent house, unlike the integrated examples cited by Black.

Late Roman RC15 used a mixture of stone foundations and post-trenches (presumably the stone foundations supported a timber superstructure). The excavators considered that the timber features revealed at the north-west end of the building formed a timber apse, although the evidence is fragmentary and far from conclusive. If correct, an apse at the end of the long axis would be a more usual arrangement, as has just been discussed.

The contemporary masonry building RC13 represents a step-change in the scale of construction on the site. Only part of the building lay within the excavation area, but if the masonry walls revealed at Goldsmith Street Areas I and III are part of the same building we can reconstruct a house of courtyard plan with a south-west range *c.* 45 m long and a north-west one *c.* 60 m long (Fig 5.17). Such a reconstruction is far from certain of course, and it is possible that the walls found at Goldsmith Street were part of a separate structure adjacent to that found at Trichay Street. In that case RC13 would have been composed of a single block of rooms orientated at right angles to Street A. However, we do need to accommodate the mosaics found in the 18th and 19th centuries (the location of the mosaics marked on Fig. 5.17 derives from the Urban Archaeological Database). The repeating design of the principal mosaic (Cosh and Neal no. 157.1) clearly shows that it adorned a corridor, of sufficient length to accommodate this treatment. Most likely the mosaic floored a corridor in front of a block of rooms parallel with Street A, and thus provides support for the reconstruction of a single building of courtyard plan with ranges on all four sides. If the reconstruction of the plan is correct, the house compares in scale to large courtyard houses found in towns such as *Verulamium* (House III.2, which measured 56 × 49 m: Wheeler and Wheeler 1936, 93–6) and Caerwent (House 2s, up to 76 m long and 36 m wide: Ashby *et al.* 1902, 121–37).

The plan of the building as revealed in the excavated area is relatively simple, with a row of three rooms with a front corridor or portico opening onto a central courtyard (the corridor appears to have been an addition to the original layout). Judging from the type of flooring and absence of painted wall-plaster, there is no evidence for high-status rooms in this part of the south-west range. Room 2 contained ovens and hearths, and could have been a kitchen within part of a range devoted to service activities (it is not clear whether the ovens were a primary feature or a later insertion). Two rooms were subsequently added to the rear of the range. Room 5 possessed a pillared hypocaust with a hypocaust arch in the wall separating Rooms 5 and 6. The stoke-hole must have lain in Room 6 therefore, although no trace of it survived. Room 6 perhaps also served as a fuel store). It is unclear whether further rooms existed to the north-west of Room 5, although the preservation of a clear western corner to this room suggests that this may not have been the case. If so, the location of Room 5 is curious, as it was built behind the main range at a point straddling the wall dividing Rooms 2 and 3 (unless that wall had already been removed when Room 5 was added). If Room 5 was a small, single, heated room presumably it was accessed via a door from Room 3 (the position of oven 767 in Room 2 would make access difficult from there). The size and location of Room 5 do not mark it out as an important reception room, nor is there any surviving evidence of good-quality flooring. Abundant plain white plaster was recovered from demolition deposits within the room, along with fragmented box-tiles and stone roofing tiles.

Activities conducted in the insula

There is little useful evidence for the nature of activities undertaken in this part of the *insula* before the 4th century AD, when a water trough was installed in the area between RC13 and RC14, and the yard covered with a dump of rubble and earth. The trough was fed by a narrow trench that presumably contained a water pipe which could have been fed from a cistern or tank beyond the limits of the excavation area. This evidence need not therefore necessarily indicate the existence of a piped water supply in Exeter in the late 4th century AD akin to that found at *Verulamium* where the pipe dates to the very late 4th century AD at earliest, and quite conceivably the 5th century AD (Frere 1983, 226; 2011). The water pipe trench was covered by a silty brown soil 0.2 m thick which contained fragments of building material (suggesting that at least part of a nearby structure had been demolished by this time), along with many coins and other finds. The excavators interpreted this area as a stockyard, and the soil as trample which had accumulated over time through the movement of animals into and out of the yard. The quantities of artefacts in this deposit suggest an origin as domestic rubbish, perhaps household food waste dumped here as animal feed. The restricted width of the yard is commensurate with its use by smaller animals, and it has been speculated previously that some pigs may have been bred in towns (Maltby 2015, 184), although until recently hard evidence was lacking. The recognition through micromorphological analysis of pig slurry in small fields or pens adjacent to 2nd-century AD houses at Vine Street, Leicester, now seemingly provides confirmatory evidence for urban pig breeding (Morris *et al.* 2011, 29) and the Trichay Street yard could conceivably have also been a piggery, as larger stock would have required imported hay and fodder for feed (see also Maltby in EAPIT1, Chapter 6). Faunal analysis demonstrates that cattle and sheep were brought on the hoof from the countryside to urban markets, where they were slaughtered and processed by specialist butchers based in the towns (Matlby 2010, 165–76, 284; 2015, 181–3). Urban livestock markets could have taken place in open spaces within or outside the town defences. A probable example of an extra-mural livestock market has been identified at Chichester (Down 1989, 69–70), and expanses of Late Roman metalled surfaces within the walls of Cirencester could have been marketplaces (Holbrook and Salvatore 1998, 23–5). A series of small ditched enclosures was found in the Goldsmith Street excavations, immediately outside the inferred north-west range of the courtyard house (Fig. 5.17). The ditches contained discrete dumps of butchered cattle bones, and if these are associated with the activities conducted within the enclosures, then conceivably these pens held small quantities of stock prior to slaughter.

Periods 4–5: The post-Roman and Middle Saxon periods

Post-Roman dark earth (5th to 10th century)

Following the abandonment of the latest Roman buildings (Period 3g), a layer of dark loam accumulated above the latest Roman deposits. It was between 0.2 and 0.4 m thick and indicates that there was some form of activity, if only gardening, cultivation or the dumping of organic waste, before the Late Saxon occupation in the 10th century. Modest amounts of animal bone, mainly of cattle and sheep, alongside residual Roman finds including Late Roman pottery and roofing slate from the demolition of RC13, were also found in the dark earth. Throughout the excavation, pottery of the 12th, 13th and 14th centuries was regularly found in this soil, and no completely undisturbed areas were encountered. It was evident that the soil was turned over, presumably in the course of cultivation or gardening, long after the foundation of the *burh*.

Dating evidence: dark earth

- 363. Glass beaker (EAR4, fig. 95, no. 56), late 4th century AD.
- 383. Single sherd Upper Greensand-Derived wares (UGSD), 10th to 13th century.
- 397. Coin 401, Magnus Maximus (AD 387–8), well circulated, one of the latest Roman coins from Exeter, and somewhat later than the latest stratified coin from the Roman sequence (coin of AD 363–7 from Period 3f layer 416). South-East Dorset BB1 cooking pot (EAR4, fig. 29, type 21.20), probably no earlier than last quarter of 4th century AD; 12th/13th-century pottery.

Period 6: The Saxo-Norman town (*c.* AD 900–1200)

The excavation examined three large tenements in St Pancras parish, with a small part of a fourth property. Their frontages were on Waterbeer Street, a lane running along the backs of the burgage plots at the centre of High Street (Fig. 5.18). Documentary evidence shows that in the period 1250–1550 this street contained a mix of properties with some surprisingly wealthy households alongside more lowly buildings including a barn and a stable (Chapter 4 above). Waterbeer Street is first documented in the 13th century but was probably part of the Late Saxon street plan (Allan *et al.* 1984, fig. 128). The rear of the

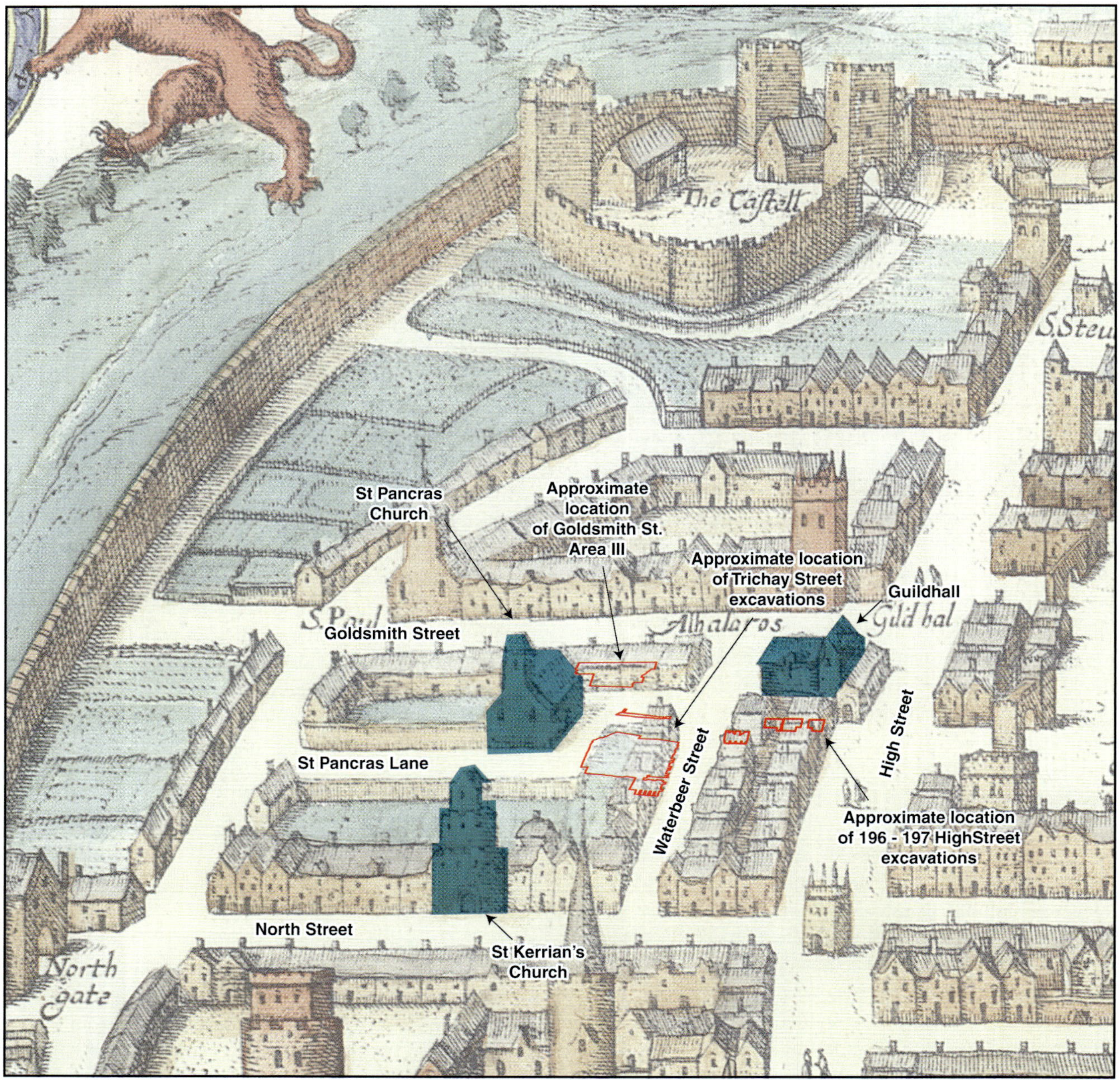

Fig. 5.18 The relationship of the excavations to the surrounding historic street plan as marked on Hooker's map of 1587 (1618 edition) (© RAMM)

excavated properties was marked by Trichay Street, a back lane running from North Street to St Pancras church, serving the Waterbeer Street tenements, first recorded in 1243 (see Figs 5.1 and 5.19).

The north-eastern boundary of the excavation was formed by the side of Pancras Lane as it was in 1972; its position resulted from late 19th-century street widening over a former medieval tenement. Pancras Lane was a side street leading off Waterbeer Street towards the church of St Pancras, skirting around the church and continuing north-west to meet Paul Street. The church is orientated east to west, rather than conforming to the alignment of the street, suggesting that it was laid out without the constraints of the tenement plots; it clearly predates Pancras Lane. Its foundation date is unknown, but it has a Norman font and it probably originated in the 12th century (EAPIT 1, Chapter 7; Allan *et al.* 1984, 398; Orme 2014, 153–4).

Although most of the medieval street system of Exeter bears no relation to the Roman one (EAPIT 1, Chapter 7, Fig. 7.1) the central part of medieval Waterbeer Street partly overlies Roman Town Street C (Chapter 3.2; cf. Allan *et al.* 1984, fig. 127). This, however, is unlikely to be more than coincidence; the medieval street bends, reflecting the slight curve in High Street, veering away from the Roman alignment at the two ends of the street.

Period 6a: The earliest Saxo-Norman features (10th/11th century)

In the absence of a stratified sequence of medieval deposits, the identification of the earliest Late Saxon contexts on Trichay Street relies almost entirely on the pottery. Unfortunately the ceramic sequence between the late 9th and late 11th centuries in the entire south-western region is not closely dated, although its general development is known in outline. In the early stages of the *burh* (?early and mid 10th century), Exeter appears to have been either aceramic or only partially ceramic – that is, pottery was not in circulation or was used in only in small quantities. The earliest groups from the *burh* are believed to be the few contexts which contain much bone and little pottery – only regional and foreign imports alongside the local wheel-thrown Bedford Garage Wares produced in Exeter (Chapter 17 below; Allan 1984a, 12, Horizon A). A larger number of pits belong to the period when the principal class of Saxo-Norman ceramics (Upper Greensand-Derived wares: UGSD) was in use alongside Bedford Garage Ware and some limestone-tempered wares; this probably began in the late 10th century (Horizon B). Many other Saxo-Norman pits can be attributed to a later period when coarse (UGSD) pottery was plentiful, after the disappearance of Bedford Garage Wares but prior to the arrival of glazed wares; this is now thought to belong to the late 11th and early 12th centuries (Horizon D). In a final stage in the Saxo-Norman sequence, glazed tripod pitchers and handmade sandy wares make their appearance (Horizon E, mid to late 12th century). Numerous other features contain only small quantities of pottery and could belong anywhere in this sequence (Horizon C).

Wells, cesspits and refuse pits

Two contexts contained pottery which shows features of the Saxo-Norman ceramic Horizon A (Fig. 5.19). The large pit 66/67/68, close to the Waterbeer Street frontage, contained a substantial group of cattle and sheep bones (281 NISP), together with fragments of a leather belt (EAR3, 327). A second group of intercutting pits, also near the frontage (7; 18; 19; 27; 77), had a similar composition, suggesting an early date in the Late Saxon sequence; the two earliest features of the group contained no pottery. These pits may date from a time when pottery was not in general circulation, possibly in the early or mid 10th century.

Three other pits (26, 29, a pair of pits *c.* 12 m behind the Waterbeer Street frontage, and 439) contained Late Saxon pottery which probably dates from the mid 10th to 11th century (Allan 1984a, 9, Horizon B). Pit 439 lay at the back of the Waterbeer Street plot close to Trichay Street. It was subcircular, 2.15 m in diameter and at least 0.6 m deep. Alongside a group of wheel-thrown Bedford Garage Wares and limestone-tempered pottery, it contained an assemblage of animal bones, including cattle bones with butchery marks, with residual Roman pottery and coins.

Pits 26 and 29 lay about 12 m behind the frontage; they were found in the bottoms of Victorian cellars. Their surviving lower parts were subcircular in shape, *c.* 1.3 m in diameter and 0.5–0.8 m deep. The Late Saxon ground surface can be estimated to have been about 1.4–1.7 m above that level; when newly dug, these features would therefore have been over 2 m deep. Cess deposits were present in the lowest fills of both pits. Their upper fills contained conjoining sherds of coarse pottery, suggesting that they were backfilled at the same time. A large assemblage of animal bones (379 NISP), including cattle bones with butchery marks, was recovered from the upper surviving fills of pit 26, showing that it was later used for dumping refuse. The other finds from this pit included a number of fragments of leather including offcuts – probably cobblers' waste (EAR3, 327).

These may be only a small proportion of the Late Saxon features. Nine pits which contained animal bone but no pottery may also represent an early stage in the development of the *burh* when little pottery was in circulation, but may equally be contexts of later date which happen not to contain pottery. Five of them (20; 94; 104; 105; 155) were isolated pits, all close to the Waterbeer Street frontage in the area of the early pits 26 and 29; they all contained primary deposits of cess. The sixth (345) was a heavily disturbed subrectangular cesspit, cut by pit 282 in which 11th/12th-century pottery was found. Two further pits containing animal bone but no pottery (655; 677, both n.i) lay close to the Trichay Street frontage, and another fragment of a cesspit (688) was found towards the rear of the Pancras Lane trench. Radiocarbon dates from bones found within these features could be instructive.

Nine further cesspits (21; 279; 280; 283; 352; 436; also 282; 334 and 382, n.i.) contained small groups of pottery which are loosely datable to the late 10th to early 12th century (Horizon C). They varied between 1.6 m and 2.9 m in diameter and between 0.3 m and 1.1 m deep. None of them showed evidence for any form of internal structure such as a plank or wattle lining. Their primary fills were generally represented by brown/green cess deposits; some were waterlogged. Their upper fills were typically mixed clays, oyster fragments, Roman tile and slate, charcoal, and occasional volcanic stones, with some residual Roman pottery. Large assemblages of animal bone, some with possible butchery marks, were recovered from the fills of pits 21 (113 NISP), 279 (109 NISP), 331 and 334, indicating that they had been used as rubbish pits once they had gone out of use. A single pit (331) contained no cess and may have been used only as a refuse pit. Six further pits in the same area each had thick cess deposits in their bottoms but yielded no finds.

Three layers of dark brown clayey silt, each *c.* 0.2–0.3 m deep (351; 424; 467, n.i.) were found along the northern edge of the site. They may represent upcast material from the excavation of the three cesspits nearby (331, 436, 334, n.i.); pottery recovered from these deposits suggests that they were broadly contemporary with the pits.

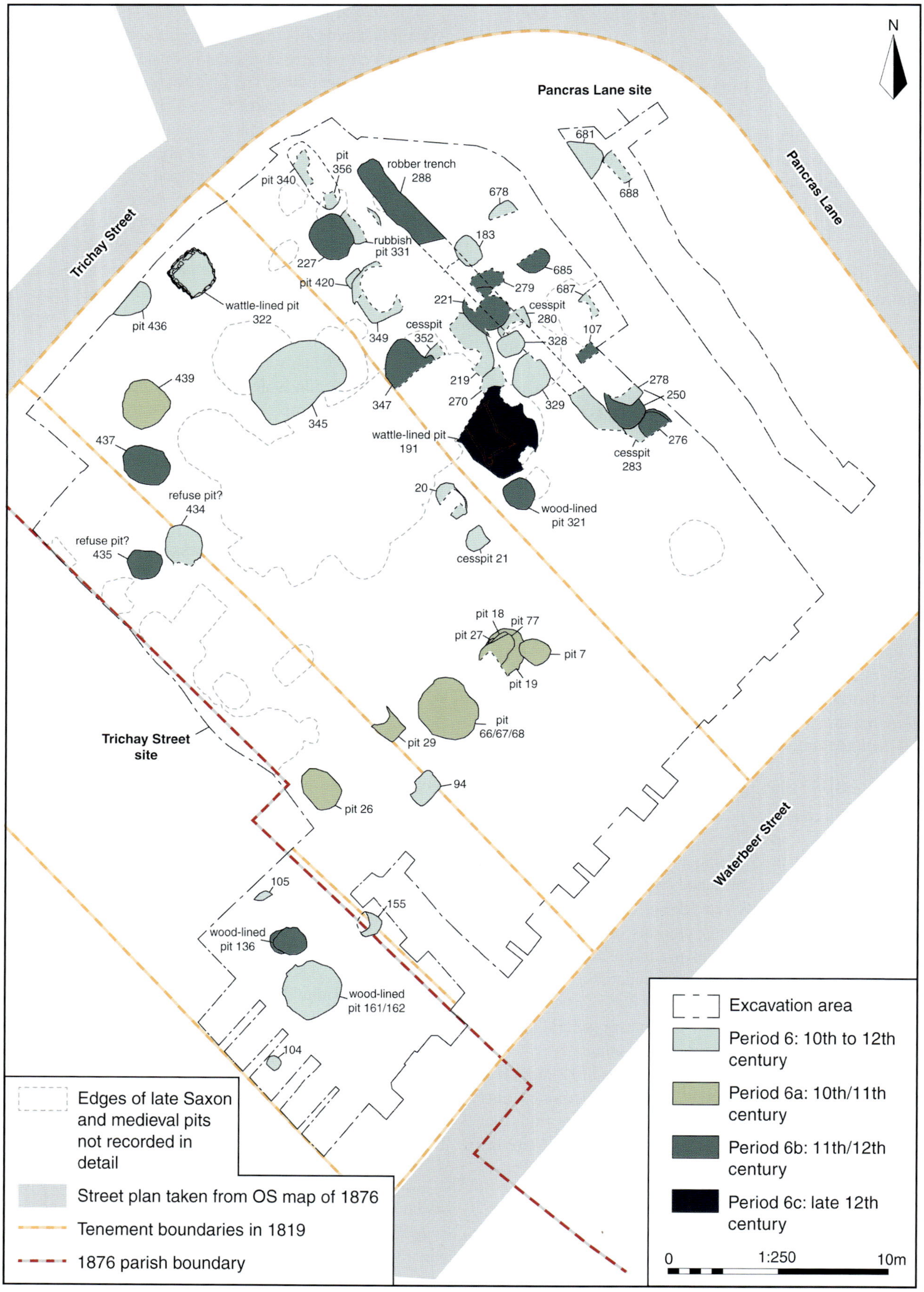

Fig. 5.19 Plan of Period 6 (10th to 12th-century) features

Finally, it should be noted that a large cluster of intercutting Late Saxon and medieval pits was found towards the centre of the north-western part of the excavation. Since time was running out towards the end of the excavation, this area was scraped down by machine to the top of Roman deposits, where the outlines of pits were recorded; the pits were not dug individually. The positions of the pits have been plotted from the plans of the Roman deposits which they cut through.

Period 6b: later Saxo-Norman features (11th century/12th century)

No fewer than 29 pits contained pottery of Horizon D, which is currently dated to the late 11th or early or mid 12th century (Fig. 5.19). They were all broadly subcircular to subrectangular in shape, with steeply sloping sides and either flat or concave bases. They measured between 1.4–2.7 m in diameter and 0.3–1.1 m deep.

Cesspits

Fifteen of these features (107; 136; 161; 183; 221; 227; 250; 276; 278; 321; 347; 678/685; 687; and 277 and 292, both n.i.) were probable cesspits, indicated by the presence of thick primary deposits of soft green-brown cess. The upper fills of some of these features contained domestic refuse. Alongside medieval coarse pottery and a large collection of animal bones (671 NISP), the finds from pit 227 included some suggestions of occupations and high-status activities: a few fragments of parchment on which no writing was visible (EAR3, 352), a fragmentary penannular finger ring (EAR3, 84, 347, M61) and a Saxo-Norman bone spindlewhorl (EAR3, 351, B25). Large quantities of sheep and cattle bone (224 NISP) were found in pit 136. Eight structural timbers, including a number of planks, possibly from a timber structure, were recovered from the late 11th or early 12th-century cesspit 347 (Fig. 5.20) (EAR3, 315 m, W80–7; Appendix 5.1), along with a bone flute (EAR3, 349, B1). Timbers from this pit were dated by dendrochronology to after AD 962±9, 1040±9 and 1056±9; no sapwood was present on the first sample (EAR 3, Mf 315–18). A second timber from the tree represented by the oak board of AD 1056±9 was found in the fill of the nearby pit 320 (EAR3, 315, W92; Mf315–18). The structural timbers from this pit, the only examples known from the region in the Late Saxon period, are discussed in Appendix 5.1.

Fig. 5.20 Pit 347 with its wattle lining and timber props, inserted to avoid collapse (© RAMM)

Two pits in the southern part of the site close to Waterbeer Street (136; 161/162) preserved their stake and wattle linings, and were probably wells. The lowest fill of pit 161/162 consisted of a thick deposit of waterlogged organic material (probably cess) containing pieces of leather. The overlying fills contained some domestic waste which indicated that it later served as a refuse pit, including a possible bucket base or cask head (EAR3, 305, W23), and an oak board, perhaps the side of a box (EAR3, 305, W23). A similar pit (321), on the edge of the main pit group, had a primary black organic fill containing seeds and other organic material. Its upper part had evidently begun to slump and had been propped with various reused timbers including a probable garderobe seat (EAR3, 313, W76). Dendrochronological dating of this timber indicated that it was felled in AD 949±9, so it was probably at least 50 years old when it was deposited in the pit (EAR3, Mf 315–18).

Robber trenches

A robber trench (288), which quarried the rubble foundation of a wall (253) of the Late Roman town house RC13, also dated to this period. Part of the trench (292, n.i.) was infilled with cess. A pit (420) also cut the wall of the Roman town house and may also represent robbing of the wall. No finds were recovered from the fill of this feature.

Wells or refuse pits?

Four pits did not contain cess fills, suggesting that they may have been used as wells or refuse pits from the outset. One in the north-western part of the site (340/356) contained a large assemblage of pottery and animal bone. Pit 219, which lay to the south-east, produced only a few finds. The other two pits lay to the west of the main group (434, 435).

Period 6c: late 12th-century wattle-lined well

Among the complex of intercutting pits towards the northern part of the site was a well-preserved wattle-lined pit (191; Fig. 5.21), cut about by later medieval features including the lime-slaking pit 193 (described below). It was formed by cutting four oak base plates (still retaining their full complement of rings in places) which formed the base of a rectangular frame into which vertical wattle poles had been inserted, with woven panels described by the excavator as being of hazel. Later the pressure of the surrounding clay had caused the structure to collapse, breaking one of the base rails and causing the wattle panel above it to fall into the pit. The finds from the fill included a large animal bone assemblage, a group of pottery of *c.* 1200 and various small finds (details in dating section below).

Dating evidence

CONTEXTS CONTAINING POSSIBLE EXAMPLES OF CERAMIC HORIZON A (EAR3, 9), ?EARLY/MID 10TH CENTURY:

- Pit 66/67/68: Almost all the pottery (37 of the 41 sherds) was residual Roman material; the Late Saxon sherds were of wheel-thrown Bedford Garage Ware, a probable imported vessel and two coarse wares which were not UGSD wares.

FEATURES CONTAINING POTTERY OF CERAMIC HORIZON B (EAR3, 9), PROBABLY LATE 10TH/11TH CENTURY:

- Pits 26 (EAR3, nos. 335–41); 29 (EAR3, nos. 342–4); 439 (EAR3, nos. 355–8).

FEATURES CONTAINING POTTERY OF CERAMIC HORIZON C (EAR3, 9–10) WITH A GENERAL DATE RANGE OF LATE 10TH TO EARLY 12TH CENTURY:

- Cesspits 21; 280; 282 (EAR3, nos. 427–9); 283; rubbish pit 331 (EAR3, nos. 420–6); cesspit 334 (EAR3, nos. 345–7); cesspit 352; pits 382; 436. Smaller groups of fabric 20, Horizon C were present in contexts 161; 183; 219; 289; 292; 320; 328; 329; 338; 356; 391; 424; 434; 467, 487, 680, 681, 684 and 687.

FEATURES CONTAINING POTTERY OF CERAMIC HORIZON D (EAR3, 9), NOW DATED TO THE LATE 11TH OR EARLY 12TH CENTURY:

- Cesspit 107: Normandy gritty ware; fabric 20; cesspit 136 (EAR3, nos. 359–67); cesspit 221 (EAR3, nos. 374–8); cesspit 227: Bedford Garage Ware, fabric 20; cesspit 250: fabric 20; cesspit 276 (EAR3, nos. 452–63); cesspit 277 (EAR3, nos. 379–419); cesspit 279: EAR3, nos. 368–73; robber trench 288 (EAR3, nos. 430–50); wood-lined pit 321: fabric 20 and dendrochronological date of after AD 949 from timber in fill; cesspit 347: EAR3, nos. 464–93; dendrochronological date of after AD 1056 from timber in fill; pits 395, 398, 402, 435, 685: all fabric 20, 435 also with Normandy gritty ware and fabric 23.

THE POTTERY RECOVERED FROM THE FILLS OF THE FOLLOWING FEATURES BROADLY CONFORMS TO CERAMIC HORIZON E (EAR3, 9), NOW DATED TO THE MID TO LATE 12TH CENTURY:

- Pit 191. Dendrochronological date for construction of AD 1180. Pottery: EAR3, nos. 888–921 (*c.* 1200); also an iron staple (EAR3, 337, M.12), a strap ornament (EAR3, 339, M.109) and a possible bone flute (EAR3, 349, B.5). An Anglo-Irish coin, dating to 1281–2 (EAR3, 24, E.12) was recovered from the garden soil post-dating the infilling of the pit.

Period 7: The high medieval city (*c.* 1200–1350)

Period 7a: Industrial activity (early 13th century)

Limekiln and associated pits

After the infilling of the wattle-lined pit 191, a limekiln was built on the north-western part of the site in the early 13th century (Figs 5.22–5.23). It consisted of a circular central chamber (360) flanked by oval stoking pits (357, 393) whose

a

b

Fig. 5.21 Wattle-lined pit 191 (Period 6c): (a) view from the north, showing the broken base plate of the collapsed eastern side and the upstanding wattles of the other sides; (b) the upstanding western side (© RAMM)

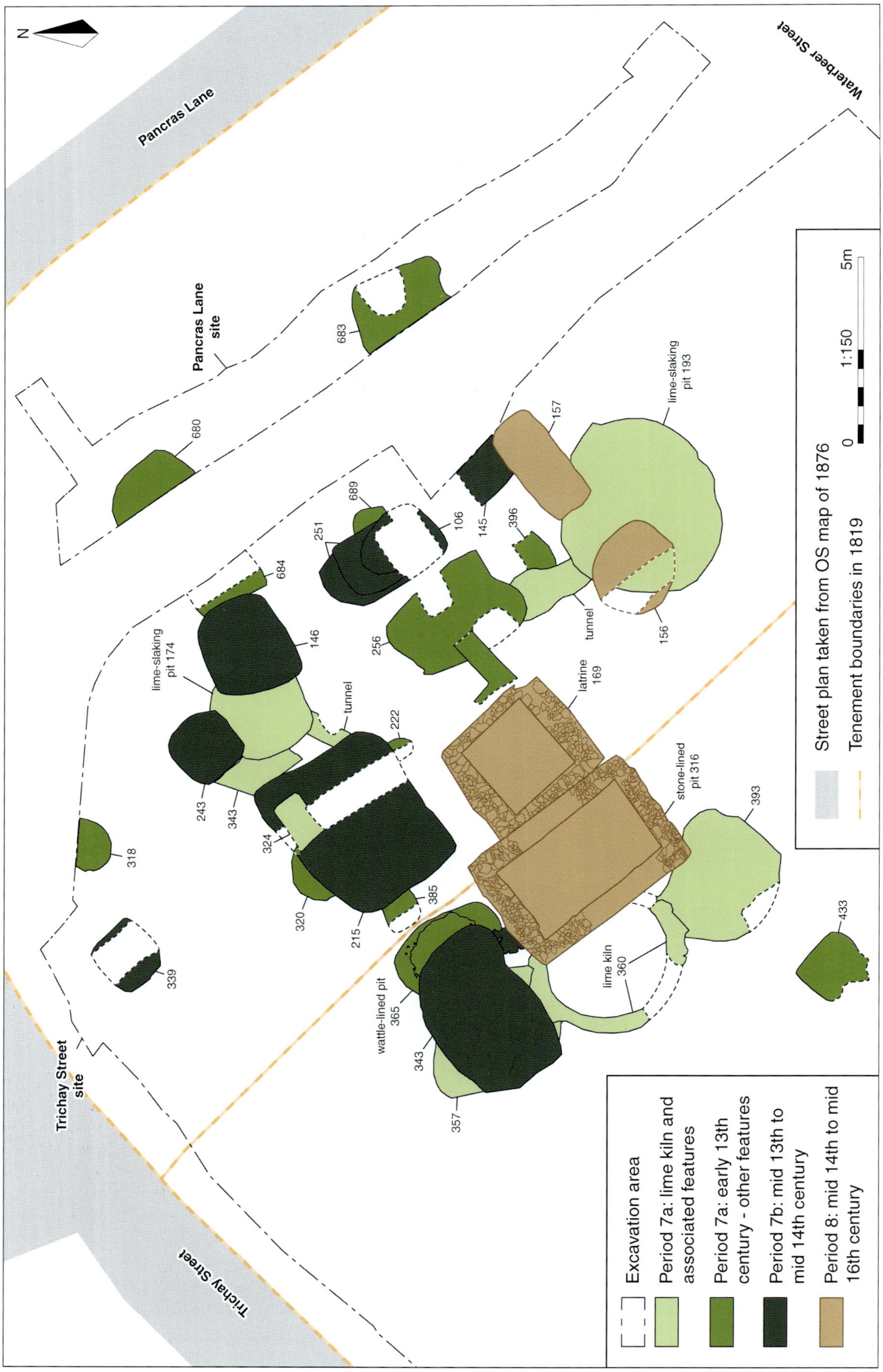

Fig. 5.22 Plan of Periods 7 (c. 1200–1350) and 8 (c. 1350–1550)

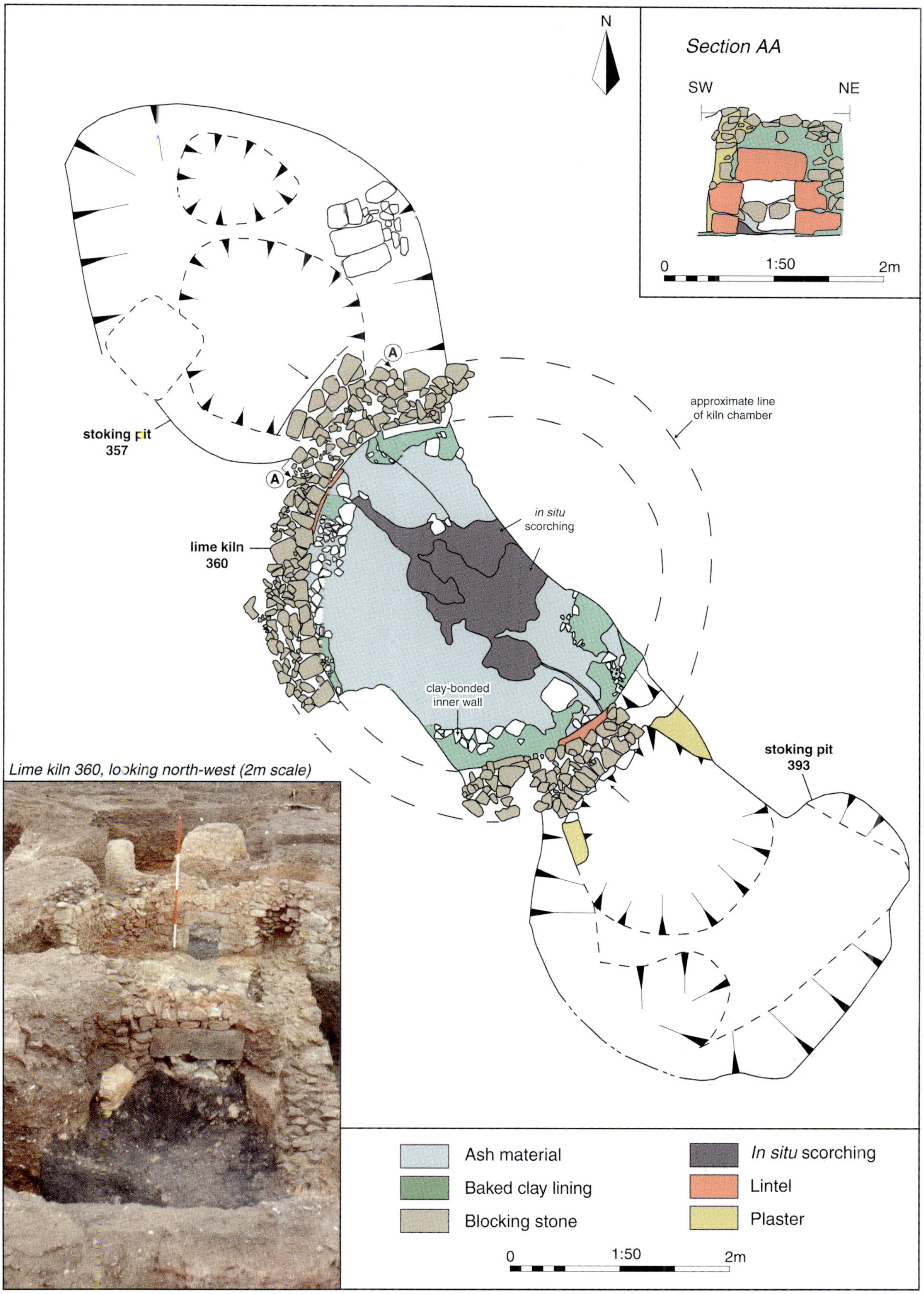

Fig. 5.23 Plan, section and photograph of the early 13th-century limekiln 360 (Period 7a). In the photograph, the 2 m long ranging rod stands at the entrance to the tunnel on its north-west side

long axes were aligned parallel to the tenement boundaries of the Waterbeer Street properties. The central chamber was dug about 0.8 m below the contemporary ground surface. It had an internal diameter of 2.8 m and consisted of a wall of volcanic stone rubble, with vertical inner and outer faces, bonded with white lime mortar (360) and surviving to a maximum height of *c.* 1 m. The kiln floor showed evidence of *in situ* burning, and was overlain by a thin layer of mixed yellow clay and lime, covered in turn by layers of wood ash and large quantities of chalk. Around the edges of the chamber floor was a secondary wall (Fig. 5.23, 'inner wall') whose top was at the same height as the kiln floor; its function is discussed below. Later features had removed about half the chamber floor, but its two opposing flues were both preserved, each *c.* 0.5 m wide and 0.5 m high, and each capped with a large rectangular dressed block of volcanic stone. They communicated with the stoking pits.

About 7 m to the east of the limekiln, two large circular pits were found (174, 193), both *c.* 1.4–1.7 m deep and containing much waste lime in their fills (Fig. 5.22). Upon excavation it became apparent that a roughly horizontal tunnel had been dug in a side of each pit, leading into a hole with vertical sides, rising to the surface about 2–3 m away. In pit 193 (Fig. 5.24) the tunnel also led into a shallow trench in the pit bottom, which in turn led to a circular depression at its centre. There were some signs of scorching in the base, but this was much more pronounced on the walls of the pits, which were heavily burnt. These features are interpreted as lime-slaking pits; they are discussed further below.

Although the kiln and lime-slaking pits must have been used together, they lie on opposite sides of the line which became the tenement boundary between 9 and 10 Waterbeer Street, which was clearly in place by the mid 14th century (see below). This appears to indicate that the tenement boundary represents the subdivision of a single large property in the course of the period *c.* 1200–1350 – a phenomenon evident elsewhere in the city at this time, for example at Rack Street (Chapter 8 below).

Period 7a: Domestic activity (early 13th century)

Well

A roughly circular wattle-lined pit (365) more than 0.7 m deep was found in the same area. Waterlogging preserved not only the woven wattle structure of the pit (Fig. 5.25) but various organic objects in the fill including oak boards (EAR3, 305, W89–91), an oak block (EAR3, 309, W33), the rim of a lathe-turned wooden bowl (EAR3, 305) and part of a leather shoe (EAR3, 327, L4). The feature was probably a well.

Cess/refuse pits

Nine cesspits (106, 145, 251, 320; also 163, 329, 402, 403, 419 which are n.i.) and eight refuse pits (146, 256,

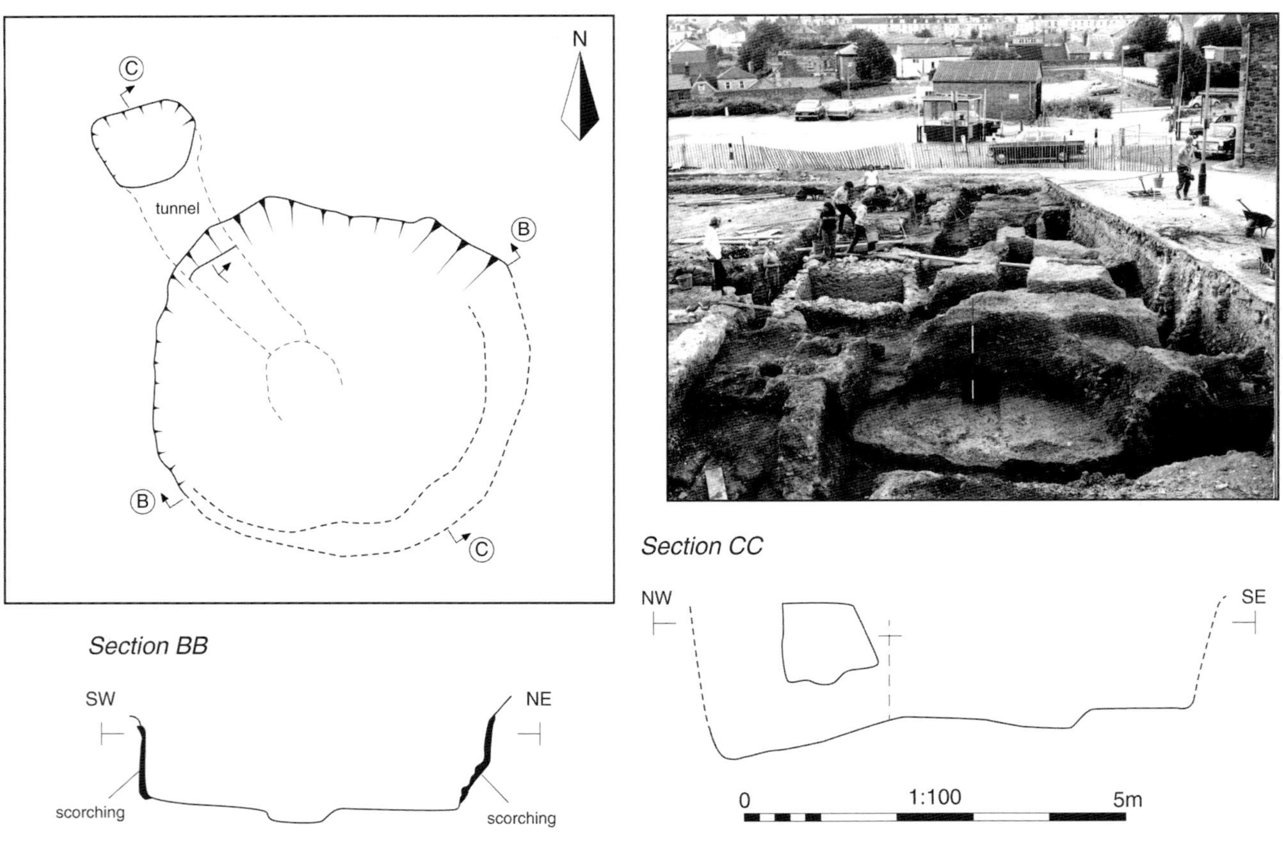

Fig. 5.24 Plan, profiles and photograph (2 m scale) of lime-slaking pit 193 (photo: © RAMM)

Fig. 5.25 The collapsed wattle lining of pit 365 (Period 7a), which was infilled in the early 13th century (© RAMM)

318, 680, 684; also 338, 398, 686 which are n.i.) in the northern part of the site contained finds of the early to mid 13th century. The marked concentration of cesspits in this area, repeating the pattern in the Saxo-Norman period, suggests that this part of the site, towards the back of the tenements, was used for lavatories and the disposal of rubbish.

Typically, the pits were *c.* 2–3 m in diameter and 0.45–1.1 m deep, square in shape and with near-vertical sides and flat bases. The cesspits had primary fills of waterlogged soft green-brown cess; some preserved organic finds. The base of a cask head (EAR3, 305, W23) and a wood panel, perhaps the side of a box (EAR3, 315, W88), were recovered from the fill of pit 163. Shoe fragments and the remains of a goatskin pouch were recovered from the fills of pits 402 and 403 respectively (EAR3, 327, L6). A large animal bone assemblage (110 NISP) was recovered from pit 145. Four cesspits (222; 385; 396; 689), similar in size and shape to those discussed above, contained no finds but have been assigned to this period from their stratigraphic relationships (for instance 222 was cut by Period 7b pit 215).

The refuse pits were generally larger, measuring 1.05–3.6 m in diameter; some contained large quantities of animal bones and pottery. Pit 256 contained layers of ash and a large assemblage of cattle and sheep bones (256 NISP). Animal bones (122 NISP) and a brooch with raised settings for green glass (EAR3, 339, M.51) were recovered from refuse pit 146. Five other pits (328; 433 and 338; 430; 487 all n.i) may also represent refuse pits, although only limited evidence for waste was recovered from their fills. During this period a robber trench (354, n.i.) was dug to recover stone from an internal partition wall of the Late Roman town house (RC13).

Dating evidence

LIMEKILN AND ASSOCIATED FEATURES:

- Infilling of limekiln 360 and associated stoking pits 357, 393: Pottery: EAR3, nos. 961–97 (1200–50).
- Lime-slaking pits 174, 193: Pottery: EAR3, nos. 1062–71, 1050–5 (both 1200–50).

THE POTTERY FROM THE FILLS OF THE FOLLOWING FEATURES CONFORMS TO CERAMIC HORIZON F (*c.* 1180–1250) (EAR3, 9):

- Cesspit 251A. Pottery: EAR3, nos. 1161–8. Refuse pit 256. Pottery: EAR3, nos. 1056–61. Refuse? pit 318. Pottery: fabric 20; Dorset sandy ware. Occupation layer 342. Pottery: fabric 20; glazed sherd. Robber trench 354. Pottery: N. French white wares; Dorset sandy wares; fabric 20. Pit 365. Pottery: EAR3, nos. 922–60; Pit 386: N. French white wares; Dorset sandy wares; fabric 60 pitcher sherds. Cesspit 403. Pottery: EAR3, nos. 624–48. Cesspit 419. Pottery: fabric 20 and ?import. Layer 423. Pottery: fabric 20, fabric 27; Normandy green-glazed. Pit 430. Pottery: fabric 20 and sandy wares. Pit 433. Pottery: fabric 20 and sandy ware. Refuse pit 686. Pottery: London ware; N French white ware; fabric 20. Cesspit 163 contained no pottery

THE POTTERY FROM THE FOLLOWING FEATURE CONFORMS TO CERAMIC HORIZON G (MID 13TH CENTURY) (EAR3, 9):

- Refuse pit 146. Pottery: EAR3, nos. 1107–46.

Period 7b: Domestic occupation (c. 1250–1350)

Cesspits and rubbish pits

The concentration of rubbish pits and cesspits in the northern part of the site is still evident in the late 13th and early 14th centuries; the repeated use of this area for this purpose into the 14th century created a very complex sequence of intercutting pits. Among the major features of this period were two large cesspits (343, 215), whose primary organic fills were later covered by a thick layer of clay; pit 343 also contained lime derived from one of the underlying limekiln stoking pits (357). A large assemblage of cattle and sheep bones (302 NISP), an important assemblage of pottery including a London ware jug and a curfew (fire-cover; EAR3, nos. 85–7) and a number of small finds including a small bell (EAR3, 341, M.138) and a key (EAR3, 345, M.184) were recovered from pit 215. This feature cut a robber trench (324), dug to extract stone from a wall of the Late Roman town house (RC13), which contained finds broadly of the same date. Pit 215 was quickly succeeded by a later pit (214, n.i.), but still of early 14th-century date. Another much shallower refuse pit (339) lay to the north-west; yet another pit (243), just to the north of pit 215, contained no dating evidence but is assigned to this phase as it cut the lime-slaking pit 174.

Dating evidence

THE POTTERY FROM THE FOLLOWING FEATURES CONFORMS BROADLY TO CERAMIC HORIZON H (*C.* 1250–1350)

- Cesspit 106: Exeter jugs, fabrics 40/42. Cesspit 145: mainly fabric 20, also Exeter jugs. Refuse pit 214: Exeter jugs fabrics 40/42. Cess/refuse pit 215: EAR3, nos. 1401–22. Upcast layer 255: Saintonge, after 1250. Robber trench 324: minor pottery group, fabric 40/42 jugs. Refuse pit 339: minor pottery group, Exeter/S. Somerset jugs. Cesspit 343. Pottery: minor group with Saintonge; Exeter jug fabrics 40, 42.

Period 8: The later medieval city (*c.* 1350–1550)

By the mid 14th century the practice of digging open cesspits, rubbish pits and wicker-lined wells in back gardens had ceased, and throughout the city there is therefore a sharp decline in the number of features represented in this period. The most notable features at Trichay Street were two large stone-lined pits, abutting each other on either side of the tenement boundary between 9 and 10 Waterbeer Street (Fig. 5.22). They may have had covering structures, no trace of which survived.

The earlier and smaller one (169) measured 3.65 × 3.05 m in plan and was more than 0.95 m deep (Fig. 5.26). Its walls were built of uncoursed local volcanic trap rubble, bonded with a sandy yellow lime mortar. The natural clay in the centre of the pit bottom had been dug to a deeper level than the bottoms of the walls. The lowest fill consisted of a large quantity of cess. The pit was subsequently backfilled with an important assemblage of domestic rubbish including pottery of the late 14th or early 15th century and much animal bone (147 NISP). The waterlogged conditions also preserved branches and a range of organic objects including a lathe-turned wooden plate and bowls (EAR3, 305, W3–4 and 13), leather finds including parts of shoes and a knife sheath in a style of typical of the late 14th/early 15th century (EAR3, 327, L17–18), and eight split oak boards (EAR3, 315, W93–101) six of which (samples 33–8) were dated by dendrochronology to between AD 1114±9 and 1249, showing that they were at least a century old when discarded. The pit may have replaced the open cesspit 215, which lay beside the same boundary about 1–1.5 m to the north-west and had been backfilled in late 13th or early 14th century.

The second stone-lined pit (316) was a massive structure abutting the other side of the tenement boundary between 9 and 10 Waterbeer Street (Fig. 5.27). Its mortar-bonded walls consisted of volcanic rubble intermixed with large coursed blocks of Heavitree stone – the building stone which came into circulation in the late 14th century and continued to be popular in the city into the 19th century. Rather more than 2 m of the pit fill was excavated, and one of the most remarkable collections of medieval and later objects ever excavated in the region was recovered. Although the final infilling of the pit did not take place until *c.* 1660, many of the finds dated from the two preceding centuries or earlier, and the lowest deposits examined (layers 23–30) were clearly of late medieval date. They contained a very large assemblage of shoes, boots, clothing fragments, belts, dagger/knife-sheaths and other leather finds (EAR3, 330–3, L65), with cask fragments, lathe-turned bowls and other wooden objects (EAR3, 305, 309), late medieval vessel glass (EAR3, 268, G41–2, 44, 46), a very large collection of animal bones, and pottery of the late 15th or early 16th centuries (EAR3, nos. 2141–3). Perhaps the most unusual find was a pair of coin forger's dies, designed for the illicit production of gold nobles and half-nobles of the period 1351–1413

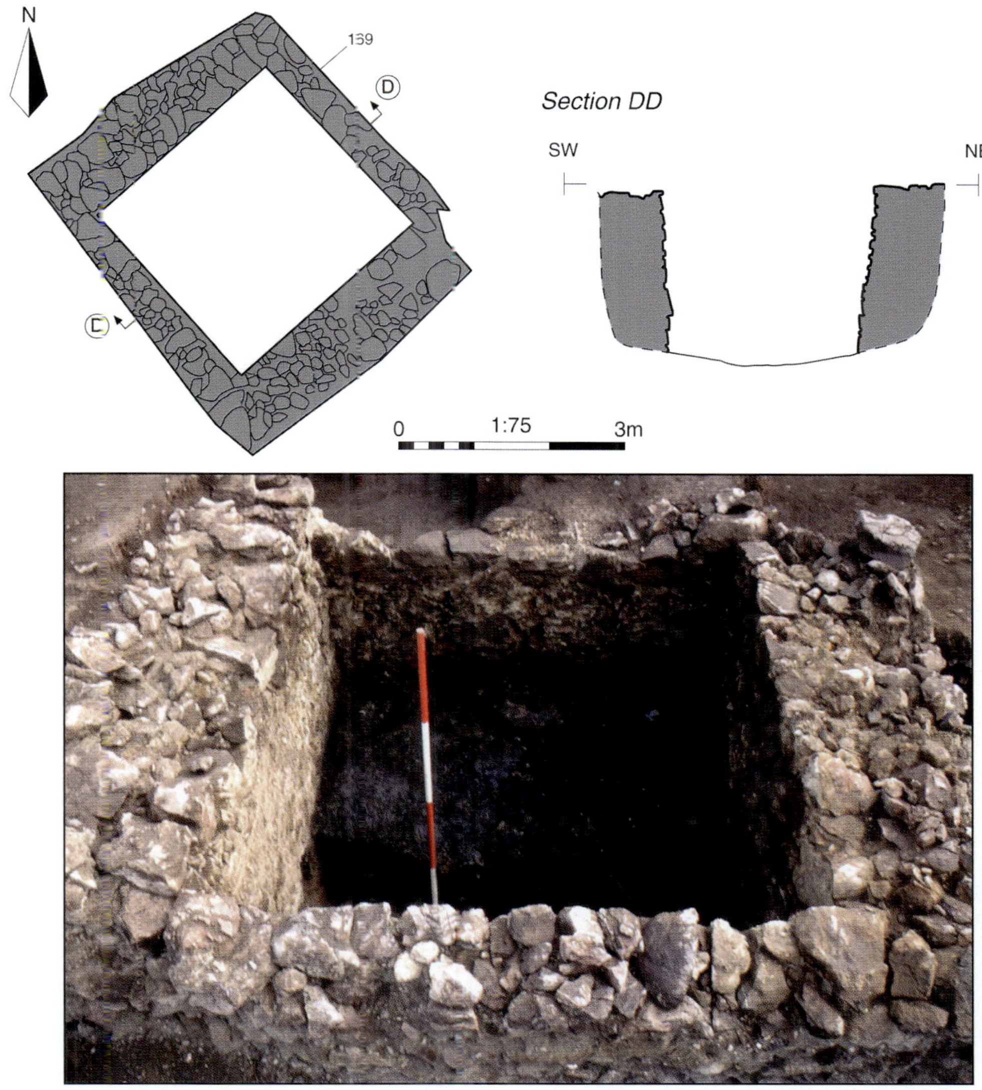

Fig. 5.26 Stone-lined pit 169 (Period 8): plan, section and photograph during excavation (© RAMM)

(EAR3, 253–4, D1–2 from layer 23). Following the excavation, the destruction of the lower parts of the pit, also in Heavitree stone, with their black organic fills, was observed from a distance when the site was bulldozed in 1974. It was then estimated that the pit descended as much as *c.* 2 m below the point where excavation had been halted. No further finds were recovered, and it was not possible to examine the lowest fills of the pit. For this reason the question of whether this was simply a large cesspit, backfilled with rubbish over a long period, is unresolved. At the time of excavation the feature was interpreted instead as an industrial pit; this is discussed further below.

Two further cesspits (156, 157, n.i.) and a pit of unknown function (599, n.i.) were also infilled in the late 15th and early 16th centuries. All structural evidence on the street frontage had been destroyed by cellars and it is likely that further late medieval features have been truncated by post-medieval activities.

Dating evidence

- Cesspit 156. Pottery: EAR3, nos. 1713–16 (1500–50).
- Cesspit 157. Pottery: EAR3, nos. 1551–5 (1450–1500).
- Garderobe 169. Pottery; EAR3, nos. 1451–62 (late 14th/early 15th century). Also leather and wooden objects (details in text).
- Stone-lined pit 316. Pottery and many other finds EAR3, 180–5, 253–4, 268, 330–3, closing date *c.* 1660.
- Pit 599. Pottery: EAR3, nos. 1818–19 (late 15th/early mid 16th century).

Discussion of the medieval evidence *by John Allan*

Introduction

The medieval features excavated at Trichay Street and on Goldsmith Street Area III (see Chapter 6 below) bore many points in common, and the two excavations yielded similar

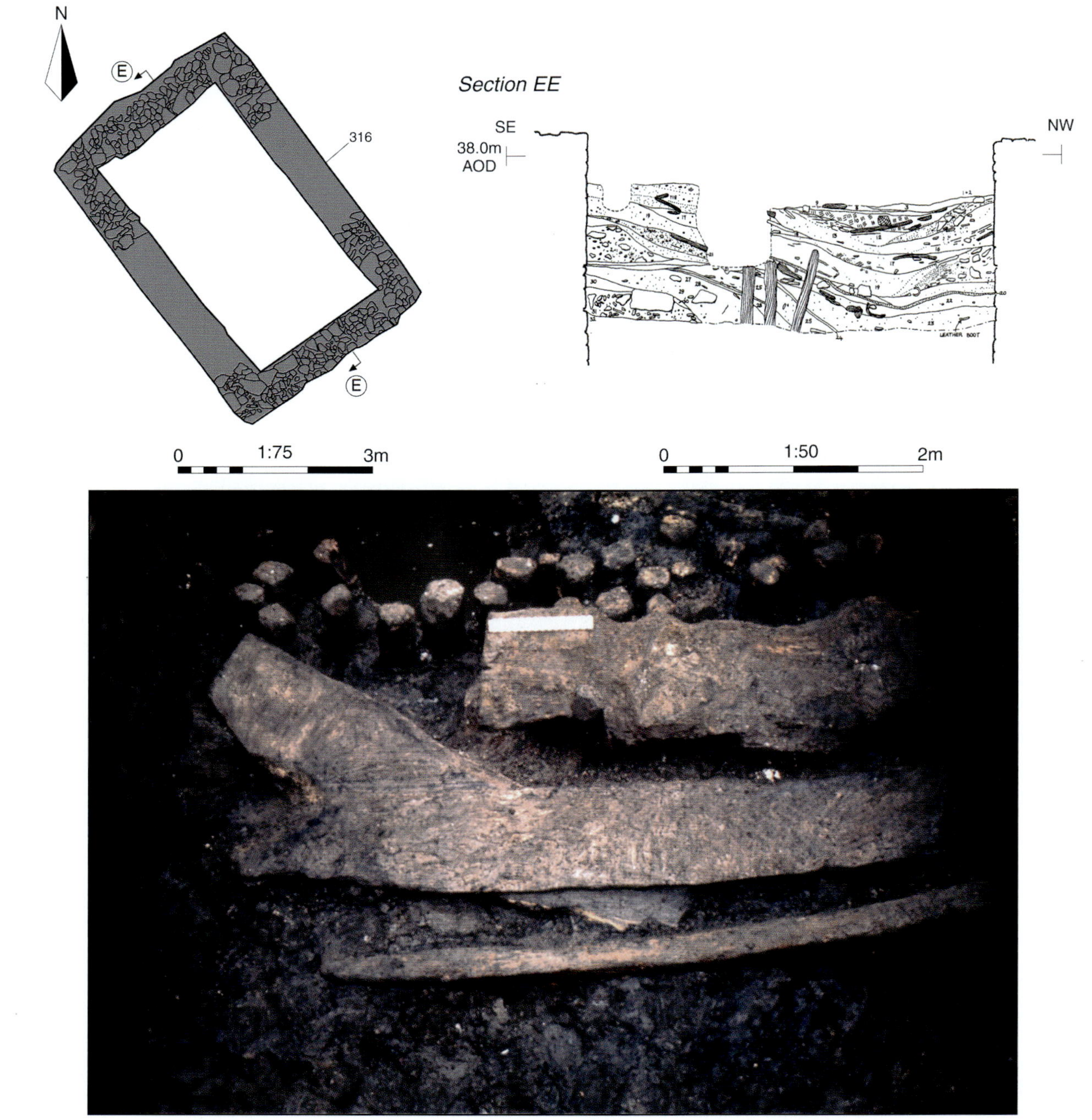

Fig. 5.27 Stone-lined pit 316 (Period 8): plan, section of excavated deposits and photograph of waterlogged timbers (with driven piles supporting a wall of a later building in top of view) (© RAMM)

evidence; they will therefore be discussed together. In order to understand the results, two fundamental aspects of these sites should first be considered: their topography (with its effect on the formation of stratified deposits) and geology.

Topography

Trichay Street and Goldsmith Street lie on a slope running down from High Street to the Longbrook to the north. Here and on neighbouring sites close to the centre of the Early Roman town, stratified deposits quickly accumulated to a depth of 1 m or more in the late 1st and 2nd centuries AD as short-lived buildings with earth floors and timber-and-clay walls succeeded one another (presumably because building materials were brought into the fortress and early town). With the change to stone houses in the Late Roman town the process of accumulation was reduced markedly, and in the Late Saxon and medieval periods there was only a modest build-up of stratified deposits. Here, as in much of Exeter, such deposits suffered erosion as the city's sloping streets developed into hollow ways, and floor levels on street frontages were terraced back into the slope in the medieval period and later. The modern road surface of North Street, for example, is now almost 1 m below the yards at the back of the tenements which flank it. Throughout this part of the city, post-Roman deposits are therefore generally thin or absent, and structural evidence usually scrappy or non-existent. Roman features are commonly surprisingly close to the modern surface. In Goldsmith Street Site III, part of the tessellated pavement of the Late Roman town house was found immediately below modern tarmac (Chapter 6 below). A section recorded in Waterbeer Street, about 25 m south-west of the Trichay Street excavation, exposed a sequence of Roman streets, the highest being only 0.40 m below the present pavement level (Site 51: 45–6 North Street; part of the section is shown at http://archaeologydataservice.ac.uk/archives/view/exeter_51_2015/overview.cfm, its position on the south-western side of Waterbeer Street marked '*via quintana*' at http://archaeologydataservice.ac.uk/archives/view/exeter_51_2015/index.cfm). Further down the slope, closer to the fringes of the walled area, no stratification survived below 19th-century house plots along Paul Street, as John Collis found in 1971 (the area of 41–7 Paul Street. For the site see Collis 1972, fig. 1; Henderson *et al.* 1993b, fig. 1; the area was cleaned but does not appear on plans because there were no archaeological features). The medieval archaeology of the Guildhall area sites therefore consists of numerous pits, often in complex relationships, with little or no horizontal stratification or structural evidence. At Trichay Street there were deep Victorian cellars on the frontage, where we might expect the principal structures. At Goldsmith Street Site III there were no such cellars, but nevertheless hardly any medieval building remains survived.

Geology

Much of central Exeter lies directly on river terrace gravel. By contrast, Permo-Triassic clays lie below Trichay Street, Goldsmith Street III and some nearby sites – yellow-brown and weathered when close to the surface but with spectacular hues of purple and mauve clays at depths below 1 m or so. These clays are water-holding, creating anaerobic conditions where features are cut below the natural surface. Thus the preservation of organic material in the lower parts of pits on these sites was especially good, providing information about the internal wooden structures of features and allowing the recovery of important assemblages of waterlogged organic artefacts and environmental samples.

At the time of excavation, some of the studies which arose from the material recovered, such as the dendrochronological analyses and the publication of textile fragments, leatherwork and wooden objects, were innovations. Had these sites been dug in recent years, however, with far greater emphasis on the analysis of organic remains, and with better provision of conservation facilities, a much wider range of analytical techniques would no doubt have been applied to this material.

Chronology

Only a very few pits containing pottery from the earliest horizon have been distinguished in the Late Saxon *burh* (EAR3, 9–10, Horizon A). In this regard the results from Trichay Street and Goldsmith Street III correspond with those from the four other sites in the Guildhall area (196–7 High Street, Queen Street, and Goldsmith Street Areas I and II; Sites 43, 68, 37), suggesting that there was little settlement in this part of the city at the very early stage in the development of the *burh* (see EAPIT 1, Chapter 7).

A striking feature of both Trichay Street and Goldsmith Street Area III was the large number of Late Saxon and Early Norman pit groups. They demonstrate the rise of urban occupation represented by wells, cesspits and the disposal of domestic rubbish. A major contribution of both excavations was the recovery of substantial collections of animal bone, pottery and waterlogged wooden objects. The few early features were followed by intensive pit-digging spanning the 11th, 12th, 13th and early 14th centuries. Given the uncertainties regarding the dating of the ceramic horizons, and of individual features, no clear signs of changes in the intensity of activity have been distinguished over this long period. Dendrochronological dating provides more precision in selected cases. Two samples from Trichay Street are likely to belong to the late 10th century (after AD 949± 9 from pit 321 and after AD 962±9 from pit 162, although an unknown number of missing rings need to be added to both samples). Ten dendrochronological samples from Goldsmith Street Area III yielded dendrochronological dates of the early 11th century, and further samples of this date came from Trichay Street (EAR3, 317, 320); both sites produced further dates in the 12th century. The interpretation of these results is discussed further in EAPIT 1, Chapter 7.

After the mid 14th century there is a sharp decrease in the number of excavated features. Although the documentary evidence does show that one of the Trichay Street site properties was vacant after the Black Death, the archaeological evidence need not be interpreted as evidence for a decline in activity on the site; the disappearance of the typical medieval open pit in the back yard from the archaeological record is a phenomenon recorded elsewhere – not only on other sites in Exeter but more widely in English towns. In the 1970s it was noted, for example, at Southampton (Platt and Coleman-Smith 1975, I, 32–5) and it was discussed in a wider context by Platt (1976, 70–2). More recently, Schofield and Vince (1998, 80–3, 232–4 and *passim*) have reviewed the subject. The change probably reflects changing patterns of water supply and waste disposal, with stone-lined garderobes within houses replacing cesspits in gardens, and the rise of urban rubbish collection. Portman illustrated some good examples of internal garderobes in late medieval town houses in Exeter, both surviving and in the documentary record, but noted that their provision seems to have been far from universal in the late medieval city, perhaps serving only a minority of households (Portman 1966, 15–16). He also quoted instances of the collection of '*gumphus*' (night soil?) from city properties in the 15th century (*ibid.*).

The pits

Types of pit

Although a wide range of shapes and sizes of medieval pit are represented on the Guildhall sites, and many do not fall readily into types, a number of distinctive forms are represented:

a. *Circular wicker-lined pits* in which quite well-made woven hurdles lined the circular shaft. They are presumed to be wells, allowing water to drain through the lining whilst supporting the surrounding soil, but were commonly infilled with domestic rubbish. (Fig. 5.20)
b. *Rectangular wicker-lined pits* with a horizontal timber on each side of the pit bottom, into which vertical rods were dowelled, with woven wickerwork between the rods, which would have prevented the sides from eroding whilst allowing water to accumulate in the pit bottom, as in type (a). TS 191 a good example (Fig. 5.21).
c. *Cask-lined pits* – circular vertical shafts, revetted by casks whose tops and bottoms had been removed, allowing water to percolate into the base from below. Goldsmith Street pit GS 281 is a well-preserved example of a single-depth cask (Fig. 6.11). A pit excavated at Paul Street in 1982 was the sole example from the city excavations of two casks placed one above the other.
d. *Plank-lined wells* – pits, roughly square in plan, with vertical corner posts holding horizontal planks. GS 315 is a good example, formed of riven oak.
e. *Stone-lined garderobes* – small rectangular-walled shafts, less than 1 m wide, some containing cess. Examples are known on various sites in the city including Queen Street (Site 68), and the National Westminster Bank, High Street (Site 62), and 38 North Street (Site 38); their infilling spanning the period from at least the early 15th to the early18th century.
f. *Stone-lined pits, possibly cisterns rather than having an industrial function* – Much larger well-built stone-walled rectangular pits, *c.* 3 m wide, 3.6–4 m long and 2–4 m or more deep, the central area of the bottom sometimes scooped out to a greater depth. These pits were a distinctive feature of the excavations at Trichay Street and Goldsmith Street Site III, where four were excavated (TS 169, 316; GS 201, 228; Figs 5.26 and 5.27). A further example was observed but not recorded in detail when the tenements to the west of the Trichay Street site were removed by machine in 1974, but such features have not been recorded on any other excavated Exeter site. The deposits which marked their final abandonment ranged in date between the late 14th and the mid 17th century. A striking feature of two of these pits was the evidence that they were infilled over very long periods: GS 228 yielded early 14th-century pottery and pewter in its lower fills but was not finally infilled until the early 16th century, whilst the lower fills of TS 316 yielded large quantities of leather, glass, pottery and other objects of the late 14th and 15th centuries, whilst the top was not finally infilled until *c.* 1660–70 (details in EAR3, 180–5, including a drawn section of TS 316). Their use is discussed below.

Pit functions: the 10th to 13th centuries

The excavations took place before the analysis of soil samples for parasite eggs became a well-established procedure; the recognition of cesspits has therefore relied simply on records of soft greenish fills in pit bottoms, recorded in the site notes. The first four types of pit described above (a–d) were cut into water-bearing clay, preserved organic remains, and gathered water when they were re-excavated. The wicker-lined examples belong to types of pit known elsewhere, for example, at Lincoln and York (Jones *et al.* 2003, 266–7). Their initial function was probably as wells, although some served subsequently as rubbish pits or cesspits. On the other hand, many of these features were simply open, unlined holes. Certainly many of them were used as cesspits, and some or many may have been had this purpose from the start. Alongside the many records of cess in pit fills, two garderobe seats were recovered – one a two-seater from a late 10th to early 12th-century pit consisting of a stout sawn oak plank, originally about 1.8 m long with two large circular holes towards the middle (EAR3, 316, W.102), the second a possible example which yielded a dendrochronological date after AD 949 ±9 had been reused to revet one side of the pit TS 321 (*ibid.*, 313, W.76).

The function of the later stone-lined pits

The purpose of the four large stone-lined pits is less clear. They were not cellars as the bottoms of some of them had been dug down below the bases of the walls, making it difficult to stand in them (this would have increased the capacity of these features and was probably too pronounced a feature to represent regular use). Neither do they seem to have been garderobes since cess was not identified in GS 201, GS 228 or TS 316, although it was noted in the bottom fills of TS 169. The site notes relating to GS 201 are very brief, and TS316 was not bottomed, but GS 228 was carefully excavated to its full depth. The black peaty organic lower fills of this feature certainly did not contain recognisable cess deposits (Chapter 6 below). It may also be significant that they were much larger than the Type E garderobes described above (up to *c.* 40 cubic metres in capacity).

When they were excavated it seemed probable that these were features connected with some specific industrial process. The wall-tops of GS 228 retained sockets representing either the joists of an overlying floor or a series of parallel horizontal timbers running over the pit. In TS 316 the excavators reported that the walls were lined with pitch, although no samples seem to have been analysed to confirm the identification. If correct, this shows that this particular pit at least was designed to retain water; the anaerobic conditions in the bottoms of all these features show that they held water.

The use of the pits for tanning was considered during the excavations and deserves discussion. In their dimensions these features bear some general similarities to stone-lined pits found in other towns which have been interpreted as tanning pits, such as the 11th-century examples at Lower Bridge Street, in Chester (Mason 1985, 23–31 – although only 1.5 m and 0.8 m deep), but the Exeter features are isolated, contrasting with the groups of pits found on definite tannery sites (for a very helpful review of the subject see Shaw 1996, 107–20). They also lack the lime or bark deposits which seem characteristic of tanneries. Neither do any of them display the characteristic faunal assemblages of tanneries (*ibid.*; Albarella 2003; Yeomans 2008; Levitan 2019). It is true that some contained waste leather fragments, but they indicate the cobbling of old shoes and are unconnected to shoe production (Friendship-Taylor 1984, 325, 327–33). Interpretation as tanning pits therefore seems unconvincing, and neither the structural nor the faunal evidence supports this interpretation.

These features, then, were designed for the bulk storage of liquids (presumably water). They were positioned in various parts of the tenements – two backing on to a boundary wall separating two back yards, one on the street frontage where, almost certainly, it lay below the floor of a house. There seems to have been one of these features in each of the larger tenements excavated in the Goldsmith Street/Waterbeer Street area. One or two possible examples of comparable stone-lined pits have also been found by chance in the cellars of properties in Cathedral Close (notably the so-called 'Roman bath' at 16 Cathedral Yard, although that might have been a medieval garderobe) but it is notable that they have not been recorded on sites excavated further from the city centre – for example in the West Quarter, Exe Bridge or in the suburbs. This may be because they were features associated with more substantial properties, but might also suggest that they were a type of feature particularly suited to the impermeable Permian clay underlying the Trichay Street and Goldsmith Street sites. The most likely interpretation, we suggest, is simply that they were used as cisterns – an alternative to the deeper wells needed where the water table was lower.

Artefacts and ecofacts

Much of the significance of the sites lay in their rich collections of artefacts and ecofacts, especially from Saxo-Norman deposits. The large assemblages of animal bone from Trichay Street and Goldsmith Street were important components of the assemblages published by Maltby, who analysed about 7,400 stratified medieval bones from Trichay Street (EAR2, 109–47). Rather more than 7,000 sherds of medieval pottery were recovered from the site, most of them likewise in stratified groups, with some excellent pit groups. Indeed the study of the medieval and later pottery from Trichay Street and Goldsmith Street was the foundation of post-Roman ceramic studies in Exeter; their intercutting pits allowing a sequence of ceramic horizons to be established (EAR3). In a regional context they remain some of the key groups for considering the pottery sequence of the surrounding area.

The medieval artefacts of wood and leather from Trichay Street and Goldsmith Street Site III remain the only substantial finds of this sort from any Saxo-Norman context in South-West England. The dendrochronological studies which arose from this material broke new ground, being the first to be undertaken in the region, and leading on to further work in Exeter houses and at the cathedral, followed some years later by the programme of dating standing Devon farmhouses, undertaken by English Heritage. Forty years later, they remain the most substantial tree ring-studies of Saxo-Norman samples in the region (see Chapter 11 below).

The limekiln and associated features

A limekiln is a structure designed to produce quicklime (calcium oxide) by burning limestone (calcium carbonate) at temperatures above 900 °C. After the quicklime is removed from the kiln, it is mixed with water to create slaked or hydrated lime (calcium hydroxide), which forms the basis of mortars and plasters (Williams 2004; Smith 2011).

Limekilns fall into two broad categories: flare kilns and draw kilns (Williams 2004). In a flare kiln, the type generally used in medieval Britain, a bottom layer of coal or charcoal was laid on the floor of the chamber, and the kiln above loaded solely with limestone. The two were separated by a temporary vault of limestone which sat on a stone or clay ledge within the walls. Fires lit in the flues burned for several days; afterwards the entire kiln was emptied of lime. By contrast, in a draw kiln, the type which came to supersede the flare kiln in the 18th and 19th centuries, the chamber was filled with layers of chalk or limestone alternating with layers of wood, coal or coke which were stacked over a grate at the base of the chamber. As the stack burnt and sank to the bottom of the chamber, lime was extracted through the draw hole at the bottom of the kiln, and further layers of stone and fuel were added to the top (Williams 2004).

The Trichay Street structure was clearly a flare kiln, having the distinctive inner ledge which would have supported the temporary internal limestone vault which separated the fuel from the charge. The broad flat bottom of the chamber is another characteristic of the type: a draw kiln needed sloping sides which would funnel the lime towards the draw hole. Although examples of flare kilns with domed roofs are known in the 19th century, it is presumed that medieval kilns would have been open-topped.

Medieval limekilns varied considerably in size; they ranged from 1–5 m in internal diameter (for comparative plans see Smith 2011). Excavated examples are known with one, two, three or four flues. The costs of construction of early 13th-century kilns, broadly of the same date as the Trichay Street example, varied accordingly from £2 10s to £20 (Salzman 1952, 150–1). The largest and most costly may have resembled the huge early 13th-century kiln excavated by Jane Hassall at Bedford, 4.1–4.5 m wide at the bottom, and with a surviving height of 2.8 m, where it was 5.8 m wide (Hassall 1979). Thus, with two flues and an internal diameter of 3.5 m, this example is rather larger than average, although appreciably larger examples are known. How high would it have stood? A basic point which has emerged from the experimental firing of updraught kilns firing pottery is that the chamber needs to be at least as high as it is broad to achieve the necessary draw to operate effectively (Dawson and Kent 1999; 2008). This is likely to be the case with limekilns, which need to reach the same temperature, and instances of medieval English kilns measuring 14 feet high and 14 feet deep, and 10 feet internally but 20 feet high, are documented (Salzman 1952, 150–1). The Trichay Street structure is therefore likely to have stood at least 3.5 m above the kiln floor; given the almost-flat site, loading its top would thus have required some form of surrounding mound or stepped approach.

The second stage in the production of lime was carried out after the removal of the burnt limestone blocks from the kiln. They were transferred into lime-slaking pits, where water was poured on them, converting them to quicklime. This was a violent and potentially dangerous process in which great heat was produced; the lime spat unpredictably when water was poured on it. The excavation examined two lime-slaking pits (174 and 193); in each case a tunnel had been dug, sloping up from the bottom of one side to ground level about 3 m away. Burnt limestone would have been placed in the pit bottom; water would then have been poured in through the tunnel without the danger of direct exposure to the bubbling quicklime. The tunnels do not seem to be a feature of all medieval lime-slaking pits; for example no such feature was noted in the large (1.8 m wide and 2.5 m deep) lime-pit dug into the back of the town defences at Roushill, in Shrewsbury, which was found half-full of slaked lime (Barker 1961).

Lime-burning generated acrid smoke and noxious fumes; it might therefore be expected that a kiln would be located some distance away from occupation. In this instance, however, several pits in this part of the excavated area produced pottery of the same ceramic horizon as the limekiln, some preceding the lime-burning (Period 6b, pit 191 and Period 7a, pit 365) and some later than it (Period 7b, pits 256 and 146, the latter only slightly later). It seems clear that the tenement was occupied when the kiln and slaking pits were used. This is unsurprising; in the recent past Cornish limekilns, for example, sometimes stood beside houses and cottages (Isham 2000, 46–7 and *passim*).

Medieval limekilns can sometimes be associated with specific building programmes, including those of major churches, town walls or castles. In this instance it is hard to make such a connection. The kiln was certainly built after 1180 and probably after 1200 (it followed the infilling of pit 191, whose structure yielded a tree-ring date of AD 1180: EAR3, 317), and was probably backfilled before *c.* 1250 (EAR3, 70–5). The kiln is some distance from the largest medieval stone building in the city – the cathedral, which was not undertaking major building works in the early 13th century, apart from the Chapter House. The city walls and the two urban friaries may all have been customers, and there may have been work at St Nicholas Priory in this period, but the kiln is not close to any of them. It seems more likely that it reflects a steady growth in stone house-building in the early 13th century as the city changed from timber to stone houses.

Although instances of the use of coal in the firing of limekilns are known in London and Corfe in the 1270s and 1280s (Salzman 1952, 150–1), the small amount of evidence at Trichay Street indicates wood-firing. Regarding the origin of the chalk, a probable source may be suggested. The nearest chalk outcrops to Exeter are in the coastal parishes of Beer and Branscombe in south-east Devon, where there is a long history of quarrying chalk for lime-burning, as well as for building stone (BGS 2017). These parishes supplied building stone to Exeter on a considerable scale, both by coastal traffic in barges and by overland carriage. They are the obvious source for the chalk, and were used into the 19th century.

Appendix 5.1

Late Saxon structural timbers

David Gould

Four timbers of radially cut oak recovered from 11th or early 12th-century cesspit 347 are of note for their unusual form (Fig. 5.28). Timbers W.80–2 are planks with tapering ends and a notched groove cut along their upper surface while W.83 has two notched faces (EAR3, 314). The timbers were subject to tree-ring dating analysis; timbers W.80–3 correspond to the dendrochronology samples TS 28–30, with W.82 not being sampled. TS sample 28 was not measured because it had less than 50 tree rings, while TS sample 29 in fact corresponds to a timber separate from this group, W.84 (EAR3, 315). Consequently, only timber W.83 can therefore be dated and had a felling date of 962 ± 9 (EAR3, MF 130). Three other timbers, of differing forms, were recovered from the same context and were dated: W.84 (TS sample 29) was felled in 1040 ± 9 and W.86–7 (TS samples 31–2) were felled in 1056 ± 9. Allan (EAR3, 315) suggested that the beams W.80–2 were originally part of a framed timber building, with the planks either being laid horizontally and held in place by corner posts, or vertically with the pointed ends placed in a foundation beam. The former scenario was considered most likely as beam W.83 with two notched faces could have held the ends of horizontal planks in a rectangular structure.

Both scenarios are possible, although a tradition of constructing outer walls of buildings using vertical planks of timber was relatively widespread across north-west Europe from the early medieval period until the 12th and 13th centuries; thereafter it was largely restricted to Scandinavian churches and to rural ancillary buildings in the Alpine region (Chapelot and Fossier 1985, 273). The technique of constructing buildings using vertical planks of timber is known by continental authors as the *Stabbau* technique, a German term indicative of the fact that the distribution of such buildings known from excavation is most heavily concentrated in northern Germany, particularly at sites where Scandinavian influence was probable, if not certain (*ibid.*, 269). However, this prominence may partly be the result of favourable conditions for the preservation of organic materials in the ground in this region and it may also reflect the development of particular approaches to medieval archaeology there (*ibid.*, 273). Documentary sources in fact suggest that *Stabbau* buildings may have had a more westerly distribution than is suggested by excavation, particularly as 5th to 10th-century references to churches described as *ecclesia ligneis tabulis fabricata* (church made of wooden planks) are relatively numerous (*ibid.*, 270). English-language texts tend to use the term stave walls rather than the German *stabbau* terminology, although early medieval stave buildings are relatively rare within the UK and Ireland (see below).

The *Stabbau*, or stave wall, technique of constructing buildings using vertical planks of timber was derived from vertical palisade walls and incorporated the development of tongue-and-grooved joints between the vertical planks. The notches cut into the Trichay Street timbers W.80–2 would appear to correspond to the tradition of constructing walls using tongue-and-grooved jointed vertical planks. Within the *Stabbau* tradition, two methods of tongue-and-grooved construction were employed (Fig. 5.29): the first used alternating double-grooved planks and thin planks; the second was quoining, using single grooved planks with a tapering thin edge (*ibid.*, 269). The profile of the Trichay Street timbers W.80–82 with their single grooves and tapering edges would therefore conform to the second method of tongue-and-groove construction; timber W.83, with grooves on two faces, would therefore represent a corner post.

Although their survival is rare in the UK and Ireland, examples of buildings of vertical tongue-and-grooved construction have been noted at excavations in waterlogged

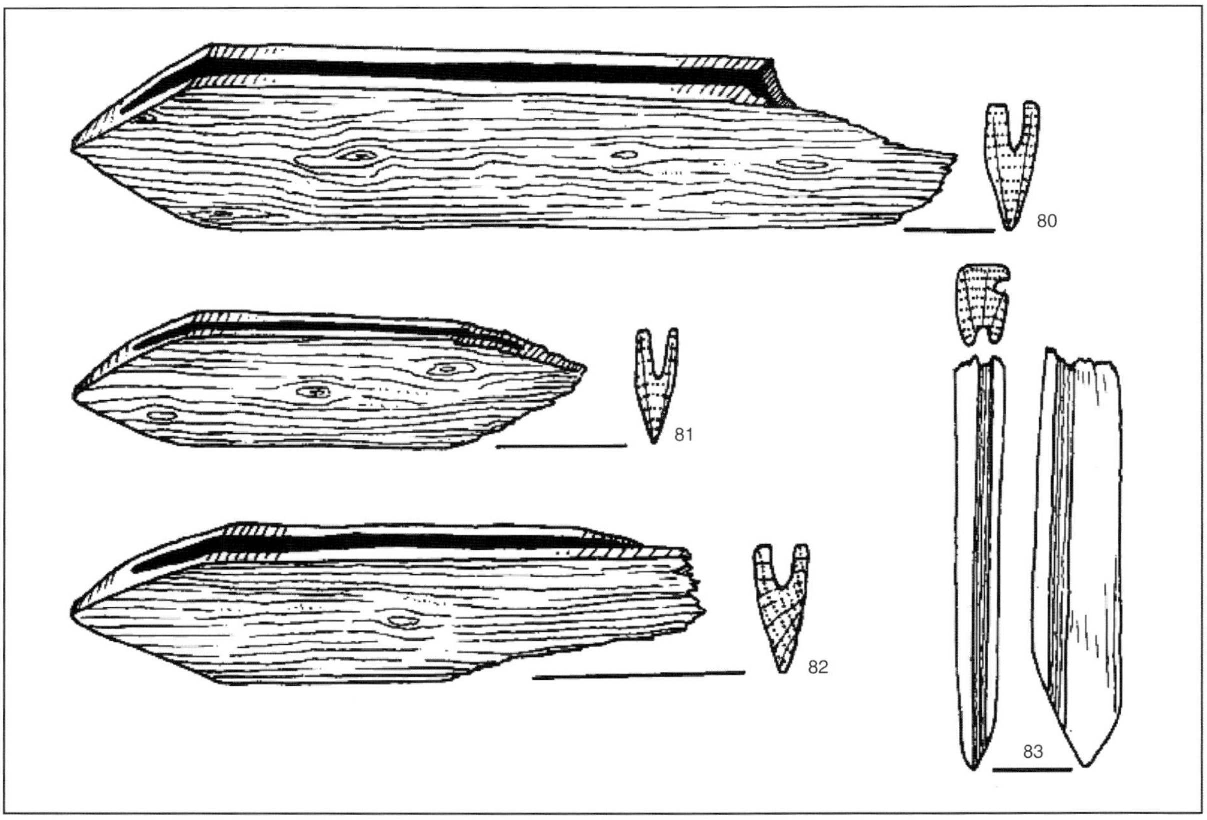

Fig. 5.28 Late Saxon timbers W.80-3, scale 1:10 (EAR3, fig. 180)

areas in the City of London and Southwark since 1988 (Goodburn 1995, 49). Although their precise provenances are not noted, a further example of a tongue-and-groove plank (timber no. 7232) was recovered from the Billingsgate Lorry Park site in London (Milne 1992, 92). Little else was written of that particular timber other than similar examples had been noted at Husterknupp and Buderick in Germany and in surviving Scandinavian churches such as at Hedared in Sweden (*ibid.*).

Although small numbers of tongue-and-groove planks have therefore been recovered from London, they remain relatively rare in England. For example, of the seven early medieval sites excavated in the Billingsgate and Cheapside areas of London between 1976 and 1985, 48 timber buildings were catalogued and while some preserved traces of vertical timber walls, no tongue-and-groove planks were recorded (Horsman *et al.* 1988). The preservation of several timber baseplates probably represent wall bases for vertical timbers, with the vertical timbers themselves surviving at buildings IRO3 and PDN3, both of which employed D-shaped timbers alternated with thinner planks rather than tongue-and-groove joints (*ibid.*, 75–6).

Building PDN3 was a particularly well-preserved example, with Horsman *et al.* (*ibid.*, 76) noting a close parallel in its form to a building excavated at Dublin. Building CP85/1, excavated at Dublin's Christchurch Place, was one of 83 buildings excavated at Dublin by the National Museums of Ireland between 1962 and 1976 and was the only one recorded whose walls were constructed using vertical timbers rather than single or double post-and-wattle or wattle with planks (Murray 1983, 19–27). Unlike the Trichay Street timbers, building CP85/1 employed alternating double-grooved planks with thin planks.

A noteworthy feature of building CP85/1 was that one of its thick double-grooved planks which had evidently fallen from its eastern wall preserved the upper end of the vertical beam: the beam was grooved up to a height of 1 m, but above this it was tapered to the same thickness as the alternating thin planks so the tops of the planks could have fitted into a wall plate, holding them in place (Murray 1983, 27). Although the Trichay Street timbers also taper beyond the edges of their grooves, they taper on their thin edges rather than on their faces and so would have been unsuited securing them within a wall plate.

However, it is also possible that the Trichay Street tongue-and-grooved timbers do represent a form of horizontal wall construction, as originally suggested by Allan. Although rare, tongue-and-grooved timbers could be employed horizontally and examples were found at

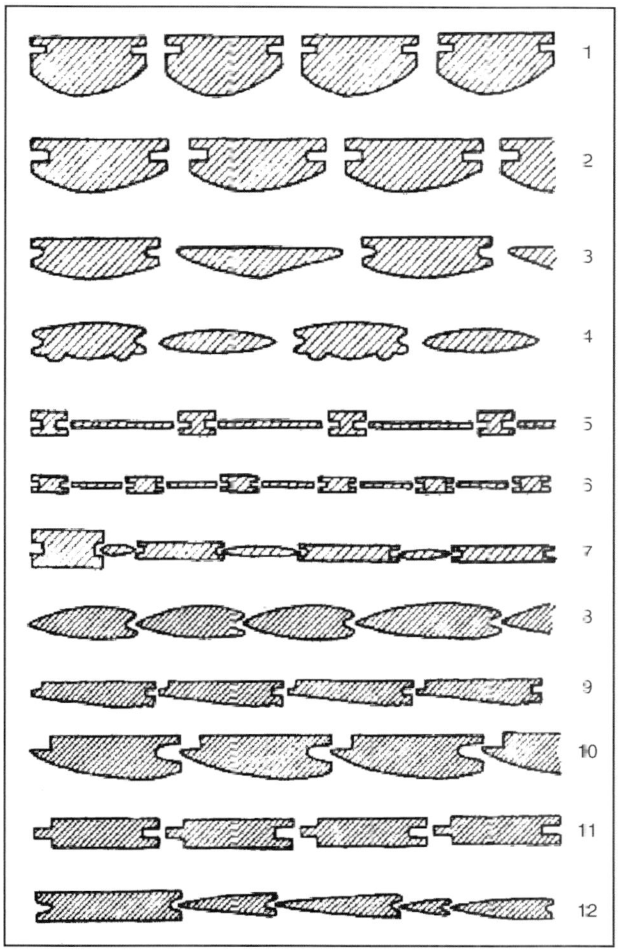

Fig. 5.29 Tongue-and-grooved construction techniques (Chapelot and Fossier 1985, fig. 91)

Wellgate in Conisbrough, South Yorkshire, and dated to the late 6th or early 7th centuries (Buckland *et al.* 2013, 12), although this would make them considerably earlier than the Trichay Street timbers. Other Early Saxon timber buildings such as those at Thirlings, in Northumberland, Charlton, in Hampshire and Maxey, in Northamptonshire, may also have had horizontal beams (*ibid.*, 14).

Although the Trichay Street timbers suggest a form of tongue-and-groove wall construction, the non-rectangular form of the planks is problematic. During the construction of vertical-walled structures, the planks could either have been placed directly into the ground or into sill beams; the pointed ends of Trichay Street's timbers would not therefore have fitted into a sill beam (the ends had suffered no decay and had not therefore been buried). Similarly, pointed timber ends would have inhibited the positioning of a roof or any other horizontal wall plates above them. If the planks instead represent horizontally-constructed walling, then again their pointed ends would have inhibited placing them within grooves in supporting uprights. At present, their true nature, though suggestive of tongue-and-grooved vertical wall planks, remains unclear. It is possible that the Trichay Street timbers represent non-load bearing vertical timbers, suggesting that they were a form of palisade wall rather than a building wall.

6

Excavations at Goldsmith Street Area III, 1971–2

Neil Holbrook, John Allan and Jonathan Hart

Introduction

Between August 1971 and May 1972 an excavation which covered an area of 26 × 15 m was undertaken on the site of two tenements in Goldsmith Street which lay less than 100 m from the centre of the High Street at SX 9194 9293 (site code GS III; Site 39 (see Chapter 2 above); Fig. 5.1). The site extended back from the former street frontage of Goldsmith Street (Fig. 5.18), and at the time of excavation it was proposed that this area would be destroyed entirely by the new Guildhall Shopping Centre. Subsequently, however, the proposal was abandoned and the site is now an open area within the shopping centre.

With the exception of disturbances caused by a small cellar on the frontage, backfilled in the mid 13th century (GS 214; for the finds: EAR3, 210–14), a few service trenches, and a well which had been infilled with many thousands of discarded sherds from an early 19th-century china shop, the preservation of medieval deposits was remarkably good for a site close to the city centre. Indeed the overall stratigraphic sequence was much fuller in Goldsmith Street Area III compared to Areas I and II, (Site 37) where the Roman civilian activity was not particularly intensive. For that reason the EAPIT project decided to concentrate its resources on the analysis of the findings in Area III rather than Areas I and II.

This chapter summarises the archaeological evidence for the Roman military period and examines in detail that relating to the occupation of the site from the beginning of the Roman civil period (*c*. AD 75/80) to the mid 16th century. No evidence for late prehistoric or earlier occupation (Period 1) was uncovered but, in order to present the account in a way consistent with the other site reports, the period divisions and numbers follow those used in the overall EAPIT project. A detailed archive report on the Roman military remains (Henderson *et al.* 1993a) forms the basis of the summary presented here. That report, along with a context register and stratigraphic matrix for the Roman civil period onwards, is available for download at https://doi.org/10.5284/1035176. Only limited analysis of the post-military stratigraphy had been carried out prior to the start of this project. Shortly after the completion of the excavation a short summary of the principal findings from work undertaken in advance of the development of the Guildhall Shopping Centre was published by Collis (1972), along with brief annual summaries of the Roman evidence (Hassall *et al.* 1972, 344; Wilson *et al.* 1973, 313). The site has figured in two city-wide Roman-period syntheses (Bidwell 1980, 36, 54, 71–2; Henderson 1988). The stratigraphic account of the Roman civilian phases presented below draws on an initial phase of post-excavation analysis undertaken by Caroline Earwood in 1992 and John Salvatore in 1993. Key deposits were described by group numbers assigned with the prefix L (Layer) or F (Feature). The system of numbering adopted for the buildings described in this report in many cases differs from any previous numbering systems used in the site notes and interim accounts. The buildings have the letter prefixes RM (Roman military), RC (Roman civil) and Me (medieval). Table 6.1 provides a concordance of the numbering used in this report for Roman streets and buildings with that adopted in the city-wide gazetteers presented in Chapter 3. In the phase plans features are shown in bold colours, while layers are shown as lighter shades. A few features are not illustrated (n.i.), as field drawings were not located in the archive.

The excavation was directed first by John Collis, followed in the wet winter months of 1971–2 by Christopher Henderson, the principal supervisors being G. Black, J. Reading, E. Wayman and D. Whipp. At that stage the Director of the Exeter Museums Archaeological Field Unit was Michael Griffiths.

Table 6.1 Concordance of the numbering of Roman buildings used in this chapter with those used in the city-wide gazetteers in Chapter 3

This report	*Gazetteers*
RMA	Barrack C2
RMB	Barrack C3
RMC	?*immunes* barracks
RMD	?*immunes* barracks
RC1	10i
RC2	11i
RC3	9i
RC4	15ii
RC5	14ii

Period 2: The Roman legionary fortress (*c.* AD 50/55–75/80)

The following account is a summary of the Roman military evidence that has been reported on previously (Henderson *et al.* 1993a). The interpretations and descriptions presented here are those found within that report, and the lettering system for the buildings is also followed with the addition of the prefix RM. The excavations at Goldsmith Street revealed the first Roman military buildings to be recognised as such in Exeter, with parts of four barracks revealed in three separate excavation areas (termed Areas I–III). In order to understand the layout and relationship of the buildings, the results from the three Goldsmith Street excavation areas are summarised below, although the description of the subsequent civilian and medieval evidence relates to Area III only. The excavation site lay on the right-hand side of the *retentura* of the legionary fortress.

Phase 1

Within Area III parts of two rectangular barrack blocks (RMA and RMB; Chapter 3.1 above, barracks C2 and C3) were found, their long axes aligned north-west/south-east (Fig. 6.1). They were built back-to-back, separated by a 1 m-wide passageway, with Barrack RMA facing north-east and RMB south-west. Barrack RMA was the more fully revealed of the two, with parts of the front and rear walls and some internal partitions surviving sufficiently to indicate a ground plan which can be reconstructed as having a length of *c.* 60–62 m if the barrack extended as far as the projected line of the *intervallum* street. The barrack was 10.7 m wide with a centurial block at the north-western end. The *contubernia* were 7.25 m deep, with the remaining width occupied by a portico along the north-eastern side. The wall lines survived as post-trenches indicating post-in-trench construction. Large quantities of daub found in post-fortress levelling deposits indicate that the barracks had clay walls as well as clay floors. Although less fully revealed, barrack RMB was of comparable dimensions to RMA and used similar post-in-trench construction. Barracks RMC and D (Chapter 3.1 above, ?*immunes* barracks) to the south-east of RMA and B were characterised by wider post-trenches than in RMA and B which has led to the suggestion that they date to Phase 2 of the military occupation, although an origin in Phase 1 is not out of the question (Henderson *et al.* 1993a, 3).

Phases 2 and 3

Phase 2 saw rebuilding of RMA and B on the same footprints and with similar post-in-trench construction. Barrack RMB fronted onto a metalled street in Area II and a putative fifth barrack may have existed on the other side of this street, although no trace of it survived. Some remodelling of Barrack RMC was also evident. Phase 3 describes the latest modifications to the south-eastern ends of RMA and B. The earlier internal walls were removed and are presumed to have been replaced by partitions based on sill beams, of which no trace survived but which were, in places, implied by the straight edges of clay floors. There were possible latrine pits in the *contubernia* at the south-east ends of the barracks.

Period 3: The Roman town

The process by which the abandoned fortress was converted for use as an urban centre has been described in Chapter 5 above and EAPIT1, Chapter 6. At Goldsmith Street Area III the earliest post-military activity was represented by the dumping of a series of deposits during the late 1st century AD (Period 3a). Following this, pits and ditches were dug (Period 3b) suggesting a period of low-intensity use prior to the construction of the first civilian structures at some point in the 2nd century AD (Period 3c). These buildings (RC1–3) were built in timber and repaired on several occasions; at least one of them was probably a house. It is unclear how long the buildings remained in use, but occupation perhaps stretched into the earlier 3rd century AD, at which time they were demolished and their sites used for the construction of two stone (or stone-founded) buildings (RC4 and 5) (Period 3d). Building RC4 was a house of some quality with underfloor heating and tessellated flooring. These buildings underwent repair and modification before their final abandonment.

Period 3a: Demolition of the military barracks and levelling (late 1st century AD)

Activity in this period is represented by a series of dumped deposits, typically formed from yellow to red clays, associated with the deliberate demolition of the barrack blocks at the end of the military occupation (Henderson *et al.* 1993a, 7). Although many of the dumps probably represent redeposited natural clays, some included organic refuse, charcoal lenses, daub and pottery. The daub was presumably derived from the walls

Fig. 6.1 Plan of Period 2: Roman military barrack blocks discovered in Goldsmith Street Areas I–III

of the former barracks, suggesting that material from the demolished structures was spread over the site as levelling. These deposits were overlaid by a thin trampled soil (L422) which may represent the initial reuse of the area. Above this was a series of thin, poorly defined spreads of ash, charcoal and slag. No hearths were recorded, however, and it is unclear whether the deposits reflect metalworking within the site, or debris imported from elsewhere. Of note amongst these burnt deposits was a layer of charcoal debris derived from burnt laths and a log (L435), perhaps contractors burning a pile of demolition debris derived from the former barracks.

Dating evidence

- Dump L419. Samian: bowl, probably Flavian.
- Dump L420. Samian: Dr. 29, AD 70–85 (EAR4, fig. 14, no. 55); Dr. 30, AD 70–85.
- Dump L422. Samian: Dr. 27g, stamp no. 4, AD 45–65

The little dating evidence from these deposits is consistent with the demolition of the fortress buildings *c*. AD 75/80, although L422 and the metalworking debris relate to the earliest civilian activity in the late 1st century AD.

Period 3b: Early civilian activity (late 1st–early 2nd centuries AD)

The levelling works undertaken in Period 3a were followed by the digging of a number of ditched boundaries (Fig. 6.2). These ditches were highly truncated but respected the general axis of the former fortress. They did not persist once the first civilian structures were built in Period 3c, indicating that they were not set out as property boundaries in anticipation of building works. Rather, this part of the town seems to have remained as essentially open ground following the demolition of the fortress buildings and the ditches perhaps defined comparatively short-lived agricultural or horticultural plots.

Fig. 6.2 Plan of Period 3b (late 1st to early 2nd centuries AD)

Ditches F528 and F486 were the best-preserved of the boundaries, yet even these survived only as short, intermittent segments less than 3 m in length. Both were aligned north-east/south-west and the largest F486 was up to 0.95 m wide, although this included several recuts; a further recut was numbered F523. Ditch F486 contained charcoal, ash, oyster shells and pottery, presumably derived from domestic occupation and potentially deposited here during manuring. Two further ditches, F202 in the north-western part of the site, and F429 in the south-eastern part, were highly truncated and of uncertain orientation.

A number of shallow scoops and postholes probably also relate to this period as they were truncated by later remains. Many of these features were not planned, especially the postholes. Three postholes (F525, F526 and F527) within the south-eastern part of the site might have formed a light-weight structure of some description. Posthole F525 was square in plan and included a lower charcoal fill, suggesting it had held a square post which had burned *in situ*. Posthole F526 also included charcoal lenses.

The scoops were generally fairly irregular, with shallow rounded profiles. Indeed, many or all of them may not have been cut features as such, but perhaps thin layers filling undulations in the underlying dumps. Another possibility is that they were caused by disturbance from pigs or chickens, animals that dig down to create dust baths. Finds from the scoops included oyster shells, animal bone, charcoal and pottery.

Dating evidence

- Ditch F486. Samian: Dr. 37, AD 70–85; Dr. 27g, stamp no. 7, AD 50–65; Dr. 15/17R or 18, stamp no. 53, AD 45–65.
- Scoop F344. Coin 58, Nero, AD 64–8, very worn. Samian: Cu. 11, Vespasianic.
- Scoop F376. Samian: Dr. 37, AD 75–90; Dr. 29, AD 70–85; Dr. 18 and 18R, Flavian?
- Scoop F449. Samian: Dr. 18, pre-Flavian.
- Scoop F450. Samian: Dr. 62 or 67, Nero-Vespasian; lagena, AD 50–65 (EAR4, fig. 10, no. 4).

This slight evidence only establishes a date after *c.* AD 75 for this activity, although much of the material is likely to be residual from the period of military occupation. Conceivably the use of these features could immediately pre-date the construction of the Period 3c timber buildings, and thus date to the early 2nd century AD.

Period 3c: Timber buildings RC1–3 (?earlier 2nd to ?earlier 3rd century AD)

The site was redeveloped with the construction of three timber buildings (RC1–RC3) in the 2nd century AD (Fig. 6.3). The building plots occupied by structures were not represented by any surviving physical remains but were long-lived as they were respected by the subsequent Period 3d stone buildings. None of the three buildings was revealed in its entirety, and so their full extent and ground plans are unknown. Building RC3, the best preserved, contained a number of rooms within which some floors survived; it was at least partially rebuilt at some point.

Building RC1

Building RC1 lay within the central part of the site, but only survived in a very partial state. An L-shaped beam slot (F508, F509, F510), 0.25 m wide, formed the eastern corner of the building. Assuming the building was contemporary with RC3 to the south-west, RC1 can have been no more than *c.* 4 m wide and of uncertain length. The narrow width of the beam slot was comparable to the internal partitions of Building RC3 rather than its external walls, which suggests that RC1 was a relatively insubstantial structure. A patch of pink clay flooring (F512) survived within the building and surrounded an oval pit F511, up to 0.9 m across (although it is possible that this pit was a later feature cut through the floor).

Building RC2

Building RC2 lay 2.4 m north-east of RC1. Only its eastern corner survived, formed by the 0.7 m-wide stone footings of walls F484/485. The wall was abutted by a hard clay surface (F491) to the north-west, which perhaps marks the site of an entrance into a further room to the north-east which lay outside of the excavation area. To the south-west of this clay surface was a patch of stone surfacing F483.

Building RC3

Building RC3 was found close to the south-western edge of the site. It is considered here to be a separate structure from RC1, although conceivably they could have formed a single building. Patches of mortar (F440, n.i.) and gravel (L423, n.i.) surfacing between the extant parts of the RC1 and 3 were recorded but not planned, and might have been internal floors or part of an external passageway. RC3 was at least 14 m long by at least 5 m wide and contained at least four rooms. The north-eastern wall was rebuilt at some point using a different constructional technique to that used in the original build.

The only external wall line to survive of the original build of RC3 was that to the north-east, F377 (also numbered F394/F478). This was a 1 m-wide trench which presumably held a sill beam. The beam itself must have been deliberately removed when the building was demolished for no trace of it survived and the trench had been backfilled. A single posthole (F388, n.i.) adjoined the outside face of the beam trench. Other postholes within the beam trench have been assigned to an episode of rebuilding but it is conceivable that these had entirely truncated earlier post settings, in which case the wall was of post-in-trench rather than sill beam construction from the outset. Demolition material (L391) derived from this building included cob and plaster fragments which suggest the nature of the superstructure. Similar material was also found in the backfills of the 0.25 m-wide beam slots which formed internal partitions (F405, F406 and F407) defining four rooms (Rooms 1–4). The slots may have held timber base plates or the bases of wattle and daub panels.

Room 1 was defined to the south-east by slot F407 and to the north-east by the projected continuation of external wall F377. Its north-western and south-western

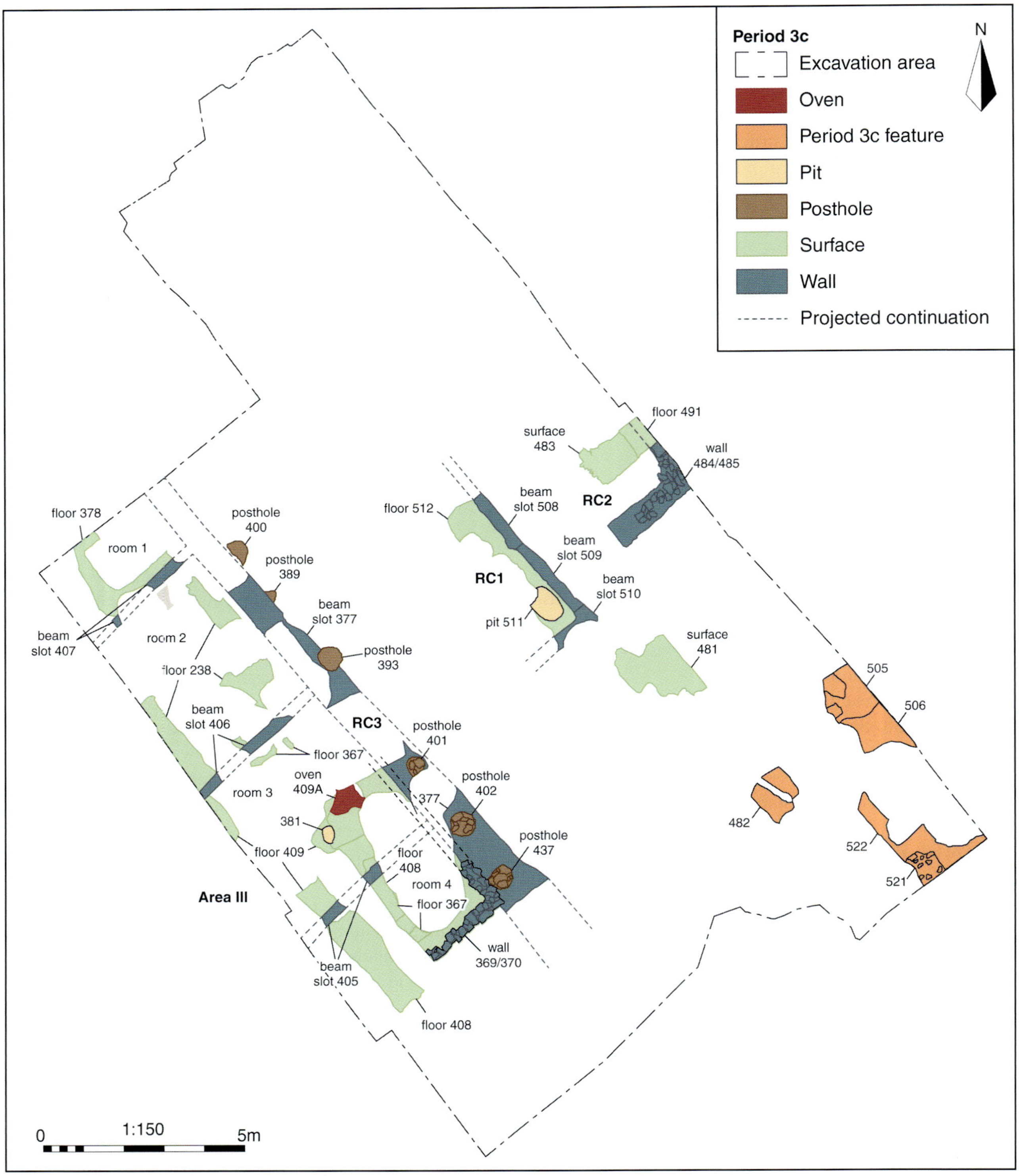

Fig. 6.3 Plan of Period 3c (earlier 2nd to ?earlier 3rd century AD) buildings RC1–3

walls lay outside the excavated area. Beam slot F407 was adjoined by a series of successive floor layers termed F378 suggestive of wear and resurfacing over the life of the building. The earliest surface was a pebble floor which was overlaid by a charcoal-rich occupation layer. This was in turn covered by a floor of crushed plaster and crushed tiles, which had been resurfaced with gravel. The latest surface was formed from crushed tile and crushed *opus signinum*, perhaps reused from elsewhere.

Room 2 lay to the south-east of Room 1 and was separated from Room 3 by partition slot F406. It was 4 m long, at least 4 m wide internally and was floored with pink mortar F238 sat upon yellow mortar make-up, in all 80 mm thick. The next room (Room 3) was of similar size to Room 2. Its south-east wall was defined by slot F405. A series of brown clay make-up layers (L393, L394, L395; n.i.) had been laid prior to the room being floored with clay (F409; also numbered L427/L429). Heaped on the floor up against the partition wall supported by slot F405 was a 0.16 m-high pile of *tesserae*. These *tesserae* were mostly white, with a few black examples, and none had any mortar adhering, suggesting that they were unused. They were perhaps originally stored in a bag of which no trace remained. This room had apparently been resurfaced (F380; n.i.), but details of this were only sketchily recorded. Room 3 contained oven F409A, which survived as a shallow cut lined with scorched clay. The base of the oven was covered with charcoal, but no superstructure survived. Posthole/pit F381 adjacent to the oven was possibly associated with it. The south-east extent of Room 4 was lost to truncation but it was 4.6 m wide and at least 2.8 m long. It was floored with *opus signinum* set upon a pitched stone make-up (F408) with quarter-round mouldings preserved along its north-east and north-west edges where it met the timber walls (Fig. 6.4). A later modification to this building might be represented by an L-shaped wall foundation F369/F370, 0.4 m wide and of drystone construction. The phasing of this foundation is uncertain: it seems to fit best with RC3, although another possibility is that it formed an outbuilding associated with Period 3d Building RC5. The foundation may have defined a south-east end wall to Room 4 which would thus have had a length of *c*. 2.2 m. To the north-west of the foundation a couple of isolated remnants of flooring were found (F367, laid on make-up layer L382/L383 (n.i.) of clay with plaster). This was perhaps a later, but very poorly preserved, floor within RC3.

Occupation layers accumulated above the floors of RC3 although these were not planned. Amongst these layer L397 was a dark soil with oyster shells and charcoal and L431, a brown clay with stones, oyster shell and charcoal. Building RC3 was repaired at some point in its life. An alignment of six postpits was found along the line of beam slot F377, but on a slightly divergent alignment (F437, F402, F401, F393, F389 and F400). The postpits were up to 0.7 m across, and a number included packing stones. They suggest that the north-eastern wall was rebuilt using a different building technique to the slots associated with the original build. The presence of cob and plaster in the backfills of the internal beam slots indicates that these remained in use until the building was dismantled; there is no evidence that they were ever replaced.

Fig. 6.4 Opus signinum *floor with quarter-round mouldings within Room 4 of building RC3. The extent of later disturbance is evident. View looking north. 2m scale (© RAMM)*

Demolition of the timber buildings

The demolition of the timber buildings appears to have been a deliberate process. The remaining (internal) sill beams of Building RC3 were lifted, presumably for reuse, and the resulting trenches backfilled with debris including cob and plaster most likely from the demolished walls. Further demolition debris was used as make-up in advance of rebuilding work, mostly dumps of pinkish clays (such as L401A, L407 and L404, all n.i.). Make-up layer L391, which also filled beam slot F405, included cob and plaster demolition debris. Extensive scorching of the upper surface of this deposit may suggest that some of the demolition debris, perhaps timbers and wattlework not suitable for reuse, was burnt. Further indications of this practice may come from a series of irregular scorched areas (F482, F505, F506, F521, F522; and F481, F487, L434, all n.i.) on the surface of the underlying dumped clays in the south-east corner of the site. These were initially interpreted by the excavators as hearths associated with metalworking but, with the exception of a possible tuyère (F529, n.i.; not included in EAR4 so identification far from certain and cannot be verified), no structural remains of hearths were found, and no metalworking slags or other residues are recorded. Charcoal and ash layers L411 and L442 were associated with this burning, whilst layers L408 and L418 may represent trample formed during this work, or immediately afterwards.

Dating evidence

BUILDING RC3

- Floors F378. Samian: Dr. 37, Trajanic.
- Floor make-up L394. Samian: Dr. 37, AD 70–85 (EAR4, fig. 14, no. 56); Dr. 30, AD 70–85 (EAR4, fig. 14, no. 57); Dr. 29, AD 70–85 (EAR4, fig. 14, no. 58). Pottery: rough-cast beaker (EAR4, fig. 23. no. 7); South-Western BB1 grooved flat-rimmed bowl type 65.1b.
- Make-up L395. Coin 55, Nero, AD 64–8, very worn. Samian: Dr. 29, AD 70–85; Dr. 15/17 or 18, stamp no. 101, Flavian. Pottery: rough-cast beaker; South-East Dorset BB1 flat-rimmed dish; South-Western BB1 grooved flat-rimmed bowl type 65.1b.
- Occupation L397. Samian: Dr. 31R, 33, Antonine.
- Occupation L431. Samian: Dr. 37, AD 125–50 (EAR4, fig. 14, no. 61); Dr. 18/31, Hadrianic. Pottery: Rhineland mortarium, type TC56, fabric FC15, *c.* AD 150–250 (EAR4, fig. 84).
- ?Secondary floor make-up L383. Samian: Dr. 80, late Antonine.
- Demolition L391. Samian: Dr. 37, Hadrianic-Antonine; Dr. 33, 2nd century AD. Pottery: South-Western BB1 plain-rimmed dish type 92.2.
- Demolition filling robbed beam slot F407. Samian: Dr. 37, AD 125–50 (EAR4, fig. 14, no. 59).

The South-East Dorset BB1 flat-rimmed bowl from make-up L395 would be consistent with a date after *c.* AD 120 for the construction of RC3. Pottery from the occupation deposits shows that the building continued in use until after *c.* AD 150/160, and conceivably into the earlier 3rd century AD, although precision is not possible with the available evidence.

Period 3d: Stone buildings RC4 and RC5 (3rd to 4th centuries AD)

At some point the Period 3c timber buildings were demolished and replaced by two stone-founded buildings (Fig. 6.5). Neither building was revealed in its entirety within the excavated area. RC4 overlay the demolished remains of RC1 and 2, and RC5 occupied the footprint of RC3 which may reflect continuity of building plots between the periods.

Building RC4

Building RC4 was built within the north-eastern part of the site. The south-western side of the building lay within the excavation area, but it extended beyond this in all other directions and its overall dimensions are therefore unknown. The provision of underfloor heating and tessellated and *opus signinum* floors suggest that RC4 was a town house. Parts of some of the wall lines had been entirely robbed of stone, but robber trenches preserved the wall lines.

The axis of the house followed the prevailing orientation of the earlier structures and indeed the *insula* as a whole. A corridor (or possibly a portico) ran along the south-west side of the house. This may have lain to the rear of a block of rooms which faced north-east, or equally the corridor could have been at the front of the range which would have then faced south-west across the open space towards RC5. Behind the corridor five rooms were identifiable on the basis of internal partition walls (Rooms 1–5), but their interiors lay only partially within the site. Some rebuilding and repair work was suggested in the preliminary post-excavation analysis undertaken by the excavators, but not all of it is clearly supported by the primary archive. That some modifications occurred over time is apparent enough, however, although the sequences are not always clearly elucidated.

Following the demolition of the Period 3c buildings, construction work for RC4 began with a cut (F384, F504; n.i.) to terrace the building platform into the natural slope, which had been raised and replicated by the earlier deposits. A stone levelling layer (F383, n.i.) made good the ground within this terrace and the walls were built within deeper foundation trenches cut into the underlying make-up layers. Wall F353 (also numbered F365 and F403), 0.8 m wide, was considered by the excavators to be the original south-western side of the building, with the corridor a later addition. Whilst this is possible, it cannot be demonstrated as the relationship between wall F353 and

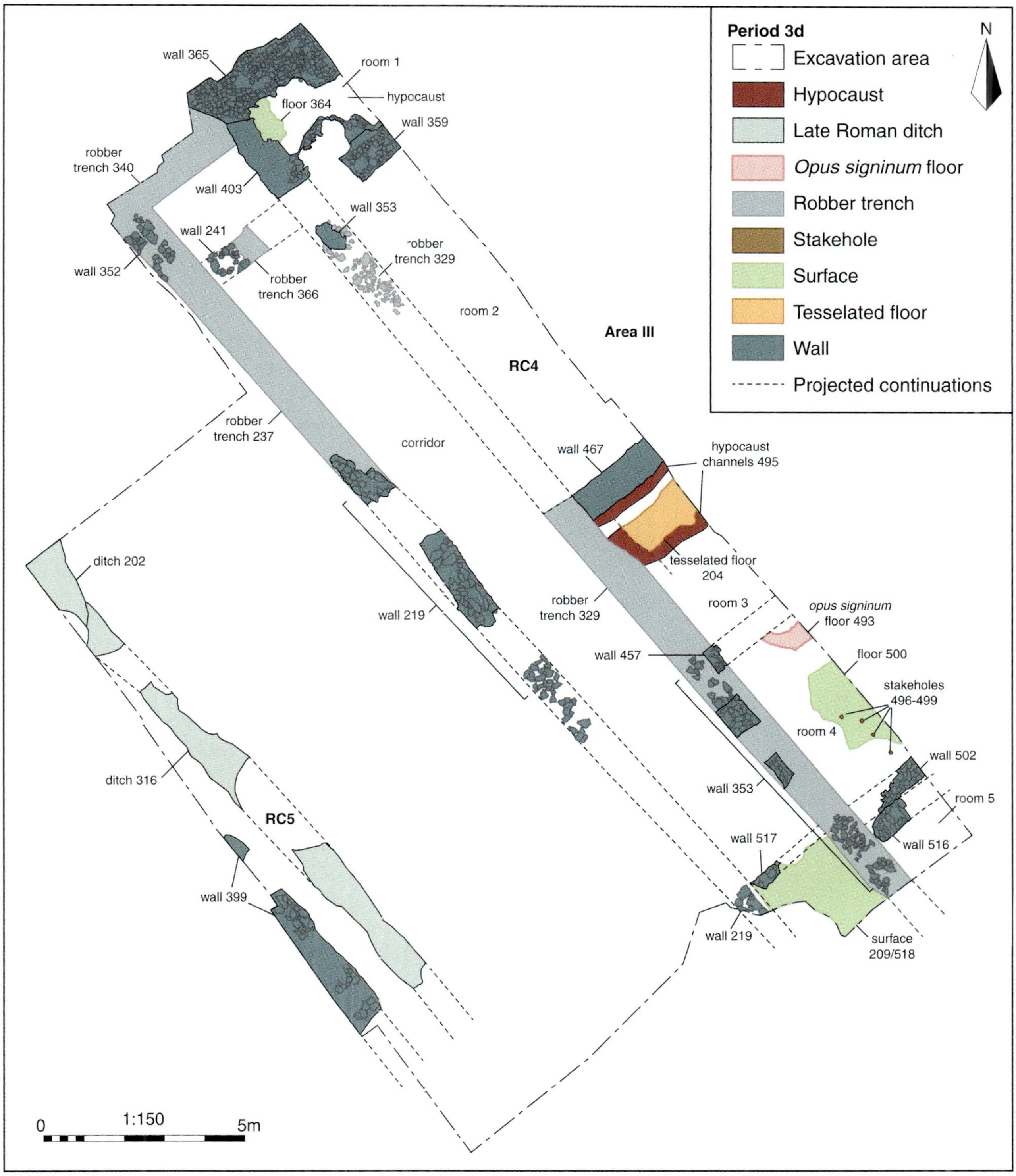

Fig. 6.5 Plan of Period 3d (3rd to 4th centuries AD) buildings RC4 and 5

the end wall of the corridor had been destroyed by later robbing and truncation. However, the corridor wall was built from different types of stones to those used in wall F353, which could support the notion that it was a later addition. Wall F353 had been extensively robbed (robber trench F329) but the surviving segments of footings were constructed from pitched volcanic trap stones.

CORRIDOR

A corridor or portico ran along the south-western side of the building. The outer wall of the corridor was formed by wall F219 (also numbered F352). Again, this wall had been extensively robbed, but its line can be traced by robber trench F237, with a return at the north-western end marked by robber trench F340 potentially defining the western corner of RC4, although this cannot be confirmed as the return was right up against the edge of excavation. Wall F219 was founded on large white stones (presumably limestone) and was 0.7 m–0.8 m wide. The corridor was 2.4 m wide internally and ran the length of the exposed part of the house. At the north-western end of the corridor there was a small room, 2.8 m by 1.8 m internally, defined by partition wall F241 which had been largely robbed out by robber trench F366. At the south-east end of the corridor there may have been a comparable room defined by stone partition wall F517, which had also been extensively robbed. The width of the room is unknown as it extended beyond the excavation area, but it is conceivable that these two rooms mark the full length of the corridor and thus quite probably the full length of this range of the building. In that case the building would not have been much longer than the 26 m exposed in the excavation, and it would have terminated *c*. 5 m away from the likely line of the street frontage. Flooring only survived within the south-easternmost room in the corridor. Here, a pinkish sandy mortar make-up layer (or possibly a primary floor surface; F501; n.i.) was overlaid by floor F209 which included a further make-up deposit of white plaster rubble beneath a 20 mm-thick pink sandy mortar floor. Floor F518 seems to have been part of this surface.

Room 1

Room 1 was 2.3 m wide and at least 2.25 m deep internally, defined by partition walls F359 to the south-east and F365 to the north-west. Partition wall F359, was 0.6 m wide and F365 at least 1.25 m wide, the full width of its footings extending beyond the edge of excavation. The reason for the greater width of this latter wall is not readily apparent, unless it supported a pavilion or tower at the end of the building? Within the room patches of flooring survived. The earliest of these, F364, was a small (up to 1.15 m across) patch of *opus signinum* floor set upon a pitched stone make-up. A layer of charcoal above the floor surface (also numbered F364) may have been an occupation deposit relating to its use. The second patch of flooring, F363 (n.i.), was a yellow-brown mortar resurfacing of the earlier floor and was covered by a demolition deposit (F348) composed of crushed *opus signinum*, tile and white-painted plaster within sandy brown soil. During the fieldwork and in the initial post-excavation analysis this room is said to have contained a hypocaust (Collis 1972, 8, fig. 3), and Bidwell (1980, 71) states that this hypocaust was a later insertion and used *pilae* (material not stated). Detail on the hypocaust is lacking in the site records but perhaps the room was originally floored with *opus signinum*, and subsequently a hypocaust of *pila*-type was inserted above it?

Room 2

Room 2 lay to the south-east of Room 1, its south-eastern extent defined by partition wall F467, 0.8 m wide. The room was 9.45 m wide and at least 3.1 m deep although, given the degree of truncation in this part of the site, it is possible that all trace of intermediate partition walls might have been lost. Internally, the only remains to have survived within this room were a floor, an occupation layer and a posthole, none of which were planned. A 40 mm-thick mortar floor F477 (n.i.) survived in patches and butted up against partition wall F467. The floor was covered by an occupation layer (L416, n.i.) composed of brown clay with charcoal and pebbles. The floor was cut by posthole F476 (n.i.), although whether this related to the Roman building or was a later feature is uncertain.

Room 3

The next room to the south-east, Room 3, was separated from Room 4 beyond it by partition wall F457. Wall F457 was built from the same level as the base of a channelled hypocaust within the room. Its lower courses of footings were clay bonded whilst the upper surviving courses were mortared. Unpainted plaster facing adhered to the internal face of the wall where it joined wall F353. It would be unusual for a hypocaust basement to be plastered, and this could be an indication that the hypocaust was a later insertion and that the room was not heated when originally constructed. It would seem that the hypocaust and wall F457 were themselves later additions, based upon different construction techniques used in partition walls F457 and F467, and the deeper level that F467 was built from relative to the construction level for wall F457 and the hypocaust. This conclusion is further supported as wall F457 forms a butt joint with corridor wall F353. On balance, F457 is likely to be a latter addition to the building, with the hypocaust added at a yet later date.

The hypocaust was built within a construction cut deeper than the finished floor level. Within this, brown soil levelling L415 (n.i.) was laid, and this formed the level from which the hypocaust channel walls (F495) were built. Wall F457 was perhaps added at this time, although its relationship with levelling L415 is not recorded. Much of the hypocaust had been destroyed by later truncation, but where the channel walls survived they were formed from square ceramic tiles bonded with red clay set out to form a central north-east/south-west aligned channel with additional channels 1.8 m wide alongside the two exposed walls of the room (Fig. 6.6). The main hypocaust channel had a basal fill of charcoal and this thickened towards the south-west. No trace of a stoke-hole was found, so this must have lain outside of the excavated area to the north-east. If so, this would support the idea that the building faced south-west with the corridor at the front. The other channels had lesser amounts of charcoal, indicating that these were spurs from the main channel. Fragments of box tile found in the corner of the room suggest that some of the heat was conducted up the walls in flues formed from these tiles. Above the hypocaust was a tessellated floor F204 laid onto a thick bedding layer of white mortar (Fig. 6.7). Only a small patch of this survived; it was

Fig. 6.6 Channelled hypocaust within Room 3 of building RC4. The charcoal fill of the main central channel is in the foreground. View looking north. 20 cm scale (© RAMM)

Fig. 6.7 Fragment of tessellated floor within Room 3 of building RC4. 20 cm scale (© RAMM)

formed from *tesserae* cut from red ceramic tiles. The channels would have been bridged with flagstones.

Room 4

Room 4 lay to the south-east of Room 3 and was separated from Room 5 beyond it by two adjacent walls (F502 and F516). Wall F502 had been built using 'spotted' volcanic trap stones and was 0.6 m wide. It was parallel and adjacent to wall F516, itself built from large 'veined' volcanic slabs. One wall presumably replaced the other, although their relative sequence is not known. Wall F516 included a square post-setting, perhaps indicating that the internal walls at least were of timber-frame construction above stone sills. The relationship between walls F502 and F516 and wall F353 had been destroyed by truncation; wall F353 had been founded deeper than the relatively slight partition walls. Room 4 was 4.75 m wide internally and contained patches of flooring which survived as 'islands' between areas of truncation. Floor F493 was a small surviving patch of *opus signinum* laid onto a pitched stone foundation (also numbered F493). To the south-east, a slightly larger patch of clay flooring survived, F500. This had been cut by a series of stakeholes (F496, F497, F498 and F499); it is uncertain what these relate to.

Room 5

Room 5 was revealed at the south-eastern end of the site, but only a small part of it fell within the limits of excavation. No internal deposits were recorded.

Building RC5

Building RC5 was built to the south-west of RC4, separated by a 6 m-wide open space, although no surfacing survived in this area. Little of this building lay within the excavation area, and where it did it had been heavily disturbed by later activity. Nevertheless, RC5 clearly lay on the prevailing alignment, and it is possible that it formed the north-east wing of the courtyard house investigated at Trichay Street (Chapter 5 above), with the northern corner of this range revealed in Goldsmith Street Area I (Fig. 5.17). The construction sequence for Building RC5 is poorly understood, but a make-up layer (L386/L390; n.i.) was laid during the construction works. The north-eastern wall of the building (F399) was 0.7 m wide and had been built using pitched slabs of volcanic trap bonded with clay in the footing courses and, above these, mortar-bonded coursing, although most of the dressed masonry had been removed by robber trench F392 (n.i.).

A steep-sided, flat-based ditch F316, 0.7 m deep, followed the alignment of RC5 and may have cut through Period 3c wall F369/370. The bottom of the ditch was filled with red clay (L369) overlaid by stone rubble, mortar and slate (L361/362) demolition debris derived from RC5. The uppermost fill, L322, was a dark deposit with mussel and oyster shells. Ditch F316 was truncated by a smaller ditch, F202, but the orientation of the latter feature is uncertain as only a small segment of it was revealed. The ditch perhaps defined a plot boundary and could be associated with the ditches which defined small plots further to the north-west in Goldsmith Street Area I (Fig. 5.17).

Dating evidence

RC4

- Make-up L410. Samian: Dr. 31, 27, both Antonine; Dr. 18/31, stamp no. 21, AD 135–60.

RC5

- Make-up L386/L390. Samian: Dr. 80, late Antonine; Dr. 33, 38, both Antonine.
- Ditch F316. Coin 430, illegible 3rd or 4th century AD. Pottery: *céramique à l'éponge* (Raimbault 1973 form VI); ?Mayen Ware; chocolate colour-coated ware pentice moulded beaker; × 2 New Forest beakers (Fulford 1975 type 27; EAR4, fig. 23, nos. 20–21); South-East Dorset BB1 bowl type 47.1.

There is no useful evidence for when RC4 and 5 were constructed. If the material in the backfill of ditch F316 relates to the demolition of RC5 then this event did not occur before the last quarter of the 4th century AD to judge from the presence of South-East Dorset BB1 bowl type 47.1.

The civil sequence
by Neil Holbrook

The Roman civil sequence at Goldsmith Street Area III shows unsurprising similarities with that revealed at Trichay Street (Chapter 5 above), although understanding is hampered here by the comparatively small size of the excavation area, the high levels of disturbance caused by later activity, and the paucity of stratified dating evidence. The site was situated off-centre within *insula* V, the south-east limit of the excavation area being *c.* 6 m back from the street frontage. Traces of timber buildings fronting on to Street C were found a little further to the north-west during excavations at Queen Street (Chapter 3.4, building 12i). The earliest activity following the abandonment of the legionary fortress and demolition of the timber barrack buildings at Goldsmith Street comprised some ditches and shallow scoops cut into the levelling deposits. There were no buildings within the site at this time, which was perhaps used for the keeping of animals and horticulture. The date of the first buildings is unclear; after *c.* AD 120, but perhaps not until some decades later in the 2nd century AD.

The Period 3c buildings survived in a highly partial state which seriously hampers an appreciation of their plan and layout. Indeed so little remained of RC1 and 2 that next to nothing can be said of them (they could even be sequential rather than contemporary structures). RC2 possessed stone footings, but this need not necessarily imply a stone superstructure. RC3 was the best preserved of the buildings. It does not appear that this was a strip building fronting onto Street C dividing *insulae* V and X as this would make for a very long building if it extended to the frontage. The presence of an *opus signinum* floor with quarter-round mouldings in Room 4 also argues against this interpretation as the residential rooms in typical strip buildings usually lay at the end of the building farthest from the street. More likely, therefore, is that the building faced south-west, perhaps with a front corridor or portico providing access to the block of rooms revealed in the excavation. In this respect RC3 recalls building RC11 at Trichay Street, which dated to the mid 2nd to earlier 3rd century AD, as that building likewise faced across an open space rather than onto the street frontage. Room 4 conceivably formed one end of building RC3, and Room 1 perhaps the other given that it also had an *opus signinum* floor. Room 3 may have performed a service function as it contained an oven.

An unusual find from this room was a pile of predominately white, unused, *tesserae*, perhaps originally contained in bag. The find testifies to the presence of tessellated pavements in 2nd or 3rd-century AD Exeter, mostly likely within timber houses. The excavators thought that the *tesserae* suggested an unfulfilled intention to construct a tessellated floor within the building (Collis 1972, 8). This need not necessarily be so, however, and it is pertinent that a builders' yard was found next to the street frontage in adjacent *insula* X. Finds from this area included a heap of white lias chips most likely derived from the preparation of *tesserae* (Chapter 3.4, building 24ii). The builders' yard dated to the mid 3rd century AD; it is not inconceivable, given the poor quality of the dating evidence, that RC3 might have continued in use as late as this. The area to the north-west of the timber buildings remained undeveloped throughout their life; the only evidence of this period found in the excavations at Goldsmith Street Areas I and II was a small number of rubbish pits (Bidwell 1980, 54, insula V(3)). Some of the demolition deposits from RC3 contained burnt material. If this is to be associated with the fire which consumed the timber buildings within *insula* IV at Trichay Street in the Hadrianic or early Antonine period then the buildings were demolished around this time. Alternatively the dating evidence would also permit the Period 3c timber buildings to have been built after this event, when *insulae* IV and V were amalgamated through the suppression of the street that separated them (Chapter 3.2, Street F).

The timber buildings were replaced by two stone buildings, but there is little precision on the date when this occurred. Only the back wall of RC5 lay within the excavation area. As discussed in Chapter 5 it is possible, but far from certain, that this was part of the same courtyard house as revealed at Trichay Street (RC13; Chapter 3.5, building 14ii). RC4 probably faced south-west across an open area towards RC5. RC4 was evidently a house of some pretension given that it had two rooms furnished with hypocausts, one of them floored with a red tessellated pavement. Two small rooms were formed within the corridor, either from the outset or as later modifications. They perhaps formed small pavilions at either end of the corridor, in which case the building would have been just over 26 m long. The only evidence for the date when the stone buildings were demolished derives from open ditch 316, parallel with the back wall of RC5 (it perhaps defined the limit of the land plot containing the building, and served to block access to it from the open space to the north-east). The ditch was backfilled with demolition debris from RC5. While it did not produce any coins, it did yield a type of South-East Dorset BB1 bowl which almost certainly does not date before the last quarter of the 4th century AD. This ditch is perhaps to be associated with the series of recut ditches which formed irregular enclosures found further to the north-west in Goldsmith Street Areas I and II (Fig. 5.17). The latest ditches there were filled after the middle of the 4th century AD and one of them contained a dump of cattle skulls (Chapter 5 above, and Bidwell 1980, 72, insula IV/V(3)). No further structures were found in Areas I and II.

Periods 4–5: The post-Roman and Middle Saxon periods

The discovery of fragments of a Late Roman tessellated floor in Room 3 of building RC4 immediately below modern tarmac shows that the latest Roman deposits will have been approximately at modern ground level and that any post-Roman dark soil had been removed entirely by later truncation.

Period 6: The Saxo-Norman town (*c.* AD 900–1200)

Pottery Horizons A and B

No features on this site contained pottery of the earliest ceramic horizon in the Late Saxon town (Horizon A, probably early 10th century), and only two (229, 333) are attributed to ceramic Horizon B (?late 10th to 11th century; Figs 6.8–6.9).

Pit 229 was a large oval feature close to the street frontage, 3 m long and more than 1.7 m deep. Alongside a group of pottery which included red-painted wares from Normandy (details below), its lower fills contained waterlogged finds, the most remarkable of which was a complete cask end with incised cross and pentacle (EAR3, 305, W16); a small hone was also recovered (EAR3, 298, S24). The position of the pit shows clearly that the frontage was not occupied continuously by buildings; this remained the case as late as the late 13th century, as was evident from the succession of pits in this area (252 cutting 243, which cut 279, which cut 297, cutting 229).

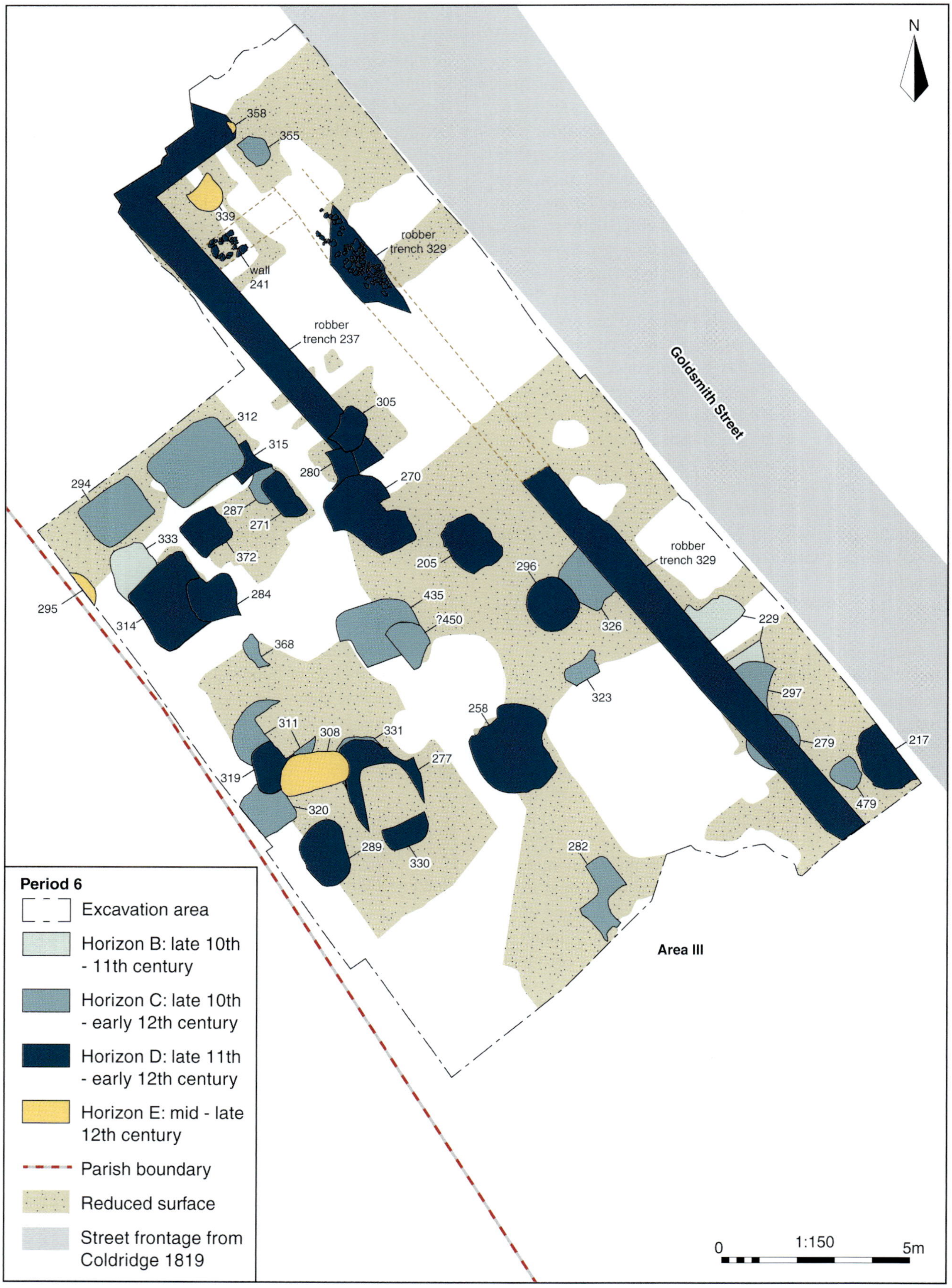

Fig. 6.8 Plan of Period 6 (c. AD 900–1200)

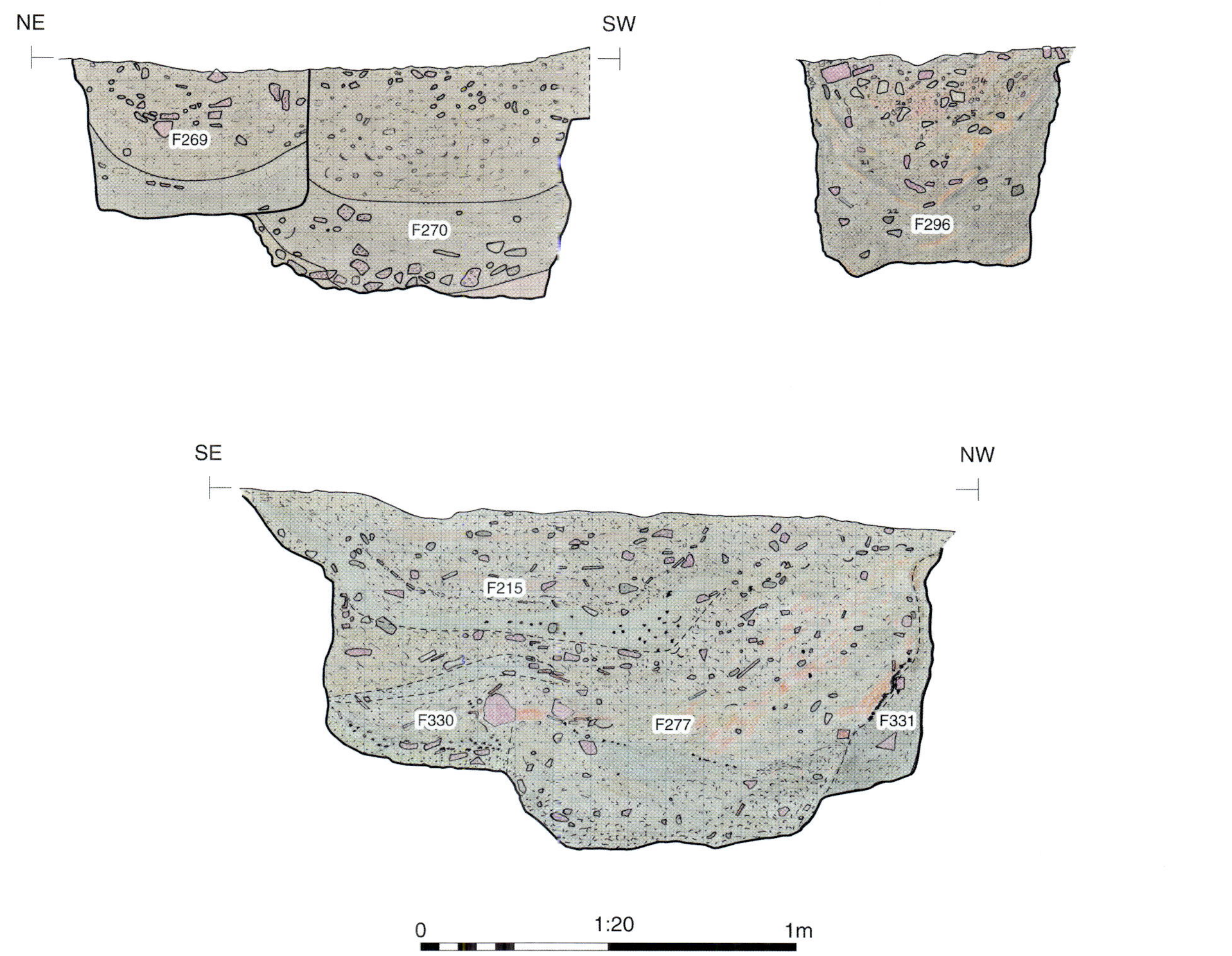

Fig. 6.9 Selection of sections of Saxo-Norman pits (original field records). Top left: Pits 270 and 269. Top right: Pit 296. Bottom: C.G. Henderson offered the following interpretation of the pit group 215/277/330/331. Two 10/11th-century pits (330, 331) are the earliest features. The cesspit 277 was cut through their fills. Most of the contents of 331 later slumped into 277 (compare plan: Fig. 6.8). About 1.8 m above the bottom of 277, a layer of cess (green in the field drawing) spilled across pit boundary with 330 and into the middle of 330. The settlement of pit fills after burial may explain this; the soft organic lower fills sometimes decayed and compacted after burial, whilst their upper fills of mixed clays did not settle so much, creating a cavity between the upper and lower fills. This happened in the case of 330; liquid cess from 227 later filled the cavity. Subsequently, the broad shallow cesspit 215 was dug; it was infilled in the mid 13th century

Pit 333, the first in another sequence of five pits which spanned the period from the 10th to the late 13th century, lay towards the rear of the site; it was a roughly oval feature measuring 1.9 × 1.2 m in plan and more than 1.4 m deep.

Pottery Horizon C

Sixteen pits (listed below in the Dating Evidence section) produced smaller groups of Saxo-Norman pottery of ceramic Horizon C, datable only broadly to the period between the late 10th and the early 12th century. Four of them (323; 326; 366; 479) had soft green lower fills and are presumed to have been cesspits; no evidence of use was noted in the others.

Pottery Horizons D and E

Sixteen Saxo-Norman pits contained assemblages of ceramic Horizon D, containing unglazed Saxo-Norman pottery with little or no Bedford Garage Ware and no tripod pitchers; they probably date from the late 11th or early 12th century.

Some of these features are interpretable as wells. The timber-lined pit 315 was square in plan, with an upright rectangular oak post driven into each corner; notches were cut in two adjacent sides of each post to accommodate a lining of horizontal boards. One such board gave a dendrochronological felling date of *c.* AD 1020, offering a *terminus post quem* for the feature's construction; nine other boards, some with sapwood, remain undated (EAR3,

320). The pit had been abandoned after its sides buckled inward under the pressure of the surrounding clay.

A second probable well was 217, a roughly circular pit on the street frontage, *c.* 2.1 m deep. If it lay within a tenement rather than encroaching into the street, its location indicates that the Late Saxon street frontage was 1 m or more further forward than its post-medieval position. The lowest 0.6 m of fill of this pit was waterlogged, yielding a substantial collection of wood including a spade (EAR3, 305, W17) and six cross-matching boards, one of which was felled *c.* AD 1040 (EAR3, 320); leather fragments including a belt and strap were recovered from the same deposit (EAR3, 325, L1–2). The same interpretation seems likely in the case of 258, a large pit, circular in plan, which yielded an important group of pottery (details below); the waterlogged lower fills contained timbers including fragments of casks (EAR3, 305, W19–21), together with a fine Beer limestone lamp (EAR3, 294, S1).

A larger number of these features are recorded as having soft green organic deposits in their lower fills and are presumed to have been cesspits, such as pit 284 ('green tinged soil'), 289 ('distinctive green edge, black inner fill'), 296 (Fig. 6.9), 314 ('green silty inner fill; brown gritty outer fill') and 319 ('green-brown fill with large charcoal flecks'). They varied in form from deep features which were roughly square in plan about 2.5 m across, *c.* 1.5 m deep ('with black cess in the bottom') to circular or oval (*e.g.* 205, 277). No evidence of function was noted in pits 271, 305, 330 or 372.

Three robber trenches of the walls of the Late Roman town house (329, 237, 241/366) also contained pottery of this period. They cut three of the earlier Saxo-Norman pits (229, 279, 326) but contained no glazed wares, and so their robbing is broadly datable to the 11th or early 12th century.

Dating evidence

CERAMIC HORIZON B, LATE 10TH/11TH CENTURY

- Pits 229 (Pottery: EAR3, nos. 190–206), 333 (EAR3, nos. 150–8).

CERAMIC HORIZON C, LATE 10TH TO EARLY 12TH CENTURY

- Pits 279 (Pottery: EAR3, nos. 210–17), 297 (nos. 207–9), 282, 287 (nos. 223–6), 294, 311 (nos. 299–301, more probably Horizon C rather than the published Horizon B), 312, 320, 323, 326, 331 (nos. 218–19), 355, 368, 435, 450, 479.

CERAMIC HORIZON D, LATE 11TH OR EARLY 12TH CENTURY

- Pits 205 (Pottery: EAR3, nos. 271–86), 217 (nos. 295–8; also timber felled *c.* AD 1040, described above), 258 (nos. 302–34), 270 (nos. 243–55), 271 (nos. 227–34), 277 (nos. 220–2), 280 (nos. 235–9), 284 (nos. 184–9), 289, 296, 305 (nos. 240–2), 314 (nos. 159–83), 315 (nos. 256–70), 319, 330, 372 (nos. 287–94); robber trenches 329, 237, 241.

CERAMIC HORIZON E, MID TO LATE 12TH CENTURY

- Pits 295, 308, 321, 339, 358.

Period 7: The High Medieval city (*c.* 1200–1350)

Period 7a: c. *1200–50*

Seven pits (227, 243, 257, 265, 283, 286, 307) were infilled with pottery of ceramic Horizon F, datable to *c.* 1180–1250 (Fig. 6.10). They were mainly roughly oval features but included one large deep rectangular feature (286, 2.5 × 2 m in plan) which was probably a cesspit of the form also seen in the Saxo-Norman period.

By this stage pit-digging had almost ceased in the north-western part of the site, the latest pit in this area (227) being of late 12th or early 13th-century date. It seems probable that after that time this part of the site was occupied by a building. It was here that the sole medieval structural feature of the excavation was found: the narrow (*c.* 0.18 m) trench 337, extending back from the frontage, which cut pit 227. It is unclear whether this would have held earth-fast posts or the footings of a timber-framed structure.

Period 7b: c. *1250–1350*

Pit-digging continued at least as late as the end of the 13th century or the early 14th (Fig. 6.10). Most pits belong to the familiar oval, roughly circular or roughly rectangular forms; some were certainly cesspits (*e.g.* the large oval pit 215, whose section is shown in Fig. 6.9). Two particularly unusual examples are described more fully below. Pit 281 was a cask-lined well, the pit lining consisting of the 24 oak staves forming the wall of a cask bound with withies (Fig. 6.11; detailed record: EAR3, 309, 312–13, W71). The lower half of the barrel survived as a waterlogged object; the impressions of the staves could be traced in the upper half of the pit, where the remains of the closely bound horizontal withies which surrounded the staves were also recorded; they survived almost to the pit top. Dendrochronological examination showed that the cask had been made after *c.* 1185 but incorporated one late 10th-century stave (EAR3, 322). The capacity of the barrel can be estimated very approximately as about 215 customary gallons (EAR3, 312). The pit was infilled in the late 13th century.

Near the southern corner of the site was an unusually large pit (256) measuring 3.0 × 4.0 m in plan; it was backfilled in the late 13th or early 14th century. Although not so deep as the later stone-lined pits in this area (although its depth is not recorded within the archive), it is possible that it was a predecessor of the Period 8 stone-lined ?industrial pits 228 and 201 discussed below.

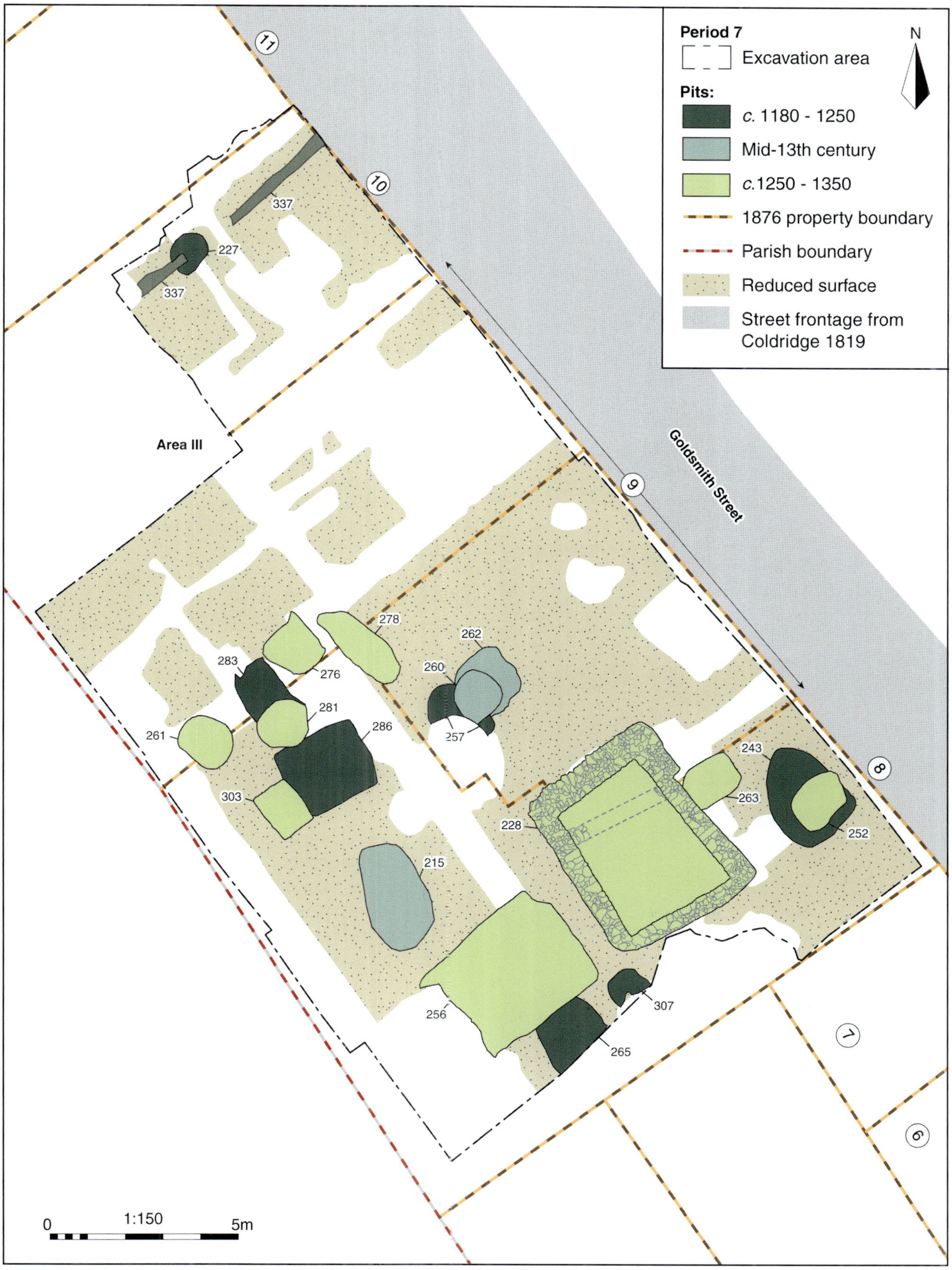

Fig. 6.10 Plan of Period 7 (c. 1200–1350)

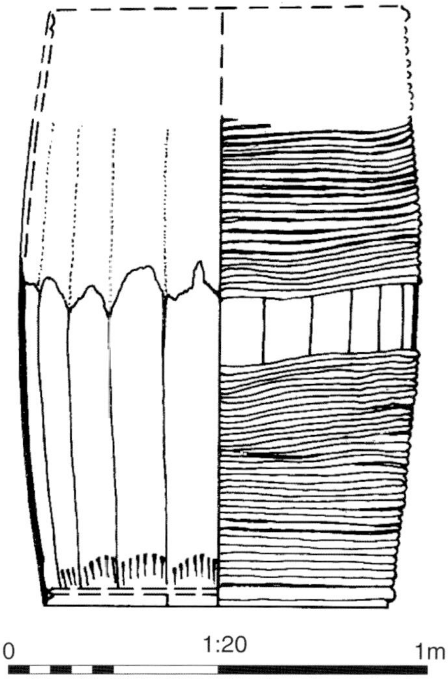

Fig. 6.11 Cask-lined pit 281: (top) drawing compiled on dismantling of the cask showing staves, external bindings remaining in pit walls after removal of the staves, and profile, its upper half restored as a mirror of the lower half; (bottom) view of interior showing oak staves (© RAMM)

Dating evidence

Ceramic Horizon F (*c.* 1180–1250)

- Pits 227, 243 (Pottery: EAR3, nos. 1018–43), 257, 265, 283 (nos. 1044–55), 286, 307 (nos. 998–1017).

Ceramic Horizon G (mid 13th century)

- Pits 215 (Pottery: EAR3, nos. 1196–1231), 260, 262

Ceramic Horizon H (*c.* 1250–1350)

- Pits 252 (with Saintonge polychrome sherds), 256 (Pottery: EAR3, nos. 1352–79), 261, 263, 276, 278. 281 (nos. 1568, 1589), 303.

Period 8: The later medieval city (*c.* 1350–1550)

On this site, as elsewhere in the city, the latest open pits and wells were broadly those with Saintonge polychrome wares, and by about the mid 14th century the practice of digging such features in back gardens had ceased. The most notable late medieval features were two large stone-lined pits (201, 228) in the south-eastern tenement (Fig. 6.12).

Stone-lined pit 228

In its primary form the earlier of these two features (228) consisted of an approximately square pit measuring *c.* 2.3 × 2.3 m internally in plan, with walls of mortared but uncoursed volcanic rubble, which lined the sides to a depth of 2.05 m (Fig. 6.13). It was later enlarged on the north-west side, whose wall was dismantled; a few stones of the ragged ends of the primary wall on this side survived in the pit bottom (Fig. 6.13b). The secondary form of the pit extended it by about 1 m; the later masonry was also of local volcanic trap rubble but was noticeably thicker than the primary masonry.

In the long sides of the pit walls there was a series of horizontal housings, comparable to joist holes, but set *c.* 1 m apart (Fig. 6.13b and f). Since the walls had been robbed to a depth of 1.3–1.4 m, these features would have been at least that distance below any floor level. They indicate the presence of horizontal timbers extending across the pit. The wide gaps between these timbers seems too great for floor joists and may show that goods were suspended below this level, or that there was some sort of internal structure in the pit. Following the removal of the lower fills, it was evident that the natural clay in the centre of the pit had been dug down to a depth of 0.75 m below the base of the walls; the maximum depth of the bottom was about 3 m below ground level (Fig. 6.13c).

The lower layers of the pit (layers 13–17) were black fibrous anaerobic deposits, rich in organic waste, in

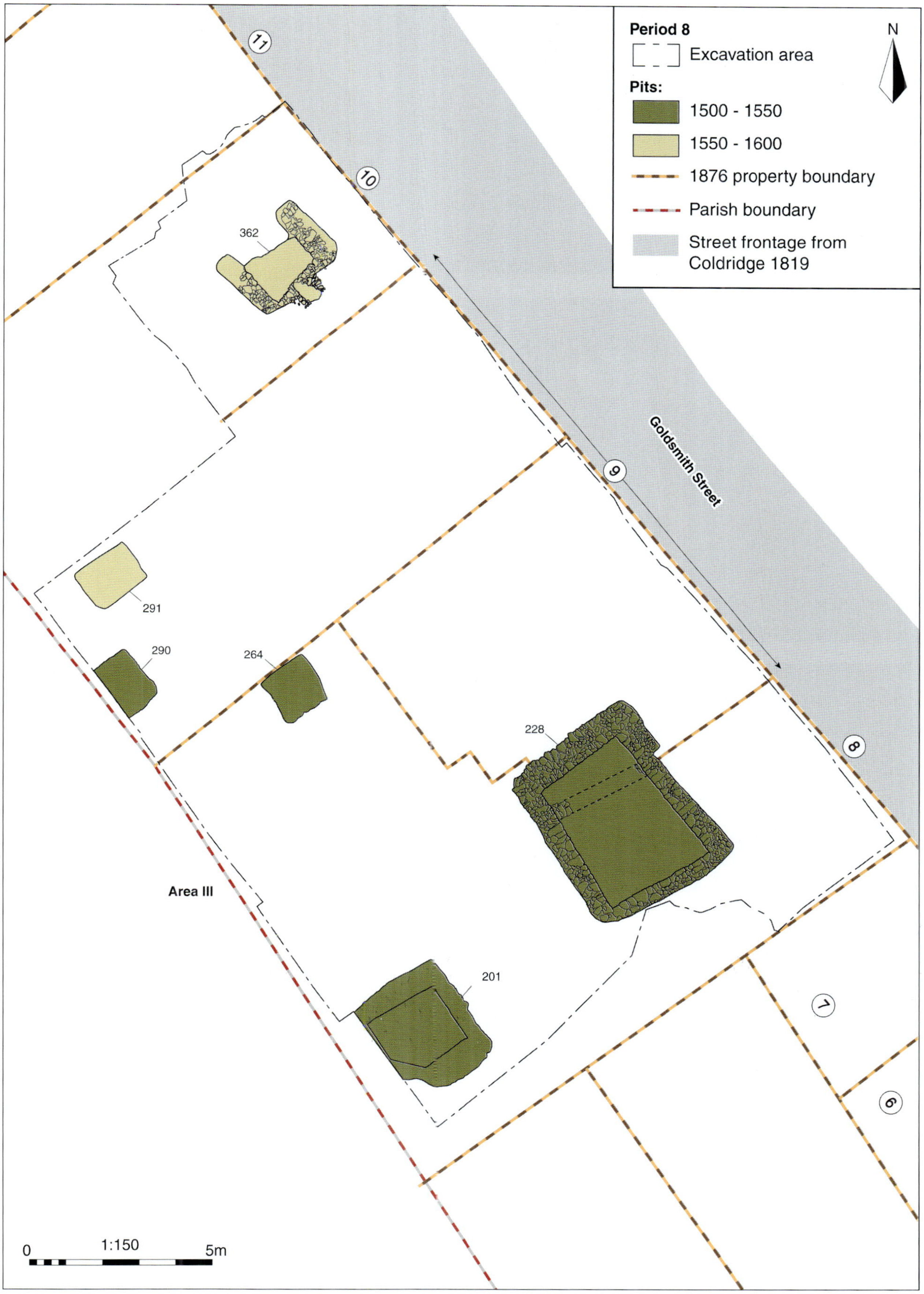

Fig. 6.12 Plan of Period 8 (c. 1350–1550)

Fig. 6.13 Pit 228: (a) excavation in progress; (b) plan; (c) profile across centre; (d–e) Saintonge green-glazed and polychrome jugs from the lower fills; (f) excavation of the lower deposits looking south-east (© RAMM)

which very large quantities of fly pupae were visible (Fig. 6.13f). One of the most important assemblages of late medieval objects excavated in the region was recovered from these deposits. The pottery included two complete Saintonge polychrome jugs and other near-complete vessels (Fig. 6.13d–e; EAR3, 1448–50). The associated finds included a crushed mass of fragments of 14th-century glass; the 24 glass vessels distinguished comprised jugs, goblets, beakers, bottles, a flask and many urinals (EAR3, G2–25). A 14th-century English pewter dish,

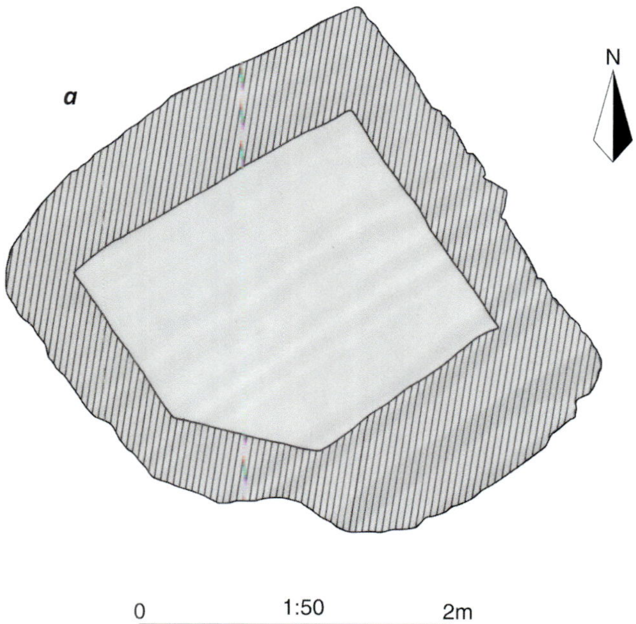

Fig. 6.14 Pit 201: (a) plan; (b) view looking south-east (© RAMM)

Fig. 6.15 The excavation after removal of modern deposits, showing early post-medieval deposits under examination (© RAMM)

comparable to a find from Southampton, was another unusual find (EAR3, 345, M157; for the Southampton find: Michaelis 1975). The waterlogged conditions also preserved branches and a range of organic objects including a lathe-turned wooden plate and bowls (EAR3, 305, W3–4 and 13), leather finds including parts of shoes and a knife sheath in a style typical of the late 14th/early 15th century (EAR3, 327, L7–16) and eight split oak boards (EAR3, 315, W93–101), six of them (samples 33–8) dated by dendrochronology between AD 1114±9 and 1249, showing that they were up to two centuries old when discarded.

The top *c.* 1.1 m of deposits (layers 1–12) consisted of waste building materials interleaved with bands of domestic rubbish; at this height the retaining walls had been robbed and the pit fill spread across their tops. The upper fills contained a second major assemblage of domestic objects. Its 115 early 16th-century pottery vessels (EAR3 160–3, 1729–83) included at least 30 stoneware drinking cups and jugs from Raeren, Cologne, Siegburg and Langerwehe (EAR3, 1729–45), as well as local ceramics used in distillation and a wide range of South-West English kitchen and tableware (EAR3 160–3, 1749–83). Four probable Venetian pieces were present in the series of 12 vessel glasses (EAR3, 268, G49–57 the drawn vessels). Layers 8–12 also included a major group of leather shoes and boots, with parts of a bag, a purse and a belt (EAR3, 327–9, L19–31). Alongside large numbers of roofing slates, the building materials also included a set of ceramic water pipes (including EAR3, 1774) and fragments of clear window glass (EAR3, 268). Three jettons (two pornographic: EAR3, J12a, 12b), with five lathe-turned wooden bowls (EAR3, 305, W6–9, 11), a yardstick for measuring cloth (W 34) and a mirror (W35) were also recovered from this deposit. A sprue from the casting of small lead objects was found in layer 6 (EAR3, 347, M236).

Other pits

The second stone-lined pit (201; Fig. 6.14) was also rectangular in plan, excepting one diagonal corner which perhaps avoided some preceding feature; it measured 2.1 × 1.9 m in plan and was 2.5 m deep. This too had mortar-bonded walls of volcanic rubble. It contained another important assemblage of early 16th-century pottery, glass, leather and textiles (details in Dating Evidence section below) and a group of four boards from a very mature tree whose rings spanned the years AD 775–1022 and whose estimated felling date was *c.* AD 1040 (EAR3, 320). These timbers were several centuries old when discarded. The site records relating to this feature are rather summary; it was first encountered at an early stage in cleaning the

Fig. 6.16 Field record of the central part of the site, showing the stone foundations of early modern buildings, with 19th-century boundaries. Inset: the excavation area in relation to the properties shown on the 1876 Ordnance Survey map (© RAMM)

site and was dug quickly because it was expected to be of much later date.

Two deep rectangular pits (264, 290) found towards the rear of the tenements were packed with an important assemblage of early 16th-century pottery wasters which display characteristics of Low Countries pottery (EAR3, 1620–1704). They are interpreted as evidence for a potter from the Low Countries operating in Goldsmith Street. The city had a surprisingly large immigrant community at this time, and immigrants from the Low Countries and elsewhere are recorded as living in the parish in the 1520s (EAR3, 136–8; Rowe 1977, 35–44; Allan 2014d). Like the nearby pit 291, they were probably cesspits.

A further stone-lined pit (362) at the north end of the site was evidently a garderobe, the stone extension on its south-west side marking the base of the chute which would have risen in the side wall of the house in which it stood. Features of this sort have been seen in other excavations in the city (*e.g.* Friernhay Street and National Westminster Bank; Sites 75 and 62) and in standing buildings (*e.g.* 41–2 High Street, mid 16th century; the Well House, Cathedral Close, ?late 16th or 17th century).

Early modern buildings

Finally, a number of walls of Heavitree and volcanic stone were recorded in the plan drawn after the first cleaning of the site (Figs 6.15–16, the original field record). Three sides of a range, *c.* 5.8 m wide and running parallel to the street, were recorded at the back of one plot, with a series of flat stone slabs abutting the outer side the north-eastern wall, presumably marking access from a yard or passage closer to the street. The walls were composed of Heavitree breccia and smaller fragments of volcanic trap rubble. The range was laid out after pit 290 had been backfilled and was therefore built after the early 16th century. On the other hand, the walls did not contain brick, which becomes universal by the end of the 17th century. The range therefore dated to the late 16th or 17th century.

Further to the north-west, one side of a building extended back from the street frontage. Although the fit to the early mapping is not perfect, this was probably a property division between sometime 6 and 7 Goldsmith Street (held jointly as 9 Goldsmith Street in the late 19th century, as shown in Fig. 6.16), and the wall is one side of the building which became 7 Goldsmith Street. Built mainly of small volcanic rubble, it seems to have abutted the rear range, and was therefore no earlier than the latter part of the 16th century.

Dating evidence

- Stone-lined pit 201. Published group of pottery (EAR3, nos. 1717–28); glass (nos. G60–2); leather (p. 330) and textiles (EAR3, 334–6), *c.* 1500–50.
- Stone-lined pit 228, layers 13–17. Published group of pottery (EAR3, nos. 1446–50), glass (nos. G14–25), leather (nos. L7–16) and textiles (p. 334–6) *c.* 1300–1500.
- Pit 228, layers 1–12. Published group of pottery (EAR3, nos. 1446–50), glass (nos. G14–25), leather (nos. L7–16) and textiles (EAR3, 334–6), *c.* 1500–50.
- Pottery waster pits 264 and 290: Published group of pottery (EAR3, nos. 1620–1704) and glass (nos. G68–70) *c.*1500–50.
- Pit 291. Published pottery group (EAR3, nos. 1862–9), *c.* 1550–80.

7

Excavations at 196–7 High Street, 1972–4

John Allan, Nicky Garland and Neil Holbrook

Introduction

Between late 1972 and early 1974 excavations were undertaken at 196–7 High Street (centre at SX 9195 9263; see Fig. 5.1) prior to the demolition of the standing buildings and their redevelopment as part of the Guildhall shopping centre. The site was chosen for two reasons. First, excavation at Trichay Street (Chapter 5) and elsewhere had shown that the cellars at the centre of the city had removed most deposits, but that Roman military features at the bottom of the stratigraphic sequence could be expected to survive below the cellar floors, and their excavation offered an efficient way of building up the fortress plan. Second, part of 197 High Street remained undisturbed, and it was realised that this represented an unusual chance to investigate post-Roman and Saxo-Norman deposits along the principal street of the Saxon *burh* and medieval city.

The excavations were undertaken in four separate cellars (Figs 7.1–7.2). Area A lay at the rear of 196 High Street, beside the Waterbeer Street frontage, while Areas B, C and D were within the tenement strip of 197 High Street, with Area D on the High Street frontage (Fig. 5.18). Owing to time pressures, Roman military deposits in Area C were not excavated. The excavations of 1972–3 were conducted by Stewart Brown under the direction of Christopher Henderson, who carried out the final stage of excavation in 1974. In addition to the excavations, a photographic record was made of the standing fabric of one of the long side walls of 197 High Street in 1972, and further building recording was carried out by John Thorp at 197 and 198 High Street in 1973 and 1975.

This chapter summarises the archaeological evidence for the Roman military period and examines in detail the evidence for occupation of the site from the beginning of the Roman civil period (*c.* AD 75/80) to the mid 16th century. The period numbers follow those used in the preceding chapters. No evidence for late prehistoric or earlier occupation (Period 1) was uncovered. A detailed archive report on the Roman military remains (Bedford and Salvatore 1993d) forms the basis of the summary presented here. That report, along with a context register and stratigraphic matrix for the Roman civil period onwards, is available for download at https://doi.org/10.5284/1035180. Only limited analysis of the post-military stratigraphy had been carried out prior to the start of this project. Two brief annual summaries of the Roman evidence have been published (Wilson *et al.* 1975, 276; Goodburn *et al.* 1976, 376), and the site has figured in the two previous city-wide Roman-period syntheses (Bidwell 1980, 53–4, 69–72; Henderson 1988, 110–18). A summary of the medieval sequence is given in EAR3, 41–5. The site archive contained detailed notes and draft texts prepared by Christopher Henderson and Stewart Brown, which provide a partial stratigraphic narrative of the Roman and medieval evidence. These accounts have informed the interpretation presented in this chapter. The system of numbering adopted for the buildings described in this report in many cases differs from any previous numbering systems used in the site notes and interim accounts. The buildings have the letter prefixes RC (Roman civil) and Me (medieval). Buildings RC1 and RC2 equate with Building 17i, and Building RC3 with 22ii, in the city-wide gazetteers presented in Chapter 3. Plans for each phase are shown in Figs 7.2–11. Features are shown in bold colours, while layers are shown as lighter shades. A few features are not illustrated (n.i.), as field drawings were not located in the archive.

A number of factors have hindered our understanding of the archaeological sequence. The excavated areas were small; none measuring more than 10 × 6 m. Preservation of archaeological deposits was variable, with one isolated upstand of stratification (Area C) between areas of later cellars. The depths of the cellars varied, causing variable preservation of the Roman deposits. Roman civil remains

Fig. 7.1 Photographs of the 196-7 High Street excavation with Area B on the left, and military posthole 120 on the right with a 30 cm scale (© RAMM)

were uncovered in Areas A, B and C, but had been truncated in Area D. Medieval remains were confined to Areas B and C. It was possible to identify some Roman structures that extended across Areas B and C, but no entire building plans were recovered. Finally, the excavations were conducted in cramped conditions and artificial light, sometimes making it difficult to see features.

Period 2: The Roman legionary fortress (*c.* AD 50/55–75/80)

The excavation site lay on the right side of the *retentura* of the legionary fortress in a block bordered by the fortress baths to the south-east and the *fabrica* to the north-west. The south-east side of the block was defined by the *via decumana* (Chapter 3.1 above, fortress Street D) and the north-west side by fortress Street C.

In Area A, the earliest feature was a single pit (140, n.i.) that contained a large quantity of burnt bone (Bedford and Salvatore 1993d, 2). Although no dating evidence was recovered from its fill, the pit was stratigraphically earlier than two postholes associated with the granaries which constituted the main phase of military occupation. Approximately 138 stakeholes were found; they can be interpreted as the supports for the raised floor of one or more granaries (Fig. 7.2). The stakeholes were *c.* 30 cm deep and covered an area of 40 × 15 m, extending across Areas A, B and D. The absence of associated postpits suggests that the posts were driven into the ground, and this was apparent when some stakeholes were sectioned. It is difficult to determine the layout of structures due to the sheer number of posts and indeed their number indicates several phases of construction, or several attempts to achieve a satisfactory grid of posts (Bidwell 1980, 37). A post-trench and small area of metalling at the north-western edge of Area A may represent part of a granary and an associated loading bay set back *c.* 6 m from the edge of the fortress street C. No evidence for the demolition of these granary structures was found.

Period 3: The Roman town

Introduction

When the Early Roman town was created within the defences of the former legionary fortress, many of the

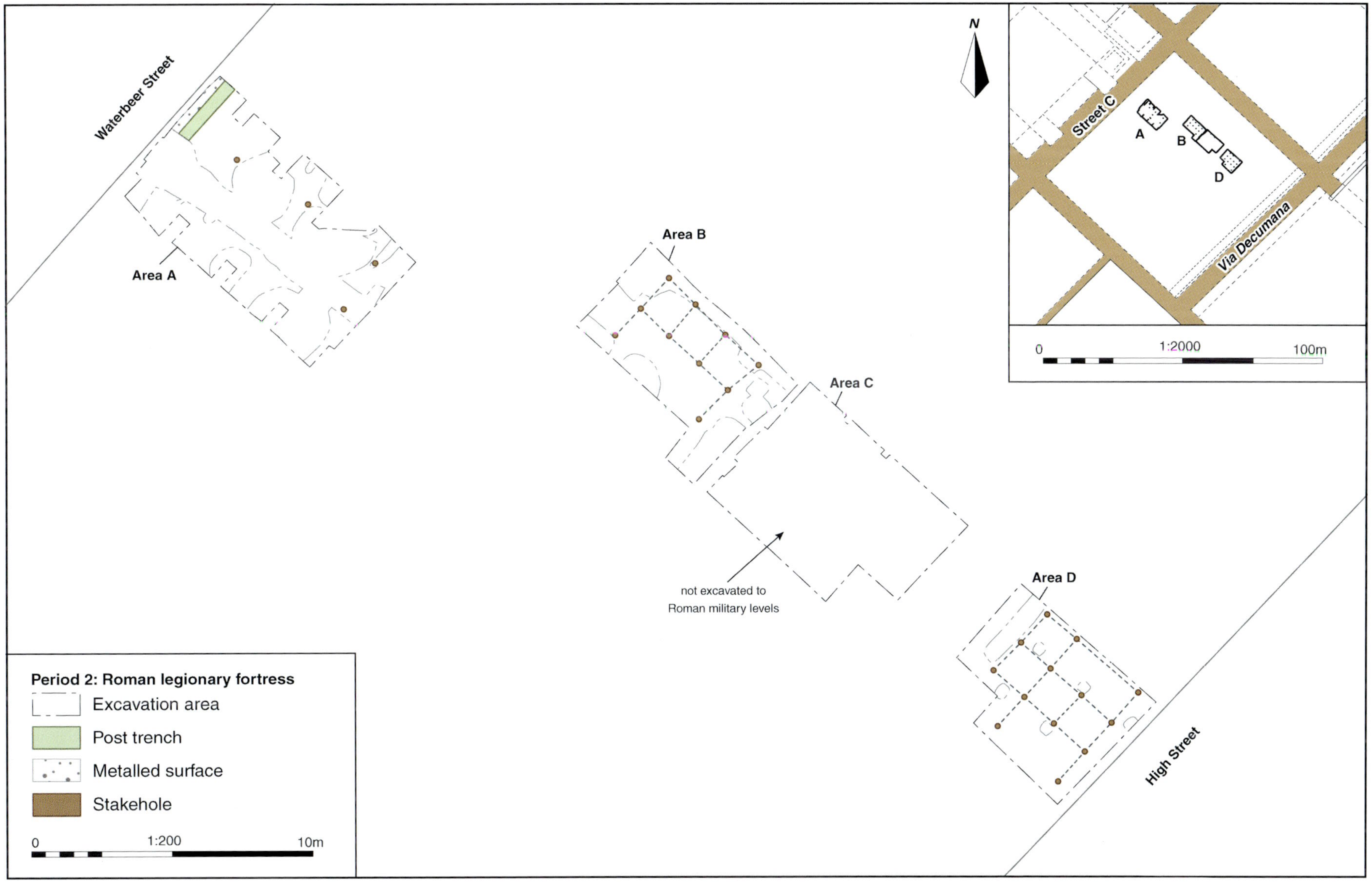

Fig. 7.2 Plan of selected Roman military features (Period 2). This plan shows a selective number of the total of 138 stakeholes revealed, and is based upon an attempt to identify a regular grid layout (after Bedford and Salvatore 1993d, fig. 3)

fortress streets were retained to delineate the *insulae* of the new town. The excavation lay within *insula* IX, which was defined to the north-west by town Street C and to the south-east by Street D which separated the *insula* from the forum and basilica. The north-west edge of this early civil street has been detected in excavation a short distance from this site (EAR1, 120). It lay 3 m to the north-west of an original military street, which was suppressed when the fortress was abandoned (Chapter 3.2, observation D2i). The earliest post-military deposits at the present site comprised a small wooden structure and several boundary ditches (Period 3a), followed in the Hadrianic or Antonine period (Period 3b) by the construction of timber-framed building (RC1) upon stone foundations. The demolition of RC1 was followed by the construction of a building (RC2) which was destroyed by fire and perhaps converted into some manner of lean-to structure (Period 3c, late 2nd to early 3rd century AD). In the final phase of Roman occupation (Period 3d), which probably dates to after the mid 3rd century AD, a possible wooden structure was flanked to the south-east by stone building (RC3), which contained at least one tessellated floor.

Period 3a: Earliest civilian activity (late 1st century to early 2nd century AD)

In the central part of the site (Areas B and C) successive layers of red-brown clay levelling (42; 43 and 381; 383, n.i.), 0.1 m deep, were laid over the site of the demolished military granaries (Fig. 7.3). The only structural evidence revealed lay in Areas B and C and consisted of two postholes (296; 297) and a possible post-trench (379). The postholes, each 0.4 m in diameter and 0.08 m deep, were spaced at a distance of *c.* 2 m along a north-east/south-west alignment, while the trench (379) was 0.5 m wide and 0.25 m deep and lay on a similar, but not precisely parallel, alignment. The trench conceivably held the base of a wattle-and-daub wall. A single posthole (382), 0.5 m in diameter and more than 0.3 m deep, lay to the south of the trench. It is impossible to determine whether the trench and postholes were associated with a single structure. No finds were recovered from these features, although they were all cut into the clay levelling deposits.

In Area A there were two small north-east/south-west aligned ditches (134; 135), each 0.4 m wide and 0.12 m deep. Both ditches truncated a thin layer of charcoal (125) associated with the Period 2 military occupation, and indicate that the levelling deposits found in Areas B and C were not laid here. The ditches were staggered at an interval of 0.35 m and lay 10 m to the north-west of the possible structure. They may have defined building plots within *insula* IX.

In the southern part of Area D a single postpit (231, n.i.) truncated the military deposits. The circular postpit was 0.65 m in diameter and 0.4 m deep and contained a packing of volcanic trap fragments. Part of the postpit lay beyond the excavation area and post-medieval cellars had truncated much of the rest of this area. It is possible that the postpit was associated with a larger structure that lay beyond the confines of Area D.

Dating evidence

There is no dating evidence for this phase of occupation. These features have been assigned to this period as they were stratigraphically later than the Period 2 military granaries and were overlaid by early to mid 2nd-century AD deposits of Period 3b.

Period 3b: Timber building RC1 and refuse deposits (Hadrianic – Antonine)

By the early 2nd century AD a series of refuse dumps, 0.1–0.3 m deep, covered the north-western part of the site. In Area A several brown clay deposits (122; 123, n.i.) contained frequent inclusions of charcoal flecks, roof tile, gravel and broken oyster shells. Similar clay and stone dumps (37; 38, n.i.) were also present in Area B. A single posthole (44, n.i.), 0.19 m in diameter, was cut into layer 38 but was overlaid by a later dump of gravel (41, n.i.). It may have formed part of a temporary structure. In Area C a layer of brown clay (378, n.i.) containing baked daub and tile fragments was overlain by small dumps of discarded oyster shells (377, n.i.). The similarity between the deposits in Areas A, B and C suggests that they represent contemporaneous refuse dumping across the site, possibly associated with nearby construction activities.

Building RC1 was aligned north-west/south-east and consisted of two postpits (40; 376) which cut the dumped refuse layers described above (Fig. 7.4). The postpits were *c.* 1.2 m in diameter and 0.7 m deep and contained large pieces of volcanic trap rubble and yellow clay packing. Although the full dimensions of the structure are unknown, a small north-east/south-west aligned wall foundation (375) was cut into the upper fills of postpit 376, possibly suggesting that it extended to the north-east. The foundation was comprised of fragments of volcanic trap bonded with a red-brown clay. The foundation might represent a later structural addition and perhaps served as a cill for a timber base plate. There was a single internal posthole (374), 0.14 m wide and 0.18 m deep, within the postulated bounds of RC1. A layer of yellow clay (373, n.i.), 0.05 m thick, to the north-east of the postpits formed an internal floor surface. The floor was overlain by a layer of black charcoal-rich occupation material (372, n.i.). A small pit (88), more than 0.7 m in diameter and 0.4 m deep, to the south-west of postpit 40 may have been contemporary with RC1, but was heavily truncated by later activity.

Dating evidence

- Dump 122. Coin no. 86, Trajan, AD 112–14, very worn; Samian: Dr. 37, *c.* AD 125–150 (EAR4, fig. 14, no. 65); Dr. 37, *c.* AD 100–20 (EAR4, fig. 14, no. 66).

Fig. 7.3 Plan of Period 3a (late 1st to early 2nd century) structure and boundary ditches

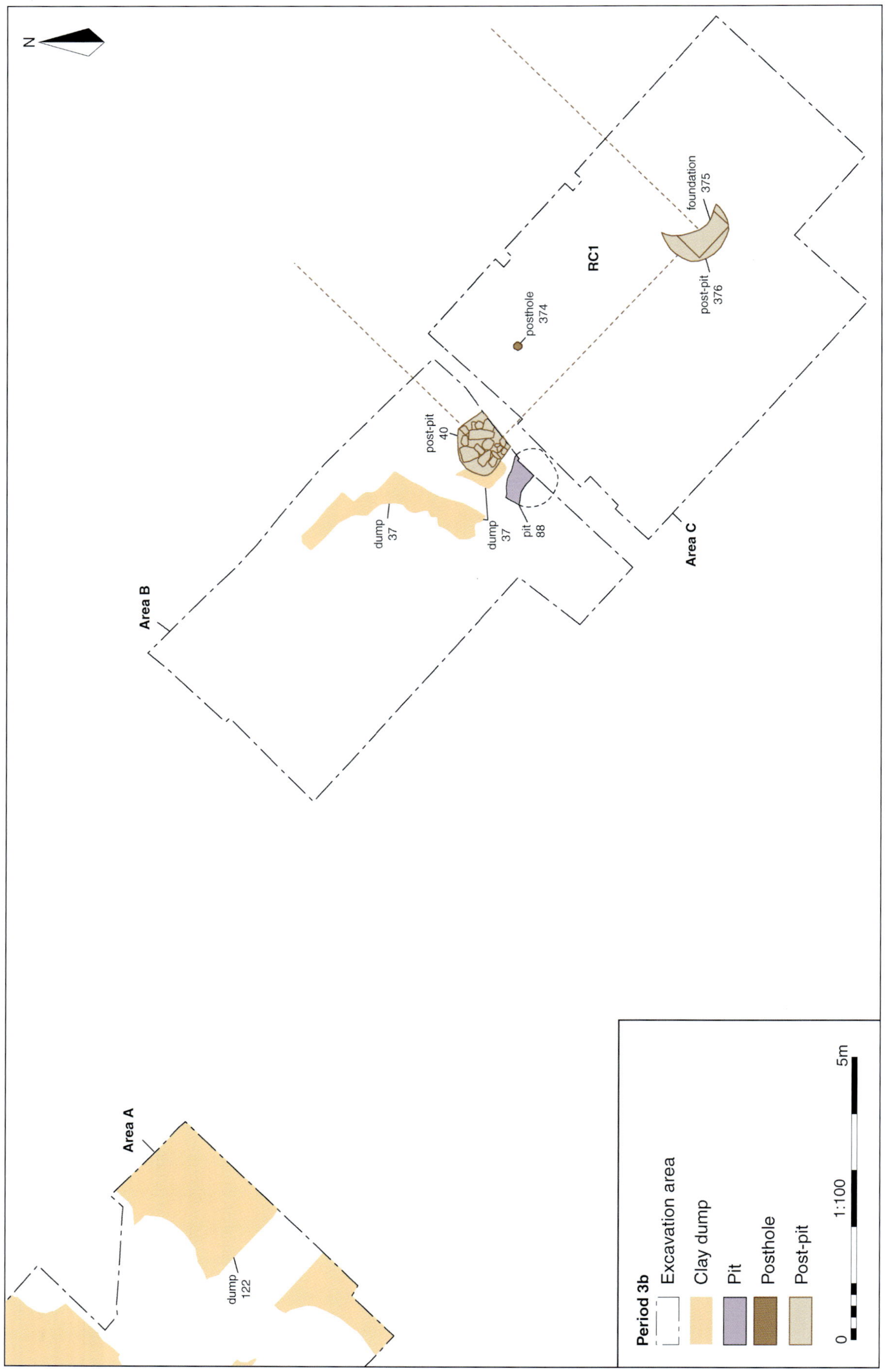

Fig. 7.4 Plan of Period 3b (Hadrianic–Antonine) building RC1

Pottery: Fine South-Western BB1 jar (EAR4, fig. 47, type 9.4).
- Dump 38. Pottery: South-East Dorset BB1 flat-rimmed dish.
- Dump 378. Samian: Dr. 18/31, Hadrianic; Dr. 37, *c.* AD 100–120 (EAR4, fig. 14, no. 67); Dr. 37, Flavian.

The presence of a very worn coin of AD 112–14, Hadrianic samian and a Fine South-Western BB1 jar suggest that the dumps were deposited in the Hadrianic or Antonine period. Although no dating evidence was recovered from RC1, the demolished structure was sealed by Period 3c demolition deposit 371.

Period 3c: Building RC2 (late 2nd to 3rd century AD)

At some point in the late 2nd or 3rd century AD building RC1 was demolished, a 0.15–0.2 m thick layer of red brown clay (371, n.i.) within the footprint of the structure in Area C presumably deriving from levelled daub walls. The deposit also contained large fragments of volcanic trap, perhaps derived from stone cill walls such as 375.

Building RC2

RC2 was defined by two parallel stone wall foundations (363; 368), each aligned north-east/south-west and *c.* 3.6 m apart (Fig. 7.5). The foundations were 0.5 m wide and constructed from fragments of volcanic trap bonded with red clay. The narrow width of the wall foundations suggests that they were cill walls supporting a timber superstructure. A layer of brown clay (370, n.i.), 0.05 m thick, survived in patches between the wall foundations and was probably an internal floor surface. A small oven (366) within the building had baked sides and was more than 0.6 m long and 0.3 m wide. The stoke-hole for the oven probably lay to the north-east, outside the excavation area. A thin layer of charcoal (367, n.i.) accumulated to the west of the oven and was doubtless associated with its use. At some point during the occupation of RC2 the oven fell out of use and was demolished. A yellow brown clay floor surface (365, n.i.), up to 0.05 m thick, sealed the oven (366) and associated charcoal layer (367). A contemporary white gravelly mortar floor (364), 0.1 m thick, survived adjacent to the south-eastern wall foundation (363). The presence of two different floors may suggest two separate rooms within RC2, or two periods of use, however, later truncation had removed all stratigraphic relationship between these two deposits.

RC2 was destroyed by fire sometime between the late 2nd and early 3rd century AD, leaving a layer of ash and burnt daub (362, n.i.), up to 0.1 m thick, covering the remains of the structure. A levelling deposit of brown clay (361, n.i.), which contained charcoal, oyster shell and pink clay lumps, formed the base for the reconstruction of RC2, which was located within a similar footprint to the earlier building. The reconstructed RC2 was defined by a small stone foundation (360), 0.3 m wide and 0.12 m deep. The foundation was constructed of volcanic trap and was built immediately adjacent to wall 363 of the earlier building. No foundation was present on the north-west side of the building, suggesting either that foundation 368 was reused or that the structure was rebuilt as a small lean-to, with the main structure lying to the south-east of wall 360. A lens of white plaster (359, n.i.), up to 0.3 m thick in places, lay to the north-west of wall foundation 360 and was likely associated with the reconstruction of this building. A deposit of charcoal and dark brown clay (357, n.i.), 0.1 m deep, was dumped over the layer of plaster. A line of three stakeholes (350; 351; 352), spaced at intervals of 0.4–0.5 m, cut through the refuse deposit and lay perpendicular to foundation 360. The stakeholes were each 0.1 m wide and deep and may have formed an internal partition or part of the lean-to.

A small oven (354) was built to the south-west of the line of stakeholes and cut through foundation 368. The oven was 0.7 m in diameter and 0.35 m deep. The interior surfaces had been burnt *in situ* and a thin layer of charcoal was present in the base of the oven. If the oven was contemporary with the building, and the wall above foundation 368 was still standing, then presumably the fire pit lay outside the building. More likely the oven post-dates the use of the wall and the foundation was utilised as a convenient stone lining for the main chamber. A layer of trampled charcoal (356, n.i.), up to 0.2 m deep, surrounded the oven. A thin truncated layer of dark brown silt containing oyster shells (349, n.i.) was deposited to the north-east of the stakehole alignment, either an occupation or abandonment deposit. At some point during this period oven 354 went out of use and a small stone cist (353) was constructed above the site of the fire pit. The cist was 0.75 m long, 0.4 m wide deep and was lined at the north-western and south-eastern ends with roughly positioned stones and tile. A contemporary surface of volcanic stone chippings (355, n.i.), 0.05 m thick, was laid around the cist. No finds were recovered from the cist and it is difficult to determine its function. Perhaps it acted as a small soakaway.

Occupation adjacent to the street

A number of features in Area A represented small-scale occupation along the south-east frontage of town Street C. A well (90, n.i.) *c.* 3.5 m from the estimated line of the street frontage was 1.9 m in diameter and 3.15 m deep and had near vertical sides and a flat base. The well was truncated by later activity and no evidence for an internal structure survived. A large assemblage of animal bone was recovered from the backfilled deposits in the well. A small posthole (97, n.i.), 0.5 m in diameter and 0.34 m deep, lay to the west of the well and may have been associated with it. A postpit (119, n.i.) 0.9 m in diameter and 0.5 m deep to the east of the well was packed with

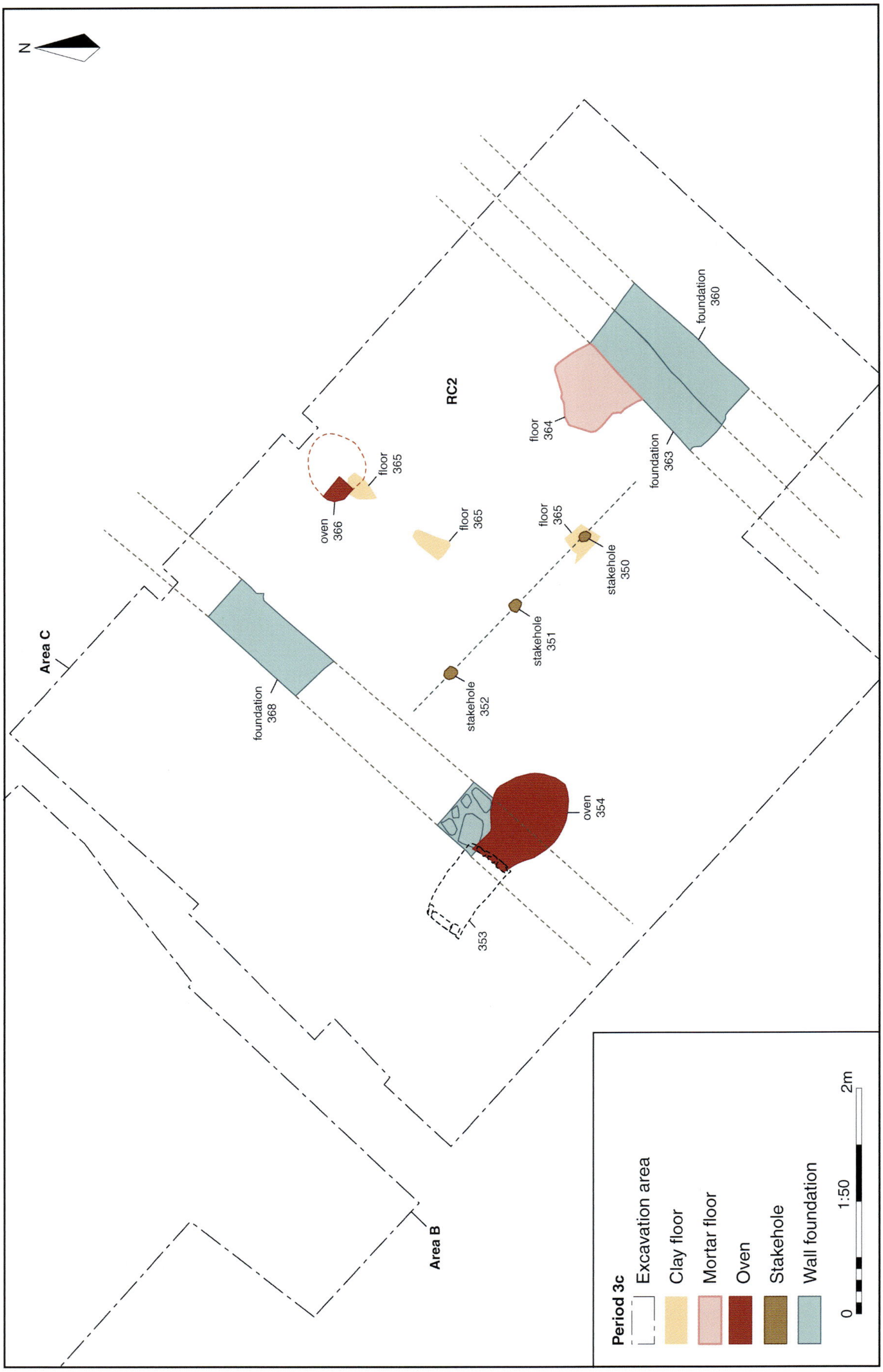

Fig. 7.5 Plan of Period 3c (late 2nd to 3rd century AD) construction and refit of building RC2

volcanic trap and brown clay, suggesting it formed part of a larger structure that lay beyond the excavation area. Although no dating evidence was recovered from these features, as they cut through Period 3b dump 122 they were presumably contemporary with RC2.

Dating evidence

- RC1 demolition 371. Samian: Dr. 18/31, Hadrianic-Antonine.
- Dump 357 associated with the reconstruction of RC2. Samian: Dr. 31, stamp no. 110, early Antonine; Dr. 30, Dr. 31 (x 3), Dr. 31R (x 2), all Antonine. Pottery: Lower Rhineland barbotine beaker; Exeter Gritty Grey Ware cooking pot with obtuse-angled lattice decoration; single sherd of South-Western Grey Ware storage jar.

There is limited dating evidence for this period of occupation, although we can assume some longevity based upon the phases of construction and reconstruction of RC2. If the pottery sherd with obtuse-angled lattice from dump 357 is assumed to follow the chronology of South-East Dorset BB1, then the reconstruction of RC2 probably dates to after *c*. AD 220. South-Western Grey Ware storage jars first appear in Exeter in the late Antonine period (EAR4, 175).

Period 3d: A possible timber building and stone building RC3 (mid 3rd to 4th century AD)

Several dumps of clay (36; 37, n.i.) were laid in Area B at some point after the mid 3rd century AD. These deposits consisted of mixed clay with inclusions of charcoal and oyster shell, were 0.2–0.3 m deep, and represent levelling ahead of the construction of new buildings. A thin layer of yellow clay (17), 0.16 m deep, was the latest of these dumps in Area B.

Structure?

Ten postholes (19–25; 28–30, Fig 7.6) cut into the top of the clay levelling (17) in Area B were considered by the excavators to be have been part of another small timber structure. The postholes varied from 0.12–0.8 m in diameter, suggesting they were used for different functions. No discernible pattern could be identified and the postholes may represent several phases of activity. An east/west aligned gully (18), 0.4 m wide and 0.6 m deep, passed through the centre of the postholes and may be contemporary with them. A layer of small pebbles laid at the base of the gully suggests it functioned as a drain or soakaway.

A layer of earth (16, n.i.) was dumped over the area of the postholes, while two gullies with irregular profiles (26; 27) were dug to the south-east of them. The gullies were aligned north-east/south-west and were 0.45–0.65 wide and 0.24 m deep. A pit (25), 1.15 m in diameter and 0.28 m deep, cut backfilled gully 27. No dating evidence was recovered from the pit and it might be associated with a later phase of activity.

Building RC3

Stone building RC3 within Area C was constructed on two levelling deposits (347; 348), 0.2 m thick, comprised of daub, mortar and charcoal. These layers sealed the latest occupation in Period 3c. RC3 was represented by two stone foundations (256/257; 340) which together formed the western corner of the building. As uncovered RC3 was more than 6 m long and 3 m wide and extended to the south-east and north-east beyond the limit of the excavation. No evidence for RC3 was found in Area D due to truncation by later activity. The wall foundations were 0.8 m wide and 0.6 m deep and consisted of volcanic trap bonded with clay. The width of the foundations is commensurate with a stone superstructure for the building, although stone cill walls supporting a timber-framed structure cannot be excluded.

There was a series of floor surfaces within the building. A rammed gravel surface (346, n.i.), 0.05 m deep, formed the initial floor and was overlaid by a thin lens of mixed clay and mortar (345, n.i.), possibly occupation debris. This deposit was covered by a 20 mm-thick layer of salmon coloured backing plaster (344, n.i.), interpreted by the excavators as the remnants of wall-plaster that was stripped during renovations of the building. Above this a dump of mortar-flecked brown soil (343, n.i.) raised the level by up to 0.6 m and formed a base for a red tessellated pavement (341) set on white bedding plaster (342, n.i.). The tessellated floor only survived in two small patches where it consisted of both square and rectangular-shaped *tesserae* made from ceramic tile, each approximately 2.5 cm thick. There was no evidence for the demolition of RC3 and it is probable that the structure was carefully dismantled once it had fallen out of use.

Antiquarians recorded fragments of tessellated pavement along the frontage of 197 High Street (Goodchild 1952, 100, site no. 4; Bidwell 1980, 73; Cosh and Neal 2005, mosaic no. 157.2). A small section of tessellated pavement was uncovered in 1777 in the area outside 196–197 High Street, and in 1874 workmen laying gas pipes underneath the pavement outside 197 High Street uncovered two pieces of tessellated pavement. The first was constructed of square brick *tesserae* while the other consisted of rectangular roofing *tegulae* laid on edge and interspersed by grey and white *tesserae* (Bidwell 1980, 79, note 16). A fragment of the latter is preserved in the RAMM; the long rectangular brick *tessera* may be from an *opus spicatum* pavement. Although located approximately 10 m to the south-east of RC3, the similarity between these pavements and that found within the structure may suggest that they form part of single building. If this were the case RC3 would have been in excess of 15 m long and may have encroached on the line of town Street D.

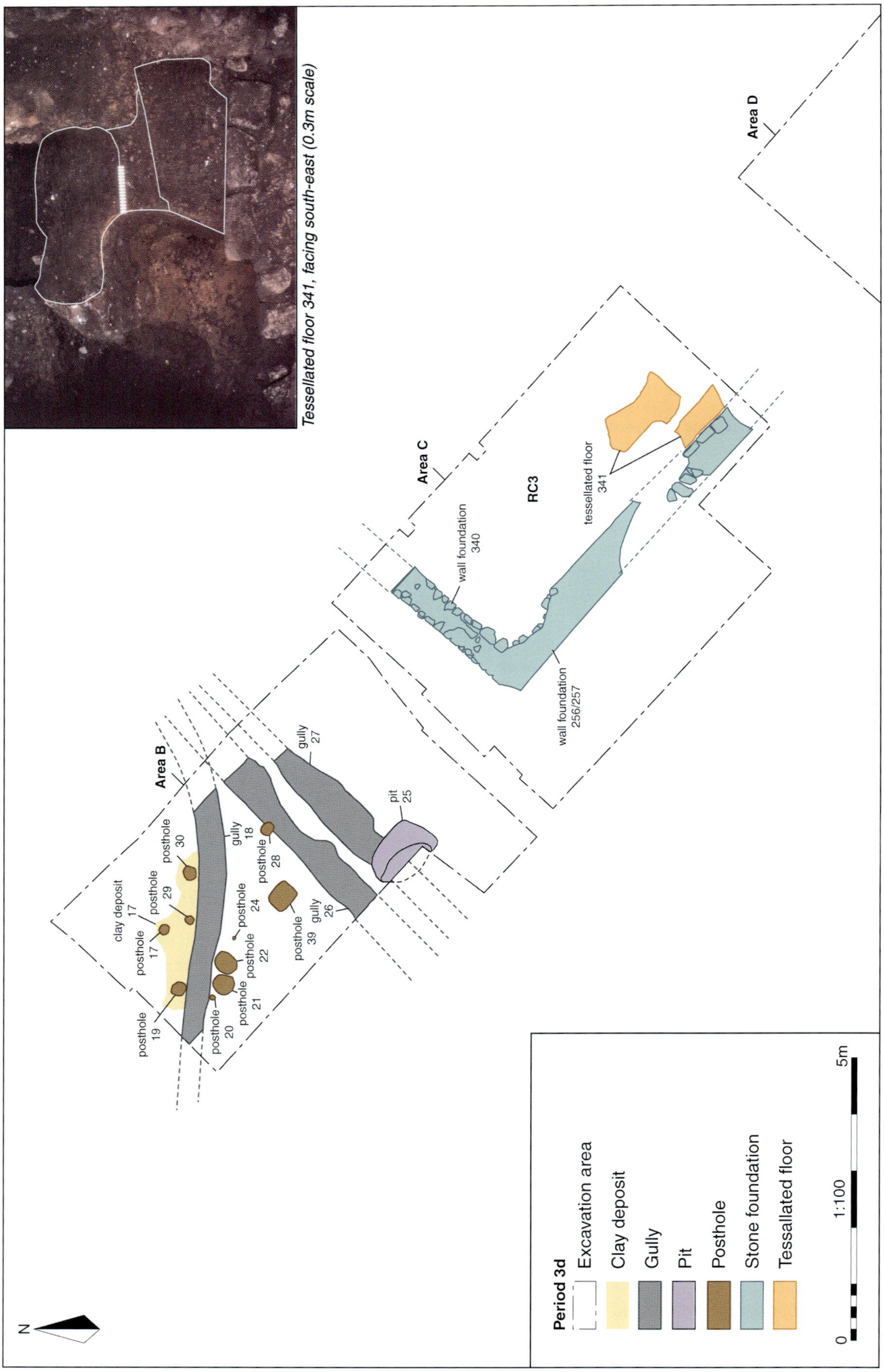

Fig. 7.6 Plan of Period 3d (mid 3rd to 4th century AD) building RC3 and possible structure

Dating evidence

- Gully 18. Pottery: South-East Dorset BB1 cooking pot with obtuse-angled lattice decoration (after *c.* AD 220).
- Dump 16 sealing possible timber structure. Pottery: South-East Dorset BB1 cooking pot with obtuse-angled lattice decoration
- Levelling 347. Pottery: Exeter Gritty Grey Ware flanged bowl (EAR4, fig. 66, type 20.1a).
- Levelling 348. South-East Dorset BB1 cooking pot with obtuse-angled lattice decoration.

Limited dating evidence for this phase of occupation has been recovered from either of the structures in Area B or C. The possible structure and RC3 were probably contemporary as both were constructed on top of levelling deposits which the flanged bowl from 347 indicates date to after *c.* AD 250. There was no evidence for the demolition of RC3.

Aspects of the Roman civil sequence *by Neil Holbrook*

The restricted extent of these excavations, exacerbated by a paucity of dating evidence, hinders an understanding of the form and chronology of early civilian activity in this part of Exeter. While Areas A to D were spread across much of the width of *insula* IX, no street frontages were investigated and the Roman evidence was largely concentrated in Areas B and C which lay in the middle of the *insula*. *Insula* IX would have been a prime site for residential occupation, close to the basilica and forum in the heart of the Roman town, and we might therefore reasonably expect some of the earliest civilian occupation in the town to have occurred hereabouts. The first traces of post-military occupation probably date to the late 1st or early 2nd century AD, although little can be said of its form. A major replanning took place in the Hadrianic or Antonine period (Period 3b) when refuse was dumped to level-up the site for the construction of building RC1 which appears to have been of timber-framed construction, with the walls supported on dry-stone foundations. RC1 is broadly dated to the Hadrianic or Antonine period, but the dating evidence is scanty. RC1 was replaced at some point in the late 2nd or 3rd century AD by RC2, a 5.5 m-wide structure of more substantial construction. Once again dry-stone cill walls probably supported a timber framed superstructure with wattle and daub infilling (burnt daub was recovered from its demolition levels). The building contained at least one oven, and so presumably served a domestic purpose. RC2 was destroyed by fire, just possibly part of the same event evidenced at Trichay Street (Chapter 5) but was reconstructed to a similar plan.

At some point after the mid 3rd century AD there was another fundamental replanning of this part of the *insula* when stone building RC3 was constructed. Presumably this building fronted on to the street that lay *c.* 15 m to the south-east, and thus only one of its rear corners was found in the excavation (unfortunately all trace of this building had been destroyed in Area D). Clay bonded wall foundations probably supported a dressed masonry superstructure, although all trace of the latter had been comprehensively robbed in the post-Roman period. The building was subsequently equipped with a tessellated floor, albeit one of crude workmanship. The antiquarian records of tessellated pavements immediately in front of 197 High Street most likely lay within other rooms of this building, which could have been of some pretension as it bordered the forum. Outside the back of the house the ditches found in Area B perhaps delimited the rear of the building plot, with postholes and a drain testifying to activity in the centre of the *insula*. There is unfortunately no useful evidence for how long RC3 was occupied as no demolition deposits survived. Indeed the site seems to have been robbed of all useable stone prior to the accumulation of dark earth in Period 4. There are hints, however, from residual Roman coins found in later deposits that occupation continued hereabouts until at least the end of the 4th century AD, if not beyond. These comprise a very worn Theodosian issue of AD 388–92 (EAR4, no. 402), the only issue of the House of Theodosius recovered from Exeter (EAR4, 34, table 7), and two very worn issues of Valentinian I (AD 367–75; nos. 387–8). How much weight should be ascribed to the very worn appearance of the Theodosian coin is open to question as these issues were often poorly-made objects with weak or partial impressions (Besly 2006, 83–5). The distribution of very late Roman artefacts within Exeter has been argued to indicate that the area of occupation within the town contracted to the central *insulae* around the forum at the very end of the 4th century AD (EAR4, 11–14), and this would have included *insula* IX.

Periods 4 and 5: The post-Roman and Middle Saxon periods

Post-Roman dark earth (5th to early 10th century AD)

Following the demolition of the latest Roman building RC3, a layer of dark loam accumulated over its site. This so-called post-Roman dark earth (249) varied in thickness from 0.2–0.4 m and must indicate some activity, if only cultivation and/or dumping, before the earliest Saxo-Norman occupation in the 10th century (Period 6). A large assemblage of animal bone and oyster shell, including residual 3rd and 4th-century AD Roman pottery and coins, was recovered from the dark earth. No other post-Roman or Middle Saxon activity was found.

Dating evidence

- Dark earth 249. Coin 302, Constantius I, AD 330–5, very worn; coin 264, illegible, AD 270–90, very worn; coin 109, Caracalla?, AD 200–17, very worn. Pottery:

Scrap of medieval fabric 20. See EAR3, 42 for listing of key dating evidence.

The dark earth contained mostly Roman artefacts, apart from a single scrap of medieval UGSD coarse ware. This implies that it was largely undisturbed by later activity.

Period 6: The Saxo-Norman town (*c.* AD 900–1200)

Evidence for Period 6 activity comes largely from Area C, where the longest sequence of Saxo-Norman deposits excavated in the city was preserved, extending uninterrupted from the 10th to the late 12th/early 13th century (EAR3, 41–3).There were also a few features of this period in Area B; in the other excavated areas, activity of this period had been truncated by later cellars.

Area C

Period 6a: Pits (late 10th to early 11th century)

The earliest features of the Late Saxon *burh* were a series of intercutting pits (Fig 7.7: 251; 254; 331; 333) which lay along the south-western edge of the excavation area and extended beyond it. They all contained layers of cess, overlain by brown earths containing charcoal and oyster shell, as well as moderate assemblages of pottery and animal bone. The character of their fills suggests that they were all used as cesspits, and later for dumping refuse. These pits may have lain behind a house on the street frontage.

The earliest pit (333) was subrectangular and more than 1.95 m wide and 0.5 m deep. After it was backfilled, it was cut by two large, subcircular pits (251; 331). Pit 251 was more than 3 m wide and 2 m deep and pit 331 more than 2.5 m in diameter and more than 0.5 m deep. An iron axe head was recovered from 331 (EAR3, 337, M.1), which was cut by a later subcircular pit (254), 1.8 m in diameter and 1.75 m deep. The backfilled pits were covered by a spread of charcoal (248, n.i.), which contained pottery and a Late Saxon penannular finger ring (EAR3, 339, M.60).

Dating evidence

Ceramic Horizon B (EAR3, 9; late 10th or 11th century)

- Pit 333. Pottery: EAR3, 42–3, nos. 1–5.
- Pit 251. Pottery: EAR3, nos. 18–23.
- Pit 254. Pottery: EAR3, nos. 6–7.
- Layer 248. Pottery: EAR3, no. 8; Late Saxon finger ring (EAR3, 339, M.60).

Period 6b: Cesspits and building Me1 (11th century)

A layer of orange clay containing charcoal, oyster shells and mortar (247, n.i.), 0.1–0.2 m thick, covered layer 248. It was cut by two pits (Fig 7.7: 250; 252). The larger one (250) was 2.3 m in diameter and more than 2 m deep; it lay partially beyond the excavation area. Pit 252 cut pit 250; both contained deposits of cess overlain by refuse including tile and oyster shell. A polished bone awl (EAR3, 351, B.19) and a bone spindlewhorl (EAR3, 351, B.25) were recovered from pit 252. Pit 255, to the north-west, was much smaller; it was 0.55 m in diameter and 0.2 m deep, and was broadly contemporary with the other two pits. A possible hearth (253), *c.* 0.7 m in diameter and 0.35 m deep, contained several layers of burnt clay, ash and charcoal, as well as deposits of oyster shell and animal bone.

These features were followed by two trenches (239; 332) which formed the eastern corner of building (Me1) in excess of 5.32 m long and 5 m wide. They were 0.8 m wide but only 0.2 m deep and contained fragments of volcanic trap rubble bonded with yellow clay. No floors or other associated features were uncovered within or surrounding the building. Since the trenches were so shallow, it seems unlikely that they represent a stone building or a timber structure with earth-fast posts. It is proposed that they represent timber buildings with ‘foundation bed’ construction (see Discussion below).

Dating evidence

Ceramic Horizon B (EAR3, 9; late 10th or 11th century)

- Pit 250. Pottery: UGSD (fabric 20). EAR3, no. 13.
- Pit 252. Pottery: Hamwic 127; Exeter Bedford Garage Ware; UGSD: EAR3, nos 14–17.
- Layer 247. Pottery: UGSD. EAR3, nos. 9–12.
- Foundation trench 332. Pottery: Exeter Bedford Garage Ware; limestone-tempered fabric 22. EAR3, nos. 24–26.

Period 6c: Building Me2 and cesspits (late 11th to early 12th century)

After building Me1 was demolished, a gully (238, n.i.) was dug through one of its foundation trenches (239); it was aligned north-east/south-west and was 0.6–0.8 m wide and 0.5 m deep. Since it lay parallel with High Street and *c.* 12 m behind the frontage, it may have marked the rear of a building running back from the frontage, or of a yard behind a house parallel to the street. A refuse pit (232, n.i.) to the south of gully 238, 1.6 m in diameter and 1.22 m deep, was overlain by further deposits of burnt clay, pebbles, gravel and oyster shell (240, 241, n.i.). The last deposit (241) contained a penny of William I struck in 1072–4. This sequence of deposits represents several episodes of activity.

At the end of the 11th century or early in the 12th, a deposit of yellow clay (214) sealed the demolished remains of Me1; it was followed by a new building (Me2; Fig. 7.8). This was represented by two partially robbed wall trenches (219; 242) and two robber trenches (225; 234) defining a structure 4.4 m wide. They enclosed a small room 3 m long and wide, with a second room to the south-east. The foundation trenches (219; 242) were

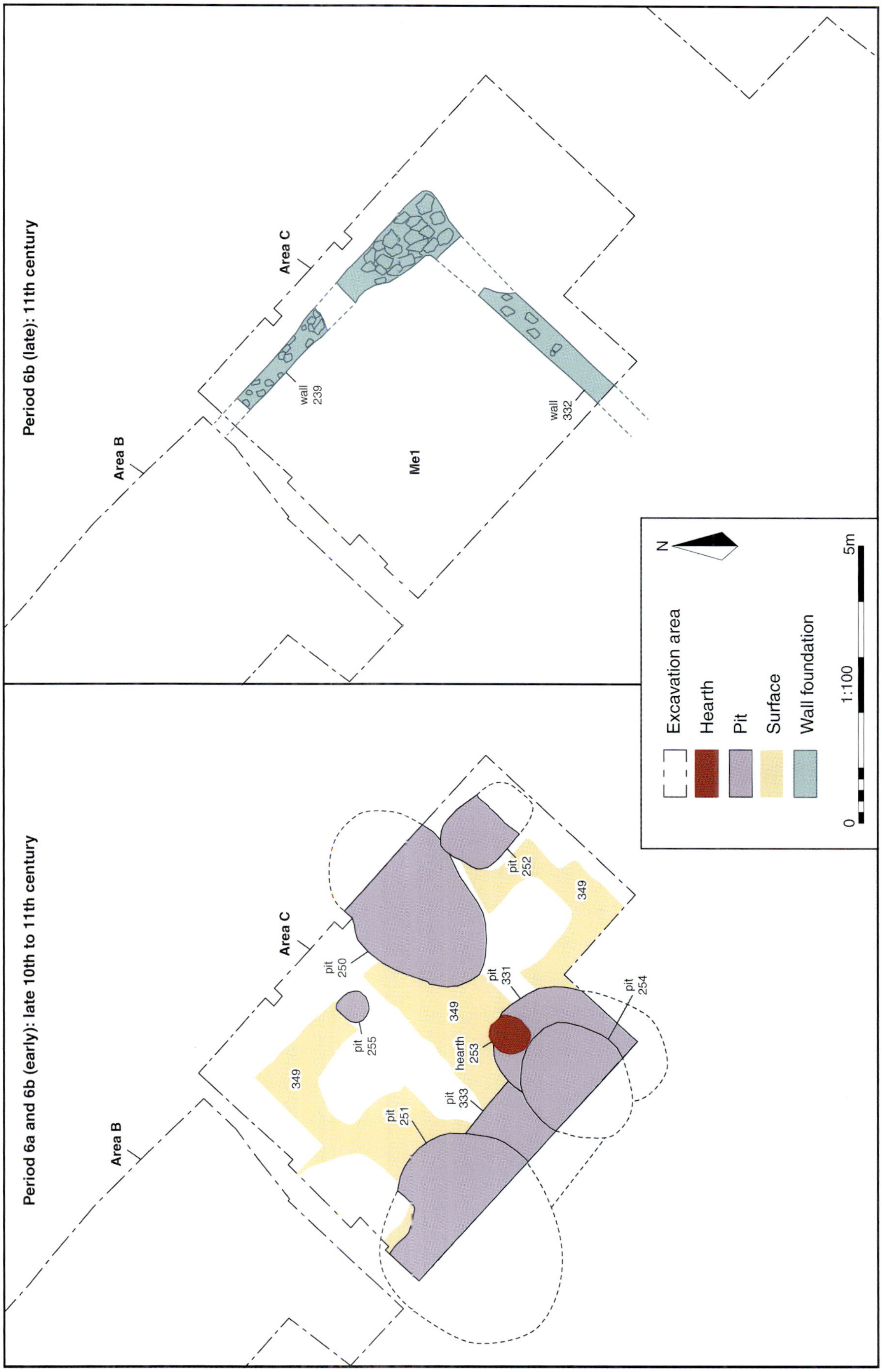

Fig. 7.7 Plan of Periods 6a (late 10th to 11th century) pits and Period 6b (11th century) building Me1

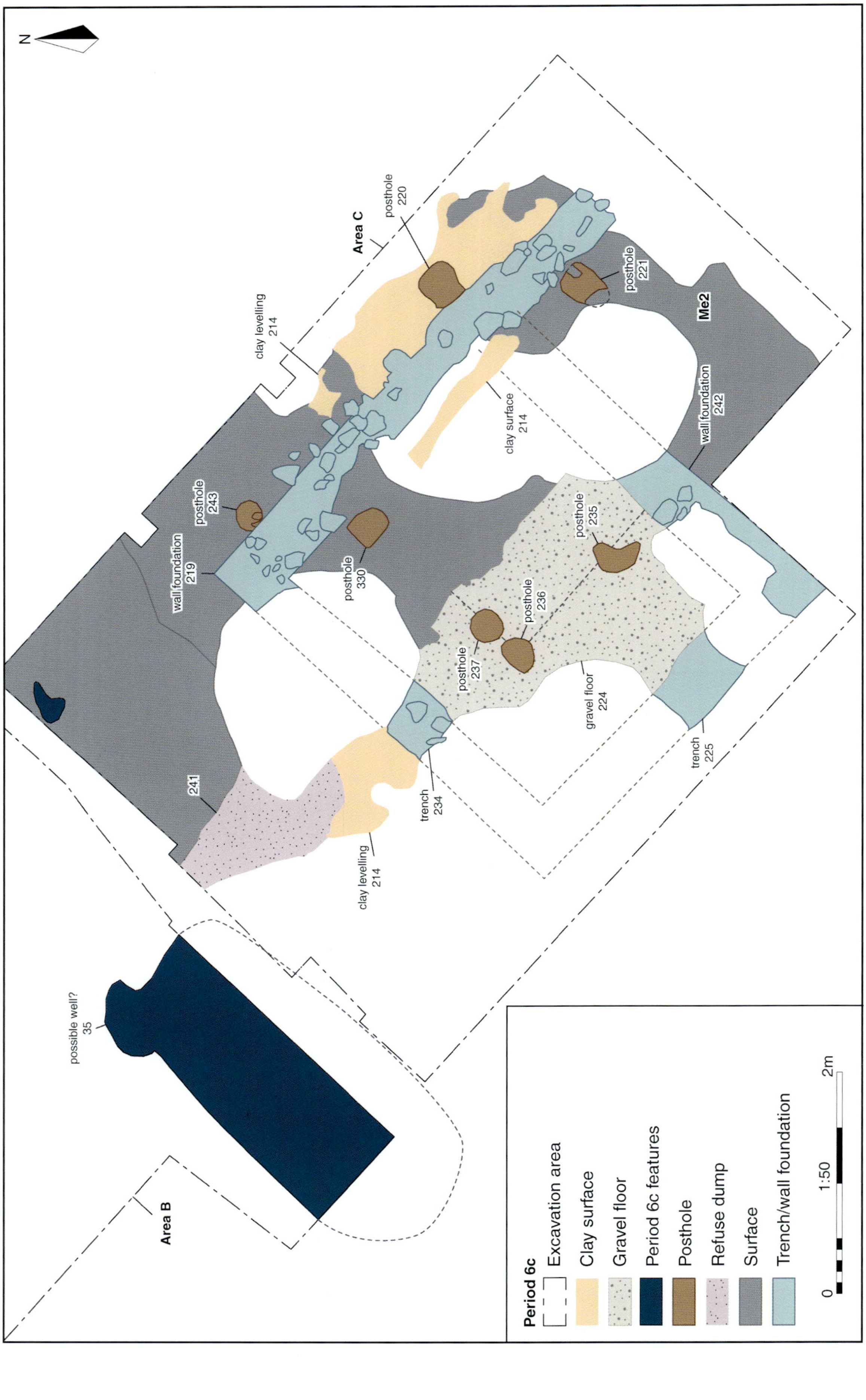

Fig. 7.8 Plan of Period 6c (late 11th to early 12th century) building Me2 and other features

0.25–0.4 m wide, 0.15–0.2 m deep and filled with volcanic trap fragments bonded with clay. The two robber trenches (225; 234) each measured 0.2 m wide and deep. The difference between their construction techniques may show that two building phases were represented. The room was floored with a layer of gravel (224) 0.2 m deep. The remains may have been elements of the rear portion of a structure on High Street, whose frontage lay 10.5 m to the south-east. Given the narrow trench widths, it seems that this was a timber building; they seem too shallow for earth-fast posts, and are interpreted as parts of a structure with 'foundation bed' construction (see Discussion below).

A secondary phase of construction saw the replacement of this room by a post-built structure. Four postholes (235; 236; 237; 330), each 0.2 m wide and 0.2–0.25 m deep, cut through floor surface (224). A small trench foundation (218, n.i.), 1.3 m long and 0.43 m wide, dug against trench 219 appeared to belong to the same phase of occupation. Part of a probable rotary quern stone was reused in the foundation (EAR3, S.21). A posthole (330) cut through the wall foundation; further postholes were found to the south-east of the room (221) and beside the external face of wall 219 (220; 243).

Dating evidence

Ceramic Horizon C (EAR3, 9–10; late 10th to 12th century)

- Boundary ditch 238. Pottery: EAR3, nos. 35–9.
- Pit 232. Pottery: EAR3, nos. 29–33.
- Layer 241. Pottery: EAR3, nos. 27–8. Coin: William I Penny (1072–4) EAR3, 248, E.1.
- Floor surface 224. Pottery: EAR3, nos. 42–5.
- Robbing of wall-trench 218. Pottery: EAR3, nos. 46–9 (12th century).
- Robbing of wall-trench 219. Pottery: EAR3, nos. 50–8 (12th century).

Ditch 238 and pit 232 were the earliest features in this phase; they probably date to the late 11th to early 12th century. The coin of 1072–4 from refuse deposit 241 provides a late 11th-century *terminus post quem* for the construction of building Me2. The pottery from wall-trenches 218 and 219 of Me2 originated from their backfill and so is associated with the demolition rather than construction of this building.

Period 6d: A yard, well and further building (Me3) (mid to late 12th century)

By the mid 12th century building Me2 had been demolished and was overlain by a patchy layer of burnt earth and charcoal (216, n.i.), 0.05 m thick. The burnt material may suggest that Me2 had burnt down. It was overlain by a layer of gravel 0.1 m deep (217, n.i.) along the south-western edge of Area C. On the eastern side of the area, a dump containing burnt clay, charcoal and a small assemblage of animal bone (210, n.i.), 0.08 m deep, overlay layer 217.

Following the demolition of Me2, Area C became an open space containing a possible fence line, two pits and a well (Fig. 7.9). Three postholes (226; 328; 329), 0.2–0.25 m in diameter and 0.3 m deep, which cut gravel surface 217, may represent a fence aligned north-west/south-east. Four smaller stakeholes (227; 228; 229; 230), 0.15 m wide and deep, adjacent to posthole 226, may have been associated with it. Pit 233 lay to the south-west of the fence. It was subrectangular, 0.95 m long, 0.65 m wide and 0.4 m deep. Pit 246 straddled the putative fence line. It was 1.9 m in diameter and more than 0.5 m deep. Charcoal, burnt clay, oyster shells and organic material were recovered from both pits, indicating that they were used for dumping refuse.

A possible well (211) and two hearths (205; 209) lay to the north-east of the fence. The well (211) was 1.8 m in diameter and more than 2.5 m deep. It had been dug below the level of the modern water table, preventing full excavation; no evidence for a timber lining was uncovered in the excavated part. Its fills indicated that, once it had gone out of use as a well, it had been reused for the dumping of cess and refuse.

The presence of two hearths at the end of this sequence suggests that a third building (Me3) was represented in Area C, but no structural remains were found. The first (hearth 209) overlay both the dump 210 and two patches of cobbles which followed (212; 213, n.i.). It was formed from volcanic trap fragments that had been burnt *in situ*, and was filled with baked clay, charcoal and ash. It lay only partially within the excavated area. The second hearth (205) was 1.6 m long, 0.95 m wide and 0.1 m deep. Its base had been burnt *in situ* and was overlain by layers of charcoal and burnt clay. Part had been cut away by later features.

Dating evidence

Ceramic Horizon D (EAR3, 9; probably late 11th or early 12th century)

- Layer 210. Pottery: EAR3, nos. 66–73.
- Hearth 209. Pottery: EAR3, nos. 74–6.
- Well 211. Pottery: EAR3, nos. 78–82.
- Cobbled surface 213. Pottery: EAR3, no. 60.
- Pit 246. Pottery: EAR3, nos. 61–5.

Period 6e: ?further phases of building (Me3) (late 12th to early 13th century)

In the late 12th century the Period 6d features were covered by soil deposit (161), succeeded by a sequence of hearths and pits (Fig. 7.10). Hearth 203 consisted of a layer of clay 0.05 m deep that had been burnt *in situ*, overlain by a dump of charcoal and burnt stone; it was covered by two successive layers of mortar (163; 164), each *c.* 0.12 m deep.

Hearth 203 was followed by hearth 176, the largest found in Area C. It was 2.15 m in diameter and 0.5 m deep, and lined with large fragments of volcanic trap, bonded in clay. A burnt charcoal spread was found

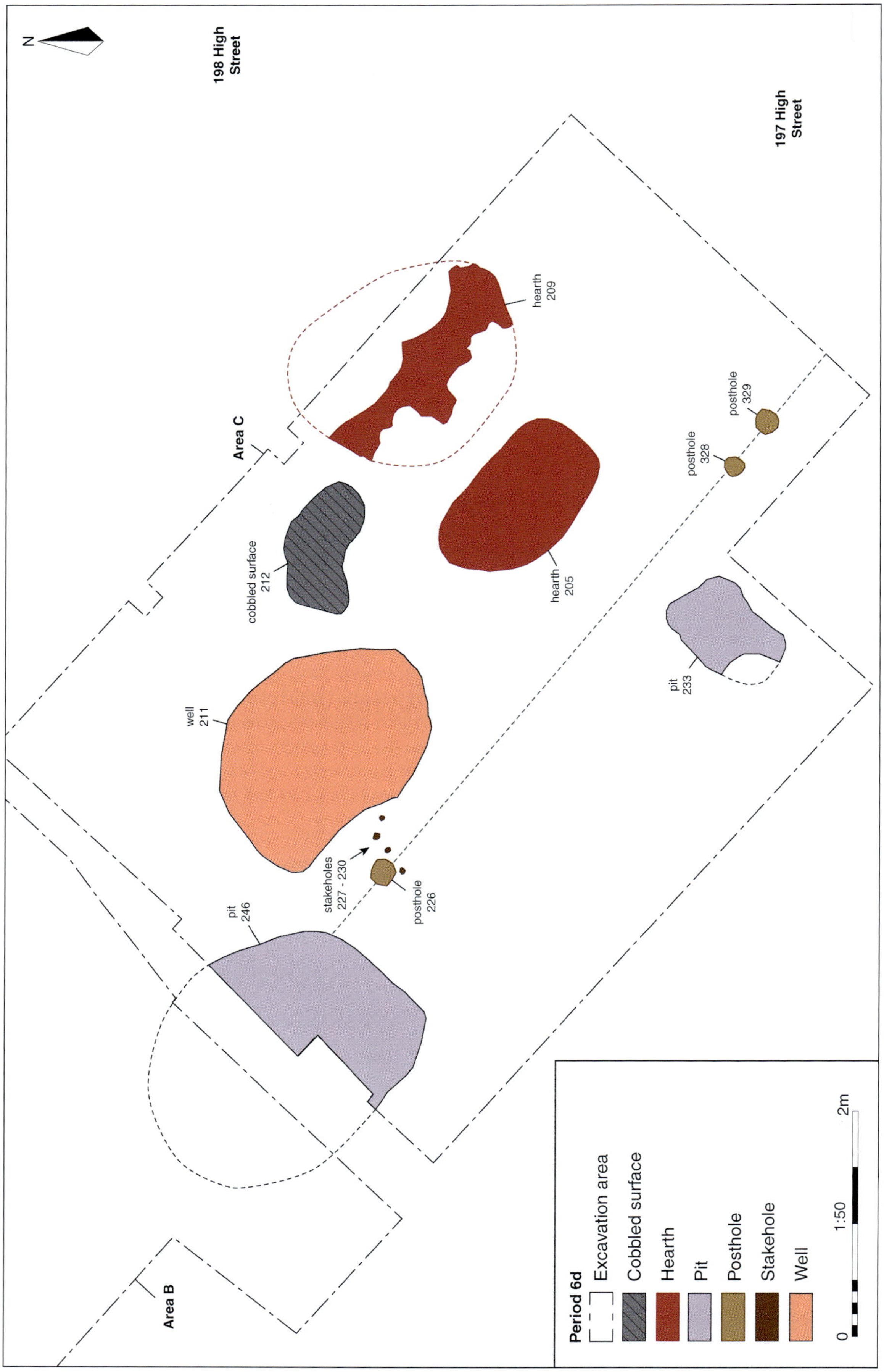

Fig. 7.9 Plan of Period 6d (mid to late 12th century)

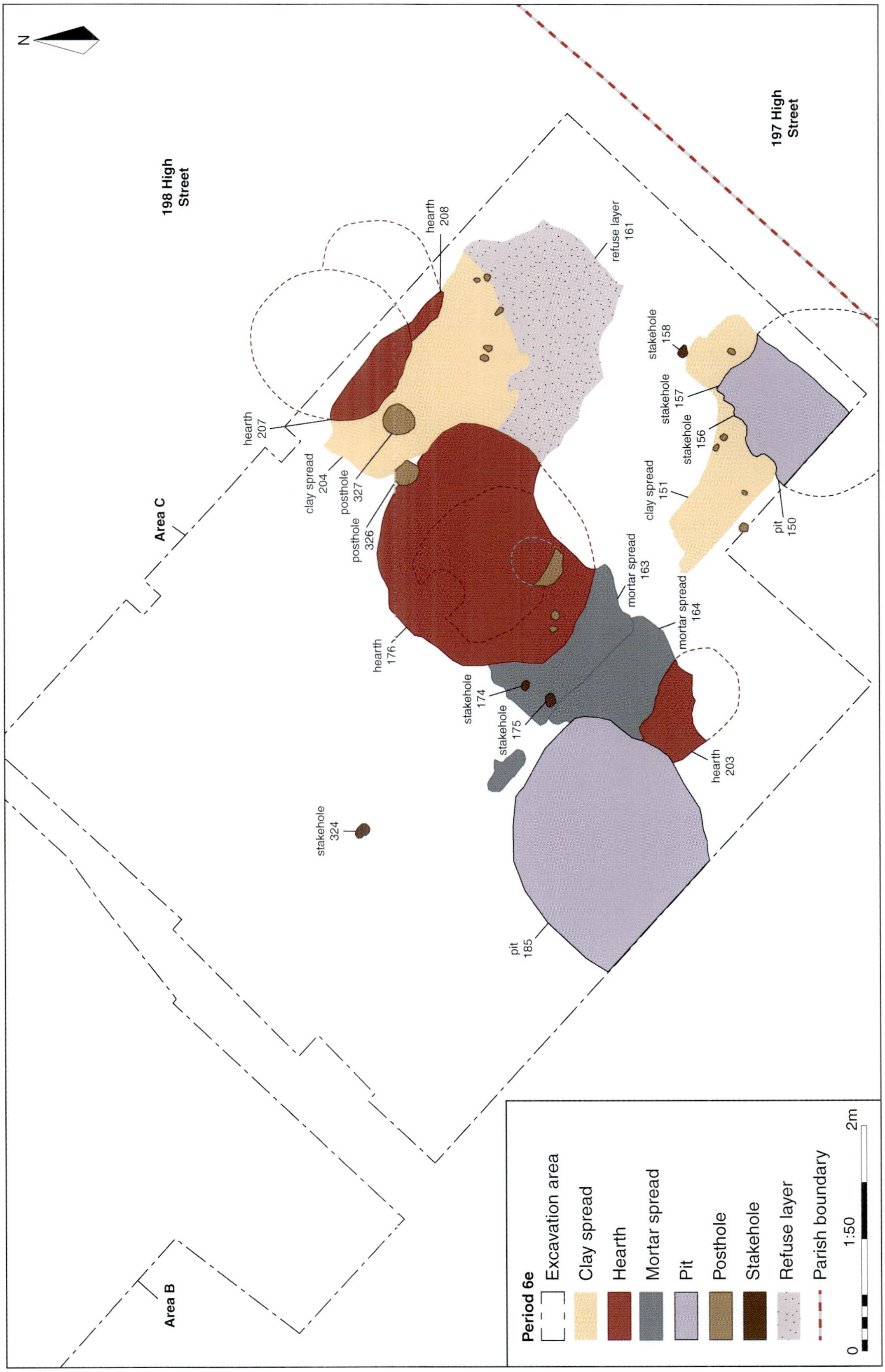

Fig. 7.10 Plan of Period 6e (late 12th to early 13th century)

on it (162, n.i.), overlain by burnt red clay containing fragments of volcanic trap derived from its demolition. A further hearth (208) lay to the north-east, only part of which lay within the excavation area. It was covered with a layer of dark earth with frequent charcoal inclusions and was replaced by a similar feature (207). Hearth 207 was 0.28 m deep; this too lay mostly beyond the excavation area. It was filled with charcoal, burnt clay and some patches of white mortar. Pit 150 was more than 1.05 m wide and 0.4 m deep and filled by a number of refuse deposits. Several dumps of clay (151), 0.09 m thick, deposited to the north of the pit, may represent upcast from its excavation.

Two postholes (326; 327) and 17 stakeholes (149; 152–158; 167–175; 324) surrounded the pits and hearths. There is no discernible pattern in their positions and consequently it is difficult to determine their functions; perhaps they formed light screens or partitions.

The final phase of activity in this period was represented by a layer of clayey soil, 0.02–0.04 m thick with a trampled top surface (147, n.i.). A large refuse pit (185) cut the edge of the former hearth 203; it was 1.77 m in diameter and more than 0.6 m deep, and contained a series of refuse deposits including charcoal, clay lumps and oyster shells. Finds included a bone spindle whorl (EAR3, 351, B.24).

Dating evidence

Broadly ceramic Horizon E (EAR3, 9; late 12th/early 13th century)

- Layer 186. Pottery: EAR3, nos. 83–8 (late 12th/early 13th century).
- Hearth 176. Pottery: EAR3, nos. 89–94 (late 12th/early 13th century).
- Pit 185. Pottery: EAR3, nos. 100–110 with tripod pitchers (late 12th/early 13th century).
- Layer 147. Pottery: Normandy white ware lamp; Exeter coarse ware fabric 20 (late 12th/early 13th century).

Features in the other cellars

A few features were found below the cellar floors of Areas A and B. No dating evidence was recovered from them, but their character and stratigraphic relationships suggest that they represent Saxo-Norman occupation.

Two cesspits (127; 139, n.i.) and a wattle-lined pit (98, n.i.) were found below the cellar floor of Area A, cut by modern foundations and drainage pipes. Pit 127 was more than 1.1 m in diameter and 0.5 m deep; pit 139 was 2.3 m in diameter and more than 0.7 m deep; both had thick primary fills of cess, covered by refuse deposits. Pit 98 was 2.8 m in diameter and more than 3.15 m deep. A collapsed stake and wattle lining was found in the lower part of the pit, indicating that initially it was a well; it was later used as a cesspit and for dumping waste.

In Area B, a cesspit (7, n.i.) and a possible well (35) were found beneath later disturbances (Fig. 7.8). The cesspit was 1.2 m in diameter and more than 0.3 m deep. It was filled with layers of green cess, clay and decomposed wood. The possible well (35) was more than 0.6 m in diameter at its bottom and 0.6 m deep; it may have been quite a substantial feature. It was backfilled with layers of gravel and dark grey clay which contained a Saxo-Norman bone pin (EAR3, B.20).

Salvage recording in the basement of 198 High Street in 1975 showed that two large oval Saxo-Norman pits (HS 500 and 501, n.i.) extended under the boundary wall between 197 and 198 High Street, implying that they did not form separate tenements at this time (Exeter Urban Archaeological Database (EUAD) 11181, Recognition Event No. (RENN) 55, 224). One contained part of an elaborate folding balance (http://www.rammtimetrail.org.uk/Object/116).

Periods 7 and 8: The high medieval and late medieval city (1200–1550)

Introduction

In the later Middle Ages and the Early Modern period 196–7 High Street formed part of the pattern of long narrow tenements in the central part of the High Street, recorded most accurately on the Ordnance Survey map of 1876. Documentary study demonstrates that the boundaries of these particular burgage plots were already in place by the mid 14th century, and some can be shown to have existed by the 1260s (see Chapter 4 above). Area A on Waterbeer Street formed the rear cellar of the important property of 196 High Street, owned by the Vicars Choral of Exeter Cathedral and the home of some of the city's richest merchants, most notably John Gist, the six-times Mayor of the city, and his descendants. Areas B–D lay within the adjacent plot, 197 High Street, another property occupied by wealthy townspeople, the most famous of whom was the notable 16th-century benefactor Joan Tuckfield.

Later medieval stratified deposits survived only in Area C at 197 High Street, where the sequence could be linked to the construction of a late medieval hall house; in 1973 late medieval fabric survived in both tenement walls flanking the site (Fig. 7.14). There were also a few features of this date below the cellar floors of Areas A and B. The significance of the cellars themselves in the late medieval houses will be discussed below.

Period 8 in Area C: Building Me4 stone hall house (late 14th/early 15th century)

After the activities of Period 6e in the late 12th/early 13th century, there is a long gap in the stratigraphic sequence in Area C (corresponding to Period 7) until the late 14th or early 15th century (Period 8). This probably represents the truncation of deposits, perhaps associated with the construction of a hall house at the start of Period 8 (Fig. 7.11).

Fig. 7.11 Plan of Period 8 (c. 1350–1550) heated room and passage

Beside the tenement boundary with 196 High Street, a sunken strip of ground 3.5 m long and 0.4 m wide was interpreted by the excavators as a side passage running towards the rear of the property. It was infilled with a clay loam containing mortar and slate (141), possibly a levelling deposit following subsidence, and perhaps associated with the construction of Me4.

Building Me4 was represented by the upstanding stone boundary wall separating 197 High Street from its neighbour to the north-east, No. 198. This was cleaned and recorded by photomosaic by Michael Griffiths, then Director of the Exeter Archaeological Unit, but his records seem not to have survived. Excavators' memories (not very reliable) recall that it was of volcanic stone rubble, suggesting that it may have dated from the period before *c.* 1350. The wall contained a stone fireplace whose projecting corbels had subsequently been trimmed back; the footprint of the two jambs is visible in the edge of excavation (Fig. 7.11). It is now uncertain whether the fireplace was a primary feature, but the presence of an early stone fireplace does show that Area C was a heated room by the 16th century, and perhaps in the later Middle Ages. Given its position behind the front block of the tenement, it was probably a ground-floor hall.

The relationship between this early wall and the stratigraphic sequence in Area C is now unclear. There were three late medieval features in the excavated area: two substantial pits (142; 165) and a small fragment of walling (222). The two pits (142; 165), both subcircular, 0.95–1.35 m in diameter and 0.3 m deep, had ragged edges, suggesting the robbing of the features they held. They may have contained timber uprights, and they may have been earlier than the tenement wall. The small fragment of walling (222) consisted of volcanic trap bonded with a cream-coloured mortar 1.1 m long and 0.4 m wide. It cut the edge of the infilled pit 142. It probably marked the division between the room occupying Area C and a side passage beside the boundary wall with 196 High Street. A floor surface composed of gravel and patches of white mortar (148, n.i.), 0.05 m thick, was preserved in the passage. It was overlain by a soil layer whose top surface was trampled (128, n.i.).

Period 8 in Area A: late 15th/early 16th-century leather-processing pits

A pit containing the remains of a pair of casks (89, Fig. 7.12) was found beneath the cellar floor of Area A. The ends had been removed from both casks before they had been placed in the pit, but the lowest parts of the vertical staves survived to a maximum height of 0.23 m, bound with hoops of halved withies (EAR3, 312–13, W.73–4; Fig. 7.12). The barrels can be reconstructed as originally touching one another and standing *c.* 1.3 m tall. The bottoms of the barrels were filled with dark anaerobic layers overlying a layer of white lime. The lime deposit suggests that the barrels were used for leather-making (discussed below). The pits were infilled in the early 16th century.

Dating evidence

Later features in Cellar C broadly conform to ceramic Horizon J (EAR3, 9; early 14th/early 15th century)

- Passageway 141. French jetton, very little wear, late 14th or early 15th century (EAR3, 251, J.4). Pottery: Spanish tin-glazed; Rouen jug (probably residual); Saintonge jugs; Exeter fabric 40 (1350–1450).
- Layer 128. Pottery: Exeter fabric 21; fabric 42 jugs. EAR3, nos. 119–120 (?1350–1450).
- Area A, Barrel pit 89. Pottery: Raeren stoneware; Coarse Sandy Ware (backfilled in the early 16th century).

The late medieval and post-medieval buildings at 195–8 High Street
by John Allan

The following summary description of the buildings at 196–7 High Street, demolished in 1973, also includes an account of the two adjacent properties, which formed part of the same group of tenements; it draws on accounts prepared for the EUAD by Stuart Blaylock in 2001.

195 High Street: front block

This property was the subject of building recording by Exeter Archaeology in 1998 and 2010 (Passmore 2011). Behind a plain early 19th-century frontage on High Street, it consists of an almost intact five-storeyed house of *c.* 1700, with a fine a staircase and large-field bolection-moulded panelling; there is a courtyard behind, crammed onto a small site. A late medieval cellar underlies the entire property. An accomplished carved wooden overmantel of *c.* 1600, acquired by the RAMM in 1928 and showing the Judgement of Paris, came from this house; it was probably imported from the Low Countries (Portman 1966, 47; Fig. 7.13a).

195 High Street: centre of tenement (formerly part of 196 High Street)

Prior to the 1970s, the central section of the burgage plot with 195 High Street on its frontage formed part of 196 High Street – an arrangement which already obtained in the 14th century, when it served as the kitchen block for the neighbouring property (for the documentary evidence see Chapter 4 above). At the start of the 20th century it retained a fine 'Elizabethan room' on the ground floor with a moulded plaster ceiling, panelling, an early fireplace of volcanic stone with a plasterwork overmantel, and an early window in the side wall overlooking Parliament Street. The room was destroyed in 1914 but was recorded in photographs now held at the Devon Heritage Centre (Fig. 7.14b). The fireplace was preserved, although heavily restored, and may be seen with its fine overmantel

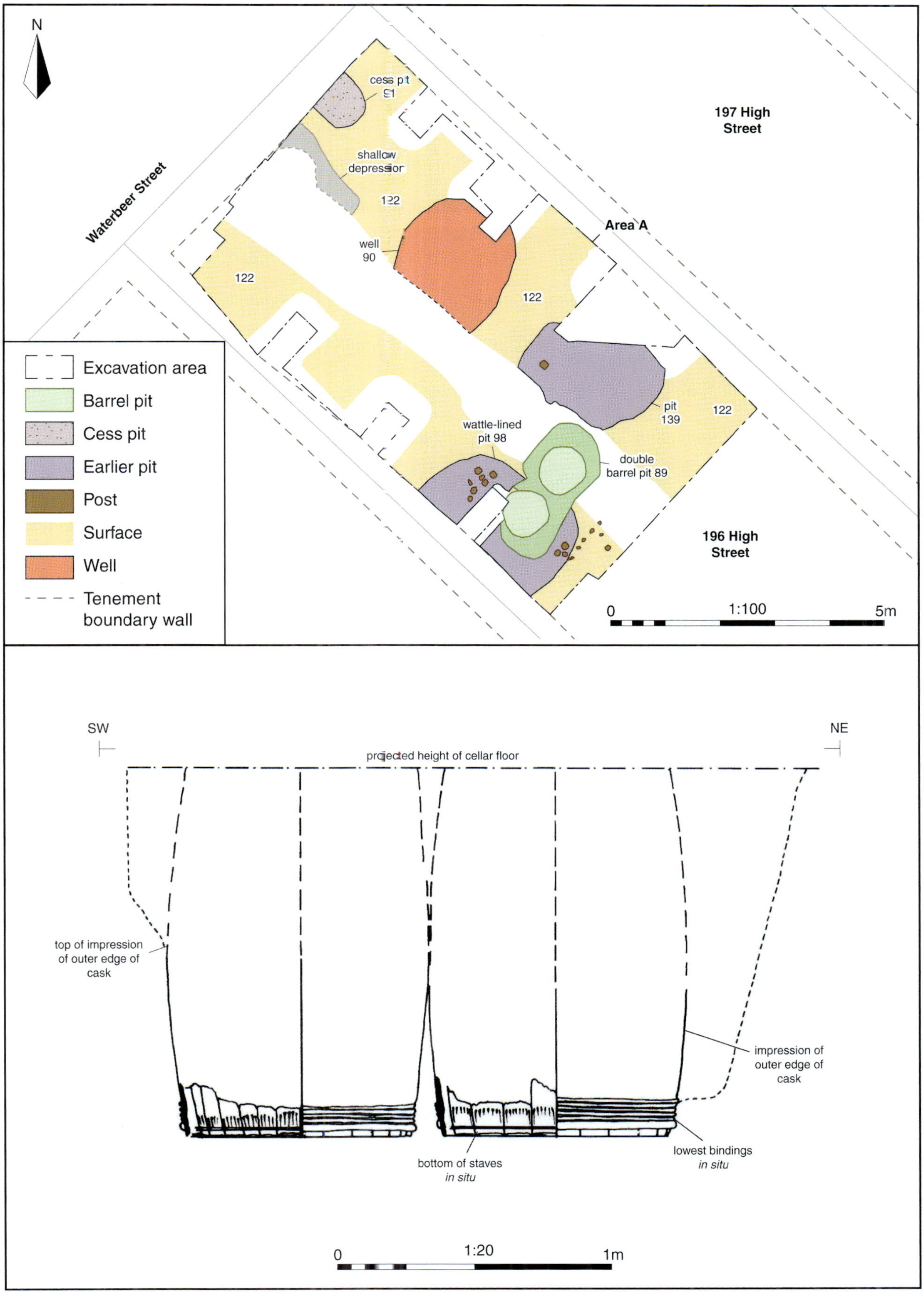

Fig. 7.12 Top: features in Area A. Bottom: cask-lined tanning or tawing pits

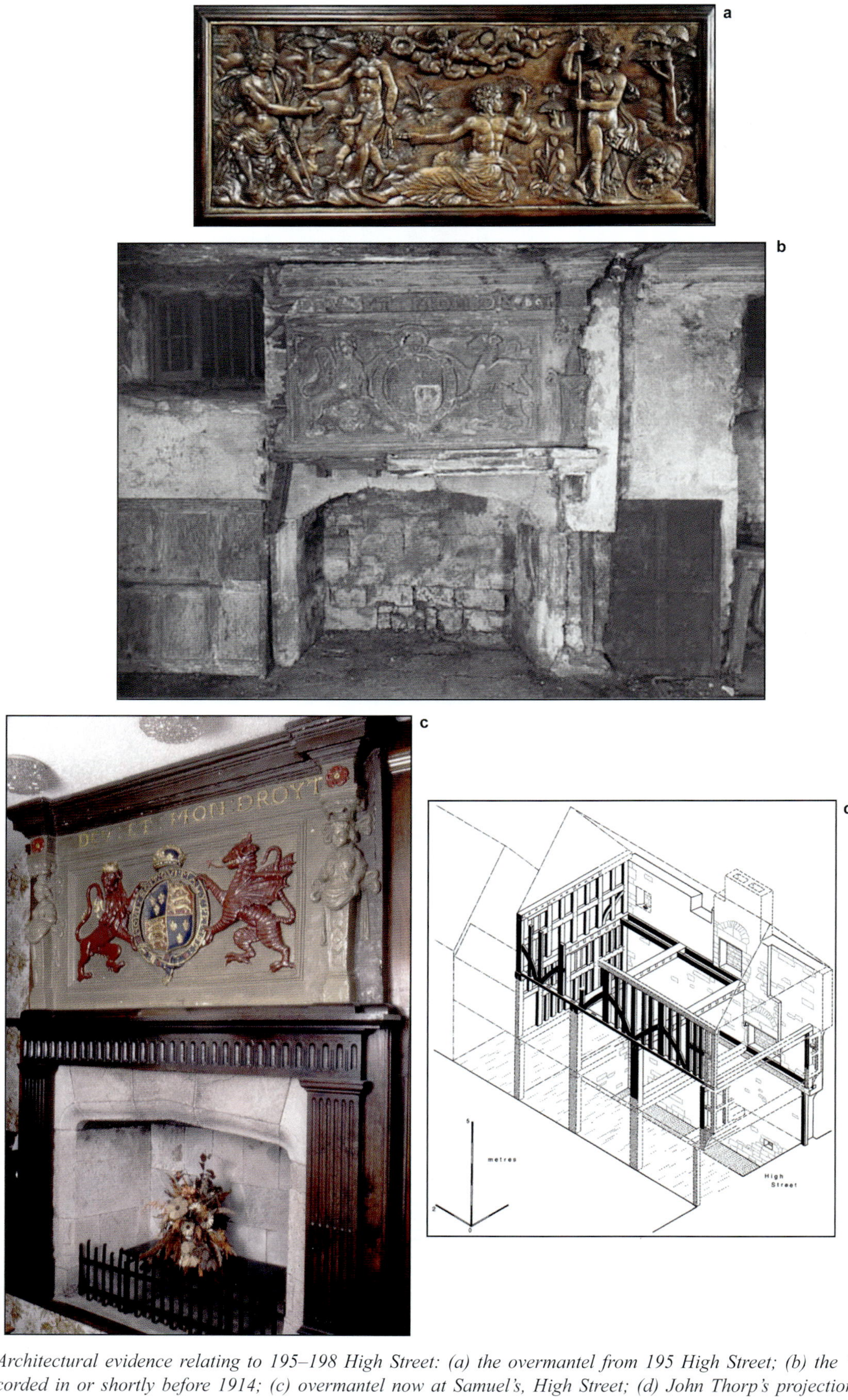

Fig. 7.13 Architectural evidence relating to 195–198 High Street: (a) the overmantel from 195 High Street; (b) the 'Elizabethan Room', recorded in or shortly before 1914; (c) overmantel now at Samuel's, High Street; (d) John Thorp's projection of the late 16th-century front block of 198 High Street (photos: (a) © RAMM; (b): © Devon Heritage Centre); (c) S. Mather photography; (d) © Exeter Archaeology archive, Exeter City Council)

in the modern shop on the site; the overmantel displays the royal arms of Elizabeth I, flanked on each side by a caryatid (Fig. 7.14c). A four-light oak window with ovolo-moulded mullions, also from the rooms dismantled in 1914, is displayed nearby. No fresh recording was undertaken in the 1970s or subsequently (Reed 1931, 277; Portman 1966, 49, n.4; EA (Exeter Archaeology) record card of 1973; EUAD Monument 11180, period MD4, RENN 43.

195 High Street: rear block (23 Waterbeer Street)

After this property was demolished without record in 1973–4, the early (probably late medieval) stone-lined cellar underlying its entire footprint was exposed. No recording was undertaken.

196 High Street

Little is known of the standing building of 196 High Street, which was demolished without record in 1973 when its distinguished late medieval and Early Modern history was unknown. The front block was presumably the 'fair brick house… lately built' referred to in 1702: see documentation collated in Chapter 4 above, but it had been at least partially rebuilt in 1914 (Reed 1931, 277). The survival of older stonework in the party wall to the north-east was seen when building recording was undertaken at No. 197 (below). The rear frontage onto Waterbeer Street was of 18th-century brickwork. The medieval cellar of the Vicars Choral which extended back to Waterbeer Street formed the excavated Area A.

197 High Street

The building was recorded by John Thorp prior to demolition in June 1973, but it was not possible to strip all the wall surfaces, so early features may have escaped record. The main range then standing on the High Street frontage was an 18th-century house of four storeys measuring 11.7 × 5.5 m, with a cellar below. Immediately to the rear was a yard 5.3 m deep which may have represented the rear courtyard of an older house. Behind it, a 7.2 m length of Permian breccia ('Heavitree stone') walling marked the tenement boundary with 196 High Street. This may have represented the rear face of a former back block or hall at 196 High Street; the building stone indicates a date after *c.* 1350. Further rubble masonry on the Waterbeer Street frontage was seen fleetingly but not recorded in the course of demolition in 1975 (EA archive record; EUAD Monument 11179; RENN 43, 222).

198 High Street

Prior to demolition in 1975, a more thoroughgoing piece of building recording was undertaken by EMAFU at 198 High Street, led by John Thorp. The building occupied a typical High Street tenement plot 11 m wide and 42 m long, with frontages both on Waterbeer Street and High Street; documentary evidence shows that this arrangement had obtained in the late Middle Ages. Prior to investigation, the structure appeared superficially to be of 18th-century date, with modern work to the rear, but stripping and examination of the fabric revealed much information about earlier structures, and showed that there were two late medieval structural phases prior to the complete rebuilding of the front block in the late 16th century (EUAD 11181, RENN 55, 224; plans of basement and standing building at https://doi.org/10.5284/1035192).

Much of the north-east wall of the property survived, and it was in this that most of the early features were recorded. The earliest fabric observed was in two sections of cellar wall, characterised as phase 1. The building was cellared throughout, although much of the fabric was of post-medieval date. These two short lengths of Permian breccia ('Heavitree stone') masonry in the north-east wall of the cellars, one towards the High Street frontage, the second towards the Waterbeer Street frontage, were dated to the early 15th century, although a late 14th-century date also seems possible. They probably represent the roughly contemporary erection of houses over small cellars, one on each frontage; since their masonry was similar, the construction may have been carried out simultaneously by one owner.

Phase 2 masonry survived in isolated patches, along with several features; it was mainly of small, roughly-squared volcanic stone blocks, with ashlar of the same material and Beer stone for dressed features; a late 15th-century date was suggested (Thorp n.d., 3). The house was evidently of mixed construction, with mortared stone side walls and timber-framed cross-walls and partitions. The side wall stood up to 7.5 m high. Notable features of this phase included a small two-light timber window frame with narrow arch-headed lights: the window was unglazed and is consistent with a late medieval date (similar windows were recorded in the adjacent 199 High Street by Reed: 1931, 278). On the party wall with 199 High Street, a fragment of wall painting in black, white and crimson was recorded at ground-floor level, behind the later front block. The design is uncertain, but included a band with the word [?]NOMEN painted in black-letter script, possibly suggesting that the composition included a scroll inscribed with a prayer or invocation (window and painting are recorded on EA archive drawing ref: 224.2). Although the evidence was fragmentary, the structure was interpreted as a late medieval hall-house with a decorated open hall behind a storeyed front range; the location of cellars suggested that there was a side passage along the south-west boundary of the site. No record survives of a rear block, although one can presumably be inferred by comparison with other houses of the period.

The phase 2 house was almost entirely rebuilt in the late 16th century, when a new front block three storeys high was built on the High Street frontage. Much of this survived, including the side wall with fireplaces and a garderobe, the massive timber frame of the rear wall of the front block, and the tension-braced framing of the boundary wall with 197 High Street, with 16th-century small-field panelling in one room (Fig. 7.13d). This was destroyed entirely in 1975.

Discussion
by John Allan

Although small in scale, the excavations at 196–8 High Street made a significant contribution to the understanding of the archaeology of Exeter, since they were the only instance where it proved possible to examine a block of Saxo-Norman stratification in the tenements at the centre of the city; indeed they remain the sole investigation of this kind of evidence in Devon and Cornwall. The highly unusual nature of the site was not fully appreciated at the time of excavation; a survey conducted by EMAFU a few years later showed that cellars had removed entirely the equivalent early medieval deposits (and most of the Roman civil deposits below them) from all the other burgage plots in the High Street, and from almost all or all the tenements in the other main streets (unpublished; evidence presented on an OS map formerly in the EMAFU archive); this was therefore a unique and precious survivor.

Area C lay behind the High Street frontage. The excavator's initial post-excavation analysis, carried out in the 1970s, identified 13 successive phases of Saxo-Norman occupation, spanning a period of perhaps 200 years from the mid 10th to mid 12th century. They are published here as five main periods of occupation (Periods 6a–6e), some of which encompass a sequence of events. They include at least three different timber buildings – more if the succession of hearths in the late 11th/early 12th century represents more than one building – interleaved with periods when the site was open ground with cesspits, yards and gullies. Although the dating evidence is imprecise, the buildings must have been short-lived, lasting on average for 50 years or less – perhaps 30 years or less, given the long sequence of events represented. It is unclear whether the buildings were aligned at right angles to High Street or parallel with it; given their position between 5 m and 12 m behind the frontage, they could represent structures extending back from the frontage, or lying behind small yards to the rear of houses arranged parallel to the street. Evidence of their building techniques is limited but Buildings Me1–2 were defined by shallow trenches which seem to have been of 'foundation bed' construction (*i.e.* with rubble-filled trenches, perhaps once capped with gravel or mortar) rather than earth-fast posts, whilst the absence of foundations in Me3 might suggest the use of 'ground-level' foundations, recorded, for example, in early medieval London (for descriptions of these two building techniques, based on excavated evidence in London, see Horsman *et al.* 1988; see Schofield and Vince 2003, 104, for examples of these techniques in other towns).

Part of the value of the excavations lay in the recovery of its unique sequence of Late Saxon and Norman artefacts. It provided the first unequivocal evidence that the wheel-thrown ceramics made at the Bedford Garage kiln in Exeter, previously dated to the 14th century (Fox and Dunning 1957), were in fact of Late Saxon date, since characteristic sherds of this type were present in the lowest phases of the Saxo-Norman sequence, below a coin struck *c.* 1072–4, but absent or almost absent from the following seven phases of Saxo-Norman occupation. The finds also included two bone spindle whorls and two bone needles, indicators of textile production.

The creation and sub-division of tenements

The block of tenements which was examined was an especially interesting one, since 197–8 High Street form the pair of tenements which intrude from St Martin's into St Pancras parish (Chapter 4 above). Thus the excavations shed some light on the important questions of whether the narrow medieval burgage plots on High Street represent the subdivision of larger properties, and whether the parish boundaries represent divisions laid out upon the foundation of the *burh*.

The excavations showed that all the tenement divisions which were examined archaeologically had come into existence after a period of Late Saxon occupation. At 198 High Street two large pits of the 11th/early 12th centuries certainly extended below the boundary wall between 198 and 197 High Street (features recorded in watching brief; details in EUAD entry for 198 High Street; for the site see Fig. 7.14). Since these two adjacent burgage plots form the block of St Martin's intruding into St Pancras parish, it is probable that they formed a single messuage *c.* 11 m wide, held by a citizen associated with St Martin's when the parish boundaries were determined in the 1220s or at an earlier date, but divided into two burgage plots by the time that documents survive in the early 14th century. Nos 195 and 196 form a pairing of similar size (14 × 42 m: Fig. 7.14) to the south-west, flanked on both sides by parish boundaries; it seems likely that they too represent a single holding of the early 13th century or earlier. In that instance the documentary evidence indicates that they had become separate properties by the 1260s.

The evidence relating to the tenement boundary between 196 and 197 is perhaps of greater interest because this was also a parish boundary and therefore a feature of the city of the 1220s. A cluster of Late Saxon pits was found in Area C; four underlay the parish boundary of 196/7 High Street and a further pit (250) was cut by the tenement wall between Nos 197 and 198 (Fig. 7.7). They show that neither boundary existed in the 11th or early 12th century. Thus 196–8 High Street appear to have formed components of a single Late Saxon property, with 195 High Street probably forming a fourth element of the holding. It would then have had

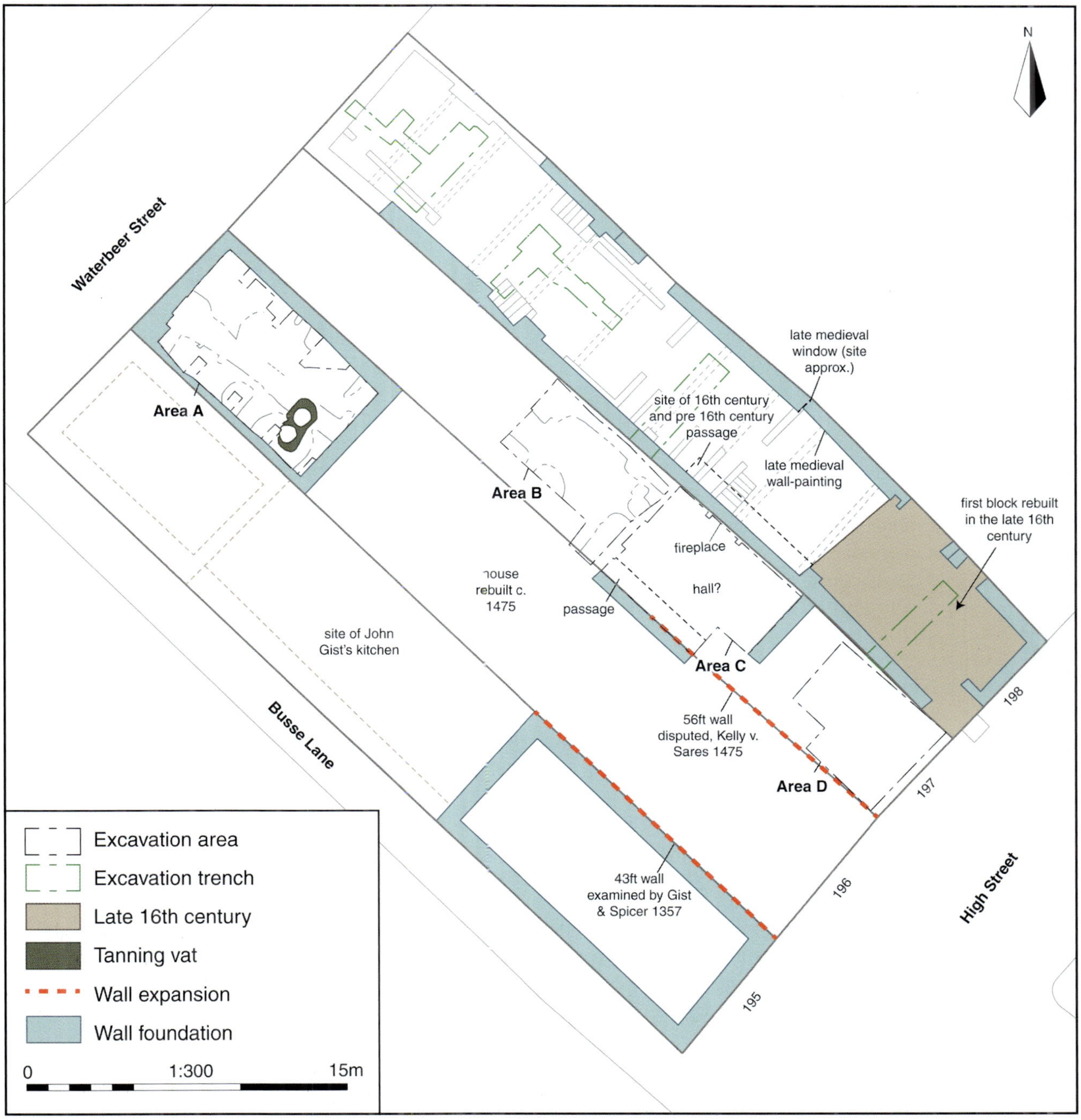

Fig. 7.14 Reconstruction of the late medieval tenements of 195–198 High Street

a length of about 42 m and a width of at least 26 m. It had been subdivided into two tenements by the time the parish boundaries were established at the start of the 13th century. By the time detailed documentation survives, there were four properties.

The high medieval and late medieval houses, c. 1250–1550

The documentary record relating to these tenements shows that by the mid 14th century 195–8 High Street were four separate narrow burgage plots, and indeed that the entire pattern of 13 narrow strips between the modern Parliament Street and Goldsmith Street (195–207 High Street), familiar from maps of the 19th and 20th centuries, was already fixed by that date. It also shows that the process of subdivision of the long burgage plots extending between High Street and Waterbeer Street, with the creation of separate tenements on the Waterbeer Street frontage, was well developed by the late 14th century, and most elements of the 19th-century pattern of properties was already in place by that stage. The Waterbeer Street houses at the rear of 195 and 200–2 High Street (perhaps also No. 199) were certainly separate holdings by the late 14th century, whilst Nos 196 and 197 remained undivided into the 19th century. More complex arrangements had already arisen in some burgage strips by the early 14th century; the home of Emma Barbour and later of John Gist at 196 High Street was served by a kitchen block which occupied the central portion of the neighbouring strip at 195 High Street – an arrangement which appears to have survived into the late 20th century, explaining the division of 195 High Street into three holdings visible on the 1910 Valuation map, and the continued use of the central portion as part of 196 High Street prior to its demolition, along with the building on the Waterbeer Street frontage, in 1973.

In the later Middle Ages and Early Modern periods the divisions between the properties were marked by stone walls. Such a wall already separated 195 and 196 High Street in 1267 (Chapter 4 above), and in 1475 the one between 196 and 197 High Street had windows 14 feet (4.3 m) above ground. They served not only as sides of buildings and markers of property divisions but also as seatings for gutters – features which receive mention surprisingly commonly in city deeds, providing water supplies as well as drainage in restricted settings, and sometimes requiring expensive maintenance. It is argued in Chapter 4 that the wall on which Thomas Gist granted his neighbour permission to set a guttering of wood and lead in 1405 was the one which marked the south-western boundary of the excavated Areas B and C at 197 High Street.

The excavated evidence relating to the period after 1250 adds one telling detail to this picture. Late medieval houses on narrow plots elsewhere in the main streets of the city were commonly designed with one party wall incorporating their fireplaces, garderobes and other features, with a plain wall on the opposite side of the tenement, backing onto the neighbour's property, flanked by a side passage which ran from the frontage to the rear of the property. Nos. 36–8 North Street are good examples of the type (Thorp 2012, esp. 148–51, 220–2). Such an arrangement is evident from the excavation at 197 High Street, where Area C consisted of a heated room whose fireplace was built in the north-eastern boundary wall with 198 High Street; evidence for a side passage (with a fragment of the wall marking the side of the probable hall) was found running parallel to the opposing tenement boundary with 196 High Street. The line of the passage evidently extended further back, as is apparent from the shape of Area B, whose cellar wall on its south-western side aligned with the excavated passage wall in Area C (Fig. 7.14). This same arrangement of a party wall with the main services on the north-eastern side and a side passage on the other side was also evident at 198 High Street, both in the house as rebuilt in the late 16th century and in its predecessor. Building recording there also found a small late medieval ground-floor window which lit the hall from the side of 198 High Street – presumably from an open space which was probably the side passage of 199 High Street. Documentary evidence implies a side passage about 2 m wide at a later date at 196 High Street (Chapter 4 above). Thus there were probably three adjacent properties, and perhaps a fourth organised in the same way, with side passages running back from the street frontage on the south-western side of each plot.

Evidence for leather-processing

Finally, a comment may be added regarding the pair of late medieval casks found below the cellar floor at the rear of 196 High Street, which are interpreted as evidence of leather-processing in the late 15th or early 16th century. The cask ends had been removed before burial; the stave-built cask walls, still bound by withies, were then lowered into a pit and buried, the lower parts of each cask being below the water table. Both contained a bottom fill of lime.

Similar evidence has been recovered from two other Exeter sites. First, in the excavation beside Exe Bridge (Site 56), the bases of a pair of late 13th-century barrels were found to the rear of Frog Street House B, a tenement which sloped down to the River Exe. In that instance, close examination of the lime deposits showed that they were laminated, indicating the casks' repeated use as lime baths (Brown 2019, 62–7, 98–9). Second, a pair of early 18th-century casks was found at Alphington Street/Shooting Marsh Stile (Site 80); they contained much lime and were packed with hundreds of horn-cores of cattle (https://doi.org/10.5284/1035217). In his review of the archaeological evidence for tanning in the British Isles and abroad, Shaw (1996) showed that small circular pits (measuring 0.7–1.5 m in diameter), very commonly lined with barrels, form the most common evidence for tanning and tawing, from the Anglo-Saxon period into the 18th century. They were used not just for small hides, since cattle hides could be cut up prior to immersion. Features of this form probably correspond to the tanners' 'vats' recorded in the Early Modern period, distinguishable from 'troughs' which may be presumed to have been the roughly rectangular pits known at some tanneries (Shaw 1996, 112–14; see also Cherry 1991; for an example from Bristol see Jones 1991, 26).

The question of whether the High Street pits represent tanning or tawing requires a brief consideration of the different processes used in these activities, which are usefully summarised by Cherry (1991, 295–7) and Shaw (1996, 107–8). Both entailed two early stages which required soaking the hides in pits: first liming, which followed the preliminary processes of washing and the removal of horns, hooves and unusable portions of the hide. In this process the tanners broke down the outer layers of hair and flesh of the hides by immersing them in a solution of lime (sometime supplemented or substituted with ash or urine), then removing the hair and flesh by scraping with knives (summaries in Cherry 1991; Shaw 1996, 107–27). This was followed by a second stage named mastering, in which the hides were de-limed and softened in an alkaline solution which contained either dog or bird dung, or barley or rye in stale beer or urine. In tawing, the hides would then be removed from the vat and transferred to a large tub where they were dressed with alum, oil and other substances. By contrast, the creation of tanned leather required further protracted soaking of the hides in pits containing first a weak solution (in pits or tubs named 'handlers'), and later strong, solutions between layers of oak bark (in 'layaways'); this lasted up to 12–18 months.

It will be apparent that all the finds of leather-processing pits from Exeter, including those from High Street, show firm evidence for only the initial liming stage of these processes. Shaw (1996, 119–20) considers the most likely explanation. Although this could indicate tawing rather than tanning, or show that the initial stages of tanning were carried out here and the later stages elsewhere, he concludes that small-scale tanneries probably used a primitive method in which the processes of liming, mastering and tanning were undertaken in the same pit, or in a pair of pits. In the case of the Exeter evidence, further light might be thrown on this by analysis of the residues in the pit bottoms, but no such samples have been located.

It might seem surprising that such an obnoxious activity was conducted in one of the most prestigious of Exeter tenements, home to mayors of the city in the Late Middle Ages and the 16th century. Although the leather trades did concentrate in the area near the River Exe in the parishes of St Edmund and Mary Steps, and were found in the extra-mural parishes of St David and St Sidwell (Kowaleski 1995, 160), tanners also operated in the crowded setting of the tenements of the main streets; the cordwainer John of Tavistock and tanner Walter of Lydford at 204 High Street are good examples (Chapter 4 above, 204 High Street).

8

Excavations at Rack Street, 1974–5 and 1977–8

Nicky Garland, Neil Holbrook and John Allan

Introduction

Between late 1974 and early 1975, and mid 1977 and early 1978, two separate excavations took place beside Rack Street (centred at SX 91900 92275; Fig. 8.1) as a number of areas in open ground to the south-west of the (then) Central Primary School were examined in advance of redevelopment. In 1974–5 two areas were investigated, with a watching brief on builders' trenches further to the north-west revealing further information (Site 52). In 1977–8 (Site 64) one principal open area was investigated, supplemented by three additional trenches (Trenches A–C). The excavations lay towards the periphery of the Roman and medieval walled city, and remains of these periods were anticipated at the start of the work. Unexpectedly, however, the first season of work encountered the defences of the Roman legionary fortress – the first time they had ever been recognised in Exeter. The excavations were directed by Christopher Henderson, and site supervisors included John Salvatore, Colin Tracy, Bruce Follansbee and Jon Hunn.

This chapter summarises the evidence for the Roman legionary fortress and presents in detail the archaeological sequence from the beginning of Roman civilian occupation (*c*. AD 75/80) to the end of the late medieval period in the mid 16th century. Detailed archive reports on the Roman military remains were produced for both excavations in 1992 (Bedford and Salvatore 1992c; 1992d) and form the basis for the summary presented here. Those reports, along with a context register and stratigraphic matrix for the Roman civil period onwards, are available for download from the Archaeology Data Service (ADS) at https://doi.org/10.5284/1035189 and https://doi.org/10.5284/1035201. Only limited analysis of the post-military stratigraphy had been carried out until the commencement of this project. Brief annual summaries of the Roman evidence have been published (Goodburn *et al.* 1976, 358; Goodburn *et al.* 1978, 459), and the site has figured in two previous syntheses (Bidwell 1980, 23–4, 46–7, 74–9; Henderson 1988, 110–18). The site archive contained detailed notes and a partial stratigraphic narrative of the Roman evidence by Christopher Henderson. That account has informed much of the interpretation presented in this chapter.

The system of numbering adopted for the buildings described in this report differs from previous numbering systems used in the site notes and interim accounts. The buildings have the letter prefixes RC (Roman civil) and Me (medieval). Table 8.1 provides a concordance of the numbering used in this report for Roman streets and buildings with that adopted in the city-wide gazetteers presented in Chapter 3. On the period plans features are shown in bold colours, while layers are shown as lighter shades. A few features are not illustrated (n.i.), as field drawings were not located in the archive.

As with the other excavations in this volume, it is important to record the considerable disturbance that had been caused to earlier deposits by post-medieval and modern features, including a number of deep sewer trenches that cut through the archaeological deposits (Bedford and Salvatore 1992c, 1). The site slopes steeply down towards the West Gate and the River Exe, which lie to the west and south-west of the excavated sites, and episodes of post-Roman erosion and terracing have removed all archaeological deposits on some sites in this part of the city. Roman deposits had been removed entirely from the western parts of the principal excavation areas, and in these zones only substantial features such as the fortress ditches survived. Although Roman structures were revealed in different parts of the site, in no case did the full plan of any building survive. Medieval features, including a small number of structures, were equally affected. The fragmented nature of the surviving stratigraphy at the Rack

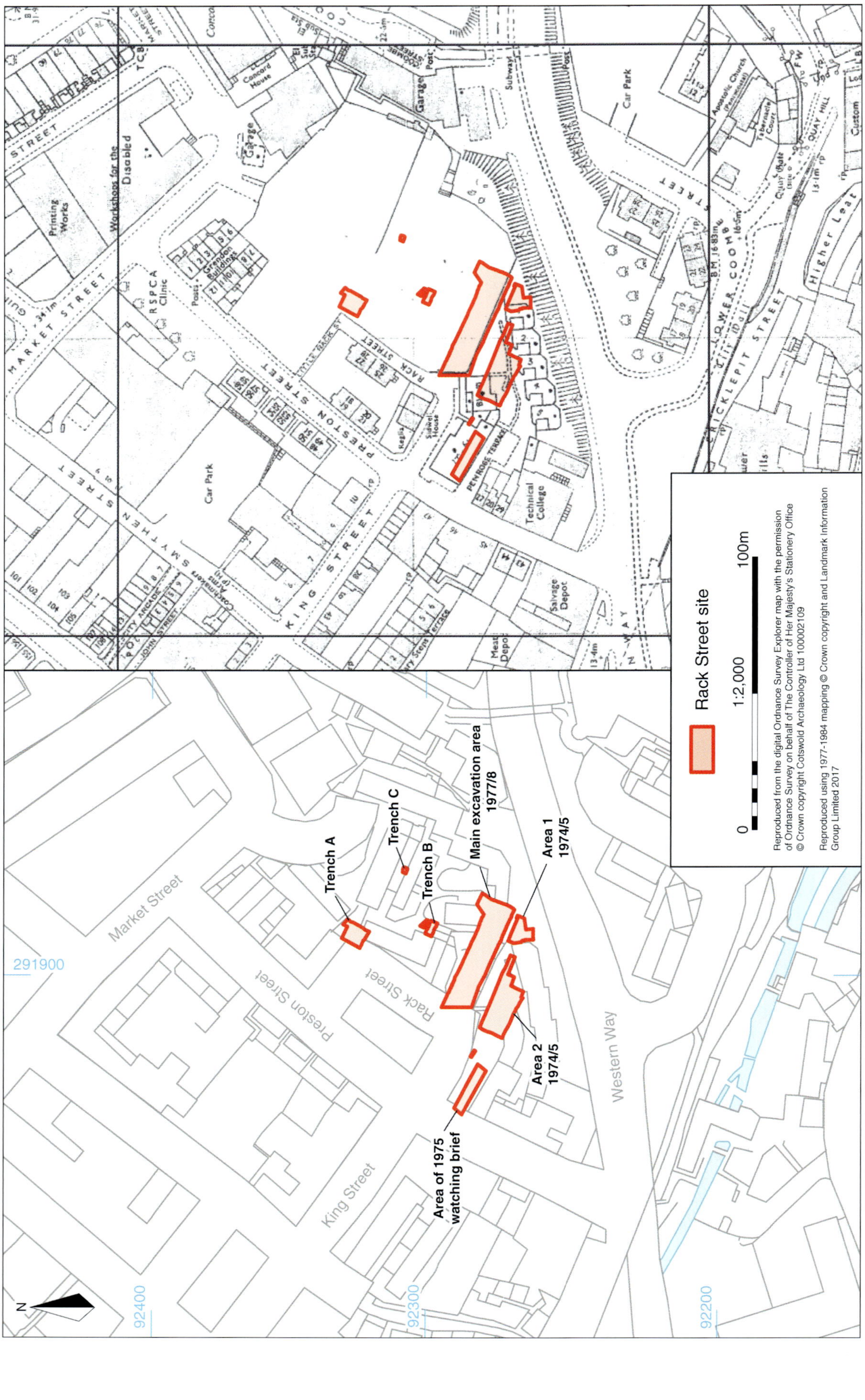

Fig. 8.1 Location of the excavation area. Left: relative to the current OS map; right: relative to the 1984 map

Table 8.1 Concordance of the numbering of Roman buildings used in this chapter with those used in the city-wide gazetteers in Chapter 3

This report	*Gazetteers*
Intervallum street	Street B
Civil street	Street M
RC1	47ii
RC2	47ii
RC3	31ii
RC4	48ii
RC5	49ii
RC6	50ii

Street excavations is therefore a major limiting factor in the interpretation and reconstruction of the Roman and medieval structural sequence. No later prehistoric (Period 1) activity was found in the excavations.

Period 2: The Roman legionary fortress (*c.* AD 50/55–75/80)

The excavations revealed the southern corner of the defensive circuit of the legionary fortress, as well as examining an area immediately outside of the defences and a ditch flanking the *intervallum* street immediately inside the rampart in Trench A (Fig. 8.2). The legionary defences were represented by two phases of ditch which have been subject to differing opinions on their chronology and interpretation. The inner ditch was undoubtedly the primary ditch associated with the construction of the fortress rampart. That ditch was originally thought to have been infilled in the pre-Flavian period, and the idea developed that the outer ditch was dug as a replacement for it during the period of military occupation (Bidwell 1980, 23; Henderson 1988, 107–10 provides some possible reasons for why this might have occurred). However, the recovery of a Dr. 29 samian bowl dated *c.* AD 75–90 from the infilling of the inner ditch at Rack Street now shows that this ditch remained open throughout the life of the fortress (EAR4, 7; fig. 10, no. 9). This therefore demonstrates that the outer ditch cannot have been dug until the very end of the military period or, much more plausibly, was in fact associated with the establishment of the early town. Thus, what has hitherto been referred to as the outer fortress ditch may actually have been a new defensive ditch associated with the establishment of the early town. This is discussed further in EAPIT1, Chapter 6, but in this chapter the ditches are referred to as the inner fortress ditch and the outer ditch.

The inner fortress ditch (240; 1013/1471) was 3.5 m wide, 1.66–1.85 m deep with a V-shaped profile (Figs 8.3–8.4). A slot at the base of the ditch suggests that it was cleaned out occasionally. The line of the ditch can be reconstructed over a distance of *c.* 48 m by its discovery in three separate excavation areas. The outer ditch (363; 1470) was much larger than the inner, 5–7 m wide and 2.5–2.9 m deep. It was of Punic profile, with a near-vertical outer face and a more gently sloping inner one. The line of the outer ditch could be traced between the two main excavation areas and further to the north-east in Trench C. A further 18 m-length of the outer ditch, this time on the south-eastern side of the fortress, was seen in a service trench to the north-west of 1974/5 Area 2 (Fig. 8.1). Here it had been heavily truncated by post-Roman erosion with only the bottom 0.8–1.0 m surviving, indicating that almost 2 m of its upper profile had been removed. Thus the outer ditch has been traced over a distance of *c.* 105 m in this southern part of the circuit.

No evidence for the fortress rampart survived in these excavations but at Mermaid Yard (Site 63), 45 m to the north-east, it was found to be *c.* 6 m wide (Bedford and Salvatore 1992f, 1–2). No metalling of the *intervallum* street (Chapter 3.2, Fortress Street B) survived in its expected location in Trench A but a small ditch in Trench A (1444) probably marked its inner edge. This ditch was 0.5 m wide and 0.36 m deep but may have been truncated by later activity. Elsewhere in Exeter the *intervallum* street was 4–6 m wide (Chapter 3.2, observations B5i–B8i).

Some 16 m beyond the outer ditch there was a curving drainage ditch (662; 1185/1472). It was 1.5 m wide, 1 m deep and had a V-shaped profile; it may have defined an extra-mural enclosure contemporary with the fortress. It had been infilled by the end of the military period.

Period 3: The Roman town

Introduction

The Early Roman town was created within the defences of the former legionary fortress. The earliest post-military activity at Rack Street comprised the digging of the outer ditch, followed quite quickly by its partial infilling, as well as some small-scale extra-mural occupation (Period 3a). The interpretation of the later history of the defensive ditch(es) surrounding the early town has been viewed in two different ways. In 1980 Paul Bidwell, based upon a consideration of the excavated sections and dating evidence recovered from the infilled ditches at Rack Street and Mermaid Yard, proposed that the outer ditch largely filled up during the earlier 2nd century AD, thereupon a new ditch was cut across the area formerly occupied by the inner and outer ditches. This was broader, but shallower, than the previous ditches whose infilled lower profiles survived beneath the base of the new ditch (Bidwell 1980, 46–7, fig. 26 (a section from Mermaid Yard)). This so-called 'early civil' ditch was infilled with dumps of refuse containing Antonine pottery. Henderson took a different view, influenced by subsequent work at Friernhay Street and Paul Street, and considered that there was no new recut ditch as such, the Antonine refuse deposits simply representing dumps above the abandoned

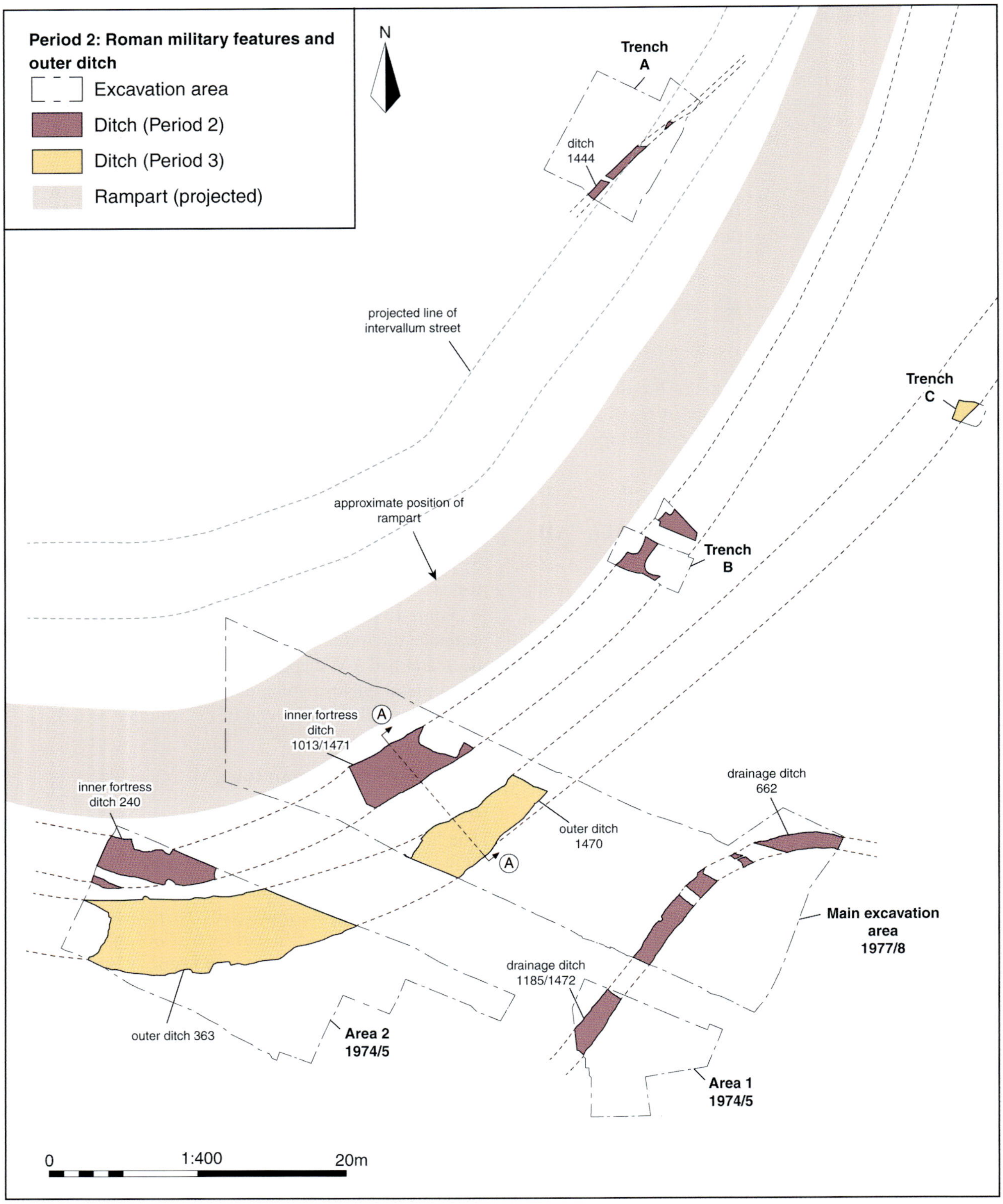

Fig. 8.2 Plan of Roman military features (Period 2)

outer ditch rather than being infills of a newly cut feature (Henderson 1988, 115–18, fig. 5.10). This matter is discussed more fully in EAPIT1, Chapter 6, but in the interpretation presented below the Antonine dumps found at Rack Street are considered to have been fills of a recut civilian ditch. The profile of this ditch is shown in the illustrated section (Fig. 8.3) where it contains the Antonine dumps shaded green.

The ditch was entirely backfilled in the mid to late 2nd century AD (Period 3b) and this event is to be associated

Section AA

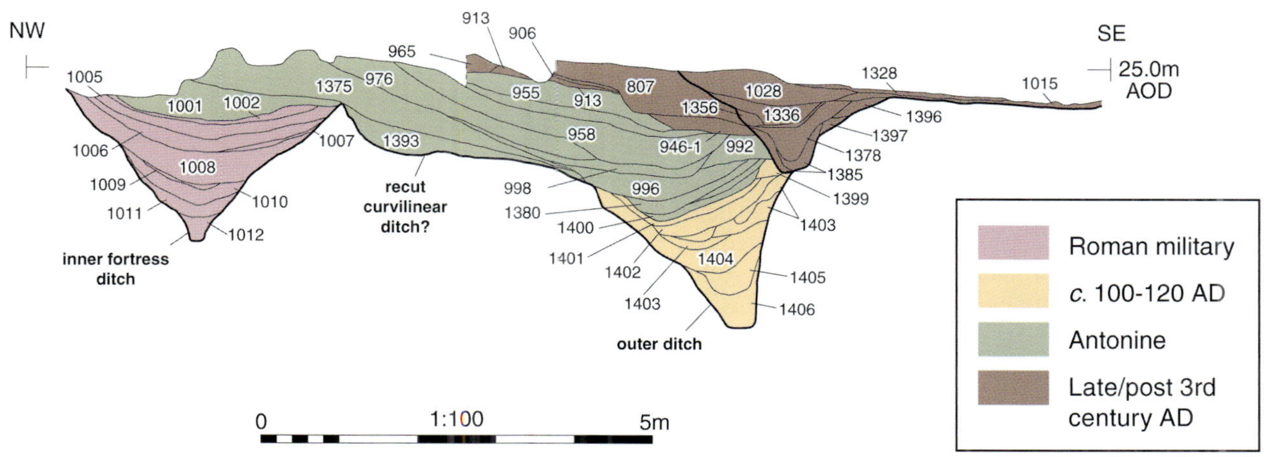

Fig. 8.3 Section AA through the inner (fortress) and outer (civil) ditches

Fig. 8.4 The inner fortress (left) and outer civil (right) ditches. 2 m scales (© RAMM)

with the construction of a new circuit of town defences and the extension of the street grid. By the end of the 3rd century AD a series of poorly preserved structures was constructed over the line of the backfilled defensive ditches as occupation expanded within the walled area.

In the late 3rd to early 4th century AD (Period 3c) two timber buildings were constructed alongside a new street. They were destroyed by fire and replaced by two (possibly three) stone structures (Period 3e) which were demolished by the end of 4th century AD.

Period 3a: Partial infilling of the outer ditch (late 1st to early 2nd century AD)

The outer ditch remained an open feature following the establishment of the town, although the lower part of the ditch was filled in the early 2nd century AD with a series of dumped refuse deposits (363.7; 649; 1382; 1383; 1384; 1393; 1394; 1398; 1399, all n.i., 1400, Fig 8.3). These dumps varied in composition but were generally represented by dark brown loams that contained broken pottery and sizeable assemblages (872 NISP) of butchered cattle bones (EAR2, 11, 14, 89). Tip lines visible in sections through the ditch fills demonstrate that the refuse was dumped predominantly from the outside face of the ditch.

A possible structure was built beyond the ditch, close to the line of the former drainage ditch 662 (Fig. 8.5). Two yellow clay levelling deposits (487; 554), 0.05–0.1 m thick, provided the base for the structure, which consisted of four postholes (553; 558; 565; 586), each 0.3–0.4 m in diameter, and a single postpit (577), 0.6 m wide. A post-pipe (552, n.i.) was visible within posthole 553. A fragment of possible post-trench (576), 0.25 m wide, partially cut postpit 577 and may represent an associated structural feature. No pattern is evident in the layout of these features and the form of the structure they represented, if a building at all, is very uncertain. Once the structure had fallen out of use, dumps of clay refuse, similar to those in the base of the fortress ditch, were deposited over its site. Clay dumps 0.1 m thick (494; 495; 582; 589, all n.i.) were laid to the south of the former structure, while mixed clays with charcoal inclusions (566; 567, both n.i.) covered postpit 577. They were sealed by a further 0.1 m-thick clay dump (451; 490; 559; 580, all n.i.).

Dating evidence

LOWER FILLS IN THE OUTER DITCH

- Ditch fill 363.7. Samian: Dr. 15/17 or 18, stamp no. 65, AD 100–20; Dr. 37, AD 100–130 (EAR4, fig. 12, no. 30); Dr. 37, AD 100–20 (EAR4, fig. 12, no. 31); Dr. 37, AD 80–100 (EAR4, fig. 12, no. 32). Pottery: Lezoux rough-cast beaker; Lezoux hairpin beaker.

POSSIBLE STRUCTURE

- Dump 490. Samian: Dr. 29, 1st century AD.

The samian shows that the dumping of refuse in the outer ditch continued into the early 2nd century AD. It is uncertain whether this was a specific event that occurred sometime in the first two decades of the 2nd

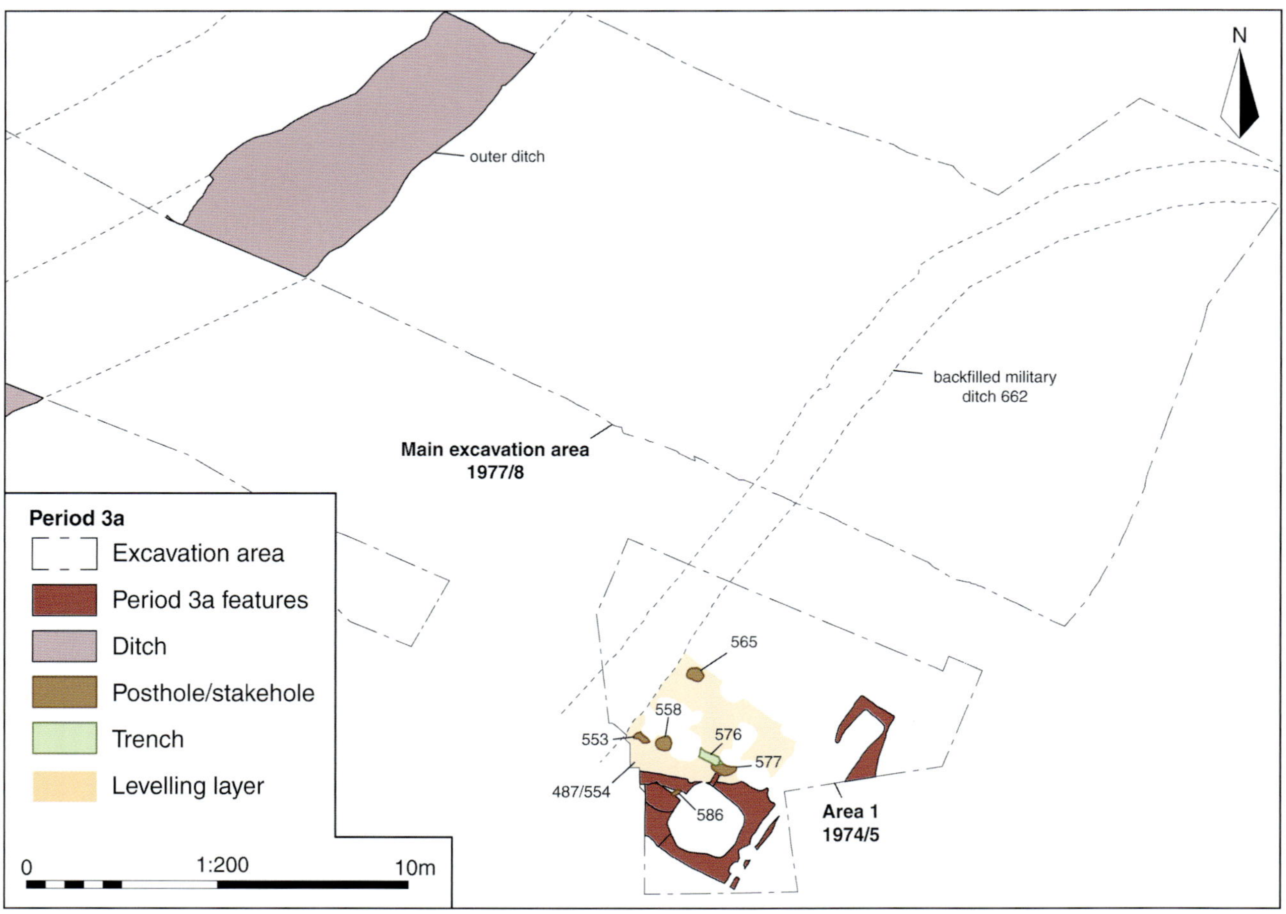

Fig. 8.5 Plan of Period 3a (late 1st to early 2nd century AD)

century AD, or whether it had been a longer process that was ongoing from the late 1st century AD. However, the presence of primary butchery waste in different layers of the lower fills lends support to a relatively short-lived episode rather than a longer process. Insufficient finds were associated with the possible structure to permit any great refinement of its date beyond the date range ascribed to Period 3a.

Period 3b: The defensive ditch is recut and infilled (mid to late 2nd century AD)

As discussed at the start of this section, it is considered that at Rack Street and nearby Mermaid Yard (at least) a new ditch was recut after the infilling of the outer ditch (1470) in Period 3a. This new ditch was broader and shallower than the previous defensive ditches, being in the order of 9 m wide and *c.* 1.6 m deep. The ditch was fully infilled by the mid to late 2nd century AD by a series of clay dumps (363.1; 363.6; 895; 956; 957; 975; 977; 993; 994; 995; 997; 1364; 1365; 1366; 1367; 1368; 1371; 1372; 1373; 1374; 1375; 1379; 1381; 1388; 1389; 1390; 1391; 1392, all n.i; 955; 958; 976; 992; 996; 998; 1001; 1380, Fig 8.3) representing discrete episodes of refuse deposal. They contained charcoal inclusions, animal bones and broken pottery as well as two coins (EAR4, nos. 61 and 90), an earring (EAR4, fig. 112, no. 69), a buckle plate from a *lorica segmentata* (EAR4, fig. 110, no. 39) and two iron pins (EAR4, fig. 120, nos. 9–10). These later refuse deposits were observed in sections dug through the filling of the outer ditch in both 1975 Area 2 and the main 1977/8 excavation area. As is apparent from Fig. 8.3, dump 958 was somewhat thicker than the other deposits; it was a fairly clean clay with charcoal flecks, some shells and yellow clay lumps. This deposit is interpreted as representing the levelling of the fortress rampart into the partially infilled ditch.

Dating evidence: Infilling of the recut civilian ditch

A full listing of the samian from these dumps can be found in EAR4, 287–8. The latest pottery is as follows:

- Ditch fill 363.1. Samian: Dr. 31R, late Antonine; Dr. 37, AD 160–90 (EAR4, fig. 15, no. 79). Pottery: South-East Dorset BB1, type 39.2b.
- Ditch fill 958. Samian: Dr. 37, late Antonine.
- Ditch fill 976. Samian: Dr. 79, later Antonine.
- Ditch fill 1001. Coin no. 90, Trajan, AD 89-117, well circulated.
- Ditch fill 1375. Pottery: South-East Dorset BB1, type 39.2b.

The date of these fills has been fully discussed in EAR4, 9–11 where a date range of *c.* AD 160–200 was proposed. Following examination of the sizeable groups of pottery from the outer ditch at Friernhay Street the authors refined this range to *c.* AD 160–80 (Holbrook and Bidwell 1992, 37–9). It is unclear whether this dumping was a protracted process or a short-lived event immediately prior to the levelling of the former fortress rampart when the expanded town defences were constructed.

Period 3c: Fragmentary traces of structures overlying the backfilled defensive ditches (late 2nd to late 3rd century AD)

Following the final backfilling of the recut civilian ditch, various features were cut into the top of the latest ditch fills (Fig. 8.6). Although no pattern is discernible, it is possible that they represent one or more structures constructed in this area prior to the establishment of a more formal building layout in Period 3d.

In the north-western corner of 1974/5 Area 2 there was a line of five stakeholes (445; 446; 447; 448; 638), each 0.1 m in diameter. They were overlaid by several 50 mm-thick layers of clay (656; 657; 658, all n.i.) into which another two stakeholes (315; 316) and three postholes (312; 313; 314) were cut. The postholes were on a broadly north-west/south-east alignment and measured 0.25–0.3 m in diameter and 0.2 m deep. A fragment of concreted gravel (318) 0.5 m to the south of the postholes may have been an associated internal floor surface. Two truncated fragments of trap wall foundation (409; 433) survived 2.5 m to the west of the possible floor. Wall foundation 433 was dug through a 50 mm-thick surface (431) composed of hard gravel chippings and pea grit laid on a clay levelling deposit (432, n.i.). To the south-east a short fragment of post-trench (538), 0.4 m deep, might be another part of this structure. Just beyond the post-trench, and outside the likely bounds of the building, was a refuse pit (540), 1.3 m in diameter and more than 0.5 m deep, filled with two deposits (535; 536; both n.i.) of mixed clay with inclusions of oyster shell, charcoal and pebbles. Nearby a cobbled surface (527) laid on a thin bedding of orange clay (533, n.i.) covered an area *c.* 6 m long and 2.5 m wide. This was covered by a thin layer of charcoal (648) and several dumps of clay (304/411; 410), each 0.2–0.4 m deep. Two postpits (436; 443/519), each 0.75 m in diameter and 0.4 m deep, lay to the south of the cobbled surface. Each had a post pipe and was packed with large pieces of clay. Between the two postpits there was a truncated hearth (528) filled with soft burnt red clay, and a small post-trench (530), 0.35 m wide, adjacent to postpit 436. A trench (537) 0.6 m wide and 0.3 m deep lay 2 m to the south of the two postpits; it is best interpreted as a robber trench for a stone wall. There was no dating evidence from these features but they were overlaid by Period 3e building RC3. It is possible that rather than dating to this period, at least some of these features were contemporary with Period 3d structures RC1 and 2 to the north-east. Two pits (1370; 1390), each 2.2–2.4 m in diameter and up to 1 m deep, were dug into the top of the infilled outer ditch. Pit 1390 was filled by two deposits

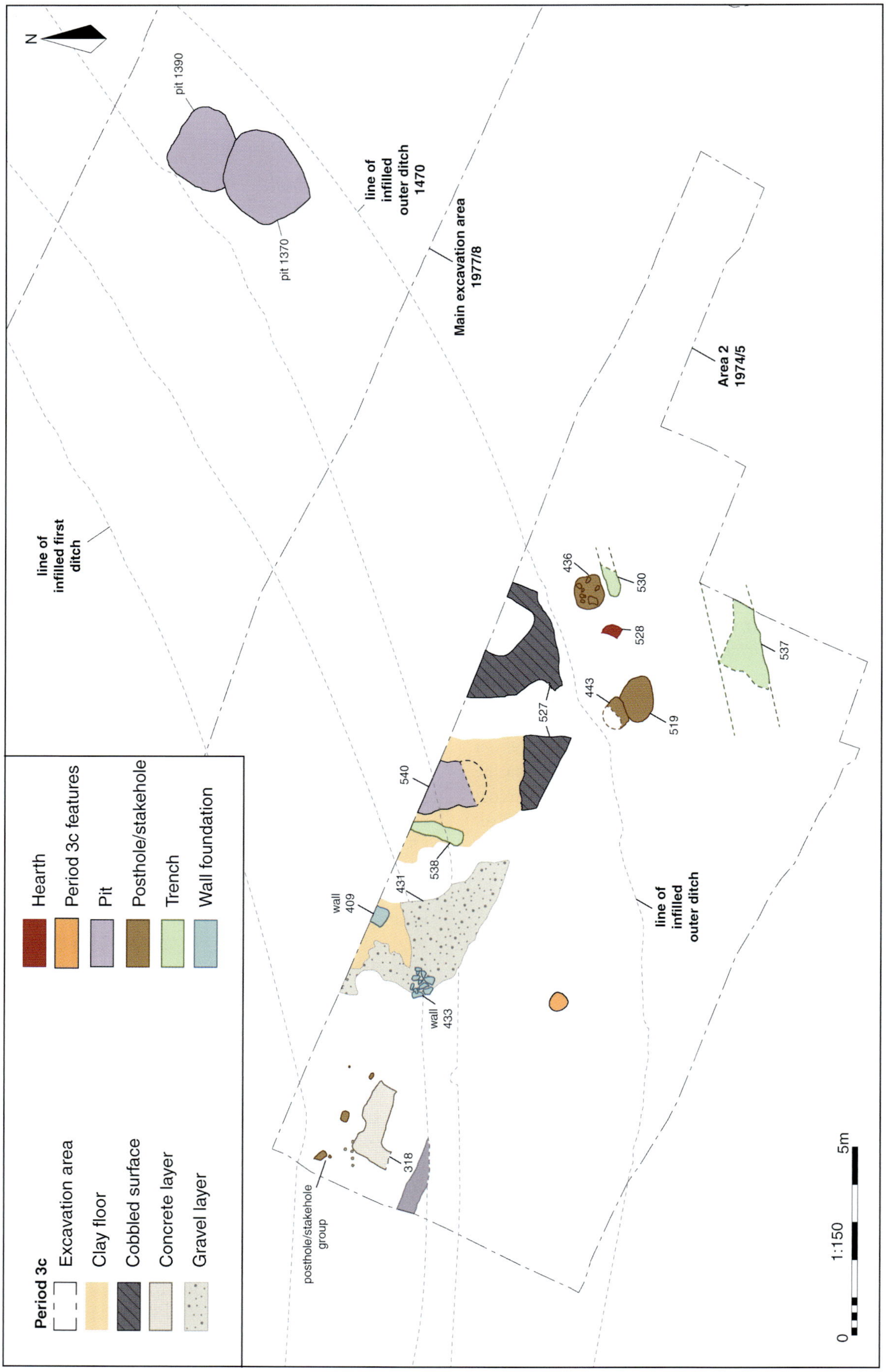

Fig. 8.6 Plan of Period 3c (late 2nd to late 3rd century AD)

of silty clay (1388; 1389) and was truncated along its northern edge by pit 1370 which contained a thick deposit of trap stones and large pebbles.

Dating evidence: Pits dug into infilled outer ditch

- Pit 1370. Samian: Dr. 33, stamp no. 70, AD 160–90; Dr. 37, AD 150–90.

There is no useful dating evidence for the structures and associated features overlying the infilled defensive ditches, other than that they were earlier than Period 3e building RC3.

Period 3d: Timber buildings RC1–2 and associated street (late 3rd to early 4th century AD)

At some point in the late 3rd or early 4th century AD the layout in this part of the town was reorganised with the construction of a metalled street on a north-east/south west alignment (Chapter 3.3, Street M). This separated *Insula* XV *et al.* to the north-west from *Insula* XXXIII *et al.* to the south-east, where two successive timber buildings (RC1–2) were constructed on the street frontage (Fig. 8.7).

Street

A series of thin clay loam refuse dumps up to 50 mm thick (842; 843; 861; 894; 945; 946; 964; 965; 990; 991; 1361; 1362; 1363; 1376, all n.i; 906; 913, Fig. 8.3) was deposited over the line of the backfilled outer ditch in the 1977/8 main area. These dumps served to level the uneven ground prior to the construction of a new street; they contained a large quantity of pottery and a number of other finds including several copper-alloy pins (EAR4, figs 118–19, nos. 130–1), a needle (EAR4, fig. 118, no. 122), a rod (EAR4, fig. 118, no. 120), a military fitting (EAR4, fig. 111, no. 52), and an iron stylus (EAR4, fig. 120, no. 11). A hoard of 26 coins, deposited *c.* AD 275, was recovered from dump 842.

The new street (430; 510; 646) was constructed just beyond the outside face of the backfilled outer defensive ditch. It was located in both 1974/5 Area 2 and the 1977/8 main area, although correlating resurfacings of the street and the sequence of recutting in a flanking ditch between the two areas could not be achieved. The street crossed the site on a north-east/south-west alignment and was constructed from small and medium-sized cobbles interspersed with fragments of tile. An incomplete copper-alloy pin (EAR4, fig. 118, no. 126) was recovered from surface 430. The surface was patched and re-made on a number of occasions (222; 236; 405; 434; 439; 440; 506; 511; 514; 647, all n.i.). A copper-alloy pin (EAR4, fig. 118, no. 125) and a military harness fitting (EAR4, fig. 112, no. 60) were recovered from the surface 236 and an incomplete medical instrument (EAR4, fig. 117, no. 110) from surface 405. Thin (50 mm-thick) dumps of sandy clay were deposited over the street surface in 1974/5 Area 2 (512; 541; 639; 640; 641; 642; 643; 644; 645, all n.i.), perhaps crude attempts at localised resurfacings. The street was thus maintained for a lengthy period.

A large ditch (311; 1387; 1474) flanked the north-western edge of the street. It was 2.05 m wide, 1.5 m deep and was filled with a series of clayey loams (1385; 1386; 1397, n.i.) that contained an assemblage of animal bone (84 NISP) which shows that the ditch was filled with refuse once it was no longer maintained. The ditch fill also yielded a copper-alloy medical instrument (EAR4, fig. 117, no. 111). Once backfilled the ditch was subsequently recut (1369/1473, n.i.) and this recut was in turn backfilled by a series of similar refuse deposits (1357; 1358; 1359; 1360, all n.i.). Several small objects were recovered from the fills of the initial cut of this ditch: an incomplete copper-alloy finger ring (EAR4, fig. 114, no. 84) and a medical instrument (EAR4, fig. 117, no. 112), two bone pins (EAR4, fig. 123, nos. 14–15), a shale bracelet (EAR4, fig. 126, no. 16), and a copper-alloy stylus (EAR4, fig. 118, no. 121) from fills of the recut. The ditch was in turn recut again (1377), and this ditch is likely contemporary with the earliest surface identified in the 1977/8 main area (1015, n.i.) which was formed of compacted pebbles 0.3 m thick (this context might in fact include more than one surface, hence the lack of corresponding layers between the two excavation areas). A glass intaglio (EAR4, fig. 107, no. 3) and a bone pin (EAR4, fig. 123, no. 16) were recovered from 1015. Ditch 1377 was backfilled with layers of silty clay (1028; 1336; 1395, n.i.) which contained a number of coins.

Three small postholes (508; 513; 517, all n.i.), 0.2 m in diameter and 0.2 m deep, were dug into the street surface in 1974/5 Area 2, although there is little further information concerning these features in the archive. A narrow drain (515/516, n.i.) flanked the south-eastern side of the street in 1974/5 Area 2. The drain was 1.6 m wide and filled with large cobbles, pieces of volcanic trap, tile and slate fragments, presumably from the demolition of a nearby building. At right angles to the street there was a metalled open space immediately to the north-east of building RC1. It was composed of cobbles (595) embedded in a thin layer of clay.

Building RC1

Timber-framed building RC1 was constructed on top of an orange clay and pebble floor surface (276, n.i.). It consisted of a row of five substantial postpits (50; 463; 464; 465; 466) defining the north-eastern wall of the structure, and a roughly parallel row of six postholes (94; 587; 592; 593; 599; 611, all n.i.) 2.15 m to the south-west (Fig. 8.7). The postpits were 0.7 m in diameter and 0.5 m deep, while the postholes were 0.2 m diameter and 0.2 m deep. It is likely that the row of postholes represented an internal division within the building that extended beyond 1974/5 Area 1 to the south-west; the 2.15 m wide room perhaps served as a corridor. Six stakeholes (296; 297; 298; 452; 454; 590), 0.1 m in diameter, on a north-east/south-west alignment across the centre of the structure presumably represent a

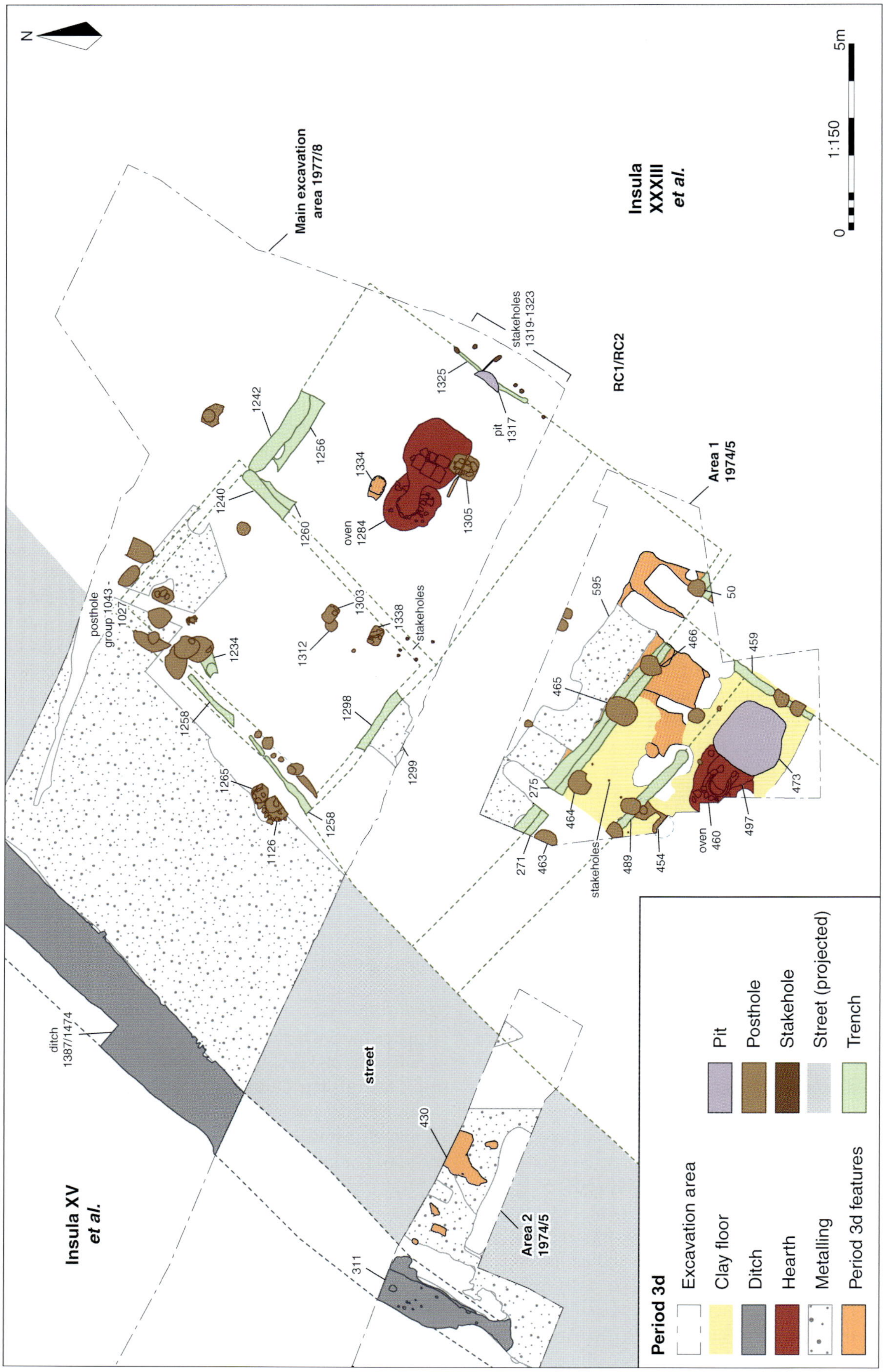

Fig. 8.7 Plan of Period 3d (late 3rd century to early 4th century AD) buildings RC1–2

further internal subdivision. A 50 mm-thick layer of occupation debris accumulated within the structure (281, n.i.), while a small hearth (497), 0.1 m deep and lined with burnt clay, lay to the south-west of the possible corridor. The hearth was later cut by a large pit (473), 1.8 m in diameter, which was in turn cut by the construction of an oven (460). Oven 460 was 1.4 m long, 0.75 m wide and was lined with large trap stones (289). A clay surface (288) surrounded the oven, while several burnt clay deposits (461; 562; 579; 581) were dumped against the oven wall. Several layers of burnt clay and daub (462; 467; 496, n.i.), 0.1–0.3 m thick, accumulated to the east of the oven.

RC1 burnt down, evidenced by several layers of burnt material (282; 283; 290–294, n.i.) which overlay the post-pits and postholes. Some of the posts appear to have been burnt *in situ*. A layer of yellow clay loam with charcoal inclusions (594, n.i.), 0.15 m deep, was dumped the over the external cobbled surface 595 to the north-east of the now demolished RC1.

Building RC2

The burnt debris of RC1 was covered with several deposits of clay levelling, 0.2–0.3 m thick (85; 269; 1327; 1355, n.i.), in preparation for the construction of RC2. RC2 consisted of a series of post-trenches (271; 275; 459; 489; 1256; 1258; 1260; 1325) that defined a building in excess of *c.* 14 m long and *c.* 12 m wide, assuming it was a single structure, which is by no means assured given the fragmentary preservation (Fig. 8.7). The post-trenches were each 0.35–0.4 m wide and 0.2–0.35 m deep and were associated with a large number of postholes and stakeholes. The trenches likely held the base of wattle and daub panels set between timber uprights. Two trenches (271; 1298) set 4.8 m apart probably formed internal partitions. A layer of plaster (270), 20 m thick, to the south-west of trench 271 indicates that at least some of the internal walls were plastered. Several of the post-trenches associated with RC2 were replaced at a later date (275; 1240; 1242), indicating that the structure was at least partially reconstructed at some point during its life. The north-western wall of RC2 underwent several reconstructions. This wall was defined by a post-trench (1258) in which 18 stakes were inserted (1489 to 1509 inclusive, n.i.), a parallel post-trench (1234), which contained two postholes (1507; 1508, both n.i.), an alignment of small postholes (1244; 1245; 1246; 1247; 1249; 1267) and two large stone-packed postholes (1126: 1265). A series of stakeholes (1319–1323 inclusive), 50 mm in diameter, also punctuated the south-eastern wall trench 1325 and point to reconstruction. A small burnt wooden partition (1329, n.i.) in this area indicates that at least part of the structure was destroyed by fire. A trench (459) suggests that RC2 extended to the south-west beyond the limit of 1974/5 Area 1.

In 1974/5 Area 1 ten postholes (133; 134; 139; 140; 450; 455; 488; 492; 550; 564, all n.i.), 0.25–0.45 m in diameter and 0.2–0.4 m deep, represented internal structural features within the south-western part of the building. Within the northern part of RC2, a series of small (50 mm diameter) stakeholes (1346–1353 inclusive) and three postholes (1305; 1312; 1338), each 0.4 m in diameter and 0.4 m deep, provide further evidence for the division of the internal space. There was an oven (1284) within the north-eastern part of RC2. It was 3.15 m long and 1.6 m wide; traces of burnt planks survived on three sides of the ash pit, which was partially floored with ceramic tiles (Fig. 8.8). Immediately to the north of it a large South-West Grey Ware storage jar had been laid on its side (1334; EAR4, fig. 68, type 1.1). The interior of the pot displayed signs of blackening so it may have been used as a small oven (Fig. 8.9). Several patches of cobbled floor surfaces survived within the structure (1299 and 135; 272; 1309, all n.i.). A group of postholes at the north-eastern corner of the RC2 (1043; 1134; 1136; 1175; 1178; 1191; 1207) may represent an extension to the structure, although they were not closely dated. The postholes were 0.4–0.6 m in diameter and 0.4 m deep. Two of them had been recut (1154; 1193).

Fig. 8.8 Period 3d oven 1284. 20 cm scale (© RAMM)

Further modifications were made to RC2 during its life, including the insertion of a new post-trench (1232, n.i.) and four postholes (1301; 1310; 1330; 1332, n.i.),

Fig. 8.9 Period 3d pottery vessel 1334 used as an oven, with oven 1284 behind. 10 cm scale (© RAMM)

each 0.4 m in diameter. Oven 1284 and pot oven 1334 fell out of use and were infilled with a series of sandy clay and charcoal-rich deposits (1282; 1283; 1285; 1288 and 1335, all n.i.). By the mid 4th century AD RC2 had been destroyed by fire, a thick layer of burnt daub and charcoal (1262; 1263; 1264; 1296; 1297, n.i.) overlying its remains.

Dating evidence

LEVELLING DUMPS OVER OUTER DITCH 1470

- Dump 842: Coins: hoard B, deposited *c.* AD 275 (EAR4, 32–3). Pottery: North African amphora.
- Dump 861. Coin: no. 87, Trajan, AD 114–17, well circulated.
- Dump 946. Coins: no. 195, illegible, AD 260–80, very worn; no. 77, Domitian, AD 85, very worn.

STREET

- Surface 430. Coins: no. 164, Tetricus I, AD 270–3, very worn; no. 100, Marcus Aurelius, AD 154–5, very worn.
- Resurfacing 236. Coins: no. 223, Tetricus I, AD 270–90, well circulated; no. 224, Tetricus I, AD 270–90, very worn.
- Resurfacing 434. Coin: no. 135, Claudius II, AD 268–70, very worn.
- Street surface 1015. Coins: no. 374, *Fel. Temp. Rep.* (copy), AD 350–60, virtually uncirculated; no. 403, illegible *minim*.

STREET-SIDE DITCH

- Ditch 311. Coin: no. 120, Postumus, AD 259–68, uncirculated. Pottery: Nene Valley Ware beaker, white paint over colour coat; Rhenish (Trier) Ware beaker.
- Primary fill 1378 of recut ditch 1369. Coin: no. 118, Gallienus, AD 260–8, uncirculated.
- Fill of recut ditch 1369. Coin: no. 163, Tetricus I, AD 270–3, little wear.
- Fill 1336 of ditch 1337. Coin: no. 121, Postumus, AD 259–68, little wear; no. 182, Tetricus II, AD 270–3, well circulated; no. 241, Tetricus II, AD 270–90, little wear; no. 213, Tetricus I, AD 270–90, virtually uncirculated; no. 246, Tetricus II, AD 270–90, little wear; no. 247, Tetricus II, AD 270–90, well circulated.

RC2

- Foundation trench 275. Pottery: Rhenish (Central Gaul) beaker.

Coins date the levelling dumps above the outer ditch to the last quarter of the 3rd century AD, and this forms a *terminus post quem* for the street. Doubt must attach to the evidential value of the coin from street surface 1015, and in particular its ability to provide a *terminus post quem* for subsequent resurfacings (which have been assigned to Period 3e). Even when well embedded in metalling, coins cannot be regarded as securely stratified in the places they were dropped. Street surfaces can be disturbed by traffic when wet, with the result that small objects such as coins can get pressed down into the body of the underlying metalling. Localised patching of potholes is also almost impossible to detect in excavation. While coin no. 374 should not therefore be regarded as a secure *terminus post quem* for the subsequent surfaces, it does demonstrate that the street was still being maintained after *c.* AD 350. RC1 and 2 pre-date the construction of RC4 in Period 3e, and overall a late 3rd or early 4th-century AD date range for Period 3d seems appropriate.

Period 3e: Stone Buildings RC3–6 (early to mid 4th century AD)

Building RC3

RC3 was a stone building on the north-west side of 1974/5 Area 2 (Fig. 8.10). Defined by three robber trenches (428; 525; 526), it was 12.3 m wide and in excess of 5.2 m long. There was no surviving evidence for the northern wall of the building within the excavation area. The robber trenches were between 0.85–1.25 m wide and 0.2–0.4 m deep; in a few places the trap stone footings survived *in situ*. A small trench 408 at the south-west corner of the

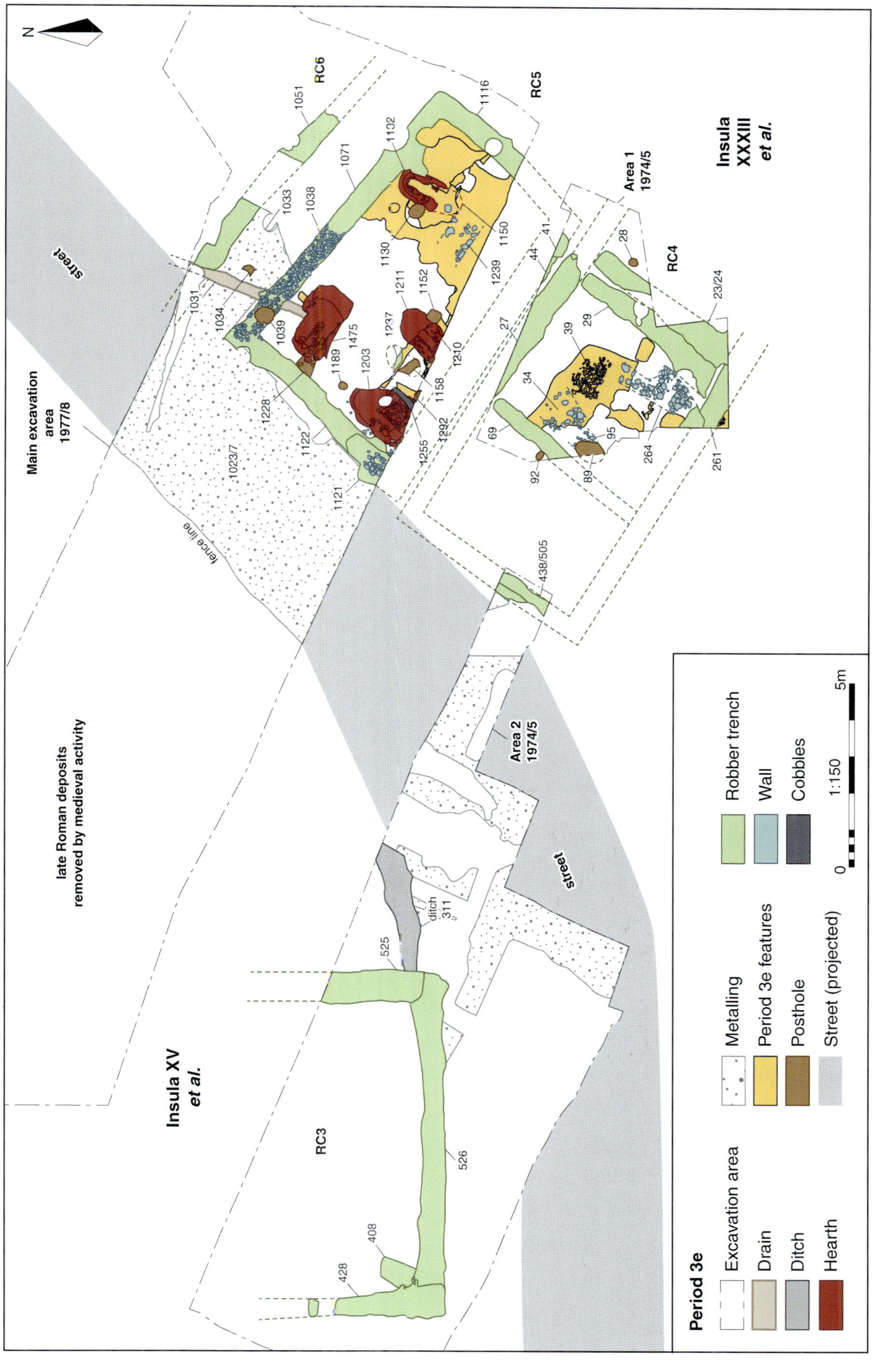

Fig. 8.10 Plan of Period 3e (early to mid 4th century AD) buildings RC3–6

building is of uncertain function. No internal features or floors survived. RC3 appears to have encroached somewhat onto the street as its front wall seemingly overlay the line of the by now infilled street-side ditch 311.

Building RC4

Following the destruction by fire of RC2, three separate stone buildings were built over its former site (Fig. 8.10). These buildings were founded on several layers of demolition material (26; 93; 1236, all n.i.) from which a copper-alloy pin (EAR4, fig. 119, no. 132) was recovered. The walls of RC4 had been entirely robbed, their lines represented by a series of robber trenches (23/24; 27; 29; 69; 261; 438/505), 0.6–0.8 m wide. The rear wall had been replaced at some stage by a new wall on a slightly different line. The excavators believed that robber trench 29 dated to the Roman period, thus indicating that this was the primary wall which was replaced by the wall represented by robber trench 23/4. It is uncertain whether this wall formed the back wall of the building or merely a partition with a further room to the south-east. If the former, the building would have been *c.* 12.25 m long and 8 m wide. In the main room fragmentary spreads of trap fragments may represent the remains of a metalled floor surface or make-up (34; 95; 264) associated with a fragment of cobbled surface (39). Two deposits (278; 279, both n.i.) of brown soil with pebbles, charcoal and mortar flecks lay to the south of the cobbled surface and might also be vestiges of floor surfaces. Three scattered postholes (28; 69; 92) were associated with the building.

Building RC5

Immediately to the north-east was a second stone building RC5, that was 12 m long by 8 m wide. As a clear eastern corner of the building was preserved, we can be confident it did not extend further to the south-east and that the full extent of this single-celled building has been recovered. Like RC4 the masonry had been heavily robbed in the medieval period, although a length of dry-stone trap footings (1038), 0.9 m wide, of the north-east wall did survive. Elsewhere its plan was marked by robber trenches 41, 44, 1071, 1116, 1121 and 1122. Scattered postholes (89; 1045; 1130; 1142; 1152; 1156; 1158; 1189; 1220; 1228; 1292), 0.3–0.7 m in diameter, across the interior of the RC5 do not form any discernible pattern. Posthole 1039 truncated wall foundation 1038 and is presumably a later modification. A sequence of floor surfaces was preserved within the building. A 50 mm-thick layer of crushed stone (1287, n.i.) was covered with a light orange clay (1286, n.i.) and in turn a cobble surface (1255, n.i.). A compacted clay surface (1291, n.i.) and a layer of crushed stone (1201, n.i.) were also revealed in another part of the room. The building contained four substantial ovens, each of them constructed in a similar manner with a stone-lined U-shaped chamber leading from a stoking-pit which displayed evidence of intense burning. Oven 1132 was 1.8 m long and 1.05 m wide and formed from burnt trap stones set in red clay. There was a stoking-pit (1150) to the south-west. Oven 1203, 2.5 m long by 1.7 m wide, lay along the south-western side of RC5. The oven walls were made from trap stones bonded with sandy red clay. Oven 1210, 1.6 m to the south-east, was also constructed from trap stones with a stoke-hole (1211) to the north-east. A tiny fragment of cobbled surface (1254, n.i.) survived to the north-west of this oven. Oven 1475 was located in the northern corner of the building; it was 2.15 m long, 1.1 m wide and built from large burnt trap stones bonded with red sandy clay. There was a layer of black clay (1196, n.i.), presumably raked out from the oven, adjacent to the stoking-pit. A 0.4 m-wide drain (1031) led from near this oven northwards and must have served to drain the building (it presumably passed through the exterior wall in a simply-built culvert). The ovens might be sequential replacements of one another and it cannot be demonstrated that they were all in use contemporaneously.

Building RC6

A 2.2 m wide cobbled alleyway (1033) separated RC5 from another building, RC6, to the north-east. The surface was 0.32 m thick and was comprised of compacted pebbles bound by a dark brown clay loam. The only evidence for RC6 was a single robber trench (1051), 0.9 m wide.

Street refurbishment

At some point the Period 3d street-side ditch 1387/1474 was recut (1337, n.i.) and a second resurfacing of the street occurred (1274; 1328, n.i.). A series of 11 stakes (1146; 1148; 1161–1169 inclusive, all n.i.), 0.1 m in diameter, were driven through the second surface of compacted gravel along north-western edge of the back-filled drainage ditch to form a fence along the edge of the refurbished street (Fig. 8.11). Following the establishment of the fence, a third street surface (1023; 1027) was laid, formed of compacted small pebbles 0.15–0.25 m thick. A foundation for a boundary wall (1022, n.i.) formed from large pieces of trap stone and fragments of ceramic tile, 9 m long, 0.65 m wide and 0.5 m deep, was constructed along the north-western edge of the street. It replaced the former ditch and fence. Although some patching of the street was still undertaken (1202, n.i.), the insertion of these features coincided, potentially, with its disuse represented by a 0.1 m-thick build-up of silty clay (1026, n.i.) along its north-west edge.

Dating evidence

RC5

- Wall foundation 1038. Coin: no. 320, *Constantinopolis*, AD 330–5, virtually uncirculated.
- Fill 1141 of pit robbing stone from oven 1475. Coin: no. 178, Tetricus I, AD 270–3, very worn.

Fig. 8.11 Late Roman surface of Street M separating insulae *XV* et al. *and XXIII* et al., *with stake-built fence to left. Buildings RC5 and 6 lay on the right-hand side of the street. 2 m scales (© RAMM)*

STREET REFURBISHMENT

- Street surface 1328. Coins: no. 227, Tetricus I, AD 270–90, virtually uncirculated; no. 230, Tetricus I, AD 270–90, virtually uncirculated; no. 245, Tetricus II, AD 270–90.
- Street surface 1023. Coin: no. 200, Gallienus, AD 265–80, well circulated.
- Wall foundation 1022. Coin: no. 242, Tetricus II, AD 270–90, well circulated.
- Street-side build-up 1026. Coin: no. 228, Tetricus I, AD 270–90, little wear.

Unless coin no. 320 was introduced during later robbing, it dates the construction of RC5 to after AD 330. Coin no. 374 for street surface 1015 has already been discussed in the consideration of the dating evidence for Period 3d. It shows that the street was being maintained after *c.* AD 350.

Period 3f: Demolition of RC3–6 (mid to late 4th century AD)

Demolition deposits (246, n.i.) containing large pieces of volcanic trap overlay the remains of RC3, and small patches of demolition material (309; 329; 341, all n.i.), probably from the demolition of RC3 or 4, overlay the uppermost street surface hereabouts. Demolition deposits covering RC5 (1021; 1109; 1110; 1160; 1171; 1174; 1197; 1206, all n.i.) varied from 0.15–0.65 m in depth and consisted of layers of clay loam, plaster, mortar and other debris including crushed stone roofing tiles (the retained samples suggest that the building was roofed with Jurassic White Lias, probably from Somerset; EAR4, 282). Four postholes (1029; 1036; 1118; 1128, n.i.), each 0.6 m in diameter and 0.5 m deep, cut through the demolition deposits covering RC5. A single posthole (500, n.i.), 0.4 m in diameter and located on the eastern edge of 1974/5 Area 2, also truncated the demolition material there. The date of these postholes is uncertain.

Dating evidence: Demolition of RC3 and 4

- Demolition 1160. Coin: no. 375, *Fel. Temp. Rep.* (copy), AD 350–60, virtually uncirculated.
- Demolition 329. Coin: no. 356, *Constantinopolis,* AD 337–41, well circulated. Pottery: North African amphora.

If the absence of later coins is regarded as significant, demolition shortly after the middle of the 4th century

AD is suggested. Well-circulated coins of AD 367–75 and 364–7 were recovered from the post-Roman dark earth and a further six coins of the House of Valentinian (AD 364–78) from medieval and post-medieval deposits on the site (EAR4, coins nos 380, 400, 384, 392, 393, 395, 396 and 397).

Discussion of the Roman civil evidence *by Neil Holbrook*

The dumps in the base of the outer defensive ditch constitute the first evidence for domestic civilian activity at Rack Street following the refurbishment of the former legionary defences. The latest pottery from this material shows that it continued to accumulate into the opening decades of the 2nd century AD, although it is less clear whether this was a specific time-limited event at that time, or an on-going process over several decades. On balance the former seems more likely as the dumps contained an exceptional deposit of animal bones composed of a minimum of 49 cattle and lesser numbers of other species (EAR2, tab. 2). The cattle assemblage was dominated by jaw, skull and loose teeth, as well as 86 metatarsi and 26 metacarpi fragments. Maltby concluded that these bones constituted those parts of the cattle carcass considered to be of no further use, and thus discarded as primary butchery waste. Where did this material come from? There is a possibility that it derives from a military-period midden that was redeposited in the outer ditch in the early 2nd century AD but given that the bones were deposited 25–40 years after the departure of the army this seems unlikely. The lack of fragmentation of the bone assemblage also indicates that it did not travel far from its original place of deposition, and nor had it been exposed to prolonged attrition from scavenging animals. Creation of the butchery waste in the early decades of the civilian occupation is therefore indicated and thus it testifies to systematic processing of cattle products in Exeter at a time when the urban population levels are likely to have been quite low (EAR2, 14, 89).

It is suggested above that by the early 2nd century AD the outer ditch at Rack Street had become infilled with refuse, and a new defensive ditch was dug, *c.* 9 m wide and 1.6 m deep. We have no information on the condition of the former fortress rampart at this time at Rack Street as all trace of it has been destroyed here. However, at nearby Mermaid Yard (Site 63) the rampart survived to a height of 0.8–0.9 m throughout the Roman period, and a similar situation is likely at Rack Street. There is no evidence from Exeter that the fortress rampart was refurbished to protect the early town, although this must remain a possibility, especially as in some places at least, the *intervallum* street just inside the rampart was resurfaced and maintained throughout the 2nd century AD (Chapter 3.2, Street B). This was most clearly shown at Friernhay Street (street observation B6i) where several civilian resurfacings were found, and the side ditch was recut, as well as at several other locations (observations B3i, B4i, B7i, B8i). At Rack Street the effects of later truncation within the small area examined in Trench A had removed any evidence for the continued use of the *intervallum* street, or of any structures that may once have fronted onto it.

Only very ephemeral traces of early civilian activity survived at Rack Street, and there is no reason to believe that the area was intensively occupied at this time. Little can be said of the possible structure beyond the outer ditch, other than it need not necessarily represent a roofed building. A date range of *c.* AD 160–80 has been proposed for the final infilling of the recut civilian ditch, based on evidence from several sites within the city (Holbrook and Bidwell 1992, 37–9). It is likely that a wedge of cleanish clay visible in one of the sections through the ditch at Rack Street (Fig. 8.3, 958) should be interpreted as evidence for the (at least partial) levelling of the old fortress rampart, a sequence observed in a number of other excavations on the defensive circuit such as Mermaid Yard (Site 63; Bidwell 1980, 47), Friernhay Street (Site 75) and Paul Street (Site 76). It is likely that the old legionary *intervallum* street fell out of use in the early 3rd century AD as a consequence of the levelling of the fortress defences and construction of the City Wall (as was demonstrated at Friernhay Street).

The Rack Street site now lay away from a street frontage in a peripheral part of the new walled town. Fragmentary traces of structures that can be broadly dated to the period from the late 2nd to the late 3rd century AD were found above the infilled outer ditch, but little can be deduced of their form or layout other than that they do not appear to have shared a common alignment. Once again, occupation was not on any significant scale until a major replanning occurred in the late 3rd century AD with the construction of a new street. Some further levelling-up of subsidence, from which a hoard of 26 coins deposited *c.* AD 275 was recovered, took place prior to the construction of the new street. If this represents a purse group lost during this process, or even a deliberate deposition, then a date of *c.* AD 275 can be proposed for the construction of the street which was also revealed 55 m to the north-east at Mermaid Yard (Chapter 3.3, street observation M1ii). There a timber building, later replaced in stone, was found on the frontage (Chapter 3.5, building 51ii). The alignment of Street M to the south-west of the Rack Street site is not certain, although the position and orientation of building RC3, as well as the course of the street-side ditch, suggest that the street turned to the west, in the general direction of the West Gate.

The addition of a new street to the town plan in the late 3rd century AD can be viewed in a number of ways. On the one hand it indicates a slow expansion of the built-up area out towards the limit set by the town defences. If occupation had been intense hereabouts the street would surely have been constructed at an earlier date in the 3rd century AD. On the other hand it does signify continued public investment in the urban fabric of Exeter at this time. Unambiguous evidence for the later addition of new streets to the established layout of Romano-British towns is not commonly attested, principally because excavation on a reasonable scale is required to prove this. However, we may note that a new side street was added in the first half of the 4th century AD at Winchester, perhaps replacing an earlier hollow way, and the creation of extensive metalled areas at Cirencester is also a late phenomenon (Holbrook and Salvatore 1998, 23–5; Ford and Teague 2011, 56, 182).

Street M separated *insula* XV *et al.* to the north-west from *insula* XXXIII *et al.* to the south-east and was flanked on the latter side with at least one timber building (RC1). There was a metalled alleyway leading off the street on the north-east side of RC1, although this probably went out of use when RC1 was destroyed by fire and replaced by another timber building RC2. Given the fragmentary level of preservation, it is unclear whether RC2 was a single structure or two contiguous ones. Both RC1 and RC2 contained a substantial oven (460 in RC1; 1284 in RC2) of typical plan (a well-preserved late 4th-century AD example was found at *Verulamium* for instance; Frere 1983, 93–4, pl. X(a)). The absence of slag or other industrial debris argues against a metalworking function, so more likely the buildings served as shops with ovens associated with food production in rooms to the rear of the retail area which fronted the street. Adjacent to oven 1284 a large storage jar set on its side into the floor (1334) seems to have served as a pot oven. A similar arrangement was found in a 2nd-century AD context at Silchester where a storage jar with scorched interior (as here) was interpreted either as a *clibanus* (a ceramic cover used in cooking) or as a quenching vessel (Cool 2006, 52; Fulford and Clarke 2011, 17–18). RC2 was itself destroyed by fire, a thick deposit of burnt daub testifying to the nature of its walls. RC2 was replaced by a row of three stone-founded buildings built end-on to the street in conventional strip building fashion. If they were built as a single operation they date no earlier than AD 330, given the recovery of a coin of this date from the foundations of RC5. On the opposite side of the street a single stone building RC3 was found; it encroached slightly onto the line of the street and overlay a now abandoned street-side ditch which had been allowed to silt up. Away from the site of the building, the north-west frontage of the street was marked by a stake-built fence which indicates that there were no buildings opposite RC4–6 (although this part of the site had been heavily disturbed by later activity, some vestiges of stone-built buildings are likely to have survived if they had existed here). The fence was subsequently replaced by a stone boundary wall which recalls the compound wall alongside the street frontage at Trichay Street (Chapter 5 above) and a stone boundary wall at Friernhay Street (Site 75) which defined two sides of a compound (or perhaps even a religious *temenos;* EAPIT1, Chapter 6). It is uncertain if buildings RC3–6 were built fully of stone or whether the foundations just supported stone cill walls for a timber superstructure. Demolition deposits demonstrate that at least some of the walls were plastered and that the buildings were roofed with White Lias limestone probably from Somerset (EAR4, 282).

RC5 was a single roomed building that contained four substantial ovens. RC4 had at least two rooms (it is unclear if the back wall was found in the excavation or whether the building extended further to the south-east). The ovens inside RC5 suggest some continuity of function in this part of the site from the activities carried out in the timber phase. Once again, the absence of slag is notable. While an association with food preparation seems likely, in the absence of diagnostic botanical remains the function of the ovens can only be guessed at. A bakery is one possibility, although there were no quern stones present to indicate the milling of flour, and MacMahon (2003, 65–6) has unsurprisingly found little conclusive evidence for bakeries in the province outside of London where there is informative environmental evidence (Hall 2005, 140). RC5 could of course have been involved in some other aspect of food production, such as the cooking or curing of meat, although the single-roomed plan suggests that this building was involved solely in the production, and not the sale, of commodities. We might note that a late Roman masonry 'bakehouse' containing at least two ovens of similar design to those at Rack Street has been explored at nearby Topsham. The building was 15.8 m long by 7.2 m wide and six quern stone fragments were recovered from the vicinity of the structure (Morris and Montague 1938; Sage and Allan 2004, fig. 21, no. 11; EAPIT1, Chapter 6).

The street continued to be maintained and used after *c.* AD 350, judging from a coin recovered from its metalling, although the stone buildings may have been demolished not long after this date. A single coin of AD 350–60 was recovered from demolition deposits, yet eight issues of the House of Valentinian were retrieved from post-Roman deposits on the site (two of them from the dark earth). This implies that the buildings were demolished shortly after the middle of the 4th century AD, with the later issues deposited after this event had occurred (perhaps these coins were contained in refuse that was dumped around the abandoned buildings, subsequently to be incorporated within the dark earth?). Five scattered postholes cut the demolition debris, and were presumably thought by the excavators to be sealed by the dark earth (although this relationship can be difficult to discern). As their date is uncertain and they make no coherent plan it would be unwise to treat them as firm evidence for post-demolition, but pre-Saxo-Norman, activity on the site.

Periods 4 and 5: The post-Roman and Middle Saxon periods

Following the demolition of the latest Roman buildings, the site appears to have remained unoccupied; a layer of dark loam 0.2–0.4 m thick accumulated above the demolition deposits of these buildings (213; 215; 302; 1014, n.i.). Residual Roman finds were recovered from this dark earth, along with a large assemblage of animal bone, including cattle and sheep. No other evidence was found for post-Roman or Middle Saxon activity. Pottery of the 12th and 13th centuries was recovered from the dark earth, doubtless introduced during subsequent cultivation, and no undisturbed post-Roman dark soil was encountered.

Dating evidence

- Dark earth 215. Coin: no. 380, Valens, AD 364–7, very worn. Pottery: medieval fabric 20 (*c.* 950–1350) and sandy wares (*c.* 1200–50).
- Dark earth 1014. Coin: no. 400, Valens, AD 367–75, well circulated. Copper-alloy penannular brooch (EAR4, fig. 193, no. 38).

The coins of AD 364–7 and 367–75 are later in date than the latest coins firmly stratified in Roman deposits.

Period 6: The Saxo-Norman town (*c.* 900–1200)

Period 6a: Robbing of Late Roman stone buildings (11th and early 12th century)

In the 11th or 12th-century robber trenches were dug through the post-Roman dark earth to extract stone from the long-abandoned Roman buildings. The excavated trenches were backfilled with cess and used for the disposal of refuse; pottery broadly of the 11th or early 12th century was found in two of them (406, n.i.; 407, Fig. 8.17).

Period 6b: The earliest domestic occupation

The earliest substantial signs of Saxo-Norman domestic occupation were two probable wells: one (1421, n.i.) backfilled with a group of over 200 sherds of mid to late 12th-century date, the other (502, Fig. 8.17) 0.9 m deep and 1.05 m in diameter with a waterlogged stake and wattle lining. Other scattered features probably of this period included a postpit (471, n.i.), and, in the 1977/8 main area, a pit (862, n.i.), a foundation slot (868, n.i.) and associated posthole (870, n.i.). None of these produced much dating evidence, and they testify to a sparse level of occupation in this peripheral part of the city.

Dating evidence

- Robber trench 400: minor group, fabric 20 (probably 11th/12th century).
- Robber trench 406: (37 sherds) fabric 20, Bedford Garage Ware (11th/early 12th century).
- Robber trench 407: (138 sherds) fabric 20 including combed wares; North French white ware (probably late 11th/early 12th century).
- Fill 863 of pit 862: (3 sherds): fabrics 20, 23 (10th to 12th century?).
- Fill 1422 of well 1421: (237 sherds): Ceramic Horizon E group (EAR3, 9) with tripod pitchers (probably mid to late 12th century).

Period 7: The High Medieval city (*c.* 1200–1350)

Figure 8.12 illustrates the broad position of the site in relation to the street layout shown on Hooker's map of 1587 (in an edition of 1618). The frontage of Rack Street marked approximately the north-western edge of the excavated areas. Building Me1 was the back of a room fronting onto Rack Street; finds from associated refuse pits to the rear of it indicate occupation broadly of the early 13th century (Period 7a). Me1 was replaced in the mid to late 13th century by a row of rooms (Me2–4), with a further structure Me5 to the north-east. These buildings had fallen out of use by the mid 14th century.

Period 7a: Building Me1 and associated pits (early 13th century)

The earliest structural evidence consisted of a group of ten postholes, each 0.2–0.45 m in diameter and 0.2–0.5 m deep, close to the Rack Street frontage, in the western corner of the excavated area (352; 398; 415–422: Fig. 8.13 'posthole group'). The surviving postholes seem to form an L-shaped plan, but this is misleading; further postholes may once have continued into the area to the west, which had been removed by a later cellar. No dating evidence was recovered from any of these features, but they were cut by building Me1.

Building Me1 consisted of a terrace (698), cut into the underlying deposits, representing a room standing on the Rack Street frontage. The north-east and south-east edges of the feature were present within the excavation area; the maximum depth of the terrace was 0.5 m. Two layers of crumby plaster (347; 387) provided a rendered white finish to the vertical north-eastern side of the terrace, similar to the plastered internal face of building Me2 (below). A potentially significant detail of the terrace was its slightly rounded corner, which was taken to suggest that the room had cob walls (but see Discussion).

Further back from the street frontage was a series of 0.1–0.2 m-thick layers of clay loam, some of which produced finds of the late 12th or the early 13th century (307, 542; 425, the last n.i.). This area was cut by two large subrectangular pits which contained useful groups of pottery (380, 402) and several smaller pits (210; 371; 394; 393, the last n.i.) with a maximum depth of 1.3 m.

Dating evidence

Evidence presented in EAR3, 67–70.

- Dump 307: fabrics 20, 62 (late 12th/early 13th century).
- Refuse pit 328: fabrics 20, 40 (after *c.* 1250).
- Refuse pit 346: fabrics 20, 23, 44, 63; French white ware jug (mid or late 13th century).

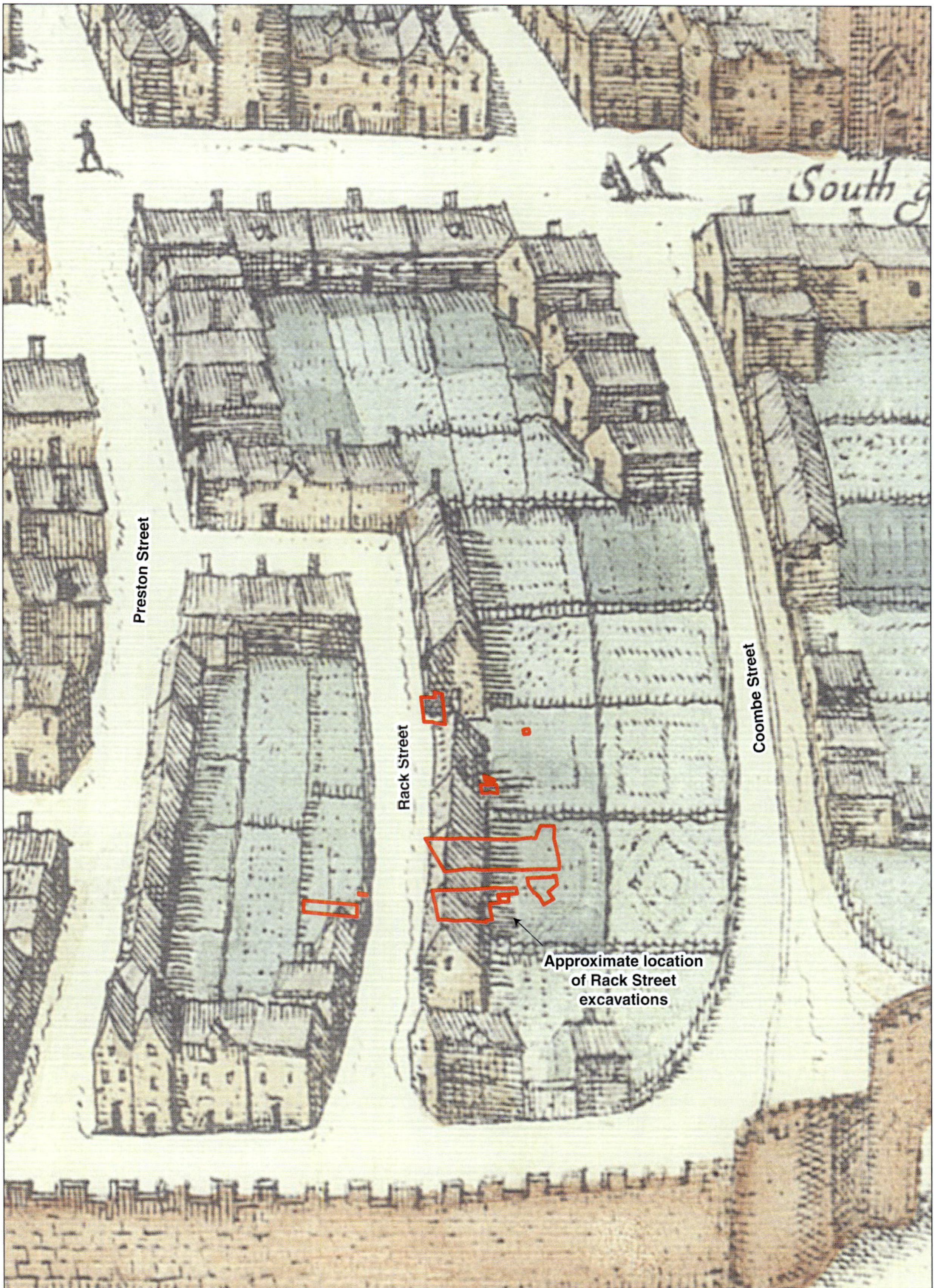

Fig. 8.12 The relationship of the excavations to the surrounding historic street plan as marked on Hooker's map of 1587 (1618 edition) (© RAMM)

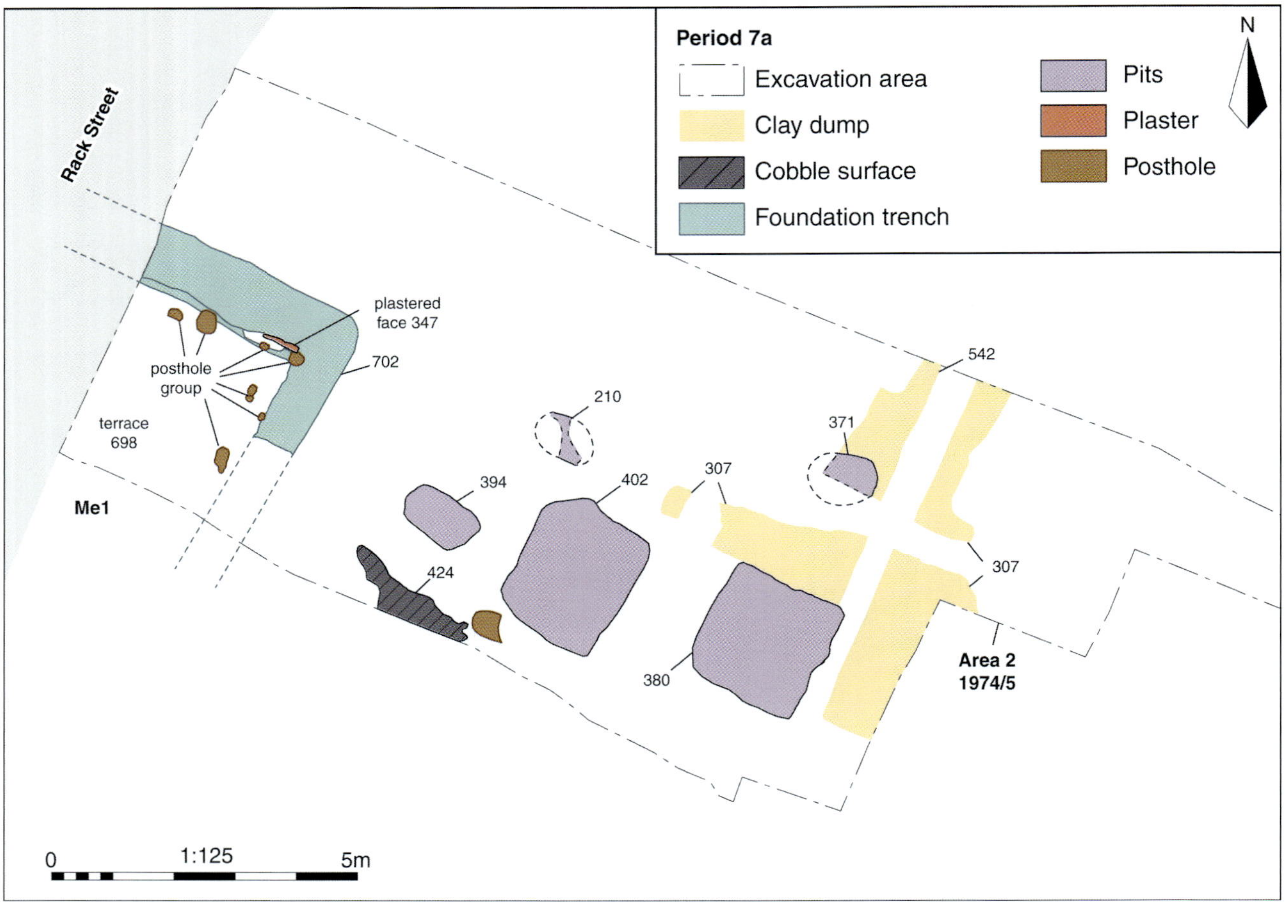

Fig. 8.13 Plan of Period 7a (early 13th century) building Me1

- Refuse pit 380: group with Rouen jug, fabrics 20, 62, including EAR3, no. 877 (*c.* 1170–1250).
- Refuse pit 402: fabrics 20, 60, 62, EAR3, nos. 868–76 (*c.* 1200–50).

*Period 7b: Domestic occupation (*c. *1250–1350)*

Building Me2 was constructed around the mid 13th century (Fig. 8.14). It was built after Me1 had fallen out of use, and it cut a patch of Period 7a clay-bonded cobbling (424) bedded in a clay layer (425, n.i.) which survived near the southern edge of the excavation. Layer 425 contained a local jug sherd, dating the sequence to after *c.* 1250.This structure consisted of three rectangular terraces extending back from the Rack Street frontage, each representing a small room with its long axis at right angles to the street.

The terrace marking the front room (Room 1) had largely been cut away by a small post-medieval cellar, but a compacted floor (369) of clay loam and gravel 0.1 m thick was preserved along its north-eastern and south-eastern sides. This incorporated a small hearth (395), covered with burnt clay and gravel. Behind this lay a second and better-preserved room (Room 2), defined by a terrace 6.4 m long and 3.3 m wide, dug into the slope of the hillside. A passage, indicated by a shallow trench (375), extended the full length of the southern side of the terrace, leaving an unheated room *c.* 1.8 m wide to the north-east. Within this a roughly-laid cobbled surface (401) floored the south-eastern part of the room, and a small patch of clay floor (382) survived in the north-western corner.

Behind Room 2, a further terrace (704) marked a third room cut into the underlying deposit. Rooms 2 and 3 were surrounded by upstands of earlier deposits (350; 354; 358/377; 383), typically *c* 0.8 m wide and standing to a maximum height of *c.* 0.3 m. A thin layer of white plaster (338) survived along the north-eastern face of cut 383. A narrow (50 mm) trench (386) continued the line of the passage seen in Room 2; it was presumably the base of a light screen. A 50 mm-thick layer of brown loam occupation (348, n.i.) overlay the floor. Five broadly sub-circular postpits (404; others 306; 390; 403; 501 all n.i.), 0.5–0.9 m in diameter and 0.4–0.75 m deep, each packed with cobbles, were dug in the area occupied by Me2.

A robbed-out foundation of a small boundary wall (319) *c.* 1.5 m to the north-east of, and parallel to, Me2 probably defined the edge of the tenement plot. The robber trench was 0.72 m wide and 0.45 m deep.

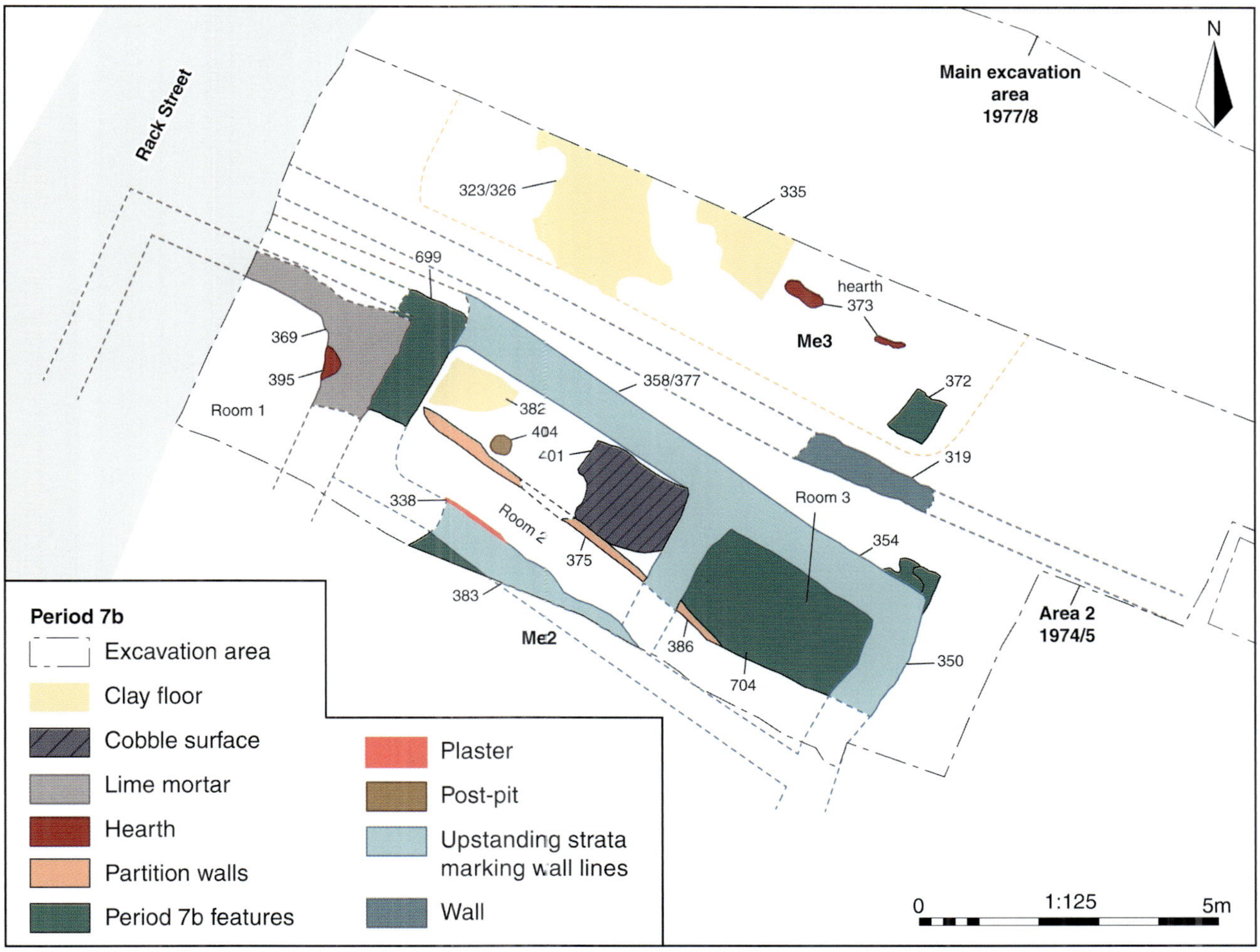

Fig. 8.14 Plan of Period 7b (mid 13th to mid 14th century) buildings Me2 and 3

Building Me3

A 50 mm-thick compacted clay floor (323; 326; 335) and two small patches of hearth (373) laid within a terrace (697, n.i.) represent a badly disturbed building (Me3) 2 m to the north-east of Me2. A clay spread in a separate part of the terrace (372) may have been a further part of the same floor. A thin layer of dark clay with frequent charcoal inclusions and occupation debris (300; 345) overlay the surface of the floor. Although this area was heavily disturbed by subsequent activity, later deposits and features suggest that the structure underwent some renovation. Two deposits of dumped clay (344; 356, n.i.) formed the base for a new compacted clay floor (326, n.i.). Features dug into the surface of the floor included a posthole (332, n.i.), a pit (340, n.i.), two stakeholes (361; 362, n.i.) and a hearth (342, n.i.).

Building Me4

To the north-east of Me3 another structure (Me4) lay close to the edge of 1977/8 main area and extended beyond the excavation area (Fig. 8.15). It was *c.* 7.7 m long and in excess of 2.15 m wide. Although only fragmentary evidence survived in this part of the site, it appears that the building was constructed within terraces (919; 920) cut into the underlying ground surface

Dating evidence

Building Me2

- Wall 358: North French green-glazed; Saintonge *pégau*; fabrics 20, 40 (jug), 42 (jug), 62 (*c.* 1250–1300).
- Partition wall 375: South-East Dorset Sandy Ware, fabric 40/42 (*c.* 1250–1300).
- Wall 377: tripod pitcher sherd (after *c.* 1150).
- Wall 383: fabrics 20, 40 (*c.* 1250–1350).
- Occupation deposit 396: fabrics 20, 62 (after *c.* 1200).
- Occupation deposit 348: Saintonge green-glazed ware; fabrics 20, 40, 42, 62 (*c.* 1250–1300).

Building Me3

- Occupation deposit 300: fabrics 20, 40 (after *c.* 1250).
- Posthole 322 and 332, floor 323: fabric 20 (after *c.* 950).
- Hearth 342: sandy ware; jug (13th century?).

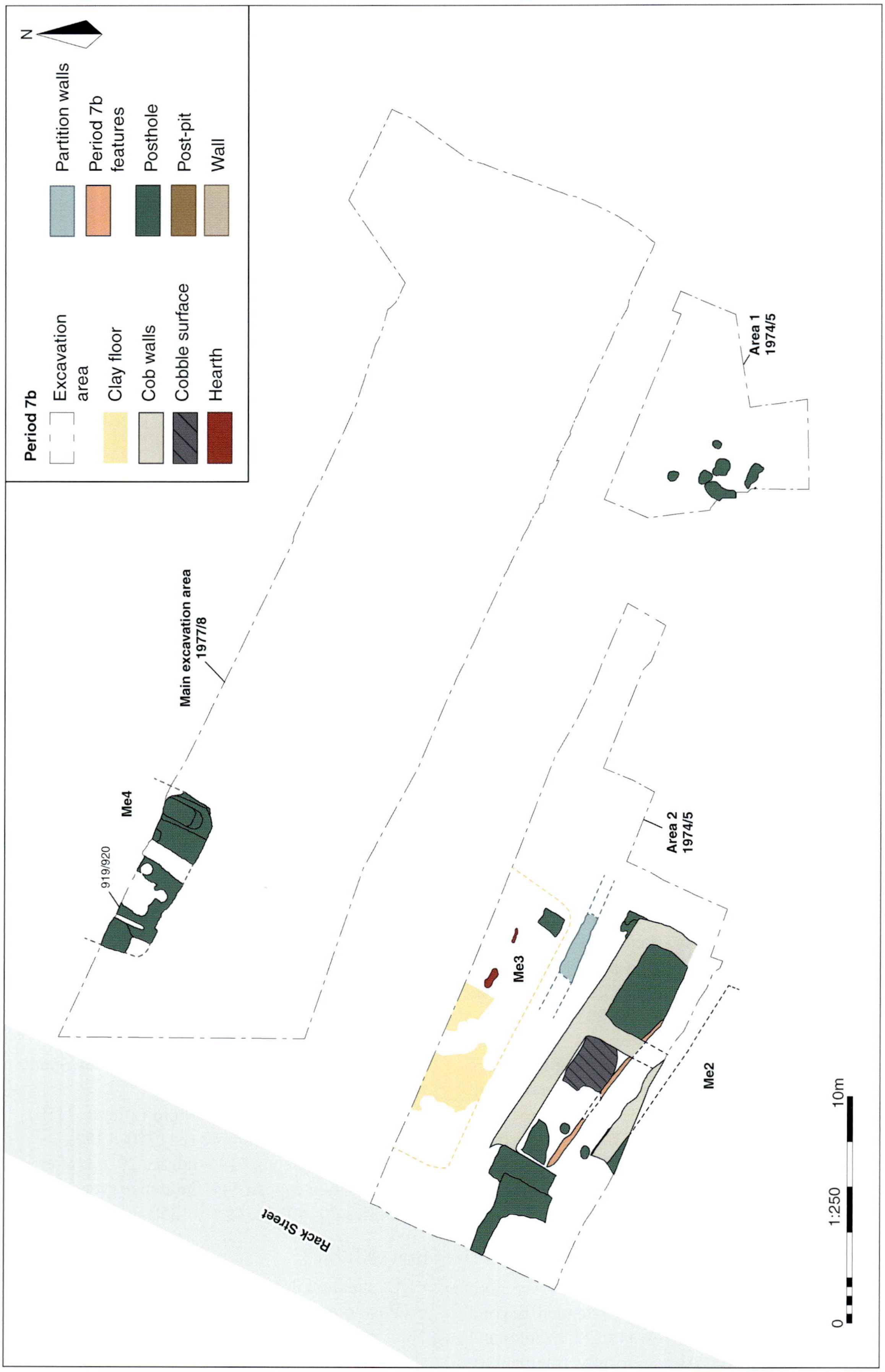

Fig. 8.15 Plan of Period 7b (mid 13th to mid 14th century) buildings Me2, 3 and 4

- Occupation debris 345: fabrics 40, 62 (*c.* 1250–1300).
- Dump 356: fabrics 20, 22, 40 (*c.* 1250–1300).
- Posthole 378: fabric 40 (after *c.* 1250).

PIT

- 902 (903): jug fabrics 40/42 (after *c.* 1250).

Dating evidence from Me2–4 broadly dates to *c.* 1250–1300, although some earlier residual material is present.

Period 8: The later medieval city (*c.* 1350–1550)

By the mid 14th century Buildings Me2–4 had fallen out of use and their terraced footprints infilled by a series of clay loams (198; 220, 305; 331; 333; 364; 384; 784; 797–8; 925 all n.i.).

Building Me5

Later medieval occupation is represented by a single building fragment Me5 in 1974/5 Area 2 (Fig. 8.16). It comprised a trap stone foundation (209), 0.9 m wide, aligned north-west/south-east. The interior of Me5 probably lay to the north-east of the foundation, as to the south-west there were pits and surfaces typical of an external area. A probable robber trench (243) 3 m to the south-west of 209, may define the line of a boundary wall to the building plot. A fragment of a cobbled surface (239) partially overlay the projected line of the robber trench 243, as did pits 216 and 217, both 2.4 m in diameter and at least 1.2 m deep. The pits were filled with brown loams. After Me5 had fallen out of use and the two pits had been backfilled, the area was covered with a series of 0.1–0.2 m-thick dumps of demolition material and refuse (158; 211; 212; 214, all n.i.) containing roofing slate, mortar, animal bone and charcoal.

Features in the back gardens

Scatters of quite substantial postholes were found in 1974/5 Area 1 (33; 43; 49; 83; 84; 130; 131; 132; 255; 277, and 45; 265; 266; 267; 273; 458; 560, all n.i), and in the south-eastern part of the 1977/8 main area (1016; 1018; 1106, and 807; 892; 902; 909; 1049; 1055; 1057; 1061; 1065; 1067; 1069; 1083/1085; 1089; 1095; 1097; 1099; 1100; 1102; 1113; 1124; 1198, all n.i.) (Fig 8.17). There is no obvious patterning in the layout of these features, although we should note that the area had been badly disturbed by later activity. The postholes probably represent several phases of activity and may have been

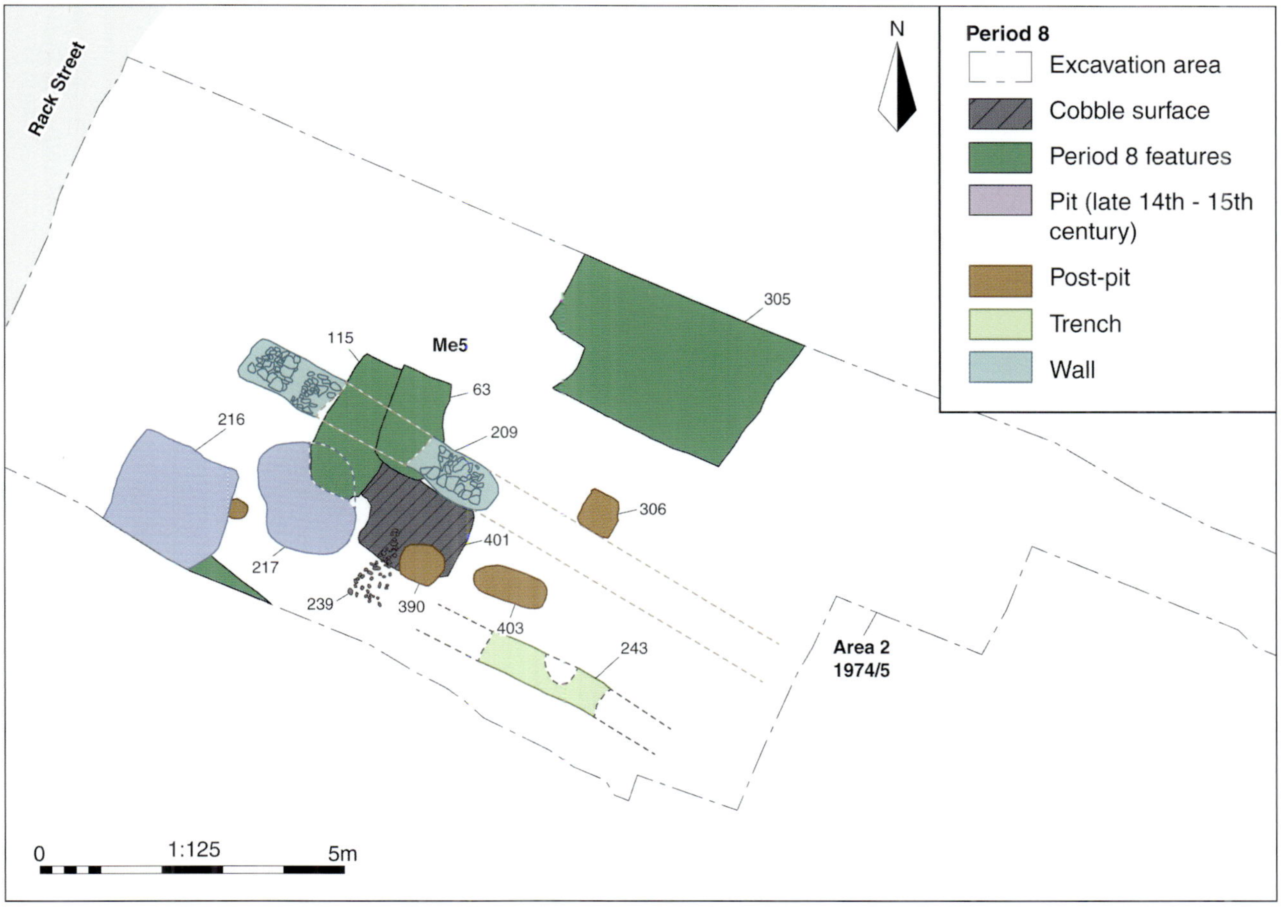

*Fig. 8.16 Plan of Period 8 (*c. *1350–1550) building Me5*

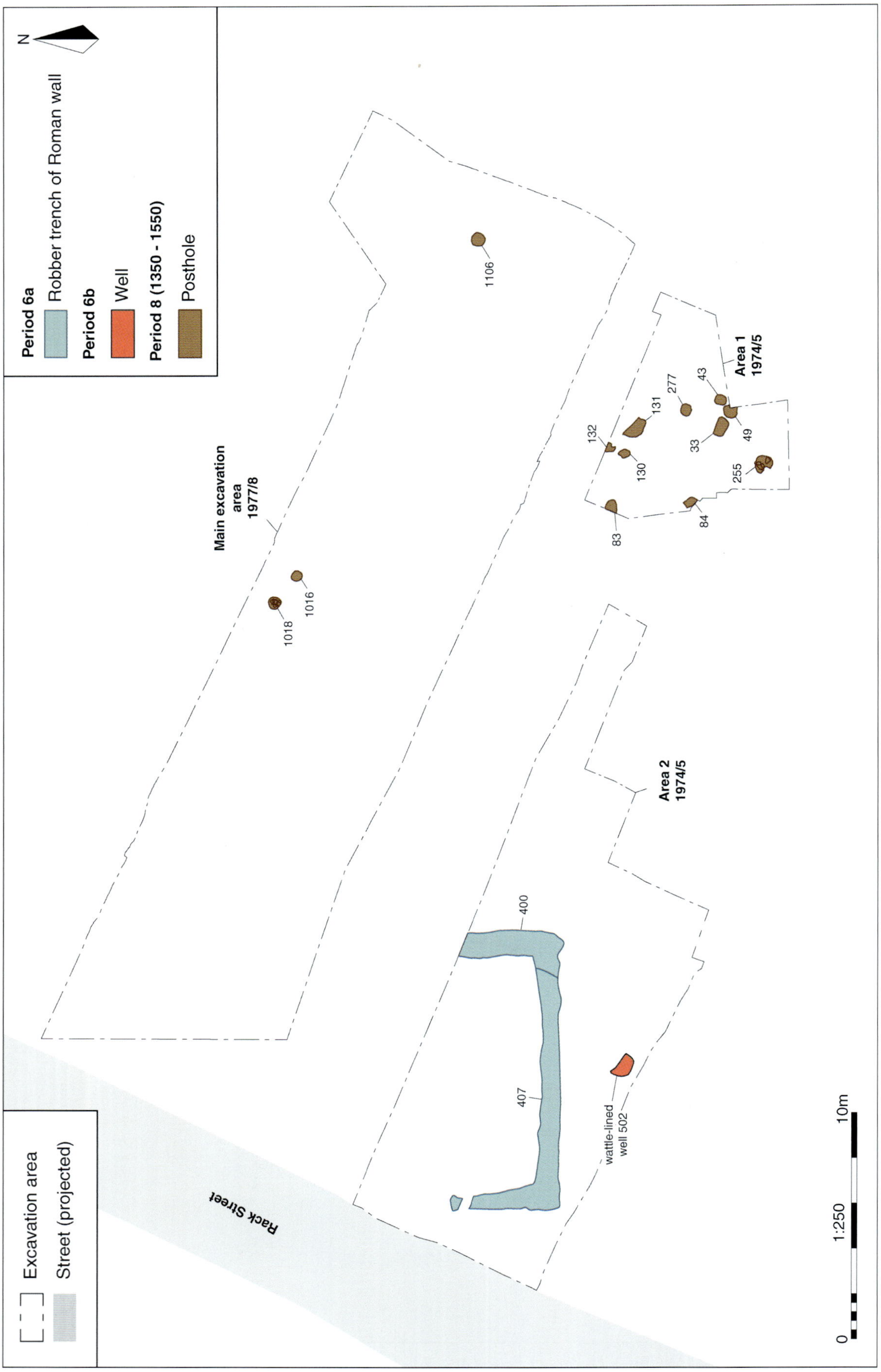

Fig. 8.17 Miscellaneous features of Periods 6, 7 and 8

associated with cloth-drying racks recorded in the documentary evidence for this site from the early 15th century (see below). Dating evidence for the postholes is poor; some post-date *c.* 1250.

Dating evidence

DEMOLITION OF BUILDINGS ME2–4

- Infill 220 of terrace 697: fabrics 20, 40, 42, 62, 63 (*c.* 1250–1350).
- Infill 331 of terrace 703: fabrics 20, 42 (after *c.* 1250).
- Infill 333 of terrace 704: fabrics 40, 42, 43, 62 (14th century).
- Infills 364 and 366 of terrace 700: EAR3, 58–9, nos. 879–87 including Saintonge polychrome of *c.* 1280–1330.
- Dump 797 infilling terrace 919/920: Saintonge green-glazed ware; fabrics 20, 23, 40 (*c.* 1250–1350).
- Dump 784. Saintonge plain ware; Rouen jug; fabrics 20, 40, 42 (*c.* 1250–1350).

Overall, the evidence indicates abandonment in the first half of the 14th century.

BUILDING ME5

- Dump 158: Saintonge green-glazed ware, fabrics 20, 21, 27, 40, 42, 62 (*c.* 1250–1300).
- Dump 211[=248]: Saintonge polychrome and all-over-green; fabrics 20, 40, 42, 62 (1280–1350). Also fragments of a roof louver (EAR3, 227, no. 2945).
- Dump 212: fabrics 20, 23, 27, 62, local jug (*c.* 1250–1300).
- Cobbled surface 239: jug sherd, (after *c.* 1250).
- Pit 216: fabrics 20, 23, 40, 42, 43 (*c.* 1300–1400).
- Pit 217: jug sherd (after *c.* 1250).

POSTHOLES

- 807 (fill 808): jug (after *c.* 1250).
- 892 (fill 893): jug (after *c.* 1250).
- 909 (fill 910): fabrics 20, 27, 40/42 (after *c.* 1250).
- 1049 (fill 1050): Saintonge green-glazed Ware (after *c.* 1250).
- 1089 (fill 1090): fabric 20 (after *c.* 950).
- 1095 (fill 1096): local jug (after *c.* 1250).
- 1102 (fill 1103): fabric 42 (after *c.* 1250).

SCATTERED FEATURES

- Pit 874 (fill 875): Redware jug (after *c.* 1300).
- Pit 941 (fill 942): fabric 20 (?medieval).
- Trench 959 (fill 960): ridge tile (late 13th to 15th century).
- Trench 1442 (fill 1443): Saintonge plain ware, local jug (*c.* 1300–1550).
- Trench 1456 (fill 1457): (14th/15th century).

The dating evidence from the infilled deposits above Me2–4 suggests that these structures had fallen out of use by the mid 14th century. The pottery from Me5 is consistent with a date range in the early to mid 14th century. These features are stratigraphically the latest medieval activity, overlying building Me2, and in turn cut by post-medieval features.

Discussion of the medieval occupation and the documentary evidence relating to the Rack Street excavation sites and their surroundings *by John Allan*

Rack Street lies in the West Quarter of Exeter, a part of the city associated in the Early Modern period and in the recent past with poor housing, overcrowding and great poverty (Hoskins 2004, 16, 110, 113). In the Middle Ages it was called *Tightstrete* (the variants including *Tygttestrete, Tittestrete, Trygestrete, Teyytestrete, Tythestrete*) – a name the editors of *The Place-Names of Devon* found difficult to explain, although they thought it might come from the trade-name *tiler* (Gover *et al.* 1931, 23). The name Rack Lane (commonly spelled Rock Lane or Rock's Lane) seems first to be recorded in the mid 16th century (*ibid.*). As we shall see, cloth-drying racks were established there in the Late Middle Ages, and it is likely that the change of name reflects their introduction.

At least 20 medieval deeds survive for the street, the earliest belong to the 1260s and 1270s. Rather more than half of them clearly relate to the tenements on the north-west side, between Preston Street and Rack Street. In the 18th and 19th centuries that side of the street was more densely occupied than the south-eastern side, as is evident on Coldridge's map of 1819 (Fig. 8.18), and the higher number of medieval deeds may indicate that the same pattern obtained in the Middle Ages. Regarding the south-eastern side, three documents relate to properties close to the City Wall beside Cricklepit Street, showing that this area was occupied by tenements in the late 13th and early 14th centuries (MCR 23–4 Edw. I, m. 16, S&J 0515; MCR 2–3 Edw III, m. 38, S&J 0476), leaving just six which may describe lands on other parts of the south-eastern side, closer to the excavated sites.

These documents give some sense of the character of this part of the city. Several mention gardens, and one a barn (*grangia*) which lay at the back of a property fronting onto Preston Street (D&C 186, S3278). The occupations recorded reflect the fundamental importance of the cloth trade; leaseholders in the street included the fuller John Bolle in 1324 and the dyer Roger Hakeworthy of Exe Island in 1430 (MCR 17–18 Edw II, m. 18, S&J 4283; D&C 186, S&J 3278), but they also mention a fletcher (a maker of arrows) and a pavior (a maker or layer of paving) in 1380–1 (D&C 269–70, S&J 3517, 3520). There are also occasional references to the character of buildings. All four of the Exeter deeds noted by the writer

Fig. 8.18 Extract from Coldridge's map of 1819 (photo: Tony Collings; © Devon Heritage Centre)

which mention thatched houses refer to properties in this part of the city, and all date to the period 1260–1300. For example, in 1262 Alice Uppahille granted to Adam of Kennford a straw-thatched house close to St Mary Steps church, with permission to bring in ladders to thatch or repair it and to draw off rainwater from it, the rent being a pair of white gloves or the payment of 1d and 3d to Exe Bridge (VC 3004, S&J 0472; see also VC 3015, S&J 0007; ED/M/177, S&J 0497; ED/M/186, S&J 0500).

Some of the Rack Street tenements owned by institutions can be identified. The Dean and Chapter of the cathedral had two tenements at the north-eastern end of the street, where Rack Lane turned north-west to join Preston Street, which they held until the 1860s (D&C 123,046), and the Vicars Choral had three messuages with three cellars projecting into the street on its north-west side (D&C 123,046). The City Chamber also held three properties there; one of them had been owned prior to the Reformation by St John's Hospital. It consisted of a pair of tenements on the south side of Rack Street, known jointly in the 15th century as 'the Ottery tenement' (*tenementum Otyry* – perhaps named after an early tenant).

The late Harold Fox has researched the history of these last two properties, tracing their tenurial history over a period of 700 years (Fox 1986). He showed that this was 'our tenement on the south side of Teyghtstrete', given by the wealthy citizens Gilbert and John Long to St John's Hospital in 1224 × 1235 (for the date of the gift see Orme and Webster 1995, 233). By 1284, when it was leased by Philip of Zelebregge, it formed one of at least three adjacent holdings, with two further properties to the rear. Later, perhaps *c.* 1300, it was divided into two tenements, held by John and Geoffrey Tyghttere; as Fox points out, this was an example of the process of splitting up properties at a time of growing population to accommodate two co-heirs (Fox 1986, 167). The St John's Cartulary, written *c.* 1420, records the subsequent downfall (*casum*) of the houses, whose probable cause was the Black Death. References

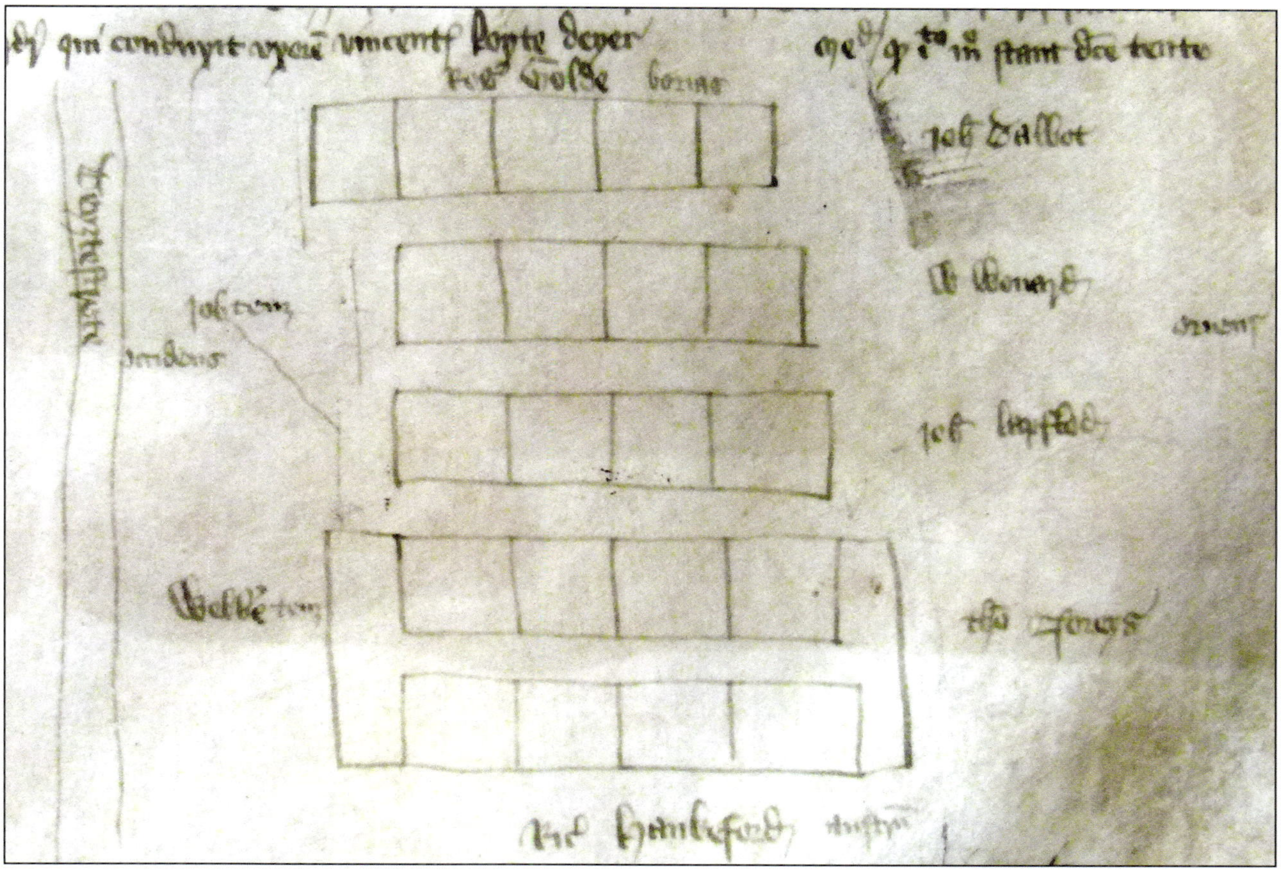

Fig. 8.19 Map in the St John's Cartulary, c. *1420, showing five racks, with the names of their owners to the right and Rack Street to the left (photo: Todd Gray; © Devon Heritage Centre)*

to vacant properties, mentioned in other late 14th-century deeds relating to this area, may have the same explanation (*e.g.* ED/M/503, S&J 3499 dated 1384, which describes the lease of a vacant property between Preston Street and Rack Street; the neighbouring property was also vacant).

The cartulary states that after the downfall of the houses the plot was divided into four equal selions of land, on each of which tenter-frames (racks for drying cloth) were built (Fox 1986, 166). Most unusually, the document includes a plan or view of these structures, annotated to the right with the names of the occupiers of the racks at the time of writing (Fig. 8.19). From top to bottom they were John Talbot, W. Wonard, John Lapflod and Thomas Noreys, with Richard Haukeford below the double rack at the foot. The first two at least were wealthy citizens: John Talbot had served as mayor, William Wonard [*alias* Wynard] held property in High Street (MCR 5–6 Hen V, m. 37d) and founded the almshouses which still bear his name in Magdalene Street. Tenter frames of the same sort were a common sight in post-medieval Exeter (Fig. 8.20a) and were still in use elsewhere in Britain in the 20th century (Fig. 8.20b)

Following the dissolution of monastic houses, which included hospitals such as St John's, the property was acquired in 1555 by the City Chamber. Fox has traced its later history through rentals and surveys of Chamber lands, showing that the city retained ownership until 1842. In the 1550s the leases on the racks were still being taken out by prominent Exeter people but by 1611 the site was described as a garden, and in 1671 'one garden, sometyme 4 sulions' – the four strips shown on the medieval map. The first post-medieval reference to a building on the site was in 1691, when the property was described as a house. This, or its successor, was pulled down in the 1930s (Fox 1986, 166).

Precisely where was this holding? The Map Book of the Chamber of the City of 1756–60 is a key source in this regard. It records only one city property on the south-east side of Rack Street (Fig. 8.21(a); ECA 5/3/37, Map 10, property 21; Ravenhill and Rowe 2000, 187); it was not planned in detail but its frontage is indicated by a number, showing that it was not then in the ownership of the city but that they charged a chief rent. The position of this property on the 1876 map is shown in Fig. 8.21(b). It will be apparent that the site includes the area excavated in 1977, whilst the sites excavated in1975 lay in the adjacent property to the south-west.

The archaeological evidence adds a number of points to Fox's account. First, it provides information about the period prior to the survival of documentary evidence.

a

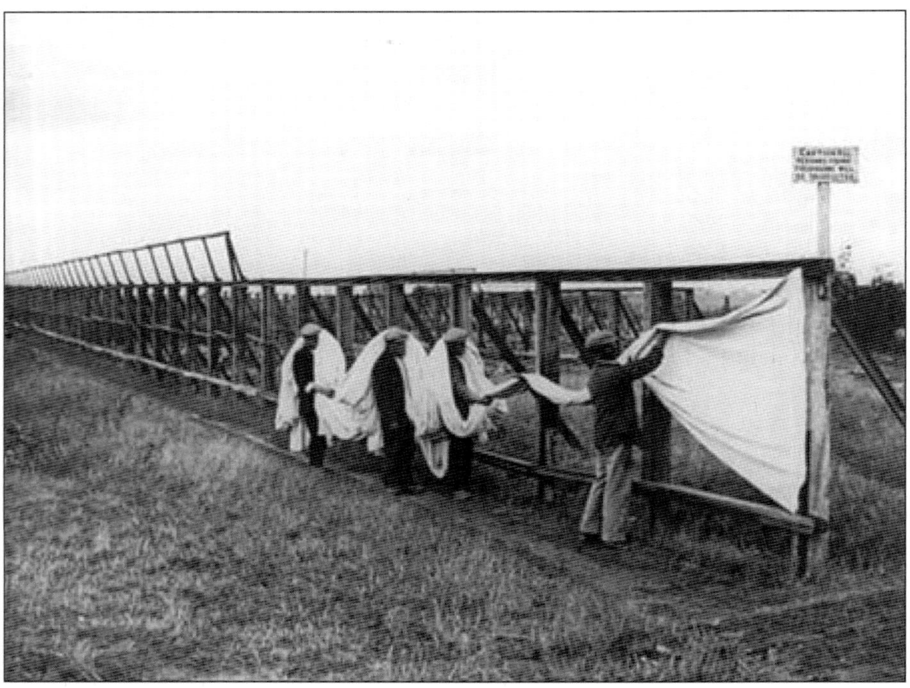

b

Fig. 8.20 (a) Tenter frames on the floodplain of the River Exe, c. *1770 (© Bodleian Library, Gough Maps 5, fol. 3B, Exeter,* c. *1772). (b) Tuckers taking down a stockfull of fabric from the Witney Blanket Mill's tenter frames in the early 20th century (courtesy of the Witney Blanket Story)*

Although small amounts of Late Saxon pottery were present in the robber trenches of the site's Late Roman town houses, no Late Saxon pits were found here, and only limited evidence of 12th-century occupation. Hardly any other Late Saxon pottery was found in the nearby excavations in Mermaid Yard, and there too only a few 12th-century pits were found. Our impression, then, is that this steeply-sloping part of Exeter was thinly inhabited in the Saxo-Norman period. This impression is reinforced by a consideration of the locations of the city's 30 or so early chapels; none were in this quarter, and the fact that this part of the walled area became an outlying part of the

a

b

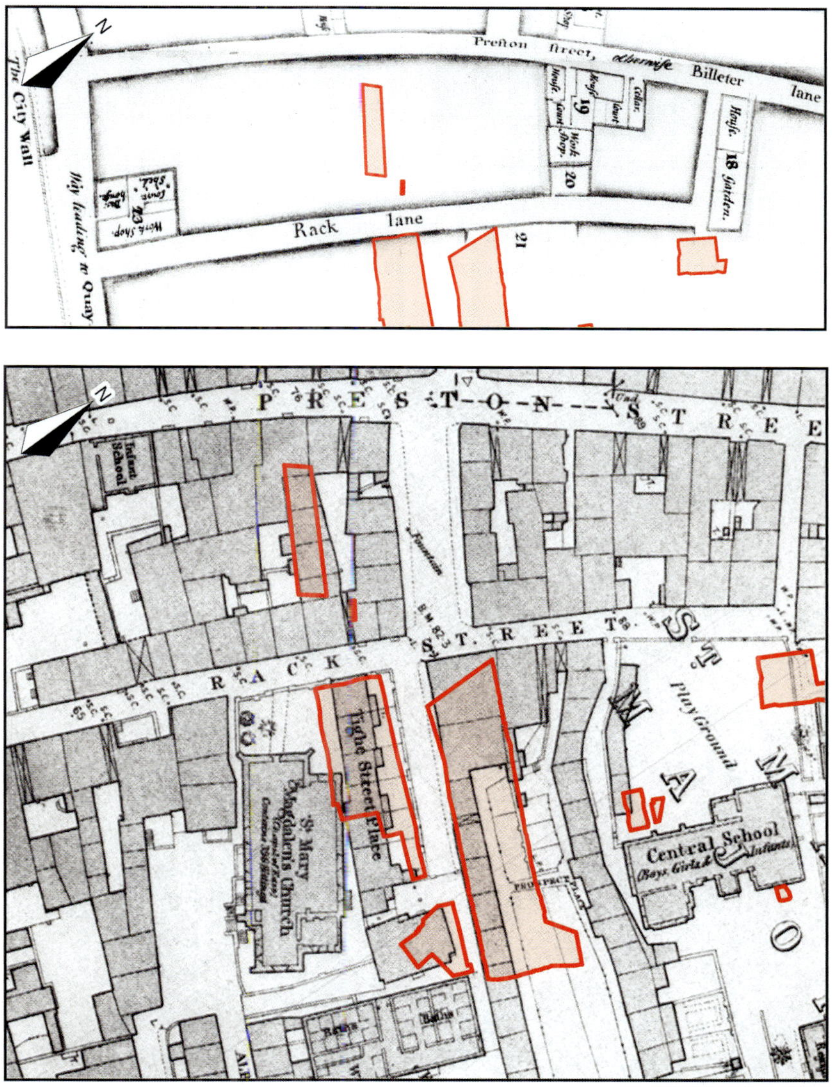

Fig. 8.21 (a) Extract from the Map Book of the Chamber of the City, Map 10, showing city properties in Rack Street (photo: Gary Young, © Devon Heritage Centre. (b) Extract from the Ordnance Survey 1:500 map of 1876, with the outlines of the excavations of 1975 and 1977 (© Devon and Exeter Institution)

parish of Mary Major has been interpreted as evidence that it was the rump of the old minster parish after the process of chapel creation came to an end (Allan *et al.* 1984, 399–400)

The evidence for occupation becomes more plentiful from the early 13th century, when a room (Me1) was built on the frontage. It is likely that this is just the corner of a larger structure on the street frontage. The building which replaced Me1 in the late 13th century (Me2) is of greater interest, since much more of its plan can be discerned. It is interpreted as a building 5 m wide and in excess of 12 m long, consisting of three rooms, all dug into the slope of the hill, with their long axis at right angles to the street. The room on the frontage was apparently heated and was plastered at the feet of the walls; each of the two rooms behind were unheated and had a narrow passage running along their south-western wall. No direct evidence survived for the form of their walls, and at the time of excavation it was suggested that they would have been of cob. One piece of evidence suggests a different interpretation: the backfilling of the room terraces contained slates and ridge tiles, and (more unexpectedly) substantial fragments of a quite elaborate ceramic roof louver. This last find would have been used with a slate rather than a thatch roof. Since cob buildings were normally thatched, whilst stone-walled buildings usually had slate roofs (Cox and Thorp 2001, 85–6, 124, where the occasional use of slate verges on thatched roofs is, however, noted), this seems significant evidence of stone building. Although very fragmentary, the other building remains add to the impression that late 13th or 14th-century buildings of similar character occupied the adjacent site to the north-east. This area, excavated in 1977, was part of the pair of properties studied by Fox, which were owned by St John's Hospital and abandoned after the calamity of the Black Death. The numerous late medieval postholes found in the 1977 excavation are therefore likely to represent the most southerly of the four rows of racks shown on the 15th-century map. It is probable that the many similar holes in Area 1 of 1975/6 represent further tenter frames behind the houses on the adjacent plot.

The plot owned by St John's Hospital remained a rack field at least as late as the 1550s, becoming a garden by the early 17th century, and was built on only in the late 17th century. The archaeological evidence fits this picture well: there are hardly any 16th or early 17th-century finds (about 15 sherds) from the site but a series of deposits including pit groups containing much domestic rubbish spanning the period of *c.* 1690–1800 (including RS 703, *c.* 1690–1720; RS 1420, *c.* 1760: EAR3, 204, 214).

The same evidence for the abandonment of houses around the mid 14th century was also found in the plot excavated in 1975/6, and the rear of this tenement also showed the clusters of postholes which probably represent late medieval cloth racks. Domestic occupation had evidently resumed on this site by the early 16th century, however, as pits of this date were found in the rear of the property. They included two interesting pit groups, the first (RS 36) containing stonewares from Raeren, Langewehe, Cologne and Beauvais (EAR3, 158–9, nos. 1705–10), the second (RS 115) a decorated drinking jug from Beauvais and a rare tin-glazed dish from Seville (EAR3, 165–6, nos. 1821–2). They provide clear evidence that a wide range of imported goods was to be seen, even in the poorer households of Tudor Exeter.

9

The Faunal Remains from Exeter, 1976–1990

Malene Lauritsen

Introduction

Exeter saw one of the seminal early studies of faunal remains from an urban settlement in Britain (Maltby 1979), but such was the pace of excavation within the city that many of the assemblages recovered over the following 15 years remained unpublished. This chapter summarises a more detailed study (Lauritsen 2019) of the animal bones from ten sites in Exeter excavated between 1976 and 1990, and covers material dating from the Roman, medieval and post-medieval periods (up until the 18th century). The findings confirm the results of previous studies of faunal material from the city – most notably Mark Maltby's (1979) analysis of the animal bones from excavations carried out between 1917 and 1975, and Bruce Levitan's (1987; 1989) study of selected medieval sites – while a new understanding has been gained of butchery practices and, most notably, fracture patterns that result from the extraction of bone marrow as well as spatial variation in patterns of animal product consumption within higher and lower-status areas, and between secular and monastic communities. A total of 40,066 bones were examined with 12,725 identified to species level. Of these 3,331 were from Roman contexts, 5,718 from medieval contexts, and 2,796 from post-medieval contexts (with a small number of the identifiable specimens from undated contexts). Almost all specimens were hand collected though a couple of contexts were wet sieved. The primary focus of this study has been on cattle, caprines (sheep/goat) and pigs while other species, such as game, have been used to draw further interpretations about the social contexts of the material. Site Numbers refer to Chapter 2 in this volume.

Methods

Recording methodology

The choice of methods was primarily guided by those used in the previous analyses of Exeter material as well as other studies of English urban faunal assemblages (Maltby 1979; Levitan 1989; Dobney *et al.* 1995; Bond and O'Connor 1999; Coles forthcoming a; b). All the mammal and bird bones were recorded in Microsoft Access and later transferred to Microsoft Excel for data analysis. Fish bones were only recorded as total numbers for each assemblage. Each specimen was listed in an Access database with the following detail: provenance of the bone; species; element; zone (Dobney and Rielly 1988); side; fusion; butchery; modification (burning, gnawing, root etching, acid damage); fracture type (Outram 2002); Fracture Freshness Index (FFI) score (Outram 2002); fracture history profile (Johnson *et al.* 2016); dental age; sex; weathering score (McKinley 2004); pathology; metrics; and other relevant notes such as photographs or observations that did not fit in any of the other database categories. Horncore bases were counted when more than 50% complete and only the articular ends of ribs were recorded. Vertebra and rib fragments were identified to medium or large mammal size as this was useful for the study of butchery, though all other specimens that could not be identified to a specific species were included in the category 'unidentifiable'. The 'minimal number of animal units' (MAU) were calculated for the main domesticates to take fragmentation and variations in the number of elements in skeletons into account (*e.g.* Crabtree 1990). The MAU was obtained using Binford's (1984) method, siding of individual elements, and Dobney and Rielly's (1988) zones to ensure the most accurate number. Similarly, assessment of skeletal part abundances was used here to determine the frequencies of individual portions of the animals to aid our understanding of issues such as dietary habits, activity areas in the city, and site status. The skeletal part abundances were achieved by using zone MAU specific to proximal and distal ends and shafts (Lauritsen 2019). All references to proportions and

Table 9.1 List of phases with their corresponding time periods and date ranges

Phase code	*Phase name*	*Date range*
1	Roman Military	55–75
2	Roman Civil	75–300
3	End of Roman to post-Roman	300–670
4	Early medieval	670–900
5	Saxo-Norman 1	900–1050
6	Saxo-Norman 2	1050–1150
7	High Medieval	1150–1300
8	Late Medieval	1300–1500
9	Post-medieval 1	1500–1650
10	Post-medieval 2	1650–1800
R	Undated Roman	
M	Undated medieval	
UdPM	Undated post-medieval	

frequencies of domesticates were based on MAU rather than 'minimum number of individuals' (MNI). Fusion data for age-at-death analysis were obtained for cattle, caprines and pigs using Silver (1969). Measurements were taken following guidelines set out by von den Driesch (1976) and analysed using Meadow's (1999) log-ratio method. The figures presented in this chapter are of breadth measurements; increases in the mean values indicate greater measurements from the given phase, and smaller mean values indicate lesser measurements suggesting smaller animals. The log-ratio standards are presented in Lauritsen (2019). Additionally, fracture analysis was undertaken using Johnson *et al.* (2016) and Outram (2001) to assess the frequency of marrow fracturing.

Phasing

The phasing system used in this study is presented in Table 9.1. There is, at present, no data from Phase 4 (early medieval) as there is very little evidence for occupation within Exeter between the early 5th and late 9th centuries (see EAPIT 1, Chapter 7).

Site groupings

The data from each individual excavation were combined in a series of period-based groups in order to gain an understanding of how the different phases and areas ('quarters') of Exeter compare (Table 9.2). The groups are described below and the quarters as used in this study are marked on Fig. 9.1.

Roman military: all assemblages associated with the Roman legionary fortress were analysed as one group.

Roman Civil: all assemblages associated with the civilian town were considered as one group as the majority of the faunal material examined in this study was recovered from the infilling of the Roman town ditch in the late 2nd century AD (which means that we do not know where in the town or with which buildings it was originally associated). The vast majority of the faunal material was excavated from Mermaid Yard (MY) and Friernhay Street (FH).

Medieval and post-medieval period: as a general rule, sites from these periods were grouped together based on their location in the four quarters of the city and their immediate extra-mural areas (Fig. 9.1), although there are some exceptions noted below:

- The North Quarter site group includes the material from Paul Street (PS) and Queen Street (QS) and is an area considered to have been of relatively high status based on its close proximity to the castle, street names, and other evidence from the archaeological investigations (Exeter City Council 1984).
- The East Quarter did not produce any medieval or post-medieval assemblages analysed as part of this project, although the Princesshay excavations (Coles forthcoming b) have produced material.
- In the South Quarter only Mermaid Yard (MY) has material from these periods, although it should be noted that this single site may not be representative of the whole district.
- The West Quarter group contains the data from Bartholomew Street East (BSE), Bartholomew Street West (BSW) and Friernhay Street (FH). The Phases 6 and 7 (1050–1300) assemblages from BSE and BSW were from within monastic precincts, while FH is regarded as having been of high status from Phase 8 (*c.* 1300–1500) onwards (Exeter City Council 1974; 1981).

Extra-mural areas: faunal material from two sites, Acorn Roundabout (AC) and Good Shepherd (GSH), were analysed and are included in this study as comparative sites for the relevant phases.

The Roman fortress and town

Major domesticates

On the sites examined in this study there is some evidence of differences in meat consumption between Exeter's Roman military phase (Phase 1) and the civilian town (Phase 2) (Fig. 9.2). In terms of the proportions of species by MAU based on this study alone, cattle were present in greater numbers in the Roman period than in any of the following phases, with their greatest frequency being during the Roman town (Phase 2) (Fig. 9.2) which is consistent with trends across Roman Britain (King 1999, tab. 3; Rippon 2012, 263). As cattle increased in frequency from Phase 1 to Phase 2, pigs decreased in numbers, while the proportion of caprines remained the same throughout these two Roman phases. Based on metrical analysis undertaken for this study (Figs 9.5–9.7), there is no evidence for the development or import of new 'breeds' during this period. There are also some shifts in what portions of the animals

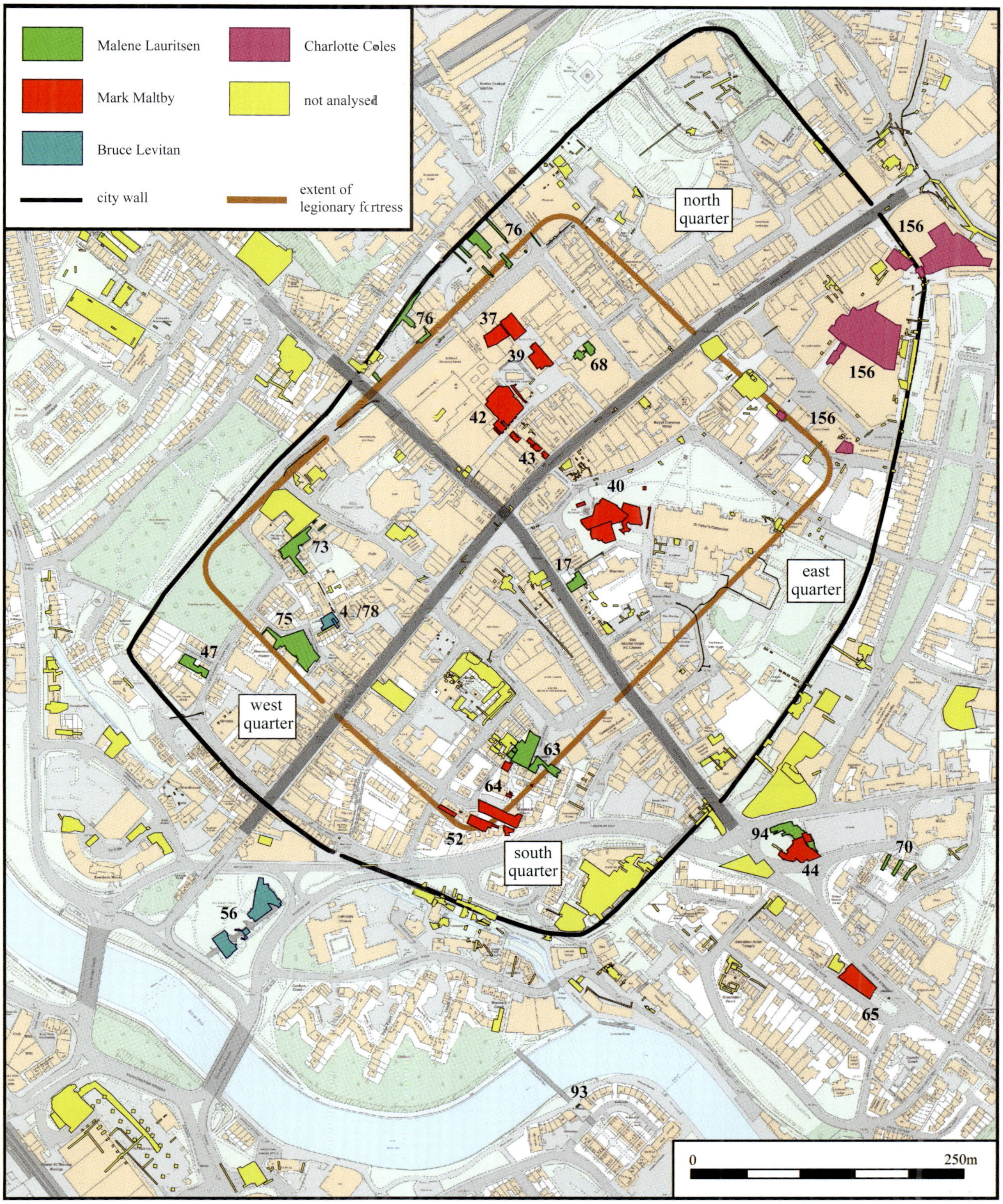

Fig. 9.1 Map of Exeter showing the Roman legionary fortress, the Roman and medieval city wall, and the four 'quarters' as used in this study. Highlighted areas represent excavations, with the colours reflecting who has studied the faunal remains (drawn by David Gould)

were favoured, with cattle shoulders being particularly numerous in Phase 2 even though they are not found in Phase 1. Cattle and caprines were equally exploited for marrow extraction during the military phase, though more data are needed to understand the use of marrow at that time (Fig. 9.3). In the Roman town (Phase 2), as cattle increased as a proportion of the overall livestock they became the primary species exploited for marrow, while equal proportions of caprine and pig bones were broken for marrow. While the proportions and preferred portions

Table 9.2 Assemblage overview with site code, site numbers on Fig. 9.1 (and see Chapter 2), presence of faunal material by phase, and total NISP by site

Site Code	*AC (94)*	*BSE (73)*	*BSW (47)*	*EDST (206)*	*FH (75)*	*GSH (70)*	*HB (93)*	*MY (63)*	*PS (76)*	*QS (68)*
Quarter	*n/a*	*West*	*West*	*East*	*West*	*n/a*	*n/a*	*South*	*North*	*North*
Phase										
1		X			X			X	X	X
2			X		X			X	X	X
3			X					X	X	X
5	X								X	X
6	X	X			X			X	X	X
7	X	X	X		X			X	X	X
8	X	X	X		X			X	X	X
9		X			X	X		X	X	X
10		X	X		X		X	X	X	
R		X	X	X	X			X	X	X
M		X	X					X	X	X
PM		X			X			X	X	X
NISP	253	1424	209	102	2308	92	147	1866	2304	4020

AC	Acorn Roundabout
BSE	Bartholomew Street East
BSW	Bartholomew Street West
EDST	The Deanery
FH	Friernhay Street
GSH	Good Shepherd Hospital
HB	Haven Banks
MY	Mermaid Yard
PS	Paul Street
QS	Queen Street

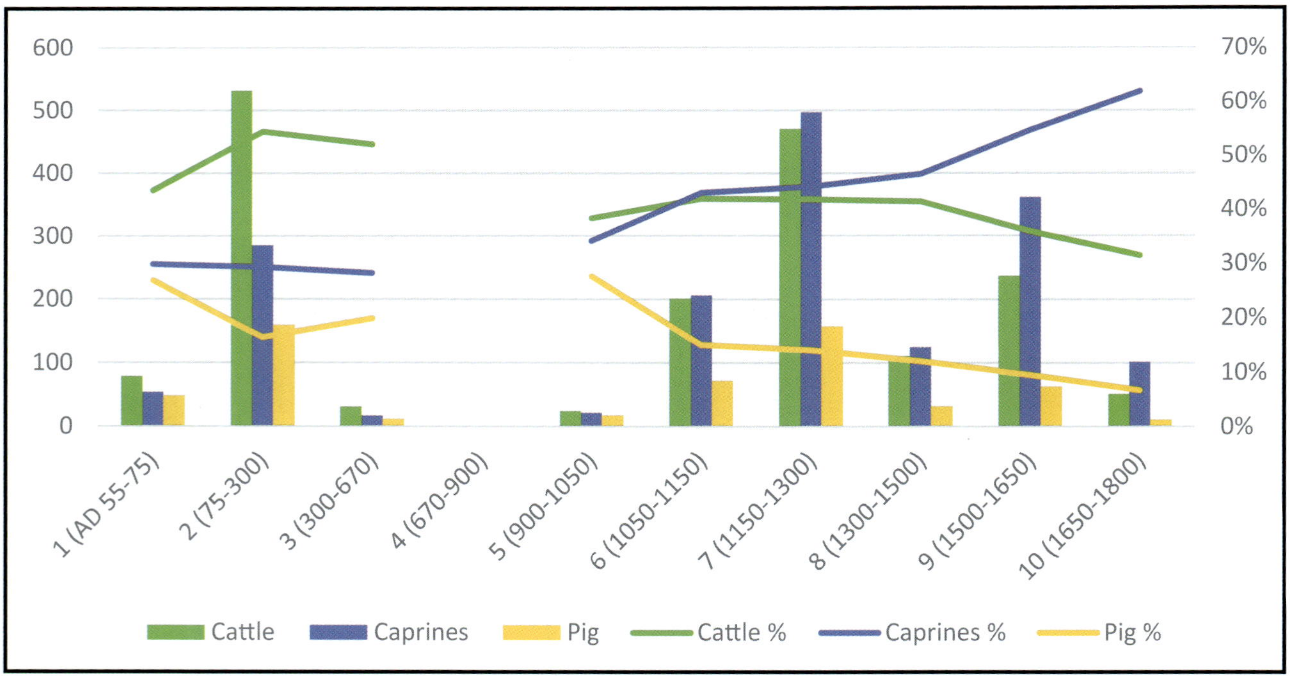

Fig. 9.2 Overview of MAU of major livestock species by absolute numbers and percent

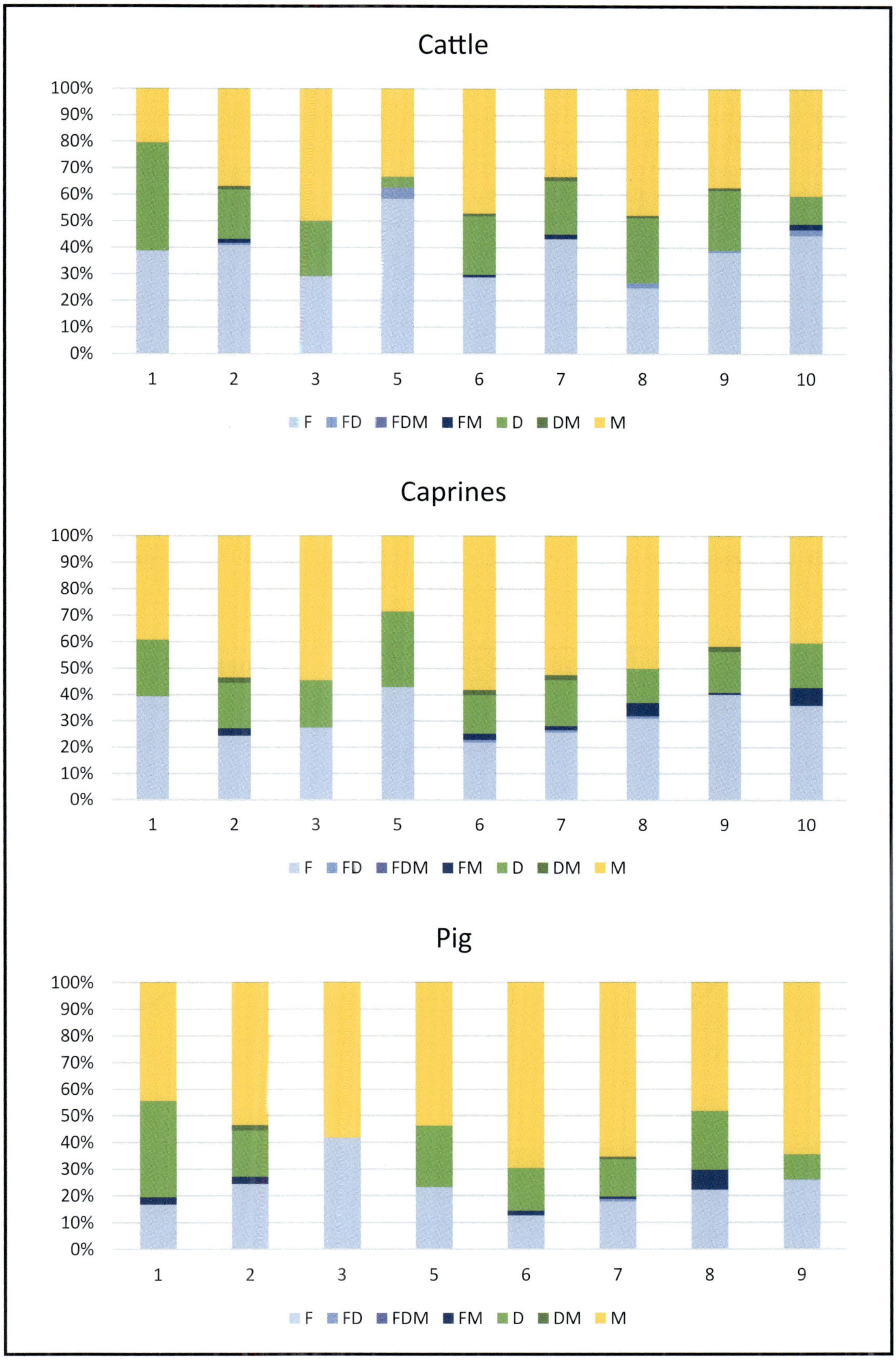

Fig. 9.3 Overview of fracture history profiles for cattle, caprines, and pig. X-axis: phase (phase 10 for pig has too little data to be included here). F: fresh fracture; FD: fresh + dry fracture; FDM: fresh + dry + mineralised fracture; D: dry fracture; DM: dry + mineralised fracture; M: mineralised fracture

and parts of these species changed, the herd management styles remained unaffected by the shifts in the popularity of cattle, caprines and pig. Similarly, procurement of the animals appears to be the same across all time periods with all animals being transported to Exeter 'on the hoof', although some or all pigs may have been reared in town, based on the representation of all skeletal elements (Lauritsen 2019, chap. 5) which was also noted by Maltby (1979). Before being slaughtered for meat, all cattle were used as working animals and kept into full adulthood while pigs were reared specifically for meat and the caprines consumed were the product of more mixed management strategies (Fig. 9.4). All major livestock were butchered in a very systematic manner consistent with trends across the Roman Empire, and particularly noteworthy are two sagittally split vertebrae from Phase 2 (Roman town): these are an unusual find in Roman Britain which provides good evidence of the presence of professional butchers in this phase of Exeter's history.

For the military material, the consistency with other Roman military sites in Britain reflects a highly organised approach towards the supply of provisions. According to Tacitus, each Roman fort was provided with enough supplies to last a full year and the basic diet during peacetime would consist of these grains, bacon and cheese probably alongside vegetables (Tacitus, *Agricola* 22,2). This diet could be supplemented in various ways such as purchasing goods from shops, gifts from family, or by hunting, the latter of which is well documented in the archaeological record (Davies 1971, tab. 1). The faunal remains from Exeter, along with a range of other studies, have also highlighted just how far from the supposed basic military diet the reality was. While pork was indeed consumed in a greater quantity in the military phase than at any other time apart from Phase 5 (900–1050), and the shift from legionary fortress to civilian town did see a drop in the significance of pig in Exeter, it was far from the main source of meat and other animal products (Figs 9.2 and 9.3).

Game consumption

As indicated by documentary evidence, the Roman military diet was supplemented with game species and in Exeter's legionary fortress 5% of all specimens are from

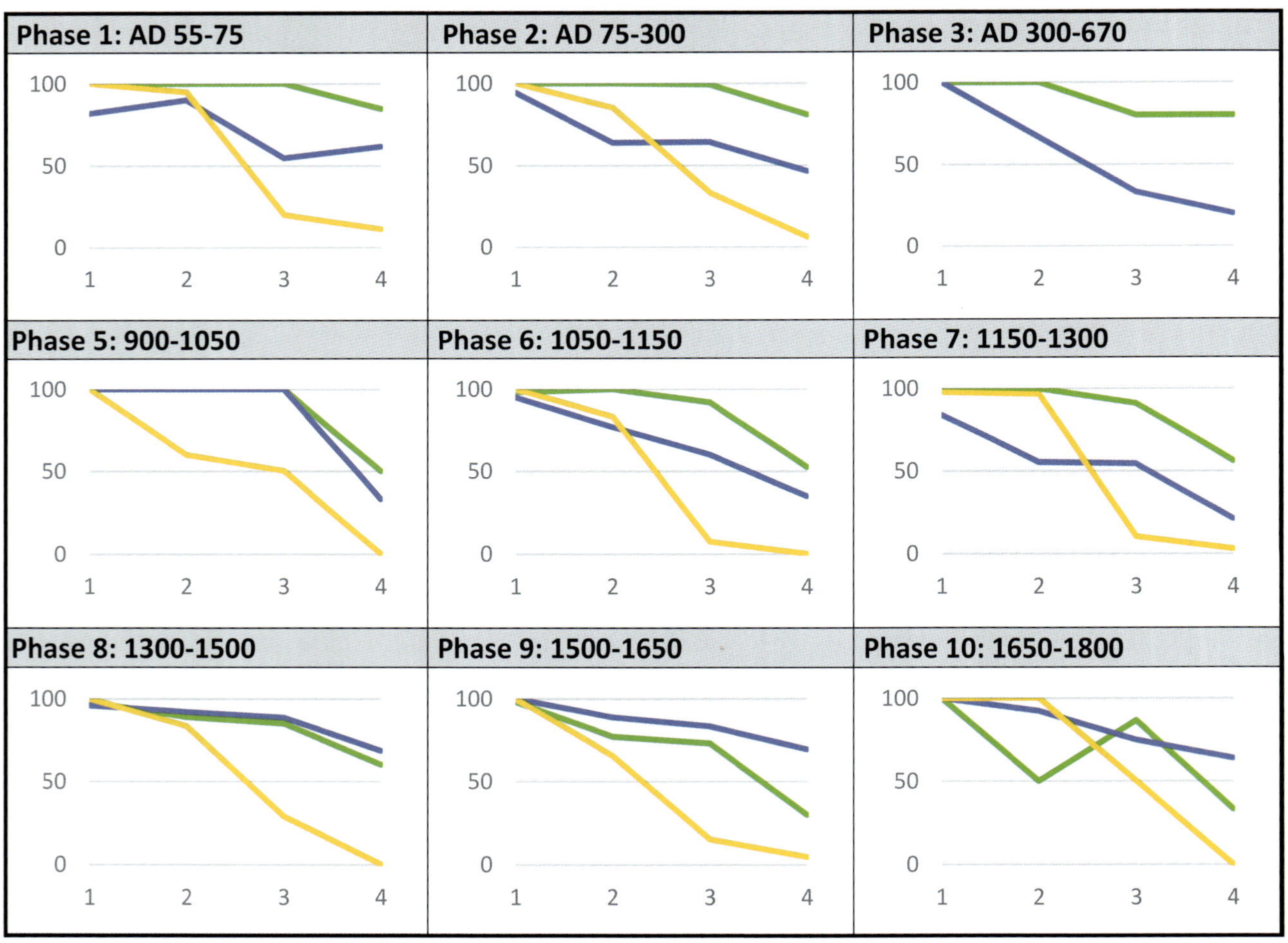

Fig. 9.4 Overview of age profiles. X-axis – fusion stage: 1: neonatal; 2: juvenile; 3: young adult; 4: adult. Y-axis – percent survival. Green: cattle; blue: caprine; yellow: pig

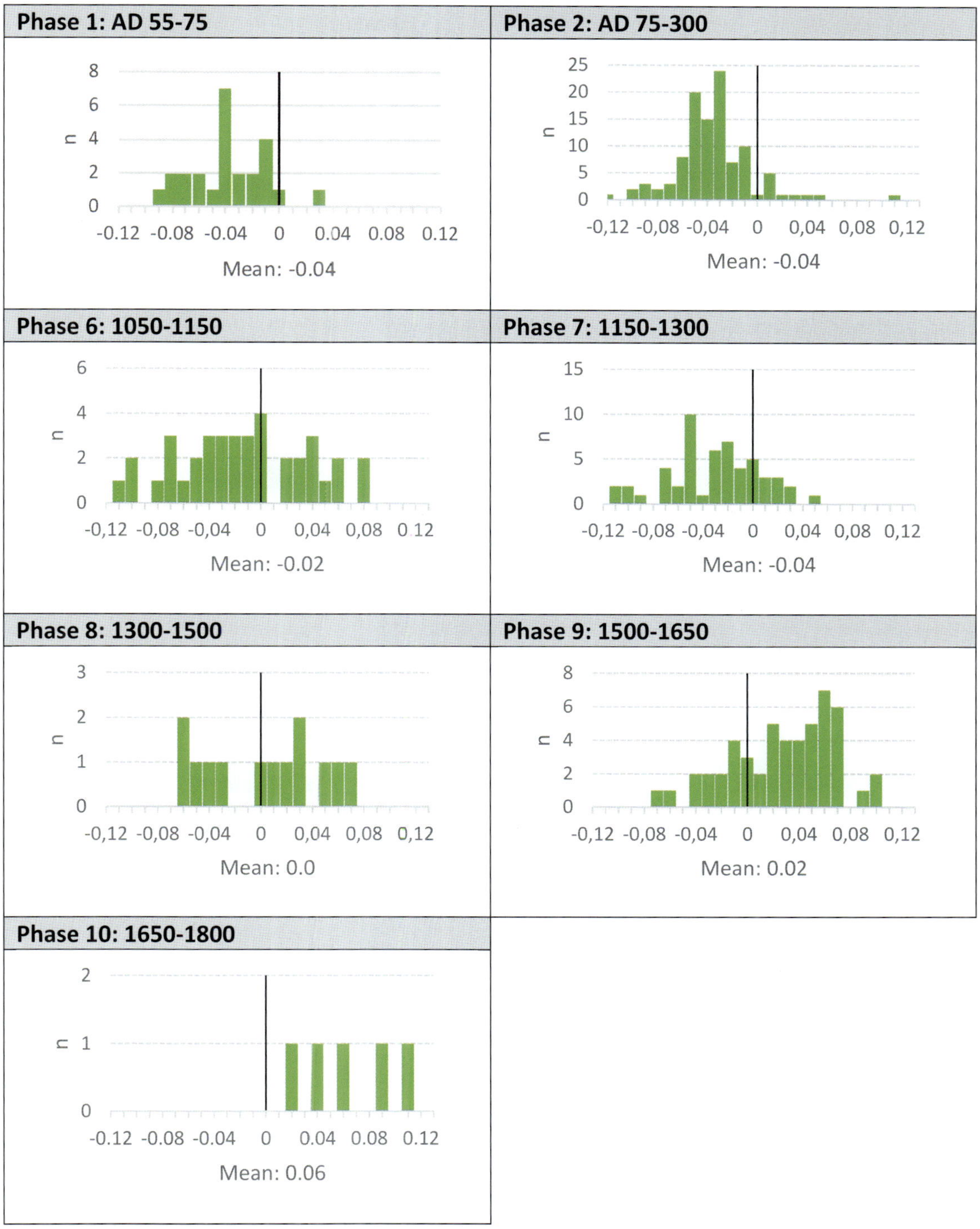

Fig. 9.5 Overview of cattle log-ratios

game, which is much greater than in any later phase. The number of game species increases from three in Phase 1 to eight in Phase 2 (Table 9.3), with the species represented showing more diverse hunting strategies, and the presence of waterfowl suggesting that the wetlands around the Exe Estuary were being exploited. There are some indications that deer, and probably hare and wild boar, hunting was linked to high-status Roman society (Maltby 2014), and all of these species have been identified in Exeter, although the wild boar identification is only a probable one (Maltby 1979). It should be noted that the deposits analysed for this study had not been sieved, and so the absence of small animals like passerines is to be expected, meaning that the full extent of hunting in the Roman or any of the later periods will remain unknown; we can only say for certain that they were, as a minimum, hunting large mammals. The proportion of game specimens in the assemblages studied here decreased from 5% in the Roman military

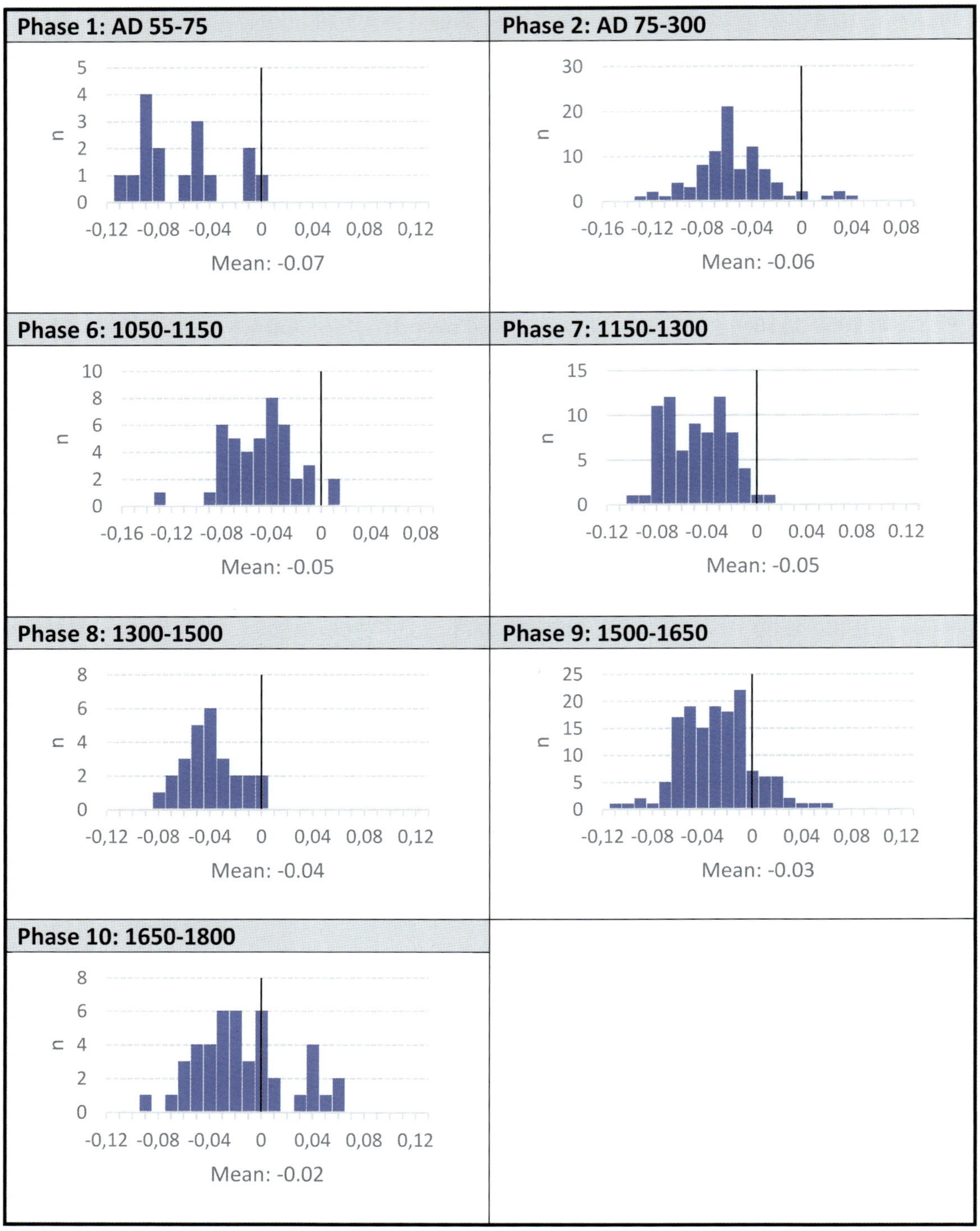

Fig. 9.6 Overview of caprine log-ratios

period to 1% in the civil phase. This probably reflects the relatively low status of urban populations at this time and their lack of access to the countryside resources.

Late Roman town

In the Late Roman town (Phase 3) there was only a small amount of new faunal material (NISP 150) available for this study. The livestock proportions seen in these assemblages (Fig. 9.2) may not be particularly reliable due to the small sample size, although cattle appear to still dominate. The skeletal part abundances show continuation of the patterns seen in the previous centuries, though with additional deposits of skull and jaw fragments which are assumed to be signs of slaughter and primary butchery occurring within the town walls. The meatier parts of the cattle carcasses are now absent while humeri from both caprines and pigs occur in higher proportions than previously. The marrow exploitation also shows

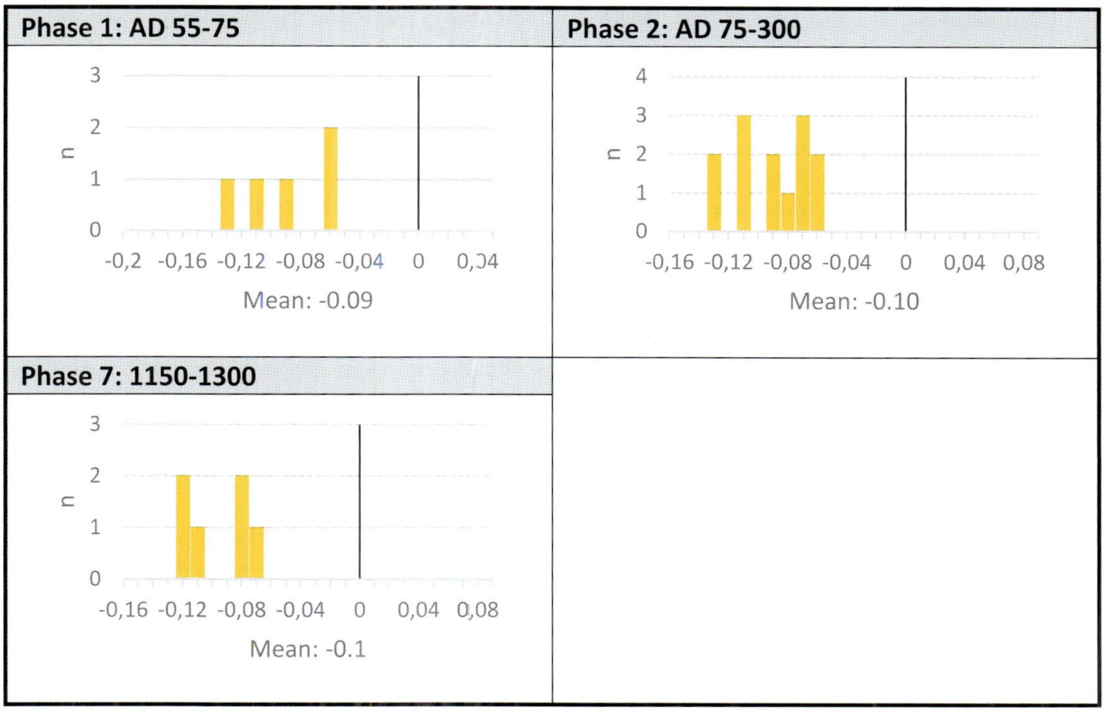

Fig. 9.7 Overview of pig log-ratios

Table 9.3 Numbers and proportions of game species in the Roman period

Phase	*1*	*2*	*3*
No. of game species	3	8	1
Proportion of total number of species	27.2%	38.1%	11.1%
Total phase NISP	398	2094	150

a decreasing reliance on cattle marrow, while fracture evidence suggests that pig marrow may have been up to twice as frequent in Phase 3 compared to Phase 2 (Fig. 9.3). The reliance on caprines and pigs for meat and marrow – despite cattle being the most frequent species – can indicate a variety of exploitation patterns. It can suggest that different fractions of the Roman population had differential access to products from these species, or alternatively, that cattle were being processed in Exeter but the products were transported elsewhere. A larger faunal sample from across the Roman town is needed to determine what interpretation is the most likely.

The medieval city

Major domesticates

From the end of the Roman period until the beginning of the 10th century there is a gap in our knowledge about what was happening in Exeter, although by Phase 5 (900–1050) pigs were relatively frequent, matching their proportion of the major domesticates seen in the Roman military phase. Pigs are easy to rear, grow fast, and can be kept within towns – in a pen living off scraps – so ensuring a reliable meat supply. Pigs then reduced in numbers after the Norman Conquest and continued to decline until the end of the 18th century. When looking at the North and West Quarters separately, there are some differences in the proportions of pigs. In the North Quarter, where pigs were generally more frequent, the decline in their numbers starts after Phase 5 but evens out after Phase 8, while in the West Quarter the continuous decline does not start until after Phase 8.

As a proportion of the major domesticates, cattle generally remain steady throughout the medieval phases but are more frequent in the West Quarter than the North Quarter. Unfortunately, the medieval sample sizes from the South Quarter are very small, and therefore may not be accurate, though they do suggest that cattle were much more frequent during Phase 7 (*c.* 1150–1300) than anywhere else in Exeter. Caprines in general increased slowly in frequency over the medieval period (Fig. 9.2), yet once again there are differences between the North and West Quarters, with caprines in the North Quarter being the most numerous livestock species from the Norman Conquest onwards, whereas in the West Quarter there is little change in proportions from Phases 6 to 8 (*c.* 1050–1500) with cattle and caprines occurring in equal numbers based on MAU throughout the medieval period. It should, however, be kept in mind that cattle are the largest of the three species, so a carcass contains a larger quantity of meat compared to a caprine or pig, and they are therefore highly likely to have supplied the majority of the meat to medieval Exeter even though caprines are more numerous in some parts of the city.

Material from extra-mural sites suggest that the livestock species occurred in noticeably different proportions compared to sites within the city wall. In the Phase 7 (*c*. 1150–1300) assemblage from the extra-mural Acorn Roundabout site, cattle represented 60% of the total livestock MAU and caprines 26%. This pattern is similar to the Roman town (Phase 2) and contemporary material from the South Quarter, but rather different to medieval phases in the North and West Quarters, although there is no immediate explanation for this difference. While the game species identified amongst the faunal remains suggests that the Acorn Roundabout area may have been home to a relatively high-status household, social status is unlikely to be the cause of this very high proportion of cattle as it is so much higher than the clearly wealthy North Quarter and similar to the South Quarter that was mostly a low-status district. The discrepancy may therefore simply be a result of the preference of the individual household, or different social factors influencing the choice of meat on either side of the city wall.

In terms of the kill-off patterns for cattle and caprines, there are some differences compared to the Roman period (pigs having always been reared primarily for meat: Fig. 9.4). During Phases 6 and 7 people living in the North Quarter consumed meat from young caprines as opposed to the West and South Quarters and in all other medieval phases where the meat came from old animals. Similarly, in all phases and Quarters, beef was acquired from old cattle except for in the West Quarter during Phase 8 where it came from younger cattle. This suggests that different herds supplied different parts of the city, with animals primarily reared for wool, or traction, being the norm, but the younger animals turning up in the North and West Quarters having been reared primarily for meat reflecting demand for more tender meat amongst the high-status citizens.

The presence of different herds and demands of the high-status citizens may also be reflected in the metric analyses of cattle and caprines (Figs 9.5 and 9.6). The mean value of cattle and caprines increase from Phase 7 to Phase 8, more so for the former than the latter, suggesting that existing stock was developed to increase the size of the animals or that new stock was introduced. Unfortunately, there is too little data from pig to determine if this species saw size developments or import of new stock.

Butchery patterns show a dramatic change from the highly systematic techniques seen in the Roman period. The medieval butchers focussed on separating a carcass by striking above, below, or through joints with a heavy blade, but there is no apparent system in how the joints were separated making the patterns appear haphazard. There is evidence for sagittal splitting being reintroduced in the second half of the 12th century (Phase 7) in the North Quarter and becoming more frequent in the West Quarter throughout Phase 8 indicating that this butchery technique is associated with the high-status households.

Fracture patterns vary both between species and areas of the city. In all phases in the North Quarter, cattle were the most heavily exploited for marrow, and caprines and pig had similar frequencies in Phases 6, 7 and 8 with a steady increase in frequencies over time. In the West Quarter, the patterns are completely different. In Phases 6 and 7, caprines and cattle have similar proportions of freshly fractured specimens, but the proportion decreases for cattle in Phase 8 while it remains the same for caprines. In Phases 6 and 7 only very small amounts of pig specimens have been broken for marrow but this increases to approximately 25% in Phase 8. Moving to Phase 7 in the South Quarter, cattle are once again the most frequently exploited. The medieval fragmentation patterns show that marrow extraction is specific to species and rather heavily influenced by social context. Assuming that the North Quarter sets a baseline for high-status living in medieval Exeter, it underlines a big difference between the high-status diets and that of the ecclesiastic areas in the Phases 6 and 7 of the West Quarter. The North Quarter population consumed marrow, particularly from cattle, in much larger quantities than in the West Quarter, which shows more of a preference for caprines and almost entirely avoids pig.

Game consumption

As with the Roman period, the presence of non-livestock species is useful when looking at the social groups represented within medieval Exeter. While game never contributed large quantities of meat to the diet, its consumption appears to have had social implications as one of the sumptuary laws restricted access to game species, meaning that only the nobility or the very wealthy consumed these meats. Tables 9.3 and 9.4 give an overview of the presence of game species in Exeter, and as the total NISP of a phase and quarter will affect the number of identified status-indicator species the proportion of game species out of the total number of identified species is listed. Based on this information, in the medieval, and probably post-medieval, periods an area is highly likely to primarily have had high-status households if the game species proportion is above 20%, though it is still important to look at the individual species to determine the nature of the households. With this in mind it becomes clear that the high-status population of Exeter primarily lived in the North Quarter from *c*. 1050 to the first half of the post-medieval period (from Phases 6–9), as there is a much higher number of game species and other high-status species indicators such as woodcock, hawk and grey heron. The material from Phase 7 (*c*. 1150–1300) in the West Quarter also appears to be from a high-status tenement, and the presence of five of these species confirms the interpretation of the household as belonging to the upper echelons of society. The find of 23 hawk bones (MNI: 3)

Table 9.4 Numbers and proportions of game species in the medieval and post-medieval periods

Phase	*5*	*6*		*7*		*8*		*9*		*10*	
Quarter	N	N	W	N	W	N	W	N	W	N	W
No. of game species	2	2	2	9	0	6	5	11	1	3	3
Proportion of total number of species	16.7%	12.5%	18.2%	39.1%	0%	30%	26%	35.5%	12.5%	25%	30%
Total phase NISP	134	427	568	1842	485	385	472	1528	134	155	191

is particularly interesting as hunting with birds of prey was limited to the elite. Finding them, and roe deer, is a very strong indicator that, at least for a while during the Late Middle Ages, a high-status household occupied a tenement on modern day Friernhay Street.

The South Quarter of Exeter is traditionally regarded as a relatively low-status area, although the excavations at Mermaid Yard lay close to a bell foundry (a high-status occupation). The presence of red deer (a complete humerus) and fallow deer (a partial metatarsal) in a single context from Phase 7 (*c.* 1150–1300) could indicate a household that was not entirely low status. There is no evidence that meat on the humerus was consumed or that the metatarsal was used for craft purposes, so we cannot determine why these specimens were located in the area, but as they were found in the same context it seems possible that a household had access to game on at least one occasion.

The skeletal part abundances at Mermaid Yard – and in particular the relatively high numbers of low utility elements – suggests that primary butchery was going on in that area, though this activity was not confined to the South Quarter but occurred in almost all areas and phases. The skeletal part abundances and presence of game species underline that the different parts of Exeter never had a single function or social status. One example is Levitan's (1989) analysis of the Exe Bridge material with its large deposits of horncores likely to have come from a nearby horn worker (Levitan 1989, tab. 2; 2019). These deposits are, rightly so, interpreted as industrial waste, yet they are still mixed with high meat utility elements showing the mixed nature of the deposits.

The monastic diet

In contrast to high-status phases and areas – notably the North Quarter – the Phase 6 and 7 material from the West Quarter, which was excavated from contexts within monastic precincts (Bartholomew Street East (site 73) and Bartholomew Street West (site 47)), has only two game species in Phase 6 and none in Phase 7, as opposed to respectively 2 and 9 in the North Quarter, showing the scarcity of game in the diet within ecclesiastical areas (Tables 9.3 and 9.4). It is important to note that lay servants may have lived within the precincts so the faunal patterns may represent multiple fractions within medieval society, although as servants were very unlikely to have had access to game these particular species are most likely to be waste from the ecclesiastical diet. Monks were prohibited from eating meat unless ill, but over the course of the 12th century meat was first allowed for those dining with the abbot in private, next, in a designated separate room for those in poor health, and finally, though still in a separate room, to all monks during certain periods of 'recreation' over the course of the year (Knowles 1963, 462; Burton 1994, 166; Harvey 2006, 220). The bending of the dietary rules may be evident in Exeter if game meat, in small quantities, was indeed consumed alongside that of livestock though we cannot determine for certain whether the livestock remains are associated with laymen or ecclesiastics. The minimal differences in the proportions of domestic livestock between the material from monastic and high-status areas indicates that the general diets were fairly similar, though within the ecclesiastical areas more cattle and less caprines were eaten than the secular North Quarter population. Furthermore, fracture patterns show that marrow consumption was different with the monastic precinct diet containing more caprine marrow and very little pig marrow. There is also some evidence for the monastic precincts receiving less 'meaty' parts of the carcass, such as the tibia and the radius, compared to the North Quarter which could suggest that these parts were eaten by poorer servants rather than monks.

The post-medieval period

Major domesticates

The transition from Phase 8 (*c.* 1300–1500) to the post-medieval period heralds some clear changes in the exploitation of livestock, with caprines becoming more frequent while cattle decline in representation across both the North and West Quarters (Fig. 9.2). Other changes are reflected in the metrical analysis (Figs 9.5–7) with log-ratios showing a marked increase in caprine breadth measurements suggesting a shape change, likely towards a stockier build, rather than overall increase in size or height in the animals. This shows a development of existing caprine types or importation of new ones along with a shift in herd structure consistent with management for wool (Fig. 9.4). This development is in line with our knowledge of the importance of the cloth industry in Exeter which had been growing since the 14th century (see EAPIT 1, Chapter 4) and when the MAUs show caprines to be increasing in numbers (Fig. 9.2): the 16th-century (Phase 9) changes are likely to reflect further growth in the woollen industry (Gray 2001).

Worthy of note is the relative scarcity of post-medieval faunal material compared to Phase 8 (*c.* 1300–1500) especially when taking the larger population into consideration, a trend which has also been observed elsewhere in Britain. In Exeter, the relative scarcity of post-medieval material is primarily evident in the South and West Quarters, whereas in the North Quarter, where the vast majority of Maltby's (1979) material similarly was recovered from, this is less noticeable. Furthermore, in this study, there are no signs of any intra-mural industrial or craft activity such as primary butchery or horn and leather working within the post-medieval faunal assemblages examined. Historical evidence, however, shows post-medieval industrial works related to tanning, horn working and wool processing in Exeter being located in close proximity to the River Exe and the Quay, and excavations at Shooting Marsh Stile (Site 80) revealed large post-medieval deposits of cattle horncores suggestive of nearby horn working. This evidence may suggest that industrial work moved outside of the city walls in later periods. The scarcity of post-medieval faunal remains outside of the North Quarter, despite the number of archaeological excavations having taken place, could be explained partly by disposal techniques similar to the industrial works and partly by truncation of the deposits by Victorian and later construction phases which has been noted in the majority of excavation reports from Exeter.

Game consumption

In the North Quarter 11 game species have been identified in Phase 9 (Table 9.4), making it the highest number identified at any point in Exeter's history, accounting for 3% of the total NISP for this area. The material from St. Nicholas' Priory, a Tudor manor house in the West Quarter, provides a contemporary comparison for the material from the North Quarter. Here six game species are represented, making up 1.2% of the total faunal and avian NISP and 30% of the total number of identified species (Levitan 1989, tab. 7) which, following Tables 9.3 and 9.4, confirms that it was a high-status household on par with those in the North Quarter.

The most substantial evidence for wealth and connections of an individual household in Exeter is the presence of three turkey bones in a context from a tenement on Paul Street (Site 76) in the North Quarter dated to 1520–1550 on the basis of its ceramics. Currently, these are the only turkey remains to overlap with the documented 1524/1526 introduction of the species to England, and it is notable that the associated contexts at Paul Street also contained the remains of imported glass and ceramics from the Netherlands, Spain, Northern Europe and Venice (EAPIT 1, Chapter 8, Fig. 30), reflecting its high status and the numerous international connections Exeter had during the expansion of the woollen industry (Lauritsen *et al.* 2018; EAPIT 1, Chapter 4).

Conclusions

The excavated sites and their associated artefacts and faunal assemblages show that the North, West and South Quarters of Exeter were occupied by different parts of urban society such as high-status households, monastic communities, and the lower status artisans. This study has shed new light on meat consumption and use of other animal products amongst these social groups, and longer-term changes over the Roman, medieval and post-medieval periods. Metrical analysis showed shape changes and size increase over larger time scales consistent with national agricultural developments. Butchery practices similarly showed broad changes over time. Roman butchery was highly systematic, whereas medieval butchery was haphazard but with systematic use of sagittal splitting becoming more and more common from Phase 8 (*c.* 1300–1500) onwards (although there were no contemporary differences within the urban setting indicating that butchery practices were not related to social standing other than the reintroduction of sagittal splitting by high-status households). The proportions of the livestock species in the diet do not appear to be related to specific social groups in contemporary material, although differences are apparent within the various settlement phases such as the high proportion of pigs in the Roman military period which decreases in favour of beef in the Roman civil phase. Pigs are also relatively frequent in pre-Norman Exeter but cattle and caprines were at all times the most frequently exploited animals, with caprines dominating from Phase 8 (*c.* 1300–1500) onwards as a result of the prospering woollen industry.

This study is the first to have examined fracture patterns in Exeter. Prior to this no detailed quantitative analysis of fractures had been undertaken on material from any of the historic periods in Britain, and likely further afield, and indeed our understanding of the importance of marrow and bone fats in the past two millennia as a whole is still in its infancy. If we want to understand the full use of animal products in the past, and how those uses varied throughout society, fracture studies are a key part of building that knowledge. In prehistoric material this type of analysis has identified periods of dietary stress that drove people towards heavy exploitation of bone grease (Outram 2001) as well as identifying the transition to milk/dairy product consumption in the Neolithic (Johnson *et al.* 2018). These same analytical techniques have the potential to identify similar dietary trends in the historic periods which may not otherwise be apparent through other faunal analyses. The results of the analysis of fracture patterns presented here – and discussed in greater depth in Lauritsen 2019 – have shown differences between monastic communities, with their almost complete avoidance of pig marrow, while the wider population only consumed it slightly less than that of cattle and caprines. As a general rule cattle and caprines bones were fractured in almost equal frequencies for marrow, although cattle varied in frequency between consecutive phases while caprines saw a steady increase in exploitation from the Norman Conquest onwards which may be linked to the overall increase of caprines in the diet.

Similar to the metrical analyses, this study shows that the herd management practices were also consistent with national trends. Cattle were at all times managed primarily for traction, and caprines for wool, before the relatively elderly animals were driven to Exeter on the hoof and slaughtered in the city. Pigs were managed solely for meat and likely to have been reared within or in close proximity to the town. There were, however, a few differences within the city itself with cattle and caprines occasionally being managed for meat to supply the high-status population in Phase 8 (*c*. 1300–1500) with more tender cuts of veal and lamb.

This study means that the assemblages from all major excavations in Exeter carried out between 1971 and 1990 have now been studied (and see Maltby 1979; Levitan 1987; and Maltby's summaries in EAPIT 1, Chapters 5–8), which means that it is important to look to the future and where research priorities now lie. While high-status secular assemblages are quite well-represented, it would be extremely useful to have more material from ecclesiastical and low status communities, notably in Exeter's South Quarter. There is also a need for a detailed study of the fish remains. As mentioned previously, fracture studies have not been undertaken on historic material prior to this analysis. It has, however, been shown that bone marrow was a valuable source of fat which was exploited by social groups in different quantities and ways in the various periods. There is now a need for comparative studies on other settlement types and within different social groups to determine how this food source has been exploited more widely in historic periods.

To support the metrical data, geometric morphometric analysis also needs to be undertaken, particularly of sheep, to gain further understanding of the development of existing types in the region and the introduction of new ones. In particular, it would be useful for testing the potential introduction of new caprine stock during the early post-medieval period to determine if there were indeed two different groups of caprines being consumed in Exeter at one time, with the group in the North Quarter disappearing or at least increasing to a similar size as the animals in the West and South Quarters by Phase 10. Furthermore, if different groups were present it would be interesting to see if they are morphometrically similar to animals elsewhere in Britain or Europe so we can determine where new stock was introduced from, and this metrical data could be compared to isotopic data.

Acknowledgements

I would like to express my gratitude towards Alan Outram and Stephen Rippon for supervising the PhD project on the faunal remains of Exeter: your guidance and advice have helped shape and improve the project from start to finish. I also wish to thank the University of Exeter College of Humanities Graduate School Doctoral Award for funding the project. I am particularly grateful to the Royal Albert Memorial Museum and Thomas Cadbury for providing access to the faunal collections.

10

Archaeometallurgy: An Assessment of Roman and Medieval Crucibles and Other Possible Metalworking Debris

Carlotta Gardner and David Dungworth

A number of excavations within Exeter have produced evidence for metalworking, including those associated with the early post-War work by Lady Fox (1952a) in South Street Area 1 (Site 15), and the redevelopment of Exeter's city centre in the 1970s and 80s (Site 42: Trichay Street, 1972–4; Sites 52 and 64: Rack Street, 1974–5 and 1977–8; Site 63: Mermaid Yard, 1977–8; Site 75: Friernhay Street, 1981): Site Numbers refer to Chapter 2 above. The South Street crucibles and slag were published by Fox (1952a, 64, 93), while unpublished Ancient Monuments Laboratory Reports (AML) were produced for the Trichay Street, Rack Street, Mermaid Yard and Friernhay Street crucibles (Bayley 1989a; 1989b), with some of the Friernhay material published in Bayley 2001. Small amounts of iron smithing slag and hearth bottoms from Trichay Street, Rack Street, Friernhay Street and Mermaid Yard were assessed by Wilthew (1986).

As this evidence for metalworking was not published in *Roman Finds from Exeter* (Holbrook and Bidwell 1991), EAPIT provided the opportunity for a re-examination of this material using modern scientific techniques, the majority of the work being carried out by Carlotta Gardner at University College London as part of her PhD on *Metalworking Crucibles in Roman Britain* (Gardner 2018). In addition, David Dungworth, formerly of Historic England, carried out an assessment of crucibles from medieval contexts.

Assessment of the Roman crucibles *by Carlotta Gardner*

Introduction

Metalworking remains from sites across Roman-period Exeter have previously been examined and published in books, papers and unpublished AML reports, as detailed in the introduction to this chapter and in more detail in Table 10.1, although little of this material has been investigated using scientific techniques. As part of the EAPIT project, material was therefore assessed from five sites – Friernhay Street (FH), Rack Street (RS), South Street (SS), Trichay Street (TS) and Mermaid Yard (MY) – and a selection, mainly crucibles, were analysed using a range of scientific techniques. The aims of this re-examination were to reveal the types of non-ferrous metallurgical processes that were taking place during this period in Exeter, to assess the types of materials that were being employed in the production of metallurgical ceramics, and to compare the results with our understanding of Roman period metalworking and crucibles elsewhere in Britain.

Abbreviations used

BSE: back scattered electron images
EOL: extra outer layer of clay
FH: Friernhay Street
H/FL: hearth/furnace lining
pXRF: portable X-ray Fluorescence
RS: Rack Street
SEM-EDS: Scanning Electron Microscopy-Energy Dispersive X-Ray Spectroscopy
SS: South Street
TS: Trichay Street
MY: Mermaid Yard

Material

Rack Street (RS)

Bayley (1989a) and Wilthew (1986) have previously assessed the metalworking debris from the Roman legionary and civilian phases at Rack Street. Most of the crucibles were from a dump of material relating to the demolition of the Roman legionary fortress in *c.* AD 75–80, although a fragment of melting hearth or furnace with a relined rim used for working gunmetal (an alloy of copper, tin and zinc) came from a late 2nd-century AD deposit (context 363–14), and a fragment of dense, lead-copper rich slag that could be from litharge (a by-product of the cupellation of silver) came from a late 4th-century AD context (Bayley 1989a, 6). A total of five crucible fragments (RS 1180, 1181, 1183c, and 1185 Nos. 1–2) from the Roman legionary phase, a piece of hearth/furnace lining (RS 363-14[a]) from the late 2nd-century AD dump, and pieces of slag and/or corroded metal (RS 1183c, 1215, 363-14[b]) were re-examined as part of this project.

Friernhay Street (FH)

An assemblage previously examined by Bayley (1989b; 2001) included material from late military dumps against the back of the legionary fortress rampart with two crucible fragments used for copper-alloy smelting (FH 778 and 882) and two shallow hemispherical crucibles (FH 883 and 1535) used for cupellation (the separation of silver from base metals). Crucibles from a 2nd-century AD roadside ditch (FH 805) appear to have been used for 'parting' (the process of separating silver from gold): four sherds were found from thick-walled, possibly hemispherical handmade vessels that appear to have had diameters of 120–150 mm. The fabrics were oxidised-fired (whereas metal-melting crucibles are reduced-fired) and have a pale olive-green or deep bottle-green vitrified outer surface that looks like a glaze. Two (FH 778 and 822) of these 12 crucible fragments were re-analysed as part of this study, as well as one piece of slag (FH 837).

South Street (SS)

Two crucible fragments (SS 62/1949.SF3a and SF3b) were sent for analysis that have previously been assessed, illustrated and published by Fox (1952a). They came from what at the time was interpreted as a 'kitchen workshop floor' (Fox 1952a, 64) but as this dated to *c*. AD 50–75 it was clearly associated with the Roman legionary fortress.

Mermaid Yard (MY)

The material submitted from Mermaid Yard was made up of fragments of vitrified ceramic, pieces of slag, and corroded copper-alloy spills. The material was analysed using surface portable X-ray Fluorescence (pXRF), but apart from the metal spills, the material was fragmentary and undiagnostic and so no further analysis was completed.

Trichay Street (TS)

Bayley (1989a) and Wilthew (1986) have previously assessed the metalworking debris from the Roman legionary *fabrica* at Trichay Street, and this material was not sent for assessment as part of this report. It mostly consisted of copper-alloy scraps and waste, mostly from brass armour fittings, along with iron smithing slag. There were a small number of handmade crucible fragments with an organic-tempered fabric that are probably derived from two or three vessels that had been used to melt brass. One had a globular form with an added layer of less refractory clay (EOL: extra outer layer), while the other was a thick-walled hemispherical form with the suggestion of a pinched-out pouring lip and a maximum diameter of *c*. 10 cm. Other material comprised corroded copper-alloy (that pXRF shows to be gunmetal in composition), and altogether this evidence appears to suggest the repair of Roman military armour within the legionary *fabrica*. Other material identified at the site includes a small ball of Egyptian blue and some undiagnostic material.

Methodology

All the material was examined macroscopically, with a focus on recording and describing any key features. For the crucibles the form, whether an extra outer layer of clay (EOL) was applied, likely forming technique, fabric characterisation, and any slaggy residues adhering were recorded. Through this study crucibles were identified from three of the five sites (SS, RS and FH), as well as some smaller pieces of slag and corroded metal spills. The material was analysed using pXRF to determine the types of processes that they are evidence of.

There are a number of limitations in using pXRF for analysing corroded metal, slag and crucibles (Dungworth 2000; 2001; Dungworth and Starley 2009; Kearns *et al.* 2010) and therefore the data was used qualitatively. The key limitations are that pXRF is a surface technique. When analysing corroded metal this can cause a number of issues as various corrosion processes can enrich or deplete surfaces of particular elements. A specific issue for porous ceramics used in metalworking is that zinc, a metal commonly alloyed with copper from the Roman period onwards (Dungworth 2001), vaporises at the temperatures required to melt the metals it is frequently alloyed with. This results in high levels of zinc being identified in XRF spectra as it is readily absorbed by the ceramic. The results of pXRF analysis have been reported to reflect the qualitative nature of the data. Tables listing the samples and the 'level' of the alloying elements are included in the results section on a simple qualitative scale: ? possible detection, + low levels, ++ medium levels, +++ high levels detected, and blank where an element was not detected.

Nine of the crucible fragments and one metal spill were sampled for further analysis using scanning electron microscopy with energy dispersive spectrometry (SEM-EDS). The fabrics were described and the vitrification level (Table 10.2) was recorded using the method developed by Maniatis and Tite (1981) and used by Freestone and Tite (1986). The same methodology for the analysis of crucible bodies outlined in Freestone and Tite (1986) and Martinón-Torres and Rehren (2009) was followed. With this method the 'bulk' and 'matrix' were analysed separately. The bulk analyses were performed at low magnification (x50 magnification) and assessed the chemical composition of the ceramic material generally, including

Table 10.1 Summary of the information available in published reports on the crucibles from Exeter and details of which material was seen and analysed in this current study

Site	Sample No.	Published information				Current study		
		Object	Description	Probable use	Reference	Seen	pXRF	SEM
RS	363-14	crucible or H/FL	Re-lined rim from crucible or H/FL	copper-alloy containing zinc	Bayley 1989a	Y	Y	Y
	1183c	crucible	Rim sherd, wheel-thrown (?), EOL	copper-alloy containing zinc	Bayley 1989a	Y	Y	Y
	1181	crucible	Rim sherd, handmade(?)	copper-alloy containing zinc	Bayley 1989a	Y	Y	Y
	1185 (No. 1)	crucible	Rim sherd, handmade(?)	copper-alloy containing zinc	Bayley 1989a	Y	Y	Y
	1185 (No. 2)	crucible	Body sherd, handmade(?)	copper-alloy containing zinc	Bayley 1989a	Y	Y	Y
	1180	crucible	Body sherd, handmade(?), EOL	copper-alloy containing zinc	Bayley 1989a	Y	Y	Y
FH	822	crucible	Rim sherd of heavily tempered refractory fabric. Hemispherical form.	copper-alloy	Bayley 1989b	Y	Y	Y
	778	crucible	Body sherd from a mineral tempered, though not very refractory.	copper-alloy	Bayley 1989b	Y	Y	Y
	883	crucible	Rim sherd from a shallow crucible with pinched lip, similar to 1535 but larger.	silver	Bayley 1989b			
	1535	crucible	Small shallow hemispherical crucible with pouring lip and distinct vitreous tide-mark.	silver	Bayley 1989b			
	805.1	parting vessel	Rim sherd, exterior very heavily vitrified with patches of bottle-green colouration.	gold	Bayley 1989b			
	805.2	parting vessel	Rim sherd, with vitrified exterior surface, bottle-green in colour.	gold	Bayley 1989b			
	805.3	parting vessel lid	Sherd from the edge of the 'lid' applied to a vessel (like 805.1 and 805.2). Outer surface vitrified.	gold	Bayley 1989b			
	805.4	parting vessel	Rim sherd, with vitrified outer surface and orange-peel texture and a patchy bottle-green colour.	gold	Bayley 1989b			
	805.5	parting vessel	Body(?) sherd with vitrified outer surface, green in colour.	gold	Bayley 1989b			
	805.6	parting vessel	Body sherd with an even bottle-green vitrified outer surface.	gold	Bayley 1989b			
	805.7	parting vessel lid	Sherd from the edge of an applied lid, similar to 805.3.	gold	Bayley 1989b			
SS	SS.62.1949.SF3a	crucible	Crucibles of coarse grey clay and sub-angular form; the base is reddened by burning.		Fox 1952a, 64	Y	Y	Y
	SS.62.1949.SF3b	crucible	Crucibles of coarse grey clay and sub-angular form; the base is reddened by burning.		Fox 1952a, 64	Y	Y	
		crucible x6	Crucibles fragments, the shape of the crucibles resembles one found in Glastonbury lake village, dated at the time as Early Iron Age 'B'.	enameling or lead	Fox 1952a, 64			
TS		crucible	Handmade, organic tempered, globular form with added outer layer.	brass	Bayley 1989a			
		crucible	Handmade, organic tempered, thick-walled hemispherical form with pinched pouring lip.	brass	Bayley 1989a			

clay and inclusions. The 'matrix' was analysed at much higher magnification (x800) and is the 'relatively continuous phase made up by the vitrified clay' (Martinón-Torres 2005). SEM-EDS was also used to analyse the chemical composition of the slaggy residues and the phases within them.

Results and discussion

Slag, metal spills and crucible residues

The majority of the Roman crucibles from Exeter have visible residues adhering to the inner and outer surfaces. The results of pXRF of these residues, and the inner surfaces of the crucibles, shows that they were used to melt a variety of alloys, with brass and gunmetal – and sometimes those alloys with added lead – dominant (results summarised in Table 10.3). SEM-EDS analysis of the adhering residues confirm the pXRF results.

Table 10.2 Abbreviations used to describe the vitrification stage of ceramics and their meaning

Abbr.	*Meaning*
NV	No vitrification
V	Vitrification
V+	Extensive vitrification
CV	Continuous vitrification
CV(FB)	CV with fine bloating pores (<10 µm)
CV(MB)	CV with medium bloating pores (10–40 µm)
CV(CB)	CV with coarse bloating pores (40–100 µm)
CV(VCB)	CV with very coarse bloating pores (>100 µm)

Precious metal working is also evident. The re-examination of the material showed the presence of silver working/refining at both Rack Street and South Street. Sometimes, due to the very low concentration of silver in the residues, slag and metal spills, pXRF was unable to detect its presence but SEM-EDS was able to. At Rack Street a piece of slag and a metal spill show the presence of silver in low concentrations and at South Street slag adhering to a crucible and a piece of slag also show the presence of silver (Table 10.4).

Other potential evidence for silver working/refining may be present at South Street. Six crucible fragments analysed by Mr. Baker (Fox 1952a), which can no longer be located, apparently had an 'opaque glassy paste adhering' to them in which Mr. Baker identified high lead concentrations giving rise to his suggestion that they were probably associated with 'enamelling or lead preparation'. Though these crucible fragments could not be reanalysed it is possible that they are actually associated with silver refining or assaying (the determination of the quantity of a given metal, normally silver or gold, in an ore or alloy). Similar lead-rich glassy slag has been identified on a number of Roman crucibles from Exeter (Friernhay Street: Bayley 1989a; 2001), London (Gardner and Marshall in prep), the Roman fort at Brough (Bainbridge cited in Gardner 2009), and further afield in Germany (Rehren and Kraus, 1999), and where this glass has been analysed (Rehren and Kraus 1999; Gardner and Marshall forthcoming) it is thought to be associated with silver refining/assaying. As mentioned in the introduction to Friernhay Street, Bayley (1989b; 2001) found evidence for silver and gold working.

Table 10.3 Qualitative results of pXRF analysis of crucibles from Exeter (?: possible detection; + low levels; ++ to +++ medium levels; ++++ high levels detected; where blank this element was not detected)

Sample	*Object type*	*Iron*	*Copper*	*Zinc*	*Silver*	*Tin*	*Lead*	*Probable alloy*
RS363-14[a]	crucible		++	++		+++	+	gunmetal
RS363-14[b]	vitrified ceramic(?)	++++	?	?		+	+	iron
RS363-14[c]	corroded iron(?)	++++	?	?				iron
RS1183c[a]	crucible		+	+++			++	leaded brass
RS1183c[b]	metal spill/slag		+++	+			+++	leaded brass
RS1181	crucible		+	+++		+	+++	leaded gunmetal
RS1185[a]	crucible		+	++++			+	brass (leaded?)
RS1185[b]	crucible		+	+++			+	brass (leaded?)
RS1180	crucible		+++	+			+	brass (leaded)
RS1215	metal spill		++				++++	?
FH837	metal spill(?)		++++					copper
FH822	crucible		++	++++			+	brass (leaded?)
FH778	crucible		++	++		+++	+++	leaded gunmetal
SS.62/1949.SF3[a]	slag		?		+	+	+++	silver?
SS.62/1949.SF3[b]	crucible		?	+			++	brass (leaded?)
MY.47.2005.1.5[a]	corroded metal(?)		++++			+	++	gunmetal
MY.47.2005.1.5[b]	undiagnostic slag(?)	++++	?					iron
MY.47.2005.1.5[c]	undiagnostic slag(?)		+++	+		++++	+	gunmetal
MY.47.2005.1.5[d]	undiagnostic slag(?)		++++			++	+	bronze

Table 10.4 Normalised composition (in weight percent) of four prills analysed within sample RS 1215 which came from a context dated to the later 4th century AD (nd = not detected)

RS 1215	Cu	Ag	Pb
Prill 1	98.2	1.8	nd
Prill 2	17.4	2.9	79.8
Prill 3	38.8	nd	61.2
Prill 4	1.3	nd	98.7

The evidence for copper-alloy working is unsurprising, with all site types often showing evidence for it. The precious metalworking, however, appears to be relatively abundant in Roman Exeter with evidence at three of the five sites investigated and with only a limited sample analysed, it is expected more evidence is present. Whilst the majority of the evidence appears to represent the refining/assaying of precious metals on a small scale, further investigation into the scale of the industry in Exeter may well be warranted due to the silver rich deposits nearby in the Tamar Valley (Smart 2014) and Combe Martin, in North Devon (Rippon *et al.* 2009).

Crucible characterisation

A total of nine crucible fragments were identified within the assemblage of material from Roman Exeter. The crucibles from the three sites, with the exception of RS 1183c[a], are all handmade and appear to be shallow hemispherical forms, some with pouring lips moulded into the rim (*e.g.* Fig. 10.1). RS 1183c[a] is the only example of a wheel-thrown crucible seen in this study, and it is probably from a narrow-necked, flat-bottomed, wheel-thrown beaker. RS 363-14[a] is an oxidised (OXID) piece of ceramic which has been involved in, or exposed to, metalworking processes as it has a thick slag layer adhering to it with visible prills trapped within. The sample also appears to have had a second layer of clay applied: Bayley (1989a) has described it as a relined crucible or piece of hearth/furnace lining (H/FL). Macroscopically the fabrics of the crucibles appear quite consistent (Table 10.5). The majority are relatively fine-grained fabrics, with mineral inclusions (SAND) and the majority have voids characteristic of burnt out organic material (ORG), like straw or chaff. All are reduced fired (RED), with the exception of RS 343-14[a] which is oxidised (OXID). Sample RS 363-14[b] is so heavily vitrified that it is no longer possible to identify the original fabric. There are two EOLs remaining on RS 1185[b] and RS 1180, with possible evidence that one was once attached to the wheel-thrown crucible RS 1183c[a]. The EOLs are typically heavily vitrified and bloated, and like sample RS 363-14[b], it is not possible to characterise the original fabric macroscopically.

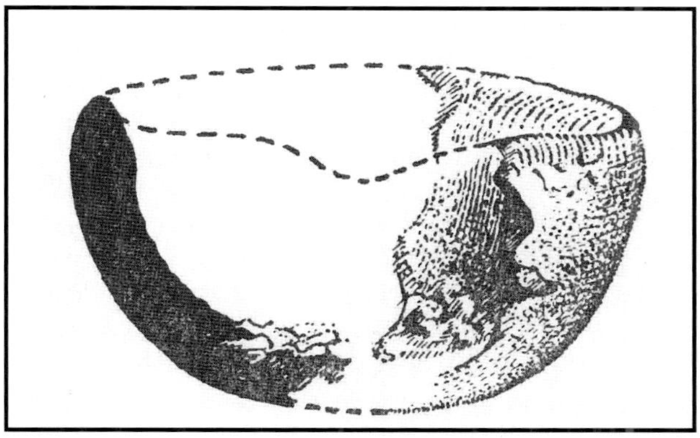

Fig. 10.1 Illustration of reconstructed crucible (SS.62/1949. SF3[a]) from South Street (drawing by R. Howard-Jones in Fox 1952a, fig. 8)

Table 10.5 Summary of crucible macroscopic fabrics

Sample	Object	EOL	Fabric
RS363-14[a]	H/FL		OXID SAND
RS363-14[b]	vitrified ceramic		–
RS1183c[a]	crucible	Y(?)	RED SAND
RS1181	crucible		RED SAND + ORG
RS1185[a]	crucible		RED SAND + ORG
RS1185[b]	crucible	Y	RED SAND + ORG
RS1180	crucible	Y	RED SAND
FH822	crucible		RED SAND + ORG
FH778	crucible		RED SAND + ORG
SS.62/1949. SF3[b]	crucible		RED SAND + ORG

Fabric characterisation

Microscopic examination of the crucible fabrics, with SEM BSE imaging, revealed four fabrics (Table 10.6 and Fig, 10.2). The majority of the crucibles fall within Fabric 1 the most distinguishing feature of which is the voids left from the burning-out of organic inclusions and the presence of argillaceous inclusions. Crucibles are often tempered with organic material. The addition of this type of material improves the desired thermal properties (Hein *et al.* 2008) and improves the reducing environment, which when strong enough produces carbon monoxide which promotes the reduction of iron oxides in the ceramic to iron metal (Martinón-Torres and Verrocchio 2008) resulting in the presence of metallic iron droplets in the fabric (Fig. 10.3). This removes the majority of the iron oxides, which act as a flux, from the ceramic matrix resulting in a more refractory material (Freestone and Tite 1986). At higher magnifications these droplets are visible (white in colour, and circular in profile). This has happened in a number of the examples of Fabric 1 from Exeter, some crucibles showing higher

Table 10.6 Fabric groups and their descriptions

Fabric	*Inclusions*	*Vitrification stage*	*Samples*
1	*Quartz: c.* 15–20%, moderately sorted, sub-angular to sub-rounded, very fine to fine sand-sized with occasional medium sand-sized grains also present. *Organic:* long voids where organic material has burnt out. Measure from 0.15mm to 2.7mm in length. Argillaceous: rare to frequent, rounded, very coarse sand-sized.	NV to V+(MB)	RS 1180, RS 1181, RS 1185[a], RS 1185[b], SS62/1949.SF3[b]
2	*Quartz: c.* 35%, bimodal. Fine fraction: well to moderately sorted, sub-angular to sub-rounded, fine sand-sized. Coarse fraction: poorly sorted, sub-angular to sub-rounded, coarse to very coarse sand-sized.	V+(FB)	FH 778, RS 363-14[a]
3	*Quartz: c.* 30–35%, moderately sorted, sub-angular to sub-rounded, medium sand-sized.	CV (F to MB)	FH 822
4	*Quartz: c.* 15–20%, bimodal. Coarse fraction: poorly sorted, sub-angular to sub-rounded, coarse to very coarse sand-sized. Fine fraction: well-sorted, sub-rounded to rounded, very fine sand-sized.	V+ to CV (F to MB)	RS 1183c[a]

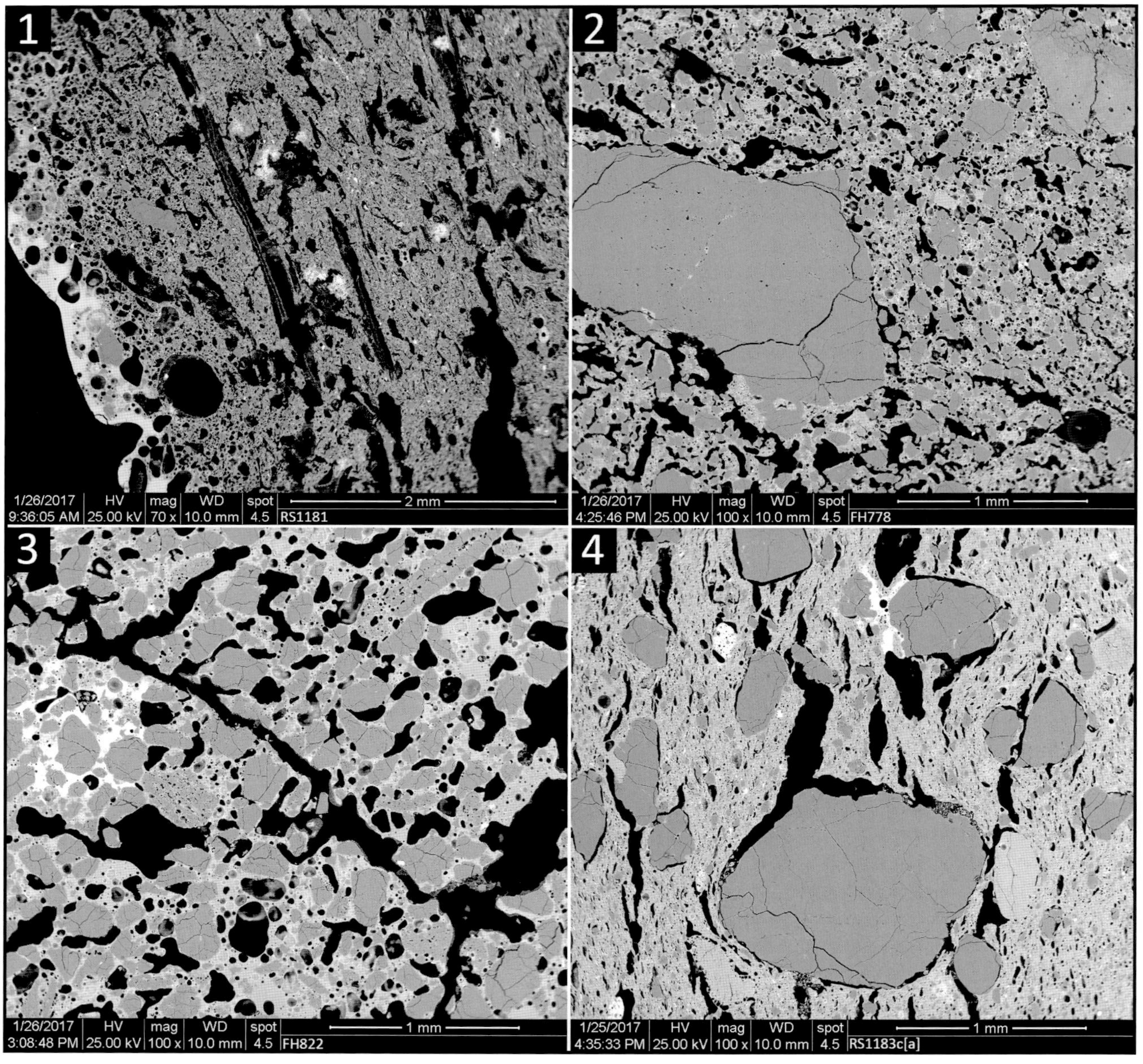

Fig. 10.2 BSE images illustrating the four fabrics identified with the Exeter crucible assemblage. 1: RS 1181; 2: FH 778; 3: FH 822; 4:RS 1183c[a]

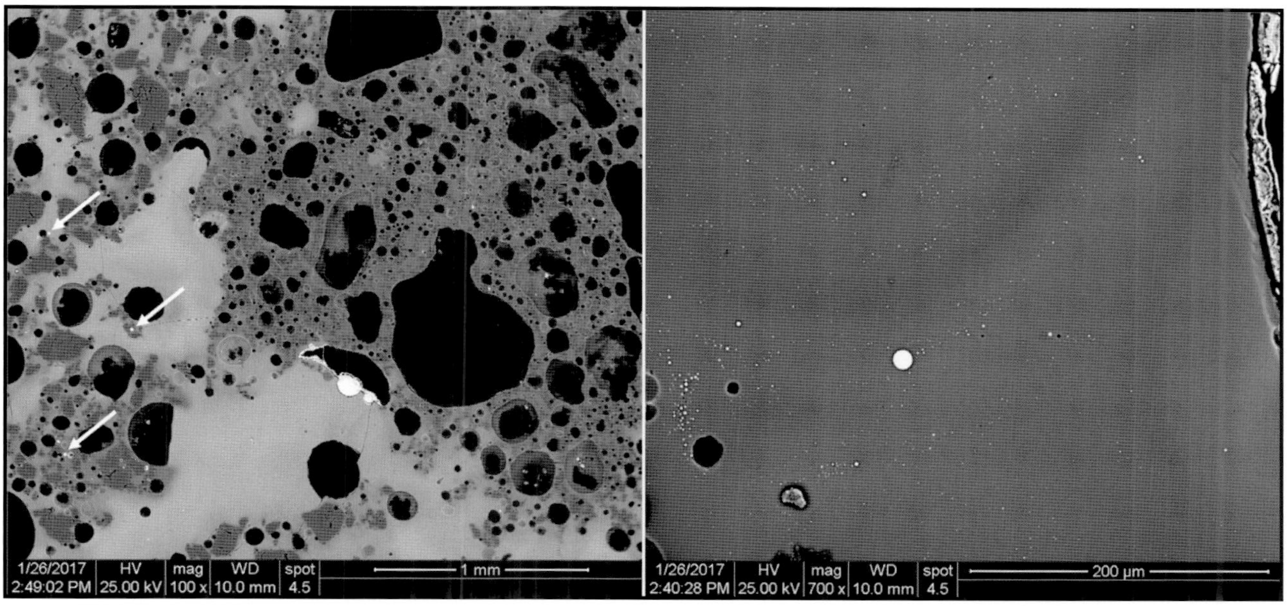

Fig. 10.3 BSE images demonstrating the presence of metallic iron droplets in the Fabric 1 crucibles. Left: iron droplets shown by white arrows; right: high magnification of rounded iron droplets within a glassy matrix (sample: RS 1180)

concentrations than others. The argillaceous inclusions do not appear to be grog but are more likely argillaceous rock fragments (ARF) or clay pellets, both suggesting poor and inconsistent clay processing as they are not always present.

Fabrics 2 and 3 are similar but differ because of the bimodality of the quartz inclusions in Fabric 2. Fabric 4 is quite distinct from the others and is represented by the only wheel-thrown sample. The quartz inclusions and elongated voids are orientated parallel to the vessel walls and there are a number of voids which run around the quartz grains. The elongate voids are likely caused by the over-firing of the fabric during use as a crucible though they may also be caused by the shrinkage of the matrix during the drying phase of production (Herz and Garrison 1998).

All the crucibles which were examined with BSE imaging show that the quartz grains have a series of cracks within them. This is due to the $\alpha \rightarrow \beta$ quartz transformation at *c.* 573 °C during firing, use and cooling (Martín-Márquez *et al.* 2008). The voids around a number of the quartz inclusions is due to their thermal expansion and subsequent shrinkage on cooling. Other thermal alterations of the fabrics include the vitrification of the ceramic matrix: in most cases there is a gradient from complete vitrification and medium to coarse bloating on the exterior to no vitrification in the middle of the crucible body. There is also evidence for the partial melting of feldspars, which occurs at temperatures exceeding 1,100–1,200 °C in oxidising environments (Rice 1987; Reedy 2008). Though this likely occurs at lower temperatures in reducing environments, it indicates that the charged crucibles were heated to around 1,100 °C to enable this partial melting, and consequently the correct temperature range required to for melting most copper-alloys.

Bulk chemical analysis (with SEM-EDS) indicates variation in the composition of the fabrics, most of which is influenced by the silica content. Although all the crucibles are abundant in quartz (silica) inclusions, there is variation in the amount of quartz in each sample and this can cause a 'dilution' effect, masking variations in the elemental composition of the ceramics. To reduce this influence the ceramic matrix was analysed. The results have been plotted in a biplot of alumina and the sum of the fluxing elements (Na_2O+MgO+K_2O+CaO+FeO) and coloured by fabric. The results show that there is one major compositional group (circled in Fig. 10.4) and three outliers. The major group comprises crucibles from all three sites and they have a medium alumina content (*c.* 13–18 wt.%) and relatively high fluxing elements (*c.* 8–11 wt.%). One outlier, RS 363-14[b], is characterised by its high silica content (82.4 wt.%) and low alumina (10.5 wt.%) and fluxing elements (3.3 wt.%). The second outlier, the only wheel-thrown crucible RS 1183c[a], is characterised by its high alumina content (22.3 wt.%) and the third, FH 822, by its high fluxing elements (14.0 wt.%) which is a result of particularly high sodium (3.4 wt.%) and potassium (7.5 wt.%) in comparison to the other material at Exeter (average sodium: 0.9 wt.%; and potassium: 2.9 wt.%).

There is some correlation between the fabric and chemical groupings with the main chemical group made up of Fabrics 1 and 2 and the outliers of Fabrics 3 and 4. The exception is RS 363-14b, which has been assigned to Fabric 1, but falls outside the main compositional group.

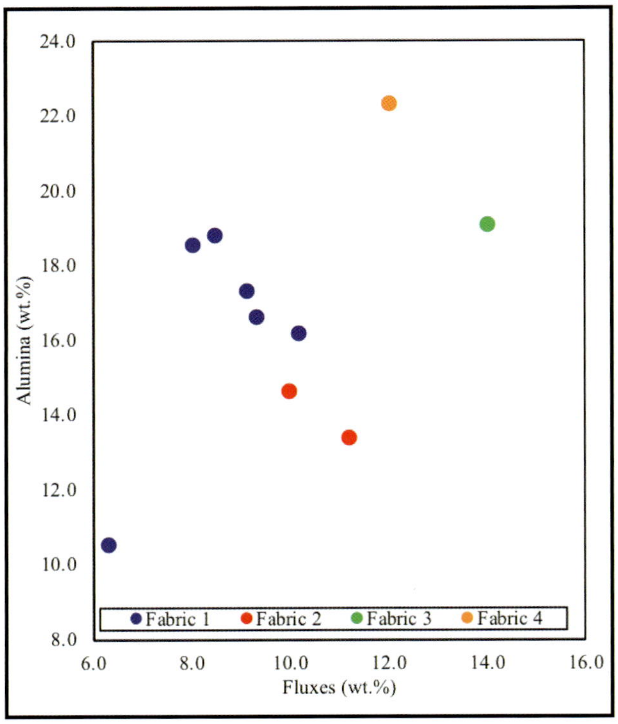

Fig. 10.4 Biplot of alumina against the sum of the fluxes (Na2O+Mg+K2O+CaO+FeO), coloured by fabric (matrix analyses)

This piece of ceramic is highly vitrified and bloated making it difficult to assign it accurately to a fabric group. Elemental analysis shows that it is likely made of different raw materials, although it is difficult to say any more about provenance due to the method of analysis and the lack of trace elemental data.

The refractoriness of ceramic materials used in metallurgical processes is an important consideration. Refractory materials are those able to withstand high temperatures without decomposition and resist various thermal and physical stresses. Clays rich in silica and/or alumina are best suited as they tend to be low in iron and alkali earth elements which act as fluxes. The use of refractory clays for crucible production really begins in the Roman period in Britain (Freestone and Tite 1986), though of course there are exceptions. However, low refractory clays are still used for their production during this period but are often adapted with the addition of sand (rich in silica (quartz)) and/or organic material. Previous work suggests that metalworkers were aware of the suitability of different clays and clay paste recipes for use as crucibles, and whilst in modern terms they may not be classed as refractory, they were fit for purpose. The material from Exeter is technically not highly refractory, with relatively low alumina and high fluxing elements (Na_2O+MgO+K_2O+CaO+FeO), although due to the large volume of quartz inclusions and in most examples also organic matter present, whether intentional or not, the ceramics appear to have been suitable for use at high temperatures.

Summary and conclusion

The assessment and analysis of metallurgical debris, both past and present, has shown that a range of small-scale metallurgical processes took place across Exeter during the Roman military and civilian phases of occupation. During the Roman legionary phase iron smithing and copper-alloy working occurred within the Trichay Street *fabrica*, copper-alloy was worked at South Street, while dumps of material against the fortress defences at Friernhay Street and Rack Street produced evidence for silver and copper-alloy working. The Early Roman town probably saw gold working at Friernhay Street, while copper-alloy was worked at Rack Street in the early Roman period, and silver cupellation is also evident there in the Roman period. The range of processes identified in Exeter is typical of the Roman period where a large increase in the use of metals sees evidence appear at most sites in the province. The significant variation in copper-alloy compositions is consistent with Roman copper-alloys (Dungworth 1996) and our understanding of the prolific recycling of metals during the period (Craddock 2009, 110).

The crucibles assessed in this study appear to be fairly consistent in form, all but one being small, shallow, hemispherical bowls with pouring spouts moulded into the rim. This is a typical handmade form of the Roman period with examples found at sites such as Doncaster and Colchester (Bayley 1992). The abundant quartz and organic matter in the fabrics used to make these handmade forms is also consistent with evidence from across the country. There is one wheel-thrown crucible which is made of a distinctive fabric and also falls away from the main group chemically. This indicates that, though handmade forms predominate, wheel-thrown forms were in use within the town, though to what extent is unclear with such a small assemblage of material. Evidence for the application and use of EOLs in Exeter is limited, with only two crucibles showing clear evidence and one potential other example. EOLs were used across the Roman empire but are largely associated with wheel-thrown forms, and Gardner (2018) has shown that this is a technology which predominates in high-status and well-connected Roman settlements such as provincial capitals and *coloniae*.

Overall, this material is representative for a site of this size and status in the Roman period. There is potential for further research into the precious metals industry in the area, which should include not only the metallurgical ceramics but also a study of the other metallurgical debris. As the analysis of a metal spill from Rack Street shows, there is potential for other materials to provide supporting evidence. Equally, a wider study including surrounding sites and a consideration of the silver rich deposits in the

Tamar Valley and Combe Martin, in North Devon, may be beneficial.

Assessment of the medieval crucibles and other archaeometalurgical debris
by David Dungworth

Each crucible fragment was examined in turn (following Historic England 2015) and a full catalogue can be found in Appendix 10.1. Although the catalogue contains 34 entries, 15 of these are probably not crucibles and in most cases the other vessels are simply sooted rather than vitrified. In addition, three of the catalogue entries are fragments of vitrified hearth lining. This leaves just 14 catalogued crucibles and one 'heating tray'. Given the limited number of crucibles from medieval contexts, the limited dating of these contexts, and the possibility that some or all of them could be residual, the potential of these crucibles to provide information on the manufacture and use of crucibles in medieval Exeter is restricted. As a result it was decided not to proceed with the detailed SEM-EDS analysis of the crucibles.

One of the items assessed does warrant more detailed reporting (Catalogue No. 9; Fig. 10.5). This large medieval ceramic object was recovered during the 2005 excavations at Princesshay (Site 156, context 1555, sf 2425). The artefact was identified during excavation as a fragment of a crucible, although the curve suggests that it had a diameter of about 300 mm (much larger than any previously identified medieval crucibles). In addition, the fabric is mostly oxidised fired, where crucibles are usually reduced fired, in order to protect the contents from oxidation. There is an opening close to the 'rim' which displays more vitrification than the other parts of the object. While there appear to be no exact parallels for this object, it is proposed that this is a portable hearth. The 'rim' would have actually been the base and rested on the ground, and the opening would have been a bellows hole.

Fig. 10.5 Fragment of large ceramic object, possibly a portable hearth, from Princesshay

Appendix 10.1

Catalogue of medieval crucibles and other archaeometallurgical debris (for Site Numbers see Chapter 2)

Lab	*Box*	*Accession*	*Site*	*Description*
1	EX186	204/1999.3	Bartholomew Street 1959 (Site 35) Area XI SF 124	Body Fragment of crucible
2	EX302	300/1988.9	196–7 High Street 1973 (Site 43) L.247 Published in Allan 1984a	Fragment of rim and body of crucible. External diameter ~80 mm. Height >38 mm
3	EX302	300/1988.10	196–7 High Street 1973 (Site 43) L.247 Published in Allan 1984a	Fragment of rim and body of a vessel. Inverted rim of large vessel (diameter ~200 mm). The body is fractured at what appears to be a carination. Probably not a crucible.
4	EX353	300/1988.1211	Goldsmith Street 215 (Site 37/39) A54.7	One of two body fragments of possible crucibles
5	EX353	300/1988.1211	Goldsmith Street 215 (Site 37/39) A54.7	One of two body fragments of possible crucibles
6	EX4354	450/2005	Princesshay (Site 156) EPH05 7940 (fill of 7898 medieval ditch 3)	Fragment of body of possible crucible
7	EX4354	450/2005	Princesshay (Site 156) EPH05 968 medieval	Fragment of body of possible crucible
8	EX4354	450/2005	Princesshay (Site 156) EPH05 3755 sf 3430 medieval	Fragment of 'heating tray'
9	EX4354	450/2005	Princesshay (Site 156) EPH05 1555 sf 2425 medieval	Portable ceramic hearth structure ?!
10	EX3143	24/2005	Cathedral Close 1971 (Site 40) F49	Fragment of body of possible crucible
11	EX4698	526/2006/12	George's Meeting House (Site 153) EGM04 601	Fragment of body of possible crucible (or hearth lining)
12	EX3127	45/2005	Rack Street 1977 (Site 64) DRSV 103 L1272	Base fragment from small rounded crucible. Appears to have been deeper than its diameter but no rim visible

Lab	*Box*	*Accession*	*Site*	*Description*
13	EX3127	45/2005	Rack Street 1977 (Site 64) DRSV 103 L1272	Body (? rim) fragment from a small rounded crucible (cf Lab#12)
14	EX3127	45/2005	Rack Street 1977 (Site 64) DRSV 103 L1272	Mould sprue cup
15	EX1795	24/2005	Cathedral Close (Site 40)	Shallow bowl with pinched spout. Approximate diameter 70 mm, height 30 mm. Biscuit fired: reduced core, oxidised surfaces. Not a crucible?
16	EX1795	53/2005	Goldsmith Street (Site 37/39) 45-44-13 F326 C11–C12	Fragment of base of crucible
17	EX1795	53/2005	Goldsmith Street (Site 37/39) F326 late C12	Fragment of flat base of vessel. Partially vitrified Crucible?
18	EX1795	53/2005	Goldsmith Street (Site 37/39) GS693 37-90-7	Fragment of body of crucible?
19	EX1795	53/2005	Goldsmith Street (Site 37/39) GS F169 31-90-20	Fragment of vessel?
20	EX1795	53/2005	Goldsmith Street (Site 37/39) 29-96-8	Fragment of possible crucible
21	EX1795	53/2005	Goldsmith Street (Site 37/39) GS 120	Fragment of possible crucible
22	EX1795	53/2005	Goldsmith Street (Site 37/39) GS 41-52-6	Three fragments of hearth lining
23	EX1795	53/2005	Goldsmith Street (Site 37/39) GS 27-92-14	Two fragments of possible crucible
24	EX1795	53/2005	Goldsmith Street (Site 37/39) GS 41-40-16	Fragment of a base of a vessel. Large base diameter (?>200 mm). Flat base?
25	EX1795	53/2005	Goldsmith Street (Site 37/39) GS 43-60-5	Seven joining fragments of crucible base. Diameter >95 mm. Rounded base. Part of #26 and #27
26	EX1795	53/2005	Goldsmith Street (Site 37/39) GS 43-60-5	Three joining fragments of crucible. Part of #25? and #27
27	EX1795	53/2005	Goldsmith Street (Site 37/39) GS 43-60-5	Fragments of crucible (rim). Diameter ~105 mm Part of #25 and #26
28	EX1795	55/2005	NatWest Bank (Site 62)	Fragment of rim and body of bag-shaped crucible. Rim diameter 75 mm max body diameter 90 mm. Base missing but probably rounded. Height >75 mm
29	EX1795	9/2005	Rack Street (Site 52) RS 74 BB	Fragment of the rounded end of a flat-bottomed vessel (a 'boat'?)
30	EX1795	9/2005	Rack Street (Site 52) RS 75 F65	Slag or vitrified clay (?crucible)
31	EX1795	29/2005	196–7 High Street 1973 (Site 43) HS 73 F250	Probably crucible fragment
32	EX1795	51/2005	Trichay Street (Site 42)	Crucible fragment (rim)
33	EX1795	51/2005	Trichay Street (Site 42)	Crucible fragment (body)
34	EX1795	51/2005	Trichay Street (Site 42) TS 72 F161	Crucible fragment? Rim diameter ~35 mm Specks of gold visible

11

Dendrochronology: The Roman and Medieval Timbers from Exeter

Cathy Tyers

Introduction

This chapter briefly summarises a re-evaluation of dendrochronological analyses undertaken on archaeological material from Exeter in the 1970s and 1980s. Those sites are placed within a more general context of dendrochronology in Exeter, and its wider environs, as well as addressing questions relating to the source of timber utilised in Devon.

Setting the scene

Dendrochronology is an independent and precise scientific dating technique that is now well established and widely used on archaeological sites and historic buildings. The information obtained is a valuable component underpinning the discovery, identification and understanding of assets in the historic environment, aiding decisions relating to protection, management and conservation, and enhancing appreciation and enjoyment of our buried archaeology and standing buildings at both national and local levels. However, whilst there is now a robust network of oak (*Quercus* spp) data in existence across much of England with the last millennium being particularly well-replicated, the situation was very different four decades ago. The potential of dendrochronology in relation to (pre)historic assets was only just beginning to be fully realised and more widely investigated, these investigations initially centring on archaeological excavations being undertaken in major urban areas. The dendrochronological work undertaken on excavated timbers from a small number of sites in Exeter during the 1970s and early 1980s was therefore at the forefront of the development of dendrochronology as a dating tool in England.

It was John Collis who initiated dendrochronological studies in Exeter, collecting samples from waterlogged medieval deposits at Goldsmith Street in 1971/2 (Sites 37 and 39; Chapter 6 above) and submitting them to his Sheffield University colleague Ruth Morgan shortly afterwards. This early initiative showed that some of the excavated material was producing long tree-ring sequences, although no dating was achieved in this earliest round of work. Collis' lead was followed in 1972/3 when a further valuable series of Late Saxon and later medieval samples was recovered from Trichay Street (Site 42; Chapter 5 above). This material formed the basis of the earliest dendrochronological work in the South-West Peninsula, undertaken by Morgan and Hillam in 1976–8 and published some years later (Hillam 1984a; Morgan 1984). At that time the network of oak reference data (chronologies) in England was only starting to be established (*e.g.* Fletcher *et al.* 1974; Barefoot 1975; Morgan 1976; Fletcher 1977; Siebenlist-Kerner 1978) and thus the successful dating of sites in the wider South-West was reliant on reference chronologies from London and the South-East, as well as from Germany and Ireland (Baillie 1977a; 1977b; Hollstein 1980). This comparative data was added to throughout the 1980s as the result of archaeological excavation and the increasing analysis of historic buildings. This resulted in the network of dated chronologies steadily becoming more widespread and better replicated, although it continued to be dominated by the South-East (including London) and Midland regions with some exceptions, notably the urban centres of York and Carlisle.

From the early 1970s the Exeter Museums Archaeological Field Unit (EMAFU) had also collected samples from historic buildings in the city, especially those in the course of demolition or alteration. Here the initial results were often disappointing as it became apparent that much of the timber was fast-grown (*e.g.* comments in Hillam 1984a). There were, however, some successes such as the dating of 41–2 High Street (Mills 1988; and see Bedford and Salvatore 1993a) and Exeter Guildhall (Bridge 1986; Mills 1988). Some material collected in those early years, such as that from 38 North Street (demolished in 1972: EAPIT 1, Fig. 1.6; Thorp 2012) has proved datable as more reference material has accumulated in recent years (Tyers 2012) and some buildings have been subsequently revisited (*e.g.* Howard *et al.* 1999; 2004).

By the early 1980s the excavations had yielded a good series of samples with felling dates ranging from the late 10th/early 11th to early 13th centuries, along with a smaller amount of later material, mainly from historic buildings, dating to the 15th century and later, but with a large gap between the two. With this in mind John Allan drew up a proposal for a partnership between the EMAFU and Sheffield University which would bridge this chronological gap by sampling the series of well-preserved medieval roofs at Exeter Cathedral, where there were very large numbers of timbers of late 13th and 14th-century date. The early work, which sampled about 180 timbers, was presented in Mills' PhD thesis (Mills 1988), and in 1999 the programme resumed with Historic England (then English Heritage) support, and it is still ongoing (Howard *et al.* 2001a; 2001b; Arnold *et al.* 2003; 2006a; 2006b; forthcoming; Hurford *et al.* 2009). With well over 300 samples examined, the cathedral is one of the most fully dendrochronologically investigated buildings in the country.

Nevertheless, Exeter and the South-West Peninsula remained somewhat isolated dendrochronologically, and by the late 1980s remarkably little progress had been made in the wider region, particularly bearing in mind its wealth of extant historic buildings. The network of dated sites across Devon and the wider South-West region in general was very sparse and the overall success rate (the number of dated timbers as a percentage of the number of timbers considered suitable for analysis) was far lower (*c.* 30–35%) than across the better represented areas of the country, where on average approximately 70–80% of timbers deemed suitable for analysis were successfully dated by dendrochronology, at least for the last millennium. It was suggested at the time that the problems encountered with respect to successful dendrochronological analysis in Exeter, and the county of Devon as a whole, were potentially related to the apparent preponderance of timbers derived from young trees with complacent growth (*i.e.* lack of variation in ring width which theoretically indicates that the growth of a particular tree is relatively unaffected by variation in climate). Other potential issues considered included the reuse of timbers resulting in multiple woodland sources being represented in a single structure, the varied topography producing differences in tree growth over quite small areas, and the possibility of importation of timber from further afield in England or elsewhere in Europe.

The 1990s saw a rapid rise in the use of dendrochronology, particularly in relation to historic buildings, and hence a substantial improvement to the network of reference chronologies across mainland Britain. This network of reference chronologies now extends back over 7,000 years but the geographical and temporal coverage remains variable and it is still, not surprisingly, dominated by material from the last millennium. Historic England (English Heritage) were exploiting the potential of dendrochronology with respect to the understanding of the historic environment and were undertaking increasing amounts of dendrochronology. This included a significant amount of work undertaken in Devon, partly through work on sites (*e.g.* Groves and Hillam 1993; Groves 1998) undertaken in support of the strategic objectives of the then English Heritage and partly through the Devon Dendrochronology Project (Groves 2005; Tyers *et al.* forthcoming). The Devon Dendrochronology Project was jointly funded by Historic England (then English Heritage) and Devon County Council with Keystone Historic Buildings Consultants being commissioned to undertake the initial selection of candidate buildings and the recording of buildings selected for dendrochronological analysis. The primary aims of the project were to address and elucidate the problematic nature of dendrochronology in Devon. It was hoped that a targeted approach through this project, in combination with casework, would enhance the network of reference chronologies in Devon, thereby increasing the success rate of dendrochronology within the county and refining typological understanding of the development of traditional building techniques.

The Devon Dendrochronology Project demonstrated, as had previously been suspected, that there is indeed a preponderance of timbers derived from young trees, certainly with respect to historic buildings dating to the 14th to 17th centuries, resulting in far more sites being considered unsuitable for dendrochronological analysis than in many other areas of England. The extensive assessments undertaken of historic buildings, or phases within, for the Devon Dendrochronology Project showed that around 30–35% were deemed unsuitable for analysis as they were constructed using timbers with too few rings (<40–50) for reliable dating purposes (*i.e.* timbers that had been derived from young trees still in their formative growth period), although recent technical advances now mean that some of these buildings would be considered suitable for analysis. This is in stark contrast to, for example, Herefordshire where fewer than 5% of buildings are rejected at assessment stage but similar to, for example, Kent. However, the work undertaken in the 1990s and subsequent decades demonstrated that in Devon, and other areas considered problematic, significantly enhancing the density of site chronologies in these peripheral/problematic areas, thereby forming a well-replicated local network of chronologies, results in a significant rise in success rates.

Re-evaluation

The archaeological sites highlighted for re-evaluation were those originally analysed in the 1970s and 1980s. The sites are listed below (with the Site Numbers referring to Chapter 2 in this volume):

- Paul Street (Site 76; Hillam 1984c; and new analysis as part of EAPIT)
- Trichay Street (Site 42; Hillam 1978a; 1984a)
- Goldsmith Street (Sites 37/39; Morgan 1980; 1981)
- Exe Bridge (Site 56; Hillam 1978b; and new analysis as part of EAPIT)
- Quay (Site 84; Mills 1988)
- 198 High Street (Site 55; Morgan pers. comm.)
- Friernhay Street (Site 75; new analysis as part of EAPIT) can now be added to this list

With the possible exception of a very limited amount of remeasuring on some of the staves from Goldsmith Street held in the Royal Albert Memorial Museum (RAMM), this project was reliant on the availability of the original ring width measurements, the majority of which were at a resolution of 0.1 mm rather than the 0.01 mm resolution now standardly used. It is worth noting that long-term storage of waterlogged samples in a waterlogged state in anything other than strictly controlled conditions results in severe degradation and thus, broadly speaking, where samples had been retained they were no longer in a state of preservation that allowed remeasurement anyway. Long-term storage of such samples remains a national issue.

A series of samples present in the RAMM stores were identified for rapid assessment but, following careful re-examination of the samples initially selected during the rapid assessment as possibly worth further investigation, only a small number of additional samples were incorporated into this project. Details of the reanalysis of each site and the newly analysed samples from Exe Bridge, Friernhay Street and Paul Street are provided in Tyers forthcoming and summarised in Figs 11.1 and 11.2 in which felling dates are given using the relevant sapwood estimates (Baillie 1995; English Heritage 1998). While the series of newly analysed barrel staves from Paul Street were proven to be coeval, they unfortunately remain undated by dendrochronology (Tyers forthcoming).

The four timbers from Paul Street remain the only ones dated from Roman Exeter. Two of the Trichay Street timbers and one of the Exe Bridge timbers are potentially the earliest dated medieval timbers from these excavations with *terminus post quem* dates for felling of AD 931, AD 944, and AD 951 respectively. A group of Goldsmith Street timbers were felled towards the mid 11th century and appear to potentially just pre-date a group from Trichay Street. A further series of timbers from Trichay Street date to just over a century later in the late 12th century, whilst a few, along with the Friernhay Street timber, date to the early or mid 13th century. A second timber from Exe Bridge probably just pre-dates the mid 16th-century 198 High Street timber, which in turn is likely to just pre-date several timbers from Goldsmith Street that were probably felled in the latter half of the 16th century. The dated timbers from the Quay represent several different felling periods ranging from the mid 16th to early 17th centuries.

In addition to the sites indicated above, samples from standing buildings, excluding the main structural material from the Cathedral which is outside of the scope of this project, also analysed in the 1970s or 1980s were re-evaluated, but apart from confirming the dates obtained for the Guildhall, 41/42 High Street and Bishop's Throne in the Cathedral (Bridge 1986; Mills 1988), no additional samples from either these or other buildings were dated.

The current state of dendrochronology in Exeter and Devon

Devon now has a well-replicated robust continuous chronology produced from the 90+ dated historic buildings

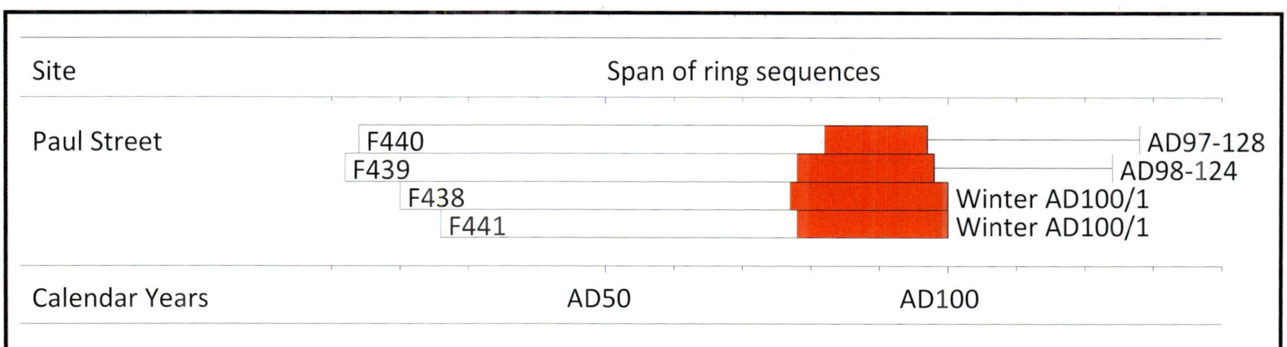

Fig. 11.1 Bar diagram showing the dated Roman timbers from Paul Street with individual felling dates/date ranges. White bars: measured heartwood rings; red bars: measured sapwood rings (© Historic England)

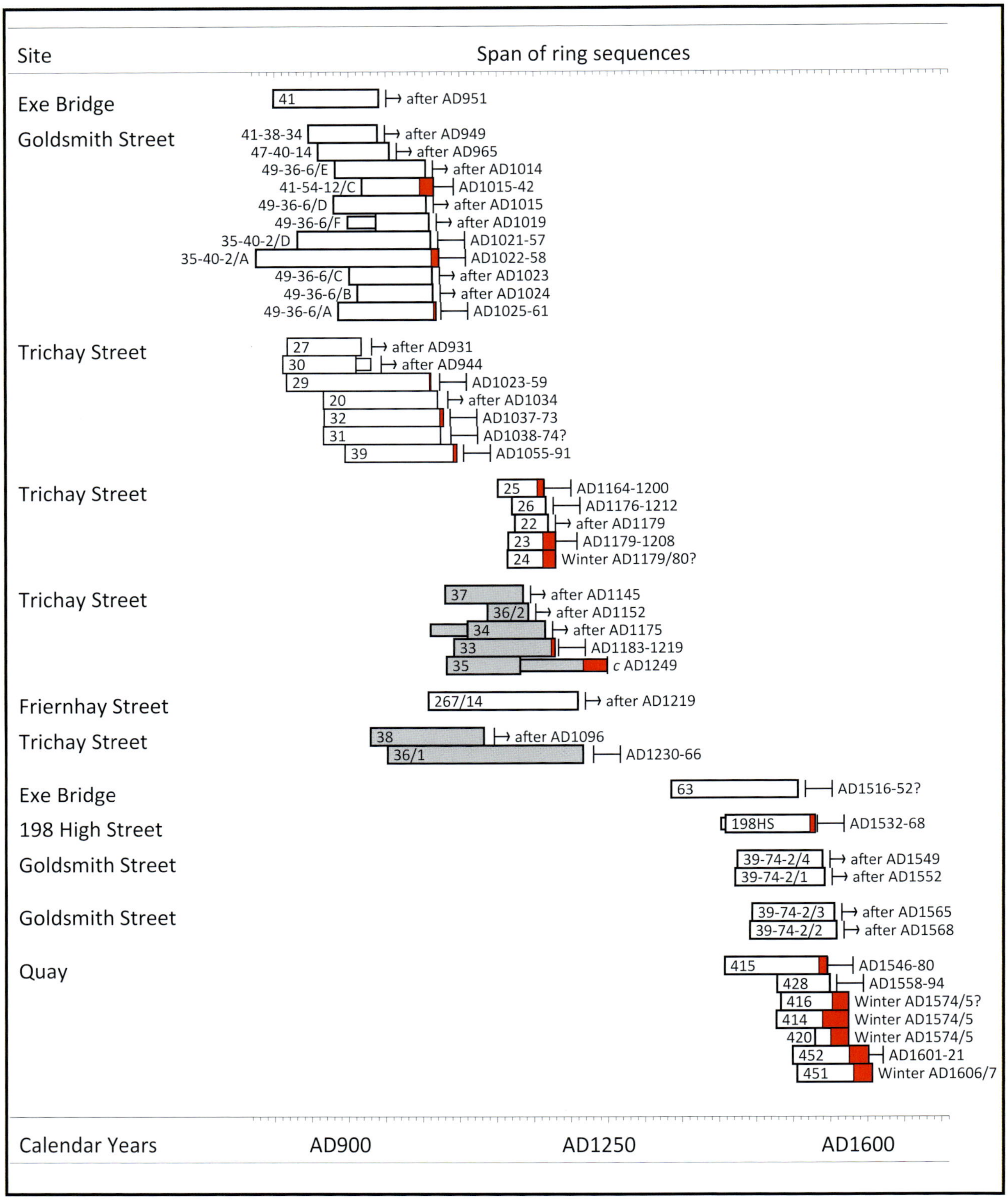

Fig. 11.2 Bar diagram showing the dated medieval timbers from Trichay Street, Goldsmith Street, Exe Bridge, Quay, 198 High Street, and Friernhay Street with individual felling dates/date ranges. White bars: measured heartwood rings (native oak); grey bars: measured heartwood rings (Irish oak); red bars: measured sapwood rings; narrow bars: unmeasured rings (© Historic England)

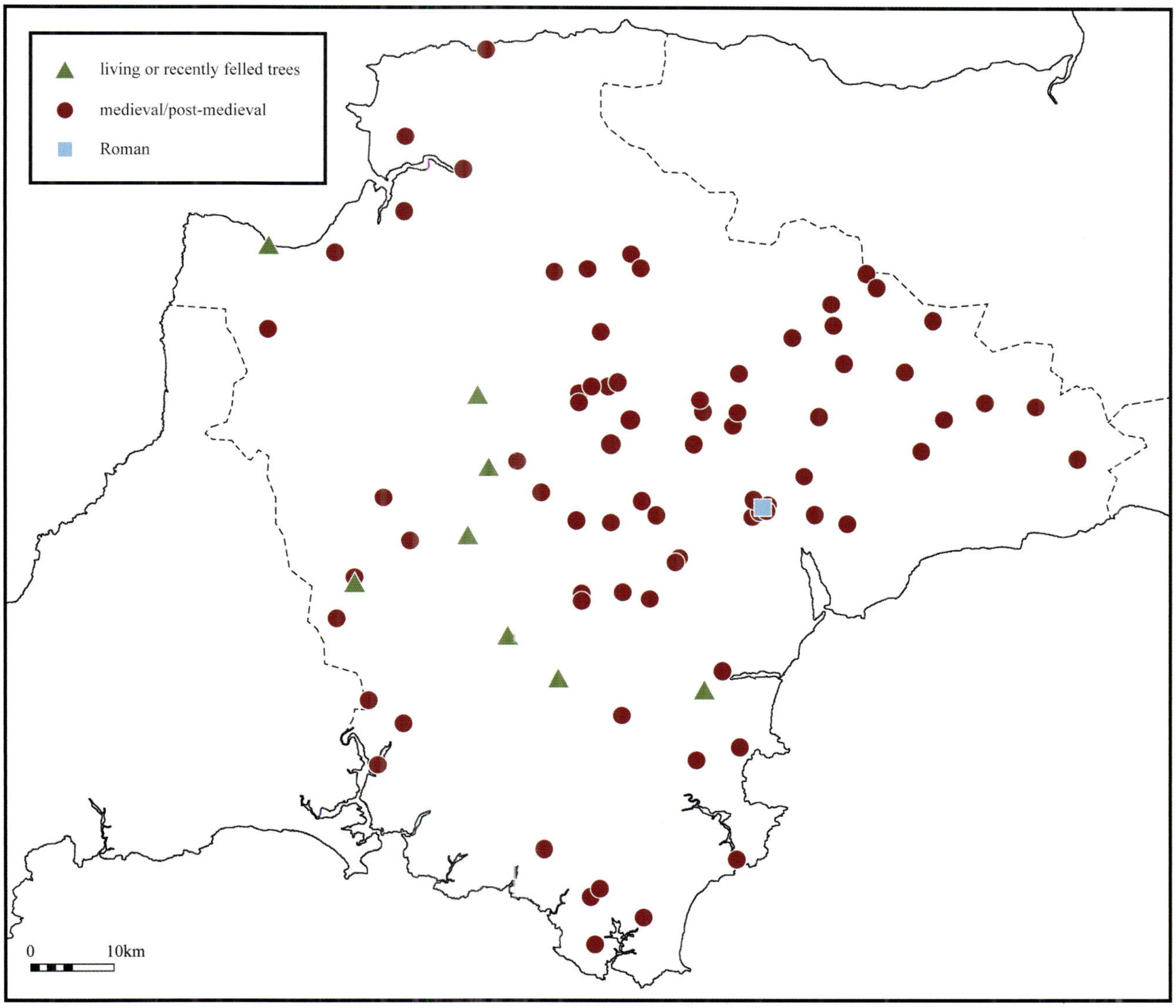

Fig. 11.3 Map showing the network of sites across Devon from which there are dated reference chronologies. Green: living or recently felled trees; red: medieval/post-medieval; blue: Roman (© Historic England)

(including Exeter Cathedral and various other multiphase buildings) and a small number of archaeological sites (see for example the Historic England Research Report Series reports http://research.historicengland.org.uk/ and the Vernacular Architecture Group Dendrochronology Database http://archaeologydataservice.ac.uk/archives/view/vag_dendro/). This continuous chronology spans the 12th to early 21st centuries and incorporates the majority of dated individual site chronologies, thought to represent local timber resources, plus the small number of woodland sites where living trees or recently felled trees were analysed to produce known local site chronologies (Fig. 11.3). There remain discrete areas within Devon that, for this period, require further targeted coverage, probably due to the varied geographical nature of the county, but Devon and the wider South-West region in general remains very poorly represented before the 12th century. Thus, whilst dendrochronology has clearly made significant advances with respect to sites dating to much of the last millennium in Devon, it has basically not advanced with respect to sites dating to the early 12th century or earlier, with the Paul Street Roman data still being the only dated chronology for the Roman period in the South-West Peninsula.

The number of dated timbers in Devon from the last millennium is approaching 1,500 and the success rate is now far closer to the national average. Approximately 40% of these dated timbers are from Exeter and 60% from the rest of the county. Within Exeter approximately 60% of the dated samples are from the Cathedral and only 40% from other sites, the latter including high status buildings with clear ecclesiastical connections such as the Bishop's Palace, the Archdeacon of Exeter's House and The Deanery. The felling periods identified for the

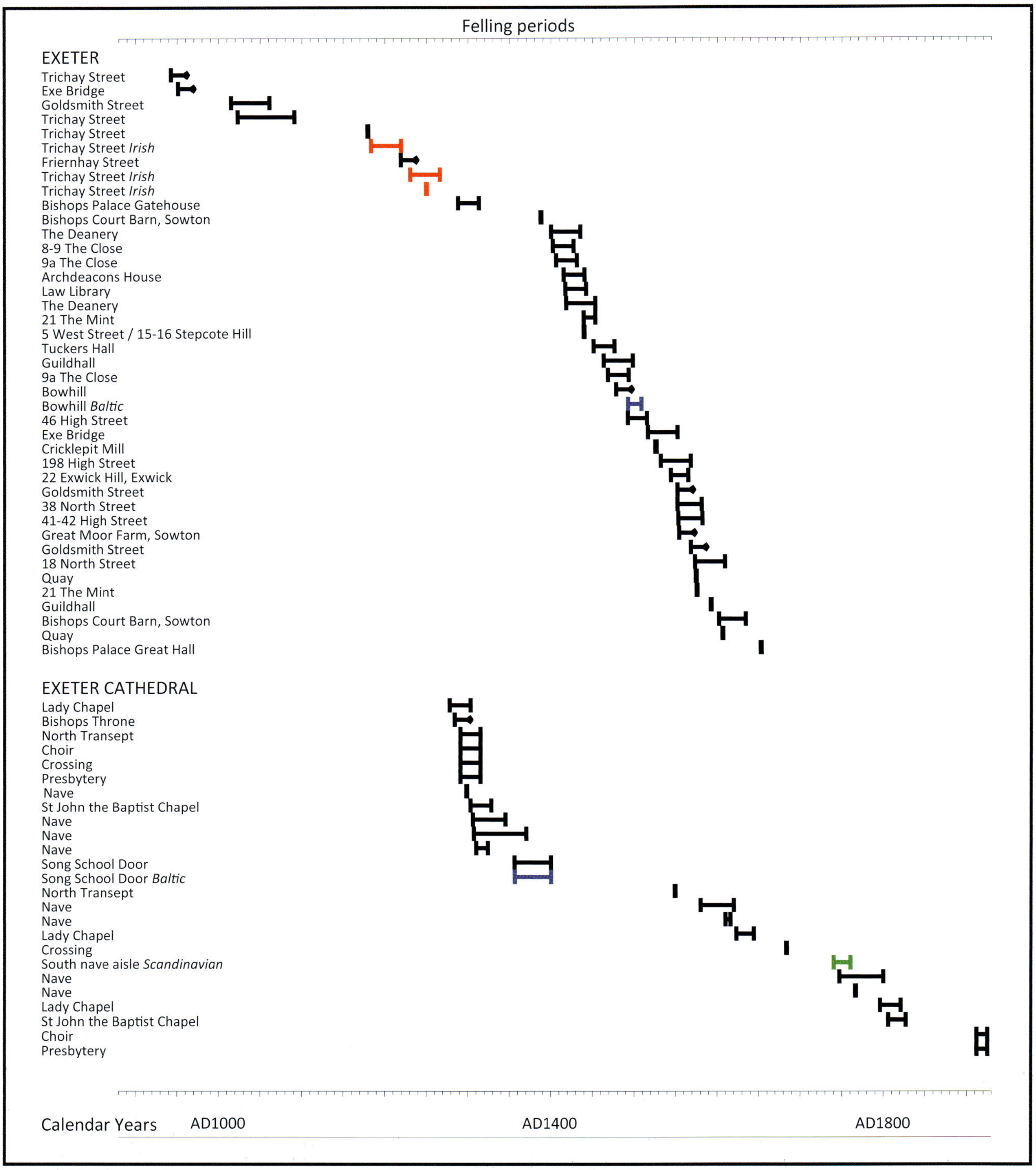

Fig. 11.4 Diagram summarising the felling periods identified from sites in Exeter for the last millennium. Note that most entries represent a series of dated timbers and that some entries represent either multiple or extended felling periods. Black: English oak timbers; red: Irish oak timbers; blue: Baltic oak timbers; green: Scandinavian conifer timbers (© Historic England)

dated sites in Exeter are illustrated in Fig. 11.4. The vast majority of the dated buildings, excluding the Cathedral, date from the early 15th century through to the late 16th century. The bulk of the dated timbers from the Cathedral date from the very late 13th century through to the mid/late 14th century and it is noticeable that the only other building with late 13th/early 14th-century timbers identified is the gatehouse to the Bishop's Palace. There are, however, timbers from the Cathedral dating to the mid 16th through to the early 20th century, while timbers dating to the mid 13th century and earlier are all from archaeological excavations.

Timber source

Documentary sources suggest that much of the timber utilised in Exeter Cathedral and civic buildings within the city was from woodland resources in Devon, generally not too far removed from Exeter (Erskine 1981; 1983; Juddery and Staniforth 1986; Mills 1988). The dendrochronological evidence, in general, accords with the documentary evidence and with the overall assumption of the predominant use of relatively local timber sources in Exeter and across the county (see below and Tyers forthcoming), although it should be noted that dendroprovenancing is a tool that is limited to distinguishing between broadly regional sources (*e.g.* Bridge 2012; Bridge and Fowler 2019). Two buildings, the Grade I listed Leigh Barton which lies approximately 1.3 km north-east of Churchstow in the South Hams (Groves 1998; 2006), and the Grade II* listed Broomham which lies approximately 3.1 km north-east of King's Nympton in North Devon (Groves 2005), are used to illustrate the likelihood of use of relatively local timber sources through the level of similarity of their site chronologies with reference chronologies produced from other individual sites (Figs 11.5 and 11.6). The level of similarity is affected by various factors including replication (sample depth) and chronology length, whilst the distribution of reference chronologies with which significant levels of similarity is shown depends on the overall distribution of contemporary reference chronologies. For illustrative purposes, the buildings chosen therefore have broadly coeval chronologies spanning 1345–1484 (Leigh Barton) and 1370–1464 (Broomham). These two examples are both thought to indicate the use of relatively local timber sources with the distribution of reference chronologies being what is considered typical of such material. Leigh Barton shows the highest levels of similarity with other sites from the South-West Peninsula but also shows a trend up the west of England and into Wales. This is more pronounced for Broomham and it is of note that both show some significant, although at a lower level, similarity with southern Ireland (and Leigh Barton with west Scotland) but no significant levels of similarity with chronologies from France, Belgium, Germany or beyond.

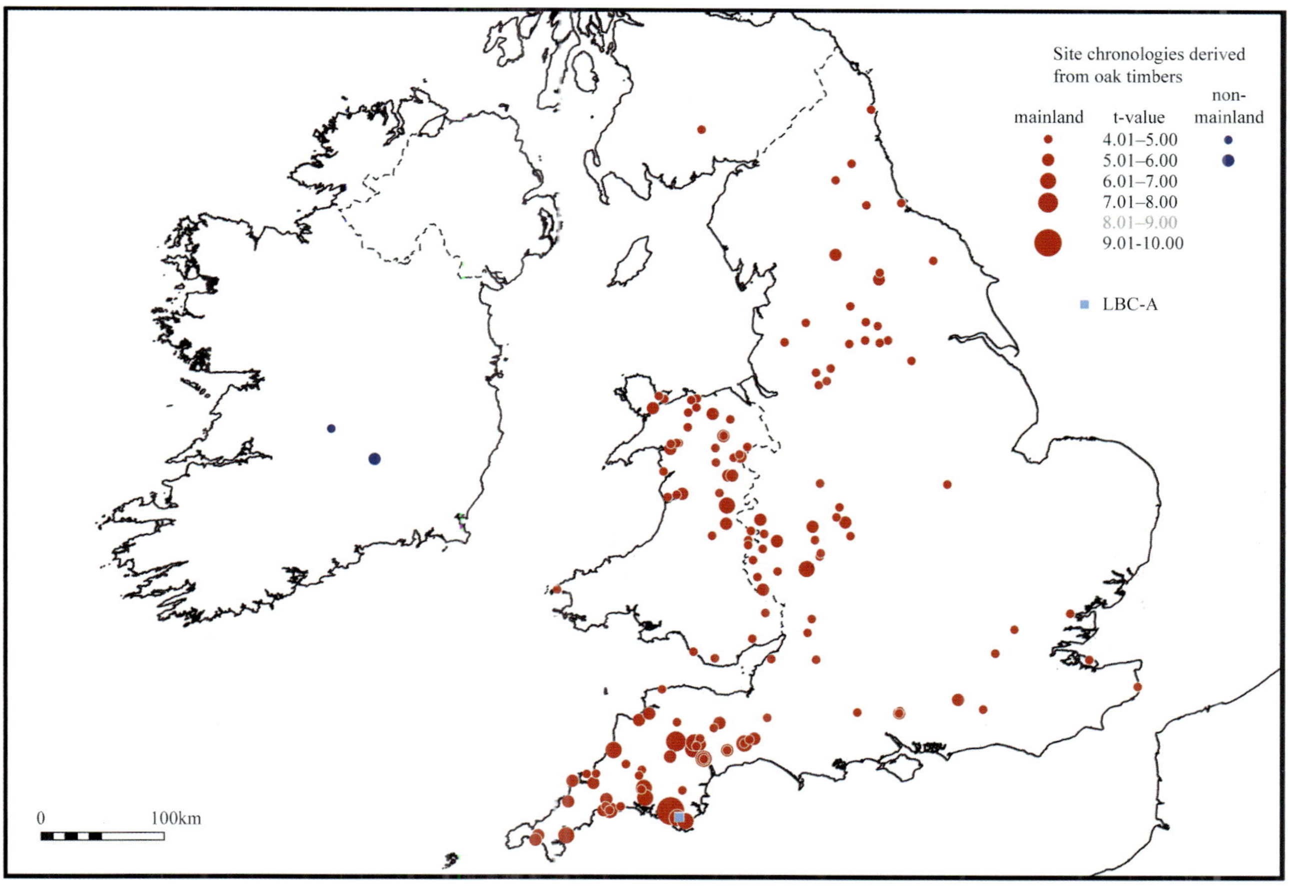

Fig. 11.5 Dendroprovenancing of the 140-year, 15-timber, site chronology, LBC-A, from Leigh Barton, in Churchstow, spanning the period 1345–1484. Light blue square: location of Leigh Barton; red circles: site chronologies derived from oak timbers of likely mainland Britain origin showing significant similarity; dark blue circles: site chronologies derived from oak timbers of non-mainland Britain origin showing significant similarity (© Historic England)

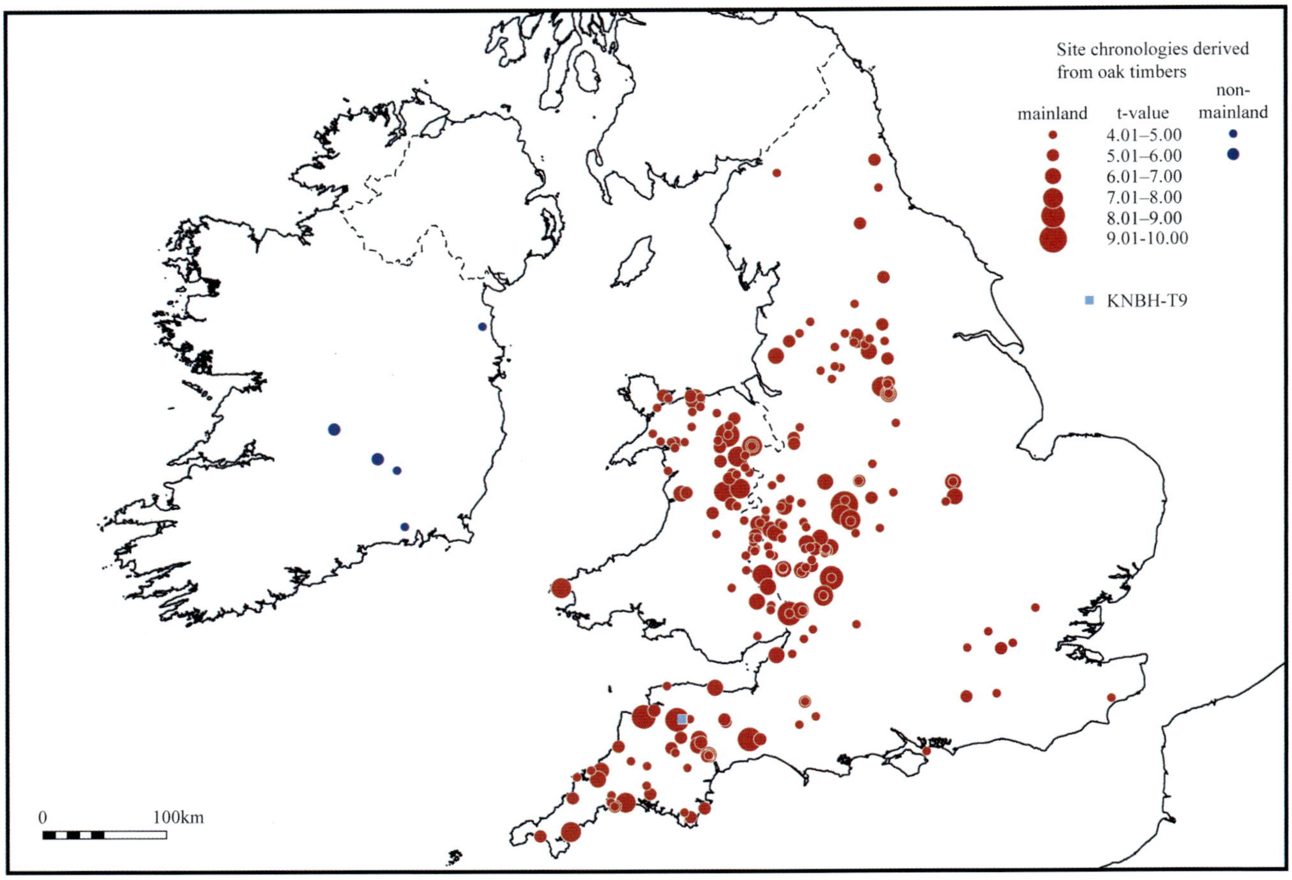

Fig. 11.6 Dendroprovenancing of the 95-year, 9-timber, site chronology, KNBH-T9, from Broomham, in King's Nympton, spanning the period 1370–1464. Light blue square: location of Broomham; red circles: site chronologies derived from oak timbers of likely mainland Britain origin showing significant similarity; dark blue circles: site chronologies derived from oak timbers of non-mainland Britain origin showing significant similarity (© Historic England)

A series of dated timbers from 46 High Street, in Exeter (Arnold and Howard 2009), the site chronology from which spans 1309–1491, show a similar trend in chronology distribution up western England and Wales, as well as some lower levels of similarity with both Ireland and right up into the west of Scotland (Fig. 11.7). This chronology is both better replicated and slightly longer than the chronologies from Broomham and Leigh Barton and it is noticeable that it shows more extensive similarity to chronologies over towards the east of England. The overall conclusion is that the dated timbers from 46 High Street, in Exeter, are likely to have been derived from relatively local sources.

Documentary evidence makes it clear that as early as the 12th century there was significant trade in European timber, operated through organised routes (*e.g.* Salzman 1952; Dollinger 1970; Kent 1973; Fedorowicz 1980; Clarke 1992; Bowett 2012). Initially this trade was predominantly timber brought in for specialist purposes, such as oak planking or deal (softwood) boards, and formed only part of the cargo, although during the mid 17th century there was a significant rise in the importation of baulks, dominated by pine (*Pinus sylvestris* L.), that is maintained throughout the latter centuries of the last millennium. By the mid 18th century a number of Baltic ports were sending cargoes consisting solely of timber to England, these being dominated by material suitable for general construction purposes. Dendrochronology has provided supporting evidence through the identification of imported timbers (Bonde *et al.* 1997; Wazny 2002; Daly 2007; Tyers 2010). In England, Irish timbers have been identified in, for example, Salisbury Cathedral (Miles 2002a; 2002b), German timbers in, for example, Peterborough Cathedral (Tyers and Tyers 2015), and numerous instances of Baltic timbers have been identified (*e.g.* Groves 1992; Tyers 1998; Tyers 2003; 2014; Miles *et al.* 2004). In Exeter the 14th-century vertical oak boards from the Cathedral Song School door and the *c.* 1500 oak ceiling boards at Bowhill have been identified as of Baltic origin (Hurford *et al.* 2009; Groves 2004), whilst the mid 18th-century pine timbers in the Cathedral nave south aisle roof have been identified as Scandinavian in origin (Arnold *et al.* forthcoming).

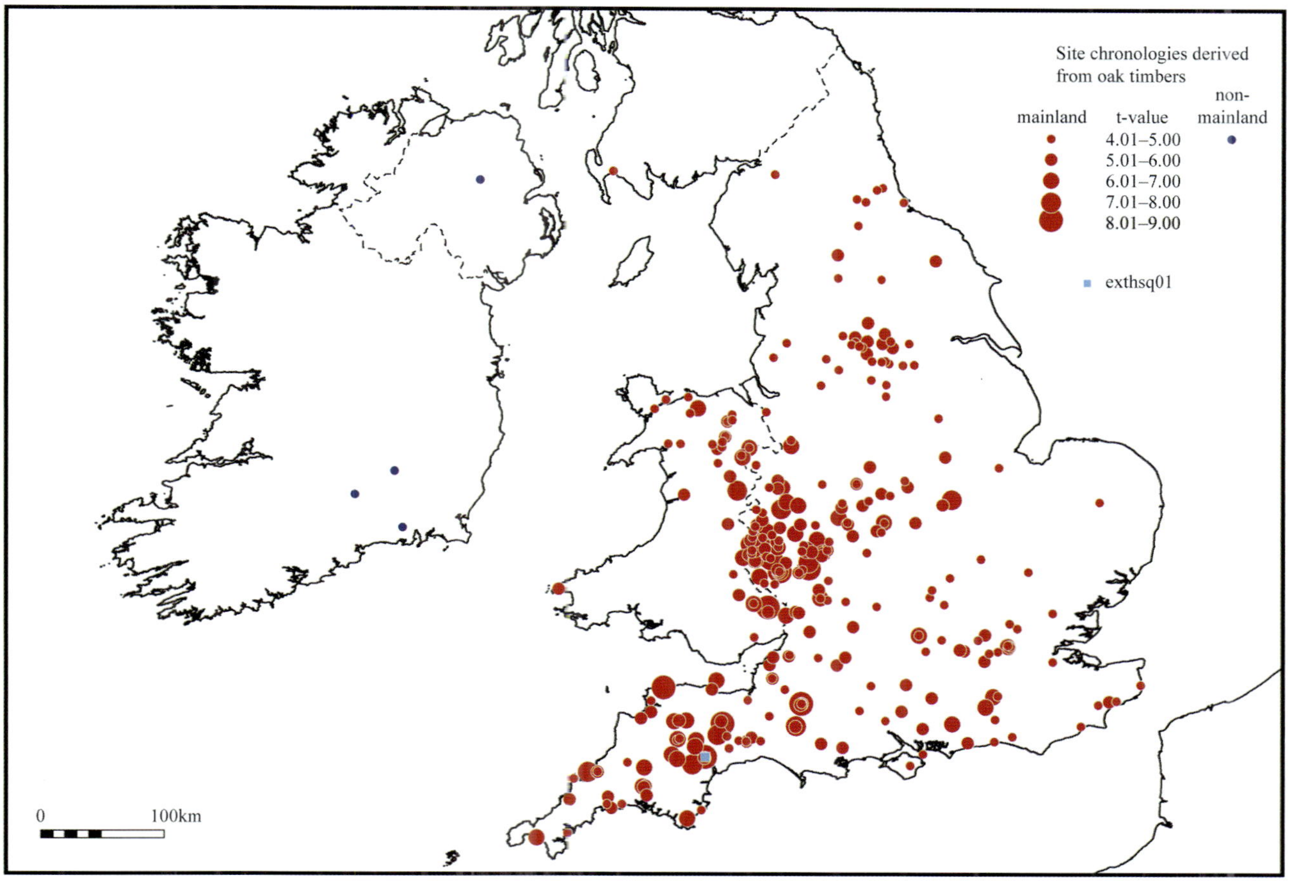

Fig. 11.7 Dendroprovenancing of the 183-year, 25-timber, site chronology, EXTHSQ01, from 46 High Street, in Exeter, spanning the period 1309–1491. Light blue square: location of 46 High Street; red circles: site chronologies derived from oak timbers of likely mainland Britain origin showing significant similarity; dark blue circles: site chronologies derived from oak timbers of non-mainland Britain origin showing significant similarity (© Historic England)

Hillam (1978a; 1984a) had originally raised the possibility that some of the Trichay Street timbers were of Irish origin but it was concluded at that time that this was relatively unlikely. It has been noted through documentary evidence, however, that there are strong links between the South-West Peninsula and Ireland and that the Exeter Cathedral accounts indicate the use of boards from Ireland and Wales in the early 14th century (Erskine 1981, 87, 89, 138). The possibility of the presence of Irish timber at Trichay Street was therefore considered worthy of reinvestigation, bearing in mind the development of the network of Irish data in the intervening decades, and this clearly demonstrates that at least some of these timbers – those dating to the late 12th and 13th centuries (Fig. 11.2) – are likely to be of Irish origin. They show the highest levels of similarity with reference chronologies from the south and east of Ireland, as well as chronologies from Salisbury Cathedral identified as representing Irish origin timber (Figs 11.8 and 11.9). These seven timbers from Trichay Street identified as likely Irish origin can therefore be added to the handful of other sites now identified in England as potentially having timber from Ireland.

The provenancing of other timbers from Trichay Street is, however, not so clear and highlights some of the problems with dendroprovenancing. The chronology from the earliest group of Trichay Street timbers, dating to the early/mid 11th century (Fig. 11.2), shows a high level (t-value = 8.0) of similarity with the chronology formed from the group of 11 timbers of similar date from Goldsmith Street (Fig. 11.2). The combined sequence from these two groups of timbers has been successfully dated but relevant reference chronologies are very sparse in the South-West Peninsula and north into Wales and the dating is therefore reliant on well-replicated long reference chronologies from further afield (Fig. 11.10). The lack of high levels of similarity with either Irish or French/Belgium/German chronologies, compared to the similarity demonstrated with southern English chronologies, albeit somewhat more distant from Exeter, is taken to suggest that this material may well be English and potentially from relatively local sources. However,

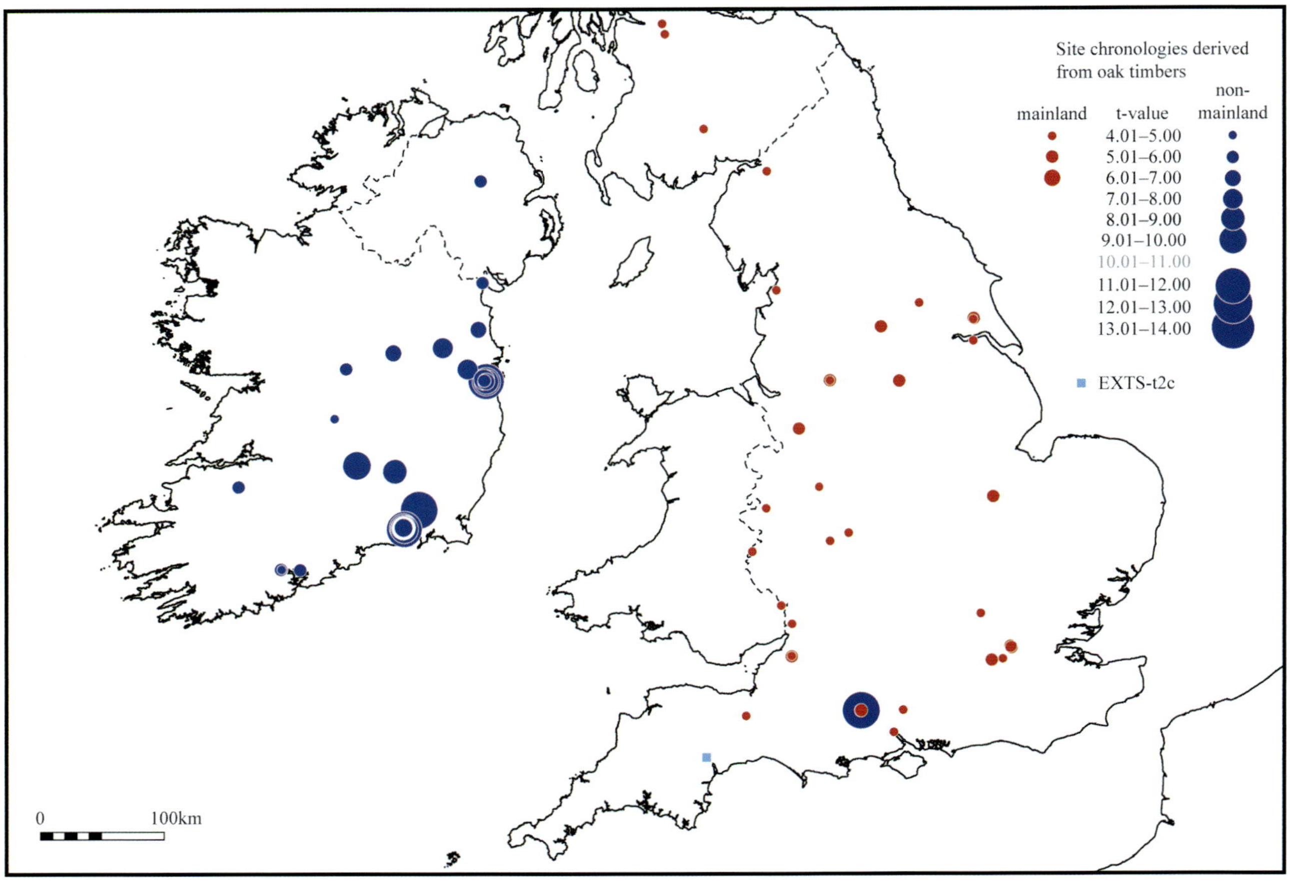

Fig. 11.8 Dendroprovenancing of the 288-year, 2-timber, site chronology, EXTS-t2c, from Trichay Street, in Exeter, spanning the period 929–1216. Light blue square: location of Trichay Street; red circles: site chronologies derived from oak timbers of likely mainland Britain origin showing significant similarity; dark blue circles: site chronologies derived from oak timbers of non-mainland Britain origin showing significant similarity (© Historic England)

due to the lack of a strong local, or even regional, network of chronologies for the relevant period, the source remains uncertain, as it also does for the group of five late 12th-century timbers from Trichay Street (Fig. 11.2) that are again thought likely to be of English origin (Tyers forthcoming).

This early/mid 11th-century probably English material and the late 12th/13th-century Irish material is predominantly radially split planks, whilst the late 12th-century probably English material is, with one exception, baulks (Hillam 1978a; Morgan 1980). The early/mid 11th-century probably English material from both Goldsmith Street and Trichay Street has a tendency to be derived from generally slower-grown and longer-lived trees than the late 12th/13th-century Irish material (Tyers forthcoming). This latter is very different from the late 12th-century material, probably of English origin, which is derived from faster-grown, younger, trees (*ibid.*). These observations are clearly based on very limited amounts of material but both the early probable English timbers and the Irish timbers are broadly similar in general characteristics to oak timbers subsequently widely imported from Germany and the Baltic region. This, combined with those apparently local timbers felled in the order of a century later used in the Cathedral *(ibid.*), suggests that the local environs did contain trees that could produce timber of a similar quality to imported material, which raises questions as to the accessibility of local resources.

A broadly comparable picture is apparent in Bristol where archaeological material dating to the mid 12th to early 13th centuries, and thus equivalent to that of the Exeter material investigated, shows similarities with respect to source and characteristics to that of Exeter. The majority of archaeological material from Bristol, at present, appears more likely to be of English origin (Tyers forthcoming) probably derived from sources in the surrounding hinterland in the South-West and West Midlands but, although this is highly probable for some material from Dundas Wharf and 1–2 Redcliff Street (Nicholson and Hillam 1987; Arnold and Howard 2016), it is less clear cut for other material from Dundas Wharf and Cabot Circus (Nicholson and Hillam 1987; Tyers 2013) and is again with the proviso noted above regarding the geographical coverage of the network of chronologies

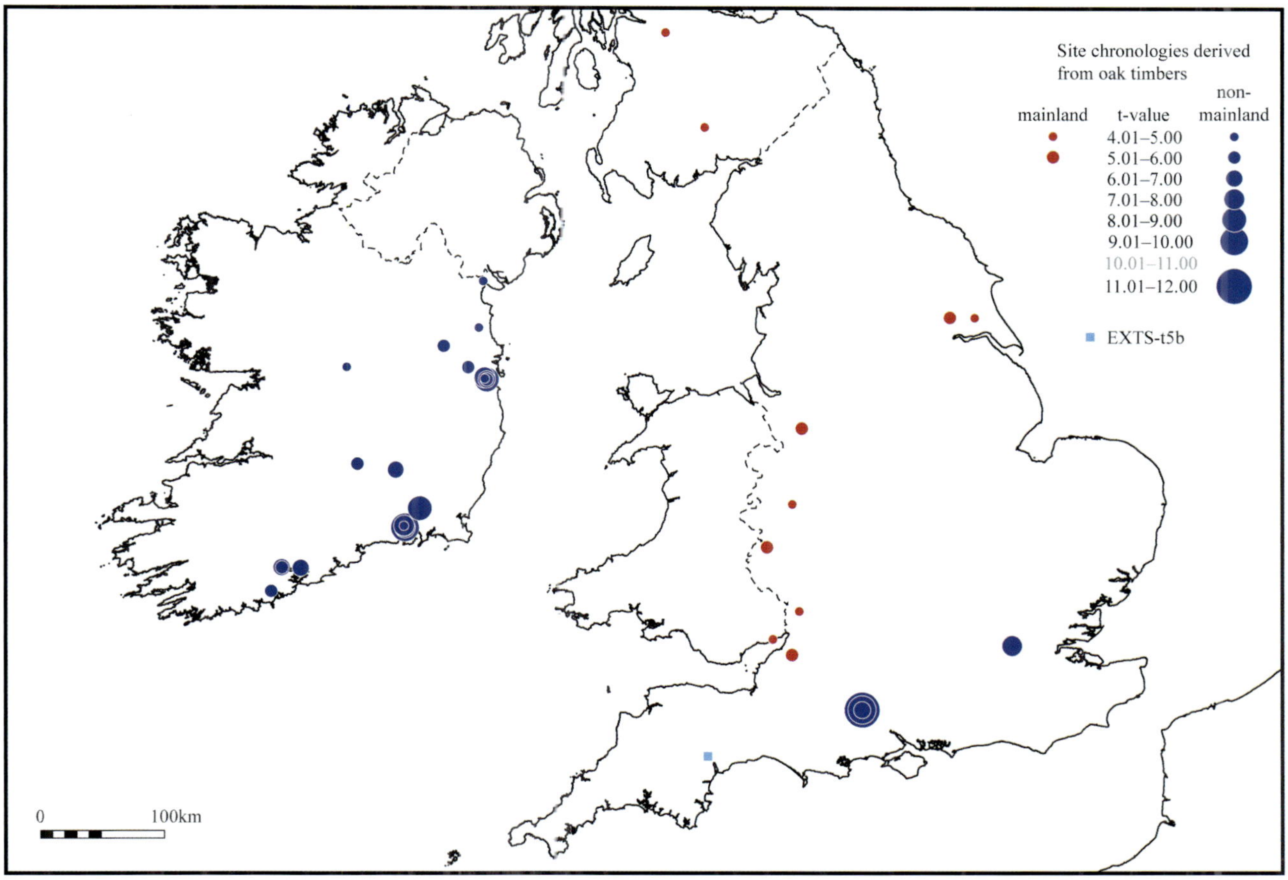

Fig. 11.9 Dendroprovenancing of the 149-year, 5-timber, site chronology, EXTS-t5b, from Trichay Street, in Exeter, spanning the period 1030–1178. Light blue square: location of Trichay Street; red circles: site chronologies derived from oak timbers of likely mainland Britain origin showing significant similarity; dark blue circles: site chronologies derived from oak timbers of non-mainland Britain origin showing significant similarity (© Historic England)

for the relevant period. However, the presence of a small amount of probable Irish origin material, dating to the mid 12th century, has now been identified at Dundas Wharf, this appearing to be derived from similar sources to the Exeter material in the south and east of Ireland (Tyers forthcoming).

Concluding remarks

The robust nature of dendrochronology has been clearly demonstrated by the validation of the original analyses undertaken on material from various sites in Exeter in the 1970s and 1980s. Dendrochronology has since progressed significantly in Devon, with numerous sites having been successfully dated from the last millennium, producing a strong local network of reference data for the 12th to early 21st centuries. This re-evaluation has also highlighted the now apparently secure provenance of some of the Trichay Street timbers as of Irish origin. These Irish timbers, along with other material in Exeter of Baltic and Scandivanian origin, do, however, appear to be the exceptions with the vast majority of dated timbers from Exeter, and the rest of the county, appearing to be from relatively local sources. It is, however, important to bear in mind that dendroprovenancing is an area of investigation under constant development with the ever-increasing network of reference chronologies and as further statistical tools are developed (Bridge and Fowler 2019). One of the key factors in relation to dendroprovenancing remains its reliance on the availability of reference data composed of local timber, as opposed to heavily replicated regional chronologies, and that this varies tremendously both geographically and temporally. This is clearly an issue with the early to mid 11th-century material from Trichay Street and Goldsmith Street whose provenance, although considered likely to be southern English, is unproven. The very importance of Exeter as a historic regional centre and its proximity to the English Channel actually increases the potential issues relating to the use of non-local timber and means that dendroprovenancing will be an ongoing part of the understanding of historic timber supply in Exeter, in spite of the apparent predominance of timber derived from relatively local sources.

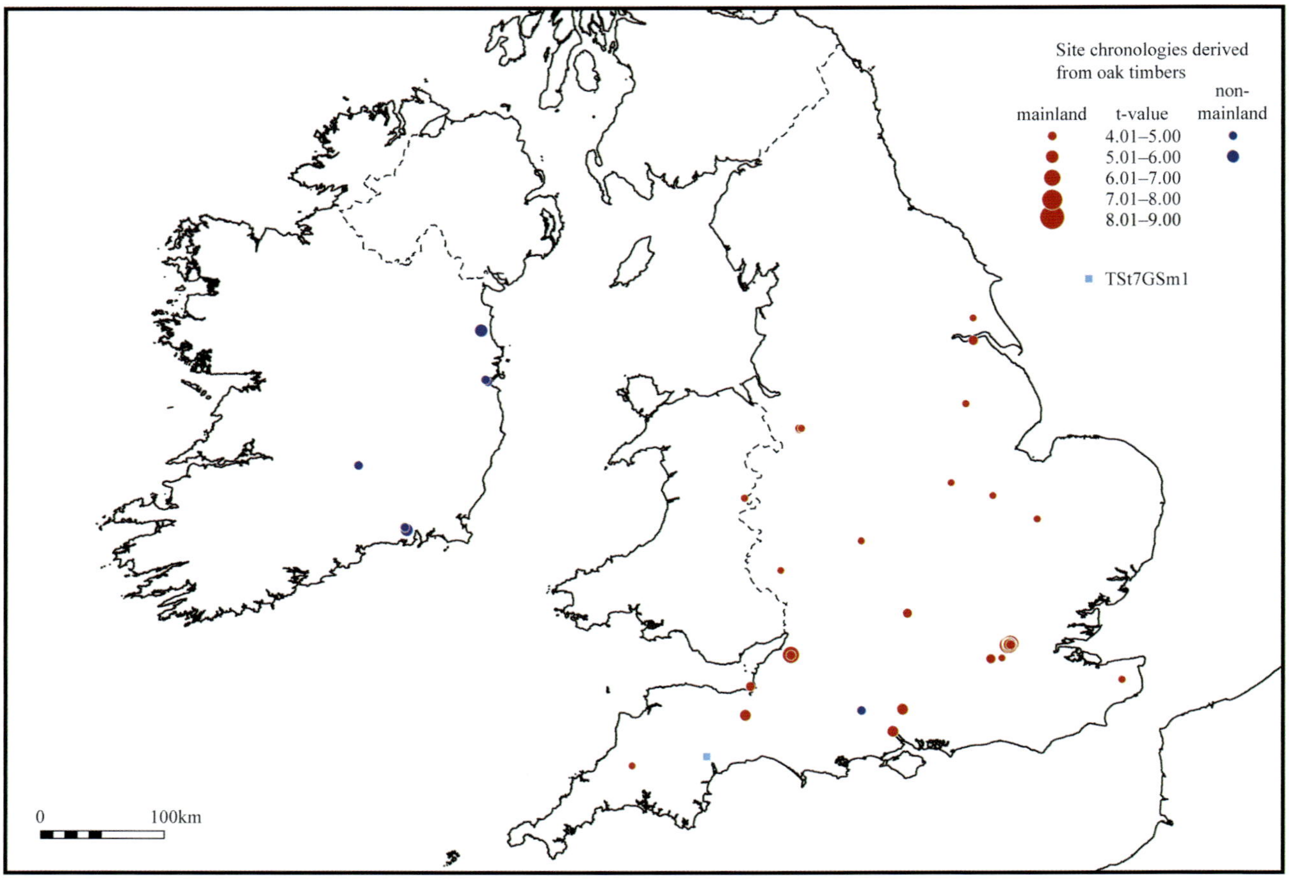

Fig. 11.10 Dendroprovenancing of the 272-year, 18-timber, site chronology, EXTS7GS1, from Trichay Street and Goldsmith Street, in Exeter, spanning the period 775–1046. Light blue square: location of Trichay Street/Goldsmith Street; red circles: site chronologies derived from oak timbers of likely mainland Britain origin showing significant similarity; dark blue circles: site chronologies derived from oak timbers of non-mainland Britain origin showing significant similarity (© Historic England)

Acknowledgements

John Allan, Ian Tyers and Martin Bridge are thanked for invaluable discussions during the writing of this chapter. Sharon Soutar (HE Graphics Officer) is thanked for her patience over the production of all of the map-based figures.

12

Pottery Supply in Roman Exeter and the South-West

Paul Bidwell

with contributions by Kamal Badreshany and Roger T. Taylor

Introduction

The most striking feature of pottery supply at Roman Exeter is the huge imbalance between the range and volume of imports in the military period and the much greater reliance on local and regional sources in the later town. The contrast is very evident in the publications of pottery from excavations in 1971–9 and from the following decade (Holbrook and Bidwell 1991; 1992). The first of these publications includes type series of the local and regional coarse wares, and also an important study by Kay Hartley (1991) of the British and imported mortaria. During the last 20 years there have been fewer excavations, but several informative pottery assemblages have been recovered. Their publications are pending; the most extensive reports will be on the pottery from Princesshay (Site 156) and St Loye's College (Bidwell forthcoming a and b).

Substantial advances in understanding pottery supply at Exeter have been made possible by studies published since the beginning of the 1990s of other pre- and early Flavian fortresses and forts, as at Usk and Lincoln, and of towns such as Dorchester. Clear differences can be seen, but varying methods of quantification often give rise to problems in making detailed comparisons. In some instances this is because the reports were prepared in the 1980s or even earlier, when there was no common approach to quantification, and then appeared in print many years later. At Exeter much of the pottery was catalogued in the later 1970s when only weights and minimum numbers were recorded, and after 1980 estimated rim equivalents (EREs) were used instead of minimum numbers; only amphorae, mortaria and fine ware sherds were counted, a method not applied to other coarse wares because of the different degrees to which their various fabrics fragmented.

The fortress at Usk is the obvious site for comparison with Exeter because both were established in the early Neronian period and have the largest amounts of published pottery amongst all the 1st-century AD military sites in western Britain. Work began on the pottery from the fortress in 1967 and was completed in 1981, but a further 12 years elapsed before the results were published (Greene 1993). Quantification of the coarse wares from selected groups was mainly by minimum numbers which prevents direct comparisons with Exeter. Fortunately, there is another way of assessing the assemblages at the two sites and determining the relative importance of various wares. From the excavations at Usk in 1965–76 there were 125 legible samian stamps on South Gaulish and early Lezoux wares (Hartley and Dickinson 1993); the equivalent figure from all sites dug at Exeter in 1971–90 but including stamps from Montans was 106. There is no reason to think that there would have been any great difference in the numbers of samian vessels in relation to those of other classes that were used at the two fortresses, and these figures might be taken to indicate in broad terms that the overall assemblage at Usk was probably only about a quarter as large again as that from the specified sites at Exeter. The demand for amphora-borne products would also have been similar. From Exeter there were 8–10 amphora stamps of 1st-century AD date (Holbrook and Bidwell 1991, 219; Williams 1992, 61–2) and 15 from Usk (Brook 1993), suggesting that the difference in the size of the two overall assemblages was perhaps a little larger than the numbers of samian stamps suggest. The nine stamps on north Gaulish mortaria at Exeter

(Hartley 1991, 221–3), as opposed to the four from Usk (Hartley 1993, 420–3), could be seen as a contrary indication, but as noted below, Exeter relied much more on imported mortaria than Usk.

There will always be reservations about these sorts of comparisons: the full legionary occupation at Exeter lasted longer than at Usk, and some of the 1st-century AD pottery at both sites is associated with later civilian occupation. Small differences in the presence of certain wares in overall assemblages can only be regarded as significant if they have been quantified using the same methods; this is almost never the case at major military sites and towns in Britain or indeed elsewhere in the north-west provinces. If, however, the differences are very large, involving factors in whole numbers rather than fractions, they can be regarded as meaningful. London has produced amounts of 1st-century AD pottery many times larger than at Exeter and Usk. More precise figures are unknown, but in simple terms if from Exeter there are the same numbers of a certain class of import as at London, at Exeter such imports can be seen to be have played a much greater part in the supply of pottery than at London. The same considerations apply of course to the pottery from the town at Exeter, though comparisons are even more difficult. Dorchester, a town of much the same size as Exeter and drawing on many of the same sources of pottery, is particularly relevant, but the only major quantified assemblage is from Greyhound Yard (Seager Smith and Davies 1993). Comparisons with Silchester and London, where there are many detailed quantifications of the pottery, are often instructive, but those towns depended on supply systems that were different from those that served the South-West.

A central theme of what follows is comparisons between sites, and the difficulties that have been outlined explain why they are necessarily laborious and unsystematic. The result, it is hoped, will be a clearer picture of pottery supply to Exeter and the general economy of the fortress and later town. There is much more that could be done with the data, already published or soon to appear, particularly in establishing the full extent to which pottery use varied at the different types of site which were dependent on the Exeter fortress. This is a field of research that depends very much on detailed quantifications, and past practices are as much a problem at Exeter as elsewhere (Rippon 2017, 337–40). Despite the repeated issue of standards and guidance since the 1980s, the latest published four years ago (Barclay *et al.* 2016), for many reasons these problems are likely to endure, not least because of slender resources and conflicting priorities in post-excavation programmes.

Note that the term 'military period' in the South-West spans the period from *c.* AD 55 to *c.* AD 80/85, applying to the area traditionally regarded as the territory of the Dumnonii. Fabric codes refer to Tomber and Dore 1998 unless otherwise stated.

The Iron Age background

Until recently no sites were known in the vicinity of Exeter where Iron Age occupation had continued into the earlier 1st century AD, and it was thus uncertain whether pottery was produced locally in the decades before the Roman conquest (Holbrook and Bidwell 1991, 15). The existence in this period of a local tradition – Late Iron Age Plain Ware (LIAPW) – has now been established following excavations at St Loye's College (Quinnell forthcoming) and Aller Cross (Quinnell 2015a, 121; and see EAPIT 1, Chapter 3). The fabric of these vessels is of Ludwell Valley type, and they were apparently from the same source as some examples of the earlier South-Western Decorated Ware. Fabric 3 in the Exeter series (Holbrook and Bidwell 1991, 181) might include examples of LIAPW and needs to be reassessed, but the fabric is very scarce in fortress and later levels.

In the Late Iron Age, regions to the east and west of Exeter produced pottery which was much more technically accomplished. Fine gabbroic ware from western Cornwall was probably traded as far east as Mount Batten, beside Plymouth Sound, where sherds of what appears to be cordoned ware have been found in pre-Roman levels (Cunliffe 1988, 24, 40). Whether gabbroic ware was distributed further along the south coast remains uncertain, but this is a question which the recently completed excavations at Mount Folly, in South Devon, might answer. The ware reached north Devon in the Late Iron Age and occurs in Early Roman contexts at Fremington, Shebbear and the fortlet at Martinhoe (Quinnell 2018b, 131–2). In the Late Iron Age, Durotrigian black-burnished ware presumably from the area of Poole Harbour (its production continuing into the Roman period as DOR BB1) is represented at Seaton by a large group (Holbrook and Bidwell 1991, 15) and at Blackhorse, 5 km west of Exeter, by a few sherds (Laidlaw and Mepham 1999, 182–3). A sherd of this ware was also recorded from the earlier of two enclosure ditches at St Loye's College which preceded the Roman settlement (Quinnell forthcoming), and it now seems that its distribution extended at least as far west as the Exe.

BB1 from South-East Dorset contributed to the supply of the fortress at Exeter and presumably arrived by the same routes as formerly, though in much larger quantities. Likewise the gabbroic ware industry served the forts in Cornwall, including Calstock; the small amounts from the Exeter fortress represented a modest extension of the Late Iron Age markets for this ware.

The supply of coarse wares in the military period

Supply to the fortress was reviewed in *Roman Finds from Exeter* (Holbrook and Bidwell 1991, 16–18), which also included type series for the four main fabric groups current in the military period: South-Western BB1 (SOW BB1: Fig. 12.2), South-East Dorset BB1 (DOR BB1: Fig. 12.2),

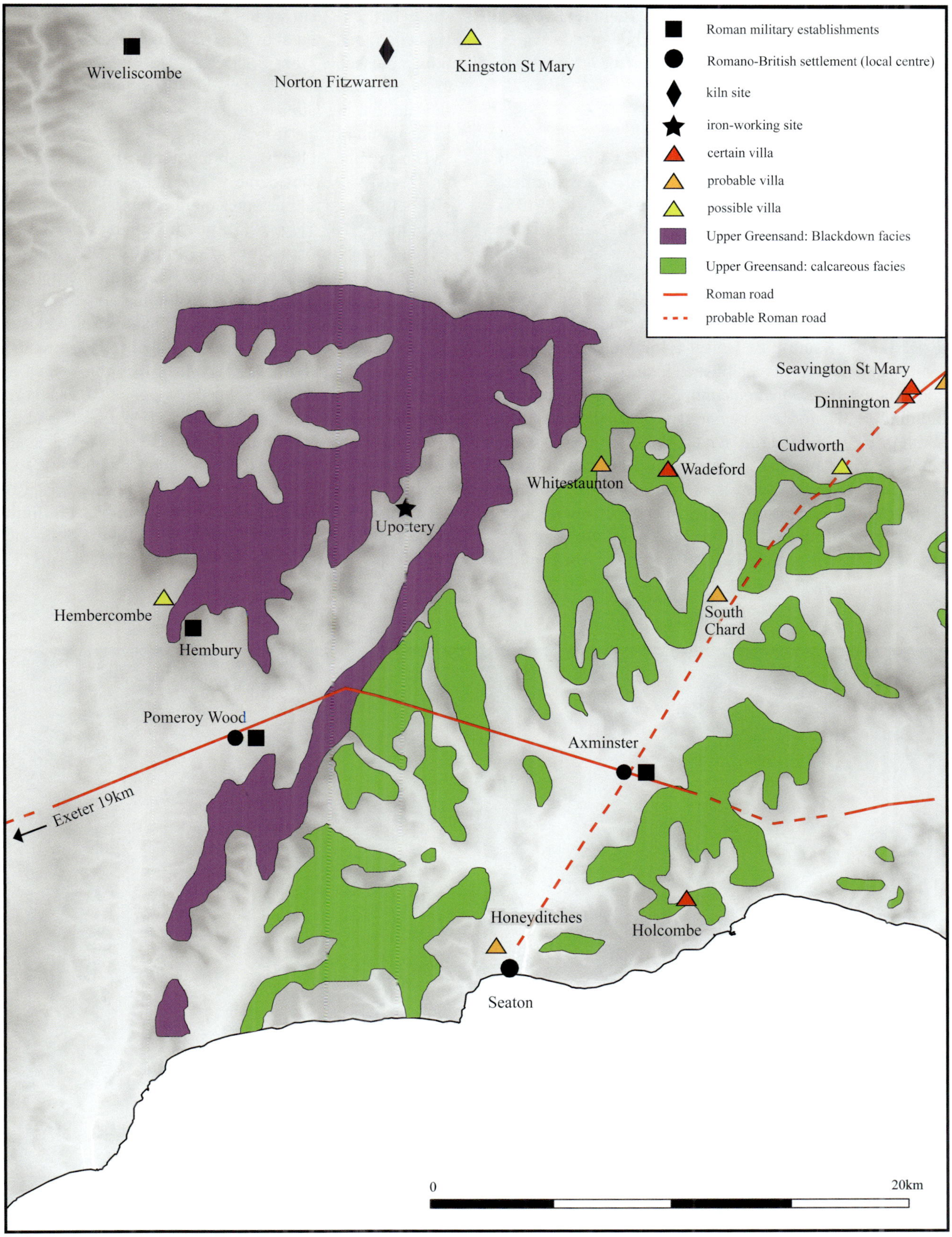

Fig. 12.1 The Upper Greensand facies in eastern Devon and the Blackdown Hills in relation to Roman major settlements and roads (drawn by David Gould)

Fortress Wares and Sandy Grey Wares. There is now more to say about South-Western BB1 and the Fortress Wares, but little that is new has been learnt about the other fabrics.

South-Western BB1 (SOW BB1)

The source of this type of black-burnished ware, formerly thought to have been in western Dorset or southern Somerset (Holbrook and Bidwell 1991, 90, 114, 135), has now been identified as the western Blackdown facies of the Upper Greensand in the Blackdown Hills, on the eastern border of Devon (Fig. 12.1; Appendix 12.1). In the fort at Waddon Hill, South-Western BB1 supplied most of the cooking wares, and was more than twice as common as BB1 from South-East Dorset (Holbrook and Bidwell 1991, 91). The fort was established in the Claudian period, and although its occupation continued for a few years after building of the fortress began at Exeter, all the South-Western BB1 could hardly have arrived during this short period of overlap. The industry was clearly established before *c*. AD 55. It lay at least 16 km west of Waddon Hill, presumably near the border of the area under direct Roman control in the Claudian period. Durotrigian pottery from Seaton (see EAPIT 1, Chapter 3), a site on the south coast *c*. 12 km south-east of the Blackdown facies, has been mentioned above. Its fabric is macroscopically indistinguishable from South-East Dorset BB1, and the absence of the South-Western version might be taken to indicate that the latter industry was not established until the beginning of the Roman period.

The amounts of the two fabrics at military sites in eastern Devon vary considerably. At Exeter South-Western BB1 is from two to four times more common than South-East Dorset BB1 (Fig. 12.5), but at Bolham in Tiverton it is six times more common (Holbrook 1991, tab. 7, 46.4% by weight as opposed to 7.4% of all the pottery with a total weight of 18.04 kg excluding amphorae and mortaria). This might be because Bolham is much closer to the Blackdown facies which lie about 10 km to the south-east, but at Pomeroy Wood, in Honiton, which is even closer to the facies, South-East Dorset BB1 is more common (Seager Smith 1999, tab. 81, phases 2 and 3, 22.4% as opposed to South-Western BB1 at 15.5%, in an assemblage weighing 20.46 kg excluding amphorae). The disparity in supply to the two forts might have arisen if the industry was located around the north-western limit of the facies, perhaps in the vicinity of Hemyock in the Culm Valley where there was pottery production in the

Fig. 12.2 Examples of later 1st and 2nd-century AD BB1 vessels from Exeter sites; back row, left and right, in South-East Dorset fabric, the other three in South-Western fabric (© RAMM)

medieval period (see Chapter 17 below); Pomeroy Wood is on the road that runs east from Exeter to Dorchester and would have had easier access to supplies of South-East Dorset BB1. One advantage of a more northerly location for the South-Western BB1 industry would have been proximity to the road which, it has been suggested, ran north-east from Exeter through Cullompton (EAPIT 1, Chapter 3).

The Fortress Wares

The Exeter Fortress Wares were made in four fabrics (A–D), ranging from a fine oxdised version to others, reduced and oxidised, which were heavily gritted to varying degrees (Holbrook and Bidwell 1991, 144–54). Some of the wide range of types seem to be derived from the pottery of South-East England while others have continental parallels (*ibid*., 144–5). The late Vivien Swan (2009, 35–6), who had an unrivalled knowledge of coarse wares in the north-western provinces, was able to be more specific. Some of the Exeter types, most notably the tripod bowls, resembled 'vessels indigenous to the area south-east of Paris, in north-west Burgundy, the Yonne and upper Loire valleys', and Swan considered that these Fortress Wares were made by 'potters craft-trained in that general region, … [who were] expected to make vessel-types which conformed to Roman military requirements as well as pots with Gaulish affinities.' Another strand in the origins of the potters was established by the presence at St Loye's College of a face pot in Fortress Ware B decorated with phalluses, a type otherwise confined to the Rhineland, apart from single examples from Kingsholm and *Novae*, a legionary fortress in *Moesia* (Bulgaria) (Fig. 12.3; Bidwell forthcoming b, nos. 8–9; Braithwaite 2007, 380–1).

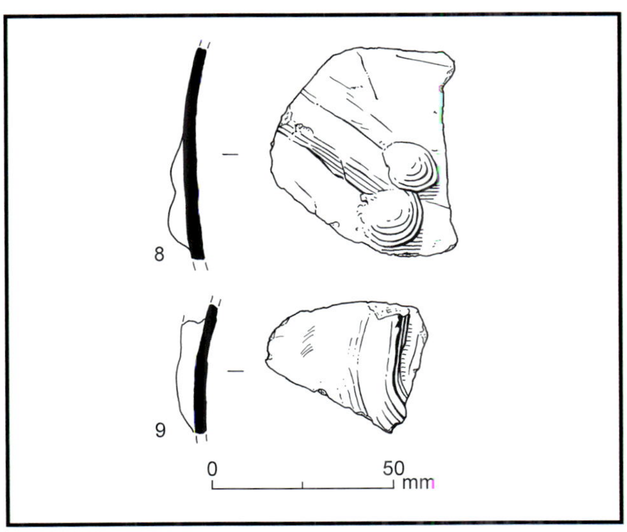

Fig. 12.3 Face pot from St Loye's College: sherds decorated with a phallus (drawing by Jane Read)

Until the studies undertaken by Taylor and Badreshany (Appendices 12.1 and 12.2), it was always assumed that the industry had been established in the vicinity of the fortress (Holbrook and Bidwell 1991, 144). At other fortresses and major military bases, the kilns were nearby, as in the 1st century AD at Colchester, Gloucester, Lake Farm and Longthorpe (Swan 1984, *passim*), and, on the Rhine in the Tiberio-Claudian period, at Neuss (Filtzinger 1972, 50, Abb. 2). To find that at Exeter the source of the clays used for the Fortress Wares lay in the Bovey Formation, some 20 km to the south-west, was thus unexpected (Fig. 12.4). However, the kilns were not necessarily located in the Bovey Formation. Major industries in Roman Britain are known sometimes to have relied on clay deposits as far as 10 km distant from the kilns (Swan 1984, 43). Nearer to Exeter in scale were the tile and pottery works at Holt, established in the Trajanic period to serve the fortress at Chester which lay some 12 km further down the River Dee. Rather than the local boulder clays, the potters used alluvial deposits occurring 11 km to the south of Holt, and for the eggshell wares an even more distant source (Grimes 1930, 10, 163). The clay deposits at Exeter were suitable for potting, and the mortaria and flagons made at Bartholomew Street West just to the north-west of the Exeter fortress at the very end of the military period were presumably made from the local clays. However, these deposits are iron-rich, and the pale to mid-grey finishes of the vessels in Fortress Wares A and B were presumably easier to achieve with the iron-poor clays of the Bovey Formation. Their potters were very skilled, apparently requiring clays of

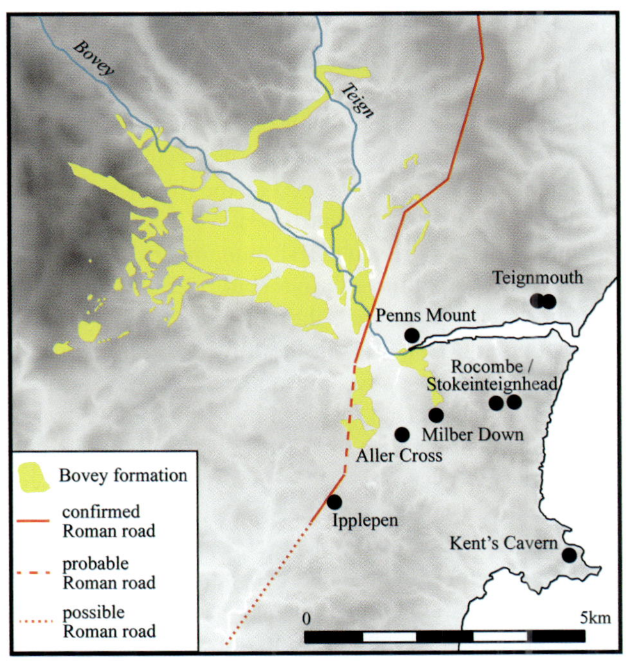

Fig. 12.4 The Bovey Formation near Bovey Tracey in relation to selected Roman settlements and roads (drawn by David Gould)

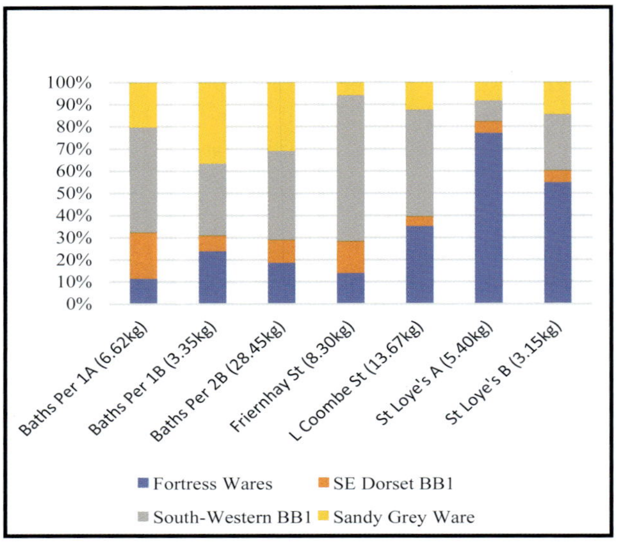

Fig. 12.5 Chart showing the relative quantities by weight of Fortress Wares, BB1 and Sandy Grey Wares at fortress and extra-mural sites. Columns 1–3: fortress baths (Bidwell 1979, tab. 9); column 4: Friernhay Street, all fortress deposits (Site 75); column 5: Lower Coombe Street, fortress period deposits (Site 97); columns 6–7: St Loye's A, upper filling of Iron Age enclosure ditch, and B, later fortress period deposits (Bidwell forthcoming b) (originated by author)

a specific character to produce vessels with the desired colours and textures.

Only traces of manufacture will determine beyond doubt whether the Fortress Wares were actually made on or near the Bovey Formation. The possibility that the clays were brought to Exeter is mainly suggested by the proximity of kilns to fortresses which has been observed elsewhere and the wider evidence for the transportation of clays. Another consideration is the frequent association of tile kilns with potteries, as seen for example at Gloucester and Holt. There have been no indications in the extensive study of ceramic building materials in Devon of production in the 1st century AD on the Bovey Formation (EAPIT 2, Chapters 13.2 and 13.3).

In the fortress at Exeter BB1 outnumbers the Fortress Wares by factors of three to four (Fig. 12.5). At St Loye's College, in sharp contrast, the Fortress Wares are much more common than BB1: in the filling of the Enclosure B ditches there is by weight almost six times more of the Fortress Wares (but the quantity is skewed by sherds from a large storage jar in Fortress Ware C), and in the later deposits twice as much. At Lower Coombe Street there are also many more Fortress Wares, relative to their occurrences in the fortress. The relevant assemblages are large enough for it to be stated with some confidence that the principal market for these wares was not the legion but rather the civilian communities in the *canabae* and in the settlement at St Loye's College. More than anything else, this is vivid testimony to the early success of BB1 potters in securing a major share in the supply of pottery to the army, a relationship which was to expand and flourish until almost the end of the Roman period. The much larger contributions which the Fortress Wares made to civilian supply surely means that their potters were also civilians.

Considering the modest contribution which Fortress Wares made to the supply of the fortress at Exeter, the wide range of types which they represented might seem remarkable, especially when compared with the limited range of locally produced wares at Usk (Greene 1993). The difference is that, even though the Usk potters met most of the legion's local need for coarse wares, their pottery apparently travelled no further afield (that at least is the implication of a statement in Webster 1992, 111). The Exeter Fortress Wares, however, were distributed throughout the South-West (Holbrook and Bidwell 1991, 16): they have now been identified at sites in an area extending from Dorchester in Dorset to Carvossa in Cornwall, which are 180 km apart (Fig. 12.6). At the military sites they occur in significant quantities but never in the amounts seen in the *canabae* at Exeter and at St Loye's College. Some finds are from civilian sites. There were five sherds of Fortress Ware B from Penns Mount, in Kingsteignton, a double-ditched enclosure 20 km south-east of Exeter which has no obvious military connections (archive report; for the site, see Pears and Smith 2016). The site lies on the Bovey Formation, but the Fortress Ware was found with samian, imported mortaria and BB1, all of the military period. Its presence does not necessarily indicate local production and might equally show that Fortress Wares were amongst the wide range of pottery used by the army that in parts of Devon also reached rural sites in small quantities during the later 1st century AD, as also at nearby Aller Cross, in Kingskerswell (Bidwell and Croom 2015, 146, tab. 5). The Fortress Wares at Dorchester were also from civilian contexts, but urban rather than rural.

The only contemporary parallels to the reach of the Exeter Fortress Wares amongst industries that were mainly supplying the army with coarse wares are the mortaria made at Kingsholm which arrived at Usk in considerable quantities and are found at Cirencester and a few other military sites in South-West England (Hartley 1993, 396–7).

At the very end of the military period in the South-West, there was another episode in the history of the Fortress Wares, when their distribution was much enlarged and included military sites in northern Britain; this is discussed further below.

Other locally made wares in the military period

There seems to have been some local manufacture of mortaria and flagons, though more of the latter were imported than once seemed likely (Holbrook and Bidwell 1991, 139–44, fabrics 401, 405, 406, 435, 440 and 451). Kilns in northern Gaul have now been recognised as major sources for Exeter, and at St Loye's College their products outnumbered other types of flagon (Bidwell forthcoming b; cf. Holbrook and Bidwell 1992, 66–7). Imported mortaria were many times more common than local products, at least until the final stage of the military occupation (Holbrook and Bidwell 1991, tab. 13; cf. 1992, tab. 1). Exeter and the South-West were exceptional in this respect. In the fortress at Usk the majority of mortaria were local products (Hartley 1993, 396), while at the military base of Kingsholm there were roughly equal numbers of local and imported mortaria (Hurst 1985, tab. 6).

Imports from Gaul in the 1st century AD

Six stamps on *terra nigra* are recorded from Exeter, all but one from sites in the fortress, and there are three from Topsham (finds from Britain up until 2006 are catalogued in Timby and Rigby 2007). There are two each from Usk and Cirencester, but none from Kingsholm and Gloucester, including the nearby site at Barnwood (Holbrook 2018, 171) which surely had military associations; there are also no stamps from Wroxeter. The general impression is that the ware is scarce on military sites in western Britain apart from those in the South-West Peninsula. This is borne out by more detailed comparisons. From the excavations in 1971–79 at Exeter there were 53 examples of *Cam.* 16 platters and 11 *Cam.* 58 cups (Rigby 1991, 77) which were by far the commonest types, as opposed to 23 of Type 10 (mainly examples of *Cam.* 16) and four of Type 8 (including examples of *Cam.* 58) at Usk (Greene 1979, 122). Kingsholm produced only five sherds of the ware (Hurst 1985, 71) and the Webster excavations in the fortress at Wroxeter only one definite *Cam.* 16 and two sherds of eggshell *terra nigra* (Darling 2002, 179–80).

Terra nigra is also common at forts in the South-West Peninsula, with 13 vessels at Calstock (Timby 2014, 45), seven vessels including two stamps at Nanstallon and five vessels including a stamp at Bolham in Tiverton. It occurs with comparable frequency at sites to the east of Exeter along the coast or a little distance inland, as at Dorchester, Chickerell, Jordan Hill in Weymouth, and Lake Farm (all in Dorset).

In south-eastern Britain, during the period immediately preceding the conquest, there was a surge in the importation of Gallo-Belgic wares and other pottery from Gaul and further afield, seen clearly at Silchester (Timby 2000, 305–9; 2018, 209–13). The westernmost site on the south coast where this is evident is the Ower Peninsula on the south side of Poole Harbour (Timby 1987; Cox and Hearne 1991, 134–5), but it is possible that before the conquest these exports occasionally found their way into Devon and Cornwall. A possible outlier from the main distribution area was at Seaton where a sherd from a cordoned beaker in micaceous grey ware was identified as an import from Gaul (Miles 1977, fig. 12, no. 15); it was found in the Durotrigian group noted above.

There were also perhaps pre-Roman imports from beyond northern and central Gaul. The occurrence at Hembury of a sherd of Arretine Ware is puzzling. It was probably Tiberian in date, and Todd (1993) preferred to see it as a survival discarded during the Roman military occupation rather than as a pre-Roman import; the hillfort was apparently not occupied in the later Iron Age. However, the ware is not known elsewhere at Roman military sites in southern Britain, except those with preceding Late Iron Age occupation from which Arretine sherds might have been displaced. Todd also pointed to the absence of the ware at Maiden Castle and Hengistbury Head, emphasising how geographically exceptional its findspot would have been in the Late Iron Age, but he overlooked the occurrence of Arretine Ware on the Ower Peninsula (Pengelly 1987). Furthermore, although he regarded its occurrence at Hembury as unique in the South-West, there is a sherd which is probably of Arretine Ware from Carvossa (Dickinson 1987) where there are some indications of later Iron Age occupation. The pottery from Hembury is shortly to be reassessed (information from Henrietta Quinnell), which might establish whether there was any occupation in the earlier 1st century AD.

The extension in this period of trade routes from Gaul along the Channel coast as far as Cornwall thus seems likely, even if the traffic west of Poole Harbour was on a very small scale. This could have been another pre-existing system which the Roman army in the South-West exploited for its pottery supply. The quantities of imported wares were of course very much greater than before the conquest, which raises the question of the extent to which the demands of the army disrupted the earlier arrangements.

Pottery reaching Exeter and the South-West from *Gallia Belgica* and other parts of northern Gaul included, in addition to *terra nigra*, butt beakers (Holbrook and Bidwell 1991, fig. 74, no. 1), North Gaulish grey wares (St Loye's College: Bidwell forthcoming b, no. 22; Okehampton: Bidwell and Croom forthcoming b, no. 2), flagons and, above all, mortaria which, as already noted, were imported in far greater numbers than in other parts of Britain. At the same time Gallo-Belgic wares reached south-eastern Britain in smaller numbers, as at London and the fortress at Colchester. Both were Claudian foundations where the pottery assemblages were free of residual material from pre-Roman occupation, a complicating factor at sites such as Canterbury, Fishbourne and Silchester, though at the last it was possible to show that by the early Neronian period Gallo-Belgic wares had become scarcer (Timby 2000, 305–9). Colchester is of particular interest because at the nearby settlement of *Camulodunum*/Sheepen, originating in the Late Iron Age, there were enormous quantities of Gallo-Belgic wares; they were far less common in the fortress and in the *colonia* which succeeded it (for the problems which this raises about the chronology at Sheepen, see Bidwell 1999, 489–91; Timby

2004, 67–8; Pitts 2014, 135). The quantities of 1st-century AD pottery from London are very large indeed, and the total of 15 stamps on *terra nigra* which they include is very modest when compared to six from Exeter and three from Topsham. The ware was certainly very rare in the Early Roman assemblages published in 1994; only 25 of the 100,187 sherds of all the pottery were *terra nigra* (Davies *et al.* 1994, fig. 174b).

Exeter and the western sea routes in the military period

There is more Spanish colour-coated ware from Exeter than from any other site in Britain (ten vessels listed in Greene 1991, 72, and an additional five sherds from the 1980–90 excavations; see Holbrook and Bidwell 1992, tab. 54). All three authors linked these relatively high numbers to Exeter's proximity to the Atlantic seaways. A type of mortarium, present in the South-West in much larger numbers than the Spanish fine ware, is probably from western Gaul or perhaps Brittany, rather than Spain as was once thought (Hartley 1991, FC1, TC2–6; Hartley and Tomber 2006, 26–70; see also Taylor 2014c, ruling out the possibility of a source in South-West England). From Exeter there are 17 vessels (Hartley 1991, 194, and four more from Friernhay Street 1981 and Lower Coombe Street 1989–90), together with two from St Loye's College (Bidwell forthcoming b). Hartley cited other examples from Carvossa, Nanstallon, North Tawton and Bolham, in Tiverton, to which can be added two from Calstock (Bidwell 2014, illus. 44, nos 18–19) and another two from Pomeroy Wood, in Honiton (Seager Smith 1999, 301–2, also identifying an example from Greyhound Yard, in Dorchester). These mortaria occur in small numbers elsewhere in Britain (Hartley 1991, fig. 77, and see below), but their main distribution was to military sites in the South-West (Fig. 12.6).

Large amounts of samian ware arrived at Exeter during the military period, most of it transported from La Graufesenque in southern Gaul via the Rhône and Rhine and then down the Channel coast or through London. A second but very minor source was Montans. Its principal market in the pre-Flavian period was Aquitania and northern Iberia, but a stamp of Cadurcus is known from Topsham (die 2a, Tiberio-Claudian; Radford 1937, fig. 9, no. 1), and from Exeter two stamps of Iullus ii have been recorded (*c.* AD 40–65; Dickinson 1991, no. 129, die 3a, Shortt Collection; die 7a, no. 39, Site 63, Mermaid Yard); in addition, there is a Claudian Dr. 15/17 from the likely *canabae* at Lower Coombe Street (Site 97, context 849; the detailed samian lists from 1971–79 excavations have not been consulted). Definite pre-Flavian examples from elsewhere in Britain, as listed by Willis (2005, sect. 6.6.2, app. 6.8; see also the Mainz Samain Research Project), are confined to five from London and a Claudio-Neronian example from Stanwick (N. Yorks), though there are a few examples which are probably of pre-conquest date from Silchester. Although the quantities are very small, in proportion to the much larger volume of finds from London, Montans Ware is commoner at Exeter, and in the fortress period might well have been imported directly from western Gaul. In later periods the ware was not particularly common at Exeter and probably reached the town from London or other areas to the east where it occurs in much larger quantities.

The three classes of pottery discussed above provide solid evidence for the direct supply of pottery to Exeter by the western seaways during the fortress period. The traffic might have been on a much larger scale than these finds indicate if amphorae had accompanied the fine ware from southern Spain (Holbrook and Bidwell 1991, 17). A study of amphora stamps from Britain suggested that the South-East, Wales and the Hadrian's Wall area were each supplied by different trade routes (Funari 1996, 86). The sample of stamps from the military period in the South-West is too small to establish whether its supply relied to a greater degree on sources different from those that served London and the South-East during the 1st century AD, but future finds might make this possible.

The findspots in Britain of Spanish fine ware and particularly the mortaria considered to have originated in western Gaul would be consistent with their redistribution from Exeter to other sites in western Britain (Fig. 12.6). There may have been a direct overland route to the lower reaches of the River Parrett, from where the mortaria could have been distributed by coastal trade around the Bristol Channel to Sea Mills and Caerleon (EAPIT 1, Chapter 3); Evans and Hartley (1997, 315) suggested that examples from the fort at Loughor had arrived via Exeter. A cross-country route used for the movement of pottery and other goods from the south coast that avoided the long voyage around Cornwall finds a parallel in the later distribution of BB1 from South-East Dorset to ports such as Crandon Bridge near the mouth of the Parrett in Somerset (Allen and Fulford 1996, 258–9; Rippon 2008, 134–7).

In the earlier 1st-century AD pottery from Aquitania and perhaps amphorae from Spain reached southern Britain via the western seaways, and this material occurred on the Ower Peninsula in South-East Dorset (Timby 1987, 73–4). At the Bucknowle villa site in Purbeck, a few miles south-west of the Peninsula, there was *terra nigra* from Aquitania (Rigby 2009, 140, nos. 16–21), all regarded as post-conquest except a tazza dating from 20 BC to AD 20 (no. 18). The supply of pottery from these sources to Exeter during the fortress period probably represents the adaptation of an earlier trading system which was still functioning at the time of the conquest.

This trade continued after *c.* AD 75 when Exeter was held for a few years by a much smaller force (EAPIT 1, Chapter 5). The mortaria from western Gaul are known from sites in southern Wales and Scotland which were established in the mid and late AD 70s (see below).

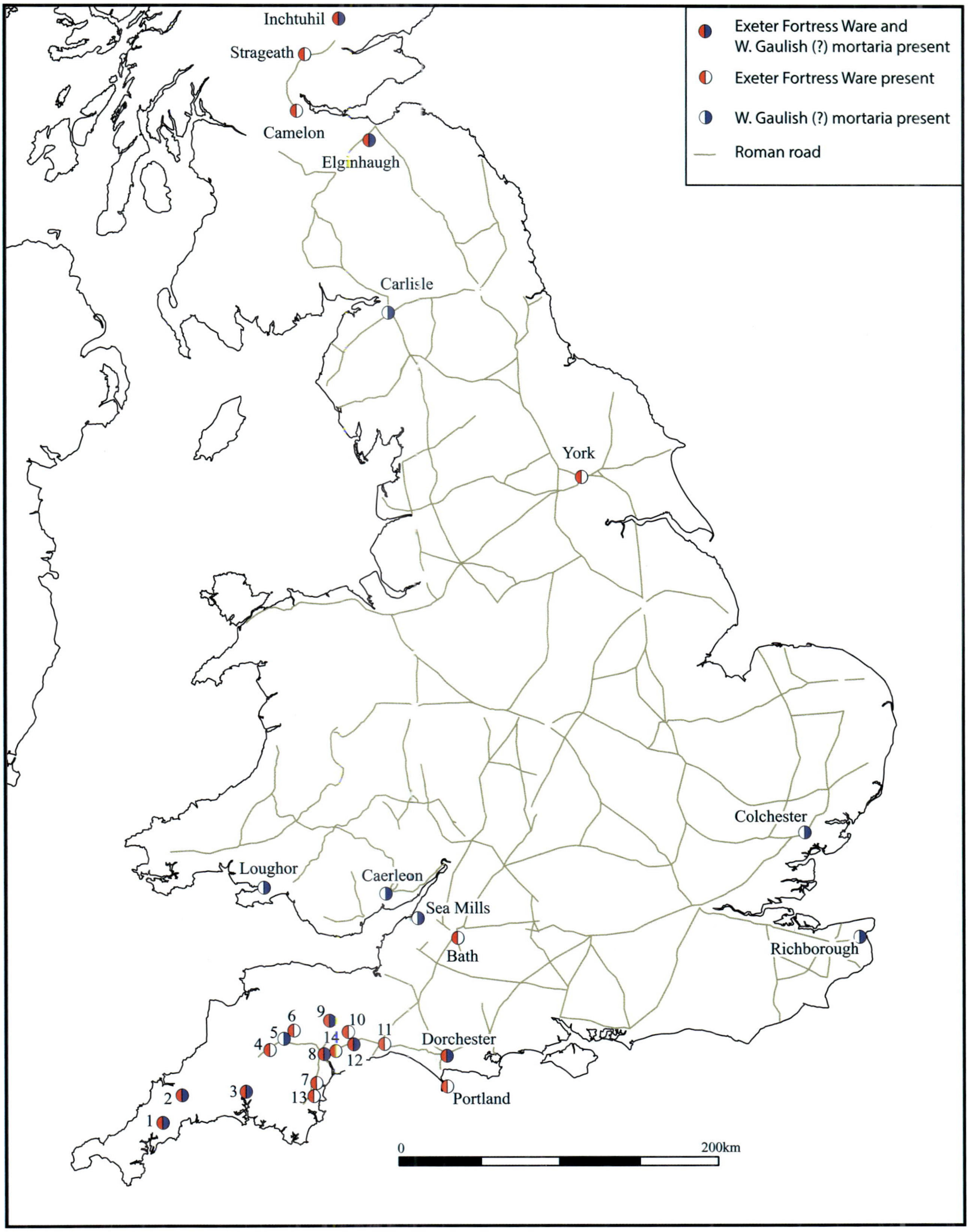

Fig. 12.6 Map showing distribution of Exeter Fortress Wares and mortaria probably from western Gaul. Key to findspots in the South-West. 1: Carvossa; 2: Nanstallon; 3: Calstock; 4: Okehampton; 5: North Tawton; 6: Bury Barton; 7: Penns Mount, in Kingsteignton; 8: Exeter/St Loye's College/Topsham; 9: Bolham, in Tiverton; 10: Hembury; 11: Woodbury, in Axminster; 12: Pomeroy Wood, in Honiton; 13: Aller Cross, in Kingskerswell; 14: Hill Barton, in Pinhoe. For details of find spots beyond the South-West, see Table 12.1 (drawn by David Gould)

Indeed, vessels categorised as Late Imitation *Terra Nigra* (Holbrook and Bidwell 1991, 86–7), which are known only from post-fortress levels, may well be imports from Brittany (Greene cited in Holbrook and Bidwell 1992, 54). Their absence from other sites on the south coast had been taken to show that they were not imports, but this no longer seems a valid objection given the exceptional number of imports from western Gaul at Exeter. Greene also noted resemblances between some of the *terra nigra* at Usk and products from Brittany, the fabric of which seems similar to vessels at Exeter, some from the fortress period (fabric 373: Holbrook and Bidwell 1991, 79).

Overview of pottery supply to Exeter and the South-West during the military period

The fortress at Exeter and the forts throughout the South-West relied on regional sources of pottery and imported wares to an extent not seen elsewhere at military sites in 1st-century AD Britain. BB1 seems to have had a great appeal to the army. It was the main type of pottery in use during the Claudian period at Lake Farm, Hod Hill and Waddon Hill (all in Dorset) and remained in demand after the early Neronian advance to the west. Its potters made virtually no attempts to imitate Roman forms at this stage and clearly realised that the limited range they were making met much of the army's needs. At the fort of Calstock in Cornwall there was much more gabbroic ware than BB1 (Bidwell 2014, tab. 4), as also apparently at Carvossa and Nanstallon, though the pottery from these two sites has not been quantified. This well-potted, dark ware, often with burnished surfaces, was just as acceptable to the army as BB1, and at the Cornish forts had the advantage of proximity to its production area.

The Exeter Fortress Wares had an extensive military market but were more popular amongst the civilian communities dependent on the fortress at Exeter. The army was already relying on BB1 by the time it reached Exeter, but this type of pottery might have been new to many of the merchants, traders and craftspeople who arrived from other parts of Britain or from the continent. They seem to have preferred pottery in the mainstream of provincial taste. Underpinning local and regional supply were large quantities of imports. Their ready availability limited the development of specialist potteries in the South-West, especially those making mortaria.

Fortress Wares in the northern frontier zone, and Exeter as an entrepot for the re-export of continental pottery

The Fortress Wares industry was clearly exceptional, but it was nevertheless surprising to find its products at York and a number of Flavian military sites in Scotland occupied in *c.* AD 80–7. Since the original publication of these finds (Swan and Bidwell 1998), further possible or probable examples have been found (Table 12.1), and the study by Badreshany as part of EAPIT has confirmed the identification of selected examples as Fortress Ware B (Appendix 12.2). Four possible reasons for the presence of these vessels in Scotland were advanced in 1998: their transport in personal baggage when units were moved from the South-West to take part in the Agricolan campaigns, their inclusion likewise in the general stores of the units, their transport by new recruits sent to northern Britain, and finally that they were objects of trade or make-weights in larger cargoes (*ibid.*, 24–5). The last of these reasons was seen as 'certainly not appropriate for the Exeter Fortress Wares' because of the distances involved and the unlikelihood, as it then seemed, that the far South-West contributed to supply of the army in Scotland. Following the full publication of pottery from Elginhaugh (Dore 2007) and later excavations at Camelon (Bidwell and Croom forthcoming a), the total number of Fortress Ware vessels has increased, and other possible examples have been identified in older publications (Table 12.1). In addition, an Exeter mortarium had been identified at Camelon (information from Kay Hartley, type as Hartley 1991, fig. 85, nos. B2 and B7). Table 12.1 probably understates the numbers of Exeter products in northern Britain: Fortress Ware B is an easily recognisable fabric, but the A and D fabrics are much less so, and unless the types of vessel are distinctive, such as the tripod bowls and jars with flat-topped rims, examples might well have been overlooked. There are the same difficulties in distinguishing possible Exeter flagons.

Products of two industries which served the army in the South-West – South-Western and South-East Dorset BB1 – are not known in Flavian Scotland, though they appeared there in the early Antonine period. Now that the dominance of BB1 in the South-West and its appeal to the army have become clear, its absence in Scotland undermines the case for the incidental movement of Fortress Wares as a result of the postings north of individuals and units: why would wares that the army relied on to a much greater extent than the other coarse wares be excluded from these sorts of movements? Trade now seems the most likely reason for the presence of Fortress Wares and other Exeter pottery in Scotland, even though it was firmly rejected by Vivien Swan and the writer in 1998.

These wares would no doubt have travelled with bulkier and more vital consignments such as agricultural produce and metals, the origins of which are much more difficult to determine. However, other types of pottery seem to have been distributed along the same route, and this is illustrated most clearly by the mortaria which probably originated in western Gaul (discussed above). In southern Britain they are almost entirely confined to military sites in the South-West and south Wales, with outliers at Richborough and Colchester (Fig. 12.6). The pattern of their distribution, with far more from Exeter and the South-West than from elsewhere in Britain, might suggest they were actually made at Exeter, though this seems to

Table 12.1 Finds of Exeter Fortress Wares beyond Devon and Cornwall. cf. Fig. 12.6

Site	Status	Exeter Fortress Wares (FW) fabric/other site fabrics	Form	Type	No.	Reference
Dorchester Greyhound Yard	Early stage of town, though military presence possible	FWB (38G)	Reeded-rim bowl	B25, cf. A17.2-3	1?	Seager Smith and Davies 1993, fig. 131, Type 601
		FWB? (38G?)	Jar	B2, cf. A10	1?	*Ibid.*, fig. 131, Type 602
		FWB?? (38G??)	Lid?	B37, cf. A29	1?	*Ibid.*, fig. 131, Type 603
		FWB?? (38G??)	Reeded-rim bowl	B25.2/	1?	*Ibid.*, fig.131, type 604
		FWB (38G)	?	Sherds	41	*Ibid.*, table 41
Dorchester County Hospital		FWB?	Not specified	?	?	Seager Smith 2008, 7, table P2
Portland	Burial	FWD?	Dish	D7.3	1	Putnam 1970, fig. 11, no.5
Bath Nelson Place	Fort?	FWC?	Reeded-rim bowl	Cf. B25	1	Bidwell and Croom forthcoming c, no. 47
York	Fortress	FWB (G12)	Jar	B2, cf. A23	1	Monaghan 1993, fig. 292, no. 2904
York	Fortress	FWB	Lid	B28	1	Monaghan 1997, fig. 407, no. 4096
Camelon	Fort	FWB	Jar	B2, cf. A10	5	Swan and Bidwell, fig. 1, B–D; Bidwell and Croom forthcoming, nos. 10 and 110
		FWB	Reeded-rim bowl	B25.2-4	2	Swan and Bidwell 1998, fig. 1, F; Bidwell and Croom forthcoming a, no. 88
		FWB	Small jar	B21.1	1	Bidwell and Croom forthcoming a, no. 88
		FWB	Jar	?	1	Swan and Bidwell 1998, fig. 1, A
		FWB	Tripod bowl	B32, cf. A23	1	Swan and Bidwell 1998, fig. 1, F
Elginhaugh	Fort	FWB	Jar	B2, cf. A10	2	Dore 2007, fig. 10.11, no. 94
		FWB	Tripod bowl?	cf. A16.1	2	Dore 2007, fig. 10.14, no. 169
		FWB	Reeded-rim bowl	B25.2	2–3	Dore 2007, fig. 10.13, no. 94 (and 147?)
Strageath	Fort	FWA?	Tripod bowl?	A16.1	1	Anderson 1989, fig. 118, no. 82; cf. Holbrook and Bidwell 1992, fig. 17, no. 117
Inchtuthil	Fortress	FWB?	Bowl	Cf. B24–5	2	Darling 1985, fig. 100, nos. 59–9

be ruled out by petrological analysis of examples from Calstock (Taylor 2014c, 54, samples 1 and 2). If they were imported, most clearly entered Britain via Exeter. In northern Britain they are known from Carlisle and Inchtuthil, and also from Elginhaugh where there were three or four examples (Hartley 2007, 326–8, types 1–2, also identifying the example from Inchtuthil); they presumably arrived with other pottery that originated in Exeter.

Much more difficult to specify are other imported wares which might have reached northern Britain via Exeter. *Vases tronconiques* in North Gaulish Grey Ware are known from Camelon and Inchtuthil (Swan 2009, 74–5, map 1) and also from St Loye's College and Okehampton; none of the examples that can be dated more broadly to the Flavian–Trajanic period, all from military sites in northern England apart from Richborough, are necessarily as early as those from Scotland and the South-West. Opinion is divided as to whether they were imported specifically to cater to the needs of Gaulish soldiers or were merely objects of a wider trade in pottery from northern Gaul (Swan 2009, 67–95; cf. Fulford 2010, 69–70), but they are perhaps further evidence of a link between Scotland and the South-West. North Gaulish flagons, particularly common in the South-West, are well represented at Elginhaugh, where there are eight examples (Dore 2007, fig. 10.7, nos. 10 (2), 14–16 (5) and 21 (2)), and they are also present at Camelon (several examples, information from the late Vivien Swan; Bidwell and Croom forthcoming a) and Red House, in Corbridge (Hanson *et al.* 1979, fig. 15, no. 3). If they were re-exported from Exeter, they were presumably accompanied by Oise/Somme mortaria (Hartley 1991, 189–90, FC2–5), at least some of which were from the same production centres as the flagons; they contributed far more to the supply of mortaria at military sites in the South-West than elsewhere in Britain. There are many other types of imported pottery, including mortaria from Italy and Central France, amphorae, samian and fine wares, which could have been redistributed through

Exeter, but none of these types occurring in Scotland is unusually common in the South-West. It can of course be clearly demonstrated that Flavian sites in Scotland were also supplied by east-coast sea routes. For example, *Verulamium* mortaria, which are very scarce at Exeter (Hartley 1991, tab. 13), are the commonest non-local mortaria at Elginhaugh (Hartley 2007, tab. 10.12).

The recovery of mortaria made at Elginhaugh from four other forts provides an instructive contrast with the distribution of the Exeter pottery (*ibid.*, 359). Two found at Camelon, 50 km to the west of Elginhaugh, could have been the objects of small-scale, fairly local trade, but the others at Carlisle, Ribchester and Castleford (the last two 'virtually certain' examples) are far more distant finds. A short-lived fort in newly conquered territory, soon to be abandoned, scarcely seems plausible as a base for long-distance trade to forts in the more settled parts of Britain, and the mortaria were presumably transported to the three forts in northern England as the possessions of individuals. They were probably civilians rather than soldiers, for when the unit was withdrawn from Scotland it seems unlikely that it would have been split between three forts or have moved to them in quick succession. Circumstances at Exeter were entirely different: the Fortress Wares already had a large regional market, and the South-West relied on a distribution system for imported pottery to a degree not seen elsewhere in pre- and early Flavian Britain. The military situation also has to be taken into account. As we have seen (EAPIT 1, Chapter 5), the early Flavian period saw a resumption of large-scale campaigning which culminated in the conquest of Scotland. Supply would have been a problem, and part of the solution would have been to draw on the resources of the South-West and its surplus capacity following the progressive withdrawal of the army from the region. From the point of view of the potters making Fortress Wares and the Exeter merchants, the long route to the north was viable economically, as it proved to be in the 2nd century AD when South-Western BB1 was sent to Hadrian's Wall and Antonine Scotland (see below).

The final stage of the Fortress Wares industry confirms what is now apparent from the recognition that its principal market at Exeter was not the fortress but the *canabae* and the small town at St Loye's College, which is that the potters were civilians and not soldiers. Production continued after the departure of the main part of the legion in *c.* AD 75 and was sustained into the AD 80s, perhaps after the complete withdrawal of the army from the South-West. Moreover, at the beginning of this period there was a surge in the manufacture of mortaria at new production sites around the former fortress. Four potters stamped their names on the mortaria: Vitanius at Bartholomew Street West (Site 47; Fig. 12.7; Hartley 1991, 214–5; Holbrook and Bidwell 1991, 285–6), and Severus, Volatus? or Volaetus? and a fourth potter with an undecipherable name at Lower Coombe Street (Hartley 1992, 63). Following the withdrawal from Scotland in

Fig. 12.7 Stamp of Vitanius from the Bartholomew Street West kiln site (Hartley 1991, fig. 88, nos. 6–8; © RAMM)

c. AD 87 and the departure of many units from Britain, the military market must have contracted, and it was probably then that the Fortress Wares and other minor industries cut their production or closed down.

Local and regional pottery supply in the early town and until the mid 3rd century AD

Introduction

Most of the regional sources of coarse pottery during the fortress period, with the major exception of the Fortress Wares, were also drawn upon to supply the town until about the middle of the 3rd century AD, when some of the potteries seem to have closed down. Using the information mainly from the 1971–79 excavations, the development of these later potteries and the range of types they produced were reviewed in 1991 (Holbrook and Bidwell 1991). Subsequent excavations at Exeter have in general not produced substantial groups or assemblages of this period; the largest was from the ditch of the early town defences which at Friernhay Street (1981, Site 75) produced 25.98 kg or 3.339% EVEs of pottery excluding the amphorae (Holbrook and Bidwell 1992, tab. 2). The stratigraphy at many of these sites still awaits full analysis; it might offer refinements of dating and insights into changes in pottery use but will probably not alter the general picture evident in 1991. Perhaps more important has been subsequent research on sites beyond Exeter and its immediate region which has been very informative about the sources of pottery that reached the town and their importance regionally and, in the case of South-Western BB1, throughout the province of Britain.

South-Western (SOW BB1) and South-East Dorset BB1 (DOR BB1)

Assessments of the relative importance of these two wares in the South-West and Dorset have always been incomplete, because in many reports they have not been distinguished despite the fact that the differences were already clear more than 30 years ago. One exception was the catalogue of pottery at Greyhound Yard, in Dorchester (Seager Smith and Davies 1993, 249–51, tab. 35), where, though the work seems to have been completed before *Roman Finds from Exeter* was published in 1991, the two fabrics were recognised. The less common fabric was subsequently identified as South-Western BB1, and at seven sites in and around Dorchester it usually represented about a third to a quarter of all the BB1 by sherd count (Seager Smith 2008, tab. P3). South-East Dorset BB1 was current until the end of the Roman period, and at Greyhound Yard the amounts of South-Western BB1, production of which had ended by the mid 3rd century AD, were larger in deposits of Period 5 (pre- and early Flavian) and Period 6 (late 1st to early 2nd centuries AD) than in the overall site assemblages.

South-Western BB1 had a larger regional distribution than was formerly apparent, and its importance is emphasised by the extent to which it was exported to 2nd and earlier 3rd-century AD military sites in northern Britain. A few definite and probable findspots were identified in 1991, in addition to those on either side of the Bristol Channel (Holbrook and Bidwell 1991, fig. 26), but there are now many more in northern Britain: Carlisle and Hardknott; along Hadrian's Wall at turrets 18b, 30a, 33b, 34a and 45a and beyond the Wall to the east at the coastal fort of South Shields; and at Bearsden on the Antonine Wall and, near its eastern end, at Camelon and Cramond. The distribution is concentrated in North-West England and the east–west corridors of the two Walls and is presumably the result of the ware being included in cargos transported up the west coast from ports on the south side of the Bristol Channel. It might have travelled overland from the Blackdown Hills, now identified as its source (Appendix 12.1) to these ports with other commodities, perhaps iron (EAPIT 1, Chapters 3 and 6).

Sandy Grey Ware

This is a general class which includes, in addition to local products, pottery from Alice Holt, south Wales and probably other industries (*ibid.*, 154–62). South Wales Grey Ware, which now has a type series (Webster 1993, 232–55), has also been found at Pomeroy Wood, in Honiton (Seager Smith 1999, 301, fig. 161, no. 202). Its presence in the South-West, and the presence at Exeter of a Caerleon mortarium (Hartley 1991, 193, FB32), can be added to the distribution pattern of South-Western BB1 as evidence for trading links with south Wales (EAPIT 1, Chapter 6).

Micaceous Grey Ware, Gritty Grey Ware and South-Western Grey Ware Storage Jars (Holbrook and Bidwell 1991, 163–77)

Micaceous Grey Ware requires no further comment. It has long been recognised that South-Western Grey Ware Storage Jars were produced at several centres, and it is now clear that the Gritty Grey Wares were likewise not from a single pottery. The evidence for this has emerged from petrographical study of samples from the 2nd and 3rd-century AD settlement at Shortlands Lane, Cullompton (Morris 2014). The results, which include study of the storage jars, can be summarised as follows (Wood 2014):

- North Devon source, perhaps the lower reaches of the River Taw: Storage Jar Type 1.1 (Holbrook and Bidwell 1991, fig. 68), cf. Croom and Bidwell 2014, fig. 50, no. 35, as Wood 2014, Storage Jar 2; Grey Ware Group 1, jar not in Exeter Type Series, Croom and Bidwell 2014, fig. 48, no. 20, as Wood 2014, 162.
- source between Bovey Tracey and Lustleigh: Exeter Gritty Grey Ware, Croom and Bidwell 2014, fig. 49, no. 25, and Reduced Ware 2, not illustrated; Wood 2014, 164 for both samples.
- source close to the borders of Devon and Somerset (Norton Fitzwarren?; cf. Timby forthcoming): storage jar not in the Exeter Type Series, Croom and Bidwell 2014, fig. 51, no. 39, cf. Wood 2014, 167.

The remaining samples were consistent with an origin in eastern Devon and Exeter. Gritty Grey Wares from Exeter need to be reappraised to see whether they display a similar range of sources. The identification of the area between Bovey Tracey and Lustleigh as one of the possible sources of the wares is of great interest because it was the source of the clays used for the Exeter Fortress Wares (see above and Appendix 12.1). The North Devon source seems less likely, but no sites with Roman pottery are known in Devon west of Exmoor.

South Devon (SOD RE) and Aller Cross Wares

Many additions can be made to the map of findspots for South Devon Ware published in 1991, but they do not extend its distribution to the east, beyond the western parts of Somerset and Dorset, with outliers at Dorchester (Holbrook and Bidwell 1991, fig. 7; cf. EAPIT 1, Chapter 3, Fig. 3.24). It should be noted that vessels with combed decoration which date to the 2nd century AD, when finds of the ware are rare at Exeter, are probably not South Devon products (*ibid.*, fig. 71, Types 11.1 and 11.2; 1992, fig. 16, no. 93): combed decoration has never been seen on other examples of the ware, and these vessels are likely to be imports, their granite-derived fabric perhaps suggesting a source in Brittany or Normandy, as with a bowl or dish with feet in a similar fabric (Holbrook and Bidwell 1991, fig. 72, Type 18.1).

Another granite-derived fabric current in the 1st to 3rd centuries AD, Aller Cross Ware, has recently been recognised in the area south of Newton Abbot, about 25 km south of Exeter (Bidwell and Croom 2015, 131–2). Although it was not identified amongst the pottery previously catalogued at Exeter, the fabric is distinctive and, even if a few sherds of the fabric were wrongly classified, it seems unlikely to have reached Exeter in significant quantities.

Mortaria production

As at towns further to the east such as Dorchester (Seager Smith and Davies 1993, 224), imported mortaria predominated at Exeter until well into the 3rd century AD, with Rhineland products being particularly common from the second half of the 2nd century AD. There was some production at Exeter or nearby (Hartley 1991, 215), and from later excavations there are local copies of Rhineland types and Oxfordshire mortaria, the latter certainly dating to the second half of the 3rd century AD (Bidwell forthcoming a, nos. 41–2, and with further discussion).

Local and regional supply in the Late Roman period

By the middle of the 3rd century AD, production of the Gritty Grey Wares was in decline, and there was increasing reliance on South-East Dorset BB1 and later also on South Devon Ware (Holbrook and Bidwell 1991, 21–3; EAPIT 1, Chapter 6). The only other local or regional product that was common in Exeter during the 4th century AD was the South-Western storage jar. The quantity of South Devon Ware relative to that of South-East Dorset BB1 increased throughout the century (Holbrook and Bidwell 1991 (MF), Groups 10–14, tabs 13–14) but never exceeded the latter (Bidwell 2016, section 3). At Aller Cross, a probable example of a complex farm 25 km south of Exeter (Hughes 2015, 178), supplies of South Devon Ware continued after South-East Dorset BB1, present in large quantities in late 3rd and early 4th-century AD contexts, seem to have no longer been reaching the site (Bidwell and Croom 2015, 153–3). Nothing suggests this was the case at Exeter, where both wares seem to have arrived until the general collapse of pottery industries throughout Britain. The only survivors were the potters making gabbroic wares in Cornwall, scarcely any of their products being exported east of the Tamar after the 1st century AD (EAPIT 1, Chapter 3, Fig. 3.22).

Late Roman imports and trade with western Gaul

In 1991 *céramique à l'éponge* had seemed to occur at Exeter in large quantities, demonstrating the strength of trading links with western Gaul in the late 3rd and 4th centuries AD (Holbrook and Bidwell 1991, 21, 83). Wider contacts during the same period were represented by numerous finds of North African amphorae, which led Williams and Carreras (1995, 237–8) to state that 'if during the late Roman period some North African amphorae cargoes were arriving in Britain from the Atlantic seaboard route round Spain or cross France via Bordeaux, Exeter would have been a convenient port-of-call'. A clearer picture of Exeter's relative importance in these overseas routes has emerged from subsequent publications.

Céramique à l'éponge (EPO MA)

These vessels, predominantly small flanged bowls resembling the samian Dr. 38, have orange colour coats applied so as to achieve the effect of marbling or, much more rarely in Britain, star-like patterns. They were the products of two centres in western France: one was in Centre-Ouest and probably the source of the single example from Exeter decorated with the star-like pattern (Fig. 12.8; Fox 1953, fig. 9, no. 11, pl. X, D); the source of probably all the other examples was at Vayres, 30 km south-east of Bordeaux from where some of its products were exported to Britain (Sireix and Convertini 2008). At Exeter the minimum number of vessels recorded until 1979 was 27, stratified in late 3rd and 4th-century AD deposits or occurring residually in post-Roman levels (Holbrook and Bidwell 1991, 83). There were also three sherds from excavations in 1980–90 (Holbrook and Bidwell 1992, tab. 4), the base of a bowl from Smythen Street/Market Street (1998, Site 134; Bidwell and Croom 2020) and three more sherds from Princesshay (Bidwell forthcoming a). The Exeter assemblage was formerly regarded as the largest from Britain (Holbrook and Bidwell 1991, 83), but perhaps there are more from *Clausentum* where nearly 100 sherds have been recorded, though how many vessels they represent is uncertain (Wood 1993, 121, n. 5). A comparison of the quantities from these two sites involves the usual difficulties, but even if the Late Roman deposits at *Clausentum*

Fig. 12.8 Sherd of céramique à l'éponge, *probably from a flagon, decorated with a star-like pattern; found in the marketplace south-west of the forum (Fox 1952, fig. 9, no. 11, pl. X, D) (© RAMM)*

were much better preserved than at Exeter, the total extent of the excavations was much smaller: *céramique à l'éponge* certainly seems to have played a more important part in the supply of pottery to *Clausentum*. Conversely, the ware seems to have been much scarcer at Dorchester, where there were two sherds from the Greyhound Yard sites and four sherds from Dorchester Hospital (Seager Smith and Davies 1993, 214; Seager Smith 2008, 3) as opposed to a minimum of 24 vessels from the excavations at Exeter in 1971–80 (Holbrook and Bidwell 1991, 83; see below for a comparison of the quantities of later Roman pottery at Greyhound Yard and Exeter). There are now finds of this ware from rural sites in Devon: one definite and one probable from Aller Cross (Bidwell and Croom 2015, fig. 27, nos. 48–9) and a flagon rim from Cullompton (Croom and Bidwell 2014, fig. 51, no. 50).

North African and Eastern Mediterranean amphorae

As was the case elsewhere in Britain, North African amphorae had already begun to reach Exeter in the 2nd century AD, but they were not common until the 4th century AD (Holbrook and Bidwell 1991, 215–8). Their contents varied. Olive oil was a principal product of the areas where these amphorae originated, but they were also used for the transport of wine, preserved fish and fruits, and also fish sauce (Reynolds 2010, 284, n. 331, 302, n. 444). An example of Keay XXVB from Trichay Street could have contained wine (Holbrook and Bidwell 1991, fig. 89, no. 9). The quantities from excavations at Exeter between 1971 and 1990 amounted to about 6.6 kg (Holbrook and Bidwell 1991, tab. 14; Williams 1992, tab. 5), excluding the excavations on the basilica and forum which produced 30 sherds (Fig. 12.9; Peacock 1979b, tab. 10); there were also ten sherds from Princesshay (*c.* 0.5 kg) and three sherds (95 g) from Smythen Street/Market Street.

Exeter has been identified as one of the four major concentrations of North African amphorae in Britain, together with London, Leicester and York (Williams and Carreras 1995, 237, tab. 1). More recent finds have widened the area of distribution or greatly increased the quantities known from sites where these amphorae have

Fig. 12.9 Amphora fragments from a 4th-century AD deposit north-east of the basilica and forum; to left, probably an example of Gauloise 4 from southern Gaul; the other sherds are from North African amphorae (Bidwell 1979, figs 67–8, nos. 208–11). Scale 10 cm (© RAMM)

already been recorded. At Shadwell, a settlement on the eastern outskirts of Roman London, there were 6,000 sherds (170 kg) of pottery mainly from deposits of the late 3rd and 4th centuries AD (Gerrard 2011, 61), including 50 sherds (4.868 kg) from North African amphorae which represented just under a quarter of all the amphorae by weight (Williams 2011). The quantity from this small site falls not far short of the total from Exeter. However, from what was by far the largest series of Late Roman deposits at Exeter, excavated in 1971–79, there were only 43.5 kg of pottery, excluding samian, amphorae and mortaria but including large amounts of residual material (Groups 10–14, last quarter of the 3rd century to end of the 4th century AD: Holbrook and Bidwell 1991 (microfiche), tabs 10–14). In these deposits, North African sherds represented 15% of all the amphorae, the remainder of which, however, was almost all residual apart from a few sherds from the Eastern Mediterranean (Holbrook and Bidwell 1991, tab. 14); on the basilica and forum site, 16.2% of all the amphora sherds from all periods, including the fortress levels, were North African (Peacock 1979b, tab. 10). Another useful comparison is with Dorchester, a town similar in size to Exeter. At the Greyhound Yard sites there were 21 sherds of North African amphorae (Williams 1993, 217), while the Dorchester Hospital excavations produced only eight sherds (Seager Smith 2008, 4), but as at Shadwell the later Roman deposits were much larger than at Exeter. Greyhound Yard in Periods 9–11 (early to late 4th century AD) produced 18,956 sherds, representing 37% of all the Roman pottery (Seager and Davies 1993, 287–9). If the average sherd weight was 28 g, as at Shadwell (Gerrard 2011, 61: 6,000 sherds weighing 170 kg), the weight of the pottery from the Periods 9–11 deposits at Greyhound Yard would have been in the region of 531 kg. From Late Roman and post-Roman contexts at Dorchester Hospital, there were 141 kg of pottery (Seager Smith 2008, 3). Given the huge disparities with the size of the Exeter deposits, North African amphorae seem to have been comparatively rare at Dorchester. They were even scarcer at Silchester: from the basilica and forum site there was only one small sherd which was possibly North African amongst 70 kg of amphorae (Williams 2000, 225), and from deposits of the late 3rd to early 5th century AD on Insula IX three sherds (weight 0.255 kg) were identified amongst all the pottery (total weight 129 kg) from the groups selected for study (Timby 2006, tab. 14).

Other imported amphorae

Much scarcer than those from North Africa were sherds from Eastern Mediterranean amphorae. They include examples probably from the Aegean and Palestine (Peacock 1979b, tab. 10; Holbrook and Bidwell 1991, tab. 14; 1992, tab. 5). The only rim was found together with a well-circulated coin of AD 346–7 in the trample layer over the yard associated with the Late Roman house at Trichay Street (see Chapter 5 above; Holbrook and Bidwell 1991, fig. 90, no. 15). It resembles rims from 2nd-century AD contexts in South-East Britain (Vilvorder *et al.* 2000, 481) and from 3rd-century AD contexts at Lyon (Lemaître 2000, fig. 9, nos. 4–8), but where in the Eastern Mediterranean these amphorae originated remains uncertain.

Discussion

Supply from western Gaul in the 1st century AD has already been discussed. Direct evidence for the continuation of trade contacts with Exeter or its region during the 2nd and earlier 3rd century AD depends solely on what appears to be a dish in South-Western BB1 with characteristic decoration (cf. Type 80.1) from the Cité Judiciaire excavations at Bordeaux (Sireix and Convertini 1997, fig. 5, no. 6, from a context dated AD 150/170). Perhaps of greater significance is the scarcity at Exeter of Gauloise 4 amphorae, generally from *Gallia Narbonensis*, which were included in the older categories, Dressel 30 and Pélichet 47 (Holbrook and Bidwell 1991, 215, tab. 14: cf. Williams 1992, tab. 5). These wine amphorae are commoner in South-East Britain which they reached via the Rhône and Rhine (Peacock and Williams 1986, 64, fig. 21). None seems to be known at Bordeaux, though there are a few other Gaulish types (Berthault 1999, 262–6). Bordeaux, then as now, was at the heart of an area producing prized wines, at least some of which was transported in locally produced amphorae. These amphorae, none yet recognised in Britain, were not made after the middle of the 2nd century AD; subsequently, all of the wine from the region was probably exported in barrels (*ibid.*, 269). It is likely that Exeter and other towns in south-western Britain where Gauloise 4 amphorae are not common received much of their wine in barrels from Bordeaux (for an overall survey of trade between Bordeaux and Britain, see Sireix 2005).

With the arrival from Bordeaux of *céramique à l'éponge* in the late 3rd century AD, the link with Exeter is more readily apparent. It is very likely that North African amphorae were also part of the commerce between the two centres; these amphorae are common in Bordeaux in the later Roman period and seem to have travelled there across the 'Gaulish isthmus', that is north-west from the Mediterranean coast and down the Garonne (Berthault 2012, 316–7). They have also been recorded in some numbers in northern Gaul and along the lower Rhine (Williams and Carreras 1995, 242; Laubenheimer and Marlière 2010, 48, 61, 70), perhaps markers for a route to eastern Britain for the importation of these amphorae which was separate from the Atlantic route. During the 5th century AD North African amphorae continued to arrive at Bordeaux, if anything in greater numbers, but it is uncertain whether the few later 5th and 6th century AD examples from south-western Britain represent continuity of trade from the late 4th and early 5th century AD (Bidwell *et al.* 2011, 115; Duggan 2018, 151).

Conclusions

In the decades before the Roman conquest, Devon and Cornwall were on the periphery of the zone in southern Britain which received a wide range of continental imports. The networks that delivered these imports were extended to serve the Roman army as it advanced into the South-West. There seem to have been fewer Gallo-Belgic wares in parts of south-east England during the Claudio-Neronian period, perhaps because supplies were increasingly diverted to a military market which proved more lucrative. Similarly, the routes that distributed South-East Dorset BB1 before the conquest were extended to serve the Roman army further to the west and indeed in south Wales. Less certain is the extent of the market for South-Western BB1 before the foundation of the Exeter fortress, though the industry was certainly functioning in the Claudian period.

Pottery supply to the fortress at Exeter and to forts in Devon and Cornwall was organised, as we have seen, on a different basis from that at Usk, with a greater reliance on imports and regional sources. At Usk the local potters, if not soldiers, were immigrants working in the traditions of the Rhineland and Upper Germany (Greene 1993); the fortress at Lincoln relied for its cooking wares on potters working in the local Iron Age tradition (Darling 2014, 305). At Exeter the Fortress Wares and other local industries only had a minor share in the military market and were apparently not operated by the army. The difference at Usk is explained by the absence of pre-existing pottery sources in its locality and what may have been the inability of production centres to its east, such as the source of Malvernian ware, to satisfy demand from the army. Distance from the sources of imports was probably also a factor at Usk, and it may have relied to some extent on re-exports from Exeter; distance from the production centres might also explain the small quantities of BB1 at Usk, and they too might have arrived there via Exeter. The reason for the difference between Exeter and Lincoln is obvious: Lincoln was in a locality with a strong pre-existing pottery tradition.

In the final years of military occupation in the South-West, the Exeter Fortress Wares, which already had a very extensive regional market, made a modest contribution to army supply in northern Britain; they might have been accompanied by other locally-produced wares and have travelled with continental imports which were first landed in Britain at Exeter. This trade was short-lived, but numerous finds of South-Western BB1 on 2nd-century AD military sites in northern Britain demonstrate a revival in trade from eastern Devon, if not directly from Exeter. The town was supplied by some locally made pottery, but depended much more on supplies of BB1, with products from South-East Dorset gradually replacing the South-Western Ware. Most of the mortaria used in the early town were from *Gallia Belgica*, but they were later superseded by imports from the Rhineland.

There was a substantial amount of trade around the South-West Peninsula in the later Roman period in which Exeter was involved (Holbrook 2001). Indirect evidence points to some links with the Atlantic seaways in the 2nd and 3rd centuries AD, and it is likely that wine was supplied to Exeter in barrels from the Bordeaux region. In the later 3rd and 4th centuries AD fine wares arrived from Bordeaux, which was probably also an entrepôt for the export of North African amphorae to Exeter. In the later 3rd century AD there was much reliance on South-East Dorset BB1, local production of pottery having largely come to an end. South Devon Ware was of increasing importance at Exeter during the 4th century AD but never replaced BB1.

A few Late Roman amphorae reached the town from the eastern Mediterranean, but none is necessarily any later than the early 5th century AD. Mediterranean amphorae and fine wares of the later 5th and 6th centuries AD, widespread finds in South-West England, are absent at Exeter. For some 350 years Exeter had been the main focus in the South-West of trade along the Atlantic seaways. The end of this connection signalled the end of the town: it no longer had anything to offer the ships which plied their trade along the coasts of Devon and Cornwall after the early decades of the 5th century AD.

Acknowledgements

I am grateful to Mike Fulford, Neil Holbrook and Stephen Rippon for comments on the text, to David Gould who prepared the maps, and to John Allan, Jane Read and the staff of the RAM Museum at Exeter for providing the other illustrations. Kamal Badreshany is warmly thanked for his scientific report, as is Roger Taylor for his contribution. Roger was indisposed while studying the pottery, and the final form of his report owes much to John Allan's assistance.

Petrological Appendices: Introduction

The following studies by Taylor and Badreshany address two questions: what were the sources of South-Western BB1 (SOW BB1), Fortress Wares, and South-Western Grey Ware Storage Jars; and can petrological study confirm that certain vessels from forts in Flavian Scotland, identified on the basis of their typology and macroscopic examination of their fabrics, are indeed Fortress Ware products? The presence of Fortress Wares in Scotland has been established by Badreshany, and Taylor proposes that their fabrics originated in the Bovey formation. Bidwell (EAPIT 2, Chapter 12 above) has raised the possibility that even if the clays came from the Bovey Formation, the place of manufacture for the Fortress Wares could still have been at Exeter which lay some 20 km to the north-east.

Appendix 12.1

Petrological Studies of South-Western BB1, Exeter Fortress Wares and South-Western Grey Ware Storage Jars

Roger T. Taylor

Methodology

Petrological examination of the three classes of Roman pottery selected for study in this project was undertaken by examining the surfaces of sherds under the binocular microscope at magnifications of x20 to x40. This procedure has the advantage of allowing the inspection of much larger areas of sherds than the limited areas visible in thin section, greatly increasing the chances of encountering rare but diagnostic inclusions. The identification of minerals was aided by the use of thin sections, viewed under a petrological microscope.

In this study 12 samples of South-Western Black Burnished Ware 1, 25 of Fortress Wares and 10 of South-Western Grey Ware Storage Jars have been described in detail. Selected descriptions of individual vessels are published here; the others can be found in online Tables 12.3.1–12.3.6, where museum accession numbers and site codes will also be seen. Components are listed in their approximate order of abundance; percentages of mineral content are estimated visually. With the exception of some of the storage jars, the samples were taken from the type-series published in Holbrook and Bidwell 1991, where illustrations of the vessels sampled will be found. All samples are now held at the Royal Albert Memorial Museum in Exeter.

South-Western Black Burnished Ware 1 (Exeter Fabric 40)

Fabric descriptions

Three of the 12 detailed descriptions of individual vessels are published here; the other nine can be found in online Table 12.3.1 along with a table summarising the inclusions in all the South-Western BB1 vessels examined in this project (online Table 12.3.2).

EAR 4, fig. 36, type 8.2

Pear-shaped jar with faint central lattice band. Reduced grey core and paler grey outer and inner surfaces.

Mineral content: less than 5% (larger grains only).

- Quartz: sparse translucent colourless, angular to sub-angular and rare polished grains, 0.5–0.8 mm. Sparse colourless, transparent sub-rounded to well-rounded, polished, grains, 0.1–0.2 mm. 0.1–0.5 mm. Sub-angular white vein quartz, 1.1 mm.
- Feldspar: rare soft variably altered sub-angular to sub-rounded grains, 0.3–0.8 mm and very rare transparent grains with traces of cleavage, 0.5 mm.
- Mica: muscovite rare flakes up to 0.1–0.2 mm.

Matrix: abundant transparent to translucent colourless quartz, generally angular to sub-angular and less than 0.1 mm, with much less than 0.05 mm and with some fine white mica.

EAR 4, fig. 36, type 6.1

Body sherd of a butt-beaker imitation, reduced with impressed concentric and lattice ornament on black-burnished exterior and pale grey bleached inner surface.

Mineral content: *c.* 60%.

- Quartz: transparent to translucent angular to sub-rounded, 0.05–0.5 mm, rarely 0.7–0.8 mm and rare rounded polished grains, 0.15–0.4 mm.
- Flint/chert: fragment with white cortex and grey core, 4 mm.
- Silicified shell: white tabular fragments, 0.2 and 0.3 mm.
- Tourmaline: black vitreous sub-angular and sub-rounded polished grains, 0.4 and 0.6 mm.

Matrix: quartz and sparse muscovite, less than 0.05 mm.

EAR 4, fig. 36, type 1.1

Flagon rim sherd with vertical burnishing; thin pale pinkish brown oxidation surfaces underlie black slip.

Mineral content: *c*. 40%.

- Quartz: Transparent to translucent, some white and opaque, angular to rounded grains, 0.1–0.5 mm. Sparse sub-rounded to rounded grains, 0.2–0.3 mm, show polish.
- Shell: White curved and tabular silicified fragments, 0.3 mm.
- Chert: Rare angular fragments, 0.5 mm.

Matrix: smooth finely micaceous clay.

Comment on South-Western BB1

These samples contain inclusions typical of wares derived from the Upper Greensand of East Devon and South Somerset. Pottery of this fabric grouping can contain a number of distinctive components, although three or four of them are usually sufficient to identify the source of the pottery. As seen under the binocular microscope the distinctive components are:

- Quartz, including well-rounded and brilliantly polished grains.
- Chert as white, grey or brownish, angular fragments.
- Silicified fossil shell as white tabular fragments, occasionally showing traces of ribbed ornament.
- Sandstone as variably silicified fragments.
- Tourmaline, var. schorl, as black, more or less rounded, and commonly polished grains.
- Feldspar as white, more or less altered grains, sometimes showing cleavage surfaces.

The silicified fossil shell is a particularly significant component as it ties the production area more specifically to the Blackdown facies at the western edge of the Upper Greensand outcrop in East Devon (Fig. 12.1). Here the Upper Greensand became decalcified and the mollusc fauna silicified in the early Tertiary. The polished grains are a further characteristic of the same facies. Collectively, this range of inclusions indicates a source derived from that area, probably taken from stream beds.

The mineralogy of South-Western BB1 therefore shows that this is part of the major and long-standing tradition of pottery production using Upper Greensand-Derived (UGSD) temper. Ceramics using inclusions from this source are represented in the Neolithic, Bronze Age and Iron Age pottery of East Devon, continuing into Roman times. Production resumed on a large scale in the medieval period (Allan *et al.* 2010; EAPIT 2, Chapter 17).

The Fortress Wares

Detailed descriptions of single examples of each of the four main groupings of Fortress Wares are described below, together with a description of a single anomalous vessel. Descriptions of the other 20 samples described in detail in this project, can be accessed in online Table 12.3.3, where a table summarising the inclusions in all the samples of this class will also be found (online Table 12.3.4). No thin sections of this class of pottery were available.

Sample descriptions of each fabric

Fortress Ware A

EAR 4, FIG. 52, TYPE 10.1

Jar, reduced, hard fired.

Mineral content: less than 5% larger grains.

- Quartz: transparent to translucent, colourless sub-rounded to well-rounded grains, tending to be polished, 0.1–0.4 mm.
- Mica: muscovite, a scatter of larger cleavage flakes up to 0.1 mm.
- Feldspar: rare soft white altered sub-angular grain, 0.5 mm.
- Tourmaline: rare black glossy grains, 0.1 mm.

Matrix: very silty/fine sandy with some fine mica.

Fortress Ware B

EAR 4, FIG. 53, TYPE 2.1

Jar, reduced medium grey with a pimply surface.

Mineral content: c. 10%.

- Quartz: transparent to translucent colourless, sub-rounded to rounded grains, tending to be polished, rather unevenly distributed, 0.1–2 mm.
- Feldspar: sparse altered white to off-white sub-angular grains, 0.2–0.5 mm.
- Composite: a quartz/feldspar grain, sub-rounded and polished, 1 mm.
- Tourmaline: black, rounded to sub-rounded glossy grains, 0.05–0.1 mm.

Matrix: silty micaceous with flakes up to 0.05 mm.

Fortress Ware C

EAR 4, FIG. 56, TYPE 10.1

Platter/dish heavily made. Oxidised light orange. Hard-fired.

Mineral content: *c*. 5%.

- Quartz: transparent to translucent colourless, sub-angular to well-rounded and some rounded polished grains, 0.3–1.2 mm.
- Rock fragments: siltstone, pale grey quartzose fragments and sandstone as rounded fine-grained fragments, 3.2 mm.

- Mica: biotite, very rare brown cleavage flakes, 0.6 mm. Muscovite, a scatter of cleavage flakes.
- Tourmaline: sparse black glossy sub-angular to sub-rounded, 0.1–0.6 mm.
- Feldspar: white to off white, variably altered, sub-rounded grains, rarely showing cleavage, 0.6–1 mm.
- Ferruginous: brownish-red, soft sub-angular to rounded pellets, 0.2–1 mm.

Matrix: silty, finely micaceous with a scatter of muscovite flakes up to 0.1 mm.

Fortress Ware D

EAR 4, FIG. 57, TYPE 9.1

Bowl, wheel-thrown, oxidised, rim, body and base sherds. Hard-fired, with external slip.

Mineral content: less than 5%.

- Quartz: rare, well-rounded, matt surfaced grains, 0.1–0.45 mm, and sub-angular translucent grains, 0.4–0.8 mm.
- Tourmaline: two black glossy sub-rounded grains, 0.2 0.15 mm.
- Mica: rare muscovite cleavage flakes up to 0.2 mm.
- Ferruginous pellets: a scatter of soft deep red mainly angular pellets 0.1–0.5 mm.
- Other fragments: rare medium to dark brownish soft angular to sub-rounded grains of uncertain origin.
- Possibly kiln debris or manganiferous material incorporated in the clay. Not apparently of igneous origin, up to 3.0 mm.

Matrix: silty, finely micaceous clay with abundant muscovite.

Fortress Ware D variant

EAR 4, FIG. 57, TYPE 1.1

Pedestal base, light pinkish buff oxidised, hard fired.

Mineral content: less than 5%.

- Quartz: angular to sub-rounded transparent to translucent, 0.05–0.5 mm.
- Feldspar: white variably altered some grains showing traces of cleavage, sub-rounded to angular grains, 0.15–1 mm.
- Tourmaline: rare black sub-rounded matt surfaced grains, 0.9 and 0.3 mm
- Mica: muscovite as cleavage flakes, 0.05–0.08 mm.
- Biotite: one cleavage flake, 0.3 mm.
- Rock fragments:
    - o Basaltic igneous, greyish with white feldspar laths enclosing dark mineral, two angular fragments, 2 mm. One part of a 4 mm rounded fragment.
    - o Aplitic microgranite, pale buff, sub-angular quartzo-feldspathic fragment, 3 mm.
    - o Siltstone, light buff, siliceous, tabular rounded, 0.9 mm.
- Ferruginous pellet: rounded, 2.5 mm.

Matrix: finely micaceous silty clay with cleavage flakes common with a continuous gradation up to 0.05 mm.

Discussion

It is apparent from the similarity of their mineralogy that the Fortress Wares have a common source. Although the fabrics are distinguishable by differences in style and physical appearance, their hard mineralogy has proved to be similar, consisting predominantly of quartz with a minor content of the black tourmaline schorl, more or less altered feldspar, and a variable proportion of muscovite mica. A limited range of other rock fragments is also present in all wares. The hard mineral content of Wares B, C and D (*i.e.* in the size range 0.05–1.5 mm) is generally low, visually estimated at *c.* 5% or less. Fortress Ware A differs from the others in having a sand content of about 10%.

In determining the origin of these wares, three key points require consideration. First, although their iron content is variable, it is noticeable that some have a notably low iron content, resulting in pale-coloured fabrics upon firing. This distinguishes them from many clay sources in South-West England, including those of the Exeter area, which typically have a high iron content, producing red earthenware when fired. Second, they all derive from clays whose mineralogy indicates some connection with a granitic source, but the wares also contain inclusions derived from the Upper Greensand. Third, some of the quartz sand is aeolian.

Among the potential clay sources in the vicinity of Exeter, those of the Palaeogene sediments of the Bovey Formation display all these characteristics (EAPIT 2, Chapter 12, Fig. 12.4). The Formation is set in a fault-controlled basin some 20 km south of Exeter. To the north, it rests predominantly on Carboniferous slate, shale and chert, and comes in close proximity with the Dartmoor Granite, resting on rocks within the metamorphic aureole. In the south, the formation rests on Devonian slates, and to the south-east on Cretaceous Upper Greensand (UGS).

The rock fragments found in Fortress Wares are consistent with an origin in the Bovey Basin. They contain chert, which occurs in the Upper Greensand and also in the Carboniferous rock succession at the west and north of the basin. The sandstone and other sedimentary fragments present in the sherds could also have a Carboniferous source. Some show evidence of contact metamorphism; the very rare occurrence of biotite mica provides a further link to the granite. There is a tendency for the quartz and tourmaline grains (particularly the quartz) to have polished surfaces.

A study by Coque-Delhuille and Gosselin-Vuilleumier (1984) which used scanning electron microscopy (SEM) to investigate the mineralogy of the Upper Greensand (UGS) and the sands of the Bovey Formation has shed confirmatory light on the Bovey Formation as the source of Fortress

Wares. They found quartz, feldspar and tourmaline in the UGS and noted the rounded and polished surfaces of some quartz grains. This surface texture, including the presence of polished quartz related to a marine environment, led them to conclude that the Bovey Formation sands had been derived from weathering from the UGS. The sands were intermixed with quartz derived from the Dartmoor granite. Some input from rocks of the granite aureole and those surrounding the Bovey Basin was also present. They also found that some quartz grains showed surface textures indicative of an aeolian environment during sand formation. These specific features are also evident in the Fortress Ware sherds; the occurrence of matt-surfaced quartz grains in some vessels is consistent with the observation of Coque-Delhuille and Gosselin-Vuilleumier (1984) that some quartz in the sands of the Bovey Formation has a surface texture characteristic of an aeolian environment.

The deposit is large enough to have supported the production of four potteries or clay sources sufficiently similar to produce wares with similar mineralogy. The higher sand content of Fortress Ware A probably indicates a variation in clay source; the sand was probably derived from the Upper Greensand, close to the eastern margin of the Formation. It is not thought that the members of the Bovey Formation containing white-firing kaolinitic clay themselves are a source of Fortress Ware clay. These clays would have been relatively inaccessible because of a substantial cover of alluvial gravel of the River Bovey. It is considered that the underlying Abbrook Clay-and-Sand and the Lappathorn Members of the Bovey Formation, which consist of a range of silty and sandy clays cropping out on the eastern side of the Bovey basin, are a more probable source. The belief that the Bovey clay deposits have been exploited since Roman times (Selwood *et al.* 1984) appears to be of longstanding but has been without firm evidence until recent work at Twinyeo demonstrated some use of Bovey clay in the Roman period (Quinnell and Taylor 2015, 234).

One sherd among the 25, however, contains basalt inclusions which appear to come from the Exeter area. It is described here as Fabric D variant and merits further research.

South-Western Grey Ware Storage Jars

Exeter Grey Ware Storage Jars are large vessels with everted rims, generally with a medium-grey reduced fabric. They commonly have impressed thumb ornament below the rim and short incised or stabbed decoration on the inner edge of the rim. The indigenous mineral content of 5–10% is relatively low. Ten examples were examined and described in detail in this study, and ten further specimens were examined more rapidly, and checked for main mineral components. A detailed description of a single typical vessel is published here; the other nine descriptions will be found in online Table 12.3.5, and online Table 12.3.6 summarises the inclusions in these vessels.

EAR 4, fig. 68, type 1.2

Storage jar, grey surfaces over lighter grey core, hard fired; thumb impressed ornament.

Mineral content: *c.* 0.5%.

- Quartz: transparent to translucent colourless, angular to sub-angular and some rounded grains, 0.2–0.8 mm, some showing some polish.
- Vein quartz: sub-rounded grain of opaque white quartz 6.7 mm and some angular grains of white quartz, 2 mm.
- Rock fragments:
    - o Fine-grained sandstone, grey rounded to sub-rounded fragments, 1.1–3 mm and one micaceous fragment.
    - o Large angular quartzitic fragment, 7 mm.
    - o Micaceous slate, silvery tabular fragments, 1.2–1.5 mm.
    - o Siltstone, medium grey rounded oblate fragment 4 mm. Microgranitic, buff altered angular fragment, 8 mm.
- Feldspar: rare, off-white, soft altered sub-angular grains, 0.5–1 mm.
- Tourmaline: black sub-rounded grain, 0.0 mm.
- Mica: rare muscovite flakes up to 0.2 mm.

Matrix: Finely micaceous clay with mica and quartz silt less than 0.05 mm.

Comment

The small content of igneous-related fragments suggests proximity to the Permian volcanic outcrops of the Exeter area, while the character of the sandstone content is suggestive of a source in the Carboniferous sandstones of the same area. The combination of minerals might be found somewhere to the south-east of the city. In an attempt to establish a more specific source, a comparison is made here between the mineralogy of the Grey Wares and that of tiles from the early Roman site at St Loye's, south-east of the city centre.

Comparison with samples from St Loye's and the Ludwell Valley

Tile from St Loye's

(2160) Curved tile from well, possibly a thick imbrex. Oxidised bright terracotta with pale buff flecks, moderately soft-fired, variable in thickness 17.5–26.6 mm. Sanded on the concave surface and unbroken edge with coarse sand, granules and small pebbles.

Mineral content: c. 5%

- Quartz: a scatter of matt-surfaced angular and rounded grains, 0.1–0.8 mm.

- Rock fragments: micaceous silvery slate sub-rounded to rounded, 0.5–1 mm; sandstone, buff to white bleached, 0.5–2.2 mm; granitic quartz/feldspar fragment, 2.5 mm.
- Feldspar: white sub-angular altered grains which rarely show reflective cleavage surfaces, 0.6–0.8 mm.
- Sanding: angular to sub-rounded mineral grains and rock fragments 0.1–9 mm.
- Sandstone: grey and buff weathered medium to fine-grained fragments.
- Shale: grey rounded oblate fragments.
- Feldspar: soft white altered sub-angular to rounded and occasional cleaved grains.
- Quartz: transparent colourless to white opaque, angular to rounded.
- Quartz: white vein quartz angular to sub-angular, partially crystalline with some larger fragments.

Clay samples from the Ludwell Valley

Two sand samples, extracted from the alluvial clays of the Ludbrook about 500 m east of the St Loye's Roman military site, show a strong resemblance to the mineralogy of the Grey Ware Storage Jars at Exeter and the St Loye's College tile, with the implication that the Ludwell Valley is the source of the potting clay:

Sample 1 (from NGR 9404 9082)

Stream incised into alluvial deposits *c.* 1.75 m thick. Sample collected *c.* 0.25 m above the base of section (25 cm above water level). Brown plastic sandy clay with an organic content. The sand content and some of the black organic content extracted by dispersal and elutriation in water.

Sand mineralogy was as follows:

- Quartz: translucent angular to rounded grains
- Rock fragments: sandstone, slate, acid igneous
- Feldspar: white sub angular to sub-rounded grains
- Tourmaline: black vitreous angular grains
- Biotite: sparse brown cleavage flakes
- Limonite: soft brown grains
- Organic: black plant fragments.

Sample 2 (from NGR 9490 9080)

From stream incised into alluvial deposits *c.* 1.5 m thick. Sample collected *c.* 30 cm above base of section. Chocolate brown (slightly reddish medium brown) very plastic, slightly sandy/silty clay treated as above.

Sand mineralogy was as follows:

- Quartz: angular to rounded, some rounded grains frosted
- Feldspar: white sub-rounded to sub-angular grains
- Tourmaline: black vitreous angular grains
- Biotite: sparse brown cleavage flakes
- Muscovite: sparse cleavage flakes
- Rock fragments: acid igneous
- Organic: black plant and insect fragments.

Comment

The Grey Wares are closely comparable to the fabric of Roman tiles from St Loye's, and to the clay samples from the Ludwell Valley. They also show similarities to the Iron Age fabrics from Exeter Law Courts and Digby sites, attributed to the Ludwell Valley, with the implication that the Ludwell Valley is the source of the potting clay. Variations in the mineral content are consistent with likely variations in the source clay related to different potting batches and clay dug over a period of time encountering local variations.

The widespread local distribution and quantities of Grey Ware Storage Jars found in Exeter and the two-century time span over which they were in use point to a large production site, presumably with an associated substantial quantity of wasters. This site has yet to be located but was outside the limits of the Roman town.

Appendix 12.2

The ICP-AES and -MS Analysis of Fortress Wares from Exeter

Kamal Badreshany

Introduction

Twenty-three samples of selected Fortress Ware fabrics A, B, C and D were analysed by both Inductively Coupled Plasma Atomic Emission and Mass Spectroscopy (ICP–AES and ICP–MS) with the aim of gaining a better understanding of aspects of their production. Most of the samples were from Exeter, with five from Camelon and two from Elginhaugh forts in Scotland.

Chemical analysis using ICP yields the inorganic elemental chemical composition of each sample, providing a chemical signature that can be used to determine whether different ceramics were made using clays from the same outcrops and can imply a shared production location (Orton and Hughes 2013, 168–83). The more closely related the chemical signature of two samples, the greater the likelihood that they are made from materials derived from the same clay outcrop. As the signature can vary even within the same clay outcrop, very close signatures suggest production from a geographically and temporally proximate batch of materials and, thus, probably indicate the same production location and a similar date.

The samples (Table 12.2) were a mixture of the coarser fabrics B and C and the finer A and D. The Fortress Wares at Exeter are well known from the excavations in the area. No work, however, has been undertaken to look at their geochemistry to gain a better understanding of their production and distribution. A few samples from Scotland that are stylistically very similar to Fortress Ware B were tested to confirm a chemical match and provide further evidence that they were produced at Exeter. This study aims to address two primary research questions:

1. To investigate whether the four known Fortress Ware fabrics (A, B, C and D) form distinct chemical groups or whether they are intermixed.
2. To see if the geochemistry of the samples points to a location near Exeter. Additionally, a comparative analysis will be made with ICP data from ceramics found associated with the Late Saxon Bedford Garage kiln, located within the city walls of Exeter itself, in the hopes of providing further evidence for a production location in Exeter for the Fortress Wares (see EAPIT 2, Chapter 17).

Analytical methods

Following the methodology employed by Hughes (1998; 2005), powders were obtained from the profile of each sherd using a 12-volt dental drill fitted with a 2 mm-diameter solid tungsten carbide bit. The samples were prepared at the Durham Archaeomaterials Research Centre. The powders were acid-digested using Hydrofluoric acid and analysed by ICP–AES and ICP–MS at the Department of Earth Sciences, Durham University by Chris Ottley. The analysis measured for 42 elements. The major elements, analysed by ICP-AES as weight percentage oxide, include Al_2O_3, Fe_2O_3, MgO, CaO, Na_2O, K_2O, TiO_2 and MnO. The minor and trace elements analysed by ICP-MS as parts per million include Sc, V, Cr, Co, Ni, Cu, Zn, Ga, Rb, Sr, Y, Zr, Nb, Cs, Ba, La, Ce, Pr, Nd, Sm, Eu, Gd, Tb, Dy, Ho, Er, Tm, Yb, Lu, Hf, Ta, Pb, Th and U. A number of elements were removed from multivariate statistical analysis as they can be affected by various processes during deposition and sample preparation, including P_2O_5, Co, Ba and Zr. P_2O_5 and Ba can be leached from the sherd differentially, depending on the depositional environment of the sample. Co can be found in tungsten carbide drills and may contaminate the sample, especially if the fabric is hard. Lastly, Zr is not dissolved completely during acid

Table 12.2 Fortress Ware samples examined using ICP-AES and -MS

ICP number	*RAMM Acc. No. (marked on sherd)*	*Publicction refs: EAR 1: Bidwell 1979 EAR 4: Holbrook and Bidwell 1991*
Fortress Ware A		
5/1	148/1993.6.1	EAR 4, fig. 52, type 6.1
5/2	148/1993.10.1	EAR 4, fig. 52, type 10.1
5/3	148/1993.20.1	EAR 4, fig. 53, type 20.1
5/4	148/1993.23.1	EAR 4, fig. 53, type 23.1
Fortress Ware B		
5/5	149/1993.1.1	EAR 4, fig. 53, type 1.1
5/6	149/1993.4.1	EAR 4, fig. 53, type 4.1
5/7	149/1993.10.1	EAR 4, fig. 54, type 10.1
5/8	149/1993.12.1	EAR 4, fig. 54, type 12.1
5/9	(no Acc. No. shown; marked CG 76 EBL)	EAR 1, fig. 64, no. 105
FV631	Camelon, Scotland	
FV675	Camelon, Scotland	
RDA6L	Camelon, Scotland	
R115	Camelon, Scotland	
R232	Camelon, Scotland	
Fortress Ware C		
5/10	150/1993.5.2	EAR 4, fig. 55, type 5.2
5/11	150/1993.7.1	EAR 4, fig. 55, type 7.1
5/12	150/1993.10.1	EAR 4, fig. 56, type 10.1
5/13	150/1993.3.1	EAR 4, fig. 55, type 3.1
Fortress Ware D		
5/14	151/1993. 2.1	EAR 4, fig. 57, type 3.1
5/15	151/1993. 7.2	EAR 4, fig. 57, type 7.2
5/16	151/1993. 7.3	EAR 4, fig. 57, type 7.3
5/17	151/1993. 9.1	EAR 4, fig. 57, type 9.1
Elginhaugh		
5/18 (CMB1)	Eliginhaugh	
5/19 (CMB2)	Eliginhaugh	

digestion and, as a result, the reported concentrations can be inaccurate. An initial survey of the geochemical data indicated that we were dealing with a regional dataset, one in which most of the samples derive from related materials. As such, CaO, Fe_2O_3 and K_2O, were removed from the multi-element analyses, as they are of little use in differentiating samples from closely related geological contexts, such as those being examined from this work. Various processes can also affect these elements during deposition and the resulting variability can serve to hinder the interpretation of results based on the analysis of materials derived from a granite derived context.

The accurate recognition of samples derived from closely related geographical and temporal contexts as belonging to various production locations requires the use of multiple strategies. The use of multivariate statistics on the full suite of elements analysed by ICP–MS, save those elements excluded for reasons given above, is one. Another useful strategy in such cases is to focus on the group of trace elements known as the Rare Earth Elements (REE). The REE are ideal for geochemical fingerprinting in clays as they are largely immobile during low-grade metamorphism, weathering and hydrothermal alteration (Rollinson 1993 2003). As such REE values, more than other elements, are a good indicator of the original composition of the parent rock. Moreover, studies show there is no fractionation of these elements as a result of the firing process (Finlay *et al.* 2012, 2389). The REE are divided by the British Geological Survey into Light REE (LREE) La, Ce, Pr, Nd, Sm, and Eu and the Heavy REE (HREE) Gd, Tb, Dy, Ho, Er, Tm, Yb, and Lu. The REE values were normalised using the values for chondritic meteorites as presented in Rollinson 1993 (online Table 12.4).

The synthesis of the data resulting from the ICP analysis of ceramic data requires multivariate statistical data reduction techniques, such as principal components analysis (PCA; Orton and Hughes 2013, 176–80). PCA examines the variation in the data and reduces the dataset to a few variables, called principal components, which serve to explain most of the differences in the chemical fingerprints of the samples. The first two principal components usually explain most of the variation in the sample. The numerical values generated for each sample in a PCA are referred to as their 'factor score'. Two samples with similar factor scores will thus have a similar chemical fingerprint and appear near each other on the plot of the results of the analysis (Figs 12.10–12.13).

Two additional strategies involving the REE were also employed to help interpret the data (Rollinson 1993 2003). The first strategy plots the ratio of LREE/HREE, as these values reflect geological inputs. The second plots the values of LREE+HREE, which can inform on the nature of the parent rock. In all cases ceramic samples exhibiting similar values, especially across multiple strategies, are likely to share a production source.

The PCA was conducted on data from the ICP analysis of the 24 ceramic samples listed in online Table 12.5. The PCA and graphing were conducted using the R statistical software package. For the PCA, the weight percent and ppm concentration values were first normalised by converting them to log values (base 10). The conversion is necessary as it removes the bias in the statistical calculations toward element concentrations that have larger absolute values but lower concentration values. For example, though 13% by weight is a higher

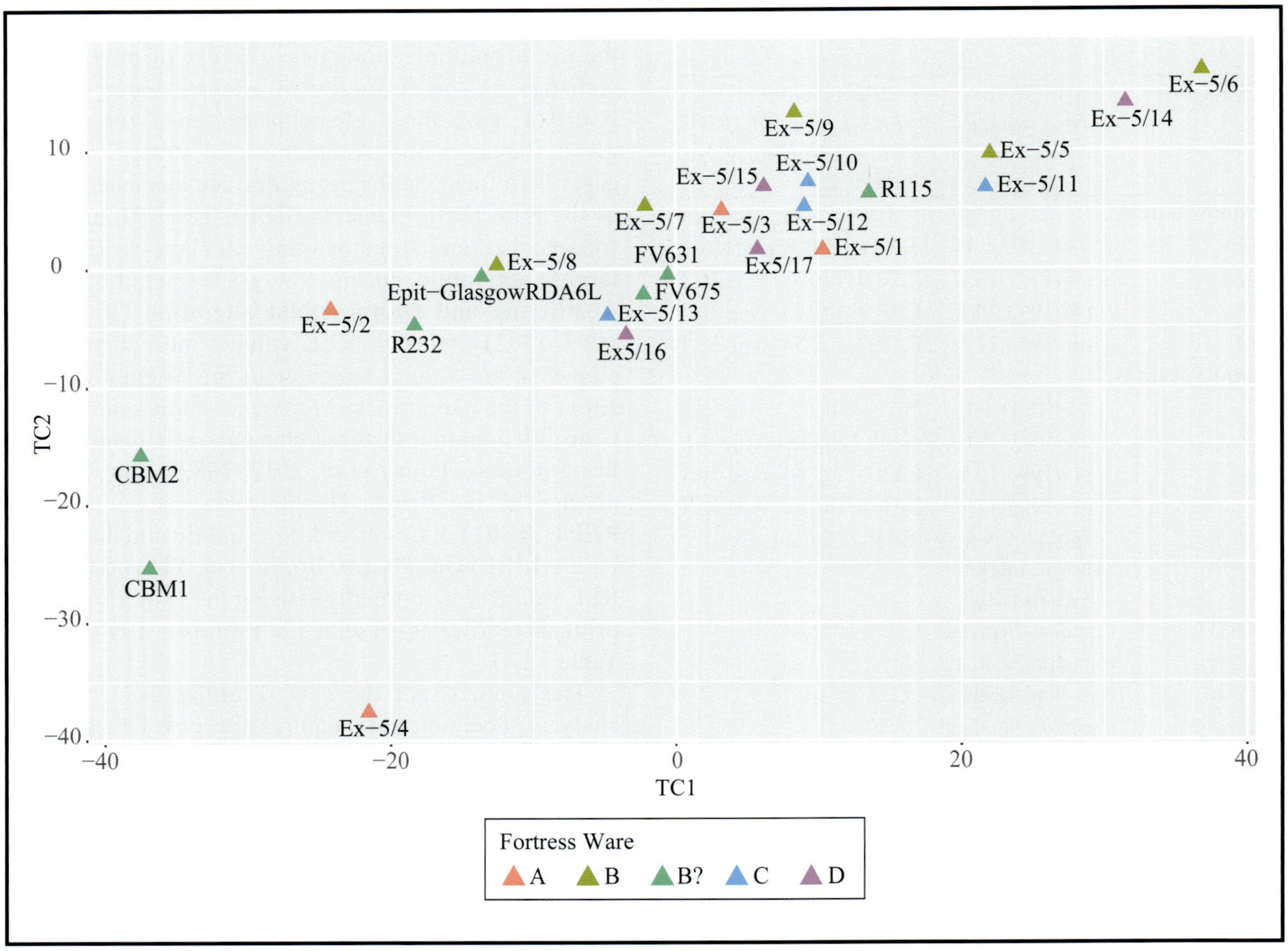

Fig. 12.10 The results of the Principal Components Analysis of all samples, labelled by sample number and ware

concentration than 420 ppm, it has a lower absolute number. The resulting values were then subjected to a principal components analysis and the first four components extracted. The first two, however, explained most of the variation in the data, and were plotted on the graphs shown in Figs 12.10–12.13. The factor scores of these components can be found in the accompanying Excel file (online Table 12.5).

Results and discussion

The graphs appear to present a picture of shared chemistry between the ware groups, though the geochemical results do show clustering amongst samples of the various ware groups. Some clustering within individual groups is evident, but overall samples exhibit a fairly similar chemical composition, making their meaningful separation into groups a challenge. This conclusion is broadly reinforced by their thin section petrography which indicated a uniform mineralogy throughout the samples, despite different shapes/wares identified in macroscale (see Taylor, Appendix 12.1). All the samples yielded results in line with values published from geochemical surveys from the Exe Valley (Ward *et al.* 1992; Rawlins *et. al.* 2003), especially the REE data. Additionally, the values are largely in line with those produced from the Late Saxon Bedford Garage kiln. The thin section petrography, however, convincingly indicates a probable source in the Bovey basin for most of the samples of the Fortress Wares, which is in line with the chemistry. The use of multiple strategies, however, has allowed for the identification of some groups that seem to be geographically linked. The samples from Scotland (FV631, FV675, RDA6L, R115 and R232) can all be chemically linked to Fortress Ware examples (often Ware B), so were likely to have been produced near Exeter. A few outliers were noted, namely sample Samples 5/4 (Ware A), and the two samples from Elginhaugh (CMB 1 and 2). These were removed and the PCA re-ran to gain a better separate the remaining, more closely related, samples into chemical groups.

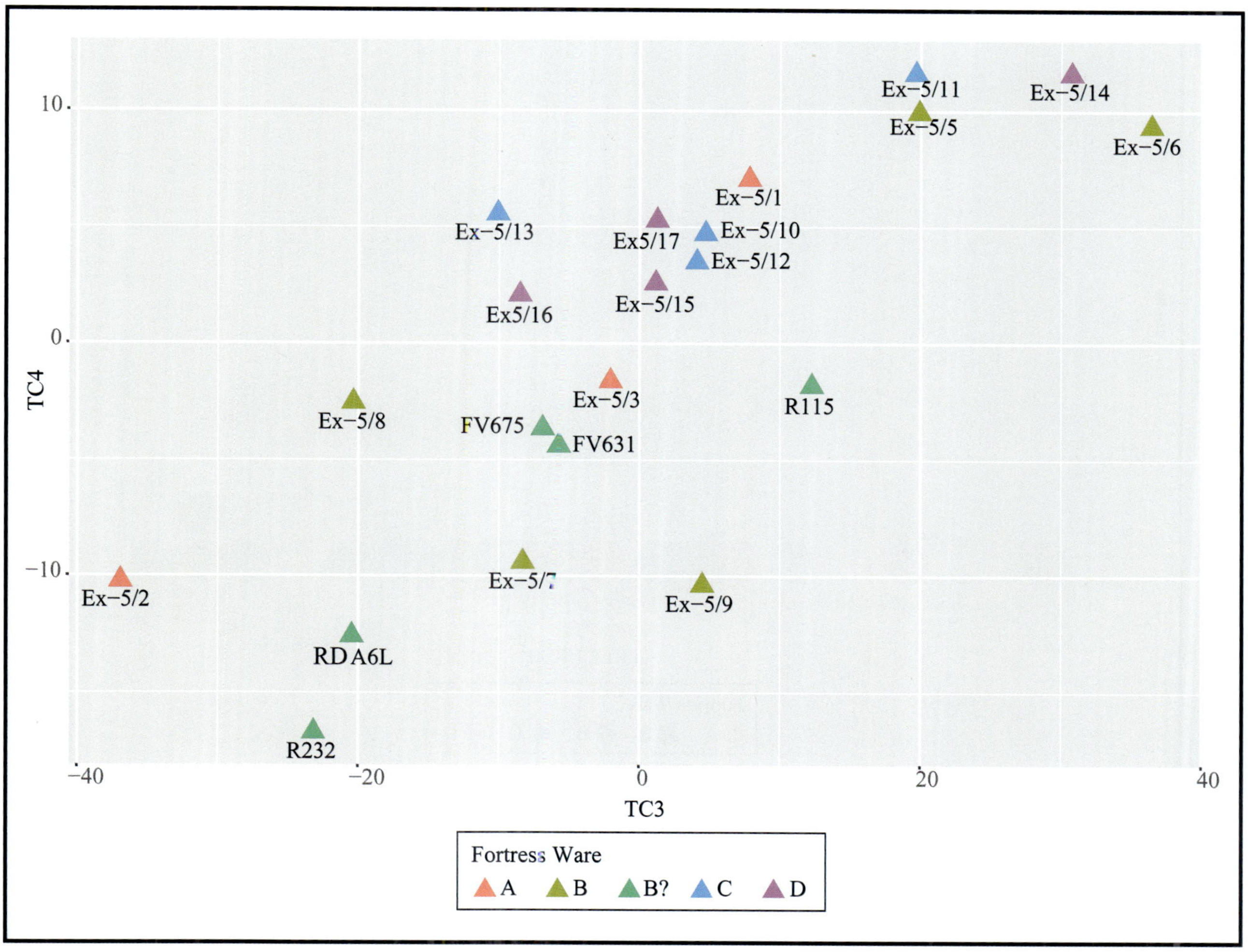

Fig. 12.11 The results of the Principal Components Analysis with outliers removed, labelled by sample number and ware

The first question asked whether the Fortress Wares form distinct chemical groups or whether they are intermixed. The PCA analysis shows clusters of samples of one or another ware type but also some intermixing. The fabrics A and B show more variability than the fabrics C and D. Their highly similar chemistry for the samples across ware groups, as reflected on the PCA and REE plots, is unsurprising, since they come from the same production location (see Taylor, Appendix 12.1). The greater variability observed for samples from groups A and B is probably due to a greater range of tempering materials used and varying degrees of coarseness. For example, according to Taylor, sample 5/5 (151/1993.1.1) is relatively fine-grained compared to other examples from this ware group. The Scottish samples and a number of examples from Wares A and B, found to the left in the PCA (Fig. 12.11), are less enriched in REE indicating they are less clay rich and probably contain more calcareous or silica rich tempering material when compared to some samples to the right of the graph. The geochemical analysis confirms that the Scottish samples are likely from the same production as Fortress Ware B. Wares C and D are, for the most part, enriched in REE indicating they are more clay rich. It is clear from the analysis that the Fortress Wares types are made from related materials, something reinforced by the petrographic analysis (Taylor, Appendix 12.1).

The second research question is aimed at understanding if the chemistry of the samples supports a source near Exeter. The values for the REE (Fig. 12.13) are all relatively low (less than 250 ppm), in line with the types of sedimentary deposits found near Exeter (Rollinson 1993). In contrast, medieval ceramics from Buckfast Abbey on the Dartmoor Granites showed nearly double the REE concentration (Badreshany 2018). The chemistry generally supports the idea of a production location on the types of deposits consistent with those located near Exeter or the Bovey Basin. A number of samples of Fortress Ware B show higher levels of Cr relative to

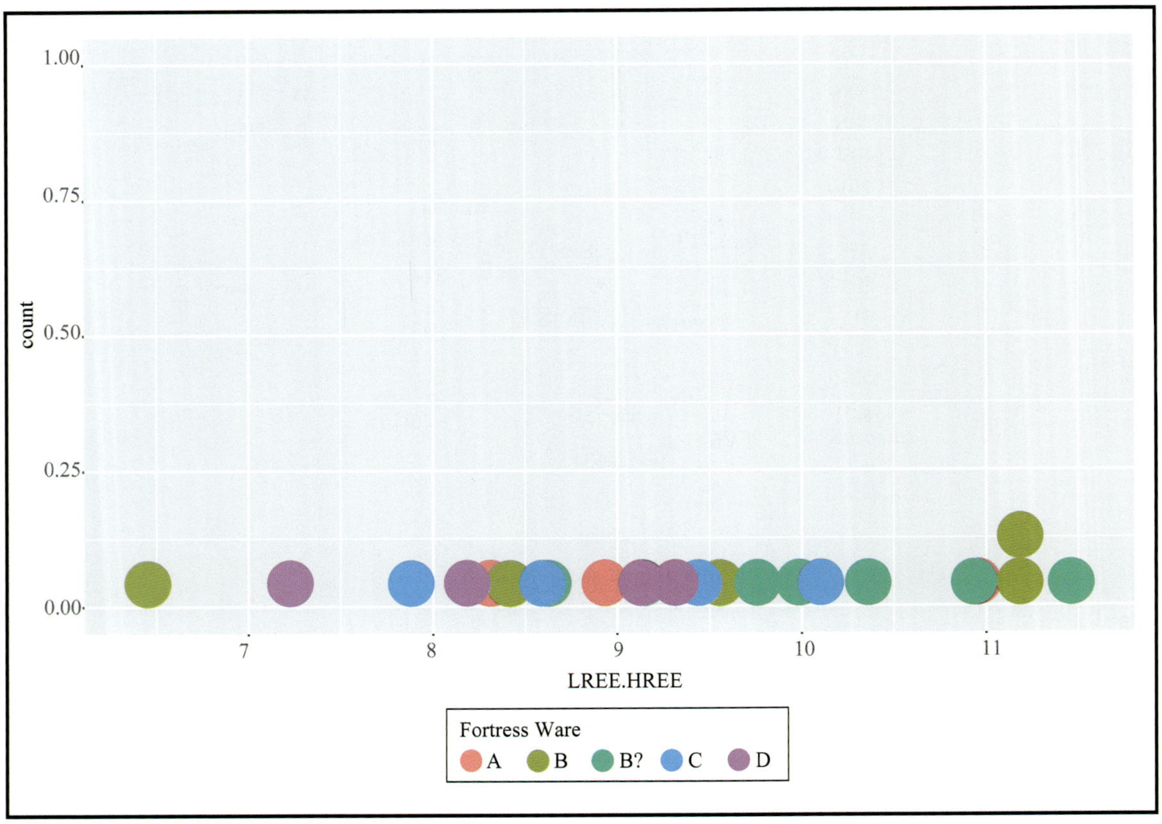

Fig. 12.12 Ratio of total ppm LREE/HREE by Ware. The values have been normalised to chondritic values

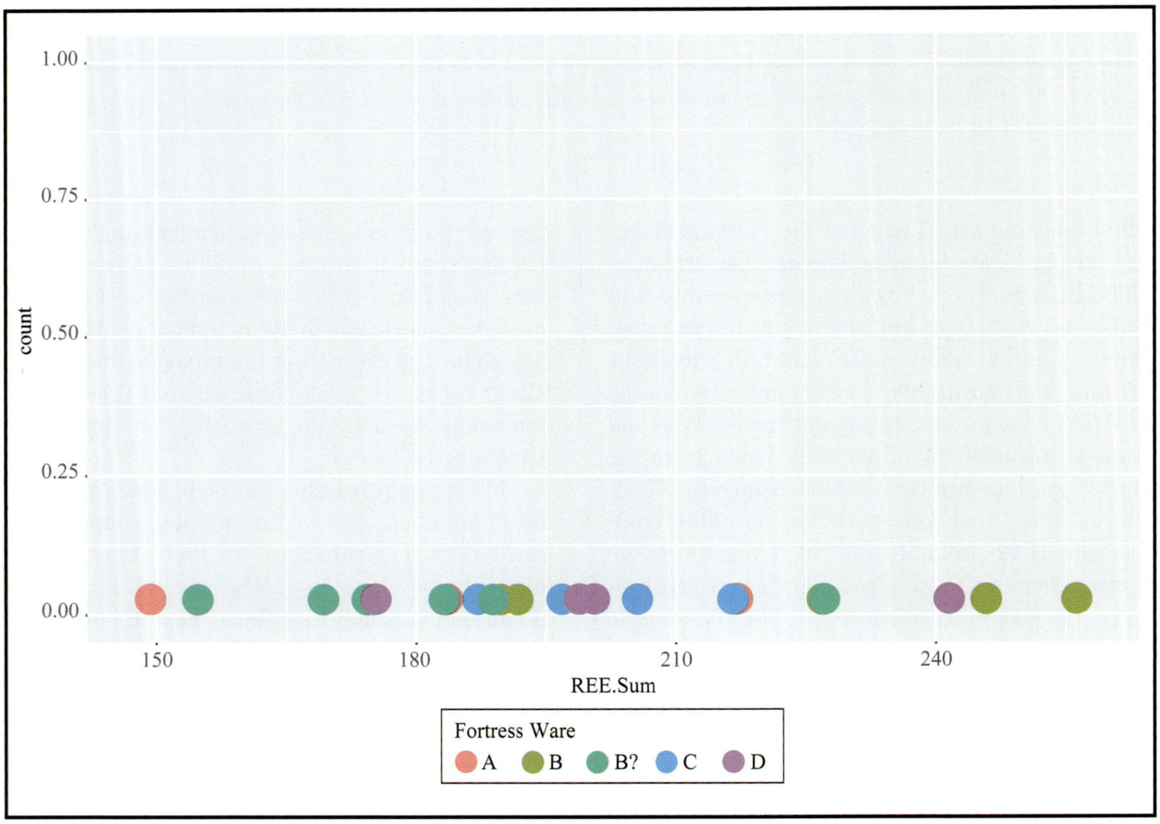

Fig. 12.13 Concentration of LREE+HREE in ppm by Ware. The values fall in line with those published for sedimentary rocks. The values have been normalised to chondritic values

the other samples, which might indicate the inclusion (whether purposeful or inadvertent) of locally available basalts as temper in some of the coarser pottery, as noted by Taylor (see Appendix 12.1) and Hughes (EAPIT 2, Chapter 17). As indicated earlier, all the samples (except those identified as outliers) derive from related materials.

Conclusions

The ICP analysis of the 24 samples of Fortress Wares indicates that the pottery has broadly related chemical signatures suggesting a shared production location, very likely somewhere in the region of Exeter (probably the Bovey basin according to Taylor, see Appendix 12.1). The data did exhibit some variability allowing for the creation of meaningful groupings based on Ware type (A, B, C or D), though many of wares cross-cut chemical groupings, something also seen with the petrofabrics in Taylor's petrographic analysis. This analysis also indicates these Fortress Wares (especially Fortress Ware B) were distributed as far afield as Scotland, as samples found there are a close typological and chemical match.

13.1

Roman Ceramic Building Material: Introduction

Stephen Rippon and Neil Holbrook

This chapter contains two papers on Roman ceramic building material (CBM) in Devon. The first, by Sara Machin, is concerned in the main with the description in thin section of the petrological characteristics of different CBM fabrics, although she also makes some use of portable X-Ray Fluorescence (pXRF). The second paper, by Peter Warry, utilises two techniques: typological study of tiles, principally *tegulae* roofing tiles, combined with a more extensive fabric analysis utilizing pXRF. Warry has researched extensively on Roman CBM in Britain, and at an early stage in the EAPIT project the editors invited him to turn his attention to the CBM from Exeter and Devon more generally. The county was considered to be of particular interest for such a study as the quantities of CBM recovered from excavations and fieldwalking in Devon are small in comparison to the assemblages recovered from Dorset and Somerset where buildings with tiled roofs were much more prevalent. It is, however, exactly this relative scarcity of CBM in Devon which makes detailed analysis a much more practicable and manageable proposition than in the neighbouring counties to the east where a researcher is confronted with a daunting quantity of material to work with. The CBM from Exeter and Devon had also attracted interest from different researchers over several decades and we sensed that it was already better studied than the material recovered from some other parts of the province, such as Paul Bidwell's (1979, 148–54) review of the CBM recovered from the excavation of the legionary bath-house and subsequent basilica and forum in 1979.

In the late 1980s RAMM invited Neil Holbrook and Paul Bidwell to formulate a written retention and disposal policy for its collection of Roman tile, which it had lacked previously, and this included the formulation of a four-fold division of the Exeter CBM fabrics. Quantification by weight according to this fabric series was undertaken during the discard process. Given that Machin and Wary have recently re-examined the retained CBM assemblages held by the RAMM it is worthwhile setting on record the criteria upon which retention and discard of the Exeter assemblage was accomplished. Following quantification by fabric, tiles that met the following criteria were retained:

1. All usefully stratified *tegula* fragments which retained flange profiles, patterns drawn with the finger, etc.
2. *Imbrices* that retained half their profile over a length of 100 mm or more
3. All box tiles from 1st-century AD contexts, along with any other fragments which had combed decoration or preserved the openings cut into their sides
4. Flat tiles (defined as tiles more than 30 mm thick) if they preserved their full length on at least one side.

Tile fragments that did not meet these criteria were discarded. The retention practice adopted for rural sites seems to have been more varied and some of the publications of these sites did not include a report on the CBM.

In their *Roman Finds from Exeter*, Holbrook and Bidwell (1991, 281–2) devised a categorisation of Exeter tile fabrics entirely on the basis of a visual inspection of colour, assessment of hardness and to a lesser extent obvious inclusions within the clay matrix. It is only fair to point out that David Williams – who subsequently carried out a programme of petrological analysis – played no part in this categorisation, and simply reported on a single sample of each fabric sent to him. In retrospect it is apparent that the differentiation between Exeter Fabrics 1–3, which were all considered to be made locally, probably owed more to variances in the firing of specific batches of tiles than to different clay sources. The buff-coloured tiles (Fabric 4) were clearly a distinct group and this is supported in the re-analyses presented by Machin and Warry below. The opportunity was also taken at that time to submit tile samples recovered from a variety of other sites in Devon for thin section description, and this was fully reported on by Williams (1991a; b).

Following the publication of *Roman Finds from Exeter* interest in Devon CBM was maintained by Jennifer Wheeler (later Durrant) who published some valuable papers, especially one concerning the likely kiln site on Hatherleigh Moor (Wheeler and Laing-Trengrove 2006). Not all of Durrant's work has yet been published, and particularly noteworthy is her analysis of the CBM recovered from the tile production site at Princesshay in Exeter, excavated between 1997 and 2006 (Site 156), and that from another likely kiln site beneath St David's church (Site 191; Durrant forthcoming a; b). The studies presented in this chapter have benefited greatly from Durrant's generosity in sharing the results of her work ahead of publication. Roger Taylor has also applied his methodology of the detailed description of the petrological inclusions contained within ceramic fabrics to selected samples of CBM (he had initially developed this method to assist in the characterisation of pottery fabrics: Quinnell 2003; Taylor and Wheeler 2006). Of particular importance was his work on the Roman tile reused in Exminster church that identified five fabrics including three further sources in southern Devon (Allan *et al.* 2008; and see Taylor forthcoming).

Warry's (2006) initial approach was to apply his typology of *tegula* cutaways to the Devon material. During this research the pXRF machine owned by the University of Exeter became available to the project and Warry enhanced his typological study with an extensive programme of fabric analysis based upon data collected by pXRF. A major challenge in the application of pXRF to archaeological ceramics, including CBM, has been to determine an appropriate method of data collection which balances consistency of sampling with time expended. Just as crucial has been the formulation of a method for the analysis of the chemical data collected to permit the discrimination of the potentially separate sources of tile production. At the time of the study there was little available literature to guide the data analysis and, for instance, we became aware that the Building Roman Britain project at Bournemouth University was grappling with very similar issues. Given the pioneering nature of pXRF analysis for the study of CBM, Warry decided that it would be valuable to commission a third method to provide an independent check on the validity of the conclusions drawn from the pXRF data. This entailed thin section petrographic description of the principal fabrics identified from Warry's analysis by Machin of the University of Reading.

In presenting these complementary approaches to the analysis of the Roman CBM from Devon it is logical to present Machin's work first (Chapter 13.2 below) as it builds directly upon the thin section descriptions published by Williams in 1991, and its conclusions are compared by Warry with the pXRF results in Chapter 13.3. Machin followed her thin section descriptions with a limited programme of her own pXRF analysis, undertaken independently of Warry's work. Machin used different equipment and adopted a different method of data analysis to those adopted by Warry. She concluded that her pXRF did not permit the isolation of potential sources of tile production, whereas Warry using typology in combination with pXRF is more confident in the ability of his analysis to provide that level of discrimination. Readers will doubtless find it instructive to compare the two methods and their slightly differing results, although it is reassuring that the thin section and typology/pXRF approaches reached broadly similar conclusions, with the differences perhaps highlighting that one approach was superior with some fabrics and the second approach with other fabrics?

Devon is now one of the best studied regions of Roman Britain in terms of the attention devoted to its Roman CBM by a variety of researchers over several decades. Hopefully the research published in this chapter will encourage future scholars to engage afresh with this material. More remains to be done. There has been no detailed typological study of the CBM from stratified deposits in Exeter, with important chronological horizons provided by deposits that can be associated with the period of 1st-century AD military occupation, and also the extensive dumps deposited *c.* AD 160–80 in the outer ditch of the early town. Securely dated evidence for the first arrival in Exeter of the imported buff tiles (Machin Fabric 4 = Warry's Topsham grouping) will also be valuable. As Exeter is subject to continued ongoing redevelopment it is surely only a matter of time before a tile kiln and its associated waster dumps are encountered within a controlled archaeological excavation. The vast majority of CBM which will be recovered in the future will doubtless be from development-led fieldwork where considerations of value for money and cost effectiveness are ever present. pXRF does potentially offer a non-destructive and rapid method of fabric analysis which is becoming an increasingly affordable tool in post-excavation analysis, although further work is urgently required to realise the full potential of pXRF for the study of Roman CBM, and for a consensus to form around the most appropriate methods of data collection and analysis. These are research topics for the future.

13.2

Roman Brick and Tile Production in Devon

Sara Machin

Introduction

This chapter comprises a macroscopic and petrographic study of the ceramic building material (CBM) from Roman sites in Devon, both from within Exeter and a selection of sites in the surrounding area. The report considers the variety of fabrics that can be identified within Roman CBM at a single site – Exeter – evidencing supply from more than one production centre in the region or further afield. In places, it serves to challenge the long-held view that CBM is a high-bulk, low-value item, made local to the demand centre and transported only over short distances. The results look to see if supply networks can be established and where possible, identify production centres or raw material resources used.

Background

Roman CBM from sites in and around Exeter were typically divided into three fabrics, recognised to be of local origin, alongside a fourth, typically later, fabric which is understood to have been imported into the region (Holbrook and Bidwell 1991). A more complex picture of tile production in south Devon began to emerge with the petrological study of Roman tiles embedded in the walls of Exminster church (Allan *et al.* 2008). This identified three further sources of tile in south Devon: one containing Dawlish sandstone, another slate, and a third ?estuarine clay (Taylor 2009, 122–4). Previous fabric studies have shown that it was not always possible to distinguish the three Exeter fabrics in hand specimen with the only difference being the proportion of coarse material, both of quartz grains and rock fragments, which can only really be determined in petrographic thin section. The fabrics were separated petrographically with Fabric 2 being described as the coarsest exhibiting a high proportion of rock fragments, which include acid igneous rocks characteristic of the geology local to Exeter. Fabric 3 is the finest textured whilst Fabric 1 is an intermediate between the two having more quartz sand present than Fabric 3 but fewer igneous rock fragments than Fabric 2. This fabric analysis concluded that the textural differences across these fabrics likely reflected variation within a single clay source, with nothing to suggest a non-local origin for the material in or close to Exeter.

Fabric 4 in Exeter is described as a calcareous fabric with curved fragments of fossilised shell and cryptocrystalline limestone (Holbrook and Bidwell 1991). Examples have also been recorded at sites elsewhere in Devon, around Southampton and the Isle of Wight, and in London. Since no kilns producing this fabric have been identified, the area of the Solent has been suggested as the origin for the material based on the distribution of examples (Fig. 13.2.1). It is also noted that there is potential for the material to have been imported from the continent (Betts and Foot 1994, 33). This fabric was introduced into Exeter in the late 3rd century AD and if produced locally, is thought to mark the end of the Exeter tile industry. It has been estimated that 25% of all *tegulae* are of Fabric 4 in deposits dated to *c.* AD 270 or later (Holbrook and Bidwell 1991, 281–2, fig. 136).

There have been two potential production centres for Roman brick and tile identified in the immediate vicinity of Exeter. Early finds suggested that tiles used in the construction of the legionary baths in Cathedral Close were produced to the north-east of the fortress in the area now known as Princesshay (Bidwell 1979, 148). These military-period tiles were made of Permian clay with acid igneous inclusions that was very similar to kiln debris and wasters excavated more recently in late 1st and 2nd-century AD civilian-period contexts at the Princesshay excavations (Site 156; Chapter 2, Fig. 2.2 above; Steinmetzer, Stead, Pearce, Bidwell and Allan forthcoming). A further possible extra-mural tile production site has also been identified at St David's Church, located to the north-west of the legionary fortress and outside the later civil town. Again, this is based on the presence of waster material,

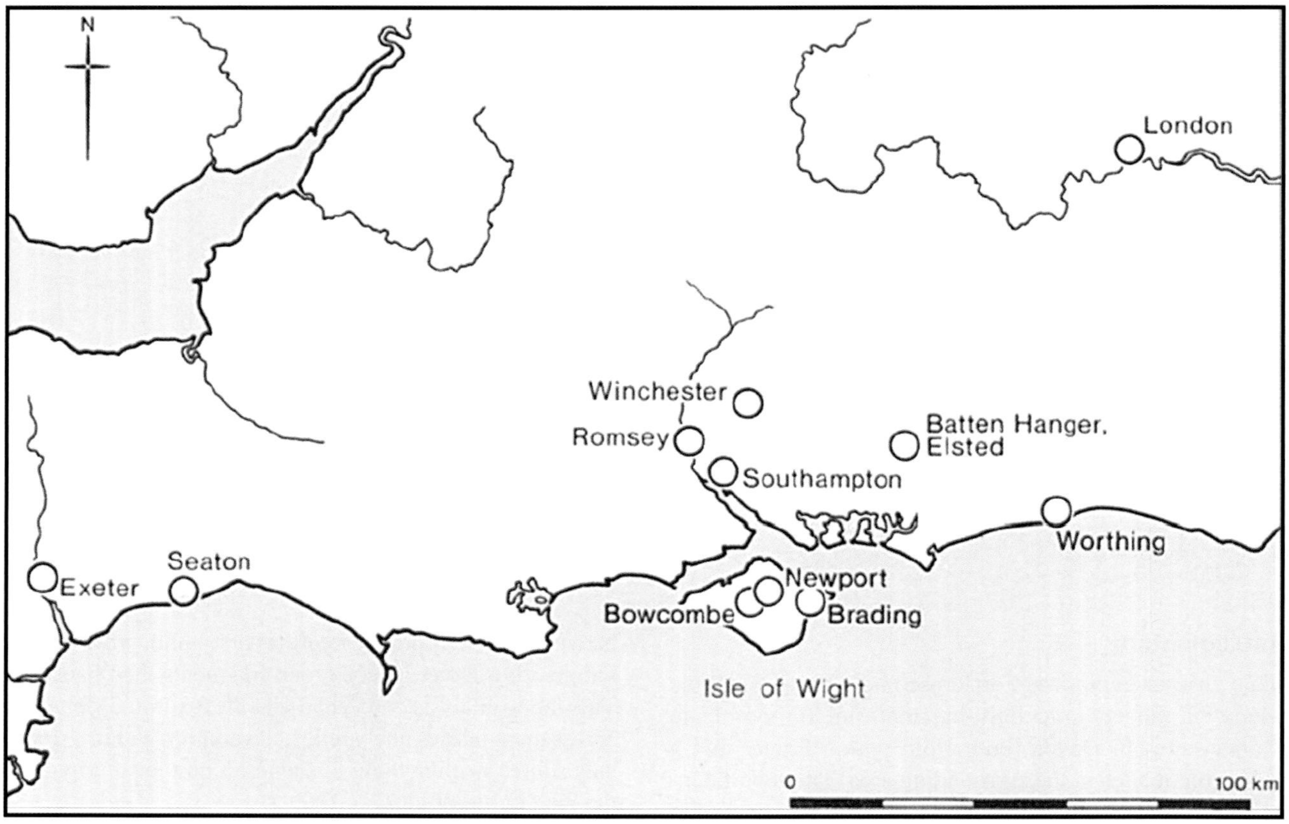

Fig. 13.2.1 Distribution of calcareous Roman brick and tile (after Betts and Foot 1994, fig. 4)

and production has been dated by a small amount of associated pottery to the mid to late 1st century AD (Site 191; Chapter 2, Fig. 2.2 above; Chapman *et al.* 2017; Steinmetzer forthcoming).

Outside Exeter, Hatherleigh Moor has been identified as another probable tilery. The site is located approximately 40 km west-north-west of Exeter where an abundance of waster material has been recovered. Gradiometer survey results also highlight some evidence of *in situ* burning (Wheeler and Laing-Trengrove 2006, 56). This evidence has led to the site being identified as a brick and tile works although no kiln structures have been identified or excavated.

Sample selection and study area

CBM was examined from two sites within Exeter along with material from three extra-mural ones, and seven rural locations (see Table 13.2.1; Fig. 13.2.2). All the retained CBM from these sites was examined and assigned to a form group. Flat pieces greater than 30 mm thick and without distinguishing features have been classified as bricks. The presence of complete dimensions meant that some bricks were able to be assigned to specific form types (*e.g. lydion, bessalis*). Flat pieces, measuring less than 30 mm thickness, and without diagnostic features are recorded as tile. Some of the fragments recorded as tile will undoubtedly be *tegulae*, *imbrices* and other forms. Flue-tiles were recorded where distinctive scoring, combing, relief-patterning or vents were present. *Tegulae* were identified where a flange is present, there is clear evidence of a flange having been removed, or where a lower or upper cutaway could be identified. Small fragments that could not to be assigned to a particular form were recorded as unidentified.

All material was examined using a x10 hand lens and assigned to a macroscopic fabric group. A number of samples were taken from each site and fabric group for preparation of ceramic thin sections. All results are based on the retained material only, which outside of Exeter was the result of often highly subjective, undocumented, retention policies. The retention policy in Exeter is outlined in Chapter 13.1 above. The volume of CBM recovered, particularly when excavating urban centres, is such as to prohibit a 100% retention policy. There is a significant lack of available space for archive deposition and repositories are under increasing pressure to rationalise existing collections. Therefore, on-site retention strategies typically tend to favour complete or exceptional examples, with no consideration of fabric, resulting in unrepresentative collections held in archives. For example, tiles with footprint impressions are typically retained, leading to them being proportionally overrepresented in collections (Machin 2018, 256). Some of the sites included in this study are

Table 13.2.1 Project sites and codes used for thin section identification numbers (TSID): for Site Numbers see Chapter 2 above

Intra-mural sites	*TSID code*	*Rural sites*	*TSID code*
Cathedral Close (Site 40)	CC	Aller Cross, in Kingskerswell	AC
Trichay Street (Site 42)	TR	Ashcombe Barton, in Ashcombe	ASH
		Bolham, in Tiverton	ASHBOL
Extra-mural sites		Bury Barton, in Lapford	BB
Princesshay (Site 156)	PH	Hatherleigh Moor, in Hatherleigh	HM
St David's Church (Site 191)	SD	Holcombe	HOL
St Loye's College	SL	North Tawton	NT
		Otterton Point, in Otterton	OTT
		Pomeroy Wood, in Honiton	PW
		Honeyditches, in Seaton	SEA
		Topsham	TOP
		Woodbury, in Axminster	WB

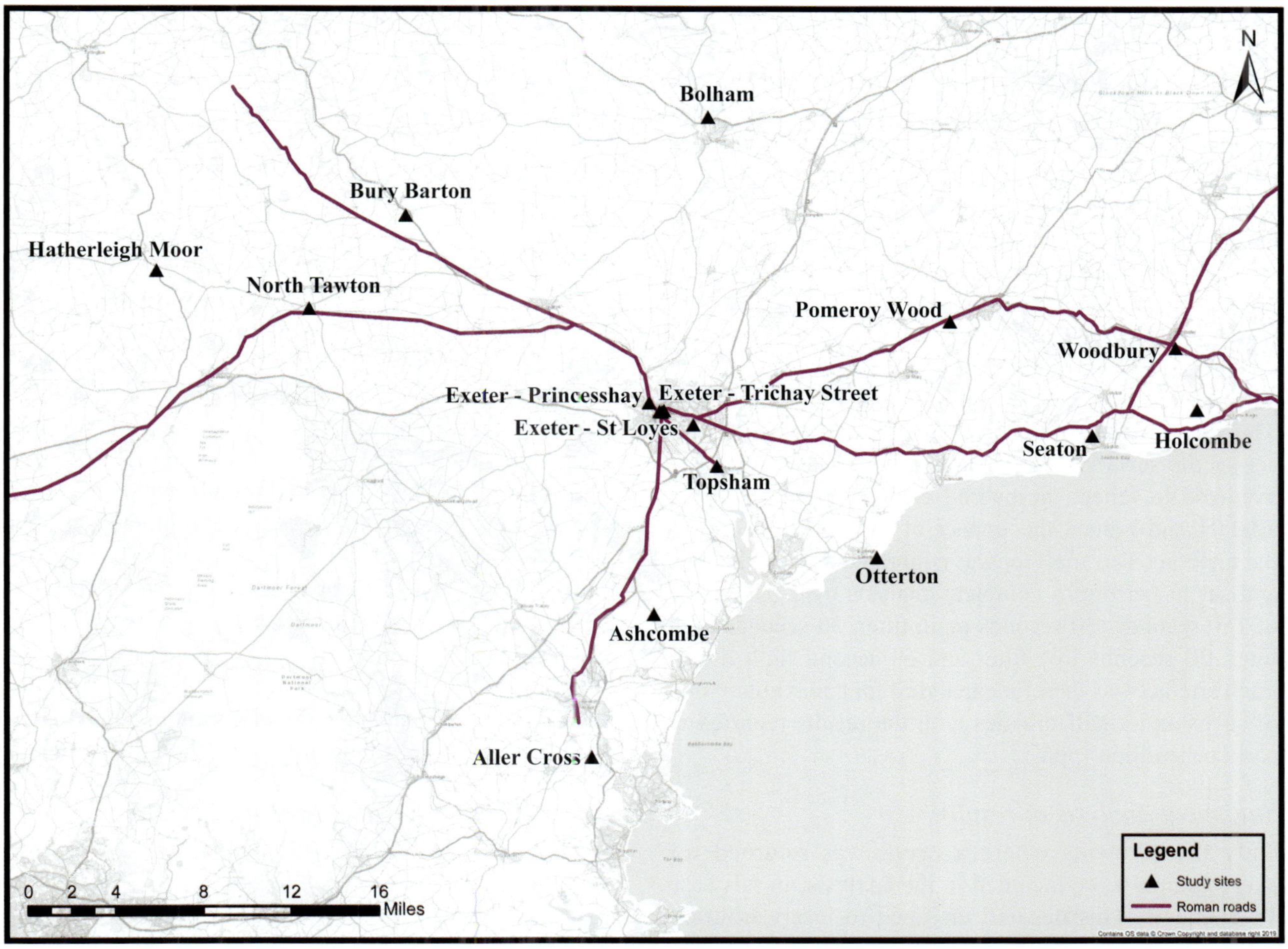

Fig. 13.2.2 Location of study sites used in Machin's study of Roman tile

clearly unrepresentative when the proportion of different forms is considered. This retention bias has often led to CBM assemblages being dismissed in the construction of site narratives.

Methods

Portable X-Ray Fluorescence (pXRF)

The first 34 samples in the study were also included in a round of analysis using pXRF.

Machine specification and calibrations

pXRF analysis was conducted using a Niton XL3t GOLDD+ spectrometer. The analyser is calibrated to calculate the chemical composition for up to 32 elements, excluding the lightest elements (H–Na). The analyser was calibrated using NIST standard reference samples with published values: JB-1 – basalt (Myokanji-toge, Japan), JG-1 – granite (Sori, Gumna-ken, Japan), FER-1 – iron formation sample (Bathurst, New Brunswick, Canada) (confirmed with additional testing on a conventional lab-based EDXRF analyser). These silicate rocks standards were chosen as they are similar in composition to ceramic artefacts.

Selection of elements and number of readings

The number of readings per sample was established by Machin (2018) following the method outlined by Potts *et al.* (1997). Ten points were analysed on a single sample of a heterogeneous fabric, at a minimum spacing of 30 mm to avoid overlapping analysed volumes (*ibid.*, 35). The results were used to calculate the number of replicate readings needed to achieve 10/5/2% standard error. The results showed that two determinations (rounded up from 1.87) are required to achieve a relative standard deviation of the mean of 10%. Eight repetitions (rounded up from 7.49) would be required to achieve a relative standard deviation of the mean of 5%. Based on the results of this analysis, the decision was taken to take three measurements on each sample in different positions.

All analysis was conducted using the 8 mm window, as opposed to the 3 mm spot analysis, in an attempt to partially compensate for variations in clay composition. The three readings were taken at different locations across the surface of each sample. These readings were averaged to reflect the overall clay composition of the artefact and reduce the impact of the heterogeneity of the material. The analyser was calibrated to mining mode and set to perform a complete analysis over the course of 150 seconds (30 seconds main filter, 30 seconds high filter, 30 seconds low filter and 60 second light filter). Each artefact was therefore analysed for a maximum total of seven-and-a-half minutes with the results reported in parts-per-million (ppm).

Statistical analysis of results

Only the elements where a result was returned for every sample were included in the analysis, in this case 14 elements. This negated the need to insert arbitrary values where the reading was below the limit of detection (Sanford *et al.* 1993). The replicate analyses were averaged for each element for each sample. The average results for each site were then log-transformed. This serves to normalise element distributions and reduce the impact of differences in magnitude for some of the major elements (Bakraji 2006, 191). For example, iron (Fe) which is highly variable because of chemical action during weathering, erosion, sedimentation and diagenesis (Degryse and Braekmans 2014, 194). The data were then processed using Principal Components Analysis (PCA) using SPSS to identify discrete compositional groups within the dataset or assess the coherence of hypothetical groups already established (Degryse and Braekmans 2014, 195). Variations in elemental concentrations may also be due to variable tempering rather than to clay source distinctions and these temper-related effects are often revealed in the first Principal Component. The dominance of silica in the samples means that variation in this compound, which is related to abundance of quartzose inclusions in the samples, is likely to exert a strong dilution effect on the relative proportion of the other elements (Baxter and Freestone 2006, 524). Therefore, principal components two and three are used in the scatterplot to eliminate this dilution effect of quartz-sand temper (Neff *et al.* 1988).

Thin section preparation

The samples were polished and mounted onto frosted microscopic slides. The samples were trimmed to approximately 2 mm thickness, lapped to a thickness of 30 μm using a Logitech LP30 and then cleaned and covered with a thin glass coverslip. Each section was given a unique identification number (TSID). The thin sections were analysed using a Leica DMEP polarising microscope at x25–x100 magnification under plane polarised light (PPL) and crossed polars (XP). Digital microphotographs were taken using a Leica DFC420 camera. A total of 86 thin sections was prepared for analysis. The thin sections were then described according to the criteria set out by Quinn (2013, 79–102, appendices A1–A3), recording to the inclusions identified, both plastic and aplastic, followed by a description of the clay matrix and a characterisation of the voids within the fabric. All photomicrographs included in the report are at x25 magnification and in crossed polars, unless otherwise stated.

pXRF results

All CBM was assigned to a fabric group primarily based on the non-plastic inclusions, and the heterogeneity and composition of the clay matrix. The fabrics in this collection have been numbered from Machin-CBM1 to Machin-CBM14. Machin-CBM fabrics 1–4 have been named according to their composition and corresponded to the established Exeter CBM fabrics (Holbrook and Bidwell 1991); all other fabrics are named according to their distribution rather than the location of their production.

An example of a PCA plot is shown in Fig. 13.2.3 which shows a large grouping of samples with the majority clustered in one area of the plot. The grouping of the results in one area of the plot, with the exception of

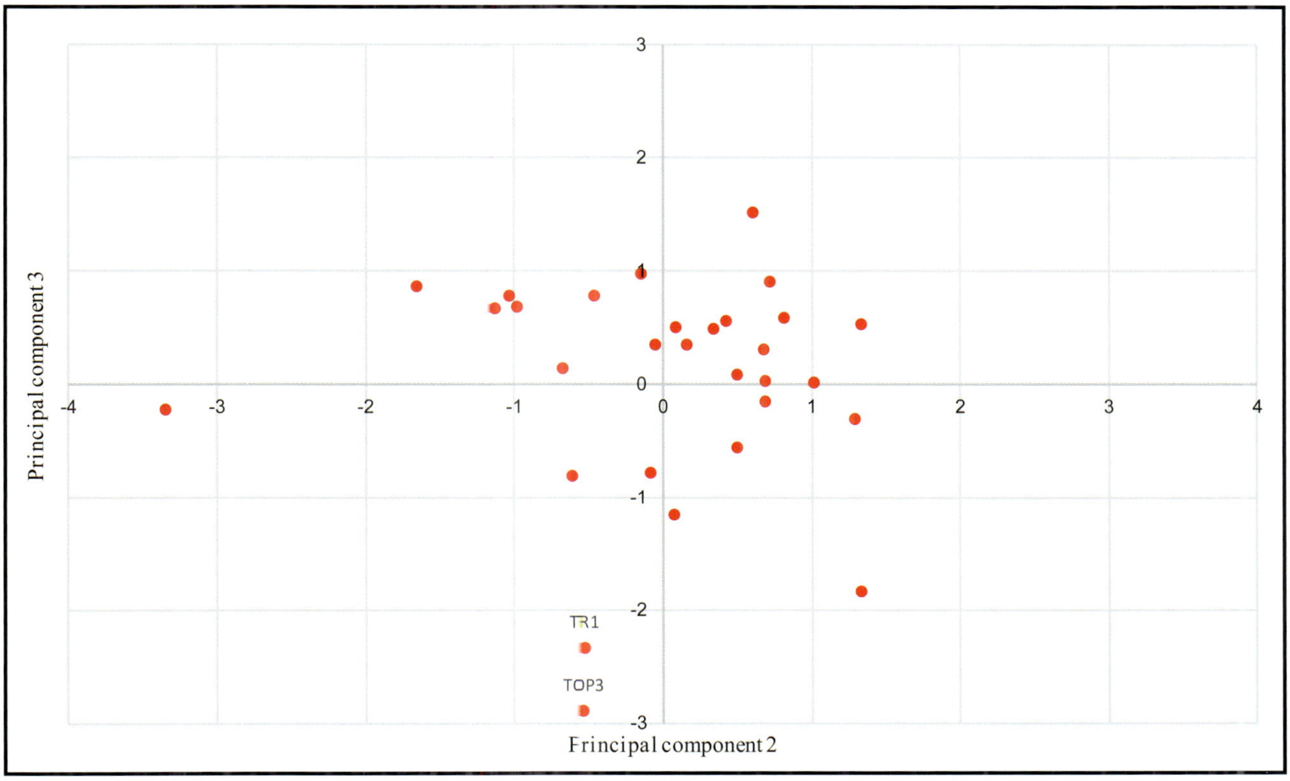

Fig. 13.2.3 Results of PCA classification of 34 CBM samples analysed, based on the normalised abundance of 14 elements

two of these initial samples (Fig. 13.2.3), shows that the geo-chemical composition of the majority of the samples is insufficiently distinct to separate the samples using the portable pXRF results. Two samples plot away from the group, which are examples of Machin-CBM4 (see below). The loading plot (Fig. 13.2.4) shows it is calcium (Ca) that is affecting the distribution into the bottom left-hand quadrant of the plot, confirming the calcareous composition of these two samples (TR1 and TOP3). This lack of distinct grouping from the pXRF analysis led to the decision not to analyse all the material in this way. Instead, the macroscopic groupings were confirmed and described in detail using thin section petrography.

Thin section results: petrographic fabric descriptions

Machin–CBM1: Exeter coarse quartz sand

(Figs 13.2.5–13.2.7)

Macroscopic description: Micaceous fabric with sparse translucent and opaque pink quartz grains visible. Slight heterogeneity noted with the presence of buff/cream clay streaks. Rare to absent rock fragments. Hard fired and oxidised throughout. Surface colours vary from reddish-yellow (5YR 6/8) to red (2.5YR 5/8).

TSID: AC3, CC9; CC10; SL1; SL2; TR3; WB6.

Petrographic description:

Inclusions: 30–35%, equant and elongate, angular to rounded, <1.825 mm, poorly sorted, double to open spaced, weak alignment, moderately bi-modal.

Predominant to Dominant: **Monocrystalline quartz**: equant and prolate, sub-rounded to rounded, <0.25 mm, mode = 0.05 mm. Fine quartz silt.

Common: **Muscovite mica**: equant and prolate, elongate, <0.125 mm, mode = 0.05 m.

Common: **Monocrystalline quartz**: equant and prolate, sub-angular to sub-rounded, <0.475 mm, mode = 0.3 mm. Fraction of medium-to-coarse quartz sand.

Few: **Fe Oxides**: equant and prolate, sub-rounded to rounded, <0.4 mm, mode = 0.225 mm. Scatted throughout the samples, iron-rich grains.

Rare: **Rock fragments**: equant and prolate, sub-rounded to rounded, <0.75 mm, mode = 0.4 mm. Including examples of sandstone, siltstone and chert.

Voids: 5% consisting of meso-planar voids exhibiting random alignment.

Matrix: 60–65%. A slightly heterogeneous fabric with some buff clay streaks visible. The matrix is Fe-rich mid orange-red in both PPL and XP. The matrix exhibits slight optical activity with a speckled b-fabric, going in and out of extinction in random zones. Where present, clay streaks are

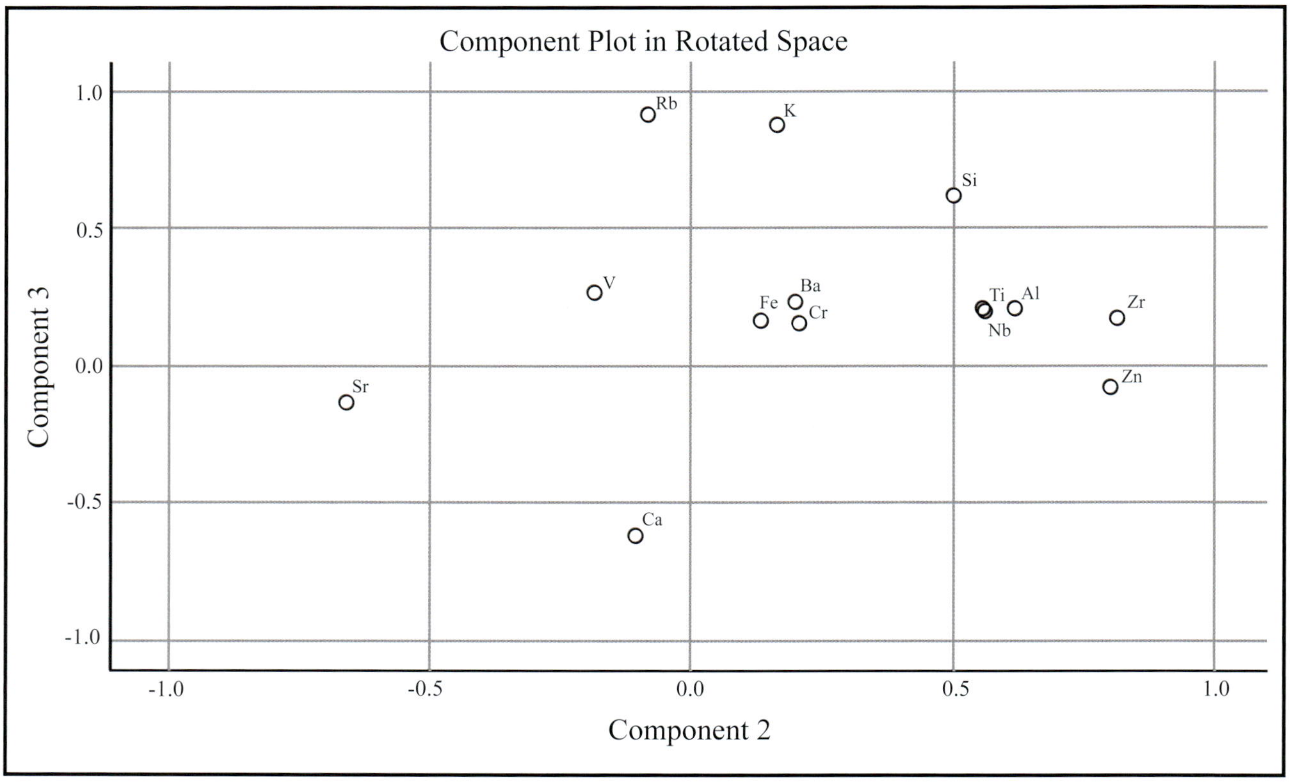

Fig. 13.2.4 Loading plot of principal components 2 and 3

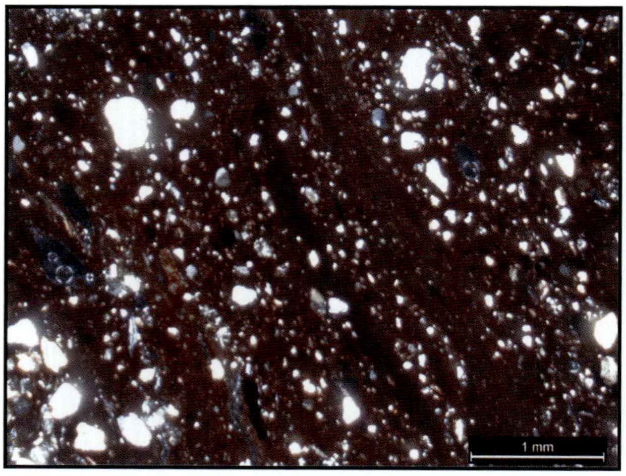

Fig. 13.2.5 Machin-CBM1 thin section AC3

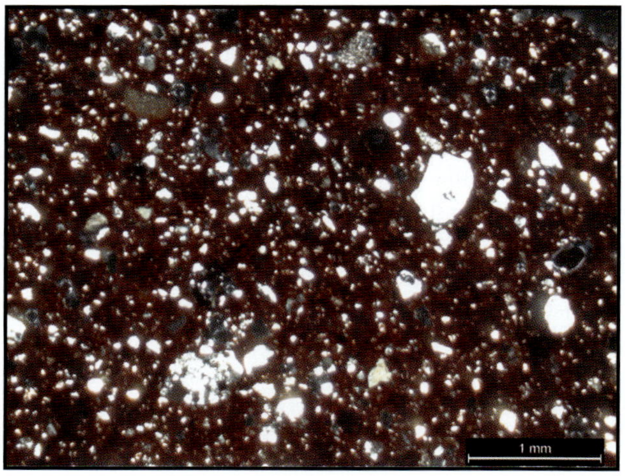

Fig. 13.2.6 Machin-CBM1 thin section CC10

Fe-poor, with merging to diffuse boundaries. They exhibit low optical density when compared to the surrounding clay matrix. There is also a number of Fe-rich clay pellets present visible in some of the samples. These are rounded with clear-to-diffuse boundaries, equant in shape with high optical density in relation to the surrounding matrix.

Summary: This is a fine iron-rich fabric with a common larger medium-to-coarse quartz grains and occasional rounded rock fragments within the same approximate size range resulting in a moderately bi-modal fabric. The rock fragments and coarser sand component are typically rounded, and found in bands throughout the matrix, suggesting that they have derived from a sand, used either as temper to improve the workability of the clay or as a moulding sand which has then become incorporated into some of the bricks during processing. This fabric corresponds with Exeter Fabric 1 (Holbrook and Bidwell 1991).

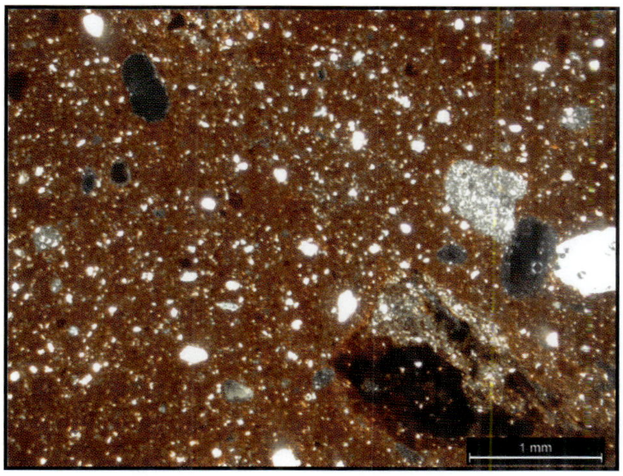

Fig. 13.2.7 Machin-CBM1 thin section SL1

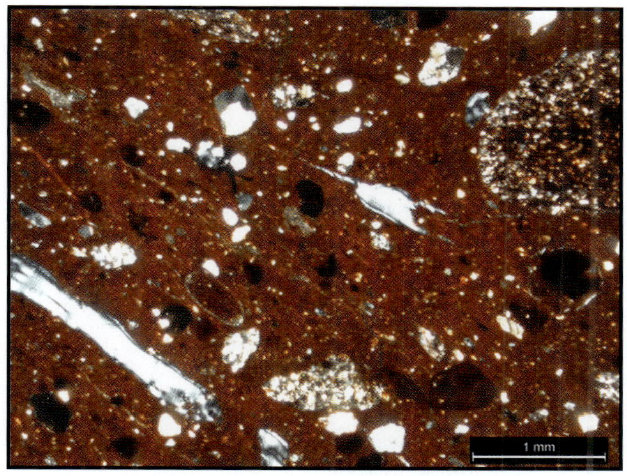

Fig. 13.2.8 Machin-CBM2 thin section BOL6

Machin-CBM2: Exeter coarse rock fragments (Figs 13.2.8–13.2.12)

Macroscopic description: Moderately heterogeneous coarse fabric with sparse quartz. Large proportion of rock fragments visible in hand specimen. Moderately micaceous. Hard fired and oxidised throughout. Surface colours vary from reddish-yellow (5YR 6/8) to red (2.5YR 5/8).

TSID: AC4; AC6; BOL6; CC1; CC2; CC7; CC11; NT; PH2; PH3; PH4; PH8; PH9; SD1; SD2; SD3; SD4; SD5; SL3; TR2; WB4.

Petrographic description:

Inclusions: 35–40%, equant and elongate, angular to rounded, <2.75 mm, poorly sorted, single spaced, weak alignment, bi-modal

Frequent to Common: **Rock fragments**: 20–25%; primarily equant, sub-rounded to rounded, <2.75 mm, mode = 1.75 mm. Mixture of rock types throughout the matrix including sandstone, siltstones, flint, porphorytic lavas and basalts.

Common: **Monocrystalline quartz**: equant and prolate, sub-angular to sub-rounded, <0.25 mm, mode = 0.1 mm. Fine quartz silt and sand fraction.

Few: **Monocrystalline quartz**: equant and prolate, sub-angular to sub-rounded, <0.7 mm, mode = 0.625 mm. Coarse quartz sand fraction.

Few: **Muscovite mica**: equant and prolate, angular, <0.15 mm, mode = 0.15 m.

Few: **Fe Oxides:** equant; rounded to sub-rounded, <0.4 mm; mode = 0.225 mm; Fe-rich grains scattered throughout.

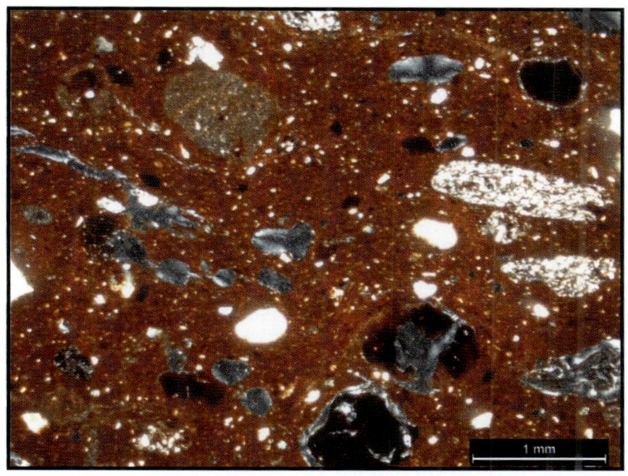

Fig. 13.2.9 Machin-CBM2 thin section CC1

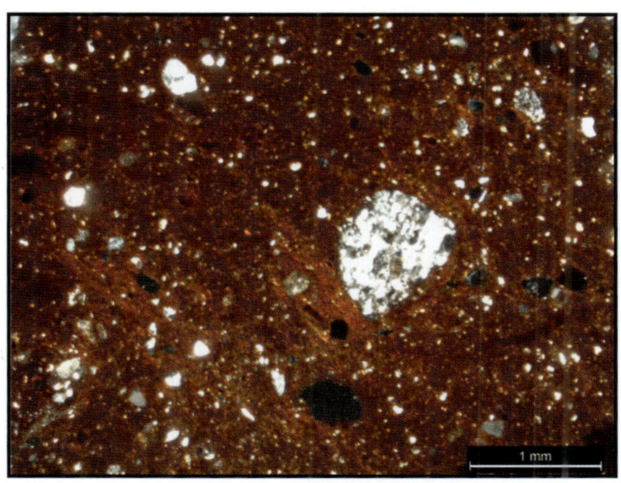

Fig. 13.2.10 Machin-CBM2 thin section SD5

Voids: 5% consisting of macro vughs exhibiting random alignment. No remnants present.

Matrix: 60–65%. A moderately heterogeneous fabric with some clay streaks visible. The matrix is Fe-rich mid orange-brown in both PPL and XP. It is moderately optically active with a speckled b-fabric. Sample PH2 exhibits reduced optical activity as a result of higher firing temperatures starting the vitrification process. Where present, clay streaks are Fe-poor, with merging to diffuse boundaries. They exhibit neutral optical density when compared to the surrounding clay matrix. There are also examples of Fe-rich pellets present. These are rounded and equant in shape with sharp to merging boundaries. The pellets exhibit neutral optical density.

Summary: This is a coarse, iron-rich heterogeneous fabric with inclusions dominated by fragments of rock resulting in a strongly bi-modal fabric. The standard deviation of the major length of the aplastic inclusions is 0.311, compared with that of the fine Exeter fabric (Machin-CBM3) at 0.094. The matrix is Fe-rich with common fine quartz throughout. There is a higher proportion of rock fragments in these samples than observed in other fabrics. This aligns to Exeter Fabric 2, described as the coarsest of the Exeter fabrics having inclusions of rock fragments including sandstone, chert, siltstone, altered igneous rock fragments and some iron ore (Holbrook and Bidwell 1991, 281). The rock fragments are of a coarser grade than those noted to have been added along with the addition of sand (Machin-CBM1). The rock fragments include volcanic rocks in the form of porphyritic lavas and basalts. These are likely to have derived from the Exeter lavas formerly known as the Exeter traps (Bristow *et al.* 1985, 21). Trap rocks were used for the facing blocks in the walls of the legionary bath-house (Bidwell 1979, 28) in Cathedral Close (Site 40). The Exeter lavas include basalts as identified in one Cathedral Close sample (CC1) and one Princesshay sample (PH4) which also contained examples of porphyritic igneous rocks (Figs 13.2.11 and 13.2.12).

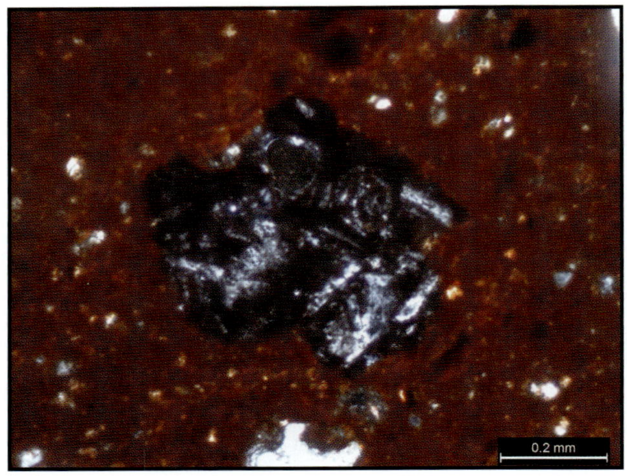

Fig. 13.2.11 Machin-CBM2 thin section CC1 showing basalt fragment (x100)

Fig. 13.2.12 Machin-CBM2 thin section PHR showing porphyritic igneous rock (x100)

Machin-CBM3: Exeter fine (Figs 13.2.13–13.2.17)

Macroscopic description: Highly micaceous fabric with sparse translucent and opaque pink quartz grains visible. Slight heterogeneity noted with the presence of buff/ cream clay streaks. Rare to absent rock fragments. Hard fired and oxidised throughout. Surface colours vary from reddish-yellow (5YR 6/8) to red (2.5YR 5/8).

TSID: CC5; PH1; SEA1; SEA4; TOP2; TOP4; TOP5; TR4.

Petrographic description:

Inclusions: 25–30%, equant and elongate, angular to rounded, <0.9 mm, poorly sorted, double to open spaced, weak alignment, weakly bi-modal

Dominant: **Monocrystalline quartz**: equant and prolate, sub-rounded to rounded, <0.25 mm, mode = 0.05 mm. Fine quartz silt.

Common: **Muscovite mica**: equant and prolate, elongate, <0.125 mm, mode = 0.05 m.

Few: **Monocrystalline quartz**: equant and prolate, sub-angular to sub-rounded, <0.475 mm, mode = 0.3 mm. Fraction of medium-to-coarse quartz sand.

Few: **Fe Oxides**: equant and prolate, sub-rounded to rounded, <0.4 mm, mode = 0.225 mm. Scatted throughout the samples, iron-rich grains.

Rare: **Flint**: equant and prolate, angular, <0.9 mm, mode = 0.5 mm.

Rare: **Rock fragments**: equant and prolate, sub-rounded to rounded, <0.75 mm, mode = 0.4 mm. Including examples of sandstone, siltstone and chert.

Voids: 5% consisting of meso-planar voids exhibiting random alignment. No remnants present.

Matrix: 65–70%. A moderately heterogeneous fabric with some buff clay streaks visible. The matrix is Fe-rich mid orange-red in both PPL and XP. The matrix exhibits slight optical activity with a speckled b-fabric. Clay streaks are Fe-poor, with merging to diffuse boundaries. They exhibit low optical density when compared to the surrounding clay matrix. There is also a number of Fe-rich clay pellets present. These are rounded with clear-to-diffuse boundaries, equant in shape with high optical density in relation to the surrounding matrix.

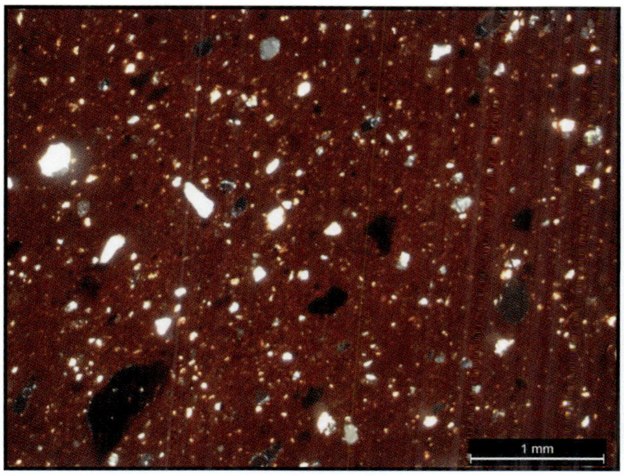

Fig. 13.2.13 Machin-CBM3 thin section PH1

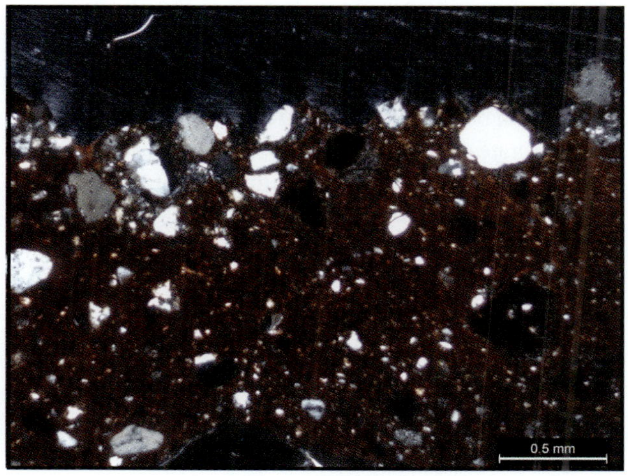

Fig. 13.2.16 Machin-CBM3 thin section PH1 showing moulding sand (x40)

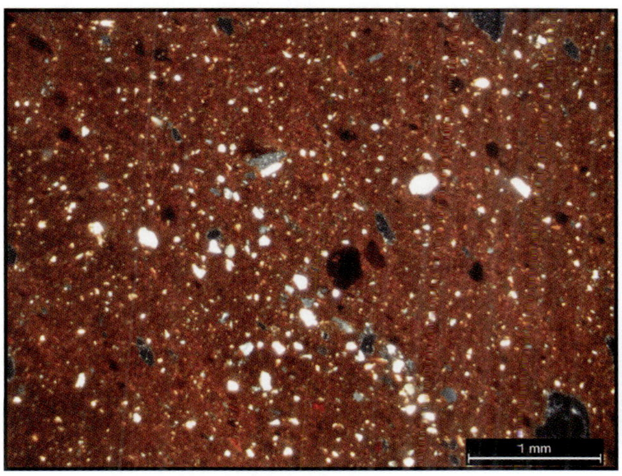

Fig. 13.2.14 Machin-CBM3 thin section SEA1

Fig. 13.2.17 Machin-CBM3 thin section TR4 showing moulding sand

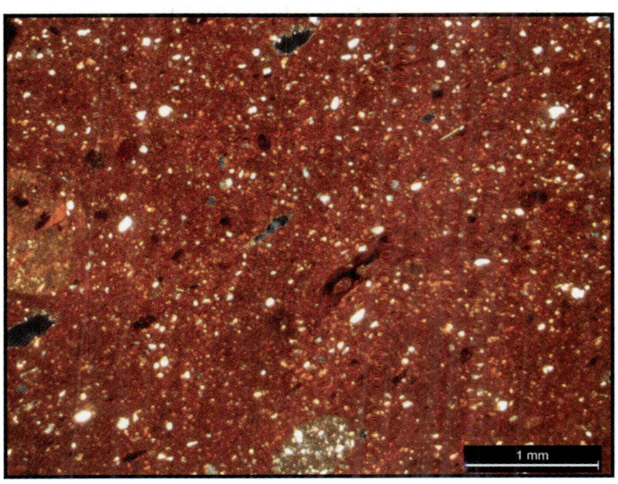

Fig. 13.2.15 Machin-CBM3 thin section TOP4

Summary: This is a fine iron-rich fabric lacking the coarse fractions of quartz and rock fragments found in Machin-CBM1 and Machin-CBM2. It can be aligned with the fine-textured Exeter Fabric 3 (Holbrook and Bidwell 1991). These samples were made from a micaceous clay with some natural heterogeneity observed. The samples in this group are unimodal with only the occasional coarser quartz grain or rock fragment. These are likely to have derived from the moulding sand: see Figs 13.2.16 and 13.2.17, showing the composition of the moulding sand present observed on PH1 and TR4.

There is nothing within Machin-CBM Fabrics 1, 2 and 3 to suggest that they were made using sources other than local clays within Exeter. The observed variation in the proportion of quartz and rock fragments is likely a reflection of the natural variation in the raw materials or the exploitation of slightly different clay beds within the same formation. Any differences in colour and texture are also not indicative of a different source clay but are more the result of different firings. The frequency of tiles in these fabrics suggests a local origin and the inclusions are consistent with exploitation of the local Permian clays (Holbrook and Bidwell 1991, 281). There is also a variable use of moulding sand and sand temper.

Machin-CBM4: Calcareous (Figs 13.2.18–13.2.20)

Macroscopic description: Heterogeneous friable fabric, oxidised throughout, showing some signs of being poorly formed with buff-coloured calcareous clay pellets throughout. Moderate quartz observed along with calcareous inclusions including shell fragments. Elongate parallel voids are likely the result of post-depositional leaching of calcareous inclusions. Pink (5YR7/4) to light red (2.5YR 7/6) in colour.

TSID: CC3; CC4; CC8; PH6; PH7; TOP3; TOP9; TR1.

Petrographic description:

Inclusions: 35%, equant and elongate, angular to sub-rounded, <1.5 mm, poorly sorted, single spaced, weak alignment, weakly bi-modal.

Dominant: **Monocrystalline quartz**: primarily equant, sub-angular, <0.3 mm, mode = 0.125 mm. Moderately well-sorted fine quartz-sand throughout.

Common: **Monocrystalline quartz**: primarily equant, poorly sorted, sub-angular to sub-rounded, <1.5 mm, mode = 0.75 mm. Moderately sorted coarse quartz sand.

Few: **Muscovite mica**: elongate, moderately sorted, <0.175 mm, mode = 0.25 mm.

Few: **Shell:** equant and elongate, <1.25 mm, mode = 0.75 mm.

Few: **Calcite:** equant, <0.75 mm, mode = 0.5 mm.

Voids: 10% consisting of meso-planar curved channels, likely resultant from leaching of calcareous inclusions predominantly shell. These exhibit random alignment.

Matrix: 55%. Highly heterogeneous calcareous fabric with a clay pellets throughout. The matrix is light yellow-brown in both PPL and XP and is optically inactive. Clay pellets account for approximately 15% of the matrix. These have clear boundaries and are equant in shape. They are buff-coloured pellets of highly calcareous clay with neutral optical density, typically concordant with the matrix.

Summary: This is a highly calcareous, heterogeneous fabric, lacking the iron-rich inclusions of the other fabrics. There is a background of fine quartz-sand throughout with the potential anthropogenic addition of the coarser quartz sand component which was also used as moulding sand. This fabric matches the calcareous fabric described by Holbrook and Bidwell (1991).

Fig. 13.2.18 Machin-CBM4 thin section CC3

Fig. 13.2.19 Machin-CBM4 thin section PH7

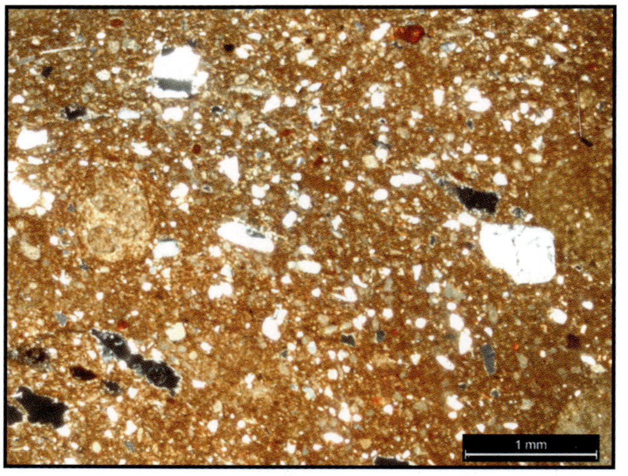

Fig.13.2.20 Machin-CBM4 thin section TR1

Machin-CBM5: Eastern (Fig 13.2.21–13.2.23)

Macroscopic description: Moderately heterogeneous fabric with a powdery texture. Hard fired and oxidised throughout. Some buff-coloured clay pellets and streaks visible. Very few quartz grains visible in hand specimen along with few iron oxides. Moderately to highly micaceous. Reddish-yellow (5YR 6/6) to light red (2.5YR 6/8) in colour.

TSID: BOL1; BOL3; BOL5; OTT3; PW1; PW2; PW3; SEA2; SEA6; SEA7; WB2; WB3; WB5.

Petrographic description:

Inclusions: 26–36%, equant and elongate, sub-angular to sub-rounded, <1.0 mm, poorly sorted, single spaced, weak alignment, weakly bi-modal.

Dominant: **Monocrystalline quartz**: primarily equant, sub-angular, <0.2 mm, mode = 0.05 mm. Well-sorted fine silt-sized quartz-sand throughout.

Common-to-few: **Monocrystalline quartz**: primarily equant, sub-angular to sub-rounded, <1.0 mm, mode = 0.75 mm. Moderately sorted coarse quartz sand.

Common: **Muscovite mica**: elongate. <0.2 mm, mode = 0.125 mm.

Very few: **Rock fragments:** <0.5 mm, mode = 0.25 mm. Rounded; comprising siltstones and sandstones and an example of greensand, see Figs 13.2.33 and 13.2.34.

Very few: **Iron Oxides:** equant and rounded, moderately sorted. <1.0 mm. Iron-rich grains.

Rare: **Chert:** <0.4 mm. Rare rounded flint fragments.

Rare: Plagioclase feldspar: <0.6 mm.

Voids: 5–10% consisting of meso-elongate channels. These exhibit random alignment. No remnants present.

Matrix: 54–69%. A slightly heterogeneous Fe-rich fabric with a clay pellets present throughout. The matrix is light yellow-brown in both PPL and XP and is moderately optically active. Clay pellets account for 10% of the matrix. They have merging to diffuse boundaries and are equant and distorted, indicating they were plastic at the time of firing. They are Fe-rich pellets of fine pure crystalline clay with high optical density, typically discordant with the matrix.

Summary: This is a fine silty fabric with a background of fine quartz silt. There is a varying proportion of coarser quartz sand present along with sparse rock fragments. Unlike fabric group Machin-CBM2, the rock fragments in this fabric group are of the same grade as the coarser quartz proportion and could therefore have been added during processing as temper or incorporated from the moulding sand. The local geology includes alluvial deposits which comprise a lower unit of sand and gravel with an upper unit of silty and sandy clay. The clay fraction varies from brown and reddish-brown silty and sandy clay to heavy from clays (Bristow *et al.* 1985, 69–70).

Machin-CBM6: Southern (Figs 13.2.24–13.2.26)

Macroscopic description: Slightly heterogeneous, soft-fired fabric with a fine powdery texture. Sparse quartz grains visible along with red iron oxides. Moderately micaceous. Typically oxidised throughout. Surface colours vary from reddish-yellow (5YR 6/6) to red (2.5YR 5/68).

TSID: AC1; AC2; AC5; ASH1; ASH2; ASH3.

Petrographic description:

Inclusions: 18%, equant and elongate, sub-angular to sub-rounded, <0.45 mm, well-sorted, double-spaced, weak alignment, weakly bi-modal.

Dominant: **Monocrystalline quartz**: primarily equant, sub-angular to sub-rounded, <0.25 mm, mode = 0.05 mm. Fine silt-sized quartz throughout the matrix.

Common: **Monocrystalline quartz**: equant, sub-rounded, <0.1 mm; mode = 0.075 mm.

Few: **Muscovite mica**: equant and prolate, elongate, <0.175 mm, mode = 0.125 mm.

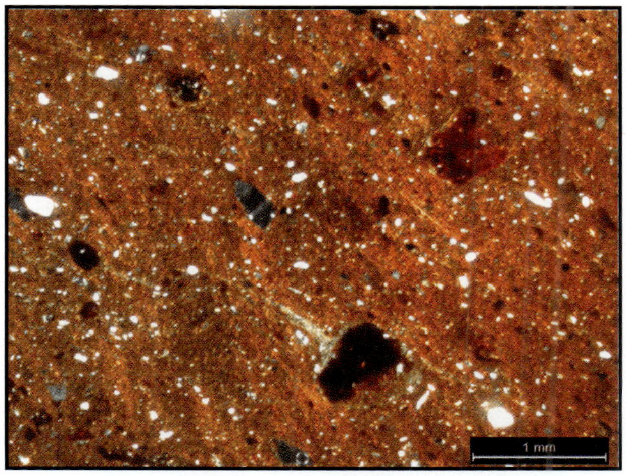

Fig. 13.2.21 Machin-CBM5 thin section BOL1

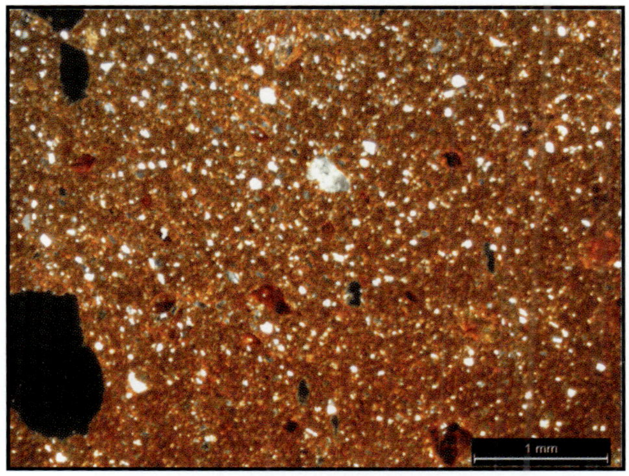

Fig. 13.2.22 Machin-CBM5 thin section PW1

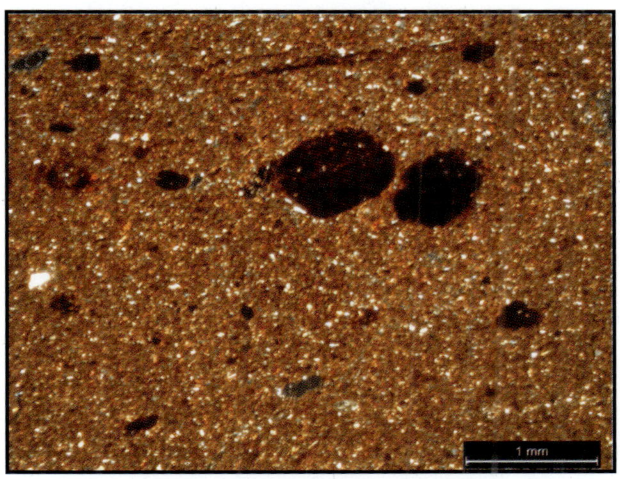

Fig. 13.2.23 Machin-CBM5 thin section SEA2

Few: **Rock fragments**: equant and prolate, rounded, <0.45 mm, mode = 0.275 mm. Siltstones, shales, and porphyritic igneous rocks.

Rare: **Flint**: equant and prolate, angular, <0.4 mm.

Voids: 5% consisting of meso vughs exhibiting random alignment. No remnants present.

Matrix: 77%. Slightly heterogeneous fabric with clay streaks present along with some clay pellets present in sample AC. The matrix is Fe-rich mid orange-brown in both PPL and XP, with little to no optical activity. Sample AC demonstrates a higher degree of heterogeneity with clay pellets present. These are rounded, iron-poor, equant and distorted. They have merging to diffuse boundaries. They exhibit neutral optical density when compared to the surrounding clay matrix.

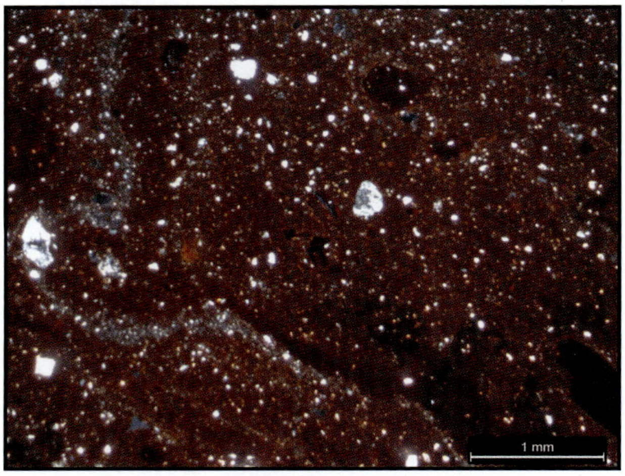

Fig. 13.2.24 Machin-CBM6 thin section AC2

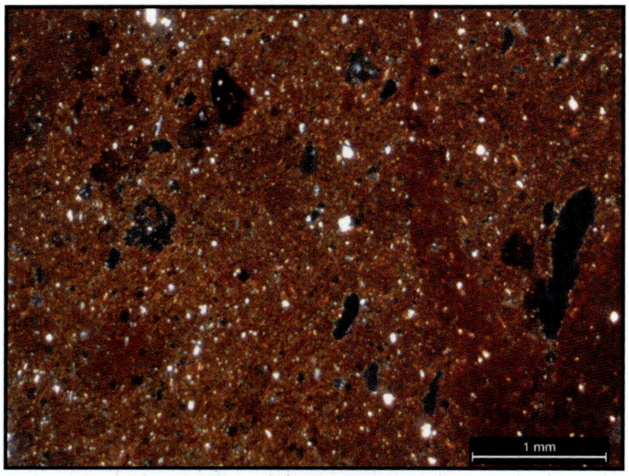

Fig. 13.2.25 Machin-CBM6 thin section AC5

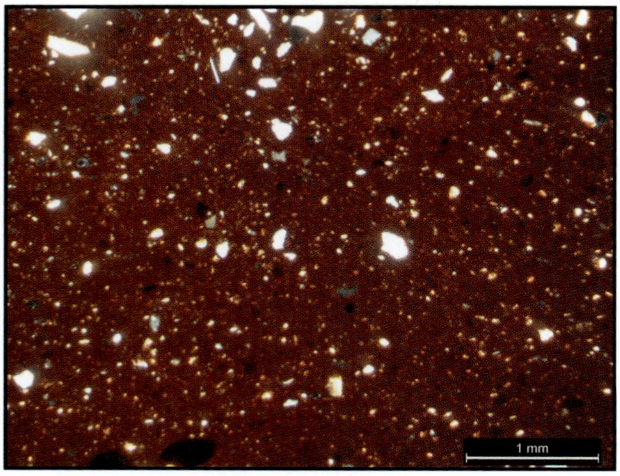

Fig. 13.2.26 Machin-CBM6 thin section ASH3

Summary: This is a fine fabric with natural heterogeneity retained in the samples. There are few inclusions greater in size than 0.5 mm. There is no evidence of the use of moulding sand on these samples, therefore the coarser fraction of quartz may be a natural phenomenon along with the sparse rock fragments. The greater heterogeneity in a number of these samples is the result of a lesser degree of processing of the clay.

Machin-CBM7: Hatherleigh Moor

(Figs 13.2.27–13.2.29)

This group comprises the samples of material from the potential tile production centre at Hatherleigh Moor.

Macroscopic description: Naturally heterogeneous clay with pale grey/white quartz-rich streaks throughout. Samples are oxidised and hard fired. HM2 is an over-fired waster which is vitrified masking some of the inclusions. There is a moderate proportion of fine quartz grains along with a sparse coarser fraction. The fabric is moderately micaceous with sparse rounded rock fragments visible. Surface colour is red (2.5YR 5/8) with the waster HM2 being dark reddish-brown (2.5YR 3/3).

TSID: HM1; HM2; HM3; HM4; HM5; HM6.

Petrographic description:

Inclusions: 30%, equant and elongate, sub-rounded to rounded, <2.5 mm, moderately sorted, single-to-double spaced, weak alignment, unimodal.

Predominant: **Monocrystalline quartz**: primarily equant, sub-angular to sub-rounded, <0.275 mm, mode = 0.05 mm. Fine silt-sized quartz throughout the matrix.

Few: **Muscovite mica**: elongate, <0.05 mm, mode = 0.04 mm.

Few: **Rock fragments**: equant and prolate, sub-rounded to rounded, <2.5 mm, mode = 1.25 mm. Comprising small rounded grains of sandstone, siltstone and granular volcanic lavas.

Very few: **Fe oxides**: equant and prolate, rounded, <0.04 mm, mode = 0.025 mm.

Voids: 5% consisting of meso channels and vughs with random alignment. No remnants present. HM2 has micro vesicles in the form of bloating pores as a result of high firing temperatures.

Matrix: 65%. Highly heterogeneous fabric with prolific quartz-rich Fe-poor streaks throughout, accounting for 25–30% of the matrix. The surrounding matrix is Fe-rich, mid orange-red in PPL and mid brown-orange in XP. The matrix exhibits minimal optical activity with HM2 being over-fired and optically inactive.

Summary: This is a highly heterogeneous fabric, Fe-rich with quartz-rich steaks throughout. The fabric has a high proportion of quartz-silt with rounded rock fragments present. This is a distinct fabric when compared to the other samples in the study. The quartz-silt-rich streaks show evidence of folding indicating minimal disturbance in the weathering of this naturally heterogeneous raw material rather than the anthropogenic mixing of two different clays.

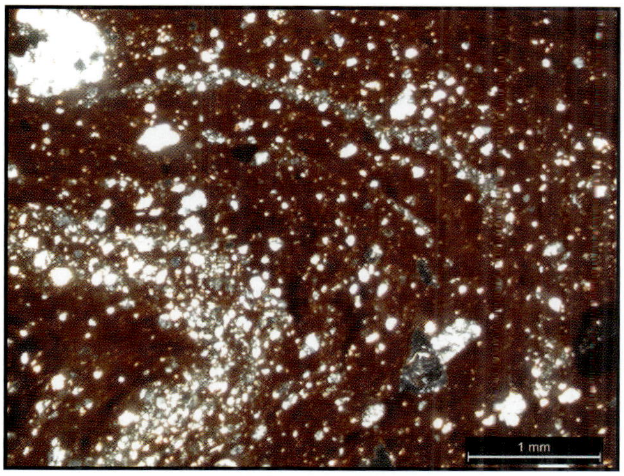

Fig. 13.2.27 Machin-CBM7 thin section HM1

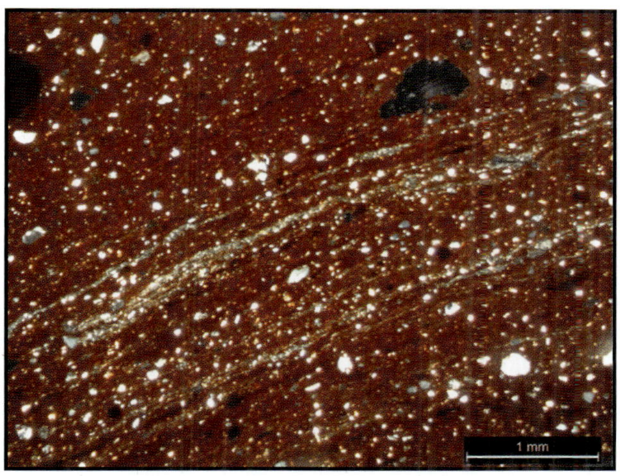

Fig. 13.2.28 Machin-CBM7 thin section HM4

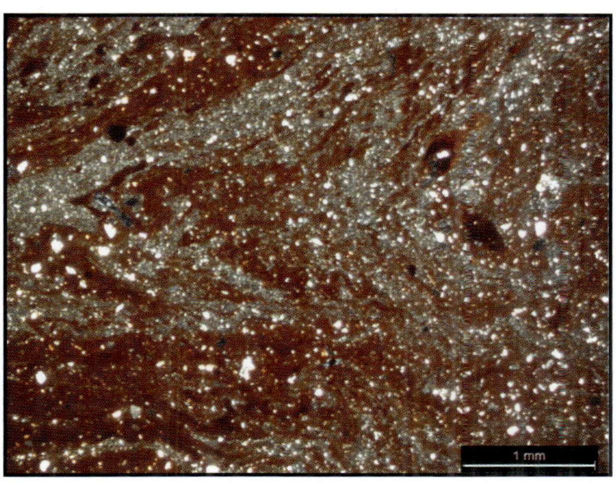

Fig. 13.2.29 Machin-CBM7 thin section HM6

Machin-CBM8 (Figs 13.2.30–13.2.32)

Macroscopic description: Homogeneous, sandy fabric typically oxidised throughout. Abundant medium-to-coarse quartz observed along with red/black inclusions and clay pellets. Voids throughout the fabric, resulting in a very lightweight material. Consistent very pale brown (10YR 7/4) colour throughout.

TSID: BB5; SEA5; TOP7; SL4.

Petrographic description:

Inclusions: 34%, equant and elongate, angular to sub-rounded, <0.5 mm, poorly sorted, double spaced, weak alignment, unimodal.

Predominant: **Monocrystalline quartz**: primarily equant, angular to sub-angular, <0.5 mm, mode = 0.15 mm. Moderately well-sorted fine quartz-sand throughout.

Few: **Fe Oxides:** equant and elongate, <0.5 mm, mode = 0.25 mm.

Very few: **Muscovite mica**: elongate, moderately sorted, <0.3 mm, mode = 0.2 mm.

Very few: **Flint:** equant and prolate, angular, <0.5 mm, mode = 0.5 mm.

Voids: 30% consisting of micro-to-macro vesicles. These exhibit random alignment with sub-parallel orientation. No remnants observed.

Matrix: 36%. Homogeneous Fe-poor fabric with scattered clay pellets throughout. The matrix is light yellow-brown in both PPL and XP and is optically inactive. Clay pellets account for approximately 5% of the matrix. These have merging-to-diffuse boundaries and are equant in shape. They are coloured the same as the matrix, with a much reduced proportion of quartz observed. The exhibit neutral optical density, typically concordant with the matrix. Example SEA5 includes a patch of calcitic material in one area of the sample.

Summary: This is a homogeneous fabric, lacking iron-rich inclusions with a background of fine quartz-sand throughout. There is the potential that this is a variant of the Machin-CBM4 fabric, being consistently iron-poor, albeit lacking the shell fragments. The high proportion of voids could be the result of post-depositional leaching of inclusions, although sample SEA5 does exhibit patches of calcareous material. This is potentially derived from the chalk found in the Holcombe area (see Machin-CBM9).

Machin-CBM9 (fabric only found at Holcombe) (Figs 13.2.33–13.2.35)

Macroscopic description: Homogeneous fabric. Hard fired and oxidised throughout. Red in colour (2.5YR 5/8).

Common quartz grains visible with fragments of rock, some of which are micaceous. Calcareous inclusions also visible in hand specimen.

TSID: HOL1; HOL2; HOL3.

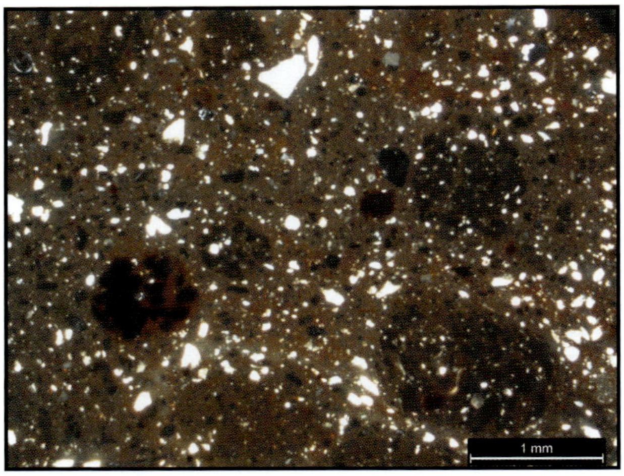

Fig. 13.2.30 Machin-CBM8 thin section BB5

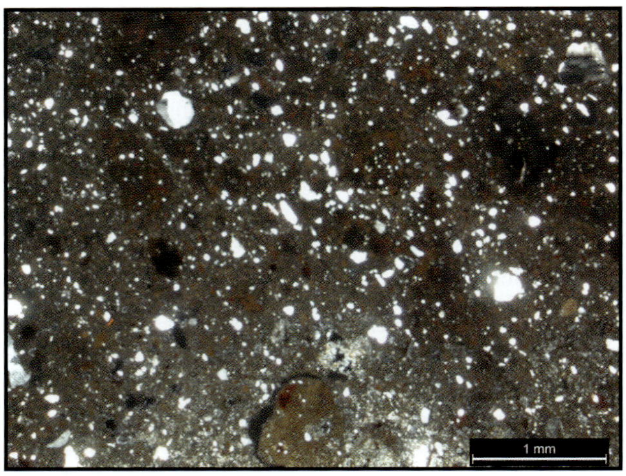

Fig. 13.2.31 Machin-CBM8 thin section SEA5

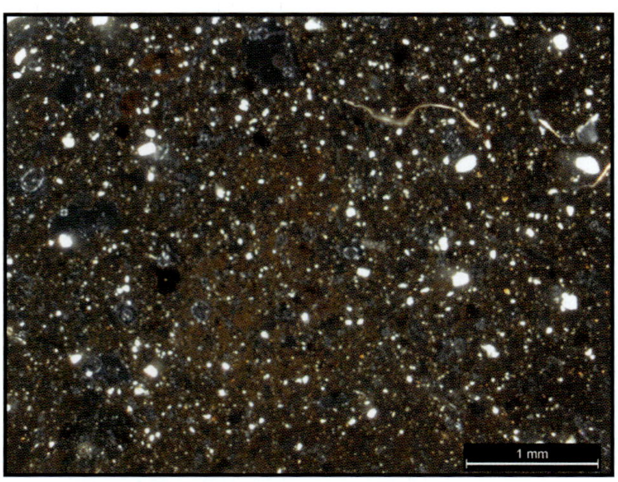

Fig. 13.2.32 Machin-CBM8 thin section TOP7

Petrographic description:

Inclusions: 28%, equant and elongate, angular to rounded, max: <1.65 mm, poorly to moderately sorted, open spaced, moderate alignment, unimodal.

Frequent: **Monocrystalline quartz**: primarily equant, sub-angular to angular, <0.25 mm, mode = 0.1 mm. Moderately well-sorted fine to medium quartz-silt throughout.

Frequent: **Calcite:** equant, sub-rounded to rounded, <1.65 mm, mode = 0.8 mm. Calcitic inclusions throughout the fabric. Potential post-depositional infill.

Common: **Flint:** equant and elongate, sub-rounded, <0.04 mm, mode = 0.03 mm. Small silt sized flint grains throughout.

Few: **Glauconite**: equant, rounded. <0.2 mm, mode = 0.175 mm. Heat-altered glauconite grains naturally occurring within the clay matrix; transformed from their natural pale green colour, to semi-opaque grains of a mid-orange in colour due to the oxidation of divalent iron. The colour changes from green to red or black depends on the firing temperature and oxidising conditions within the kiln (Basso *et al.* 2008, 95).

Rare: **Rock fragments**: equant, rounded. <0.5 mm. Rare rock fragments throughout including micaceous sandstone and chalk.

Voids: 5% consisting of meso-planar voids. These exhibit random alignment, primarily sub parallel to the surfaces with no remnants present. There is evidence of some calcite infill to voids.

Matrix: 67%. Typically homogeneous fabric with a few clay pellets present. The matrix is Fe-rich mid orange-red in PPL and mid red-brown in XP. The matrix is generally moderately optically active with a speckled b-fabric. Clay pellets have merging to diffuse boundaries indicating they were plastic at the time of firing. These are rounded, equant and exhibit neutral optical density when compared to the surrounding clay matrix. The pellets are Fe- and quartz-rich and mid-brown in colour.

Summary: This moderately heterogeneous fabric exhibits bands of quartz-silt. This could be a natural phenomenon, where bands of quartz are present in the raw clay or the result of an anthropogenic addition of quartz during processing, distributed unevenly throughout the matrix. The calcareous infill to the voids has the potential to be a post-depositional alteration, but some examples are shell-shaped and therefore may be calcareous inclusions within the matrix (Figs 13.2.33 and 13.34), along with the potential fragment of chalk within the calcareous material. The quartz component compares with the description of Holcombe 1 (Williams 1991a, 22). Holcombe lies in an area of Upper Greensand formation overlain by a layer of chalk and itself overlying a continuous layer of clay-with-flints (Gallois 2004, 35).

Machin-CBM10 (Figs 13.2.36–13.2.38)

Macroscopic description: Heterogeneous fabric with buff-coloured clay pellets and streaks throughout. Hard fired and oxidised throughout. Common opaque and translucent quartz grains visible along with iron oxides. Moderately micaceous. Reddish-yellow in colour (5YR 6/6).

TSID: PH5; PH9; WB1.

Petrographic description:

Inclusions: 25%, equant and elongate, angular to sub-rounded, <1.0 mm, moderately sorted, double spaced, weak alignment, weakly bi-modal.

Frequent: **Monocrystalline quartz**: primarily equant, sub-angular, <0.25 mm, mode = 0.125 mm. Moderately well-sorted fine quartz-sand throughout.

Frequent: **Monocrystalline quartz**: primarily equant, sub-angular to sub-rounded, <0.5 mm, mode = 0.35 mm. Moderately sorted coarse quartz sand.

Few: **Flint:** equant, sub-angular to angular, <1.0 mm, mode = 0.5 mm.

Few: **Muscovite mica**: elongate, <0.25 mm, mode = 0.15 mm.

Very few: **Fe-oxides**: equant and rounded, moderately sorted, <0.5 mm, mode = 0.15 mm.

Voids: 10–15% consisting of meso-planar voids. These exhibit random alignment. Subparallel. No remnants present.

Matrix: 60–65%. Heterogeneous Fe-rich fabric with clay pellets present throughout. The matrix is light yellow-brown in both PPL and XP and is optically active. Clay pellets account for 20% of the matrix. They have merging to diffuse boundaries and are equant and distorted. They are buff-coloured pellets of fine pure crystalline clay with low optical density, typically concordant with the matrix.

Summary: This heterogeneous fabric has naturally occurring clay pellets resulting from a variegated clay being used. The coarser quartz component is of the same grade as the moulding sand observed on the edge of the Woodbury, in Axminster, sample (Fig. 13.2.39), so it is therefore possible that the coarser quartz component is an anthropogenic addition, either deliberately as temper or accidental incorporation of moulding sand during forming.

This highly heterogeneous micaceous fabric does not appear to match any of the four fabric descriptions included in the Woodbury, in Axminster, report (Silvester and Bidwell 1984). The geology in the vicinity of Woodbury comprises Head: a mixture of clay, silt, sand and gravel, and a poorly-sorted and poorly-stratified member which can include rock debris, clayey hillwash and soil creep with local lenses of silt and/or clay (McMillan and Powell 1999, 19). There are similarities between this fabric and the Exeter Machin-CBM1/2/3 fabrics, albeit, exhibiting a greater degree of heterogeneity.

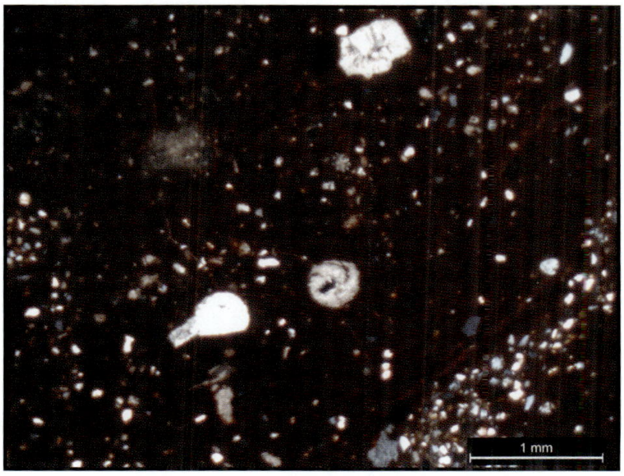

Fig. 13.2.33 Machin-CBM9 thin section HOL1

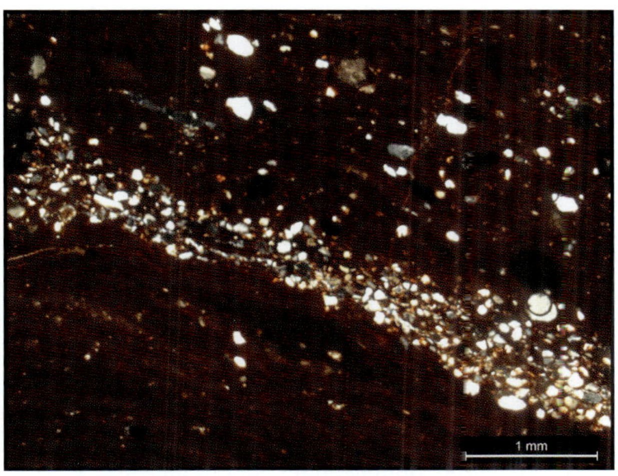

Fig. 13.2.34 Machin-CBM9 thin section HOL3

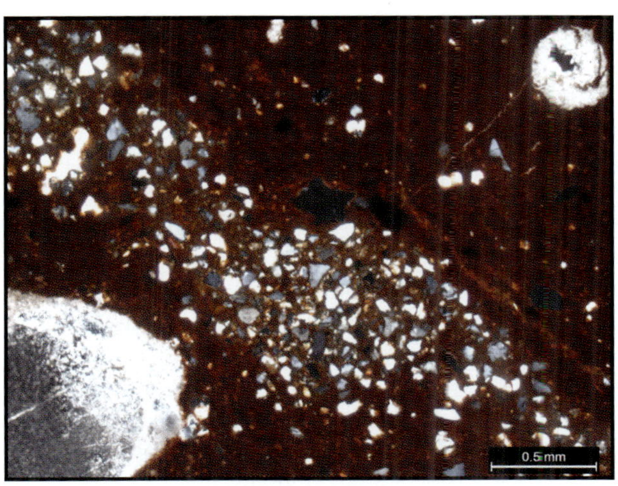

Fig. 13.2.35 Machin-CBM9 thin section HOL1 showing chalk (x40)

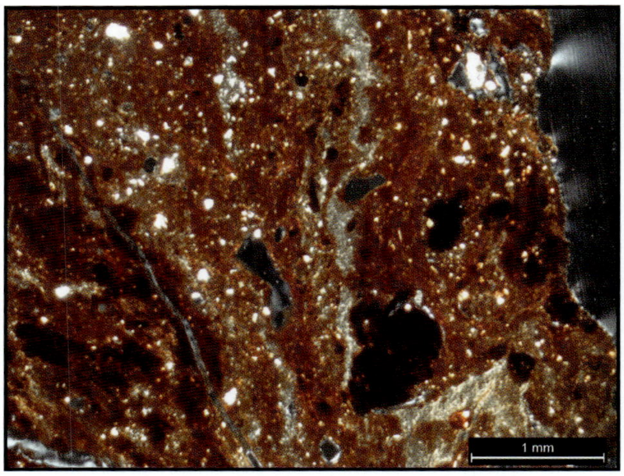

Fig. 13.2.36 Machin-CBM10 thin section PH5

Fig. 13.2.37 Machin-CBM10 thin section PH9

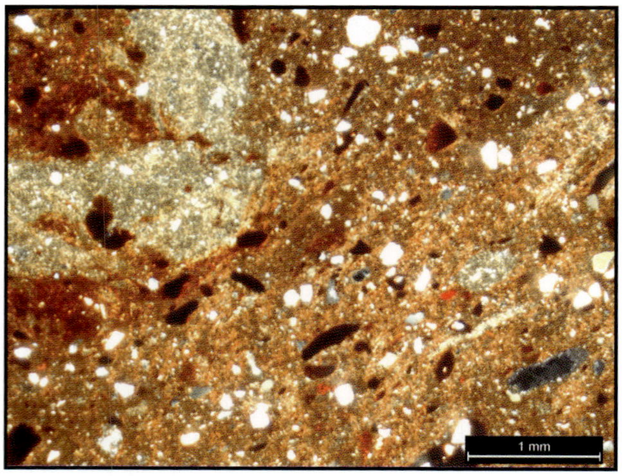

Fig. 13.2.38 Machin-CBM10 thin section WB1

Machin-CBM11 (fabric only found at Honeyditches, in Seaton) (Fig. 13.2.40)

Macroscopic description: Highly heterogeneous, fine-grained fabric. Soft-fired and oxidised throughout. Sparse

Fig. 13.2.39 Machin-CBM10 thin section WB1 showing moulding sand (x40)

quartz present with abundant clay pellets throughout. Yellowish-red colour to surfaces (5YR 4/6) with a light reddish brown core (5YR 6/4).

TSID: SEA3.

Petrographic description:

Inclusions: 11%, equant and prolate, angular to sub-angular, max: <0.4 mm, well-sorted, open-spaced, weak alignment, unimodal.

Predominant: **Monocrystalline quartz**: equant, angular, <0.15 mm, mode = 0.05 mm. Well-sorted very fine quartz-sand. Observed in bands following forming fractures.

Few: **Monocrystalline quartz:** equant, angular to sub-angular, <0.4 mm, mode = 0.3 mm. Small proportion of larger quartz grains.

Voids: 15% consisting of mega channel voids. These exhibit preferred alignment, parallel to the surfaces with no remnants present. These voids appear to follow fractures within the fabric and are remnants of the forming process.

Matrix: 74%. Heterogeneous fabric with a large proportion of clay pellets visible. The matrix is Fe-rich, light orange-brown in PPL and mid yellow-brown in XP. The matrix is moderately optically active with a speckled b-fabric. Clay pellets of two types are present. Some are iron-rich, mid red-brown in colour, with merging to diffuse boundaries. These pellets are rounded, equant, and rich in fine quartz sand. They exhibit high optical density when compared to the surrounding clay matrix. The other pellets are iron-poor pale yellow-brown in colour, also with merging to diffuse boundaries. They are highly micaceous and exhibit neutral optical density. The clay pellets account for approximately 30% of the matrix.

Summary: This is a heterogeneous, quartz-poor fabric with a fine silty matrix and no coarse component present. This is potentially an example of Silvester's Fabric 1 (Silvester 1981b, 57) described as having frequent ferrous and soft white inclusions.

Machin-CBM12 (fabric only found at Bury Barton) (Figs 13.2.41–13.2.42)

Macroscopic description: Moderately heterogeneous fabric with a powdery texture. Soft fired and oxidised throughout with sparse highly micaceous buff-coloured streaks visible. Sparse quartz grains visible in hand specimen along with a few larger iron oxides. Highly micaceous. Reddish-yellow (5YR 6/6) in colour.

TSID: BB1; BB4.

Petrographic description:

Inclusions: 27%, equant and prolate, sub-angular to sub-rounded, <0.4 mm; moderately to well- sorted, open spaced, weak alignment, unimodal.

Fig. 13.2.40 Machin-CBM11 thin section SEA3

Dominant: **Monocrystalline quartz**: primarily equant, sub-angular to sub-rounded, <0.06 mm, mode = 0.02 mm. Well-sorted fine silt-sized quartz throughout.

Frequent: **Muscovite mica**: elongate, <0.05 mm, mode = 0.02 mm.

Few: **Monocrystalline quartz**: primarily equant, sub-angular to sub-rounded, <0.4 mm, mode = 0.25 mm. Moderately sorted fine-medium quartz sand.

Voids: 5–10% consisting of meso-elongate channels. These exhibit preferred alignment with parallel orientation. No remnants present.

Matrix: 68%. Moderately heterogeneous Fe-rich fabric with clay pellets present throughout. The matrix is yellow-brown in both PPL and XP and is moderately optically active. Clay pellets account for 10% of the matrix. They have merging to diffuse boundaries and are equant and distorted, indicating they were plastic at the time of firing. They are Fe-rich pellets of fine pure crystalline clay with high optical density, typically discordant with the matrix.

Summary: This is a very fine silty fabric with a background of fine quartz silt along with a small coarser quartz component, potentially derived from the moulding sand. This fabric bears many similar characteristics to those of fabric Machin-CBM5 and it may well have been exploiting the same raw material source.

Machin-CBM13 (fabric only found at Topsham) (Fig. 13.2.43–13.2.45)

Macroscopic description: A fine highly heterogeneous, quartz-rich fabric with iron oxides visible. Hard fired and oxidised throughout. Light red in colour (2.5YR 6/6).

TSID: TOP1; TOP6; TOP8.

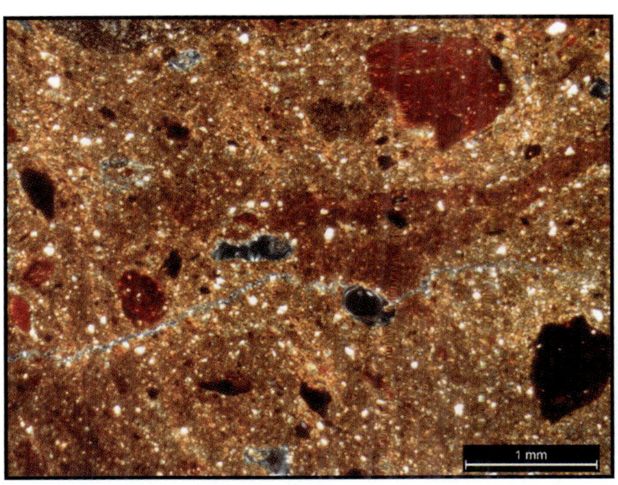

Fig. 13.2.41 Machin-CBM12 thin section BB1

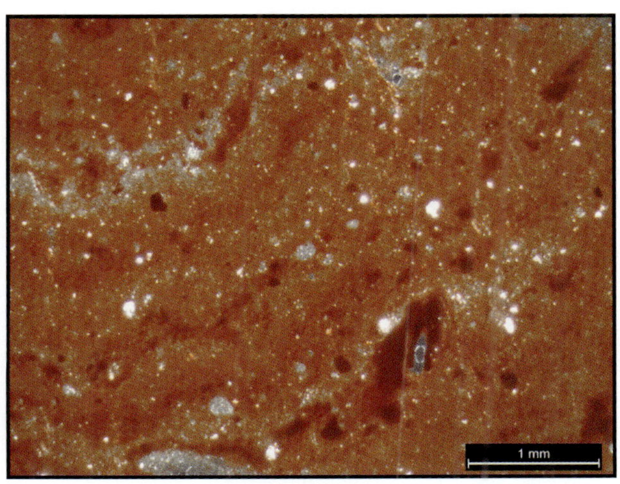

Fig. 13.2.42 Machin-CBM12 thin section BB4

Petrographic description:

Inclusions: 35%, equant and prolate, angular to rounded, <0.5 mm, poorly sorted, single spaced, moderate alignment, unimodal.

Predominant: **Quartz:** primarily equant, typically sub-angular to angular, poorly sorted, <0.5 mm; mode = 0.2 mm. Medium to coarse quartz sand.

Few: **Fe-oxides**: equant; rounded to sub-rounded, <0.5 mm, mode = 0.2 mm, Fe-rich grains scattered throughout.

Few: **Glauconite**: equant, rounded. <0.2 mm, mode= 0.1 mm. Heat-altered glauconite grains naturally occurring within the clay matrix; transformed from their natural pale green colour, to semi-opaque grains of a mid-orange in colour due to the oxidation of divalent iron. The colour changes from green to red or black depends on the firing temperature and oxidising conditions within the kiln (Basso *et al.* 2008, 95).

Few: **Muscovite mica**: equant and prolate, angular, <0.15 mm, mode = 0.10 m.

Very few: Plagioclase feldspar: <0.1 mm.

Voids: 5% consisting of macro channels exhibiting preferred alignment with parallel orientation. No remnants present.

Matrix: 60%. A highly heterogeneous fabric with clay pellets present throughout. The matrix is Fe-rich and mid orange-brown in both PPL and XP. It is moderately optically active with a speckled b-fabric. Clay pellets are both Fe-poor and Fe-rich, with sharp to merging boundaries. They are rounded and equant in shape with neutral optical density when compared to the surrounding clay matrix. They are both concordant and discordant with the matrix.

Summary: This is a coarse, quartz-rich heterogeneous fabric. The material is lacking the rock fragments observed in other fabrics. It is highly heterogeneous with clay pellets and Fe-rich grains throughout.

Machin-CBM14 (fabric only found at Otterton Point) (Fig. 13.2.46)

Macroscopic description: Homogeneous fabric. Soft fired with a powdery texture. Oxidised throughout. Sparse quartz grains visible with fragments of quartz-based rocks in a micaceous matrix. Reddish yellow in colour (5YR 6/8).

TSID: OTT1.

Petrographic description:

Inclusions: 35%, equant and elongate, angular to sub-rounded, max: <1 mm, poorly to moderately sorted, close to single spaced, weak alignment, weakly bi-modal.

Dominant: **Monocrystalline quartz**: primarily equant, angular to sub-rounded, <1 mm, mode = 0.75 mm. Poorly sorted coarse quartz sand.

Few: **Monocrystalline quartz:** equant, sub-angular to sub-rounded, <0.15 mm, mode = 0.1 mm. Moderately sorted quartz-silt.

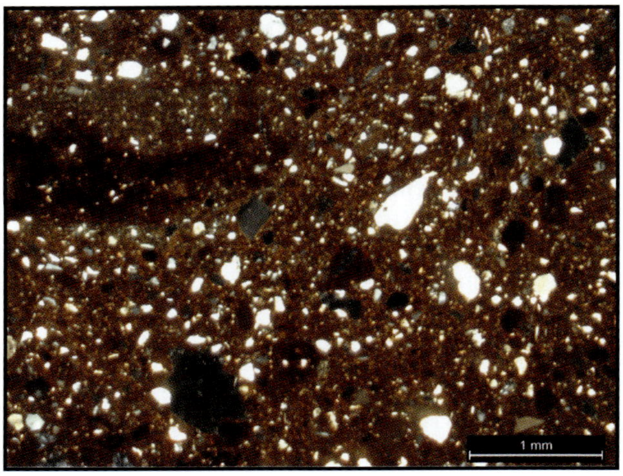

Fig. 13.2.43 Machin-CBM13 thin section TOP1

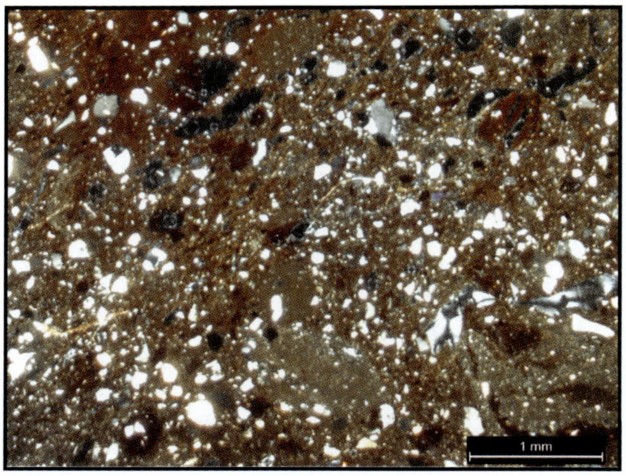

Fig. 13.2.44 Machin-CBM13 thin section TOP6

Fig. 13.2.45 Machin-CBM13 thin section TOP8

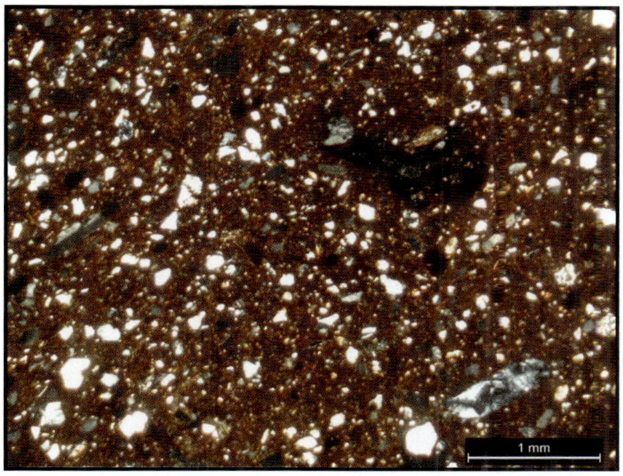

Fig. 13.2.46 Machin-CBM14 thin section OTT1

Few: **Muscovite mica:** equant and elongate, <0.25 mm, mode = 0.15 mm.

Few: **Rock fragments:** equant and elongate, sub-rounded, <1 mm, mode = 0.3 mm. Scattered sub-rounded fragments of sandstone, siltstones and shale.

Few: **Pyroxenes**: equant and elongate, sub-rounded. <0.25 mm, mode = 0.2 mm. Scattered pyroxenes showing steeply inclined extinction, not uncommon phenocrysts in lavas.

Voids: 5% consisting of meso-planar voids. These exhibit random alignment, primarily sub parallel to the surfaces with no remnants present.

Matrix: 60%. Typically homogeneous fabric with a few clay pellets present. The matrix is Fe-rich mid yellow-brown in both PPL and XP. The matrix is generally moderately optically active with a speckled b-fabric. Clay pellets have sharp-to-merging boundaries indicating they were plastic at the time of firing. These are rounded, equant and exhibit neutral optical density when compared to the surrounding clay matrix. The pellets are quartz-rich and mid-brown in colour.

Summary: This is an inclusion-rich homogeneous fabric with scattered larger quartz grains and rock fragments. The rocks are of the same size range as the larger quartz fraction and were likely introduced at the same time. This could have been an addition of temper or the accidental incorporation of moulding sand during processing.

Results by site

Intra-mural sites

Cathedral Close (CC): This is the site of the legionary bath-house, and forum and basilica (Bidwell 1979). A total of 117 fragments of CBM was retained from the excavation. The archive for this site is dominated by flue-tiles, representing 35.6% of the retained material. The majority of the material in the Cathedral Close collection, 115 items, has been assigned to Machin-CBM1/2/3 (Exeter fabrics). The other two fragments are of the calcareous Machin-CBM4, that is probably the buff fabric described in the report, which included a large quantity of roofing material (Bidwell 1979, 153).

Trichay Street (TS): Only 37 items of CBM have been retained from the Trichay Street excavation. Of these 22 are fragments of flue-tile, representing 59.4% of the material. The archive is made up of 32 examples of Machin-CBM1/2/3 along with 5 examples of calcareous Machin-CBM4.

Extra-mural sites (close to Exeter)

Princesshay (PH): A total of 106 items of CBM was recorded from the Princesshay archive, which included a small number of wasters, from the potential 2nd-century AD tile kiln (Steinmetzer, Stead, Pearce, Bidwell and Allan forthcoming). Again, almost 50% of the retained material is made up of flue-tile, whilst flue-tile only accounted for 16% of the recovered material. The material is dominated by Machin-CBM1/2/3 accounting for 86 of the items with 13 examples of calcareous Machin-CBM4 and seven pieces assigned to Machin-CBM10 (possibly related to Machin-CBM1/2/3). At Princesshay all CBM was assigned to fabric before discard. The report assigns all material to Exeter fabrics 1/2/3 with the exception of 19 examples of Fabric 4. A fifth, fine, fabric is also described and could potentially be fabric Machin-CBM10 which exhibits a fine heterogeneous fabric with iron oxides visible (Durrant forthcoming).

St David's Church (SD): This site includes another potential tile production centre and the archive included a large proportion of material categorised as kiln furniture or kiln waste, accounting for 29 of the 79 retained items. Of the remaining material, roofing material (*tegulae* and *imbrices*) accounts for 31 of the pieces. All the material from St David's Church was assigned to Machin-CBM1/2/3. As reflected in the St David's report (Durrant forthcoming) the majority of the material, 71 of the 79 retained fragments, was assigned to Machin-CBM2 (Exeter coarse rock fragments).

St Loye's College (SL): this site has been regarded as military base demolished *c.* AD 75, but recently re-interpreted as a civilian settlement contemporary with the legionary fortress and succeeded by a period of civilian occupation (Holbrook 2015, 96; Salvatore and Steinmetzer 2018; EAPIT 1, Chapter 5). Only 48 items have been retained from the St Loye's College excavation, of which 13 were recorded as brick, 23 items of roofing, six tiles, five flue-tiles and an antefix. *Tegulae* and *imbrices* also dominated the material recovered, representing 20% of the assemblage (Coles and Allan forthcoming). All but one of the pieces were assigned to Machin-CBM1/2/3 with a single example of Machin-CBM8 (possibly related to Machin-CBM4).

Rural sites

Aller Cross (AC), in Kingskerswell: The Aller Cross assemblage was recovered during the excavation of an enclosed settlement with occupation evidenced from the late 1st century AD into the late 4th century AD (Hughes 2015; and see EAPIT 1, Chapter 3 for the site's interpretation as a possible complex farmstead). *Imbrices* represented the majority of the identified forms, albeit only 36% of the recovered material (Kerr-Peterson 2015, 153). The site report describes five different fabrics within the material, three of which correspond to Exeter Fabrics 1/2/3 along with examples of the calcareous fabric Williams' Exeter Fabric 4, described in the site report as Fabric 5 (Kerr-Peterson 2015, 153–154). Of the retained material, 69 items were assigned to Machin-CBM1/2/3, with a single example of Machin-CBM4 recorded. The remaining material, 12 fragments, was assigned to Machin-CBM6 (the southern group). This fabric can be aligned to Aller Cross Fabric 4, which was described a bright orange, powdery fabric with white/buff streaks and clay lumps with moderately well-sorted quartz sand (*idem.*).

Ashcombe Barton (ASH), in Ashcombe: The material from Ashcombe Barton derives from a fieldwalking survey in 1996 when a small assemblage was recovered. The archive comprised of only 15 items, of which ten are flue-tile. All the Ashcombe Barton material has been assigned to Machin-CBM6 (the southern group) with the exception of a single example of Machin-CBM1/2/3.

Bury Barton (BB), in Lapford: The site at Bury Barton has also been identified as an Early Roman fort occupied between *c.* AD 55 and AD 70–80, but with later Roman occupation contained within an outer earthwork (Todd 2002). The CBM assemblage is described as being the typical orange-red fabric (Todd 2002, 51) with a single example of the pale cream-buff fabric described by Betts and Foot (1994) and assumed to be Exeter Fabric 4. Only six items of CBM have been retained from the site. These are categorised as five tiles and a single brick. Of these, two are examples of Machin-CBM12 (only seen at Bury Barton) along with two examples of Machin-CBM8 (possibly related to Machin-CBM4) and single examples of Machin-CBM1/2/3 and Machin-CBM4.

Bolham (BOL), in Tiverton: The fort at Bolham dates to the period *c.* AD 65–85/90 (Maxfield 1991, 55). Building material has been described as being consistent with the date of the fort with the majority of the assemblage recovered from demolition deposits. The Bolham assemblage comprised only five examples, three tiles and two *tegulae*. Of these, one can be assigned to Machin-CBM1/2/3 and the remaining four to Machin-CBM5 (the eastern group).

Hatherleigh Moor (HM), in Hatherleigh: This site has been identified as a brick and tile production centre based on the presence of overfired wasters on the site and results of a gradiometer survey which showed evidence of *in situ* burning characteristic of kilns or concentrations of fired debris (Wheeler and Laing-Trengrove 2006, 56). Devon Group 1 tiles are described in the report as having the presence of streaks of white clay with sparser white inclusions. All Hatherleigh Moor fragments examined were found to be of fabric Machin-CBM7. A potential raw material source of the material has been identified as the exposed heterogeneous clay deposits at Beckamoor Brook approximately 2.5 km south-east of Hatherleigh Moor (Greene 1978). The scale and longevity of production has not been established. No other examples of this fabric were identified from other sites in this study, although it has been reported that Hatherleigh Moor products have been identified at North Tawton, Monkokehampton and Okehampton Castle (Taylor 2006).

Holcombe (HOL), in Uplyme: This is the site of a Romano-British villa, whose original construction has been dated to the late 2nd century AD with later extensions in the later 3rd and 4th centuries AD, the latest including mosaic floors and a connected bath-house of unusual octagonal design (Pollard 1974, 94). The Holcombe archive contains 18 items of CBM, comprising nine pieces of flue-tile, seven items of roofing and two bricks. Only three items could be assigned to Machin-CBM1/2/3 (Exeter group) with the remaining 15 comprising Machin-CBM9 (only identified at Holcombe), akin to the Holcombe-1 fabric described by Williams (1991a, 22).

North Tawton (NT): The site report describes the material from North Tawton as comprised of Roman brick and tile recovered following the ploughing of a field. The material included fragments of combed box flue-tiles along with roofing material (Woolner *et al.* 1959). Williams (1991a) examined a fragment of tile from North Tawton and assigned it to Williams' Exeter Fabrics 1/2/3. All nine fragments of CBM held in the North Tawton archive were categorised as brick and assigned to Machin-CBM1/2/3, more specifically all including frequent coarse rock fragments and therefore examples of Machin-CBM2.

Otterton Point (OTT), in Otterton: The site at Otterton Point has been identified as the potential location of a villa. The report describes a total of 121 fragments of recognisable type recovered from the excavations, with a further 26 fragments from fieldwalking. The types represented were *tegulae*, *imbrices*, box flue and *pilae* (Brown and Holbrook 1989). There is no mention of fabrics in the site report. A total of 42 items has been retained from the site, 32 (72.6%) of which are *imbrices*, along with eight *tegulae* and two flue-tiles. With the exception of five examples of *tegulae* which were in Machin-CBM5 (eastern group), all the remaining material has been assigned to Machin-CBM14 (only identified at Otterton Point), a lightweight, soft-fired fabric.

Pomeroy Wood (PW), in Honiton: A total of 65,745 g of CBM was recovered from the site of a small 1st-century AD fort and later roadside settlement, including *tegulae*, *imbrices* and flue-tile, as well as undiagnostic fragments of brick and tile (Fitzpatrick *et al.* 1999). Six fabric groups were identified macroscopically (Laidlaw 1999) and the report describes these, divided by coarseness and colour along with hardness. Differences in colour and hardness of the fabrics are more likely to be the result of varied firing conditions rather than actual fabric differences. The site archive contains 29 items of CBM, including 19 categorised as roofing, along with three bricks and seven tiles. Five of the fragments were assigned to Machin-CBM1/2/3 with the remainder being Machin-CBM5 (eastern group). This fabric is potentially a match to Laidlaw Fabric 1 in the report (Laidlaw 1999, 327), described as a soft, fine, orange sandy fabric.

Honeyditches (SEA), in Seaton: The site of unknown character previously interpreted as villa or mansio with a bath-house, and fort (discussed in EAPIT 1, Chapter 3; Miles 1977; Silvester 1981b). The Honeyditches archive comprises a total of 66 items, of which 58 (87.9%) are flue-tiles, recovered during the excavation of the site approximately 50 years ago (Miles 1977), with a single example of brick and seven roofing fragments. There is a range of fabrics present in the Honeyditches material. Machin-CBM1/2/3 accounts for 24 of the pieces, with 12 examples of Machin-CBM5 (eastern group). Calcareous fabric Machin-CBM4 accounts for eight examples, along with nine examples of Machin-CBM8 (possibly related to Machin-CBM4) and 13 of Machin-CBM11 (only identified at Honeyditches, in Seaton).

Topsham (TOP): This assemblage was derived from a masonry aisled building, with construction dated to the mid 2nd century AD with potential earlier activity in the area (Rainbird and Farnell 2019). This excavation recovered 287 kg of CBM, only 12 items of which were available for examination. These comprised nine *tegulae*, along with two flue-tiles and one brick, which has potentially been used as a gaming board. The assemblage was made up of three fabrics, with five examples of Machin-CBM1/2/3, four examples of calcareous fabric Machin-CBM4, and three of Machin-CBM13 (only identified at Topsham).

Woodbury (WB), in Axminster: The site of a potential Early Roman fort excavated in the 1980s and later roadside settlement. Abundant brick and tile fragments were recovered from rubbish deposits located within a pond (Silvester and Bidwell 1984). The majority of material was roofing, along with *pila*-tiles and box-tiles. Fifteen examples of CBM are held in the Woodbury archive, of which nine examples have been assigned to Machin-CBM1/2/3 along with five of Machin-CBM5 (eastern group), and one fragment of Machin-CBM10 (possibly related to Machin-CBM1/2/3. Machin-CBM5 corresponds with the description of Fabric 3 in the report on the Woodbury material (Silvester and Bidwell 1984, 47), one of four fabrics described. These samples would also correspond with Woodbury 3, the coarser of the Woodbury fabrics identified by Williams (1991a, 22).

Discussion

Machin-CBM1/2/3

Exeter fabrics (Machin-CBM1/2/3) are of the same background clay with varying amounts of the coarse components of quartz-sand and rock fragments. These were all made in the Exeter area – including at the Princesshay and St David's Church kilns – and exploited the same local raw material source. The differences between the three fabrics reflect variation within the same clay beds along with some potential anthropogenic alteration with the use of moulding sand and/or tempering sand. It is difficult, if not impossible, to always distinguish between these fabrics in hand specimen. Figure 3.2.47 shows that the sites within Exeter were heavily reliant on locally produced material with only a very small proportion of imported material (the calcareous Machin-CBM4 and 8). Holbrook and Bidwell (1991, fig. 136) showed that *tegulae* in Fabric 4 only appear within Exeter after *c.* AD 270 (Fig. 13.2.48).

There is, however, evidence for the export of Exeter-produced material (Machin-CBM1/2/3) to sites outside of the town, including to North Tawton where all the material is assigned to this fabric group (albeit only nine fragments were examined; Fig. 13.2.49). Only the collections from Hatherleigh Moor, Holcombe and Otterton Point have no Exeter Machin-CBM1/2/3 material present. The proportions of Exeter material identified in assemblages from sites outside the town range from approximately <1% at Ashcombe Barton, to 84% at Aller Cross and 100% at North Tawton. As Fig. 13.2.50 shows, all sites were located on or near to the Roman road network therefore facilitating the movement of building materials as and when needed. It has been shown in a number of previous studies that CBM was not always made close to the site at which it was needed (*e.g.* Finlay *et al.* 2012; Betts 2017; Machin 2018). There were clearly networks in

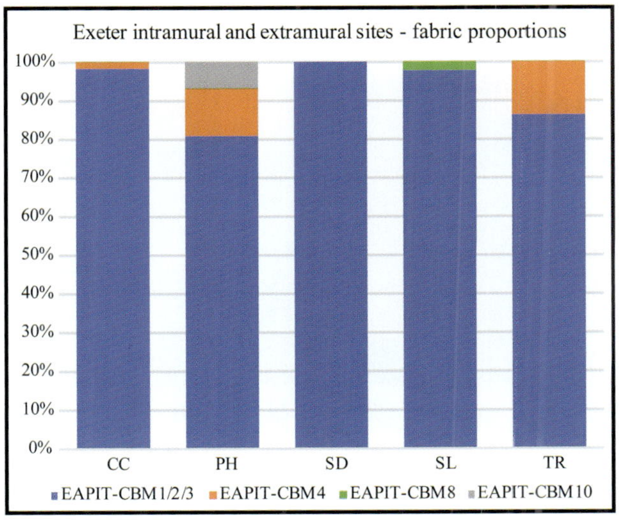

Fig. 13.2.47 Proportions of Machin-CBM fabrics within the retained museum collections from Exeter intra-mural and extra-mural sites

place to move material to the building sites when demand arose. Material was moved north, to Bolham a distance of 22 km, west to North Tawton 27 km away and east to Honeyditches a distance of 32 km.

Machin-CBM4

This material is found at a number of sites within Exeter (Cathedral Close, Princesshay and Trichay Street), as well as three of the rural sites (Aller Cross, Bury Barton and

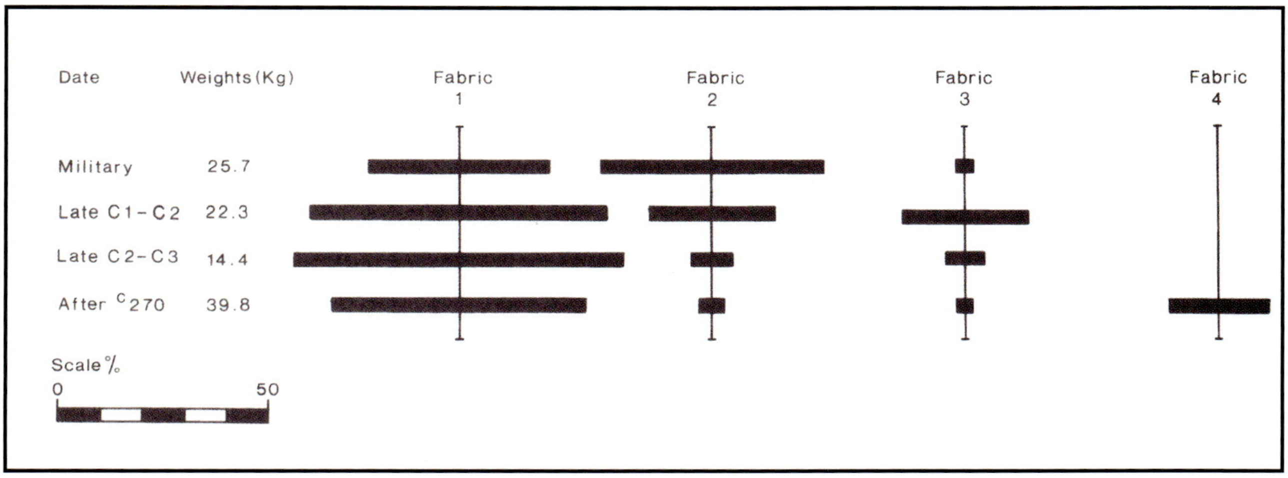

Fig. 13.2.48 Quantities and proportions of tile fabrics used for tegulae *in Exeter (after Holbrook and Bidwell 1991, fig. 136)*

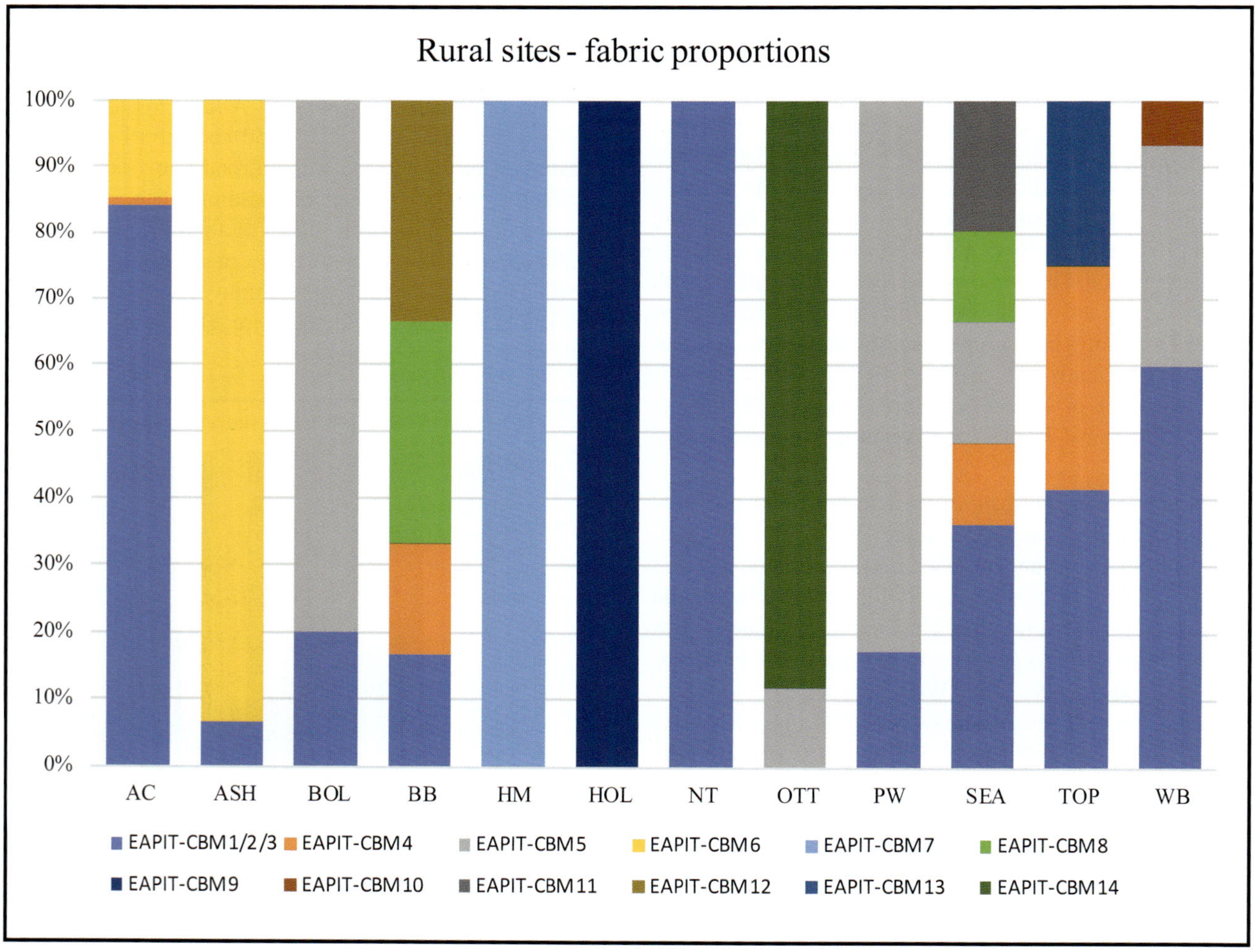

Fig. 13.2.49 Proportions of Machin-CBM fabrics in the retained museum collections from rural sites

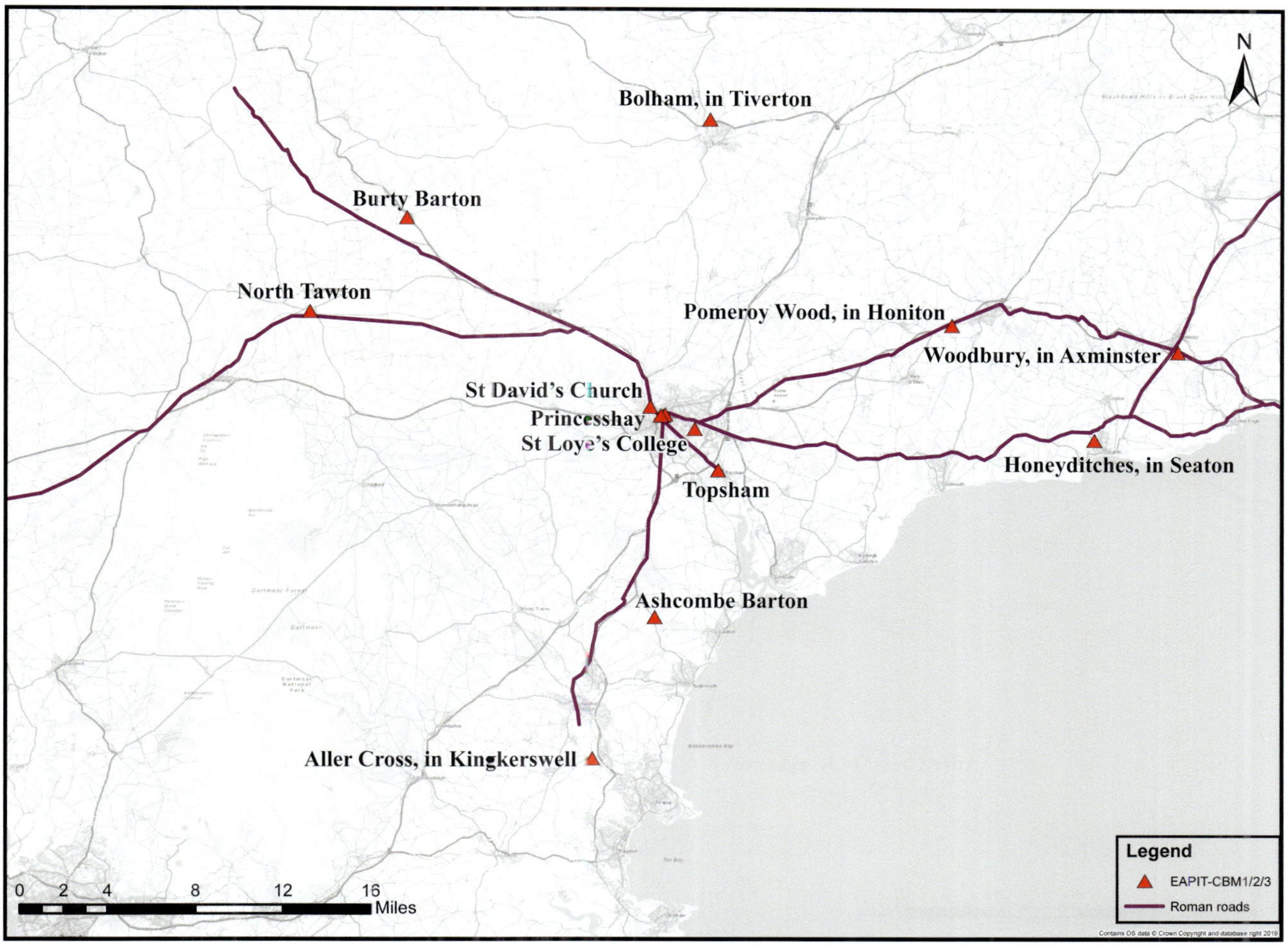

Fig. 13.2.50 Distribution of Machin-CBM1/2/3

Honeyditches; Figs 13.2.49 and 13.2.51). The presence of this 'new' fabric, from the late 3rd century AD onwards has been seen as an indicator of the end of the Exeter roofing tile industry with material being imported from further afield (Holbrook and Bidwell 1991, 281), for example, to Bury Barton, which is situated around 26 km from Exeter and 29 km from the assumed port at Topsham (Holbrook 2015, 96; EAPIT 1, Chapters 5 and 6). The majority of the examples of Machin-CBM4 recorded were roofing material (*imbrices* and *tegulae*). As mentioned above, it is possible that Machin-CBM8 is also an imported fabric, exploiting a similar source to Machin-CBM4. Of the three sites where Machin-CBM8 was identified – Exeter-St Loye's College, Bury Barton and Honeyditches, in Seaton – two also have examples of Machin-CBM4 within their collections.

Machin-CBM5 and Machin-CBM6

The eastern material, Machin-CBM5 and the southern group Machin-CBM6, exploit raw material sources which are very different from the Exeter samples. Whether these sites had individual kilns or shared production centres it is not possible to confirm. The Machin-CBM5 examples show evidence of mineral content derived from the Upper Greensand including plagioclase feldspar, rounded fragments of chert and rare examples of Greensand (Figs 13.2.53 and 13.2.54). There are distinct similarities between the mineralogy of this and that of the pottery from the 16th-century production centre at Hemyock (Allan, Dawson and Langman. 2018, 134). Here the pottery industry was exploiting the Permian marls underlying the Greensand in the area and it seem likely that the Roman brick and tile production was exploiting the same clay source.

The southern group, Machin-CBM6 (Fig. 13.2.55), features fragments of porphyritic rocks and shales, consistent with a source on the Alphington Breccia on which both Aller Cross and Ashcombe Barton are located. Soils overlying the Alphington formation are typically fine-grained, clayey with fragments of Culm sandstone, black chert and quartz porphyry and weathers to a soft-to-stiff, sandy clay (Bristow *et al.* 1985, 83). The poorly cemented, finer-grained parts of the Alphington Breccia were formerly extensively worked for brickmaking in the Exeter area (Scrivener 1983, 14).

Sites producing fabrics Machin-CBM5 and Machin-CBM6 (Figs 13.2.52 and 13.2.55) demonstrate the exploitation of local clay sources alongside some importation of material from the urban centre in Exeter.

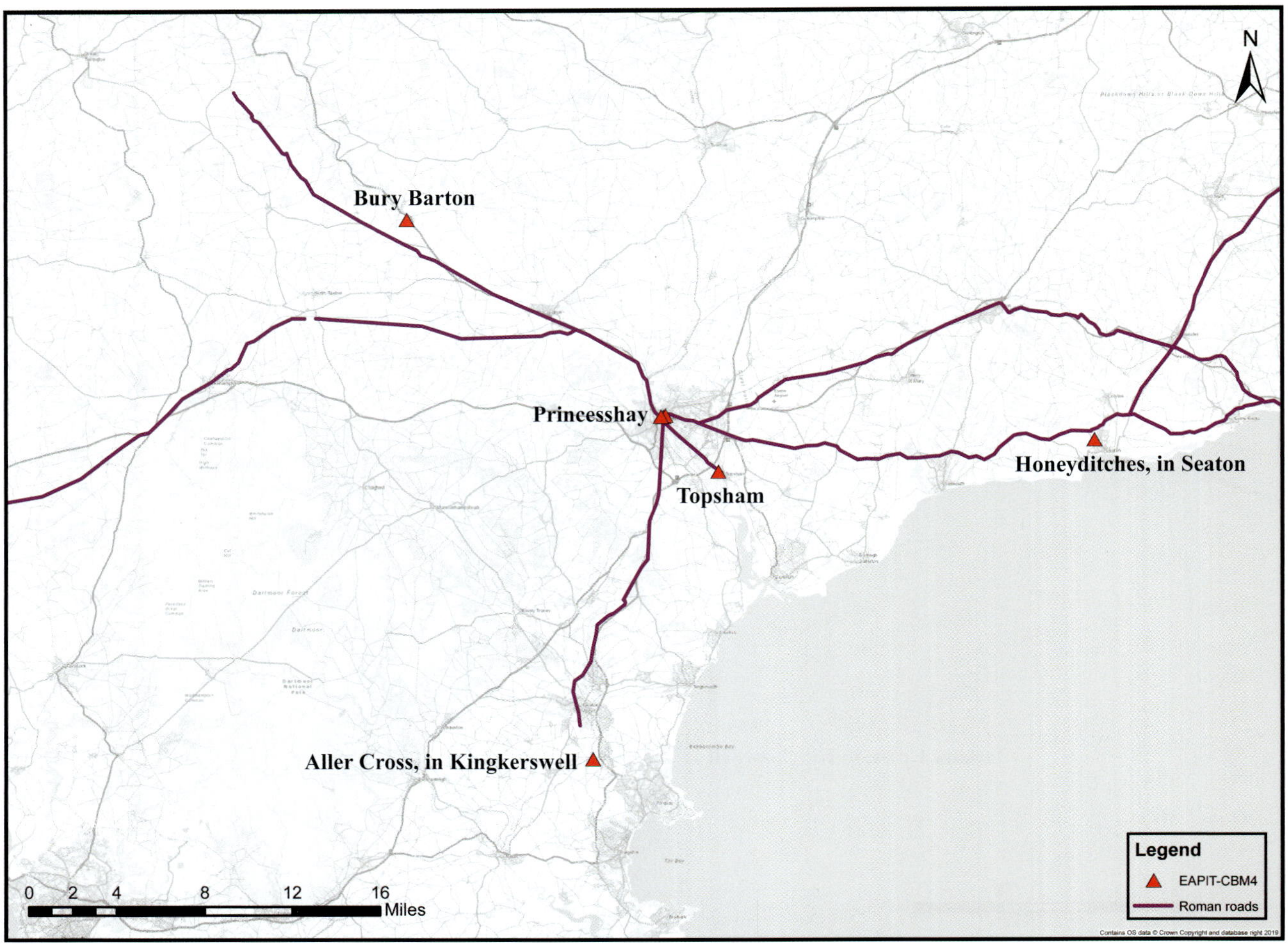

Fig. 13.2.51 Distribution of Machin-CBM4

Whilst no chronology has been applied to the material in this study, a change in brick and tile supplies has been demonstrated at other sites which may also be the case at these rural sites. A lower overall demand for building materials in the later Roman period often meant that production centres went out of use and material had to be sought from further afield. The establishment of a tilery, even for a small building project, required a large outlay of resources which could be avoided if a ready supply of material was available from elsewhere, albeit some distance away. A change of supply of building materials in London is evidenced in the fabrics of the CBM. It illustrates a change in supply from the local kiln sources, to more distant production centres, which also coincided with the cessation of production at the local pottery kilns (Betts 2017, 376). At this time, there was also an increase in the reuse of material from local demolition projects. A change in supply of building materials can also be identified at Silchester. The Neronian tilery at Little London had ceased production by *c.* AD 70, and the occurrence of Little London fabrics within the town declines markedly from *c.* AD 125 (Machin 2018, 218) leading to a reliance on other, mainly local, sources and along with the reuse of existing building materials. The fabric of CBM from Roman London suggests that a mid 2nd-century AD decline of CBM kilns within a 30 km radius of the capital allowed opportunities for new manufacturers to meet *Londinium's* needs (Unger 2009, 110–111). The change in CBM fabrics also coincides with local pottery kilns ceasing production (Betts 2017, 376), and the reuse of brick obtained from the demolition of existing buildings. Local tile production may have temporarily restarted sometime around AD 190–220 (Milne 1995, 77), the probable date of the 3 km-long Roman town wall which is in the main constructed of Kentish ragstone using a considerable volume of tiles set in a horizontal string courses. It seems unlikely that there would have been sufficient existing brick and tile available to reuse for such a vast building project (Betts 2017, 377). A tilery at St Martin-in-the-Fields was excavated in 2009 (Tefler 2009) and based on the results of archaeo-magnetometry dating of the last firing of the kiln, is estimated to have been in use between AD 400–450. This suggests that after a prolonged hiatus, fresh supplies of ceramic tiles were needed for building construction or repair, with

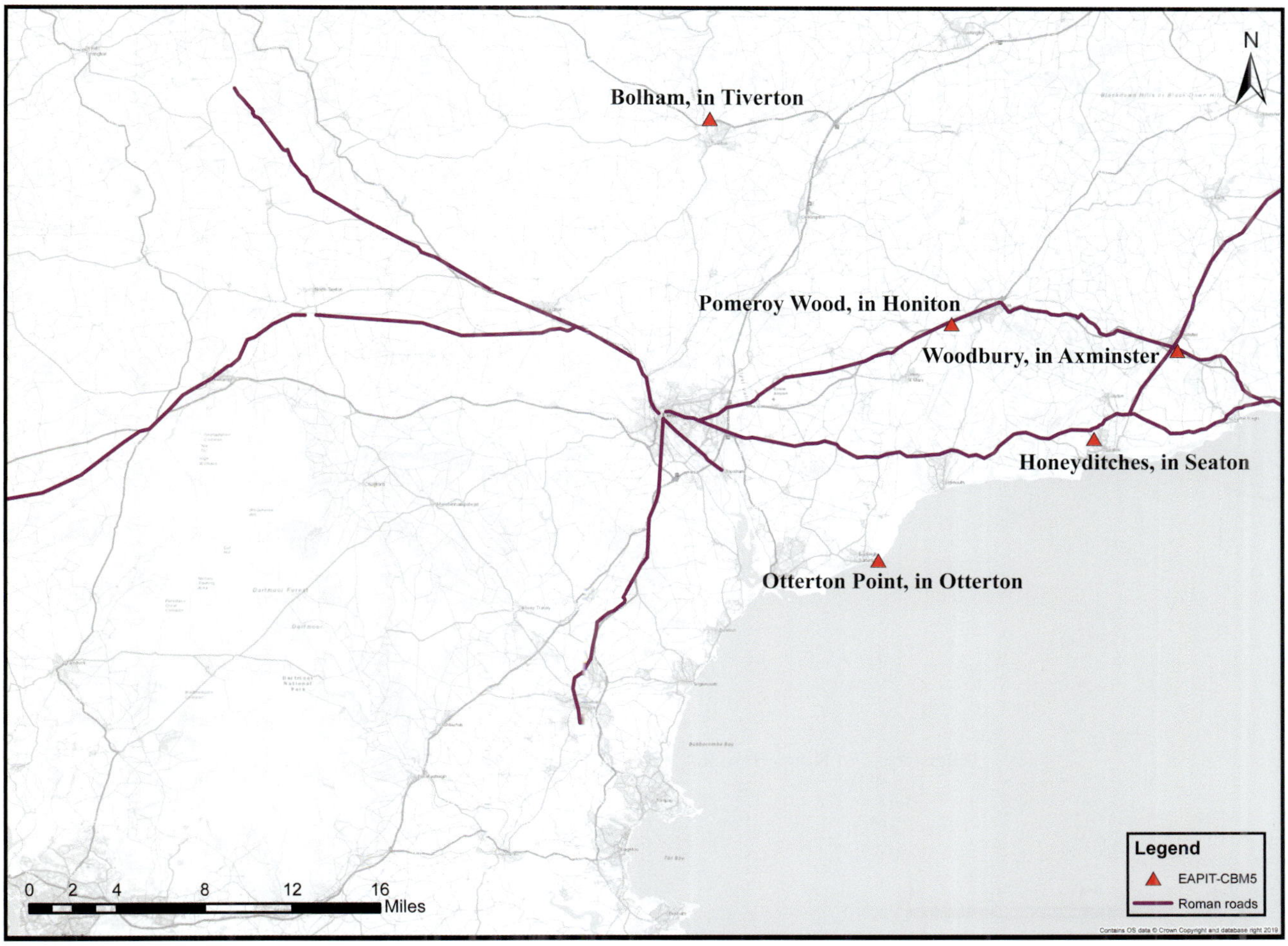

Fig. 13.2.52 Distribution of Machin-CBM5

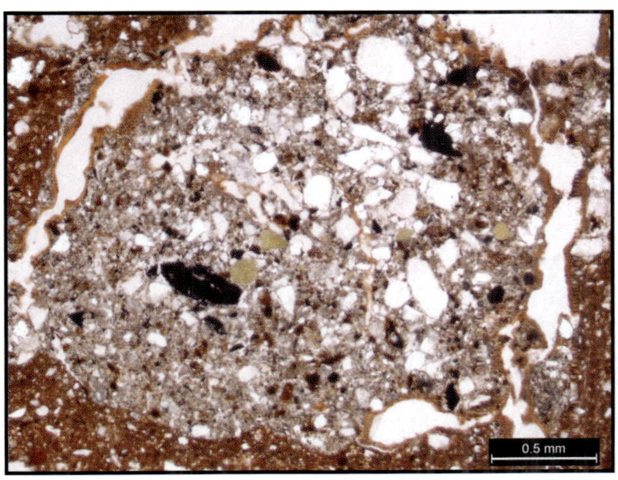

Fig. 13.2.53 Thin section PW01 showing greensand fragment (x25; PPL)

Fig. 13.2.54 Thin section PW01 showing greensand fragment (x25; XP)

no awareness of the imminent collapse of the market for which it had been established (Betts 2017, 381). Evidence of 4th-century AD tile production is also known from St Swithins Yard, Walcot Street, in Bath where a probable tile kiln was archaeomagentically dated to *c*. AD 320 (±30) (Fitzpatrick 2001, 369).

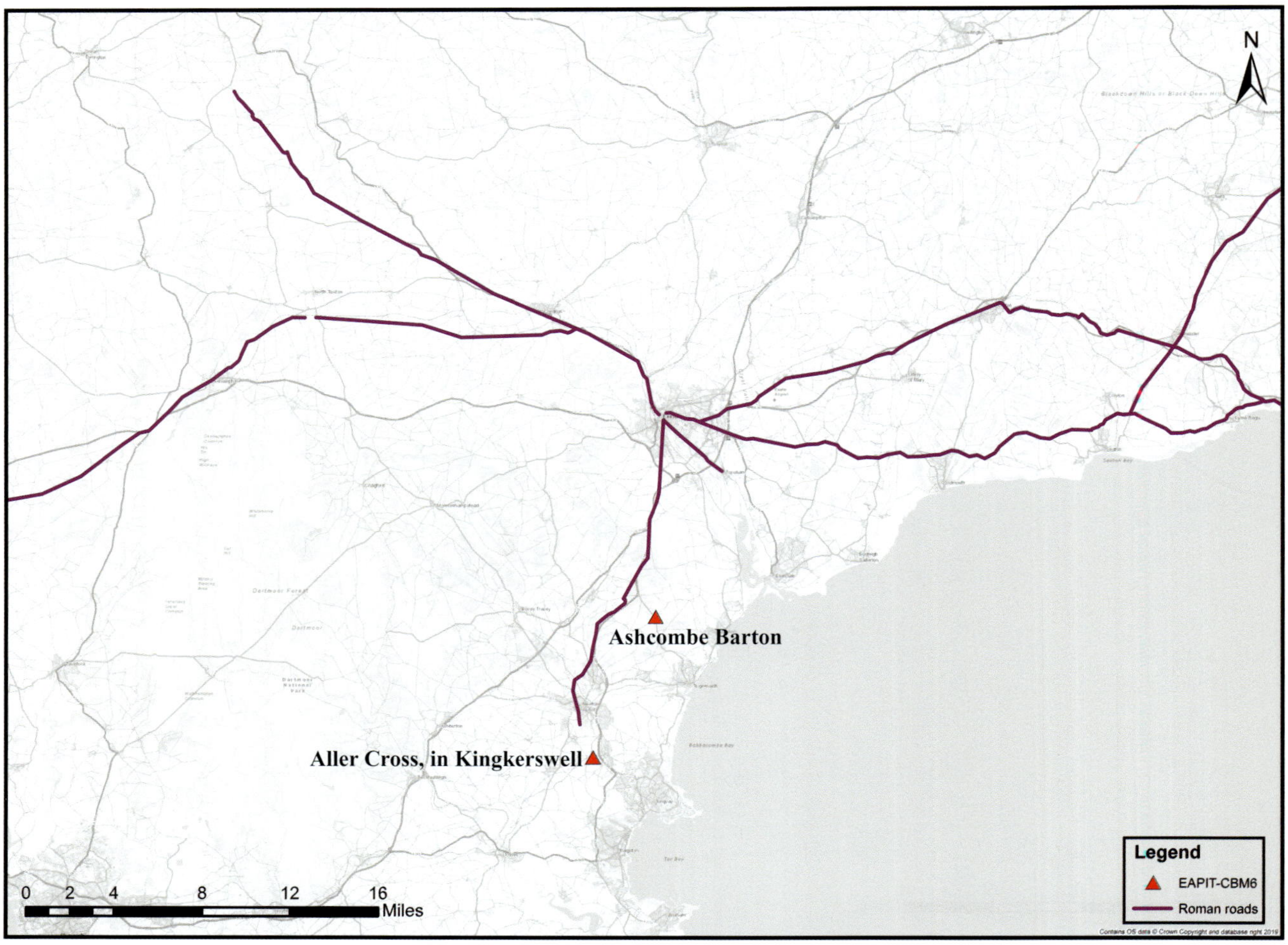

Fig. 13.2.55 Distribution of Machin-CBM6

Machin-CBM 7, 9, and 11–14

Within the material included in this study, the only examples of the very distinctive Hatherleigh Moor fabric Machin-CBM7 have been found at the site of Hatherleigh Moor itself (Fig. 13.2.2). Its rural location would suggest, if it is a kiln site, that it was established for local, short-lived demand, with large-scale, long-distance movement of the material from such a remote centre unlikely.

Machin-CBM fabrics 9, 11–14 are all found at a single site only (Holcombe, Honeyditches in Seaton, Bury Barton, Topsham and Otterton Point respectively; Fig. 13.2.56). These are likely to have been made locally to the site, to serve a short-lived high-demand or for a specialist building project which necessitated the establishment of a tilery. Based on the material examined for this project, Holcombe would appear to have exploited the local clays and to have been self-sufficient with no material imported from elsewhere.

Discussion

At the time of publication of McWhirr's (1979a) corpus of kilns, 60% of the known tile kilns from Roman Britain were located more than 20 km from a *civitas* capital, in rural areas away from centres of population (Peacock 1979a, 5). Colchester, London and *Verulamium* have produced small clusters of tile kilns, and some others are known to have been on local estates supplying these urban centres. However, most major Roman towns have produced little evidence of brick-making from their immediate environs though many may have been destroyed by subsequent urban development as may be the case at Exeter. Peacock (1979a, 9) suggests that rural tile makers migrated to the towns and fired bricks using clamp kilns located outside of town walls. Despite a marked increase in archaeological work in the extra-mural areas of Romano-British towns, very few examples have been discovered (Fulford and Holbrook 2015) and what is certain is that there must be many production sites yet undetected. Williams' (1991a) results showed, and this report confirms, that the CBM from the sites across Devon did not come from one or two large production centres. Instead it was made in many different places, resulting in a variety of different fabrics and a number of sites obtaining material from more than one source.

The skewed nature of some of these assemblages, in favour of particular forms, along with very small amounts retained at some sites, makes the archives unrepresentative

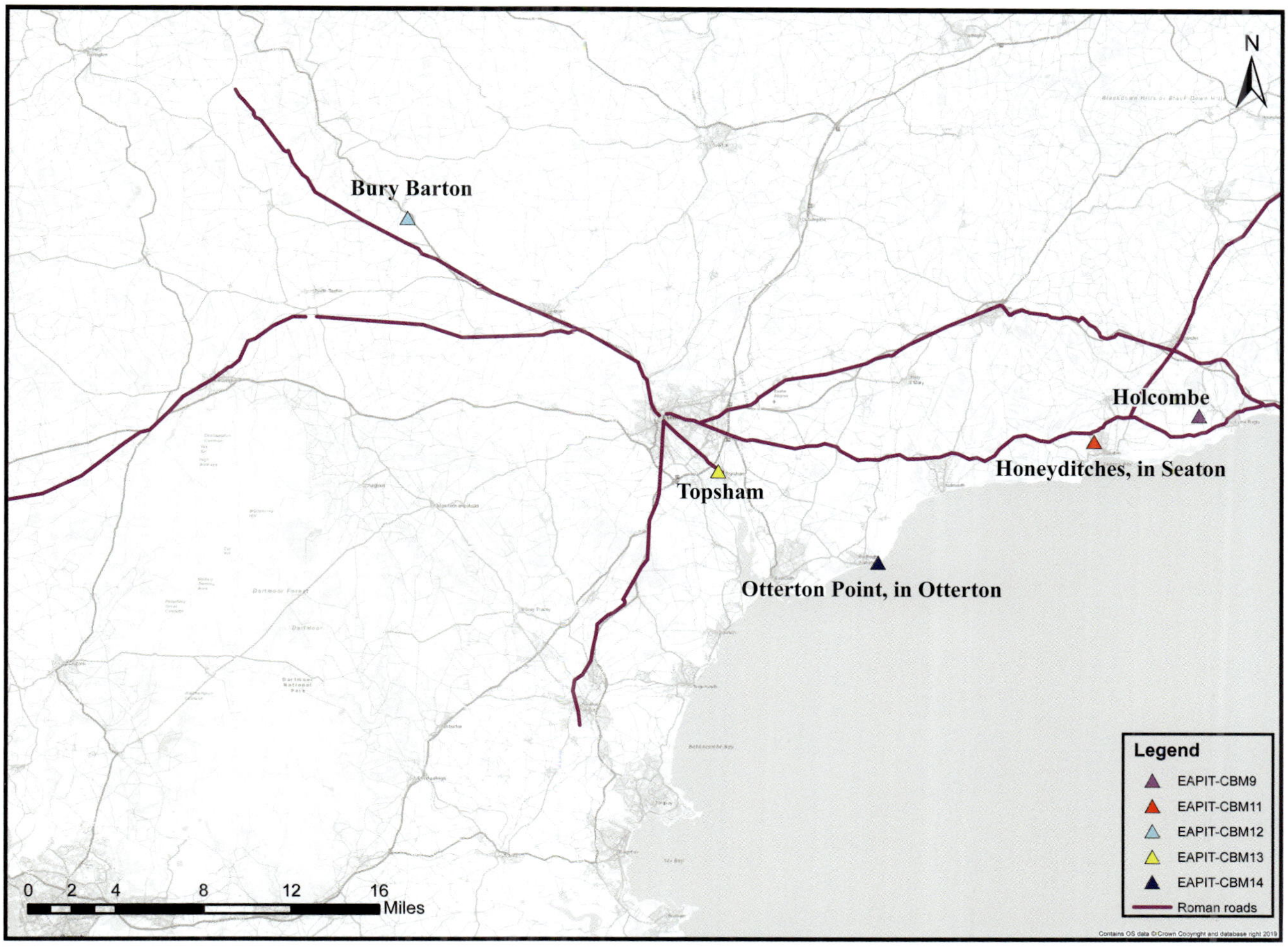

Fig. 13.2.56 Distribution of Machin-CBM fabrics 9, 11–14

of the material that would have been used at these sites. This therefore makes it difficult to confidently extrapolate results from analyses of retained samples to the recorded assemblages, which itself is a sample of the material used. This however does not negate the insights that can be gained from the detailed analysis of existing archives to add to the understanding of the brick and tile industry in Roman Britain. During the later Roman period there will undoubtedly be an increase in reuse of material for incidental repairs, renovations or new building projects, leading to a skewing of the incidence of fabrics over time. Whether recovered from fieldwalking or securely dated contexts, analysis of CBM fabrics provides an insight into the range of fabrics present at the site and a broad understanding of the reliance of local or more distant source of building materials.

Acknowledgements

I am very grateful to Dr Peter Warry for suggesting analysis of the Devon material and for providing initial support for this project. I would like to thank Jennifer Durrant and Tom Cadbury for facilitating access to the CBM collections and supporting this programme of petrographic investigation. All thin sections will be deposited within the museum archive. Grateful thanks also to Professor Michael Fulford for his comments on an earlier draft of this paper.

13.3

An Analysis of the Roman Ceramic Building Material Industry in Devon Using pXRF

Peter Warry

Introduction

Objectives, approach and structure

This chapter has two objectives: the first is to explore the evolution of the Ceramic Building Material (CBM) industry in Devon during the Roman period; how it developed, how many tileries there were, how long they operated, the market dynamics between them, the impact of imports, and the extent to which Devon was connected with and influenced by changes in CBM design and usage in the rest of Britain. Additionally, it will explore what the tiles can tell us about the evolution of Romano-British Devon more generally, and in particular, the transition from military occupation to a civilian economy.

The second objective is to test whether portable X-Ray Fluorescence (pXRF), which already makes a contribution to pottery studies, can be helpful in CBM analysis and if it can be delivered using a simplistic methodology that could be performed by a commercial archaeology unit using a basic pXRF machine. The analysis will use tile morphology, principally the shape of *tegula* lower cutaways, to help distinguish between different kiln sources and periods of production. It will then test these tentative results using pXRF to see if the postulated kilns based on morphology are supported by different chemical signatures, and finally these conclusions will be checked with reference to selected thin sections presented in Sara Machin's chapter above to confirm (or otherwise) the results. The validity of the pXRF methodology employed in this work will be determined by the credibility of the resulting conclusions.

A detailed catalogue of all the tiles examined and the project data set is available in the online Appendix 13.1.

Sites examined

The South-West Peninsula has fewer complex farms and villas and comparatively more military sites than the rest of southern England (Smith *et al.* 2016, 393; EAPIT 1, Chapter 3). This study examines a selection of 11 of the more significant excavations within Exeter and 27 sites outside of the city which constituted all of the extra-mural locations producing CBM that had been retained by the Royal Albert Memorial Museum (RAMM) in Exeter, together with additional sites not held by the Museum that were made available to the author. The complete CBM assemblage retained from each of the extra-mural sites, and a majority of the CBM assemblage from the chosen intra-mural sites, were examined (see Chapter 13.1 for details of the retention policy adopted by the RAMM for CBM excavated in the city up to the late 1980s). The sites are identified on Fig. 13.3.1. The study is limited to the modern county of Devon; whilst it would have been interesting to explore neighbouring counties, it was not practical as this is already a significant study, *inter alia*, involving a large logistical effort on the part of the RAMM to extract around half a tonne of tiles for inspection and subsequent analysis. Indeed it is the restriction of the study to Devon that has made the project feasible.

The extra-mural sites divided into nine military or former military sites, ten sites characterised by farming or industrial activities, two probable kiln sites, one villa site, the settlement at Seaton whose character is unclear (but which may also have had a military presence: see EAPIT 1, Chapter 3), three sites where no structures were found, and two sites where CBM was incorporated into later medieval buildings. The *legio II Augusta* left Exeter in the late AD 70s/early 80s and all military activity in Devon is considered to have ceased before the end of the 1st century AD (see EAPIT 1, Chapter 5), although this paper explores the possibility of military/official return in the 2nd century AD, perhaps to support the exploitation and transportation of local minerals. Some of the military sites appear to have been subsequently reutilised as either farmsteads or for official purposes such as *mansiones*.

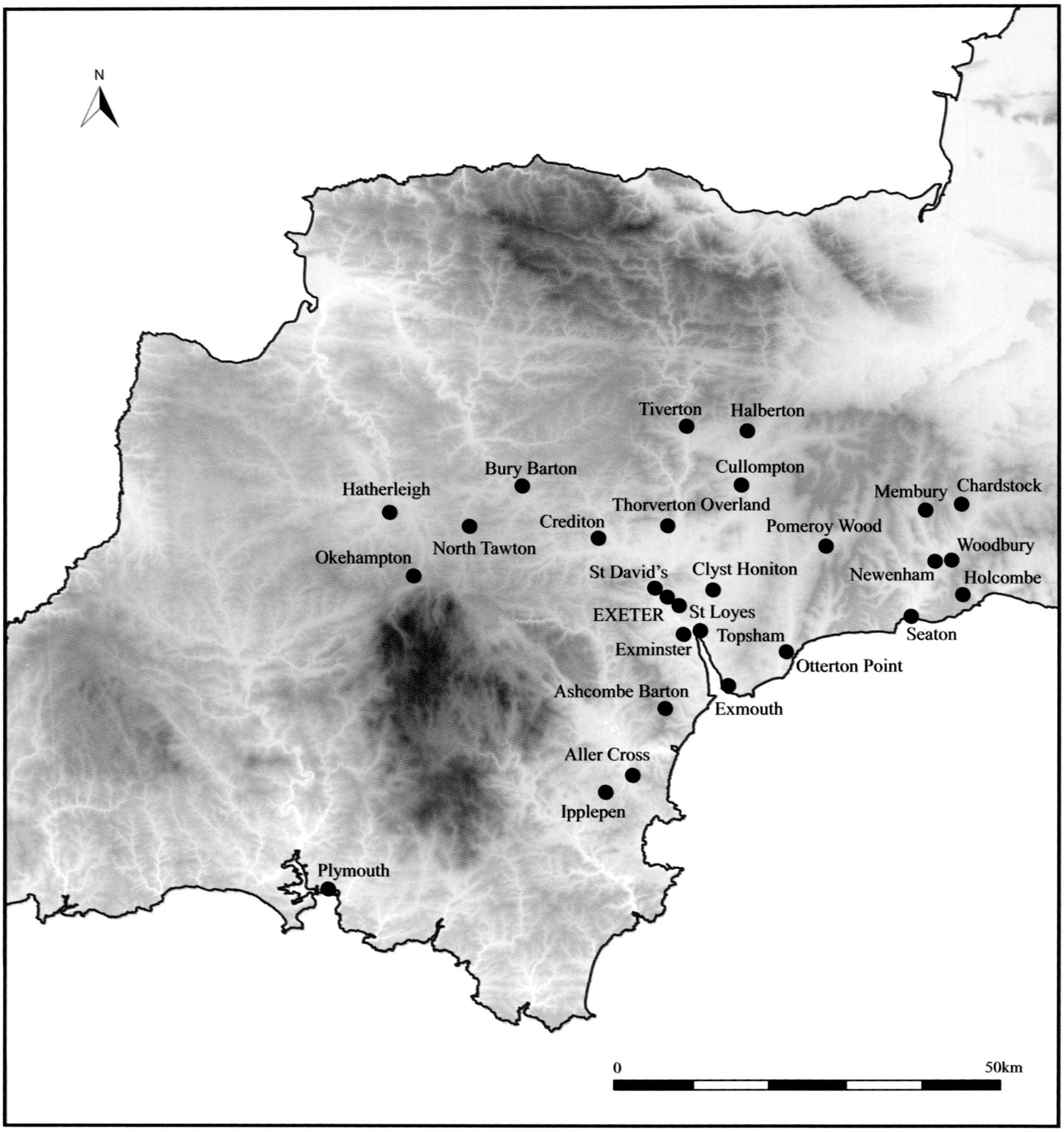

Fig. 13.3.1 Sites examined in Peter Warry's analysis of Roman tile (drawn by David Gould)

Roman tile remained a valuable commodity for lesser constructional purposes, for example drains, walls or floors, after it had served its primary function. As a result CBM was actively recycled and redistributed such that its presence on a site is not necessarily conclusive that it was originally used on that site. In particular, flue-tile appears in small amounts on many sites throughout Britain that will never have had a bath-house or even a hypocaust (author's observations).

There are three known probable kiln sites in Devon, at Princesshay, St David's church, and Hatherleigh Moor:

- Princesshay (Site 156) lies immediately outside the original fortress and Early Roman town but within the larger area encompassed by the later town defences which brought an end to the tilery *c.* AD 160–80 (Steinmetzer, Stead, Pearce, Bidwell, and Allan forthcoming). The kiln site – only known from a spread of wasters (no actual kilns have been discovered) – is known to have operated for most of the 2nd century AD and whilst there is no hard evidence for the presumed legionary kiln being in the same general area north-east of the fortress and early town, Bidwell (1979, 148) and others have suggested that the possibility should not be ignored.

- St David's church (Site 191) lies 0.5 km to the north-west of the town walls. Only a very limited excavation was possible and, whilst this did not reach any kiln structures, there were sufficient wasters and tiles to give confidence that this was the site of a tilery. The excavators (Chapman *et al.* 2017; Steinmetzer forthcoming) believe it only operated during the 1st century AD but the evidence discussed in this paper argues for this continuing well into the 2nd century AD.
- Hatherleigh Moor in north-west Devon which is evidenced by wasters, tile debris and a pronounced magnetic anomaly characteristic of intense burning (Wheeler and Laing-Trengove 2006). No dating has previously been attributed to this probable site although this paper will argue that it was in operation in the 3rd and 4th centuries.

The fabrics produced by these three kilns do not encompass all the different fabrics observed in this study and so this paper also postulates the existence of three further tileries that operated mainly in the 2nd and 3rd centuries AD referred to as Eastern, Central and Southern on the basis of the distribution of places where those fabrics have been recognised. Inevitably there will also have been other, probably smaller and more local, tileries that this analysis has failed to capture.

Previous fabric analysis

Historically, the fabrics found in Exeter have been divided into four, identified as Exeter Fabrics 1–4, as analysed by Williams (1991b, 281–2) using both macroscopic and thin section examination. Based on a sample of just over 100 kg of *tegula* fragments, Fabric 1 was the most common followed in diminishing quantities by Fabrics 2, 3 and 4. The first three fabrics were present in contexts throughout the Roman period but Fabric 4 was only seen in Exeter after *c.* AD 270. Fabrics 1 and 2 were differentiated purely on the basis of colour which Williams suggested may have simply been due to the level of oxidation in the firing; Fabric 3, which was deep reddish-brown and occasionally purplish, could also have been from the same clay source, but Fabric 4 was distinct. Fabric 1 exploited the local red (Permian) clay which may also have been the case for Fabrics 2 and 3. Betts and Foot (1994) have postulated that Fabric 4 could have come from their conjectured Solent source. This chapter supports the idea that Fabric 4 was imported but suggests that it originally arrived in the 2nd century AD (based on typologically dated 2nd-century AD *tegulae* found at Wessex Close, in Topsham, made of a fabric with the same unusual XRF signature as the Fabric 4 tiles from Exeter) and was subsequently moved to Exeter where it was recycled for other construction purposes. Williams found similarities in the fabrics from the military sites of Okehampton, Bolham in Tiverton, and North Tawton with those from Exeter but could not be sure that they were actually from the same source. He was also able to identify a rare tile from Seaton as being in Fabric 4 and to show that the tiles from Newenham Abbey, in Axminster, were different to those at neighbouring Woodbury (also in Axminster), although he obtained no other conclusive results from his thin section analysis of a further six extra-mural sites suggesting that they came from many different sources with several of these often occurring on the same site.

More recently Taylor and Wheeler (2006) have conducted a small survey of sites which divided their fabrics into five groupings on the basis of petrological inspection as summarised in Table 13.3.1. Other fabric commentary from the sites in Devon has either generated local fabric groups that have not been correlated with those from other sites, or attributions, with varying degrees of certainty, to the Exeter fabric series, normally to Fabrics 1–3. Exeter Fabric 4 has been identified at Plymouth (Bidwell 1986, 13), Aller Cross, in Kingskerswell (Kerr-Peterson 2015, 153), Bury Barton, in Lapford (Todd 2002, 53–4), and Seaton, the latter two being rare isolated examples on those sites.

In general there has been a tendency to attribute fabrics to known types leading to the assumption that most of extra-mural Devon obtained tiles from the same pool as Exeter, albeit this is not a conclusion that is supported by the analysis in this chapter. There is also an emphasis on fabric colour which may not be a good differentiator between fabrics (as Williams has already suggested in the case of Exeter Fabrics 1 and 2). Ceramic tiled roofs were status symbols, *inter alia* used as a qualification for membership of the town *ordo*, and there is evidence to show that the roofs were embellished with different coloured tiles. In particular a number of site assemblages

Table 13.3.1 Summary of Taylor and Wheeler (2006) fabric analysis

	Source	*Sites*
1	Hatherleigh Moor	Hatherleigh Moor, North Tawton, Bury Barton, Okehampton Castle, Monkokehampton
2	Taw Valley?	North Tawton, Bury Barton
3	Okement Valley?	Okehampton Fort
4	Upper Greensand	Bury Barton
5	Unknown source	Bury Barton

in southern Britain, *inter alia*, Silchester, Marcham and Druce Farm, Dorchester, have just a few tiles (almost always *tegulae*) that were made of an almost pure white fabric that were presumably used to pick out designs on the roofs. Even today some tile-makers vary the degree of oxidation such that their roofs can be differentiated with blue and red patterns. Moreover colour is not necessarily fixed: for example, the author photographed tiles from Market Street/Smythen Street (Site 115) in 2003 at Exeter Archaeology a couple of years after they had been excavated when they had a drab orange colour and then photographed them again in 2017 in the RAMM store by when they had taken on a strong orange-red colour, perhaps reflecting a difference in humidity between the two stores.

Methodology

Tile morphology

The first step used in this analysis is tile morphology, that is to examine the shape and form of the tile for clues to its date and possible source. For example, we know that the antefixes (the decorated terminations to columns of *imbrices*) with either faces (see Fig. 13.3.43 in online Appendix 13.1) or dolphins (EAPIT 1, Fig. 5.3) were produced by the legion in the 1st century AD as they were found in the construction phases of the legionary bath-house (Bidwell 1979, 149). With slightly less precision we know that certain types of signatures (very large double loops and linear squiggles) are normally military and so should also be 1st century AD in Exeter, and that half-box flue-tiles will normally be 1st or early 2nd century AD (Warry 2015b, 10). However, the most useful dating evidence comes from *tegulae* where cutaways were used to facilitate the overlapping of the *tegulae* on the roof and over time the design of the cutaway was improved to enhance the fitting and simplify the manufacture. Fragments containing the lower cutaway may be divided into five main groups; A, B, C, D and R with dating as shown in Fig. 13.3.2 which displays the shape of the cutaway when viewed looking up the right-hand flange from the bottom of the tile (Warry 2006). In the major towns of Caerwent, Cirencester, Silchester and Colchester the Group C cutaways start in the 1st century AD but this has not been observed anywhere else and there is no evidence for it in Exeter or Devon.

The quantities of the different cutaway forms observed during this study are listed in Figs 13.3.31 and 13.3.33. With one exception, the Group A *tegulae* were only found in Exeter; some of these came from the 1st-century AD fortress bath-house and the others, which appear similar, presumably also originally came from the baths. The exception is a single possible Group A tile from the St David's church kiln. Exeter had larger numbers of Group B and C *tegulae* but only two possible Group D *tegulae* as a consequence of the change to stone/slate tiles on roofs in that period. The majority of the tiles from rural sites were Group B with lesser numbers of Group C and D. The only examples of Group R (in Type 7 form) came from Wessex Close, in Topsham.

The predominance of the group B cutaway in the countryside, and to a lesser extent in Exeter, justifies

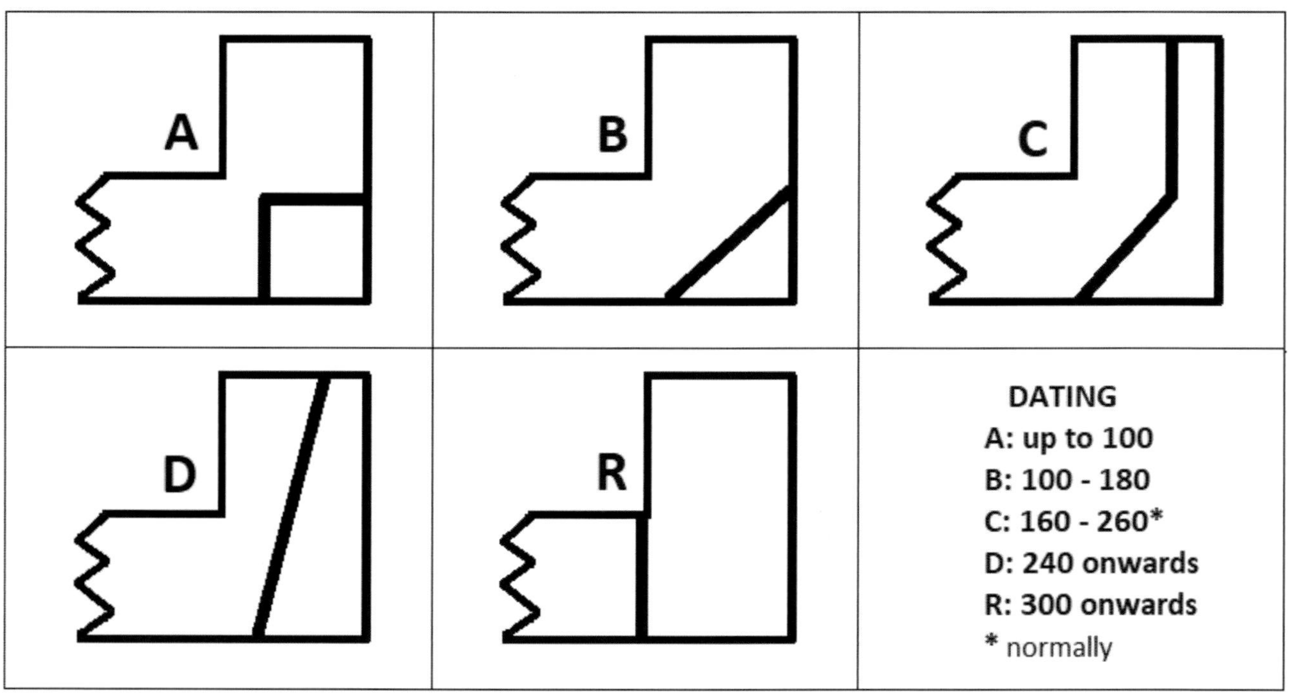

Fig. 13.3.2 Tegula *lower cutaway groups viewed looking up the right-hand flange*

rehearsing the dating evidence for this form which is set out in detail in Warry (2006). The best evidence comes from stamped tiles: there are ten Group A but only three Group B *tegulae* stamped by *legio IX Hispanc* consistent with its presence in Britain during the 1st century AD before moving to Nijmegen, in Holland, early in the 2nd century AD. It was replaced by *legio VI Victrix* not later than AD 126 (RIB 1427) for which there are no 1st-century AD Group A *tegulae* but abundant 2nd-century AD Group B ones. At Caerleon Boon has estimated the date of each of the *legio II Augusta* die groups based on contextual evidence which strongly correlate with the cutaways found on these dies (Warry 2006, 75–8). Turning to civil evidence, Gloucester was founded as a *colonia* at the end of the 1st century AD and the civic tilery started producing stamped *tegulae* at the start of the 2nd century AD all of which have Group B cutaways (Warry 2017). More generally, there were some dies that were in use as the *tegulae* transitioned from one cutaway form to the next and so they are found with both Group A and B cutaways or Group B and C cutaways or Group C and D cutaways but never with Group A and C cutaways or Group B and D cutaways, demonstrating that the cutaway forms were sequential. Finally, provided the cutaways are sequenced A, B, C, D, then the overall size of the *tegulae* and indeed all the subsidiary dimensions reduce uniformly through time. The non-conformity of some Group C *tegulae* in the towns of Caerwent, Cirencester, Silchester and Colchester has already been noted but there are no examples in the author's database of over 4000 *tegula* cutaways from some 200 different sites that undermine the sequencing or dating of the other cutaway groups although the precise dating of the Group D and R cutaways is affected by their lesser numbers in the database.

Originally *tegulae* were produced upright in an open four-sided mould or 'former' placed on a palette or table. This continued until the middle of the 3rd century AD when some tileries adopted a new technique whereby the *tegulae* were produced in a five-sided box (*i.e.* including a base) shaped in the form of a negative image of the tile such that, once filled with clay, a *tegula* was created lying face down or inverted. These two different manufacturing methods leave tell-tale indications on the *tegulae* (in particular, smoother undersides and squarer flanges on inverted *tegulae*) which can be used as a further aid to dating (Warry 2006, 34).

The dimensions of the lower cutaways, in particular the length of the cutaway and the height of the flange, tend to be specific to the formers used and hence to specific tileries and periods of production. As a result when the dimensions from a mixed assemblage of *tegulae* are plotted on a graph, *tegulae* made in the same former or same kiln tend to group together. Provided the assemblage does not contain too many different sources then very useful separation of sources can often be achieved (*e.g.* Warry 2013; 2015a; see also Warry 2010 for a similar analysis but based on the overall dimensions of the *tegulae*), but if too many sources or periods of production are present then the distributions tend to overlap too much and differentiating between them becomes problematic (*e.g.* Warry 2012). Using the cutaway types and dimensional data from the various Devon assemblages we can identify groups of *tegulae* that appear to come from a common source and then validate this morphological data by identifying the same sets of tiles on the XRF plot to see if they also form groupings there. As these are two entirely independent methodologies any correlation between them is likely to indicate that the results are meaningful.

The use of pXRF

Williams's 1991 work based upon a combination of thin section and macroscopic examination was only able to produce limited conclusions. Taylor (2006), using macroscopic examination, was successful in identifying a number of potential recipients of Hatherleigh Moor product but three of his four other potential kiln sources were only represented by single tiles that mainly came from Bury Barton. Thin section analysis is time-consuming and therefore not ideal for the large number of samples required for the countywide survey entailed in this project, although it will be practicable to use as a confirmatory test on a smaller selected sample of tiles once the basic analysis is done. Moreover, all of these approaches generate descriptive analyses of fabrics which do not easily facilitate comparison across a number of sites. In contrast pXRF, which analyses the concentrations of the constituent elements of the fabric, offers the prospect of a much quicker test with numerical rather than descriptive output which readily facilitates graphical analysis for comparison across sites. The technique has been tested on the finer fabrics used for pottery production with some success (*e.g.* Wilke *et al.* 2016) but is yet to be proven with the much coarser and less homogeneous fabrics employed to make tiles.

The pXRF analysis for this project was undertaken using a Skyray Genius 5000 portable machine on the 'mineral' setting using the manufacturer's preset internal calibration for all readings. Different exposure durations were trialed leading to a choice of thirty second exposure as longer durations added little extra precision. No special sample preparation was undertaken. This approach, which should be within the compass of commercial archaeology units, will only generate 'broadbrush' results which will not be comparable with those that would be expected of a scientific laboratory. The pXRF machine recorded 32 elements but only eight of these were consistently present across all the samples. Generally, three separate pXRF readings were taken from each tile and the average of these readings was used in the subsequent analysis. The standard deviation of the three readings for each element in each tile has been calculated and then averaged across all the tiles. The results are shown in Table 13.3.2 for three of the most important elements expressed as an absolute figure and as a percentage of the average value for that element. Strictly these are not true standard deviations for the full dataset of each element, but they give an indication of the inherent variability in the data and therefore a guide as to how far the measurements of a particular tile might vary from the average of a proposed kiln grouping.

These are large standard deviations which will produce quite a spread of results when the data are plotted and they raise the question whether better preparation of the tiles before the readings were taken could have produced tighter results. To test this, readings were taken from interiors of six tiles that had been cut through with a diamond tipped saw producing very smooth clean surfaces that would have been unaffected by surface imperfections and contamination. The average percentage standard deviation of these tiles is shown in the column headed 'perfect' percentage at the right of Table 13.3.2. With the exception of potassium where the variation was rather less, the other results show that there is little improvement in the variability of the readings, even when taken from a perfect surface. There is, however, also the danger that tiles made of the same fabric but buried in different environments will have different chemical characteristics due to the leaching of particular elements into or out of the soil. For example, Freeth (1967, 109–10) showed that sherds from a highly calcareous pot contained three times as much calcium oxide when deposited above the water table as sherds from the same pot that were found below the water table. The impact of leaching is considered further in the section on 'Dolphin antefixes and consideration of leaching effects' (below).

In all 141 tiles were sampled by pXRF. At least one fragment that was representative of the main fabric present was selected from each site assemblage, as were representative examples of any datable components such as *tegula* cutaways. The rarer fabrics were generally ignored because many Roman sites have acquired small amounts of material from other sites which do not help inform the main development of these sites. These rarer fragments may have arrived as recycled material for use in filling walls, etc., either during the Roman period or later, or as replacement tiles for roof repairs (*e.g.* Warry 2006, 88–90 shows how the repair process, mainly utilising *imbrices*, was responsible for the long tail of reducing frequency of different *Classis Britannica* tile-stamps at Beauport Park in Sussex).

Table 13.3.2 Standard deviation of XRF sample readings

Element	*Standard deviation*	*% deviation*	*"Perfect" %*
potassium	0.45	22	13
calcium	0.42	34	25
titanium	0.09	29	31

An accepted method of analysing the pXRF output is through the use of Principal Component Analysis (PCA; *e.g.* Thorn and Glascock 2010; Wilke *et al.* 2016), which reduces the multiple element concentrations into two dimensions albeit with the loss of precision. These data can then be plotted on a scattergram as shown in Fig. 13.3.3 which compares the tiles found in Exeter with those recorded from all the extra-mural sites. The PCA analysis used the natural logarithms of the concentrations of the eight elements found in all the tiles: calcium, iron, lead, manganese, nickel, niobium, potassium and titanium. The graph, and all subsequent PCA graphs, plot the first principal component (X axis) against the second (Y axis). The approach is discussed further in the section on 'Overall results and application of PCA' below.

Figure 13.3.3 clearly indicates that the fabric(s) used for the tiles from Exeter, which cluster in the centre and left of the plot, differ from the vast majority of fabric(s) used on extra-mural sites which mainly cluster on the right, although there are no obvious sub-groupings to signpost the presence of individual kilns. The lack of obvious groupings is exemplified in Fig. 13.3.4 which shows that the tiles found at Wessex Close, in Topsham, spread across the entire PCA plot. Clearly other methods will be required to break down these data into their constituent fabrics and kiln sources.

Combining pXRF and tile morphology

In searching for further fabric groupings the PCA dataset is not ideal for detailed analysis (although it will be useful for confirming the validity of the overall result once the groupings have been identified). Michelaki and Hancock (2011, 1276) recommend the use of bi-plots involving just two elements as a precursor stage to PCA analysis, although an alternative approach is possible with our dataset using three elements based upon the observation that the proportion of calcium in the samples varied substantially with a strong bias towards intra-mural sites as shown in Fig. 13.3.5. This histogram has a point of inflexion around 0.5% concentration: almost all the readings to the left of this point are extra-mural and almost all of those to the right are intra-mural with rapidly increasing proportions of calcium. In all the subsequent analysis tiles with levels of calcium below the inflexion point are referred to as calcium-light and those above it called calcium-rich.

The four elements with the highest average concentrations were iron (Fe), potassium (K), calcium (Ca) and titanium (Ti) in that order (the pXRF setting did not test for aluminium or silicon). Iron, however, showed relatively little variation between tiles and therefore would not have been a useful discriminator between different kiln sources. So, having explored alternative pairs of elements, it was decided to create a bi-plot using potassium and titanium for the X and Y coordinates respectively but with each data point distinguished by whether it was calcium-rich

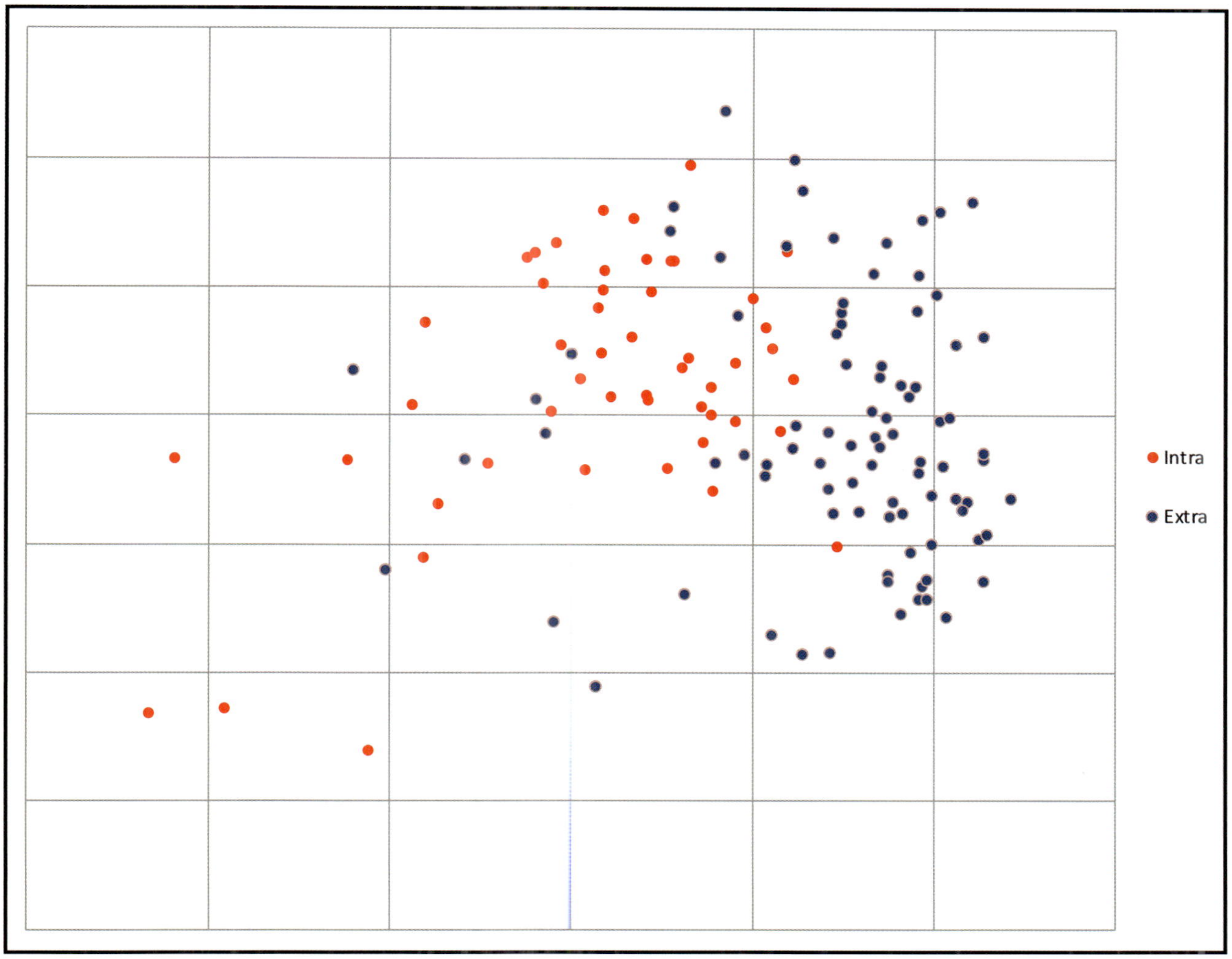

Fig. 13.3.3 Eight-element PCA plot for intra-mural and extra-mural sites

or calcium-light. Figure 13.3.6 shows all 141 tiles with the calcium-rich ones identified as red squares and the calcium-light ones as blue diamonds. This is used as a template for all the subsequent analysis in the section on 'Tile Morphology and Bi-Plot Analysis' below.

Some caution will be required in the interpretation of the XRF data because of the risk of leaching as both calcium and potassium are particularly mobile elements which may pass into or out of the tiles in different soil conditions (*e.g.* Tite 2008, 225). The natural variability in shape and size, characteristic of any handmade artefact, and the statistically random variation inherent in pXRF technology, which may be exacerbated by surface contamination and chemical leaching, complicates the analysis. These issues and variabilities could potentially frustrate the generation of useful results, so the findings from this study need validation before they can be accepted. This is inherent in the methodology adopted because the tile groupings based upon form and dimensional analysis will be independently verified by the requirement for them also to produce meaningful groupings on the XRF bi-plots. Further confirmation is provided by the PCA analysis in the section on 'Verification Using PCA and Thin Sections' below, and by the geographic distributions of kiln output that these yield. A final check is then made by thin section analysis of a carefully selected representative sample of tiles. So as not to undermine the integrity of this validation process, there has been no retrospective back-fitting of results – thus although the thin section analysis leads to some revision of the final kiln groupings, the initial findings in the section 'Tile Morphology and Bi-Plot Analysis' have not been changed (however the site catalogue has been updated to reflect the final revisions: see online Appendix 13.1). Each of the groupings identified below has been given a reference code that describes the probable source and period of the member tiles (*e.g.* P1 for Princesshay 1st century AD and T2 for Topsham 2nd century AD), however, so as not to anticipate the results before they have been validated, these codes are not expanded until the section on 'Verification Using PCA and Thin Sections' below.

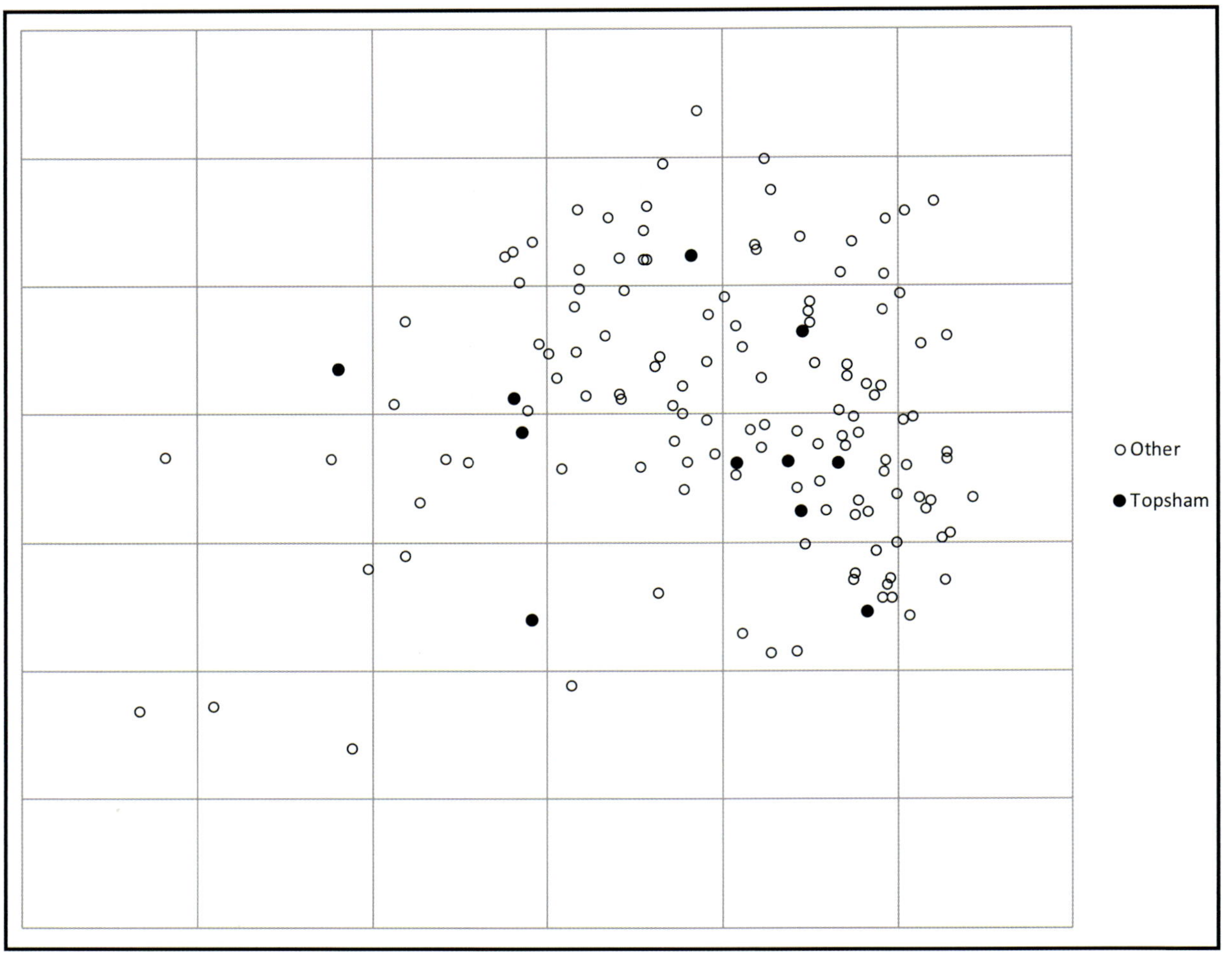

Fig. 13.3.4 Eight-element PCA plot of tiles found at Wessex Close, in Topsham

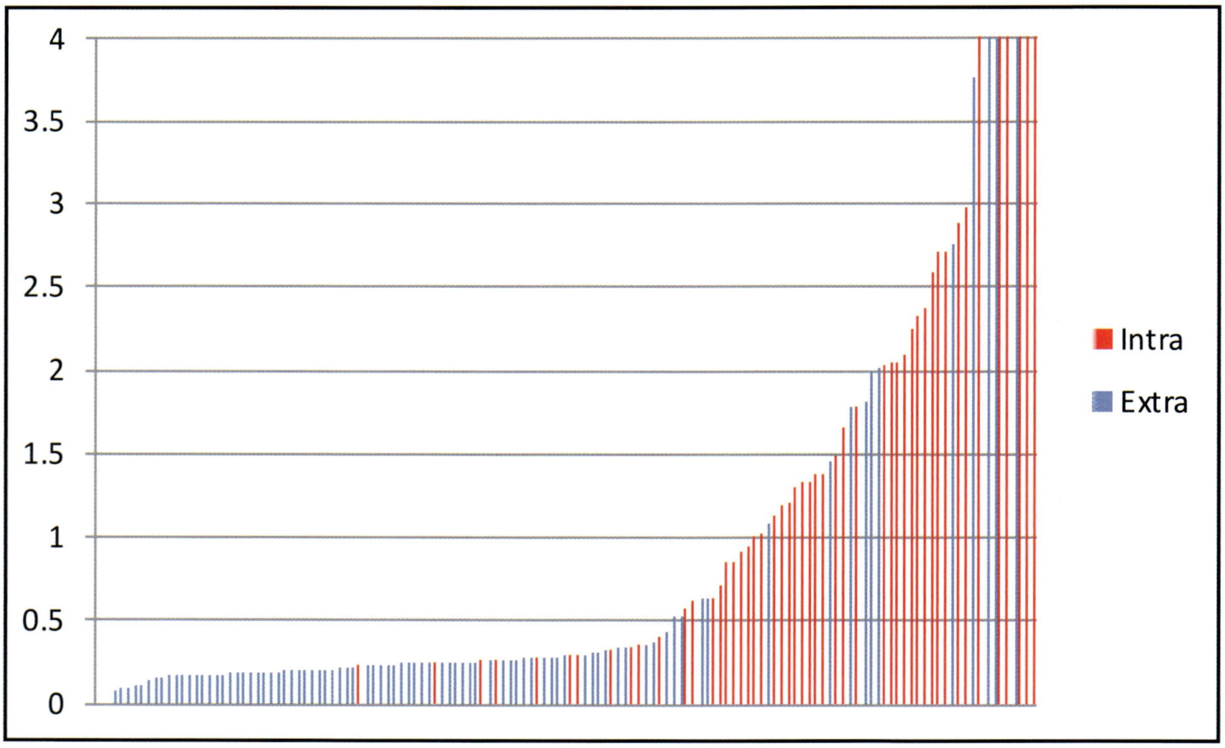

Fig. 13.3.5 Comparison of calcium percentage between intra- and extra-mural sites

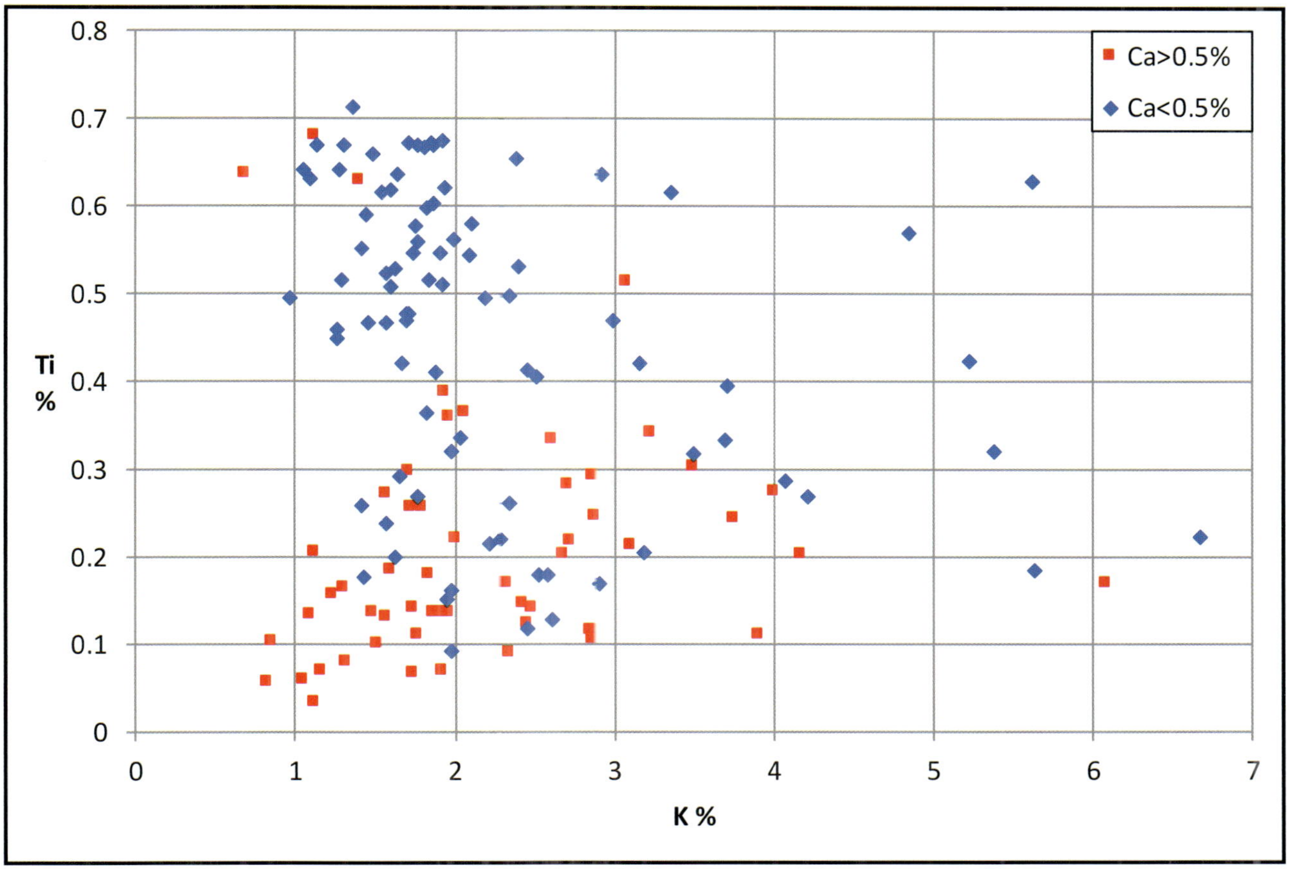

Fig. 13.3.6 All pXRF readings, basic bi-plot analysis template

Tile morphology and bi-plot analysis

1st century AD

As discussed in the section on 'Tile morphology' above, 1st-century AD tiles can be confidently recognised by Group A cutaways on *tegulae*, antefixes with either face or dolphin motifs, or, with less certainty, military style signatures (very large loops or linear squiggles as shown in Fig. 13.3.39 in the online Appendix 13.1) and half-box flue-tiles. There were 17 tiles which met these criteria. The pXRF readings from all of these tiles have been plotted on Fig. 13.3.7 and are shown against the background of the readings from all the other tiles. Ten of them were calcium-rich and are shown as red points and seven of them were calcium-light shown as blue points (one of the blue points, Tile 192, a dolphin antefix, is hidden by one of the calcium-rich points at the bottom of the plot which had almost identical potassium and titanium readings).

It can be seen that, with one exception, the calcium-rich tiles form a tight cluster at the bottom of the plot which has been bounded by the red circle (circles and ellipses will be used to highlight groups of tiles throughout the analysis; they should not be interpreted as confidence limits on the distributions). This distribution is designated as P1 for reference purposes as discussed earlier. The fact that the P1 cluster is so tight strongly suggests that the pXRF readings confirm the grouping provided by the tile morphology. The outlying red point is Tile 38 which nevertheless falls within the expected statistical limits of variation (as reported in Table 13.3.2) that we might expect if the centre of the distribution is enclosed by the red circle. Having established the P1 distribution, we can now consider whether any of the other calcium-rich tiles that lie within the red circle may also be part of the P1 distribution. As will be shown in the next sub-section, most of these belong to the T2 distribution but three, shown in yellow on Fig. 13.3.7, are probably part of the P1 distribution. One of these, Tile 187, came from the 'Exeter *thermae*' (presumably the public baths excavated in the 1930s) and the other two, Tiles 184 and 177, come from the Princesshay and Exeter (1971–1980) retained fabric collections respectively (see Table 13.3.16).

Table 13.3.3 lists all of the tiles contained within the P1 calcium-rich distribution, with the three probable tiles shown in yellow on the scattergram listed in non-bold font in the table. The P1 distribution also includes three calcium-light tiles: Tiles 192 and 211 which are dolphin antefixes (the other dolphin antefix, Tile 212,

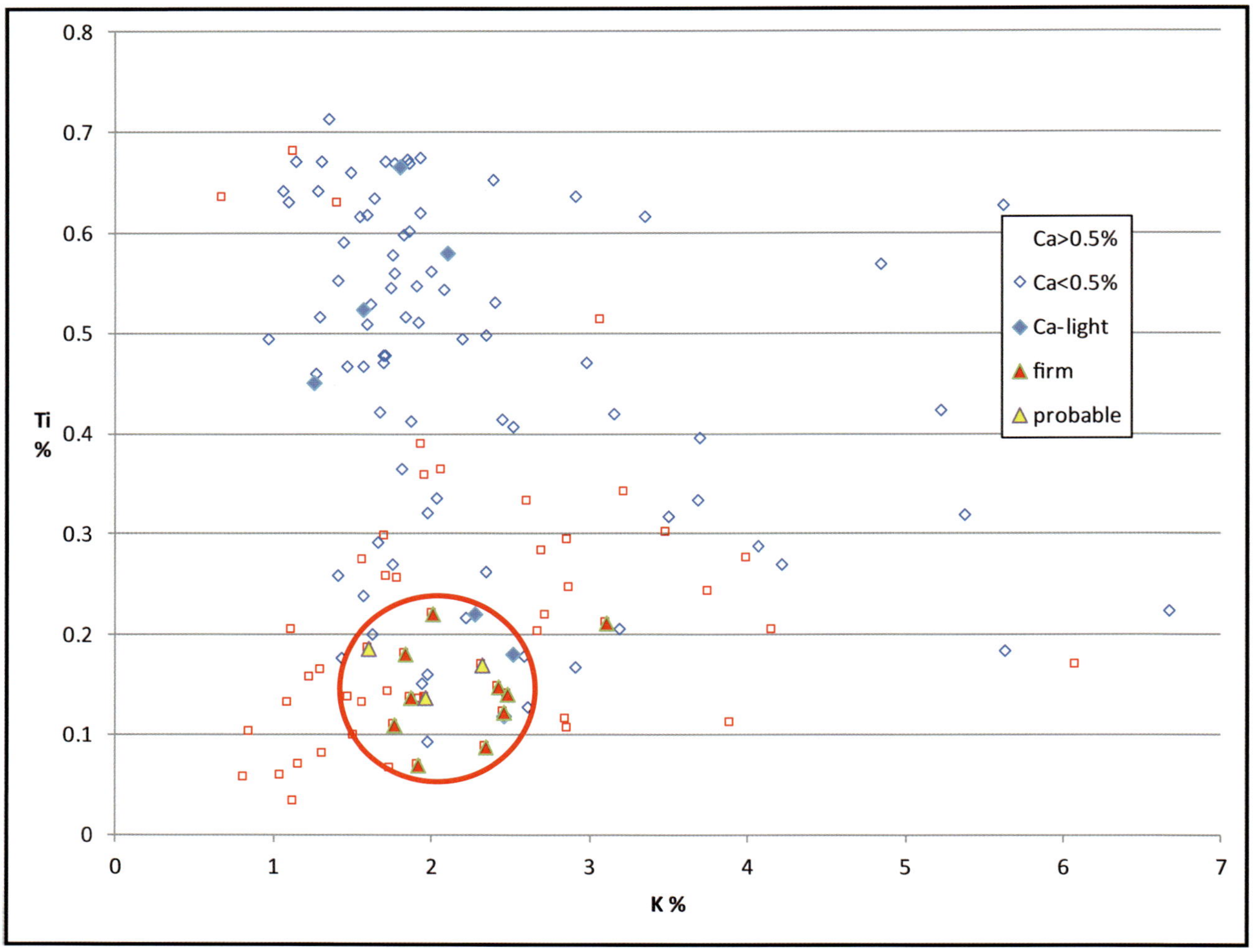

Fig. 13.3.7 P1 1st-century AD calcium-rich tiles

Table 13.3.3 1st-century AD P1 distribution of mainly calcium-rich tiles (non-bold entries are the yellow probable points on Fig. 13.3.7. For Exeter site numbers see Chapter 2 of this volume. Contexts are as recorded on the tiles or on the boxes/bags that they came from

Tile	*RAMM Code*	*Site name and number*	*Description*	*Context*
38	**24/2005**	**Exeter, Cathedral Close** (Site 40)	**Gp A *tegula***	**WM72 XM**
101	**24/2005**	**Exeter, Cathedral Close** (Site 40)	**Gp A *tegula***	**PX**
174	**24/2005**	**Exeter, Cathedral Close** (Site 40)	**half box flue tile**	**CG76EMZ**
190	**403/1990**	**Exeter, Cathedral Close** (Site 40)	**antefix face**	**25**
189	**403/1990**	**Exeter, Cathedral Close** (Site 40)	**antefix face**	**19**
211	**403/1990.2**	**Exeter, Cathedral Close WM** (Site 40)	**antefix dolphin**	**WM72 AHC 1162**
212	**403/1990.1**	**Exeter, Cathedral Close WM** (Site 40)	**antefix dolphin**	**WM72 ADP**
192	**4/2005**	**Exeter, Lower Coombe Street** (Site 71)	**antefix dolphin**	**2029**
128	**450/2005**	**Exeter, Princesshay** (Site 156)	**half box flue tile**	**6852**
129	**450/2005**	**Exeter, Princesshay** (Site 156)	**loop sig**	**2883**
184	450/2005	Exeter, Princesshay fabric collection (Site 156)	Princesshay Fabric 1 C	2883
210	**9/2005**	**Exeter, Rack Street (Site 52, Chapter 8 this volume)**	**antefix face**	**RS75**
142	**171/2008**	**Exeter, Smythen Street** (Site 115)	**Gp A *tegula***	**2548**
187	ATEMP846	Exeter, *thermae*	*opus spicatum*	
188	**448/2009**	**St Loye's College**	**antefix face**	**223**
177	EAR4	Exeter Fabric Collection	Exeter Fabric 2	

was calcium-rich) and Tile 210 which was a face antefix. These will be discussed further in the section on 'Dolphin antefixes and consideration of leaching effects' (below). The other calcium-light 1st-century AD tiles which appear to form a grouping at the top of Fig. 13.3.7 are discussed in the next section.

Later 1st to mid 2nd century AD

Second-century AD CBM is harder to discern than 1st-century AD material, particularly as we can no longer rely on the military tiles in Devon, although 2nd-century AD *tegulae* can be recognised by the presence of the Group B cutaway which was present on 29 of the tiles tested by pXRF. *Tegulae* from different sources/time periods can also be distinguished by their cutaway dimensions where sufficient of the tile remains for these to be measured. All of the tiles with measurable Group B cutaways (including many which were not included in the pXRF sampling) are plotted in Fig. 13.3.8. Three overlapping groupings of tiles can be recognised: those found at Wessex Close, in Topsham, are bounded by the green ellipse, those from rural sites bounded by the blue ellipse, and those from Exeter bounded by the red ellipse. Note that there were four examples from Exeter (shown as red diamonds) that were identified as Exeter Fabric 4 which fall into the green Topsham ellipse rather than the Exeter one. There is one 'stray' Topsham Wessex Close tile (from Context 106) that lies firmly in the red ellipse at the top of the plot which appeared to be in a different fabric and had a square flange rather than the rounded version found on the rest of the Group B Topsham tiles.

pXRF readings were only taken on a minority of the tiles in Fig. 13.3.8 and these readings, together with readings from some of the Group B *tegulae* that were too incomplete to be included in Fig. 13.3.8, are shown on the XRF plot Fig. 13.3.9. The *tegulae* which appear in both Figs 13.3.8 and 13.3.9, having both pXRF readings and measurable cutaways, are described as 'firm' and shown in the stronger colours whilst the Group B *tegulae* with pXRF readings but were not measurable are described as 'prob' and shown in the fainter colours. It can be seen that there are two separate groupings of calcium-rich tiles, one enclosed by the green circle at the bottom left of the plot (identified as T2) and the other by the red ellipse in the centre (identified as P2), whilst the calcium-light *tegulae* form a rather more amorphous grouping surrounded by

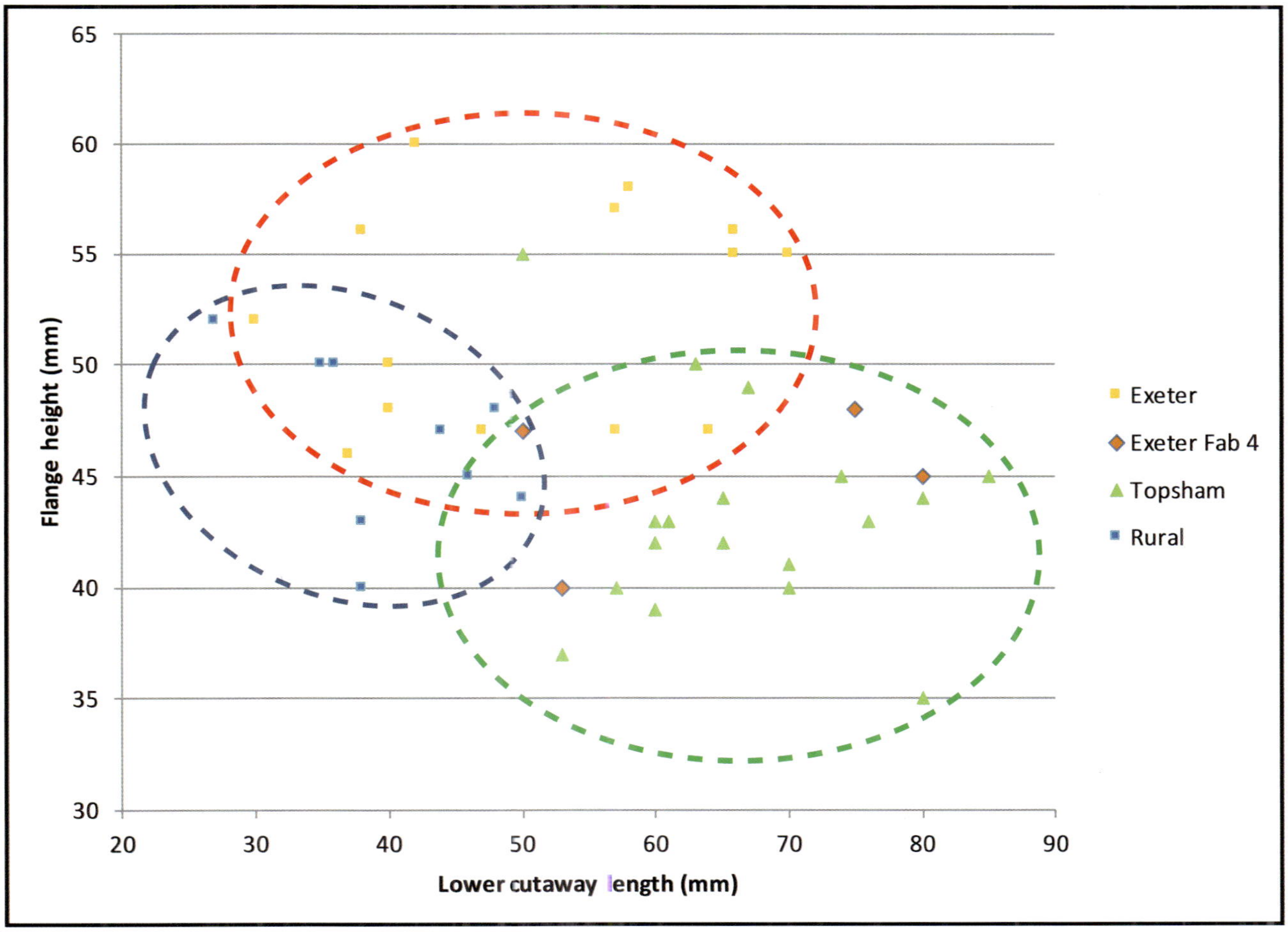

Fig. 13.3.8 Dimensions of tegulae *with Group B cutaways*

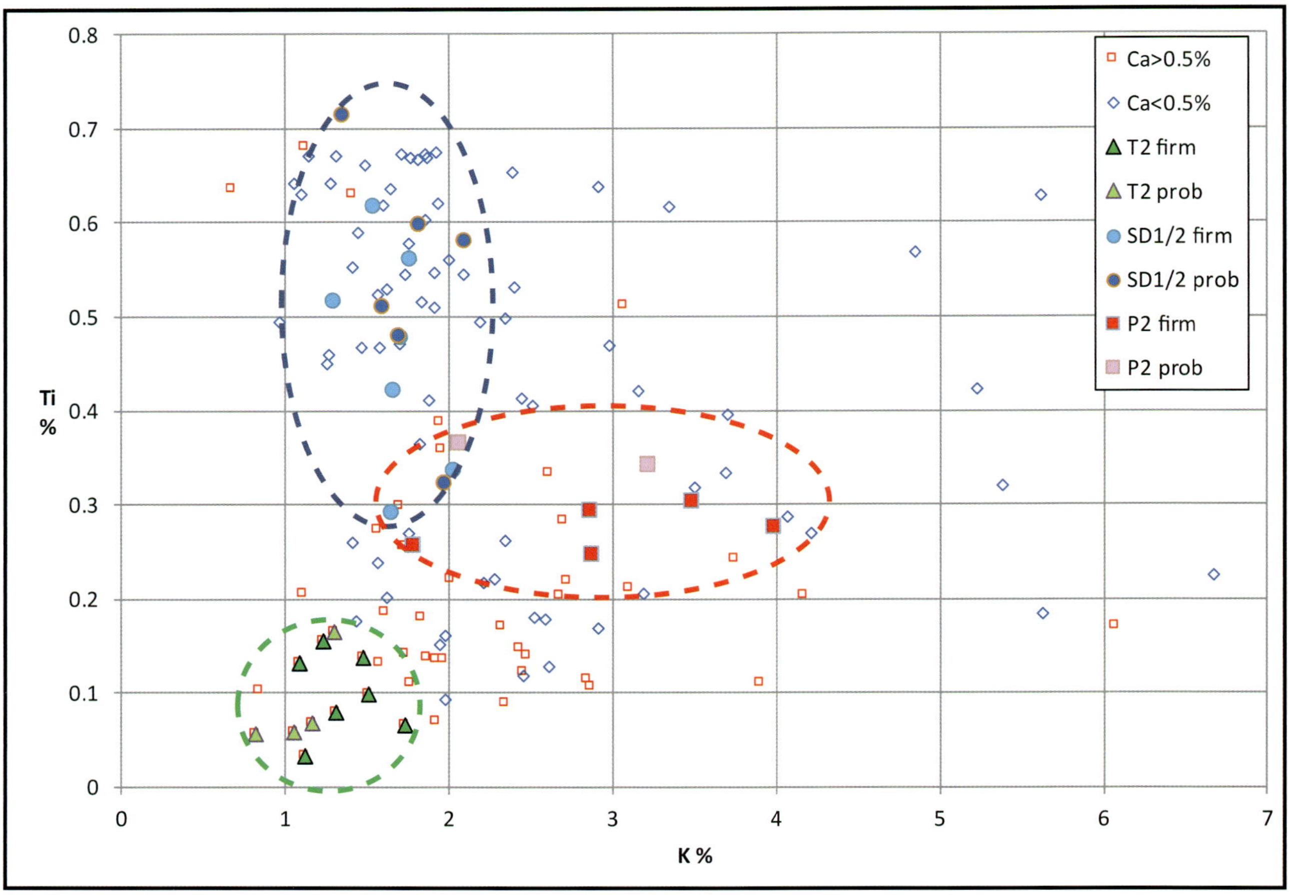

Fig. 13.3.9 Group B early to mid 2nd-century AD pXRF plot

the blue ellipse (identified as SD1/2). These pXRF groupings represent real differences in the kiln sources of these tiles because they correspond directly with groupings found in the dimensional plot (Fig. 13.3.8). As shown in Fig. 13.3.10, all of the *tegulae* that are common to both the pXRF and cutaway plots track exactly between their individual groupings in the two plots. So, for example, all of the *tegulae* in the green dimensional ellipse in Fig. 13.3.8 which were tested by pXRF also appear in the green ellipse in the pXRF plot, Fig. 13.3.9, and likewise for the *tegulae* in the red and blue ellipses.

Having demonstrated how the results of the tile morphology are also replicated in the pXRF analysis, we can now consider these results in more detail. Figure 13.3.11 repeats the pXRF plot shown as Fig. 13.3.9 which, in addition to the *tegulae*, now includes all the other pieces of CBM that may also be attributable to the three kiln sources. It also includes the four calcium-light tiles from the 1st-century AD plot Fig. 13.3.7. The 1st-century AD P1 mainly calcium-rich grouping is outlined in pink for reference purposes. The tiles comprising the SD1/2 grouping are listed in Table 13.3.4. The additional tiles which are described as 'SD1/2 other' in Fig. 13.3.11 are made up of pieces of CBM that have similar pXRF signatures and/or are associated with Group B *tegulae* already within the grouping. For example, two *tegula* fragments from Bolham, in Tiverton, which had pXRF readings that matched the grouping but did not incorporate cutaways are included because there is a further Bolham fragment with a probable Group B cutaway. There is also a tile from Milbury Farm, in Exminster (Tile 163) with an anomalous pXRF reading (see explanation in the Exminster catalogue entry in the online Appendix 13.1) that has been included in the listing because its cutaway dimensions match the other cutaways in the grouping and a second tile from the site (Tile 162) matches both the pXRF and the cutaway criteria. The 'firm' tiles that met both the pXRF and cutaway dimension criteria are shown in bold in Table 13.3.4.

Compared to the very tight 1st-century AD P1 distribution and the equally tight T2 distribution to be discussed shortly, the SD1/2 distribution, particularly the range of titanium values, seems very wide. The range equates to plus or minus two standard titanium deviations so it is at the extreme of what is reasonably probable. To gain more comfort, Fig. 13.3.12 compares just the St David's

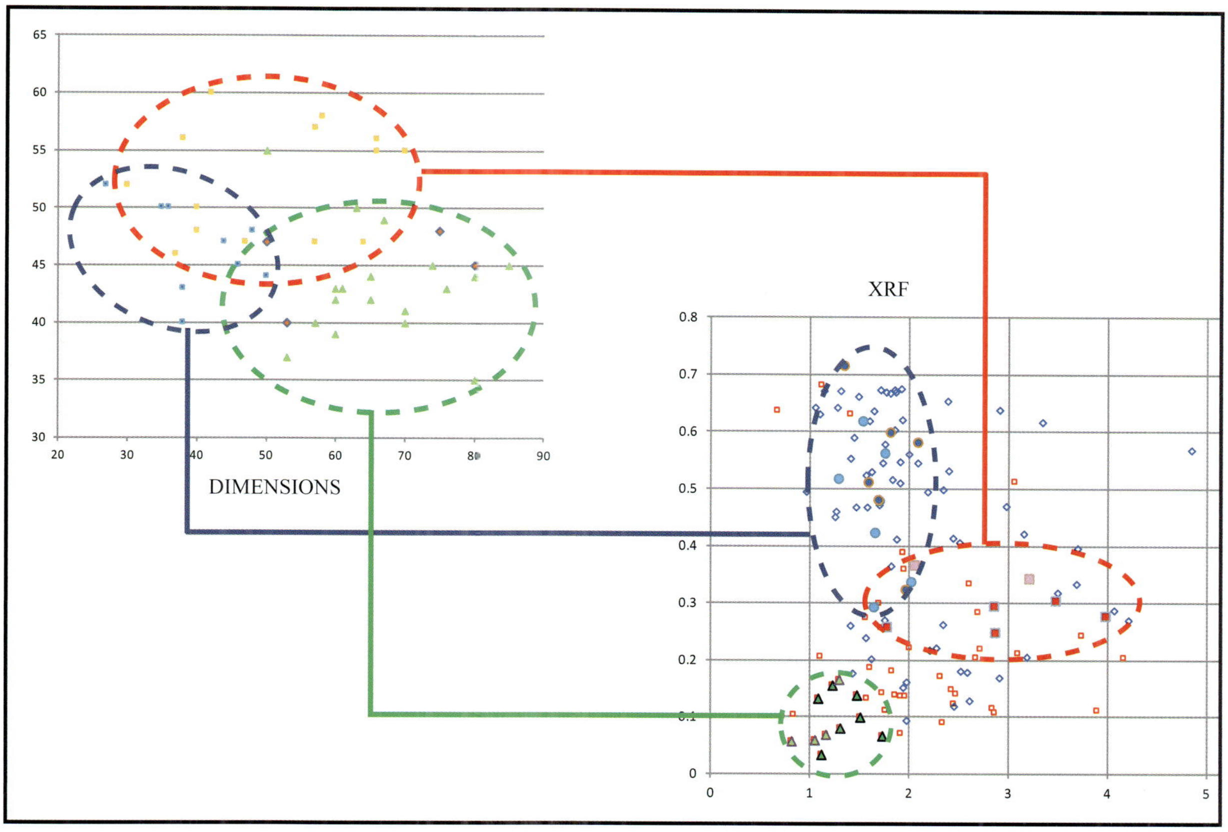

Fig. 13.3.10 Correspondence of Group B dimensional data with pXRF data

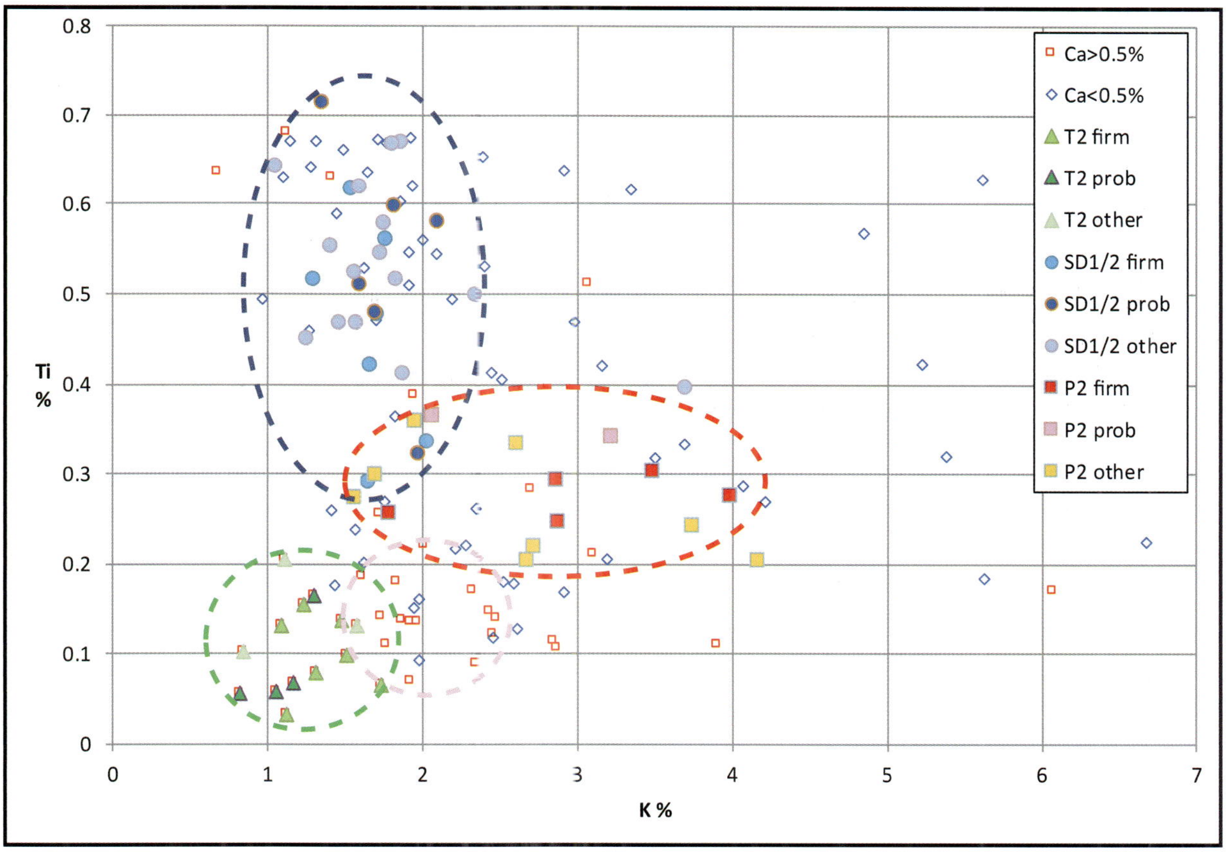

Fig. 13.3.11 All late 1st to mid 2nd-century AD tiles

Table 13.3.4 SD1/2 distribution. For Exeter site numbers see Chapter 2 this volume. Bold font denotes tiles that met both the pXRF and cutaway dimension criteria

Tile	*RAMM Code*	*Site name*	*Description*	*Context*
122	**450/2005**	**Exeter, Princesshay** (Site 156)	**Gp B *tegula***	**4933**
162	**ACD478**	**Exminster, Milbury Farm**	**Gp B *tegula***	**216**
163	ACD478	Exminster, Milbury Farm	Gp B *tegula*	254
175	530/2006	Plymouth, Woolster Street	*tegula*	
150	**3/2004**	**Pomeroy Wood, Honiton**	**Gp B *tegula***	**3849**
12	120/1975	Seaton, Honeyditches	*teg* diag upper cutaway?	212
13	120/1975	Seaton, Honeyditches	*teg* diag upper cutaway	
14	120/1975	Seaton, Honeyditches	flat tile, square nail hole	186
156	**120/1975**	**Seaton, Honeyditches**	**Gp B *tegula***	**69, 150**
25	OA1265	St David's church (Site 191)	flat tile	105
26	OA1265	St David's church (Site 191)	brick	105
157	OA1265	St David's church (Site 191)	pilaster	118
158	OA1265	St David's church (Site 191)	squiggle signature	105
159	OA1265	St David's church (Site 191)	Gp A *tegula*?	118
160	OA1265	St David's church (Site 191)	Gp B *tegula*	105
161	OA1265	St David's church (Site 191)	Gp B *tegula*	119
35	448/2009	St Loye's College	*tegula* comb signature	2156
130	**448/2009**	**St Loye's College**	**Gp B *tegula*, comb signature**	**2160**
131	448/2009	St Loye's College	squiggle sig	2160
132	448/2009	St Loye's College	brick with hole	2160
133	448/2009	St Loye's College	massive *tegula*	1778
134	**448/2009**	**St Loye's College**	**Gp B *tegula***	**2160**
135	**448/2009**	**St Loye's College**	**Gp B *tegula***	**2160**
136	448/2009	St Loye's College	squiggle signature	2160
140	35/1990	Overland, in Thorverton	Gp B *tegula*?	T22/XA1/18
15	30/1993	Bolham, in Tiverton	*tegula*	TV86LY
172	30/1993	Bolham, in Tiverton	Gp B *tegula*?	11,7
191	30/1993	Bolham, in Tiverton	*tegula*	TV86ML

church and St Loye's College data which are represented by seven and eight tiles respectively and which comprise half of all of the tiles in the SD1/2 distribution. It includes all of the St David's church tiles and all but two of the St Loye's College ones, the missing ones being the 1st-century AD face antefix (which had presumably been curated) and an isolated example of Exeter Fabric 3. If, with these two exceptions, all of the tiles came from the same source then we would expect the St David's church and St Loye's College tiles to be randomly distributed throughout the SD1/2 grouping. This is precisely what is shown in Fig. 13.3.12 which supports the idea that both sets of tiles were supplied from a single source that had a wide range of titanium values. This is reinforced by the observation that tiles with highly distinctive squiggle signatures have been found at both St Loye's College and St David's church. As will be discussed later, the kiln could have been in operation for a hundred years from *c*. AD 80–180 so it would not be surprising if over this time that there was more variation in the clay that was exploited than in less long-lived kilns.

Turning to the other tiles in the SD1/2 distribution listed in Table 13.3.4, the evidence for the Plymouth tile rests mainly on the pXRF results and is therefore weaker than the other associations. Tile 122 from Princesshay, which fits both the pXRF and dimensional plots, is the only tile from the SD1/2 source that has been recorded from within the later town defences of Exeter, although it came from a late 3rd-century AD context and may have entered the city as hardcore (consistent with similar imports from Topsham around the same time). The colour of the tiles in the SD1/2 grouping varied from bright orange (St David's church) to a dull almost greyish orange (Honeyditches, in Seaton): this may well have been caused by the different ground conditions in which the tiles had been buried but, if so, then it does not appear to have impacted the potassium, titanium and calcium concentrations in these tiles.

Next is the T2 grouping which is outlined in green on the pXRF plot (Fig. 13.3.11) with the individual tiles being listed in Table 13.3.5. As for the SD1/2 distribution, additional tiles that can be associated with this

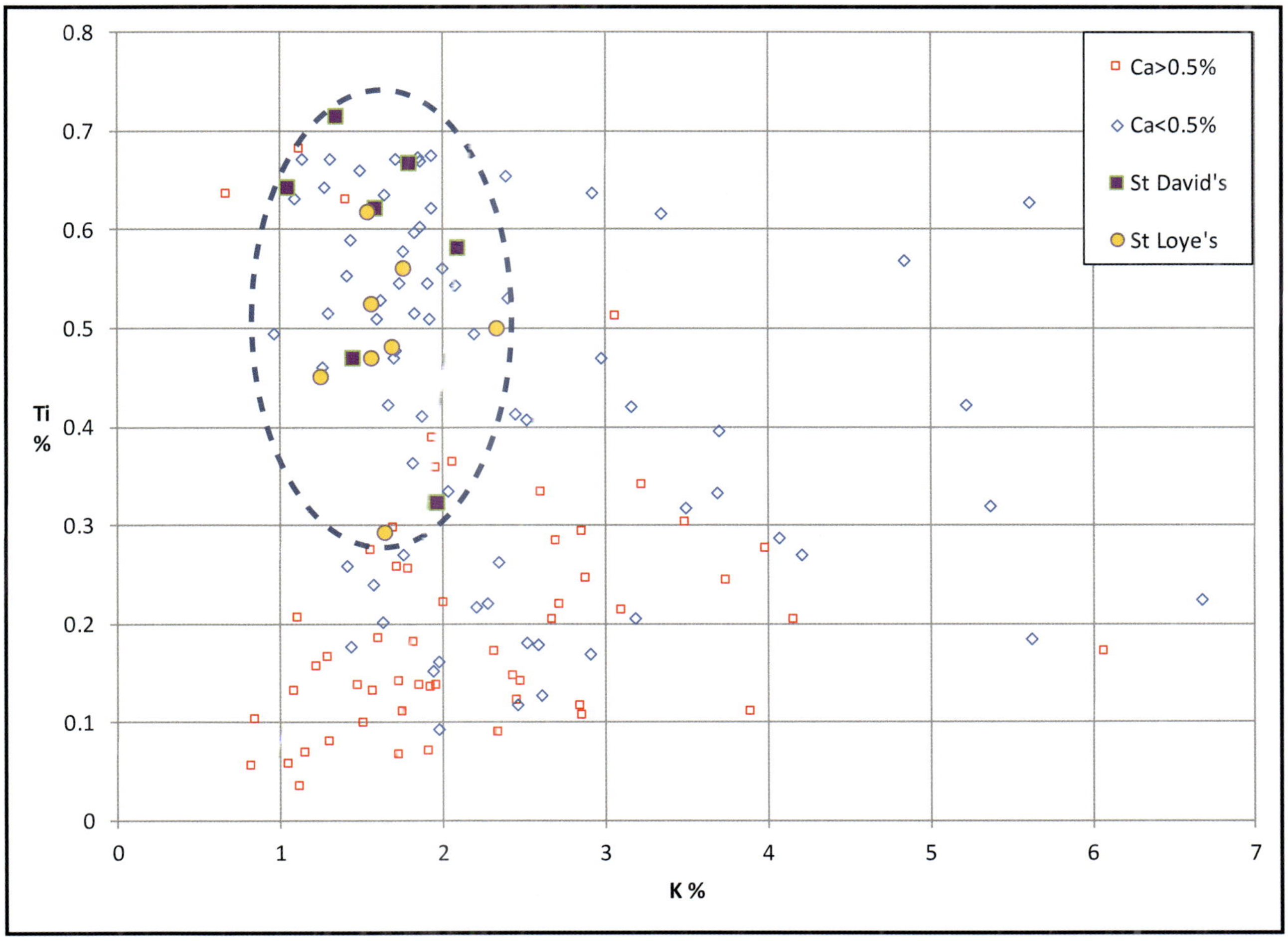

Fig. 13.3.12 Comparison of St David's church and St Loye's College tiles within the SD1/2 distribution

Table 13.3.5 T2 2nd-century AD distribution. For Exeter site numbers see Chapter 2 this volume. Bold font denotes tiles that met both the pXRF and cutaway dimension criteria

Tile	*RAMM Code*	*Site name*	*Description*	*Context*
144	**269/1990**	**Newenham Abbey, in Axminster**	**Gp B *tegula***	
37	45/2005	Exeter	Exeter Fabric 4	1357
102	**24/2005**	**Exeter, Cathedral Close WM** (Site 40)	**Gp B *tegula***	**PP**
116	24/2005	Exeter, Cathedral Close WM (Site 40)	Gp B *tegula*? Buff fabric	INT22NN
33	**88/2005**	**Exeter, Catherine Almshouses** (Site 89)	**Gp B *tegula***	**919**
34	20/2005	Exeter, Exe Street (Site 83)	*tegula*	
115	31/2005	Exeter, Holloway Street (Sites 50/65)	Gp B *tegula*? Buff fabric	F72-1
30	**450/2005**	**Exeter, Princesshay** (Site 156)	**Gp B *tegula***	**2660**
114	9/2005	Exeter, Rack Street (Site 52, Chapter 8 this volume)	Gp B *tegula*? Buff fabric	KZ
179	**51/2005**	**Exeter, Trichay Street** (Site 42, Chapter 5 this volume)	**Gp B *tegula***	**TS72AYJ**
23	ACD1360	Wessex Close, in Topsham	*tegula*	497
24	**ACD1360**	**Wessex Close, in Topsham**	**Gp B *tegula***	**497**
170	ACD1360	Wessex Close, in Topsham	flue tile	1300
171	**ACD1123**	**Wessex Close, in Topsham**	**Gp B *tegula***	**443**

grouping have been added as possibles whilst the firm tiles that feature in the cutaway dimension grouping (Fig. 13.3.8) and pXRF plot are listed in bold. These tiles produce an extremely tight pXRF grouping that just intersects with the 1st-century AD P1 grouping outlined in pink. With the exception of the tiles within the intersection, there are no unexplained calcium-rich tiles in this grouping. The grouping includes nine tiles from Exeter, seven of which have previously been identified as the buff coloured Exeter Fabric 4 and two (Tiles 102 and 179) which had not because they were not noticeably buff coloured. Exeter Fabric 4 is normally found in Exeter in late 3rd or 4th-century AD contexts so, as these tiles have 2nd-century AD cutaways, they presumably represent recycled material. There was also a single example from the medieval Newenham Abbey that had a similar rounded flange to those found on Group B *tegulae* at Topsham which presumably also arrived as hardcore in either the Roman or medieval period.

The final 2nd-century AD grouping is the calcium-rich tiles bounded in red on both the dimensional and pXRF analysis (Figs 13.3.8 and 13.3.11) as listed in Table 13.3.6. Of the four calcium-rich tiles that are not highlighted within the red ellipse on the pXRF plot, two belong to the 1st-century AD P1, one to the later 2nd-century AD P2-late distribution, and one is unallocated. Tile 112 from St Catherine's Almshouses, in Exeter, was provisionally judged to have a Group D cutaway which when damaged can appear similar to a Group B cutaway, but this tile sits better in this 2nd-century AD distribution. The Newenham Abbey, in Axminster, material was almost certainly hardcore from elsewhere introduced during the construction of the medieval abbey (Allan and Silvester 1981, 169). Like the SD1/2 grouping, the red ellipse is quite long but it broadly equates to plus or minus two potassium standard deviations and therefore just falls within the bounds of probability.

Later 2nd to mid 3rd century AD

Turning next to the late 2nd to mid 3rd-century AD period identified by the Group C *tegula* cutaway, the dimensional data as shown in Fig. 13.3.13 are less easily interpreted as most of the distributions overlap so alternative interpretations to the ones offered below are clearly possible. There is just one distinct grouping demarcated in red consisting exclusively of Princesshay tiles and this is matched by the calcium-rich P2-late grouping also defined in red on the pXRF plot (Fig. 13.3.14). A new, calcium-light, source (C2/3) also contains Exeter tiles and is represented by the tiles encircled by the black ellipses on Figs 13.3.13 and 13.3.14. Table 13.3.7 lists the constituents of the P2-late grouping using the system of bold lettering for tiles present in both the dimensional and pXRF plots and Table 13.3.8 lists the constituents of the C2/3 source. In addition to supplying Exeter, the C2/3 source probably also supplied Overland, in Thorverton, Otterton Point, Exmouth St Margaret's and Wessex Close, in Topsham, all located in the neighbourhood of Exeter, as well as Dainton Elms Cross, in Ipplepen, to the south. It contains both the tested examples of Exeter Fabric 3.

Table 13.3.6 P2 2nd-century AD distribution. For Exeter site numbers see Chapter 2 this volume. Bold font denotes tiles that met both the pXRF and cutaway dimension criteria

Tile	*Code*	*Site name*	*Description*	*Context*
16	269/1990	Newenham Abbey, in Axminster	*Tegula*	new 77
145	269/1990	Newenham Abbey, in Axminster	Gp B *tegula*	
108	**9/2007**	**Exeter, Cathedral Close** (Site 40)	**Gp B *tegula***	**540**
31	88/2005	Exeter, Catherine's Almshouses (Site 89)	Gp B *tegula*?	1112
112	88/2005	Exeter, Catherine's Almshouses (Site 89)	Gp D *tegula*?	1119
104	**3/2005**	**Exeter, Friernhay Street** (Site 75)	**Gp B *tegula***	**F339**
105	**3/2005**	**Exeter, Friernhay Street** (Site 75)	**Gp B *tegula***	**915-5**
103	3/2005	Exeter, Friernhay Street (Site 75)	column	799
29	450/2005	Exeter, Princesshay (Site 156)	flat tile	6915
119	450/2005	Exeter, Princesshay (Site 156)	flue voussoir	6852
120	450/2005	Exeter, Princesshay (Site 156)	waster	2883
121	450/2005	Exeter, Princesshay (Site 156)	brick with hole	2883
185	450/2005	Exeter, Princesshay (Site 156)	Princesshay Fabric 1F	6883
137	**9/2005**	**Exeter, Rack Street** (Site 52)	**Gp B *tegula***	**1289**
180	**51/2005**	**Exeter, Trichay Street** (Site 42)	**Gp B *tegula***	**TS72BDW**

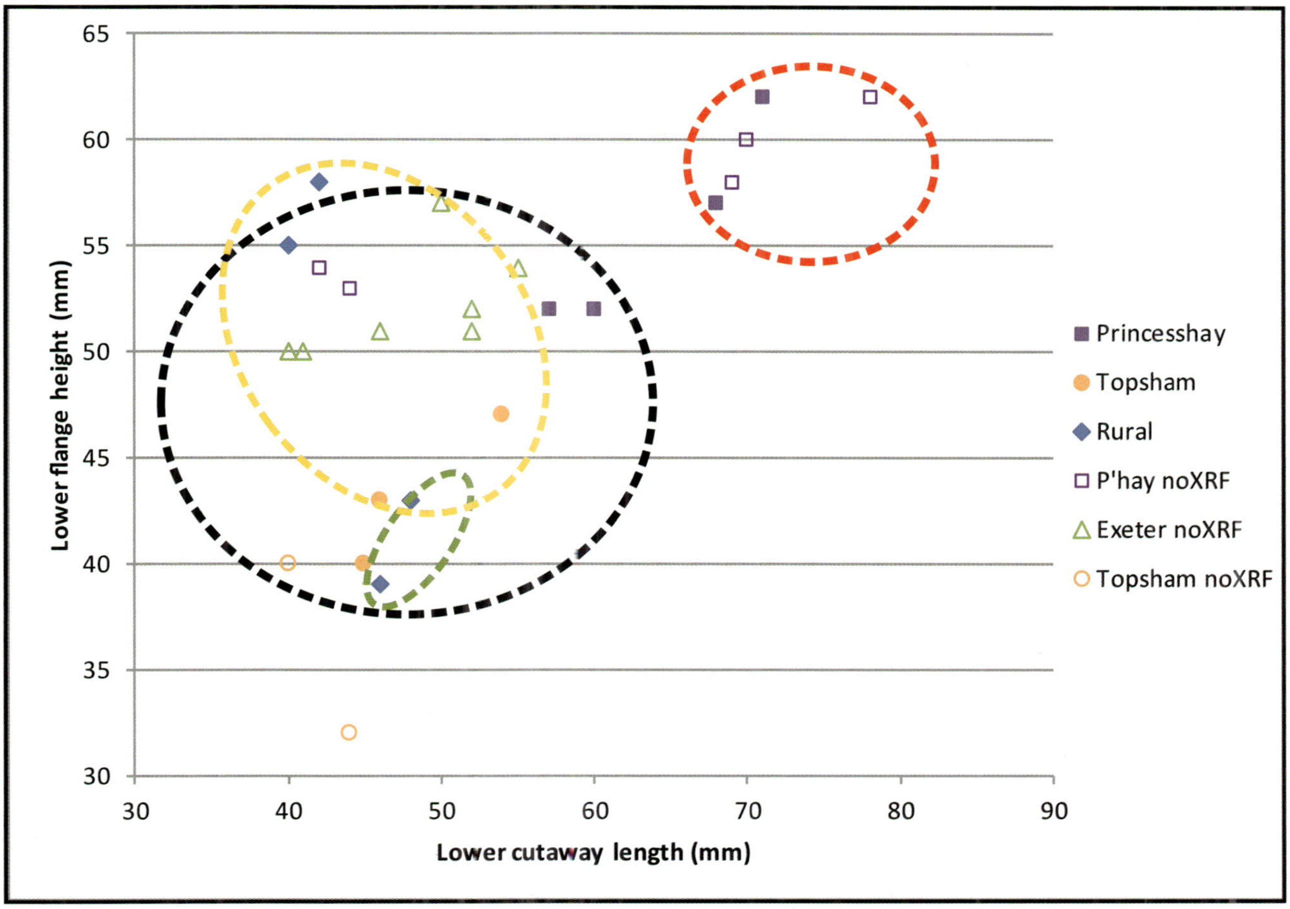

Fig. 13.3.13 Late 2nd to mid 3rd-century AD tegula *dimensions*

The remaining two groupings are also calcium-light. The E2/3 distribution is identified by the green ellipses that encompassed just two very similar *tegulae* on the dimensional plot which translated into a much more dispersed grouping on the pXRF plot. These tiles are listed in Table 13.3.9. Most of these tiles come from a compact area in the east of the county which adds credibility to the grouping. The exception is Dainton Elms Cross, in Ipplepen, in the south of the county that lay on a major Roman road that appears to have headed towards Exeter, and whose pottery and other material culture indicates was a small roadside settlement with likely economic links with the *civitas* capital (EAPIT 1, Chapter 3).

The final S2/3 distribution defined by the yellow ellipses is listed in Table 13.3.10 and only contains tiles from Aller Cross, in Kingskerswell, and Topsham. The Aller Cross assemblage was unusual, *inter alia*, being dominated by *imbrices*, so it is possible it may have been recycled material delivered from another site. The pXRF distribution shown on Fig. 13.3.14 is almost identical to that for the SD1/2 distribution and the cutaway dimensions are also similar, albeit they were Group C rather than Group B cutaways: it is therefore conceivable that this grouping is a continuation of the SD1/2 kiln.

Later 3rd/4th century AD

Late tiles can be recognised either by the cutaway form or by the new method of inverted manufacture that some tileries had adopted which, *inter alia*, produced smooth undersides and squarer flanges (Warry 2013, 149). There were only six *tegulae* with late cutaways and only two of these were measurable, with the result that significant reliance has to be placed on the identification of tiles as being made by inverted manufacture which can be difficult when only a small portion of the original tile can be examined. Tiles that appear to be inverted manufacture or have late cutaways are identified as 'firm' in the pXRF plot Fig. 13.3.15 and listed in bold on Tables 13.3.11 and 13.3.12. Tiles missing the identifying late characteristics but from sites where other tiles with late characteristics were present have been shown as 'probables'. This produces two groupings of calcium-light tiles: the one with low potassium (H3/4)

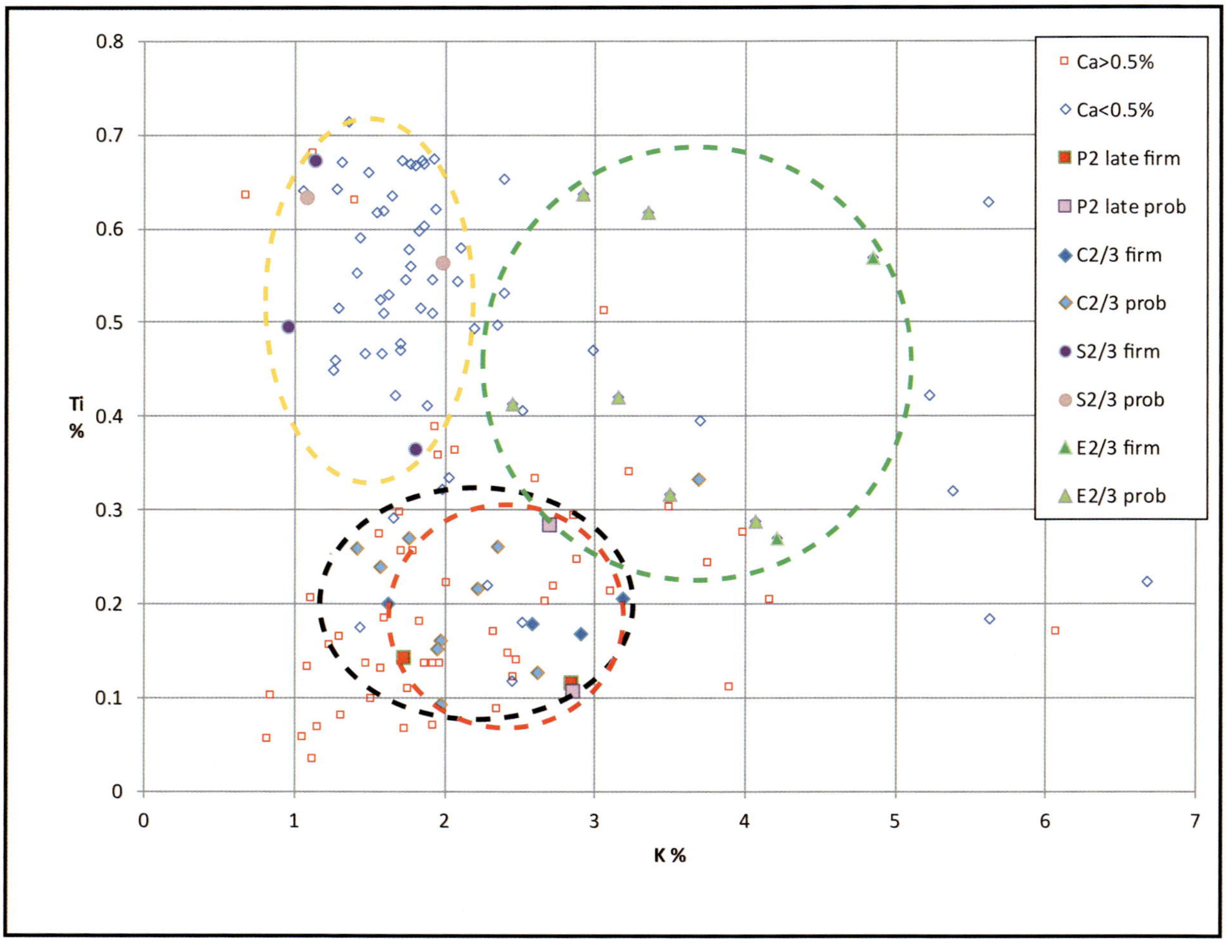

Fig. 13.3.14 Late 2nd to mid 3rd-century AD pXRF groupings

Table 13.3.7 P2-late calcium-rich distribution grouping. For Exeter site numbers see Chapter 2 this volume. Bold font denotes tiles that met both the pXRF and cutaway dimension criteria

Tile	*Code*	*Site name*	*Description*	*Context*
123	**450/2005**	**Exeter, Princesshay** (Site 156)	**Gp C *tegula***	**3583**
124	**450/2005**	**Exeter, Princesshay** (Site 156)	**Gp C *tegula***	**585**
107	9/2007	Exeter, Cathedral Close (Site 40)	Gp C *tegula*	540
113	88/2005	Exeter, Catherine Almshouses (Site 89)	Gp C *tegula?*	1115

Table 13.3.8 Late 2nd to mid 3rd-century AD C2/3 calcium-light distribution. For Exeter site numbers see Chapter 2 this volume. Bold font denotes tiles that met both the pXRF and cutaway dimension criteria

Tile	*Code*	*Site name*	*Description*	*Context*
109	9/2007	Exeter, Cathedral Close (Site 40)	Gp C *tegula*	540
125	**450/2005**	**Exeter, Princesshay** (Site 156)	**Gp C *tegula***	**4636**
126	450/2005	Exeter, Princesshay (Site 156)	flue tile	3717
127	**450/2005**	**Exeter, Princesshay** (Site 156)	**Gp C *tegula***	**6852**
183	450/2005	Exeter, Princesshay (Site 156)	Princesshay Fabric 2FB	4627
186	450/2005	Exeter, Princesshay (Site 156)	Princesshay Fabric 2F	700
3	277/1990	Exmouth, St Margaret's	flat tile	
47	452/2007	Dainton Elms Cross, in Ipplepen	tile	604
39	**839/1989**	**Otterton Point, in Otterton**	**Gp C *tegula***	**36**
28	448/2009	St Loye's College	UC *tegula* Fabric 3?	2160
139	35/1990	Overland, in Thorverton	Gp C *tegula*	T22/346
168	**ACD1123**	**Wessex Close, in Topsham**	**Gp C *tegula***	**397**
176	EAR4	Exeter Bartholomew Street East (Site 73)	Exeter Fabric 1	BSE80
178	EAR4	Exeter Fabric Collection	Exeter Fabric 3	805

Table 13.3.9 Late 2nd to mid 3rd-century AD E2/3 distribution. Bold font denotes tiles that met both the pXRF and cutaway dimension criteria

Tile	*Code*	*Site name*	*Description*	*Context*
118	**88/2009**	**Woodbury, in Axminster**	**Gp C *tegula***	**u/s**
9	276/1990	Chardstock	only *tegula*	
146	276/1990	Chardstock	flue tile	
46	ACD1307	Dainton Elms Cross, in Ipplepen	flat tile	105
181	MEMCT13	Membury	Gp C *tegula*?	108
2	3/2004	Pomeroy Wood, in Honiton	flat tile	
151	3/2004	Pomeroy Wood, in Honiton	flue tile	3344
152	**3/2004**	**Pomeroy Wood, in Honiton**	**Gp C *tegula***	**733**

Table 13.3.10 Late 2nd to mid 3rd-century AD S2/3 distribution. Bold font denotes tiles that met both the pXRF and cutaway dimension criteria

Tile	*Code*	*Site name*	*Description*	*Context*
20	ACD570	Aller Cross, in Kingskerswell	flat tile	1095
21	ACD570	Aller Cross, in Kingskerswell	flat tile	144
110	**ACD570**	**Aller Cross, in Kingskerswell**	**Gp C *tegula***	**745**
166	**ACD1360**	**Wessex Close, in Topsham**	**Gp C *tegula***	**1353**
167	**ACD1360**	**Wessex Close, in Topsham**	**Gp C *tegula***	**1041**

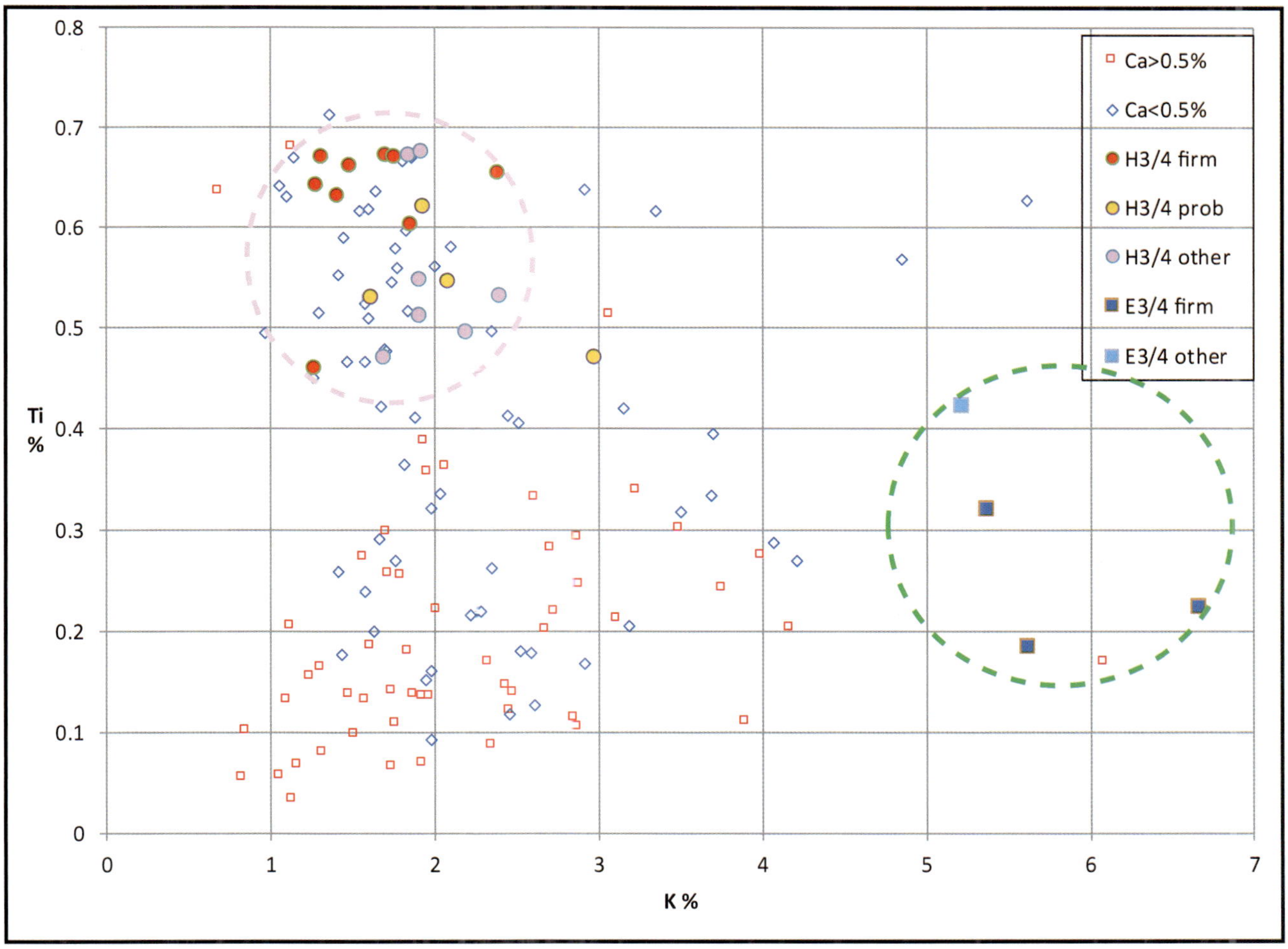

Fig. 13.3.15 pXRF groupings of late tiles

Table 13.3.11 Late H3/4 distribution. For Exeter site numbers see Chapter 2 this volume. Bold font denotes tiles that met both the pXRF and had either later cutaways or were inverted manufacture

Tile	*Code*	*Site name*	*Description*	*Context*
8	**184/2000**	**Ashcombe Barton**	**flat tile, invert mfr**	
17	**88/2009**	**Woodbury, in Axminster**	**Gp D *tegula*?**	**u/s**
10	**244/2003**	**Bury Barton, in Lapford**	**UC *tegula*, invert mfr?**	**T4/F15**
11	244/2003	Bury Barton, in Lapford	flat tile	T12/F15
18	172/1999	Hayes Farm, in Clyst Honiton	*imbrex*	205
32	88/2005	Exeter, St Catherine's Almshouses (Site 89)	thin flat tile	1186
4	**212/2007**	**Hatherleigh Moor, in Hatherleigh**	**UC *tegula*, invert mfr**	**G4**
40	212/2007	Hatherleigh Moor, in Hatherleigh	waster	G4
147	**30/2004**	**Hatherleigh Moor, in Hatherleigh**	**UC *tegula*, invert mfr**	**25**
148	30/2004	Hatherleigh Moor, in Hatherleigh	flue tile	1
153	**35/1943**	**Hatherleigh Moor, in Hatherleigh**	**UC *tegula*, invert mfr**	
154	30/2004	Hatherleigh Moor, in Hatherleigh	waster	14
48	452/2007	Dainton Elms Cross, in Ipplepen	fragment	604
182	MEMCT13	Membury	flue tile	u/s
143	839/1989	Otterton Point, in Otterton	flue tile	35
45		Halberton	flue tile	BF/213/1A
22	**ACD1123**	**Wessex Close, in Topsham**	**Gp R, T7 *tegula***	**105**
164	ACD1123	Wessex Close, in Topsham	gaming board	101
165	**ACD1123**	**Wessex Close, in Topsham**	**Gp R, T7 *tegula***	**141**
169	**ACD1123**	**Wessex Close, in Topsham**	**Gp D *tegula*?**	**539**

Table 13.3.12 Mid 3rd century AD onwards E3/4 distribution. Bold font denotes tiles that met both the pXRF and had either later cutaways or were inverted manufacture

Tile	*Code*	*Site name*	*Description*	*Context*
27	**79/1995**	**Woodbury, in Axminster**	***tegula*, Invert mfr**	**635**
19	172/1999	Hayes Farm, in Clyst Honiton	*tegula*	428
1	**3/2004**	**Pomeroy Wood, in Honiton**	**Gp D *tegula***	**4607**
44		Halberton	**Gp D *tegula*?**	**BF/213/1F**

incorporates all of the tiles from Hatherleigh Moor which was therefore the likely source, whilst the source of the high potassium grouping (E3/4), which consists entirely of tiles found in the east of the county, may be a continuation of the late 2nd to mid 3rd-century AD E2/3 kiln, albeit now accessing clays that were slightly richer in potassium (Topsham Tile 169 is just calcium-rich with 0.53% calcium but it makes sense to include it in the calcium-light H3/4 grouping).

Having defined the groupings, further weak 'possible' tiles have been added to the Hatherleigh grouping on the grounds that their pXRF signatures match and the sites from which they come are probably late. The outlier from the distribution is Tile 154 which was a waster from Hatherleigh Moor where presumably the more intense firing created a slightly different chemical composition (although another waster from the site, Tile 40, lies within the distribution).

Unallocated tiles

Table 13.3.13 lists the 12 *tegulae* that could not satisfactorily be allocated to any of the above groupings, which are plotted in Fig. 13.3.16. The seven calcium-rich tiles (5, 36, 111, 117, 138, 149 and 155) are spread out across the graph and all but Tile 5 are well distant from the P1, P2, P2-late and T2 calcium-rich groupings. In principle they could signify four further sources of tile but this is unlikely, especially as they would each be represented by a single tile. Four of these tiles are flue-tiles so it is possible they may have suffered chemical contamination from the smoke that will have permeated the flue system or that the fabric used for flue-tiles differed from that used for roof tiles. The five calcium-light tiles, four of which come from former military sites, are also widely separated and could possibly represent a further four kiln sources unless chemical leaching has masked the original composition of the tiles.

Table 13.3.13 Unallocated tiles. For Exeter site numbers see Chapter 2 this volume

Tile	*Code*	*Site name*	*Description*	*Context*
5	284/1989	Holcombe Villa	flat tile, square nail hole	
6	524/2006	Okehampton Fort	only fragment retained	
7	524/2006	Okehampton Castle	UC *teg*, only fragment	
36	24/2005	Exeter, Cathedral Close (Site 40)	pentagonal tile	Mid 4C
49	ACD 670	North Tawton	flat tile	191
106	190/2010	Cullompton	*imbrex*	538
111	88/2005	Exeter St Catherine's Almshouses (Site 89)	flue tile	919
117	88/2009	Woodbury, Axminster	flue tile	905
138	40/1989	North Tawton	*tegula*	3
141	272/1990	Crediton Villa	*tegula*	
149	284/1989	Holcombe Villa	flue tile	
155	120/1975	Honeyditches, in Seaton	flue tile	67

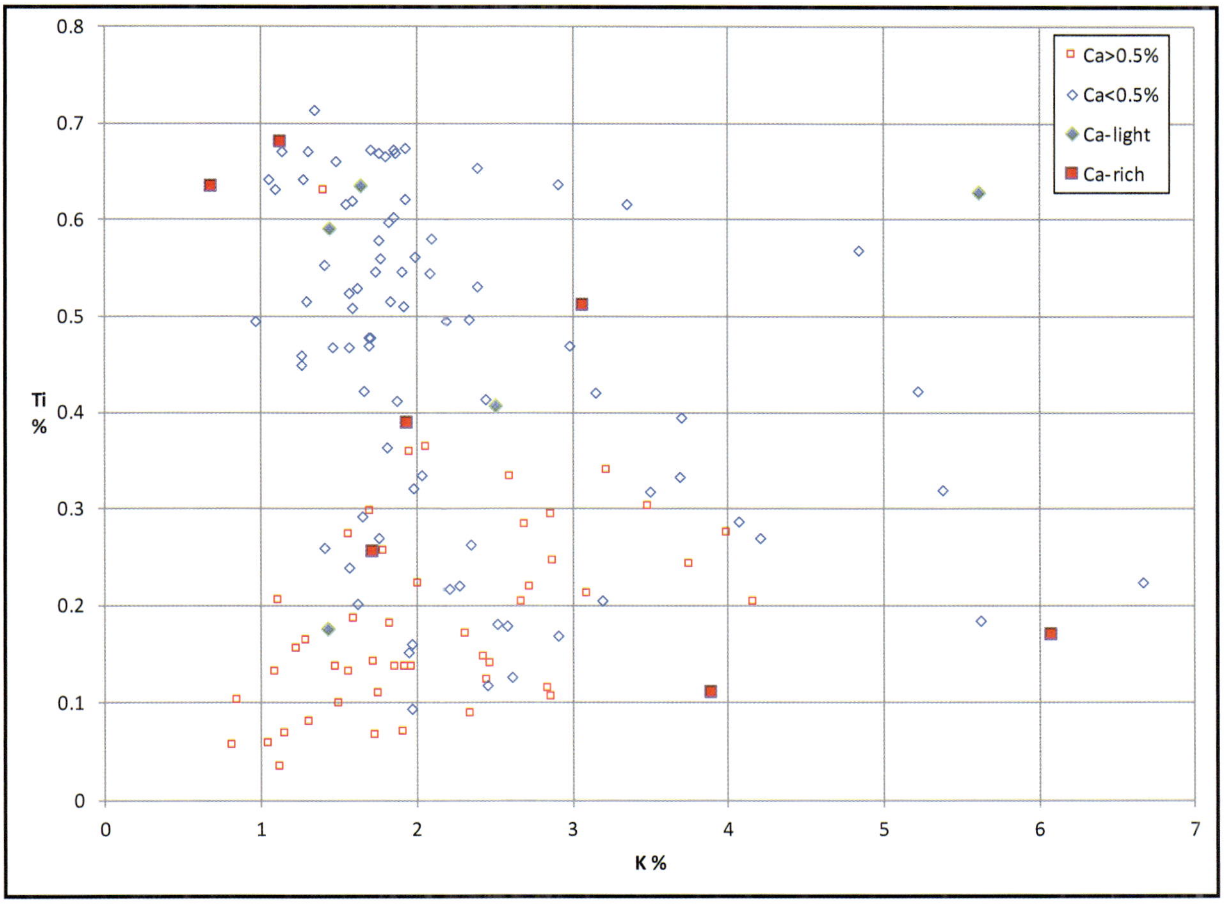

Fig. 13.3.16 Unallocated tiles

Verification using PCA and thin sections

Overall results and application of PCA

This section takes the groupings identified through tile morphology and pXRF bi-plots in the section on 'Tile Morphology and Bi-Plot Analysis' above and checks them firstly against the evidence from PCA and then tests the key conclusions against the results of the thin section petrography.

In designing a PCA there is a trade-off between the number of elements used and the clarity of results obtained: too few elements and useful information will be omitted, too many elements, especially non-diagnostic elements, and definition will be lost as it becomes harder for the PCA to adequately represent all of the elements in a two-dimensional plot. As Michelaki and Hancock (2011, 1273) comment 'the addition of more diagnostic elements can mask the presence of distinct chemical groups'. One measure of this can be gleaned from the proportion of the variation in the readings that is explained by the pair of principal components that have been plotted. With our dataset a PCA of all 21 elements using the first and second principal components explained only 25% of the variation, whilst a PCA using eight elements explained 50% and with six elements 64% was explained. In practice eight elements appeared to give the best definition and also coincided with the number of elements that were present in all of the samples. For this next section of PCA analysis, however, only six elements will be used in order to provide an extra degree of independence by removing one of the coordinates used in the potassium vs titanium bi-plots above. As potassium is known to be susceptible to leaching it was chosen to be the key element omitted, while Manganese tends to give erratic readings so was the second element to be omitted. Calcium is also highly mobile and susceptible to both leaching and accretion but was retained in the PCA analysis because of the very strong differentiation between intra-mural and extra-mural sites shown in Fig. 13.3.5.

Figure 13.3.17 shows how these distributions look when converted onto a six element PCA chart. The chart is a bit busy for easy interpretation but the crucial observation is how the different coloured points, which equate to the distributions identified in the section on 'Tile Morphology and Bi-Plot Analysis' above, create satisfactory and, in the main, distinct groups in the PCA analysis. The very tight T2 distribution in Fig. 13.3.11 is more spread out but still clearly distinct, while some of the previously overlapping groupings are now distinct although the SD1/2 and H3/4 distributions still overlap to a significant extent. All of these groupings are examined in more detail in the following sub-sections using exactly the same six-element PCA plot (and same tiles) as shown in Fig 13.2.17 but with different areas highlighted for discussion.

Princesshay kiln

The PCA plot, Fig. 13.3.18, picks out the three calcium-rich distributions P1, P2 and P2-late that consisted almost entirely of tiles found in Exeter. Collectively these appear to represent a reasonably coherent grouping with few

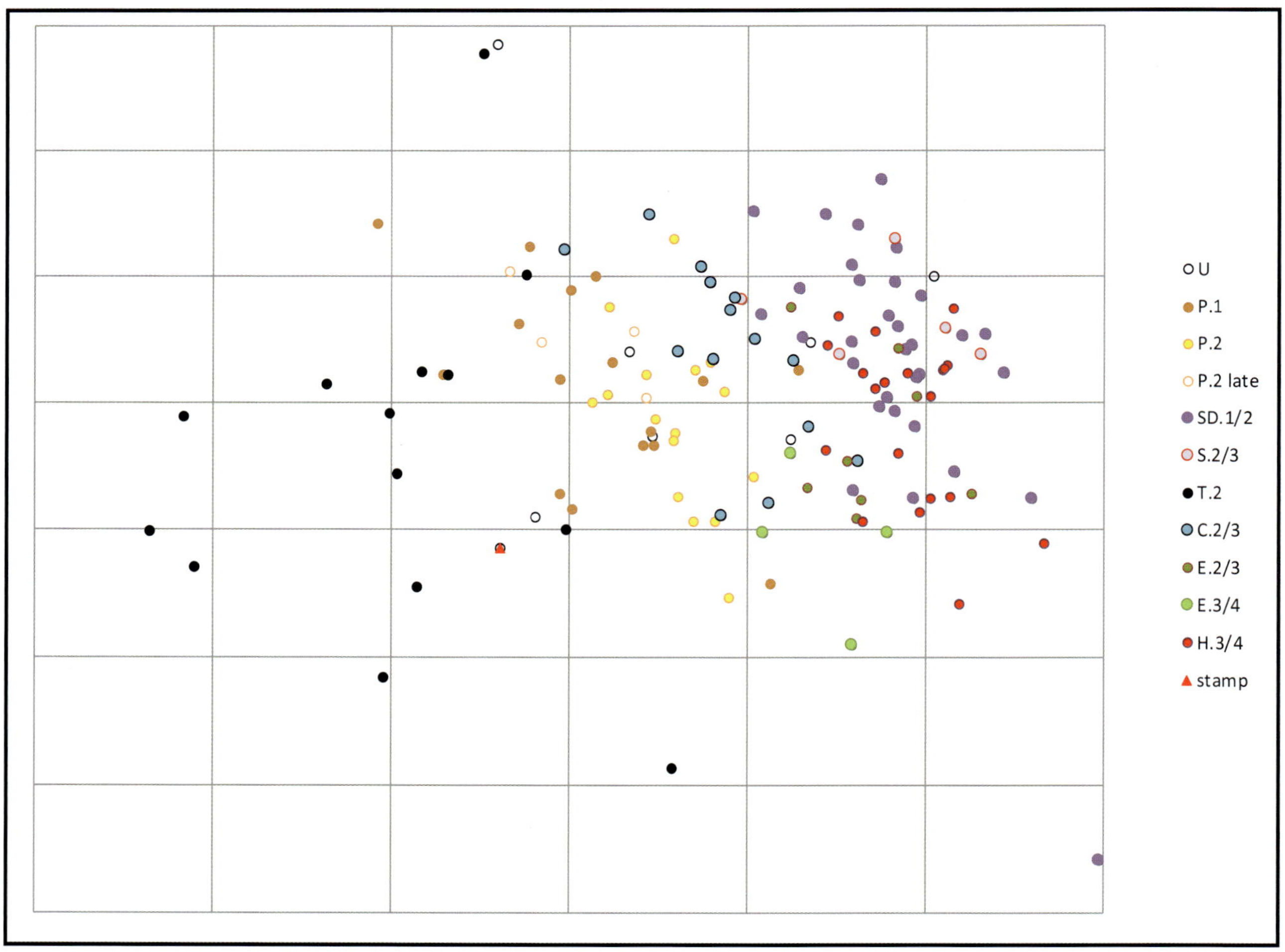

Fig. 13.3.17 Six-element PCA analysis showing groupings identified in the section 'Tile Morphology and Bi-Plot Analysis' above

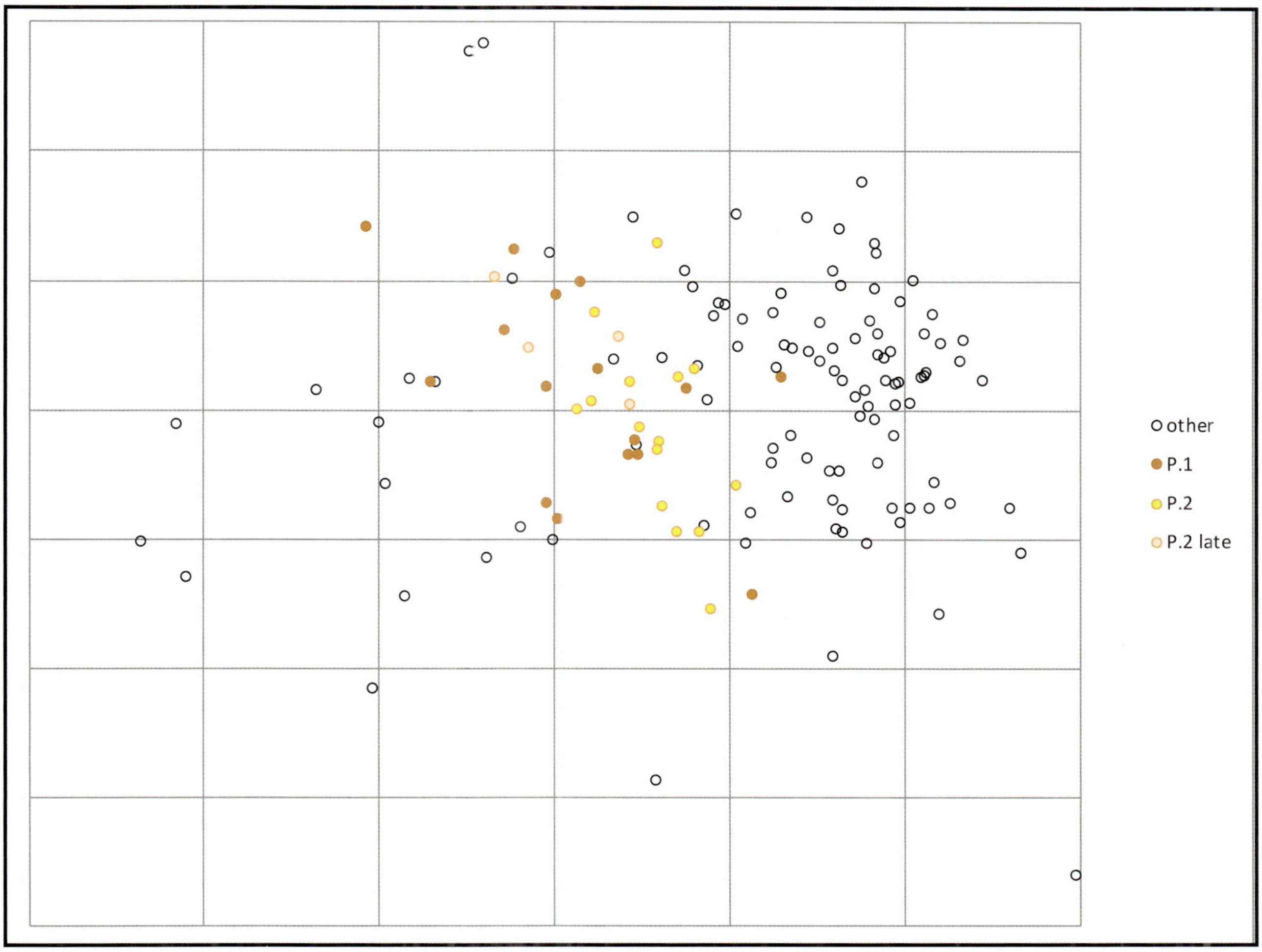

Fig. 13.3.18 Six-element PCA plot for Exeter calcium-rich tiles

inclusions into the distribution from other sources. It seems likely that all of these tiles, which represent over 100 years of production, could have exploited the same clay albeit with small changes as successive areas of the clay seam were exhausted. As almost all of the tiles were found in Exeter, the most likely production centre for the 2nd-century AD tiles must be Princesshay and in the absence of other arguments, this general area north-east of the town may also be the production centre for the legionary tiles.

At Gloucester, where the legionary fortress was followed by a *colonia* within the same walls, the legionary tilery (as evidenced by the presence there of 1st-century AD military-style tiles: Warry 2017, 79) was passed over to the civil authorities who continued production in the same facility. Without any good reason for the contrary, it would be peculiar if the legionary tilery at Exeter did not also pass into the hands of the Exeter civil authorities once the legion departed which also appears to be paralleled by the continuity of certain pottery styles (Chapter 12 above). The Princessshay kiln site lies immediately outside the legionary fortress, and while the excavator's interpretation is of a 2nd-century AD date as there were no tile wasters recovered from military-period deposits (Steinmetzer, Stead, Pearce, Bidwell and Allan forthcoming), it is likely that this general area north-east of the town was also the location of the original legionary tilery (as postulated by Bidwell 1979, 148 and Holbrook 2015, 99) for a number of reasons. The Princesshay site was heavily truncated by later activity, making it quite possible that other kilns have been destroyed (or lie outside the excavated area). If, instead, the Princesshay tilery was indeed newly established by the civic authorities then it would imply that the investment in the original legionary tilery and its infrastructure was simply abandoned as there is no evidence for the legionary tilery supplying tiles outside of Exeter at any stage, and therefore nowhere else for any subsequent legionary kiln production to go. Furthermore, in this scenario, the continuing existence of a redundant legionary tilery would make the foundation of the St David's church kiln, probably constructed when the legion left and as a result of its departure (as will be discussed in the section on the 'Military to Civil Transition' below), even more difficult to explain. Unless another kiln accessing the same calcium-rich clays is found in the Exeter area then it must be probable that the general area north-east of the town including Princesshay also encompassed the legionary tilery. This would mean that the tileries were in operation for in excess of 100 years leading to the relatively wide range of pXRF results. However, the three phases of production as denoted by the different coloured points do form sub-groupings of their own, presumably reflecting changes in the clay seam as it was exploited. The codes P1, P2 and P2-late denote that the source of the tiles is the general (Princesshay) area north-east of the town and the tiles were produced in the 1st, 2nd and late 2nd century AD respectively.

Prior to the construction of the new town defences *c.* AD 160–80, tile supply into Exeter seems to have been exclusively from the Princesshay general area: there is a single example of the SD1/2 fabric found in a 3rd-century AD context and a number in T2 fabric, recognised as Exeter Fabric 4, which come from late 3rd or 4th-century AD contexts, but all of these tiles will probably have been recycled from elsewhere. The destination of the output of the St David's kiln, which does not appear to have been into Exeter, is discussed in the section on the 'Military to Civil Transition' below. The 2nd-century AD Gloucester (and also probably Cirencester) civic authorities seem to have exercised a monopoly such that only tiles from the municipal kilns could be used within those towns (Warry 2017, 103–4) and it appears likely the Exeter *ordo* must have operated a similar rule. The two Princesshay fabric tiles found at Newenham Abbey were most likely later dispersions of hardcore as discussed in the results for the 'Later 1st to mid-2nd century AD' above.

Dolphin antefixes and consideration of leaching effects

Included in the Princesshay 1st-century AD tiles were three dolphin antefixes. All of these fitted within the very tight P1 distribution shown in Fig. 13.3.7 but Tiles 192 and 211 were calcium-light (as was Tile 210, a face antefix) whilst Tile 212 was calcium-rich like all of the other tiles in the P1 distribution. Potentially this could bring the attribution of these antefixes to the legionary kiln into doubt, especially as dolphin antefixes were produced from the same mould after the legion moved to Caerleon

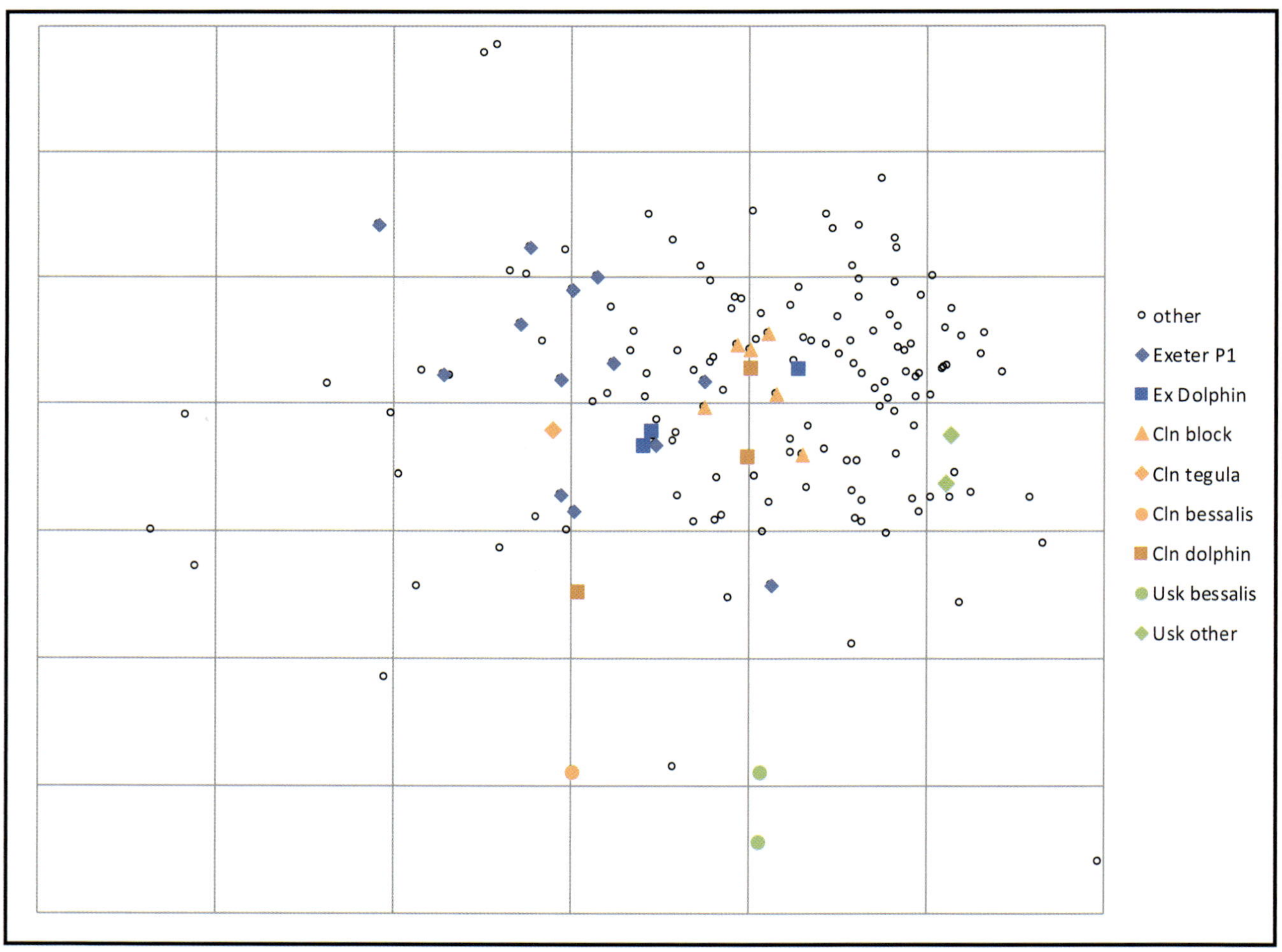

Fig. 13.3.19 Six-element PCA of military tiles from Exeter, Caerleon and Usk

(Bidwell and Boon 1976). Figure 13.3.19 adds a selection of military tiles from Caerleon and Usk to our existing Exeter and Devon data and highlights the 1st-century AD 'Princesshay' tiles as blue diamonds (research in collaboration with Dr Mark Lewis, Senior Curator, National Roman Legion Museum, Wales). The three Exeter dolphin antefixes are shown as blue squares; two of them – Tile 192 (calcium-light) and Tile 212 (calcium-rich) – fit comfortably within the distribution but the third antefix (Tile 211, calcium-light) is an outlier. Another outlier, the blue diamond at the bottom right of the distribution, is Tile 210, the calcium-light face antefix, which must surely have been made in the legionary kiln at Exeter as well.

The Caerleon tiles are shown in orange and all of these carried legionary stamps with the exception of the three dolphin antefixes (two of which have modern repairs) that are shown as orange squares. Six of the Caerleon tiles had been sawn through in modern times to separate the stamp from the rest of the tile (that was then discarded) which allowed the pXRF measurements to be taken from smooth surfaces on the interior of the tiles. These readings, which should be free of surface contamination and potentially unaffected by leaching, are shown as yellow triangles and referred to as blocks. They form a satisfactorily tight grouping distinct, and slightly offset from, the 1st-century AD 'Princesshay' tiles. Sitting within this grouping is the unrepaired Caerleon dolphin antefix represented by an orange square. The more distant placing of the two repaired Caerleon antefixes may have been caused by the liberal amounts of filler used to repair them contaminating the readings. As a result a good case can be made for the Exeter and Caerleon dolphin antefixes to have been the product of their respective kilns, consistent with the findings of Bidwell and Boon (1976, 279), but with the exception of Tile 211, one of the Exeter antefixes from a 1st-century AD context. This tile is an outlier from the Exeter grouping and fits closely with the Caerleon output based upon six-element PCA (eight-element PCA gives a similar result). However, as the other Exeter dolphin antefixes appear to be Exeter production, it is probably best to treat the fabric of this tile as an aberration.

The tiles recorded from Usk are shown in green. Based upon contextual evidence, two of these were probably made in the original Usk kiln and are the green diamonds on the right of Fig. 13.3.19; one of these was a *tegula mammata* and should therefore be from the Flavian phase of the fort. Two were *bessales* (the flat tiles used to form hypocaust *pilae*) stamped with identical legionary dies and therefore made at Caerleon, which are shown as green circles at the bottom of the chart. Adjacent to the Usk *bessales* is an orange circle representing a *bessalis* with the same legionary die but this time found at Caerleon. The three *bessales*, two from Usk and one from Caerleon, form a clearly distinct group, well away from all the other Caerleon and Usk tiles. This is surprising because the acidity of the soil varies significantly between Usk and Caerleon yet there is no evidence for differential leaching between the Usk and Caerleon *bessales*, nor is there evidence for leaching between the stamp blocks and other tiles found at Caerleon. Why the *bessales* should then form a separate distribution is unclear. Superficially the easiest explanation should be that the *bessales* were contaminated with wood smoke in the hypocaust that will not have affected other types of tiles. However, wood smoke primarily deposits potassium and carbon but neither of these elements have been used in the PCA analysis, so this cannot be the explanation. Alternatively we could hypothesise that a different clay formulation has been used for the manufacture of *bessales*, or was in use during the existence of the die that was used to stamp all of these tiles. These explanations seem somewhat unlikely, but some support for the varying treatment of different types of tiles can be drawn from the observation that the only calcium-light tiles made by the legionary kiln at Exeter that we have identified are the antefixes: two dolphins and one face (tiles 192, 211 and 210). This could suggest that a stiffer clay formulation or finer moulding sand was required for use with the more intricate moulds used for these products.

2nd/early 3rd-century AD sources

Following construction of the new town defences, Exeter supply appears to have switched to the C2/3 fabric from a postulated new 'Central' 2nd/3rd-century AD tilery accessing calcium-light clays probably sited somewhere in South-Central Devon based on the locations of the recipient sites. The PCA plot of this fabric is somewhat diffuse as shown in Fig. 13.3.20 and while it is clearly distinct from the calcium-rich fabrics from the Princesshay area, it is possible that it could represent two separate kiln sources. The C2/3 fabric would appear to be the last source of new tiles used in Exeter because within the next fifty years fashion dictated that the town switched from ceramic to stone/slate roof tiles as discussed in the section on 'Economic and architectural development' below.

All of the tiles from the St David's church excavation fall within the SD1/2 distribution so it is sensible to equate SD1/2 fabric as output of the St David's church kiln. The distribution of sites supplied by St David's church and the function of the tilery is discussed in the section on the 'Military to Civil Transition' section below. The similarity of the PCA distributions of SD1/2 and S2/3 as shown in Fig. 13.3.20 could suggest that the St David's church kiln continued in operation into the 3rd century AD. However, the absence of any Group C *tegulae* within the St David's church assemblage and the continuing absence of its product from Exeter makes this unlikely because surely, once the Princesshay kiln closed, the Exeter authorities would have been prepared to accept the output of a kiln right on their doorstep. So, despite the pXRF correlation, it seems likely that S2/3 represents a new source, postulated as the Southern kiln, accessing similar clays to St David's church.

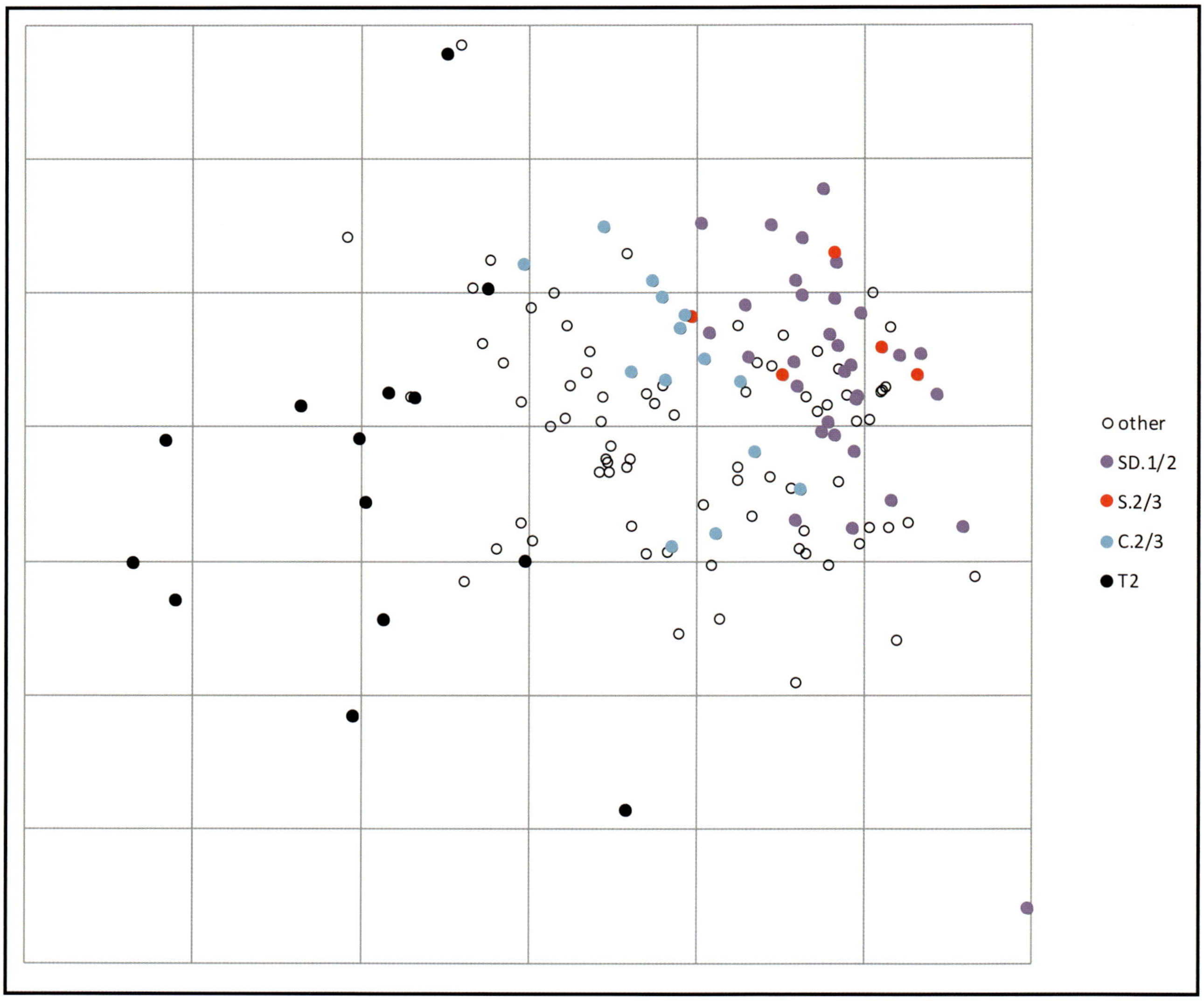

Fig. 13.3.20 Six-element PCA of 2nd-century AD fabric distributions

The third source of 2nd-century AD tiles is the T2 distribution. This appears as a discrete but well spread out grouping on Fig. 13.3.20 and contrasts with the very tight but equally discrete grouping shown on the potasium vs titanium bi-plot (Fig. 13.3.11). The distribution is mainly composed of 2nd-century AD tiles from Wessex Close, in Topsham, and tiles recognised as being in Exeter Fabric 4 which are normally found in late 3rd or 4th-century AD contexts within Exeter. As many of the Exeter examples have 2nd-century AD cutaways, it seems probable that they were transported from Topsham into Exeter as hardcore in the later 3rd century AD after the original 2nd-century AD roofs were dismantled. There is also one example at Newenham Abbey, in Axminster, which must also have arrived there as hardcore, possibly in a secondary move from Exeter. As yet there is no evidence for a tile kiln within Topsham and its port location makes it an ideal place for importing tiles by sea. The absence of good evidence for a contemporaneous distribution of this fabric outside of Topsham, and the fabric only occurring with Group B cutaways when a local kiln might have hoped to have had a longer existence, reinforces importation as the favoured explanation. This would be consistent with the Betts and Foot (1994) suggestion that Exeter Fabric 4 tiles were imported from a postulated Solent source. The T2 tiles have rounded flange tops and scarce finger grooves which match the Betts and Foot description (although other details differ), so it is probable that these tiles are further examples of their calcareous fabric. For convenience these tiles will be referred to as 'Topsham tiles' even though they were most likely imported.

Finally, the E2/3 distribution, which is shown in Fig. 13.3.21, is primarily made up of tiles found in the east of the county is evidence for a new tilery ('Eastern') that was established to supply sites in that area. That kiln also appears to have supplied Dainton Elms Cross, in Ipplepen, in the south utilising trade connections between the areas.

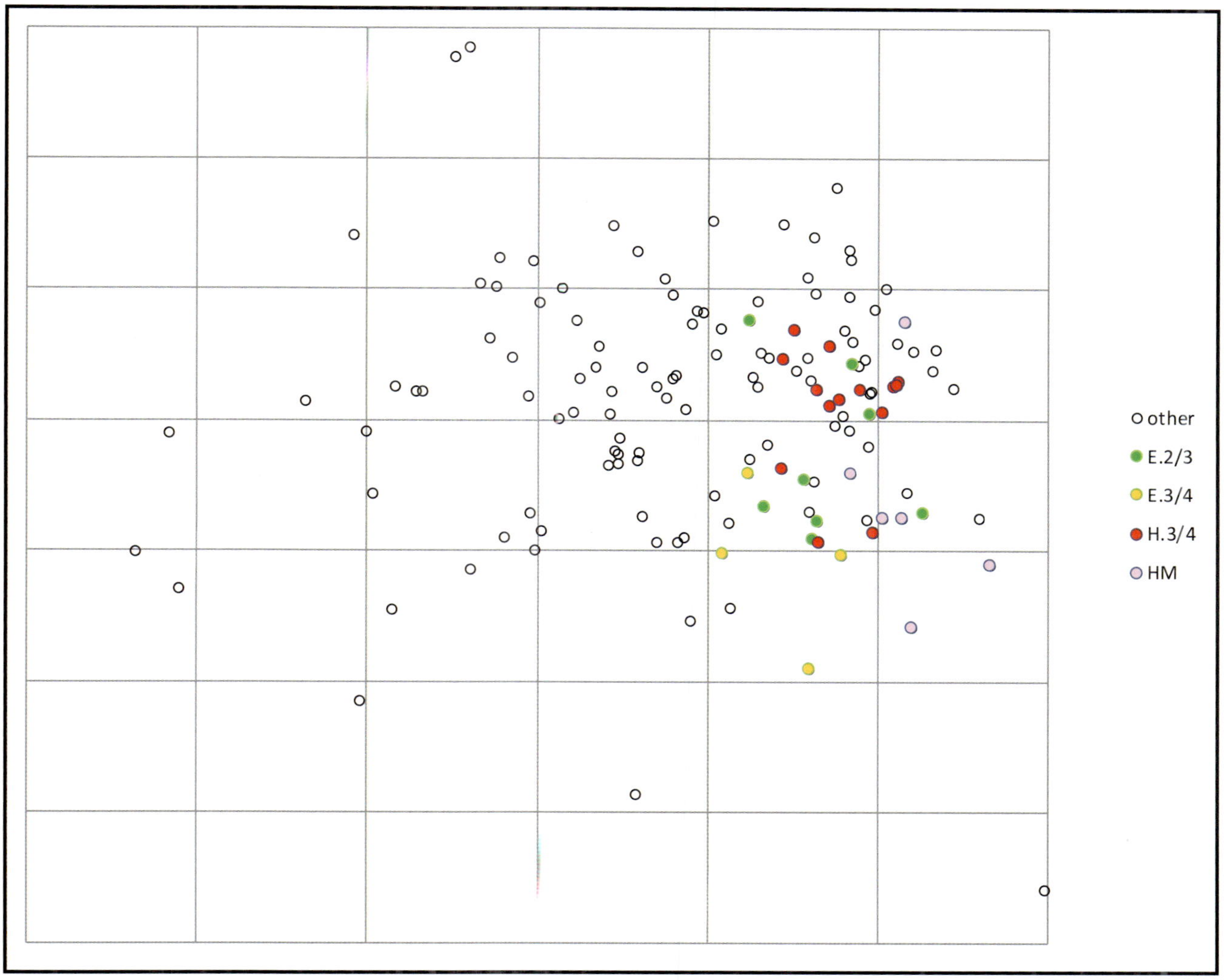

Fig. 13.3.21 Six-element PCA distributions of later tiles

Later sources

By the mid 3rd century AD the Southern and Central kilns appear to have ceased production although the Eastern kiln probably continued to supply its local market for a time as evidenced by the E3/4 distribution shown in Fig. 13.3.21. At roughly the same time a new, somewhat diffuse, H3/4 source appears in the potasium vs titanium plot which includes all of the tiles from Hatherleigh Moor and so may represent the output of that kiln. Figure 13.3.21 shows these tiles in red tones with the pink being tiles found at Hatherleigh Moor itself and the darker red other tiles attributed to the same source. With one exception, all of the Hatherleigh Moor tiles lie at the bottom right of the plot so it is probable that they are, in fact, a separate source, especially given the distance of the kiln from most of its mooted sites. In which case the other (red) tiles have been produced by a different unknown kiln.

Thin section results

Having completed the analysis based upon pXRF and morphology, we now compare those results with thin section petrography. To test the key fabric questions 34 tiles were chosen for analysis. Seven tiles were selected from Exeter to explore the calcium-rich distribution and to check that the calcium-light tiles were indeed different, five were drawn from St David's church and St Loye's College to test their relationship, seven were chosen to examine the diffuse possible late H3/4 grouping, and then smaller numbers to test the other potential groupings. Dr Sara Machin of the University of Reading was commissioned to undertake the thin section analysis of these selected tiles and her summary results are given in Table 13.3.14. She identified 13 different fabric groups hereinafter referred to as M1 to M13. Dr Machin's findings are presented in full in Chapter 13.2 above which also includes some further tiles and one additional fabric (M14) that do not form part of this report.

The calcium-rich tiles identified by pXRF are listed in red in Table 13.3.14 and it can be seen that these closely correlate with Machin's fabric groups: all of the calcium-rich tiles are assigned to her fabrics M2, M4 and M9 and all of the other fabrics are comprised of exclusively

Table 13.3.14 Thin section results (calcium-rich tiles from pXRF shown in red). Warry kiln groups are the kiln groups identified in this and the preceding section

Machin	*Warry kiln group*	*Tile no.*	*Site name*	*Description*
1	SD.1/2	35	St Loye's College	*tegula* comb sig
1	SD.1/2	134	St Loye's College	Gp B *tegula*
2	P.2 late	123	Exeter, Princesshay	Gp C *tegula*
2	P.2	185	Exeter, Princesshay	Princesshay Fab 1F
2	P.2	120	Exeter, Princesshay	waster
2	P.1	38	Exeter, Cathedral Close	Gp A *tegula*
2	P.1	190	Exeter, Cathedral Close	antefix face
2	U	138	North Tawton	*tegula*
2	SD.1/2	160	St David's church	Gp B *tegula*
2	SD.1/2	131	St Loye's College	squiggle sig
3	SD.1/2	158	St David's church	squiggle sig
3	SD.1/2	156	Honeyditches, Seaton	Gp B *tegula*
3	S.2/3	166	Wessex Close, in Topsham	Gp C *tegula*
3	C.2/3	168	Wessex Close, in Topsham	Gp C *tegula*
3	C.2/3	125	Exeter, Princesshay	Gp C *tegula*
4	T.2	179	Exeter, Trichay Street	Gp B *tegula*
4	T.2	24	Wessex Close, in Topsham	Gp B *tegula*
5	E.2/3	118	Woodbury, in Axminster	Gp C *tegula*
5	E.3/4	27	Woodbury, in Axminster	*tegula*, Invert mfr
5	E.3/4	1	Pomeroy Wood, in Honiton	Gp D *tegula*
5	E.2/3	152	Pomeroy Wood, in Honiton	Gp C *tegula*
5	E.3/4	44	Halberton	Gp D *tegula*?
5	H.3/4	45	Halberton	flue tile
5	SD.1/2	172	Bolham, in Tiverton	Gp B *tegula*?
6	H.3/4	8	Ashcombe Barton	flat tile
6	S.2/3	110	Aller Cross, in Kingskerswell	Gp C *tegula*
7	H.3/4	40	Hatherleigh Moor	waster
7	H.3/4	4	Hatherleigh Moor	UC *tegula*
8	C.2/3	39	Otterton Point, in Otterton	Gp C *tegula*
9	U	149	Holcombe Villa	flue tile
10	H.3/4	17	Woodbury, in Axminster	Gp D *tegula*?
11	SD.1/2	12	Honeyditches, in Seaton	*tegula* diag UC?
12	H.3/4	10	Bury Barton, in Lapford	UC *teg*, invert mfr?
13	H.3/4	22	Wessex Close, in Topsham	T7 *tegula*

calcium-light tiles. Indeed, as will be proposed later, if the two tiles (131 and 160) identified as St David's church output are excluded from the M2 fabric list then all of Machin's fabrics become either exclusively calcium-rich or calcium–light. Overall there appears to be relatively good correspondence with most of the kiln sources identified by pXRF and morphology with the exception of the weak Hatherleigh Moor group which is not supported by the thin section analysis. Given this correspondence, and recognising that both the methodology used in this chapter and that employed for the thin section analysis involve judgement, especially for borderline tiles, it is worth exploring what revisions would be necessary to completely align the two analyses (the 'idealised analysis') and the arguments that could be made to support such revisions.

Machin's first four fabrics (M1–M4) are intended to match Exeter Fabrics 1 to 4 as described by Williams. Like Williams (1991b, 281), she has noted that there is not a great difference between the first three Exeter fabrics and that they all derive from the same basic clay source. All five of the tiles attributed by pXRF to the Princesshay kiln in its various phases are identified as M2 fabric in thin section; two other tiles from Exeter were also examined in thin section and allocated to M3 and M4 which match the Central and Topsham import kilns respectively, consistent with the pXRF findings.

Most of the St David's church kiln output identified by pXRF and all of the five tiles found at St David's church and St Loye's College are attributed to the three broadly similar fabrics M1, M2 and M3 in thin section (*i.e.* Williams' 1991a and b, Exeter Fabrics 1–3). If the excavators' dating of St David' church is correct then these tiles should relate to a short period in the latter part of the 1st century AD, so it is surprising that these tiles are spread across the three fabrics M1–3 whilst the Princesshay tiles, representing over 100 years of production, are all attributed to M2. It is also slightly surprising that given the geographic separation of the two sites that St David's was also apparently accessing, in part, the same M2 fabric as Princesshay. Two of the tiles, one found at St David's and the other at St Loye's College, carry the same unusual squiggle signature but are attributed to different thin section fabrics (M3 and M2 respectively). These arguments, coupled with the fact that all of the St David's church output is calcium-light and all of the Princesshay output is calcium-rich, suggest that these tiles, whose fabrics appear very similar in thin section, could be candidates for revision in the idealised analysis. This is reinforced by the PCA analysis, Fig. 13.3.22 (now based on the preferred eight elements), which shows that the Princesshay M2 tiles form a tight cluster in the centre of the plot and the St David's church and St Loye's College tiles (shown in red) form an entirely separate cluster at the lower right of the plot. It might also be noted that Roger Taylor thought that the St Loye's College fabric differed from that found in Exeter on the basis of a detailed visual inspection of the inclusions contained within the clay matrix (Taylor forthcoming). It therefore seems appropriate to reallocate all of the St David's church output and the squiggle signature from St Loye's College to M1 as a first step for the idealised analysis.

There were three tiles (in green) from other sites in Fig. 13.3.22 that were attributed to the St David's kiln in the pXRF analysis; one of these, Tile 156 from Honeyditches, in Seaton, is also a strong candidate for revision to M1 in the idealised analysis as the thin section confirms it to be of the Exeter area fabric type and it has a Group B cutaway similar to the examples from St Loye's College and St David's church and is calcium-light. The other two tiles shown in green will be discussed later.

Tiles 166, Topsham, and 39, Otterton Point, were weak on the pXRF/morphology and Machin's attributions to fabrics M3 and M8 are adopted for the idealised analysis. This leaves three tiles in the M3 fabric in the idealised analysis, all of which can be attributed to the Central kiln.

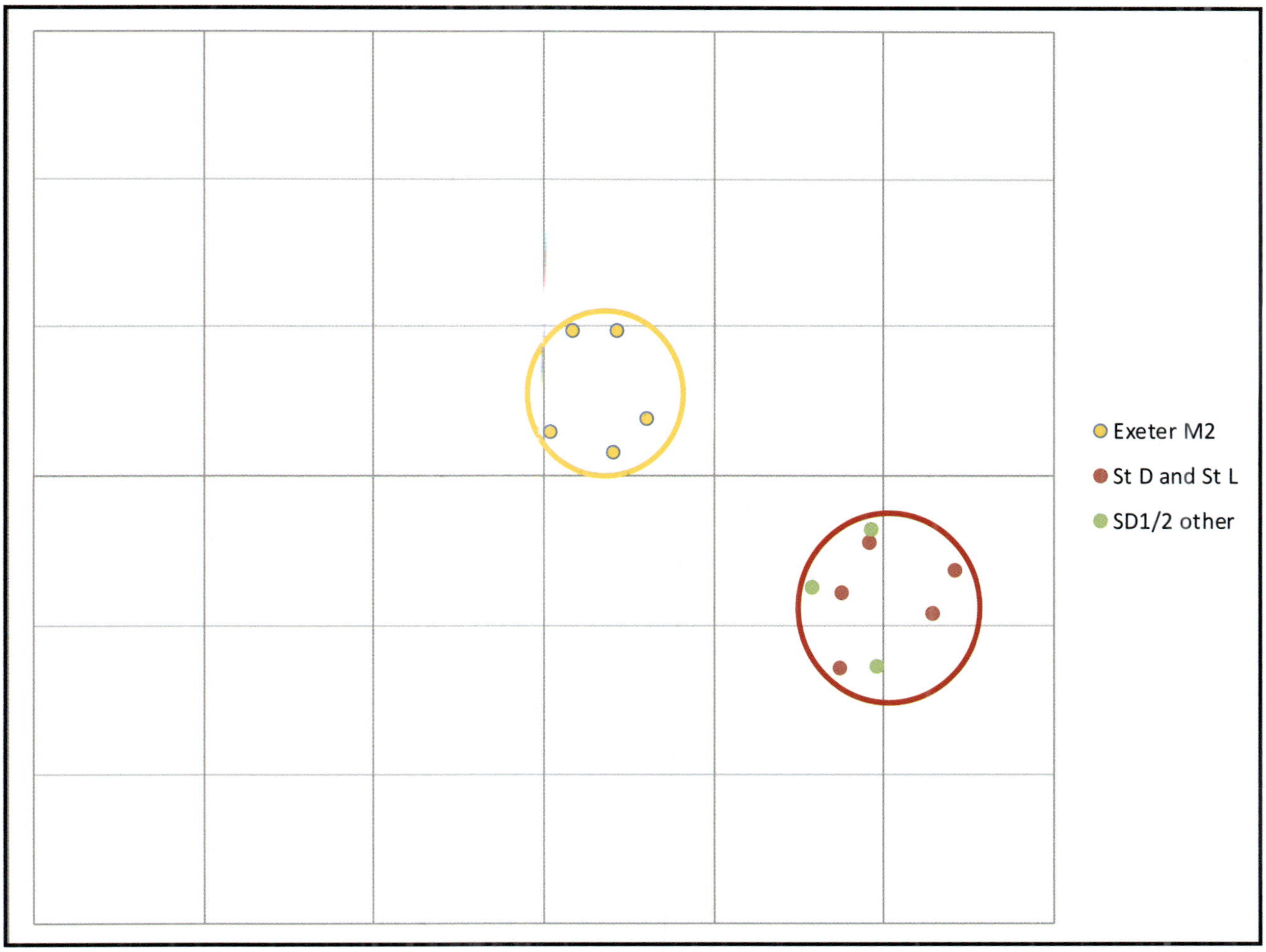

Fig. 13.3.22 Subset of eight-element PCA highlighting Princesshay M2 tiles vs St David's church and St Loye's College tiles

Machin assigned both the tiles from the Topsham grouping to her M4 fabric in line with the pXRF/morphology. The inclusions identified in the thin sections confirmed that these tiles could not have come from Devon and must have been imported.

Machin attributed seven tiles to her M5 fabric, five of which corresponded with the Eastern kiln on the pXRF. One of the two other tiles was from Halberton and was originally assigned to Hatherleigh Moor but can be reassigned to M5 as the pXRF evidence was not compelling. The other tile, from Bolham, was one of those clearly shown in the St David's church kiln group in Fig. 13.3.22 and it lies below all the other M5 tiles on the overall PCA plot (Fig. 13.3.23). This tile appears to have a 2nd-century AD cutaway whereas all the Eastern kiln output is later, and so it appears appropriate to assign this tile to the St David's church group in the idealised analysis.

The M6 thin section group corresponds to the Southern kiln. Machin has assigned the Ashcombe Barton tile to this group which makes sense geographically and is credible on the PCA plot.

The M7 thin section group consists of the two tiles from Hatherleigh Moor but no others. As discussed under 'Later sources' in the section on 'Verification Using PCA and Thin Sections', the PCA plot of the Hatherleigh Moor kiln output (Fig. 13.3.21) suggested that it could represent two different sources but it is nevertheless surprising that there are no tiles from other sites attributed by thin section to this fabric. Taylor had assigned one of the tiles from Bury Barton to the Hatherleigh Moor kiln but the example tested by thin section (Tile 10 assigned to H3/4 in the section on 'Tile Morphology and Bi-Plot Analysis' above) was seen as the unique M12 fabric (possibly similar to the M5 Eastern Group). It would suggest that there were many small production centres in Devon in the later Roman period at a time when the transition to stone roofing materials might have led to a consolidation of tileries rather than a proliferation.

There are two probable military tiles that require further consideration. The first, from the 1st-century fort at North Tawton was identified as M2 fabric consistent with the 1st-century AD military tiles from Princesshay which were also M2. However, both of the North Tawton tiles tested by pXRF were very different to the Princesshay tiles on both the K v Ti and PCA plots (both North Tawton tiles are unclassified and lie on the extreme right of Fig. 13.3.24) so this apparent affinity with Princesshay should be treated with caution. It should also be noted that tiles from the

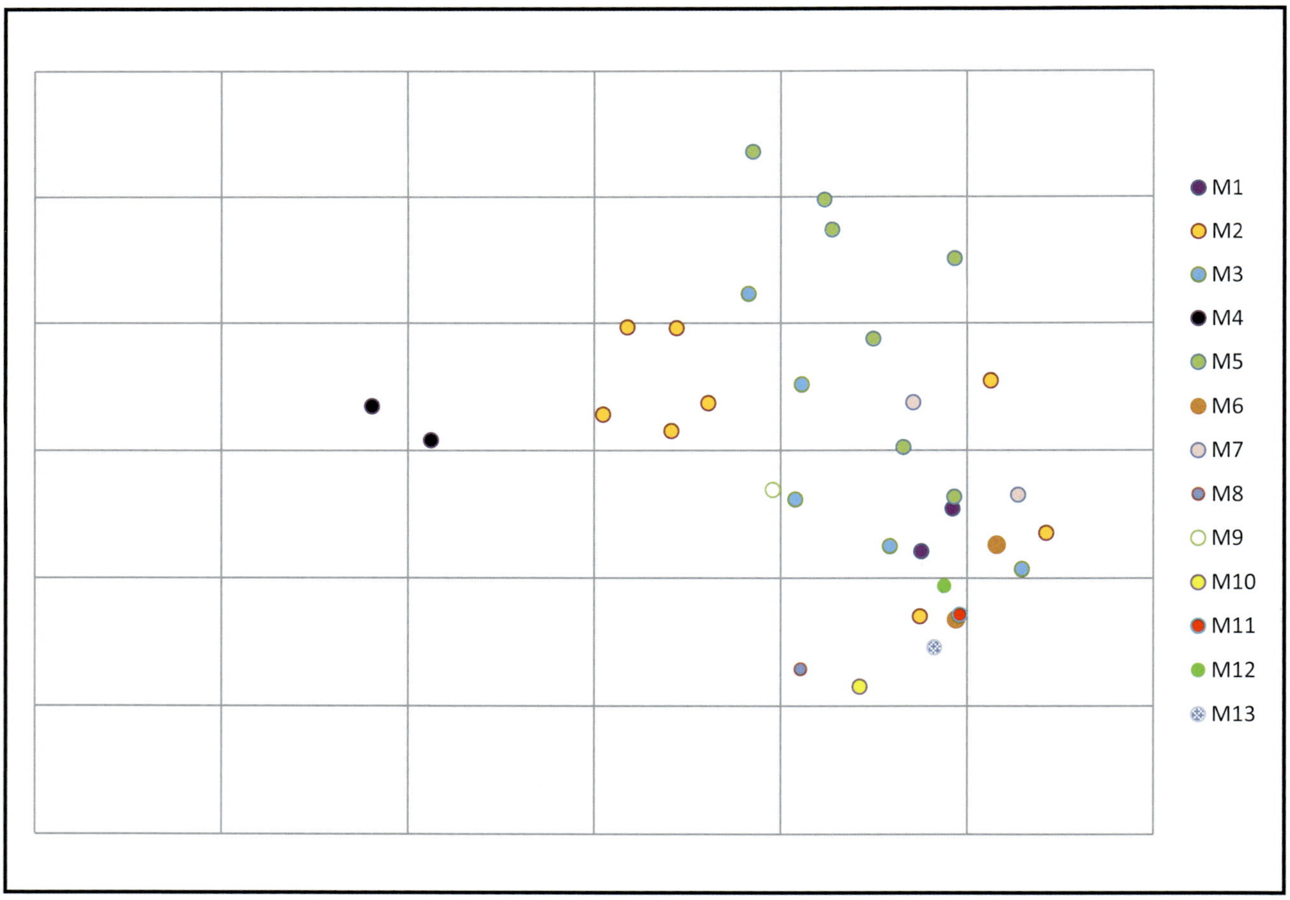

Fig. 13.3.23 Subset of eight-element PCA highlighting Machin's thin section fabrics

newly excavated 1st-century AD *vicus* at Okehampton (which could not be included in this analysis) have a fabric that visibly differed from Princesshay.

The second probable military tile (Tile 12) is one from Seaton that had a diagonal upper cutaway which is emblematic of military production (Warry 2006, 21), another example of which is illustrated as Fig. 13.3.38 (in the online Appendix 13.1). It was identified as being in the unique M11 fabric and Machin's fabric description is close to Williams (1987, 72–3) description of the fabric of the stamped tile from Seaton. Williams noted that the stamped tile had similar inclusions to one of the other tiles from Seaton which he had thin sectioned but was unable to confidently assert that it was the same fabric. By contrast Machin placed the other, probably non-military, example from Seaton (but not necessarily the same tile that Williams examined) as M3. The two Seaton tiles examined by Machin are green dots shown in Fig. 13.3.22 which lends support to them also being from the St David's church kiln. However, as the military example is definitely seen as different by Machin, and possibly by Williams, the attribution of this tile to the unique M11 fabric is accepted for the idealised analysis but is further discussed in the section on 'The source of the Seaton stamped tile' below.

Table 13.3.15 summarises the revisions proposed for the idealised analysis. In addition consequential changes will be required for tiles that were not thin sectioned but

Table 13.3.15 Idealised fabric analysis (entries in red type were calcium-rich on the pXRF)

Machin		*Warry kiln group*		*Tile no.*	*Site name*	*Description*
Revised	*Original*	*Revised*	*Original*			
	1		SD.1/2	35	St Loye's College	*tegula* comb signature
1	2		SD.1/2	131	St Loye's College	squiggle signature
	1		SD.1/2	134	St Loye's College	Gp B *tegula*
1	3		SD.1/2	158	St David's Church	squiggle sig
1	2		SD.1/2	160	St David's Church	Gp B *tegula*
1	3		SD.1/2	156	Honeyditches, in Seaton	Gp B *tegula*
1	5		SD.1/2	172	Bolham, in Tiverton	Gp B *tegula*?
	2		P.1	38	Exeter, Cathedral Close	Gp A *tegula*
	2		P.1	190	Exeter, Cathedral Close	antefix face
	2		P.2	120	Exeter, Princesshay	waster
	2		P.2	185	Exeter, Princesshay	Princesshay Fabric 1F
	2		P.2 late	123	Exeter, Princesshay	Gp C *tegula*
	2		U	138	North Tawton	*tegula*
	3		C.2/3	125	Exeter, Princesshay	Gp C *tegula*
	3	C.2/3	S.2/3	166	Wessex Close, in Topsham	Gp C *tegula*
	3		C.2/3	168	Wessex Close, in Topsham	Gp C *tegula*
	4		T.2	179	Exeter, Trichay Street	Gp B *tegula*
	4		T.2	24	Wessex Close, in Topsham	Gp B *tegula*
	5		E.2/3	118	Woodbury, in Axminster	Gp C *tegula*
	5		E.2/3	152	Pomeroy Wood, in Honiton	Gp C *tegula*
	5		E.3/4	27	Woodbury, Axminster	*tegula*, Invert mfr
	5		E.3/4	1	Pomeroy Wood, in Honiton	Gp D *tegula*
	5		E.3/4	44	Halberton	Gp D *tegula*?
	5	E.3/4	H.3/4	45	Halberton	flue tile
	6	S.2/3	H.3/4	8	Ashcombe Barton	flat tile
	6		S.2/3	110	Aller Cross, in Kingskerswell	Gp C *tegula*
	7		H.3/4	4	Hatherleigh Moor	UC *tegula*
	7		H.3/4	40	Hatherleigh Moor	waster
	8	U	C.2/3	39	Otterton Point, in Otterton	Group C *tegula*
	9		U	149	Holcombe Villa	flue tile
	10	UL	H.3/4	17	Woodbury, in Axminster	Group D *tegula*?
	11	U	SD.1/2	12	Honeyditches, in Seaton	*teg*, diag UC?
	12	UL	H.3/4	10	Bury Barton	UC *tegula*, invert?
	13	U	H.3/4	22	Wessex Close, in Topsham	T7 *tegula*

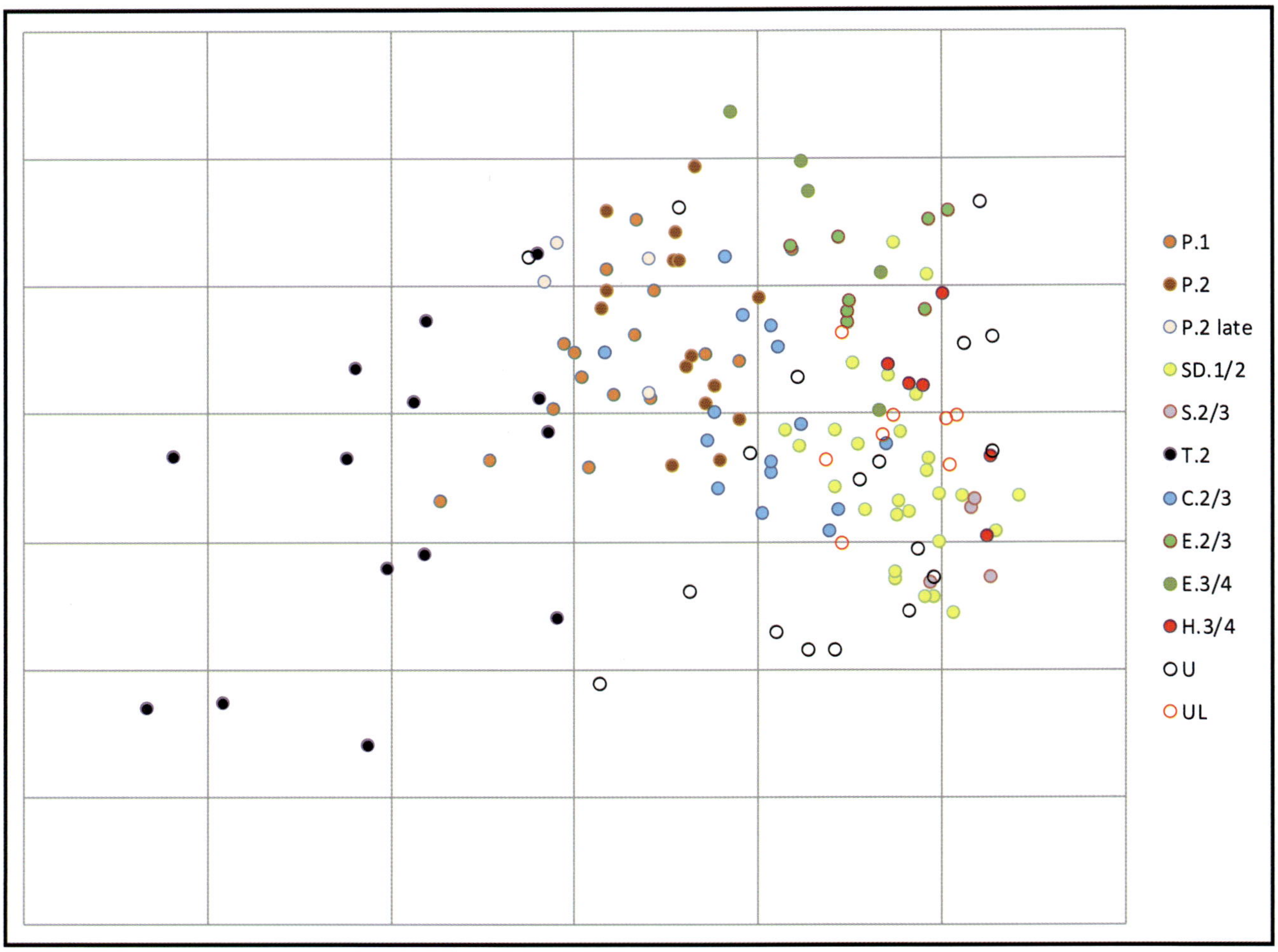

Fig. 13.3.24 Eight-element PCA of idealised fabric analysis

were similar to ones that were. Most of these relate to the H3/4 distribution that can no longer be attributed to Hatherleigh Moor and becomes unclassified, however, as these tiles still have similar pXRF signatures and some appear to be late, they will be denoted as UL (unclassified late) to distinguish them from the other unclassified tiles where no commonality with other tiles is suspected. Additionally Seaton Tile 13 which has a diagonal upper cutaway like Seaton Tile 12 and should therefore be fabric M11 will be classified as U (was SD1/2), Topsham Tile 167 should move from S2/3 to C2/3 in line with Tiles 166 and 168, and Topsham Tile 165 which has a Group R, T7 cutaway should be classified U in line with Tile 22. Fig. 13.3.24 shows the resulting PCA plot for all 141 tiles examined in this study which yields a satisfactory differentiation between the kilns. Figure 13.3.25 shows the resulting geographic distribution of the Central, Southern and Eastern kiln sites, while the St David's church geographic distribution is shown in Fig. 13.3.29.

Recycling and flue-tile

It was concluded above that the tiles imported into Topsham in the 2nd century AD were recycled in Exeter in the later 3rd century AD and that Newenham Abbey acquired hardcore, possibly from Exeter, presumably in the medieval period, but how extensive was this practice and how much might it have contributed to the perceived kiln distributions? In Gloucestershire the stamping of tiles provides a means of tracking their movement and, as a result, several possible CBM recycling centres have been identified (Warry 2017). The distribution of the stamped tiles shows that they travelled up to 70 km from their production centres but not necessarily as new tiles or in single journeys. A 2nd-century AD stamped (probable) *tegula* made at Minety, in Wiltshire, travelled some 50 km to Dings villa, in Stoke Gifford, South Gloucestershire, where masonry construction did not begin until the 3rd century AD and stone tiles were used on the roofs (Warry forthcoming) which suggests that it must surely have been recycled material. Devon only has a single stamped tile so we cannot use this approach. Instead, to get some measure of the significance, we can look at flue-tile. Figure 13.3.26 shows the 19 sites within Devon where flue-tile has been recorded (as noted in the online Appendix 13.1) and contrasts it with the three sites known to have had a bath-house, and therefore to have needed a reasonable

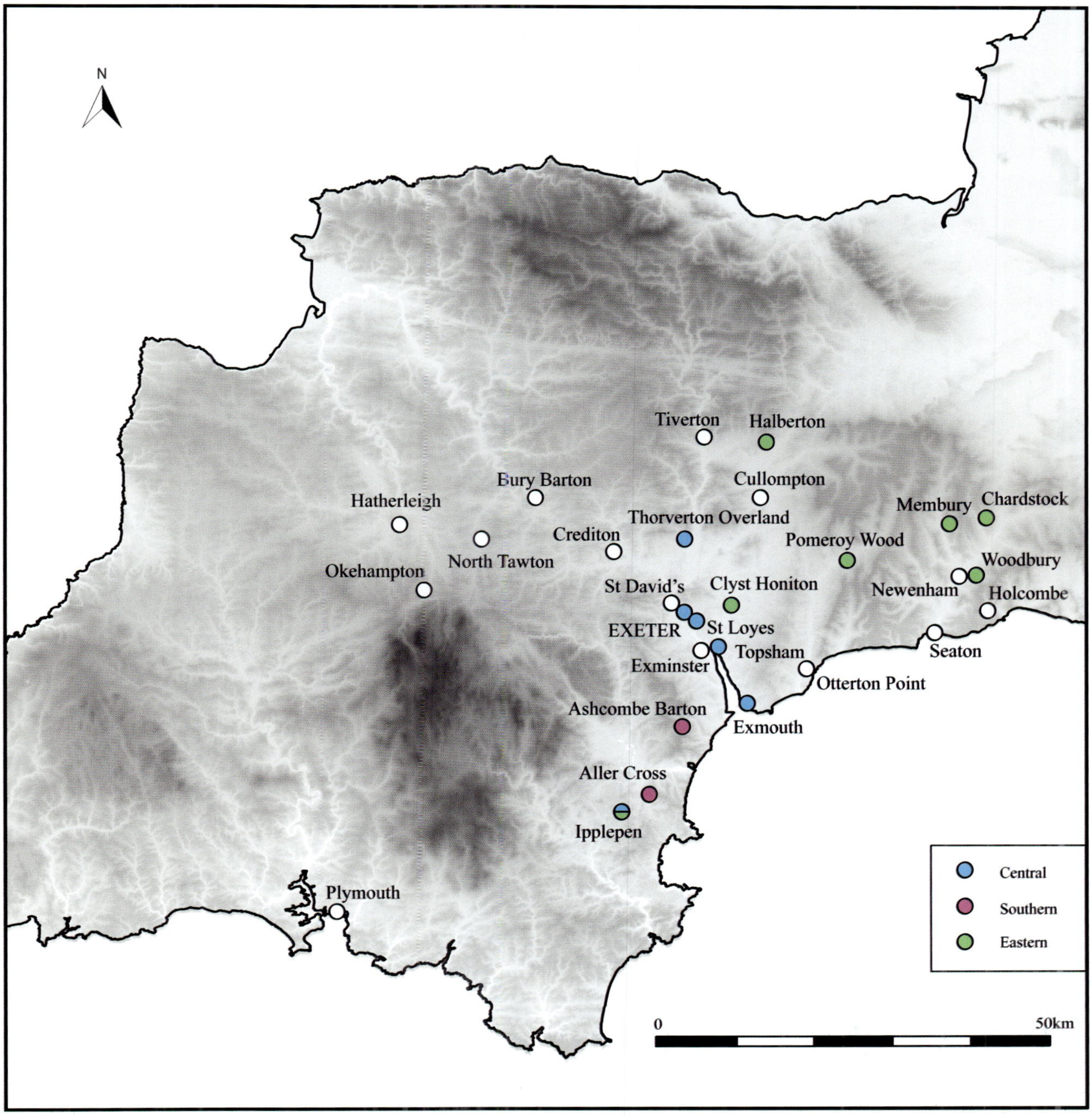

Fig. 13.3.25 Distribution of tiles produced at the Central, Southern and Eastern kiln sites (drawn by David Gould)

quantity of flue-tile for heated walls (hypocausts *per se* do not need any flue-tiles). While some of the sites reporting flue-tile may well have had bath-houses that are yet to be discovered, the mismatch is too great, and demonstrates that there must have been a widespread movement of recycled material in both Roman and medieval times. A probable further flue-tile from Totnes castle (Rigold 1954, 250), not included in this study, where again no bath-house has been discovered, could also be mentioned. This phenomenon is seen across Roman Britain, and one possible mechanism behind this movement is that goods travelled on carts to markets where, instead of travelling back empty, the opportunity was taken to bring old CBM back to the farmsteads which would always have proved useful, if only for consolidating muddy gateways. As a result considerable caution is required in equating flue-tiles with villa or bath-houses (*e.g.* Bidwell 1980, 58, note 49).

Comparison with previous fabric analyses

It is now possible to compare the results of this analysis with the fabric series established by Holbrook and Bidwell, and described in thin section by D.F. Williams in 1991, and the more recent Princesshay excavations

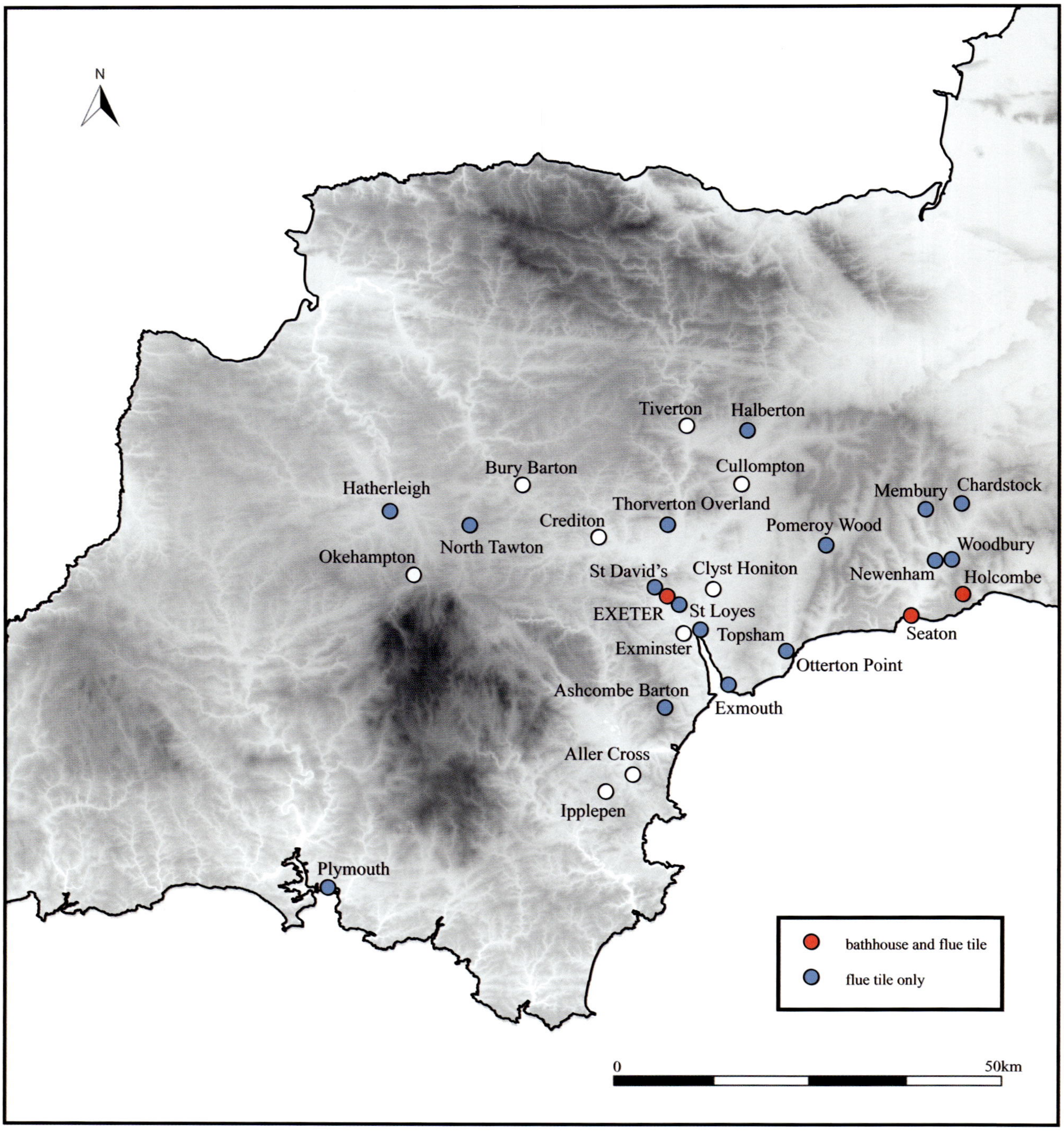

Fig. 13.3.26 Incidence of flue tile and known bath-houses (drawn by David Gould)

(Durrant forthcoming a); a comparison with Taylor and Wheeler's 2006 work is not possible because that was related to individual tiles, few of which have been sampled by pXRF. The results are tabulated in Table 13.3.16 and, as can be seen, there seems to be limited correlation with Williams 1991, however the Princesshay fabric series does appear to differentiate between the Princesshay and Central kilns postulated in this study which are not just different in date but use slightly different clay.

Table 13.3.16: Comparison of fabric analysis results

pXRF (this paper)	*Holbrook and Bidwell 1991*	*Princesshay (Durrant)*
Princesshay 1	2	1C
Princesshay 2		1F
Topsham	4	
Central	1 and 3	2F and 2FB

Military to civil transition

Introduction

Its high density of military installations (EAPIT, Chapters 3 and 5) suggests that 1st-century AD Devon was one of the more heavily garrisoned parts of Britain at that time. The current understanding is that after the legion left the Exeter fortress in the late AD 70s/early 80s, some of the outlying forts remained in use for a number of years but all were abandoned before the end of the century. However, this leaves unexplained a *legio II Augusta* stamped tile reputedly found at Seaton which must post-date these events, not least because the legion did not start stamping tiles until *c.* AD 90–100 after it was established at Caerleon (Zienkiewicz 1993, 127–9).

The authenticity of the Seaton stamped tile

A 'large Roman (?) tile' (Anon. 1859, 47), presumably the *legio II Augusta* stamped tile (Fig. 13.3.27) now in the Taunton Museum and attributed to the Roman site at Honeyditches, in Seaton, was presented to the museum by Sir W. Trevelyan in 1859 (in advance of excavations in 1864). The stamp reads L||GIIAVG in retrograde with the A and V being ligatured. The || symbol after the initial L is the cursive form of the letter E such that the stamp really reads LEGIIAVG (for the Roman cursive alphabet see, for example, Tomlin 2016, 19–22). The tile bears the impressions of multiple boot marks with the stamp being impressed onto the tile after the boot marks were made. There are a number of features about this episode that have created uneasiness over the authenticity of the tile and its attribution to Seaton, not least its apparent presence in a 2nd or 3rd-century AD site long after the *legio II Augusta* moved to Wales. Specifically, could the tile be a forgery or, if genuine, could it be an antiquarian relocation?

The Seaton stamp was until recently the only known example of this die. It certainly looks Roman and the die is very similar to *Roman Inscriptions of Britain* (RIB) 2459.42 (see Fig. 13.3.27) which is one of the more

Fig. 13.3.27 Seaton stamped tile (RIB 2459.41) and similar design (RIB 2459.42) from Caerleon (photo: John Davey; die drawings: Roman Inscriptions of Britain *II.4)*

common dies found at Caerleon. These dies are perhaps the ugliest and least impressive produced by the *legio II Augusta*; they are also retrograde and use the cursive form of the letter E which would be an odd choice for a forgery. This is compounded by the die being impressed onto a tile that has already been stepped on by several Roman boots. Taken together these arguments make forgery seem unlikely, and this possibility can now be ruled out because another stamp with this die was found at Llanwern, near Caerleon, in South Wales, at the end of 2019. This also adds weight to the pXRF results, discussed in the section 'The source of the Seaton stamped tile', which suggest that, contra Williams 1987, 72–3, the fabric could have come from Caerleon rather than Devon. Antiquarian relocation may be a better possibility for the Seaton tile. This certainly occurred as, for example, there is a *legio* XX stamp from the north-west of England in the York Museum collection and a *legio* IX stamp, probably from the east coast, in the Chester collection.

At Caerleon, six of the legionary dies (out of 72 different dies) are associated with *tegulae* where almost all of the upper cutaways have been finished with diagonal cuts rather than the normal orthogonal ones, presumably reflecting the habit of an individual tile-maker or the practice of a particular cohort (Warry 2010, 128–34). This manufacturing idiosyncrasy is only found on military, normally legionary, sites; out of the 50 known examples in the author's survey of Romano-British *tegulae*, 47 come from definite military sites and the remaining three can be associated with the military. Both of the complete *tegulae* stamped with the similar RIB 2459.42 die at Caerleon had diagonal cutaways and, most unusually, two out of the three identifiable upper cutaways at Seaton had also been cut diagonally. Thus, if this was a Victorian misattribution and Seaton was not a military site, then it would be an extraordinary fluke that an antiquarian accidentally relocated this particular die which just happened to coincide with a unique example of diagonal cutaways appearing on what would therefore have been a civil site (equally it would be an extraordinarily fortuitous forgery). As the actual die attributed to Seaton is one of only two examples of this die ever found, it would also be a singular chance if this was the tile inadvertently translated from Caerleon to Seaton.

Of course it may be argued that it is surprising that Trevelyan only found this single example of the stamped tile but, as we have no further information from him, we do not know whether having found one complete stamp, he would have discarded any others he found with similar but incomplete stamps. By way of comparison, in the case of the somewhat later 1910 excavation of Hucclecote villa, just outside Gloucester, all of the stamped tiles retained that were thought worthy of retention and reporting were complete or near complete which almost certainly means that fragmentary stamps were neither retained nor merited reporting (Warry 2017, 98). Moreover, the paucity of stamped tiles is likely to result from the small quantities being supplied coupled with CBM survival rates which are typically of the order of 1–2%. For example, in Wales three *legio II Augusta* outstations have each yielded a single stamped tile (and many others none, even though some were probably supplied with stamped tiles), whilst there are 13 further instances of single examples of individual dies being found on sites where other dies have also been found. Together this evidence makes a persuasive case for treating the Seaton stamped tile as genuine and the presence of the *tegulae* with diagonal cutaways suggests that at least some of the CBM assemblage from the Seaton site(s) is also military in origin.

The date of the Seaton stamped tile

Boon (1984, 30–1) dated the similar die (RIB 2459.42) together with two further broadly similar dies found at Caerleon, all using the cursive form of the letter E, as *c.* AD 200 based upon contextual evidence. The *tegulae* stamped with the similar RIB 2459.42 die had Group B and Group C cutaways suggesting that the die was in use in the latter half of the 2nd century AD, slightly earlier than Boon's dating. Further collateral evidence comes from incuse (*i.e.* impressed into the stamp rather than in relief as was normal for legionary dies) *legio II* stamps found on a grave at Carlisle with a die that reads L||GIIAVG; the only other example of a cursive E found on a stamped tile in Britain. Also on the same grave was an incuse *legio XX Valeria Victrix* tile, the only incuse die made by that legion. These tiles were most likely made at Scalesceugh in Cumbria and probably date to the end of the 2nd century AD when the two legions appear to have been operating together in the north-west (Warry 2010, 142).

The life of a typical legionary die has been estimated at 15–20 years (Warry 2006, 74–5) but this is likely to have extended out in the later 2nd and 3rd centuries AD when far fewer new dies were being created. So, to be consistent with all the evidence, the original RIB 2459.42 die should have been created around AD 160–70 and fallen out of use soon after AD 200. The Seaton die is very similar to RIB 2459.42 so it must have been made at the same time, *i.e.* AD 160–70, or very close to it.

Holbrook (1987) has identified Couchill, some 500 m from the site at Seaton Honeyditches, as a possible masonry-built Roman fort. A 1st-century AD date is ruled out by the use of masonry, and Holbrook suggested the early 3rd century AD on the basis of Boon's dating of the die although, as discussed above, AD 160–70 may be better and would be consistent with the dating of the Group B *tegulae* from Seaton. A 2nd-century AD fort such as this would be expected to have a bath-house but the one excavated at the Honeyditches site superficially looks too far away (Miles 1977). However, as the purpose of the fort must have been to overlook and control the seaborne approaches to the Axe Estuary, locating the bath-house within the viewing arc that the fort was to supervise would have impeded the sight lines, even if the bath-house was downslope. So the bath-house location makes military sense and, as it was at the same contour level as the fort, it would not have been too inconvenient. The first phase bath-house is relatively small compared to the likely number of troops it was to serve but not excessively so. By way of comparison, the 2nd-century AD fort at Hardknott in the Lake District is also positioned on the side of a steep hill and is almost exactly the same size as Couchill, while its (external) bath-house is only slightly bigger (Ferguson 1893, 384). Holbrook goes on to suggest that the Seaton site might have been a *mansio* which, on this analysis, would identify with the second expanded phase of the bath-house. These military/official scenarios are reinforced by the presence of a 3rd-century AD military vulvate stud from a cavalry harness fitting (EAPIT 1, Chapter 3).

The source of the Seaton stamped tile

The fabric of the Seaton stamped tile is shown in green on Fig. 13.3.28. Williams (1987, 72–3) believed that the fabric could have been the same as the other tiles at Seaton without being able to be definitive but that it differed from the Caerleon stamped tiles that he tested. This differs from the PCA results which show that a Caerleon *tegula* (red dot) with the sister die RIB 2459.42 is very similar to the Seaton stamped tile whilst all the unstamped tiles from modern excavations at Seaton (blue dots) are significantly separated from these two tiles. The sawn Caerleon stamp blocks (yellow dots) discussed in the section on 'Dolphin antefixes and consideration of leaching effects' (above) lie in between these sets of tiles. So, contrary to Williams, it is possible that the Seaton stamped tile was made at Caerleon and was part of a small initial despatch of tiles provided by the legion to Seaton, while the bulk

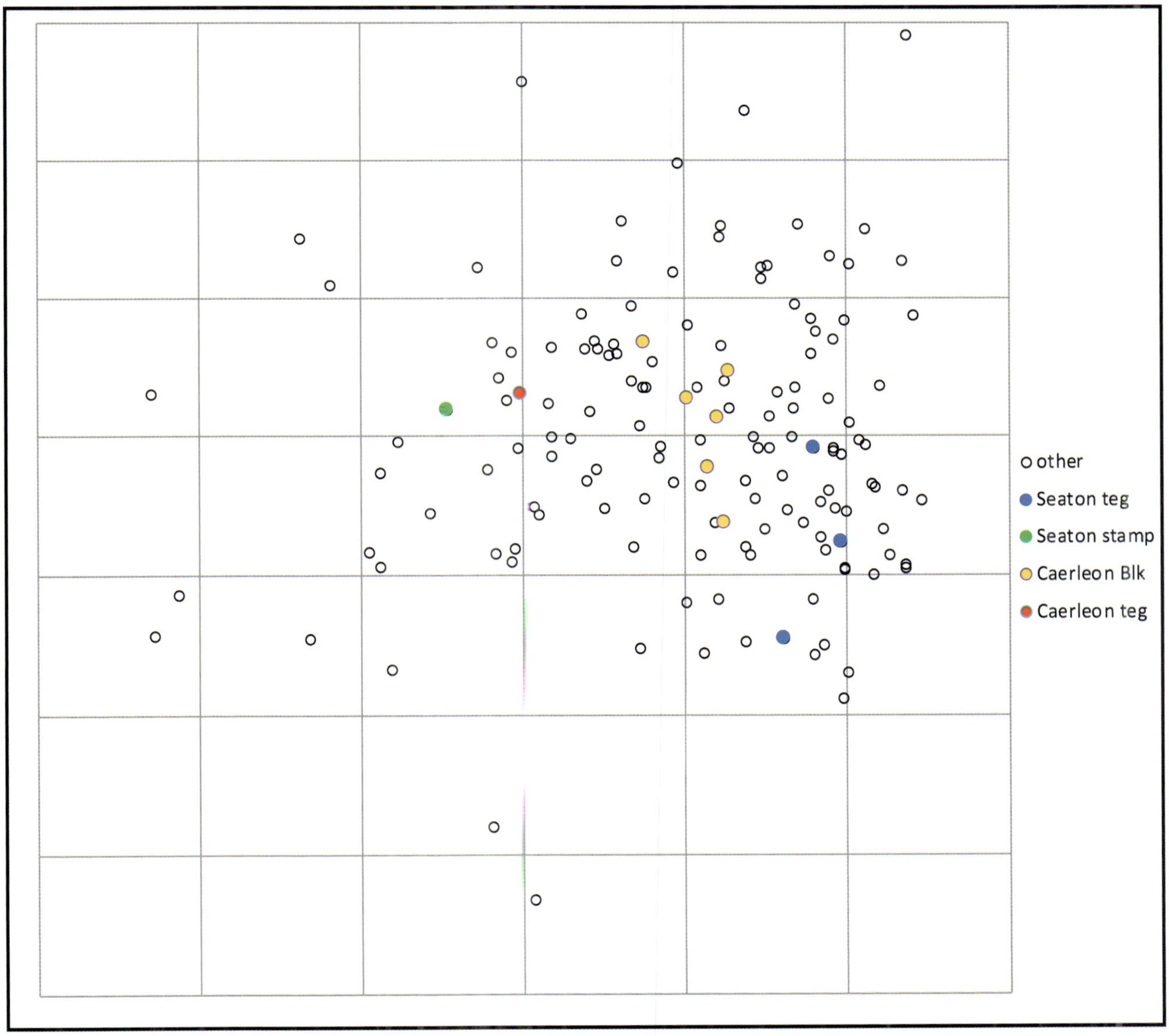

Fig. 13.3.28 Eight-element PCA comparing Seaton tiles with Caerleon

of the tiles, represented by the blue dots, must have been made locally in Devon. Machin's identification of one of the *tegulae* with diagonal cutaways as being in a unique fabric, and not the product of the Exeter clays, is difficult to explain as it would imply that there were three sources of tile supply to Seaton: the initial stamped tiles from Caerleon, an Exeter source (most probably St David's church) and a third unique source.

Some auxiliary units produced their own stamped tile, such as *cohors IIII Breucorum* at Grimescar, in West Yorkshire, but there are very few known examples of legionary stamped tiles being made away from their main kiln site and none specifically for a small outstation. Now that a second example of the Seaton die has been found at Llanwern it is clear that tiles with this die were originally made at Caerleon after which a military detachment either with the die or an initial batch of stamped tiles was despatched to Devon. Once in Devon the military detachment may have used the St David's church tilery for further supplies as opposed to the more distant Caerleon, and the presence of *tegulae* with diagonal cutaways does suggest that the St David's church kiln was being operated by military tile-makers when these tiles were made. Alternatively, if Machin's identification is correct, we need to interpose a separate military tile-works producing the *tegulae* with diagonal cutaways and a civilian tile-works at St David's church meeting other needs.

The function of the St David's church tilery and its likely dating

To better understand the context of these 2nd-century AD military tiles at Seaton we need to consider the St David's church tilery in more detail. The kiln site lies 0.5 km outside the town (EAPIT 1, Fig. 5.2) which, based on the evidence of 57 sherds of pottery from a very limited excavation that did not come down onto the kiln itself, the excavators dated to the 1st century AD (Chapman *et al.* 2017; Steimetzer forthcoming). This is inconsistent with the CBM dating from the site which included both 1st and 2nd-century AD *tegulae*. As kilns do not in general generate much if any unrelated ceramic detritus, it is possible that this ceramic evidence establishes a *terminus post quem* for the construction of the kiln with the pottery perhaps originating from sites within the vicinity (*e.g.* as noted by Goodchild 1952, 103). To explore the dating further we need to consider the circumstances that led to its construction and the customers it was intended to serve.

If the St David's church kiln had been in operation at the same time as the legion was based at Exeter then it would have supplied only the military establishment because there was no private demand at that time and, given its proximity to the fortress, we would have expected to find some of the St David's church tiles within Exeter. However, the single tile attributed by pXRF to St David's church that had been found in Exeter had a 2nd-century AD cutaway and probably arrived as hardcore in the 3rd century AD. It should be noted that there are two rare pilaster tiles that have been found in Exeter which were similar to an example found at St David's church (Durrant forthcoming b) and, although the Exeter examples were not tested by pXRF, it seems likely that they all came from the St David's church kiln. Nevertheless they may also have arrived as hardcore as neither of the Exeter pilaster tiles are known to have come from a 1st-century AD context nor is there any known use of such pilasters within 1st-century AD Exeter. Tiles may have been required for the legionary outstations/auxiliary forts within Devon (although this would be unusual in the 1st century AD) but the practice of the *legio II Augusta* when in Wales, and of all the other British legions, was to meet these demands from the main legionary tile kiln. It therefore seems probable that the St David's church kiln must have been established *after* the fortress and its kiln passed into civilian hands (or was shut down) and, perhaps as a consequence of that transfer, the St David's church kiln was constructed to supply any continuing military needs and any nascent civil demand. This civilian demand does not appear to have come from within Exeter as the absence of St David's church tiles from within the town shows that the civic authorities were effective in maintaining a monopoly for the Princesshay kiln. In fact there is no evidence for St David's church supplying anywhere in the 1st century AD, although in the first half of the 2nd centuryAD it was the *only* identified source of supply for Devon beyond Exeter, other than the imports into Topsham which did not appear to travel further afield as new tile.

Sites supplied by the St David's church tilery

The eight sites that appear to have received tiles from the St David's church kiln are listed in Table 13.3.17 and shown on Fig. 13.3.29. Of these, Princesshay may be disregarded as the solitary St David's church tile appears to represent later recycled tile. Of the remaining seven sites, six contained Group B *tegulae*. Two of the sites also had later *tegulae* in different fabrics and Woolster Street in Plymouth also had 2nd-century AD *tegulae* in the Topsham fabric. Seaton and St Loye's College had single examples of other fabrics. Little further is currently known about Milbury Farm, in Exminster, and Woolster Street, in Plymouth, although, given its location, Plymouth might possibly have been military. Overland, in Thorverton, was a farmstead or small villa (Uglow 2000, 242). Each of the remaining four sites had originally been established by the military. Of these Honeyditches, in Seaton, has evidence for masonry buildings which would probably have been roofed with *tegulae* and *imbrices*. Bolham fort, in Tiverton, was discovered by aerial photography but excavation has been limited to validation of the defences although the presence of stone (Maxfield 1991, 54) hints at the possibility of masonry structures in the vicinity. Although no masonry structures were discovered at

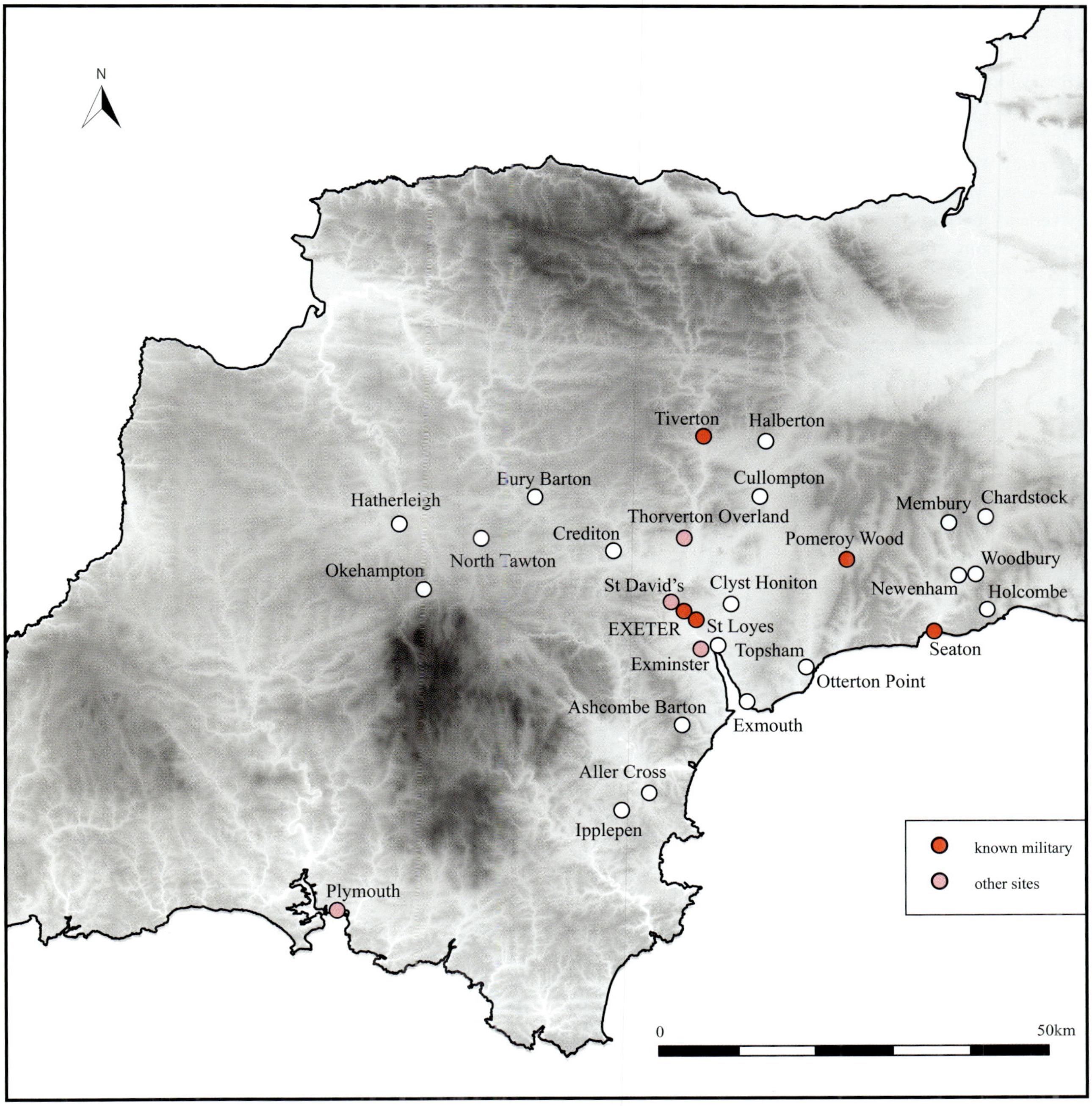

Fig. 13.3.29 Distribution of St David's church kiln output (drawn by David Gould)

Pomeroy Wood, in Honiton, the excavators were confident that they must have existed due to the presence of substantial amounts of stone and tile (Fitzpatrick *et al.* 1999, 402). Surprisingly there was no evidence for masonry structures at St Loye's College and this is discussed next.

Bidwell (EAPIT 1, Chapter 4) argues that the 1st-century AD site at St Loye's College was a civilian settlement, while Holbrook (EAPIT 1, Chapter 5) believes that a 2nd-century AD roadside settlement may have existed on the Topsham Road frontage which lay outside the excavated area. A large amount of CBM was recovered (mainly from wells capped in the later 2nd century AD) and although the majority of this was too fragmented for identification there were still nearly 600 recognisable pieces which split 62% *tegulae*, 19% *imbrices*, 16% flat tiles (possibly from *pilae*), 3% box flue-tile, and one complete face antefix (Coles and Allan forthcoming). The ratio of *tegulae* to *imbrices* is roughly consistent with the ratio by weight of a complete roof. All of the identifiable *tegula* cutaways took the Group B 2nd-century AD form. We have already seen that most of the sites with CBM in Devon have small amounts of flue-tile even though few of them are likely to have had a hypocaust or bath-house. St Loye's College is no exception although 17 pieces of

Table 13.3.17 Analysis of sites receiving St David's church fabric

	Tegulae	*Group B*	*Other* tegulae	*Other fabrics*	*Military site*	*Masonry present*
Honeyditches, in Seaton	Yes	Yes	No	Isolated	Yes	Yes
St Loye's College	Yes	Yes	No	Isolated	Yes	No
Bolham, in Tiverton	Yes	Yes?	No	No	Yes	Poss
Pomeroy Wood, in Honiton	Yes	Yes	Yes	Yes	Yes	Poss
Plymouth, Woolster Street	Yes		Yes	Yes	Poss	No
Overland, in Thorverton	Yes	Yes	Yes	Yes		No
Milbury Farm, in Exminster	Yes	Yes	No	No		
Exeter, Princesshay	Yes	Yes	Yes	Yes	Yes	Yes

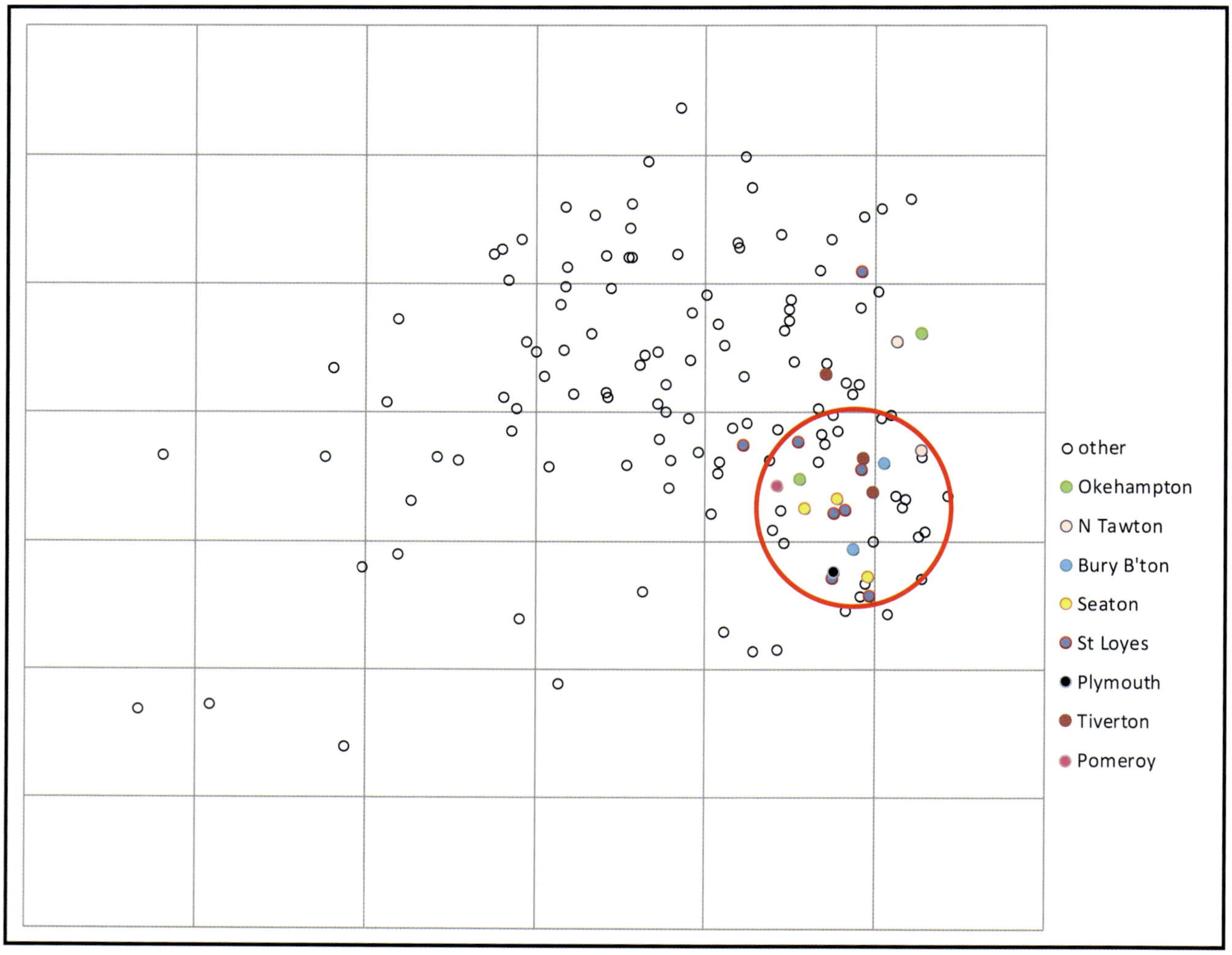

Fig. 13.3.30 Eight-element PCA of tegulae *from rural sites with military origins*

flue-tile is more than most and more significant is the presence of 90 pieces of flat, possibly *pilae*, tiles. Such brick was normally used for tiling courses in stone-built walls and for the floors and *pilae* of hypocausts, neither of which were apparent at St Loye's College. Whilst it is possible that some brick could have been used for industrial hearths, the overall CBM assemblage does not seem to be consonant with a 1st-century AD wooden building but could be entirely consistent with a 2nd-century AD roadside settlement.

One further consideration worth examining is the source of the tiles supplied to some of the other former military sites in Devon, namely Okehampton, North Tawton and Bury Barton. Figure 13.3.30 shows the PCA plot for all the tiles tested from these sites together with the 2nd-century AD tiles from the former military sites listed in Table 13.3.17. It is curious that *all* these former military sites should have similar fabric as seen by pXRF and raises the possibility that all of these sites could have been supplied by the St David's church kiln (although it should be noted that the tiles from the Okehampton *vicus* looked visibly different to the other Devon tiles). Encouragement for this possibility comes from Williams (1991b, 281–2) whose thin sections showed similarities between Okehampton, Bolham in Tiverton, and North Tawton.

2nd-century AD development in rural Devon

To provide some context for these developments within Devon, it is useful to compare the timeline of construction activity in Devon against the rest of southern Britain using *tegulae* cutaways as a proxy. Figure 13.3.31 presents the *tegula* cutaways in sequence for the rural sites in Devon and compares them against the 46 rural sites from the rest of southern Britain that have been examined by the author. Just over half the Devon cutaways come from Topsham, but excluding them from the analysis makes virtually no difference to the proportions of cutaway groups other than for the exclusion of the Type 7, Group E cutaways, which have not been found elsewhere in Devon. There is little 1st-century AD (Group A) activity in either category but the 2nd-century AD profile in Devon differs radically from that of the rest of southern Britain, with Group B cutaways representing 61% of the Devon cutaways compared to 11% in the rest of the South. Of course, the over-representation of Group B *tegulae* in Devon could be due to an under-representation of later villas and hence later *tegulae*; but to reduce the Devon proportion of Group B *tegulae* down to the 11% of the rest of the South would require an additional 253 later *tegulae*, equivalent to an improbable 12-fold increase in late tiles in the county. Other than Topsham, these rural Devon Group B cutaways were found on eight sites which, with the exception of the hardcore at Newenham Abbey, in Axminster, are all attributed to St David's church fabric.

This substantial anomaly requires explanation and it seems likely that the answer must be linked with the unusual distribution of 2nd-century AD St David's church

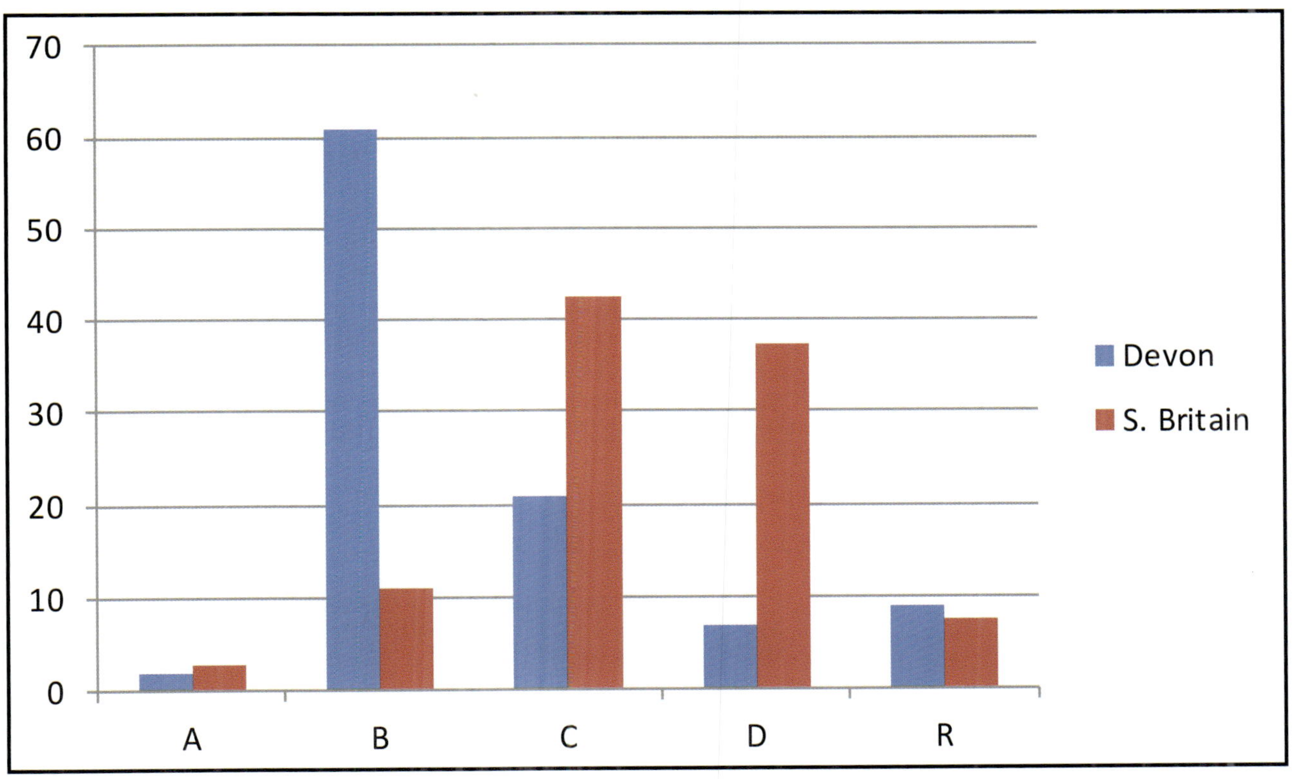

Group	*Devon* *No*	*%*	*S. Britain* *No*	*%*
A	1	2	24	3
B	34	61	83	11
C	12	21	350	42
D	4	7	308	37
R	5	9	61	7
Total	56		826	

Fig. 13.3.31 Comparison of proportions of tegulae *in Devon and southern Britain*

fabric, much of which was sent to former military sites. The obvious explanation is that these were farmsteads, industrial premises or villas that were simply re-utilising abandoned 1st-century AD forts because the ground had already been cleared and transport links were already established. If so, this relative boom compared to the rest of southern Britain dissipated quickly as most of the sites fail to show any continuation into the 3rd century AD. Given that we already believe that Seaton was a 2nd-century AD military, or possibly official, site then an alternative hypothesis would be that a number of former military sites were reoccupied in the 2nd century AD for policy reasons, for example to better supervise mineral extraction in the area, or possibly because of civil unrest. This would fit better both with the unusual upsurge in 2nd-century AD activity within Devon and also explain why this did not continue into the 3rd century AD. It might also explain the pilaster tile noted at St David's church (see online Appendix 13.1) which would have been more appropriate in a *mansio* or military building than a farmstead. In this regard it is worth noting that lead pigs from neighbouring Somerset were still being impressed with imperial stamps at least into the AD 160s (RIB II.1 2404.19–2404.22).

The answer to the above question will also determine whether we should imagine that St David's church was a private tilery established by legionary veterans (based on the style of some of their output) which started by supplying tile to the remaining forts in the period *c*. AD 80–90 and then to the evolving civilian market which was predominately centred on old military bases. Or whether it was a military/official kiln that supplied the immediate post-legionary requirements and was then mothballed until new military/official needs emerged in the middle of the 2nd century AD (EAPIT 1, Chapter 5). Hopefully future excavation on these sites will help elicit whether there actually were masonry structures on some of these sites and, if so, whether they were civil or military/official in character.

Summary and conclusions

Evolution of kiln sources

The conclusions of this work have to be caveated by warnings of the smallness of the sample (just 141 tiles tested by pXRF) and the very broadbrush data that this testing has yielded. Caution is also necessary because of the uncertain impact of chemical leaching both in absolute and relative terms across the county. Nevertheless, the leaching impact seems to be surprisingly small, and the data from Caerleon and Usk in the section on 'Dolphin antefixes and consideration of leaching effects' (above), and the general consistency of results, provides some assurance.

Figure 13.3.32 brings the analysis together in the form of a chart with time along the X axis and locations up the Y axis. The general area north-east of the town incorporating Princesshay was where the first postulated kilns were, initially supplying the legion and then the later civil town. As a result of the new town defences, Princesshay was replaced towards the end of the 2nd century AD by the postulated Central kiln using calcium-light clays which continued the supply to Exeter as well as to a number of sites positioned mainly along the River Exe, whilst the new postulated Eastern kiln supplied a growing number of sites in the east of the county. The St David's church kiln started production towards the end of the 1st century AD after the departure of the legion. It is unclear whether it was a private works run by military veterans or a military kiln replacing the legionary kiln that had been passed over to the civic

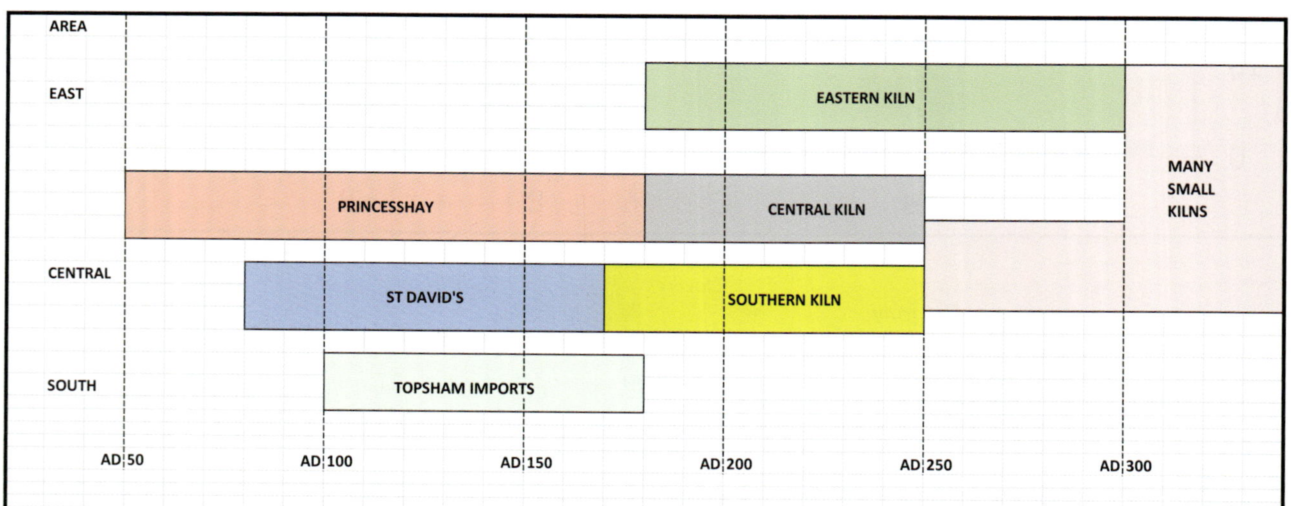

Fig. 13.3.32 Summary of kiln evolution in Devon

authorities. In either event it mainly supplied former military bases some of which may have continued to have a military or official role for example as *mansiones*. It, in turn, was superseded by the postulated Southern kiln, accessing similar clay to St David's church, which supplied some sites in the south of the county. Topsham received imports of tile by sea in the 2nd century AD but later received tiles from the Central kiln. These three kilns continued through the first half of the 3rd century AD but only the Eastern kiln continued production into the second half of the 3rd century AD. By the 4th century AD all of these larger kilns had been superseded by a multiplicity of smaller kilns, including Hatherleigh Moor, some of which appeared to displace or duplicate supplies from the Eastern kiln.

It is perhaps surprising that tile production in Devon appears to be represented by just five tileries until the latter half of the 3rd century AD but this figure probably understates the true number as minor fabrics have generally been ignored in the analysis. Imports also appear to have been restricted and are mainly represented by the 2nd-century AD Topsham tiles. However, consideration should also be given to five *tegulae* found with the regional Group R Type 7 cutaways at Topsham (see Fig. 13.3.44 in online Appendix 13.1) and the late pentagonal tiles found in Exeter. The Type 7 cutaway is a 4th-century AD form that has only previously been found in Hampshire and Sussex together with an isolated pocket in Northamptonshire (Warry 2016, 63). The polygonal ceramic tiles are also very rare 4th-century AD artefacts only previously found in Hampshire and Sussex and neighbouring counties to the north. As neither Type 7 cutaways nor polygonal tiles have been found in the half dozen late sites examined by the author in Dorset, this would suggest that either these tiles or a tile-maker have been imported into Devon.

Villa production of tiles is often cited as a likely source of CBM but there is limited evidence for this in Devon other than the apparent proliferation of small late tile fabrics and, indeed, not a great amount of evidence for it in Britain more widely. Piddington, in Northamptonshire, is probably the best example of a villa type structure with a kiln attached but many of the other candidates may be better described as tileries with farmsteads attached (as evidenced by the number of impressions of farm animals' feet found on the tiles). With the exception of Princesshay we actually know very little about the Devon tileries. The St David's church kiln lies beneath the modern church and the minimal excavation that was possible did not reach the kiln structure or any associated buildings. At Hatherleigh Moor we have the probable location of the kiln but none of the associated infrastructure. The locations of the three postulated kilns – Central, Southern and Eastern – have yet to be pinned down but Dr Machin's thin sections Chapter 13.2 help to identify the geological areas where they are likely to lie.

Economic and architectural development

There are a number of features of Exeter's development that match those of Gloucester as each civil administration assumed control of a vacated legionary fortress towards the end of the 1st century AD and also took possession of the former legionary kiln. Both appear to have excluded the products of other tile makers by granting exclusivity to their own tileries. In the case of Gloucester we know from tile stamps that the tilery was either owned, or at least sponsored, by the civic authorities (Warry 2017) and it would not be unreasonable to assume a similar arrangement in Exeter.

Figure 13.3.33 compares *tegula* lower cutaways recorded in Exeter and Gloucester. Five times as many lower cutaways have been recorded in Gloucester as Exeter which is probably mainly indicative of the number of excavations and retention policies pursued in the two towns rather than the relative number of tiled buildings. Nevertheless, it still suggests that Exeter was less endowed with such buildings than Gloucester, despite the significant size of the town once the new defences were constructed (Holbrook and Bidwell 1991, 282, fig. 136 shows that only 102 kg of *tegulae* had been recovered from Exeter prior to 1991 which compares with over a tonne from Gloucester by that stage).

The relative proportions of the different cutaway forms are instructive: both towns have slightly more than twice the number of Group B cutaways compared to Group A cutaways which demonstrates a significant survival of the legionary roofing stock followed, theoretically, by twice as many early domestic or civic roofs. However, the bigger difference is in the Group C cutaways: only 6% of the Gloucester cutaways were Group C compared with 37% of the Exeter cutaways. The Gloucester data indicate that the town switched from ceramic to stone tiles close to AD 200, if not slightly before, whereas the equality of Group B and C forms at Exeter would suggest that the transition to stone/slate tiles did not occur until nearer AD 250. Although Selwood (1991, 282) states that stone tiles start in Exeter from the late 2nd century AD, he notes they are absent from large dumps of material in the outer fortress ditch dated *c.* AD 160–180. The only evidence for new ceramic tiles entering Exeter in the later 3rd and 4th centuries AD is two damaged but possible Group D *tegulae* at St Catherine's Almshouses and a couple of pentagonal ceramic tiles from Cathedral Close which were intended to imitate the stone tiles. Thus it is probable that Exeter houses were normally wholly covered in stone/slate tiles from the later 3rd century AD onwards (as demonstrated at Trichay Street and Rack Street: Chapters 5 and 8 in this volume). This can also be inferred to be the practice in Gloucester.

It was not possible to quantify the proportions of different CBM product types found within Exeter in any scientific manner but the general impression was that, like Gloucester, there was relatively little flue-tile

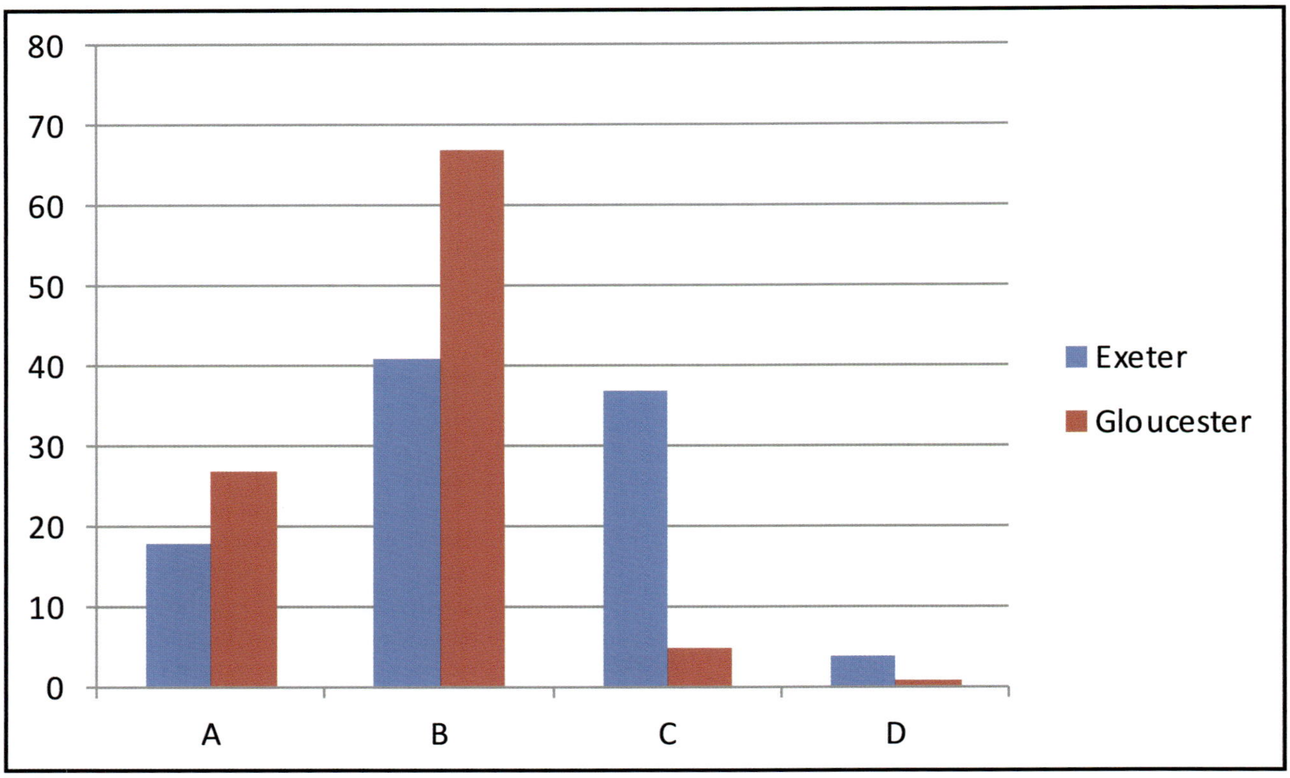

Group	Exeter No	Exeter %	Gloucester No	Gloucester %
A	10	18	76	27
B	22	41	190	67
C	20	37	16	5
D	2	4	2	1
Total	54		284	

Fig. 13.3.33 Comparison of proportions of tegula *cutaway in Exeter and Gloucester*

(say 10%) suggesting a limited number of hypocausts and bath-houses. There also appeared to be a minimal quantity of flat tile that could have been used as bonding courses in Exeter, especially when compared to Gloucester, which could suggest that fewer Exeter houses had two storeys.

Gloucester and Cirencester were amongst the first towns in the country to move away from ceramic roof tiles and the trend away from ceramic use would seem to have gradually radiated out to other towns from there. However, the tide in the countryside was less strong: some buildings continued to use ceramic tile while others moved to a combination of stone tile on the main roofs and ceramic tile on the aisles, for example as at Meonstoke (King 1996, 64–6); this combination of stone and ceramic tiles is also confirmed by miniature models of buildings – one from Titelberg and another in a private French collection. Roofs in rural Devon would appear to have been consistent with this arrangement.

The evolution of rural Devon, discussed in the section on '2nd-century AD development in rural Devon' above, showed that there was an apparent boom in 2nd-century tile use, primarily on former military sites, which was not sustained into the 3rd century AD. The CBM evidence best fits with a military/official explanation rather than agricultural/industrial cause, but is not conclusive. Also notable in Fig. 13.3.31 is the relative paucity of Group D and R *tegulae* in rural Devon compared to the rest of southern Britain which, even after compensating for the unusual 2nd-century AD peak, supports the often-made observation that villas and other buildings with tiled roofs were much scarcer here than in neighbouring *pays* further east.

Validity of morphology/pXRF methodology

In this chapter the initial analysis was based on tile (mainly *tegula*) morphology. These tentative results were then validated in a series of pXRF bi-plots and these results were checked by PCA analysis omitting the potentially mobile potassium element used for the bi-plots, thereby creating a further independent dataset. A further layer of corroboration has been provided by selected thin section analysis. A final check is provided by examining whether the fabric distributions make sense on the ground in terms of geography.

The initial results from the morphology/pXRF bi-plots have largely been sustained through each of the validation steps. Some minor adjustments have been made as a result of combined idealised analysis as shown in Table 13.3.15 where, *inter alia*, the thin sections did not support the tentative Hatherleigh Moor grouping. However, the pXRF was able to differentiate between the 1st and 2nd-century AD phases of Princesshay and the two phases of the Eastern kiln, both of which were indistinguishable in thin section. It also provided strong evidence to identify the St David's church kiln output that thin section analysis did not pin down.

Potassium, titanium and calcium may not be the most appropriate elements to use in bi-plot analysis in other geographic regions with different geologies, but the basic methodology used in this research should be applicable to CBM studies more generally and ought to be within the compass of many archaeological organisations. Considerably greater precision and more chemical elements could have been obtained with a superior machine, regular recalibration, longer duration and more sophisticated analytical techniques. However, this paper demonstrates that useful 'broadbrush' conclusions can be achieved with a less precise approach. A more exacting approach would generate more accurate readings but these would not necessarily deliver a sufficiently improved analysis to justify the extra cost and time taken. PCA software is widely available and straight forward to use so this could be added to the analytical arsenal but there should be no need to regularly use thin sections. However, attempting to interpret pXRF or PCA data blind – that is without the morphological analysis employed in this paper – is unlikely to be successful as exemplified by Figure 13.3.4.

Potential future work

This study has only examined the assemblages contained in the RAMM together with an opportunistic sample of those held elsewhere. Future work to discover and examine assemblages from further rural sites and in particular from Topsham and its environs would be helpful, especially in elucidating the 2nd-century AD position. Further pXRF analysis could be undertaken of the existing assemblages to reinforce (or otherwise) the conclusions reached in this chapter.

It would be helpful if more attention was paid to stone/slate assemblages and their interaction with ceramic tiles, in particular to quantify the relative weights of these materials from each site. It would also be interesting to look further into Cornwall, Somerset and Dorset to identify at what point tiles from sources outside of Devon begin to appear.

Finally, there would be value in undertaking pXRF on tiles found at Fishbourne and Lake Farm, Dorset to see if the close similarities (same dimensions, same lower cutaway, same rare diagonal upper cutaways) noted between *tegulae* from the early abortive trenches of the Fishbourne villa and the Exeter legionary bath-house reflect tiles made in the same kiln or simply using the same former.

Acknowledgments

This chapter would not have been possible without the generous assistance of Tom Cadbury, Jenny Durrant and Naomi Payne in flagging potential assemblages and extracting them from store; John Davey with pXRF testing; David Gould for production of the maps, context data and also with the pXRF testing; and the wise counsel and advice of Stephen Rippon, Neil Holbrook and Paul Bidwell. I am also grateful to Mark Lewis for access and advice on the tiles held at Caerleon.

14

The Querns and Millstones of Roman Exeter: Supplying and Feeding the Fortress and Town

Ruth Shaffrey

Introduction

This chapter provides a corpus of all the known rotary querns and millstones from in and around Roman Exeter and incorporates evidence from the wider region. Part 1 considers querns as a commodity: what they are made from and how these items were manufactured and distributed. The geology of the South-West Peninsula is different to any other part of England and this is reflected in the choices of stone for making querns. The evidence indicates a strongly local bias in the exploitation of stone even where it was not of high quality for grinding, while there also appears to be no link between the extraction of stone for major building projects (*e.g.* the town walls) and the working of stone for querns. This section also considers the chronology of rotary quern use and the morphology of the querns. Part 2 uses the data on quern distribution to investigate how grain processing and flour supply was organised in and around the town. By examining the density of quern use and the occurrences of millstones – the only evidence of centralised and intensified milling that consistently survives in the archaeological record – this chapter looks at where grain processing occurred. Comparison is made with the organisation of grain processing for other Roman towns.

Rotary querns are important artefacts for archaeological study because they can tell us about patterns of manufacture and supply as well as the organisation of food production. However, one could be forgiven for thinking that the residents of Roman Exeter never ate bread or drank ale, such is the disregard for rotary querns and millstones as a class of material culture in the study of the town. Until recently, the only published examples of Roman querns were a few examples made from German lava found at Friernhay Street, Rack Street and Holloway Street, published in a petrographical study (Bell and Bradshaw 1983), and no report was included in Holbrook and Bidwell's (1991) *Roman Finds from Exeter*.

This study into the use of querns in and around Exeter was based upon the examination of examples held at the Royal Albert Memorial Museum (RAMM) in Exeter, Topsham and Torquay Museums, AC Archaeology, Cotswold Archaeology, Wessex Archaeology, and the University of Exeter. To the best of the author's knowledge, this assessment includes all the Roman querns found in Exeter to date. It is not intended to provide exhaustive coverage of all the querns and millstones of Devon, because that was not within the remit of this research, but it is hoped that it will serve as an introduction to the subject and to highlight the benefits of studying these under-appreciated artefacts.

A total of 183 fragments representing 124 items were recorded for this survey. Those that were from certain pre-Roman contexts were omitted from further analysis (although are mentioned in the text where relevant) and only querns and millstones of likely rotary form are included, and so this report analyses 163 fragments from 104 querns and millstones from Exeter and Devon. These were recovered from 41 sites in total. Of these, 11 sites are from inside Exeter's town walls, five are just outside the walls (termed extra-mural in Table 14.1), 11 sites are in Exeter's wider hinterland (within 20 km as the crow flies, see below) and the remaining sites are from further afield in Devon (termed county in Table 14.1). The majority of these sites produced only a single quern each (Table 14.1).

Saddle querns were in use from the Neolithic onwards for the grinding of grains and other foodstuffs. They were superseded by the rotary quern, which was introduced during the Middle Iron Age but it is not uncommon to find saddle querns and rubbers in Roman contexts in southern England. We cannot rule out their continued use

Table 14.1 Romano-British sites in Devon with rotary querns and/or millstones (for excavations within Exeter, the 'Site Number' refers to Chapter 2 above)

Site	*Category*	*No. rotary querns*	*No. millstones (>50cm)*	*Reference/location*
Aller Cross, in Kingskerswell	county	4		Quinnell 2015b, 158
Berry Meadow, in Kingsteignton	county	1		Allan 1987, 94
Billany Farm, in Dartington,	county	3		Mudd and Joyce 2014
Bray Valley Quarries, in Brayford	county	2		Best 2005, 4
Chagford	county	1		RAMM
Choakford Farm, in Sparkwell	county	2		Tyler 2009, 13
Clanacombe, in Thurlestone	county	1		Greene and Greene 1970, 134
Dainton Elms Cross, in Ipplepen	county	6		Shaffrey pers. obs.; to be deposited in Torquay Museum
Exeter, Arts Centre	intra-mural	1		RAMM
Exeter, Crematorium	hinterland		1	Payne and Passmore 2016, 3
Exeter, Bishop's Court	extra-mural	2		Payne 2017b, 15
Exeter, Brickfields	hinterland	1		RAMM
Exeter, Exe Street (Site 83)	extra-mural	1		RAMM
Exeter, Friernhay Street (Site 75)	intra-mural	3		RAMM
Exeter, Goldsmith Street (Site 37/ 39)	intra-mural	1		RAMM
Exeter, Holloway Street (Site 50/65)	extra-mural	1	1	RAMM
Exeter, Princesshay (Site 156)	intra-mural	3		RAMM
Exeter, Rack Street (Site 52)	intra-mural	3	1	RAMM
Exeter, St Loyes College	hinterland	2		RAMM
Exeter, St Luke's School	hinterland	1		RAMM
Exeter, St Stephen's High Street	intra-mural		1	RAMM
Exeter, Trichay Street (Site 42)	intra-mural	1		RAMM
Exeter, Valiant Soldier (Site 44)	extra-mural		1	RAMM
Hill Barton, in Heavitree	hinterland	4		Shaffrey 2017a
Hill Barton, in Heavitree	hinterland	1		Payne 2016, 12
Holcombe Villa, in Uplyme	county		2	Pollard 1974, 152
Honeyditches, in Seaton	county	1		Pollard 1972, 226
Langford Barton/Springfield, in Ugborough	county	2		Mudd and Joyce 2014, 113
North Tawton	county	3		RAMM
Overland, in Thorverton	hinterland	1		Uglow 2000, 227
Penns Mount, in Kingsteignton	county	1		Weddell *et al.* 2016, 5-6
Pomeroy Wood, in Honiton	hinterland	22+	1	Loader 1999
Rocombe, in Stokeinteignhead	county	1		Torquay Museum
Shepherd's Lane, in Teignmouth	hinterland	1		Haines 2013, 21
Sherford New Community, near Plymouth	county	4		G. Jones pers. comm.
Shortlands Lane, in Cullompton	county	1		Watts and Taylor 2014, 201
Tithe Barn Green, in Monkerton	hinterland	2		Shaffrey 2016
Yarde's Field, in Topsham	hinterland	5	2	Morris *et al.* 1938
Wessex Close, in Topsham	hinterland	5		Quinnell 2018a, 46

in the processing of grain without developments in residue analysis on the surfaces of querns, which has the potential to give us much needed information on what querns were used for. However, saddle querns were omitted from this study because the original aim was to investigate the production and use of rotary querns and millstones only.

Part 1: Querns as a commodity

Any analysis of querns and millstones such as this can be divided into two parts. The first is an examination of querns as a commodity – a product that was made, distributed, owned, used, often recycled, and eventually discarded. This investigation considers the distribution of querns and millstones of different stone types, both spatially and chronologically, with a view to understanding quern production and supply in the region around Roman Exeter. The second part of this research uses querns and millstones to help us understand how grain processing (and the resulting flour and malt production) was organised in and around the Roman town.

In this section, querns and millstones have been grouped together and are discussed under the following broad lithological groupings: granite, greisen and elvan; Greensand; local basalts from the Exeter Volcanics; other South-Western rocks; and lava imported from the continent. Querns need to be studied in terms of stone type because this helps us identify likely points of stone extraction and quern manufacture. In turn, this provides information about how these tools were supplied.

Granite, greisen and elvan (Fig. 14.1A)

Granite, greisen and elvan rotary querns have been found on 14 sites. The granite used for rotary querns in and around Roman Exeter is variable and clearly from multiple sources. It includes non-megacrystic biotite granite, coarse megacrystic granite containing tourmaline, and medium-grained granite with biotite and muscovite (known locally as moorstone). Querns were also made from quartz-porphyry (known colloquially as elvan), and rarely an altered granitic rock known as greisen. Some of the granite could have been sourced on Dartmoor and the elvan may have come from the Roborough elvan, although varieties of both may also have been brought into Devon from Cornwall. There is clearly much work to be done on the provenancing of granite querns in the region, but some observations can be made nonetheless.

Granite querns were used to the west and south of Exeter and within relative proximity to the sources in Dartmoor and Cornwall. Querns of granite have been found at Aller Cross, in Kingskerswell; North Tawton, Clanacombe, in Thurlestone; Choakford Farm, in Sparkwell; Bitbeare Farm, in Winkleigh (which is Iron Age and therefore not listed in Table 14.1); Billany Farm, in Dartington, and Langford Barton/Springfield, in Ugborough. The most easterly point of use appears to have been in Exeter itself, where they have been found at Rack Street, Valiant Soldier, Friernhay Street, St Stephen's High Street, and St Luke's College (Fig. 14.1A). There is virtually no evidence for the export of granite, greisen and elvan querns to the rest of lowland Roman Britain, although a granite rubber and saddle quern from Bronze Age contexts at Bunford Hollow, in Yeovil (Somerset), probably originated in Devon or Cornwall (Shaffrey pers. obs).

The presence of granite, greisen and elvan querns in Roman Exeter evidences the movement of people and goods from the west, but their absence to the east of the town suggests that the few querns found in Exeter were personal belongings, rather than having been brought into the town for sale or exchange. If the town had functioned as a distribution point in this way, we might reasonably expect to see a different, more evenly spread, distribution pattern around the town. The lack of evidence for secondary distribution of querns via Exeter is in keeping with the idea that towns were not market centres for such goods.

Few of the granite, greisen and elvan querns were recovered from features dated more closely than 'Roman' so establishing a chronology for their production and use is problematic, although the morphology of granite rotary querns suggest that production of them began during the Iron Age and continued through the Roman period. A small bun-shaped quern with lateral handle socket at Bitbeare Farm, for example, was found in an Iron Age context, whilst a rounded quern from North Tawton is probably also of Iron Age origin. Rounded querns of elvan from Berry Down, in Kingsteignton, suggest that rotary querns were also being made from this stone before the Roman period (Fig. 14.2a; Berry Down is an Iron Age site and therefore not listed in Table 14.1). In most of southern Britain, the transition from partly perforated to fully perforated lower stones occurred during the later 1st century BC to 1st century AD. Partially perforated lower stones of elvan and granite with convex grinding surfaces and partially perforated spindle sockets were found at Aller Cross, in Kingskerswell (Fig. 14.2g, h), as well as a similar elvan example at Berry Down (Fig. 14.2i). More certainly Roman forms include examples of disc type with flat parallel faces (as at Friernhay Street, in Exeter). Greisen querns are rare but include one of probable Late Roman date with a projecting collar at Billany Farm, in Dartington (Mudd and Joyce 2014, 110–12).

Three of the querns are on the large size for hand operation at 50 cm, 53 cm and 54 cm, and these examples – from Rack Street, the Valiant Soldier and St Stephens respectively (all in Exeter) – might well have required additional power. Whilst their sizes are at the lower end of what can be classified as a millstone, they are large for the region generally, and large for querns of granite and associated stone types, which measure 29–45 cm diameter and average around 35 cm. This suggests that they might belong to a different class of quern or millstone.

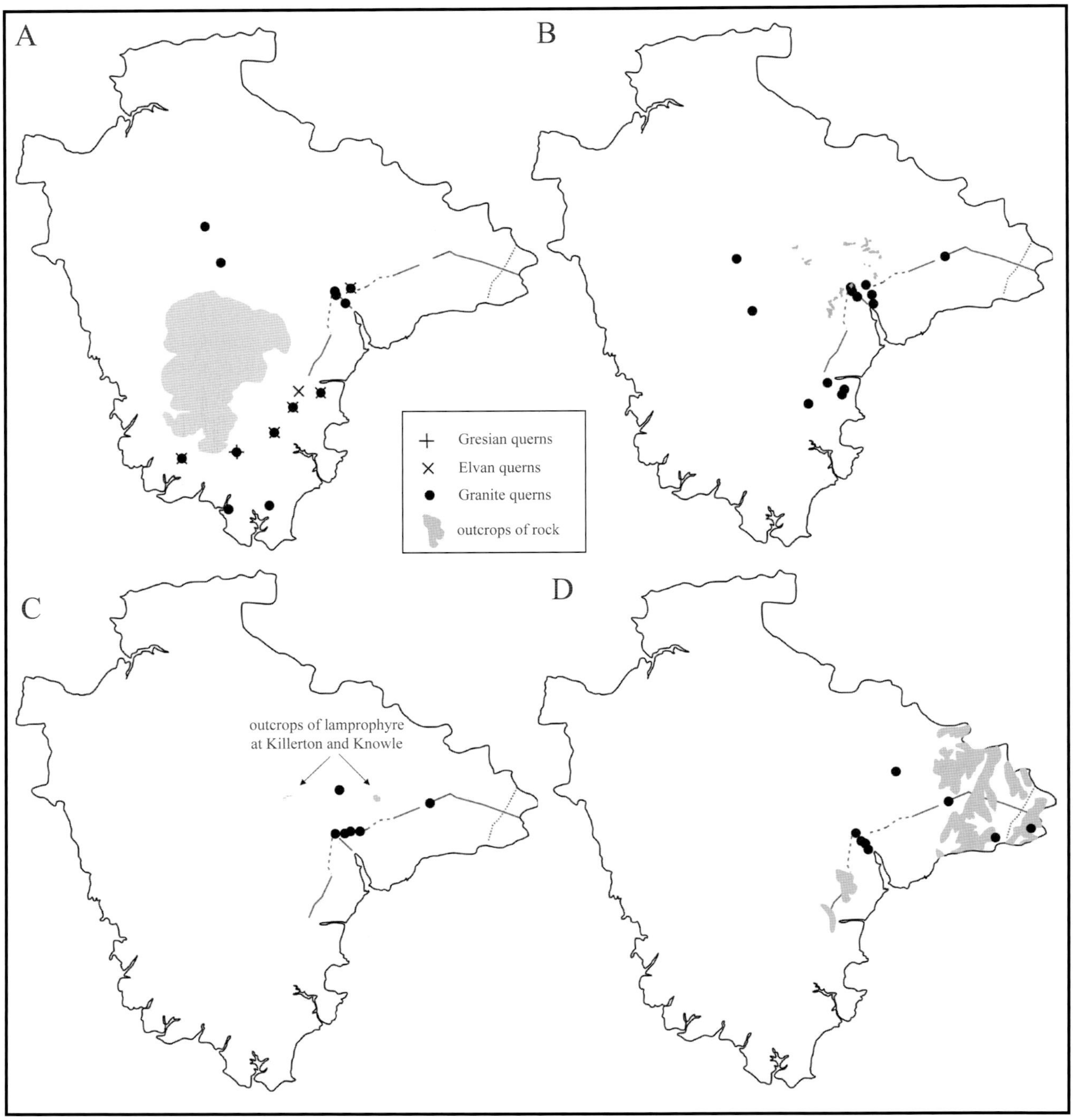

Fig. 14.1 Distribution of querns by lithology. A: granite, greisen and elvan; B: amygdaloidal basalt; C: lamprophyre; D: Upper Greensand

The Exeter Volcanics

By far the most popular choice for querns in the Exeter area are the Exeter Volcanics. Figure 14.1B maps all Permian rocks in this region. The Exeter Volcanics occur as extrusive and intrusive rocks at the base of this succession and typically occur as small outcrops, with notable exposures to the north of Exeter around Silverton (at Killerton), Thorverton and Budlake, to the south and west of Exeter near Ide and Dunchideock (Horner *et al.* 2017), as well as well-known exposures close to or in the town itself at Rougemont and Pocombe. Two distinct rock types were used for querns during the Roman period.

Amygdaloidal basalt

The most popular choice for rotary querns in the Exeter area was a reddish-purple porphyritic basaltic lava with feldspar phenocrysts and some quartz filled amygdales, from the Exeter Volcanics (Fig. 14.1B). Although it resembles stone from Pocombe on the western edge of modern-day Exeter, it lacks the distinctive quartz veins of that rock and it does not precisely match any samples collected during fieldwork for this paper. A precise source has therefore not yet been determined, but it is certainly from the Exeter Volcanics and its source is therefore likely to be within proximity of Exeter, to the north, west or south-west. It accounts for 36 querns from 16 sites.

Most of the lower stones have partially perforated sockets indicating likely Late Iron Age production, for example at Topsham, Pomeroy Wood, in Honiton, Bishop's Court near Exeter, and Penns Mount, in Kingsteignton, but an example from Pomeroy Wood is fully perforated which is more typical of Roman querns (Fig. 14.2j). Upper stones are of very varied form suggesting long lived production. They include bun-shaped querns with concave grinding surface and blind side handle socket (Fig. 14.2c) which are typical of Iron Age querns and flat-topped types, sometimes with a kerbed upper surface or wide shallow hopper (Fig. 14.2d) and disc type querns with parallel faces, more typical of Roman querns. Querns in this basalt typically range in size from 30 cm to 40 cm diameter and up to 55 cm diameter, the larger examples possibly representing mechanically powered millstones. As with querns of granite, greisen and elvan, there is almost no evidence for the movement of querns of stone from the Exeter Volcanics outside the local area, although there is a small fragment of bun-shaped upper rotary quern from a context of currently unphased date at Bunford Hollow in Yeovil, Somerset (Shaffrey pers. obs.).

Lamprophyre

Lamprophyre is a fine-grained, dark, greyish-red or bluish-grey vesicular rock (a minette) containing, in the case of the variants used for the querns, frequent biotite (Fig. 14.1C). The most likely source for the querns is in the area of Killerton but while samples from there show a strong resemblance to the querns (Shaffrey 2017a), the possibility remains that other exposures of lamprophyre were also exploited. Querns from five sites are made of lamprophyre, all in the vicinity of Exeter: Hill Barton, in Pinhoe; Tithe Barn Green, in Monkerton; Pomeroy Wood, in Honiton; Overland, in Thorverton, and Exeter Brickfields.

The most closely dated of these querns were found in features of Late Iron Age to Early Roman date (100 BC–AD 100) at Hill Barton, 4 km to the east of the town. In form, the lamprophyre querns tend towards an Iron Age shape, with rounded profile and sloped or flat grinding surface (Fig. 14.2e). At least two examples have basin-shaped hoppers and one has a blind side handle socket. Lower stones are typically partly perforated (Fig. 14.2k). These querns suggest a Late Iron Age phase of production of lamprophyre querns, but the example from Pomeroy Wood of a flat-topped Roman type indicates that production extended beyond the Late Iron Age. The small number of querns indicates a probable ad-hoc exploitation of this rock, rather than an organised industry and the limited distribution reflects this.

Vesicular lava

A very vesicular type of lava was used for querns at Pomeroy Wood. Most only survive as fragments with part of a pecked surface, but at least one substantial fragment of thick flat quern was also recovered. This seems a poor choice for a quern material as the vesicles in the rock are so substantial in size that flour and grain are likely to have fallen into the holes, necessitating regular removal of the upper stone, so that the lower stone could be cleaned. Its presence is difficult to explain.

Upper Greensand

Although the majority of querns in the Exeter area were made from igneous rock types, sandstone was also used to manufacture querns and the main source of these is in the Upper Greensand (Fig. 14.1D). The Greensand used is typically greyish-brown in colour due to the weathering of the glauconite and can have obvious traces of silicified shell. It is likely that this rock originates in the Blackdown Hills of eastern Devon (Pollard 1974, 152; Watts and Taylor 2014) but fieldwork to collect samples for comparison has not been carried out and it is not possible to be more precise on provenance at present. The Blackdown Hills were an area rich in natural resources, with an important iron industry (Griffith and Weddell 1996) and recently recognised Romano-British pottery (Chapter 12 above) and tile production (Chapter 13 above). A link between the production and export of querns and other natural resources is a logical conclusion. In the Forest of Dean, quern manufacture was associated with ironworking at the Chesters Villa, and distribution patterns of the iron and the querns from the area suggest similar mechanisms of distribution (Fulford and Allen 1992; Shaffrey 2006). A link might also be postulated between quern production and lead extraction in the Mendips (Shaffrey 2006, 77).

Rotary querns of Upper Greensand have been identified at seven sites: Princesshay, in Exeter; Exeter Crematorium and St Loye's College just to the east of the town; and Shortlands Lane, in Cullompton; Holcombe, in Uplyme; Honeyditches, in Seaton and Pomeroy Wood, in Honiton. All these sites are near to or east of Exeter, reflecting the easterly location of the outcrops. No rotary querns of Upper Greensand have been recovered from pre-Roman contexts in Devon and those that are securely dated were found in features of 3rd to 4th-century AD date as at Holcombe, in Uplyme and Pomeroy Wood, in Honiton, suggesting that a minor industry manufacturing querns from Upper Greensand was operating during the Late Roman period. The querns are also of Roman or Late Roman form, being large in diameter (ranging from 40–95 cm in diameter) and typically either of flat-disc type, or projecting-hopper type (Fig. 14.2b). One example from Honeyditches in Seaton is unusual in that it has a kerbed upper surface, a feature not common on native-made querns, and is probably an imitation of continental lava querns. Examples from Holcombe, in Uplyme, and

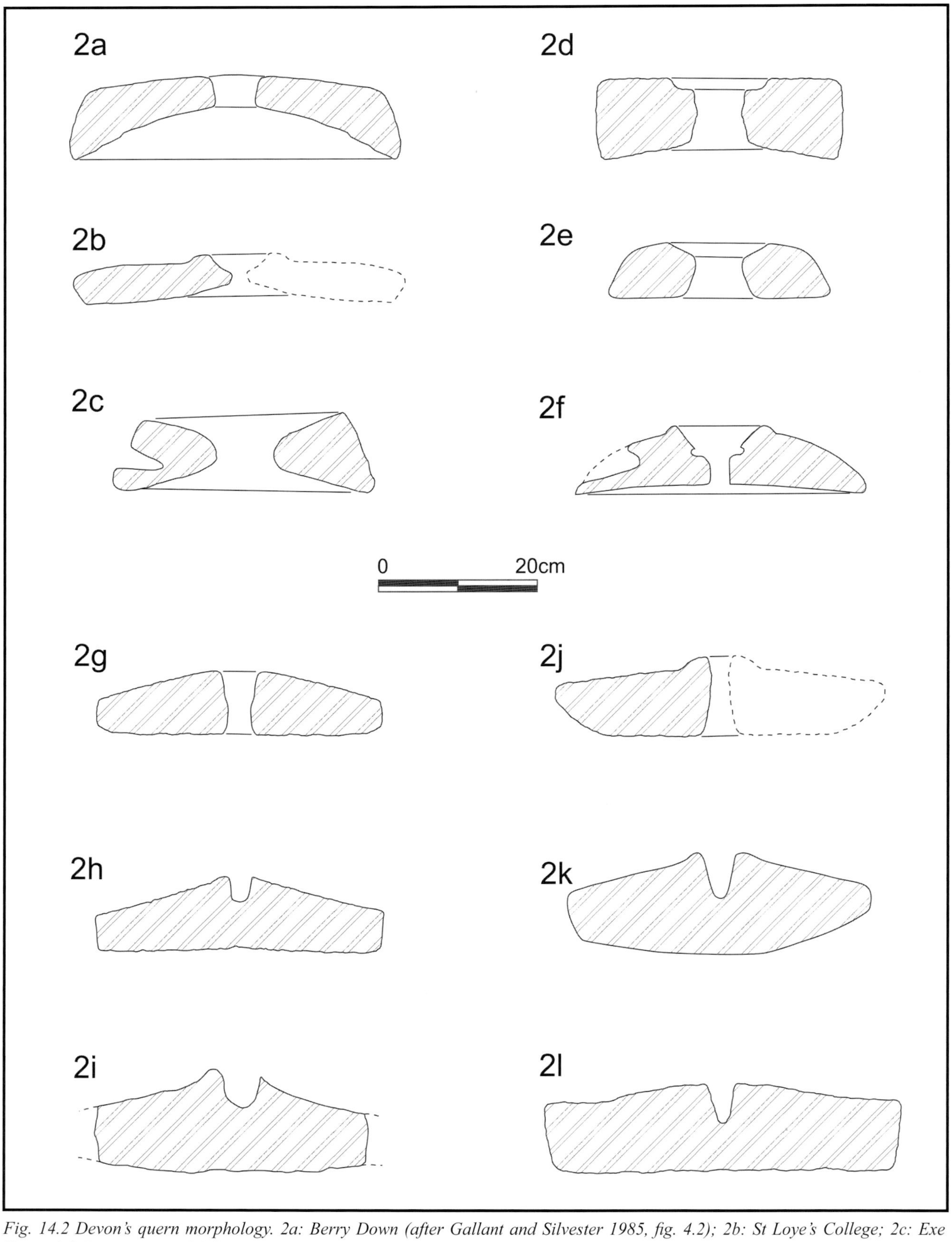

Fig. 14.2 Devon's quern morphology. 2a: Berry Down (after Gallant and Silvester 1985, fig. 4.2); 2b: St Loye's College; 2c: Exe Street; 2d: Pomeroy Wood (after Loader 1999, fig. 148.3); 2e: Hill Barton (after Mudd 2017, fig. 24d); 2f: Tithe Barn Green; 2g and h: Aller Cross (after Quinnell 2015b, fig. 34); 2i Berry Down (after Gallant and Silvester 1985, fig. 4.1); 2j Pomeroy Wood (after Loader 1999, fig 148.4); 2k Hill Barton (after Mudd 2017, fig. 24c); 2l: Pomeroy Wood (after Loader 1999, fig. 148.2)

Exeter Crematorium are large enough to have required additional power (Pollard 1974, 152; Payne and Passmore 2016, 3).

Other South-Western sources

A number of other minor sources were also used for the production of querns. One probable quern fragment of Dawlish sandstone was found at Pomeroy Wood, in Honiton. Dawlish sandstone outcrops in a band running north-south to the north and east of Exeter as well as either side of the River Exe south of Exeter towards the coast. Dawlish sandstone is typically quite soft and not particularly well suited to use for grinding, but this stone was presumably selected as an usually well-cemented variety, suitable for grinding. Two querns of Hangman Grit were found in 2nd-century AD contexts at Bray Valley in Brayford. They are of Late Iron Age/Early Roman form with partially perforated sockets. Hangman Point (from where the stone came) is located some 16 km north-west of the site (Best 2005, 4). Querns of other sandstones include typical partially perforated lower stones (Fig. 14.2l) and less typical forms such as one from Tithe Barn Green, in Monkerton, of rounded form but with a rynd chase set into the hopper (Fig. 14.2f).

Continental lava

Lava from the continent is a grey vesicular rock that was in use in Roman Britain from the time of the Conquest (Fitzpatrick 2017). It is light and easy to transport and was therefore a popular choice, particularly among the military. Analysis during the 1980s suggested that most of the lava used in Britain was imported from the Eifel region of Germany and that is the assumption made here, although French sources in Volvic, in Auvergne, and elsewhere in Europe should not be ruled out. No further analysis has been carried out for this chapter, but the most advanced XRF (X-ray fluorescence) analysis is now able to provenance lava querns precisely, not only to a region, but to a specific lava flow (Gluhak and Hofmeister 2011) and the potential exists for the Exeter querns to be subjected to this analysis in the future.

Lava querns have been found on seven excavations in Devon, five of which are within Exeter (Trichay Street, Rack Street, Friernhay Street, Goldsmith Street and Holloway Street). Outside of Exeter, lava querns have been found only at Wessex Close, in Topsham, and at Pomeroy Wood, in Honiton. Few of the lava querns have been found in closely dated contexts but one quern from Pomeroy Wood (in ten fragments), one from Rack Street, and two from Friernhay Street were found in contexts dating to the military occupation (Bell and Bradshaw 1983, 130). Lava querns were noted during the excavations at Goldsmith Street and Trichay Street (Paul Bidwell pers. comm.) but these were either never retained or are now missing. Lava querns from Rack Street, in Exeter, and Wessex Close, in Topsham, are from 2nd and 3rd-century AD contexts but all are fragmentary (Quinnell 2018a, 46) and so may be residual rather than providing evidence for the continued use of imported lava into the 3rd century AD. Fragments of quern identified as possibly Mayen lava were also found at an 8th-century AD site at Berry Meadow, in Kingsteignton (Allan 1987, 94): it is possible they are residual Roman material but were found in an 8th-century AD ditch.

The recovery of lava querns from predominantly military sites, or civilian sites with military origins, is striking, although survival of lava querns is poor in the acidic soils of the South-West, and they often survive as undiagnostic fragments, recognisable only by the stone type. The possibility that these are missed during excavation or not retained due to a perception that little can be learned from them is therefore high and we should perhaps be careful not to read too much into their 'absence'.

Few of the lava querns survive in large enough pieces for much to be said about their form, but one from Friernhay Street has the kerb and elbow-shaped handle socket typical of these querns (Crawford and Röder 1955, Type 4). Interestingly the grinding surface of this quern was worn right down to the underneath of the handle socket by the time it was deposited – during the latest occupation of the fortress now dated to the late AD 70s/early 80s (EAPIT 1, Chapter 5) – illustrating the relatively short life-span of these querns. Three examples – the querns from 1st-century AD contexts at Rack Street and Friernhay Street – have measurable diameters, and these are 38, 38 and 40 cm diameter.

Discussion

The pattern of stone exploitation for querns in the Exeter area and wider region indicates a number of small-scale industries each producing and distributing only over a relatively limited area. Although there was clearly movement of querns from Cornwall into Devon (*e.g.* elvan and probably some granite), no querns were brought into Devon from the rest of southern Britain and none of the major quern producers of the south are represented (Greensand from Pen Pits in Somerset, Lodsworth in West Sussex, or Folkestone in Kent; Old Red Sandstone from the Mendips, Bristol or Wye Valley; puddingstone from Hertfordshire or Worms Heath near Croydon in Surrey). There are also no querns of Millstone Grit, which were widely used across the rest of southern England during the Roman period. Millstone Grit outcrops extensively across a wide geographical area in Derbyshire and South Yorkshire. Rotary querns and millstones are known to have been manufactured during the Roman period at Wharncliffe in South Yorkshire, at Rivelin on the outskirts of modern-day Sheffield, and at Blackbrook in Derbyshire (Pearson and Oswald 2000; Palfreyman and Ebbins 2007; Newman 2016, 29). Not all querns can be directly provenanced to these quarries, however, and it is likely that many more quarries were in operation during the Roman period. Some of these absences are a result of geography: querns of Folkestone Beds Greensand were manufactured in eastern Kent and puddingstone from Hertfordshire and Surrey are not found in any of the westernmost counties; greensand querns from Pen Pits in Somerset are absent because these reached only a relatively small area of Somerset and Wiltshire; and Lodsworth Greensand querns from West Sussex, although distributed widely across the south, have been found only as far west as Devizes and Wanborough in Wiltshire (Buckley 2001). Both Millstone Grit and Old Red Sandstone, the two principal British stone types used for querns in southern Roman Britain, are, however, also absent. Millstone Grit querns occur on a number of sites in Somerset including at Bath (Bath Museum Acc: BATRM 1986.116), while Old Red Sandstone, which outcrops in Somerset, is the most common quern material in that county (Shaffrey 2006). Its absence in Devon is particularly noteworthy since its distribution northwards and eastwards is much greater.

In addition, with the exception of Mayen lava querns, continental imports are also absent. Querns of rocks sourced on mainland Europe or the Channel Islands are not common in Britain but are increasingly being identified, with Alderney sandstone and French puddingstone querns now known to have been used. These almost certainly arrived in Britain at ports along the south coast with French puddingstone querns being used south of the River Thames, and Alderney sandstone querns and ballast of the same rock found on the Isle of Wight and at Fishbourne palace harbour respectively, as well as further inland at Wantage in Oxfordshire (Watts 2003; Allen 2013; Green 2017; Shaffrey pers. obs.). The absence of querns from continental Europe in Exeter is therefore potentially noteworthy.

At an individual site level there seems to be broadly much less interplay between the different stone types. This is at least partly a reflection of the very small assemblage sizes; the larger assemblages at sites such as Pomeroy Wood, in Honiton, or Dainton Elms Cross, in Ipplepen, contain querns from multiple sources, and it is noteworthy that both were roadside settlements. However, it is also clear that even at these two sites with a larger number of querns, the people followed the broad pattern of choosing querns from local suppliers or those passing through, so the querns from the civilian phases at Pomeroy Wood are of Greensand/sandstone, rock from the Exeter Volcanics (those described as Permian lava and Permian volcanic in the published report) and Mayen lava. Fragments of possible quern of other sandstones were recorded in the published report (Fitzpatrick *et al.* 1999, tab. 79) but these are not certainly from querns. Those at Dainton Elms Cross, in Ipplepen, to the south-west of Exeter are all of granite, elvan or basalt from the Exeter Volcanics. Whilst it is clear, however, that in Roman Devon querns were being produced for local use, it is likely that the user of the quern had some choice over which material their

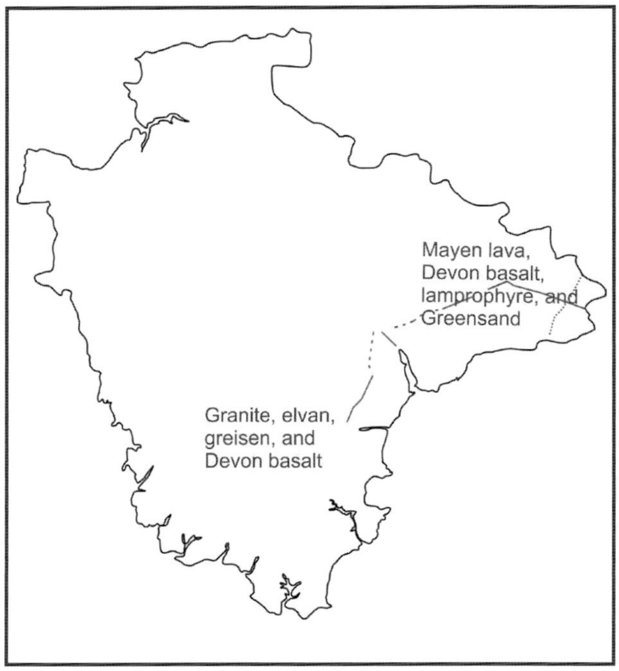

Fig. 14.3 Map showing broad distribution areas of quern lithologies

quern was made from. In southern and western Devon, households typically had a choice of querns from the range of granite examples being produced as well as those of elvan, greisen and basalt from the Exeter Volcanics. North and east of Exeter, households had the choice of using querns of Greensand, lamprophyre or basalt from the Exeter Volcanics (Fig. 14.3). A single quern of continental lava was found in a Late Roman Phase 4i context at Pomeroy Wood, in Honiton, but may be residual from earlier, military phases.

Analysis of the use of different stone types in the immediate proximity of Exeter itself is also very revealing (Fig. 14.4). The only querns found within the defences of the fortress (in both stratified military phase deposits and in later contexts associated with the Roman and medieval towns) are made of Mayen lava, a lithology scarcely seen outside the fortress. In contrast, within the town walls and just outside the town walls there are querns of granite, greensand and basalt from the Exeter Volcanics. Unfortunately, the dating of few of these querns is sufficiently close for an assessment to be made of how much of this pattern represents chronological differences and the sample sizes are small. The absence of other stone types, and the overall distribution patterns of querns of different stone types also indicates that Exeter did not function as a secondary distribution point for querns. Since most querns were used 'locally' to their point of manufacture, an additional step in their distribution process was presumably not required. Interestingly, it is also worth noting that the production of querns seems not to have been connected to other more intensive stone exploitation. The town walls

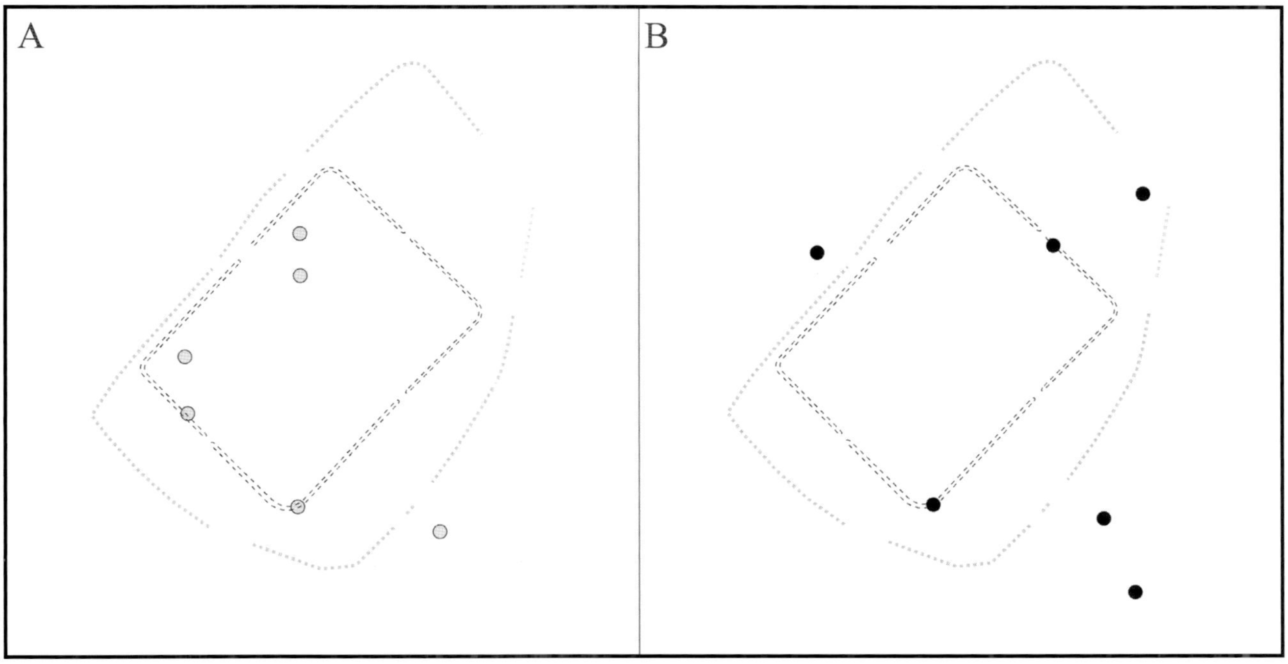

Fig. 14.4 Map of all rotary querns and millstones by number. A: Mayen Lava; B: other stone types

in Exeter, for example, are made of Rougemont stone, but so far no querns of this stone have been found nor of Pocombe stone, which outcrops to the south-west of Exeter and its distinctive quartz veins are not observed in other types of rock from the Exeter Volcanics.

Conclusion

Analysis of the querns from Exeter and across Devon reveals a pattern of mainly local exploitation that is in stark contrast to the rest of the Roman south. The centre of Exeter has seen as much excavation as many other Roman towns, and so the relatively small numbers of querns could be a genuine phenomenon (albeit possibly exacerbated by non-rigorous retention of quern fragments in the 1970s). Even factoring this in, however, the number and variation in the typology of querns of each lithology suggest long-lived and probable ad-hoc exploitation, rather than organised quarries and quern makers. The limited evidence for the exporting of Devon-made querns outside the region supports this conclusion. The absence of querns imported from other sources in Roman Britain may be the result of a lack of engagement with the wider quern distribution networks, and the occurrence of Mayen lava querns almost exclusively on sites with military origins could indicate that a reluctance to move away from local quern sources extended to lava querns, which in other parts of the Roman south appear to have filtered down into general circulation.

Part 2: Querns as comestibles

In addition to their ability to inform us about the movement and trade of goods, querns and millstones also provide important details about where and how grain was processed, which in turn is a crucial strand of evidence in our quest to understand how the supply of food and drink to towns was structured. The more grain that was processed into flour within the town, the less processing was required in the surrounding environs and vice versa. Grain could be processed using hand-powered rotary querns or mechanically powered millstones. Millstones are simply rotary querns that were too unwieldy to be operated by hand and required additional operational power (such as water, animals, or multiple people) and more leverage than a simple handle. In southern England, they are classified as being stones greater than 57 cm diameter. In practice, however, stones over 50 cm diameter are also likely to have had mechanised power if they do not retain evidence for a handle socket (Shaffrey 2015), and so the threshold of 50 cm is used here. Since structural evidence for watermills is scant, and rarely found, and we are still uncertain as to the precise nature of the structure of animal powered mills in this country, millstones are the most reliable archaeological evidence for the existence of mills.

At a simple level, the larger the quern or millstone, the greater the quantity of grain that could be processed but estimating the amount of flour that could be produced is virtually impossible. Output would depend on the type of power being used, the number of stones in operation, the size of the stones, and the duration each day in which the stones were running. However, the recovery of rotary querns at a site is evidence of the processing of grain at a household level, or, perhaps, at a small commercial premises, such as a bakery or brewhouse. A very high number of rotary querns is likely to indicate a significant level of grain processing, depending on the size of the excavated area and the nature of the site. The appearance of millstones during the 1st century AD, but more commonly from the 2nd century AD, is evidence for the intensification of arable production and the associated centralisation of grain processing (Booth *et al.* 2007, 298; Rees 2011, 112; Shaffrey 2015), both consequences of the development of urban communities. Their recovery is therefore particularly important to our understanding of how grain processing and supply of the resultant products was organised.

Current evidence suggests that some towns had urban mills at which a portion of their flour supply was centralised, but that other towns sourced some or most of their flour externally (Cruse and Heslop 2015; Shaffrey 2018). These conclusions have been drawn based on the distribution of mills, as evidenced by the millstones. However, some of the grain processing indicated by the millstones might have been concerned with the crushing of sprouted grains (malt) for brewing, and querns and millstones were probably also used to process other substances such as legumes and animal feed. Unfortunately, it is difficult to determine what was being ground on querns and millstones as we currently rely on the analysis of charred and waterlogged plant remains to distinguish between flour and malt production. In the case of Exeter, there are few plant remains to help with this issue, and where they do exist, there is scant evidence for the processing of cereals (Straker *et al.* 1984; and see EAPIT1, Chapter 3). Whilst we could also turn to phytolith or starch analysis of deposits preserved on the surfaces of querns, this is in its very early stages and not yet commonplace. In the absence of these strands of evidence, we can therefore only make an assumption that the querns and millstones of Exeter and the surrounding areas mainly represent flour production, but we must consider and remember the other functions to which they could have been put.

Cereal processing in and around Exeter

The lack of close dating for many querns from Exeter and its hinterland hinders a chronological consideration of the organisation of grain processing. Querns associated with military phases of activity, for example, have only been identified at Rack Street and Friernhay Street in the city and at Pomeroy Wood, in Honiton, but this apparent lack of early querns is most likely a reflection of the absence of context information associated with many of the other known querns, rather than an actual absence of Early Roman querns. Using querns and millstones as direct evidence for the processing of cereals, it is still possible to make several observations.

Previous studies looking at the distribution of querns and millstones around urban centres have calculated 20 km as a reasonable distance that might have been travelled in a day (Cruse and Heslop 2015; Shaffrey 2018; in prep). Whilst it is accepted that this is a simplification

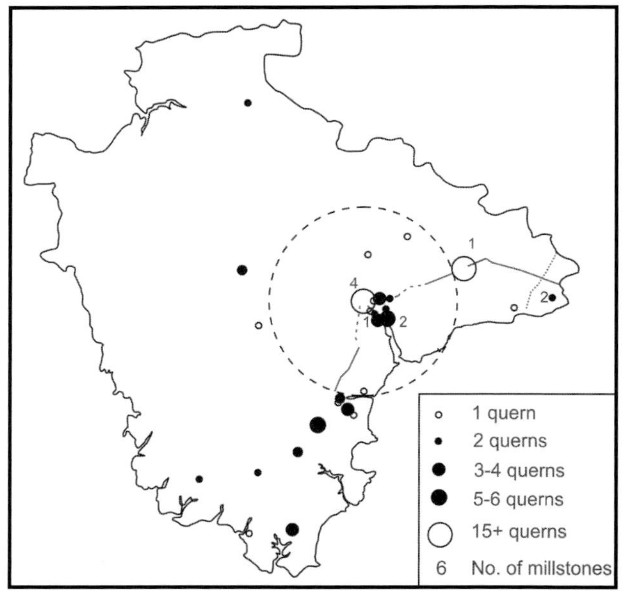

Fig. 14.5 Density of rotary querns and millstones found at Late Iron Age and Roman sites in Devon

that does not take topography into account, it is a useful tool allowing a study area to be defined. It is hoped that over time the distribution of rotary querns and millstones will be sufficiently well understood that such artificial divisions will not be necessary. The geographical area represented by the 20 km mark is indicated by the circle on Fig. 14.5.

Despite the relatively poor recovery of quern fragments from Roman Exeter, 1st-century AD military phase grain processing in the town is represented by the small number of closely dated lava querns from Rack Street and Friernhay Street. These querns provide clear evidence of grinding within the fortress and as querns were a component of military equipment, essential to feed the army and associated personnel, their recovery from sites with military occupation is to be expected. Additionally, four fragments of probable Roman millstones have been identified from Rack Street, St Stephens High Street, Valiant Soldier and Holloway Street. None of the millstones exceed 55 cm diameter (at 50, 53, 54 and 55 cm), but they are noticeably larger in size than typical rotary querns in the town (usually measuring 30–40 cm diameter) and therefore likely to have required greater power. Their presence suggests that some centralisation of grain processing occurred in the Roman town. Unfortunately, it is not possible to be sure at what time this occurred because none of the millstones are closely dated (other than having been found on Roman sites).

During later, civilian, phases of activity there is strong evidence for grain processing at Exeter as well as at nearby Topsham and Pomeroy Wood, in Honiton, with millstones and/or numerous querns from all three locations. Two millstones were also found at the Late Roman bakery site at Topsham (Morris *et al.* 1938, 77–8). At 51 and 55 cm diameter, these are similar in size to the millstones from the town. The small town at Topsham (see EAPIT 1, Chapter 6) was evidently a centre for crop processing, as in addition to these two millstones a relatively high number of querns have been found at sites in or close to Topsham including five at the bakery and a probable five at two phases of excavations at Wessex Close (Kendall 2014, 7; Quinnell 2018a, 46) where a substantial building was probably used for crop processing amongst other things (Quinnell 2018a; Rainbird and Farnell 2019). The combined evidence suggests that during the later Roman period cereals were brought into Topsham and that some of these were ground there, and the flour (and malt?) subsequently used in its bakery or bakeries. Some of these baked (or brewed?) products may have been distributed onwards to Exeter although it is likely that baking and brewing also occurred in the city, as indicated by a comparable Late Roman bakery at Rack Street. Querns and millstone were also found at Rack Street, although the absence of context information means it is impossible to determine if they were connected to a possible bakery there.

A further millstone was also found at Exeter Crematorium – adjacent to the excavated site at St Loye's College (EAPIT 1, Chapters 5 and 6) – where it had been used in a 19th-century surface associated with a mill leat. It was interpreted as probably Roman, and because of its large size at 95 cm diameter, if it was Roman it indicates the existence of a substantial, probable water-powered, mill between Topsham and Exeter. Medieval corn mills were in operation at Countess Wear (Martin Watts pers. comm.) and it is possible these reflect a long-running tradition of milling that extends back to the Roman period. Millstones measuring in excess of 90 cm are, however, not common from Roman contexts, with only 4% of millstones in the author's database exceeding 94 cm diameter, and it is therefore doubtful that the millstone from the Crematorium is Roman in date.

As well as the likelihood that Topsham was a centre for crop processing throughout the Roman period, the roadside settlement at Pomeroy Wood, in Honiton, was also important for the processing of agricultural produce. This site is located just outside Exeter's arbitrary 20 km zone but was on the main road between Dorchester and Exeter, and all the archaeological evidence points towards significant cereal processing there. The site has produced the single largest assemblage of querns from any Roman site in Devon, including 23 identifiable querns in 52 fragments plus a further 58 fragments thought to derive from rotary querns (Loader 1999, 281). One of these may be from a small millstone, which would indicate further intensification of crop processing. It is of a comparably small size to all the millstones from Exeter and Topsham (50 cm).

The emphasis on grain processing in the roadside settlement at Pomeroy Wood suggested by the high number of querns and small millstone is supported by the structural remains of corn driers associated with the civilian phases (Fitzpatrick *et al.* 1999, 255–9). Corn dryers are generally scant in Devon (EAPIT 1, Chapter 3; Brindle 2016) but might have been used for both drying grain and the roasting of sprouted grains for malting (Van der Veen 1989, 316). As the dearth of corn dryers across the South-West Peninsula suggests that arable farming was practiced at more of a subsistence level than in other parts of central-southern England (Lodwick 2017, 21), we can assume that crop processing was an important activity where they are found (especially in conjunction with querns and millstones). Further evidence for an emphasis on crop processing in the civilian phase at Pomeroy Wood is provided by two 4-post structures interpreted as having been used for grain storage, and by the archaeobotanical evidence. Analysis of the charred plant remains indicated that semi-cleaned spikelets were brought onto site for the final stages of processing and that spelt wheat was the most dominant crop (Clapham 1999, 370). Some contexts contained mostly sprouted grains, which were assumed to be for animal feed (Clapham 1999, 346), but could plausibly represent the production of ale or malted drinks, the necessary sprouted grains being crushed using querns, some of which may have been sent on to the city.

Relatively few millstones have been found in the Roman town of Exeter, and the area surrounding it, and, with the exception of the unstratified example from Exeter Crematorium, they are all small stones. It seems unlikely that any of these would have required a substantial water source to power them. It is possible that some or all of them were powered by two or more people instead, as for the 50 cm+ sized pushing mills seen in Iberia (Alonso and Frankel 2017). If so, the increase in output compared to rotary querns is likely to have been low, but significant nonetheless and their presence does indicate a greater emphasis on crop processing in the area close to which they were found than would have been achieved with rotary querns alone. Using these, and concentrations of rotary querns, it would appear as though the main areas for crop processing were inside the town itself, in the small town of Topsham, and at the roadside settlements at Pomeroy Wood and Dainton Elms Cross. Flour (and baked products), plus possibly ale (and malted drinks) would have been produced inside Exeter for immediate consumption and outside the town for both local consumption and possibly for transfer to the urban population.

The generally low numbers of querns and millstones seen in Exeter and close by is mirrored in the rest of Devon. The only other site with evidence for centralised crop processing is the villa at Holcombe, in Uplyme, which has produced fragments from two separate local Greensand millstones, including one of comparably small size to the other Devon examples, and one larger millstone of 74 cm diameter. Overall, the occurrence and form of the quern and millstones from across Devon gives the overall impression that crop processing was not a major activity in the region.

Conclusions

The querns and millstones from Exeter and Devon demonstrate a range of forms that is typical of the Roman south, but a much more limited range of stone types. Here, very local stones were typically used to manufacture querns but in small numbers over relatively long time periods, so that production appears to have been generally ad-hoc. There are only three sites – Topsham, and the roadside settlements at Pomeroy Wood and Dainton Elms Cross – with a clear emphasis on crop processing and the quern assemblages from these, although significant, are not as substantial as from comparable sites in other regions. In addition, most other rural sites have produced only one or two quern fragments and together the evidence suggests that crop processing was not a major activity in the region. If this data is a genuine reflection of the levels of activity, the lack of imported querns from the rest of southern Britain may be a result of simple economics. The low numbers of querns required could easily be met by ad-hoc manufacture locally, meaning that there was little market for imported querns other than the lava querns initially brought by the military and their associated personnel.

Acknowledgements

Research on querns is heavily dependent on access to museum archives and the author is extremely grateful to all the museums and their staff who helped with this paper. Thanks must go to Thomas Cadbury of the Royal Albert Memorial Museum in Exeter for arranging access to the museum's collection. Also to Claire Howe and Barry Chandler at Torquay Museum for access to the Rocombe querns and to Anna Adcock of Topsham Museum who kindly opened up the museum during the closed season so that querns in their care could be examined. Thanks also to Naomi Payne of AC Archaeology who allowed examination and sampling of the querns in their possession, and to Susan and Martin Watts for helpful comments on the text. Particular thanks must go, however, to Roger Taylor who used his considerable expertise to advise on petrographical matters. All errors, of course, remain the responsibility of the author. All figures are by the author, with the geology based on Devon County Council's 2004 'Devon County Minerals Local Plan'.

15

Can Analysis of Claudian Bronze Coins Found at Exeter Usefully Contribute to the Debate for an 'Earlier' or 'Later' Claudio-Neronian Origin for the Legionary Fortress?

Robert Kenyon

Introduction

This chapter sets out to consider whether the supply of bronze coins of Claudius I (AD 41–54) issued as part-payment of salary to Roman troops in newly-invaded Britain, with their subsequent dispersal in circulation at military bases and attendant *vici* or *canabae*, can offer a primary feature to the discussion for determining a date of origin and occupation of a particular site.

Scholars inspecting excavated and stray coin-finds have commented frequently, since the early 19th century in Britain, on the occurrence of bronze coins struck in imitation of orthodox issues of Claudius I. In addition, it has been long recognised that the widespread and common occurrence of crude imitations of bronze coins in Britain contrasted with the limited presence of orthodox Claudian *aes*, that is bronze coins struck in the imperial mint of Rome. More recently, an exhaustive study – employing stylistic and metallographic analyses – of an enormous deposit of Roman coins found in the riverbed at Gué de Saint-Léonard, in France (Besombes 2004), identified Claudian *aes* that the author proposed were struck at Roman imperial subsidiary mints located in Gaul and on the Iberian Peninsula. These coins were of comparable size and weight to those struck at the mint of Rome, but were stylistically 'provincial' in appearance: many of these imperial bronze coins would previously have been described as 'good' copies. Those provincially-struck imperial coins, issued in AD 41–2, soon became the subject for imitation, first in Gaul and then in Britain after the invasion by legionary and auxiliary troops in AD 43: those bronze imitations have long been described as 'Claudian copies'.

Excavated and stray coin-finds in Britain suggest that the proposed imperial subsidiary mints, operating in the early years of the reign of Claudius I, provided the bronze coins necessary to pay troops stationed in Britain and the North-Western provinces of the Empire. The extreme rarity, among British coin-finds, of Claudian *aes* bearing legends ending *P(ater) P(atriae)*, an honorific title bestowed by the Senate on Claudius in AD 42, would suggest that payment for troops in the early years following the invasion was with coins of the first Claudian issue only, that is those struck AD 41/42.

The scarcity in Britain of the second issue of Claudian *aes*, *i.e.* those struck in AD 42–43, with legends ending *P(ater) Patriae)*, provides strong numismatic and archaeological evidence for the cessation of supply of Claudius *aes* from the imperial subsidiary mints to Roman troops and administrative officials in Britain. Furthermore, it has long been recognised that Claudian *aes* struck at the central mint of Rome rarely occur as coin-finds in Britain; this absence can be seen as corroborating evidence for the supply of coins from provincial subsidiary mints.

It is feasible that those official supplies, struck in the Gallic and Hispanic imperial subsidiary mints, were stockpiled as part of the advance preparation for the invasion of Britain (cf. Kemmers 2004, 45–7 where she suggests forts on the Lower Rhine as possible locations for a supply line in support of the Roman invasion). However, once payment to troops exhausted the stockpile – and in an absence of supplies of further orthodox *aes* – 'unofficial' coins, whether from military or civilian sources, would be required to provide the wherewithal for the small change. This was to be the state of affairs in Britain and Gaul for more than 20 years. The belated first issue by Nero (AD 54–68) of bronze coins from the mint of Lyon, *Lugdunum*, in AD 64/66 addressed the hiatus in supply of fresh imperial bronze coins to pay troops and officials in Britain, Gaul and Lower Germany.

With regard to the supply of Claudian *aes* in the 20-plus years following the invasion of Britain, it may be conjectured that an 'unofficial' moneyer's requirement for a ready and constant supply of copper to produce new copies locally would lead to the removal and melting down of early imperial and Claudian *aes* from a fort's or town's circulation pool. In order for this operation to be profitable, larger coins would need to be withdrawn, melted down and a higher number of new (slightly) smaller blanks to be cast from the molten copper as fresh blanks ready for striking with 'unofficial' dies. Inspection of Claudian bronze coin-finds in Britain shows that coining dies were often freshly cut to a reduced module to better suit the size of the blank. The progressive reduction of the coin-module over time throughout the Claudian period, and without doubt into the Neronian period, would account for a lower number of larger coins and a higher number of smaller coins occurring as finds at sites that were being developed in the later Claudio-Neronian period. Conversely, a higher proportion of larger module coins and very few coins of medium/smaller module would indicate a period of origin and occupation limited to the early Claudian era. It is therefore worth considering whether the relative relationship of Claudian copies of different modules (large, medium and small) might offer a secondary aid to determining a proposed date for a site's Roman occupancy.

A method

Hypothetically, in the absence of knowledge of a coin's archaeological context and in ignorance of any other form(s) of archaeological evidence at a site, it would be interesting to consider whether analysis of finds of Claudian *aes* might suggest a narrower date of loss and deposition at a fort or town than the broad 'Claudio-Neronian/early Vespasianic period' generally attributed to circulation of those early coins. This would offer a contribution to the discussion for determining a probable date for a site's Roman origin. The varied appearance of Claudian *aes* (size, weight, design, etc.) found in Britain encourages a view that analysis of such coin-finds at a site might allow further refinement in determining its period of Roman origin and occupation.

Analysis of 124 stratified Claudian bronze coin-finds from excavations in the 1970s at Colchester (Kenyon 1987) offered the opportunity to compare those coins with Colchester's clear archaeological contexts for: the foundation and development of the Roman fortress established near the Trinovantian tribal-centre Camulodunum (AD 43/4–49); the conversion of the fortress into a *colonia* for retired legionary soldiers (AD 49–50+); the destruction of both the Roman *colonia* and the Trinovantian settlement during the Boudican revolt (AD 60/1) and the rebuilding of the Roman town shortly afterwards. A high level of confidence may be attributed to stratified Claudian coin-finds at Colchester where 'In contrast with other coins listed … over half the Claudian coins (54 percent) turn out to be in their expected levels…Many of the pre-Boudican levels were very substantial and well preserved, with comparatively few later features cutting into them' (P. Crummy 1987, 13).

The large majority of Claudian *aes* found at Colchester, from excavations of the 1970s and earlier, may be described as tolerably accurate copies that are generally of reduced module. A similar, simple description would apply also to the profile of Claudian bronze coin-finds from other Claudio-Neronian sites across Britain. Conversely, those tolerably accurate coins, with their literate legends, were complemented from the earliest period by locally-produced, much less accurate copies with incomplete or malformed legends that would be struck in increasing number in the later Claudio-Neronian period.

The very large number of broadly accurate, but undersize, Claudian copies occurring as excavated site-finds and metal-detector finds across Britain would suggest that the necessary casting of copper-alloy blanks and striking of coins must have taken place collectively on an industrial scale. Furthermore, the vast output of coins of competent workmanship would suggest that an organised, rather than *ad hoc,* arrangement would have been required for the manufacture and supply of coins on such a large scale.

Analysis of the better-preserved Claudian *aes* from excavations at Colchester, informed by their stratified context, suggested that there were principally three phases or periods of production (early/mid AD 40s, mid/late AD 40s and early/mid AD 50s) of imitations at progressively reduced module, with a fourth period (mid/late AD 50s) for even smaller module coins that are invariably local copies. The regular requirement for fresh supplies of bronze coins at Colchester, and other Roman military centres, may be attached to the demand for lower denominations to function as small change at the beginning of January, May and September when the three instalments of pay, or *stipendia*, were made to troops across the new province of *Britannia*. An outline of the sizes/weights of coin-modules, predominant at Colchester, and their suggested corresponding periods of manufacture is offered as a framework against which Claudian *aes* from Exeter and other sites may be compared. For the purpose of this exercise, it is presumed that troops stationed at different centres across the new province received fresh bronze coins of similar module at approximately the same time. Of course, troops and their followers may well have carried older, larger coins with them from their previous station, and undoubtedly those coins would have entered the pool of currency in circulation alongside the newly supplied coins in what was becoming an increasingly monetised background.

A complementary factor that might be of relevance when considering the possible date of loss of a coin is the amount of wear of the surface of the coin. It is generally held that assessing the degree of wear evident on a coin offers a broad guiding influence in determining its period of loss: for example, little wear on a coin would suggest it was lost relatively soon after being struck and introduced into circulation; conversely, a heavily-worn coin would suggest many years of frequent use in circulation before its loss. However, for Claudian *aes*, many of which are 'copies' and the products of clandestine mints in Britain and Gaul, a degree of caution is advised as not all coins would have been produced to the same high standard as those from an orthodox mint: for example, a weakly-struck copy, with its shallow impression, might exhibit the misleading appearance of having been in circulation for very many years when that was not the case.

Notwithstanding that cautionary note, with particular regard to Claudian copies, the derivative nature of imitation both in terms of the size/weight of coins and the quality of reproduction of imagery may offer further guidance to determining the period of loss. A coin that is approximately full-size/weight (*e.g.* an *as*, *c.* 30 mm in diameter and weighing 11.0 g) and accurate in design is likely to be a product of one of the imperial subsidiary mints in Gaul or the Iberian Peninsula and will have been struck in AD 41–42 (cf. Besombes and Barrandon 2000). A slightly smaller contemporary copy of those coins is likely to have been struck within two or three years of the Roman invasion of Britain. Both the orthodox coin and its close copy can be designated as being of 'early' manufacture, whereas a coin of greatly reduced module (*c.* 20–25 mm in diameter and weighing 4.5–6.0 g) that purports to be a Claudian issue can be appropriately described as a 'later' copy, struck from the early AD 50s (see Kenyon 1987 for evidence of stratified coin-finds at Colchester to support this chronologically-based observation). It follows that coins of medium-size module (*c.* 26–27 mm in diameter and weighing 8.0–9.5 g) were struck in the intervening period, that is from the *c.* mid AD 40s to the early AD 50s. In addition, the less accurate and stylistically more rudimentary copies, those that have been described elsewhere as 'Native Copies' (Bowsher and Kenyon forthcoming), can generally be considered as 'later' issues. It should be noted that 'early' copies, described above, can often be difficult to separate stylistically from coins of orthodox issue.

It might be argued that it is difficult to imagine a smaller *as* being accepted at the same value in the market place as a larger *as*. Clearly, these coins were tolerated and accepted, unless one views all coin-finds as discards, but we have no evidence for appreciating what value might have been placed upon an individual coin in the marketplace. However, it is not beyond reason to expect that haggling would take place with the trader, perhaps not only over the given price for goods or services but also over an acceptable value for the coins being offered.

Bronze coins were essential not only for the payment of troops and officials, but also for exchange in the developing extra-mural settlements and market-places. It is suggested that this demand for bronze coins would have been met primarily in two ways:

1) by large-scale minting of coins, in unidentified clandestine mints in Britain and Gaul, that were modelled on *aes* struck at the subsidiary mints of the north-western provinces in Gaul and the Iberian Peninsula, and
2) by local striking of imitative coins.

On a smaller scale, locally produced coin-dies were also used to overstrike existing coins.

Recent chemical analysis of 35 bronze coins of Claudius I from excavations at the Bloomberg site in London by Dr. Matthew Ponting (University of Liverpool) indicates the use of metal from different sources for the imitative *aes* of Claudius I: zinc-rich copper was used to strike the competent copies at unidentified clandestine mints, and recycled metal, that certainly included bronze coins, was employed for the local imitations (Ponting forthcoming). These findings confirm those arrived at by J.-N. Barrandon for similar Claudian bronze coins from the very large deposit at a river-crossing near Saint-Léonard, in Brittany (Besombes and Barrandon 2000).

It is pertinent to note that a likely source of zinc-rich copper at this time was the mines of Anglesey and North Wales. The results of the metallurgical analyses, referred to above may therefore encourage the view that the zinc-rich copper used for coins minted by the clandestine mint-operators in Britain and Gaul may have been obtained from the independent copper mines of Anglesey and North Wales in the territory of *Ordovices* before Roman assimilation there in AD 60/61 placed the mines under Roman control.

It might be expected, as described above, that the use of recycled copper would involve the removal of larger coins of each denomination from circulation for melting down and re-coining in local 'mints'. The extraction of full-size and full-weight coins from the circulation pools at forts and towns of Britain in the years following Roman occupation together with the cessation of Claudian *aes* from imperial subsidiary mints in Gaul and the Iberian Peninsula would explain the relative paucity of orthodox coins struck by Claudius I. Their replacement with issues of 'unofficial' coins of gradually diminishing size soon entered the money-stream in and around the military bases either as part of the pay issued to troops or via *nummularii* exchanging a soldier's *denarii* for small change.

Relating the visible wear of a coin's surface to the length of time a coin has been in circulation is perhaps certain to produce an inexact result: an estimate of a period of years at best rather than a specific year for a coin's loss. However, inspection of the wear evident on Claudian *aes* found in hoards that include relatively little worn Neronian and/or Vespasianic bronze coins may help to indicate what wear might be expected for Claudian coins that circulated for a lengthy period until at least the Neronian/Vespasianic period. This evidence-informed approach, limited in scope though it may be, provides an initial standard for wear against which other excavated coin-finds might be compared.

The more accumulations of this type that are inspected, the better the evidence-base that can be built for comparison. In the case of this note, two hoards will be reviewed: Lincoln's Castle Hill hoard (Petch 1958, 104–6; Robertson 2000, cat. no. 53) and the dispersed hoard found during excavations at the Valiant Soldier and Acorn Roundabout sites, Exeter (Sites 44 and 94; Shiel 1991, 32; Robertson 2000, cat. no. 52). Each of these two groups, located geographically at opposite ends of the strategic Fosse Way, are found in legionary bases: at Exeter where *legio II Augusta* maintained overview of the South-West and at Lincoln where *legio IX Hispana* were based in the north-eastern Midlands.

The Castle Hill 'purse group', found by workmen in 1957, is one example of a hoard of mixed Claudian, Neronian and Vespasianic *aes*. It provides clear evidence for the continued use of Claudian *aes* into the reign of Vespasian (AD 69–79) at Lincoln, if one accepts that those coins were taken from circulation at the same time. The hoard comprises seven Claudian *aes* (a *dupondius*, five *asses* and a hybrid (Tiberius/Minerva) *as*), one Neronian *dupondius* and two Vespasianic *aes* (a *dupondius* and an *as*) and one illegible bronze coin. The Claudian *aes* are all copies and, as might be expected, all exhibit signs of significant wear, whereas the Neronian and Vespasianic *aes* do not: the detail of hair of the emperor on the latter three coins may be clearly seen and the lettering of the legend is sharp, particularly on the Vespasian *dupondius* struck AD 71/72. The most worn coin, a Claudian copy *dupondius*, (*RIC* Ceres reverse-type*)*, at 27 mm diameter, a 'medium'-sized coin, is in a state of wear that may be described as 'poor/very poor'. No detail features are discernible and only the outline shapes of both obverse and reverse designs remain. The 'large' Claudian copy *as* (*RIC* Minerva reverse-type*)*, at 29 mm, is in 'very worn/poor' condition and is, unusually, a large example of a 'Native Copy', *i.e.* a coin bearing crudely-rendered images/lettering in the obverse and reverse designs. The last-mentioned coin is possibly an 'overstrike' (*i.e.* where coin-dies were used on an existing coin rather than a new blank disc of metal). This would account for its large size as 'Native Copies' are mostly 'smaller' sized coins. The remaining four Claudian copy *asses* are also of the Minerva reverse-type: three, at 23–25 mm diameter are what may be described as of 'small' size and one, at 26 mm, as of 'medium'-size. They are all 'very worn' and generally of rudimentary fashion in terms of design and production. The least worn of the Claudian *aes* is the hybrid copy *as* with its laureated Tiberius obverse (presumably copied from the *Lugdunum* Altar series) and Minerva reverse design. This last coin is in 'worn' condition.

Using photographs of this Lincoln 'purse group' as a sample standard measure of the relationship of a coin's wear to its length of time in circulation, it is possible to observe that larger coins that had circulated for perhaps almost 30 years became so worn that the obverse designs were worn flat, while the smaller coins that were in circulation for less time up to loss/burial(?) exhibited signs of less, but still significant, wear.

Exeter's dispersed group of 13 bronze coins of Claudius, Nero and Vespasian excavated at the Valiant Soldier and Acorn Roundabout sites is available for visual inspection at the Royal Albert Memorial Museum's (RAMM) database https://rammcollections.org.uk, accession number: 1/1991 (unfortunately, only the obverses of these coins can be clearly seen due to accession numbers obliterating the reverse images of each coin). The composition of this group suggests it should be considered as a savings group of ten higher-value brass coins (three little worn *sestertii* – one of Nero and two of Vespasian – and seven little-worn *dupondii* of Vespasian) and three very worn copper *asses* of Claudius I. This dispersed accumulation, originally hidden as a group of 14 bronze coins (although currently one Claudian copy *as* is mislaid), differs in the composition of its featured denominations from Lincoln's purse-group that was perhaps lost while in use rather than after being hidden. However, there is a similarity in the degree of wear on the Claudian-Vespasianic *aes* of the two groups suggesting they were both deposited/lost at a similar period during Vespasian's reign.

The above guiding factors – sizes/weights, degree of wear, and type of copy – offer indicators that can contribute to the discussion for the attribution of a probable period of loss for excavated Claudian *aes* found at a British site, but taken separately they are not compelling. Other contributory factors should also be considered such as the relative proportion of Claudian denominations found and the presence/absence of pre-Claudian imperial *aes*. The characteristics outlined above and those following are intended to offer guidance for determining a narrower period when the Claudian coins were lost rather than the broad 25 year 'Claudio-Neronian period' that is usually ascribed to their use.

Typically, sites of the 'earlier' (military) Claudian period (*c*. AD 43–late 40s) are likely to have coin-lists that include some or all of the following:

- full-size/weight Claudian *aes,* struck at imperial subsidiary mints in Gaul and the Iberian Peninsula that exhibit some signs of wear from circulation;
- close to full size/weight accurate copies of Claudian *aes*, and those of a slightly reduced module (reduced by up to 2 mm/3 g), exhibiting some wear;
- greater proportion of full-size/medium-size copies in comparison with smaller copies;
- both Claudian *sestertii* and *dupondii*;
- earlier imperial *aes* (Augustus-Gaius) and/or their full-size/weight (reduced by up to 2 mm/3 g) copies;
- Claudian *sestertii,* with the early Claudian countermark *PROB* (Kenyon 1988), exhibiting little sign of wear

(it is generally thought that the countermark *PROB* is a brief version of *PROB(atum)* denoting the coin has been 'approved' for (continued?) use in circulation. However, it is difficult to appreciate why newly-struck coins issued at the beginning of Claudius's reign by an imperial subsidiary mint should require approval. Nevertheless, it is beyond the scope of this brief note to begin to consider alternative expansions for this countermark);
- Republican and early imperial *denarii*.

Sites of 'later' (military/civilian) Claudian/Neronian/Vespasianic period (*c*. AD 53–75) are likely to have coin-lists that include some or all of the following:

- full-size copies of Claudian *aes* exhibiting considerable wear;
- worn Claudian *aes* of medium module;
- smaller copies of Claudian *aes* exhibiting at least some wear;
- predominantly Claudian *asses*;
- significant proportion of medium-smaller copies in comparison with larger *aes*;
- a noticeable proportion of the crudely-rendered 'Native Copies';
- less commonly, hybrid Claudian copies (*e.g.* Claudius obverse/reverse of Antonia's *dupondius*);
- less commonly, worn Claudian *aes* with the late Claudian/early Neronian countermarks such as *BON*;
- less commonly, occurrence of plated *denarii* of Augustus-Claudius I and/or well-circulated copies of earlier imperial *aes* (Augustus-Gaius).

Analysis

Fifty bronze coins (*aes*) of Claudius I (AD 41–54) were found during excavations at Exeter in the 1970s-early 80s. Those coins, together with 16 bronze coins of Claudius of local provenance in the collection of the RAMM, were recorded in 1983 on a visit to Exeter. Thirty-five of those coins were photographed and these were complemented by a photograph, taken by a member of RAMM staff, of a countermarked *sestertius* of local provenance that had been on display on the occasion of my visit. A summary of that recorded information and photographs of those coins can be found in the author's thesis (Kenyon 1992).

In addition, four other earlier imperial bronze coins – two copy *asses* of Augustus (27 BC–AD 14), an *as* of Agrippa issued by Gaius (AD 37–41), and a copy Agrippa *as* – were noted as excavated finds Site-finds elsewhere show that examples of those bronze coins often occur in the same archaeological contexts as Claudian *aes*. It is perhaps useful to note that *asses* of the Agrippa type, in particular, and also Augustan *asses* were subject to copying, and that hybrid coins (*e.g.* coins that have an obverse of Claudius and a reverse of Neptune from an Agrippa *as*) indicate that pre-Claudian prototypes were also copied in the Claudio-Neronian era. The wear evident on these coins indicates that they had circulated for a considerable time before being lost or discarded.

Recent re-inspection of those photographs and records allowed the opportunity to reappraise the bronze coins of Claudius I (AD 41–54) and consider whether they can make a useful contribution to the discussion about the origin of Roman Exeter. All 67 Claudian *aes*, with the exception of one *as*, from Exeter Museums Archaeological Field Unit's (EMAFU) assemblage of excavated coins exhibit clear evidence of wear from circulation; a copy *as* (noted above) in 'excellent', virtually unworn condition and three copy *asses* in 'good' condition; nine are described as 'worn'; 16, as 'very worn'; 12 are described as being in 'poor' condition and 26, in 'very poor' condition. All 67 coins have legible features with sufficient detail to be readily identifiable. Eight illegible bronze coins were judged by appearance and fabric to be 'probably copy *asses* of Claudius', but they are not included in this analysis.

If wear on a coin is to be considered as a factor in determining a date for its loss, then a broadly defined period (*e.g.* three to six years) might be considered a more tolerable observation than an exact date. And it may be assumed that *asses* and *dupondii*, being of the lower denominations, were used more frequently than *sestertii* in any marketplace serving a military post (the lowest denomination is the *quadrans*, worth a quarter of an *as*, but the rarity of finds of *quadrantes* of Claudius I in Britain indicates they were not issued to Roman troops and officials in this new province). It may reasonably be assumed therefore that the wear on a *sestertius* would be less than that recorded on the surface of a *dupondius* which in turn would be less than that evident on an *as* for any given length of time in circulation.

The four coins that are in better than 'worn' condition are all copy *asses* of the most common reverse type, Minerva advancing right.

1. The almost unworn coin, in 'excellent' condition, exhibits the rudimentary design features attributed to 'Native Copies' and belongs to the smaller-size and -weight group (20–25 mm, 4.5–6.0 g). These coins are identified as 'later' copies and are likely to have been struck in the first half of the AD 50s. The coin's excellent condition suggests that it may have been lost shortly after being introduced into circulation and at most it would be unlikely to have seen more than one/two years in circulation (mid AD 50s).
2. Three copy *asses* were lost when still in 'good' condition.
   i One coin, also, exhibits the rudimentary design features attributed to 'Native Copies', and may also be identified as a 'later' copy that was likely to have been struck in the first half of the AD 50s. Its condition suggests it was lost after perhaps 4–8 years of circulation, *c*. AD 57–61, that is during

the emperor Nero's reign, but before his issues of *aes* from *Lugdunum* (Lyon) were struck and issued to troops in Britain.

ii The other two coins having seen limited circulation are copies of products of the subsidiary mints in Gaul and the Iberian Peninsula and at 26 mm/6.5 g and 27 mm/8.25 g may be attributed to the middle period of issue (late AD 40s to early AD 50s) with four–eight years of circulation suggesting loss in *c*. AD 52–60.

The above observations regarding the four least worn coins from Exeter would suggest a 'later' Claudio-Neronian' origin (mid AD 50s-early 60s) with perhaps more emphasis on an early Neronian origin based on the copy *as* in 'excellent' condition excavated by EMAFU.

This proposal for an early Neronian origin at Exeter is supported by the following observation. Of the remaining 63 coins: nine have been described as 'worn' and 16, as 'very worn'; the others, as 'poor' or 'very poor'. While close analysis of the amount of wear on those coins cannot contribute much to dating the origin of Exeter, their degraded condition, supported by a further reduction in module of coin to 21 mm/3.75 g for the latest issues of copies suggests their continued circulation at Exeter into the reign of Vespasian (AD 69–79).

Other notable features of Exeter's list of bronze coins of Claudius I are:

- three very worn *sestertii*, with two bearing the countermark *PROB* – one of which can be identified as having been struck at the proposed imperial subsidiary mint at León, Spain – which distinguish them as early issues originally supplied to occupying troops but having seen perhaps more than twenty years of circulation;
- 11 copper-alloy *dupondii* which with the three copper-alloy *sestertii* (both higher denominations of the bronze currency) account for 21% of the Claudian *aes* suggesting a military context for these finds;
- 53 *asses* (79% of the Claudian *aes*), of which only one is full-size but too heavily-worn to determine whether it is of orthodox origin or a good copy;
- the remaining *asses* and *dupondii* are copies with 34 of them (53%) having diameters less than or equal to 25 mm and therefore of 'later' issue;
- 23 (34%) of the *asses* and *dupondii* are 'Native copies' and also of 'later' issue;
- four very worn earlier imperial *aes*, mostly copies.

A further noteworthy and pertinent feature of Exeter's coin list, recently brought to my attention, is the hoard of 22 early imperial bronze coins excavated in 2008 at Mount Dinham, Exeter (Site 154; Leins 2013). Nine Claudian *aes* and one probable Augustan *as* are identified among this heavily-mineralised group; the remaining 12 coins are too corroded to allow identification but are considered likely to be pre-Neronian issues. Of the nine Claudian *aes*, one is confirmed as an *as* and four are *dupondii*, with another almost certainly a *dupondius* described as 'seated figure, left' among the three 'Illegible (head of Claudius)' coins. Furthermore, it would not be stretching credibility to suggest that at least one, at 9.18 g, of the remaining two of those particular illegible coins is also a *dupondius*. A 'possible Claudius' coin completes the list of identified coins. Among the 12 unidentified, extremely fragile and illegible bronze coins are others whose weights are comparable with the identified Claudian *dupondii* and therefore may also be *dupondii*, but that cannot be confirmed here. What can be said is that this is a mixed *dupondii/asses* group deposited before Neronian bronze coins were issued (*c*. AD 64/66) and available at Exeter.

Conclusion

The above observations and analysis of the classification and metrology of the excavated 67 Claudian *aes*, together with the Mount Dinham group of 22 pre-Neronian *dupondii* and *asses* that includes low weight coins (*c*. 3 g) of probable Neronian issue, indicate the legionary base at Exeter was unlikely to have been established in the Claudian period. Furthermore, the observations regarding the general degree of wear from circulation evident on the Claudian bronze coins suggest a 'later' period of coin-use. This is supported by Exeter's coin-list profile (*i.e.* the relationship between full-, medium- and small-size copies at 5%:33%:62% respectively, the occurrence of very worn, countermarked *sestertii* and the relationship between orthodox coins and their copies and also between accurate and rudimentary copies) which better fits a 'later' period of coin-use such as might be expected of a military establishment at Exeter, and its attendant *vici* or *canabae*, operating during the early Neronian to mid Vespasianic era (*c*. AD 55–75).

The result of the above reconsideration of Exeter's bronze coins of Claudius I complements and confirms the summary evidence, previously published (Kenyon 1987, 36–9), suggesting a profile of later circulation for those coins than that for Claudian *aes* from the Early Roman sites of Colchester and Richborough. That evidence was set out in scatter-diagram form of the sizes and weights of coins in worn or better condition and was used as comparative material – along with similar diagrams for coin-finds from Wroxeter, Gloucester, Cirencester and Sea Mills – against finds of Claudian *aes* from those earlier Roman sites in south-eastern Britain.

Recent reanalyses of the different 'modules' (*i.e.* size and weight of flan) used for 'Claudian copies' found at the above-mentioned Roman centres in the neighbouring territories of the Dobunni and Cornovii to the north of that of the Dumnonii (Table 15.1) provide some comparative data for the coins from Exeter. Those reanalyses offer a narrowly-focused survey of just one element of the

Table 15.1 Classification of 'Claudian copies' from sites in the territories of the Dumnonii, Dobunni and Cornovii by module (Kenyon, 1987, 36–40). Coins in better condition are noted alongside their relevant 'module' in the Table

		Module 1, c. *AD 43–44*	*Condition*	*Module 2,* c. *AD 44–49*	*Condition*	*Module 3,* c. *AD 50–54*	*Condition*	*Module 4,* c. *AD 55–60*	*Condition*	*Total*
i	*Wroxeter Cornovii*									
	Imitation *Aes*									
	Sestertius	–		–		–		–		0
	Dupondius	3	*1 worn*	9	*2 good*	2	*1 good*	–		14
	As	–		26	*1 good*	18	*2 good*	6	*3 worn*	50
	Total	3		35		20		6		64
	%	5%		55%		31%		9%		
ii	*Kingsholm & Gloucester* Dobunni									
	Imitation *Aes*									
	Sestertius	1	*good*	–	–	–		–		1
	Dupondius	–	–	14	*6 worn*	4	*1 v. worn*	–		18
	As	1	*v. poor*	17	*3 worn*	20	*2 good*	5	*2 worn*	43
	Total	2		31		24		5		62
	%	3%		50%		39%		8%		
iii	*Exeter* Dumnonii									
	Imitation Aes									
	Sestertius	–		–		–		–		0
	Dupondius	2	*1 poor*	3	*1 worn*	5	*1 v. worn*	–		10
	As	1	*v. poor*	18	*1 good*	26	*1 excellent*	8	*3 v. worn*	53
	Total	3		21		31		8		63
	%	5%		33%		49%		13%		
iv	*Cirencester* Dobunni									
	Imitation Aes									
	Sestertius	–		–		–		–		0
	Dupondius	1	*good*	1	*v.poor*	2	*1 good*	–		4
	As	2	*1 worn*	12	*1 worn*	17	*1 good*	5	*1 good*	36
	Total	3		13		19		5		40
	%	8%		33%		48%		13%		
v	*Sea Mills* Dobunni									
	Imitation *Aes*									
	Sestertius	–		–		–		–		0
	Dupondius	–		1		2	*1 worn*	–		3
	As	1	*worn*	27	*1 v.good*	39	*2 good*	14	*2 worn*	81
	Total	1		28		41		14		84
	%	1%		33%		49%		17%		

Module 1, issued *c.* AD 43–44: Size and weight close to that of an official *as* (*c.* 30–31 mm, 10–11.5 g), *dupondius* (30–31 mm, 13–15 g) and *sestertius* (34–36 mm, 27–30 g)
Module 2, issued *c.* AD 44–49: Size and weight of an *as* (*c.* 26–28 mm, 8–9.5 g), *dupondius* (*c.* 27–28 mm, 10–11 g) and *sestertius* (*c.* 31–33 mm, 20–23 g)
Module 3, issued *c.* AD 50–54: Size and weight of an *as* (*c.* 25 mm, 4.5–6 g), *dupondius* (*c.* 23–25 mm, 8–9 g) and *sestertius* (*c.* 28–30 mm, 16–18 g)
Module 4, issued *c.* AD 55–60: Size and weight of an *as* (*c.* 20–23 mm, 3.5 g)

archaeological evidence, *i.e.* the metrology of the bronze coins of Claudius I found at the particular sites, without the contextual information that can be gleaned from the close inspection of individual coins, as demonstrated above, and therefore should be treated with some caution. However, with that *caveat* strongly underlined, this 'snapshot' of coin-supply and use would seem to suggest that Claudian bronze coins were supplied to a military presence at Exeter at about the same time as they were being used at Cirencester and the port of Sea Mills, but perhaps at some time after coins were supplied to troops at Wroxeter and Gloucester/Kingsholm.

Finally, and to give a broader view of Roman military presence in the territory of the Dumnonii, it is worth setting the Neronian-Vespasianic period of coin-use at Exeter against what seems to be clear evidence for much earlier Claudian coin loss further south-west along the Peninsula in the area approaching Plymouth. The Claudian hoard of nine *sestertii* found at Roborough, near Plymouth (Holbrook and Shiel 2002), is a superb example of an early Claudian bronze coin group with its inclusion of a *sestertius* of the emperor Gaius (Caligula) (AD 37–41), rarely found in Britain, together with a *PROB* countermarked specimen among the eight 'little worn' *sestertii* of Claudius I that were issued by the provincial subsidiary mints operating in Gaul and on the Iberian Peninsula in AD 41–42. The little amount of wear evident from the illustration of these coins in that excellent report indicates an early post-invasion date for the group's deposition or loss that would pre-date the legionary presence in Exeter (see Chapter 16 below).

Acknowledgements

I am grateful to Richard Reece for recently asking a question that prompted me to think about how close consideration of the bronze coins of Claudius I (AD 41–54) found at an excavated site might suggest a date of origin for that site, and to Neil Holbrook for later asking me to consider applying the approach that developed from that consideration to the excavated Claudian coin-finds from Exeter.

16

The Roman Coins from Exeter and its Hinterland

Andrew Brown and Sam Moorhead

Introduction

In recent years there have been an increasing number of studies of Roman coin finds in different parts of the country. Most of these have been in the core territory of the Province, or the Lowland Zone as some scholars call it. The South-West, beyond the Blackdown Hills, and Exeter itself, however, present a very different pattern of coin-loss from the heartlands of *Britannia* which demands rigorous interrogation to understand why this region diverges from other parts of the Province. Many of the Roman coins from Exeter have been discussed by Norman Shiel and Richard Reece, notably in *Roman Finds from Exeter* (Holbrook and Bidwell 1991, 24–38) which listed 1,625 examples found across the modern city. Since then, Shiel has catalogued another substantial assemblage of 146 coins from the 1997–2006 excavations at Princesshay (Site 156; Steinmetzer, Allan and Orme forthcoming) and a hoard of 22 early imperial *aes* has been recovered from excavations at Mount Dinham (Site 154; Leins 2013; 2008T102/PAS: DARCH-4072D1).[1] In addition, it is now possible to gain a comprehensive overview of all the Roman coin hoards from Exeter as a result of a Leicester University and British Museum project investigating Iron Age and Roman hoards.[2] Probably the major contribution this chapter can make is in providing a much broader context for the Exeter coin finds by using the British Museum's Portable Antiquities Scheme (PAS; finds.org.uk) Roman coin data from Devon and the broader South-West (*i.e.* including Dorset and Somerset). The PAS data include a substantial number of the detector finds from the excavations at the roadside settlement at Dainton Elms Cross, in Ipplepen, which now provides a major numismatic assemblage which can be compared to Exeter's. It is therefore now possible to discuss Exeter in relation to its immediate hinterland and the wider South-West, rather than seeing the town as an island of Roman activity in a region largely devoid of significant comparative data.

This chapter therefore consists of two major sections. The first will consider the coins from Exeter and compare them with a selection of other urban sites in Roman Britain, while the second will introduce the PAS data for Roman coins from Devon and discuss the county's profile in relation to Exeter. This will then enable a series of broad conclusions.

The coins from Exeter

Excavation and stray finds

At present, there appear to be 1,769 Roman coins available for study, which can be summarised as follows (the lettering of each group corresponds to the columns in Tables 16.1 and 16.2, and Figs 16.1 and 16.2):

A: 1,053 coins found before 1942 and recorded by R.G. Goodchild (in Fox 1952a, 104) and listed by Reece (1991a, 34, tab. 7 column 1). These coins come from a variety of sources, a number of which appear to be detailed in a listing by Shiel and Reece (1979, 165–79). The overall profile of these finds appears entirely plausible for high level analysis.

B: 64 coins, catalogued by B.H.St.J. O'Neil, from the 1945–7 excavations in Second World War-damaged areas (Fox 1952a, 64). To these, Reece added a variety of other groups found in Exeter: 26 coins from Chapel Street (Greenfield 1964, 14), 2 from the South Gate (Fox 1968, 14), and 6 from Bartholomew Street (Holbrook and Fox 1987, 38). From these coins, Reece was able to use 81 coins in analysis (Reece 1991a, 34, tab. 7 column 2).

C: 90 coins from the excavations of the legionary baths, basilica and forum at Exeter, 1971–77 (Shiel and Reece 1979, 162–4) and listed in Reece (1991a, 34, tab. 7 column 3)

D: 1 Iron Age and 445 Roman coins, catalogued by Shiel (1991, 24–31) from excavations in Exeter in 1971–9

Table 16.1 Groups of excavation coins and stray finds from Exeter (frequency): for Site Numbers see Chapter 2 above

Site / Reece period	*Date range*	*A* *Excavations pre-1942 (Fox 1952a)*	*B* *Excavations by Fox 1945–7 (Sites 15–30; Fox 1952a)*	*C* *Excavations of the fortress baths, and basilica 1971–7 (Site 40; Shiel and Reece 1979)*	*D* *Excavations in Exeter (excluding the baths/ basilica), 1971–9 (Shiel 1991)*	*E* *Excavations at Princesshay 1997–2006 (Site 156; Shiel forthcoming)*	*Total all*	*Total B–D*
1	Pre-41	14	2	3	6	0	25	11
2	41–54	82	6	11	45	1	145	62
3	54–69	73	4	6	20	2	105	30
4	69–96	95	5	14	20	3	137	39
5	96–117	54	–	5	9	1	69	14
6	117–38	22	3	–	4	0	29	7
7	138–61	42	1	1	1	5	50	3
8	161–80	20	–	1	2	0	23	3
9	180–92	8	–	–	3	0	11	3
10	193–222	21	1	–	4	2	28	5
11	222–35	7	–	–	1	0	8	1
12	235–60	13	–	–	–	0	13	0
13	260–75	63	12	11	89	47	222	112
14	275–94/6	85	11	14	76	11	197	101
15	294/6–317	23	–	3	3	1	30	6
16	317–330	39	4	3	12	7	65	19
17	330–348	251	22	13	75	36	397	110
18	348–64	50	3	2	11	15	81	16
19	364–78	89	7	3	25	6	130	35
20	378–88	2	–	–	1	0	3	1
21	388–402	–	–	–	1	0	1	1
Total		1053	81	90	408	137	1769	579
Uncertain					35+5	9		

Table 16.2 Groups of excavation coins and stray finds from Exeter (frequency) (per mill)

Site / Reece Period	*A* *Excavations pre-1942 (Fox 1952a)*	*B* *Excavations by Fox 1945–7 (Sites 15–30; Fox 1952a)*	*C* *Excavations of fortress baths, and basilica 1971–7 (Shiel 1979)*	*D* *Excavations in Exeter (excluding the baths/ basilica), 1971–9 (Site 40; Shiel 1991)*	*E* *Excavations at Princesshay 1997–2006 (Site 156; Shiel forthcoming)*	*Total All*	*Total B–D*
1	13	25	33	14.7	0	14.65	19
2	78	74	122	110.3	7.3	82.8	107.1
3	69	49	67	49	14.6	60.3	51.8
4	90	62	156	49	21.9	77.4	67.4
5	51	0	56	22.1	7.3	38.9	24.2
6	21	37	0	9.8	0	16.3	12.1
7	40	12	11	2.45	36.5	28.2	5.2
8	19	0	11	4.9	0	12.95	5.2
9	8	0	0	7.4	0	6.2	5.2
10	20	12	0	9.8	14.6	15.8	8.6
11	7	0	0	2.45	0	4.5	1.7
12	12	0	0	0	0	7.3	0
13	60	148	122	218.1	343	125	193.4
14	81	136	156	186.3	80.3	111	174.4
15	22	0	33	7.4	7.3	16.9	10.4
16	37	49	33	29.4	51.1	36.6	32.8
17	238	272	144	183.8	262.8	223.7	190
18	47	37	22	27	109.5	45.6	27.6
19	85	86	33	61.3	43.8	73.2	60.4
20	2	0	0	2.45	0	1.7	1.7
21	0	0	0	2.45	0	0.6	1.7
Total	1000	1000	1000	1000	1000	1000	1000

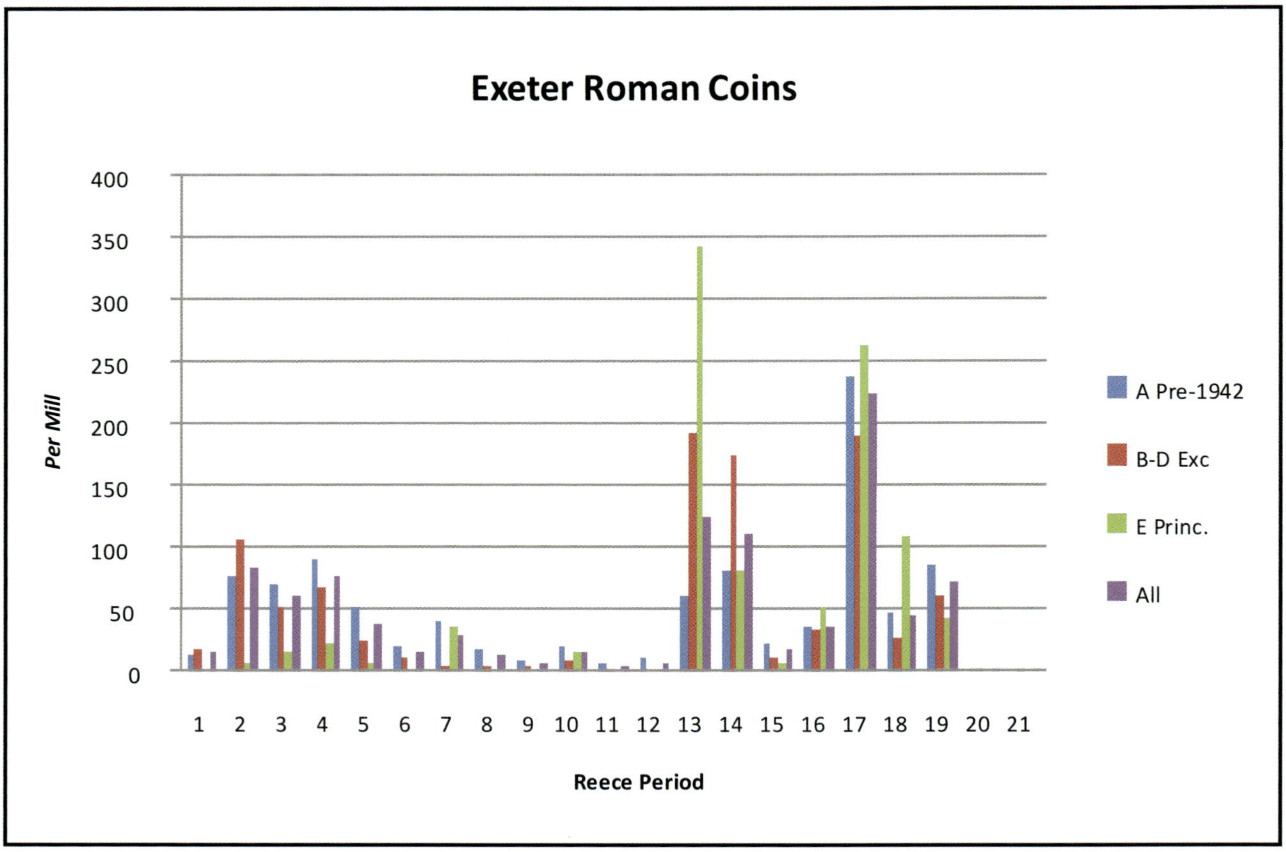

Fig. 16.1 Bar chart (per mill) *showing Group A (pre-1942 coins), Groups B–D, Group E (Princesshay excavations), and profile for all coins from Exeter*

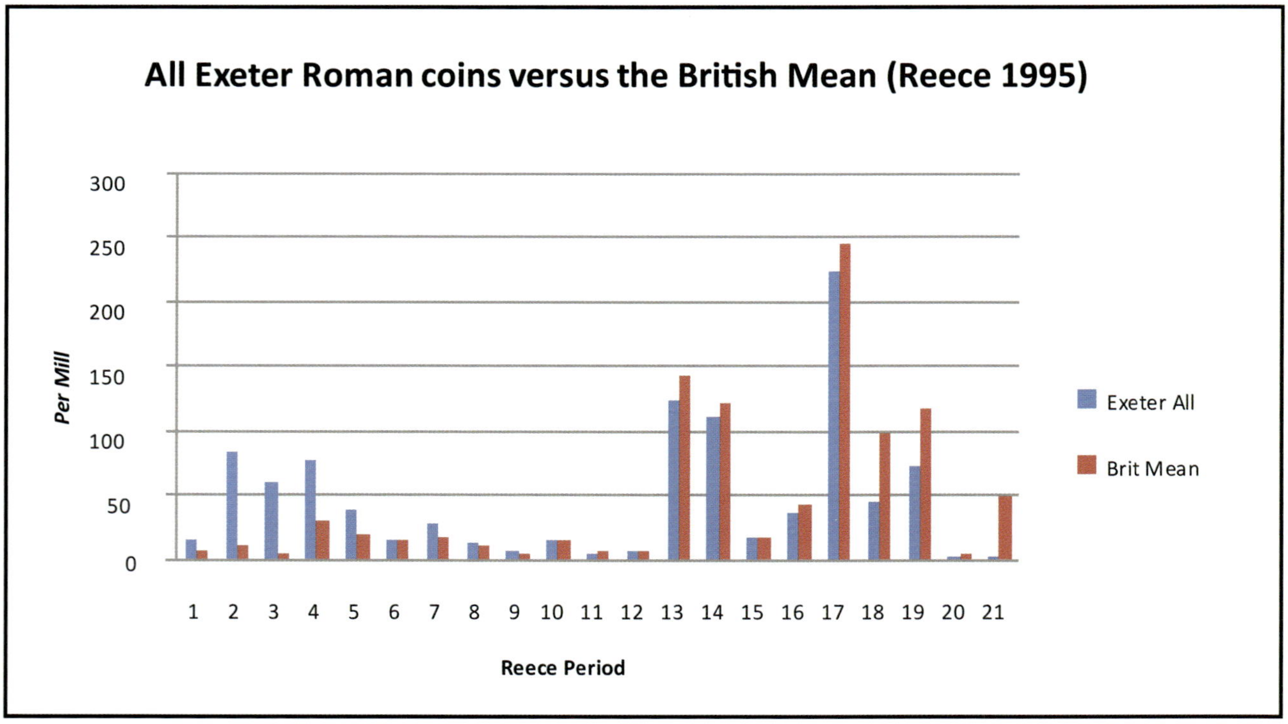

Fig. 16.2 All Exeter Roman coins versus the British Mean (Reece 1995) (per mill)

which includes an *addenda* not used in Reece's listing (Reece 1991a, 34, tab. 7 column 4). In this article, 408 coins are noted which can be assigned to Reece Periods.

E: 146 coins, catalogued by Shiel (forthcoming) from the 1997–2006 excavations at Princesshay, in Exeter (Site 156), of which 137 can be assigned to Reece Periods. Some of these coins come from within the fortress, some within the town defences, and others from outside the town walls.

It should be noted that Reece (1991b, sites 10–12) lists three groups of coins from Exeter in his *Roman Coins from 140 Sites in Britain*: No. 10 is 102 coins from Exeter excavations 1971; No. 11 is 128 coins from Exeter excavations 1972; and No. 12 is 99 coins from various sites in Exeter. These listings are superseded by the totals listed in Reece 1991a. Also note that in this chapter we follow the convention introduced by Reece of expressing coin finds as *per mill* (thousand) rather than percent (see Reece 1987, chapter 5).

Roman coin hoards from Exeter

As a result of the Leicester University/British Museum project (see above), we are able to list nine (or possibly ten) potential hoards from Exeter (Hoards 9 and 10 might actually be two different records of the same find),

Table 16.3 Roman coin hoards from Exeter (Site Numbers refer to Chapter 2 above)

No.	*PAS IARCH no.*	*Robertson 2000*	*Date of discovery*	*Location*	*tpq*	*Contents*	*Other References*
1	IARCH-70DAA5	p. 2, no. 9	1774	St Catherine's Lane	Uncertain, but early	Some Roman coins, including one of Augustus Caesar	Lysons 1822, cccxi
2	IARCH-4072D1	–	2008	Excavations at Mount Dinham (Site 154)	Prob-pre-AD 69	22 *asses*, Augustus to Claudius, *tpq* prob pre-Flavian	Treasure number: 2008T102; Leins 2013
3	IARCH-33EE7C	p. 11, no. 52	1973	Dispersed hoard disturbed from a building within an extra-mural military-period compound (excavations at the Valiant Soldier and Acorn Roundabout sites: Sites 44 and 94); apparently post-AD 73	AD 72/73	11 Claudius to Vespasian *aes*; poss 4 more Claudius to Vesp (Shiel 1991)	Shiel 1978; N. Shiel, in *Coin Hoards* V (1979), 48, no. 112, omitting *As* of Nero; Shiel 1991, 32
4	IARCH-246EE6	p. 13, no. 65	Before 1891	Taphouse Road, that runs through Tedburn St. Mary, Whitestone and Holcombe Burnell	AD 70s or later?	40 silver, Tiberius to Vespasian etc	Worth 1891, 82
5	IARCH-309EBB	p. 35 no. 175	Before 1630	St David's; near the Castle	AD 161 or later	30+ gold and silver to Ant. Pius or later	Lysons 1822, cccxi; Westcote 1630
6	IARCH-972D46	pp. 107–8, no. 483	1715	St David's; cellar of bakehouse in Cathedral Close	AD 260–9	*c.* 310+ silver Trajan to Postumus	Shiel 1978
7	IARCH-FFC19C	p. 139–40 no. 616	1977	St David's; excavation on Rack Street (Site 64)	AD 285	26 radiates, AD 261–285 (incl 20 barbarous)	Shiel, 1978, 256–8; 1991, 32–3
8	IARCH-B30D59	p. 272 no. 1138	1778	St David's, near Broadgate	AD 330–48	7, Carausius to House of Constantine (AD 330–48) – hoard?	W.T.P. Shortt in *Gent. Mag.*, 1836, II, 156
9 (same as 10?)	IARCH-E18FBB	p. 297, no. 1242	1874	St Thomas'; Freehold Land Societies property	AD 348	33 *nummi* AD 330–348	N. Shiel, in *Coin Hoards* IV (1978), 42, no. 166
10 (same as 9?)	IARCH-9BCE88	p. 277, no. 116	Before 1891	St Thomas'	AD 348 or later	30 *nummi* including Constans and Constantius II	Worth 1891, 82

although the information for individual finds varies enormously. The hoards are listed in Table 16.3 in probable chronological order, according to the *terminus post quem* of the coins (although in many cases an exact *tpq* is not possible to ascertain).

A study group of Roman towns as comparanda for Exeter

It is interesting to compare Exeter's coin profile with those of other urban centres in the South and West of the province, and Colchester in the South-East (Tables 16.4–16.5 and Figs 16.3–16.5). Of course, every Roman town has a different history and one is not necessarily comparing like with like. Colchester, Cirencester and Gloucester are similar to Exeter in having Roman military origins. Silchester has pre-Roman origins, whilst Dorchester, and possibly Winchester, appear to be foundations carefully placed to supplant existing British centres. Caerwent is a later, 2nd-century AD, foundation, whereas Ilchester only really thrives as a town in the 3rd and 4th centuries AD. Patterns do, however, emerge in coin-loss across these urban centres and they provide useful comparanda for Exeter. For this purpose, statistics for the seven towns (listed below) have been taken from Reece's listing (Reece 1991b),[3] and while he often provides several different assemblages for each town, in this study all finds have been amalgamated to provide a single profile.

Discussion of the Exeter coin assemblages, making comparison with other urban centres

The largest single group of coins is that of the pre-1942 pieces, collated by R.G. Goodchild and published by Lady Aileen Fox in 1952a (Group A). An initial comparison of this group with the others does suggest that it is quite plausible as a reliable sample of coins found in Exeter. However, without extensive research, we cannot be sure which coins were found inside the confines of the legionary fortress and early town, and those which were discovered within the larger later town perimeter or even in its environs (see Fig. 16.1). The finds do immediately warn us that different excavations will often produce very different chronological coin profiles.

There are 25 pre-Claudian coins from Exeter, pieces which would have arrived with the military after the Claudian invasion. To these coins, one can add an *as* of Augustus found in a hoard with Claudian coins at Mount Dinham (Hoard 2). Figure 16.1 shows how the majority of coin groups display high proportions of issues from the Claudian to Flavian periods. Robert Kenyon has fully explained the nature of the Claudian coins from Exeter in this volume (see above, Chapter 15), arguing for a foundation of the fortress *c*. AD 55. That the fortress remained in use into the early Flavian period is suggested by the coin finds and by a dispersed hoard with a *terminus post quem* of AD 72/73 found during excavations at the Valiant Soldier and Acorn Roundabout sites (Sites 44 and 94; Hoard 3). There appears to be another hoard of 40 silver *denarii* secluded in the Flavian period, but details are lacking (Hoard 4).

There is a drop in coin-loss during the Trajanic period and a lower coin-loss for most of the 2nd and 3rd centuries AD, up until AD 260. This needs to be examined a little closer. Firstly, if one considers the major excavations from 1945–79 (Groups B–D) there are very few coins between AD 96 and 260 (36 from 579 = 6.2%). It is a similar picture at Princesshay (8 from 137 = 5.8%) although there is a peak in Period 7 (AD 161–80) which interestingly mirrors many rural sites across Britain (Moorhead 2013, 92). In the pre-1942 group, however, there are many more coins from AD 96–260 (187 from 1053 = 17.7%), and when these coins are considered they do bring Exeter to around the British Mean for Reece Periods 5–12 (see Fig. 16.2). Furthermore, Exeter has a generally similar profile for this Period as many other towns in Roman Britain (see Tables 16.4 and 16.5, and Figs 16.3–16.5). The discrepancy between the different groups in Exeter is hard to explain: it could be a problem with the reliability of the pre-1942 sample, but it could also be that coins were found across a wider range of sites, thus providing a more balanced picture than that provided by excavation in the region of the legionary fortress. Antonine hoards are quite common in Britain, but there is only one poorly recorded find of 30 or more gold and silver coins, buried sometime after AD 161 (Hoard 5). We have to be careful about reading too much significance into the dearth of coins for Periods 11–12 (AD 222–260) because pieces from this Period are scarcer across the entire province, the graph effectively reflecting a fall in coin supply to *Britannia*.

The major upturn in coin-loss for 'radiate' coins in Periods 13–14 (AD 260–75) is typical on sites across Britain and should not be seen as indicating any significant activity or change at Exeter; the coins in question were increasingly debased and were struck in copious quantities. However, although there is a notable peak at Princesshay in Period 13 (343 *per mill*), the averages for Periods 13 (125 *per mill*) and 14 (111 *per mill*) are just below the national average (see Fig. 16.2). When compared to other towns, Exeter does lag behind Dorchester, Silchester and Winchester, but compares favourably with the other towns in the study group (see Tables 16.4 and 16.5, and Figs 16.3–16.5). There are only two radiate hoards (numbers 6 and 7) from Exeter which is not a large number when one considers that there are over 650 hoards from this Period from across the province. The coin record for Periods 15–17 (AD 294–348) is quite in line with sites across Britain (see Fig 16.2) and with most of the towns in the study group (Tables 16.4 and 16.5, and Figs 16.3–16.5). The highest peak in Period 17 (AD 330–48) is seen at sites across Britain, it generally

Table 16.4 Coin finds from Exeter and other selected Roman towns in Britain: frequency (Reece 1991b)

Reece Period	*Date (AD)*	*Exeter*	*Ilchester*	*Dorchester*	*Caerwent*	*Gloucester*	*Cirencester*	*Silchester*	*Winchester*	*Colchester*
1	Pre-41	25	0	7	4	0	66	21	1	52
2	41–54	145	0	12	2	11	135	79	19	133
3	54–69	105	0	4	1	13	59	22	4	49
4	69–96	137	0	19	39	24	279	187	21	138
5	96–117	69	0	10	24	4	120	107	14	46
6	117–38	29	0	11	20	3	98	125	16	53
7	138–61	50	3	16	15	4	139	158	12	83
8	161–80	23	0	13	15	1	92	102	16	51
9	180–92	11	1	4	6	0	32	42	3	12
10	193–222	28	0	11	18	8	137	100	8	67
11	222–35	8	0	3	11	1	73	55	5	30
12	235–60	13	0	6	11	1	105	71	8	29
13	260–75	222	14	358	93	46	1076	2144	450	354
14	275–94/6	197	12	451	102	86	819	1483	419	410
15	294/6–317	30	4	20	8	2	123	168	22	26
16	317–330	65	6	51	42	20	543	592	54	62
17	330–348	397	23	525	354	80	2242	2901	358	605
18	348–64	81	3	141	46	57	1073	1068	146	239
19	364–78	130	26	115	59	69	1320	1570	143	172
20	378–88	3	0	7	12	1	82	48	11	8
21	388–402	1	34	90	16	20	1368	673	106	11
Totals		1769	126	1874	898	451	9981	11,716	1836	2740

Table 16.5 Exeter and other selected towns in Roman Britain: per mill *(Reece 1991b)*

Reece Period	*Date (AD)*	*Exeter*	*Ilchester*	*Dorchester*	*Caerwent*	*Gloucester*	*Cirencester*	*Silchester*	*Winchester*	*Colchester*
1	Pre-41	14.65	0	3.7	4.4	0	6.6	1.79	0.5	19
2	41–54	82.8	0	6.4	2.2	24.4	13.5	6.74	10.3	48.5
3	54–69	60.3	0	2.1	1.1	28.8	5.9	1.88	2.2	17.9
4	69–96	77.4	0	10.1	43.4	53.2	27.95	15.96	11.4	50.4
5	96–117	38.9	0	5.3	26.7	8.9	12	9.13	7.6	16.8
6	117–38	16.3	0	5.9	22.3	6.65	9.81	10.67	8.7	19.3
7	138–61	28.2	23.81	8.5	16.7	8.9	13.9	13.49	6.5	30.3
8	161–80	12.95	0	6.9	16.7	2.2	9.2	8.71	8.7	18.6
9	180–92	6.2	7.94	2.1	6.7	0	3.2	3.58	1.6	4.4
10	193–222	15.8	0	5.9	20	17.7	13.7	8.54	4.4	24.4
11	222–35	4.5	0	1.6	12.25	2.2	7.3	4.69	2.7	10.9
12	235–60	7.3	0	3.2	12.25	2.2	10.5	6.06	4.4	10.6
13	260–75	125	111.11	191	103.6	102	107.8	183	245.1	129.2
14	275–94/6	111	95.24	240.7	113.6	190.7	82	126.58	228.2	149.6
15	294/6–317	16.9	31.75	10.7	8.9	4.4	12.3	14.34	12	9.5
16	317–330	36.6	47.62	27.2	46.8	44.3	54.4	50.53	29.4	22.6
17	330–348	223.7	182.54	280.1	394.2	177.4	224.6	247.61	195	220.8
18	348–64	45.6	23.81	75.2	51.2	126.4	107.5	91.16	79.5	87.2
19	364–78	73.2	206.35	61.4	65.7	153	132.25	134	77.9	62.8
20	378–88	1.7	0	3.7	13.4	2.2	8.22	4.1	6	2.9
21	388–402	0.6	269.84	48	17.8	44.3	137.1	57.44	57.7	44.2
Totals		1000	1000	1000	1000	1000	1000	1000	1000	1000

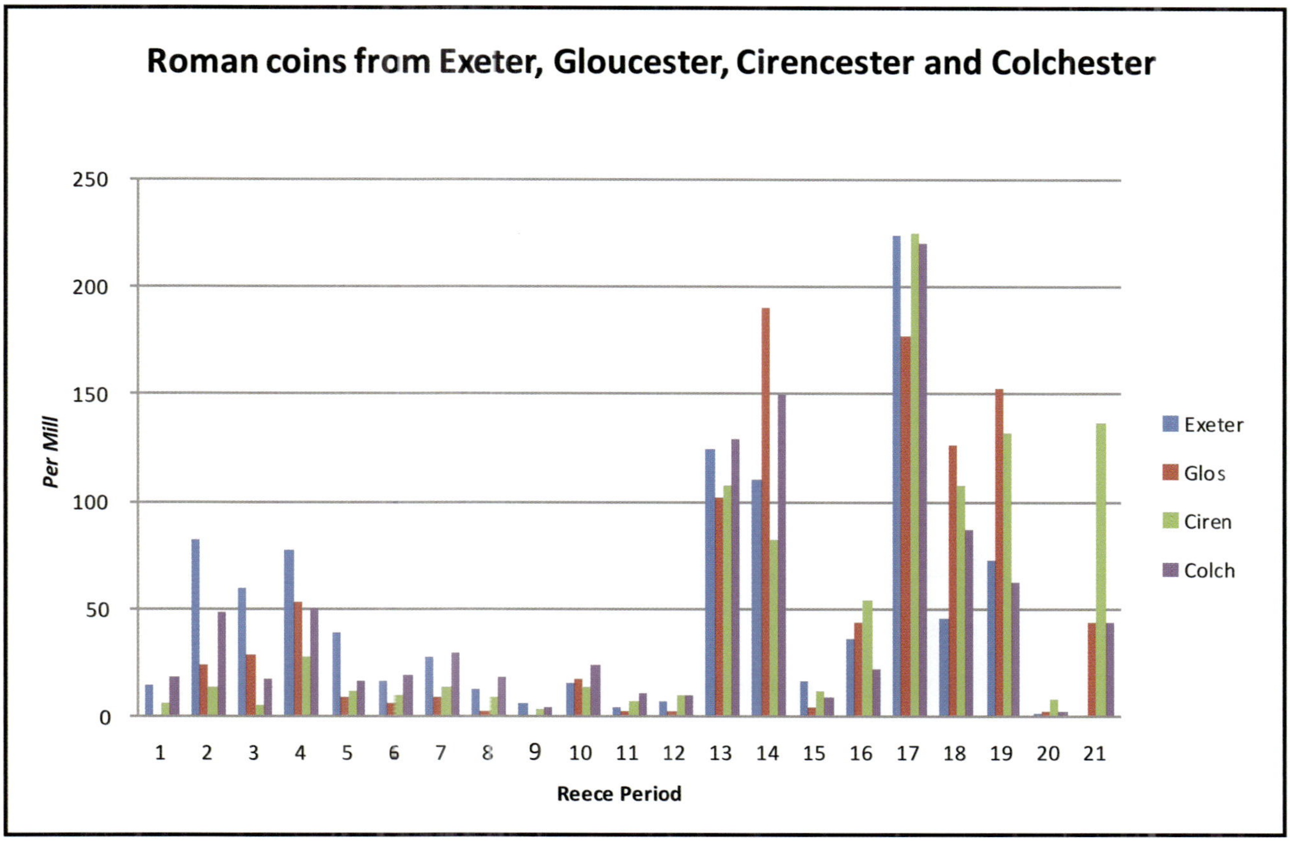

Fig. 16.3 Roman coins from Exeter, Gloucester, Cirencester and Colchester (per mill). *These are towns with Roman military origins*

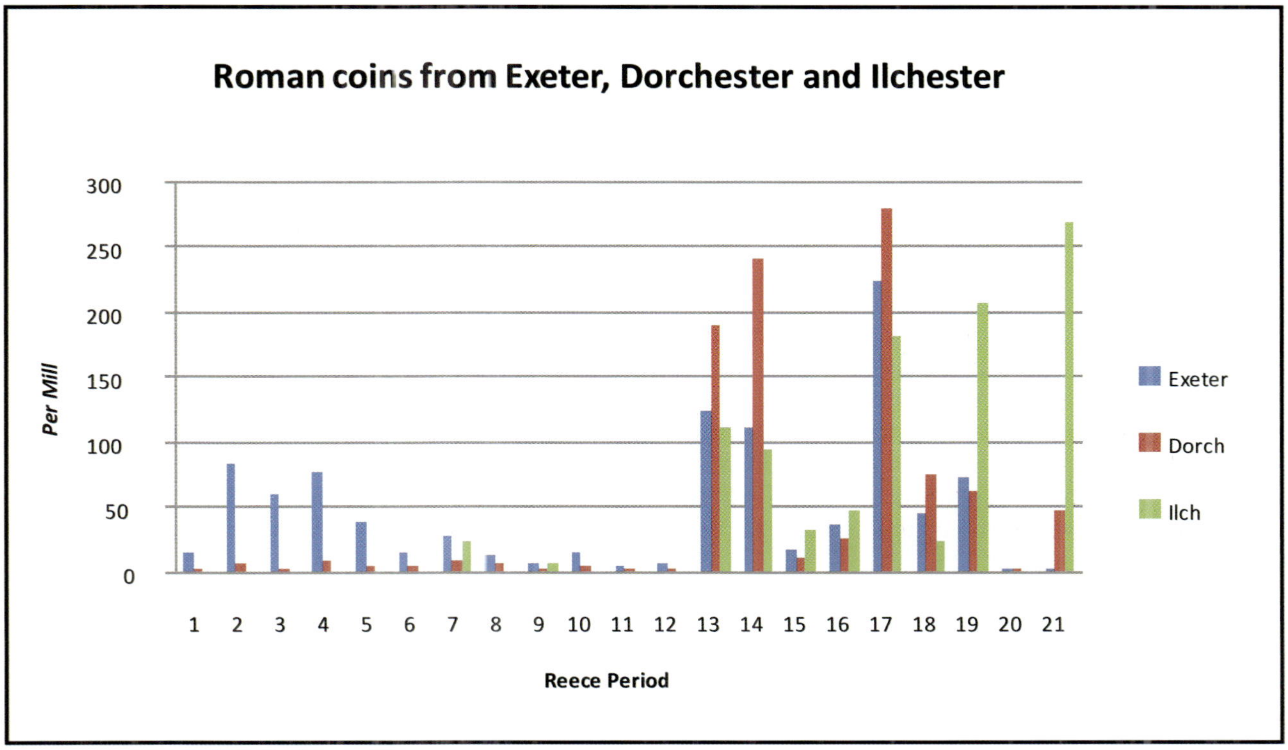

Fig. 16.4 Roman coins from Exeter, Dorchester and Ilchester (per mill). *These are the two closest major towns to Exeter*

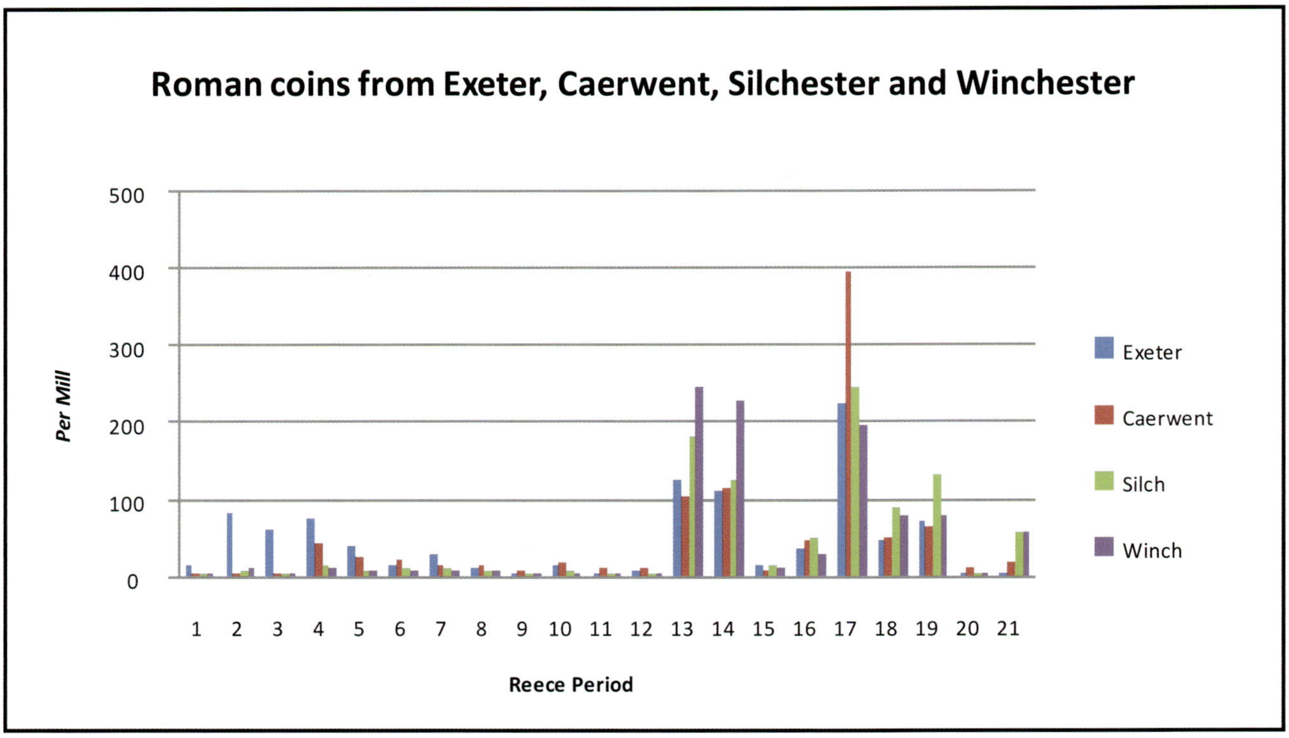

Fig. 16.5 Roman coins from Exeter, Caerwent, Silchester and Winchester (per mill). *Caerwent is a 2nd-century AD foundation; Silchester has Iron Age antecedents*

being the period of most coin-loss on British sites. It is possible that two or three hoards (numbers 8–10 below) belong to this Period, one possibly being slightly later (Hoard 10).

Exeter does, however, show a marked decline in Periods 18–19 (AD 348–78) and then a near total collapse in coin-loss (only one coin recorded!) for Periods 20–21 (AD 378–402). Although this does happen at a number of rural sites in Britain, it is most unusual for urban sites. Dorchester, Caerwent, Silchester, Winchester and Colchester also experience a drop in coin-loss after AD 348, but they all have quite a strong showing in Period 21 (AD 388–402) indicating more monetary activity at these towns in the last decades of Roman Britain. Caerwent only has 17.8 *per mill* coin loss for single finds in Period 21 (AD 388–402), but over 10,000 Theodosian *nummi* of this period in several hoards were found in excavations at the site (see IARCH-B91A6A; IARCH-92308D; IARCH-E8BAE4; IARCH-50AC09; IARCH-762A25; IARCH-A20516; IARCH-58FB56). Indeed, Caerwent is second only to Richborough (over 22,800) for the number of Theodosian coins found, a stunning contrast to the one coin found at Exeter. At Ilchester, the pattern is quite the opposite from Exeter with coin-loss in Periods 19 (AD 364–78) and 21 (AD 388–402) exceeding that of Period 17 (AD 330–48). This locks Ilchester into a network of sites with high coin-loss in the Valentinianic Period (19: AD 364–78) which appear to be connected with official activity, probably the extraction of taxes in kind, much of which was probably exported to the continent (Moorhead 2001, 90–5; Moorhead and Stuttard 2012, 206–8, 226–7; and see discussion below in 'Chronological review' section on AD 364–378, Reece Period 19). Gloucester and Cirencester also belong to this group with Ilchester and Cirencester also showing a very high coin-loss in Period 21 (AD 388–402). For coin-loss after AD 378, Exeter stands alone with its single Theodosian coin. It has been shown how, in this Period, bronze coin use shrunk down to military and urban centres, and nodal points on the road network, probably reflecting that base metal coinage was only used in quantity by the military and officials (Walton 2012, 109; Moorhead and Walton 2014, 104–112). It does seem that the general population were prepared to go on using silver *siliquae*, but eschewed the bronze *nummi*, as *siliquae* are proportionally much more common on rural than on military and urban sites (Moorhead and Walton 2014, 112, tab. 2). This strongly suggests that Exeter had ceased to be an important centre for the late Roman administration.

To summarise the coin finds from Exeter and their comparison with other similar urban sites, it is clear that Exeter has two distinct characteristics, separated by a long phase of relative normality. In the 1st century AD, from the Claudian to Flavian periods, Exeter has the highest proportional coin-loss of any settlement in Britain, reflecting the legionary presence from *c.* AD 55 into the Flavian period. If the pre-1942 coin records are reliable, we can say that the coin records for the 2nd century AD up to *c.* AD 348 are relatively consistent with other towns in the study group. However, after a decline in coin-loss from AD 348 to 378, there is an almost complete collapse after AD 378 which singles Exeter out as the only town with next to no coin-loss in the Theodosian period. The lights appear to go out early.

Portable Antiquities Scheme Roman coins recorded for Devon

The data set

The landscape of Roman coinage in Britain has changed dramatically since Reece (1991b) published his 140 sites in 1991. The increase in metal detected finds recorded as a result of the introduction of the new Treasure Act (1996) and subsequent advent of the PAS has resulted in an exponential rise in the numbers of Roman coins recorded annually. As of December 2019, the PAS contains almost 319,000 Roman coins in 287,547 database records covering all periods of Roman coin use and loss in Britain (Fig. 16.6). To this can be added more than 3,000 Roman coin hoards ranging in size from single precious metal coins to the largest Roman coin hoards known from Roman Britain: the Cunetio Hoard of 54,951 coins (Besly and Bland 1983) and the Frome Hoard of *c.* 52,500 coins dating to the 3rd century AD (Moorhead *et al.* 2010).

At a very general level, Devon is a notable area of low coin use and loss, particularly in comparison with regions further to the north and east. Some of this is likely affected by access to the landscape itself, for example in the two National Parks where metal detecting is illegal, but the paucity of material elsewhere is striking and appears to represent a definite lack of coin use in the South-West Peninsula generally. The PAS records 1,012 single Roman coins for Devon in 1,007 database records, with additional examples from the Unitary Authorities of Torbay (6 coins) and Plymouth (5 coins), to give a total of 1,023 coins. This number includes 234 recently discovered coins from Dainton Elms Cross, in Ipplepen, that will be added to the PAS in due course (at present, only the early detector finds are on the PAS database). It should be noted that only 772 coins in Devon have been assigned a Reece period, but a significant proportion that remain impossible to closely identify are of 1st to 2nd-century AD date. *Denarii* of the second half of the 2nd century BC (*e.g.* DEV-0E6CE2, DEV-2F6E66, and SOM-C5DB54) are the earliest Roman types represented, with nine Theodosian coins from AD 388–402 (Reece Period 21) marking the end of coin use in the region. In addition to the single finds, over 45 coin hoards of Roman date have been recorded, the largest being the Seaton Down Hoard of *c.* 22,000 4th-century AD *nummi* (PAS-D7EA4C). The focus of PAS material is for the most part to the east and south of Dartmoor, and south of Exeter, with only sparse coin finds around the western edge of the National Park, and fewer examples still in the northern and western regions of the county (Fig. 16.7). This is not simply a reflection of where metal detecting is most prevalent, possible, or reported in Devon but appears to be a genuine representation of the Roman landscape, since if we plot all PAS finds for the County (Fig. 16.8) the range of finds is much more widespread, particularly in the north-west.

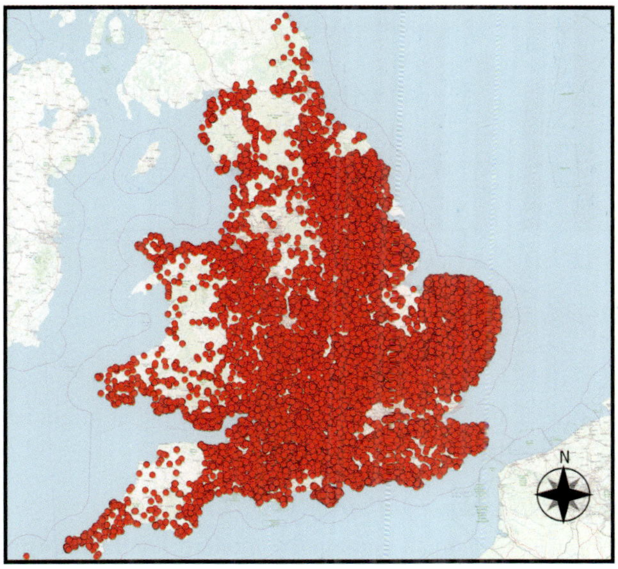

Fig. 16.6 Roman coin finds on the PAS as of 2019 (map data: © OpenStreetMap contributors)

Of the 1,023 Roman coins recorded in Devon, 772 have been assigned Reece Periods that allow for the reconstruction of Devon's coin loss profile (Fig. 16.9). The Early Roman period is well-attested, notably with relatively high numbers of coins (*per mill*) recorded up to the end of the Flavian period (AD 69–96) and then with large increases into the Antonine period of *c.* AD 138–180 (Reece Periods 7 and 8). Spikes in coin usage are seen in the mid 3rd century AD (Reece Period 13), the Constantinian period (AD 330–348; Reece Period 17), and the Valentinian period (AD 364–378; Reece Period 19). A small, but not negligible, spike is seen at the end of the Roman period with the Theodosian coinage (AD 388–402; Reece Period 21).

The Devon profile demonstrates very clear differences when considered alongside neighbouring counties (Figs 16.9–16.12). Compared to the 791 Roman coins recorded through the PAS in Cornwall, Devon has comparatively fewer coins *per mill* in the Flavian through Antonine periods but is considerably better attested in the Late Roman period when Cornwall rapidly tails off (Fig. 16.11). Both of these profiles are notably different to, for example, Dorset and Somerset whose very similar

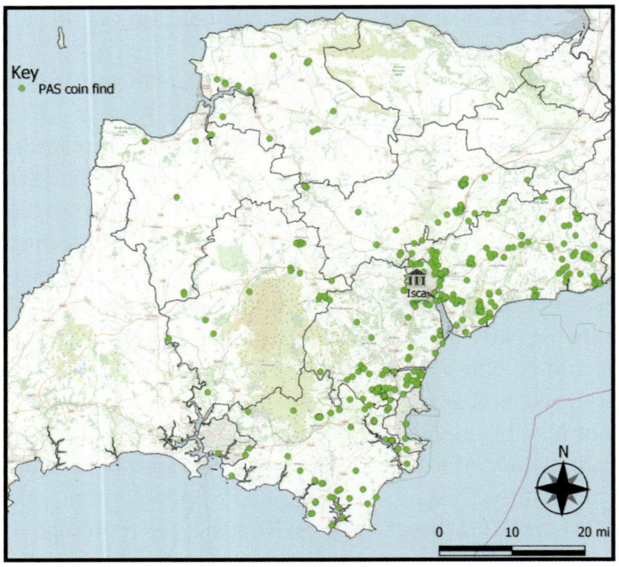

Fig. 16.7 Roman coin finds in Devon recorded through the PAS (map data: © OpenStreetMap contributors)

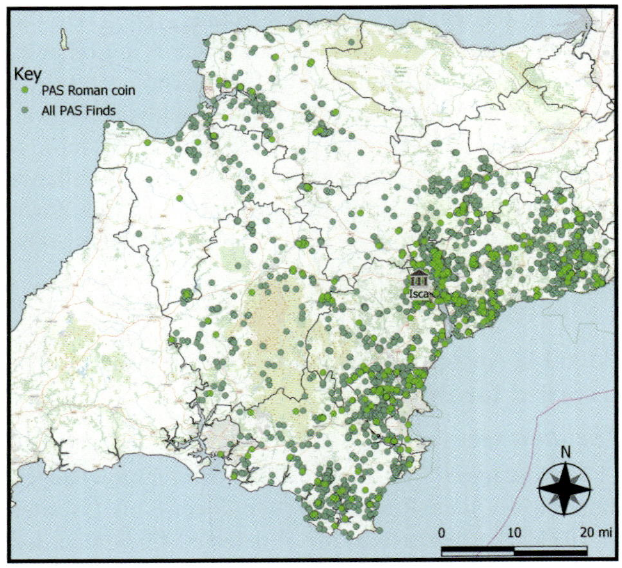

Fig. 16.8 All finds recorded in Devon through the PAS. Dark green indicates all Devon PAS finds; light green indicates all Roman period finds (map data: © OpenStreetMap contributors)

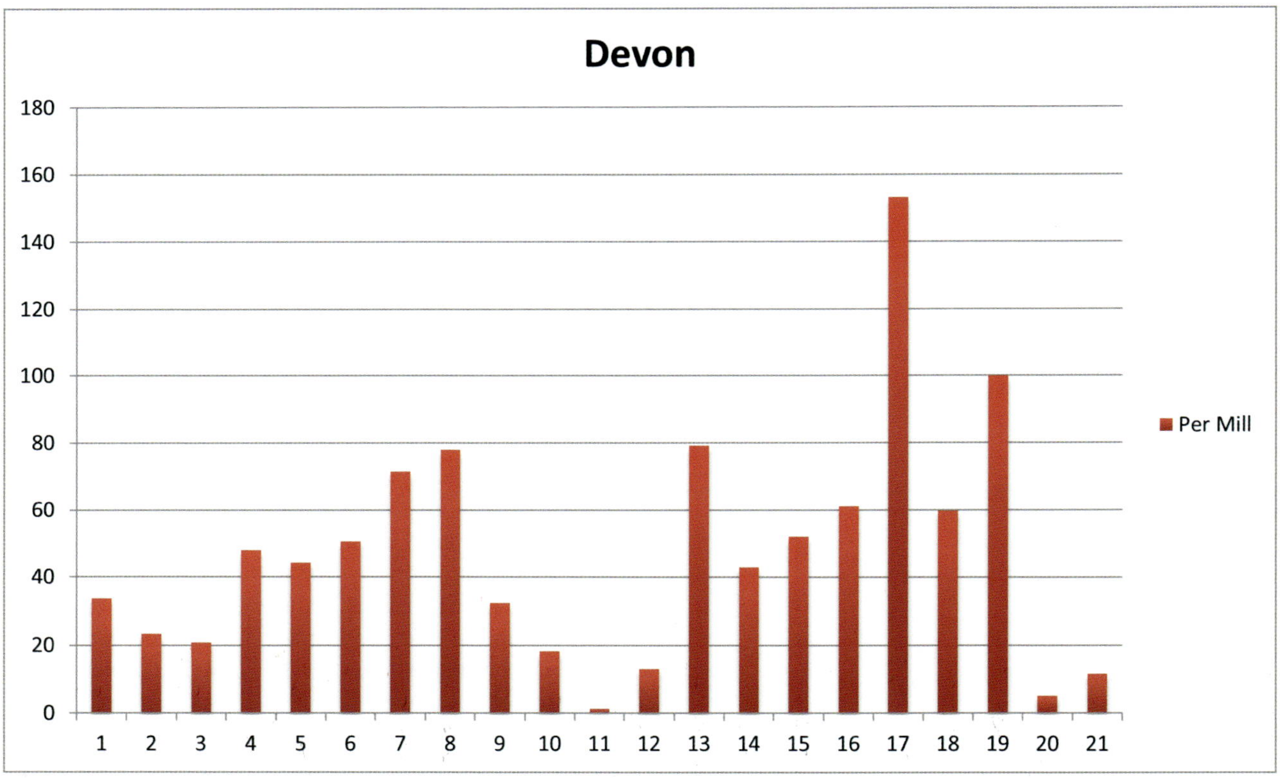

Fig. 16.9 Reece Period analysis for Devon

coin profiles demonstrate little activity in the Early Roman period but intensive coin use in the 3rd and 4th centuries AD between *c.* AD 260–378 (Reece Periods 13–19; Fig. 16.12). This is much closer to the national picture given by the British Means defined by Richard Reece (1991b), Philippa Walton (2012, 36–7) and the PAS dataset (Walton 2012, 31–37). At a regional level, Devon and Cornwall are both clearly divergent from what might be generally expected.

The PAS coins by district[4]

Analysis of Roman coinage by modern local authority district within Devon highlights clear differences around the County (Table 16.6). The very small numbers of PAS

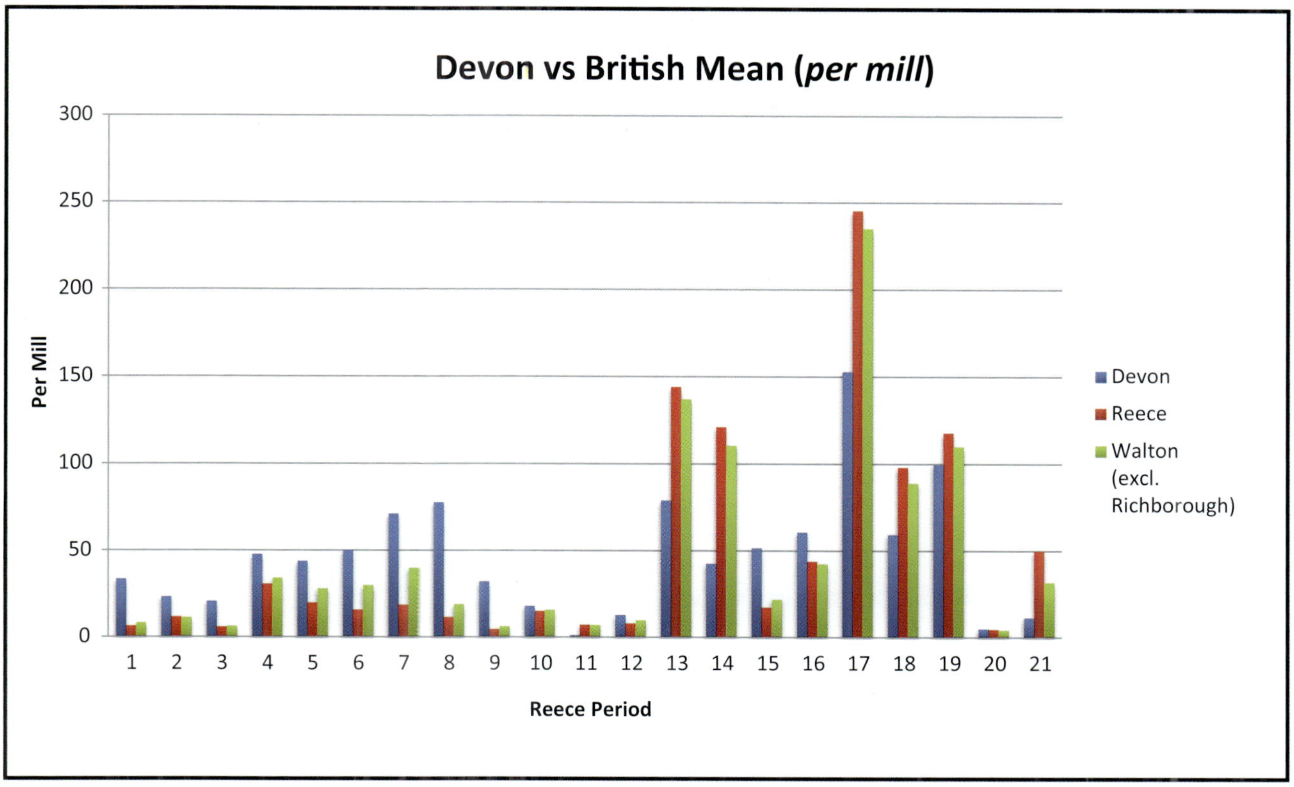

Fig. 16.10 The Devon PAS coin profile against Reece's British Mean (Reece 1995) and Walton's British Mean (Walton 2012, 233, tab. 7) excluding Richborough which skews the overall picture enormously because of its huge volume of Theodosian coinage, likely to be the result of dispersed hoarding, which gives a false impression for the province as a whole

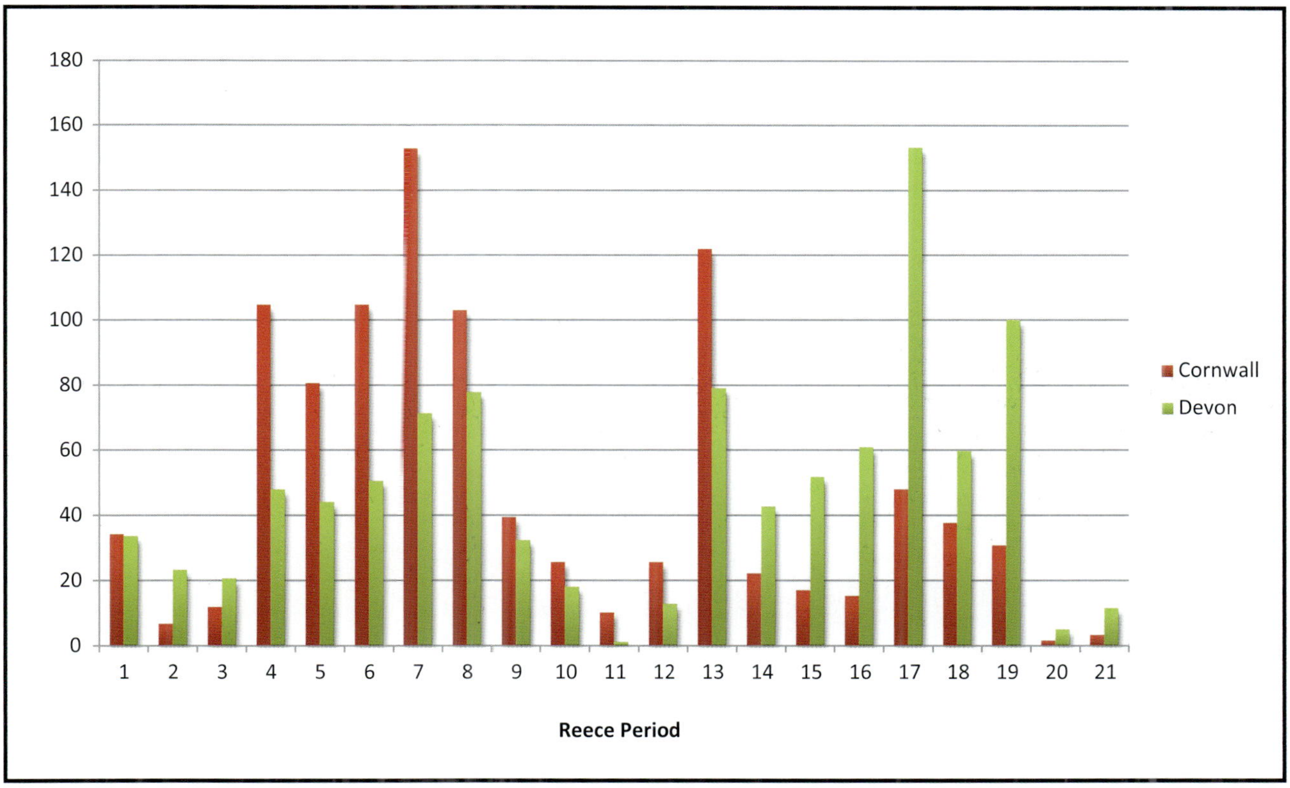

Fig. 16.11 Reece period analyses of Cornwall and Devon combined

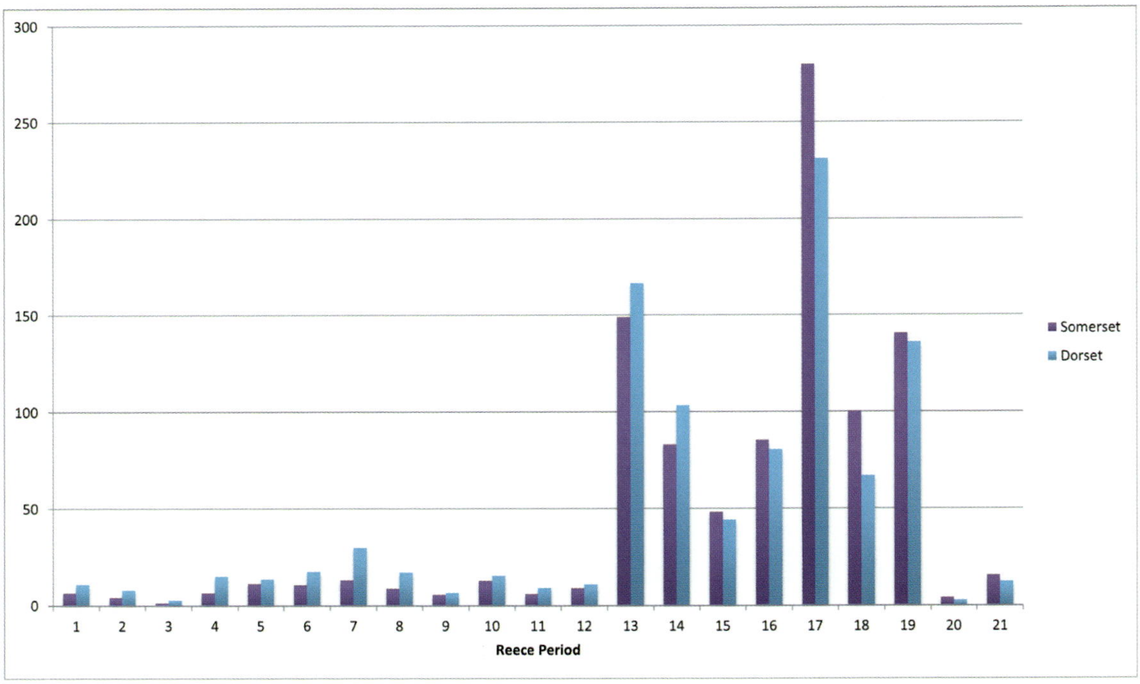

Fig. 16.12 Reece Period analyses of Dorset and Somerset

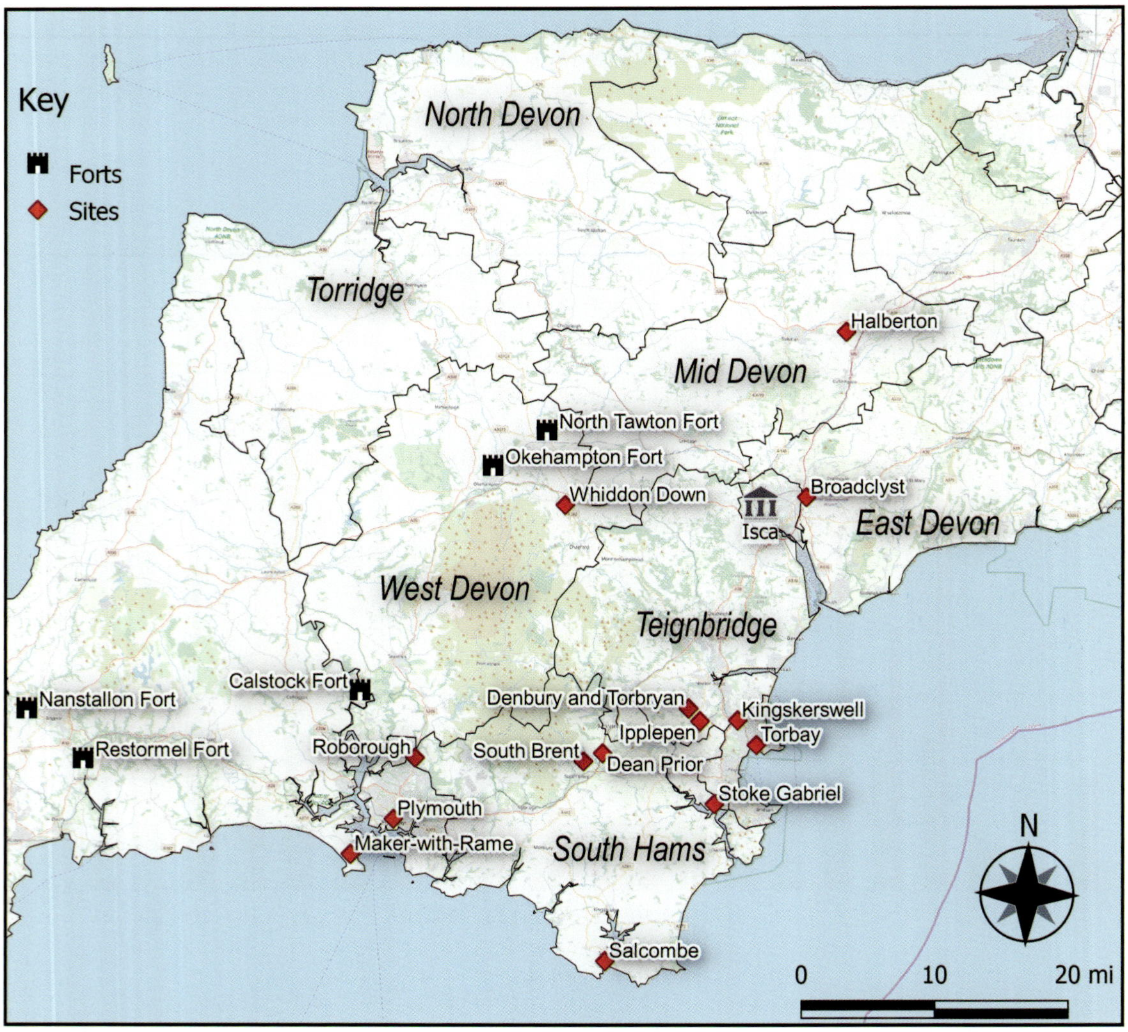

Fig. 16.13 Map of Devon districts and sites mentioned in the text (map data: © OpenStreetMap contributors; Boundary data: Office for National Statistics licensed under the Open Government Licence v.3.0, Contains OS data © Crown copyright and database right 2017)

Table 16.6 Number of PAS coins by Devon district

Reece Period	*East Devon*	*Exeter*	*Mid Devon*	*North Devon*	*South Hams*	*Teignbridge*	*Torridge*	*West Devon*	*Totals*
1	4	0	7	1	3	7	1	1	24
2	1	0	0	1	7	7	0	0	16
3	2	0	1	0	2	11	0	0	16
4	8	1	2	0	3	20	0	0	34
5	6	2	4	1	4	16	0	0	33
6	5	0	1	1	14	16	0	2	39
7	11	2	3	1	14	22	0	1	54
8	14	2	3	1	15	17	1	4	57
9	9	0	1	0	9	3	0	2	24
10	5	1	1	0	2	7	0	0	16
11	0	0	0	0	1	0	0	0	1
12	3	0	1	1	1	3	0	0	9
13	6	2	19	2	11	19	1	0	60
14	1	1	5	0	5	19	0	0	31
15	14	0	3	0	5	15	0	3	40
16	1	0	12	0	2	32	0	1	48
17	13	3	12	0	10	79	0	0	117
18	9	0	3	0	7	23	3	0	45
19	7	2	2	0	7	60	0	0	78
20	2	0	0	0	0	0	1	0	3
21	0	0	0	0	6	3	0	0	9
Total	121	16	80	9	128	379	7	14	754

coins in Exeter, North Devon, Torridge and West Devon are not statistically useful in defining coin use and loss here, although they do highlight the comparative paucity of material in the north and west of the region. In contrast, the 80 coins from Mid Devon demonstrate some activity in the first half of the Roman period, followed by clear peaks in the mid 3rd century AD (Reece Period 13: AD 260–75; Fig. 16.14) and again in the Constantinian period (Reece Periods 16 and 17: AD 317–348).

The most notable assemblages are focussed in the east and south of the county. The 628 coins from East Devon, South Hams and Teignbridge clearly highlight a substantial early phase of activity, most notably a gradual increase in coin use and loss running up to a peak in the Antonine period, *c.* AD 161–180 (Reece Period 8; Fig. 16.15). The South Hams has notable coin losses in Reece Period 2, *c.* AD 41–54, as well as in the entire Antonine period (Reece Periods 7–8), the mid 3rd century AD (Reece Period 13), and a surprising late showing in the Theodosian period (Reece Period 21). East Devon and Teignbridge have broadly similar trends in the Early Roman period, but the very obvious difference lies in the comparatively huge numbers of Constantinian and Valentinianic coins represented in Teignbridge during Reece Periods 17 (AD 330–48) and 19 (AD 364–378).

PAS sites with major Roman coin assemblages

There are few parishes in Devon with discrete coin scatters recorded through the PAS that are statistically viable for analysis and which might point towards more clearly defined Roman settlements (Table 16.7). Ipplepen is clearly the largest after Exeter, but several smaller sites have increasing numbers of coins that help fill out the picture (Fig. 16.13). What is notable is that the sites in the north (Halberton and Broadclyst; Fig. 16.16) generally reflect Late Roman activity in the 3rd to 4th centuries AD, a profile not dissimilar to the combined material from Exeter with its peaks in Reece Periods 13, 14, 17 and 19 (this is not surprising as they lie relatively close to Exeter). Further to the south, the two nearby sites of Dainton Elms Cross, in Ipplepen, and Denbury/Torbryan have evidence for early activity, particularly in the Antonine period, but still with notable Late Roman phases, most obviously in the Constantinian period (Reece Period 17) at Dainton Elms Cross and the Valentinian period (Reece Period 19) at Denbury/Torbryan (Fig. 16.17). The most notable difference lies with the remaining three south-eastern sites of Salcombe, South Brent and Stoke Gabriel, and the comparable site just over the Tamar from Plymouth near Maker-with-Rame (Fig. 16.18). There is a clear emphasis on the late 1st to 2nd centuries AD through to the late Antonine period (Reece Period 9) at Stoke Gabriel. South Brent behaves perhaps more like Ipplepen

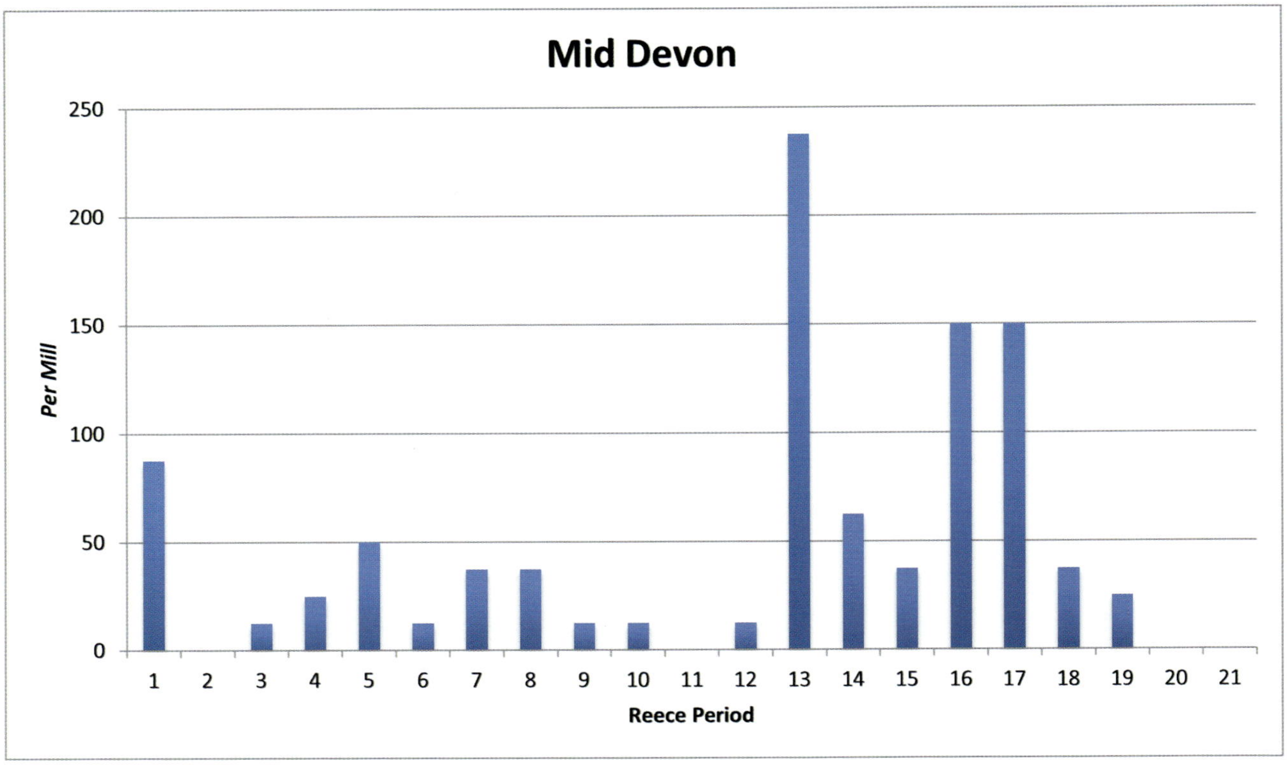

Fig. 16.14 PAS coins from Mid Devon (per mill)

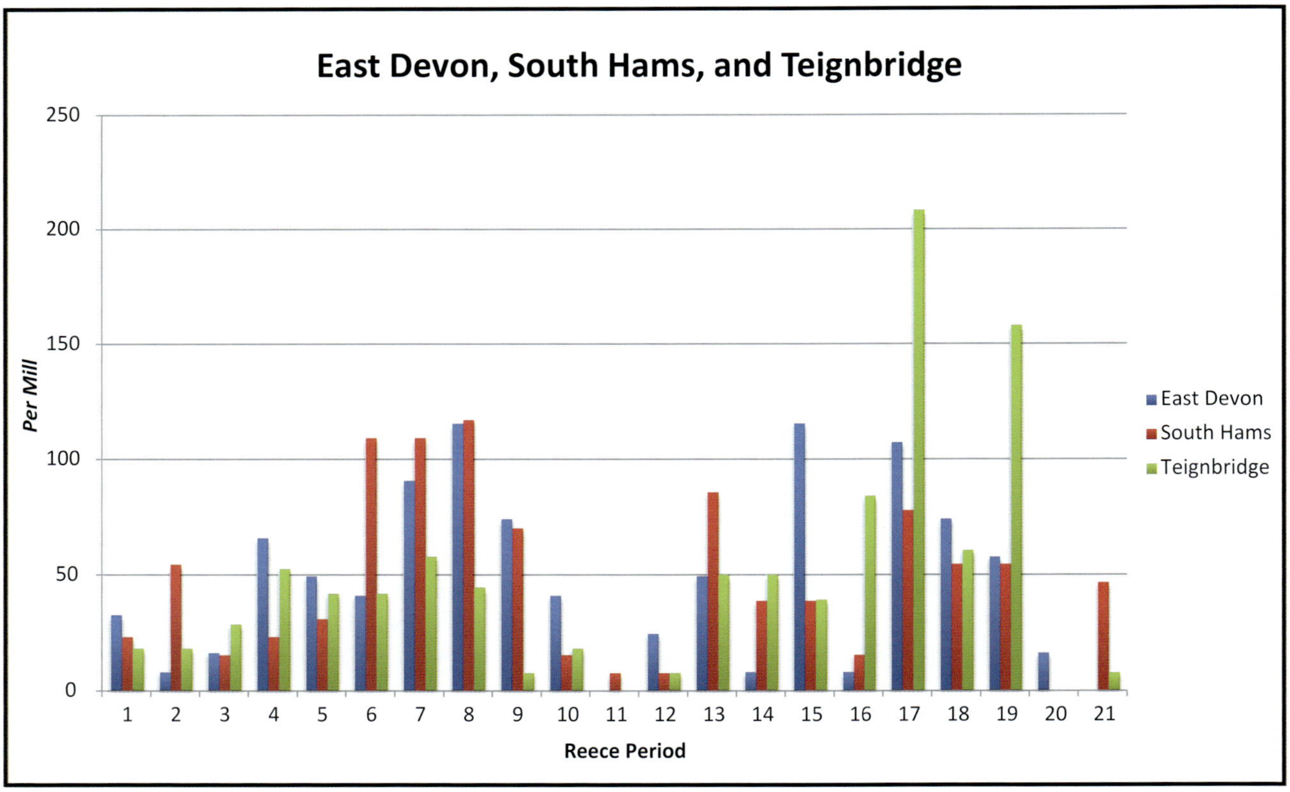

Fig. 16.15 PAS coins from East Devon, South Hams and Teignbridge (per mill)

Table 16.7 PAS sites with significant assemblages of Roman coins

Reece Period	Dainton Elms Cross, in Ipplepen	Broadclyst (26)	Denbury and Torbryan (85)	Halberton (66)	Salcombe (31)[1]	South Brent (48)	Stoke Gabriel (42)	Maker-with-Rame (Cornwall)[2] (52)
1	5	0	0	0	0	0	0	0
2	3	1	0	0	0	1	0	0
3	5	0	0	0	0	0	1	0
4	16	0	1	0	0	0	1	0
5	9	1	3	1	2	0	2	1
6	4	0	6	1	4	1	3	3
7	11	0	3	1	4	4	4	4
8	7	0	7	1	5	1	8	4
9	1	0	2	1	0	1	7	0
10	4	0	0	1	0	0	1	2
11	0	0	0	0	0	0	1	0
12	2	0	0	1	0	0	0	1
13	11	2	6	18	0	8	1	1
14	16	1	2	5	0	5	0	1
15	14	1	0	3	0	0	2	0
16	29	0	0	10	0	2	0	1
17	64	3	5	12	0	9	0	1
18	17	1	1	2	0	4	1	0
19	13	3	45	2	0	4	1	3
20	0	0	0	0	0	0	0	0
21	3	0	0	0	0	2	0	1
Total	234	13	81	59	15	42	33	23

[1]The remaining 16 coins from Salcombe that could not be attributed to one Reece period are all early bronze issues of the 1st or 2nd centuries AD.

[2]A number of coins have been recorded near Maker-with-Rame in Cornwall, on the opposite side of the Tamar estuary to Plymouth. Their proximity to other southern and eastern Devon sites makes them an interesting comparison, especially given that modern county boundaries would not have been a factor in antiquity.

and Denbury with less emphasis on the early period and peaks in the late 3rd century AD (Reece Periods 13 and 14) and Constantinian period (Reece Period 17). It is worth noting, too, that both South Brent and Maker-with-Rame have very clear Theodosian spikes in Reece Period 21 (AD388–402) that are only hinted at in Ipplepen but seemingly nowhere else. South Brent has also produced one of just two Late Roman crossbow brooches recorded through the PAS (DEV-E1A6A8, the other from Exeter: LEIC-EEE688), again hinting at activity here towards the end of the Roman period.

The individual sites, much like the regional distributions, demonstrate what seems to be a shift in Roman coin use and loss within Devon during the Roman period. In the north and west, and at least as far as Exeter, coin use is sparse, but with an apparent greater emphasis on the latter stages of the Roman period in the 3rd and 4th centuries AD. South and east of Exeter, perhaps as far as South Brent, this late 3rd and 4th century AD presence is clear, but increasingly with larger volumes of early material most notably of the Flavian through to the Antonine periods. In the most southern and eastern sites, however, the situation is almost reversed and the emphasis is clearly on early coinage with large peaks in the Antonine period more reminiscent of the general coin profile for Devon as a whole. Of course, this may be a slight chicken and egg scenario in that the Devon coin profile is substantially populated by material from the southern and eastern assemblages.

A broad comparison of the Devon PAS data with Exeter

The PAS data provides a significant and useful background that enables Exeter to be placed in its regional setting from a Roman numismatic perspective (Figs 16.19–16.21). It should be noted, though, that the total number of coins from each region is significantly smaller than for Exeter and that any new finds could significantly change the proportions. Of immediate interest is that pre-AD 43 coins (Period 1) make up a higher proportion of finds

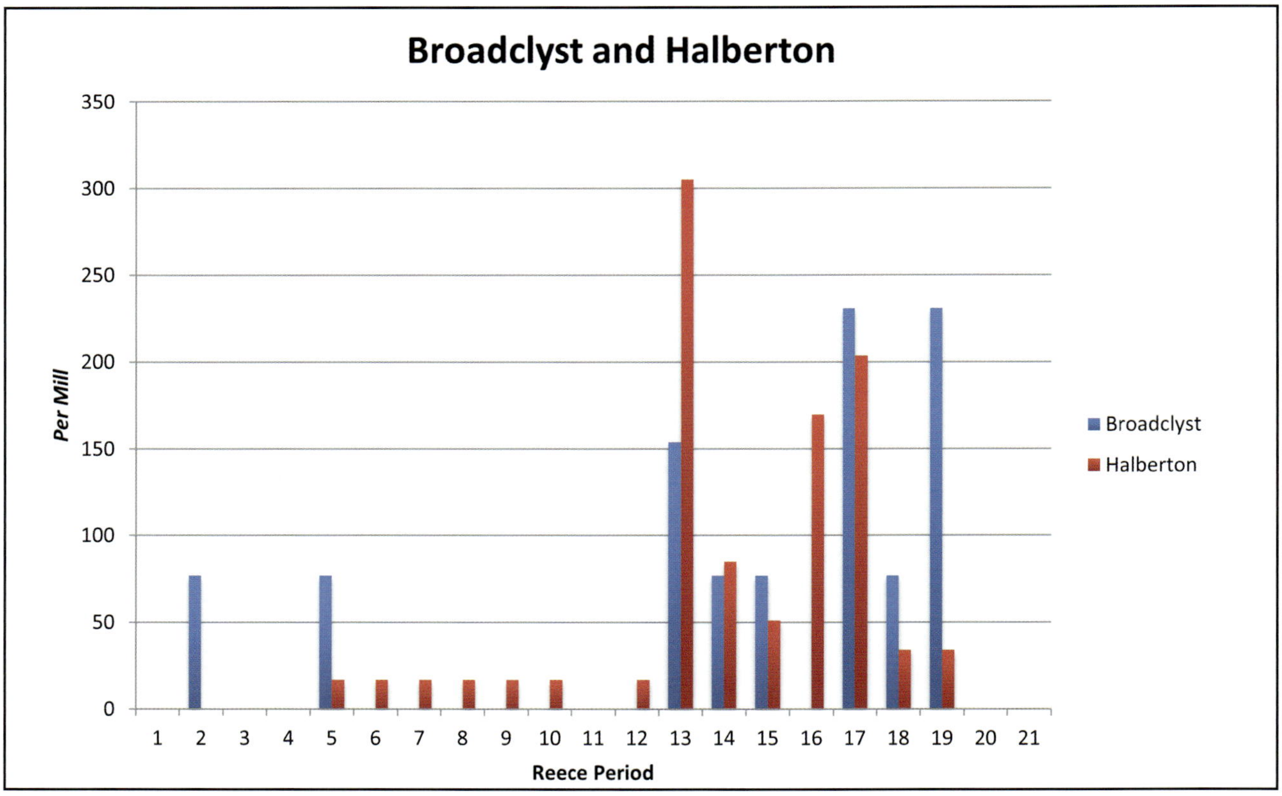

Fig. 16.16 PAS Roman coins from Broadclyst and Halberton (per mill)

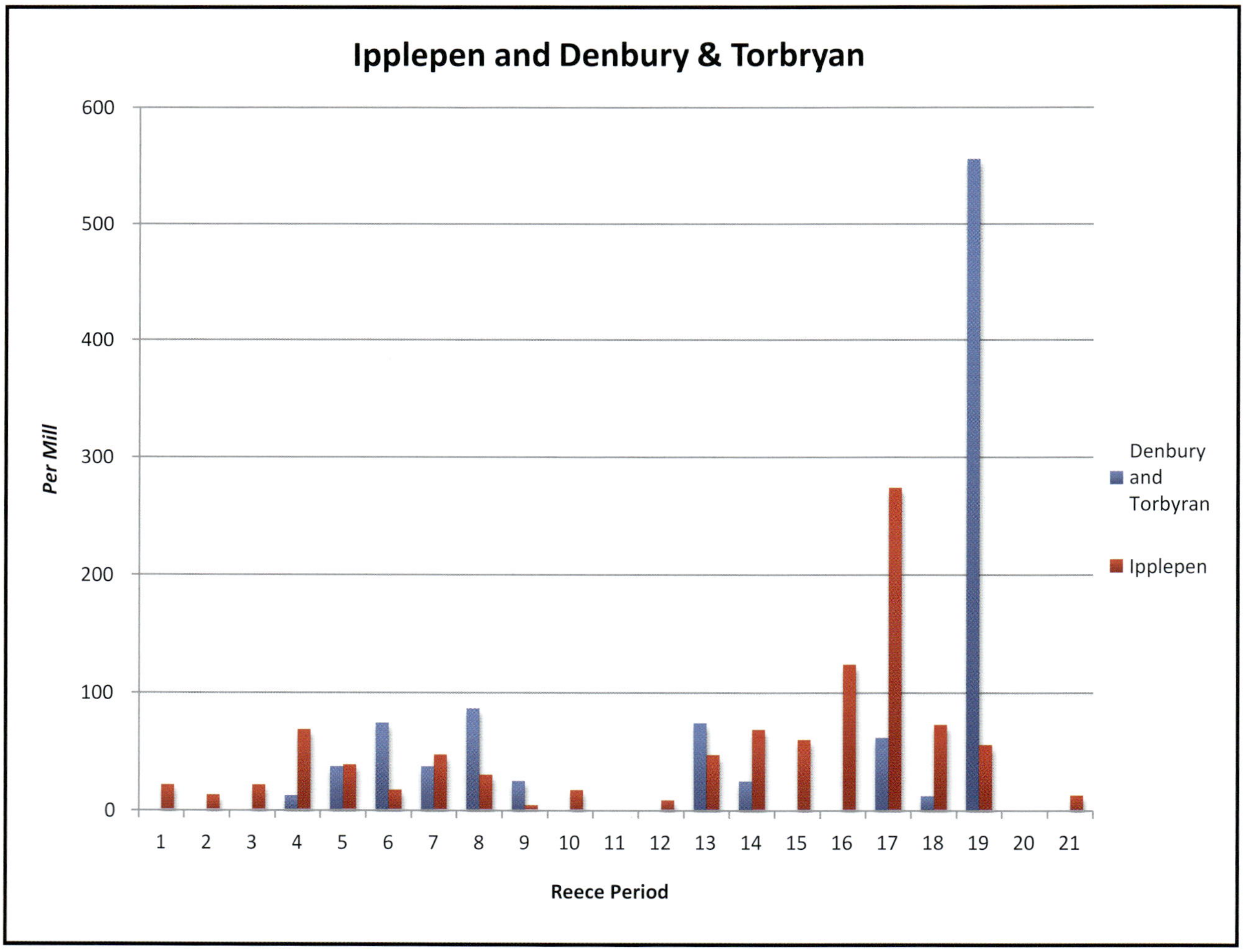

Fig. 16.17 PAS Roman coins from Ipplepen and Denbury/Torbryan

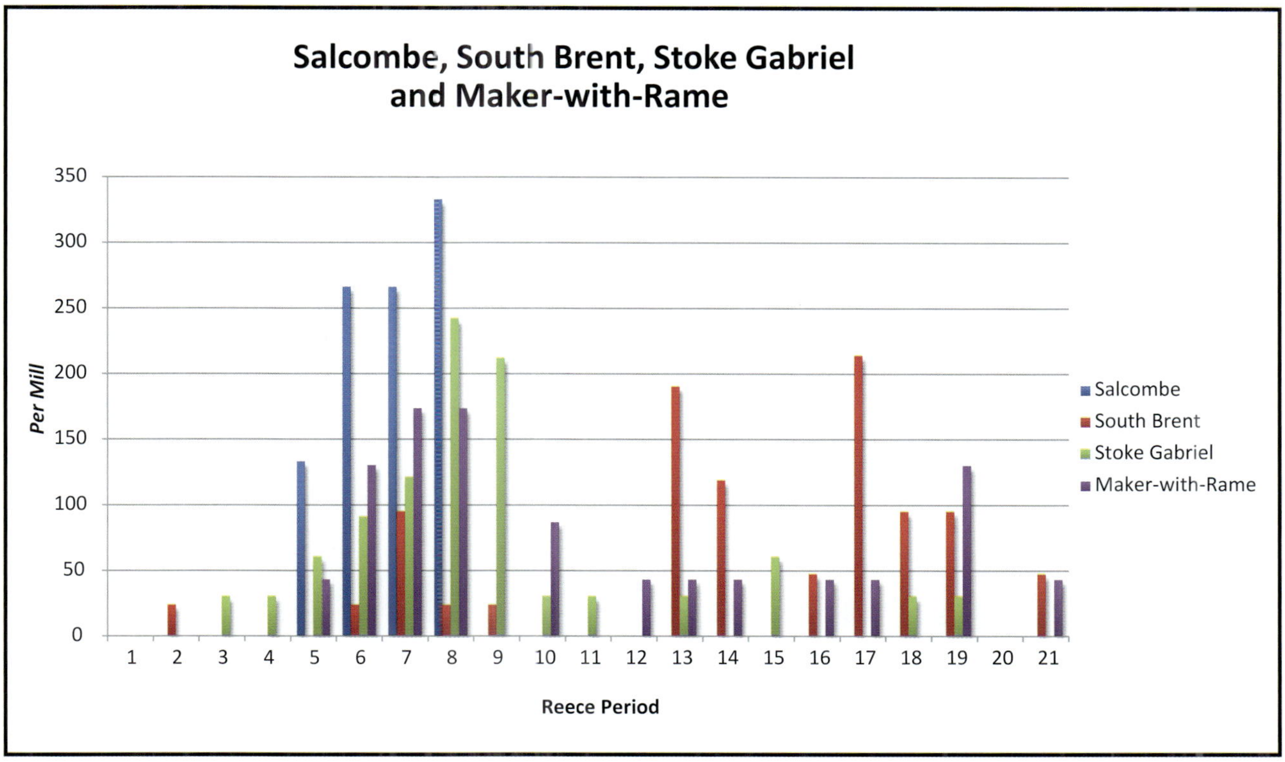

Fig. 16.18 PAS Roman coins from Salcombe, South Brent, Stoke Gabriel and Maker-with-Rame (East Cornwall)

in the regions than in Exeter, although they are all, bar one *sestertius* of Agrippina (see below), Republican and Augustan *denarii* that could have been lost at any time in the 1st century AD or later. Exeter, as expected, is much better represented in the Claudian and Neronian Periods (Reece Periods 2 and 3: AD 41–54), but in the early 2nd century AD (Hadrianic and Antonine periods, Reece Periods 6–9: AD 96–192) is superseded by Devon as a whole. Both demonstrate slight peaks in the later 3rd century AD (Reece Periods 13 and 14: AD 260–75), but the higher totals at Exeter are to be expected as urban centres tend to have a higher proportion of radiates than rural ones (Reece 1987, 94). Periods 15 and 16 (AD 294–330) are much better represented in Devon than at Exeter, although it should be noted that these coins are quite prolific at Dainton Elms Cross and Halberton (a large number of Period 15 (AD 294–317) and Period 16 (AD 317–330) coins have been found on the southern part of the site at Dainton Elms Cross: it is possible that they are a dispersed hoard, moved over significant distances by the plough, but no epicentre has been found to prove this hypothesis). In Period 17 (AD 330–48), Exeter has a higher total than Devon, but in the last periods (Reece Periods 18–21: AD 348–402), Exeter falls behind. It is notable that there are nine Theodosian coins of Period 21 (AD 388–402) in Devon, as compared to the single specimen at Exeter.

A chronological review of Roman coin-finds from Devon

The Claudian conquest, AD 43–late 40s (Reece Period 2)

Evidence for the Claudian invasion in Britain is increasingly attested from a numismatic perspective, most notably in hoards like the find of 37 *aurei* datable to AD 41–2 from Bredgar in Kent (IARCH-75460A; Robertson 2000, 6, no. 22) and mixed conquest-period coin groups like the Owermoigne Purse Hoard from Dorset (PAS-6AA253; 2010 T404) that contains Early Roman silver and bronze issues alongside local Iron Age (Durotrigan) types. In Britain, Claudian and earlier *sestertii* are typically scarce but invariably associated with areas of military activity. The around 50 examples recorded through the PAS (Fig. 16.22) include findspots along the south coast as far as Devon and may plausibly indicate the early movement of the Roman military in south-western Britain in the years immediately following the Claudian invasion.

Small clusters of Claudian bronze coinage are apparent in Devon, most notably between Exeter and Plymouth and particularly in the area around South Brent/Dean Prior (Fig. 16.23). The nine *sestertii* dating to *c.* AD 42 from the Roborough hoard (Plymouth: Holbrook and Shiel 2002) and four *sestertii* from the Dean Prior hoard, probably dating to around the same period as Roborough[5] (see

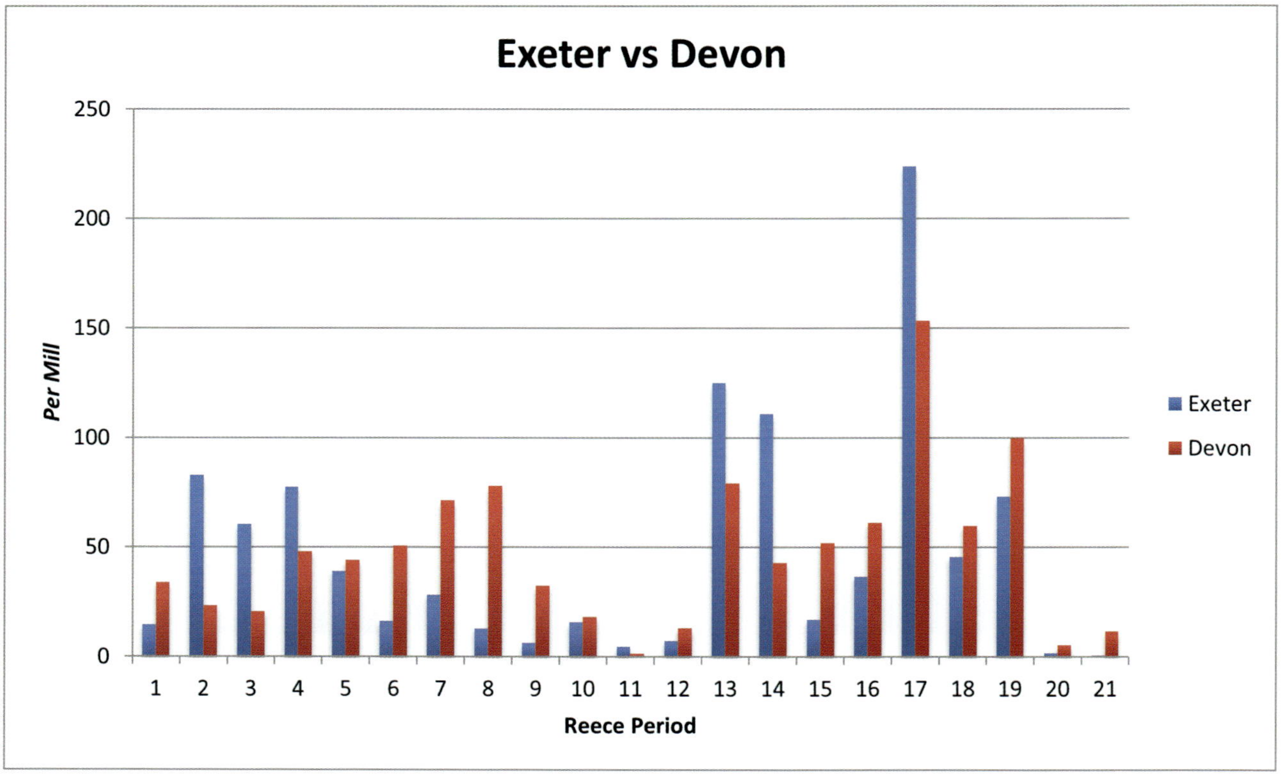

Fig. 16.19 Exeter (all coins) versus the PAS Devon totals (per mill)

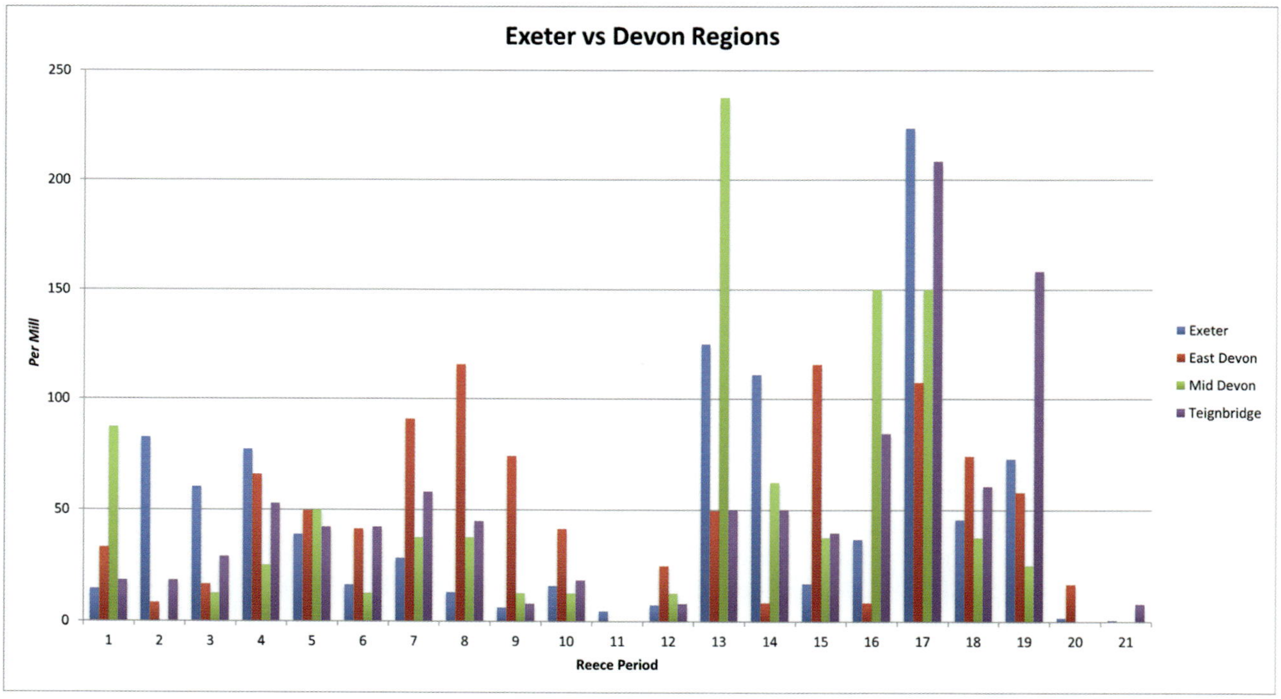

Fig. 16.20 Exeter (all coins) versus the Devon regions: East Devon, Mid Devon and Teignbridge

PUBLIC-562CF9, PUBLIC-56C92E, PUBLIC-56D8E3, and PUBLIC-FE2AC1), are significant contributions to this number and potentially quite revealing. Within the Roborough hoard was an earlier *sestertius* of Gaius (AD 37–41), and it is interesting to note that a PAS find, a *sestertius* struck by Gaius for Agrippina the Elder, was found near Torquay (DEV-EEA7E1).[6] If we consider the Claudian bronzes as any form of indication for early

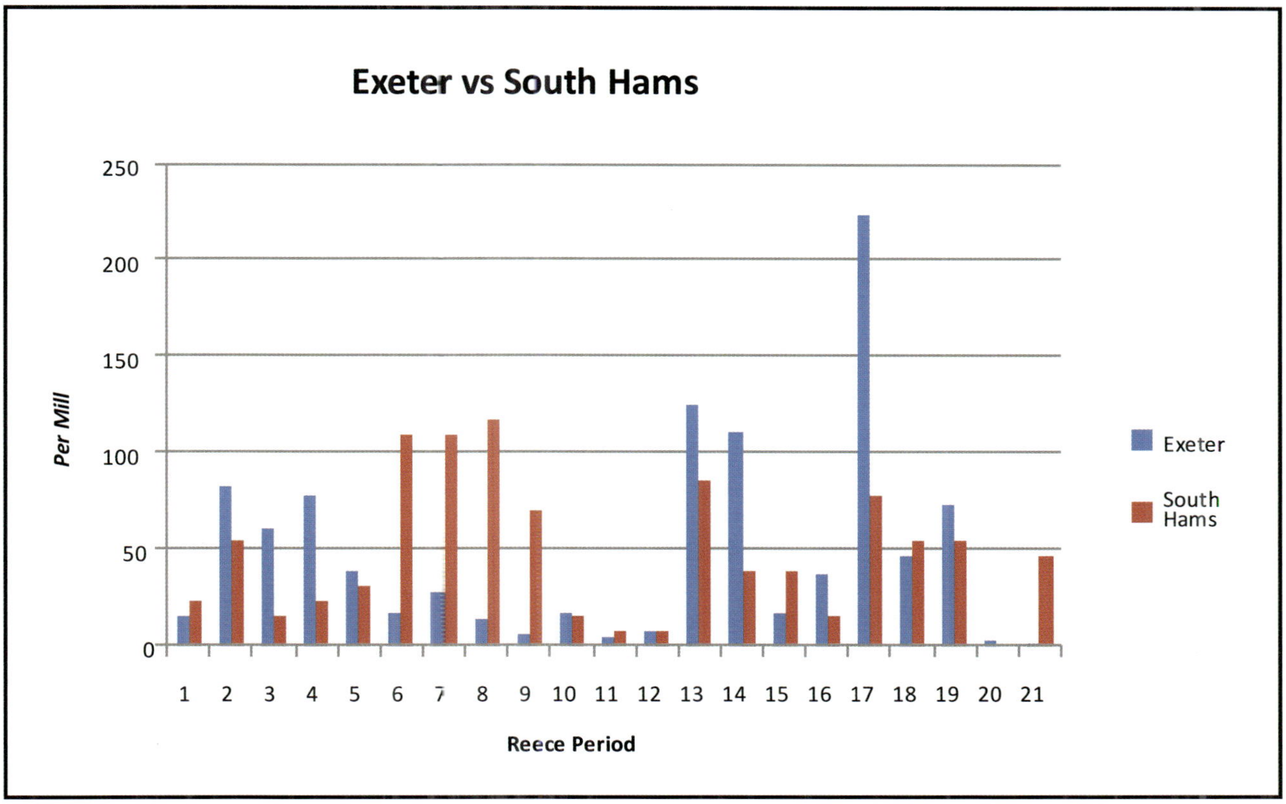

Fig. 16.21 Exeter (all coins) versus the Devon region of South Hams (per mill)

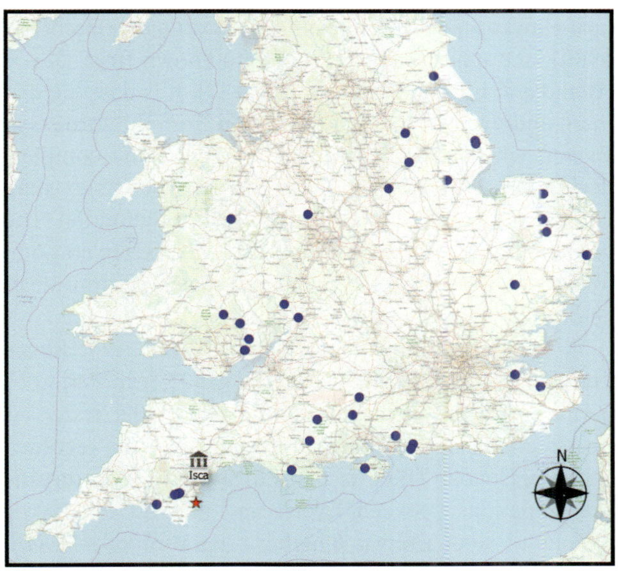

Fig. 16.22 Claudian sestertii *recorded through the PAS with a* sestertius *of Agrippina (in red; DEV-EEA7E1) (map data: © OpenStreetMap contributors)*

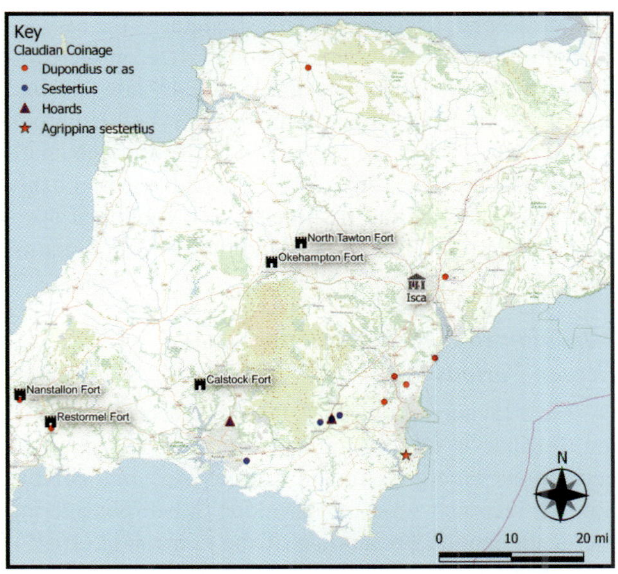

Fig. 16.23 PAS Claudian coins in Devon with key hoards and later military sites (map data: © OpenStreetMap contributors)

military activity, the location of the Devon examples might point to military activity south of Exeter. It might be argued that as commander of *legio II Augusta*, the future emperor Vespasian or his successors advanced well beyond Exeter, south and east of Dartmoor, perhaps as far as Plymouth or further still towards the (later) military emplacements at Calstock, Restormel and Nanstallon (Fig. 16.24). It is interesting to note that there are only three *sestertii* of Claudius found in Exeter (Kenyon 1988, 54-5, nos. 4, 14, and 18). Kenyon, in this volume (Chapter 15,

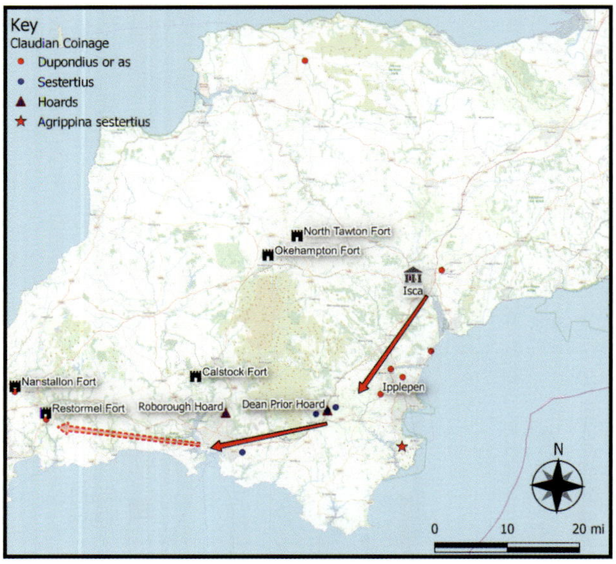

Fig. 16.24 Putative direction of advance by legio II Augusta *in the AD 40s as shown by Claudian and earlier coins, with later forts (map data: © OpenStreetMap contributors)*

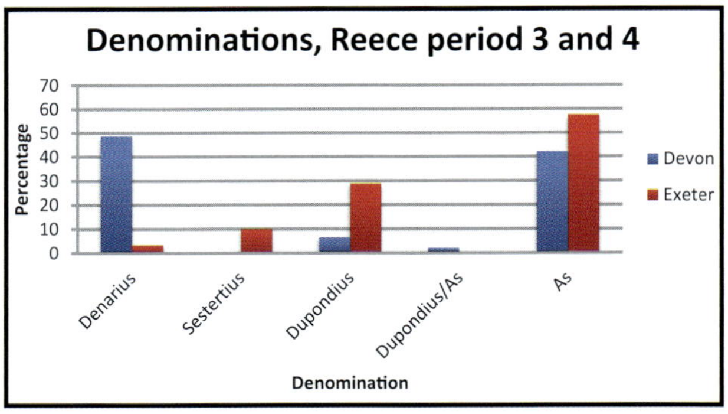

Fig. 16.25 Denominational breakdown of coins comparing PAS Devon (45 coins) with Exeter (59 coins). Note that the data for the Exeter denominations in this part of the chapter come from the 1945–7 to 1997–2006 excavations (Fox 1952; Shiel 1979; 1991; forthcoming; see Table 16.1, Groups B–E), although the majority of 2nd-century AD coins from Exeter are in the pre-1942 coin list (Fox 1952a) which come from a wide variety of sources, making the specific information difficult to access

above), differentiates between sites of earlier military activity in the Claudian period (*c.* AD 43–late 40s) and later military/civilian sites of the Claudian to Flavian periods (*c.* AD 53–75). With a high incidence of Claudian and earlier *sestertii,* South Devon very much fits into Kenyon's first group, although as he states, Exeter falls into the second, later, group. This strengthens the case for Roman military activity well beyond Exeter in the early phases of the Claudian invasion, *c.* AD 43–late 40s, and appears to vindicate suggestions made by Neil Holbrook and Norman Shiel in their report on the Roborough hoard (Holbrook and Shiel 2002, 217). This advance probably involved both land and sea forces, such combined operations being used later in Scotland by Agricola (Tacitus, *Agricola,* 25, 28).

Neronian to Hadrianic periods, AD 54–138 (Reece Periods 3–6)

By the Flavian period (AD 69–96; Reece Period 4), the distribution of coinage in Devon fills out with concentrations emerging in the Torbay area but notably nothing recorded west of Dartmoor. When considering the denomination breakdown of the coins (Fig. 16.25), it is striking how there are proportionally many more silver *denarii* found in Devon (*c.* 48%) than in Exeter (*c.* 3.4%). Given that soldiers were largely paid in silver, one would expect more silver from Exeter, although note the apparent Flavian *denarius* hoard of 40 coins found on Taphouse Road (see Table 16.3, no. 4). This might reflect continued military activity south and west of Exeter and then into Cornwall. Restormel was likely in use and the archaeology of Nanstallon suggests it was functioning by this stage prior to being dismantled when the *legio II Augusta* departed for *Isca Augusta* (Caerleon) from *c.* AD 74 (Fox and Ravenhill 1970; 1972; Bidwell 1980, 12–14). The sole gold Roman coin on the PAS for the South-West Peninsula, an *aureus* of Nero dating to AD 66–67 from the Bodmin area in Cornwall (CORN-DE6541), belongs in this period. A second *aureus* of Nero was identified near Hawkesdown Hill hillfort, near Axminster (Holbrook 1989), and other Neronian *aurei* are known from Devon (Bland and Loriot 2010: nos. 136–137). It is possible that the withdrawal of most of the legion from the fortress at Exeter, which started in *c.* AD 74, led to the complete drying up of a silver supply to Exeter, whereas existing coins continued to circulate in the rest of the region. The preponderance of *dupondii* and *asses* at Exeter do point towards a thriving local economy, dependant on small change.

A change occurs in the Trajanic (AD 98–117; Reece Period 5) and Hadrianic (AD 117–138; Reece Period 6) periods with the increasing dominance of the *sestertius* over the *denarius*, making up over 60% of the recorded coins in Devon. There is more of a parity with regards denominations between Exeter and the rest of Devon, although Exeter still has a higher proportion of *dupondii* and *asses* suggesting a greater need for small change in an urban environment (Fig. 16.26).

The Antonine and early Severan periods (AD 138–222; Reece Periods 7–10)

The overwhelming proportion of bronze coins appearing in the Antonine period in the South-West Peninsula marks a clear change in coin use patterns within the region. The *denarius* is almost non-existent, with the *sestertius* making up over three quarters of the finds

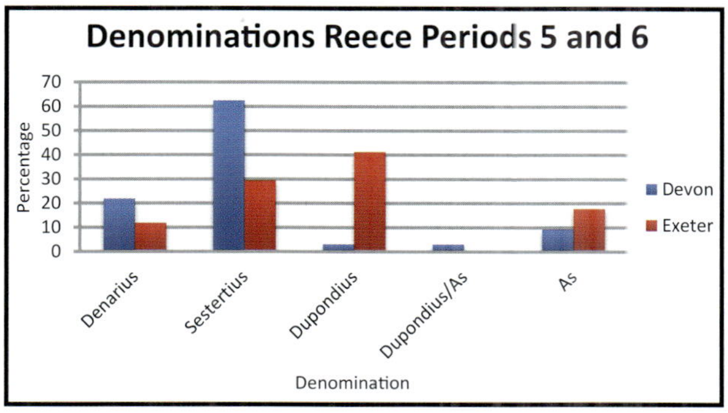

Fig. 16.26 Denominational breakdown of coins in the Trajanic and Hadrianic periods: PAS Devon (64 coins) vs Exeter (17 coins)

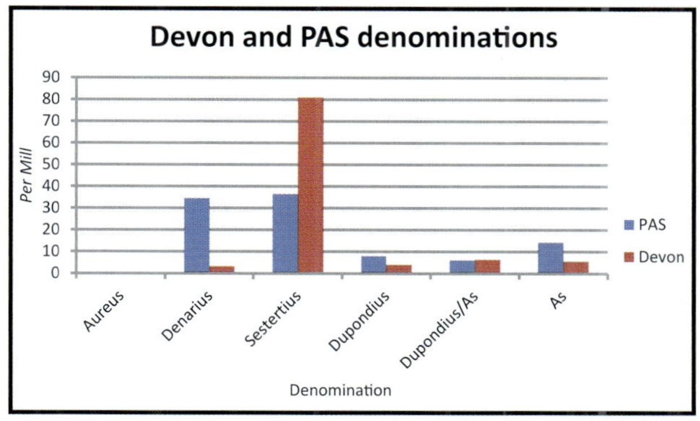

Fig. 16.28 Denominational breakdown of coins for the Antonine Period: PAS National (15,959 coins) versus PAS Devon (126 coins)

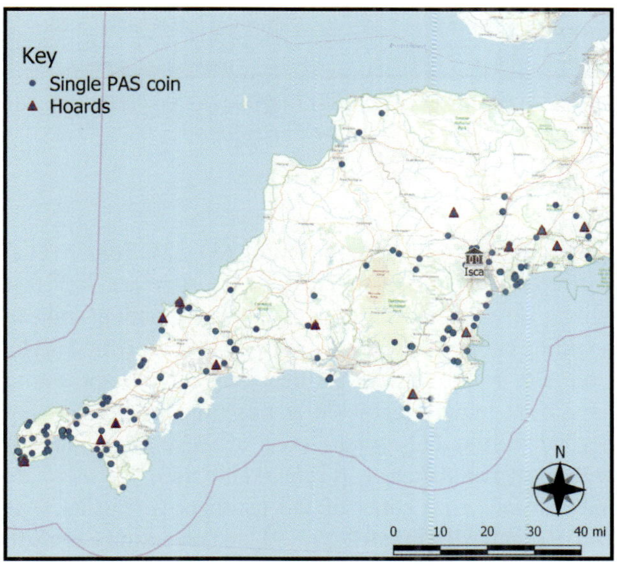

Fig. 16.27 Antonine (AD 138–92; Reece Periods 7–9) coinage on the PAS database in Devon and Cornwall (map data: © OpenStreetMap contributors)

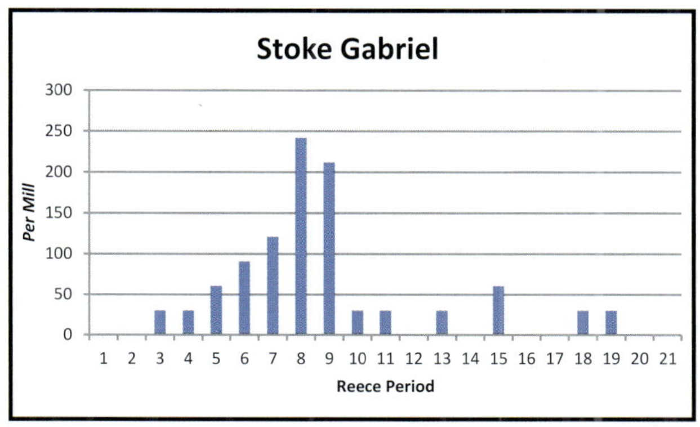

Fig. 16.29 Coin profile of the 33 PAS coins from Stoke Gabriel (this does not include the eight Reece Period 17 nummi *found on excavation)*

(Fig. 16.28), suggesting that silver was simply not being used in any substantial quantity after the end of the Flavian period. This is also in contrast to the PAS data nationally, which shows more of a parity between *sestertii* and *denarii*. The highest proportions of coin finds are in East Devon and the South Hams and to a lesser extent Teignbridge, showing the coastal nature of coin distribution in this period (Fig. 16.27). In the South Hams, Stoke Gabriel is an important site overlooking the River Dart. The metal detected coin record from the site suggests activity throughout most of the Roman period, but has distinctive peaks in the Antonine period. It has one *denarius* and 22 *sestertii* from Reece Periods 7–9 (AD 138–92) (Fig. 16.29). Excavation, though, produced eight *nummi* of Constantinian date, *c*. AD 340s–50s (Masson Phillips 1965, 25).[7] The peak in the Antonine period is duplicated in other finds like the Kingskerswell Hoard (2007 T134; IARCH-77C224) of 13 coins dating to the late Antonine period and the emperor Commodus (AD 180–192; Reece Period 9). This phenomenon is quite unlike Exeter and the authors have noted from initial investigation that this Antonine peak is shared with the overall PAS data from the Isle of Wight.[8] These finds do suggest access to South Devon, probably via the River Dart and the Salcombe Estuary rather than ingression via Exeter. It is also interesting to note that coin finds begin to appear around the northern and western fringes of Dartmoor, perhaps indicative of increased movement around the north of Dartmoor and then south towards Cornwall. A recent hoard of 412 bronze and 5 silver coins at Whiddon Down (DEV-F03C57; 2008 T168 and 2016 T324) dating to *c*. AD 198 (Reece Period 10) exemplifies increasing monetarisation north of Dartmoor.

This distribution does engender discussion about the function of coinage in Devon during the Antonine period. It might reflect an element of Roman control over the landscape possibly to extract minerals (notably tin) and agricultural produce, but the lack of silver coinage does suggest little or no military presence. Another interpretation might be that the Roman authorities controlled the territory, potentially as an imperial estate (*e.g.* Mattingly 2006, 262, fig. 10), which could explain the predominance of base metal coinage.[9]

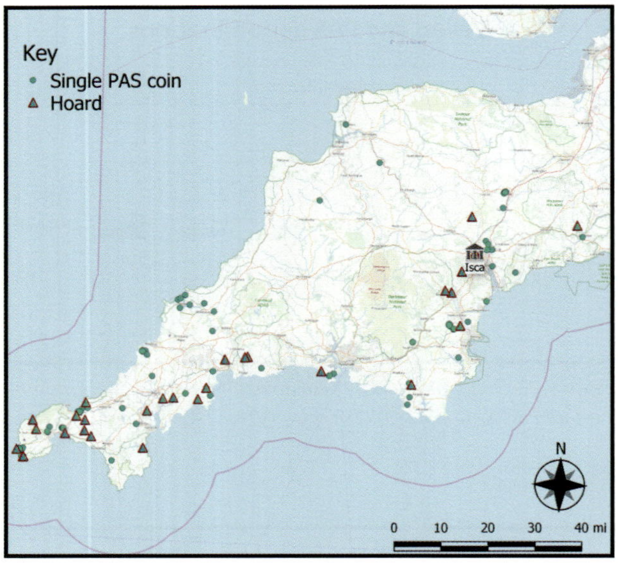

Fig. 16.30 Roman radiates on the PAS in Devon and Cornwall, AD 260–96 (Reece Periods 13–14) (map data: © OpenStreetMap contributors)

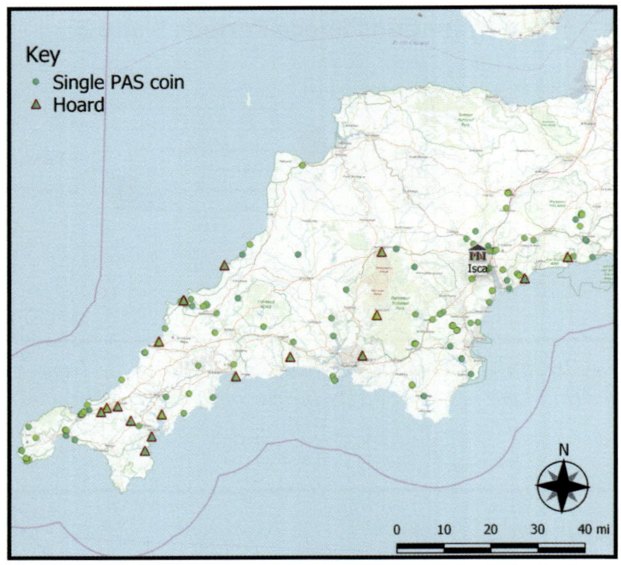

Fig. 16.32 PAS nummi *in Devon to AD 364 (Reece Periods 15–18) (map data: © OpenStreetMap contributors)*

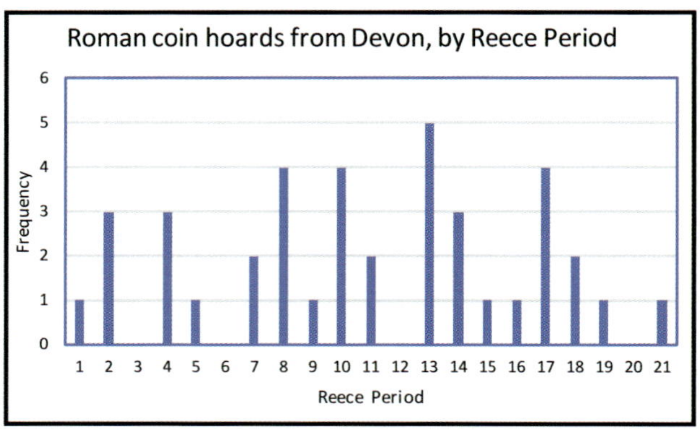

Fig. 16.31 Roman coin hoards from Devon by Reece Period (tpq) (source: PAS:IARCH records for Devon)

The 'Radiate' period (AD 260–96; Reece Periods 13–14)

Compared to earlier phases of activity, the radiate period of the later 3rd century AD (*c.* AD 260–96; Reece Periods 13–14) is quite poorly represented in the coin data from Devon. The emphasis is again along the coastline in the Torbay area south of Exeter, but less than 100 coins from these two periods combined is much lower than we might expect (Fig. 16.30). Exeter on the other hand demonstrates more substantial coin loss and this is perhaps to be expected, since Reece (1987, 94) highlights the preponderance of radiate coinage emergent in urban centres at precisely this time in contrast to a corresponding paucity within the rural landscape. To a degree, we can see this reflected in the hoarded assemblages within Devon. The late 3rd century AD witnesses the peak of hoarding in Roman Britain with almost 700 known hoards. While several small radiate hoards are known from Devon, for example the 43 coins dating to *c.* AD 274 from Aveton Gifford (DEV-A0BD4A; 2014 T331), they are very few and far between and there is not the corresponding spike in hoarding noted elsewhere within the province (Fig. 16.31). Coin use in the South-West Peninsula simply appears to have been hugely restricted at this time, or perhaps not needed for the daily transactions of Devon's indigenous with local population. It is remarkable, too, that there are only around nine coins of the usurpers Carausius (AD 286–93) and Allectus (AD 293–96) in Devon and Cornwall combined, suggesting there may have been other factors at work within this region during their reigns.

The 4th century to AD 364 (Reece Periods 15–18)

The picture generally fills out in the 4th century AD, with coinage more common and again focussed on the eastern and southern coastlines (Fig. 16.32). Exeter and the South-West Peninsula share a general upward trend from Period 15 (AD 294–317) to Period 17 (330–48) with different places peaking at different times: East Devon peaks in Period 15 (AD 294–317), Mid Devon in Periods 16–17 (AD 317–30 and AD 330–348) and Exeter, South Hams and Teignbridge in Period 17 (AD 330–48). The greatest peak in coin loss within the county is in Period 17 (AD 330–48) and on the east coast in the Teignbridge District this almost matches the proportion of *nummi* found at Exeter. Hoarding is resurgent to a degree, for example with the more than 200 *nummi* to AD 324 from Plympton near Plymouth (DEV-8A5096; IARCH-463F35; 2011 T579) and reflects a general return to coin use within the rural landscape. It is interesting to note that site finds from Reece Period 16 (AD 317–30) are common at Dainton Elms Cross and Halberton, which might suggest an overall increase in supply to the region in this period.

The 4th century: AD 364–378 (Reece Period 19)

There is a fairly uniform decline in coin-loss after AD 348, except in Teignbridge where there is a major peak in the Valentinianic period (Reece Period 19: AD 364–78). Most Valentinian finds tend to be in coastal districts, notably at the two sites of Dainton Elms Cross and Denbury/Torbyran, which together have produced 58 of the 77 examples recorded in the entire county (Fig. 16.33). Indeed, if all the single finds of Valentinianic coinage combined are plotted with a schematic heatmap[10] (Fig 16.34), the concentrations in the Teignmouth area are glaringly obvious. To the single finds can also be added the hoard of 243 *nummi* from Newton Abbot, the majority of which date to between *c.* AD 364–78 (DEV-7B17D0; IARCH-928E3A; 2007T209). Exeter, although demonstrating a slight peak in the Valentinianic period (Reece Period 19), has a substantially lower proportion of coins than the Teignmouth region.

What we are possibly witnessing here is a shift in the use of the landscape reflected in the Roman coinage recorded in the region. Britain at this time was a key grain exporter to the Rhine and concentrations of Valentinianic *nummi* like this appear to be linked with the exploitation of the rural landscape by the Roman authorities within the province. This is more readily evident further north and east, for example around Ilchester (see above), and in regions like Wiltshire, around the Wash and north to East Yorkshire, where an emergence of fortified towns, like *Cunetio*, and a correlation with Late Roman military fittings, suggests high concentrations of Valentinianic *nummi* represent activity relating to the collection of the *annona militaris* (Moorhead 2001, 90–5; Moorhead and Stuttard 2012, 206–8, 226–7). It is highly plausible that the rural landscape of Devon was exploited in a similar fashion. Indeed, concentrations of coins from the Valentinian period along the rivers and coastlines of eastern Devon make a lot of sense in this regard. Raw materials (mineral and agricultural) could have been very easily shipped by boat to other parts of the province and the continent from here without the need for extensive overland movement of goods or people. It is plausible that the distribution of Valentinianic *nummi* along the coastline, in particular, perhaps reflects the authorities continuing to dip into the region with exchange and payment taking place in centres close to where any shipments would have occurred leading to Exeter being bypassed. This might well be the case in Cornwall, too, with concentrations of Valentinianic *nummi* from Hayle and Padstow (on the PAS database) and Trevelgue (Reece 1991b: site 79).

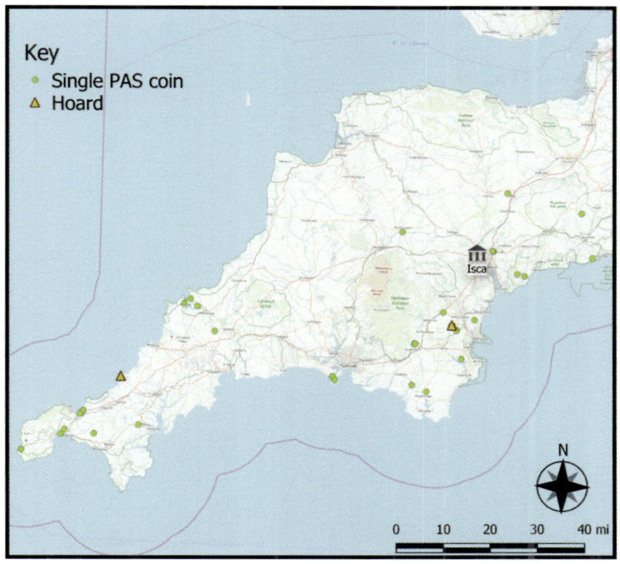

Fig. 16.33 Valentinianic nummi *on the PAS in Devon and Cornwall, AD 364–78 (Reece Period 19) (map data: © OpenStreetMap contributors)*

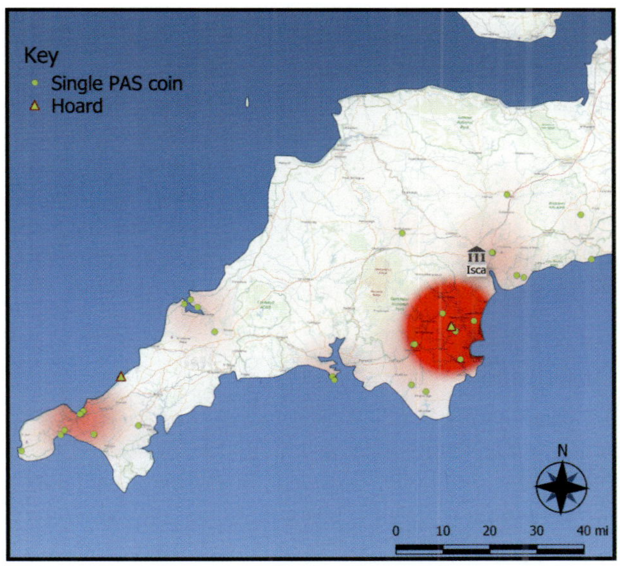

Fig. 16.34 Heatmap highlighting the distribution of Reece Period 19 coinage in the South-West Peninsula (map data: © OpenStreetMap contributors)

The end of Roman Britain, AD 378–402 (Reece Periods 20–21)

The last stages of Roman coin use in Britain are poorly represented within Devon, with just a dozen coins recorded to date. Exeter, with only one coin in Reece Period 21, appears to have largely fallen out of the monetary sphere at this stage and it is again in the coastal southern and eastern regions that most coins are to be found (Fig. 16.35). Most notable are peaks in coin loss in Teignbridge (Dainton Elms Cross has three coins) and the South Hams (which has nine coins). The low number of pieces in general reflects a trend within the province that sees the cessation of supply of base metal coinage by *c.* AD 402. Almost half of the coins in Devon are silver denominations, which is perhaps to be expected to a degree given that silver would have continued to circulate for some time after the Roman formal withdrawal in AD 409. It might well be that official interest was greater in the Teignbridge and South Hams regions in the

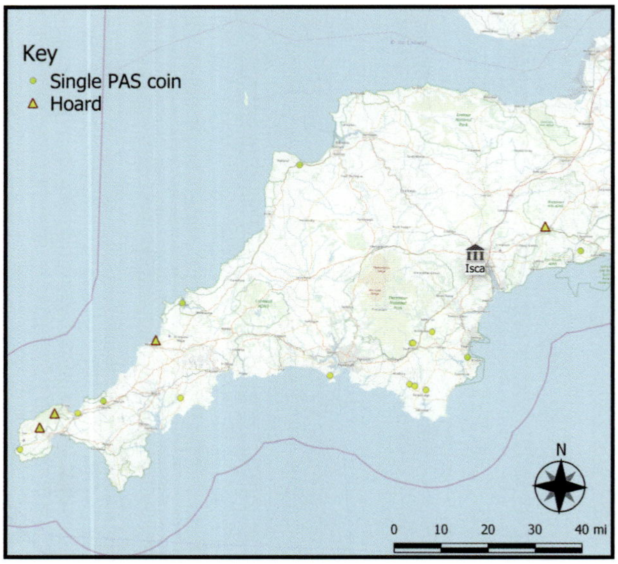

Fig. 16.35 Theodosian coinage on the PAS in Devon and Cornwall (Reece Periods 20–21) (map data: © OpenStreetMap contributors)

Late Roman period, rather than at Exeter and its northern and eastern hinterland. Access would have been gained via rivers such as the Teign, Dart and Avon, and via the Salcombe Estuary. Indeed, many Theodosian coin finds across the province, both from sites and hoards, are found in coastal and riverine regions (Moorhead and Walton 2014, 104–12). In this case, it could be argued that parts of Devon had contact with Roman officialdom until the collapse of Roman government in around AD 409.

Conclusion

It is clear that the South-West Peninsula was not as heavily monetised as the regions beyond the Blackdown Hills to the north-east. Exeter, however, does share a tolerably similar profile to other urban centres except for its very high coin loss in the Claudian to Flavian periods (that can be accounted for by its origins as a legionary fortress) and its almost total collapse in the importation of new coinage after AD 378. Although more PAS data are required for the Devon regions to gain a more valid picture, it does seem that the currency pool in Devon was not necessarily dependent on, or very closely related to, that of Exeter. The evidence does not suggest that Exeter was a currency nodal-point for the region, unlike other centres in the province such as *Verulamium* in Hertfordshire (Moorhead 2015, 157). The arrival of coin in the region does seem to have often been directly to coastal regions in East and South Devon, probably via rivers such as the Teign, Dart and Avon and up the Salcombe Estuary. This does question the administrative and economic role of Exeter in the region and might suggest that contact between Roman officials and traders with the local population was made at a more local level. Finally, the dearth of silver in 2nd-century AD Devon does suggest that Roman officialdom was not necessarily reinforced by a military presence.

Acknowledgements

The authors would like to thank the finders the late Philip 'Jim' Wills and the late Dennis Hewings for reporting, and Danielle Wootton for recording, the initial finds of Roman coins from Ipplepen and for all of their subsequent help. We would also like to thank Stephen Rippon for all his support and patience during the writing of this piece.

Notes

1 Special mention should be made of Norman Shiel who has been the key numismatist working on the Roman coins from Exeter since the 1970s.

2 *Crisis or continuity: hoarding in Iron Age and Roman Britain with special reference to the 3rd century AD* is an AHRC-funded research project which involved the addition of all hoards to the PAS Database (finds.org.uk) by Eleanor Ghey using the prefix IARCH. For more information, see https://www2.le.ac.uk/departments/archaeology/research/previous-research-projects/hoarding-in-iron-age-and-roman-britain and refer to the publication Bland *et al* 2020.

3 Caerwent: Reece 1991b, 51–2; Cirencester: ibid., 39–43; Colchester: ibid, 34–8; Dorchester: ibid, 17–19; Gloucester: ibid, 13–15; Ilchester: ibid, 33; Silchester: ibid, 45; Winchester: ibid, 20–2.

4 Not all coins can be assigned a Reece period for this analysis. Eight coins have Reece periods but no findspots. The 10 coins with Reece periods from the Unitary Authorities of Plymouth and Torbay are not included here.

5 The Dean Prior coins are heavily corroded, but do not appear to be heavily worn.

6 This is one of only two of this type recorded in Britain; see PAS BERK-6C41FC for the other.

7 At Ipplepen it has been shown that there is a larger proportion of earlier bronze denominations found by detectorists but fewer Late Roman bronze coins. In contrast, the excavations have produced a higher proportion of smaller Late Roman bronze coins. Stoke Gabriel appears to demonstrate a similar phenomenon.

8 The Isle of Wight coins are being worked on by Stephanie Smith at Kings College, London as part of an MPhil/PhD thesis.

9 It is interesting to note that coin profiles for the Isle of Purbeck and the Isle of Wight could suggest that these regions were also imperial Estates.

10 Individual findspots for each coin of Valentinian date were mapped using the Geographic Information System (GIS) software QGIS (https://qgis.org/en/site/). Through the heatmap plugin available with QGIS, the findspots were analysed based on their spatial relationship to one another, producing a 'heatmap' that highlights where the greatest densities or concentrations of coins are located (darker red indicates greater density of finds). The circular appearance of these hotspots is a product of both the relatively sparse dataset (greater numbers will produce more overlapping radii and therefore a more amorphous plot) and the manner in which QGIS processes the data as a radius around an individual point or findspot.

17

The Local, Regional and Other North European Pottery, 900–1550

John Allan

with contributions by Michael Hughes and Roger T. Taylor

Introduction

The medieval pottery excavated in Exeter forms one of the most important collections of such material in the British Isles. At a regional level it is an especially valuable sequence, with a high proportion of securely stratified and relatively well-dated material, and its evidence is fundamental to the dating of many medieval sites in Devon and Cornwall, and thus to the archaeology of the two counties. It includes one of the major collections of imported pottery in the British Isles, the Saxo-Norman imports being an especially significant series, and is rich in evidence for regional trade.

About one tonne of post-Roman ceramics was published in the early 1980s, that included almost 20,000 sherds of Saxo-Norman pottery and more than 17,000 fragments dating from the years 1200–1550 (Allan 1984a: EAR [Exeter Archaeological Report] 3). In the period of about 35 years which has elapsed since that volume was published, there has been a steady accumulation of new finds including some important pieces, although the growth of the collections has been slower, especially for the Saxo-Norman pottery, since fewer opportunities have arisen for excavation in the city centre. Full inventories of most of the ceramics excavated since 1980 have been compiled (Langman and Allan 1991; 1999b covering all finds to 1990; individual archive listings for most subsequent sites). Quantification of selected classes of imported pottery using these lists suggests that whereas the volume of later medieval material has almost doubled since 1980, the Saxo-Norman collection has increased by only about 10–20%.

The picture has changed more fundamentally in the surrounding region. In the early 1980s Exeter was the only urban place in Devon and Cornwall which had seen a sustained programme of archaeological work. Since then, far more exploration has taken place in other Devon towns, notably Totnes, Exmouth, Newton Abbot, Crediton and Barnstaple, and there are now many more rural samples from the county. Although many gaps remain, the elements of regional patterns are now emerging, giving a wider context for the city collections.

The same period has also seen much publication outside the region, both in other parts of Great Britain and Ireland, and in continental Europe, providing the student with much more readily accessible information about many classes of finds. Equally important, fresh approaches have been developed to the study of material culture in the medieval and early modern eras, encouraging those engaged in the field to think about their material in new ways.

Aims of the project

An initial purpose of this chapter is to offer a brief guide to current understanding of the principal classes of medieval pottery represented in the Exeter collection, providing descriptions and illustrations of the various wares and reference to some of the principal finds, with the intention of helping those working on comparable material.

In considering the most valuable ways in which fresh progress might be achieved in understanding the collection as part of EAPIT, we have given priority to petrological and chemical studies of selected classes of ceramics. Since the Saxo-Norman imported pottery is an especially significant aspect of the collections, we have invited Michael Hughes to undertake chemical analysis of about 50 examples of these wares from the city, using ICP-MS. We have also taken this opportunity to invite Hugo Blake and Alejandra Gutiérrez, the leading specialists in the fields of Italian and Iberian medieval ceramics respectively, to review the Exeter finds which fall within their fields of interest (see Chapter 18 below).

A particular reason for pursuing the petrology and chemistry of the local wares has been the recognition that the region around Exeter, with its varied and distinctive geology (see EAPIT 1, Chapter 2), is very suitable for these forms of study, and collaborative exercises with Roger T. Taylor and Michael Hughes, carried out over the last 20 years and more, have provided a body of comparative data from sites elsewhere in the South-West which help place the Exeter material in a regional context. We have not had the resources to tackle the full range of English ceramics in the collection, so have concentrated our attention on major classes of material whose definition or sources have been in doubt, notably Exeter fabrics 40 and 42, and on wares which seemed especially suitable for further petrological work, such as those relating to the Upper Greensand and the probable Breton sherds. Further chemical analyses on other classes of material would certainly be valuable in the future, such as the Saintonge pottery from the city, or on the range of 13th-century English redwares. Nevertheless, with about 125 vessels analysed, the programme will amount to one of the largest bodies of chemical analyses carried out on one of the ports of the British Isles.

Saxo-Norman pottery, *c.* 900–1200

English pottery

Chronology and the ceramic sequence

In 1984 it was proposed (EAR 3, 9–13) that most of the Saxo-Norman pottery of Exeter could be divided into three main chronological groupings, as follows:

- *Horizon B*, in which the local pottery consists of a mix of the coarse, unglazed, hand-made 'Upper Greensand-Derived' (UGSD) pottery with wheel-thrown 'Bedford Garage' Wares (both types described below).
- *Horizon D,* in which unglazed UGSD is the only local ware in use. Elaborately combed and decorated wares are a feature of this horizon.
- *Horizon E,* in which glazed tripod pitchers made their appearance alongside the unglazed wares.

A fourth grouping (Horizon C) was proposed in those instances where the presence of just a few Bedford Garage Ware sherds left uncertainty as to whether a context belonged to the period when this ware was in use.

The chronological succession of these horizons was evident, for example, from the sequence from 196–7 High Street (Site 43), where Phases 2–6 contained pottery of Horizon B, Phases 7 and 8 of Horizon C, Phases 8–9 of Horizon D, and Phases 12–13 of Horizon E (EAR 3, 42; the sequence of events is unchanged but the phase numbers are different in Chapter 7 above).

It remains possible that a few Late Saxon pit groups are earlier in date than Horizon B, but the evidence for this is not clear-cut. These contexts contain animal bone but either lack pottery entirely (perhaps indicating an aceramic phase, perhaps short-lived) or pottery types which could precede the use of UGSD (Bedford Garage Wares, or regional and foreign imports). Two pits on Trichay Street (Site 42, pits 66–8, described above in Chapter 5) contained large quantities of animal bone but no medieval pottery. An isolated pit at Queen Street (Site 68, pit 360) contained only an imported Hamwic fabric 127 vessel (10th/11th-century plain white ware jars with simple everted rims, made in the Lower Seine Valley) and animal bone. A small pottery group on the Valiant Soldier site outside the South Gate (Site 44, pit 199) contained Bedford Garage Wares, a possible import and ?limestone-tempered ware but not UGSD (EAR 3, 44–7, nos. 131–4).

It was hoped that the present project would submit animal bone samples from these potentially early contexts for radiocarbon dating, but none of the associated animal bone met the Historic England criteria for undertaking such analysis. The date of the earliest medieval occupation encountered in the excavations therefore remains as uncertain as it was 35 years ago. It seems clear, however, that pottery did not circulate in the early days of the *burh* in the quantities used in later centuries. Comparisons of the relative numbers of animal bones and pottery sherds show that the earliest contexts contain only about a quarter of the pottery used in the late 11th or 12th centuries (EAR 3, 12). The early *burh* may not have been completely aceramic but could be regarded as partially ceramic. The dating of Bedford Garage Ware and UGSD is discussed further below.

Bedford Garage Ware

Background

Bedford Garage Ware is a class of high-quality wheel-thrown pottery, usually fired red or orange but sometimes orange/pink and rarely pale grey, not very different in appearance from the post-medieval flowerpot. A few rare vessels have patches of thick glaze, which can be either olive green or yellow (Fig. 17.1). A kiln producing this ware was discovered when the Bedford Garage (so named after the nearby town house of the Dukes of Bedford) was built in 1935 (Site 5; Montague 1935, 188); it was dug into the tail of the Roman rampart at the back of the city wall in the area which has since been renamed Princesshay. The find was re-excavated by Lady (Aileen) Fox in 1955 and published by Fox and Dunning (1957). So accomplished was the pottery that Dunning proposed a late medieval date; it was only with the excavation of stratified Late Saxon deposits in the 1970s that it became apparent that this was in fact a class of Late Saxon wheel-thrown pottery (Hurst 1977b, 77; EAR 3, 27–30).

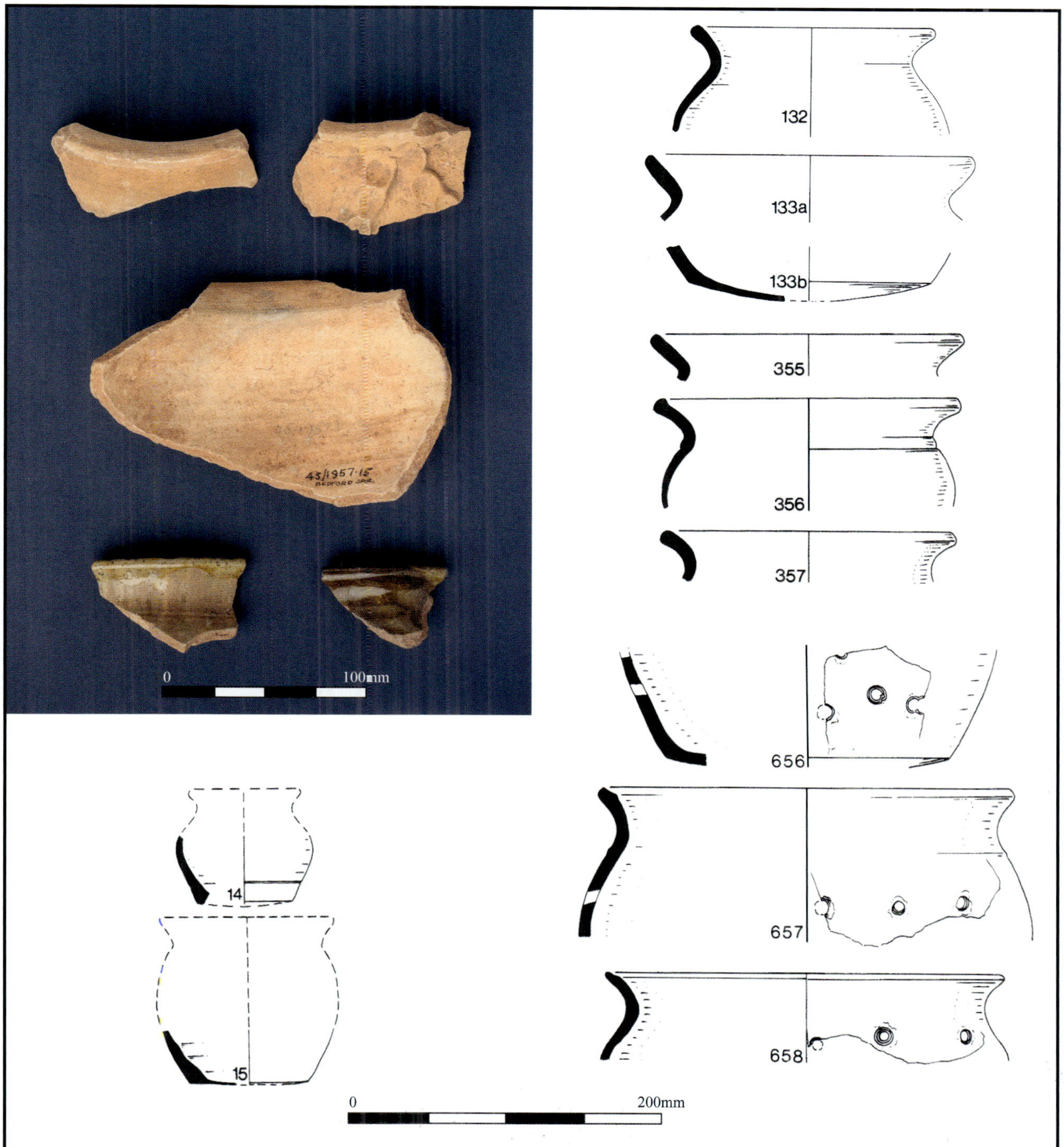

Fig. 17.1 Bedford Garage Ware (© RAMM, the line drawings from Allan 1984a)

Forms

Most of the vessels are plain unglazed rounded jars with flat or sagging bases and simple everted rims, thrown in two main sizes (Fig. 17.1): small (bases with diameters of 80–100 mm) and medium-sized (most commonly with bases of *c.* 140–180 mm wide). A few other forms are also known: larger perforated jars, storage jars with applied strips (type 5), a plain wide-mouthed form (type 4), lamps and a ?jug (types 6 and 7). Perhaps the most interesting are the large perforated jars (Fig. 17.1, nos. 656–8), which belong to a class of vessel discussed by Moorhouse, who has shown that they were used for a variety of purposes including the production of white lead, distillation and fermentation (Moorhouse 1972; 1981, 117; 1986, 112). Comparable finds, although of rather later date, are known from Glastonbury Abbey (Kent 2015). Vessels of this form have not been found outside the kiln.

Petrological and chemical analyses

A petrological description of this fabric was published by Vince (1984b, 32) and need not be repeated here; his identification of small quantities of acid igneous rock fragments and even a rounded fragment of granite, alongside the more commonplace quartz, chert and sandstone, may be noted. No samples have previously been subjected to chemical analysis, so seven examples of Bedford Garage Ware from Exeter were analysed by ICPS as part of the present project and compared with two later medieval redwares whose origins are probably in the Exeter area. The results are presented below (see Hughes, Appendix 17.3 below, fabrics 40 and 42).

Dating

The dating evidence from excavations prior to 1980 was presented in EAR 3, 27–8; the sequence from 196–7 High Street (Site 43), where Bedford Garage Ware was found in the first six stages of Saxo-Norman occupation, the sixth of which contained a coin of 1072–*c.* 1080, remains an important piece of evidence. No further dating evidence has been recovered since that time. At present, quite a long period of production and use seems likely (pre–*c.* 950 to *c.* 1100), and this would explain the numerous Saxo-Norman pit groups containing this fabric.

Distribution

Although it is found commonly in Saxo-Norman deposits in the city, Bedford Garage Ware rarely makes up more than 10–15% of a group (by weight or sherd count). Although hundreds of vessels have been recovered from the city, it has proved very rare elsewhere in Devon, being known from just three places: the *burhs* of Totnes and Lydford, and Stockland (Fig. 17.2). At Totnes there are several vessels, at the other two sites just a single find (unpublished finds from 39 Fore Street, Totnes (1985) and King's Thatch, Stockland, all at RAMM; for Lydford: Allan 1981, 133, no. 1).

Interpretation: an immigrant potter from Normandy?

The refined fabric, wheel-throwing, rich glazes and use of kiln technology mark Bedford Garage Ware out as pottery in a completely different tradition from the coarse, handmade, bonfire-fired and unglazed pottery seen throughout south-western England in the Late Saxon period. The potter(s) must have come from somewhere outside the region. Traditions of making high-quality wheel-thrown wares are features of the ceramics of northern France, the Low Countries and various centres in eastern and south-central England, the nearest of which is Winchester. In 1984 the writer proposed that an English source was as likely as a French one (EAR 3, 29–30), but this ignored the strong similarity of this material to northern French pottery. The close correspondence in form to the 10th/11th-century plain white ware jars with simple everted rims, made in the Lower Seine Valley (Adrian *et al.* 1999, nos. 187–8, which would be classified in Britain as Hamwic fabric 127) strongly suggests that this is the output of a potter from Normandy.

One example of a potter from Normandy has previously been postulated in south-western England: the vessel forms of some of the late 11th or early 12th-century pottery from Castle Neroche, in Somerset, are clearly northern French in origin, notably the jars with collared rims and the large storage jars with applied thumbed strips (Davison 1972). There is a major difference between the Exeter and Castle Neroche finds, however; whereas the Bedford Garage sherds correspond to northern French wares in all but their local red fabric, the Castle Neroche vessels are handmade coarsewares, tempered with inclusions from the Upper Greensand, and were presumably bonfire fired.

A much closer parallel to the Bedford Garage kiln is that found at Pound Lane, Canterbury, published with a full discussion by Cotter (1997). This too was a single-flue kiln making wheel-thrown wares in the northern French tradition, but at a slightly later date (*c.* 1145–75). Its products – plain jars and larger storage jars with thumbed strips – were broadly of the same vessel types, although its most distinctive products were jars with collared rims. The location of the kiln, dug into the back of the city rampart, was also precisely similar to that of the Bedford Garage kiln. The Canterbury kiln was published as the work of an immigrant potter, and this has now been widely accepted; precisely the same arguments apply at Exeter. The locations of these two kilns, immediately inside the city walls when most kilns were rural or suburban, raises the possibility that these were the operations of valued foreign craftsmen, offered protection by civic authorities.

Upper Greensand-Derived pottery (UGSD)

All Late Saxon and Norman assemblages from the city consist mainly or entirely of a single fabric grouping, initially named Exeter fabric 20 (EAR 3, 3–12). This fabric continued in use into the early 14th century. Examples are shown in Figs 17.3 and 17.4. It was apparent by the 1970s and 1980s that this was a major class of Saxo-Norman ceramics, widely distributed across south-western England; for example, it was noted that some of the Exeter finds were very similar to examples excavated at Ilchester, in Somerset, published by Pearson (1982). Their source was not, however, established in a number of programmes of thin-sectioning undertaken at that time, since most of the inclusions in the fabric proved not to be diagnostic of a specific geology.

It was Roger Taylor's more detailed petrological study which distinguished a number of rare but much more indicative inclusions in this fabric group, derived from the Upper Greensand of the Blackdown Hills in eastern

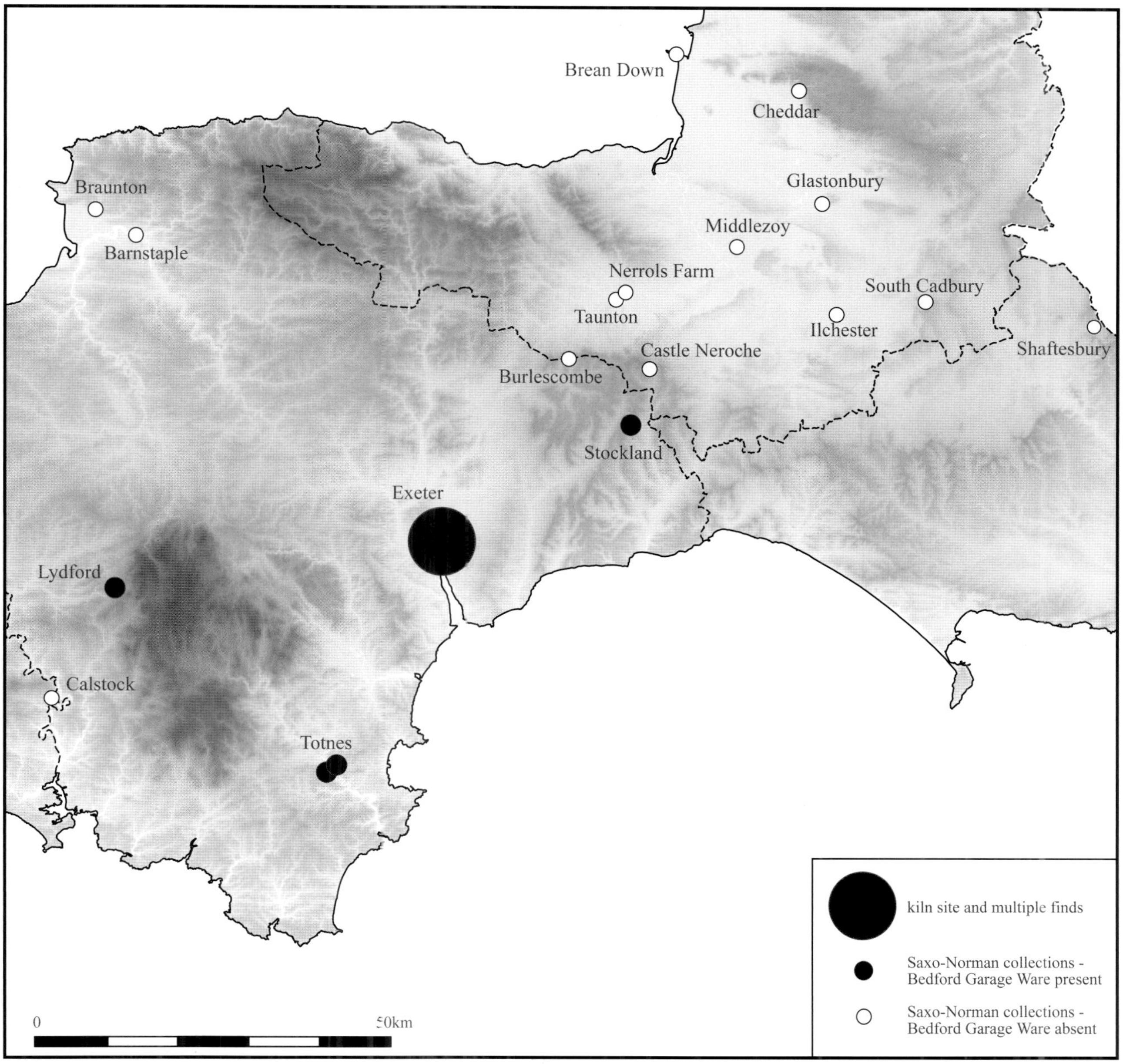

Fig. 17.2 The distribution of Bedford Garage Ware (drawn by David Gould)

Devon and southern Somerset. His work was published as part of a general discussion of this class of material which also included ICP analysis of a range of samples from sites in Somerset (Allan, Hughes and Taylor 2010). Now known as 'Upper Greensand-Derived' (UGSD) ware, it is believed to represent a number of potteries using temper derived from deposits around the fringes of the Greensand.

Petrology by Roger T. Taylor

Following the examination of a large number of samples of this fabric from a range of sites in Somerset, Dorset and Cornwall (Taylor 2003a; 2010; 2014a, 69–70), nine samples from Exeter (Allan 1984a, nos. 303, 304, 306, 309, 311, 317, 321, 322, 330) were examined under the binocular microscope at x20 magnification. Since these are clearly a single fabric group, an overall description is presented here. Inclusions are described in approximate descending order of frequency. Typically, the temper forms *c.* 5–10% of the fabric, a common percentage in this kind of pottery. Sample descriptions of individual vessels are available in online Appendix 17.1; an overall description is as follows:

- Quartz: translucent and transparent, colourless to white, frequently well-rounded and polished. Grains up to 1.5 mm.

Fig. 17.3 Upper Greensand-Derived pottery from Exeter (© RAMM)

- Chert: white, angular, 0.5–2.0 mm, one 6 mm; sparse in some sherds. Also uncommon flint.
- Silicified sandstone: sparse, white, sub-angular, mainly up to 0.3 mm, one 1 mm.
- Tourmaline: black, polished, sub-angular to well-rounded, sparse, mainly up to 0.5 mm.
- Silicified shell: white, tabular fragments, up to 2 mm.
- Ferruginous pellet: occasional, in some sherds, rounded, reddish, 1.5 mm.
- Clay matrix: finely micaceous.

These inclusions clearly derive from the Upper Greensand and correspond to other examples of this broad fabric grouping examined in Cornwall, Devon, Somerset and Dorset. The silicified shell seen in nos. 303 and 304 is a firm indicator of the Blackdown facies of the Upper Greensand, and probably of a fairly restricted area within it. The silicified sandstone seen in no. 309 is also a pointer to the Blackdown facies, but not conclusive evidence of this specific origin. The fabrics of six other samples (nos. 306, 311, 317, 330, 321, 322) are all very similar to these vessels (they all contain the polished quartz, black tourmaline, sparse white angular chert), but no silicified shell was seen in them.

Within the broad UGSD grouping are at least two sub-groupings: one calcareous, the other non-calcareous. The former grouping is well represented in Somerset, where the calcareous component is probably derived from Liassic clays forming the vessel body; the presence of fossil ammonite fragments in some specimens supports this conclusion (Taylor 2010, 171). Allan's testing of a large sample of Exeter sherds in the 1970s showed that more than 95% of them are non-calcareous. It is reasonable to conclude that all the samples examined are from the Blackdown facies, as are the other specimens analysed by the writer from Devon and Cornwall.

Chemical analysis by Michael J. Hughes

Examples of this fabric (UGSD) from Exeter have been included in the recent programmes of ICP/ICPS analysis for Sherborne Old Castle in Dorset, and Calstock in Cornwall (Hughes 2003a; 2004c). In view of the considerable body of chemical analyses undertaken on this class of ceramics in recent years, no fresh sampling was undertaken in this research programme.

Chronology

It is certain that this fabric has a long life and was still in production in the early 14th century. The start date, however, remains rather uncertain, since there are few closely dated contexts of the 9th and 10th centuries in the region. The Exeter evidence offers only a general indication of a start date: there are very few groups from the early life of the *burh* which appear to precede the use of this pottery (end 9th/early 10th century?) but it occurs in every pit on sites such as Trichay Street, Goldsmith Street and 196–7 High Street (Sites 39 and 42–3; see Chapters 5–7 above) which were probably occupied by the late 10th century (note the tree-ring dates from Goldsmith Street, for example: see Chapter 11 above).

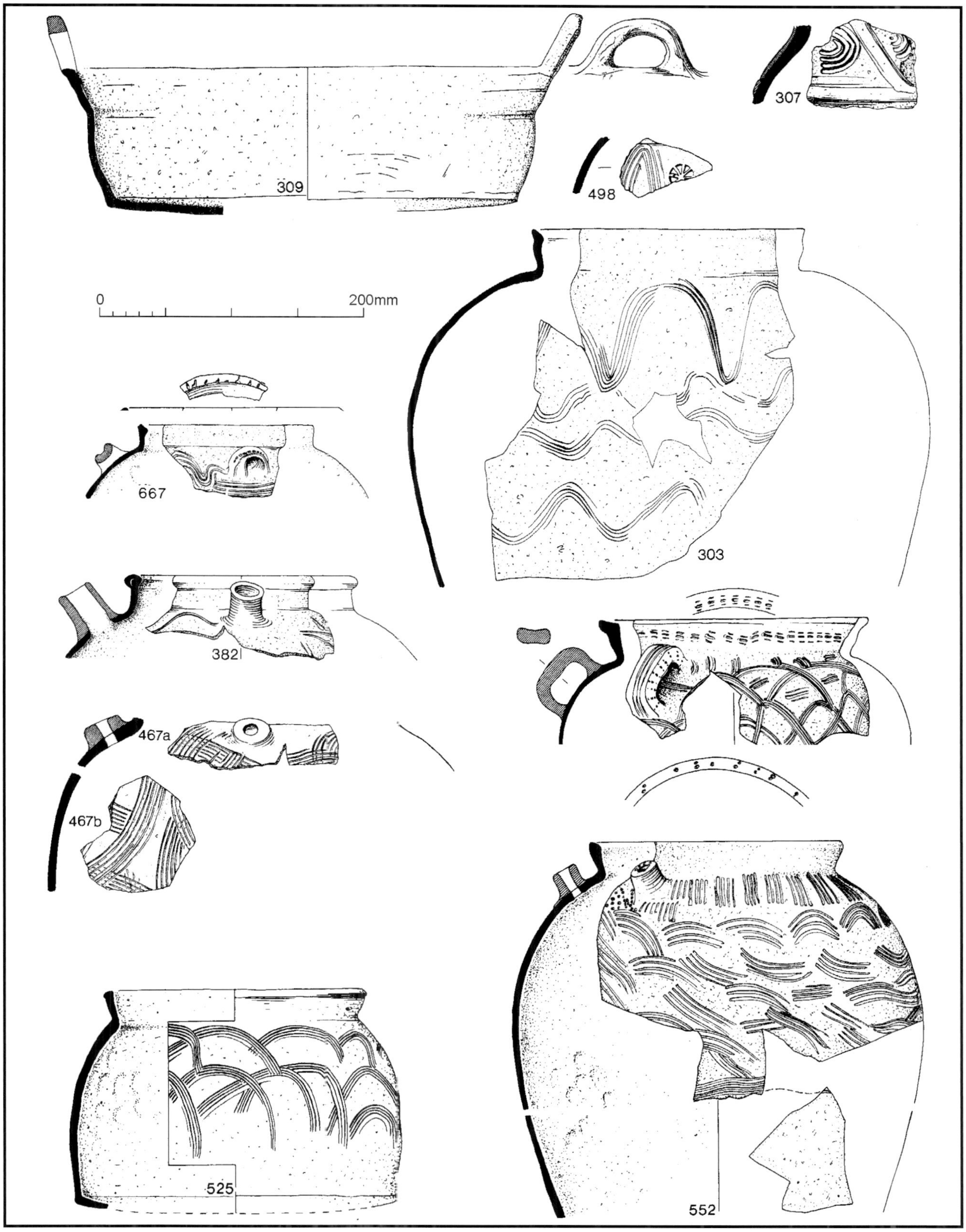

Fig. 17.4 Upper Greensand-Derived pottery from Exeter: decorated vessels characteristic of Horizon D, probably late 11th/early 12th century (from Allan 1984a)

The best evidence for the start of this tradition comes from Somerset and has been discussed several times in the last few years (Allan, Dawson and Kent 2015, 254; 2018a, 132; 2018b). It seems probable that this fabric came into use *c.* 930/950, although two radiocarbon determinations from Hemyock, modelled to indicate a date of *c.* 900–30, may indicate a slightly earlier start of production (*eid.* 2018a, 132).

Distribution

The overall distribution of UGSD is shown in Fig. 17.5. This ware is now known from seven sites in eastern Cornwall, where it forms the bulk of 11th and 12th-century assemblages, alongside small quantities of gabbroic pottery from western Cornwall (Brown *et al.* 2006, 269–70, 283–4; Allan 2014). Its most westerly distribution points are Par, Lamanna at Looe, and Tintagel (O'Mahoney 1989; further finds will be published by Quinnell and Thorpe).

UGSD was almost the sole class of pottery used on many sites in Devon in the 11th and early 12th centuries. In the 1970s and 1980s the only examples known in West Devon and Cornwall were from high-status sites, notably the castles of Launceston, Okehampton and Lydford, whilst there were no sherds in this fabric from most of the Dartmoor longhouses. This raised the possibility that distribution was restricted to high-status sites. This idea is now untenable; the recovery of a small

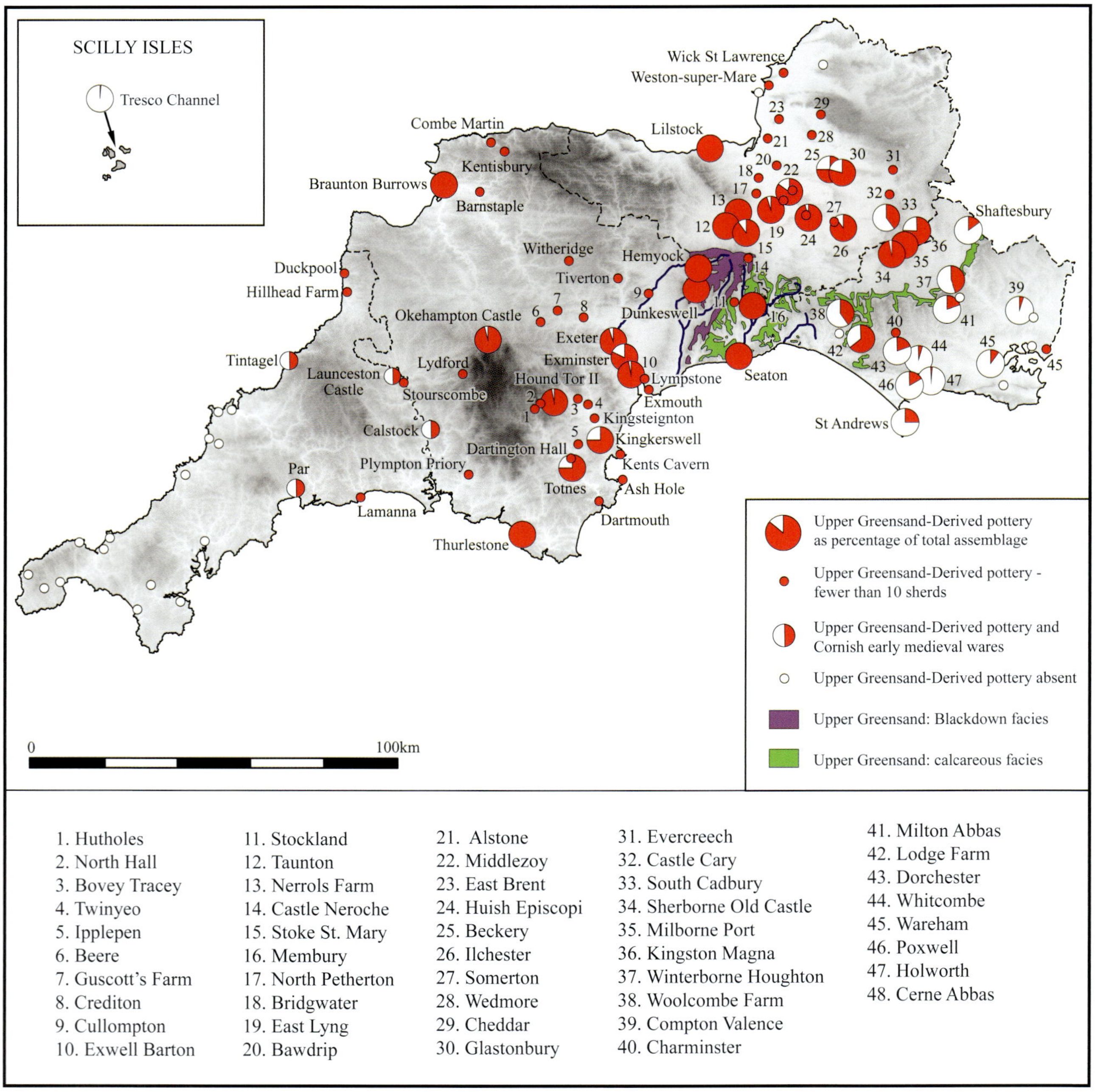

Fig. 17.5 The distribution of Upper Greensand-Derived pottery (drawn by David Gould)

group of this material from AC Archaeology's excavation at Stourscombe on the fringe of Launceston, and the Duckpool find, show that its distribution is not restricted to high-status places. In fact the claim that much of the county was aceramic, or only partially ceramic, in the 11th and 12th centuries is slowly being eroded by finds on distant rural sites such as Braunton Burrows, Thurleston, Kentisbury, Combe Martin and Hound Tor. Nevertheless, no examples have yet been recorded over a large area of north-western Devon, even in the substantial programme of excavation at Roadford Reservoir.

This general fabric grouping also dominates assemblages on many sites in the southern parts of Somerset, forming a declining proportion of assemblages further north (Allan, Hughes and Taylor 2010; Allan, Dawson and Kent 2015). It seems to be very rare on, or to the north of, the Mendips, but a systematic search is needed to reassess some sites such as Cheddar. It should be noted here, however, that in contrast with the majority of finds in Devon, some of the Somerset wares in this general fabric grouping – in Taunton, for example – are calcareous, indicating that they do not come from the Blackdowns facies of the Greensand.

As a fine group from Sherborne Old Castle illustrates, UGSD was also the predominant fabric in northern Dorset in the years around 1200 (Allan 2003). The proportions for other sites in Dorset shown in Fig. 17.5 are taken from Spoerry's (1990, 8, figs 5, 6) study. It should be noted that these proportions are not directly comparable to those shown in the other counties, since they show UGSD as a percentage of all the ceramics on sites where occupation extended into the 13th and 14th centuries, when other local potteries supplied the market. Nevertheless, his figures do bring out the sharp decline in the market share taken by this fabric group in the eastern half of the county. On the eastern fringe of the distribution, he found that they made up only 3–4% of the sample which he examined from Christchurch, for example, but he also noted the presence of sherds of this type as far away as Salisbury and Southampton (*ibid.*).

Finally, it may be noted that very small quantities of UGSD have now been recognised in South Wales: petrological examination by Roger Taylor at the National Museum of Wales in 2016 confirmed the identification of two sherds from Castle Tower, Penmaen (for the collection: Talbot 1966). This raises the possibility that it may be found further along the southern Welsh coast, and even in Ireland.

Other Saxo-Norman coarsewares

Limestone-tempered wares, ?from Hampshire/ Dorset

A few limestone-tempered wares have been recovered in the earliest contexts from the *burh* (fabric 22); since they do not occur in later deposits it now seems more probable that they date from the late 9th/10th century rather than the 10th/11th century as suggested in the past (EAR 3, 5). When they were published in the 1980s it was thought most likely that they came either from south-eastern Devon or from further east (Brown and Vince 1984, 33). Since no centre for the production of limestone-tempered pottery in eastern Devon has emerged, and no comparable finds have been made in that area, it now seems probable that these sherds are regional imports from central Wessex, where similar vessels – with their deeply sagging bases and vesicular fabrics – are known (cf. Hodges 1981, 6–7, Class 2).

Wheel-thrown glazed wares

No examples of Late Saxon or Norman glazed wares of English origin have so far been recognised from Exeter, although examples have been identified elsewhere in the region: Winchester ware at Glastonbury, Ilchester, Bath and Beckery chapel, and Stamford ware at Launceston Castle (Allan, Dawson and Kent 2015, 255; for Beckery: Allan 2016; for Launceston: Brown *et al.* 2006, 278).

Saxo-Norman imported pottery, 900–1200

Introduction

The series of over 230 Saxo-Norman imported wares from Exeter is the only substantial collection of this sort in the region, and one of a small number of such series in the British Isles, others being at Southampton, London and Dublin. This material reflects the city's status among the leading six or seven towns of Late Saxon England, and as one of its two major south coast ports. The imports make up only about 1.5% of sherds in the major stratified contexts of this period (by sherd count: EAR 3, 8–17, Horizons A–D), a noticeably lower proportion of the total than at Southampton, where imports account for 6.7% of sherds in the sample of *c.* 1066–1250 which Brown (2002, 97) analysed. Some allowance should be made for the fact that his figures group the early 13th-century material with the Norman, and this will include a higher proportion of imports; nevertheless, Normandy gritty ware alone formed 4.5% of sherds in the entire Southampton assemblage of 1066–1250, a notably higher figure. The overall composition of the Exeter material, quantified by sherd counts and minimum numbers of vessels (which are close to actual numbers, since most individual pots are recognisable), is shown in Table 17.1.

Imported pottery from the Low Countries and the Rhineland

Imports from the Low Countries

The small collection of Saxo-Norman imports from the Low Countries was re-examined by Wolfram Giertz with John Hurst in 1995, and Giertz examined one further fragment in 2019. There are so few vessels that they may be described individually. Sherds from a yellow-glazed pitcher (EAR 3, no. 127; Fig. 17.6A), found in the robbing of the apse of

Table 17.1 Imported pottery from Exeter, 900–1200

	Sherds/vessels published in EAR 3	*Total sherds/vessels 2019*
Belgium/Low Countries		
Huy-type, 11/E12C	[2/1 but not named as such].	4/3
Andenne, L12/E13C	1/1	1/1
Greywares, possible	1/1	1/1
Rhineland		
Blau-grau	10/4	11/5
Normandy		
Hamwic fabric 127	25/11	29/15
Other Normandy buff wares	12/10	17/15
Unglazed Normandy gritty	109/59	142/89
Red-painted	10/6	12/8
Gritty glazed redwares	14/8	17/10
Gritty glazed white wares	14/13	17/15
Yellow-glazed white wares	31/20	34/22
Early Rouen-type	4/4	4/4
Beauvais		
Red-painted	30/4	37/6
Unpainted	9/4	9/4
Beauvais or Normandy		
Red-painted	13/4	16/6
Brittany/W Normandy		
Micaceous buff ware	12/3	12/3
Source unknown /misc.	40/24	44/28
Total	337/178	407/235

the Late Saxon minster (Site 40), were first discussed by Verhaeghe and Janssen (1984, 18–20). They believed them to be from a pitcher of Low Countries (probably Belgian) origin, although the kiln source was then unknown. This vessel can now be identified specifically as a late 11th/early 12th-century Huy-type vessel from Middle Meuse Valley; the proposed date fits well with the site context date of 1089–1133. Giertz compared the fragments to a pitcher from Dowgate, London (Giertz 1996, 55).

Giertz confirmed the identification of a second yellow-glazed pitcher sherd, found in a late 12th/early 13th-century pit at Trichay Street (Site 42; EAR 3, no. 624; Fig. 17.6B), as Andenne Ware; he attributed it to Andenne Period IIB (late 12th/early 13th-century), the very hard sand-tempered fabric and rich iron-flecked glaze being typical features.

Two other sherds from different vessels, both excavated at Bartholomew Street East in 1980 (Site 73), were identified by Giertz as further examples of Huy-type ware from the Middle Meuse Valley, datable to the 11th century. He attributed one of them, an unstratified yellow-glazed body sherd (Fig. 17.6C), to the early 11th century; this is therefore the earliest piece of evidence for the importation of ceramics from the Low Countries in south-western England. He regarded the other (Fig. 17.6D), an untempered white ware with iron-blotched yellow glaze, as broadly of 11th-century date.

Giertz did not think that a white ware pitcher which had been suggested as a possible Low Countries product (Fig. 17.7, no. 675) was from that area; the relation of the spout and rim is apparently different from that seen in Meuse Valley products.

Imports from the Rhineland

Sherds from five *blau-grau* ladles have been recorded from the city including one complete profile from a mid to late 12th-century context (EAR 3, no. 649; Fig. 17.6E). Only one other find of this type is known to the author in the region: the example of early 13th-century 'pseudo-Pathrath' ware from Buckfast Abbey, in Devon (Allan 1988, 81, no. 1).

Imported pottery from northern France

The publication of the imported Saxo-Norman pottery from excavations in the 1970s concluded that pottery from northern France, especially from Normandy, made up the bulk of the collection (Hodges and Mainman 1984). It was also pointed out, however, that the quantity of published material from northern France was limited, and hardly any medieval kiln waste was available from Normandy to compare with the imported wares being studied in England.

The principal type of imported pottery in the earliest of these contexts (10th and ?early 11th century) consists

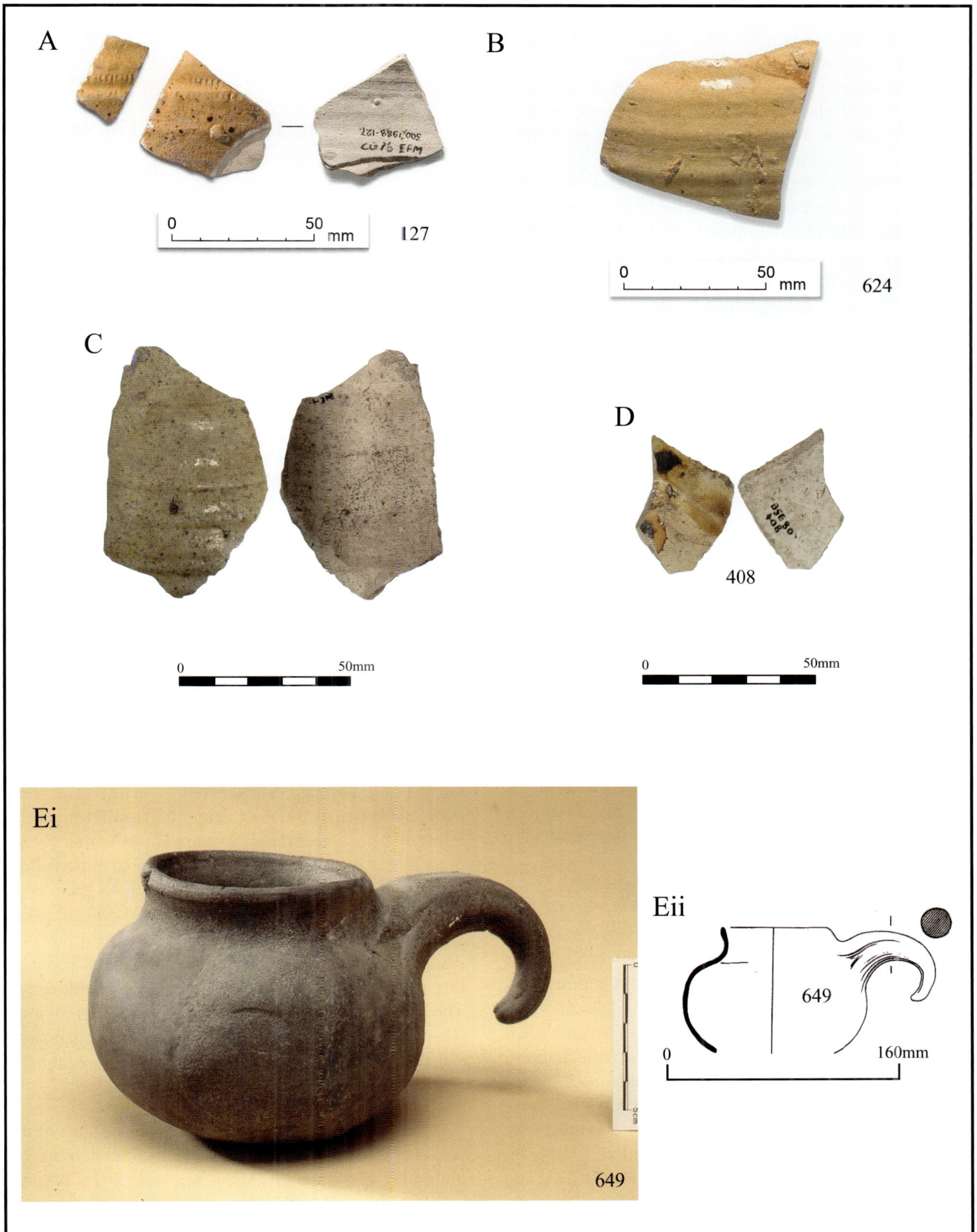

Fig. 17.6 Imported pottery from the Low Countries and the Rhineland, c. *1000–1200. (A, C–D) Huy-type ware from the Middle Meuse Valley; (B) Andenne-type ware; (E)* Blau-grau *ware (photos © RAMM; line drawing from Allan 1984a)*

of small unglazed wheel-thrown jars in sand-tempered white ware (Hamwic fabric 127; Fig. 17.7). In later Saxo-Norman contexts (post *c.* 1050?), Normandy gritty ware is the most common class of import, but there is also a range of glazed white ware and redware pitchers and jugs, some of which are hard to identify simply by visual examination and thin-sectioning.

Since Hodges' and Mainman's publication, there has been a modest increase in the Exeter finds (Table 17.1). This changes the picture only a little; the higher proportion of Normandy gritty wares in the new sample simply reflects the fact that few sites excavated since 1980 have encountered Late Saxon deposits. An initial project to explore the chemistry of this collection and compare it with material from Late Saxon Southampton was published about 20 years ago, but resources were limited and only six Exeter vessels were analysed (Hughes 2002–3). A key feature of the EAPIT programme has been the chemical analysis of a much larger sample of the Saxo-Norman pottery in the city collection, increasing the total number of analysed Saxo-Norman imports to 55 (Fig. 17.8). The results are presented in Appendix 17.2. This provides a much more reliable means of identifying the origins of the imported sherds. The programme confirms the conclusion of Hodges and Mainman that the bulk of the collection comes from northern France, especially from Normandy, but puts this key finding on a firmer footing. A key conclusion of the ICP study is that a high proportion of the imports sampled, including sherds with different fabric textures and colours and glaze colours, show strong chemical similarities with ceramics made close to Rouen; they appear to have been made in the Lower Seine Valley. It should also be noted that three different sources were distinguished among the Normandy gritty wares, suggesting that they were supplied from several sources.

Distribution of imported pottery in the region

Figure 17.9 shows the distribution of imported pottery in south-western England in the period *c.* 900–1150. Exeter has the only substantial collection of this sort in the region. The only other place with several finds is Totnes, where about ten examples are now known, mainly unpublished (but see Rigold 1954, 242–9; Allan 2014c). With their predominance of French wares, including red-painted sherds, Normandy gritty wares and yellow-glazed white wares, these finds are very similar in overall character to the Exeter pieces. A recent find at Lympstone on the Exe Estuary by AC Archaeology in 2018 (unpublished) adds a third site on the South Devon coast to the pattern. Elsewhere, only about three further finds of the period have been recorded from the entire region, including a single find of Hamwic fabric 127 from Barnstaple and another from Padstow, in north Cornwall (Allan and Langman 2002–3). The virtual absence of continental imported ceramics of this period is particularly striking in Somerset, where there are major pottery collections of this date (mapped on Fig. 17.9). The interpretation of this material is discussed further in EAPIT 1, Chapter 7.

Pottery of the late 12th and early 13th centuries

Local wares

During the early or mid 12th century, local potteries began producing handmade glazed wares, principally tripod pitchers. There is no specific evidence for the date of this innovation at Exeter, or indeed elsewhere in the region until we reach Bristol, where dendrochronological dates indicate the introduction of local jug production before *c.* 1130 (Ponsford 1991, 95–8), or Winchester, where tripod pitchers were in use before the end of the 11th century (Biddle and Barclay 1974, 151–4). Tripod pitchers remained in circulation into the early 13th century in Exeter, and probably after 1250, some of the later examples being associated with Saintonge pottery (*e.g.* EAR 3, 70–6, although it is possible that the late finds are residual).

Analysis of a selection of these pitchers by Roger Taylor for this project has confirmed that the most common tripod pitcher fabric (fabric 60) has the same petrology as the Upper Greensand-Derived wares, and was therefore made in the pottery industry around the Blackdown Hills. Figure 17.10 shows a typical specimen.

Regional imports

With the growing demand for glazed ceramic tableware in the late 12th and early 13th centuries, a range of wheel-thrown jugs also supplied the Exeter market, and these mark the onset of the next ceramic phase (Horizon F). Some of them were certainly imported from Normandy and other places in northern France, but regional imports from London, South Dorset and north-eastern England were also identified in EAR 3. Examples of South Hampshire redwares and perhaps Southampton pottery can now be distinguished among this material, and it is probable that other sources of English jugs await identification. The English regional imports become much less common when potteries producing good-quality local jugs were established in the Exeter area in the mid 13th century.

Dorset and Hampshire

The most significant source of ceramics in groups of this period at Exeter is Dorset and Hampshire. Scratch-marked pottery is very rare in Exeter, represented by a single substantial find (Fig. 17.11, no. 595) and a mere handful of other sherds, but it was marketed in other places in Devon, notably Totnes, where it is more common (Rigold 1954, 248; Allan 2014c, 3, 20).

The class of sand-tempered pale-bodied ceramics now named 'Wessex Coarsewares' (Mepham 2018, 17) is much more common (Fig. 17.11). Specimens of this

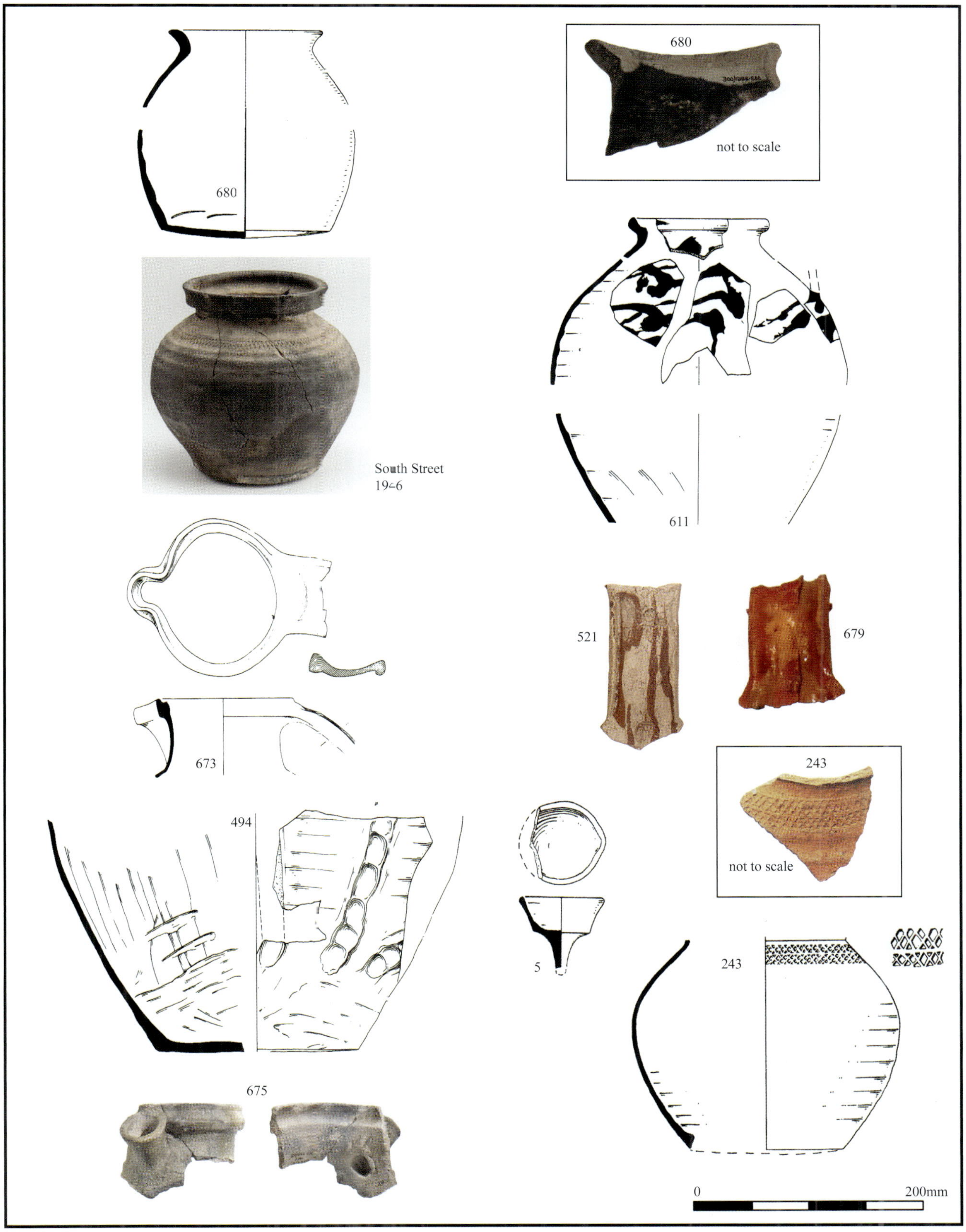

Fig. 17.7 Imported pottery from northern France, c. *900–1200 (photos © RAMM; line drawings from Allan 1984a)*

Fig. 17.8 Imported pottery from northern France: vessels analysed by ICP-MS. The bold numbers are the EAPIT sample numbers; those in italics are their drawing numbers in EAR 3 (photos © RAMM)

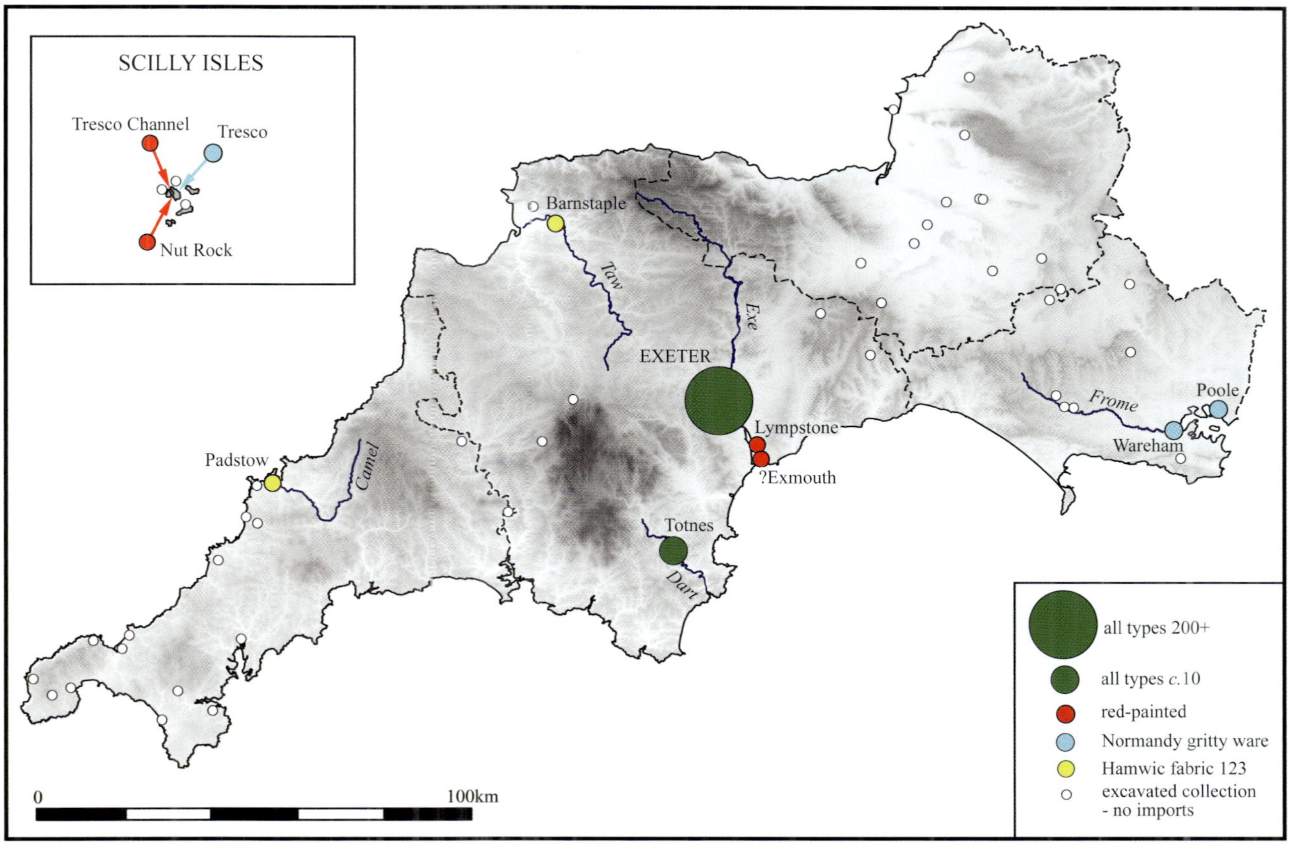

Fig. 17.9 The distribution of Saxo-Norman imported pottery in south-western England (drawn by David Gould)

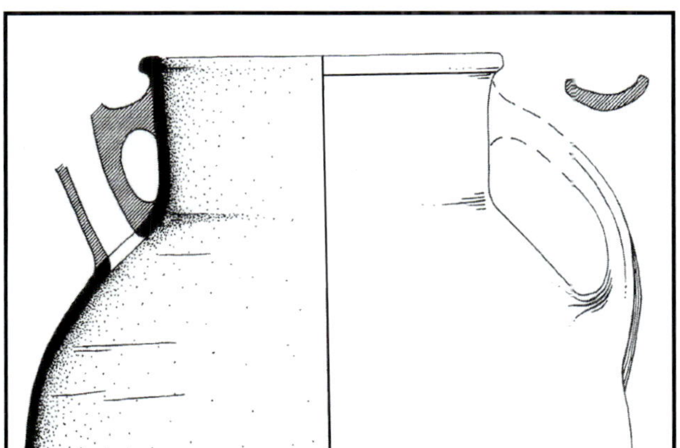

Fig. 17.10 Tripod pitcher in Upper Greensand-Derived fabric (from Allan 1984a)

type were attributed to south-eastern Dorset in EAR 3, but it was not then appreciated that they represent a significant trade, or that there were further sources of this fabric, extending into Wiltshire. The earliest consist of handmade jugs, supplemented later by pitchers and jugs. Mepham has shown that this class of pottery was also produced in south-eastern Wiltshire and eastern Dorset, which are therefore possible sources of the Exeter finds, although less accessible than the Poole Harbour area of south-eastern Dorset.

I suggest that a number of Exeter finds in early and mid 13th-century deposits with fine red or pink sand-tempered bodies and blotchy orange-green glazes (named Exeter fabrics 44 and 45 in EAR 3) are South Hampshire redwares. Samples are illustrated in Fig. 17.12. A few examples of scale-decorated jugs similar to those produced in Southampton whiteware have also been found, but it is not certain that they are Southampton products (Fig. 17.12, no. 1611; also EAR 3, nos. 1073, 1124; for Southampton kiln finds see Brown 2002, 13–14; a selection of Exeter sherds of this type was inspected by Bob Thomson, who noted several possible examples but no definite one). Further similar fragments have been seen in other excavations in Devon, for example at Newton Abbot and Totnes; this class of ceramics needs more work, including chemical analysis.

Fig. 17.11 Wessex coarsewares from Exeter (photos by Gary Young, © RAMM)

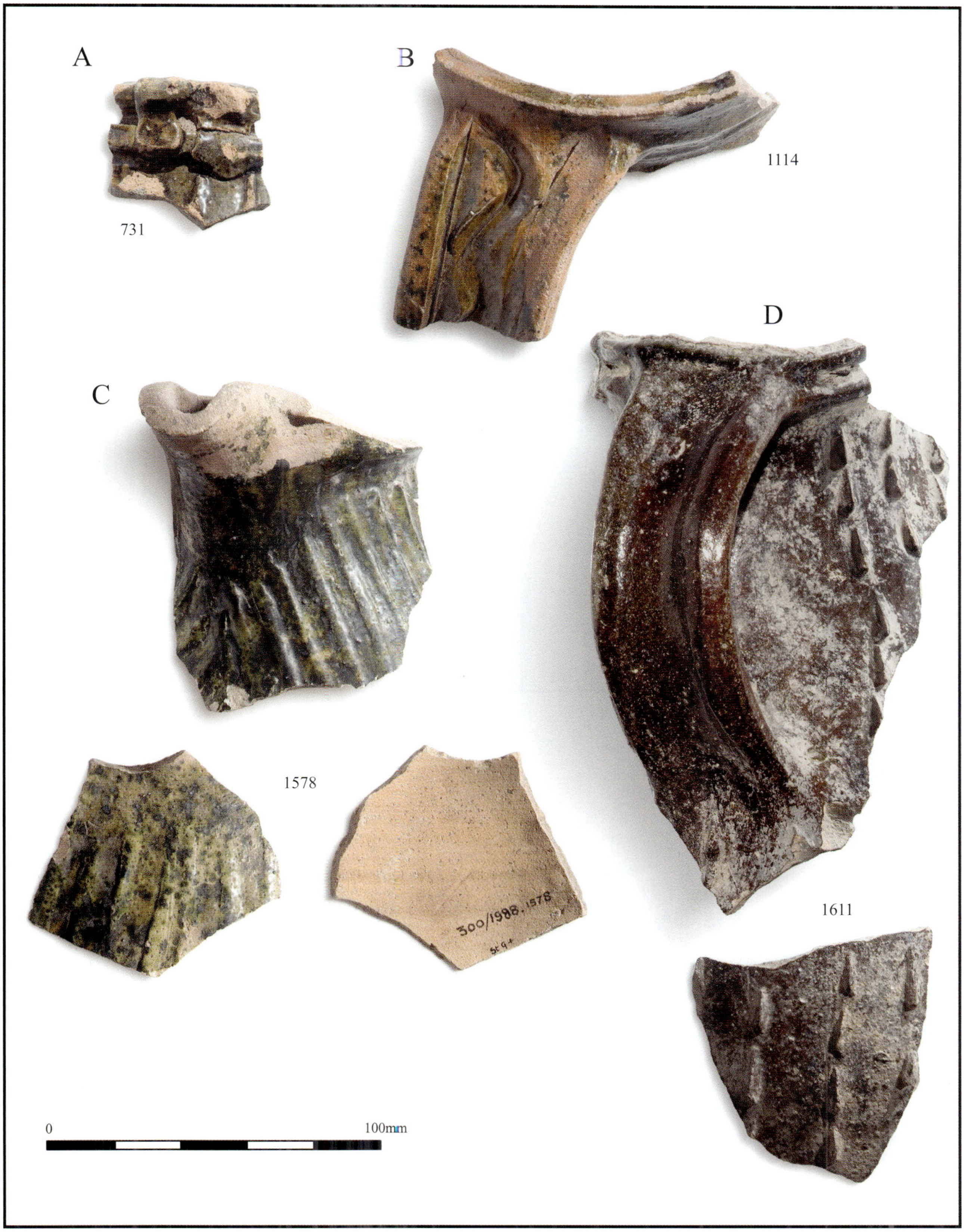

Fig. 17.12 (A-C) Proposed examples of Hampshire redwares; (D) possible Southampton jug from Exeter (photos by Gary Young, © RAMM)

London

The late 12th century also saw the emergence of a trade in London-type wares – both early rounded jugs (first identified in the Exeter collection by Alan Vince) and the readily recognisable vessels in 'north French style' including both Rouen copies and sgraffito-decorated wares (Pearce *et al.* 1985). Eighteen vessels of London ware were recorded in EAR 3; Fig. 17.13 shows the principal examples.

In the 1980s these Exeter finds formed an isolated grouping of London wares, separate from the main concentration of finds in the vicinity of the capital (Pearce *et al.* 1985, figs 4–5). In the last 30 years, however, there have been further single finds of this type in southern Devon, with examples extending along the coast into western Cornwall, forming a small spread of finds distant from those around London (Fig. 17.14, based on Pearce *et al.* 1985, figs 4–5). For the other published finds from South-West England see Allan and Langman (1998–9, 180–2; 2010, 162, no. 87). A second and larger group of London wares is present in Scotland, where it has been suggested that their presence may be related to the trade in fish to the capital (George Haggarty pers. comm.). Both in Scotland and the South-West Peninsula the bulk of the trade preceded the emergence of a local jug-making tradition.

Bristol

Both in the early and late 13th century, a few Ham Green ware jugs circulated on the Exeter ceramics market, with seven examples recorded in 1984 (EAR 3, 22; Fig. 17.15). These wares are rare on inland sites in Devon; it seems likely that they came overland through Somerset, where Ham Green wares circulated extensively, rather than via north Devon, where I have not seen examples.

North-eastern England

An unexpected feature of the Exeter pottery has been the identification of at least eight vessels from North-East England; they included two from Scarborough, two from Doncaster, two from Lincoln and one from Nottingham (EAR 3, 22; reports on the last two centres by Coppack (1984) and Hayfield (1984)). These finds lie far beyond the normal range of the north-eastern potteries, although Scarborough ware is known from Southampton (Brown 2002, 17). The principal examples are shown in Fig. 17.16.

Northern French imports

Normandy

The trade in green-glazed white ware jugs from Normandy was evidently well established when the earliest deposits

Fig. 17.13 London-type wares from Exeter and Crediton (photos: Gary Young, © RAMM)

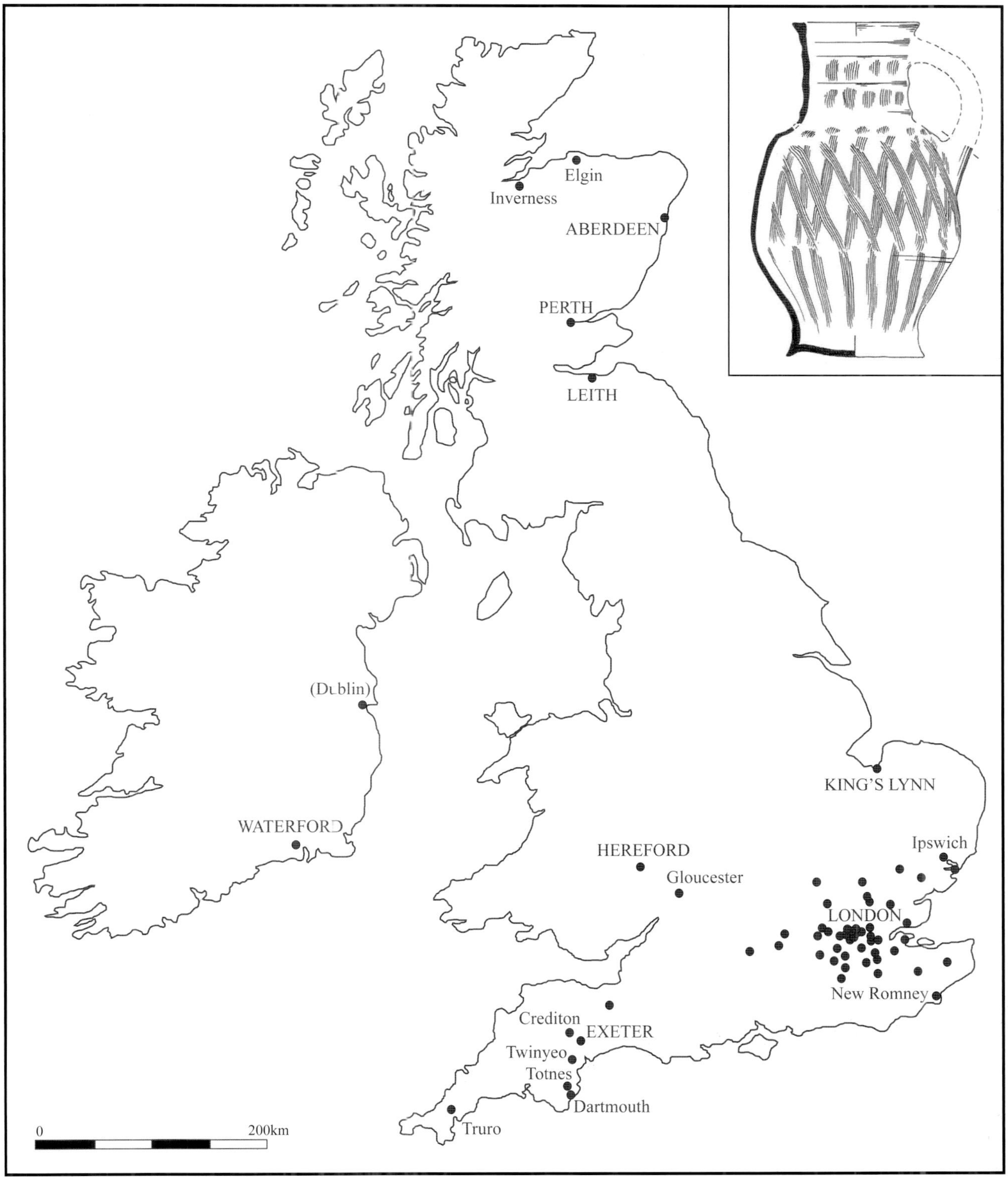

Fig. 17.14 The distribution of late 12th and 13th-century London-type ware in the British Isles (Pearce et al. *1985 with additions in Scotland (George Haggarty and Derek Hall pers. comm.), Ireland (McCutcheon 2006, 54, 56 and pers. comm.) and the South-West Peninsula. Sites in capitals outside South-East England have produced more than one vessel (drawn by David Gould)*

Fig. 17.15 Ham Green and Bristol wares from Exeter (photos © RAMM)

Fig. 17.16 Pottery from north-eastern England from Exeter (photos: Gary Young, © RAMM)

at Exe Bridge (Site 56) were laid on the riverbank at the start of the 13th century (EAR 3, 60–3), but Exeter offers no specific evidence regarding the emergence of this trade in the preceding period. These vessels are common in the city, with more than 300 vessels identified from the excavations to 1980 (EAR 3, 22). ICP-MS analysis shows that many of these wares have a chemistry consistent with products of the Lower Seine Valley (Appendix 17.2). Figure 17.17 illustrates the range of green-glazed white wares; Fig. 17.18A–B show examples of the Rouen-type jugs from the city, and Fig. 17.18D a rare yellow-glazed white ware costrel which was sampled in the ICP programme. The distribution of these wares in the region is shown in Fig. 17.19, where it will be evident that they are confined largely to the ports and high-status sites: castles and monastic sites.

Château de Bretagne

Figure 17.18D shows the handsome jug with a white fabric tempered with fine quartz sand, its body with incised decoration and copper-green glaze, found in the fill of a wattle-lined pit at Trichay Street (Site 42; EAR 3, 70, pit 191, no. 888). For some time the origin of this vessel remained uncertain until a kiln producing pottery in this style was found at Château de Bretagne in the arrondissement of Rennes, northern France, where an isolated deposit of white clay outcrops (I am grateful to Francoise Labaune-Jean for information about this recent find).

This rare class of pottery is represented in south-western England by three other vessels from Exeter and a further find from Glastonbury Abbey, in Somerset (Allan, Dawson and Kent 2015, 259, no. 69). There is another from Southampton, but the finest series of such vessels in the British Isles is from Dublin, in Ireland (McCutcheon 2006, 99–102).

Here we may have a problem with dating: the near-complete example from Exeter was found in the fill of a pit which was constructed from timbers dated by dendrochronology to AD 1180, offering a *terminus post quem* for its deposition; a date around 1200 is probable (EAR 3, 70–1). This is at variance with the dating from Tours, where the vessel type is placed in the 11th century (Husi 2003, chronolo-typologie tabl. Tours 3, Pichet 9).

Brittany: sherds with metamorphic inclusions

Introduction

Fragments of 22 medieval vessels of probable Breton origin were recorded from the excavations of 1971–80. Eight of them formed a clear fabric grouping (fabric 103) with a highly distinctive pale yellow-cream fabric containing abundant white and golden mica, and with a characteristic glaze (typically blotchy yellow-green with black spots of iron bleeding) and decoration (either with applied scales covering most of the body or with impressed knife-stabbing). It seemed probable that they come from a single source.

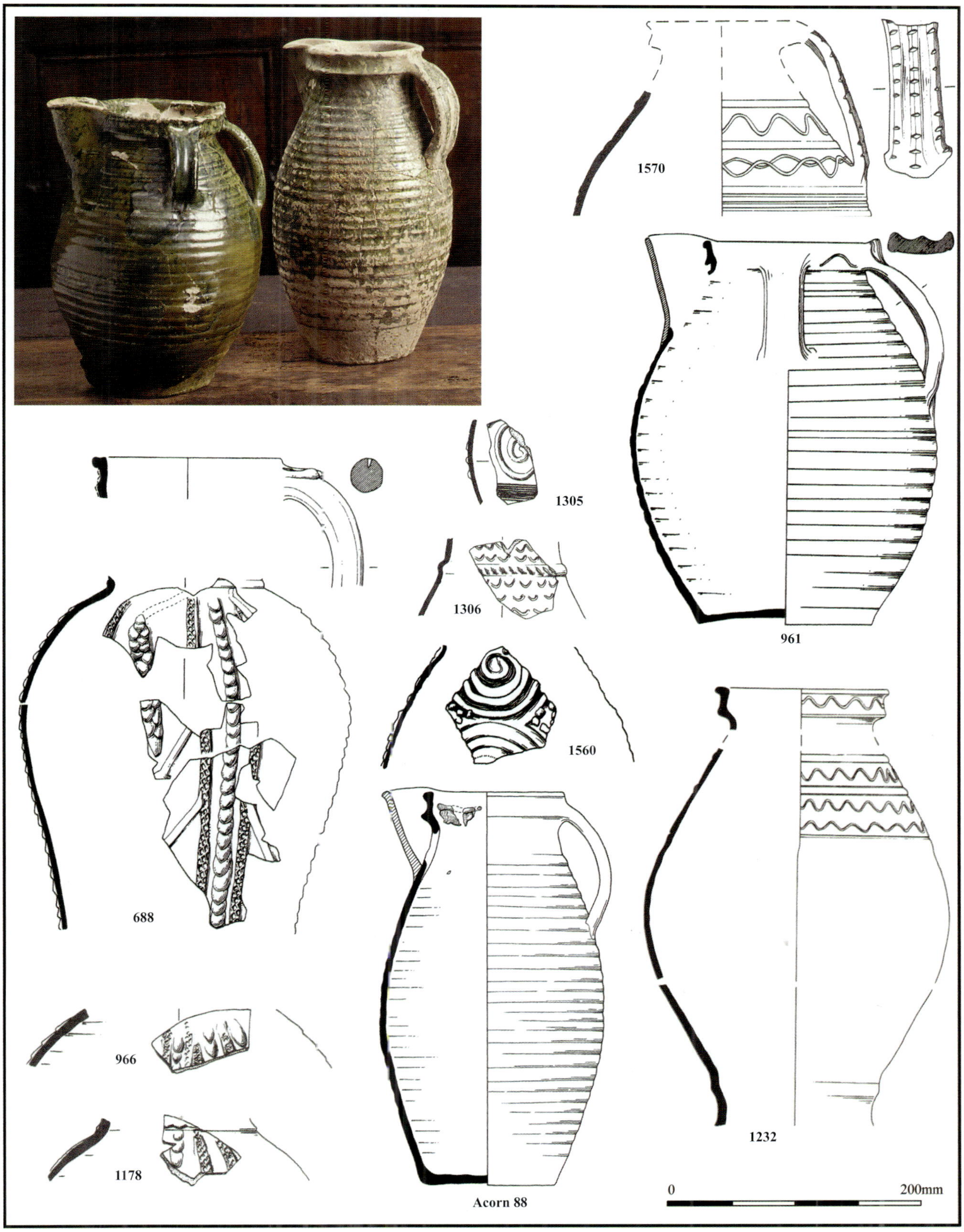

Fig. 17.17 Northern French highly decorated pottery from Exeter (Photo © RAMM; line drawings from Allan 1984a)

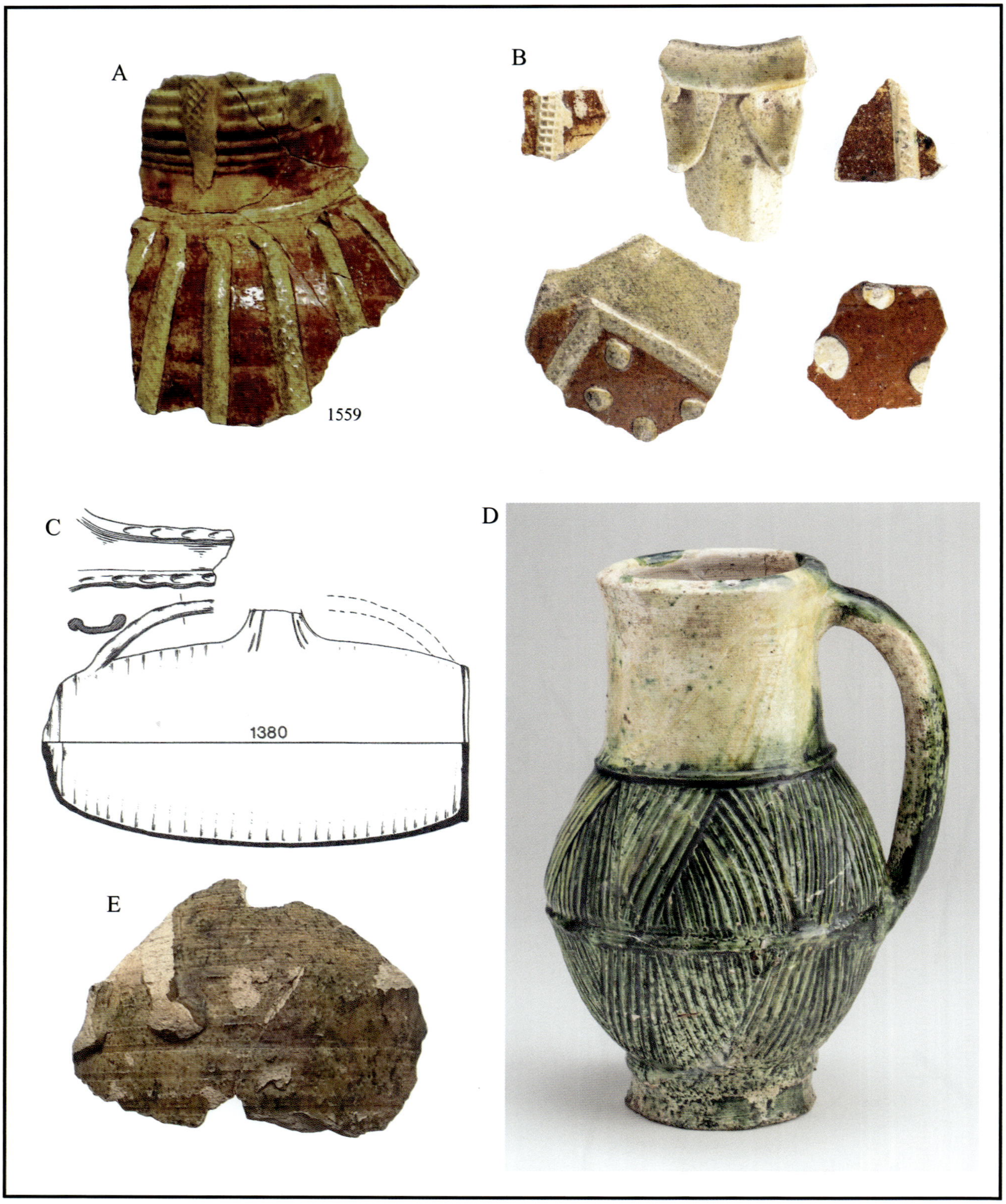

Fig. 17.18 Imported pottery of the late 12th and early 13th century. (A–B) Rouen jugs; (C) yellow-glazed costrel from the Lower Seine Valley; (D) jug matching kiln waste from Château de Bretagne; (E) an example of Exeter fabric 10 (with the feet and legs of an applied stick-man?), attributed to Brittany (photos © RAMM; line drawing from Allan 1984a)

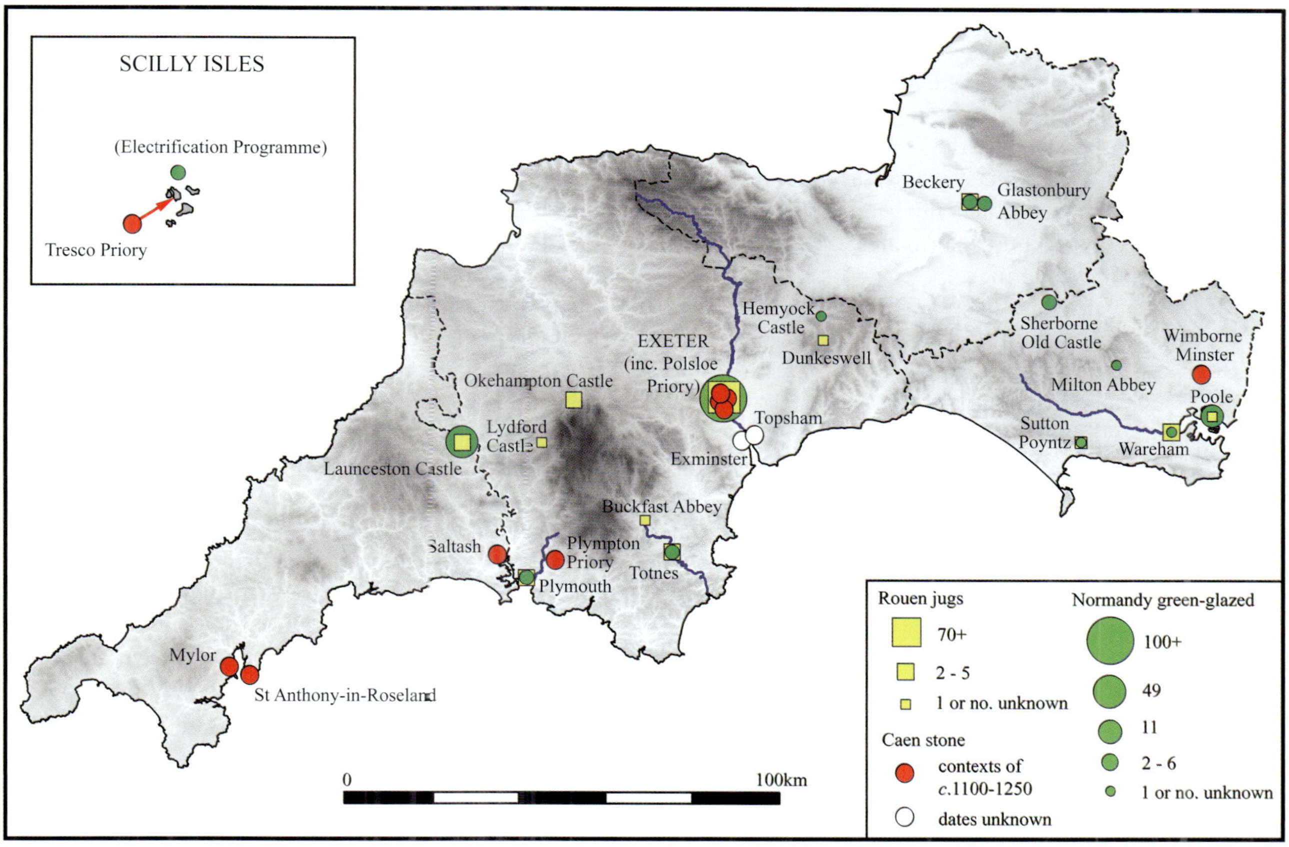

Fig. 17.19 The distribution of northern French pottery of c. *1150–1250, with Caen stone,* c. *1100–1300, in south-western England (drawn by David Gould)*

The 14 other vessels were seen as a second fabric grouping (fabric 104); these too are wheel-thrown wares, contrasting with the handmade south-western English products.

One example of fabric 103 and six of fabric 104 were thin-sectioned by David Williams, and a further vessel was thin-sectioned by Alan Vince (Williams 1984b, 37; EAR 3, 63, no. 807). Both Williams and Vince identified metamorphic mica schists among the inclusions in these fabrics. Williams noted that the nearest large source of such rocks to Exeter is in Brittany, but pointed out that the possibility of a source in the South-West Peninsula could not be dismissed, since outcrops of mica schist can be found in the region, for example at Bolt Head on the South Devon coast and on the Lizard peninsula of south-western Cornwall (Williams 1984b, 37). In view of their high quality, their early and mid 13th-century date preceding the emergence of local glazed jug production in South Devon, and their difference from all known Cornish and South Devon pottery, a Breton source has seemed much more probable. The petrology of the collection was therefore re-examined by Roger Taylor (below).

The petrology of the Breton wares by Roger T. Taylor

Fabric 103

Four vessels were examined as part of EAPIT, and the writer's report on a further example from Exwell Barton, in Powderham has also been published recently (Taylor 2014a). Since they are all very similar to one another, a single overall fabric description is presented here:

Table 17.2 The dating of Breton pottery at Exeter

Ceramic horizon	*A–D*	*E*	*F*	*G*	*H*	*Later*
Date	Pre-1150	Late 12C/ early 13C	Early 13C	Mid 13C	Late 13– Early 14C	Later
Fabric 103	–	4	7	5	–	1
Fabric 104	–	–	6	5	–	1

Abrasion 1–2; surface erosion 1; temper (larger grains) forms about *c.* 10% of the fabric. The body in almost all examples is fired to a pale creamy-buff to very pale pink.

- Quartz: transparent colourless to opaque white, angular to sub-angular abraded grains, 0.1–0.5 mm. Some grains are composite and finely granular, one in a lenticular group 3 mm long which could indicate a metamorphic source rock.
- Muscovite: cleavage flakes common, mainly 0.05–0.8 mm, rarely 2 mm.
- Biotite: rare brown cleavage flakes, 0.3 mm and rare flakes altering muscovite.
- Feldspar: white soft altered sub-angular to sub-rounded grains 0.1–0.3 mm.
- Rock fragments: reddened weathered slate or possibly muscovite schist, some with visible mica flakes, 1.0–2.5 mm.
- Matrix: silty finely sandy clay with much fine muscovite.

The fabric is derived from a granitic or metamorphic terrain. Although it is difficult to be certain that this ware does not have a Cornish/Devon source, there is noticeable absence of the black tourmaline schorl, which is particularly characteristic of the granites of the South-West Peninsula. It is likely that the mineral content is entirely indigenous and not an added temper.

Fabric 104

Nine vessels from Exeter including EAR 3, nos. 807, 970, 1161, 1203, 1205, 1236 were re-examined. A single fabric description is offered here; detailed descriptions of individual sherds are available online in Appendix 17.5. The fabrics of all these vessels display a very consistent appearance and temper.

EAR 3, no. 807 (Exe Bridge 1976)
Glazed, ribbed jug handle.
Temper:

- Quartz: sub-angular to sub-rounded, abraded
- Mica: muscovite flakes abundant
- Mica: biotite, flakes common
- Rock fragments: white to transparent fine-grained quartz, some grains with small flakes of biotite.

Comment: Rock fragments probably quartz-rich segregations from mica schist. Metamorphic derived grains with river sand.

Provenance

Fabrics 103 and 104 have similar petrological features and probably come from the same source. The abundance of mica and schistose rock fragments points to a metamorphic terrain. Areas in the South-West Peninsula previously considered as possible sources by Williams (1984b, 37), such as the Lizard and Start Point, are unlikely to provide such material. The area of schistose on the Lizard, located at the south-western tip, is extremely small; it consists of quartz-chlorite muscovite schist but with substantial areas of hornblende schist. Further east in Cornwall, the Dodman is largely sandstone and chlorite schist. These mineral associations are not represented in Fabric 103.

Although Jean Le Maho has suggested a probable source around Rouen (Brown 2002, 25), this is inconsistent with the petrology of the sherds. The Armorican metamorphic terrain of Brittany, where there are extensive tracts of metasedimentary schists, is much more probable. The fine grain size of quartz and mica, and the presence of metamorphic fragments, tend to preclude a greissenised granite source for the mica and quartz. The high proportion of muscovite in this fabric is unusual; local superficial kaolinisation of metasediments could account for this, and it could also account for the low iron content of the clay indicated by the pale-firing colour. It should also be noted that there is a noticeable absence of the black tourmaline schorl, which is particularly characteristic of the granites of the South-West Peninsula. It is likely that the mineral content is entirely indigenous and not an added temper.

Discussion

The total quantity of fabrics 103 and 104 from Exeter has now increased to 60 sherds from 42 vessels and 14 sites. All the recognisable vessels are jugs; the typical features of blotchy iron-spotted green-yellow glaze, applied scales or bosses, and impressed knife-marks, have been noted above. An example is shown in Fig. 17.18E.

Dating

These vessels first appear in groups containing tripod pitchers and UGSD sherds which probably belong to the late 12th century (no. 923), but are most common in contexts of the early and mid 13th century. They may extend into the period 1250–1350.

Other finds of Breton pottery

Exeter is one of three south coast ports with small collections of medieval Breton wares. At Plymouth, four examples were published from Dung Quay (Taylor 2003b, 62–3), and finds of *céramique onctueuse* (a Breton coarseware tempered with talc) have been recorded from Woolster Street (Preston 1986, 26); there are probably unidentified sherds on other sites. Fabric 104 is present in Southampton, where an example from an early 13th-century context at the Wool House was published by Platt and Coleman-Smith (1975, vol. 2, 73, no. 337, 'sandy cream-buff fabric'), and at least two jugs, one of them with the characteristic scale decoration, have been published by Brown (2002, 25, fabric 1711, 'North French micaceous whiteware'). An unpublished example from West Hall may also be noted (marked 70:2:33d).

Elsewhere in the South-West Peninsula a single find of fabric 103 has been recorded from Exwell Barton, in Powderham, not far from Exeter, and a Breton coarseware from the Althea Library, in Padstow, Cornwall, may also be noted (Allan and Langman 2002–3; Allan 2014b, 151, no. 2).

Pottery of the High Middle Ages, *c.* 1250–1350

The sequence of ceramic horizons

The arrival of Saintonge pottery in the English ports, traditionally dated *c.* 1250, was adopted in EAR 3 in marking a key horizon in the Exeter sequence. In a number of instances the local jug fabrics appear in the same horizon, suggesting that they too came onto the Exeter market *c.* 1250. Two stages in the pottery sequence of this period are discernible (EAR 3, 8–10):

- *Horizon G,* with a mixture of small quantities of Saintonge pottery and local jugs with types of the preceding period, handmade UGSD jar sherds still being by far the most common type, *c.* 1250–80.
- *Horizon H,* broadly of *c.* 1270–1350, in which the local jug fabrics 40 and 42 are associated mainly with Saintonge imports including polychrome wares. UGSD coarseware jars still make up about half the pottery.

Local jug fabrics 40 and 42

Introduction

From the mid 13th century until the mid or late 15th, good-quality red earthenware jugs form the predominant general class of wheel-thrown pottery at Exeter (Fig. 17.20). Upon close visual examination, Allan (1984a) distinguished two main fabric groups within this material, named 40 and 42. The separation was made initially on the basis that the matrix of fabric 40 appeared finer-bodied, but with clay pellets, typically with fine glistening inclusions, later confirmed by petrological examination as muscovite (Brown and Vince 1984, 33).

Since these wares were a common feature of the city assemblages and there were few finds elsewhere, they were initially named 'Exeter jugs' or 'Exeter-type jugs'. An unexpected result of the programme of thin-sectioning undertaken in the early 1980s, however, was the observation that fabric 40 appeared to contain glauconite, and this appeared to preclude an origin in the Exeter area and suggested production at least 15 km to the east of the city on the Blackdown Hills (Brown and Vince 1984, 33).

Commenting on the general similarity of these two fabrics in thin section, Alan Vince suggested subsequently that the distinction between fabrics 40 and 42 was not entirely convincing and that this basic aspect of the Exeter classification needed reviewing (pers. comm. to John Allan *c.* 1997). The present account starts with that review, and consists of Roger Taylor's detailed petrological examination of a range of samples, followed by Michael Hughes' chemical analysis.

Petrological examination of Exeter fabrics 40 and 42 by Roger T. Taylor

EXETER FABRIC 40

This distinctive fine redware fabric was described in thin section by Brown and Vince (1984, 33). The most

Fig. 17.20 Examples of local pottery. The five jugs on the right are of fabric 40, the roof finial in the centre a granite-derived vessel (© RAMM)

abundant inclusions are angular to sub-angular quartz (up to 0.4 mm but mainly much smaller), but clay pellets and muscovite are also typical features. Twelve of the vessels from Exeter published in 1984 (EAR 3) were re-examined under the binocular microscope at x10, x20 and x40 magnification, alongside thin sections of the original type-samples. Since the collection of thin sections made in the early 1980s, then held in the Museum of London, cannot be found at present, new thin sections have been prepared.

General fabric description

A dozen examples from different Exeter excavations were examined, together with a number of finds from outside the city including Cleeve Abbey, in Somerset. All the vessels have a fine clay matrix, typically fired red or dark pink, although some sherds are reduced to dark grey. A summary fabric description based on a series of examples, with the inclusions listed in descending order of frequency, is as follows:

- Quartz sand: abundant, fine, distinctly angular, fine grains, both clear and stained pinkish-brown, with a scatter of rare larger rounded grains (up to 0.5 mm) with polished surfaces, indicating an origin in a modern marine or beach sand.
- White mica: a little, very fine, up to *c.* 0.2 mm.
- Dark crystalline grains: very sparse, small. They appear to be basic igneous rock fragments.
- Vein quartz: rare white fragments.
- Shell: occasional soft platey fragments.

Discussion

Although vessels in this fabric show close similarities of potting, form and decoration, there is some variation in the inclusions present; the fine sands are a common factor, but the relative proportions of the components of the temper vary considerably from vessel to vessel. Very sparse, small, dark, crystalline grains, which appear to be igneous, are discernible in some samples. These rare inclusions tie this ware to the Exeter area, where there are potential source rocks for such material, particularly in the Permian Breccias in the hinterland of the Exe Estuary, or to the Teign Valley, where such minerals might also be found. Among the fine sand grains, many vessels also contain sparse inclusions of larger angular quartz sand (up to 0.5 mm) which have a polished surface, indicating an origin in a marine or beach sand such as one would expect on a coastal or estuarine site. The presence of shell fragments in some specimens could also be consistent with a source in an estuary, where estuarine molluscs would provide a source. Other vessels, however, contain coarse rounded quartz grains associated with the fine-grained sand, indicating a source higher up the estuary, where some coarse river-founded sand is present. Some caution may also be expressed, both about the identification of glauconite in the report of 1984, and about the conclusion that it indicates an origin well to the east of Exeter. This mineral can be hard to identify with certainty. No definite examples were found in the range of specimens examined here.

The overall implications are that, rather than being made in eastern Devon/southern Somerset, Exeter fabric 40 was produced in either the Teign Valley or the Exeter area, but not in the city itself. The distribution of this fabric on archaeological sites favours the latter source. The base clays could be Permian marls around the city, or possibly clays weathered from the Carboniferous shales, although there are no indications of residual sandstone fragments or of vein quartz which might be likely from the Carboniferous shales.

Exeter fabric 42

Eight published vessels from Exeter were inspected which form a distinctive fabric type. The mix of temper in each sample is quite complex, with constituents derived from the Permian and Carboniferous sandstones. All the components can be found in the Permian rocks of the Exeter area, where the breccias contain Carboniferous fragments. A potential source area lies to the south-east of the city, where Permian Dawlish sandstone overlies Heavitree Breccia; an appropriate mix of ingredients could be found in the Mincinglake Valley, which runs within the city's eastern suburbs. The proposed origin in south-eastern Devon or southern Somerset (Brown and Vince 1984, 33) now seems unlikely.

Sample descriptions

1. EAR 3, no. 1431 (Fabric 42 type specimen)

Wheel-thrown jug from Queen Street (Site 68) pit 112, *c.* 1280–1320. Oxidised pink-red fabric, all-over external slip and copper-green glaze.

- Quartz: a few well-rounded, frosted, grains are present. Two larger angular quartz grains with conchoidal fractures have very distinctive frosted/etched surfaces. This points to a short distance of transport from the source rock.
- Rock fragments: reddish mudstone grains, more common than in most samples of this fabric.
- Sandstone: fine-grained sandstone grains are quite rare.
- Fine-grained quartzo-feldspathic igneous grain.
- Feldspar: a single white cleaved grain, 1.5 mm.
- Fine-grained white mica: present in the matrix, a few grains reaching 0.1 mm.

2. EAR 3, no. 1409

Large wheel-thrown jug from Trichay Street (Site 42) pit 215, *c.* 1280–1350. Orange-pink body with vertical iron stripes alternating with bands of brushed white slip, the glaze speckled green-brown on the body. Temper forms *c.* 0.5–1% of the body.

- Quartz: mainly angular to sub-rounded grains; a few very well-rounded grains with frosted surfaces. Quite a high proportion of the quartz grains are stained pinkish-brown. One area, apparently a potter's patch to an over-thinned area of the body, contains a high proportion of reddish-brown sub-rounded quartz grains, mainly 0.2–0.3 mm, with a few larger grains.
- Sandstone rock fragments: fine-grained (*c.* 0.1 mm) grey sandstone, probably Carboniferous sandstone. Irregular rounded to sub-rounded grains, 1.5–3 mm.
- Mudstone: a scatter of reddish-brown grains, mainly rounded, 1–2 mm.
- Ferruginous grains: rare, soft, brownish-red, 1–2 mm.
- Fine-grained white mica: present in the matrix.

Correction to published identification

Upon petrological examination, one of Allan's identifications of 1984 did not fall into the fabric group described above, and is described separately:

3. EAR 3, no. 1406

Highly decorated globular jug with a red fabric.

- Quartz: sub-angular to well rounded, quite commonly polished, up to 1 mm.
- Chert: white, angular, sometimes cavernous suggesting former glauconite, up to 2 mm.
- Beckite (concentric silica development associated with the replacement of calcareous bodies including fossil material).
- Matrix: distinctively micaceous (flakes up to 0.1 mm).

Comment: Upper Greensand-Derived, as indicated by the beckite, *contra* EAR 3, 87.

ICP analysis of Exeter fabrics 40 and 42

Michael Hughes' report on the chemical analysis of these fabrics forms Appendix 17.3. It concludes that fabrics 40 and 42 are indeed different fabrics.

Dating

The dating evidence assembled by the early 1980s showed that fabrics 40 and 42 are first recorded in stratigraphic sequences in the horizon in which Saintonge green-glazed wares are first found, indicating that production started *c.* 1250. No further evidence has been brought to bear on this conclusion, other than the evidence from elsewhere (notably London) that the traditional estimate of *c.* 1250 for the first arrival of Saintonge jugs in Britain was indeed around 1250 (Vince 1985, 47–56).

Regarding the date at which production of this ware ceased, the only significant evidence to add to that in EAR 3 is Taylor's confirmation (in Steinmetzer *et al.* forthcoming) that several complete jugs in the large group from well 8685 at Princesshay (Site 156) are certainly in this fabric. The group is probably of early 15th-century date. This confirms that Exeter fabric 40 still formed a significant component of assemblages in the city at that time, suggesting that production continued into the mid/late 15th century.

Forms

The most complete examples of fabrics 40 and 42 are assembled in Figs 17.21–2. The principal vessel form is the narrow baluster jug, typically decorated with vertical iron-rich stripes, sometimes with dot-and-circle decoration, but larger globular jugs are not uncommon (Fig. 17.22). The close similarities between many of the jugs are obvious. The rare forms include costrels (Fig. 17.22, no. 26), bottles and pans with handles (EAR 3, 5, forms 2–5).

Distribution

Figure 17.23 shows the distribution of fabrics 40 and 42, revising the map published in 1984 (EAR 3, 6, fig. 5). Since the proportion of wheel-thrown jugs increases steadily through the period of 200 years or more when these fabrics were in circulation, variations in the proportions of assemblages made up by these wares may show either chronological changes or differences in marketing this class of pottery on broadly contemporary sites. Since much of the material outside the city is poorly dated, a map showing pie diagrams with precise percentages of wares at each site would be misleading; instead, a simpler presentation of the material is shown here. The picture in southern Devon has filled out since the last publication, especially in the area to the south-west of the city, where there have been substantial excavations both in towns and on rural sites. There has been less excavation in south-eastern Devon, where the picture is still poorly understood, and north and north-western Devon remain complete blanks despite the excavation of much new material. Examples remain rare at Plymouth (about 20 sherds among about 4400 late medieval sherds at Woolster Street, for example: Preston 1986, 26–7). The sherds which were thought to be of Exeter fabric 40 from Cleeve Abbey, in Somerset (Allan 1998, 46, 51, 57–8), have therefore appeared an isolated occurrence. Despite the fact that they appear very similar in fabric under the microscope, these should be regarded as doubtful examples of the Exeter fabrics.

Among the generally low totals from more distant sites, the finds from the castles of Okehampton, in western Devon, and Launceston, in Cornwall, stand out. Those from Okehampton (71 sherds from at least 13 vessels, forming 2.25% of the later medieval sherds) contrast with the near-complete absence of finds of these jugs from neighbouring farms and peasant hamlets, even those with large collections such as the 10,000 sherds from Okehampton Park (Allan 1978; cf. Allan and Perry 1982, 92). More striking is the quantity from

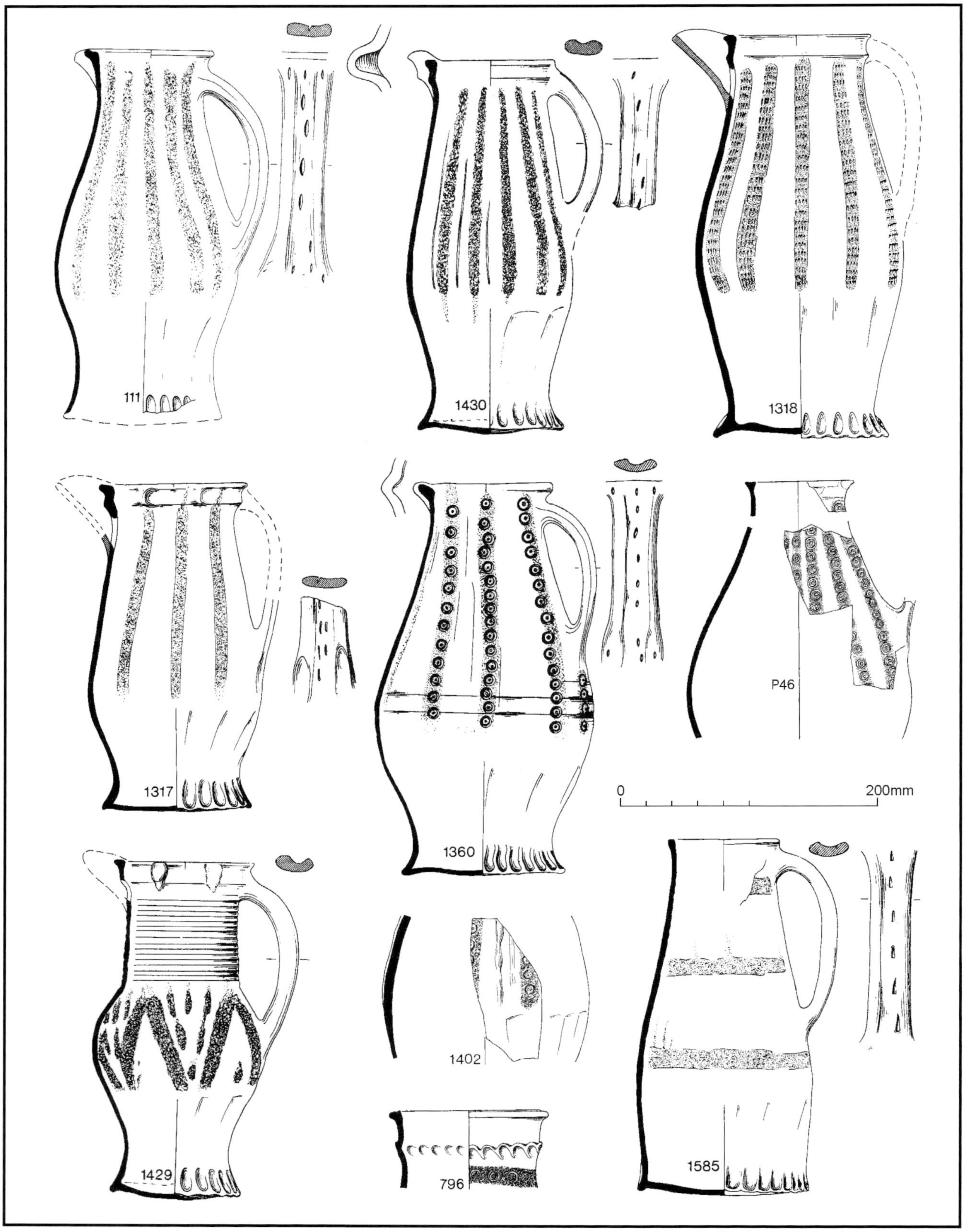

Fig. 17.21 Exeter fabric 40 baluster jugs from Exeter and (P46) Launceston Castle (P46 redrawn from Brown et al. *2006; the others Allan 1984a)*

Fig. 17.22 Exeter fabric 40: jugs and other forms (photo: © RAMM; drawings by John Allan and Sandy Morris)

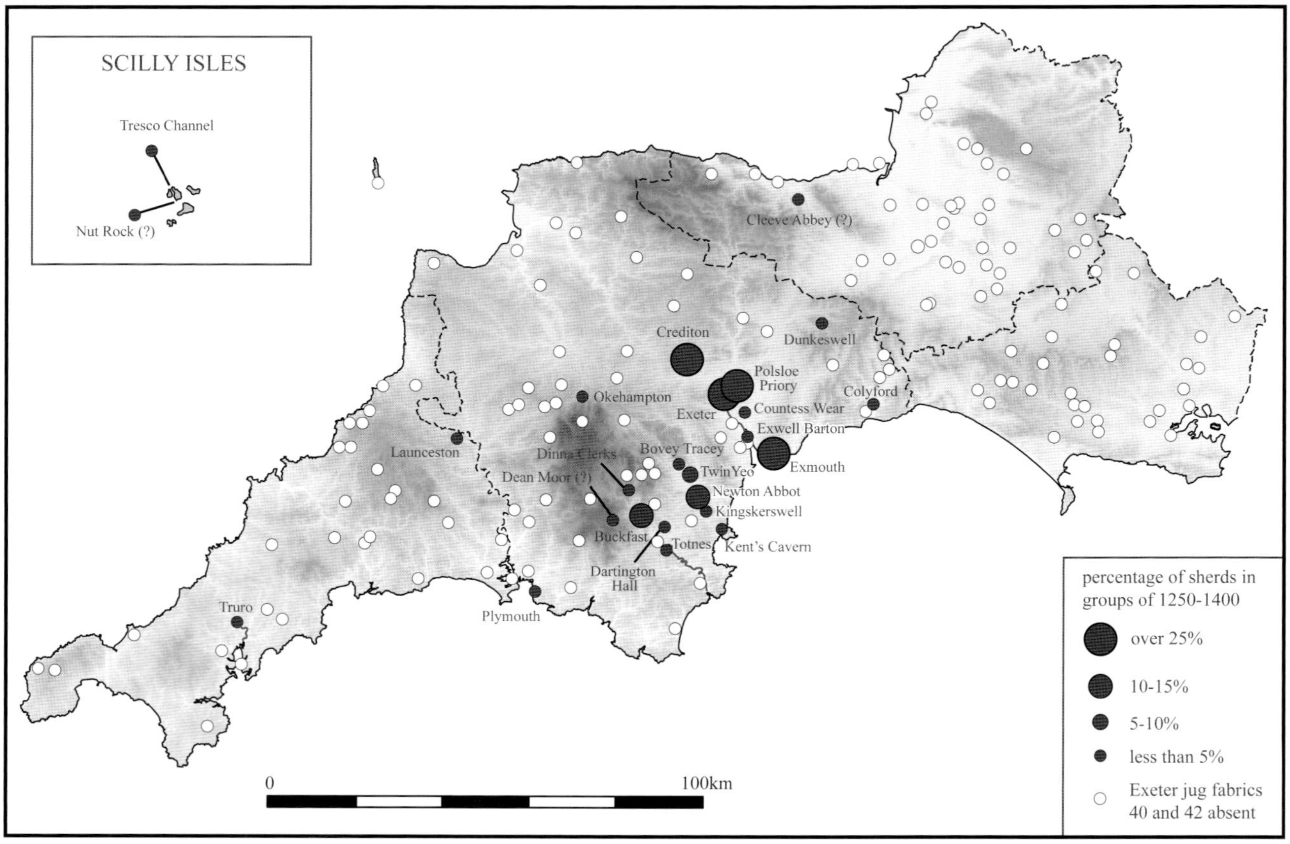

Fig. 17.23 The distribution of Exeter fabrics 40 and 42 (drawn by David Gould)

Launceston Castle, where at least 835 sherds of these two fabrics were identified, fabric 42 being rather more common; they formed about 5.8% of the later medieval sherds recorded (Brown *et al.* 2006, 274–5). At both castles the explanation for these finds may lie partly in the much stronger demand for decorative tableware on high-status sites, but these finds may also reflect the movement of goods in peripatetic aristocratic households. Okehampton was a castle of the Courtenays, whose more favoured household was Tiverton, nearer Exeter in the Exe Valley.

The most unexpected aspect of the new pattern is the evidence for distribution much further to the west than was known in the 1980s, with finds from Pydar Street in Truro (Allan and Langman 1998–9, 183, no. 7) and Tresco Channel on the Isles of Scilly (Allan *et al.* 2019).

Other wares

North Devon coarseware

By the late 13th century, North Devon Medieval Coarseware, a handmade, unglazed fabric tempered with angular clear quartz inclusions, dominated the ceramics market throughout mid and north Devon, often being the only class of pottery seen on a rural medieval site in that part of the county (Fig. 17.24). A striking feature of these wares is the sharp boundary of the area in which they were marketed. On a number of sites about 25 km from the city this is the main or only class of medieval pottery. At Crediton, only *c.* 14 km from the city, they made up something like 40% of the later medieval pottery. In the city they form only 1% of the total later medieval assemblage (Allan and Langman 2010, 154; EAR 3, 128).

Granite-derived wares including Totnes-type ware

The late 13th century saw the emergence of a pottery at Bridgetown Pomeroy, the new town on the River Dart opposite Totnes, where pottery production continued into the early 18th century (Allan 1984c, 79–80). Its products are highly distinctive, being tempered with sands washed down from Dartmoor, rich in micas and other granite-derived minerals. A second documented South Devon pottery at Dodbrooke near Kingsbridge, and other potteries at Plympton and Bere Ferrers whose products are known only in the post-medieval period, probably made very similar wares, but there is currently no medieval archaeological evidence for these sites (details in Allan *et al.* 2018b, 82–3). Like their North Devon competitors, these potteries enjoyed very limited success in the Exeter market, despite the possibilities of coastal transport (Fig. 17.25). Sherds from Seaton show that a few of these products also travelled further east along the South Devon coast.

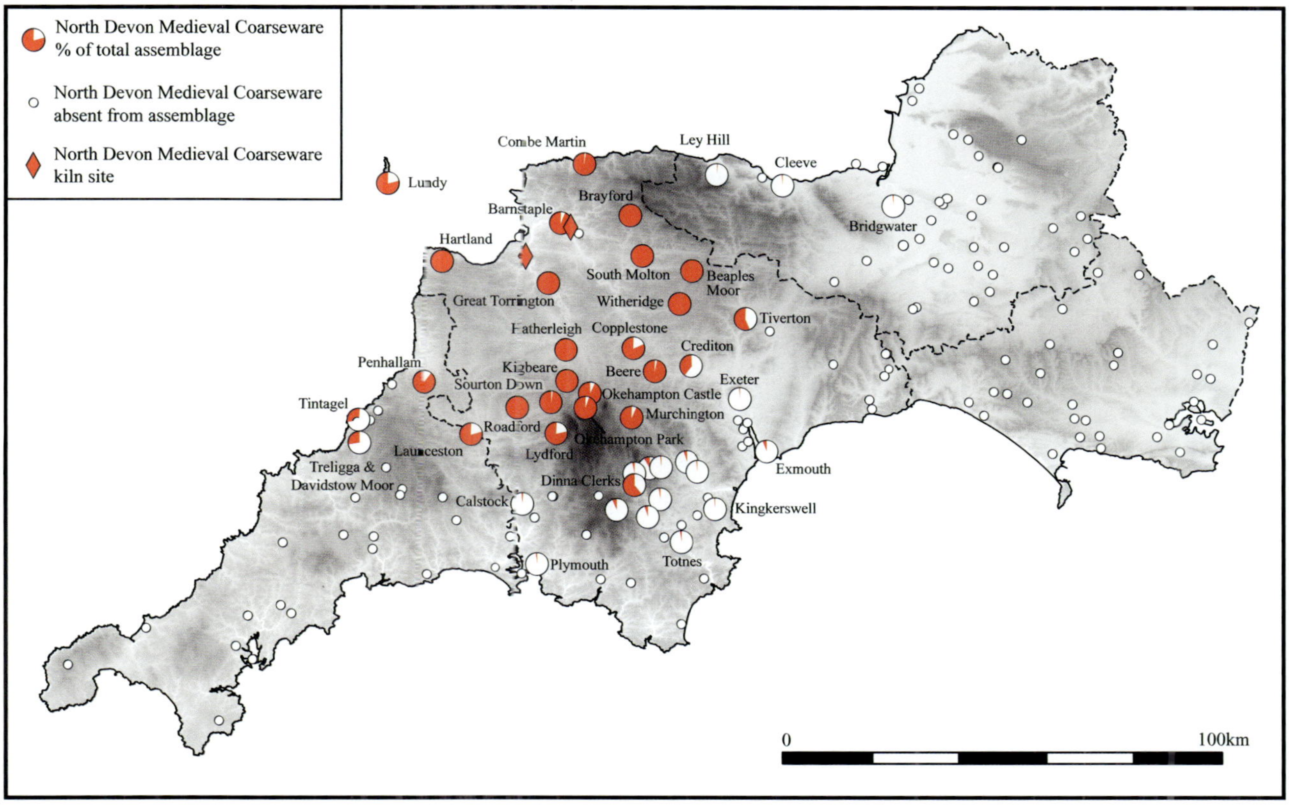

Fig. 17.24 The distribution of North Devon pottery in south-western England, c. 1200–1500 (drawn by David Gould)

Regional imports

It has been noted that the trades in pottery from other English centres declined after the mid 13th century. No later 13th-century or later wares from the London area have been recognised. We have yet to see a definite example of a Laverstock (Salisbury area) jug from Exeter, and the splendid Poole-type white ware jugs of the late 13th and 14th centuries are also unknown here, although they are represented in several excavations in Plymouth. There are a few examples of wheel-thrown Bristol (Redcliff) pottery at Exeter (Fig. 17.15, no. 1602 is one example which was not recognised in EAR 3), but they are generally scarce.

Saintonge imports

In total, at least 424 Saintonge vessels were recorded from the excavations up to 1980, and a further 320 French green-glazed white ware vessels were deemed too fragmentary for firm attribution (EAR 3, 22). I have not thought it profitable to count every sherd found since then, but it can be estimated that somewhere between 600 and 1000 Saintonge vessels are represented in the Exeter collection. Nearly all of them are jugs; there is just one horn, with one mortar and about five *pégaux* (large three-handled pitchers). The Exeter puzzle jug (Fig. 17.26A–C) remains a unique object. A wide range of other decorative types is represented: polychrome (23 vessels in 1980), all-over-green (17 examples in the same sample), sgraffito (three) and mottled green-glazed jugs with combing, applied vertical thumbed strips, rouletted horizontal bands, and applied bosses (Figs 17.26–7).

Saintonge wares formed between 7% and 11% of the assemblages of *c.* 1250–1350 on a range of city sites, without obvious signs that they were used in greater numbers on richer sites. Saintonge polychrome pottery is even recorded in the groups of ceramics from the small houses of Rack Street (EAPIT 2, Chapter 8) that must surely have been homes of the poor.

Distribution in the region

Exeter is one of three ports in the south-western region with substantial collections of Saintonge pottery, the others being at Plymouth and Poole. Finds of this type are most frequent in the Plymouth assemblages, where Saintonge wares commonly make up about a quarter of stratified groups by sherd count, and individual groups sometimes contain more than 40% Saintonge wares (detailed figures in Allan 1994). We do not have much statistical information for Poole, but Saintonge wares formed about 5% of a sample of more than 4000 sherds examined there in the 1980s (also by sherd count: Allan 1983b, 196). All these collections, of course, are dwarfed by that at Southampton. It has been noted that not only the proportion but the types of Saintonge vessels represented

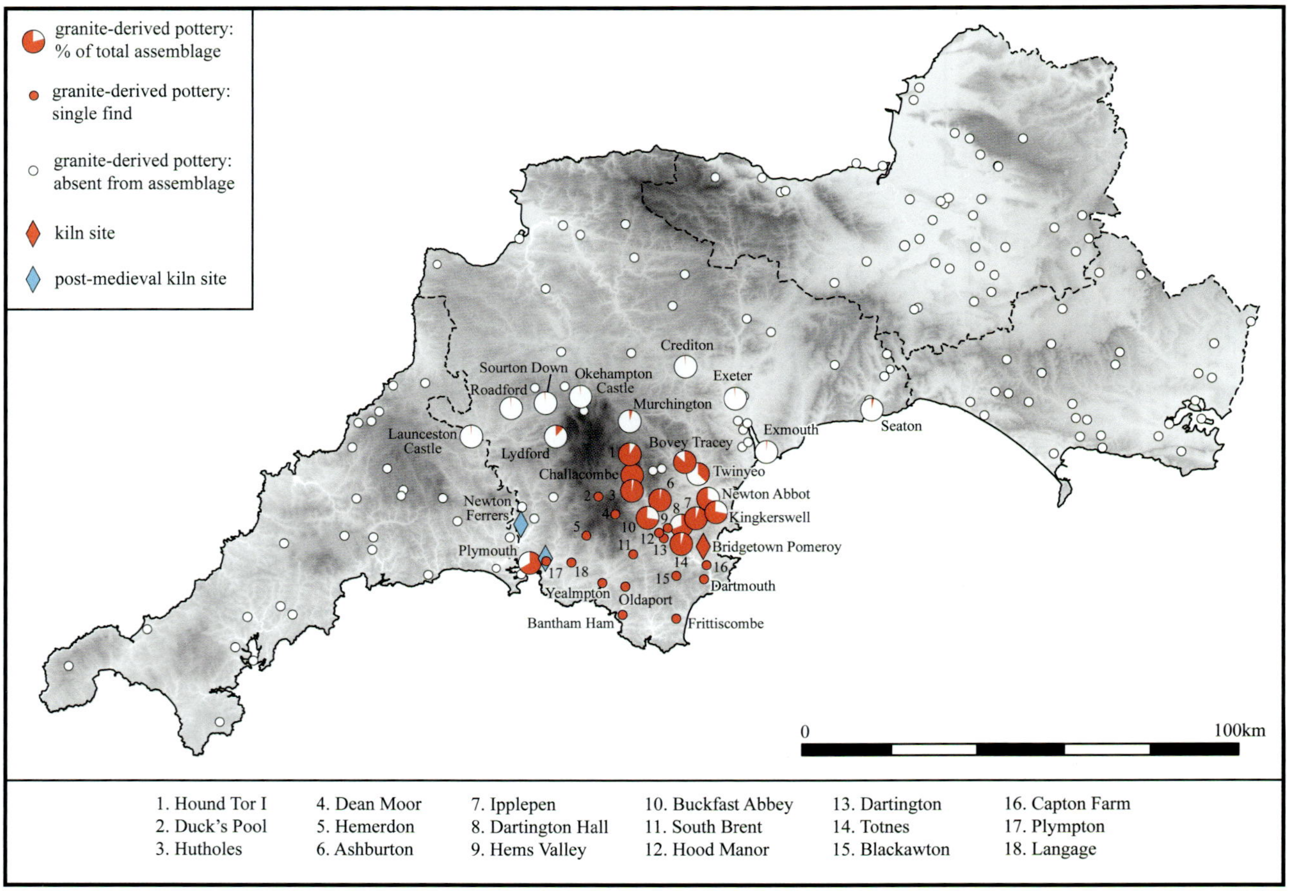

Fig. 17.25 The distribution of South Devon granite-derived pottery in south-western England (drawn by David Gould)

in these collections varies. The Plymouth material consists almost entirely of green-glazed white ware jugs; the Southampton finds include a wider range of vessel types, such as redwares, mortars, costrels, lids and gritty wares (Brown 2002, 26–8).

An attempt to map all the findspots of Saintonge pottery in the region is shown as Fig. 17.28. Coverage is likely to more complete in Devon and Cornwall than in Somerset and Dorset. Despite the map's imperfections, it is likely to be accurate in showing that occurrences are much more common on or near the south coast, with concentrations of finds around the ports of Exeter, Dartmouth and Plymouth, with a probable group of sites emerging around the Fal Estuary. The other big concentration of finds is on the Isles of Scilly, where Saintonge wares made up about 10% of sherds on a range of sites on land but a much higher fraction of pottery in the assemblages from offshore sites (Allan *et al.* 2019; Allan and Stevens forthcoming). In Somerset, finds are restricted mainly to the port of Bridgwater and high-status inland sites like Glastonbury Abbey and Wells Cathedral Close (Allan, Dawson and Kent 2015; Dawson *et al.* 2015). The inland towns have few imports; the five examples from Taunton form a minor part of a large sample.

The Late Middle Ages, *c.* 1350–1550

The sequence of ceramic horizons

After the period of highly decorated wares the quantity of pottery available for study declines markedly with the disappearance of urban rubbish pits and cesspits, a phenomenon evident across southern England (see Chapters 5–7 above). Four ceramic horizons are now distinguished in the city, introducing one subdivision of those proposed in the 1980s (EAR 3, 10):

- *Horizon J*: groups in which the jug styles of the highly decorated period were still in use, but the handmade UGSD jars were largely replaced by wheel-thrown wares. Trichay Street pit 169, in which pottery of this horizon was associated with shoes of the late 14th or early 15th century, remains the best-dated example of this period (*ibid.*, 10, 89, 327).
- *Horizon K:* groups with no jars, consisting almost entirely of wheel-thrown jugs, in which there is a change to brushed slip and sgraffito as the main form of decoration. The only imports are examples of late medieval Saintonge jugs. Two major groups of this horizon have been published (from Exe Bridge layers

Fig. 17.26 Saintonge pottery from Exeter. (A–C) The Exeter puzzle jug; (D) polychrome jugs from Goldsmith Street pit 228 (Site 39); (E) green-glazed jugs from Smythen Street (Site 115); (F–G) later medieval bib-glazed jugs (photos © RAMM)

459–61 and Queen Street well 350: EAR 3, 90–3; Allan 2019, 120–2); a very large group of jugs of very similar character has more recently been excavated at Princesshay (Site 156; Fig. 17.29A).

- *Horizon L:* groups in which the local wares typical of the early 16th century such as Donyatt Group 3 (Coleman-Smith and Pearson 1988, 80–1) are in circulation alongside many of the typical late 15th/early 16th-century imports such as Raeren stonewares and Beauvais earthenwares, but there are no bowls, which become universal after *c.* 1500. The group from Polsloe Priory (Site 59) contexts 1582–3, stratified below two early 16th-century pre-Dissolution deposits, remains the best example of this horizon (EAR 3, 91–3).
- *Horizon M*: groups with typical imports of the early 16th century, including groups from Dissolution deposits and contexts with numismatics, leather and glass of *c.* 1500–50 (*ibid.*, 154–67).

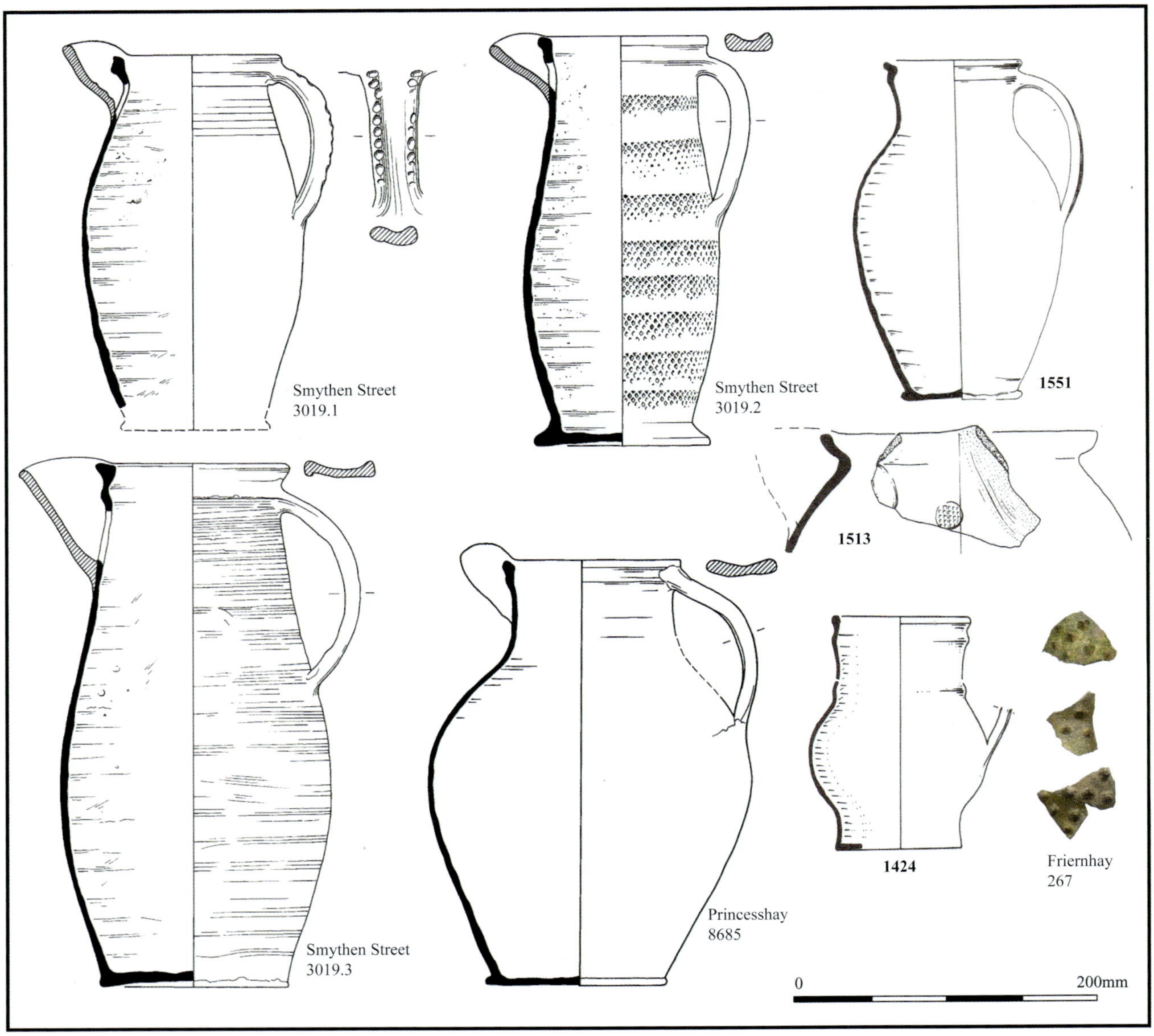

Fig. 17.27 Saintonge pottery from Exeter (drawn by Jane Reed and John Allan, © RAMM)

Local pottery

One uncertainty here is the point at which production of Exeter fabrics 40 and 42 ceased. These wares are present in Horizons J and K but had certainly disappeared by Horizon M; whether they were still in use in Horizon L is less clear, but an end date of *c.* 1450 is suggested on the present imprecise evidence.

The late medieval jug fabrics contain few inclusions and their sources can be hard to establish, even with petrological study. In the future it would be worthwhile to carry out a programme of ICP analysis to distinguish the sources represented, which probably include products of Donyatt in South Somerset (Coleman-Smith and Pearson 1988), Hemyock in eastern Devon (Smart 2018), and other related centres. Figure 17.29B shows a typical example of these late medieval jugs.

Low Countries and Rhenish stonewares

A significant feature of the pottery of Exeter and other sites in Devon and Cornwall is the striking rarity of stonewares dating before *c.* 1450, notably those from Langerwehe and Siegburg, which are common in the east coast ports of England and Scotland (compare *e.g.* Vince 1985; Evans 2019; Haggarty 2019). It is only with the arrival of Raeren-type vessels in the late 15th century that the market in stoneware develops. At present the starting date for these wares at Exeter is derived from evidence of customs accounts showing that the importation of 'stone cups' was underway here by the 1470s (EAR 3, 117). This seems to correspond well with the earliest reference to the importation of stonewares *(cruses)* in Southampton, dated 1470 (Brown 2002, 132).

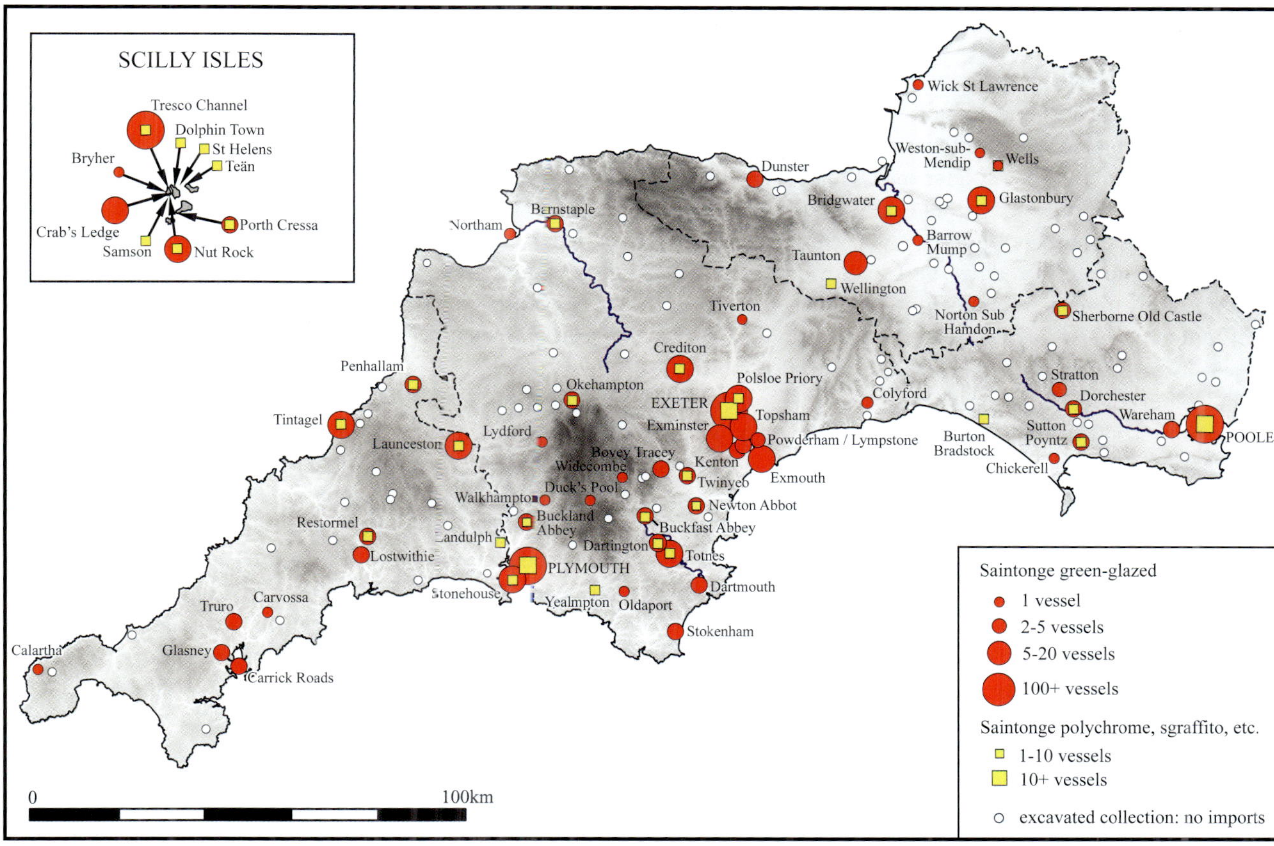

Fig. 17.28 The distribution of Saintonge pottery in south-western England (drawn by David Gould)

Fig. 17.29 Later medieval pottery at Exeter. (A) The Princesshay (Site 156) well group during conservation, probably early 15th century; (B) South Somerset jug from Friernhay Street (Site 75), mid or late 15th century (© RAMM)

In the last quarter of the 15th century stonewares rapidly became the principal class of imported ceramics in the city. This was a trade conducted on a considerable scale; the evidence of the Exeter customs accounts can be used to calculate that more than one million stoneware pots arrived in the port of Exeter over the post-medieval period (Allan 1983a, 39–45; 1984a, 125–6). Fragments of more than 333 examples of early 16th-century imported stonewares were recovered by 1980, and every collection of household rubbish sampled from this period, both in rich and poor parts of the city, contains several such vessels. Stonewares form 64% of the imported pottery of that date (EAR 3, 103). They form an appreciably higher proportion of the Exeter imports than they do in contemporary deposits at Plymouth *(*Allan 1994, 48–9), and the proportion is somewhat higher than on other major collections in south-western England and southern Wales (cf. figures for Carmarthen, Penhow, Acton Court and Glastonbury Abbey in Allan and Wrathmell 2016, 61).

The principal type of imported ceramics at Exeter in the late 15th and early 16th century is Raeren stoneware (47% of all imported vessels in early 16th-century contexts) followed by products from Cologne (11%), Siegburg (2%), Langewehe (2%) and Beauvais (1%: figures in EAR 3, 113). Figures 17.30 and 17.31 show characteristic examples of the first three types.

The rich documentary evidence for the port of Exeter shows that the sudden rise in stoneware imports does not reflect a significant reorientation of the city's trading pattern with the development of shipping trade to the Low Countries but instead the development of an indirect trade via London; in the late 16th century fully 90% of the Rhenish stonewares arriving at Exeter had come by indirect trade through the capital (Allan 1983a, 37–40; 1984a, 113–26). This shows that that in the late 15th century Devon rapidly adopted the practice of using ceramic drinking equipment for storing and drinking at table. In this regard the county was old-fashioned; much of eastern England and the ports of Scotland had adopted these customs in the course of the 14th and 15th centuries.

Northern French imports

In the late 15th century the potteries of northern France also took advantage of the region's novel demand for decorated tableware, and for specialist items such as albarelli (drug jars) and flasks. The principal classes of imported ceramics from this region have been described elsewhere: stonewares, monochrome-glazed and sgraffito-decorated earthenwares from the Beauvaisis, flasks from Martincamp, and white ware floor-tiles from Normandy (Hurst *et al.* 1986, 102–16; Allan, Hunt, Keen and Taylor 2016).

Beauvais wares

At Exeter the Beauvais white ware drinking jugs with their brilliant yellow or green glazes are especially common, represented by at least 64 examples in Exeter (Fig. 17.32C–I; the yellow-glazed more common than

Fig. 17.30 (A) Late 15th-century Siegburg jug with pewter lid from Goldsmith Street (Site 39). (B) Raeren stonewares from various Exeter sites (photos © RAMM)

Fig. 17.31 (A) Three early 16th-century Cologne stonewares from Goldsmith Street pit 228 (Site 39): oak leaves and acorns, plain jug and rosettes. (B) Cologne Bartmann *jugs of the mid 16th century (photos © RAMM)*

the green), compared with 15 sgraffito-decorated wares (mainly dishes and albarelli), two monochrome-glazed combed wares and 17 stonewares; the total minimum vessel count is currently 98. The predominance of drinking jugs over the better-known sgraffito wares is also evident at Southampton, and in Wales (Brown and Thomson 1996, 45; Papazian and Campbell 1992, 19–21). Beauvais wares are even more strongly represented at Plymouth, where 101 vessels have been recorded from a smaller sample of late 15th/early 16th-century ceramics (published examples from St Andrews Street, Woolster Street, Kitto Institute, Dung Quay, and many unpublished finds: Broady 1979, 7; Preston 1986, 28–30; Allan and Barber 1992; Allan 2000a; Allan and Langman 2003, 58–61). Elsewhere in the region there are also substantial finds at Barnstaple, Totnes and Poole (respectively 33, 20, and more than 14 vessels: many unpublished but see Allan 1984a; Barton and Thomson 1992). In total, 311 Beauvais vessels have been noted by the writer from sites in south-western England (Fig. 17.33). This seems a high figure, but Beauvais pottery is also well represented in Wales and Scotland, for example (Papazian and Campbell 1992; Haggarty 2019), and the entire south-western region could not match the 20 or so complete profiles or substantial fragments from Southampton (Brown and Thomson 1996).

There are also interesting differences in marketing patterns within the region. The drinking jugs are generally the most common (at least 152 examples, cf. 97 sgraffito vessels, 50 stonewares and 12 comb-decorated dishes with monochrome glazes) but in Barnstaple, for example, sgraffito-decorated wares have proved consistently more common than the drinking jugs on several sites (27 vessels, cf. six of the latter).

Normandy floor-tiles

Introduction

EAR 3 published a distinctive class of late 15th and early 16th-century plain white ware floor-tiles (some with streaks of red clay, others in a pink fabric with white clay lumps or streaks), glazed either yellow or green, found on several sites in the city, which had also been recognised by Dr Christopher Norton at Winchester (Allan and Keen 1984, 240–2). It seemed probable that they were imports from Normandy, where Norton had noted comparable tiles at Rouen, and the publication related them to references in the Exeter customs accounts to the importation of tiles from Normandy (probably Rouen) in the period 1490–1540.

The evidence for the distribution of tiles of this type in the British Isles was brought together in a discussion of the floor of the chapel of Cotehele, in Cornwall, which seems to be the only intact pavement composed of such tiles surviving in Great Britain and Ireland (Allan, Hunt, Keen and Taylor 2016). Figure 17.34 reproduces the distribution map prepared for Cotehele, with the additional sites of Ottery St Mary, in Devon, and Kilkenny, in Ireland, found since 2016. It shows that the marketing pattern was strongly weighted to the south-west of England, and especially to south Devon, where there are numerous examples, both in churches and on secular sites (*ibid.*). They are now known from 16 sites in Exeter, and from several other sites around the Exe Estuary, including Kenton, Topsham, Exmouth and Withycombe Raleigh. By contrast, they are very rare in south-eastern England, where the rival products from the Low Countries, imported in their thousands, dominated the market.

An interesting point emerged from this mapping: the tiles have a quite different distribution pattern from the Beauvais wares. Beauvais imports circulated not just in southern England but up the east coast and in Scotland, whereas Normandy floor-tiles have a much more restricted distribution, being largely excluded from the markets of south-eastern England and the North Sea ports. This difference illustrates the snares of drawing conclusions about trading patterns based on single classes of artefact.

EAPIT offered a context for carrying out chemical analysis of some examples of these tiles, alongside other ceramics from Normandy (described above), and by chance the submission of these specimens coincided with the discovery of examples at Kilkenny, in Ireland, described by Michael Hughes (Appendix 17.4).

Saintonge wares

Finally, Exeter offers some evidence for the decline in the importation of Saintonge pottery in the later Middle Ages. In two of the three principal deposits of Horizon K (probably early 15th century) there are only a few examples of Saintonge jugs (including Fig. 17.27, Princesshay (Site 156) context 8685), but in the third context, from Exe Bridge (Site 56), fragments from these jugs are just as common as they were in the late 13th and early 14th centuries (EAR 3, 90–1; Allan 2020, 119–22). A few examples of the bib-glazed jugs typical of the later Middle Ages have been recognised (Fig. 17.26G), and one unusual vessel with a pink fabric and applied grid-stamped pads may also be noted (Fig. 17.27, no. 1513, not recognised in EAR 3).

By the late 15th century, there had clearly been a decline in the importation of Saintonge jugs in Exeter, although there are a few unglazed vessels in early 16th-century contexts (EAR 3, no. 1784). A few Saintonge chafing dishes are also in the same deposits (*ibid.*, 111–12), but all the late Saintonge types are much less common than at Plymouth and Southampton, and probably than at Poole (figures in Allan 1994).

Fig. 17.32 Beauvais earthenwares from Exeter. (A and C) Yellow-glazed drinking jug from Fore Street; (B) albarello with double slip and sgraffito decoration; (D–I) other yellow- and green-glazed drinking jug fragments; (J–K) sgraffito dish and albarello, both with single brown slip (© RAMM, line drawings from Allen 1984a)

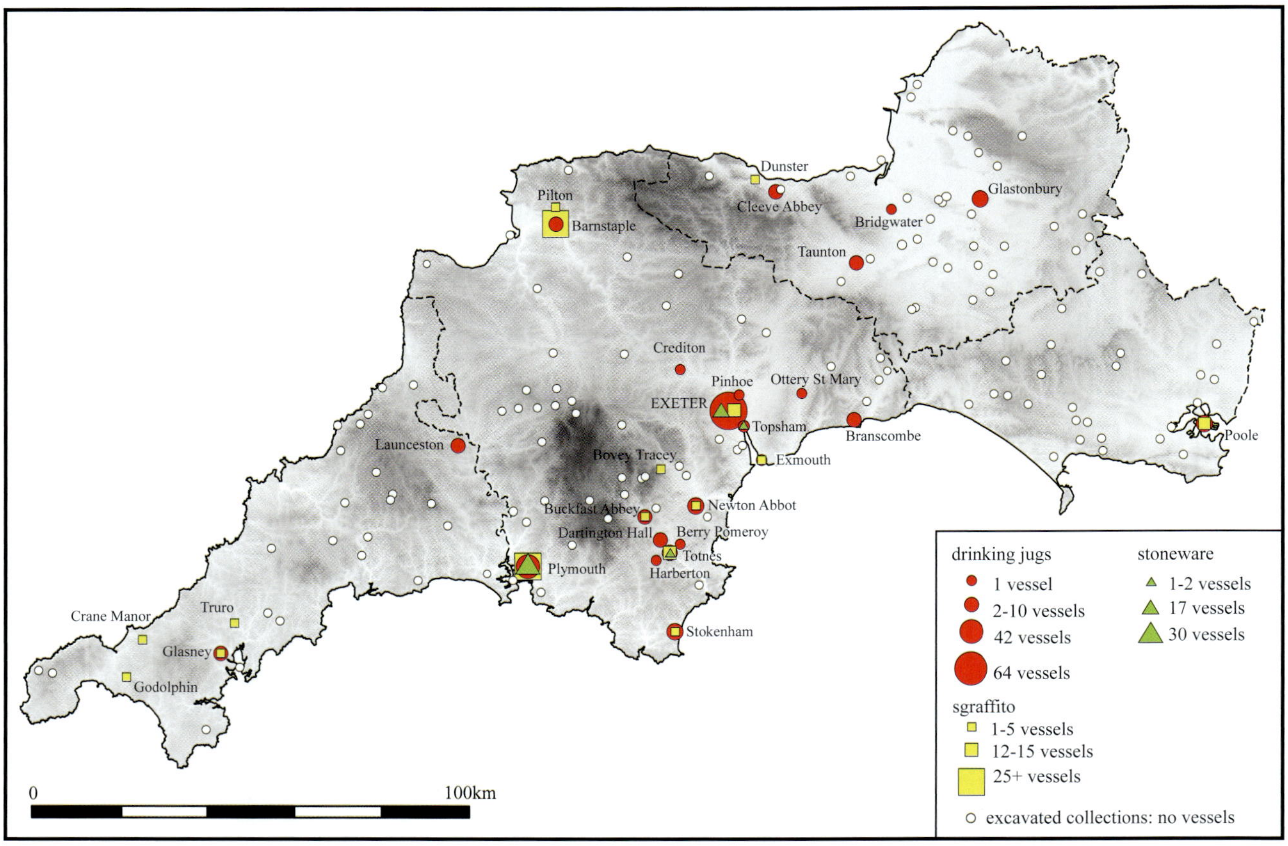

Fig. 17.33 The distribution of Beauvais wares in south-western England (drawn by David Gould)

Acknowledgements

My chief debt is to Graham Langman, who catalogued most of the pottery from Exeter Archaeology's excavations of 1981–2012. I am grateful to Henrietta Quinnell (Cornish pottery), George Haggarty and Derek Hall (Scotland), Clare McCutcheon and Joanna Bird (Ireland), Naomi Payne (recent finds by AC Archaeology), David Dawson and Mike Ponsford (Somerset and Bristol), and Lyn Blackmore (London). All the sherds have been examined by the writer.

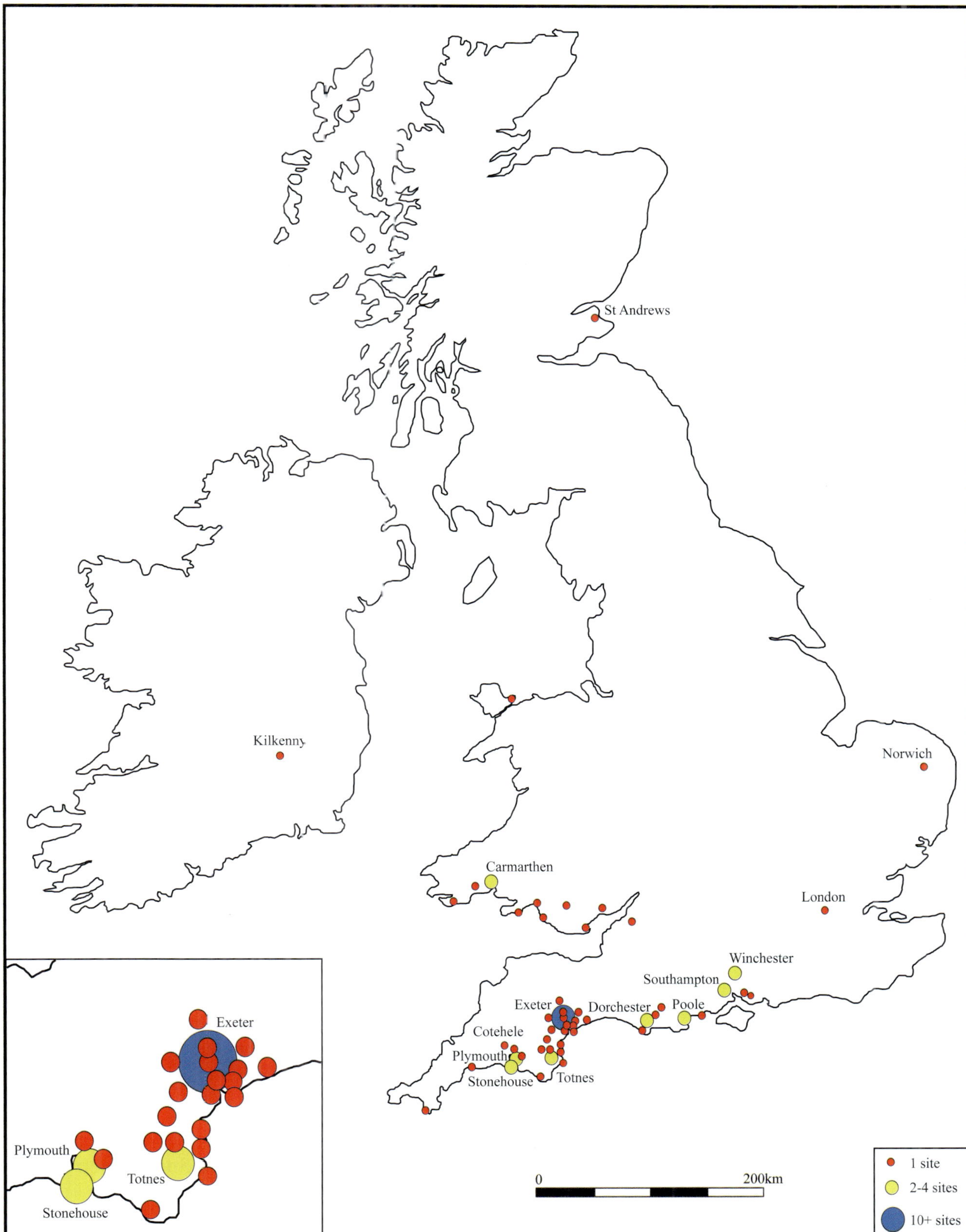

Fig. 17.34 The distribution of Normandy floor-tiles in Great Britain and Ireland (drawn by David Gould, from Allan, Hunt, Keen and Taylor 2016 with subsequent additions)

Appendix 17.2

Plasma Spectrometry Analyses of North French Wares

Michael J. Hughes

Introduction

Inductively-coupled plasma spectrometry (ICPS) analysis, which examines the chemical elements in a sample, is currently one of the most widely used analytical techniques applied to pottery fabrics to determine their possible source. This report presents the results of ICPS analyses of a range of imported Saxo-Norman vessels found in Exeter which are believed to be of northern French origin. The project was specifically chosen to address lacunae in the analyses of several significant French pottery types. Part of the justification for analysing French imports is the relative scarcity of systematic data on many of the well-known types of such pottery, and the need to address this lack. Without a sufficient database of analyses of ceramics of approximately the same period from a range of possible sources, it is not possible to determine the source of a particular item of pottery.

Earlier analyses of northern French wares by ICPS have shown a range of different chemical patterns, which typically appear to represent the products of individual workshops or closely associated groups working the same or similar clay resource. However, the numbers analysed have been quite limited, and for some pottery types no analyses exist, which handicaps attempts to assign imported northern French wares to their source. While mostly older analyses of a few specific types of this pottery have existed for some time, they were carried out by other analysis techniques, principally X-ray fluorescence (XRF), and most often for a much restricted range of chemical elements compared to ICPS. There is value in attempting to make a comparison against these, where they have been published in sufficient detail, but often the numbers of elements analysed in common with ICPS are too few to make statistical comparison a possibility, although visual comparison of the data has proved of some limited value.

In recent years, a survey and summary of the principal ICPS investigations on French white wares was made by the late Alan Vince; his work forms a convenient starting point for understanding the range of chemical patterns found – in the present case for northern French wares (Vince 2011). Earlier analyses of northern French wares by other methods have included XRF of the local clays of the region (Dufournier 1981), northern French white wares from the Bryggen in Bergen (Deroeux *et al.* 1994), and highly decorated wares from a number of sites (Boivin *et al.* 1996). Most of these include analyses for only the major elements – aluminium, iron, titanium, calcium, magnesium, sodium and potassium – considerably fewer than ICPS analyses, which include these. Vince (2011) compared the Bryggen data against his analyses of early Rouen glazed wares, and found a close correlation between the samples from the kiln site at La Londe (the only kiln for which ICPS analyses exist of its products) and Rouen-style jugs found at Bergen (assigned by Deroeux *et al.* 1994 to their Groups 1 and 2). Further, comparing the Bergen analyses with those of a series of imports from sites in the British Isles analysed by ICPS seemed to indicate that in addition to the well-known highly decorated jugs, the Lower Seine Valley was also producing and exporting green-glazed jugs, unglazed jugs and glazed lobed cups (Vince 2011, 201).

Inductively Coupled Plasma Spectrometry analysis

Forty-nine vessels from Exeter, all believed to be northern French wares of 10th to 13th-century date, were selected for analysis. Sherds of each vessel were sampled by Kamal Badreshany at the University of Durham Archaeomaterials Research Centre (DARC). A powder sample of each vessel was obtained by drilling, then analysed using a

Table 17.3 List of northern French imported ceramics from Exeter selected for analysis by plasma spectrometry (ICPS). For Site Numbers see Chapter 2 above

Description	*Project sample No.*	*Publication No. (EAR 3)*	*Site and context*
1. Hamwic fabric 127			
Jar	1	Unpublished	Princesshay (Site 156) 3523
2–4. Beauvais-type sand-tempered wares			
Red-painted	2	39	High St (Site 55) 238
Red-painted	3	553	Queen St (Site 68) 49
Red-painted	4	611	Preston St (Site 60)
5–16 Unglazed Normandy white wares			
Lamp	5	95	High St (Site 55) 147, L12/E13C
Rouletted	6	190	Goldsmith St (Site 39) 229
Spout	7	192	Goldsmith St (Site 39) 229
Rouletted	8	348	Trichay St (Site 42) 334
Storage jar with strips	9	494	Goldsmith St (Site 37) 691
Red-painted jug	10	521	Goldsmith St (Site 37) 56
Handle with applied strip	11	545	Queen St (Site 68) 57
With applied strips	12	557	Queen St (Site 68) 49
Rim	13	558	Queen St (Site 68) 49 & 82
Rim	14	559	Queen St (Site 68) 49
With applied strips	15	669	Goldsmith St (Site 37) F38, 16C
16–19: Normandy gritty wares			
Body sherd, applied strip	16	147	Friars Gate (Site 45) unstrat.
Body sherd with bosses	17	672	Goldsmith St (Site 37) 34
Body sherd	18	Unpublished	Goldsmith St (Site 37) 156
Jug/pitcher sherds	19	Unpublished	Goldsmith St (Site 39) 286
20–30: Glazed white wares & redwares			
Redware with rouletting	20	Dunning and Fox 1951	South Street Area I (Site 15)
Glazed white ware handle	21	58	High St (Site 55) 219
Glazed rouletted strip	22	256	Goldsmith St (Site 37/39) 315
Red/brown-glazed sherd	23	53/2005	Goldsmith St (Site 37/39) 328
Rouletted & ye. gl.	24	287	Goldsmith St (Site 37/39) 372
Rouletted buff ware	25	379	Trichay St (Site 42) 277
Rouletted sherd, ye. gl.	26	556	Queen St (Site 68) 49 & 82
Spouted pitcher	27	675	Trichay St (Site 42) 742
White ware	28	676	Goldsmith St (Site 37/39) unstrat
White ware	29	677	Goldsmith St (Site 37/39) 98
Redware with strip	30	1573	Goldsmith St (Site 37/39) 286
Green-glazed white ware	31	125	Cathedral Close Pit 8
32–38: Rouen-type wares, late 12C/early 13C			
Base	32	728	Exe Bridge (Site 56) Phase 1
Handle	33	1197	Goldsmith St (Site 37/39) 215
Decorated body sherd	34	1198	Goldsmith St (Site 37/39) 215
Body sherd with strip	35	1559	North Street pit 9
Body sherd with dots	36	1562	Goldsmith St (Site 37/39) 247
Body sherd with strip	37	1019	Goldsmith St (Site 37/39) 243
Handle	38	962	Trichay St (Site 42) 360/393
39–41:Normandy highly decorated/scale-decorated, green-glazed, L12/E13C			
Rod handle	39	688	Exe Bridge (Site 56)
Scale-decorated, green glazed	40	966	Trichay St (Site 42)360/393
Scale-dec.	41	1178	Trichay St (Site 42) 432
42–49: North or west French white wares			
Strap handle	42	689	Exe Bridge (Site 56)
Jug rim, strap handle	43	963	Trichay St (Site 42) 360/393

(Continued)

Table 17.3 List of northern French imported ceramics from Exeter selected for analysis by plasma spectrometry (ICPS). For Site Numbers see Chapter 2 above (Continued)

Description	*Project sample No.*	*Publication No. (EAR 3)*	*Site and context*
Green-glazed rim	44	964	Trichay St (Site 42) 360/393
Green-glazed with wavy lines	45	1232	North St (Site 38) 11
Yellow-glazed costrel	46	1380	Knott's, South St 1899
Green-glazed jug with wavy lines	47	1570	Goldsmith Street (Sites 37/39)
Rod handle with red clay pellets	48	1563	Goldsmith Street (Site 37/39)
Jug rim	49	1572	Goldsmith St (Site 37/39)

combination of inductively-coupled plasma atomic emission spectrometry (ICP-AES) and -mass spectrometry (ICP-MS). Both the techniques of analysis and the statistical processing were the same as those used for the other ICPS investigations on pottery from the EAPIT project, described below (see 'Exeter jugs') and in Chapter 18. The sherds analysed are listed in Table 17.3, and the results of analysis for a total of 39 chemical elements in online Table 17.4). Figures 17.7–17.9 illustrate the range of wares. Throughout the following text, vessels are referred to by the project sample numbers shown in Table 17.3, which are given in bold in the text).

Interpretation and discussion of the results using Principal Components Analysis

While an initial examination of the data using plots of pairs of element concentrations can often differentiate between pottery groups with significantly different chemical patterns, the northern French wares analysed do not show major differences, so interpretation moved directly to the use of Principal Components Analysis (PCA), as in the other studies of EAPIT ceramics. As a multivariate statistical technique, this is much better able to cope with subtle inter-group chemical patterns.

PCA on the Exeter northern French wares against similar wares from Tresco Channel

A relevant recent set of analyses to the Exeter study is an investigation of finds of northern French wares recovered from underwater sites in the Isles of Scilly in the vicinity of Tresco Channel (Hughes 2019). These included red-painted Normandy wares (seven samples), French green-glazed rouletted pottery (three samples), Bristol Pottery Type (BPT) 192 (six examples), and other suspected northern French wares. It was particularly valuable to see the chemical patterns for the first three of these groups, which complemented the vessels selected for the Exeter study.

The results from the Exeter samples were combined with those from the northern French wares from Tresco Channel and examined statistically using PCA. Both projects used ICPS atomic emission and mass spectrometry, so a large element dataset could be used for the statistical test. PCA simultaneously considers the concentrations of many elements in each sample and the results are conveniently displayed in graphical form.

The plot of the first two principal components showed that the first component did not differentiate sufficiently between the groups, but the plot of the second and third components did (Fig. 17.35). None of the Exeter sherds fell outside a general chemical pattern for the wares as a whole. Of the Tresco Channel sherds, one green-glazed rouletted ware appeared to have suffered a problem during analysis and one of the suspected northern French wares seemed from its analysis more likely to be a western French white ware; these two were excluded from the re-run statistical tests. Many of the Exeter pottery types formed consistent chemical groups, separated or closely related to each other, which indicates a range of clay compositions used for their manufacture, consistent within each group but differing (for the most part) between groups, and indicating typical clay chemistries for northern French white ware pottery. All the sherds discussed here from Tresco Channel and from the other sites on Scilly fall within a range of composition patterns of the Exeter samples.

Many sherds fall into a general cluster (Fig. 17.35), indicating very probably closely related origins. The French green-glazed rouletted wares from Tresco Channel form a particularly compact cluster on the second component, in the middle of the Fig. 7.35, suggesting the same production centre for this group.

There are some fairly dense clusters of points suggesting the use of some common clay resources. Two of the Tresco Channel type groups, however, are clearly chemically different from the Exeter samples. These are of the Bristol Pottery Type 192 and the green-glazed rouletted white ware; they form compact self-contained groups in the lower centre of Fig. 17.35 (*i.e.* low on the second principal component), close to each other but not overlapping, suggesting different workshops, clay sources or chronological periods. The finding of a series of quite similar chemical groups present among the products of a single centre or production area is quite common in ceramic provenancing such as London delftwares (Hughes

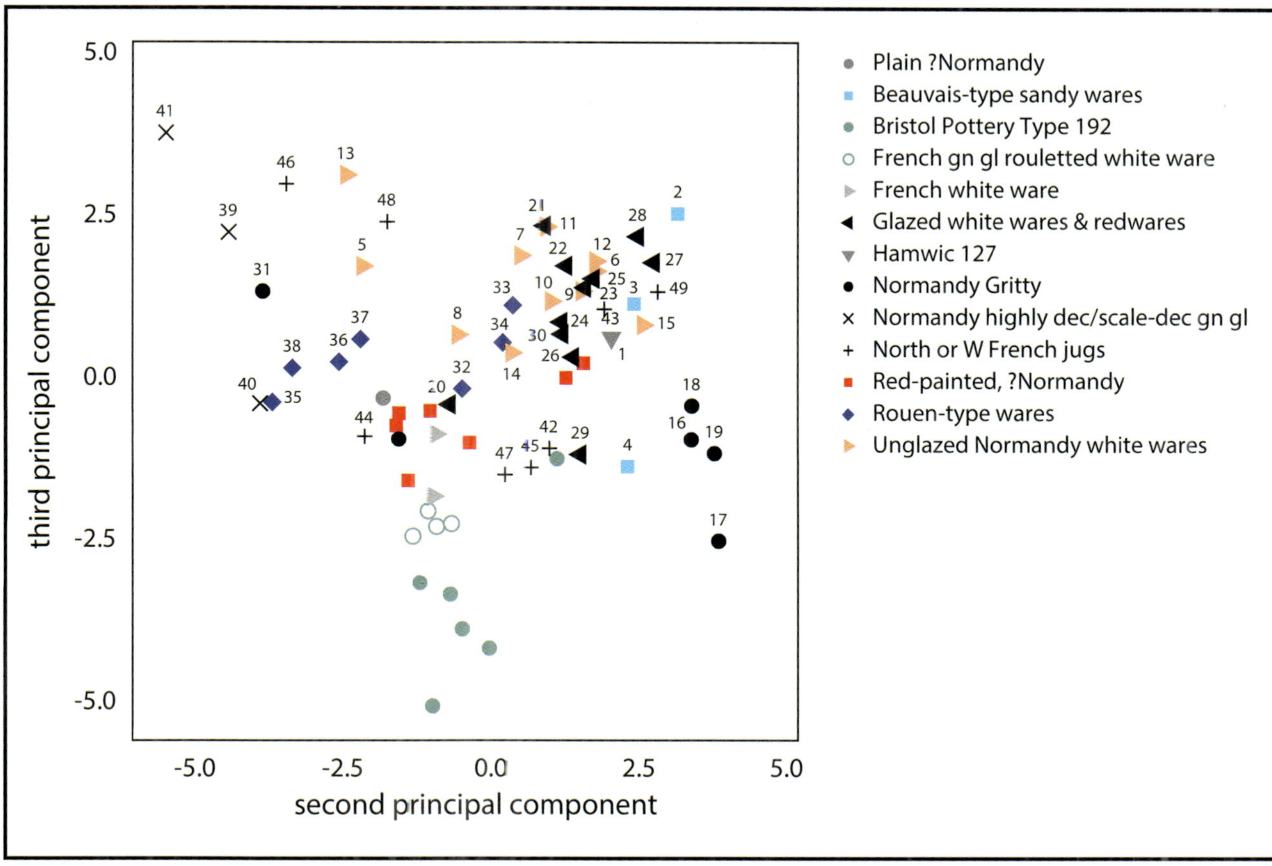

Fig. 17.35 Principal Component Analysis of the ICPS results on northern French white wares from Exeter and Tresco Channel and other sites on Scilly: plot of the second and third components, with individual catalogue numbers as labels. Unnumbered samples are from Tresco Channel and other sites in the Isles of Scilly and will be marked in the relevant reports (drawn by Michael Hughes)

2008) and tin-glazed wares produced at Antwerp (Hughes and Gaimster 1999).

Five of the Bristol Pottery Type 192 sherds form another group separated from the Exeter sherds, and just below the rouletted wares. The sixth example is further up and to the right, near three north or west French jugs from Exeter, though slightly separate from the central cluster of points and the Normandy Gritty wares from Exeter (on the right-hand side of Fig. 1). Vince (2011) also considered the analysis of Bristol Pottery Type (BPT) 192, known from sites in western England and Ireland, and examined ICPS analyses of four examples in relation to a possible south-western or western French origin. The four showed considerable variation in composition; factor analysis of the ICPS data against various groups of lower Seine valley, south-western French and western French origins found one pair closer in one test to the south-western French group but another test where the latter was omitted and a fuller element list used found the closest parallels in western France. A third example fitted with Rouen wares and a fourth was an outlier. By contrast, the BPT 192 sherds from Tresco seemed to have a consistent chemical pattern suggesting a common source.

Four of the Normandy gritty wares from Exeter, namely samples **16–19**, are also distinct, but in a different part of the PCA graph (Fig 17.35, lower right), while another (**31**) is more comparable to the three highly decorated wares on the left. It would appear that the general class of 'Normandy gritty' ware contains within it either quite distinct or geographically separate workshops, or at least three different clay resources.

The Exeter glazed white wares and redwares (samples **21–8** and **30**) form a major grouping on the upper right side of Fig. 17.35, suggesting a common workshop or workshops, intermixed with examples of the northern or western French jugs (**43** and **49**), an example of Hamwic fabric 127 (**1**) and two of the three Beauvais-type sandy wares (**2** and **3**). Also overlapping with the Exeter white ware group are all but two of the unglazed Normandy white wares (**6–12**, **14** and **15**). Two of the red-painted Normandy wares from Nut Rock, in the Isles of Scilly, are part of this same clay chemical pattern.

Three of the Rouen-type jugs from Exeter, which are thought to represent local production in the vicinity of Rouen, are also associated with this group, though four others form a separate but close chemical group to left of the main group. All those pottery types which fall into this central grouping seem to share a common origin; it seems a significant finding that so many types appear to be using the same clay resource. Although Dufournier (1981) carried out initial work on the clay resources of this area, we do not unfortunately have sufficient analyses to say whether the same clay chemical pattern exists over a small or wide area, that is whether a single clay source was used or there were multiple sources at different locations.

Apart from the two red-painted wares from Tresco that form part of the main chemical group, another five form a dense cluster to the lower left of it, partly overlapping the pair of French white wares also from Tresco Channel and one of the western or northern French jugs from Exeter (**44**). Three other Exeter jugs share a common clay pattern just below the centre of Fig. 17.35 (**42**, **45** and **47**); two others are part of the main group (**43** and **49**), while two others differ chemically from them and from each other (**46** and **48**). This selection of jugs therefore appears to include the products of several quite different locations/ workshops.

Separate from the main Exeter group, sherds in the upper left of Fig. 17.35 may represent another clay pattern and source, shared in common. All three highly decorated wares are in this group (**39–41**), together with four Rouen-type wares (**35–8**): the other three form a small cluster in the main group (**32–4**). Two unglazed Normandy white wares also belong (**5** and **13**), while the rest are in the main group. Likewise two north or west French jugs are present (**46** and **48**), again with other examples having a different clay chemistry.

Comparison by PCA of the Exeter sherds, the northern French wares from Tresco Channel, and earlier ICPS analyses of such wares from other sites

While the analyses of wares found on the Isles of Scilly have provided a significant database against which to compare the Exeter data, there exist analyses carried out previously by ICP-atomic emission only (*i.e.* not including a significant number of trace elements measurable only by ICP-mass spectrometry). Principal among these previous analyses have been those by the late Alan Vince on northern French white wares (summarised in Vince 2011), and those of the author arising from the find of a sherd of Hamwic fabric 127 from Padstow, in Cornwall (Hughes 2002–3), and small projects on pottery found in Scotland (Hughes 2015c).

The database of ICPS analyses on northern French white wares made by Alan Vince (2005; 2011; Hall *et al.* 2012) included: 'Rouen' early glazed wares (EGW: analyses V1289–1297 in the online ICPS database Vince 2010); wasters from the 8th-century kiln at La Londe, near Rouen (La Londe: analyses V2220–30); northern French unglazed wares and early Rouen wares from Perth, in Scotland (Hall *et al.* 2012; PERTH205–9, 218, 224 and 245); northern French white wares from Aberdeen, in Scotland (Hughes 2015c); and Normandy gritty ware from Leith, in Scotland (Vince and Jones 2005, LRW1–9).

In the Padstow project the following were analysed: three further examples of Hamwic fabric 127 from the South-West Peninsula (two from Exeter and one from Barnstaple; Hughes 2002–3, nos. 6–8); three Normandy gritty wares (nos. 10–12) and one red-painted sand-tempered vessel of Beauvais type (no. 13) from Exeter; and five examples of Late Saxon north French white ware from Southampton (nos, 1–5).

Whereas the initial principal components analysis on the Exeter sherds arose from both atomic emission and mass spectrometry ICPS, these comparative analyses by atomic emission reduced the statistical tests to 28 elements. PCA was applied, and the first principal component accounted for 36% of the variation in composition, correlated positively with most elements but negatively with titanium and to a lesser extent calcium and chromium. Such positive correlation is very common in archaeological ceramics studies, with the first principal component representing broad differences in clay chemistry caused by different proportions of diluting temper in the body fabric (natural or added, often quartz silt or sand). The second and third components contained a further 12% and 12% respectively of the chemical variation, so a cumulative 60% of the chemical variation in the pottery was summarised in just these three components.

While the plots of both the first and second components, and of the second and third, were examined to interpret the results, and the first two showed significant patterning in the various pottery groups represented, it was felt that the plot of the second and third components would provide a more realistic interpretation of the ICPS results since the 'temper dilution' effect was no longer a part of it. This again showed a main grouping of the Exeter samples, including the Exeter glazed white wares and redwares, and the unglazed Normandy white wares. The three additional Hamwic fabric 127 sherds formed a small group within this main group, close to the other example from Exeter (**1**), and also to two glazed white wares and redwares (**20** and **23**) and two northern or western French jugs (**48** and **49**).

There were some differences between the Exeter samples and some of the extra data added for this test, including the unglazed wares from the kiln at La Londe analysed by Alan Vince, which were distinctly higher on the second component. These overlapped with many of the Normandy gritty wares from Ronaldson's Wharf, in Leith, but were quite distinct from any Normandy gritty wares from Exeter. They also overlapped with seven of the eight examples on northern French imports analysed from Aberdeen (Hughes 2015c), and the northern French wares from Perth analysed by Vince (Hall *et al.* 2012). The Leith gritty wares fell into two chemical groups, the larger one containing 23–9% alumina, for which a suggested origin is in the area around the Cotentin Peninsula, where a kiln has been located, although no kiln samples have been analysed to confirm this suggestion. The smaller group from Leith contained over 30% alumina and were Normandy products, but it was concluded that they were not from Lower Seine Valley (Vince and Jones 2005). The Exeter Normandy gritty wares are significantly lower in alumina (15.0–17.9%), and among the other Exeter types only two exceed 20%: **41**, a highly decorated ware, and **46**, a northern or western French jug. The principal components plots of this combined dataset confirm that the Exeter Normandy gritty wares are not related chemically to the Leith examples.

The early glazed wares analysed by Vince (2011: ROUEN EGW), however, formed a chemical sub-group on the edge of the main group which also included some of the Exeter and Tresco groups, namely on the second and third components they overlapped with some of the red-painted wares from Tresco, one of the Normandy gritty wares from Exeter (**31**), two of the Normandy highly decorated wares (**39** and **40**), two of the unglazed Normandy (**5** and **8**), two of the northern or western French jugs (**42** and **46**) and two of the Rouen-type wares (**36** and **38**). These all appear to share a very similar clay chemistry.

Conclusions

The ICPS analyses of the northern French pottery from sites in Exeter shows a general composition pattern consistent with production within a specific region but with separation into distinct groups by pottery type and chronology. Comparison of results with northern French wares found in Tresco Channel, and other sites in the Isles of Scilly, has complemented the Exeter samples, throwing further light on the chemical relationships between the many types of pottery produced in northern France.

Further comparison against earlier ICPS analyses of northern French pottery by several authors have added further chemical groups to the pattern. Among the groups which did show significant chemical differences from the rest of the northern French wares were Bristol Pottery Type 192 and the green-glazed rouletted white wares; they formed compact self-contained groups suggesting that these particular sherds each came from an individual source. Normandy gritty ware showed three composition groups, suggesting either quite distinct or geographically separate workshops, or at least three different clay sources. The glazed white wares and redwares from Exeter form a single composition group, to which also belong examples of the northern or western French jugs, the Hamwic 127 vessel and two of the three Beauvais-type red-painted wares. Including other examples of Hamwic 127 in the second statistical test showed that all the known analysed examples have a similar clay chemistry, corresponding to the main chemical group. Also part of the main group are all but two of the unglazed Normandy white wares, as were two of the red-painted Normandy wares from Nut Rock, in the Isles of Scilly. Three of the Rouen-type wares from Exeter are also included in this group, though four others form a close but separate chemical group. All those pottery types which fall into the main chemical group seem to share a common origin or clay resource. The early glazed wares analysed by Alan Vince formed a sub-group within the main group which also included most of the red-painted wares from Tresco, and of the Exeter sherds one Normandy gritty ware, two each of the highly decorated wares, unglazed Normandy wares, north or west French jugs, and Rouen-type wares.

Some other types are slightly different from this major chemical group: five red-painted wares from Tresco group together, but apart from the two from Nut Rock, partly overlapping a pair of French white wares from Tresco Channel. Three of the Exeter northern or western French jugs share a common clay pattern just separated from the main chemical group which includes two others; yet another two differ chemically from them and from each other. The Exeter samples of this type of jug appear to include the products of several quite different locations/workshops. Also different from the Exeter samples were unglazed wares from the kiln at La Londe, a site close to the river Seine, about 25 km from Rouen. These were analysed by Alan Vince and overlapped chemically with many of the Normandy gritty wares from Ronaldson's Wharf, in Leith, but were quite distinct from any Normandy gritty wares from Exeter.

Some of the pottery types exhibited a single chemical profile (*e.g.* Hamwic 127, Rouen early glazed wares, highly decorated wares, and glazed white wares and redwares). While these appear to be products of a single kiln or group of kilns, it may be that examples from other consumer sites might differ, suggesting multiple kilns producing the same ware. Many types do show more than one chemical profile and may be examples of this: Normandy gritty wares, Rouen-type wares, red-painted Normandy wares, and unglazed Normandy white wares. There were also single chemical profiles for two types which fell slightly outside the main group and overlapped no others: Bristol Pottery Type 192, and the green-glazed rouletted wares.

It will be interesting to see, now that the chemical profiles of many types of northern French wares have been established in the course of this project, whether analyses of more examples of these import types from other sites conform to the present patterns or indicate new profiles (*i.e.* sources).

Appendix 17.3

Chemical characterisation of Exeter fabrics 40 and 42 by ICP

Michael J. Hughes

Introduction

Fabrics 40 and 42 were first distinguished as distinct wares in the large collections of medieval pottery from Exeter; they evidently represent a production centre or centres supplying the Exeter market (above). The two fabrics are described by Taylor (Chapter 17, above).

The three aims of this investigation were to see whether chemical analysis using Inductively Coupled Plasma Spectrometry (ICPS) would confirm or refute the proposal that these are separate fabric groupings; to establish whether the two fabrics were related; and to try to shed light on their place of production. The study forms one of a series of ICPS projects undertaken by the writer on the medieval ceramics of South-West England (Hughes 1998; 2002; 2003a; 2005; 2010a; 2014a; 2015b; 2019).

Sixteen samples of these two fabrics (ten of fabric 40, six of 42) were selected for ICPS analysis, together with four samples found at Exwell Barton, in Powderham (Allan 2014) and a single fragment of a jug from Launceston Castle, in Cornwall, which was chosen to check the reliability of the identification of one of the more distant points in the distribution of these wares (Brown *et al.* 2006, 288, fig. 9.6, P46). One further sample of fabric 40 (EAR 3, no. 1402) had been analysed previously as a comparative sample in the report on pottery from Haycroft Farm, in Membury (Hughes 2002). The methodology employed was that described in EAPIT 2, Appendix 17.2.

A possible indicator of production in Exeter itself might be similarity to the Late Saxon pottery made in the Bedford Garage kiln in the city, and seven samples were analysed as comparative samples. Thin-sectioning of Bedford Garage Ware by Brown and Vince (1984, 32) identified a small quantity of acid igneous rock fragments alongside quartz, chert and sandstone. The full list of samples analysed is given in Table 17.5 and their ICPS results in online Table 17.6. The average concentrations of elements in the Exeter fabric samples and comparative analyses are given in online Table 17.7.

Results of the ICPS chemical analyses

The examples of fabrics 40 and 42 analysed from Exeter formed two entirely consistent and different composition groups, each group containing examples of only one fabric. The two fabric groups contained similar levels of iron, calcium, titanium, manganese and the trace elements chromium, lanthanum and cerium (online Table 17.6). However, they differed in that fabric 40 had significantly less aluminium, sodium and strontium than fabric 42, but more magnesium, potassium and the trace element zirconium (which occurs in the heavy mineral zircon). The differences support the contention that the two fabrics are distinct, although the chemical differences are such that fabric 42 does not appear to be simply a coarser version of fabric 40, since in that case the elements would usually all be systematically lower.

A notable feature of both Exeter fabrics is the relatively high concentration of potassium, highest in the fabric 40 sherds. The presence of mica has been noted in fabric 40 sherds, and this is probably the mineral responsible for the increased potassium content: the weathering of feldspar (present in many igneous rocks including granites) results in the formation of mica and clay minerals (Krauskopf and Bird 1995, 98). Ferromagnesian minerals are also significantly present in granites, contributing large amounts of iron and magnesium to the resulting clays. Both fabric 40 and 42 contain significant amounts of iron, and fabric 40 also has elevated levels of magnesium, supporting the suggestion that the clays from which it is made derive from the weathering of granite.

The four Exwell Barton sherds and the Launceston Castle sample match consistently in terms of chemical

Table 17.5 Samples examined by ICPS. Samples are from Exeter unless stated otherwise

Sample No.	*Fabric*	*Site and context*	*Publication No.*
1	Exeter 40	Goldsmith St (Site 39) 256	EAR3, no. 1362
2	"	Trichay St (Site 42) 215	*Ibid.*, no. 1404
3	"	Trichay St (Site 42) 215	*Ibid.*, no. 1405
4	"	Trichay St (Site 42) 215	*Ibid.*, no. 1408
5	"	Queen St (Site 68) 112	*Ibid.*, no. 1427
6	"	Queen St (Site 68) 112	*Ibid.*, no. 1430
7	"	Goldsmith St (Site 37/39) 214	*Ibid.*, not drawn
8	Exeter 42	Wyman's Well 1950	*Ibid.*, no. 1394
9	"	Queen St (Site 68) 112	*Ibid.*, no. 1431
10	"	Queen St (Site 68) 112	*Ibid.*, no. 1434
11	"	Goldsmith St Site 37/39) 256	*Ibid.*, no. 1359
12	Bedford Garage Ware	Cathedral Close (Site 40), unstrat.	Unpub.
13	"	Trichay St (Site 42) unstrat	"
14	"	Preston St (Site 42) unstrat	"
15	"	Princesshay (Site 156) 3909	"
16	"	Princesshay (Site 156) 2744	"
17	"	Princesshay (Site 156) 5856	"
18	"	Princesshay (Site 156) 3797	"
19	Exeter 40	Exwell Barton, in Powderham 194	Allan 2014b, not drawn
20	"	Exwell Barton, in Powderham 062	*Ibid.*, 151, no. 3
21	Exeter 42	Exwell Barton, in Powderham 243	*Ibid.*, not drawn
22	"	Exwell Barton, in Powderham 033	*Ibid.*, not drawn
23	Exeter 40	Launceston Castle 2391	Brown *et al.* 2006, 46

composition with the respective sherds from Exeter in the two fabrics, so these sherds do appear to be typical examples of these fabrics, and not just apparently similar visually.

Interpretation of the ICP analyses using Principal Components Analysis and Discriminant Analysis

To make more progress with understanding the relationships between fabrics 40 and 42, and to compare them with pottery made at known production centres, it was necessary to use multivariate statistics, which simultaneously considers the concentrations of many elements in each sample. For this investigation, Principal Components Analysis (PCA) and Discriminant Analysis (DA) were used (Tabachnick and Fidell 2007); descriptions of their application to archaeology have been given elsewhere (*e.g.* Baxter 1994; 2003; Shennan 1997). The statistical package SPSS Version 15 was used for this work (Pellant 2007). For interpreting the statistical plots produced in this project (Figs 17.36 and 17.37), each individual item analysed has been shown by a symbol for either the fabric group to which it belongs, or the site where it was found. The colour of the symbol denotes its fabric type or site. Such plots are effectively chemical 'maps' for the items analysed, and if the ceramics within a group are made of the same clay, they will plot in the same part of the Figure.

Discriminant Analysis

The ICPS analyses of Table 17.5 were combined with previous analyses of material from sites in this part of south-western England, including Bedford Garage kiln wasters from Exeter and pottery from four sites in southern Somerset and eastern Devon: Donyatt and Castle Neroche (southern Somerset) and Hemyock and Haycroft Farm, in Membury (eastern Devon). Sixteen elements were used for Discriminant Analysis (indicated in online Table 17.6) and the results can be shown as a two-dimensional plot (Fig. 17.36). From the Fig. 17.36, it is immediately clear that the vessels from three southern Somerset/eastern Devon sites, namely Haycroft Farm, Castle Neroche and Donyatt, are chemically similar to each other.

The relationships between the fabric 40 and 42 sherds and these comparative groups are rather interesting but slightly unexpected. The fabric 42 sherds lie in the lower part of the Discriminant Analysis plot between the three southern Somerset sites, which are closely clustered, and the Bedford Garage kiln sherds. The bedrock geology within Exeter itself is Permian, though alluvial deposits cover extensive areas of the city, and were probably the source of the Bedford Garage material. The distinction

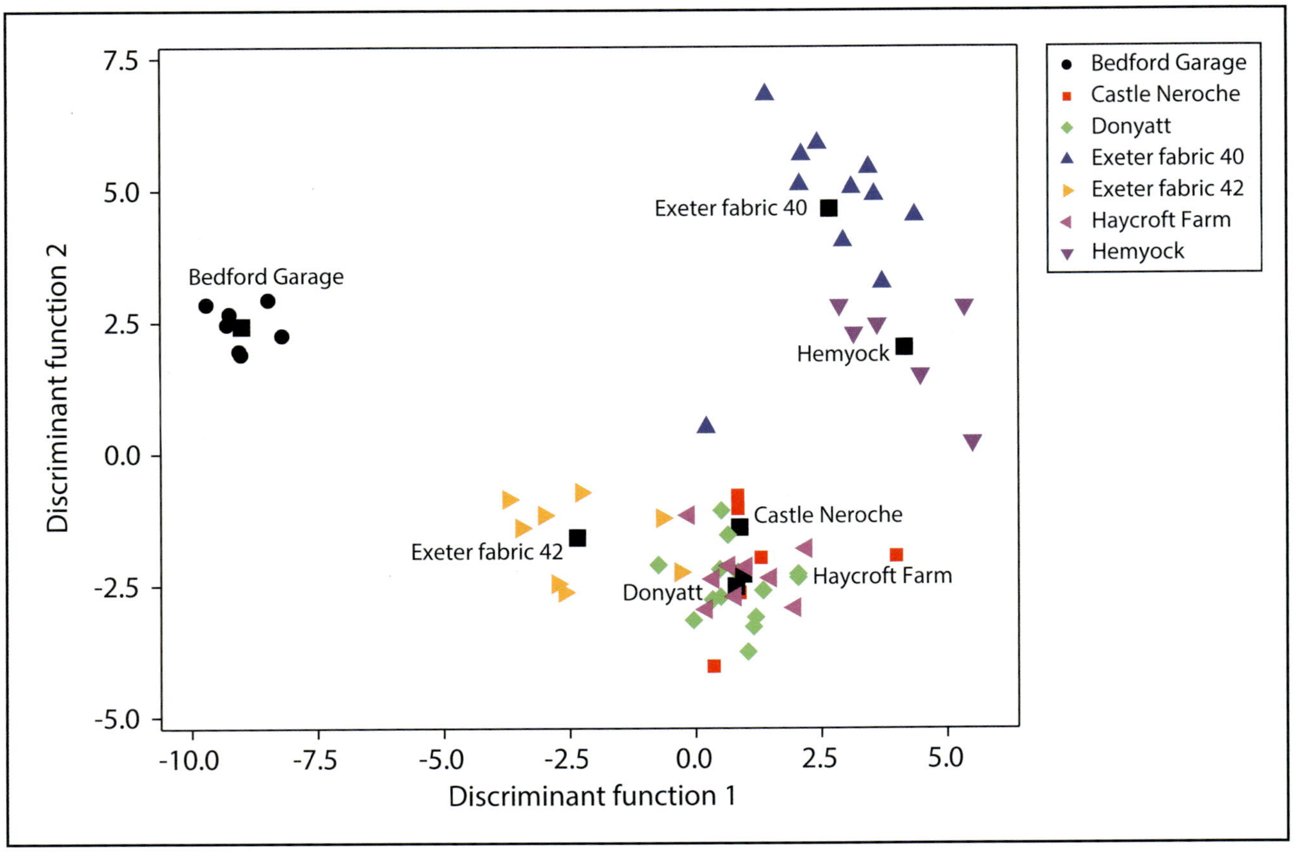

Fig. 17.36 Discriminant Analysis of the ICPS data on Exeter fabric 40 and 42 sherds, and comparative material from other sites. The horizontal axis plots the first discriminant function (containing 54% of the difference between groups), and the vertical the second function (a further 32%). The dark numbered squares mark the centre of the distribution of each group. There are close chemical similarities between the pottery of the southern Somerset sites of Donyatt and Castle Neroche, as well as Haycroft Farm, in Devon (prepared by Michael Hughes)

from the Bedford Garage material would suggest that the origin of fabric 42 is not in the immediate vicinity of Exeter. If the relatively close distance on this plot between the fabric 42 sherds and the southern Somerset sherds is taken as an indication of closer chemical similarity to the latter, a possible interpretation (not the only one) for this intermediate chemistry would be that the fabric 42 source is not in Exeter itself, but more in a direction towards southern Somerset. A caution to be noted is the current lack of data from comparative material made around Exeter and the Exe Valley; if samples from more sites in the area were analysed, any variation in local clay chemistry would be clearer, so the present interpretation remains a working hypothesis. However, the chemical differences between the fabric 42 sherds and Bedford Garage Ware are clear: the Exeter fabric 42 sherds have more aluminium, iron, magnesium and sodium but less strontium, so they are not closely related chemically.

The fabric 40 sherds were equally puzzling as a group. They are chemically distinct from the fabric 42 sherds, something that first emerged some time ago as two pairs of fabric 40 and 42 sherds were analysed by ICPS in the study of the pottery from Haycroft Farm, in Membury, where they separated clearly in a Discriminant Analysis plot (Hughes 2002, 69, fig. 4). The present Discriminant Analysis of the ICPS results places the fabric 40 sherds closest to the Hemyock group, though it is clear they are not overlapping in chemistry. The chemical difference between fabric 40 and the Bedford Garage sherds would argue for different geological deposits for the two, suggesting a source distinct from the volcanic outcrop in central Exeter which is probably responsible for much of the chemical signature of the Bedford Garage Wares.

The ICPS analysis shows the fabric 40 sherds to be chemically of a similar pattern to the Hemyock sherds, though that site is distant from Exeter. Hemyock lies on the slope below Upper Greensand deposits of the Blackdown Hills, from which its clay has weathered (BGS 2009). Less than 4 km north-east of Hemyock is Clayhidon, from which four clays were analysed by Vince (2010: analyses V0738–9 and V0741–2). The average of the samples from Clayhidon Wood on similar deposits to Hemyock (Table 17.5) shows similarities in the pattern of major and trace elements to the Hemyock average (including notably high potassium and iron), though distinguishable from the Hemyock average. Clay from Clayhidon churchyard, by contrast, lies on different deposits (BGS 2009: clay with flints) and differs in containing significantly more aluminium, titanium and rare earths but less potassium.

The same Upper Greensand geological formation at Hemyock and Clayhidon (the Blackdown facies) has, however, a westerly outlier forming the highest parts of the Haldon Hills just to the south-west of Exeter (BGS 1975, 67 (fig. 18), 70; BGS 2001). A larger outcrop lies around Great Haldon, with a smaller outcrop near Little Haldon. Clays derived from these deposits would, like the Hemyock and Clayhidon material, be rich in potassium and other characteristic elements. It is possible therefore that clays formed on the eastern down-slope below the Haldon Hills down to the Exe Estuary and towards Exeter (the slope lies on Permian deposits of granite debris), could have a similar type of chemistry to those formed at Hemyock below Upper Greensand deposits. Further investigation would be needed whether this hypothesis based on the ICPS analysis alone was supported by the actual mineralogy described for Exeter fabric 40. Taylor (above) has noted that fabric 40 contains larger rounded quartz grains (*i.e.* traces of beach sand) which would be consistent with an origin in either the Teign or Exe Estuary; the distribution of finds of the fabric favours the latter (see below). An alternative source for the fabric 40 material in the region of Exeter could be Carboniferous deposits further north in the Exe Valley (BGS 1975, 676, fig. 18), different from the alluvial deposits on which Exeter itself lies.

Principal Components Analysis

All the samples included in the Discriminant Analysis were subjected to a PCA using the same chemical elements. This showed, as expected, small 'spreads' for the individual types of pottery, while still maintaining a clear separation of Exeter fabric 40 and Hemyock sherds from all the rest. The Bedford Garage sherds intermingled with the fabric 42 samples. The principal components analysis mainly reflected the major element differences between the respective groups, whereas

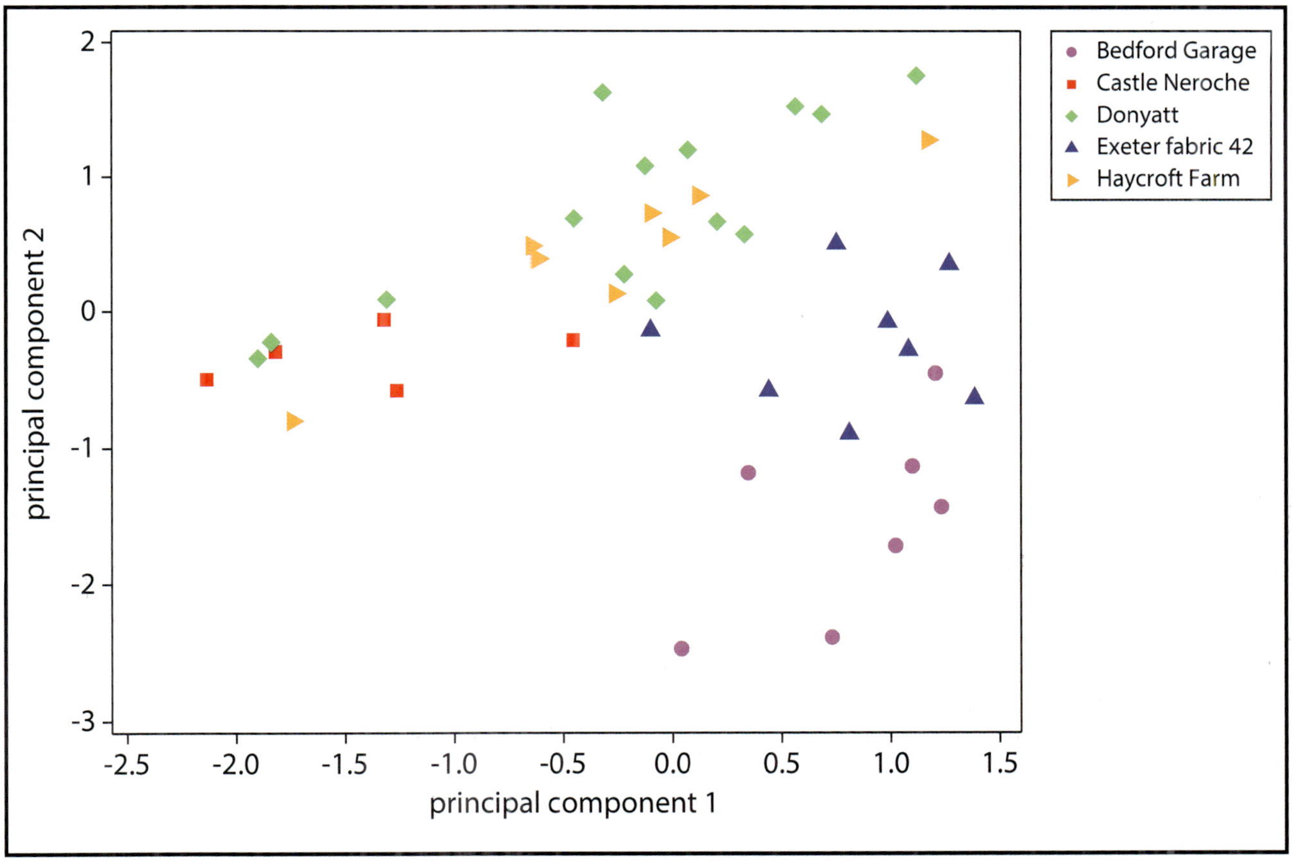

Fig. 17.37 Plot of the first two principal components in samples of Exeter fabric 42 and other comparative sites. Principal component 1 (containing 38% of the variation in all samples) had pottery richer in all elements except calcium and iron (towards the right of the plot).Principal component 2 (26% of the variation) had pottery which was richer in the elements magnesium, iron and calcium but lower amounts of zirconium (towards the top of the plot). The two sherds of fabric 42 from Exwell Barton are closest to the Donyatt/ Haycroft Farm samples (drawn by Michael Hughes)

the discriminant analysis (looking for elements which distinguished between groups) tended to reflect specific trace elements.

Since the statistical tests on all the samples and comparative material showed a similarity between the fabric 40 sherds and the sherds from Hemyock, these samples alone were included in a second stage of PCA. This showed a chemical distinction between fabric 40 and the Hemyock samples, though they share some distinctive features compared with the other pottery, including significantly higher amounts of magnesium (3–4% average) and potassium (4–5%) (Fig. 17.37).

A third principal components test was carried out on all the samples not included in the second test, to see the relationship between the Exeter fabric 42 samples and the comparative material. In this test (Fig. 17.37) the Bedford Garage Wares plotted closest to the Exeter fabric 42 samples (mid to lower part of the right side of Fig. 17.37). Curiously, however, the two sherds from Exwell Barton plotted closest to the Donyatt and Haycroft Farm samples, though still on the fringes of the Exeter fabric 42 sherds. On this figure, the Donyatt, Haycroft Farm and Castle Neroche samples are distributed in approximately that order in a series of overlapping spreads running diagonally from left to upper right across the upper part of the plot, indicating a chemical similarity between these three sites all of which are on Lias clays.

Conclusions

Exeter fabric 40 samples showed a consistent chemical composition in all the sherds of this type analysed so far by ICPS. The fabric has a chemical composition similar to the pottery analysed from Hemyock in the Blackdown Hills on the borders of Devon and Somerset, in the region of Upper Greensand deposits. There is, however, a westerly outlier of these same deposits not far from Exwell Barton on the west bank of the Exe Estuary, in the Haldon Hills. It appears a working hypothesis that clays derived ultimately from the area below the Haldon Hills may have been used to make the Exeter fabric 40 sherds. It would explain the chemical difference between the fabric 40 sherds and the local Exeter clay chemistry, as exemplified by the Bedford Garage Ware, which is chemically different from fabric 40 and very probably made of alluvial clays.

Exeter fabric 42 has a different but also consistent chemical composition in all the sherds of this type analysed so far by ICPS. Its chemical composition is similar to sherds of Bedford Garage Ware from Exeter, although not identical. The analyses might suggest that its place of production was somewhere between Exeter and the south Somerset production sites of which the nearest was Donyatt. Chemically it is more likely that the fabric 42 production site was located on a geologically similar clay to the Bedford Garage sherds, which would imply somewhere associated with Permian deposits rather than the Lias to the east of Exeter (*e.g.* Donyatt).

Appendix 17.4

Comment on the plasma spectrometry (ICP) analyses of 'Normandy' tiles from Devon in relation to tiles from Kilkenny

Michael J. Hughes

Introduction

Three typical examples of the white ware floor-tiles from sites in South Devon were submitted for analysis in the EAPIT project. They came from Princesshay in Exeter (Site 156; sample 3.50), Ashburton church (sample 3.51, Marc Steinmetzer excavation) and West Alvington churchyard (sample 3.52, AC Archaeology watching brief), and were analysed though the University of Durham. All three were of the typical white ware fabric rather than the pink/red clay which the tilery also used. A recent report on the analyses of two late medieval floor-tiles of the same sort from Kilkenny, Ireland, concluded that they were very probably of 'Normandy' origin (Hughes 2018); the Devon analyses used the same plasma spectrometry (ICP) technique, but with some additional chemical elements.

Results and discussion

The results are given in online Table 17.8, which shows the Devon tiles with those from Kilkenny, alongside comparanda cited in the Kilkenny report. The additional chemical elements analysed in the Devon tiles but not in the Kilkenny tiles or comparanda are cited at the end. In the earlier report the results for the major elements were cited as the element, but here they have been converted into oxides (the normal format for citing data on geological materials, which has been adopted for analyses of archaeological ceramics too).

The overall chemical patterns of the three Devon tiles are very similar to each other, and to the two Kilkenny tiles, confirming the latter's identity with the medieval 'Normandy' tiles in the typical white ware fabric. Two of the Devon finds – those from Princesshay and West Alvington – are closer chemically to each other than the third, from Ashburton. The latter has slightly higher concentrations of almost all elements, both the major and minor/trace elements, including the extra elements cited at the foot of the table. These include many of the rare earth elements, and again the Princesshay and West Alvington tiles have comparable concentrations of these elements, while the Ashburton fragment shows slightly elevated levels of all of them. The first two Devon tiles are close to the analyses of the Kilkenny tiles, sharing their slightly lower concentrations of many elements. The alumina levels of the Devon tiles are low like those from Kilkenny, and the previous discussion relating this to probable high levels of diluting temper in the clay fabric applies here as well.

All the features of the Kilkenny tiles noted in the previous report are shared by the three Devon tiles, including the very low concentrations of almost all the major elements except aluminium, and with very characteristic and unusually low concentration of potassium. This pattern was cited in the previous report as very similar to analyses of northern French white wares including several examples of wasters from a kiln at La Londe in the Rouen *arrondissement* on the west bank of the Seine, which had potassium contents of 0.4–0.6% (Vince 2005). Analyses by Dufournier (1981, 86, tab. 4) of numerous clay samples collected across Normandy showed that Rouen lay at the centre of a wide region of silica-rich clays dominated by kaolinite, with potassium levels below 1%; one particular group of clays was prospected around La Londe and these are cited in online Table 17.8. Apart from having lower aluminium (and higher iron which could have come with addition of an impure sand), the Kilkenny and Devon tiles fit the pattern of the clays exactly, while the analyses of wasters from the La Londe kiln cited above fits even closer (Vince 2005).

Conclusions

The analyses of the three late medieval 'Normandy' tiles from sites in Devon share the characteristics and unusual chemical pattern of the two floor-tiles from Kilkenny. It can therefore be concluded that the Kilkenny tiles are of the same 'Normandy' type and of the typical white ware fabric used by the tilery. The Devon tiles from Princesshay and West Alvington churchyard are closer chemically to each other and to the Kilkenny tiles than the third from Ashburton church. The latter has slightly higher concentrations of almost all elements and may lie in its fabric containing less diluting temper. This suggests slight differences in chemical profiles among these tiles, but the close similarity of the four samples from Kilkenny, Princesshay and West Alvington which belong to one specific chemical profile confirms production in a common source.

18

The South European Pottery, AD 1250–1550

Alejandra Gutiérrez and Hugo Blake, with contributions from Kamal Badreshany and Michael J. Hughes

Introduction

This chapter comprises four sections. The first is a discussion by Alejandra Gutiérrez of the Spanish and Portuguese ceramics found in Exeter, reviewing the city collection in the light of recent research on this subject. The second, by Hugo Blake, describes and discusses the examples of Italian and Low Countries tin-glazed pottery dating before 1550 excavated in the city. Both accounts are supported by reports on the programmes of ICP-AES and ICP-MS analysis which have formed part of the EAPIT project; Kamal Badreshany undertook the study of the Spanish and Portuguese ceramics, and Michael J. Hughes the Italian and Low Countries maiolica. Their reports form Appendices 18.1 and 18.2; detailed catalogue descriptions of individual sherds will be found online in Appendices 18.3 and 18.4.

Spanish and Portuguese ceramics found at Exeter
by Alejandra Gutiérrez

Pottery imports from southern Europe, with their distinctive colours and shapes, attracted the early attention of medieval researchers and archaeologists in Britain, such as Gerald Dunning (1961), but it was John Hurst who first published a complete corpus of British finds, later updated and complemented by those from the Netherlands (Hurst 1977; Hurst *et al.* 1986). Given the limited and in many cases non-existent data available in Spain and Portugal at the time, almost 50 years ago, this was a remarkable achievement. John Hurst was also the motor behind the beginnings of a major country-wide programme of fabric analysis, first by Neutron Activation Analysis at the British Museum, then by Inductively Coupled Plasma Atomic Emission (ICP–AE), which would help identify pottery not only in northern Europe, but also in the production areas themselves. In Exeter imported ceramics have been systematically identified and recorded both from the city and the surrounding region by John Allan during the last few decades. His detailed catalogue published in 1984 is still an exemplary and invaluable companion which was completed and updated in 1995 in a regional survey of Spanish imports in South-West England (Allan 1984a, hereafter EAR 3; Allan 1995). The *Exeter: a Place in Time* project presented the opportunity to re-examine these finds and consider them in the light of more recent discoveries regarding production made both in Spain and Portugal.

The text presented here uses John Allan's catalogues as a starting point, although all the pottery has been visually re-examined by the author (excepting some of the scattered finds of Seville containers and Portuguese coarseware, and a few other sherds, which were not readily accessible in the collections), and some sherds have been analysed as part of this project (Appendix 18.1 and online Appendix 18.3). This fresh analysis of the assemblage has in some cases produced changes in the identification, form, date or drawing which are included below without cross-reference to earlier works. All the sherds examined have been numbered individually (ID number) in order to populate the database with unique finds entries, but they are ordered below according to source and date. All catalogued sherds are from Exeter.

Spain

A wide range of Spanish pottery has been found in Exeter and Devon in general. A total of 203 different Spanish vessels (444 sherds) is recorded on the Exeter Archaeology inventories, which record more than 90% of the finds from excavations in the city (Allan and Langman 1997; Langman and Allan 1991; 1999b; listings for later sites). These can be divided broadly into glazed wares (35 vessels) and coarsewares (168 vessels); two wall tiles

Fig. 18.1 Map of the main places mentioned in the text (drawn by Alejandra Gutiérrez)

have also been recovered. Coarsewares are vessels that do not have a glazed surface and in this context the term has nothing to do with the quality or use of the pot. The vessels are listed below by production area (Fig. 18.1).

Málaga area

Only tin-glazed pottery is thought to have been imported to England from the Málaga region of southern Spain. Most of these vessels are covered in a white glaze which served as a background for painted decoration, although this rarely survives. In fact, one of the characteristics of these early imports is their badly preserved glaze, and more often than not, the absence of any decoration. When decoration does survive it consists of motifs painted in gold colour, or in gold and blue. This type of decoration is termed 'lustreware' and those from the Málaga region are traditionally dated to the 13th and 14th centuries. When no decoration is preserved, vessels found in British excavations are generally assumed to have been lustrewares.

During the 13th and 14th centuries Málaga formed part of the Islamic Kingdom of Granada, the last area in Spain under Muslim control, until it was reconquered by Christians in 1487. The port city was famous for its lustrewares and contemporary sources refer to its production there (and in Murcia and Almería) in the middle of the 13th century (described by Ibn Said in 1240–1; Llubiá 1967, 93); Malagan pottery had 'no rival', according to Fedel Allah (in 1320; *ibid.*, 96). More specifically, 14th-century sources claim that there was 'no lustreware like the one produced in Málaga', according to Ahmed Ben-Hayha in 1337; 'all countries competed to acquire the lustreware made in Málaga', according to Aben al-Jatib and the lustreware from Málaga was 'exported far away' according to Ibn Batuta in the middle of the 14th century (Osma 1912, 33–4). These exports in the late 13th and early 14th century are confirmed by written sources, such as taxes at Collioure recorded on the south-east coast of France, where Malagan pottery (*obra de terra de Malicha*) is documented in 1297 or 1316, according to various authors (Gual Camarena 1976, 167; López Elum 1986, 173).

Early exports are also recorded in England, where Malagan dishes and jugs (*discorum et picherorum terre de Malyk*) arrived at Sandwich in 1303 (Salzman 1931; Childs 1995, 27). In all these instances pottery from Málaga is recorded by name, but there is little doubt that the arrival of pottery 'of strange colours' (*olle terrene extranei coloris*) for Eleanor of Castile in 1289 must refer to lustrewares (Childs 1995, 26); the consignment arrived in Southampton and its look and colours were apparently so different from any other kind of pottery that the customs official did not have the vocabulary to describe it in his list. This is still the earliest reference to lustrewares recorded in England, and probably in northern Europe as a whole.

There has been some progress in recent years in documenting archaeologically the production of lustrewares in Málaga itself. Excavations prior to building development in the city have uncovered kilns of both medieval and later date, which produced pottery of different sorts, including lustrewares (Pineda 2004; Sabastro 2011). So far these discoveries do little more than confirm the local production of lustrewares, without helping to refine our understanding of forms, decoration or dating. Most of the material is still under study, and assemblages are mostly small and very fragmented, at least those published so far. Nevertheless, this is the first time that the well-known documentary references to local lustreware mentioned above can be matched by physical remains of workshops of the same date.

Recent research also suggests that lustreware production began in Spain much earlier than has previously been thought, and was manufactured at a wider range of centres. There are indications of 11th-century production in the south and even the centre of the country, with workshops now known in Murcia (Navarro Palazón 1990; Navarro Palazón and Jiménez 1995; Zozaya *et al.* 1995; Barceló and Heidenreich 2014). Although examples are found in the Mediterranean, for example in Italy, none of these earlier types seems to have reached northern Europe.

So far nothing has come to light to prove that lustrewares might have been manufactured nearby at Granada. Local production of lustreware-and-blue wall tiles has been documented there, but tiling was an itinerant job and does not imply that it co-existed with the manufacture of tablewares.

Strictly speaking, 'Málaga lustreware' refers in the UK to tin-glazed wares manufactured with fabrics containing schist inclusions, these appearing as dark red, shiny, hard, rounded grains. Variation in fabric colour (from orange to dark red, pink or greenish-grey) and occasional absence of inclusions might suggest that the group includes products from more than one centre or area in the region of Málaga, if not chronological disparities, but given the lack of well-characterised material at source, these differences are impossible to unravel at present; this is why some authors prefer to use the term 'Andalusian' or 'Málaga-type' instead. Málaga lustreware forms quite a distinctive group among Spanish imports and can be told apart from lustrewares manufactured at other Spanish centres, such as Valencia or Seville. It is characterised by a thin white glaze that decays very easily, often retaining the appearance of a dull white slip rather than a shiny glaze. The glaze covers the vessel all over, and decoration is usually painted in both gold and blue colours, although the lustre is often lost due to deposition processes. It appears in contexts of the late 13th (rare) and 14th centuries (more frequently). Although production is suspected until the end of the 15th century, when the city fell to Christian troops, few lustrewares have been found that can be dated securely to the 15th century, either in Málaga itself or abroad. By this century, the city was already receiving lustrewares from Valencia (for example, Puertas Tricas 1992) and the extent and volume of local production is unclear.

Only six sherds have been found in Exeter (Fig. 18.2; Table 18.1). They are all small, and only two preserve any decoration. To confirm their identification, three were subjected to chemical analysis as part of EAPIT; the results do not produce a tight group, but they certainly place these sherds apart from other places of manufacture such as Valencia (Appendix 18.1).

Although the assemblage is small, it does include some of the earliest dated examples found in Britain. Two sherds from two different pits from Goldsmith Street have been dated by their associated pottery to the second half of the 13th century (ID6, ID151). A further vessel is securely stratified in a pre-Dissolution context of the early 16th century (ID7); not enough decoration survives to find parallels and confirm whether this might be a late example, or an earlier vessel retained for a long time, or a residual sherd.

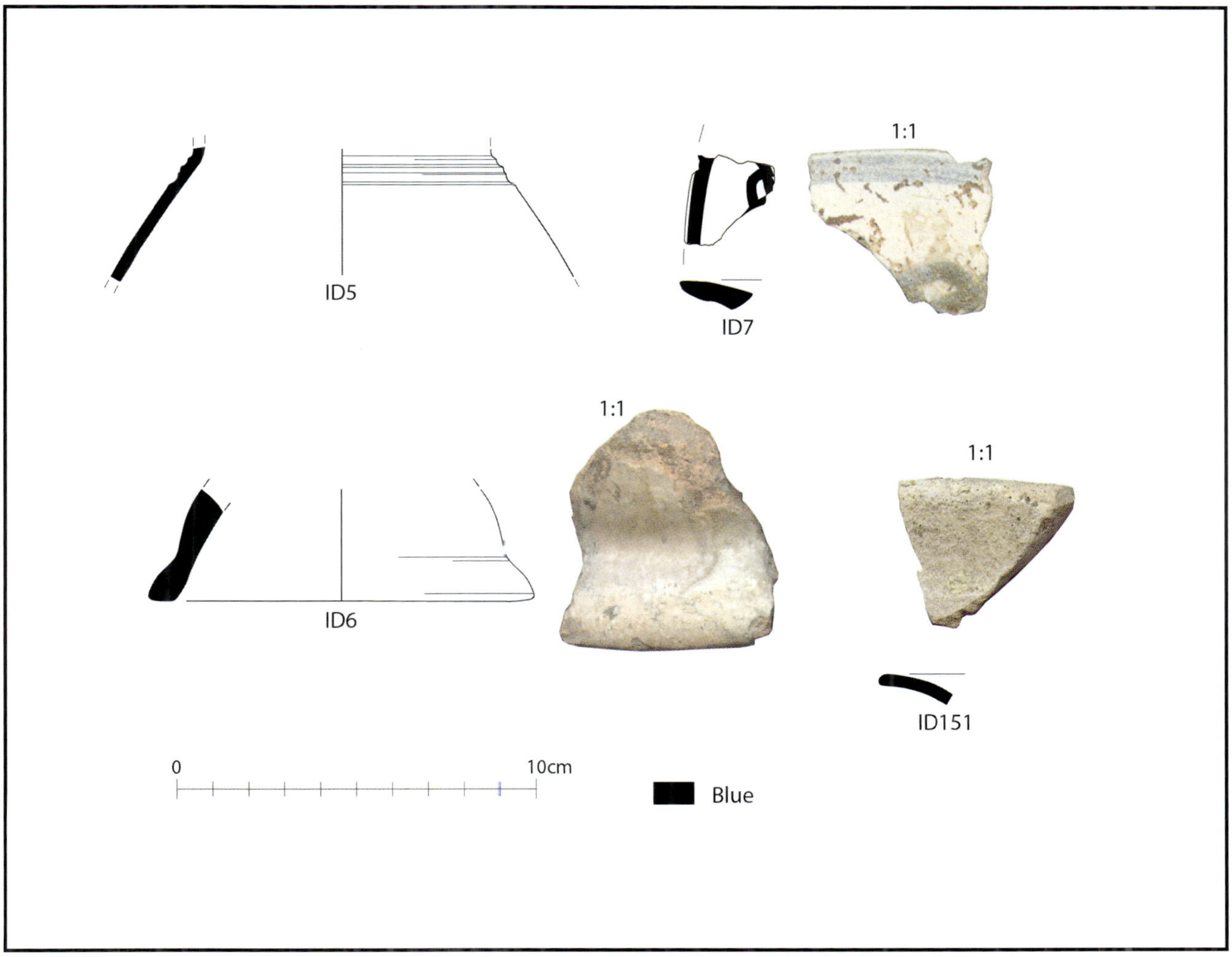

Fig. 18.2 Málaga lustreware (© Alejandra Gutiérrez)

Table 18.1 Málaga lustrewares found in Exeter (= sherds not drawn; E=early, L= late); for Site Numbers see Chapter 2 above*

ID	*Site No.: name and context*	*Context date*	*Nos. in EAR 3; Allan 1995*	*No. sherds/ vessels*	*Wt(g)*	*Durham ICP No.*
5	Site 43: High Street layer 141	L14/E15C	113; 3	1/1	8	EX18005: Málaga
6	Site 39: Goldsmith Street pit 215	Mid–L13C	1196; 1	1/1	9	EX18006: Málaga
7	Site 59: Polsloe Priory 1582/3	*c.* 1500	1553; 12	1/1	3	
151	Site 39: Goldsmith Street pit 247	Mid–L13C	22; 2	1/1	2	
152*	Site 37: Goldsmith Street pit 703	13/14C	Not listed; 4	1/1	2	
293*	Site 60: Preston Street pit 402	E16C	Listed p. 109; 134	1/1	17	EX18293: Málaga
Total				6/6	41	

Valencia area

With the exception of a single vessel, all the ceramics arriving in Exeter from the Valencia area are lustrewares. They all have a fine, light orange fabric with buff margins (larger, thicker forms may have a darker, reddish, fabric) and rare visible inclusions; under the microscope small limestone grains, clay relics and tiny spots of mica (never as large as flecks) may be visible (Vince 1982; Gerrard and Gutiérrez 1991, 129). The tin glaze is white and applied to both surfaces, including under the base. In contrast to similar ceramics from Málaga, Valencian glaze usually survives well, even when the lustre decoration is faded or lost.

Valencia gives its name to both the port city and also the modern province in central eastern Spain. A number of centres of production have been identified in the region from both documentary and archaeological evidence. Manises and Paterna, just outside Valencia city, are the best known because of the early publication of documentary evidence (*e.g.* Osma 1906; 1912; 1923; González Martí 1944). Kiln remains in Valencia itself confirm that the city also produced pottery, including lustrewares (Serrano 1994), but given the proximity of all these workshops and the uniformity of the local geology, identifying exact locations of production is complex at the moment. This might not be too relevant when trying to understand major trends in trade and exchange in the medieval period across Europe. Results from chemical analyses of Valencian pottery have produced sub-groups which might represent spatial or chronological groupings within the Valencia area, but without more reference material from kiln sites it is impossible to fine-tune the results. More importantly, this evidence can be used to distinguish Valencian ceramics from those manufactured at other Spanish centres, especially contemporary lustrewares from the Málaga area and 16th-century lustrewares from Seville, both in the south of the country, which are also regularly found in northern Europe (Hughes 1995; and see Appendix 18.1). Chemical data are more problematic when attempting to differentiate products from Valencia and Muel (Zaragoza) as their signature seems to be similar. Muel only started to produce lustrewares in the 16th century, some 200 years later than Valencia, but some decorative motifs seem to be shared between both centres (and also with Catalonia) in the earliest phases of production. A wider range of samples needs to be compiled before the issue can be fully resolved through fabric analysis.

The general framework for dating decorative motifs on lustrewares, largely derived from art historians, remains applicable (Gutiérrez 2000, fig. 2.16). In very general terms, Valencian lustrewares can be divided by centuries so that 'early lustreware' was produced in the 14th century, 'classic lustreware' in the 15th, 'late' in the 16th, and 'overall lustreware' in the 17th, with some overlap between these. Identification and dating is, however, rarely a simple matter in the UK. The size of fragments can impede the identification of forms and decoration or both. Although blue survives well, lustre motifs – which sit on the glazed surface – can be lost due to deposition processes and any patterns are then rendered invisible; although the decoration can sometimes still be identified as a 'ghost', matt, outline on the shiny glazed surface. The 12 vessels found at Exeter are illustrated in Figs 18.3–18.4 and described and listed in Table 18.2.

There are no early examples in the 'Málaga style' (with minute painted motifs and light blue decoration), nor in the 'Pula style' (with radial motifs), both typical of the 14th century. The earliest vessel is a large dish decorated with crowns (ID157), typical of the late 14th or early 15th century. Most of the remaining assemblage dates to the 15th, and displays typical decoration of the period such as Gothic writing (IHS and Ave Maria; ID127 and 153), ferns and dotted flowers (ID161), thistles and criss-cross lines (ID171). Only three vessels are any later than this, dating to the 16th and 17th centuries (ID160, 290 and 373). The latest lustreware preserves little visible decoration (ID373).

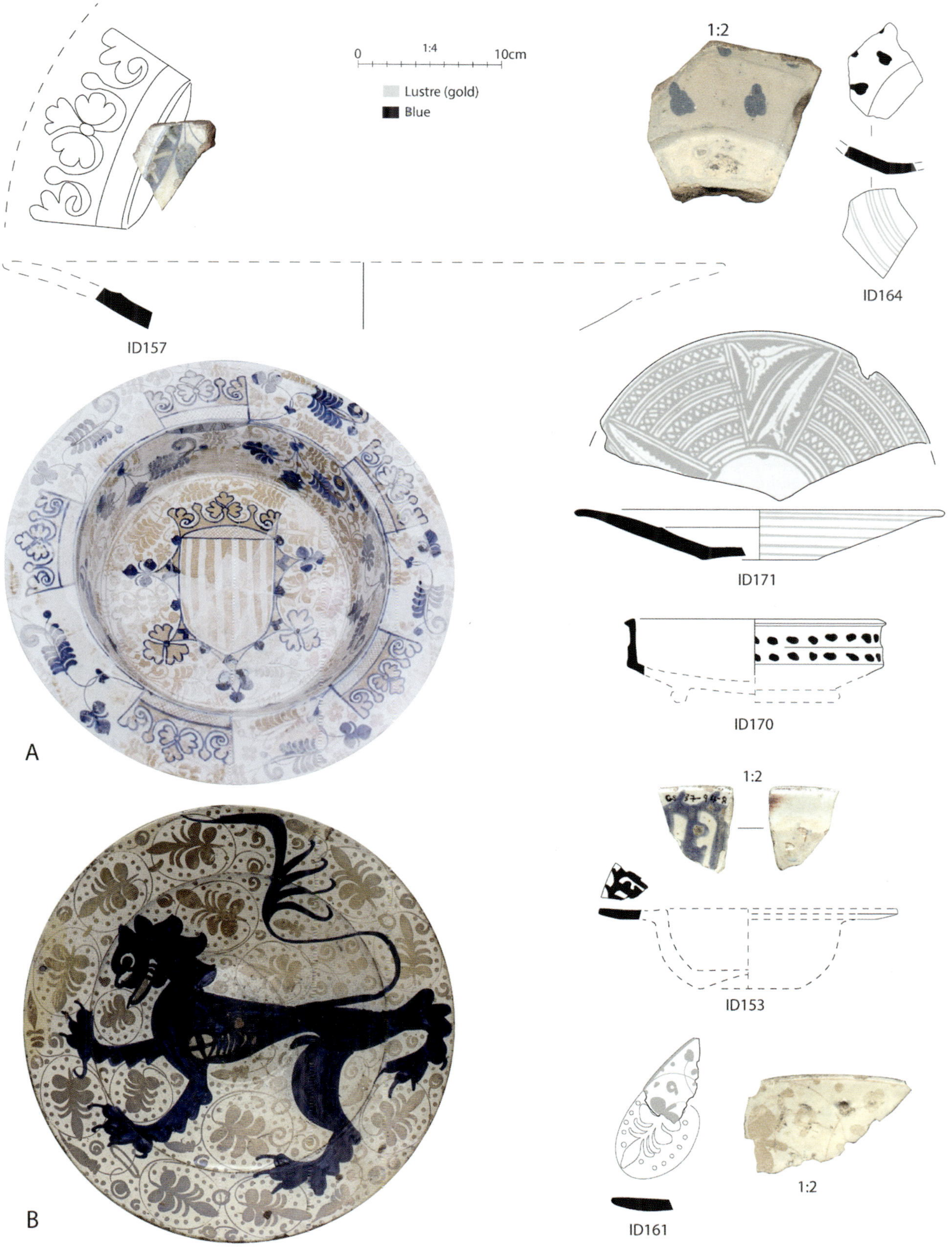

Fig. 18.3 Valencian lustrewares from Exeter. Line drawings at 1:4, with photographs at 1:2 except ID157 and (A–B) complete examples of dishes in museum collections illustrating the patterns of ID157 and ID161, not to scale (drawings: John Allan/Alejandra Gutiérrez; photos: Alejandra Gutiérrez except A: © Museo Nacional de Cerámica y Artes Suntuarias "González Martí", no. CE1/01554; B: © Lyon MBA, Photo Alain Basset)

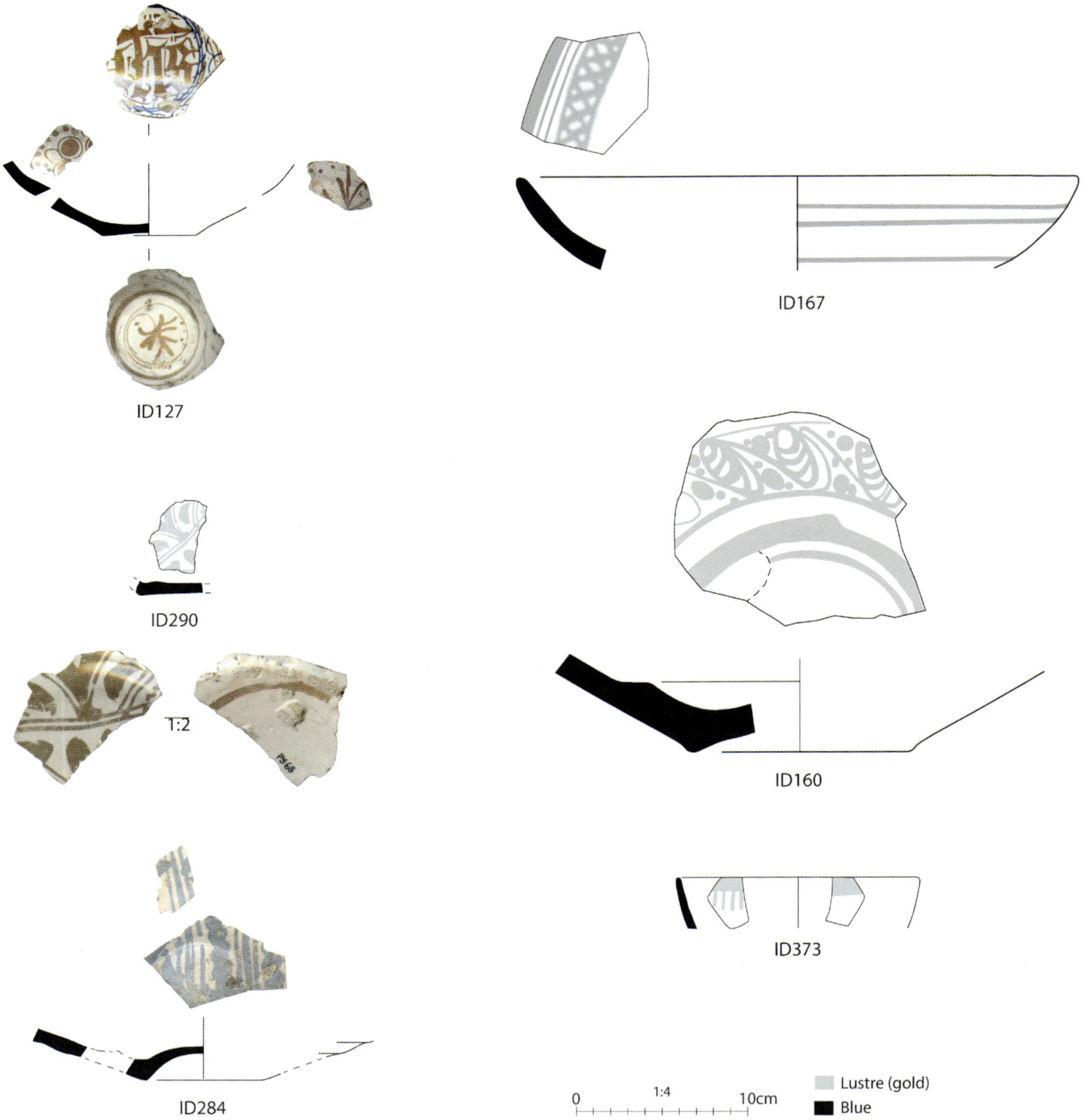

Fig. 18.4 Valencian lustreware (© Alejandra Gutiérrez)

One sherd (ID290) is of more interest, as it might have been manufactured at either Valencia or Muel (Zaragoza); the results of chemical analysis of this sherd were inconclusive (Appendix 18.1). It is decorated with the motif of split flowers and double-outlined lines, in a characteristic golden-brown colour. Both the colour and the motifs are typical of the lustrewares made at Muel. The production of lustrewares only started here at the beginning of the 16th century and seems to have been restricted mainly to dishes, lugged bowls and jugs. The decorative repertoire at Muel did share some motifs with Valencia and Catalonia during the 16th century (Almagro and Llubiá 1952; Álvaro 1981) as well as fine fabrics, so identification is sometimes difficult. Even surviving examples currently in museums can be ascribed to one or the other centre depending on who is describing the vessel. A wider reference collection of chemical signatures is needed before determining conclusively the provenance

Table 18.2 Valencian wares found in Exeter; for Site Numbers see Chapter 2 above

ID	Site No., name, and context No.	Context date	Nos. in EAR 3; Allan 1995	Sherds/ Min. No. Ve.	Wt (g)	Pottery stylistic date	ICP Durham No.
157	Site 50, Holloway Street, 63	After c. 1500	2735; 15	1/1	38	c. 1380–1450	
164	Site 68, Queen Street, 8–15	E16C	1841; 22	1/1	34	c. 1450–1500	EX18164: Valencia
171	Site 42,Trichay Street, pit 156	E16C	1713; 29	5/1	231	c. 1450–1500	EX18171: Valencia/ Muel
170	Site 37, Goldsmith Street, L8–9	c. 1550–80	1879; 28	2/1	15	15C	EX18170: Valencia
127	Site 74, Greyfriars	c. 1538	1615; 14	2/1	46	15C	
153	Site 37, Goldsmith Street, 686	L15C	2737; 17	1/1	7	15C	
161	Site 37, Goldsmith Street, pit 96	c. 1660	2179; 18	1/1	17	15C	
167	Site 59: Polsloe Priory, 1582/3	c. 1538	1547; 25	1/1	9	15C?	
160	Site 79, Albany Road, 20	c. 1570–1624	2738; 16	1/1	60	1500–25	EX18160: Valencia
290	Site 76, Paul Street, 68	c. 1550–1600	not published	1/1	13	16C	EX18290: Valencia/ Muel
373	Site 37, Goldsmith Street	17/18C	not drawn	1/1	3	17C	EX18373: Valencia
284	Site 37, Goldsmith Street, pit 93	L16C	2740; 119	2/1	71	–	EX18284: Valencia(?)

of this Exeter sherd, but the possibility that it could have been made at Muel is intriguing. Muel lustrewares had a wide regional distribution and have been recorded right across Aragón and Valencia, but while the occasional example has also appeared in the Americas (Straube 2017), so far only a single example has been identified from the UK (see below).

Remarkably, all the lustrewares found at Exeter are open forms, being exclusively dishes and bowls; no albarelos (*botes*) or jugs are present. Some fragments are residual in contexts of later date (ID160), but a couple were found in Dissolution debris of *c.* 1538 from the Greyfriars (ID127) and the nunnery at Polsloe (ID167). The rest appear mainly in pits about 50 or 70 years after they were manufactured (ID153, 157, 164, 171, 290).

One further fragment, not a lustreware, but also tin-glazed and decorated solely with painted blue (ID284), was analysed by ICP. The result lies within the Valencia chemical signature, although the vessel is far from typical of the blue-decorated wares produced there. These vessels were only made during the 14th and 15th centuries and had characteristic profiles, including bases with foot-rings, and motifs (for an English summary see Gutiérrez 2000, 29, 32–3). The profile of the Exeter dish is closer to the wares made at Seville in the 16th century, with the raised concave base and freer hand-painted decoration. Whether the dish was made at Valencia, Seville or at a different centre near them, a wider range of chemical results is needed to investigate this fragment further and ascertain its provenance.

Seville area

A wide range of the imported ceramics found in Exeter came from the Seville area in southern Spain. They include both glazed and unglazed vessels, those which were exported commercially and also rarer types of pottery which are found only occasionally in Britain. Ceramics from Seville make up the largest group of all the Spanish ceramics identified so far from medieval Exeter.

Tablewares

Tin-glazed pottery from the Seville area only seems to arrive in northern Europe after the late 15th century and becomes more frequent during the following century, once production increases in order to supply the Spanish colonies in the New World. Tin-glazed ceramics manufactured during this time are still grouped under the term 'Morisco ware', a name first used by Goggin (1968). Whether the ceramics were made by *moriscos* (former Muslims converted to Christianity and living under Christian rule) or not, the term has been retained for its well-defined characteristics, which are quite distinctive and different from later phases of production.

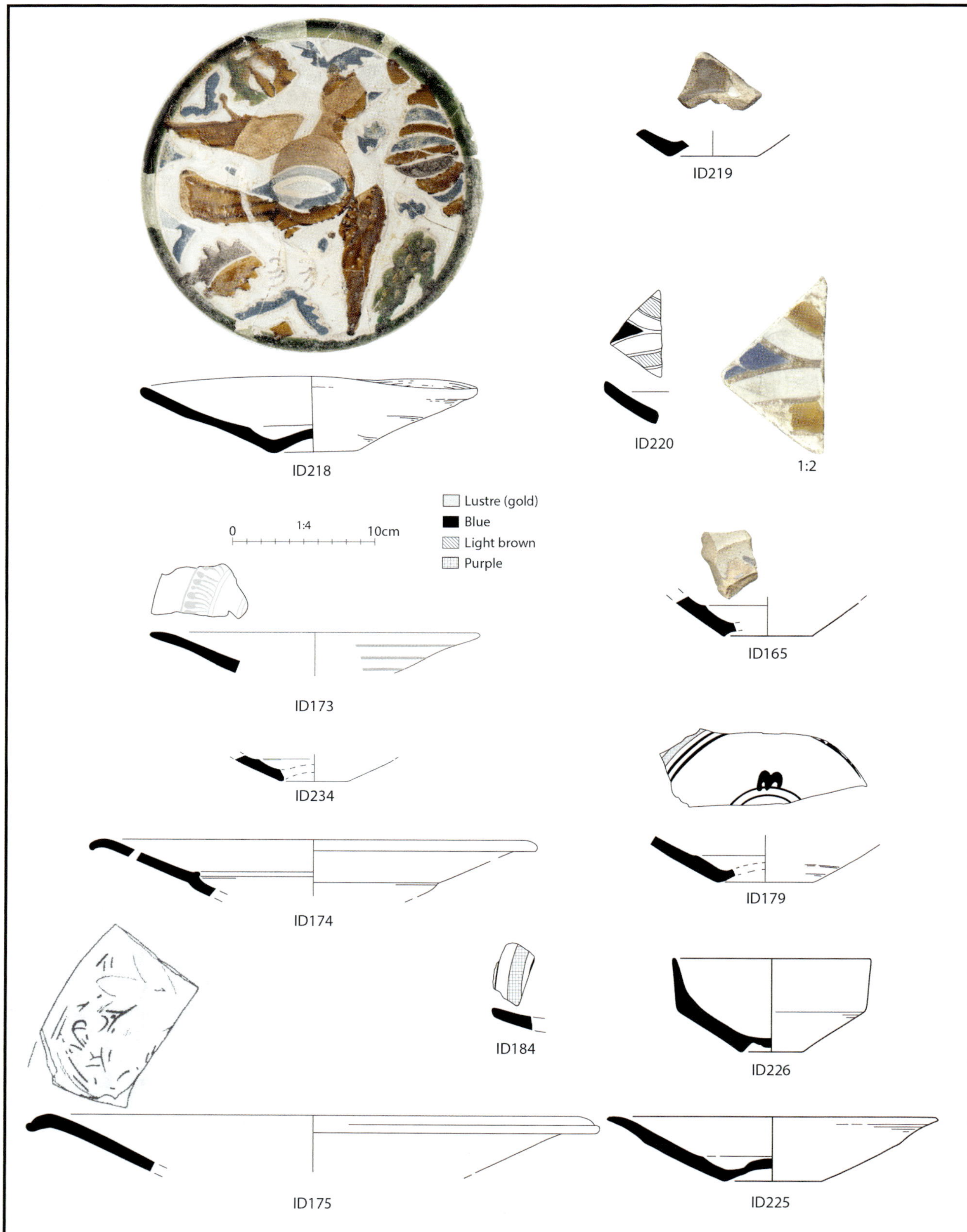

Fig. 18.5 Seville area: tin-glazed wares from Exeter (© Alejandra Gutiérrez)

'Morisco wares' are characterised by a fine light-cream fabric with no visible inclusions, although under the microscope some mica, clay relics and elongated voids are sometimes seen; vessels are glazed all-over (except for jugs and jars), always in white tin glaze, except for a single case where green has been added to the glaze to produce an opaque, emerald green glaze (quite different from lead-glazed wares). This group is traditionally subdivided according to the range of colours and motifs used in the decoration, as this can carry significance for dating. They were produced between the late 15th and 17th centuries. The terminology used here is the English system devised with Seville colleagues to accommodate Spanish types and names, rather than the North American groupings named after sites of the former Spanish colonies in America, which have now been superseded by more recent finds at Seville city itself (Gerrard *et al* 1995; Gutiérrez 2000, fig. 2.27).

Fourteen examples of Morisco ware are recorded from Exeter. They include four examples of *cuerda seca*, a technique that does not apply the glaze over the vessel, but is instead applied individually to patterns drawn out on the surface of the ceramic; these are outlined using manganese or grease, as the second function of the outline is to keep the glazes from running and keeping them confined within their pattern (Fig. 18.5; Table 18.3). The decoration is thus achieved by blocks of glazes of different colours, rather than being painted over a background (ID220). The technique, with Islamic roots in the 11th/12th centuries, was used in Seville during the second half of the 15th century but it does not seem to have survived beyond the early 16th century.

This group also includes lustrewares (Fig. 18.5). Their recognition in archaeological assemblages in the UK is quite recent; all 16th-century examples from northern European sites had previously been identified as Valencia products. Chemical analyses have been instrumental in helping reassign individual pieces, as these are visually similar and even share decorative motifs (Gutiérrez 2003). Four lustrewares were found during excavations at Exeter, all in well-dated contexts of the 16th century (Fig. 18.5). All the vessels found are dishes, some with badly preserved decoration; they all have the characteristic concentric lines on the back of the dish and plain rims. Some of the sherds listed below were analysed as part of a study into 16th-century lustrewares in Britain and their sources, which has helped to confirm their provenance from the Seville workshops (Gutiérrez 2009), while further examples were also analysed as part of the present study (Appendix 18.1). Exeter provides some good dating evidence for this type of product. The dish recovered from Polsloe Priory (ID173) was found in a pre-Dissolution context in the fill of a cistern infilled *c.* 1500. Seville seems to have produced lustrewares for a limited period only, during the 16th century; these well-stratified finds from Exeter help place production by *c.* 1500 already, especially those motifs of musical notes (*solfas*). These are very similar to those used on lustrewares made at Valencia from the end of the 15th century. Large dishes with broad brims where impressed decoration has been added do also appear in Dissolution contexts of the 1530s, such as ID174.

The Seville area also presents challenges when identifying its wares. Well-known types are traditionally said to come from 'Seville', but it is clear that similar-looking vessels were manufactured across the south of Spain and beyond. Wasters from Lebrija, for example, attest to the local production of tin-glazed wares similar to those from Seville, including plain and blue-decorated bowls (Galván and Sánchez 2005). Lebrija is some 60 km away from Seville and closer to the sea than the capital, but still inland. There is little doubt that main ports along the south coast might have also produced comparable pottery that could have been exported, as was the case with coarsewares (see below). similar-looking tin-glazed wares were also produced in Portugal, but here manufacture seems to have been limited to plain dishes and bowls in white, sometimes decorated with parallel concentric lines in blue (see below, ID204 and ID208).

Commercial containers

Besides tin-glazed wares, commercial containers in the form of unglazed jars (only occasionally glazed on the interior) also arrived in Exeter (Fig. 18.6). Most of the ceramic commercial containers involved in shipping goods found in the UK are assumed to have been made at Seville, but large transport jars were made at all major ports around the coast from the medieval period onwards, including Valencia, Alicante and Barcelona, for example (Coll 1993; Saranova and Borrego 1993; Borrego and Saranova 1994; Beltrán de Heredia 2012). Their fine fabrics can make their identification and dating at consumption sites difficult if no diagnostic sherds are found.

The Valencia area produced fine, large jars with distinctive rims and necks, but their fine fabrics can go largely unrecognised and so far only a handful of examples are known from Britain (Gutiérrez 2000, 248 and fig. 5.10, no. 8). They have flat bases and thick rims, and were between *c.* 70 cm and 100 cm tall. They were used for transport and also for storage at home, with written records referring to their holding oil and wine, sometimes with their interior sealed with pitch, whereas archaeological finds confirm that they were also used to transport smaller ceramic vessels (López Elum 1984, 46, 69; Amigues and Mesquida 1987; Amigues *et al.* 1995, fig. 3).

Products from the south of Spain have more distinctive fabrics and profiles that changed in form between the 15th and 18th/19th centuries. The earlier types include what Hurst termed 'ribbed amphorae' (Hurst 1977, fig. 33) – sizeable jars with marked grooves and slightly convex bases; they appear only rarely in the UK and they seem to predate Spanish trade with the Americas. They do

Table 18.3 Seville: Morisco wares found in Exeter

ID	*Site No., name, and context*	*Context date*	*Nos. in EAR 3 & Allan 1995*	*Sherds/Min. No. Ve.*	*Wt (g)*	*Date of pottery type*	*ICP Durham No.*
Cuerda seca							
218	Site 60, Preston St, 179	1500–50	2741; 65	12/1	560	E16C	
219	Site 52, Rack St, pit 115	1500–50	1821; 66	1/1	21	E16C	
220	Site 58, Magdalene St, pit 7	1720–50	p. 209; 67	1/1	15	E16C	
Not seen	Site 76, Paul St	E16C	–;–	1/1	–	E16C	
Lustrewares							
173	Site 59, Polsloe Priory, 1582	*c.* 1500	1534; 31	1/1	21	Very E16C	Gutiérrez 2009 sample 4
174	Site 41, St Nicholas Priory	*c.* 1536–50	1785; 33	3/1	48	1st half 16C	Gutiérrez 2009 sample 6
175	Site 76, Paul St, 34	*c.* 1500–50	34	1/1	120	1st half 16C	Gutiérrez 2009 sample 5
234	Site 59, Polsloe Priory, 1582	*c.* 1500	1535; 81	1/1	15	Very E16C	
Blue and purple							
165	Site 37, Goldsmith St, F33–8	*c.* 1556–80	1883; 23	1/1	17	1450–1550	
179	Site 40, Cathedral Close	Unstrat.	2739; 40	1/1	89	1450–1550	
184	Site 52, Rack St, 188	Undated	45	1/1	11	1450–1550	
Plain white							
225	Site 76, Paul St, 1494	E16C	72	3/1	534	E16C	
226	Site 76, Paul St, 1494	E16C	73	9/1	340	E16C	
254	Site 156, Princesshay, pit 4745	E16C	Unpub.	1/1	24	E16C	EX18354: Seville

appear in sites along the Spanish coast but their place of manufacture is still unconfirmed there. A single sherd from an early 15th-century context at Exe Bridge (Site 56) has been identified as an example of this early type (ID122). It was thin-sectioned by David Williams (1984a, 145), who commented: 'Similar to olive jars from Southampton. Fragments of quartz-mica schist, sandstone, quartzite and limestone, plus discrete grains of quartz, plagioclase and potash feldspar'. The vessel still preserves a black residue (pitch?) on the interior surface.

In 1503 Seville obtained the trade monopoly with the Spanish colonies in America and trade and transport of goods with the New World was greatly facilitated by the use of ceramic containers with a repetitive range of shapes which were later standardised according to their capacity and volume. These *botijas* were first identified on American sites and termed 'olive jars' there (Goggin 1968). Their shape changed through time and three broad groups exist between the late 15th and 18th centuries. The earliest ('early style') are small, spherical jars with two handles and a narrow rim; they gave way to globular or elongated containers with round bases in the 16th century ('middle style') (Fig. 18.6). Smaller, pointed jars only appear after the 18th century ('late style'). Although much discussion has been based around the shape of the rims, there is no definite proof to indicate that they are a reliable means to date the jars. They are sometimes glazed on the inside, either emerald green or light brown, and more rarely in white, but this does not seem to be directly related to the contents: most jars must have carried oil or wine, but most examples in Britain are unglazed. They are also known to have been identified with merchant marks, which were sometimes impressed on the rim before the jar was fired and sometimes painted or scratched on afterwards (Pleguezuelo 1993), but such marks are infrequent and rare among the examples recovered from the UK.

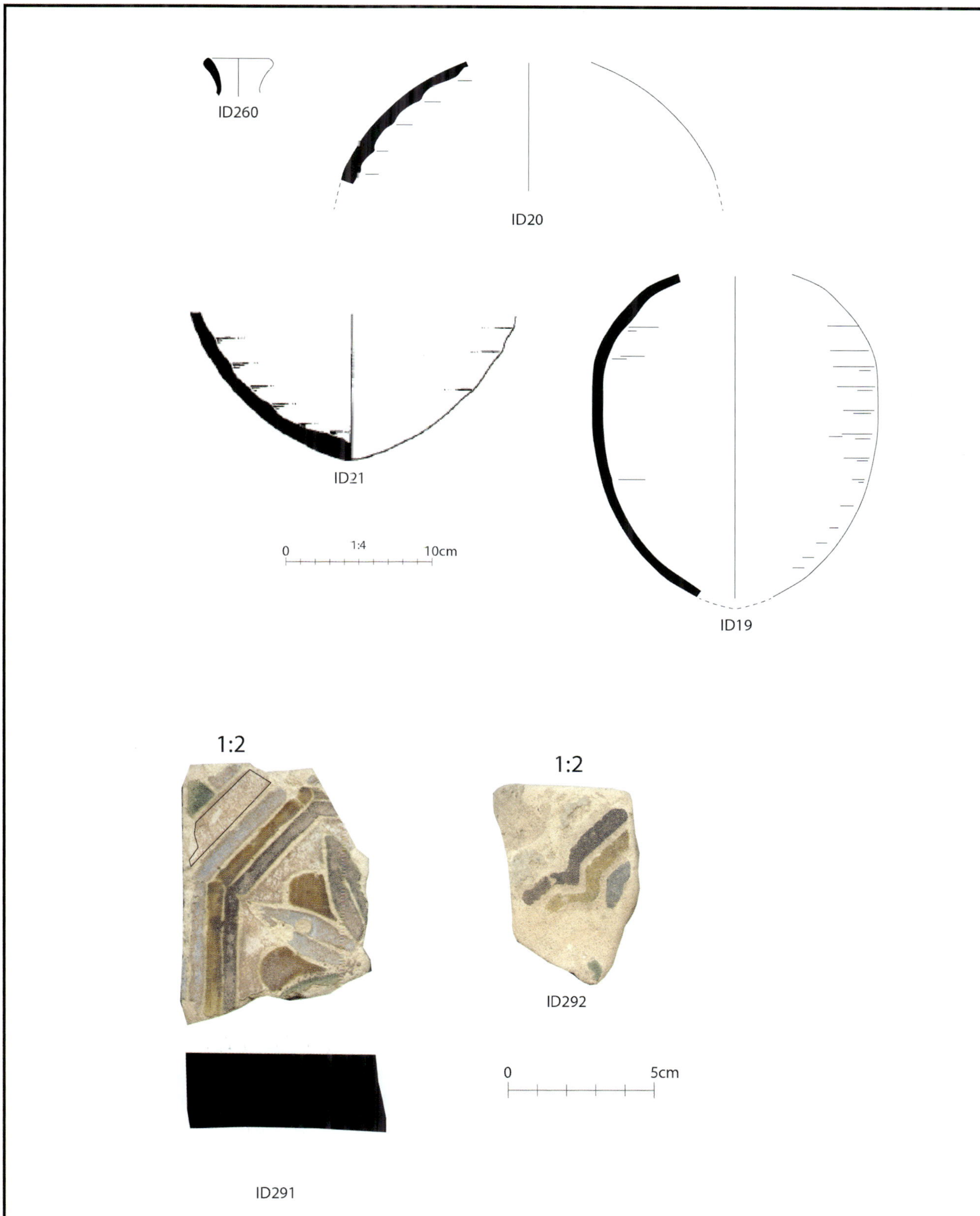

Fig. 18.6 Seville: olive jars and cuenca *tiles (© Alejandra Gutiérrez)*

The variety of fabrics seen in Britain must suggest the existence of different centres of production around and beyond the city of Seville, especially along the River Guadalquivir. In spite of Seville's trade monopoly, other ports at the mouth of the Guadalquivir, such as San Lúcar de Barrameda, and further south, such as Puerto de Santa María and Cádiz, formed part of its commercial and legal sphere (Ball 1977, 78) and no doubt must have also produced similar transport jars, although local manufacture is still not characterised.

Jars in the early style have characteristic thin walls and profiles and are easier to identify, but unless diagnostic sherds are found, it is difficult to differentiate between containers from the middle and late styles.

The assemblage of 'olive jars' found at Exeter totals 381 sherds, representing a minimum number of 168 vessels from 35 sites, although most are single sherds. I am grateful to John Allan for quantifying all the sherds; the data for the containers is in online Appendix 18.3, where descriptions of 41 vessels and a full listing of all the Exeter finds will also be found.

Tiles

Besides pottery, Seville also produced wall and floor tiles (Fig. 18.6) and these are found only rarely in the UK and the rest of Europe, with a major group known from Bristol (Gutiérrez 2012). Two examples are known from Exeter (online Appendix 18.3); other finds identified in the South West are recorded in Allan 2009–10.

Portugal

Considerable numbers of excavations over the past 20 years are slowly transforming medieval and later pottery studies in Portugal, with repercussions for the study of material culture abroad. From the point of view of ceramic studies, evidence for the production of pottery types which were first identified outside the country (for example, green-glazed vessels aboard the Armada shipwrecks: Martin 1979; Hurst *et al.* 1986) have now finally been documented in Portugal; the range and chronology of the former 'Merida-type wares' can also be fine-tuned with well-stratified Portuguese finds; and, more importantly, some wares which were thought to have been produced solely in southern Spain are also being documented in Portugal. Besides all these, whitewares covered in bright yellow or green glazes (not dissimilar in appearance to French examples), are thought to be a local manufacture at Coimbra. Data are still patchy both spatially and chronologically, and many questions remain, but we are starting to understand better the wares that were produced and exported from Portugal from the medieval period onwards.

Assemblages from consumption sites dominate the Portuguese literature (*e.g.* papers in Teixeira and Bettencourt 2012; Caessa *et al.* 2017) while remains associated with centres of production are still scarce and few, especially outside Lisbon. Apart from excavations, doctoral theses are contributing to our understanding of local production, although the field has been more thoroughly pursued for tin-glazed decorated wares, especially those of the early modern age. The lack of systematic and thorough application of scientific analyses poses a problem in that the identification of many different wares remains somewhat subjective, both for glazed and unglazed wares; so far analyses have not been used to characterise local productions but some encouraging results have already been published (*e.g.* Castro *et al.* 1997; Sousa *et al.* 2003; Vieira Ferreira *et al.* 2013a; 2013b; 2016).

The assemblage of Portuguese wares from Exeter totals 45 vessels (Fig. 18.7; Table 18.4) and it is clearly dominated by unglazed wares, although tin- and lead-glazed vessels are also found. They are discussed below according to type.

Tin-glazed wares

Portuguese colleagues are currently splitting the production of medieval and modern tin-glazed wares in Portugal into two distinctive groups: early production (*malegueira*, or 'in the Málaga style') of the second half of the 16th century, and later (*faiança*, or tin-glazed wares) from the 17th century onwards. This coincides broadly with the distinction observed in the Seville area between 'Morisco ware' and 'Seville ware', the latter being a more refined manufacture (both in technology and repertoire of forms) introduced by Italian potters arriving in Spain whose influence can be seen in workshops across the country (Pleguezuelo and Lapuente 1995, 240; Álvaro 1999). The use of saggars for firing pots, rather than cockspurs used in earlier phases, has been documented in Lisbon, and this suggests a change in technology that might also imply the arrival of foreign potters. Complete saggars with dishes still inside, all stuck together, have been recovered at Mouraria (Lisbon), for example (Castro *et al.* 2017).

Written records distinguish between potters who used glaze (*malagueiros*) and those who did not (*oleiros*), implying that the production of tin-glazed and lead-glazed wares was a specialist craft. This division appears in the middle of the 16th century (Carvalho 1918; Formigo 2014).

Later records do mention 'potters of white glaze', but this is only recorded in the 17th century (Dórdio *et al.* 2001, 146). By that date tin-glazed wares had started to be produced in quantities and at present three production centres have been located archaeologically: Lisbon, Coimbra and Vila Nova de Gaia (Porto) (Dordio *et al.* 2001, 139, 143). Researchers have tried to describe materials from each of these, but since the transport of clay between them is documented (Dórdio *et al.* 2001, 150; Leão 1999, 25), it may be challenging to distinguish between them macroscopically. Tin-glazed wares use white clays, mainly from the Lisbon area, but sometimes potters mixed these with local red clays, hence the variations in fabric

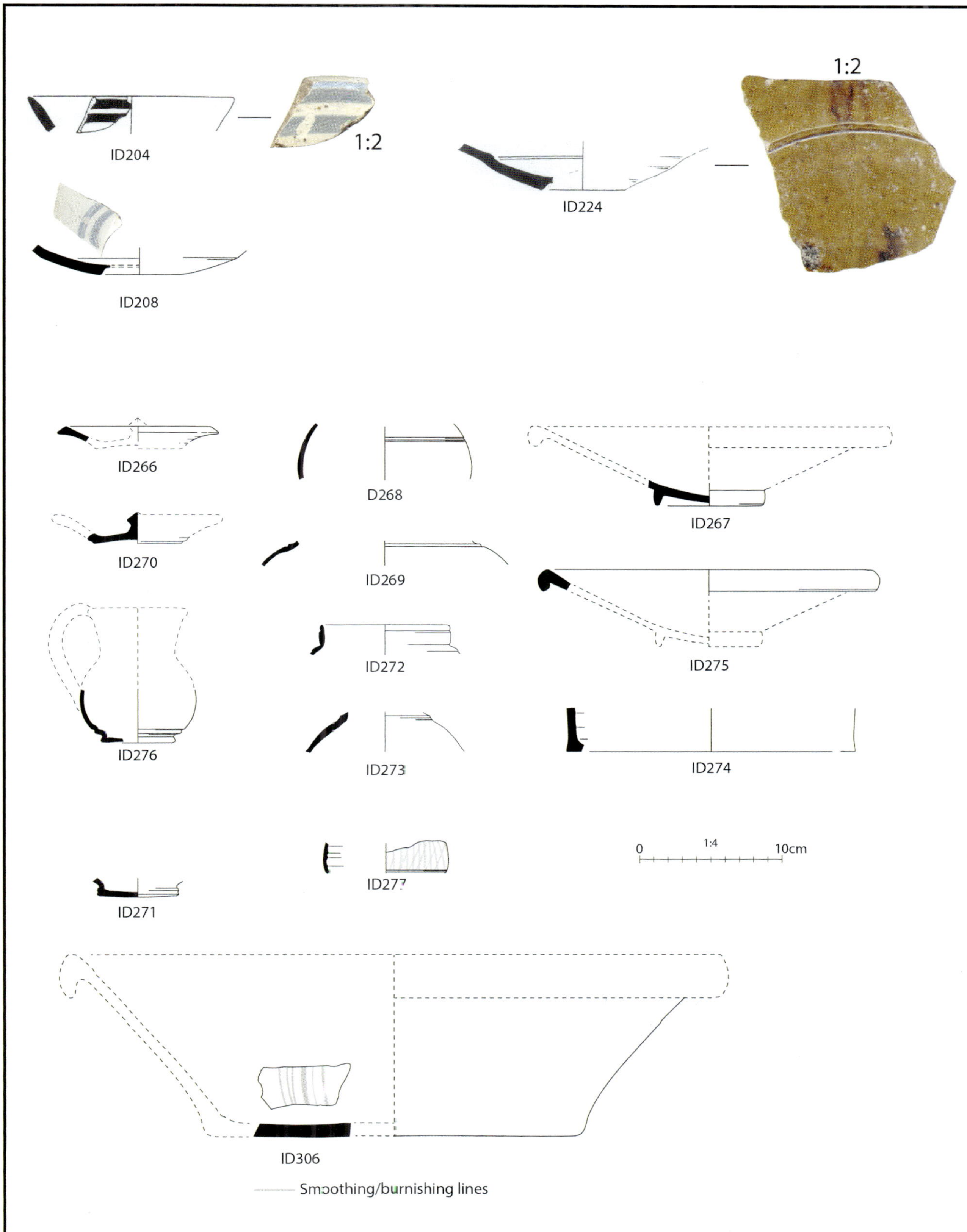

Fig. 18.7 Portuguese wares from Exeter (© Alejandra Gutiérrez)

Table 18.4 Portuguese tablewares found in Exeter

ID	*Site No., Site name, and context*	*Context No. and date*	*Nos. in EAR 3; Allan 1995*	*No. sherds/ vessels*	*Wt (g)*	*Durham ICP No.*
Tin-glazed: Portuguese Linear Blue						
204	Site 60, Preston Street, 206	19/20C	Not drawn; 58	1/1	5	EX18204: not Spain
208	Site 45, Friars Gate, unstrat.	–	2742; 62	1/1	16	EX18208: not Spain
Lead-glazed						
224	Site 37, Goldsmith Street, unstrat.	–	2743; 71			EX18224: not Spain

colour. White kaolinitic clay is available south of Lisbon in the Vale of Zebro (Viana 1989). All the fabrics are fine, sometimes with a little quartz sand and mica, generally cream, light pink or light orange in colour. As in other countries, the range of textures, colour hues, pigment density, etc. are not necessarily linked to specific places of manufacture, nor are there enough discriminatory factors to assign products to one workshop or another with any confidence (Sebastian 2011, 484), at least until such differences are confirmed by complementary methods, such as chemical analyses. Dating and classification of 17th-century tin-glazed wares is mainly based on the identification of decorative motifs through a traditional art historical approach (for example Casimiro 2013). This modern production falls outside the scope of this project and finds from Exeter have already been recorded (Allan 1984a; Casimiro 2011).

Pre-17th century phases of production are still poorly documented and unclear but they are of relevance here. References to the presence of *malagueiros* (or 'makers of Málaga work') in documents has been taken to mean the production of tin-glazed wares, although the term may be more complex and include lead-glazed wares (Sebastian 2011, 49–90). Nevertheless, wasters from this early phase have also started to be recovered and they are now known from both Lisbon and Coimbra. Rescue excavations of a huge waster dump by the river close to the workshops in Coimbra have produced coarsewares, lead-glazed and tin-glazed wares. This material is unstratified and the dating is not clear, however (I am grateful to Helena Moura, IGESPAR, for allowing me to see this material). For the moment the earliest documented reference to local manufacture of tin-glazed wares here is 1608 (Silva 2016).

The situation in Lisbon is rather confusing at present. The pottery kilns excavated at Mata de Machada, Barreiro, near Lisbon, have been dated to *c.* 1450 and 1530 based on coin evidence (Carmona and Santos 2005, 5). Among the infill of the kilns were plain tin-glazed wares (Torres 1990) similar looking to 'Morisco wares' from Seville, and these have been identified as a local product manufactured in that kiln in the early 16th century (Casimiro 2013, fig. 2). These items, however, are not wasters (Coelho and Texeira 2018), and so far there is no other evidence for the manufacture of tin-glazed wares at Lisbon before the end of the 16th century. Nevertheless, it seems now that any plain dish or bowl found locally is identified as Lisbon-made, even when it occurs alongside other Seville Morisco wares which were not made locally in Portugal (for example blue and purple).

Further research is needed to clarify the earliest phase of local tin-glazed production, although at the moment this seems to be firmly placed at the very end of the 16th century or early 17th century. Contemporary written documents refer to the manufacture in Lisbon of 'white earthenware of Talavera' (*louça branca de Talavera*) in 1572 (Fernandes 2012, app. B8); this is Talavera in Spain, which transported 'white pottery' over land to be sold in Lisbon (Brandão 1990, 50). The lack of a 'proper' local name in the documentation of the period must surely indicate that production was still a recent occurrence at this time in Lisbon.

The relevance of this phase of production for the UK is that the dishes and bowls being produced are very similar to the Morisco wares being manufactured in the Seville area, although so far only 'plain white' or sometimes 'linear blue' types with blue concentric lines seem to have been manufactured in Portugal. A couple of bowls in this linear blue style have been recovered from Exeter (ID204, ID208); although they look like Morisco wares, chemical analysis of their fabrics confirms that they were not produced in Spain, with signatures well outside the cluster of reference samples (Appendix 18.1). Most distinctive is the blue decoration, which is dull and greyish, rather than the typical bright cobalt blue used in southern Spain. The difference in colour seems to be due to the lack of arsenic in the cobalt used on Portuguese wares, which was extracted locally from the Alentejo area of central and southern Portugal, at least during these early phases of production (Vieira Ferreira *et al.* 2013a; 2013b). None of the sherds is well stratified, one being residual in a 19th to 20th century context, the other being unstratified.

Lead-glazed wares

Recent discoveries of wasters, cockspurs and other kiln material make it now possible to confirm the production in Lisbon of lead-glazed wares, covered in green or in brown, which had only been known from documentary references dating to the end of the 16th century (Diogo and Trindade 2000, 204). Although only a few workshops have been located so far, production must have been extensive across the country and local manufacture is suspected at major towns. As with other types of ceramics, production was clearly concentrated on both sides of the Tagus mouth, in and around Lisbon. The *Livro dos Regimentos dos Oficiais Mecânicos da Mui Nobre e Sempre Leal Cidade de Lixboa* includes the potters guild and mentions the production of green-glazed wares (Correia 1926, 142–7; Fernandes 2012, app. B8).

In Lisbon itself, wasters and cockspurs have been found in the former Islamic quarter of the city; they have been dated to the 16th and 17th centuries and are mainly bowls (Nunes and Filipe 2012). The Lisbon fabrics, both for the city and the region, have been described as containing quartz, mica, clay relics, iron ore and small linear cracks (Silva *et al.* 2012, 81). Interestingly among the lead-glazed wares made here are the typical green-glazed *lebrillos* or pancheons produced in the Seville area in the 16th century; these are now thought to have also been produced in Lisbon, where the fabrics are mainly red, as opposed to the cream colours of Seville. At Lisbon production of bichrome lead glazes has also been recorded, with green on the exterior and light-brown on the interior (Silva *et al.* 2012, 81).

A kiln has been excavated in Santo António da Charneca (Setúbal) and it has been dated to the 15th and 16th centuries. It produced tablewares and sugar moulds. Worthy of note is the production not only of *arista* tiles similar to those made at Seville, but also of green-glazed pancheons, bowls and dishes (Barros *et al.* 2012).

Only three vessels were found at Exeter, two of them unstratified. The *melado* dish (ID224) is lead-glazed all-over with a light brown lead glaze; this type of dish is a typical group within the Morisco wares from Seville, where the fine, cream fabrics are characteristic. The Exeter dish has a red fabric with visible inclusions and the chemical analysis confirms it was not manufactured in known Spanish centres.

Coarsewares

Understanding of coarseware production is improving all the time as new evidence comes to light. Very few manufacturing sites have been excavated so far, however, although they must have been numerous across the country, all producing similar-looking vessels. At Santarém, for example, local production of red coarsewares is documented and is described as similar to those from other sites in the country, from Lisbon and Silves to Palmela (Mendes *et al.* 2002).

Excavations at Lisbon have produced some evidence for the manufacture of coarsewares, mainly in the form of discarded wasters (*e.g.* Marques *et al.* 2012). Local production is described as having a range of colours, from orangey-red to light orange and cream, often with surfaces of different colour (pink, light orange), many times including a surface wash (rather than a slip) in a different, darker colour to that of the fabric; surfaces are usually smoothed, and only open forms and large jugs are burnished. Forms produced at Lisbon are similar to those made not only in the region but also in the north (*e.g.* Aveiro: Marques *et al.* 2012, 128). The materials associated with the kiln from Mata da Machada, Barreiro, Lisbon, are not available for study at present (A. Teixeira, pers. comm.) although they have already been published (Torres 1990; Coelho and Teixeira 2018).

More recently kilns and wasters have been excavated in Tavira in 2017 in the south of the country (Moreno 2017), and in Aveiro (in the north), with both assemblages still under study. Aveiro seems to have been a major production site, favoured by being a port. The discovery and excavation of two shipwrecks full of pottery near the port has led to the identification of a range of wares being produced here, although so far most of the assemblages date to the late 16th and 17th centuries and earlier phases remain undocumented.

Most of the redwares produced in Portugal used local granitic clays and a similar range of forms. There are, however, different fabrics in existence, but variations seem to depend on a number of factors, not only on the place of manufacture; the date when vessels were made, and probably also the size and function of the pot must also influenced manufacture. The author has examined examples at Lisbon where a single vessel may have a virtually inclusion-free body together with coarse handles full of granitic temper.

Portuguese unglazed wares (formerly 'Merida wares')

It was John Hurst who first identified these imports as a distinctive group in northern Europe and termed them 'Merida wares' at a time when the production was still unknown in Portugal itself; he subsequently corrected and explained the problem with this name (Hurst 1977a; Hurst *et al.* 1986, 69). British archaeologists have since battled to offer a range of alternative names, including 'red', 'Iberian', 'undecorated', etc. Although granitic fabrics extend well into the north and west of Spain, there is little doubt that this group of red/brown micaceous fabrics, in this range of forms, were produced in Portugal. Variation in colour, from black to cream, makes the use of 'red' redundant, and although unglazed, these vessels can be highly decorated with complicated moulded designs, inlays, etc. The term 'Portuguese unglazed wares' seems more appropriate and it is used here as an alternative to the former 'Merida wares'.

The assemblage from Exeter totals 83 different vessels, all wheel-thrown. The Exeter sherds have been divided into fabrics with the help of a microscope (x10). As a result, seven different fabrics have been identified (Fig. 18.8):

Fabric 1 (ICP: ID271 = Durham EX18271)

Orange throughout.

Well-sorted sand (quartz and black inclusions) with:

- occasional large grains of quartz <1 mm (white or transparent, rounded)
- large black shiny feldspar grains <1 mm (rounded); variable quantity from sherd to sherd
- abundant mica flecks, from spots to flecks <1 mm

These vessels have distinctive very micaceous surfaces, greyish exterior surfaces, tool-smoothed vertically, without being a proper burnishing, and uneven sanded bases, mainly quartz and mica. One base seems to be stuck to surface, rather than cut off.

At least two glazed (ID 297, 299) and 12 unglazed vessels (ID217, 294, 296, 298, 300, 301, 304, 306, 308, 309, 320, 323) are present. They range in date from the early 16th century (ID271) to *c.* 1700 (ID298). The identifiable forms are a lid (ID270), a ?standing costrel (ID308), a *pucaro* (ID271), a pancheon (ID296), a bowl/plate (ID306) and a jug (ID309).

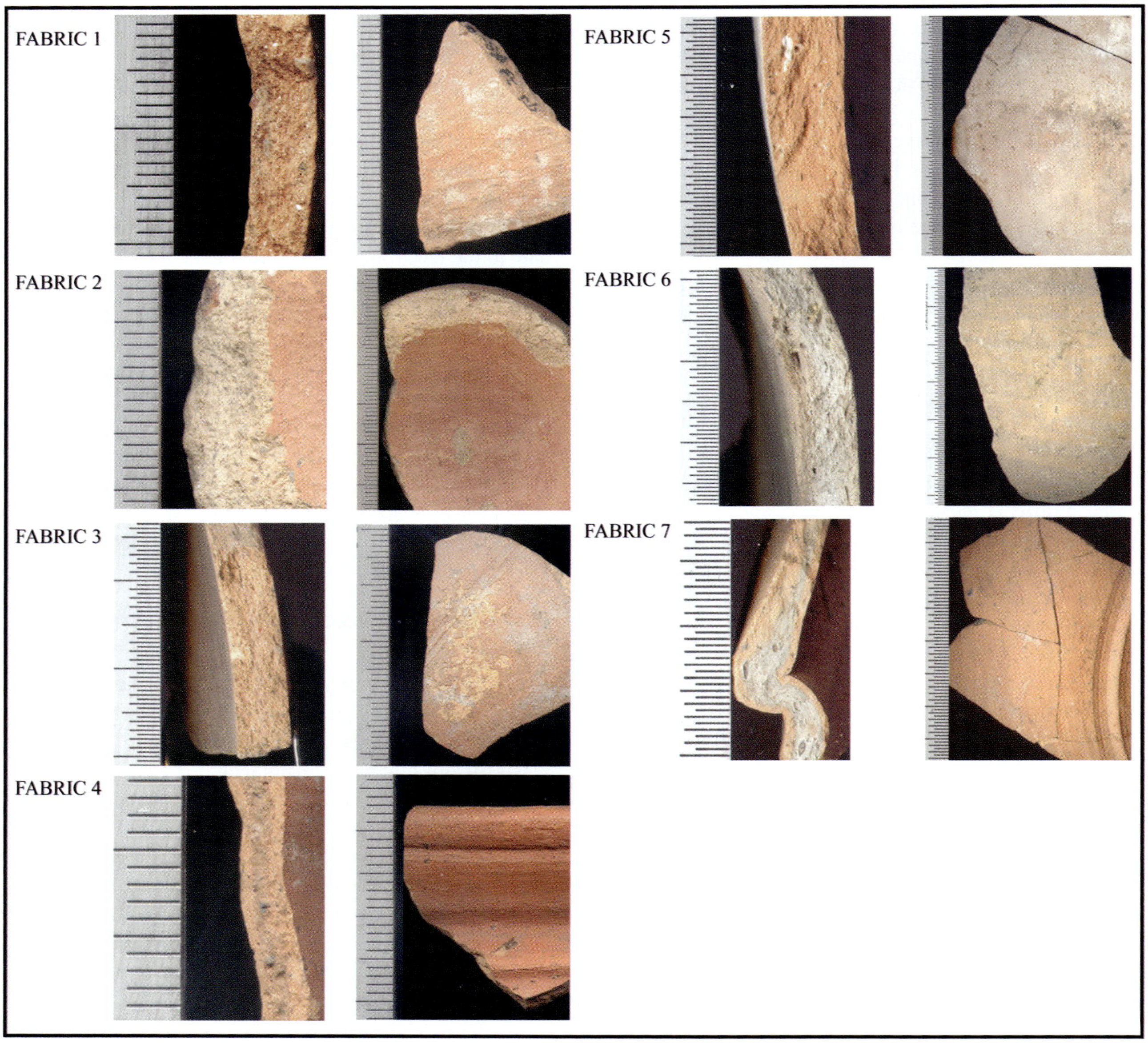

Fig. 18.8 Portuguese unglazed wares: fabrics (© Alejandra Gutiérrez)

Fabric 2 (Lisbon) (ICP: ID267 = Durham EX18267)

Dark cream fabric with orange slip on interior and exterior surfaces.

Poorly sorted sand with:

- abundant white and transparent and orange quartz 0.2–1 mm, rounded
- occasional large quartz grains <4 mm
- rare clay relics <0.5–4 mm
- abundant black shiny inclusions (feldspar?), spots and grains, 0.1–1 mm

Micaceous surfaces; thick covering of slip. Some vessels carefully potted.

At least five vessels, all unglazed, are represented (ID267, 270, 301, 314, 315), ranging in date from *c.* 1500 to the late 16th century. The recognisable forms are a bowl (ID267), a lid (ID270) and a jug (ID314).

Fabric 3 (ICP: ID 268 = Durham 18268)

Light brown fabric with slip, brighter orange interior, reddish-brown thick slip on exterior. No smoothing, or burnishing seen.

Medium size sand of:

- white and transparent quartz 0.2–1 mm, rounded
- rare angular clay relics <1 mm
- rare black shiny inclusions (feldspar?)
- abundant flecks of mica
- occasional limestone, white, well rounded, <0.3 mm.

Matrix is sandy. Micaceous surfaces with a thick covering slip.

This is the most common fabric, represented by at least 15 vessels, all unglazed (ID268–9, 275, 303, 307, 310, 312–13, 317, 430–5). The contexts of the 11 dated examples range in date from *c.* 1500 to the 16th century; no later examples were recorded. The forms are a bowl (ID275), a dish (ID313), and possible standing costrels (ID307, 310).

Fabric 4 ('pseudo terra sigillata') (ICP: ID272 = Durham EX18272)

Similar to Fabric 3, but with additional black/grey round inclusions. Orange fabric with brown core.

Very fine orange slip that recalls the colour and texture of samian bowls and it is smoothed and burnished. Medium-size sand of:

- white and transparent quartz 0.2–1 mm, rounded
- rare black shiny inclusions (feldspar), abundant in some sherds
- abundant flecks of mica
- rare, hard, well rounded black/grey inclusions (often split through the middle)
- occasional round (balls) of cream ?clay relics, very soft
- rare sandstone (x1).

Matrix is not sandy. Micaceous surfaces. Made on the wheel.

Five unglazed vessels were recognised (ID272, 277, 316, 319, 322). Two (ID272, 277) come from contexts of *c.* 1550–80; the others are from undated deposits. The recognisable forms are two *pucaros* (ID277, 319) and one jug (ID322).

Fabric 5 (ICP: ID305 = Durham EX18305)

Similar to Fabric 1, but much less sandy. Orange fabric with thin white slip (uneven) on exterior surface. Medium-size sand of:

- white and transparent angular quartz 1–2 mm
- scarce round clay relics <0.2 mm
- abundant voids <0.2 mm
- some white slip blobs mixed in with the fabric (appearing as white, elongated blobs or thick lines) 1–4 mm.

Matrix is not sandy. Micaceous surfaces (with visible flecks of mica on surfaces).

The fabric is represented by a single unglazed olive jar from an 18th-century context (ID305).

Fabric 6 (ICP: ID 311 = Durham EX18311)

Greyish brown fabric. Medium-size sand of:

- white and transparent quartz <2–3 mm
- abundant clay relics <1 mm
- rare hard, angular grey ?rock <3 mm
- very abundant mica flecks
- abundant voids <5 mm.

Micaceous surfaces (with visible flecks of mica). Sandy matrix.

Only one unglazed vessel in this fabric is present: an unstratified jug (ID311).

Fabric 7 (ICP ID276 = Durham EX18276)

Light grey core, orange margins and cream surfaces. With an orange wash over surfaces. Very fine, dense clay. Medium size sand of:

- occasional white and transparent quartz <0.3 mm
- rare voids <1.5 mm.

The fabric is represented by one vessel: a *pucaro* from an early 16th-century context (ID276).

Further work in Portugal will be needed before the provenance of these fabrics can be identified with any certainty, but it is clear that place of manufacture alone does not account for variation in fabrics. Specific forms and productions ('pseudo *terra sigillata*', for example) requires a distinctive texture and colour, and variation in fabric through time also needs to be defined locally. The assemblage from Exeter is composed mainly of small and undiagnostic sherds, making the identification of forms difficult or even impossible.

Discussion

For a city such as Exeter with so much archaeological excavation, imported pottery from Spain and Portugal is not common, accounting for 569 sherds from 273 vessels among about 76,000 sherds on the Exeter Archaeology database. Nor is it a common find among the recorded imports. The seven vessels of the period 1250–1450 represent less than 1% of the city's imported pottery of that period, almost all the other imports being French whitewares, mainly from the Saintonge (Allan 1984a, 22; above, Chapter 17). The numbers from the late 15th and 16th centuries are greater: the 28 vessels stratified in deposits of that date from excavations up to 1980, for example, form 8.6% of the imported vessels of that date by minimum vessel count. This total, however, amounts to little more than 1% of the total of at least 2164 vessels in those deposits, and less than 1% of sherds (Allan 1984a, 110, 115). Spanish and Portuguese ceramics, then, are few. They do include examples of all the major types of imported pottery seen on sites in Great Britain and Ireland, but there are no atypical finds, which are characteristic of international ports. This reflects the limited role that Exeter played in direct trade with the Mediterranean in the Late Middle Ages, with Dartmouth and Plymouth being the principal ports in the region involved in this trade at this time as attested in the material culture recovered there, especially at Plymouth (Allan 1995; Kowaleski 1995, 27). The city's involvement in trade with Spain and Portugal did grow, however, in the 16th and 17th centuries (Stevens 1958).

Malagan lustrewares

Some of the finds from Exeter are strikingly early: the two Malagan lustrewares from contexts dated to the second half of the 13th century at Goldsmith Street are still among the earliest stratigraphically recorded not only in the UK but in northern Europe. They must have been broken, lost or discarded 'soon' after their arrival, within 20 years or so.

Eleanor of Castile was no doubt responsible for bringing white ceramics painted in gold and blue from Islamic Spain to northern Europe and to English tables. She married Edward I of England in 1254 and is renowned for having introduced many Spaniards to the English court, together with other aspects of her country's tastes and fashions. All of these were evidence of a Spanish culture, itself influenced by Islamic culture, which arrived in northern Europe now for the first time. The three finds from Goldsmith Street belong to this first wave of imports (ID6, 151, 152). The jug from 197 High Street (ID5) is in a late 14th/early 15th-century context which suggests that it was discarded within a generation or so. The single dish from Polsloe Priory (ID7), and the dish from Preston Street (ID293) are small sherds, most likely residual in early 16th-century contexts rather than having been kept safely for a period of time. Except for a single jug from the High Street, all the Malagan lustrewares are open forms, such as dishes and bowls, which had no parallel in the local ceramic repertoire in South-West England at this time. They might have been display pieces in themselves – rarities to be shown off and also vessels of beauty – but they could just as easily have been used at the table, perhaps to present delicacies or other imported foodstuffs (Gutiérrez 2012, 47–8).

This type of early lustreware is found at only 20 sites in Britain, with a greater density of finds close to London and Southampton. Its distribution is limited only to certain groups in society, and outside cities they appear only in monasteries, manor houses and castles. In Exeter it is rarely possible to link these finds to individuals or even to a very specific period of use of the tenements, but one vessel – the jug from 197 High Street – was certainly found on a site where well-to-do citizens resided. This tenement was the home of a series of prominent Exeter merchants in the 14th century, among them Thomas Forbour and John Bridlegh (Chapter 4 above).

Valencia

Exports of lustreware from Málaga to northern Europe are rare, but by the 15th century lustrewares from Valencia had become very popular and are found across Europe in variable quantities. Of the 12 vessels from Exeter, most were made in the 15th century, at the peak of these exports, with just two later examples. Almost half of them were found in Goldsmith Street (Sites 37 and 39); there is a clear concentration here, not only of fine wares but also of later Seville commercial containers and Portuguese unglazed wares (Fig. 18.10). The proportion of Spanish and Portuguese pottery, however, is not unusually high in any of these groups; the large number of Iberian finds simply reflects the abundance of 16th-century groups on these sites.

At Exeter there are no examples of the early lustrewares of the 14th century made at Valencia, but these are rare and only a handful of sherds have been found in Britain. The 15th-century lustrewares are more common in Britain but are thinly distributed across the country, in more than 100 sites, including not only coastal but also inland ones (Gerrard *et al.* 1995, 286–7). It seems that this type of pottery arrived in some quantities and had little difficulty in finding a home away from ports. Two of the Exeter lustrewares come from religious houses: the bowls from Polsloe Priory (ID167) and at the Greyfriars (ID127). The latter has the motif of the 'IHS' on the base which stands for *Iesus Hominum Salvator* (Cope 1959, 41). The popularising of 'the name of Jesus' is traditionally linked to the work of Bernardino of Siena (1380–1444) and later his disciple Mateo de Agrigento in the middle of the 15th century, when he was known to have preached at Valencia (Arechaga and Manglano 1986). From this date onwards the trigram appears on Valencian ceramics and tiles as part of the decorative schemes used there. The meaning of the trigram was also known in England, where it gained widespread popularity from the mid 14th century and into the 15th century (Blake *et al.* 2003). Although the motif may convey a religious message, there is no obvious link between such decoration on imported pottery (Spanish lustrewares or Italian maiolica) and religious houses in Britain. Vessels with the motif have been found in urban contexts (such as at the High Street or the Woollen Hall in Southampton), whereas other imports found at monastic sites (for example, the abbeys at Romsey and Winchester, the priories at Christchurch and Selborne, or the friaries at Guildford, Salisbury and Southampton) have no explicit religious content (Gutiérrez 2000, 192). Nevertheless, it is interesting to note that the bowl from the Greyfriars seems to have been kept safely for a while, as it was manufactured in the second half of the 15th century but was not discarded until the Dissolution of *c.* 1536. This vessel was one of the longest in circulation among the Exeter assemblage.

The other lustrewares are single vessels from Rack Street and Trichay Street, and four examples from Goldsmith Street. When intact, the dish found at Rack Street (ID157), at around 50 cm in diameter, would have been the largest lustreware from Exeter. It is decorated with the motif of the crown, which is typically surrounded by ferns and clovers, dotted flowers or early ivy leaves. Although this design combination does appear in smaller dishes and bowls (*e.g.* Villanueva *et al.* 2009), the large plates are rarer, and they generally have a large central motif, usually a coat of arms, in the centre of the base; the coat of arms indicates that they were made to order and kept for longer periods of time, with examples still seen at museums nowadays (*e.g.* Museum García Galdiano in Madrid: Martínez Caviró 2011, no. 110, 318). Sadly there is no surviving lustreware on the front of the Exeter dish, with only a ghost for the gold on the back is still visible – the typical fern in a circle. It is striking that this dish was recovered from Rack Street, an area of the city which is known to have housed the poor and suffered great poverty, although a few wealthier citizens are also recorded in this area (Chapter 8 above), and they seem more likely owners of the dish. The fragment was found in a minor and poorly dated 16th-century context. Given its small size and wear it may have been a residual sherd.

The dishes and bowls from Trichay Street, Goldsmith Street and Queen Street include popular patterns that were exported in numbers and are not uncommon on English sites, including the lattice decoration alternating with thistles (ID171), the bryony (ID161), Gothic writing (ID153) and stylised ivy leaves (ID164) (*e.g.* Worcester and Southampton: Morris 1978, F41; Gutiérrez 2000). The shape of the partially glazed carinated bowl (ID170) is less common, although examples are also known from France (Carru 1995, 64, nos. 99–101).

After the 15th century the number of Valencia lustrewares arriving in England fell markedly, and just a handful of later sherds are known from Britain. Only two are from Exeter: a 16th-century dish found at Albany Road and a 17th-century fragment from Goldsmith Street. The identification of this type of later lustreware has had to be reassessed, as it is now clear that Seville was making almost identical-looking wares within the Morisco ware range. A re-examination and analysis of a selection of 16th-century lustrewares from English sites, including examples from Exeter, has allowed them to be re-identified as having been made at Seville, not Valencia. This means that earlier identifications of Late Valencia Lustrewares as defined by Hurst (1977) need revising across the country and numbers and distribution are likely to change.

Muel?

A single 16th-century lustreware decorated with split flowers (ID290) is intriguing, as it was not made at Seville and might not have been made at Valencia either. Both visual identification and chemical analysis suggest tentatively that it came from Muel (Zaragoza), where lustreware was produced only in the 16th century and until *c.*1610 when the *moriscos* were expelled from the country (Almagro and Llubiá 1952). Production must have been considerable, with 24 potters working there by 1575 (Álvaro 1981, 122), supplying the local area in north-east Spain. Although Muel is far from the Spanish coast and it is not known to have exported internationally, a similar lustreware bowl was also found in Cook Street, in Southampton, and another decorated in blue came from excavations at Upper Bugle Street, also in Southampton (Gutiérrez 2000, 241, fig. 5.20, no. 5); further away, another lustreware bowl has also been found at Jamestown, its provenance confirmed by Neutron Activation Analysis (Straube 2017, fig. 13). These are likely to be personal acquisitions or gifts and although the first vessel from Southampton was found in a rubbish pit with refuse derived from within the walled town, the second is firmly linked to the house that Roger Machado occupied between 1486 and 1497 (Kaye 1976, 290). This was a high-status dwelling; among other posts, Machado acted as ambassador to the courts of Naples, Spain and France (Bochaca 2012; Watson 2013). Judging from the ceramics and glass (more than 100 Venetian vessels) found during excavation, he must have collected items during his trips, including types which are rarely found on British sites (Gutiérrez 2000, 183). In contrast to this, the lustreware from Exeter was found in an unremarkable pit at Paul Street, with no other imports and it is more difficult to explain the context for its arrival.

Seville: Morisco wares

By the 16th century the largest production of pottery in Spain was centred at Seville. With the discovery of the Americas and the establishment of colonies there, the needs of the new settlers were met by the city, which obtained a monopoly for such trade during the 16th century (Serrera 2008). Huge amounts of Morisco wares were produced for both the local populations and for the New World. Such demand seems to have had an impact on the types of pottery produced, and those with more complex decoration were sidelined in favour of simpler or plainer vessels which were quicker to produce.

One of the types that seems to have been abandoned is *cuerda seca*. There are only a handful of vessels known from Britain, including four from Exeter. Of these, that from Preston Street (ID218) is broken but quite complete; it was found in a pit of *c.*1500–50 and looks as if it was discarded within a generation. The same was the case for the dish from Rack Street (ID219) which is small and worn but from an early 16th-century context. The third vessel, from Magdalen Street (ID220), is also a dish. This was found in an 18th-century context, but interestingly the sherd seems to have been cut into a triangular shape, and it might have survived for longer as a colourful counter or game piece fashioned from a discarded broken sherd.

Cuerda seca wares seem to predate the increase in ceramic output and mass production at Seville; with so few examples having been found locally in Seville as well as in northern Europe, the arrival of this type of ceramic in Britain might either represent very small numbers coming as part of other consignments, special gifts or personal belongings of Spaniards or other merchants travelling to and from the south of Spain.

Within the group of Morisco wares from Exeter are also lustrewares from the first half of the 16th century; dishes with blue and purple decoration which were produced until around the middle of the 16th century; and also plain 16th-century white-glazed wares. It was traditionally thought that, given the low numbers found in northern Europe and their concentration around ports, these vessels might have arrived through direct contact with Spaniards (Hurst 1991, 48). Nevertheless, there is some evidence to confirm that small amounts of pottery did arrive, perhaps as part of an opportunistic trade, involving quantities and an exchange mechanism that was clearly in sharp contrast to those established between Seville and the Americas (Gutiérrez 2003, 35). The finds are widely, if thinly, distributed across Exeter, appearing in all quarters of the city, in sharp contrast to the distribution of the Valencian products from the previous century (Fig. 18.9). Three of the four Seville lustrewares are from religious sites: a large (*c.* 35 cm diameter) dish from St Nicholas Priory (ID174) is in a post-Dissolution context of *c.* 1536–50 and must have been used as a serving dish given its size. Here it should be noted, however, that the finds from this context may represent rubbish from neighbouring tenements rather than from the priory itself. The other two dishes were found together in a fill at the Benedictine nunnery of Polsloe Priory, just before the Dissolution (*c.* 1536) and they must have been discarded very soon after arrival (ID173 and ID234); they are dishes of small size (*c.* 22 cm diameter) that would have been used for individual consumption of food. Similar examples are also known from other monastic sites across Britain, for example Mount Grace Priory, in North Yorkshire, where a set of a dish and a bowl, this time undecorated and also from Seville, was found (Hurst 1987). Mount Grace belonged to the Carthusian order, whose monks lived in individual cells and had their own belongings. The Benedictine order ate together at the table so that the finds from the priories at Exeter could have simply been used as smaller serving dishes and shared at the table, unless they belonged to a visitor, lay or religious, passing through Exeter who either left them behind or broke them and discarded them there.

The only Seville lustreware not from a religious site was found in Paul Street (ID175), also in a context of the first half of the 16th century. This is a large serving dish, and interestingly a matching set of undecorated dish (ID225) and bowl (ID226), both almost complete, were also recovered from the same site. The large group of early 16th-century glass from the same context may show that this was the tenement of a shopkeeper selling glass and other goods.

Seville: commercial containers

There is something of an overlap between the distribution of the Morisco wares and the Sevillian commercial containers across Exeter. These containers appear in greater numbers than any of the previously discussed decorated wares. A single sherd with a ribbed wall (ID122) came from an early 15th-century context, predating the mass-produced types of the 16th century onwards. Thin-sectioning of this sherd has confirmed that it came from the south of Spain and had a fabric very similar to the later types (Williams 1984). Without any diagnostic features, wall sherds such as these are difficult to date, but at Exeter there is a good group of 33 jars of middle style (16th–18th centuries), 11 of them stratified in 16th-century contexts and 9 in 17th-century contexts.

As already mentioned above, these jars were used as containers for products exported from the south of Spain. They were preferred given their versatility; they could carry almost anything, liquid or solid, from oil, wine and olives to chickpeas, turpentine and lead shot (James 1988; Pleguezuelo 1993; Sánchez Cortegana 1996). A residue analysis of one of the jars from Exeter confirmed that it had once contained olive oil (ID23; Evans and Elbeih 1984). John Allan (1995, 317) has already remarked on the importance that olive oil had

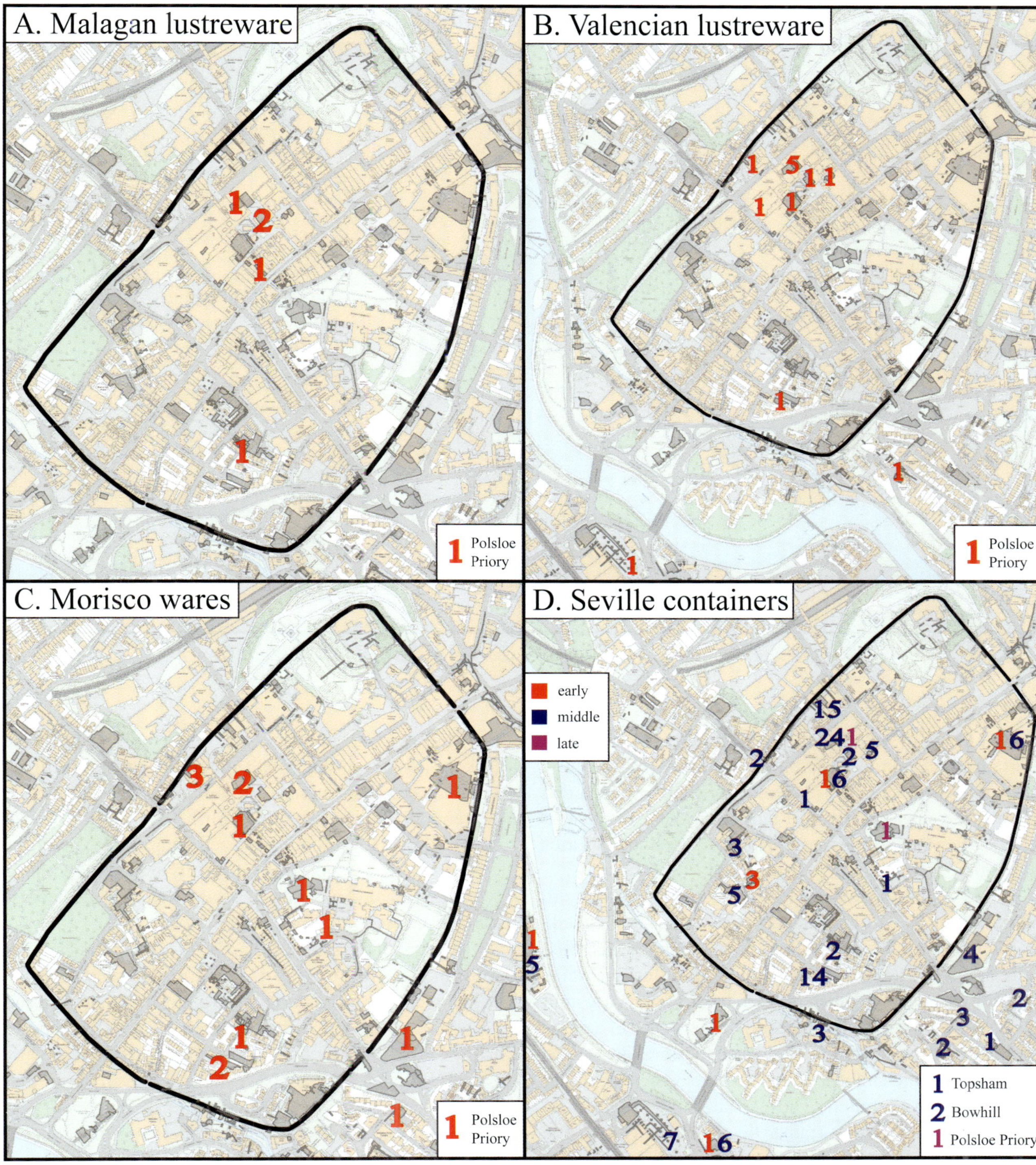

Fig. 18.9 Distribution of Spanish pottery on sites in Exeter (drawn by David Gould)

in the woollen industry, a major industry at Exeter. Oil (or butter or grease) had to be used to replace the natural oils lost through the scouring of the wool and in order to protect it from damage during carding, spinning, warping and weaving. Quantities required must have been impressive: documents specify the use of one gallon (4.5 litres) of oil for every 32 pounds (14.5 kg) of wool (Munro 1987; weight for a single fleece in the medieval period is around 2 pounds: Bischoff 1983).

Portugal: coarsewares and glazed wares

At first glance the distribution of Portuguese ceramics is not dissimilar to that of the Spanish commercial containers, and they are also of similar dates (Fig. 18.10). The understanding of this pottery is still ongoing, with much debate about sources and identifications which will not be resolved until further discoveries, studies and analyses are completed in the country. Nevertheless, the assemblage from Exeter allows us to note some interesting points.

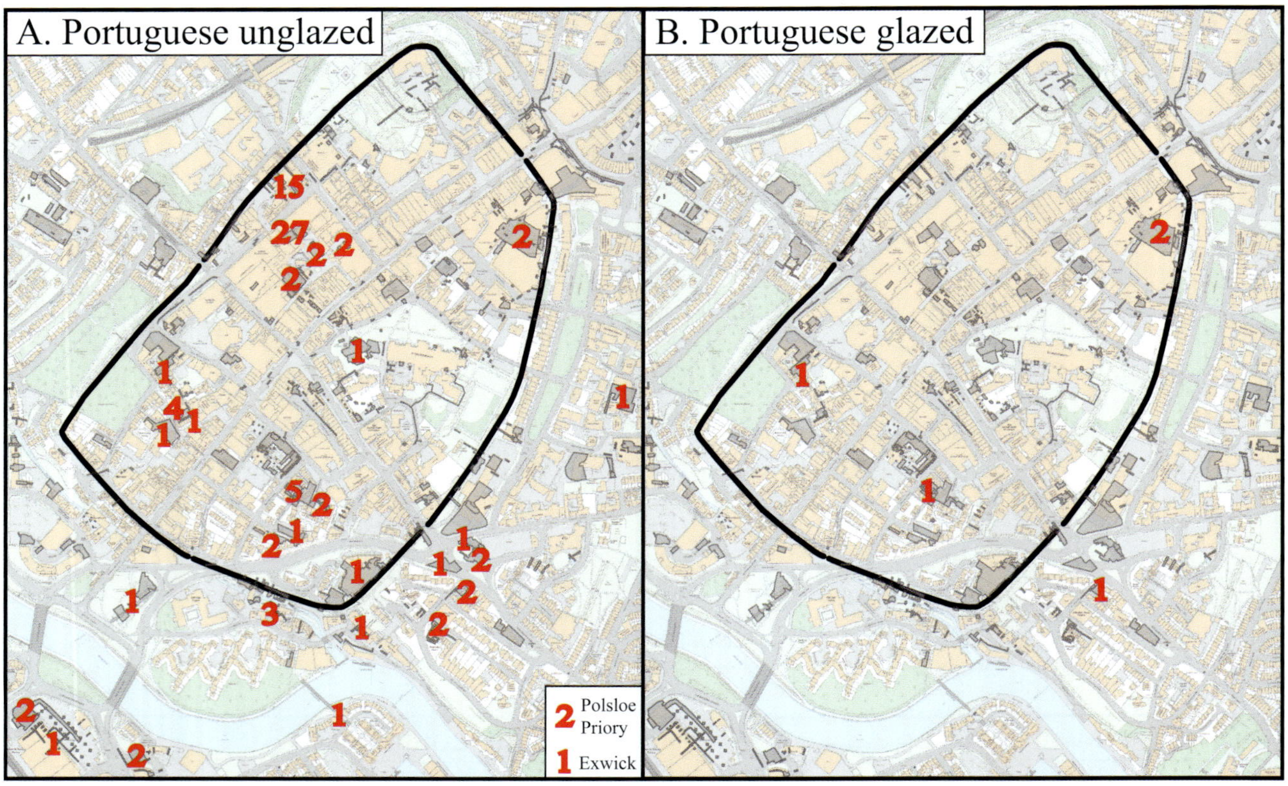

Fig. 18.10 Distribution of Portuguese pottery on sites in Exeter (drawn by David Gould)

As Allan (1995) has already noted, there are no Portuguese ceramics at Exeter before the 16th century, although finds from the 14th century onwards are recorded from other sites in Britain. Finds from the city are also scarce after the 17th century, with just three coarsewares among those which are well stratified.

Some of the glazed sherds of the 16th century are identified in Britain here for the first time. They include Portuguese *melado* dishes which are traditionally identified only as one of the sub-groups within the Morisco wares made at Seville; the diversity of fabrics observed within this group across the sites indicates the existence of a range of different centres of production, and they are likely to be both near Seville and in Portugal, where dishes of similar shape have been found. Those made at Portugal have orange or brown fabrics (rather than cream), with visible mica inclusions. The chemical analysis carried out as part of EAPIT places this dish (ID224) from Exeter as an outlier from the Seville examples, and a suspected Portuguese product, although more data and reference samples are needed to confirm this (Appendix 18.1). This has implications for vessels identified in the past across Britain.

The two early tin-glazed wares with blue concentric lines of the late 16th century were made in Portugal, perhaps at Lisbon or Coimbra, where the earliest phases of tin-glazed production are still under study. Given the number of coarsewares also arriving in Exeter at this date, they might have arrived together. The dull tone of the blue used on these vessels might be related to the lack of arsenic in the cobalt mined locally in Portugal, in contrast to that mined at Spain and Germany (Vieira Ferreira 2013a). Nevertheless, further research is needed in this area, as it has already been demonstrated that the composition of cobalt used on pottery may vary within a workshop, within a period of production, and also across time (Coll 2009; Pérez Arantegui *et al.* 2009).

Two green-glazed vessels (ID297, 299) are similar to examples found onboard the Armada ships of 1588, which were provisioned with ceramics from Seville and Lisbon. The fabric of these glazed vessels, sometimes with white slip under the glaze, was already identified by David Williams as possibly Portuguese, given the similar fabric composition to the unglazed wares (Williams 1979; Hurst *et al.* 1986, 69). More parallels are now known from Portugal itself.

Most of the Portuguese pottery in Exeter is unglazed. It arrived mainly in the 16th century. Since most vessels are represented only by one or two fragments, it is difficult to assess the range of forms in the assemblage (some have been reconstructed with parallels from Lisbon or Aveiro: Fig. 18.7), but among them are three dishes and two pancheons, nine possible standing costrels, three lids, five jugs, five small drinking jugs or *pucaros* and one olive jar. They are mostly domestic vessels. The olive jar was used in commercial exchanges and is rare both in Portugal and in Britain, with only 18 known from

Poole, eight from Southampton, and single examples from Winchester, Wareham and Romsey, Totnes and Topsham (Horsey 1992, 78, 82, 126; Gutiérrez 2000; Allan pers. comm). The standing costrel might have had a range of functions and might have arrived empty, have been used as a container for a different product to be traded, or have been used aboard the ship in which it travelled across the Atlantic (Gutiérrez 2012).

Portugal: sugar moulds

The principal exception to the sharp decline in imports of Portuguese coarsewares after 1600 is the very large collection of sugar moulds from Goldsmith Street (Site 37), which are probably of Portuguese origin (Allan 1984a, 138–41: *c.* 25 kg from at least 85 vessels; thin-sectioning by D. Williams). They fall outside the date-range of the present study. Ceramic sugar cones were essential to process the semi-refined sugar arriving from the Caribbean colonies in the 17th century. Although local potteries met with demand in England, it is clear that, when needed, moulds would be acquired wherever they were available. The importation of the ceramic moulds is already noted at Plymouth in 1594 (1,060 moulds) and in 1600 (Willan 1959, 315). Further references include the transport of 300 moulds from London to Exeter in 1673, again without specifying their provenance (London, Low Countries or Portugal perhaps); a few years later the moulds are arriving from Rotterdam (Allan 1984a, 139). At Southampton a group of at least 100 Portuguese sugar moulds were found in the quay, broken while they were waiting to be sold off or transported to the refinery (Gutiérrez 2007). This assemblage is of interest as it demonstrates that the arrival of Portuguese coarseware included a mixed range of forms; all this pottery (all 6,961 sherds) has a very similar fabric and it probably came from the same workshop in a single consignment.

Sugar moulds were produced in Portugal in several places, including Lisbon and Aveiro (Torres 1990; Morgado *et al.* 2012). In the late 16th and 17th century there is a well-organised trade in ceramic moulds with large volumes being exported from the Aveiro region through the port there. The industry in the area of Aveiro-Ovar seems to have been fuelled by the need to supply moulds to the colonies, especially Madeira, the Azores, Brazil and occasionally also to the Spanish Canary Islands. Ceramic exports were well organised, with boats exclusively filled with pots for export; a couple of such examples have been excavated, providing a glimpse at the range of forms being exported together (Alves *et al.* 1998; 2001; Bettencourt and Carvalho 2007; Carvalho and Bettencourt 2012).

Conclusion

In the Late Middle Ages Exeter played little part in commerce with the Iberian Peninsula, and relied instead on coastal trade with Dartmouth, Plymouth – the main Devon ports involved in this trade – and Southampton (Kowaleski 1995, 27). Its location 6 km from the port of Topsham will also have been an important factor affecting the quantity and range of imports, since the volume of imported pottery declines sharply outside of ports. Pottery assemblages from ports are characterised not only by high numbers of imports, but also by a wider variety of sources, forms and vessel types; the distance these travelled once they had been landed was usually very short. Among the atypical finds from Devon is a chafing dish found at Plymouth (Allan 1995, no. 95). It was made at Seville and is best paralleled by that painted by Velázquez in *An old woman frying eggs*. These are utilitarian small portable stoves to cook or heat up individual pots, of identical function to those made at this date in Somerset and in France, for example. The French examples were exported regularly, whereas the example from Seville is not known to have travelled except for this Plymouth example.

The assemblage from Exeter is not dissimilar to the range of Spanish and Portugese finds from other sites in Devon, which include Barnstaple, Cheriton Fitzpaine, Chudleigh, Chittlehampton, Dartington, Dunkeswell, Newton Abbot and Totnes (Hurst 1977, 93; Allan 1995). Pottery from these sites includes Valencian lustrewares, Morisco wares, olive jars and Portuguese coarsewares. The Devon finds include a near-complete Seville lustreware dish, found in the 1930s in Bideford (unpublished: Museum of Barnstaple and North Devon). The decorated finds are clearly concentrated in the 15th and 16th centuries, whereas the coarseware reach into later periods. The only exceptional find from the county is a sherd of an albarello of Malagan lustreware found at the Bishop's Palace at Chudleigh (Gutiérrez 2006). Although similar in fabric to the examples found at Exeter, this belongs to a type of vessel which is not only earlier but also rare, with a very limited distribution in the country, perhaps reflecting its exotic contents. The way in which rarer types of pot were acquired does seem to depend on other circumstances other than proximity to international ports (Gutiérrez 2006).

Italian and Italian-influenced maiolica found in Exeter

by Hugo Blake[1]

Introduction

In total, eight Italian vessels and 21 examples of Italo-Netherlandish maiolica dating before 1550 have been recorded from excavations in Exeter. These finds belong entirely to the period *c.* 1480–1550; there are no examples of the preceding types of medieval Mediterranean Maiolica, which are now known from more than 36 sites in the British Isles (Hurst 1991, 213; Blake and Hughes 2015, 149–51; 2019; Blake forthcoming a). They fall into four groups: the more numerous Italo-Netherlandish Maiolica (INM), so-called because the type was made in both Italy and the Low Countries; South Netherlands

Maiolica (SNM) which are undoubted Low Countries products; a single example of early Ligurian Maiolica; and seven from Montelupo in Tuscany. They were all covered with a tin-opacified lead glaze decorated with designs developed in northern Italy, whose manufacture was introduced to North-West Europe by 'Venetian' emigrant potters in the early 16th century. Our understanding of this transmission has been advanced significantly by finding out where examples found in Great Britain were made. For this reason, the chemistry of 22 tin-glazed pottery fragments of presumed Italian or Low Countries origin excavated in Exeter was determined by ICPS as part of EAPIT (Appendix 18.2).

Detailed descriptions of each vessel sampled, presented in the order of their ICP Laboratory number (prefix **DF**), will be found in online Appendix 18.4. All the Italian and South Netherlands maiolica from Exeter analysed by ICPS – which also include the earlier analyses distinguished by their Laboratory prefix **V** – are listed in Table 18.8 in Appendix 18.2 with the sites where they were found and their likely place of manufacture. This section of this chapter discusses the characteristics and chronology of the types, and the relative significance of the vessels in this country and their likely function.

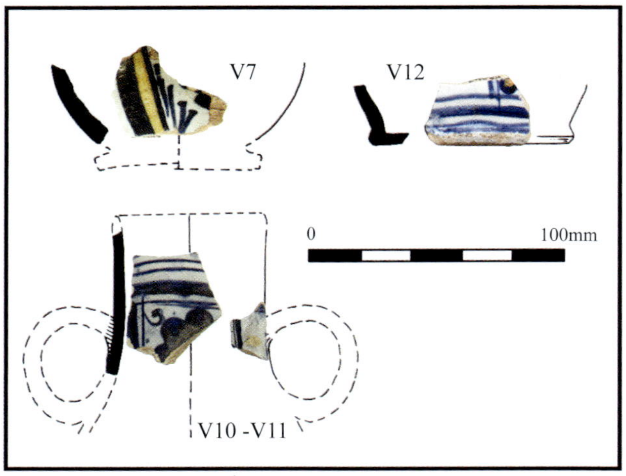

Fig. 18.11 Italo-Netherlandish Maiolica: samples attributed to Montelupo (V7, V10–V12) (graphic John Allan/David Gould, © RAMM)

Italo-Netherlandish Maiolica

The INM excavated in Exeter form one of the four largest collections of this type of pottery in the British Isles, smaller than the major collections from Southampton and London, the major ports of the Italian trade in the Late Middle Ages, but the same number as that from Winchester (Figs 18.11–13; Hurst 1999, 92, 99; 2002, 315, 325). The 21 vessels are scattered among 13 different sites, an indication that they circulated widely in urban communities. Three were excavated from each of the same sites in Goldsmith Street, Preston Street and Queen Street.

Early Netherlands Maiolica was first defined by Bernard Rackham almost a century ago as the first tin-glazed ware made in the Low Countries in an Italian Renaissance style but on closed shapes then unparalleled in Italy (Rackham 1926, 29–31, 96–7, 101–3).[2] In the post-War period John Hurst called the many he identified from archaeological excavations South Netherlands Maiolica (SNM; Hurst *et al.* 1986, 117). Laboratory analyses undertaken in the 1990s established that some examples found in Buckinghamshire, London and Southampton have a chemical signature similar to pottery from the Lower Arno Valley. In the proceedings of the British Museum colloquium on 16th-century tin-glazed pottery in North-West Europe where the analyses had been presented, Rackham's term 'Netherlandish' was revived to refer to the [late] 15th and 16th-century products of 'the Italian influenced maiolica industry operating in the Low Countries' (Gaimster 1999a, vi; cf. Rackham 1926, 15–17). In that publication some called the type Italo-Netherlandish Maiolica (INM; Gutiérrez and Brown 1999; Gutiérrez 1999; followed by Blake and Hughes 2015, 151; *pace* Hurst 1999, 98). As SNM includes types made later in the 16th century in shapes derived from German stoneware and with decoration which is easier to distinguish from the Italian prototypes, it would be appropriate to limit the term INM to the characteristic early forms produced before about 1540 (Hurst 1970, 362; Hurst *et al.* 1986, 117–18).[3]

Since the revelatory analyses 20 years ago, research commissioned by John Allan has shown that other items of this ware from South Wales, Somerset and Devon are also of Tuscan origin (Blake and Hughes 2015, 151–3). The EAPIT project has provided the opportunity to examine nearly all the remaining Exeter INM listed in the 1999 catalogue (Allan 1999b, 160–1).[4] In contrast with the five already analysed and shown to be Tuscan, the 15 now investigated were made in Antwerp. The analyses from Exeter and elsewhere in South-West Britain now exceed the number of INM examined in the 1990s for the British Museum colloquium (Gaimster 1999a). Then 14 – to which should be added two identified later – were found to be Tuscan and 13 from the Low Countries.[5] The more recent work has identified another ten as Tuscan and 18 (or 22, if the blue-glazed bodysherds – some of which could be from Malling mugs (see below) – are included) as Antwerp products.[6] The enlarged sample provides an opportunity to reconsider whether those produced in Italy can be distinguished from the ones made in the Low Countries and when they were made.

The best-known – if not the most common – shape is the double-ring-handled mug (Hurst 1999, 92).[7] 'Jugs' with a round mouth were also used in the 16th century for drinking (Gaimster 1997, 118). Because jugs with a pinched spout seem more suited for pouring into another vessel than into a human mouth, I suggested in the first report that they may be Tuscan (Blake 1999, 28,

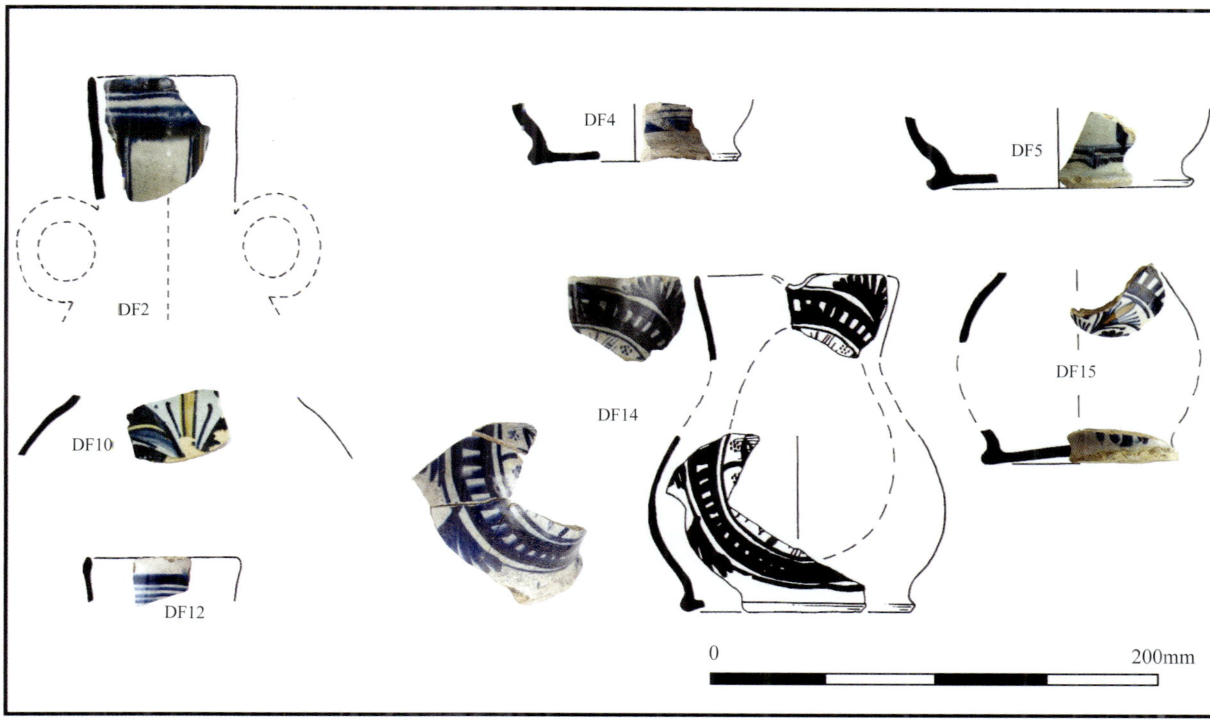

Fig. 18.12 Italo-Netherlandish Maiolica: samples attributed to Antwerp subgroup 1 (DF2, DF4, DF5, DF10, DF12, DF14, DF15) (graphic John Allan/David Gould, © RAMM)

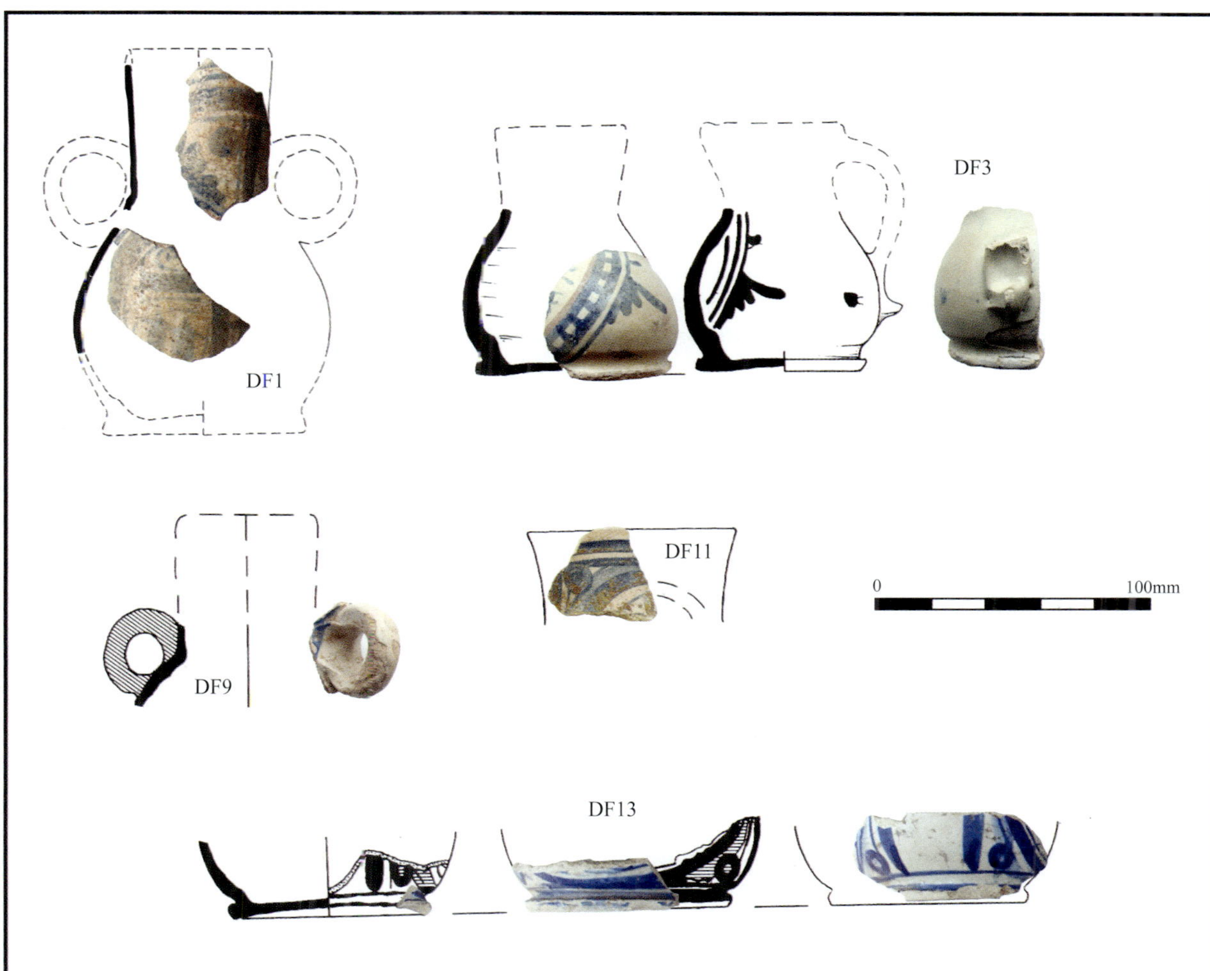

Fig. 18.13 Italo-Netherlandish Maiolica: samples attributed to Antwerp subgroup 2 (DF1, DF3, DF9, DF11, DF13) (graphic John Allan/David Gould, © RAMM)

n. 159); but DF14 shows that this small shape was also made in the Low Countries. The wide-bodied fragment DF10 appears to have been part of a much larger vessel, probably a Faenza-type jug, examples of which from London and Southampton were shown to be Tuscan, a provenance recently confirmed for another from Penhow (Blake 1999, CITG 7, CITG 16; Blake and Hughes 2015, 153, 176, Penhow 1). The earlier analyses, the larger jug's standard decorative frame and the absence of obviously religious motifs suggested that this form was imported from Italy. However, DF10 demonstrates that it – despite being much larger than any other INM shape – was also made in the Low Countries. The only forms which may still be exclusively Italian in manufacture are the handleless vases and the mugs with a pair of pinched lower handle terminals (Blake 1999, 24, types 4, 5b). Ten or 11 of the Exeter samples are classic INM shape or decoration (V7?, V10–V12, DF1–DF2, DF4–DF5, DF9, DF11–DF13), three or four jugs decorated with a ladder medallion (DF3, DF10?, DF14, DF15), and two or three blue-glazed (DF6–DF8–DF7 Malling mug? (see DF16 below)).

In 1997 Belgian colleagues observed that the dull glazes on some Exeter samples are typical of 'SNM' (Allan 1999b, 160, no. 9). Allan then described four of them as dull, all of which have now been confirmed by the EAPIT analyses as made in the Low Countries (DF1, DF3, DF11, DF13).[8] The external glaze of three which have recently been shown to be Tuscan were considered glossy or very glossy (V7, V10–V11), but so were two that we now know were made in the Low Countries (DF2, DF15). As well, part of dull DF13 is glossy. Glossiness was it seems caused by covering the tin glaze with a thinner lead glaze. As some painted colours are more soluble in a lead glaze, the blurring on V10–V11, DF2 and DF5 may be additional evidence of this extra layer (Blake 1999, 27, nos. 110–15). It may be significant that all those noted as having a dull glaze belong to SNM subgroup 2, whereas as all the glossy and blur-decorated items made in the North fall into subgroup 1, suggesting that this characteristic may distinguish different workshops in Antwerp or different production periods of the same workshop (Appendix 18.2).

Unsurprisingly the decorative parallels cited at the end of the Appendix 18.4 descriptions of the analysed EAPIT items show analogies with other Low Countries or Tuscan items found in London, some even to both sources. It is noteworthy that DF2, DF10 and DF15 are as well executed as the Italian prototypes and include orange elements. The less well-executed ladder medallion of DF14 encloses fine details. All these lie in SNM subgroup 1.

One reason why it was observed in 1999 that no distinction could be seen between Italian and Low Countries products was because it was then assumed that the few ring-handled mugs found in Italy were made there.[9] An item sold in Florence was attributed to Tuscany and the analysis of a close match found in London revealed it had been made in Antwerp (Blake 1999, 25, 32, 24, no. 48, 137, fig. 2.4 bottom right; Hurst 1999, 94, cf. fig. 4.1.2.1; Hughes and Gaimster 2002, 233, no. 123; Blake and Hughes 2003, 449, fig. 13 left). However, it was later established that the item sold in Florence had been acquired in London. The large published colour illustrations show that it shares with DF1, DF11 and DF13 the application of a paler blue to fill, or to flank, the main roundel surround and the circles within the corners of the frame (Wilson and Sani 2007, 308, illus. on 301–3). Two INM from Glastonbury are similar but decorated with a dot within the circle or with an unfilled circle and a paler band around the roundel (Allan *et al.* 2015, 268–70, fig. 8.18, nos. 202–3; colour images kindly supplied by John Allan). All of these Exeter and Glastonbury items were made in the Low Countries. The disk in a similar position on a Tuscan ring-handle mug is solid, but a paler blue was used alongside dark blue on six of those shown to be Italian in 1999 and on one in Southampton (Blake 1999, 24, fig. 2.3.1; Blake and Hughes 2015, 177, Southampton 8; Brown 2002, pl. 6.369). However, Exeter V12 of Tuscan clay has within the frame of its lower corner a blue ring filled with moderate orange yellow and there is a circle in a similar position on an Italian fragment in London (Allan, 1999b, fig. 12.1.6; Blake 1999, 44, CITG 13, fig. 2.4.13; Blake and Hughes 2015, 173, Exeter 4). The Low Countries ring-handled mugs lack the fine lines and dots on the ground between the roundel and the frame evident on some Tuscan examples (V10; Blake 1999, figs 2.3.1, 2.4.13). The paler blue bands applied around the roundel of DF13 are slapdash and the pointed end of its darker vertical bands touching the lower frame also shows haste.

Despite similarities and overlaps, the Exeter INM samples suggest that the SNM subgroup 2 items – with which the Glastonbury INM items 'overlap' (Hughes below) – with larger pale blue-filled circles dominating the corner spaces and with broader paler bands associated with the main roundels on a dull glaze can be distinguished from Italian products.

As some INM were made in Italy apparently for export to North-West Europe, it is likely that the Italian items preceded those produced in the Low Countries. Because the Spanish prototype is represented in a Book of Hours executed between 1477 and 1490, the style of the INM decoration was current in north-central Italy from towards the end of the 15th century, and the earliest known Italian workshop in Antwerp was already operating in 1508, *c.* 1490 may mark the start of Italian INM and *c.* 1500 the threshold between the imports and the Low Countries products, with the immigrants and those they trained still painting in the 1530s motifs which by then may have been out of date in Italy (Dumortier 1987, 166; 2002, 22, 164–5; Blake 1999, 27, 37, 41, nos. 168, 232; Hurst 1999, 95). As it is likely that in the early phase the immigrants' products would resemble closely those they made in their homeland and only later would their pottery become more distinctive and less well executed, it could be that the INM attributed to SNM subgroup 2 is later. However, as we will see below, the better-quality South Netherlands Maiolica jug DF18 also belongs to this subgroup and is in a style and shape associated with the first Italians to emigrate to Antwerp. It reached Exeter by the beginning of the 16th century.

Of the five Tuscan vessels in this style excavated in Exeter, four are INM, one from a context datable to *c.* 1500, two 1500–50, and the other 1550–1600 (Blake and Hughes 2015, 173; Allan 1999b, 159). Most of the 15 EAPIT items from Antwerp may have been deposited in the first half of the 16th century, two of these *c.* 1538 and *c.* 1536–50. The contexts of the others are later or not datable. As for the contexts of the Antwerp subgroups, DF2 of SNM subgroup 1 is *c.* 1500–50 and the earliest SNM subgroup 2 item DF9 is *c.* 1538 Although only two instances they would appear to confirm the proposed subgroup sequence and would seem to preclude that SNM subgroup 2 was only made later.[10] Only one Tuscan item (V7 from a *c.* 1500 context) fits the hypothetical overall chronology; but a blue-glazed fragment – which is also Tuscan – from Bridgwater, in Somerset was found with late 15th-century pottery and may thus be the earliest context so far identified in Britain for INM (Blake forthcoming b).[11] But we have to bear in mind that archaeological dating is usually imprecise and at best indicates the moment of discard, which in the case of relatively high-quality exotic products may be many years after their acquisition.

South Netherlands Maiolica

The fine and remarkable restored jug DF18, which was excavated in Paul Street, belongs to Antwerp subgroup 2 (Fig. 18.14; online Appendix 18.4). Because three similar vessels are painted with the names of syrups within a cartouche, it may have been used to contain a wet drug. Similar ornament occurs also on cylindrical jars with a slightly concave body and a constricted neck and foot, which are often called by their Italian name *albarelli*. These complete pots now in museums or private collections in North-West Europe presumably came from pharmacies in the Low Countries (Drey 1978, 116–7, pl. 59A; Dumortier 2002, 216–17, 219–20, jugs: cat. 85, 87–8; jars: cat. 79–80). They have been dated on analogy with similarly decorated tile pavements at The Vyne, in Hampshire, and from Herkenrode abbey, in Belgium. The Tudor house at the former 'must have been substantially completed between 1515 … and 1526' and the inscriptions on some of its tiles are in Middle Dutch (Rackham 1926, 65–6; Howard 1998, 44; cf. Blanchett 2000, 6, 8–9, 14–6, designs H1a–b, SS1a, H2a, Ra-g, k; Dumortier 2002, 162). In 1532 tiles were ordered for the Belgian abbey from an Italian resident in Antwerp (Dumortier 2002, 16, 163–5, 253, cat. 2; cf. figs 26, 38). In the 1960s an *albarello* wall fragment painted with a 'rosette' and a hexagonal tile decorated also with a profile 'flower' were excavated on the site of Whitehall Palace, in London. The drug jar came from a pit sealed by the Palace's construction in 1532 and the tile either from 'Cardinal Wolsey's 1520s lodgings or Henry VIII's rebuild of 1532' (Gaimster and Nenk 1997, 176; Hurst 1999, 94, fig. 4.4.7; Hurst and Le Patourel 1999, 181, fig. 17.1 centre). Analysis of the tile showed 'similar chemical features' to one examined from Herkenrode (Gaimster and Hughes 1999, 176, table 1). A syrup jar dated '1546' may provide a *terminus ante quem*. It appears to be executed in a different palette of paler blue and includes a purple-brown band and fill. The scrolls are simpler and the stems with sessile lanceolate leaves are unlike those on DF18 and its parallels (Dumortier, 2002, 220, cat. 87). If indeed the Exeter drug jug was 'deposited…at the very beginning of the 16th century', it would be the earliest known example of SNM (Willmott 2015, 325).

The main motif enclosed by the running scroll on the body of DF18 is called in Italy a 'Persian palmette', in the Exeter case seen in flower in profile and from above (the 'rosette'), rather than in the canonical 'pinecone' form. All three versions appear on floor tiles in a Bologna church. One pavement tile bears the date '1487' and another an image of a man painting a tile, identified on a notice tied to the column by his chair as 'Petrus Andrea de favencia'. Although most of the illustrated Persian-palmette tiles and pottery found in Faenza are painted in dark blue with elements filled in orange brown, some also feature green fill, and fewer yellow too. However, both the pinecone and flowering variants on a ground of small curls and spirals were painted on a plate, whose reverse is covered with an *alla porcellana* design and bears the date '1524'. A blue spout with an invected lower border occurs on a Faentine jug fragment decorated in this latter style (Bojani 1997, **1**, 71, pl. 26.291; **2**, 32–33, 103, pls 29.56/3, 78; Ravanelli Guidotti 1998, 15–6, 169–90, 206–7, 269, fig. 23; 2004, 89, 124–6, pls 3–4, cat. 4).

The North-West European tiles and similarly decorated jars are considered to have been made by the 'Venetian' Guido Andries – the best-documented early Italian potter in Antwerp who was working there by 1508, because before 1524 he was commissioned by the Bishop of Utrecht, the Duke of Burgundy's half-brother, to supply a pavement and because in 1540 he had to recover pottery in Paris (Dumortier 1987, 166, 168, 170; cf. 2002, 226). A 1532 document mentions a Venetian 'maker of apothecary pots' at a house identified as that bought by Guido in 1520 (Gaullieur 1876, 125; Dumortier 2002, 165, 167–8). Some of the pavements attributed to his workshop were painted in various designs, ascribed to 'many hands of unequal quality'. 'Hybrid' combinations are known on pots. For example, a two-handled Italian jug is decorated under its tubular spout with the lion of St Mark enclosed

Fig. 18.14 South Netherlands Maiolica: jug attributed to Antwerp subgroup 2 (DF18). (graphic: Sandy Morris: photographs © RAMM)

by a flower-and-fruit wreath on a ground of Persian-palmette type (Alverà Bortolotto 1981, pl. 81; Morazzoni 1955, pl. 49). However, the northern version of the latter design is 'often coarser in execution' than the others and the Italian prototypes, and thus unmistakably South Netherlands Maiolica (Alverà Bortolotto and Dumortier 1990, 94). Perhaps Guido Andries employed local painters or shared his commissions with other workshops. Apart from the exceptionally early context of DF18, it is striking that the only other early SMN drug jar I know in England came from Cardinal Wolsey's residence in London, an indication of the outstanding quality of the Exeter find.

The variety of coloured glazes on the small fragment DF16 from St Nicholas Priory is typical of 'Malling' mugs which have a globular or ovoid body and a cylindrical neck. They are named after an example once in a church in Kent. The early British Museum analyses confirmed that they were produced in Antwerp, where an order was made in 1549 for 20,000 'marbled pots' from five potters. English silver mounts and a Danish pewter lid show that they were in use between 1548 and 1618 (Hurst *et al.* 1986, 126–7; Hurst 1999, 96–7; Hughes and Gaimster 1999, 61; Dumortier 2002, 32, 96, 136, 209, 247, fig. 29). As 'jars and jugs with a monochrome or mottled blue or purple surface' were reported from one excavation in Antwerp and a plain blue-glazed one from Glastonbury has 'a wide upright neck…favour[ing] identification as a Malling jug', it is possible that a blue-glazed fragment could belong to this type rather than to an INM vessel (Dumortier and Veeckman 1994, 195; Oost and Veeckman 2002,

54; Allan *et al.* 2012, 8, no. 208; also Honey 1962, 35; cf. Museum Boijmans Van Beuningen, inv. no. A 3431). However, because the analysed Malling mugs fall in the SNM subgroup 2, it is likely that a blue-glazed fragment belonging to subgroup 1 is INM. If so, DF6 and DF8 are INM, whereas DF7, Newton Abbot 1008 and Totnes RN8 could be either INM or Malling (Appendix 18.2). Malling mugs have been found at 34 or more sites in Britain, but many of these may have been made after 1550 (Hurst 1999, 100; 2002, 323). However, the context of DF16 is earlier and thus falls within the scope of the EAPIT project. Like the INM mugs, it was made for drinking (Wilson *et al.* 1988, 399).

Ligurian Maiolica

Fragments of the fine and remarkable dish DF19 were recovered from a mid 16th-century pit in Goldsmith Street (Fig. 18.15). Chemical analysis shows that it was made in Genoa (Appendix 18.2). It is an example of *berettino* (greyish-blue) glazed *maiolica ligure* (Ligurian Maiolica) with *calligrafico a rabesche* (calligraphic arabesque) decoration.

Many examples of this design were found amongst production waste in a 16th-century clay quarry in via San Vincenzo, Genoa (Farris and Ferrarese 1969, 27–36, pls 1.1, 6–8, 9.7–8, 11.2; Mannoni 1969, 80–2; Marzinot 1979, 174, figs 180, 188, 205; cf. elsewhere in Genoa, *e.g.* Pessa and Ramagli 2010, 78, no. 86). The type was present in a 1544 demolition layer in Savona, where it formed 5.3% of the Ligurian Maiolica (Lavagna 1992, 135–6, fig. 10; 2011, 33–4, no. 15). An identical dish was excavated from a mid 16th-century context in Middelburg in the Netherlands (Jaspers 2011, 17, fig. 11).

The '*rabesche*' design was illustrated by Piccolpasso in *c.* 1557, which he described as 'more in use at Venice and Genoa than elsewhere' (Farris and Ferrarese 1969, 15–8, pl. 1.1; Piccolpasso 1980, vol. 1, xxi–xxiv, 66; vol. 2, 111). By 1528 Francesco da Camerino and Francesco da Pesaro (both 'from' towns in the Marche in north-east Italy) had established pottery workshops in Genoa. In 1532 Tommaso Pesaro agreed to supply 25 dozen cups 'worked *alla venetiana*' (Milanese 1980, 338). Some dishes in *alla porcellana* style recording the unions of Nuremberg and Augsburg families were made between 1515 and 1525 presumably in Venice, where the best-documented workshop of Jacomo da Pesaro was active between 1507 and 1546 (Alverà Bortolotto 1981, pls 46–7; 1988, 17; Wilson 1987, 185; Leonardi 2002, 62; Thornton and Wilson 2009,

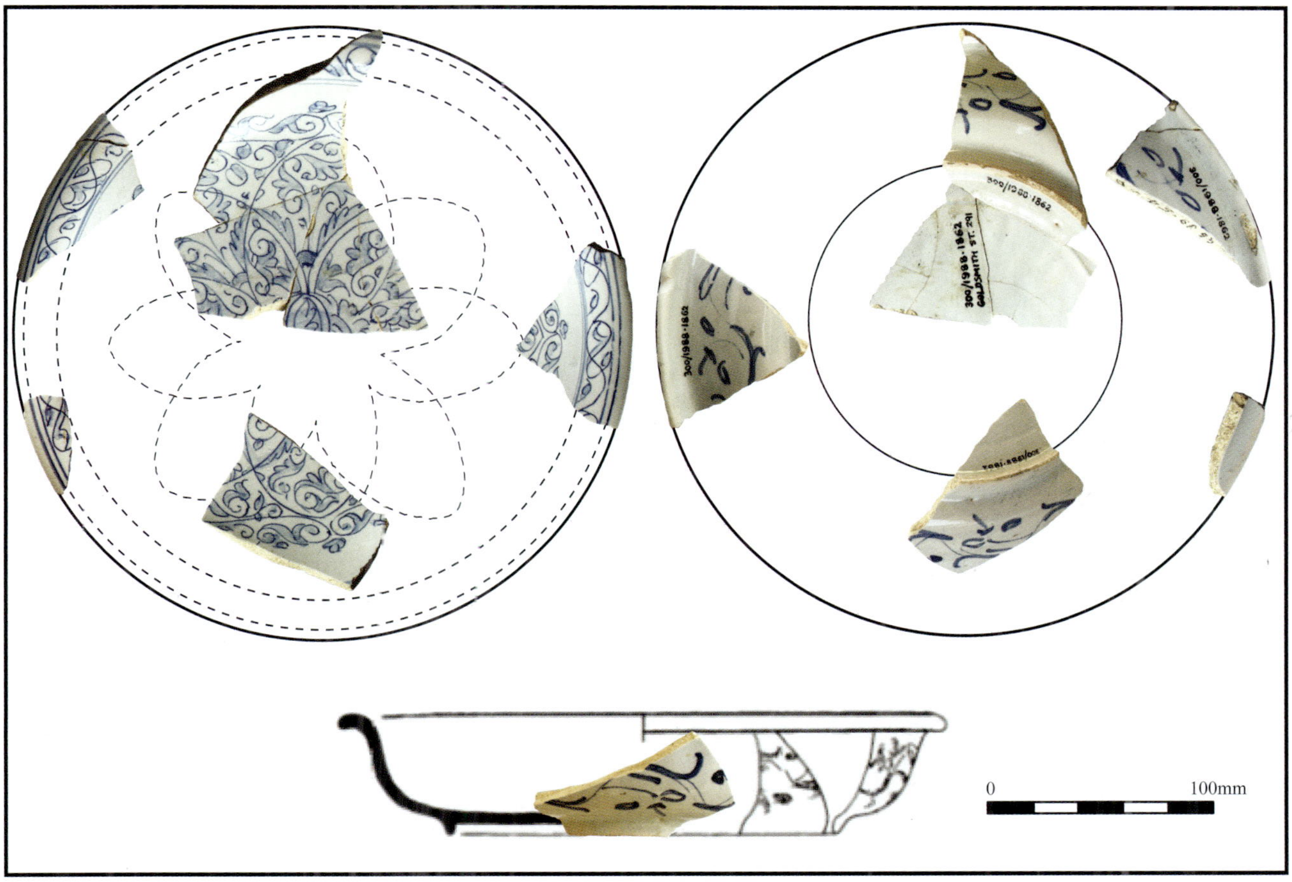

Fig. 18.15 Ligurian Maiolica: sample attributed to Genoa (DF19). (graphic John Allan/David Gould)

90–1).[12] However, although DF19's rim ornament and the schematic branching spiral scroll on its reverse resemble those on a pale *berettino* example of this 'Venetian' type, arabesques as the principal ornament occur on a dish dated 1543 (Alverà Bortolotto 1981, pl. 47d, 48e; Sani 2012, pl. 75). So, the link between the maiolica production in the two metropolitan city ports and their relative priority are at the moment unclear.

Ligurian Maiolica was the first distinctive Renaissance type of tin-glazed pottery made in Liguria. Established in the second quarter of the 16th century as a ware to rival Turkish fritware and Chinese porcelain, it and the related blue on white *alla porcellana* produced across north-central Italy introduced an aesthetic quite distinct from that of Italian polychrome maiolica and, along with the *bianchi* (white ware) of Faenza created by 1540, enjoyed a remarkable success elsewhere in Europe (Ravanelli Guidotti 1996, 6; Ostkamp 2006, 71–2; Thornton and Wilson 2009, 89–90, n. 8; Jaspers 2011, 20–4; Sani 2012, 61–4; Blake 2016, 79–80;). The quality of the excavated early Genoese products is exceptional in its potting, refined decoration – on the outside as well as within – and in the subtlety of its bluish-grey glaze. The commoner Ligurian *berettino* is more thickly potted and decorated with a broader brush on a darker blue ground, exemplified by a find from Totnes (Allan 1984c, 84–5, nos 7–8, fig. 2.7; Hurst 1991a, figs 10a–b).

Few others like DF19 have been found in Britain. One from Quilter's Vault in Southampton appears to be of the same arabesque design (Brown 2002, 87, fig. 34.371).[13] Another from the High Street belongs to the *calligrafico a volute tipo A* (calligraphic spirals type A) variant, as do eleven or fewer dishes from Acton Court in Gloucestershire (Farris and Ferrarese 1969, 22; Mallet 1972, 254–5, figs 13 top, 14 photos; Platt and Coleman-Smith 1975, 179, no. 1360, fig. 210.1360 drawing; Hurst 1991a, 214, fig. 11a–b photos; Vince and England 2004, 308, fig. 9.9.221,224, pls 8–11).[14] This design is derived from the *tuğrakeş* spiral style of Iznik pottery, an example of which bears the date 1529, although to judge from a Ligurian drug jar bearing the date '1572' its Italian imitation was still made later (Morazzoni 1951, pl. 13; Atasoy and Raby 1989, 108–13, fig. 133; Carswell 1998, 47, fig. 25). Analysis of a fragment from Acton Court shows that it – like DF19 – was made in Genoa (Vince and England 2004, 308; Appendix 18.2).

The High Street find is from a pit whose other ceramic contents were almost all made about a century later (Platt and Coleman-Smith 1975, vol. 2, 32, 42). The 'exceptional' group 'in quantity and quality' including a 'staggering…range of imports' from Quilter's Vault has been interpreted as representing 'a single phase of activity' closed '*c.* 1490–1510' (Brown 2002, 80–7, 149–50). If so, the arabesque dish, the late Siegburg stoneware mug of *c.* 1550 and the Montelupo 'lozenge net design' datable to the second half of the 16th century are intrusive (Brown 2002, 85–6, nos 318, 359, figs 30, 35; Blake 2012, 31–2; forthcoming c, fig. 5). The pottery excavated at Acton Court is also considered 'exceptional'. It has been suggested that its set of Ligurian dishes – which were along with the other Italian wares 'undoubtedly…the most highly prized' – were acquired for a royal visit in 1535, for which the east range was built (Rodwell 2003, 160–6; Vince and England 2004, 302, 308, 329–30).

Montelupo maiolica

Eight examples of Montelupo maiolica dating before *c.* 1550 have been recorded from the city. Seven are illustrated here (Fig. 18.16); a recent discovery of a plate with chequered decoration has been published elsewhere (Allan and Langman 2009, 169–72; Allan 2015, 133). The Exeter finds of this centre's products seem to show a similar pattern of rare 15th-century imports and a more significant presence *c.* 1500 and in the first half of the 16th century, evident elsewhere in the British Isles and in the Low Countries (Hurst 1991a, 213–14; Brown 2002, 40–1, 73, fig. 35; Blake 2012, 27–30; 2019, 272; Jarrett and Blackmore 2015, 105).

In Allan's recent review of Italian ceramics in South-West England the earliest type – but not necessarily the oldest item – of Tuscan maiolica excavated in Exeter is a basin fragment with a base diameter of about 200 mm from Goldsmith Street (Fig. 18.16.1; Allan 1984a, 217 fig. 123, no. 2725; 2015, 118, fig. 2.2). It may belong to Berti's *maiolica arcaica tricolore* (three-colour archaic maiolica) decorative type, the relevant variant of which he dates to the 1480s (Berti 1997, 160–1, subgroup 6.1.5, pl. 54).[15]

The earliest Renaissance maiolica are brimmed bowls. One related to Tuscan INM from a *c.* 1500 or earlier context in Polsloe Priory has painted on its brim – which terminates in an upright rim – Bernardine-type wavy sun rays and within the bowl cavity plant motifs, both comparable to those painted on north-east Italian items (Fig. 18.16.V8–V9; Berardi 1984, fig. 36b–c; Allan 1999b, 160, nos 2–3; 2015: 118, fig. 2.5–6; Blake and Hughes 2015, 154, 173, Exeter 2–3; cf. Ciaroni, 2004, fig. 144, pl. 32.3, 6, 13). The other from Goldsmith Street is decorated in a Montelupo style of *alla porcellana* called by Berti *motivi vegetali della 'famiglia bleu'* (blue family plant motifs; Fig. 18.16.2; Allan 2015, 118–19, fig. 2.7). It belongs to the variant characterized by the 'toothed half-moon' motif, the Exeter version of which may date to *c.* 1500–20, because a syrup jar with comparable ornament may have been ordered in 1507, a plate bears the coat of arms of a Florentine who was a cardinal from 1513 to 1531, and the form of the motif seems typologically early in its presumed development (Berti 1998, 135–41, 222, n. 39, type 40.1, pl. 142; jar: Marini in Wilson and Sani 2007, 46–51; motif development: Moore Valeri 1984b; cf. form and roundel frame: Vannini 1977, pl. 15). Similar vessels have been excavated in Holland at Alkmaar and Dordrecht from contexts datable to the second half of the

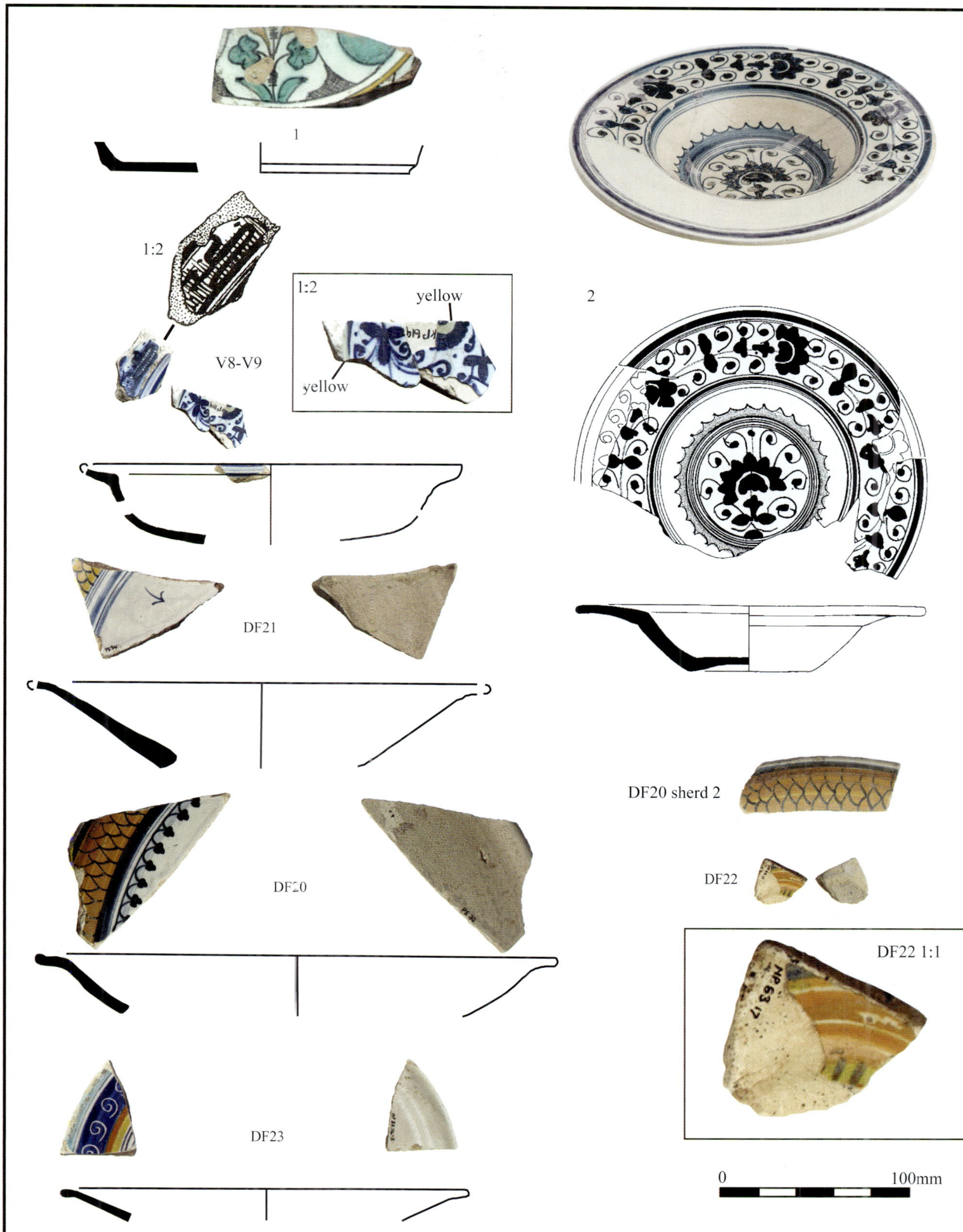

Fig. 18.16 Polychrome maiolica: Montelupo types (7.1–2) and samples attributed to Montelupo (V8–9, DF20–3) (graphic John Allan/David Gould)

16th century and between 1525 and 1575 (Ostkamp *et al.* 2002, 460, figs 20, 35).

DF20–DF23 may also have been made in the early 16th century. DF20 and DF21 from Paul Street are of the Montelupo form Aa 2.3.2, which was common in the 16th century (Fornaciari 2016, 82, 100–102, 198). The *contorno a ghirlanda* ([stylized] wreath border) decorative subtype 23.4.3 has been assigned by Fausto Berti to *c.* 1480–95 and 1480–90, because the type was found amongst kiln waste including a potter's mark, coat of arms and nickname datable around 1490, although within 1480–1520 is suggested by Fornaciari for type 23 (Berti 1998, 116, pls 53–4; 2008, 289, pl. 29i; Fornaciari 2016, 36–7, 112, 305). The small fragment DF22 from St Nicholas Priory probably came from a brimmed hemispherical bowl (Vannini 1977, pls 28, 30; Fornaciari 2016, 87, 225–9, form Bb 2). DF23 from the same site belongs to Berti's *fascia con 'bleu graffito'* (incised blue band) decorative type 34, assigned to *c.* 1510–20, because one is dated '1514' and another bears the papal insignia and the Medici coat of arms, which could, however, be of either Leo X (1513–21) or Clement VII (1523–34). According to Berti, the type only 'disappears in Montelupo kiln waste at the end of the 1530s' (Berti 1983, 212, n. 18; 1998, 131–3, pls 114–26; 2008, 304–6). There is no close parallel in the published illustrations, which are of finer items featuring figures, heraldic motifs, grotesque ornament and more elaborate concentric borders. A green band occurs on the rim of at least four and an incised anti-clockwise curl alternates with a crossed square on another (Vannini 1977, pl. 23; Berti 1983, 209; 1998, pls 121, 124–5; 2008, 304–5, pls 35b, d–e).

Concluding discussion

Chemical analysis has been critical in enlarging our understanding of the diffusion of Italian maiolica in North-West Europe. By showing that the earliest – confirmed by the dates of a context in Exeter and another in Somerset – INM was made in Tuscany in a style not yet recognised in the Arno Valley and in forms rarely found in Italy, it indicated that the type was made for export before the emigration of Italian potters. The latest EAPIT analyses suggest that a possible second phase of Low Countries INM production can be distinguished by eye by its poorer quality. Strangely this poor quality INM belongs to the same Antwerp chemical subgroup as the higher quality SNM jug DF18 which was probably made by 'Venetian' immigrants and their descendants. The apparently earlier better-quality Low Countries INM was made in other workshop(s) perhaps run by different Italian migrants (Blake and Hughes 2003, 451–3). Until sufficient waste not only from Antwerp and Montelupo but also from a wider range of production sites in the Low Countries and the Arno Valley are examined by ICPS, we are unlikely to refine our knowledge further of where INM was made and how it spread. At the moment it is possible that DF4 and DF11 were made in a known Antwerp workshop and that early INM and related types were made in the Arno Valley (Appendix 18.2; Blake and Hughes 2015, 151–4, 156, 159, 163, 184). We are on surer ground with Montelupo maiolica, which is easily identifiable, found in copious quantities where it was produced, and has been extensively analysed by another method. However, it is possible that similar types may have been made in, and exported from, other centres nearby (Blake and Hughes 2015, 161). The EAPIT and Acton Court analyses indicate that two variants of the early refined type of Ligurian Maiolica were made in Genoa, presumably before the centre of production of that class shifted to Albisola and Savona. But, two analyses are too few to exclude that they were also made in the latter communities.

Maiolica production spread across the west Mediterranean from Islamic to Christian countries around AD 1200 (*Le vert & le brun* 1995). Two centuries later Spanish blue-decorated – with or without lustre – types, Chinese porcelain, and Italian textile designs inspired by oriental prototypes transformed tin-glazed production in northern Italy (Moore Valeri 1984a; 1984b; Berti 1997, types 10–13; 1998, 40–3, 45; Ravanelli Guidotti 1998, 118–27, 265–83). Within Italy Renaissance maiolica was spread by potters moving to bigger cities from in many cases the Marche region. In the early 16th century some potters from North-East Italy introduced the technique to Antwerp.[16] Despite that, increasing numbers of South European products reached North-West Europe peaking around 1600 (Blake 2019, 272–3). The white surface of the tin-opacified lead glaze served as a ground for a new variety of bright colours (Gaimster 1999c, 1). Although metalware could be enamelled and similar effects could be reproduced in glass, maiolica cost less, glass is more fragile and the gold paint on the copper dishes 'wears off easily' (https://collections.vam.ac.uk/item/O129203/dish-unknown/; Clarke 1974; Caselli 2011; Higgott 2014). As long as its rarity and the quality of its decoration assured its exclusivity, maiolica was a desirable category of tableware in its own right and not just because pottery is more likely to be discarded and to survive better in the ground. Two outstanding examples of prized items excavated in Exeter are the Antwerp jug DF18 and the Ligurian dish DF19.

As well as introducing a new aesthetic, the shapes of the three classes reflect various functions related to dining. Because of the high proportion of 'yhs' trigrams on INM mugs, I suggested that they were related to the cult of the Name of Jesus and may have been used in the feasts of Holy Name fraternities (Blake 1999, 29; Blake *et al.* 2003, 175–7, 186, 191–3). As expressions of a popular devotion, artefacts marked with the abbreviation of Christ's name come from both lay and 'religious' contexts (Allan 1999b, 159; Jarrett and Blackmore 2015, 96; Gutiérrez above). Both the INM ring handle DF9 and a Spanish lustreware bowl decorated with an 'ihs' ID127 were excavated in

Exeter's Greyfriars, where a Jesus Mass was celebrated (Blake *et al.* 2003, 196, n. 87, fig. 3.1; Gutiérrez above). Feasting may have occurred where many have been found; single finds may have served as devotional aids or talismans (Blake 1999, 29).

The three-colour archaic maiolica basin is called in Tuscany a cooler, in which filled glasses were kept in water on the buffet (Fig. 18.17). The small size of the Exeter example, however, suggests it may have been used to serve solid food (Degasperi 2016, 87–93, esp. 91, pl. 4.12), as may have the *alla porcellana* brimmed bowl (Allan 2015, 118–19, fig. 2.7; Fig. 18.15.2) and its analogue DF22. As the Montelupo plates DF20, DF21 and DF23 are too large to have served as a diner's own dish, they too may have been used to support food on the table or buffet or been displayed upright there.[17]

Fig. 18.17 Cooler on sideboard (detail of Welcoming pilgrims *in fresco cycle of the* Works of mercy *by Domenico Ghirlandaio workshop, c.1480, in San Martino dei Buonomini oratory, Florence, Degasperi 2016, fig. 41)*

The early Ligurian Maiolica dishes found in North-West Europe are of the same shape and – except for those from Acton Court – of similar size,[18] whereas in Genoa closed forms decorated with calligraphic spirals type A are common (Grosso and Morazzoni 1939, pl. 12; Morazzoni 1951, pl. 13; Farris and Ferrarese 1969, 22; Atasoy and Raby 1989, 266–7, fig. 589; Pessa 2014, 67, 84–6, cat. Nos. 23–6).[19] In 1514 the Venetian Giovanni Bellini painted a larger version of a similarly shaped bowl – presumably Chinese porcelain – filled with fruit served at an informal *Feast of the Gods* (Spriggs 1964, 74, pl. 59a–b). In the 1599 edition of a Spanish-English dictionary published in London 'Porcellána' is defined as 'a kinde of earthen vessel painted, costly fruit dishes of fine earth painted' (Perciuale and Minsheu 1599, 193; for 16th-century fruit consumption in London: Forsyth 1999, 24). Post-mortem inventories drawn up in the 1600s in Antwerp list porcelain, imitation porcelain and maiolica fruit bowls (Dumortier 2002, 96). The Genoese maiolica may too have been used as serving dishes, perhaps one provided to each group of diners, who at the royal feast at Acton Court would have been many (Rodwell 2003, 166).

Although later Italian and Dutch paintings illustrate bowls and dishes containing an abundance of food – reflecting a new interest in representing 'Still Life' – a domestic scene datable to 1530 of a Haarleem patrician's family at table shows no ceramics or similar forms in other materials comparable to those featured in later Italian pictures of the *Supper at Emmaus* (Schneider 2003, 118; cf. Ravanelli Guidotti 2019, figs 1a, 2a). With the possible exception of the notable 'drug' jug DF18, the few vessels of Italian and Italian-influenced maiolica found in Exeter datable to the later 15th and to the first half of the 16th century may instead have been used on special occasions such as feasts.

Appendix 18.1

The ICP-AES and ICP-MS analysis of medieval Spanish and Portuguese ceramics from Exeter

Kamal Badreshany

Introduction

Samples of selected medieval pottery of Spanish and Portuguese origin were analysed at the DARC lab (Durham University) by both Inductively Coupled Plasma Atomic Emission and Mass Spectroscopy (ICP-AES and ICP-MS) with the aim of understanding their provenance. These were compared with data available for products from some of the major Spanish production centres of the time including Seville, Valencia and Málaga. In order to increase and improve the existing reference data for the Spanish production centres, some reference samples were also included from both Granada and Muel (Zaragoza). The two samples of 'Málaga' lustreware from Granada were provided in 1995 by Isabel Flores, but were not analysed at the time and they have been included here to better characterise the earlier lustrewares from this area. Eleven samples of kiln wasters from Muel (Zaragoza) are analysed for the first time in the UK (five as part of this project, six financed by the Department of Archaeology, Durham University). Muel was also a major manufacturer of lustrewares, very similar to those from Valencia, but have never been included in analyses carried out in northern Europe in the past.

The sherds from the Exeter excavations selected for analysis include both tin-glazed wares, mainly from Spain, and coarsewares, mainly from Portugal (former 'Merida wares'). The latter were analysed in part to provide a chemical signature for these vessels, but also to see if any chemical differences could be listed among the fabrics identified by Gutiérrez (above).

For comparison purposes, the ICP data were compared to previously analysed samples, mainly by Mike Hughes (Hughes and Vince 1986; 1991; 2003; 2005), who kindly provided results from previous analyses and made them available for this study.

Chemical analysis using ICP yields the inorganic elemental chemical composition of each sample, providing a chemical signature that can be used to determine if different ceramics were made using clays from the same outcrops and can imply a shared production location (Orton and Hughes 2013, 168–83). The more closely related the chemical signature of two samples the greater the likelihood that they were made from materials derived from the same clay outcrop. As the signature can vary even within the same clay outcrop, very close signatures suggest production from a geographically and temporally proximate batch of materials and, thus, likely the same production location and a similar date.

The aim of the present research is to supplement currently available data to provide a more robust reference dataset to facilitate provenance determinations for medieval ceramics from Spain and Portugal found in the UK, thereby enabling a better understanding of the strength and orientation of trade networks in the South-West during the medieval and later periods.

Integration of all the chemical analyses for the Spanish samples carried out in the past has proven difficult, because a range of different of methods have been used previously, including Neutron Activation Analysis (NAA) and ICP-AES (Hughes 1986; 1995a; 1995b; 2003b). In each case the results have provided a different list of elements to compare against and few overlapping elements between each different method of analysis, and this limits their use in typical multivariate analysis. The quality of the analysis of particular elements is also variable depending on which method is utilised. Still, average data for key elements (Sr, Fe, Ca, etc) have been used here to gain an understanding of the typical chemical profile from different production sites, for example at Málaga (Hughes 1986).

Analytical methods and results

Geochemical analysis is usually focused primarily on the rare earth elements (henceforth REE). REE are ideal for

Table 18.5 Samples of Spanish and Portuguese wares from Exeter and elsewhere submitted for analysis

Sample	*Site*	*Type (by eye)*
EX18005	Exeter	Spanish tin-glazed
EX18006	Exeter	Spanish tin-glazed
EX18160	Exeter	Spanish lustreware
EX18164	Exeter	Spanish lustreware
EX18170	Exeter	Spanish lustreware
EX18171	Exeter	Spanish lustreware
EX18204	Exeter	Portuguese? early tin-glazed
EX18208	Exeter	Portuguese? early tin-glazed
EX18224	Exeter	Spanish/Portuguese lead-glazed; 'melado'
EX18284	Exeter	Spanish tin-glazed
EX18285	Exeter	Spanish, Italian or Low Countries Plain Blue?
EX18290	Exeter	Spanish lustreware
EX18293	Exeter	Spanish tin-glazed
EX18334	Totnes	Spanish tin-glazed
EX18354	Exeter	Spanish tin-glazed
EX18373	Exeter	Spanish lustreware
EX18283	Totnes	Portuguese coarseware olive jar, Aveiro-type
EX18267	Exeter	Portuguese coarseware fabric 2
EX18268	Exeter	Portuguese coarseware fabric 3
EX18270	Exeter	Portuguese coarseware fabric 2
EX18271	Exeter	Portuguese coarseware fabric 1
EX18272	Exeter	Portuguese coarseware fabric 4
EX18276	Exeter	Portuguese coarseware fabric 7
EX18277	Exeter	Portuguese coarseware fabric 4
EX18294	Exeter	Portuguese coarseware fabric 1
EX18295	Exeter	Portuguese coarseware fabric 3
EX18305	Exeter	Portuguese coarseware fabric 5
EX18311	Exeter	Portuguese coarseware fabric 6
EX18325	Totnes	Portuguese coarseware fabric 8 lead glazed; Lisbon?
GR1801	Granada	Málaga lustre-and-blue reference sherd
GR1802	Granada	Málaga lustre-and-blue reference sherd
MU1801–11	Muel	wasters

geochemical fingerprinting in clays, as they are largely immobile during low-grade metamorphism, weathering, and hydrothermal alteration (Rollinson 1993). As such, REE values, more than other elements, are a good indicator of the original composition of the parent rock. Moreover, recent studies show that there is no fractionation of these elements as a result of the firing process (Finlay *et al.* 2012, 2389). Only a few of the REE elements were available due to the mix of methods used to generate the comparative data. The analyses focused on other elements as highlighted below.

The synthesis of the data resulting from the ICP pottery analysis requires multivariate statistical data reduction techniques, such as principal components analysis (PCA) (Orton and Hughes 2013, 176–80). PCA examines the variation in the data and reduces the dataset to a few variables or principal components that serve to explain most of the differences in the 'chemical fingerprint' of each sample. The first two principal components usually explain most of the variation in the sample. The numerical values generated for each sample in a PCA are referred to as their 'factor score'. Two samples with similar factor scores will, thus, have a similar chemical fingerprint and appear near each other on the plot of the results of the analysis (Figs 18.18–18.19).

The PCA was conducted on data from the ICP analysis of 61 ceramic samples in total (detailed results in online Table 18.6). Data from 10 samples of tiles from Seville and Valencia were also available but have been left out of the main statistical analyses as their composition is known to be different to pottery vessels (Hughes 1995a, 58).

The PCA was conducted using the SPSS (v.22) statistical software package. The weight percent and ppm concentration values were first normalised by converting them to log values (base 10). The conversion is necessary as it removes the bias in the statistical calculations toward element concentrations that have larger absolute values but lower values. For example, though 13% by weight is a higher concentration than 420 ppm, it has a lower absolute number. The resulting values were then subjected to a principal components analysis and the first three components extracted. The first two, however, explained most of the variation in the data, and were plotted on the graphs shown in Fig. 18.18. Given the limitations of the comparative data described above, x, y plots of selected elemental values were made and found to display and explain important variation in the data very well.

Comparative chemistry of key medieval production centres from Spain and Portugal

The Portuguese wares analysed here present, unsurprisingly, a different chemistry from the Spanish samples and form a clearly distinct group (Fig. 18.18); these are vessels found in Exeter and reference material from kilns in Portugal is not available at the moment for comparison.

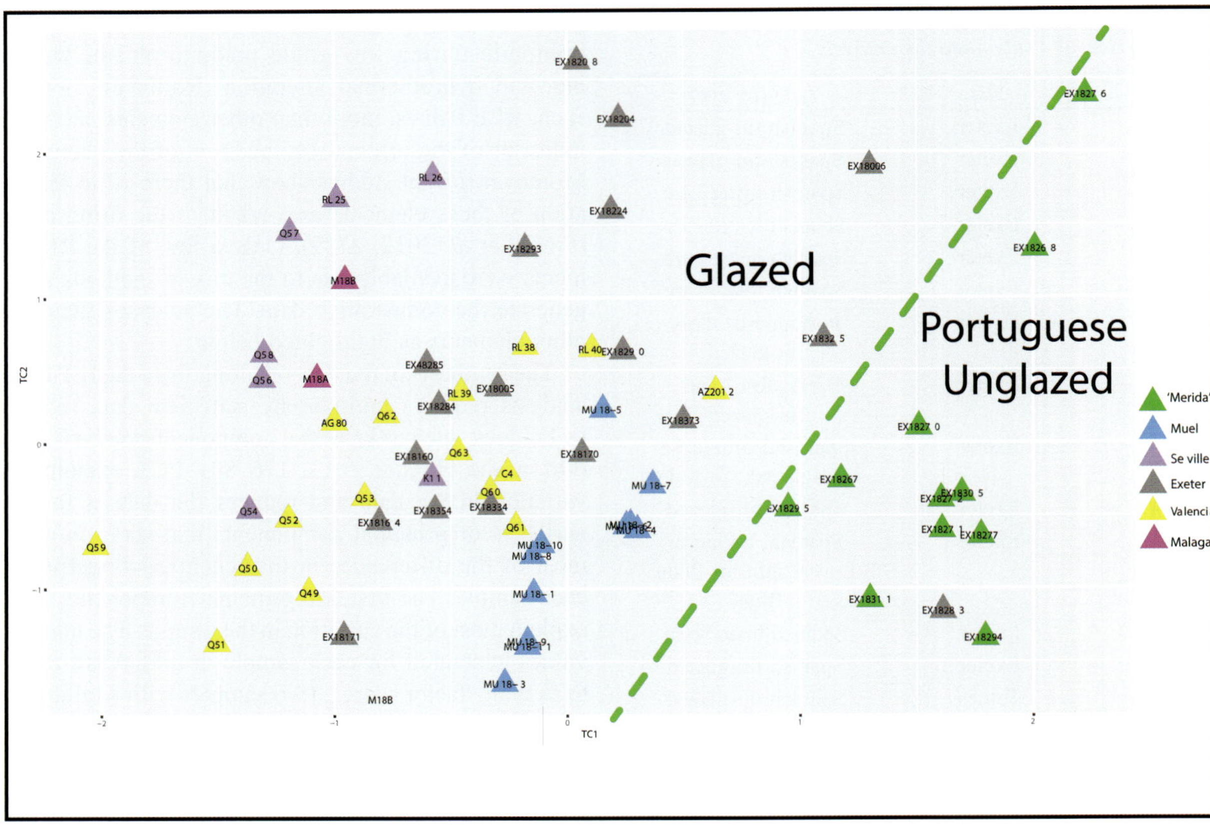

Fig. 18.18 Graph of the results of a Principal Components Analysis labelled by sample number including samples analysed by ICP-AES and ICP-MS as part of this study (EX) and samples analysed by ICP-AES and NAA in earlier studies. The Portuguese redwares (former 'Merida wares') are included in this graph ('Portuguese unglazed') which skews the results, making the Spanish samples more difficult to differentiate (graphic: Kamal Badreshany)

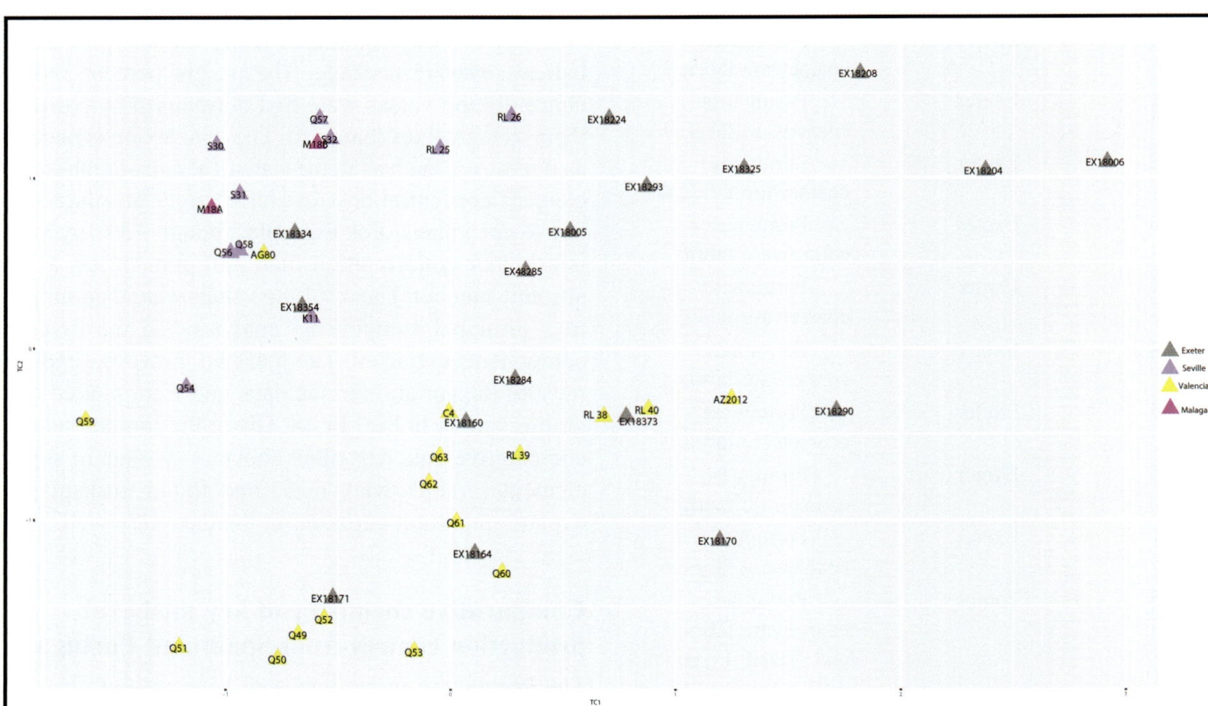

Fig. 18.19 Graph of the results of a Principal Components Analysis labelled by sample number including samples analysed by ICP-AES and ICP-MS as part of this study and samples analysed by ICP-AES and NAA in earlier studies. Portuguese redwares are excluded to help differentiate the various Spanish ceramics. To make the plots even clearer samples from Muel were excluded as only a couple the Exeter sherds were suspected to possibly originate in Muel. Sample AG80 (late lustreware dish from Southampton) previously identified by Alan Vince as Valencia seems to plot with Seville here (graphic: Kamal Badreshany)

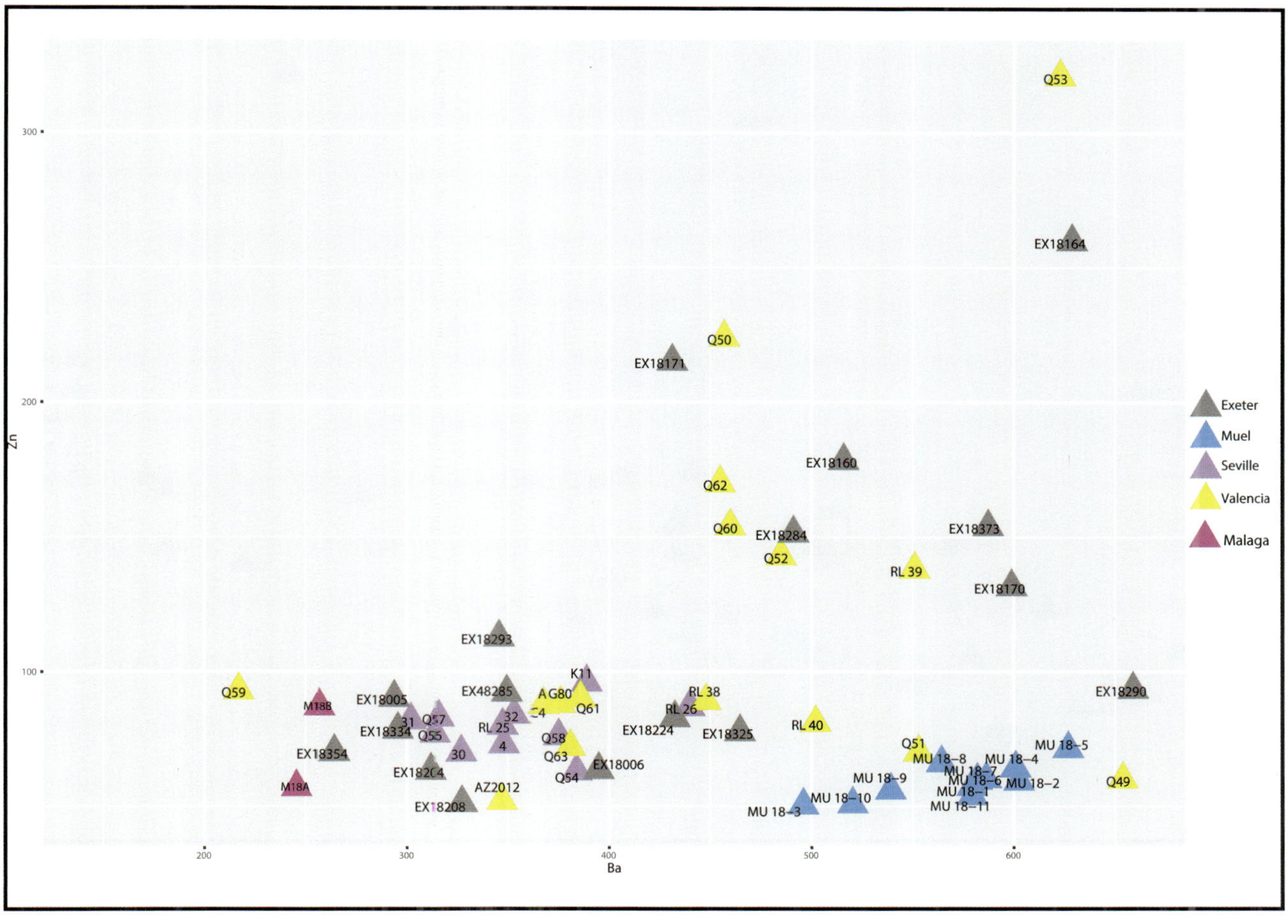

Fig. 18.20 Graph of Ba and Zn values which shows a clear cluster of samples from Muel (graphic: Kamal Badreshany)

The data published for medieval Spanish ceramics present a fairly uniform chemistry, indicating a broad unity in the clays being used across the region for potting and tiles. Still, key differences in the levels of certain elements allow for distinguishing between the production centres of Seville, Valencia, Muel and Málaga. The key elements that distinguish Spanish production sites will be discussed below. The comparative chemical data used to highlight the patterns explained below was published by Hughes (1991; 1995a; 1995b; 2003), Hughes and Vince (1986), and Iñañez *et al.* (2008). Given the limited nature of the dataset (depending on the type of analysis carried out in the past), Ba, Ca, Cr, Fe, K, Sc, Sr and Zn are the most useful elements for distinguishing the ceramics from the production centres investigated in this study, though other minor variations in composition, especially in the REE, exist. Plotting the principal components, Ba and Zn (Fig. 18.20), and Sc and Cr (Fig. 18.21), were generally the most useful way of distinguishing between the various production centres.

Seville

Values published for sherds from Seville show that they tend to be high in Sr (*c.* 350–500 ppm) relative to the other Spanish production sites considered in this research. They also tend to be high in Fe (*c.* 4.5–6%) relative to other production centres, but similar to values established for Valencia. The published data show sherds from Seville tend to be moderately high in Cr (*c.* 60–75 ppm), and slightly higher than values published for Valencia. Samples from Seville also tend to be higher in Na, when compared to those from Valencia.

Valencia

Values published for Valencia tend to be lower in Sr (*c.* 220–300 ppm), when compared to Seville and in line with values from Muel. Sr can often be positively correlated with Ca, although samples from Valencia tend to be higher in Ca than those from Seville. The Sr values, thus, are not strongly correlated with Ca for these sherds making Sr useful for differentiating between samples from these production centres. Vessels from Valencia do show similar Fe levels to sherds from Seville, but are slightly lower in Cr.

Muel

Samples from Muel analysed in this study tend to be low in Fe (*c.* 1.5–3.0%) compared to samples from the other production centres considered as part of this study. Muel samples also tend to be low in Al and Cr. They tend to be high in Ba and low in Zn (Fig. 18.20).

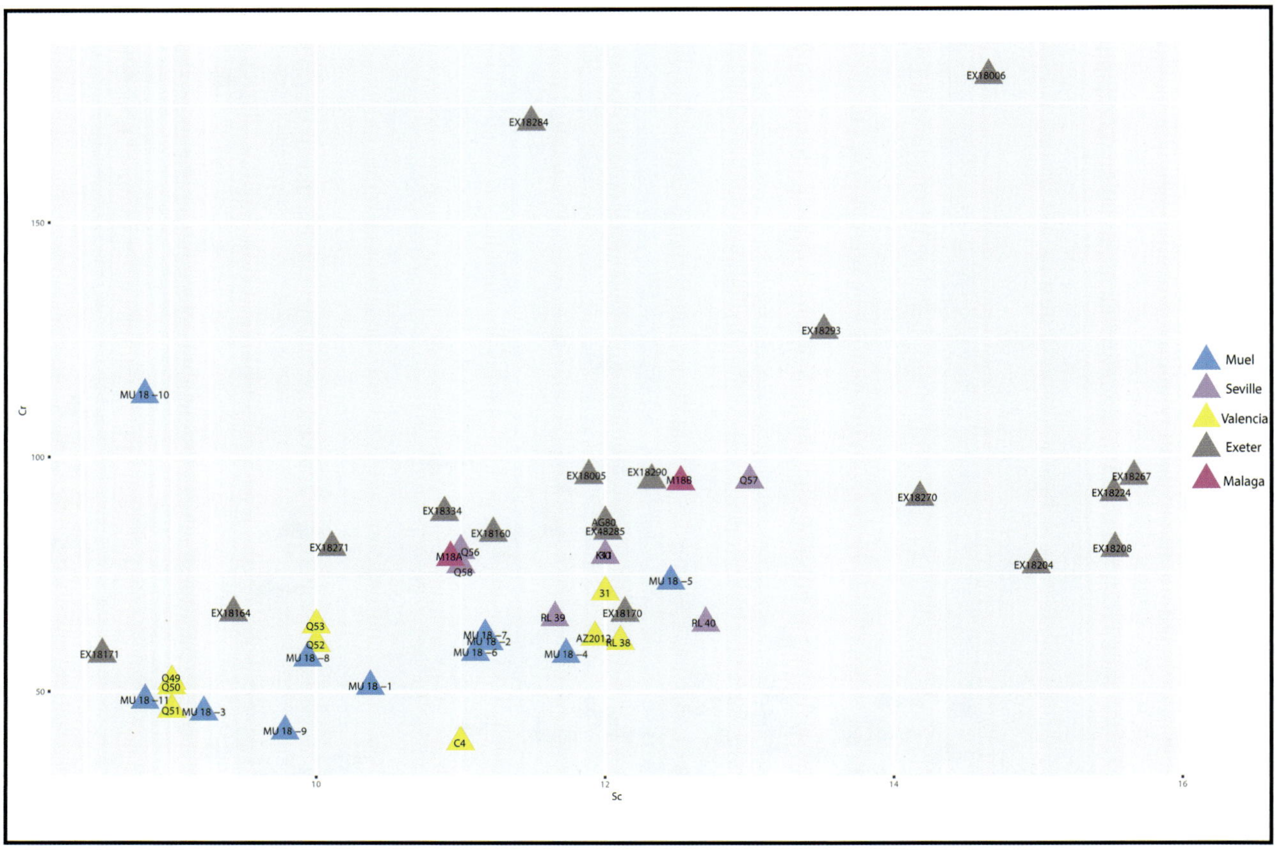

Fig. 18.21 Graph of Sc and Cr values. Hughes (1986) published a similar graph, which showed the usefulness of these elements for differentiating samples from Málaga from other Spanish centres (graphic: Kamal Badreshany)

Málaga

Based on published information, samples from Málaga tend to be high in Sc (*c.* 13–17 ppm) and Cr (*c.* 100–150 ppm) (Fig. 18.21), relative to other samples considered in this study. Two of our reference samples (GR1801 and GR1802) fell slightly below these ranges for both elements, showing that there is more chemical variability in the Málaga samples than previously thought. Our Málaga samples are very similar chemically to those from Seville, something which was also noted by Hughes (1995a).

Barcelona

Published data for Barcelona show samples from that centre are also high Sc, showing similar levels to Málaga, but tend to be lower Cr (*c.* 80–90 ppm) than samples from the latter site (Hughes 1986). None of the Exeter samples analysed here could be linked to published data from Barcelona.

Portugal

Our analysis shows that the Portuguese samples tend to present a fairly uniform group. They are all very low in Ca (less than 1% wt) and Sr (which is likely correlated with the Ca values), relative to other samples considered in this study. They tend to be elevated in K as well (*c.* 3.75–4% wt) and Sc (Fig. 18.21), though some samples are lower in Sc (see below). The generally show higher levels of the REE when compared to Spanish samples.

Results and discussion

A key aim for this analysis is to provide a chemical basis for the differentiation of samples produced in different locations. The chemical differences described in the previous section provide one way to identify the samples from the various Spanish and Portuguese production centres. Some of the identifications are only tentative at present as only a limited set of elements could be used due to different analytical techniques being applied across the dataset in the past. The study of Spanish and Portuguese medieval ceramic production centres would benefit from the creation of a new chemical database using ICP-AES and ICP-MS that provides a broader range of elements for each of the production centres discussed in the text.

Portuguese wares

The samples included in this study are representative material of the different fabrics identified during the study of the assemblage (above). The main aim of the analysis was to understand whether the Portuguese fabrics (thought to have come from several production areas in Portugal) can be subdivided into different chemical groupings. Sample EX18283, an olive jar of a type so far only found in the Aveiro region, was to provide a chemical reference for possible Aveiro products and to provide a signature for future reference. In Fig. 18.18 the PCA shows the unglazed wares from Portugal as a largely uniform group; there is some chemical similarity by type, especially with Portugal fabrics 2 and 4. Portugal fabric 7 (EX18276) exhibits slight differences than the other samples, as it is very low in Ca and much higher in Cr. EX18283 fits well within the Portuguese group and is most closely related in terms of its chemistry to fabric 1 (EX18294) and fabric 6 (EX18311). More chemical data from the country are needed to confirm the precise sources of these samples.

Spanish wares

As mentioned earlier, the samples from the Spanish production centres, though broadly similar, present some key differences. Aside from defining these differences, an aim of this study was to lend evidence to the identification of the production centre associated with Spanish ceramics found in Exeter. Table 18.7 shows the PCA based on the available elements. The PCA does split the samples into definable two groups: one composed mostly of samples from Seville and the other samples from Valencia. Most of the Exeter samples can be fit into one of these two groups. There are, however, some outliers, and these represent samples of uncertain origin and probably not from either Seville or Valencia. More helpful for differentiating samples from various production centres are graphs of specific elements. Figures 18.20 (Ba and Zn) and 18.21 (Cr and Sc) plot key elements which help us differentiate various production centres as described above. It must be emphasised that the mixed nature of the data makes the identifications of Málaga and Barcelona a bit less certain than Muel, Valencia and Seville, where the available data fit better into this kind of analysis with the range of elements available at the moment.

Table 18.7 shows the possible identifications based on the chemical data for all samples; further analysis and a fuller range of elements would help to make identifications more secure. The samples analysed from Exeter are in some cases poor chemical matches for published datasets from Seville, Valencia, Málaga or Muel. Each of these areas had a variety of centres of production working across space and time, and samples analysed so far are limited and might come from a specific kiln only. Variations in clay sources or production locations around these major centres could yield samples that are visually attributable to a well-known production centre but fail to match the published chemistry. EX18006 for example, fits reasonably well with some published data for Málaga, though it is higher in Cr than most published examples. Furthermore, it is not a good fit with the two Málaga reference samples (GR1801 and GR1802) analysed as part of this study. A larger geochemical dataset of Spanish samples, from good contexts and well differentiated chronologically, is required to firmly contextualise samples found throughout Europe and the Americas.

A couple of suspected early tin-glazed Portuguese wares (EX18204 and EX18208) do not plot with any of the known Spanish centres and this might confirm they are from Portugal; they do present a fairly tight group and, therefore, likely originate from the same location. A further lead-glazed vessel which was thought might have come from Seville (EX18224) is an outlier but samples from Seville tend to be of tin-glazed, rather than lead-glazed wares and further data is needed to secure this identification. Nevertheless these samples fit quite well with samples of unglazed Portuguese wares in terms of their Cr and Sc values and this might indicate these vessels could be attributable to some as of yet unidentified Portuguese production centre, though they differ from them in other respects.

Conclusions

The ICP analysis of the 42 samples indicates the Spanish samples present a variable group, although clear groupings can be identified between samples from Seville, Valencia, Muel and Málaga. The Portuguese unglazed wares are also distinctive, and the data indicate some chemical differences linked to several fabrics identifiable macroscopically. There is, however, too little data at present to pinpoint further production sites in finer detail.

The analysis of the Spanish samples highlights the need for a more comprehensive geochemical dataset with samples from good contexts drawn from the main production centres across the whole of the medieval period. Currently, the data are too dispersed both across space and time and in terms of technique utilised. Increasing our understanding of medieval Spanish ceramic production requires agreement from interested scholars to move towards a larger dataset produced using standardised methodologies, ensuring comparability of results.

Table 18.7 Samples of Spanish and Portuguese wares from Exeter and their likely production centres (based on the available chemical data)

Sample	*Site*	*Type*	*Results*
EX18005	Exeter	Spanish tin-glazed (contains schist)	Málaga (likely)
EX18006	Exeter	Spanish tin-glazed (no visible inclusions)	Málaga (likely)
EX18160	Exeter	Spanish lustreware	Valencia
EX18164	Exeter	Spanish lustreware	Valencia
EX18170	Exeter	Spanish lustreware	Valencia
EX18171	Exeter	Spanish lustreware	Muel (likely)
EX18204	Exeter	Portuguese? early tin-glazed	Portugal?
EX18208	Exeter	Portuguese? early tin-glazed	Portugal?
EX18224	Exeter	Spanish/Portuguese lead-glazed; '*melado*'	Portugal?
EX18284	Exeter	Spanish tin-glazed	Valencia
EX18285	Exeter	Spanish, Italian or Low Countries Plain Blue	Low Countries
EX18290	Exeter	Spanish lustreware	Valencia or Muel
EX18293	Exeter	Spanish tin-glazed - it contains schist	Málaga (likely)
EX18334	Totnes	Spanish tin-glazed - sandy fabric	Málaga (likely)
EX18354	Exeter	Spanish tin-glazed	Seville
EX18373	Exeter	Spanish lustreware	Valencia
EX18283	Totnes	Portuguese coarseware olive jar, Aveiro-type	Portugal
EX18267	Exeter	Portuguese coarseware fabric 2	Portugal
EX18268	Exeter	Portuguese coarseware fabric 3	Portugal
EX18270	Exeter	Portuguese coarseware fabric 2	Portugal
EX18271	Exeter	Portuguese coarseware fabric 1	Portugal
EX18272	Exeter	Portuguese coarseware fabric 4	Portugal
EX18276	Exeter	Portuguese coarseware fabric 7	Portugal
EX18277	Exeter	Portuguese coarseware fabric 4	Portugal
EX18294	Exeter	Portuguese coarseware fabric 1	Portugal
EX18295	Exeter	Portuguese coarseware fabric 3	Portugal
EX18305	Exeter	Portuguese coarseware fabric 5	Portugal
EX18311	Exeter	Portuguese coarseware fabric 6	Portugal
EX18325	Totnes	Portuguese coarseware fabric 8 lead-glazed; Lisbon?	Portugal
GR1801–2	Granada	Málaga-type lustre-and-blue	Málaga reference sherds
MU1801-11	Muel	Wasters	reference sherd

Appendix 18.2

Plasma Spectrometry Analysis (ICPS) of Italian and Low Countries pottery

Michael J. Hughes

Introduction

The body fabrics of examples of presumed Low Countries and Italian tin-glazed pottery found at several sites in Exeter were analysed for the concentrations of their chemical elements by inductively coupled plasma spectrometry (ICPS) to try to determine their place of production. Such provenance studies require the comparison of analyses from the 'test' items against databases of analyses of material from the presumed sources, such as wasters or biscuit wares from known and dated production sites. Although no ICP analyses exist from known workshops of South Netherlands Maiolica (SNM), there are instead analyses of pottery and tiles from consumer sites which can be confidently assigned as SNM (see for example Allan *et al.* 2012 for a recent project which references these), and from an earlier neutron activation analysis (NAA) project on pottery from other Low Countries sites and three workshops in Antwerp (Hughes and Gaimster 1999; 2002). The situation is similar for Italian ceramics, with consumer-site material assignable to Tuscany and Liguria (Blake and Hughes 2015; 2019) and an ICP project is underway on production waste from these regions. Thus databases of analyses exist against which the Exeter sherds could be compared. The items tested for this project and six other sherds from Exeter previously examined are listed in Table 18.8. The detailed results of the analysis are tabulated in online Table 18.9.

ICP analysis and statistical methodology for interpretation of the results

The chemical analysis and statistical procedures are the same as described in earlier investigations of pottery from the South West (*e.g.* Allan 2009–10; Allan *et al.* 2012), including the advantages of using a combination of atomic emission and mass spectrometry ICPS. Table 18.8 summarises the conclusions drawn from the interpretation of the results.

Visual inspection of the data shows that they fall into two groups. One with the most samples contained low aluminium, iron, magnesium, sodium and chromium and seems to conform closely to previous analyses of South Netherlands Maiolica (samples DF1–16 and DF18). The second group, with four examples (DF20–DF23), has higher concentrations of these elements and is consistent with identification as Montelupo-style polychrome wares produced in Tuscany. These were initial impressions, and previous work has shown that the differences between these regional groups extend into other elements which are revealed when multivariate statistics are applied to the analyses.

Statistical interpretation of the chemical analyses

The aim of the statistical tests was to look for patterns of similar chemistry among the samples, which indicate similar origin, and to compare them with the relevant databases of previous analyses. In the discussions which follow, the Exeter pottery is labelled with its laboratory sample number V or DF (Table 18.8), G: pottery from Glastonbury Abbey (Allan *et al.* 2012), JSE: Jeffrey Street in Edinburgh (Franklin 2011; Hughes 2014a), MIN: London (Hughes and Gaimster 2002, 230–41).

Low Countries, South Netherlands Maiolica (SNM)

Principal components analysis on the Exeter results combined with other ICP analyses of SNM

The items which visual inspection of the ICP results suggested were SNM comprised DF1–16 and DF18. Although a blue-glazed sherd from Goldsmith Street (DF7) has a slightly different chemical composition, it was initially included in the tests. These 17 analyses formed part of a principal components analysis, including

Table 18.8 All Italian and South Netherlands Maiolica sherds from Exeter analysed by ICPS

ICP lab. no.	*Allan 1999b no.*	*Site (Site number)*	*Provenance subgroup*
V7	1	Polsloe Priory (59)	Montelupo A
V8–V9	2–3	Polsloe Priory (59)	Montelupo B
V10	4	Queen Street (68)	Montelupo B
V11	5	Queen Street (68)	Montelupo B
V12	6	Preston Street (60)	Montelupo B
DF1	7	Preston Street (60)	Antwerp 2
DF2	8	Goldsmith Street (37)	Antwerp 1
DF3	9	Exe Bridge (56)	Antwerp 2
DF4	12	Goldsmith Street (37)	Antwerp 1
DF5	14	Queen Street (58)	Antwerp 1
DF6	15	Preston Street (60)	Antwerp 1
DF7	16	Goldsmith Street (37)	Antwerp 2
DF8	17	Trichay Street (42)	Antwerp 1
DF9	18	Lucky Lane (74)	Antwerp 2
DF10	19	St Nicholas Priory (78)	Antwerp 1
DF11	20	Paul Street (76)	Antwerp 2
DF12	21	Exe Street (83)	Antwerp 1
DF13	22	Exe Street (83)	Antwerp 2
DF14	23	Magdalen Street (88)	Antwerp 1
DF15	24	Acorn Inn (94)	Antwerp 1
DF16	64	St Nicholas Priory (78)	Antwerp 2
DF18	83	Paul Street (76)	Antwerp 2
Unpublished RAMM list (Allan 2000b)			
DF19	102	Goldsmith Street (39)	Genoa
DF20	127	Paul Street (76)	Montelupo D
DF21	128	Paul Street (76)	Montelupo D
DF22	135	St Nicholas Priory (78)	Montelupo C
DF23	136	St Nicholas Priory (78)	Montelupo B

the available previous SNM analyses for which the larger set of elements had been analysed by both atomic emission and mass spectrometry. Other earlier analyses using only atomic emission were excluded in order to obtain maximum clarity in differentiating between pottery of different source groups using the combined ICP data. The resulting database comprised 37 examples of imported SNM pottery and tiles from many sites in Britain including four examples of SNM and three Malling 'jugs' from Glastonbury Abbey (Allan *et al.* 2012, 7–8, 21–4, samples 2, 4–7, 9–10; 2015, 268–70, fig. 8.18, nos. 204, 207–9), two Herkenrode-type tiles, and two sherds of SNM and seven other Low Countries wares from Jeffrey Street in Edinburgh (Hughes 2014a), four sherds of SNM from Totnes (Allan 2014b), an SNM sherd from Crediton Vicarage (Allan and Langman 2010, 155, fig. 29, no. 13; Hughes 2009–10, sample RA26, pl. 13); the tiles are from Godolphin House in Cornwall (Allan 2009–10, 280–2, 290–2), London (Hughes 2010b) and Surrey (Hughes 2013; Betts 2016, 1–3, 14–5, 27–8). The earlier neutron activation analysis (NAA) project on SNM by the British Museum in the 1990s indicated a variety of chemical profiles for products from different workshops in Antwerp, suggesting different clay sources and mixing practices (Hughes and Gaimster 1999, 58, 61).

The resulting principal components analysis – using data on 36 chemical elements – shows that the Exeter sherds split into two chemical subgroups, which can be interpreted as made at one production centre in different chronological periods, or at two production centres. The two subgroups separate on the first and second principal components. On the first component, which principally reflects the proportion of non-clay material in the fabric, one subgroup which comprise samples DF2, DF4–DF6, DF8, DF10, DF12, DF14 and DF15 has higher concentrations of most elements apart from significantly lower rare earth elements than the other. However, on the second principal component it shows low values of rare earths, which are associated positively on this component but negatively with most other elements.

This first subgroup contained less than 18% lime (as calcium oxide), while the second subgroup consisting of items DF1, DF3, DF9, DF11, DF13, DF16 and DF18 has low concentrations of most elements (and higher rare earth elements), but some occasional high lime (>20%), and accordingly plots higher on the second principal component. For the second subgroup the low concentrations are mainly caused by a high quartz content and to a lesser extent by a high lime content (both have a diluting effect), but quite low values on the second principal component. The blue-glazed sherd DF7 is also associated with this subgroup on the plot. It has higher concentrations of most elements than the subgroup, which can be an indicator of a higher clay mineral content and less silt and sand-sized quartz.

The first, high-concentration subgroup, falls into an area of the plot of the second and third principal components otherwise occupied by only five Low Countries sherds found at Jeffrey Street, in Edinburgh (Hughes 2014a, 52, samples JSE 16–20; Masser 2014, 28, 31, 33–4, 38–9). The second, lower concentrations subgroup (which could possibly be subdivided further) is overlapped by sherds from Glastonbury Abbey and Totnes, and some maiolica tiles from sites in the South West, including Godolphin House. DF7 is on this plot a typical member of this subgroup. Relabelling the components plots to indicate which were pottery or tiles shows that most of the SNM pottery samples separate out from the tiles on the second component, apart from eight examples including DF3. This suggests systematic though not exclusive differences in clay fabric between these two material types. The finding that the Exeter sherds show probably only two main chemical patterns suggests a relatively small number of workshops for this SNM, which were also responsible for exporting to other British sites.

Although there exist ICP analyses of SNM by atomic emission only, most are of tiles (*e.g.* Hughes 2009a which references other examples) and are less relevant to interpreting the analyses of the Exeter pottery. The few pots examined include Malling 'jugs' found at Southampton (Vince and Brown 2002, 468–9; MPRG 2010, sample V357) and Shapwick House, in Somerset (MPRG 2010; Vince and Brown 2002: 469, sample AG136), and a SNM bodysherd from Cleeve Abbey, in Somerset (Allan 1998, 54, fig. 1, no. 18; 1999b, 161, fig. 12.2, no. 48; Hughes 1998, 68–72, no. 18). All three have quite similar analyses (Hughes 2009a, 376, fig. 261), and a later comparison of them with SNM from Glastonbury Abbey showed that the Shapwick and Southampton Malling 'jugs' were close to the composition of the Godolphin House tiles, whereas the Cleeve Abbey SNM sample was intermediate between the latter and the Glastonbury samples G4, G6 and G10 (Hughes in Allan *et al.* 2012, fig. 1). The Malling 'jug' (sample G7) is almost exactly identical chemically, apart from slightly higher rare earth elements, to the average clay chemistry of Malling 'jugs' found in London analysed by NAA (Hughes and Gaimster 1999, 61–2).

The earlier major investigation of SNM by NAA provided valuable data on waste from three maiolica workshops at Schoytestraat, Steenhouwersvest and the National Museum of Navigation in Antwerp (Hughes and Gaimster 1999, 61) and on Antwerp products from consumption sites in that city and Britain. Before comparing these analyses with the ICP results, the NAA dataset was adjusted by inter-laboratory standardisation factors obtained by repeat analysis by ICPS and NAA of the same international standard materials (Orton and Hughes 2013, 174–6; an example is given in Gutiérrez 2003, 38, table 1 – the factors have been slightly updated since then). In addition, element to oxide conversion factors were applied for the major elements iron, calcium, sodium and potassium. The NAA data used for comparison with the Exeter analyses included the three Antwerp workshops, SNM vessels found in London (Hughes and Gaimster 1999, 69–70, 73–4, nos. 1, 2, 4, 7–9, 14, 62, 65, 66), Malling 'jugs' from London, Antwerp and Amsterdam (Hughes and Gaimster 1999, 62; Hughes and Gaimster 2002, 232–4, 237–40, nos. 70–77, 97, 98, 108, 110, 154), two stove tiles from St Mary Graces (Gaimster and Hughes 1999a), and floor tiles from London and Surrey (Gaimster and Hughes 1999b; Hughes 2010b, 44–8; Nenk and Hughes 2019, 135–40). All the ICP data in the previous second-stage statistical test were combined with the adjusted NAA data – 130 items in all – using, however, only the 15 chemical elements analysed in common by the two methods.

The first principal component is strongly correlated positively with most elements, that is a '% temper' proportion; it does nevertheless echo the earlier statistical tests in identifying the same two Exeter chemical subgroups, although this time superimposed on a much larger number of other SNM. The second and third components shows much of the detail of the chemical differences and also allows examination of the relationship of the Exeter items to the Antwerp production samples, and to other SNM (Fig. 18.22). Again, the Exeter sherds split into the same two broad subgroups along the second principal component; they are not completely differentiated along the third component although five (DF5–DF6, DF8, DF10, DF12) are significantly lower on this compared to the subgroup on the right. Samples higher up Fig. 18.22 have generally lower transition metals chromium, cobalt and iron, plus sodium, but higher caesium and rubidium and rare earth elements.

Exeter SNM subgroup 1

The Exeter subgroup in the lower left of Fig. 18.22 (comprising DF2, DF4–DF6, DF8, DF10, DF12, DF14, DF15) has, with the exception of DF4, no other SNM overlapping it, although the top of the subgroup is near the two clusters of Steenhouwersvest sherds. This subgroup of SNM mugs could represent yet another production site. The chemical patterns established by NAA for the National Museum of Navigation and Schoytestraat workshops are clearly different to any of the Exeter sherds, in contrast

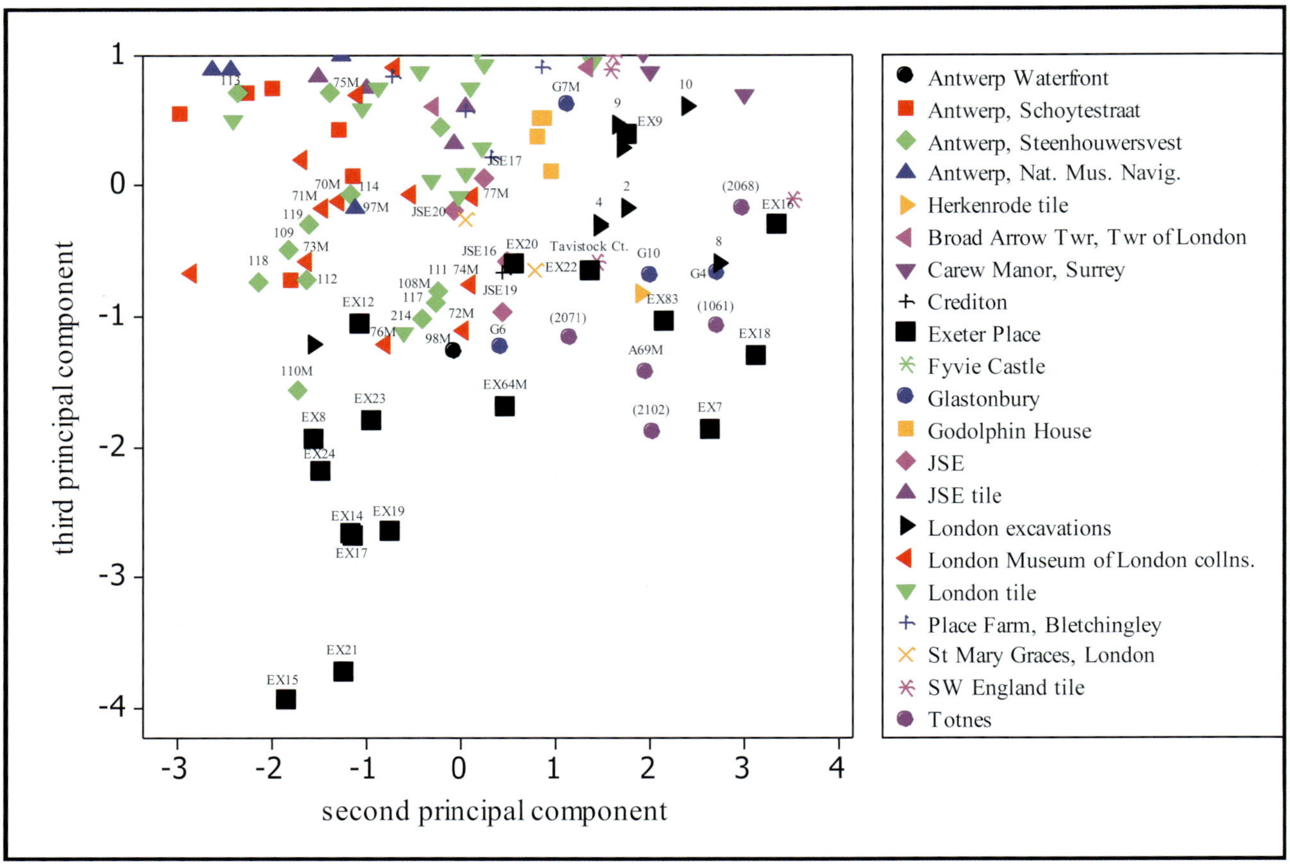

Fig. 18.22 Plot of the second and third principal components arising from a test including the Exeter samples, ICP analyses of Antwerp tiles and pottery, and NAA of wasters and biscuit from three dumps and of SNM from consumption sites in Antwerp. Sample numbers are: DF: this project; MIN (without letters prefix on plot): London (listed in Hughes and Gaimster 2002, 230–41); G: Glastonbury; JSE: Jeffrey Street, Edinburgh; M suffix: Malling jug. The Exeter ceramics appear to split into two broad chemical subgroups: 1) on the left decorated mugs (DF2, DF4–DF5, DF12, DF14–DF15), blue-glazed (DF6, DF8), and a large jug (DF10); 2) on the right a Malling 'jug' (DF16), 'drug' jug (DF18), decorated mugs (DF1, DF3, DF9, DF11, DF13), and blue-glazed (DF7) (graphic: Michael J. Hughes)

to the Steenhouwersvest site, which is much closer to, and partly overlaps some of the Exeter SNM. Two other SNM waste dumps have been excavated in Antwerp, *c.* 50 m from the Schoytestraat site, to the south-east at Aalmoezeniorstraat (Oost and Veeckman 2002, 52, fig. 1) and to the north-west under the church of St Augustine in Kammenstraat (Veeckman 2010), but no ICP data is available for them. There therefore remain workshops as yet untested analytically to be matched to most of the Exeter sherds.

Exeter SNM subgroup 2

The Exeter subgroup on the right of Fig. 18.22 (containing lower concentrations of most elements but higher rare earths as in the ICP-only principal components test) comprise SNM mugs (DF1, DF3, DF7, DF9, DF11, DF13), the early 'drug' jug (DF18) and a Malling 'jug' (DF16). Within the spread of this subgroup and mirroring its boundaries in the figure are all five examples of SNM excavated in Totnes including a Malling 'jug' (Hughes in preparation; DF17) and three SNM mugs from Glastonbury Abbey (Allan *et al.* 2012, 7, samples G4–6, 10; idem 2015, 268, fig. 8.18, nos. 202–4). As a group it is also adjacent to but not overlapping a fairly close-knit group containing three Malling 'jugs' from London (MIN72, MIN74, MIN76), another from Antwerp's waterfront (MIN98), and five samples from the Steenhouwersvest workshop (Hughes and Gaimster 2002, 232–3, nos. 109, 112, 114, 118–19). That one Exeter sherd (DF4) – despite being in subgroup 1 – is close to this group raises the possibility that it and the four Malling 'jugs' were made in the Steenhouwersvest workshop. If so, it would be the only one from Exeter which corresponds to any of the three production sites investigated by the NAA project. Sherd DF11, which does belong to subgroup 2, may also be associated with the Steenhouwersvest sherds, although it lies just outside their spread. The other Malling 'jugs' from consumption sites appear elsewhere in Fig. 18.22: on the upper left is a close-knit set of three from London (MIN70–1, MIN73) and one from the National Museum of Navigation workshop (MIN97), associated with five other samples from the Steenhouwersvest site (Hughes and Gaimster 2002, 232–3, nos. 70–1, 73, 97, associated with 109, 112, 114, 118 and 119). There is no information as yet why two chemical patterns are present within the analysed sherds from this workshop; however, the two groups are quite close chemically and could represent different batches of clay or manufacture at different dates. Although the jug was found at the National Museum of Navigation site, chemically it is unlike the other sherds from there and appears to have been made in the Steenhouwersvest workshop. Other Malling 'jugs' are close to SNM from Glastonbury (G7 – top centre); London (MIN75 – top left); two other Malling 'jugs' from Glastonbury (G2 and G9) are just off the top of the Figure, accompanied by a SNM mug from Glastonbury (G5). Close to an Exeter SNM mug (DF3: top right in Fig. 18.22) are two London SNM mugs (MIN7, MIN9) while three other London SNM vases (MIN2, MIN4 and MIN10) are also nearby. The occurrence of SNM mugs and Malling 'jugs' in the Exeter subgroup on the right of Fig. 18.22 suggests a common origin, not a random occurrence, and suggests production of these two forms of SNM in a limited number of workshops using slightly different clay resources or mixtures. Other Malling 'jugs' on the left of the Figure – sometimes accompanied by SNM mugs or in separate chemical groups – seem to form clusters. As already noted, two clusters of SNM seem associated with the Steenhouwersvest site. SNM mugs and Malling 'jugs' thus appear to have been made in several places in the city. There is a chronological distinction between the two forms: SNM mugs were made in first half of the 16th century whereas Malling 'jugs' belong to the second half of that century (Hurst 1999, 91, 96). However, their clay chemistry reveals that similar clay sources and pottery production processes were used for both types.

Labelling the items in the principal components plots as production waste, tiles or pottery shows a similar pattern to the statistical tests on the ICP analyses alone, namely the first principal component again showed no systematic difference between the types. In Fig. 18.22 which plots the second and third components, all the tiles lie either above the zero value of the third principal component, or off the top of the figure; very few pottery samples overlap their distribution. The production waste can be seen on the left, mostly the upper region (Antwerp). All the rest are vessels, showing a partial overlap with the production samples to the left and centre, whereas no workshop or tile samples overlap with the pottery to the right of centre and below the zero on the third principal component. This useful distinction between Antwerp pottery and tiles has not been reported before; it parallels ICP analyses of London delftware, where most of the products of each pothouse show chemical differences between pottery and tile fabrics (Hughes 2008).

Comparing Fig. 18.22 with the corresponding principal components plot for the ICP-only dataset does show that the latter has a noticeably greater separation between the two Exeter subgroups along the horizontal axis. This is probably a function of the lower discriminating power within the combined NAA and ICP test, because it is based on less than half the number of chemical elements compared to the ICP-only dataset.

Summarising the results of the SNM analysed from Exeter: the samples split into two chemical subgroups, characterised generally by higher and lower concentrations of elements, but with additional differences between them in the chemical patterns for specific elements. Thus they do not simply represent two levels of tempering of the same clay but rather two different clay sources. The similarity of two Exeter sherds to the NAA results for the Steenhouwersvest waste, and the closer similarity of that workshop's products chemically to the other Exeter SNM, in contrast to the National Museum of Navigation and Schoytestraat sites, may indicate that it lies closer to the unknown places which produced most of the Exeter SNM. There are precedents for finding a series of closely similar chemical patterns for the ceramic products of one city, the most relevant being London delftwares, where there are distinct chemical patterns for pothouses in Lambeth, Southwark and Aldgate (Hughes 2008). It has also emerged that the chemical patterns for the tiles produced in the city are consistently different from those of the pottery and are not simply caused by the use of a different proportion of lime to clay in the fabric.

Italian

Tuscany

The second group in the analyses, with four examples (DF20–DF23), appears consistent with analyses of typical Montelupo-style polychrome wares produced in Tuscany, while DF19 is identified as Ligurian maiolica. Relevant ICP studies have been undertaken on Italian pottery which provide comparative analyses to the probable Tuscan sherds (references in Blake and Hughes 2015). Earlier analyses of six presumed SNM vessels from Exeter showed that they were made in Tuscany (Allan 1999b, 160, nos. 1–6; Blake and Hughes 2015, 153–4, 173, Exeter 1–6). The ICP results on DF20–DF23 together with the six 'SNM' from Exeter were compared by principal components analysis against a database of 36 ICP analyses of Montelupo-style maiolica and Mediterranean Maiolica from British sites – the latter is a variant of Archaic Maiolica, most of which appear to be Tuscan (Blake and Hughes 2015, 149–51; 2019, 74, tab. 1) – and 20 typical examples of pottery and clay from Montelupo analysed by X-ray fluorescence (Baldi 2003: Morzano (Montespertoli) clays [4]; marbled group C [MAR: 2]; slipped group B [ING: 6]; and high lime maiolica ('smaltate e decorate' (tin-glazed and decorated group)) [8].

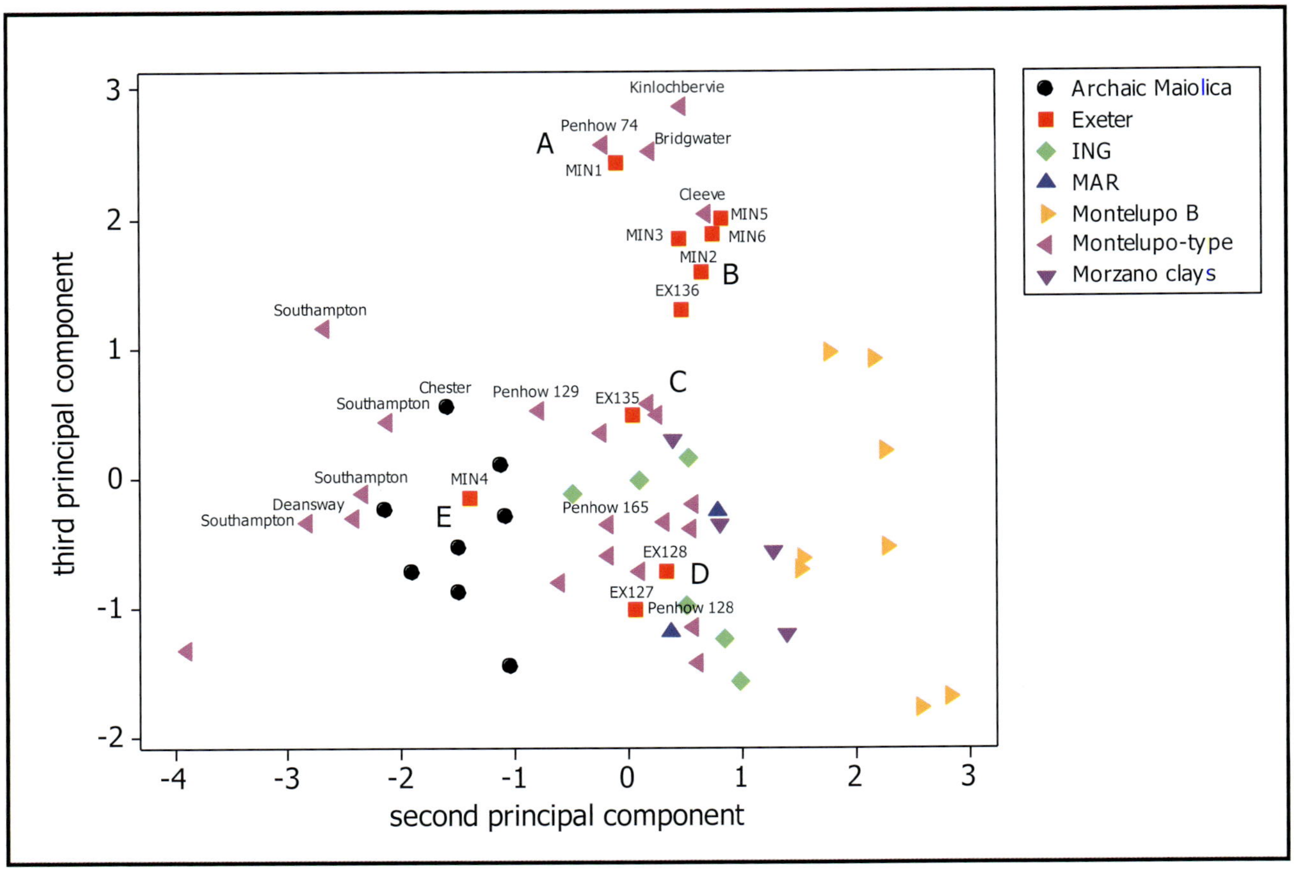

Fig. 18.23 Principal Components Analysis of four Montelupo-style items from Exeter (DF20–DF23) and six previously identified as Tuscan (V7–V12), against a 'Tuscany' database of ICP analyses which include Montelupo-style and Mediterranean Maiolica samples from consumption sites in Britain, and XRF analyses of 16th-century pottery from Montelupo (ING: slipped group B; MAR: marbled group C; high-lime maiolica ('smaltate e decorate' ('tin-glazed and decorated') group) and clays from Morzano (Montespertoli; Baldi 2003). (graphic: Michael Hughes)

The results are shown in Fig. 18.23, where all ten Exeter samples are within the range of chemical compositions represented in this Tuscan ICP and XRF database. They fall within several previously recognised chemical subgroups within this database (*e.g.* Hughes 2016, 71–2; Blake and Hughes 2015, 153, fig. 13). In this report the subgroups into which the Exeter sherds belong have been assigned letters (A–E) to aid discussion of the ICP results. Some are quite distinctly separate, such as A, B and E while C and D might be part of a larger group. Subgroups A–D all fall within a quite narrow range on the second (horizontal) component, but separate into subgroups on the third (vertical) component. Subgroup E has a spread on the third component which matches the C and D subgroups, but has a lower score than either on the second component (*i.e.* lies to the left of them), though some sherds are close to C and D. Each subgroup may represent production from a particular workshop at a specific period, but it is equally possible that the same clay source (and similar clay processing) was used by different potters over an extended period. Thus, for example, the four clays from Montespertoli (Morzano) analysed by Baldi (2003) all fall within the larger group containing C and D and give a preliminary indication of the range of compositions found within the same source. The range of chemical composition groups into which the Exeter sherds fall indicates a range of sources for these imports.

Turning to the individual Exeter sherds, a mug painted dark blue and yellow from Polsloe Priory (V7) is at the top of Fig. 18.23 in subgroup A, which also contains a sherd of grotesque maiolica from Kinlochbervie off the Sunderland coast, a glossy blue tin-glazed sherd found in a late 15th-century context in Bridgwater, in Somerset, and a Montelupo-style sherd from Penhow Castle, in Gwent (Blake and Hughes 2015, 172–4, 176, Bridgwater 1, Exeter 1, Kinlochbervie 1, Penhow 1). This subgroup is slightly separated from another immediately below it (B) from the remaining sherds from Exeter which had been analysed earlier: a bowl from Polsloe Priory (V8–V9 – initially thought to be from two separate vessels) and three SNM-type mugs (V10–V12; Blake and Hughes 2015, 173, Exeter 2–6), a blue-glazed handle from Cleeve Abbey, Somerset (Blake and Hughes 2015, 173, Cleeve 1), and a Montelupo dish from St Nicholas Priory (DF23).

These two subgroups are slightly separated from the main spread of points to the left of the centre in the lower half of the figure, and within this spread is a small subgroup (C) at the top containing the other Montelupo-style fragment – probably from a bowl – from St Nicholas Priory (DF22), two samples of late 19th-century revival maiolica made by Cantagalli in Florence with the clay used by Montelupo (Blake and Hughes 2015, 158, 169, National Museums of Scotland 1–2), and a recognizable Montelupo type from Glastonbury (*ibid.*, 173, Glastonbury 2). Below this is another group (D) containing DF20 and DF21, a brim fragment from Godolphin House in Cornwall (*ibid.*, Helston 1), a Cantagalli ewer from Plymouth, and a bowl fragment from Glastonbury (*ibid.*, 173, 176–7, Glastonbury 2, Plymouth 2). Slightly above them are three other Montelupo-style polychrome decorated items from Barnstaple, Glastonbury and Godolphin House (*ibid.*, 172–3, Barnstaple 2, Glastonbury 3, Helston 2). Baldi's slipped ware (ING) and marbled ware (MAR) types fall exclusively within the spread of subgroups C and D. Finally, group E consists of a SNM-type mug from Exeter (V10) and Penhow Castle, and Mediterranean Maiolica from the Millennium Bridge site in London, and Chester (*ibid.*, 175–6, London 18–24, Penhow 2; *idem* 2019, 85, fig. 8).

Liguria

A dish was recognised as Ligurian *berettino*, decorated with intersecting arabesque leaf and floral patterns (DF19). Previous analyses of Ligurian wares showed two distinctive chemical profiles: one with an unusually high chromium content (300–500 ppm), high nickel, low rubidium and low rare earths characteristic of Albisola and Savona pottery, although it has proved difficult to distinguish chemically between their products The other chemical profile is characteristic of Genoese ceramics and, while it shares some of the same features as those of Savona and Albisola, it differs significantly in having a lower chromium content (below approximately 200 ppm) and also lacks the high magnesium content of ceramics from the latter sites (Blake and Hughes 2019, 75, 86, 88, tab. 2). DF19 has a chromium content within the Genoa range, and visual comparison of its ICP data against previous analyses of Genoese ceramics supports this attribution chemically; there are as yet too few ICP analyses of Ligurian ceramics to make a principal components analysis meaningful. A current ICP project sets out to characterise typical products of three Ligurian (Savona, Albisola and Genoa) and two Tuscan production centres (Montelupo and Pisa) – 20 samples from each centre, although only three from San Vincenzo in Genoa have been analysed to date.

Conclusions

The imported maiolica from Exeter analysed in this project showed the chemical patterns for three sources: South Netherlands Maiolica, Montelupo-style polychrome and Ligurian *berettino*. The South Netherlands Maiolica falls into two chemical subgroups, one consisting of a large 'jug' bodysherd as well as the typical SNM-type mugs, while the other includes mainly mugs, the early 'drug' jug and Malling 'jugs'. The occurrence of the first two and Malling 'jugs' in the first subgroup is significant, even though they are of chronologically different periods, and suggests continuity of potting practice for such wares over an extended period of time. Not all of the SNM mugs and Malling 'jugs' analysed from consumer sites, including Exeter, fit into these two subgroups and some may be from other yet-to-be-analysed workshops in Antwerp. DF4 (and less clearly DF11), however, appears consistent with the chemical pattern for the production waste excavated at Steenhouwersvest in Antwerp. The Tuscan imports analysed here all appear to be have been made in Montelupo, but fall into five chemical composition subgroups previously known from analyses of examples from other British consumer sites. These subgroups may be contemporary but from different workshops within the small town. The one Ligurian *berettino* dish examined has the chemical pattern characteristic of Genoese ceramics.

Acknowledgements

Hugo Blake thanks John Allan, Duncan Brown, David Gaimster, Michael Hughes, Beverley Nenk, Dan Nesbitt and Elisa Sani for providing information, Claire Dumortier, Sharon Pearce and Timothy Wilson for assistance in accessing publications, and Angelica Degasperi for Fig. 18.17.

Notes

1. Department of History, Royal Holloway, University of London hugo.blake@royalholloway.ac.uk. As this contribution was revised after peer review during the first Covid-19 lockdown, I have been unable to consult some publications, particularly in relation to the early SNM jug DF18.
2. Rackham did not discuss the small globular jugs with a trefoil mouth and a pinched lower handle terminal, which are well known in Italy (Blake 1999, 25).
3. The distinction between South and North Netherlands Maiolica, corresponding to the present states of Belgium and the Netherlands, is also no longer applicable now that the early forms have been found amongst kiln waste in Bergen op Zoom and Utrecht (Hurst *et al.* 1986, 119; Baart 1999, 125, 127, figs 7.1, 7.2.1, 7.6–7, 7.24, 7.29). The *c.* 1540 end date reflects an assumption that the English Reformation suppressed the demand – or at least impeded the supply of – Catholic cult objects (Blake *et al.* 2003, 188, 192). Dumortier divides Antwerp's maiolica production into three phases: 1508–1541 from when the Italian Guido Andries is first recorded in the city until his death; 1541–1573 to the death of his son Lucas Andries; 1573–1630 by when most of the workshops had closed (Dumortier 2002, 17, 27, 41).
4. Of the three omitted in the 1999 corpus, nos. 10–11 may have been made after 1550 and the earlier bodysherd no. 14 did not merit illustration (Allan 1999b, 160).

5. Tuscan: (Hughes and Gaimster 2002, NAA nos. 3, 5–6, 11–13, 58, 61, 63–4, 78–81); described and illustrated by Blake (1999, CITG 1–6, 8–15; Blake and Hughes 2015, 177, Southampton 2, 6, fig. 11).
Low Countries: Hughes and Gaimster 2002, NAA nos. 1–2, 4, 7–9, 59–60, 65, 67–8, mentioned and illustrated: NAA 2 (Hurst 1999, 94, n. 29; Hughes and Gaimster 1999, fig. 3.2.2); 4 (Hurst 1999, 94, n. 28); 7 (Hurst 1999, 94, n. 30); 8 (Hughes and Gaimster 1999, fig. 3.2.8 photo.; Hurst 1999, 93, n. 26, fig. 4.2.2 drawing); 9 (Hurst 1999, 94, n. 30; Hughes and Gaimster 1999, fig. 3.2.9); 59–60 (Hughes and Gaimster 1999, 62–3; Hurst 1999, figs 4.3.3–4); 65 (Hurst 1999, 93, n. 23, fig. 4.1.2.3); 67 (Hurst 1999, 93, n. 22, fig. 4.1.2.2); 68 (Hurst 1999, 93, n. 21, fig. 4.1.2.1). To judge from the images and measurements kindly supplied by Dan Nesbitt of the Museum of London Archaeological Archive, NAA 1 (BOY86[288]) is a fragment (70 high by 47 mm wide) of the upper front left side of a small jug, decorated with a dark blue ladder medallion flanked by a narrower line, supporting without, tuft sprays at *c.* 9 and 11 o'clock, with a filled circle on the ground in between, and within a more irregular spray, one of which terminates in an orange triangular flower. Trace of thick blue upright element in centre. Crackled white glaze on both sides. The larger Faenza-type jugs are excluded from the count, but two INM not identified in 1999 are included (Blake and Hughes 2015, 153, Southampton 2, 6). Hurst (1999, 94, nos 29–30) wondered whether NAA 2 and 9 were from the same vase. The analyses show that they belonged to two different vessels (Hughes pers. comm.).
6. Tuscan: Blake and Hughes 2015, 171–3, 176–7, Bridgwater 1, Cleeve 1, Exeter 1, 4–6; Penhow 2, Southampton 7–9. Antwerp: Cleeve (Allan 1998, 54, fig. 1, no. 18, 1999b: 161, fig. 12.2, no. 48; Hughes 1998, 68–72, no. 18); Crediton (Allan and Langman 2010, 155, fig. 29, no. 13; Hughes 2009–10, sample RA26); Exeter: EAPIT DF1–DF5, DF9–DF15; blue-glazed INM or Malling?: DF6, DF8; Glastonbury (Allan *et al.* 2012, 7, samples 4–6, 10; 2015, 268, fig. 8.18, nos. 202–4); Newton Abbot (Hughes 2019, 2, sample 1008 – 'all-over blue' sherd [INM or Malling?]); Southampton (Vince and Brown 2002, 469, 473, sample V063); Totnes (Allan 2014c; Hughes 2014b, Totnes 2 [= RN8], context 2102: 'all-over blue' sherd [INM or Malling?]). The related bowl is excluded (Allan 2015, 118, fig. 2.5–6; Blake and Hughes 2015, 154, 173, Exeter 2–3 – it is one pot macroscopically as well as analytically).
7. There is no evidence that it was ever used as an altar vase. Flower vase is also an inappropriate name, because a wide variety of shapes and types of closed forms were represented containing flowers in this period in the Low Countries. Instead its prime function was as a drinking vessel (Blake 1999, 28–9) – borne out too by the 13 different ring-handled vases represented in the exceptional Quilter's Vault clearance deposit in Southampton and by the later use of a similarly shaped silver vessel (Brown 2002, 149–50; pers. comm.; Schroder 2009, 164–6, no. 61, fig. 32).
8. The glaze of DF5 described as dull, is not (Allan 1999b, 160, no. 14; cf. DF5 description online). DF11, although perhaps altered, may not be dull.
9. Two have secure provenances in Sicily and the Venetian lagoon and I saw a third in Feltre, *c.* 70 km north of Venice (Blake 1999, 34, n. 137; Blake and Hughes 2003, 449, fig. 13 centre and right; 2015, 151).
10. In note 3 it is suggested that the 1540 end date for INM is an outcome of the English Reformation. There is, however, some evidence of continued support of the Holy Name cult, which was also revived in Mary's reign (1553–8; Blake *et al.* 2003, 186–8). It is also noteworthy that the Belgian colleagues who identified 'dull' glaze as being characteristic of Antwerp maiolica did so when very few finds 'which clearly date to the first half of the 16th century' had been made in that city (Oost and Veeckman 2002, 52).
11. One Tuscan INM from Southampton was found with pottery datable to after *c.* 1480 (Blake and Hughes 2015, 177, Southampton 2).
12. I owe the Leonardi 2002 reference to Elisa Sani.
13. A defining characteristic is the absence of a concentric line enclosing the central ornament.
14. To judge from the drawing – which shows *inter alia* traces of an interlocking arcade on the outer wall – it is unlikely that a find from Narrow Street in London bears calligraphic spirals type A ornament (Jarrett and Blackmore 2015, 108, fig. 7.7).
15. Its 'pink-buff fabric' suggests a 'mid-Arno' rather than Pisan origin. A distinguishing characteristic of the Montelupo type is its unglazed outside (Berti 1997, 159).
16. For a period around 1300 painted pottery had been made in North-West Europe. The best-known example of the lead-glazed Saintonge Polychrome from South-West France is the puzzle jug found in Exeter (Fox and Radford 1933, 130–2) [above, Chapter 17, Fig. 17.26A–C]. Archaic maiolica drug jars were produced in the Low Countries. Rare – so presumably experimental – instances of painting stoneware and unglazed earthenware have also been recorded (Blake forthcoming a).
17. Shown in Italian late 16th and early 17th-century paintings (*e.g.* Ravanelli Guidotti 2019, figs 1a, 2a, 7, 17a).
18. Exeter DF19 rim diam. 220 mm, base diam. 145, height 39; Middelburg RØ 230, BØ 139, H 45; Southampton High Street RØ 236, BØ 136, H 44; Quilter's Vault incomplete H 33; Acton Court no. 221 RØ 192, BØ 122, H 36; no. 224 RØ 176, BØ 100, H 40. A comparable shape found in Genoa measures RØ 219, BØ 123, H 40.5. All except DF19 and Middelburg RØ and H calculated from published drawings (Ostkamp and Kottman 2006, 323, cat. 131; Jaspers 2011, fig. 11; Platt and Coleman-Smith 1975, vol. 2, fig. 210.1360; Brown 2002, fig. 34.371; Vince and England 2004, fig. 9.9.221, 224; Farris and Ferrarese 1969, pl. 11.2).
19. There was too an earlier preference in Exeter for bowls and dishes of Spanish lustreware (Gutiérrez above).

19

Exeter's Medieval Cemeteries: A Bioarchaeological Analysis

Mandy Kingdom

Introduction

Since the 1970s, several of Exeter's medieval cemeteries have been excavated, most notably in the Cathedral Close (Site 40), the Dominican friary (Black Friars) in Princesshay (Site 156) and the extra-mural St Katherine's Priory, in Polsloe (Site 59). This chapter summarises the detailed research carried out on the excavated medieval human remains (463 individuals) and focuses on the skeletal health and socio-economic status of those analysed (a fuller account of the bioarchaeological analysis can be found in Kingdom 2019).

To achieve a full understanding of the research material it was considered important to use an holistic approach, combining osteological analysis with archaeological and historical information. This integration establishes a 'contextual' view of the evidence and is known as the biocultural or bioarchaeological approach (its origins and development having been discussed in detail in a number of publications: Bush and Zvelebil 1991; Larsen 2002; Wright and Yoder 2003; Buikstra and Beck 2006; Katzenberg and Saunders 2008; Agarwal and Glencross 2011; Martin *et al.* 2013). The bioarchaeological process involves the detailed recording of skeletal information such as age, sex and metrical data along with pathological lesions and trauma. This data is then combined with scientific analysis such as radiocarbon dating and stable isotope analysis along with historical and archaeological contextual information to create a synthesised and comprehensive study. By concentrating on the bioarchaeological approach, this study illustrates how the lives of those buried at Exeter did or did not change through time and across socio-economic status.

Archaeological and historical context

There is little archaeological or historical evidence for the continued occupation of the Roman town into the 5th century (EAPIT 1, Chapter 7), although excavations within Cathedral Green in 1971–6 exposed two burials on a NW–SE alignment within the area of the Roman basilica and later minster church that were radiocarbon dated to the 5th to 7th centuries (OB278: 390–650 cal. AD, HAR-1614; and OB486: 410–710 cal AD, HAR-1613, OB486 being re-dated in 2015 428–618 cal. AD, SUERC-57530). The original number of graves identified on this alignment was six (Bidwell 1979, 111) although subsequent radiocarbon dating has reduced this number to two with a possible third from which no skeletal remains survive (a full table of radiocarbon dates from Exeter's excavated human remains is presented in Appendix 19.1). The two 5th to 7th-century burials are unlikely to have been in isolation, and may have been associated with an early church, shrine or accepted burial site. The excavations also revealed large numbers of later burials that appeared to be on two alignments, referred to at the time as Cemeteries II and III, along with foundations of a Late Saxon minster (Henderson and Bidwell 1982, 148; Allan *et al.* 1984, 389; Orme 2009, 7; EAPIT 1, Chapter 7). Although no structural evidence has been found, the Cemetery II burials were believed to be associated with a Middle Saxon church/monastery documented in the late 7th century (attended by St Boniface), which is thought to have been replaced by the minster founded by King Æthelstan in AD 932 and represented by the foundations found during excavation. Although a couple of radiocarbon dates relating to the change in burial orientation from Cemetery II to Cemetery III (the latter being on the same alignment as the new minster), support this long held view, the latest radiocarbon dated burial in Cemetery II (OB2) could not have been buried any earlier than 898 (cal. AD 898–1036, SEURC-39395), whilst CB66 – the earliest radiocarbon dated burial on the Cemetery III alignment – could not have been buried any later than 946 (cal. AD 729–946, SEURC-57533). The majority of radiocarbon dates from the two cemeteries suggest they are more or less contemporary (EAPIT 1, Chapter 7). The remaining 226 burials excavated in the Cathedral Close were post-Conquest through to the early 17th century (including those in Fig. 19.2).

Post-Conquest Exeter saw several new ecclesiastical foundations including St Nicholas' Priory founded in 1090, its sister house the Benedictine priory at Polsloe which existed by 1160 (Crick 2014; Orme 2015a, 185), and the new cathedral in 1114 (Orme 2009, 39). The Dominicans came to Exeter in 1232 followed by the Franciscans by 1240 (Harvey 2011, 30; Orme 2014, 102). There were other monastic foundations within or just outside of Exeter during the medieval period but those sites, like St Nicholas' Priory, have not seen excavations producing human remains that could be included in this study. For most of the medieval period the cathedral held a monopoly over the burial of Exeter's population. Although, this was conceded in some degree post 1300 to the popularity of intra-mural burial as indicated in Lepine and Orme (2003) and burial at the monasteries and hospitals. Following the Reformation, the discontinuation of a number of these additional burial sites including the charnel chapel (situated above a crypt containing disarticulated human remains), along with the thousand years of use of the Cathedral Green cemetery, contributed to its overcrowding and eventually the rising ground level necessitated its closing. A new burial ground, St Bartholomew's, was consecrated in 1636 (Jenkins 1806, 156; Orme 2009, 22) and this date also ends the period on which this study focused.

Burial sites associated with the research material

The human remains analysed in the project were sourced from a total of 11 excavations, covering four burial sites situated in or just outside of Exeter's city walls (Fig. 19.1; Table 19.1). Cathedral Green is situated at the heart of Exeter (NGR SX 920925), positioned south-east of the

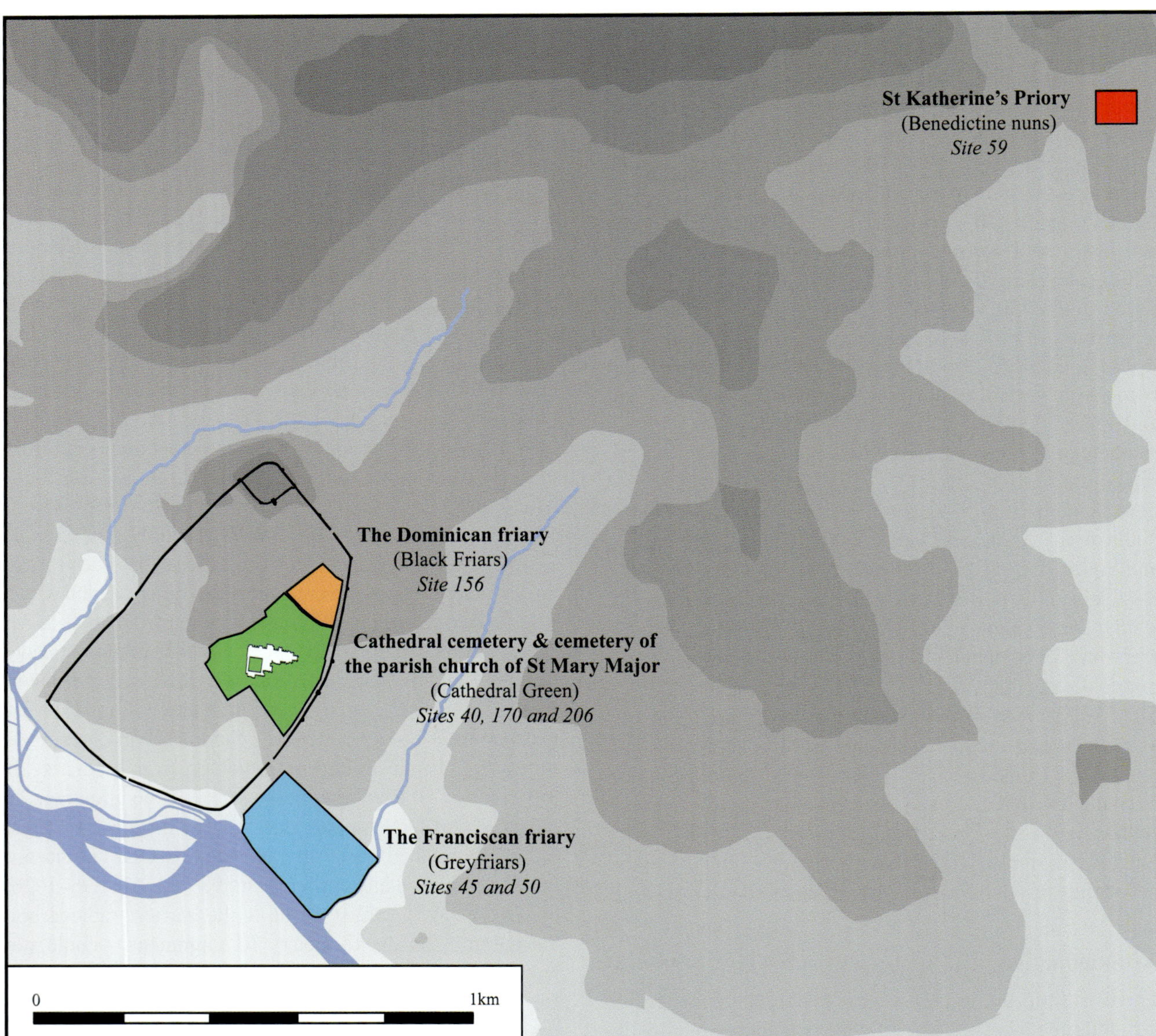

Fig. 19.1 Location of the places referred to in the text (drawn by David Gould)

Table 19.1 Sites, excavations and number of individuals analysed (for Site Numbers see Chapter 2 above)

Site	*Excavation and date*	*No. of individuals analysed*
Cathedral Green: Cathedral cemetery and cemetery of the parish church of St Mary Major	Mary Major 1971 (Site 40)	29
	War Memorial 1972 (Site 40)	49
	Cathedral Green assessment 1975 (Site 40)	5
	Cathedral Green 1976 (Site 40)	245
	Deanery 2005 (Site 206)	8
	Cathedral Green 2012 (Site 170)	2
The Dominican friary (Black Friars)	Exeter Princesshay assessment 1998 and	3
	Exeter Princesshay 2006 (Site 156)	69
The Franciscan friary (Greyfriars)	Friars Gate 1973 (Site 45)	5
	Holloway Street 1974 (Site 50)	20
St Katherine's Priory (Benedictine Nuns)	Polsloe Priory 1976 (Site 59)	30
Total individuals		463

Fig. 19.2 Later medieval burials in densely populated area of Cathedral Green (source: Exeter Archaeology Archive, © Exeter City Council)

High Street and south-west of modern day Princesshay. Human remains have been studied from six separate excavations carried out there between 1971 and 2012. A great many medieval and early post-medieval graves (Fig. 19.2) were found overlying the Roman bath-house, basilica and forum, but as a high proportion of the later burials were re-interred at the time, only a sample of those excavated (329) remained available for study. The planned and retained burials were placed into four phases determined by different alignments (Henderson and Bidwell 1982, 148) as described above. As no bone survives from the Cemetery I burials after they were radiocarbon dated they could not be included in this analysis. A total of 88 burials were assigned to Cemetery II and Cemetery III and are believed to be Mid to Late Saxon in date (Fig. 19.3B). Following the building of the new cathedral in the 12th century there was a change to the use and status of the old Saxon minster and its burial ground: it was rededicated to St Mary and became one of Exeter's many parish churches, retaining its own graveyard with burial continuing on a NE–SW alignment, whilst those burials associated with the Cathedral reverted to an E–W alignment.

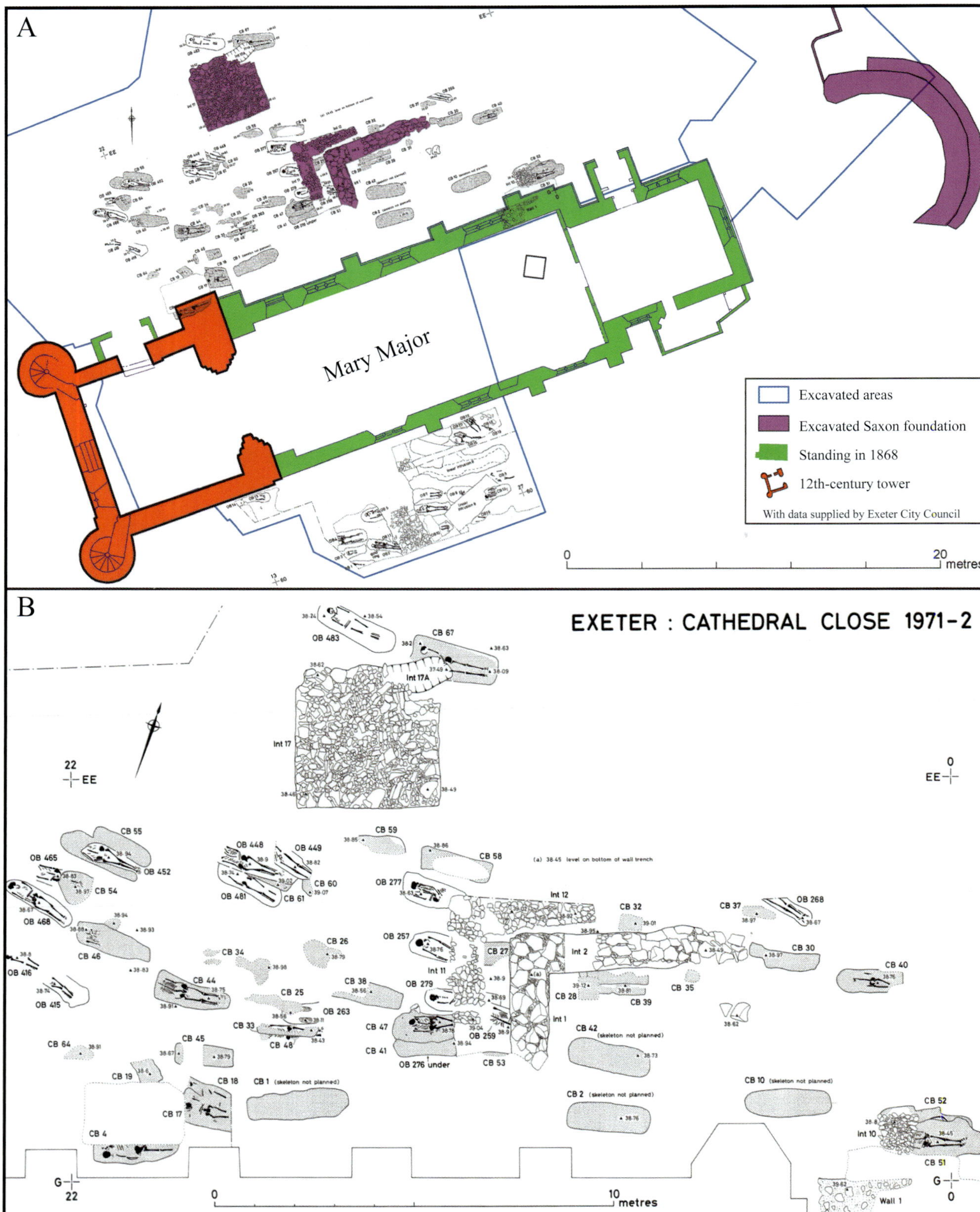

Fig. 19.3 (A) The cemetery associated with the Late Saxon minster, overlain by the later church of St Mary Major. (B) A closeup of the Saxo-Norman burials north of Mary Major church (Exeter Archaeology Archive,© Exeter City Council)

By the 14th century, burial of Exeter's lay population was also carried out at the Dominican friary situated to the north-east of Cathedral Green and south of the High Street. Burials would have taken place within the church, the cloisters and the cemetery of the friary between its foundation *c.* 1232 and its dissolution in 1538. In 1997–99 Exeter Archaeology carried out an assessment of the area with a trial trench placed in the documented area of the lay cemetery and five inhumations were recovered (Henderson *et al.* 1999), the remains of three being available for study. This was followed by large-scale excavations in 2006–7 that uncovered parts of the chancel, nave and north aisle of the friary church (Steinmetzer, Allan and Orme forthcoming; Fig. 19.4). Seventy-nine graves were identified in the excavated areas, 69 with articulated remains suitable for analysis, suggesting that the church alone would have held in excess of 500 burials, a large number of which are assumed to be of local gentry, merchants and their wives who would have paid for the privilege of this burial location.

The Franciscan friary – situated just outside of the South Gate on the south-west side of Holloway Street – would also have seen secular burial within the church, cloisters and cemetery. In 1973 six burials were excavated from the robbed remains of a chapel, possibly Wynard's chapel on the north side of the friary church (Bedford and Salvatore 1994d; Allan *et al.* 2016, 238); they may have been members of the religious community although as there were both male and female individuals present they are more likely to have been wealthy lay benefactors. In 1974 an additional 21 burials were excavated from what would have been an extensive lay cemetery associated with the friary.

The fourth burial site which produced primary research material for this study was St Katherine's Priory, in Polsloe. St Katherine's lies approximately 2.5 km north-east of the centre of Exeter in the parish of Heavitree, with the residents referred to as 'the nuns of Exeter' (Orme 2015b, 189). St Katherine's Priory was founded around 1160, as on March 1st of that year it was granted permission by the cathedral canons to have a cemetery for the burial of its sisters and priests (Orme 2015b, 185). In 1976–8 excavations exposed areas of the church, cloisters and east cemetery, along with the south and east ranges and the chapter house with approximately 53 graves recorded. Burial in the church was possibly reserved for

Fig. 19.4 Excavation of the Dominican friary showing a large number of burials (Exeter Archaeology Archive, © Exeter City Council)

the prioresses, senior members of the order and their priests, whilst the sisters and secular members would have been buried in the cemetery, cloisters and chapter house.

Burial practices in medieval Exeter

A variety of burial practices are evidenced in the past that can be separated out into grave types and grave variation (Buckberry 2007, 117). Grave types relate to grave structure and the container for the body such as plain earth, coffined and stone-lined (all of which are found in Exeter: Fig. 19.5), while grave variation can be found with any of the above for example in the use of grave markers, grave covers, grave layers (charcoal, chalk and lime) and stone head supports or foot rests.

Over the thousand years covered by this study a number of burial practices were carried out in Exeter. During the Late Saxon period there were two grave types evident: plain earth graves (70%) and coffined graves (30%). Plain earth graves – as the name suggests – are bare graves with no evidence of a coffin or lining, with the grave cut usually only slightly larger than the corpse with rounded ends and/or irregular sides. It is suggested that these graves received simple shrouded burials, although it should not be assumed that all of these burials are of low status. Coffined graves contained a burial within a wooden coffin or receptacle, and having such a grave would indicate additional expense and therefore suggest higher status. Coffins ranged from simple ones held together with wooden dowels, through those with a few nails, up to examples with nails, straps and fittings. While Hadley (2001, 105) states that due to its variety of forms the presence or absence of a coffin does not necessarily indicate status, iron was an important commodity in the Late Saxon period (Waldron 2007), and it is therefore suggested here that the more iron used in a coffin's construction the wealthier the purchaser and therefore the higher the assumed status of the individual buried. In addition to the grave types there are two grave variations found at Exeter during the Late Saxon period: charcoal burials (that account for 39%, 24/61, of the Late Saxon burials) and a burial with head support stones (1.6%, 1/61). Head support stones were stones arranged around the head to provide comfort for the deceased, support and protection, and by keeping the head upright it enabled the individual a direct line of sight to the risen Christ at Judgement Day (Daniell 1997, 181).

A charcoal burial is defined as one having a layer of charcoal in association with the inhumation and appears with both plain earth and coffined graves, examples of which are both present at Exeter where they account for 46% (11/24) of the Late Saxon coffined graves (*e.g.* Fig. 19.6). In Exeter and nationally, they mainly occur between the 9th and the 12th centuries with radiocarbon dates centred on the 9th to 11th centuries (Daniell 1997, 158; Holloway 2010, 86). Charcoal burials are thought to be high status as the majority are found at high status urban cathedrals or minsters, such as Winchester, Durham, York and Exeter and in association with elaborate coffin-fittings (Holloway 2010, 85). The rationale behind using charcoal is still not fully understood and suggestions for both practical and symbolic reasons have been proposed (Dawes

Fig. 19.5 Grave types in Exeter: from left to right, plain earth, coffined and stone-lined graves (source: Exeter Archaeology Archive, © Exeter City Council)

Fig. 19.6 A Late Saxon charcoal burial from Cathedral Green (Exeter Archaeology Archive, © Exeter City Council)

Table 19.2 Grave types from Exeter's later medieval cemeteries

Grave type	Cathedral Green (n275)		Holloway Lane (Greyfriars' cemetery) (n20)		St Katherine's Priory (east cemetery & cloister) (n17)		Total	
	No.	%	No.	%	No.	%	No.	%
Plain earth	212	77%	–	–	6	35%	218	70%
Coffined	14	5%	20	100%	4	24%	38	12%
Stone-lined	48	17.5%	–	–	1	6%	49	16%
Unknown	1	0.5%	–	–	6	35%	7	2%

and Magilton 1980; Kjølbye-Biddle 1992; Daniell 1997; Richards 2002; Thompson 2004; Holloway 2008; 2010).

At the time of the Norman Conquest, there was no obvious change in burial practice at Exeter with a continuation of plain earth and coffined graves, as well as charcoal burials. However, as the charcoal burials began to fade out during the transition between the Late Saxon and post-Conquest period we see the appearance of stone-lined graves. These are graves lined in stone with or without a 'head niche' and appear to increase in popularity during the 12th and 13th centuries (Gilchrist and Sloane 2005, 134–7), gradually dying out in the 14th century due to more wealthy individuals increasingly preferring an intra-mural church burial (burial within a church). The row of stone-lined graves outside the west front of the cathedral – a prime location – confirm that this was a high status form of burial and as with charcoal burials, this grave type was given to both men and women equally.

Following the end of the cathedral's monopoly on interment (post 1300) church burials became a mark of social and spiritual elevation and all of the monastic sites studied had a mix of plain earth, coffined and stone-lined intra-mural burials. It is evident from Table 19.2 that plain earth graves are the most dominant grave type from later medieval Cathedral Green suggesting that a high proportion of the town's laity had a simple shrouded burial (shroud pins were commonly found amongst the burials). The proportion of coffined burials appears to be different in all three cemeteries, with only 5% of the later medieval Cathedral Green burials having coffin nails recorded but much higher rates being found at the monastic sites. The sparsity of coffins may be due to the greater use of simple dowel coffins or use of a parish bier/coffin. In contrast, all those excavated from the Greyfriars' cemetery had a coffin burial.

The majority of intra-mural burials studied outside of Cathedral Green come from the Dominican friary (70 burials), with five from the church of the Greyfriars and 13 from St Katherine's Priory. As with the Cathedral cemetery burials there are plain earth, coffined and stone-lined grave types: all the stone-lined graves at Princesshay and Friars Gate belonged to males, whilst the only two intra-mural male burials at St Katherine's Priory were stone-lined graves positioned in the choir.

The Reformation would have had a major effect on burial practices in Exeter particularly with the reduction in burial sites. The Dominican friary, the Franciscan friary, St Katherine's Priory, St John's Hospital and the charnel chapel were all lost. Burial was now restricted to the remaining parish churches, the cathedral and the cathedral cemetery. With Exeter's population continuing to grow burial of the dead would have started to become a significant problem, but it took another hundred years before the Cathedral Green cemetery was closed and levelled, and the new cemetery at Bartholomew's was consecrated.

Materials and methods

The total skeletal assemblage analysed comprised of 463 articulated individuals and consists of all known medieval and early post-medieval individuals dating from between the 8th century and 1636 (Table 19.1). These were separated into four groups: the Late Saxon burials, the later medieval burials from the Cathedral Green and the various monasteries, and the later medieval stone-lined graves found in both these periods. The early post-Roman burials from the Cemetery I could not be included as very little skeletal material survived following earlier radiocarbon dating (Table 19.3). The stone-lined burials were separated out from the two key chronological groups as many were not securely dated and also to explore the higher status suggested by the grave type.

To enable the exploration of health and status within Exeter's past population standard osteological analysis was carried out including the recording of demographic information (age, sex and adult stature), along with the presence and absence of dental disease, specific and non-specific infection, nutritional and metabolic indicators of stress, trauma, and congenital, circulatory and miscellaneous conditions. All of the osteological information was considered alongside dietary information (from stable isotope analysis and zooarchaeological data), environmental factors (from historical information on disease, housing and water supplies) and burial practice (location, grave type and variation). The methodologies used followed standard osteological guidelines and are described in detail in Kingdom (2019).

Osteological analysis

Demography

Both sex and age of death estimation are important for understanding the population being studied. Creation of mortality profiles enable comparisons between the site(s) being analysed and other sites or populations, while sex and age of death estimations can facilitate the exploration of nutritional or pathological stress between different sexes or age groups. Final adult stature and body mass calculations can also be used as an indicator

Table 19.3 Separation of Exeter's medieval burials into groups (for Site Numbers see Chapter 2 above)

Excavation and date	*Site Number*	*Pre-Conquest*		*Later Medieval*		
		Post-Roman (excluded from study)	*Late Saxon burials*	*Later medieval Cathedral Green*	*Friaries and priory*	*Stone-lined burials*
Mary Major 1971–2	40		29			
War Memorial 1972	40	2	24	20		5
Cathedral Green 1975	40			5		
Cathedral Green 1976	40			199		44
Deanery 2005	206		8			
Cathedral Green 2012	170			2		
Exeter Princesshay assessment 1998	156				3	
Princesshay 2006	156				65	4
Friars Gate 1973	45				3	2
Holloway Street 1974	50				20	
Polsloe Priory 1976	59				24	6
Total		2	61	226	115	61

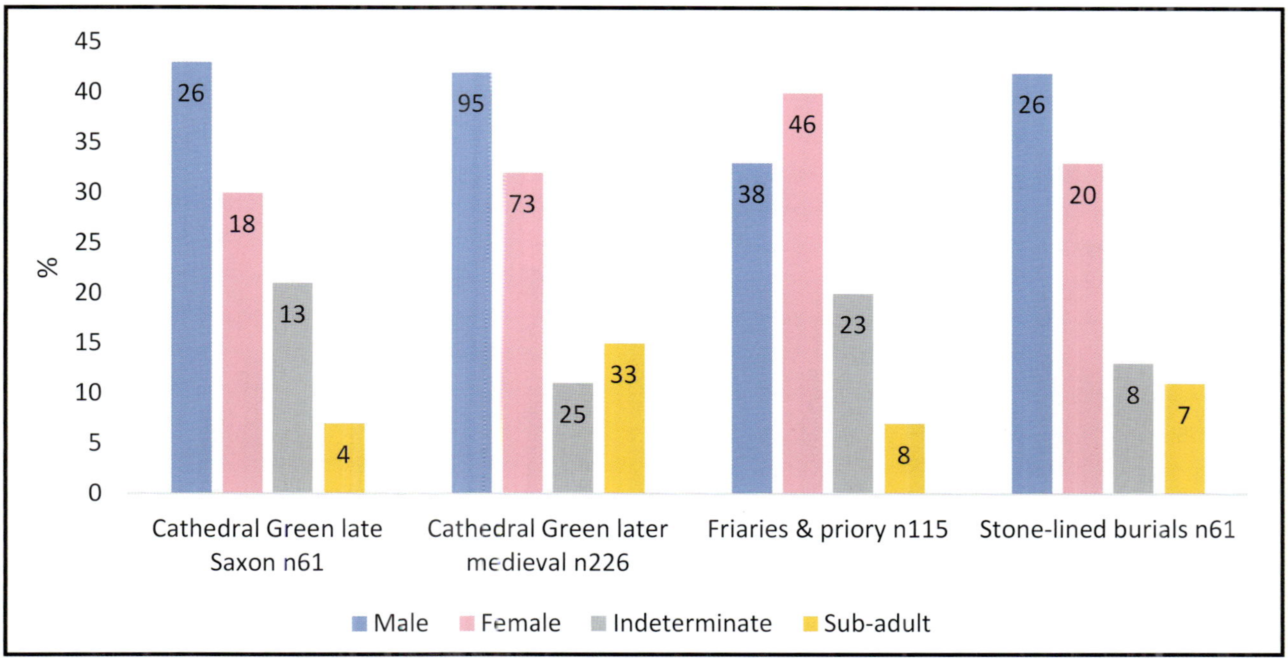

Fig. 19.7 Percentage of sex estimation by group (source: author)

of socio-economic status (Larsen 1997, 18; Gowland and Tompson 2013, 125), as they are affected not only by genetics but also environmental factors such as inadequate nutrition and poor health.

A total of 83% (342/411) of adult individuals could be sexed, with 40% (185/463) male, 34% (157/463) female, 15% (69/463) indeterminate, and 11% (52/463) sub-adults. The sex estimation for the different Exeter groups is presented in Fig. 19.7 and indicates that both males and females were buried at all four city sites and were afforded both graveyard and church burial. This suggests that the excavated areas at the friary sites included secular burial, whilst the majority of the friars were probably buried in the cloisters, areas not excavated at either site (EAPIT 1, Fig. 8.6).

A total of 346 individuals (75%) could be allocated to an age-of-death category. Only 11% (52/463) of the individuals are sub-adults resulting in a 7.9:1 ratio of adults to sub-adults. Of the adults placed in age categories, 39% (115/463) are young adults (18–25 years) or young middle adults (26–35 years), whilst 61% (179/463) are older middle-aged adults (36–45 years) or mature adults (over 46 years). This indicates that once an individual had reached adulthood, a high proportion could expect to live beyond 36 years and over half of those to 46 years and older (Fig. 19.8). The Late Saxon group has the highest prevalence (36%, 22/57) of individuals with an age-of-death under 35 years, whilst the stone-lined burials has the lowest (19%, 10/54), the pattern difference between the two groups being statistically significant (χ^2=5.4, df=1 p=0.02). The analysis also found there was the same proportion of males and females in the adolescent age group (13–17 years), but almost twice as many females than males represented in the young adult group. This high percentage is in part due to the number of young adult females (5/18) in the St Katherine's Priory collection, compared to males (0/4) – not surprising as it was a nunnery – although if these are removed the percentage for females (19%; 27/144) is still nearly double that for males (10%; 18/187), the difference once again being statistically significant (χ^2=5.8, df=1 p=0.02). This is of interest as it is the main child-bearing age group suggesting that childbirth was a significant factor in mortality.

The mean estimated stature height for Exeter males is 171.4 cm (5' 6") and 158.7 cm (5' 2") for females. Kruskal-Wallis statistical tests were carried out for males and females to ascertain if there was a significant difference in stature between the four burial groups. No significant difference was indicated between the females, although significant differences were found between the Late Saxon males and the later medieval Cathedral Green (p=0.01) and Friaries and Priory (p=0.02) males, indicating a reduced height in later-medieval males. For Exeter there appears to be no significant change in mean body mass between any of the groups, males or females. Therefore, although there is a decrease in height between the Late Saxon and the later medieval males, indicating a possible decline in socio-environmental conditions, the body mass remains constant. This suggests that the population became shorter and stockier rather than suffering from a prolonged decrease in health status or poor nutrition.

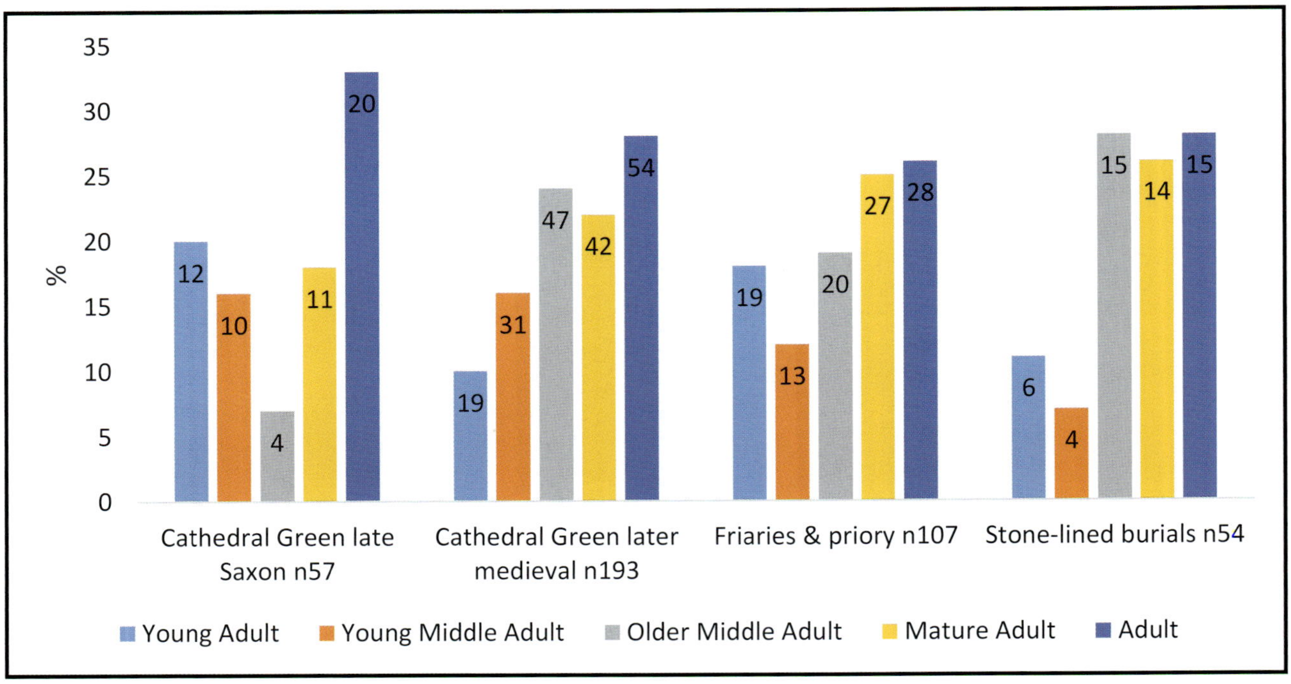

Fig. 19.8 Adult age-of-death at Exeter by group (source: author)

Dental health

Teeth are the most robust structures in the body and will often survive burial and excavation where other elements do not. They provide a wealth of information on areas such as diet, oral hygiene, stress and infection, making them a good indicator of individual and population health, which in turn is strongly related to economic and social status (Knüsel and Ogden 2008, 1798; Ogden 2008, 283; Novak 2015; Griffin 2017). Although attrition (tooth ware) is a multi-factorial process (Hillson 1996, 242), by comparing the attrition rate between Exeter's populations a difference in diet can potentially be inferred and related to socio-economic status. On assessment of the analytical data it could be ascertained that the Late Saxon sample had the highest attrition rate for individuals under 35 years and the Friaries and Priory group the lowest. This suggests a coarser diet in the Late Saxon period, containing unsieved flour and tougher vegetables and meat cuts, than in Exeter's later medieval period with the Friaries and Priory individuals having a softer more refined diet than the other groups (Fig. 19.9).

Teeth also retain permanent indications of disease linked to diet and illness, especially when the teeth are developing. The oral and dental health of Exeter's past population was ascertained by recording ante-mortem tooth loss, carious and periapical lesions along with the presence of calculus (mineralised dental plaque), periodontal disease and linear enamel hypoplasia (Table 19.4). The dental disease data indicate an increase in carious lesions, periodontal disease, ante-mortem tooth loss and periapical lesions in the later medieval groups and no obvious decrease in calculus through time. For calculus the Friaries and Priory group have the highest crude prevalence rate (CPR) (82%, 50/61) as well as having the highest CPR for the most severe deposits (80%, 49/61). This may be due to greater amounts of protein in this group's diet and/or poor oral hygiene, as all but the young adults (18–25 years) appear to have a high CPR. Another possible factor, however, is that as the Princesshay individuals – that form the main collection of the Friaries and Priory group – are the most recently excavated and have had less handling, calculus may have been better preserved.

Periodontal disease is the inflammation of the periodontal tissues supporting the teeth (*i.e.* gums), resulting in destruction of the periodontal ligament and eventual tooth loss (Ogden 2008, 289). This was found to be a common condition particularly amongst the later medieval population. The lower prevalence of periodontal disease 59% (10/17) in the Late Saxon burials, compared to 72% (101/141) in the combined later medieval groups, is likely to be associated with this group's younger age-of-death profile, as severity is seen to increase with age (Hillson 1996, 266).

Ante-mortem tooth loss is classed as a degenerative disease of the jaw and can result from a number of conditions including severe attrition, periapical lesions, carious lesions and periodontal disease. The increased ante-mortem tooth loss seen in the later medieval groups at Exeter may be due to three factors: the increased occurrence of carious lesions, increased periodontal disease, or a greater age-of-death structure.

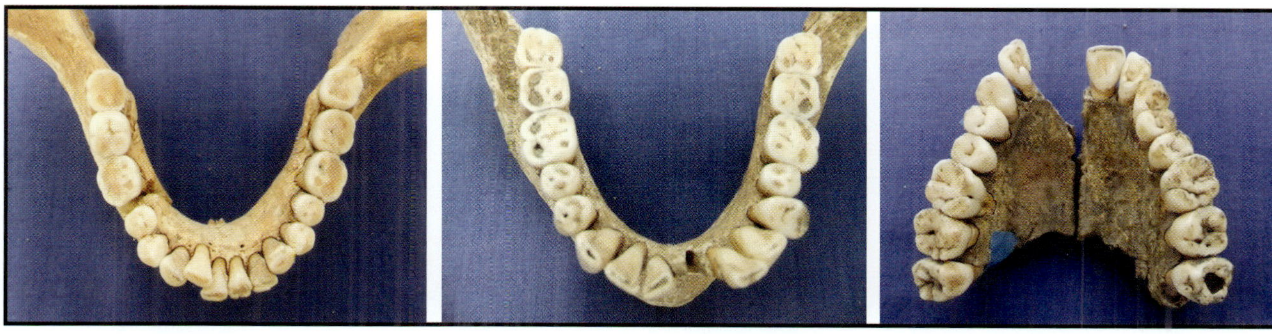

Fig. 19.9 The difference in molar wear, in older middle adults, from three of the Exeter groups, with greater attrition observed in the Late Saxon individual (left) than in the later medieval Cathedral Green individual (centre) and the least observed in the individual from the Dominican friary (right) (source: author)

Table 19.4 Crude prevalence rates of dental disease in the Exeter groups

	Calculus	*Periodontal disease*	*AMTL*	*Carious lesions*	*Periapical lesions*	*Enamel hypoplasia*
Late Saxon	78% (18/23)	59% (10/17)	16% (4/25)	17% (5/30)	20% (17/86)	27% (8/30)
Later Medieval Cathedral Green	70% (47/67)	75% (46/61)	(76%, 65/86)	70% (58/83)	20% (17/86)	40% (33/83)
Friaries & Priory group	82% (50/61)	63% (32/51)	56% (39/70)	51% (34/67)	31% (22/70)	45% (30/67)
Stone-lined burials	68% (17/25)	79% (23/29)	36% (10/28)	43% (12/28)	14% (4/28)	39% (11/28)

Carious lesions are commonplace amongst past populations and are generally caused by the lowering of the pH level in the mouth due to acid production from the breakdown of dietary carbohydrates and sugars (Hillson 1996, 260; Temple 2016, 433). Of the four Exeter groups later medieval Cathedral Green has the highest rate of carious lesions followed by the other later medieval groups, whilst the Late Saxon group had the lowest, the difference in patterning between the groups being statistically significant (χ^2=26.6, df=3 p<0.01). Although the CPR for the Friaries and Priory group (51%, 34/67) is low in comparison to the later medieval Cathedral Green group (70%, 58/83), the true prevalence rates (TPRs: 11.6%, 134/1152; and 12.1%, 133/1103 respectively) are very close with the Friaries and Priory individuals appearing to have a greater number of carious lesions per person than the other groups.

Periapical lesions occur when the pulp cavity of a tooth is exposed to the oral environment, enabling bacteria to invade the pulp and cause infection (Nelson 2016, 473). As with the other dental conditions this increases in the later medieval period with the Friaries and Priory group having the highest CPR (31%, 22/70) and TPR (1.7%, 24/1449).

Linear enamel hypoplasia (lines, pits or grooves of decreased enamel thickness on the surface of the tooth crown) are regarded as non-specific indicators of stress and occur during childhood whilst the teeth are developing (Hillson 1996, 165; King *et al.* 2005). The Exeter data show that there is a higher TPR during the later medieval period (12.3%, 342/2789) compared to the Late Saxon period (2.8%, 14/503). It is also evident that 100% (8/8) of the Late Saxon individuals with linear enamel hypoplasia and 62% (21/30) from later medieval Cathedral Green are under 35 years of age, whilst only 39% (11/28) from the Friaries and Priory group are in this age group (the difference between later medieval Cathedral Green and the Friaries and Priory group being statistically significant: χ^2=5.5, df=1 p=0.02). As linear enamel hypoplasia is an indicator of poor health in childhood this may indicate that more individuals from the Friaries and Priory group – although exposed to the causes of metabolic or nutritional stress whilst young – were able to survive to mature adulthood.

Joint disease

Excluding the skull, the adult body has over 200 joints, all of which are put under differing degrees of pressure during an individual's lifetime. The most commonly found joint diseases observed in skeletal remains are osteoarthritis (OA), degenerative disc disease, and Schmorl's nodes and rotator cuff disease (Ortner 2003, 545; Waldron 2009, 26). All of these conditions in differing degrees will affect the health of an individual.

The Cathedral Green medieval group has the highest CPR (29%, 56/191) of extra-spinal OA and the Late Saxon group the lowest (CPR 8%, 4/53) (Fig. 19.10). In all

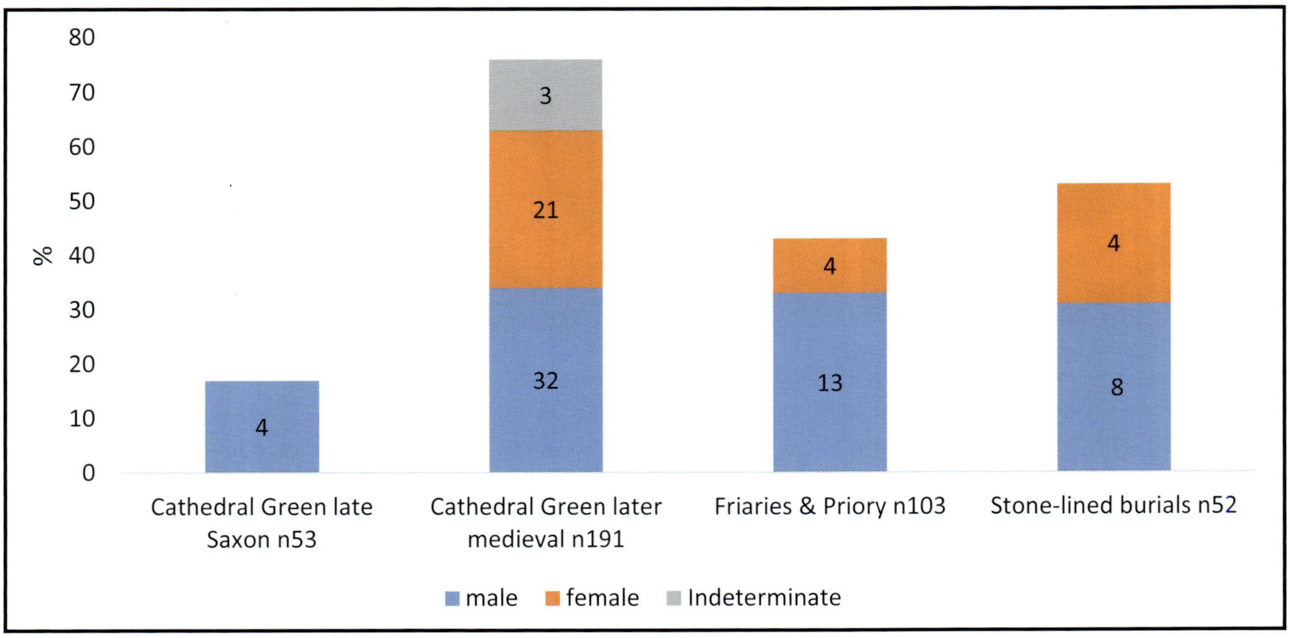

Fig. 19.10 CPR of extra-spinal joint disease for all groups (source: author)

groups males have a higher CPR than females, although the difference between males and females in the later medieval groups is only significant for the Friaries and Priory group (χ^2=0.8, df=1 p=<0.01).

The stone-lined burials have the highest CPR (36%, 15/42) and TPR (9.1%, 60/656) for spinal OA, whilst the Late Saxon group has the lowest TPR (6.3%, 15/239), although the pattern difference between the four groups is not statistically significant. For the Late Saxon group and the later medieval Cathedral Green group females (7.1%, 7/99; and 8.7%, 88/1010) have a higher TPR for spinal OA than males (3.9%, 5/128; and 5.7%, 72/1255), whilst for the Friaries and Priory and stone-lined burials males are more frequently affected. The stone-lined burial group has the highest CPR for degenerative disc disease (CPR 55%, 22/40; TPR 29.9%, 198/663) whilst the Late Saxon group has the highest TPR (39.8%, 94/236; CPR 45%, 14/31) followed by later medieval Cathedral Green (CPR 41%, 60/147). The Friaries and Priory group has the lowest (CPR 27%, 19/71; TPR 12%, 127/1058) which is similar to the results for spinal OA, the pattern difference between the groups being statistically significant (χ2=9.33, df=3 p=0.02).

A number of other joint diseases were also observed in the Exeter collections including diffuse idiopathic skeletal hyperostosis (DISH), gout, and seronegative spondyloarthropathies. DISH is a condition commonly seen in medieval skeletal material. It is a bone forming condition diagnosed by the observation of new bone in the anterior longitudinal ligament, giving a candle wax appearance, along with calcification or ossification of extra-spinal enthese and ligaments (Waldron 2009, 73). Although the direct cause is not fully understood, in modern populations DISH is associated with obesity and type II diabetes (Mays *et al.* 2007, 158; Waldron 2009, 74). Kiss *et al.* (2002) also found that patients with DISH had a greater body mass index (BMI), were heavier in younger as well as later life and were more likely to have diabetes mellitus. A total of 18 individuals from the Exeter groups were diagnosed with DISH, or probable/possible DISH: 15 males, 2 females and 1 indeterminate adult. The CPR ranges from 2.3% (1/44) in the stone-lined burials to 6.8% (10/148 and 5/73) in the later medieval Cathedral Green and Friaries and Priory groups. In addition a total of four individuals from later medieval Exeter were observed to have gout with one of these (CG636) also presenting with DISH. Gout is an erosive osteoarthropathy often associated with obesity, excessive alcohol intake and a diet rich in red meat and seafood (Resnick 2002a, 1520; Ragab *et al.* 2017). Seronegative spondyloarthropathies are a group of joint diseases with similar morphological and immunological features including ossification at insertion sites of tendons and ligaments along with sacroiliac and spinal fusion (Rogers and Waldron 1995, 70). Eight individuals in the collection (CPR 2.9%, 8/274), show one or more signs of undifferentiated spondyloarthropathy and are classified as having an erosive arthropathy of the seronegative type. Seven are from the later medieval Cathedral Green group (CPR 3.8%, 7/186) and one from the Friaries and Priory (CPR 1.1%, 1/88).

Figure 19.11 shows that later medieval Cathedral Green has the highest CPR of all joint disease (60%,115/193) and the Late Saxon group the lowest (31%,17/54), the difference between the four groups being statistically

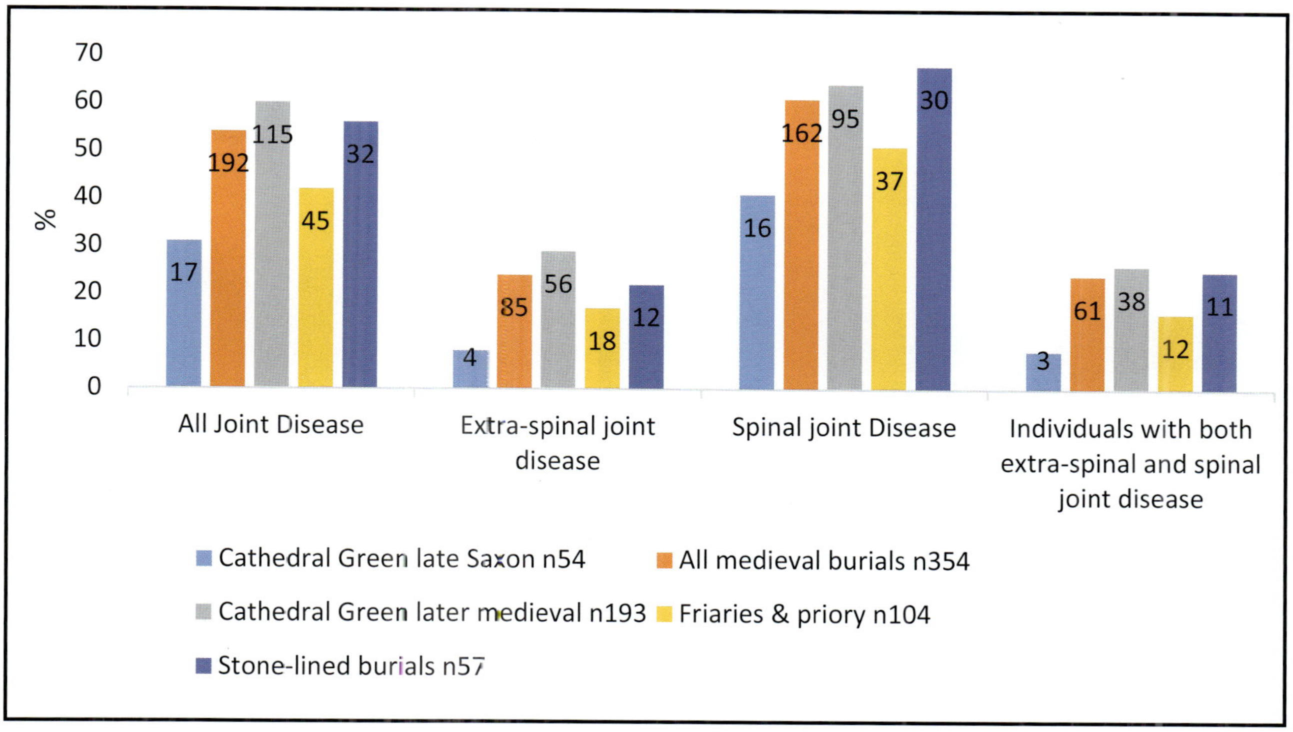

Fig. 19.11 A summary of CPR of adult joint disease for the Exeter groups (source: author)

significant (χ^2=17.67, df=3 p=<0.01). For individuals that have both extra-spinal and spinal joint disease the later medieval Cathedral Green group has the highest CPR (26%, 38/148) followed by the stone-lined burials (25%, 11/44). For the later-medieval groups it is noted that the CPR for all sections is lower for the Friaries and Priory group than the other two groups. This is unlikely to be due to age as the CPR of individuals under 35 years is similar for all groups. All areas of joint disease increase from the Late Saxon to the later medieval period, and there is a higher CPR of males with each of the different joint diseases than females. The difference between the sexes is statistically significant when all groups are combined (χ^2=8.8, df=1 p=<0.01; M = 64%, 121/188; F = 48%, 73/151), although within the separate groups there is only a significant difference between males and females in the Friaries and Priory group (χ^2=4.5, df=1 p=0.03).

Infectious disease

Infectious disease is the result of illness due to micro-organisms such as bacteria, viruses, fungi or parasites. The outcome of the infection depends upon an individual's immune status and their response to the disease process. This can differ from individual to individual and will depend on a number of factors including age, genetic predisposition and environment (Roberts 2000, 146). Infections can be acute or chronic. An acute infection such as the plague, typhoid or cholera will occur over a short period of time, during which the patient will either die or recover, leaving little or no evidence on the skeletal system (Ortner 2008a, 191). A chronic infection develops over a longer period and may have acute phases but can reoccur once or many times being more likely to leave evidence on the skeletal remains. Specific diseases that fall into the chronic infection category include tuberculosis, leprosy and treponematosis. As well as specific diseases there are also many infections which cause more general changes to the skeletal system making identification problematic. These are classed as non-specific infections. When considering infectious disease it is important that the osteological paradox (Wood *et al.* 1992) should be taken into account as it is the stronger individuals, with a healthy immune system, that will be able to resist and fight infection long enough to develop skeletal changes.

A total of 52% (213/411) of the adult population studied had active, chronic or healed lesions of non-specific infection when they died. As the maxillary sinuses are one of the body's first lines of defence against airborne particles, sinusitis is a common health condition in contemporary society (Brook 2009) and would also have been a common problem in the past. The Friaries and Priory group (58%, 14/24) and the stone-lined burials (53%, 8/15) have the highest CPR of sinusitis, with the later medieval Cathedral Green group having the lowest (30%, 10/33), the difference between the later medieval Cathedral Green and Friaries and Priory groups being statistically significant (χ^2=4.5, df=1 p=0.03).

It was found that the majority of Exeter's individuals exhibiting non-specific infection (periosteal new bone formation) elsewhere in the body had healed or healing lesions (Fig. 19.12). The stone-lined burials have the greatest percentage of active periosteal lesions (23% 7/30)

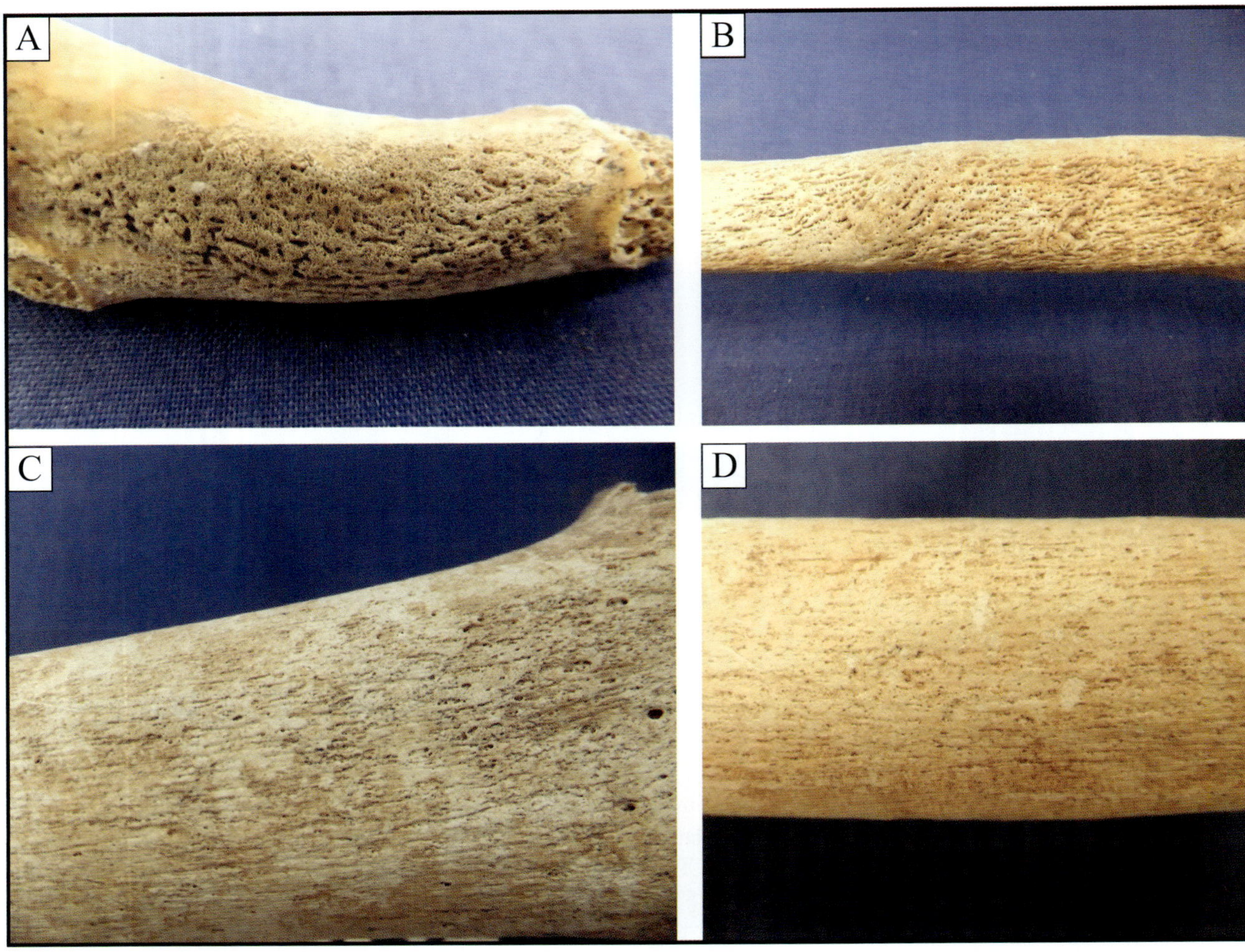

Fig. 19.12 Forms of PNB: (A) active and remodelling (CG Sk 746 left MT5); (B) chronic (CG Sk709 left tibia); (C) remodelling (CG Sk 677 right femur); (D) remodelled (CG Sk00 right femur (this bone had been loaned out for a display many years ago and has lost its original excavation number) (source: author)

whilst the Friaries and Priory group has the highest remodelled percentage (84% 38/45). The difference between the groups for those with remodelled periosteal new bone is statistically significant (χ^2=10.6, df=3 p=0.01). When examined by group there is no significant difference between the Late Saxon period and the later medieval period although there is a statistical difference between the later medieval Cathedral Green and the Friaries and Priory groups (χ^2=5.9, df=1 p=0.02).

Only 1.7% (7/411) of Exeter's adult individuals exhibited bone changes that could relate to a specific infection: 4 for treponematosis, 2 for leprosy and 1 for poliomyelitis (Fig. 19.13). These are all serious illnesses, requiring care of the individual to enable them to live long enough for skeletal changes to occur.

Overall, it would appear that at least half of Exeter's individuals were infected by pathogens that resulted in a bodily response. For many this response was no longer active at the time of death with others living long enough for bone changes to occur.

Nutritional and metabolic diseases

Nutritional and metabolic diseases are a range of disorders which include vitamin and mineral related deficiencies, and skeletal evidence of these conditions can help give important insights into adequate dietary health in past populations (Ortner 2008b). The main nutritional and metabolic bone diseases studied are scurvy, rickets/osteomalacia and osteoporosis along with cribra orbitalia and porotic hyperostosis (*ibid.*). It does not appear that Exeter's past populations suffered greatly from these dietary deficiencies, with an approximate CPR of 10% (46/463) of individuals showing evidence for the above conditions. The highest CPR (15%, 9/61) is for the stone-lined burials with five adults and four sub-adults; the lowest CPR is for the Late Saxon group (7%, 4/61) with three adults and one sub-adult. The majority of those affected appear to be suffering from non-specific metabolic stress, possibly anaemia, which may have been in part due to intestinal problems. Non-specific metabolic stress is also linked to linear enamel hypoplasia and infection;

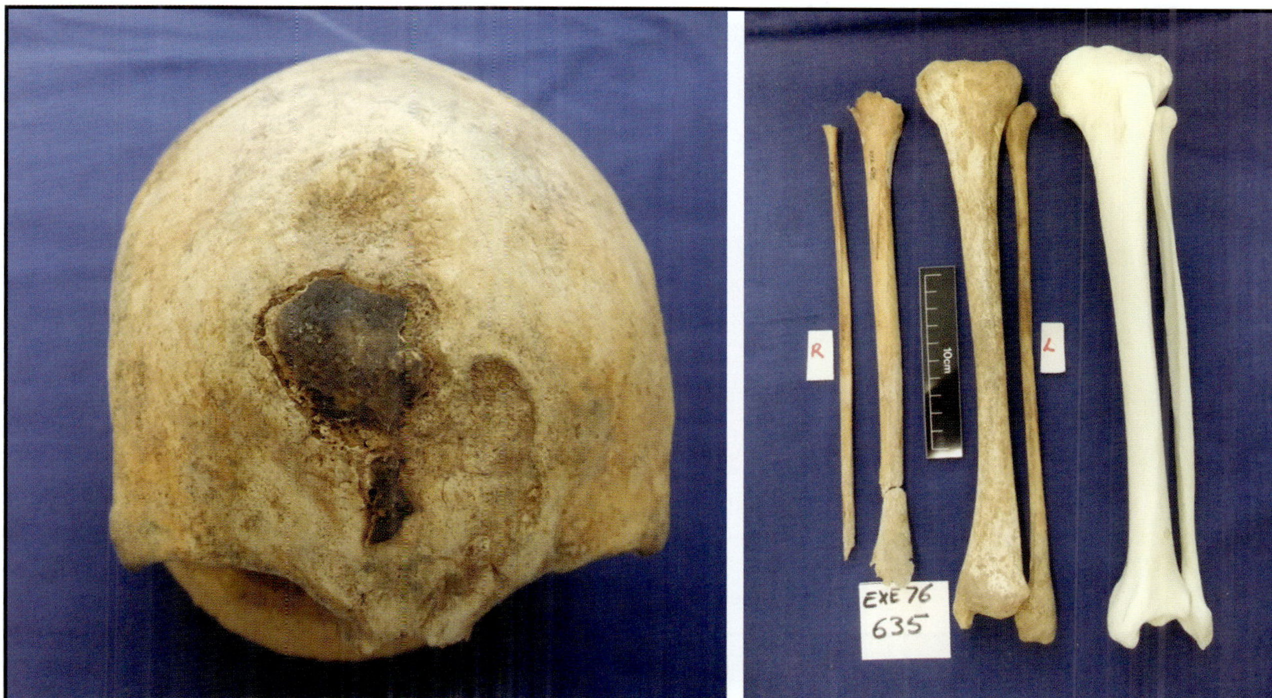

Treponematosis (venereal syphilis) indicated by healed and healing carries sicca (EPH9511)

CG635 possible poliomyelitis, indicated by atrophy of lower limbs

Fig. 19.13 Specific infection from later medieval Exeter (source: author)

it would appear that the majority of those at Exeter with metabolic stress also suffered from reduced resilience and previous bouts of illness.

Trauma

There are four ways trauma can affect the skeleton: partial or incomplete break of the bone, abnormal displacement or dislocation of joints, disruption in nerve or blood supply, and artificially induced abnormal shape or contour of bone (Ortner 2003, 120). Trauma may be intentional or accidental, end life, or cause life changing disabilities or short-term discomfort. A total CPR of 17.3% (71/411) of adult individuals from Exeter exhibit some form of trauma (Fig. 19.14) including fractures, dislocations, neurological trauma, *myositis ossificans traumatica* and osteochondritis dissecans (Fig. 19.15). Males have a higher CPR (23.8%, 44/185) than females (16.6%, 26/157), suggesting that overall males were more likely to be involved in activities that could result in intentional or accidental trauma. The stone-lined burials have the highest CPR (24.1%, 13/54) whilst the Late Saxon group has the lowest (10.5%, 6/57), although the difference between the groups or periods is not significant. The stone-lined burials also have the highest CPR for both males (30.8%, 8/26) and females (25%, 5/20), whilst the late Saxon group has the lowest male CPR (15.4%, 4/26) and the Friaries and Priory group the lowest female CPR (10.9%, 5/46). That the Friaries and Priory males have the second highest CPR (26.3%, 10/38) but the females the lowest is interesting and may indicate that the females buried in this group led a more genteel and less physically active lifestyle.

Dietary isotope analysis

Carbon and nitrogen stable isotope analysis of bones and teeth enables the exploration of diet in past populations (Katzenberg 2000, 305). Food classes differ in their stable isotope ratios allowing dietary sources of carbon and nitrogen found in bone collagen, tooth dentine or enamel bioapatite, to be measured (Richards 2004). Differences can be established between C_3 plants (temperate zone vegetation) which give lower carbon and nitrogen signatures, and terrestrial and marine sources which give mid to high signatures (Mays 2000, 425). Through collaboration with Charlotte Scull from Reading University (and the 'Foodways of Religious Women in Anglo-Saxon and Medieval England' project), along with the suite of radiocarbon dates obtained to aid phasing of the Cathedral Green cemetery it was possible to study 66 stable dietary isotopes results for Exeter. Figure 19.16 shows very scattered ranges of isotope values indicating that both the Late Saxon and later medieval populations of Exeter had mixed terrestrial and

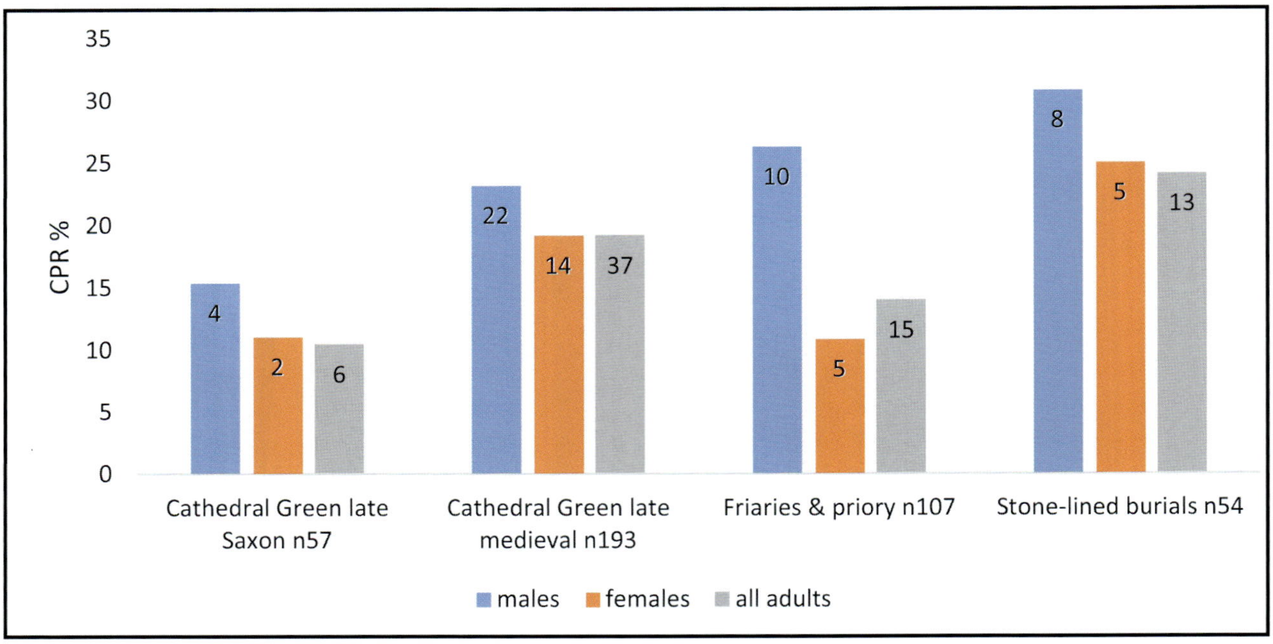

Fig. 19.14 CPR of trauma (source: author)

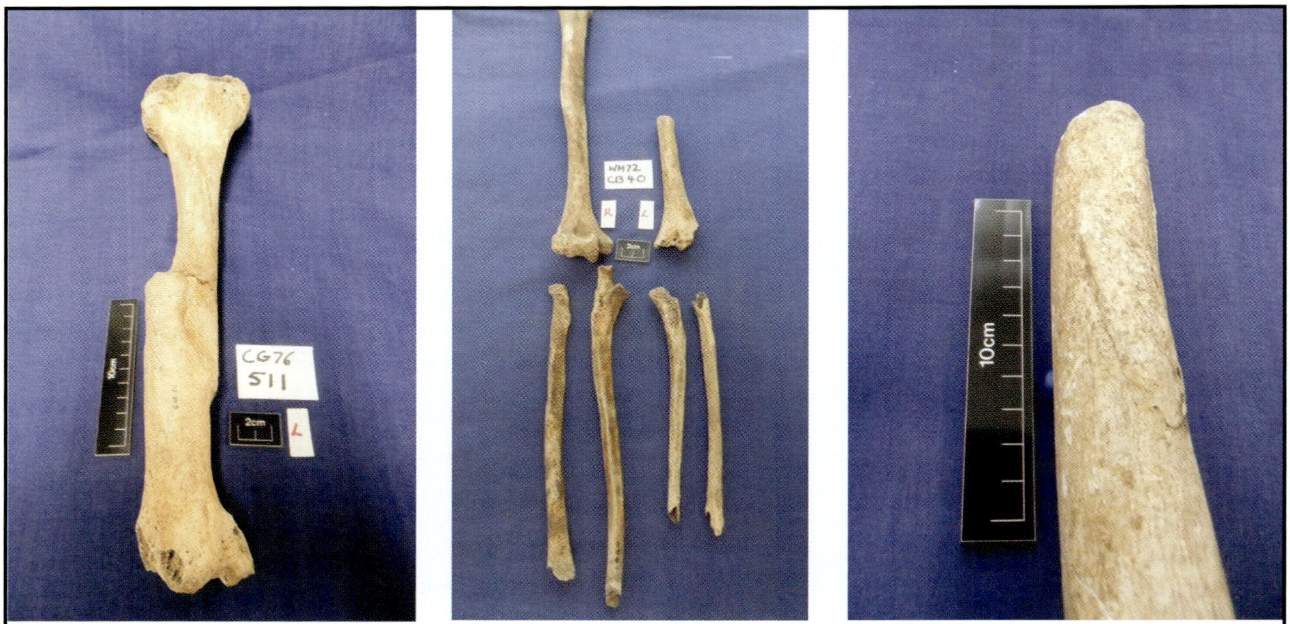

Healed, spiral/comminuted fracture of tibia (CG51)

A possible case of Duchenne-Erb's palsy (WMCB40)

Myositis ossificans traumatica (CG632) lateral left mid femur diaphysis

Fig. 19.15 Examples of trauma from the Exeter's Cathedral Green (source: author)

marine diets. The later medieval groups and particularly the Friaries and Priory and stone-lined burials, however, have higher values for both carbon and nitrogen stable isotopes, suggesting an increased proportion of both terrestrial protein and marine resources in their diets. Only in the later medival Cathedral Green group does there appear to be a clear demarcation between male and female diet. This may be due to the majority of males' sampled being Cathedral clergy, with burials close to the west front of the Norman cathedral. As the numbers analysed here are low and were not specifically targeted samples, the isotope information on diet and status is restricted, although it highlights areas of interest that would benefit from more in-depth targeted research.

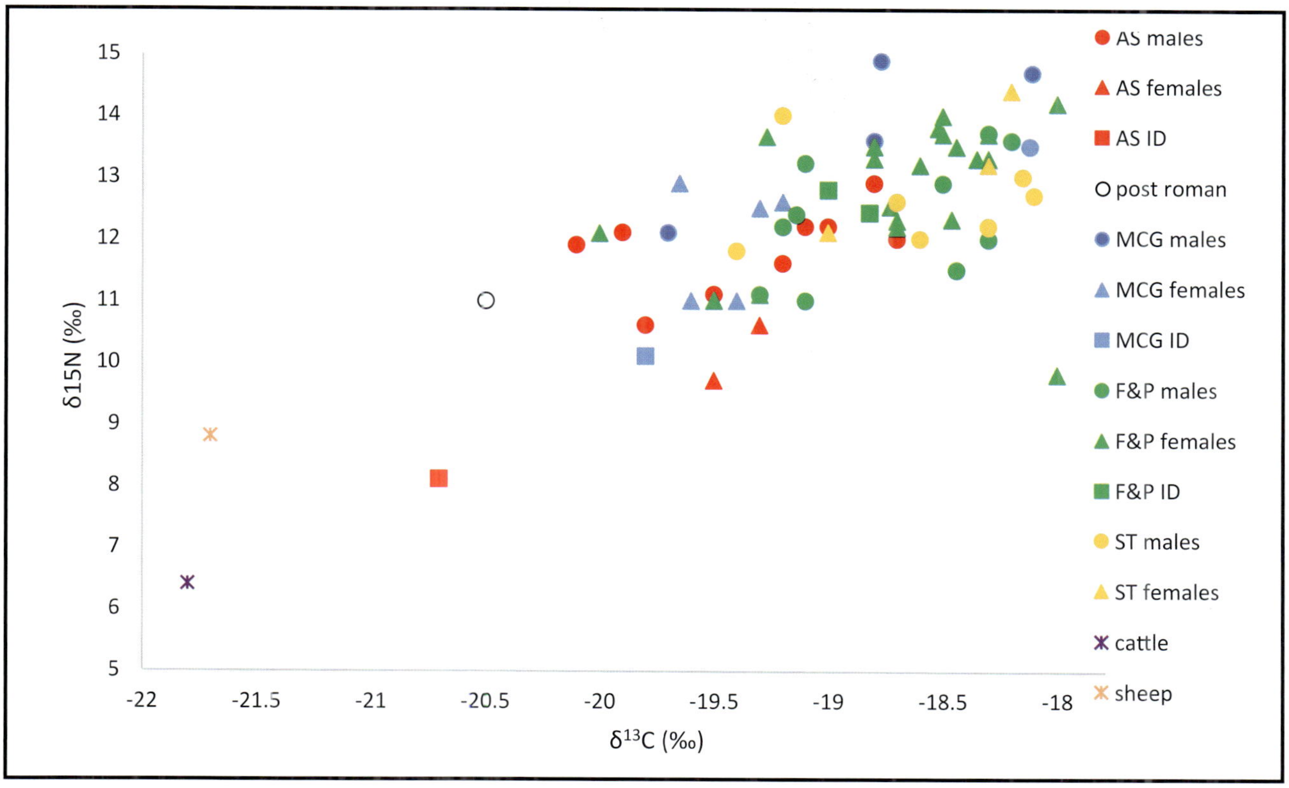

Fig. 19.16 The stable isotope data for the four Exeter groups and fauna (source: author)

Discussion

The central aim of the research summarised in this paper was to investigate skeletal health and socio-economic status across Exeter's medieval population, using a bioarchaeological approach. By bringing together the osteological findings of skeletal health with known historical and archaeological information, it explored the similarities and differences in health and status across time and between burial sites.

When considering how skeletal health differs between the Late Saxon and later medieval periods, it has become evident that the preservation and small sample size of the Late Saxon group made comparison problematic, although it appears that the majority of those analysed from both periods had access to adequate nutrition. The stable isotope values from Late Saxon Exeter are not as raised as those from the later period, although they still indicate a diet containing terrestrial protein with a contribution from marine resources. Although the later medieval population were shorter than in the Late Saxon period their body mass ratio, dietary isotope levels, older age-of-death profile and increase in skeletal indicators of affluence, indicate adequate if not good nutrition across the life course. The difference in prevalence of infection may have been affected by small sample size or poor preservation. The increases seen in dental disease, infection, joint disease and trauma in the later medieval period can all be associated with the higher age-of-death profile of this group, along with better resilience and resources to fight disease. What is seen in Exeter are small but not significant increases in skeletal indicators of stress during the later medieval period, which may be associated with gradual population increase and urbanisation.

Exeter, in common with all medieval towns, had extreme inequalities in wealth (Kowaleski 1995; Dyer 1998, 194), and so it is therefore important to consider both archaeological and historical context when interpreting and comparing skeletal evidence of health. The separate levels of Exeter's later medieval society would have experienced very different living conditions. Comparing the health and status between the later medieval groups from Exeter has proved informative with only marginal differences in the age-of-death profile, stature or body mass found, along with minor differences in dental pathology, cribra orbitalia and the prevalence of infection or trauma. There was also little difference in the dietary isotope levels between the males of the groups. The assumed higher status of those buried at the Friaries and Priory, however, is supported by them having less molar attrition and more sinusitis, those with linear enamel hypoplasia living longer and more individuals having remodelled periosteal new bone formation compared to the other groups. The females in this group also have noticeably less in the way of osteoarthritis and trauma, these differences all being associated with access to good nutrition and/or living conditions/life style. In contrast, the range of paleopathology including osteoarthritis and trauma evident at later medieval Cathedral Green is possibly an indication of the greater diversity in health and socio-economic status of those buried in that cemetery.

The osteological analysis appears to show only a marginal difference in assumed socio-economic status and skeletal health between the different later medieval groups, and a number of possibilities for this are suggested. Firstly, the city was always considered to be fairly prosperous even when other towns and cities declined (Dyer 1998, 188) suggesting the gap between wealthy and poor, enfranchised and disenfranchised, was not as large in Exeter as in other bigger, more prosperous towns like Bristol or London (Kowaleski 1995, 215). Secondly, upward social mobility was possible through trade, wealth or a fortunate marriage (Kowaleski 1990b, 213) meaning childhood status and environmental conditions may have been very different to those in later life. A third possibility is that the majority of individuals analysed were from burial sites or areas of burial, favoured by people of a similar status. It is generally accepted that those buried at monastic cemeteries, either the monastic community or wealthy lay benefactors, are of higher status (Müldner 2009). Documentary evidence indicates that as well as the friars, members of the nobility were buried in the Dominican friary, along with other rich and influential individuals. Fourthly, this analysis is likely to be missing both ends of the socio-economic scale with the majority of the nobility and oligarchy being buried inside the Cathedral (Kowaleski 1990b, 195; Lepine and Orme 2003, 116) whilst the very poor and sick would have been buried in the hospital cemeteries and less popular areas of Cathedral Green, sites not included in the study.

When compared to other sites Exeter's medieval residents appear to have fared favourably. Exeter's Late Saxon population had an older age-of-death profile, less dental pathology, cribra orbitalia, trauma and degenerative joint disease than a similar population from Winchester. This may reflect a difference in size and population density between the two towns, Winchester being the West Saxon capital from the early 700s, with manufacturing and commerce taking place by 865 (Ottaway 2017). For the later medieval period despite having a higher prevalence of linear enamel hypoplasia and non-specific infection when compared to Winchester (Molleson *et al.* 2016), St James' Priory in Bristol (Loe 2006) and St Andrew's Fishergate in York (Stroud and Kemp 1993), Exeter has an older age-of-death profile indicating that once adulthood was reached, the majority of the population had adequate nutrition and resilience, enabling them to manage the increased pathogen risk associated with urbanisation. In addition, although Exeter's population have a similar age-of-death profile to the more rural site of Wharram Percy in Yorkshire (Mays *et al.* 2007) they had a lower prevalence of joint disease and trauma suggesting a less physical life style.

Conclusion

This study has revealed important new information about Exeter's medieval residents. Many of the Late Saxon individuals buried close to the Late Saxon minster were of relatively high social status being afforded charcoal burials. They also appear to have had an adequate diet, were taller and had fewer indicators of skeletal stress than the later-medieval population, but have a lower age-of-death profile. This may indicate an urban population exhibiting good generational health but lower resistance to pathogen risk, due to environmental change and an increase in population density. Environmental changes over a period of approximately 250 years may have contributed to a gradual decrease in stature but an increase in immunity as demonstrated by the intermediate mean height, increased longevity and higher protein consumption among the stone-lined burials. The Friaries and Priory group have more healed or remodelled lesions and a greater age-of-death profile than the later medieval Cathedral Green group, suggesting that although they were exposed to the same pathogens and skeletal stress factors, they were more resilient. In addition, the females from this group have noticeably less trauma or activity related conditions suggestive of a more genteel and less physically demanding lifestyle. If these findings are combined with the burial information then it is possible to state that a difference in health and status between these two groups does exist, although this difference is in no way marked and more marginal than expected. Most of the individuals studied exhibited some form of skeletal pathology, although the majority was minor, healed or remodelled and unlikely to have impacted greatly on the daily lives of those analysed, with many reaching middle age and beyond. Overall, it has become apparent through the course of this research that the majority of Exeter's medieval population studied had adequate to good nutrition, health and longevity.

Appendix 19.1 Table of Radiocarbon Dates for Exeter Burials

Lab ID	Date sampled organisation	Context no./ skeleton no.	Site & cemetery phase	Context description [Sample ID]	Material	$\delta^{13}C_{AMS}$ (‰)	$\delta^{13}C_{IRMS}$ (‰)	$\delta^{15}N$ (‰)	C:N	Radiocarbon age (BP)	94.5% probability	68.2% probability
HAR-1614	27.06.1978 Exeter Arch Field Unit	SK OB278 Cathedral Green	Cemetery I	Supine inhumation of an adult male aged 40–50yrs (Wells, 1979). On a SSE-NNW alignment, cutting across the SW wall of the Roman *basilica* nave.	Human bone – element unknown	−21.4	*	*	*	1530±70	390–650cal AD (100% of area)	440–600cal AD (100% of area)
HAR-1613	27.06.1978 Exeter Arch Field Unit	SK OB486 Cathedral Green	Cemetery I	Supine inhumation of an adult male aged 30–40yrs (Calvin Wells, 1979). On a SSE–NNW alignment (cemetery I), cutting across the SW wall of the Roman *basilica* nave.	Human bone – element unknown	−21.4	*	*	*	1460±80	410–710cal AD (100% of area)	460–480cal AD (7.0% of area) 530–660cal AD (93.0% of area)
SUERC-57530	2015 Kingdom (University of Exeter)	SK OB486 Cathedral Green	Cemetery I	Re-dating of supine inhumation OB486 above.	Human remains os coxae	−20.5	***	11.0	3.3	1514±31	428–495cal AD (24.4% of area) 507–521cal AD (2.4% of area) 526–618cal AD (68.7% of area)	474–485cal AD (5.5% of area) 536–601cal AD (62.7% of area)
SUERC-57531	2015 Kingdom (University of Exeter)	SK OB205 Cathedral Green	Cemetery II	Supine inhumation of young adult F aged 18–25yrs, 25–50% present. E–W orientation, North of excavation trench 8 below CB68.	Human remains long bone fragment	−19.3	***	10.6	3.3	1191±31	720–741cal AD (3.5% of area) 766–899cal AD (88.3% of area) 924–945cal AD (3.6% of area)	778–794cal AD (11.2% of area) 799–878cal AD (57.0% of area)
SUERC-40322	2012 Cotswold Archaeology	Context (1401) Cathedral Green	Position and date suggest Cemetery II/III	Disarticulated adult human remains from burial deposit overlying wall foundation in Kalenderhay, South of the Saxon minster/Mary Major church.	Human bone right distal femur	−19.8	***	10.2	3.2	1190±30	722–740cal AD (2.9% of area) 766–899cal AD (89.0% of area) 924–945cal AD (3.5% of area)	778–793cal AD (11.0% of area) 800–878cal AD (57.2% of area)
SEURC-39396	2012 Exeter Archaeology	SK OB20 Cathedral Green	Originally assumed Cemetery I Dated to Cemetery II	Supine inhumation of adult, sex ID, <25% present mainly lower limbs. Originally believed to be on NW–SE orientation, From lower levels beneath Mary Major church full grave cut not established.	Human remains long bone fragments	−20.7	***	8.1	3.2	1175±30	774–900cal AD (83.1% of area) 917–965cal AD (12.3% of area)	782–790cal AD (6.1% of area) 809–891cal AD (62.1% of area)

(Continued)

Appendix 19.1 Table of Radiocarbon Dates for Exeter Burials (Continued)

Lab ID	Date sampled organisation	Context no./ skeleton no.	Site & cemetery phase	Context description [Sample ID]	Material	$\delta^{13}C_{AMS}$ (‰)	$\delta^{13}C_{IRMS}$ (‰)	$\delta^{15}N$ (‰)	C:N	Radiocarbon age (BP)	94.5% probability	68.2% probability
SUERC-40360	2012 Exeter Archaeology	SK CB67 Cathedral Green	Cemetery II	Supine inhumation of young adult male 18–25yrs, 50% present. Charcoal burial on E–W orientation, north of excavation cut by later feature.	Human remains femur fragments	−19.5	***	11.1	3.2	1165±35	775–972cal AD (95.4% of area)	782–790cal AD (5.0% of area) 809–896cal AD (54.9% of area) 924–939cal AD (8.3% of area)
SUERC-57532	2015 Kingdom (University of Exeter)	SK CB44 Cathedral Green	Cemetery II	Supine inhumation of mature adult male aged 50+, 25–50% present, presents with DISH (Diffuse idiopathic skeletal hyperostosis). E–W orientation, west of porticus.	Human remains fibula fragments	−19.1	***	12.2	3.3	1134±31	777–792cal AD (4.3% of area) 803–845cal AD (8.2% of area) 857–987cal AD (82.9% of area)	885–970cal AD (68.2% of area)
SUERC-39399	2012 Exeter Archaeology	SK CB7 Cathedral Green	Cemetery II	Supine inhumation of an adult, sex ID, <25% present. Charcoal burial E–W orientation, west end of excavation on north side of Mary Major church.	Human remains femur fragments	−19.9	***	12.1	3.2	1130±30	782–789cal AD (1.0% of area) 811–846cal AD (5.5% of area) 857–989cal AD (89.0% of area)	888–905cal AD (14.5% of area) 912–971cal AD (53.7% of area)
SEURC-39395	2012 Exeter Archaeology	SK OB2 Cathedral Green	Cemetery II	Supine inhumation of a mature male 45+ years. E–W orientation on south side of Mary Major church. Buried with gold ring dated to the 9th Century	Human remains long bone fragments	−19.8	***	10.6	3.2	1035±30	898–920cal AD (5.7% of area) 949–1036cal AD (89.7% of area)	987–1022cal AD (68% of area)
SUERC-57533	2015 Kingdom (University of Exeter)	SK CB66 Cathedral Green	Cemetery III	Supine inhumation of adult F 26–35yrs, 25–50% present. Charcoal burial on NEE–SWW orientation, far west of trench ten/excavation, descends into Roman layers.	Human remains long bone fragment	−19.5	***	9.7	3.3	1184±29	729–737cal AD (1.0% of area) 768–899cal AD (89.6% of area) 924–946cal AD (4.8% of area)	778–793cal AD (11.4% of area) 801–885cal AD (568% of area)

(Continued)

Appendix 19.1 (Continued)

Lab ID	*Date sampled organisation*	*Context no./ skeleton no.*	*Site & cemetery phase*	*Context description [Sample ID]*	*Material*	$\delta^{13}C_{AMS}$ (‰)	$\delta^{13}C_{IRMS}$ (‰)	$\delta^{15}N$ (‰)	*C:N*	*Radiocarbon age (BP)*	*94.5% probability*	*68.2% probability*
SUERC-40358	2012 Exeter Archaeology	SK CB40 Cathedral Green	Cemetery III	Charcoal from base of grave of SK CB40. Supine inhumation of young adult male 17–30yrs. NEE–SWW orientation, east of first porticus and cut by later porticus wall.	Oak Charcoal	−25.9	***	***	***	1150±35	779–794cal AD (5.5% of area) 800–976cal AD (89.9% of area)	784–787cal AD (1.6% of area) 823–842cal AD (8.4% of area) 861–903cal AD (25.3% of area) 916–968cal AD (32.9% of area)
SUERC-39398	2012 Exeter Archaeology	SK CB2 Cathedral Green	Cemetery III	Supine inhumation of young adult male 17–25yrs. <25% present. Charcoal burial on NEE–SWW orientation, inside porticus on north side of Mary Major church.	Human remains long bone fragments	−19.0	***	12.2	3.2	1140±30	781–790cal AD (2.2% of area) 808–982cal AD (93.2% of area)	879–905cal AD (20.0% of area) 912–971cal AD (48.2% of area)
SUERC-40362	2012 Exeter Archaeology	SK OB264 Cathedral Green	Cemetery III	Supine inhumation of mature adult male 40+yrs, 50–75% present. NEE–SWW orientation, just west of porticus.	Human remains femur fragments	−20.1	***	11.9	3.2	1105±35	870–1019cal AD (95.4% of area)	895–925cal AD (27.0% of area) 937–983cal AD (41.2% of area)
SUERC-39403	2012 Exeter Archaeology	SK CB8 Cathedral Green	Cemetery III	Supine inhumation of a young adult 18–25yrs, <25% present. Charcoal burial on NEE–SWW orientation, from aisle of Victorian church outside west end of Saxon minster.	Human remains femur fragments	−18.7	***	12.0	3.2	1100±30	887–1014cal AD (95.4% of area)	897–923cal AD (25.6% of area) 941–985cal AD (42.6% of area)
SUERC-40320	2012 Cotswold Archaeology	Context (1401) Cathedral Green	Position and date suggest Cemetery II/III	Disarticulated juvenile remains from burial deposit overlying wall foundation in Kalenderhay, South of the Saxon minster/ Mary Major church.	Human bone right proximal femur	−18.8	***	11.9	3.3	1090±30	892–1014cal AD (95.4% of area)	899–924cal AD (24.2% of area) 945–990cal AD (44.0% of area)
SUERC-40321	2012 Cotswold Archaeology	Context (1425) Cathedral Green	Position and date suggest Cemetery II/III	Disarticulated adult human remains from burial deposit overlying (1401) centre of trench 14 in Kalenderhay, South of the Saxon minster/Mary Major church.	Human bone right femur shaft	−19.3	***	11.6	3.2	1075±30	894–930cal AD (24.2% of area) 938–1020cal AD (71.2% of area)	902–919cal AD (15.0% of area) 964–1015cal AD (53.2% of area)

(Continued)

Appendix 19.1 Table of Radiocarbon Dates for Exeter Burials (Continued)

Lab ID	Date sampled organisation	Context no./ skeleton no.	Site & cemetery phase	Context description [Sample ID]	Material	$\delta^{13}C_{AMS}$ (‰)	$\delta^{13}C_{IRMS}$ (‰)	$\delta^{15}N$ (‰)	C:N	Radiocarbon age (BP)	94.5% probability	68.2% probability
SUERC-40361	2012 Exeter Archaeology	SK CB40 Cathedral Green	Cemetery III	Supine inhumation of young adult male 17–30yrs, <25% present. Charcoal burial NEE–SWW orientation, east of first porticus and cut by later porticus wall.	Human remains femur fragments	−19.2	***	11.6	3.1	1030±35	896–923cal AD (6.7% of area) 941–1045cal AD (84.9% of area) 1095–1120cal AD (3.2% of area) 1141–1148cal AD (0.7% of area)	982–1027cal AD (68.2% of area)
SUERC-57539	2015 Kingdom (University of Exeter)	SK CB52 Cathedral Green	Cemetery III	Supine inhumation mature male 50+yrs. <25% present. Charcoal burial, NEE–SWW orientation, east end of excavation close to north wall of Mary Major and sealed by CB51.	Human remains long bone fragments	−18.8	***	12.9	3.3	1010±28	978–1047cal AD (86.0% of area) 1092–1122cal AD (7.9% of area) 1140–1148cal AD (1.5% of area)	994–1030cal AD (68.2% of area)
SUERC-40316	2012 Cotswold Archaeology	Context (1401) Cathedral Green	Position and date suggest Cemetery II/III	Disarticulated adult remains from burial deposit overlying wall foundation in Kalenderhay, South of the Saxon minster/ Mary Major church.	Human bone right proximal femur	−19.1	***	12.0	3.2	990±30	989–1053cal AD (57.4% of area) 1080–1153cal AD (38.0% of area)	999–1002cal AD (1.5% of area) 1013–1045cal AD (43.8% of area) 1095–1120cal AD (19.6% of area) 1142–1147cal AD(3.3% of area)
SUERC-40319	2012 Cotswold Archaeology	Context (1425) Cathedral Green	Position and date suggest Cemetery II/III	Disarticulated adult human remains from burial deposit overlying (1401) centre of trench 14 in Kalenderhay, South of the Saxon minster/Mary Major church.	Human bone right proximal femur	−20.6	***	9.4	3.3	985±30	990–1056cal AD (51.3% of area) 1076–1154cal AD (44.1% of area)	1016–046cal AD (39.6% of area) 1093–1121cal AD (23.7% of area) 1140–1147cal AD (5.0% of area)

(Continued)

Appendix 19.1 (Continued)

Lab ID	*Date sampled organisation*	*Context no./ skeleton no.*	*Site & cemetery phase*	*Context description [Sample ID]*	*Material*	$\delta^{13}C_{AMS}$ (‰)	$\delta^{13}C_{IRMS}$ (‰)	$\delta^{15}N$ (‰)	*C:N*	*Radiocarbon age (BP)*	*94.5% probability*	*68.2% probability*
HAR-1611	27.06.1978 Exeter Arch Field Unit	SK OB485 Cathedral Green	Originally assumed Cemetery I Dated to Cemetery III	Supine inhumation of an adult male aged 30–40yrs (Calvin Wells, 1979). Assumed to be on a SSE–NNW alignment, cutting across the SW wall of the Roman *basilica* nave but grave cuts not definite	Human bone – element unknown	−20.7	*	*	*	880±70	1020–1260cal AD (100% of area)	1040–1220cal AD (100% of area)
SUERC-39397	2012 Exeter Archaeology	SK OB480 Cathedral Green	Originally assumed Cemetery I Dated to Cemetery III	Supine inhumation of adult female, 25–50% present. Originally believed to be on NW–SE orientation from far west of excavation full grave cut not established.	Human remains left rib	−19.4	***	11.0	3.3	795±30	1185–1278cal AD (95.4% of area)	1221–1262cal AD (68.2% of area)
SUERC-83738	2018 John Allan Exeter Cathedral	Kalendarhay 2018 trench length B	Cathedral cemetery	Disarticulated human remains from service trench length B in Kalendarhay, South of the Saxon minster/Mary Major church.	Human bone	−19	***	10.9	3.3	1136±27	880–1060AD 1090–1120AD (95.4% of area)	900–920AD 950–1030AD (68.2% of area)
SUERC-57534	2015 Kingdom (University of Exeter)	SK OB591 Cathedral Green	Cathedral cemetery	Supine inhumation of mature adult male 50+yrs, 25–50% present. On E–W orientation (CII alignment), grave lined with volcanic and Salcombe stone, cut by chancel of the later medieval church at east end of excavation.	Human remains long bone fragments	−18.3	***	12.2	3.3	1012±31	971–1050cal AD (82.9% of area) 1084–1125cal AD (9.9% of area) 1136–1151cal AD (2.6% of area)	990–1032cal AD (68.2% of area)
SUERC-13959	2006 Exeter Archaeology Report No. 7.72	(SK509) Cathedral Close – Little Stile	Cathedral cemetery	Partial remains of a supine inhumation orientated NE–SW containing two tibia and two fibula. Biological sex and age estimation unknown.	Human bone – tibia	**	**	**	**	885±35BP	1010–1160cal AD (95.4% of area)	
SUERC-83737	2018 John Allan Exeter Cathedral	Kalendarhay 2018 trench length D	Cathedral cemetery	Disarticulated human remains from service trench length D in Kalendarhay, South of the Saxon minster/Mary Major church.	Human bone	−18.8	***	12.1	3.2	1024±27BP	1020–1210AD (95.4% of area)	1040–1160AD (68.2% of area)
SUERC-13958	2006 Exeter Archaeology Report No. 7.39	(SK512) Cathedral Green – Deanery Garden	Cathedral cemetery	Inhumation of a young adult, F 18–25yrs of age in a supine position orientated on an E–W or SE–NW alignment. Individual is partial and fragmentary <25% present.	Human bone – femur	**	**	**	**	885±35	1030–1220cal AD (95.4% of area)	1050–1090cal AD (19.2% of area) 1120–1140cal AD (4.7% of area) 1150–1220cal AD (44.3% of area)

(Continued)

Appendix 19.1 Table of Radiocarbon Dates for Exeter Burials (Continued)

Lab ID	*Date sampled organisation*	*Context no./ skeleton no.*	*Site & cemetery phase*	*Context description [Sample ID]*	*Material*	$\delta^{13}C_{AMS}$ (‰)	$\delta^{13}C_{IRMS}$ (‰)	$\delta^{15}N$ (‰)	*C:N*	*Radiocarbon age (BP)*	*94.5% probability*	*68.2% probability*
SUERC-83739	2018 John Allan Exeter Cathedral	Kalendarhay 2018 trench length C	Cathedral cemetery	Disarticulated human remains from service trench length C in Kalendarhay, South of the Saxon minster/Mary Major church.	Human bone	−19.6	***	12.1	3.2	879±27	1050–1090AD 1120–1140AD 1150–1290AD (95.4% of area)	1180–1270AD (68.2% of area)
SUERC-40359	2012 Exeter Archaeology	SK OB448 Cathedral Green	Cathedral cemetery	Supine inhumation of mature male 45+yrs, 50–75% present. E–W orientation (CII alignment) north of Mary Major church.	Human remains right rib fragment	−18.8	***	13.6	3.2	630±35	1286–1400cal AD (95.4% of area)	1295–1320cal AD (26.2% of area) 1350–1391cal AD (42.0% of area)
SUERC-14930	2006 Exeter Archaeology Report No. 7.72	(SK577) Cathedral Green	Cathedral cemetery	*In situ* truncated inhumation of an adult individual consisting of the tibia, fibula and some of the tarsals and metatarsals of the left leg. On a probable SW–NE orientation, biological sex and age estimation unknown.	Human bone – element unknown	**	**	**	**	430±40BP	1410–1530cal AD (83.9% of area) 1570–1630cal AD (11.5% of area)	1420–1490cal AD (68.2% of area)
SUERC-40317	2012 Cotswold Archaeology	(SK2901) Cathedral Green	Cathedral cemetery	Supine inhumation of an adult individual, sex ID, <25% present. E–W orientation, north of present day Cathedral cemetery boundary.	Human bone left scapula	−19.8	***	10.1	3.2	420±30	1427–1515cal AD (87.9% of area) 1598–1618cal AD (7.5% of area)	1438–1479cal AD (68.2% of area)
SUERC-40318	2012 Cotswold Archaeology	(SK2902) Cathedral Green	Cathedral cemetery	Supine inhumation of young adult male 18–24yrs, <25% present. E–W orientation, north of present day Cathedral cemetery boundary.	Human bone left rib	−19.7	***	12.1	3.2	375±30	1446–1526cal AD (58.2% of area) 1556–1633cal AD (38.2% of area)	1453–1516cal AD (51.3% of area) 1597–1618cal AD (16.9% of area)
SUERC-57538	2015 Kingdom (University of Exeter)	SK OB323 Cathedral Green	Cathedral cemetery	Supine inhumation of adult female 26–35yrs, 50–75% present found with mercury on right os coxae and buried with neonate by left shoulder. NEE–SWW orientation, east of excavation.	Human remains rib fragments	−19.3	***	12.5	3.3	365±31	1449–1529cal AD (50.8% of area) 1544–1635cal AD (44.6 of area)	1458–1521cal AD (45.5% of area) 1579–1582cal AD (1.6% of area) 1591–1620cal AD (21.1% of area)

(Continued)

Appendix 19.1 (Continued)

Lab ID	*Date sampled organisation*	*Context no./ skeleton no.*	*Site & cemetery phase*	*Context description [Sample ID]*	*Material*	*$\delta^{13}C_{AMS}$ (‰)*	*$\delta^{13}C_{IRMS}$ (‰)*	*$\delta^{15}N$ (‰)*	*C:N*	*Radiocarbon age (BP)*	*94.5% probability*	*68.2% probability*
SUERC-13966	2006 Exeter Archaeology Excavation at Exeter Castle, 1984–2009	Sk118 Rougemont Castle	Late Saxon cemetery Rougemont Castle	One of two fragmented inhumations in grave (106) disturbed by a later medieval wall (110). Consists of vertebrae, scapula and right humerus. Orientated ENE–WSW with a concentration of charcoal at the west end of the grave.	Human long bone	−20.0	**	**	**	1155±35	770–980cal AD	780–790calAD (2.4% of area) 810–900calAD (39.6%of area) 910–970calAD (26.25 of area)
SUERC-13964	2006 Exeter Archaeology Excavation at Exeter Castle, 1984–2009	Sk426 Rougemont Castle	Late Saxon cemetery Rougemont Castle	Grave (427) partially exposed and not fully excavated fragmented inhumation consisting of skull, left arm and pelvis. Orientated ENE–WSW no obvious charcoal in grave.	Human long bone	−20.2	**	**	**	1070±35	890–1030cal AD	890–920calAD (15.4% of area) 960–1020calAD (52.8 of area)
SUERC-13965	2006 Exeter Archaeology Excavation at Exeter Castle, 1984–2009	Sk116 Rougemont Castle	Late Saxon cemetery Rougemont Castle	Grave (102) Inhumation of fragmented human remains consisting of skull, pelvis, legs & ribs. Orientated ENE–WSW on a bed of charcoal.	Human bone – element unknown	−19.8	**	**	**	1030±35	890–930calAD (6.6% of area) 940–1050calAD (85.5% of area) 1090–1120calAD (3.3% of area)	980–1030calAD (68.2% of area)
UBA-33485	2016 Archaeology department University of Exeter	Context (8849) Dominican Friary – Princesshay	Intra-mural burial	Disarticulated tibia with sharp force trauma to shaft, robust muscle attachments suggest male individual, grave backfill of (8871). From nave of Dominican Friary church.	Human bone tibia	−19.0	***	10.9	3.17	640±28	1284–1327cal AD (42.4% of area) 1341–1395cal AD (57.5% of area)	1293–1313cal AD (39.4% of area) 1357–1388cal AD (60.6% of area)
UBA-33487	2016 Archaeology department University of Exeter	Context (8849) Dominican Friary – Princesshay	Intra-mural burial	Disarticulated male skull with sharp force trauma to right orbit and peri-mortem fractures to occipital, age 30+, grave backfill of (8871). From nave of Dominican Friary church.	Human left lateral maxillary incisor	−19.8	***	10.8	3.15	489±33	1399–1454cal AD	1417–1440cal AD

(Continued)

Appendix 19.1 Table of Radiocarbon Dates for Exeter Burials (Continued)

Lab ID	*Date sampled organisation*	*Context no./ skeleton no.*	*Site & cemetery phase*	*Context description [Sample ID]*	*Material*	$\delta^{13}C_{AMS}$ (‰)	$\delta^{13}C_{IRMS}$ (‰)	$\delta^{15}N$ (‰)	*C:N*	*Radiocarbon age (BP)*	*94.5% probability*	*68.2% probability*
UBA-33484	2016 Archaeology department University of Exeter	Context (8849) Dominican Friary – Princesshay	Intra-mural burial	Disarticulated male skull with sharp force trauma to right orbit and peri-mortem fractures to occipital, age 30+, grave backfill of (8871). From nave of Dominican Friary church.	Human bone right occipital	−19.7	***	11.8	3.17	496±28	1405–1447cal AD (100% of area)	1416–1436cal AD (100% of area)
SUERC-57529	2015 Exeter City Council	EHP SK9511 Dominican Friary – Princesshay	Intra-mural burial	Supine inhumation of mature adult female with syphilis. 50–75% present but fragmentary and fragile due to pathology. From nave of Dominican friary church.	Human bone right femur	−18.4	***	13.1	3.4	472±29	1410–1455cal AD (95.4% of area)	1424–1445cal AD (68% of area)
UBA-33486	2016 Archaeology department University of Exeter	(SK8871) Dominican Friary – Princesshay	Intra-mural burial	Supine inhumation of a probable F, age 30–40yrs, 50–75% present but with poor preservation. From nave of Dominican Friary church, burial displaced material in context (8849)	Human left lateral maxillary incisor	−18.0	***	9.8	3.17	322±30	1482–1645cal AD (100% of area)	1517–1595cal AD (79% of area) 1618–1638cal AD (21% of area)

Bibliography

Primary documents and abbreviations

CMB	Chamber Map Book, 1756–60 (in DHC)
CRA	City Receivers' Accounts (in DHC)
CRB	City Rent Book (in DHC)
D&C	Dean and Chapter deeds, court rolls, account rolls, D&C 4536 and 7370: Schedule of Deeds and Documents Handed over to the Ecclesiastical Commissioners in 1862 (in ECLA)
DEI	Devon and Exeter Institution
DHC	Devon Heritage Centre
EAAP	Exeter Archaeology Archive Project (2015)
EAR 1	Exeter Archaeological Report 1 (Bidwell 1979)
EAR 3	Exeter Archaeological Report 3 (Allan 1984a)
EAR 4	Exeter Archaeological Report 4 (Holbrook and Bidwell 1991)
EBW	Exe Bridge Wardens' Accounts (in DHC)
ECA	Exeter City Archives (in DHC)
ECLA	Exeter Cathedral Library and Archive
ED	Exeter deeds (in DHC)
ERA	Exeter Receivers' Accounts (in DHC)
Fursdon	Fursdon transcription of Exeter Church Rates (in DHC)
Goad	Goad Fire Insurance Plan, Exeter, No. 5, Sheet 3, 1888 (in DHC)
HMC	Historic Manuscripts Commission: 'Catalogue of the Records of the Custos and College of the Vicars Choral' (in ECLA)
Hooker's Antique description	John Hooker's *The Antique Description and Account of the City of Exeter* (Brice 1765)
Hooker's Chroncicle	John Hooker's *Chronicle* (Gray 2005)
Inland Revenue 1910 Account Book	3201V/2/35 (in DHC)
John Coldridge's map of Exeter, 1819	(in DHC)
MCR	Mayor's Court Rolls (in DHC)
MMHC	Cartulary of the St Mary Magdalene Leper Hospital ED/MAG/99 and 100 (in DHC)
Moore, S.A. n.d	'MS calendar of archives of the Dean and Chapter of Exeter Cathedral' (in ECLA)
OS	Ordnance Survey 1:500 Sheet LXXX 6.17 maps with 1910 Land Register annotations (in DEI)
PCR	Provosts' court rolls (in DHC)
RAB	Receiver's Account Books (in DHC)
RIB	Roman Inscriptions of Britain
S&J	transcribed medieval deeds (Staniforth and Juddery 1991a–d)
SJC	St John's Cartulary (in DHC)
TNA	The National Archives
Valuation, 1910	3201V/2/32 (in DHC)
VC	Vicars Choral deeds, court rolls, and account rolls (in ECLA)
Wynards Rental, Ladyday 1838, 58/9 Box 9 (9)	(in DHC)

Secondary sources

DOI Abbreviations

ADS:	Archaeology Data Service
CA:	Cotswold Archaeology
IA:	Internet Archaeology

Adrian, Y.-M., Calderoni, P. and Cartier, J. 1999 *Pots de terre, fragments d'histoire* Rouen, exhibition catalogue of the Musée departmental des Antiquités

Agarwal, S.C. and Glencross, B.A. 2011 *Social bioarchaeology* Chichester, Wiley-Blackwell

Albarella, U. 2003 'Tawyers, tanners, horn working and the mystery of the missing goat', in P. Murphy and P.E.J. Wiltshire (eds) *The environmental archaeology of industry* Symposium of the Association for Environmental Archaeology 20, Oxford, Oxbow Books, 71–86

Alcock, L. 1966 'Castle Tower, Penmaen: a Norman ringwork in Glamorgan', *Antiquaries Journal* 46, 178–210

Alexander, J. and Binski, P. (eds) 1987 *Age of chivalry* London, Royal Academy of Arts

Alexander, M. (ed.) 2016 *Medieval and post-medieval occupation and industry in the Redcliffe suburb of Bristol: excavations at 1–2 and 3 Redcliff Street, 2003–2010* Cirencester, Cotswold Archaeology Monograph 8

Allan, J.P. 1978 'The pottery', in Austin 1978, 226–34

Allan, J.P. 1981 'The pottery', in Weddell 1981, 128–35

Allan, J.P. 1983a 'Some post-medieval documentary evidence for the trade in ceramics', in Davey and Hodges (eds) 1983, 37–45

Allan, J.P. 1983b 'The importation of pottery to southern England, *c.* 1200–1500', in Davey and Hodges (eds) 1983, 193–207

Allan, J.P. 1984a *Medieval and post-medieval finds from Exeter, 1971–1980* Exeter, Exeter City Council and the University of Exeter

Allan, J.P. 1984b *Medieval and post-medieval finds from Exeter, 1971–1980: microfiche* Exeter, Exeter City Council and the University of Exeter

Allan, J.P. 1984c 'The pottery; the glass', in Griffiths and Griffith 1984, 79–95

Allan, J.P. 1987 'Medieval and post-medieval finds', in Weddell 1987b, 94–5

Allan, J.P. 1988 'The pottery', in Brown 1988, 80–6

Allan, J.P. 1994 'Imported pottery in south-west England, *c.* 1350–1550', *Medieval Ceramics* 18, 45–50

Allan, J.P. 1995 'Iberian pottery imported into South-West England, *c.* 1250–1600', in Gerrard *et al.* (eds) 1995, 299–314

Allan, J.P. 1998 'Cleeve Abbey: the pottery', *Somerset Archaeology and Natural History* 142, 41–75

Allan, J.P. 1999a *St Nicholas Priory, Exeter* Exeter, Exeter City Museums

Allan, J.P. 1999b 'South Netherlands maiolica in south-west England', in Gaimster (ed.) 1999a, 157–66

Allan, J.P. 2000a 'Stonehouse Quay: pottery and trade, 1500–1800', in Gardiner (ed.) 2000, 78–84

Allan, J.P. 2000b *List of Italian vessels from Devon submitted to M. Hughes for possible ICP analysis* Unpublished list, circulated privately

Allan, J.P. 2003 'A group of early 13th-century pottery from Sherborne Old Castle and its wider context', *Proceedings of the Dorset Natural History and Archaeological Society* 125, 71–82

Allan, J.P. 2005 *An introduction to the Roman legionary fortress at Exeter* Exeter, Exeter City Council

Allan, J.P. 2009–10 'Pottery and tiles from Godolphin', *Cornish Archaeology* 48–9, 277–94

Allan, J.P. 2010 *Archaeological recording of the Western Power distribution trench, Cathedral Close, Exeter* Exeter Archaeology report 10.46

Allan, J.P. 2014a 'Post-Roman pottery: Gabbroic, Upper Greensand-derived and later medieval wares; discussion', in Smart 2014, 64–7, 82–3

Allan, J.P. 2014b 'Medieval and later pottery', in Mudd and Joyce 2014, 148–54

Allan, J.P. 2014c *The Lamb, Totnes: the pottery* John Allan Archaeology report 6/2014

Allan, J.P. 2014d 'Breton woodworkers in the immigrant communities of south-west England, 1500–1550', *Post-Medieval Archaeology* 48/2, 320–56

Allan, J.P. 2015 'Italian ceramics in south-west England, 1400–1750', *Archeologia Postmedievale* 19, 117–35

Allan, J.P. 2016 *The Beckery pottery: a reconsideration* John Allan Archaeology report 45/2016

Allan, J.P. 2018 *Archaeological recording of a service trench in Kalendarhay, Cathedral Close, Exeter, 2018* John Allan Archaeology report 65/2018

Allan, J.P. 2019 *An archaeological assessment of the excavations at St Nicholas Priory, Exeter, 1971–2001* Unpublished report

Allan, J.P. and Barber, J. 1992 'A seventeenth-century pottery group from Kitto Institute, Plymouth', in Gaimster and Redknap 1992, 202–24

Allan, J.P. and Blaylock, S. 2005 'Medieval pottery and other finds from Pig's Paradise, Lundy', *Proceedings of the Devon Archaeological Society* 63, 65–91

Allan, J.P. and Henderson, C.G. 1984 'St Nicholas Priory excavation', *Archaeology in Exeter, 1984–5* Exeter Archaeology unpublished report, 14–18

Allan, J.P. and Keen, L. 1984 'The floor-tiles', in Allan 1984a, 232–7

Allan, J.P. and Langman, G.I. 1998–9 'The pottery', in Stead 1998–9, 178–89

Allan, J.P. and Langman, G.I. 2002 'A group of medieval pottery from Haycroft Farm, Membury', *Proceedings of the Devon Archaeological Society* 60, 59–73

Allan, J.P. and Langman, G.I. 2002–3 'The pottery', in Manning and Stead 2002–3, 97–104

Allan, J.P. and Langman, G.I. 2003 'The Dung Quay pottery', in Stead 2003, 47–63

Allan, J.P. and Langman, G.I. 2010 'The pottery', in Allan *et al.* 2010, 152–62

Allan, J.P. and Perry, I. 1982 'Pottery and tiles', in Higham *et al.* 1982, 86–101

Allan, J.P. and Silvester, R.J. 1981 'Newenham Abbey, Axminster', *Proceedings of the Devon Archaeological Society* 39, 159–71

Allan, J.P. and Stevens, T. forthcoming 'A find of medieval and later pottery from Nut Rock, Scilly', *Cornish Archaeology*

Allan, J.P. and Wrathmell, S. 2016 'Discussion of the pottery', in Wrathmell 2016, 55–63

Allan, J.P., Henderson, C.G. and Higham, R.A. 1984 'Saxon Exeter', in Haslam (ed.) 1984, 385–414

Allan, J., Durrant, J., and Taylor, R. 2008 'Roman tiles in Exminster Church', *Proceedings of the Devon Archaeological Society* 66, 117–26

Allan, J.P., Blackmore, S. and Passmore, A.J. 2010 'Archaeological investigations around Crediton parish church', *Proceedings of the Devon Archaeological Society* 68, 113–198

Allan, J.P., Hughes M.J. and Taylor, R.T. 2010 'Saxo-Norman pottery in Somerset: some recent research', *Somerset Archaeology and Natural History* 154, 165–84

Allan, J.P., Dawson, D. and Kent, O. 2012 'The post-Roman pottery: online report', *Glastonbury Abbey: archaeological excavations 1904–1979* York, Archaeology Data Service

Allan, J.P., Alcock, N. and Dawson, D. (eds) 2015 *West Country households 1500–1700* Woodbridge, Boydell and Brewer

Allan, J.P., Dawson, D. and Kent, O. 2015 'The post-Roman pottery', in Gilchrist and Green 2015, 250–78

Allan, J.P., Henderson, C. and Weddell, P.J. 2016 'A summary of the archaeological evidence for the late medieval friary', *Proceedings of the Devon Archaeological Society* 74, 235–48

Allan, J.P., Hunt, R., Keen, L. and Taylor, R.T. 2016 'The late medieval tile pavement in the chapel of Cotehele', *Cornish Archaeology* 55, 205–18

Allan, J.P., Dawson, D. and Langman, G. 2018 'The pottery industry', in Smart 2018, 99–197

Allan, J.P., Dawson, D. and Mepham, L. 2018 'Medieval and post-medieval pottery studies in south-west England: a review', *Medieval Ceramics* 39, 75–102

Allan, J.P., Brown, D., Camidge, K. and Hughes, M.J. 2019 *A find of medieval pottery in Tresco Channel, Isles of Scilly* John Allan Archaeology report 82

Allason-Jones, L. (ed.) 2011 *Artefacts in Roman Britain. Their purpose and use* Cambridge, Cambridge University Press

Allen, J.R.L. 2013 'Rotary querns of Alderney sandstone from Brading and Silchester in Roman Britain: a new and rare import', *Britannia* 44, 247–50

Allen, J.R.L. and M.G. Fulford 1996 'The distribution of south-east Dorset black burnished category 1 pottery in south-west Britain', *Britannia* 27, 223–81

Allen, M., Lodwick, L., Brindle, T., Fulford, M. and Smith, A. 2017 *The rural economy of Roman Britain* London, Society for the Promotion of Roman Studies, Britannia Monograph 30

Almagro, M. and Llubiá, L.M. 1952 *CERAMICA Aragón* Barcelona, Muel

Almeida, S., Silva, R.C. da, Dias, V. and Perpétuo, J. 2012 'O lugar da Torre dos Sinos (Convento Velho de S. Domingos), Coimbra: notas para o estudo da formação dos terrenos de aluvião, em época moderna', in Teixeira and Bettencourt (eds) 2012, 483–8

Alonso, N. and Frankel, R. 2017 'A survey of ancient grain milling systems in the Mediterranean', in Buchsenschutz *et al.* 2017, 461–78

Álvaro, M.I. 1981 'La cerámica de Muel: su etapa mudéjar', *I Simposio Internacional de Mudejarismo* (Teruel 1975), 121–9

Álvaro, M.I. 1999 'La emigración de ceramistas ligures a Aragón (España) en el siglo XVII y la influencia de sus repertorios decorativos en la producción de alfares locales', *XXXI Atti Convegno Internazionale della Ceramica*, Albisola, 151–69

Alverà Bortolotto, A. 1981 *Storia della ceramica a Venezia: dagli albori alla fine della Repubblica* Florence, Sansoni

Alverà Bortolotto, A. 1988 *Maiolica a Venezia nel Rinascimento* Bergamo, Bolis

Alverà Bortolotto, A. and Dumortier, C. 1990 'Les majoliques anversoises "à la façon de Venise" de la première moitié du XVIe siècle', *Revue belge d'archéologie et d'histoire de l'art* 59, 55–74

Alves, F., Paulo, R., Garcia, C. and Aleluia, M. 1998 'A cerâmica dos destroços do navio de meados do século XV Ria de Aveiro A e da zona de Ria de Aveiro B: Aproximação tipológica preliminar', *Actas das 2as Jornadas de Cerâmica Medieval e Pós Medieval* Câmara Municipal de Tondela, Tondela, 185–210

Alves, F., Rodrigues, P., Aleluia, M., Rodrigo, R., Garcia, C., Rieth, E. and Riccardi, E. 2001 'Ria de Aveiro A, a shipwreck from Portugal dating to the mid 15th century: a preliminary report', *International Journal of Nautical Archaeology* 30 (1), 12–36

Amigues, F. and Bazzana, A. (eds) 1990 *Fours de potiers et "testares" médiévaux en Méditerranée occidentale* Madrid, Publications de la Casa de Velázquez

Amigues, F. and Mesquida, M. 1987 *Un horno medieval de cerámica: el testar del Molí, Paterna (Valencia)* Madrid, Publicaciones de la Casa de Velázquez Série études et documents 4

Amigues, F., Crusselles, D., González Villaescusa, R. and Lerma, J.V. 1995 'Los envases cerámicos de Paterna/Manises y el comercio bajo medieval', *V CICMMO*, 346–61

Anderson, A. 1989 'The other pottery', in Frere and Wilkes 1989, 243–61

Anderson, A.S., Wacher, J.S. and Fitzpatrick, A.P. 2001 *The Romano-British 'small town' at Wanborough, Wiltshire* London, Society for the Promotion of Roman Studies, Britannia Monograph 19

Anon. 1859 'The museum, part 1', *Somersetshire Archaeological and Natural History Society* 9, 45–8

Arnold, A.J. and Howard, R.E. 2016 'Tree-ring analysis of timbers', in Alexander (ed.) 2016, 93–5

Arnold, A.J. and Howard, R. 2009 *46 High Street, Exeter, Devon: Scientific dating report – tree-ring analysis of timbers* English Heritage, Research Department Report Series 71–2009

Arnold, A.J., Howard, R., Laxton, R.R. and Litton, C. 2003 *Tree-ring analysis of timbers from Exeter Cathedral, Exeter, Devon: part 3 (western roof Bays 1–4)* English Heritage, Centre for Archaeology Report 49–2003

Arnold, A.J., Howard, R. and Litton, C. 2006a *Exeter Cathedral, Exeter, Devon: tree-ring analysis of timbers of the Chapel of St John the Baptist* English Heritage, Research Department Report Series 62–2006

Arnold, A.J., Howard, R. and Litton, C. 2006b *Exeter Cathedral, Exeter, Devon: tree-ring analysis of timbers from the roof of the Retrochoir* English Heritage, Research Department Report Series 63–2006

Arnold, A.J., Howard, R. and Tyers, C. forthcoming *South nave aisle, Lady Chapel and Chapels of St John and St Gabriel, Exeter Cathedral, Exeter, Devon: tree-ring analysis of timbers from the roofs* Historic England, Research Report Series

Ashby, T., Hudd, A.E. and Martin, A.T. 1902 'Excavations at Caerwent Monmouthshire on the site of the Romano-British City of Venta Silurum in 1901', *Archaeologia* 58, 119–52

Ashby, T., Hudd, A.E. and King, F. 1911 'Excavations at Caerwent, Monmouthshire on the site of the Romano-British City of Venta Silurum in the years 1909 and 1910', *Archaeologia* 62 (2), 405–8

Atasoy, N. and Raby, J. 1989 *Iznik: the pottery of Ottoman Turkey* London, Alexandria

Austin, D. 1978 'Excavations in Okehampton Deer Park, Devon 1976–1978', *Proceedings of the Devon Archaeological Society* 36, 191–239

Austin, J. and Evans, D. 2019 *Project Sofia (Phase 1), Belgrave Road, Exeter, Devon* Cotswold Archaeology Report 880197_1

Ayre, J. and Wroe-Brown, R. 2002 *The London Millennium Bridge: excavation of the medieval and later waterfronts at Peter's Hill, City of London, and Bankside, Southwark* London, Museum of London Archaeology Service

Baart, J.M. 1999 'North Netherlands maiolica of the sixteenth century', in Gaimster (ed.) 1999a, 125–36

Baatz, D. 1977 'Review of von Petrikovits 1975', *Germania* 55, 267–70

Badreshany, K. 2018 'The ICP-AES and -MS analysis of medieval ceramics from Buckfast Abbey and other sites in Devon', in Brown 2018, 254–72

Baillie, M.G.L. 1977a 'The Belfast oak chronology to AD1001', *Tree Ring Bulletin* 37, 1–12

Baillie, M.G.L. 1977b 'Dublin medieval dendrochronology', *Tree Ring Bulletin* 37, 13–20

Baillie, M.G.L. 1995 *A slice through time – dendrochronology and precision dating* London, Batsford

Baker, D., Baker, E., Hassall, J. and Simco, A. 1979 'Excavations in Bedford 1967–1977', *Bedford Archaeological Journal* 13 [whole volume]

Bakirtzis, C. (ed.) 2003 *VIIe Congrès International sur la Céramique Médiévale en Méditerranée, Thessaloniki, 11–16 Octobre 1999* Athènes, Caisse des Recettes Archéologiques

Bakraji, E.H. 2006 'Application of multivariate statistical methods to classify archaeological pottery from Tel-Alramad site, Syria, based on x-ray fluorescence analysis', *X-Ray Spectrometry* 35 (3), 190–4

Balaam, N.D., Levitan, B. and Straker, V 1987 *Studies in palaeoeconomy and environment in south west England* Oxford, British Archaeological Reports British Series 181

Baldi, G. 2003 'Indagine archeometrica sulle ceramiche di Montelupo', in Berti 2003, 87–114, 125

Ball, J.N. 1977 *Merchants and merchandise: the expansion of trade in Europe 1500–1630* London, Croom Helm

Barber, J. 1965 '28th report on archaeology and early history', *Report and Transactions of the Devonshire Association* 97, 88–109

Barber, J. 1967 '29th report on archaeology and early history', *Report and Transactions of the Devonshire Association* 99, 314–24

Barceló, C. and Heidenreich, A. 2014 'Lusterware made in the *abbadid taifa* of Seville (eleventh century) and its early production in the Mediterranean region', *Muqarnas* 31, 245–76

Barclay, A., Knight, D., Booth, P., Evans, J., Brown, D.H. and Wood, I. 2016 *A standard for pottery studies in archaeology* London, Medieval Pottery Research Group

Barefoot, A.C. 1975 'A Winchester dendrochronology for 1635–1972 AD – its validity and possible extension', *Journal of the Institute for Wood Science* 7 (1), 25–32

Barker, P. 1961 'Excavations on the town wall, Roushill, Shrewsbury', *Medieval Archaeology* 5, 181–210

Barovier Mentasti, R. and Tonini, C. (eds) 2014 *Study days on Venetian glass: approximately 1700's* Venice, Istituto Veneto di Scienze, Lettere ed Arti

Barreira, P., Dordio, P. and Teixeira, R. 1998 '200 anos de cerâmica na Casa do Infante: do século XVI a meados do século XVIII', *Actas das 2as Jornadas de Cerâmica Medieval e Pós-Medieval*, Tondela, Câmara Municipal, 145–84

Barros, L., Batalha, L., Cardoso, G. and Gonzalez, A. 2012 'A olaria renascentista de Santo António da Charneca, Barreiro: a louça doméstica', in Teixeira and Bettencourt (eds) 2012, 699–710

Barton, K.J. and Thomson, R.G. 1992 'Catalogue of the pottery', in Horsey 1992, 65–127

Bassett, S. (ed.) 1992 *Death in towns: urban responses to the dying and the dead, 100–1600* London, Leicester University Press

Basso, E., Capelli, C., Riccardi, M.P. and Cabella, R. 2008 'A particular temper: mineralological and petrographic characterisation of ceramic fabrics with glauconitic inclusions', *ArchaeSciences Revue d'archéométrie* 32, 93–7

Baxter, M. 1994 *Exploratory multivariate statistics in archaeology* Edinburgh, Edinburgh University Press

Baxter, M. 2003 *Statistics in archaeology* London, Arnold

Baxter, M.J., and Freestone, I.C. 2006 'Log-ratio compositional data in analysis in archaeometry', *Archaeometry* 48, 511–31

Bayley, J. 1989a *Some evidence for non-ferrous metalworking from Roman Exeter, Devon* Ancient Monuments Laboratory Reports 54/89

Bayley, J. 1989b *Evidence for non-ferrous metalworking from Frien Hay, Exeter, Devon* Ancient Monuments Laboratory Report 55/89

Bayley, J, 1992 *Non-ferrous metalworking in England: late Iron Age to early medieval* Unpublished PhD thesis, University of London

Bayley, J. 2001 'Precious metal refining in Roman Exeter', *Proceedings of the Devon Archaeological Society* 59, 141–7

Beaverstock, K. and Socha-Paszkiewicz, A. 2018 *Land at Honiton Inn, Paris Street, Exeter, Devon* Thames Valley Archaeological Services report 18/58c

Becker, G., Manhart, H., Peters, J. and Schibler, J. (eds) 1999 *Historia animalium ex ossibus* Rahden/Westfahlen, Marie Leidorf

Bedford, J.B. 1995 *Archaeological recording of the Quay House, Exeter 1985–6* Exeter Archaeology report 95.40 [ADS: https://doi.org/10.5284/1035221]

Bedford, J.B. 1997 *Archaeological recording of groundworks at no. 2 Broadgate, Exeter 1995–96* Exeter Archaeology report 97.17

Bedford, J.B. 1998 *Archaeological recording at Acorn Roundabout, Exeter 1988–89* Exeter Archaeology report 98.74 [ADS: https://doi.org/10.5284/1035231]

Bedford, J.B. 2001 *Archaeological evaluation at Southernhay East Car Park, Exeter* Exeter Archaeology report 01.55

Bedford, J.B. and Hall, M.E.P. 1994 *Archaeological excavations in advance of sewer repairs in The Close, Cathedral Green, Exeter, 1994* Exeter Archaeology report 94.99

Bedford, J.B. and Hall, M.E.P. 1995 *Archaeological evaluation of a proposed development site at 51 Bartholomew Street West, Exeter* Exeter Museums Archaeological Field Unit report 95.11

Bedford, J.B. and Salvatore, J.P. 1992a *Excavations at St Nicholas Priory Exeter, 1983–84. Part 1: Roman military* Exeter Museums Archaeological Field Unit report 92.34 [ADS: https://doi.org/10.5284/1035215]

Bedford, J.B. and Salvatore, J.P. 1992b *Excavations at Friernhay Street, Exeter, 1981. Part 1: Roman military* Exeter Museums Archaeological Field Unit report 92.35 [ADS: https://doi.org/10.5284/1035212]

Bedford, J.B. and Salvatore, J.P. 1992c *Excavations at Rack Street, Exeter, 1974–75. Part 1: Roman military* Exeter Museums Archaeological Field Unit report 92.36 [ADS: https://doi.org/10.5284/1035189]

Bedford, J.B. and Salvatore, J.P. 1992d *Excavations at Rack Street, Exeter, 1977–78. Part 1: Roman military* Exeter Museums Archaeological Field Unit report 92.37 [ADS: https://doi.org/10.5284/1035201]

Bedford, J.B. and Salvatore, J.P. 1992e *Excavations at Preston Street, Exeter, 1976–77. Part 1: Roman military* Exeter Museums Archaeological Field Unit report 92.38 [ADS: https://doi.org/10.5284/1035197]

Bedford, J.B. and Salvatore, J.P. 1992f *Excavations at Mermaid Yard, Exeter, 1977–78. Part 1: Roman military* Exeter Museums Archaeological Field Unit report 92.39 [ADS: https://doi.org/10.5284/1035200]

Bedford, J.B. and Salvatore, J.P. 1992g *Excavations at Mary Arches Street, Exeter, 1975, Part 1: Roman military* Exeter Museums Archaeological Field Unit report 92.40 [ADS: https://doi.org/10.5284/1035191]

Bedford, J.B. and Salvatore, J.P. 1993a *Excavations at 41–42 High Street (Star Jeans) Exeter, 1980. Part 1: Roman military* Exeter Museums Archaeological Field Unit report 93.07 [ADS: https://doi.org/10.5284/1035209]

Bedford, J.B. and Salvatore, J.P. 1993b *Observations at 228 High Street (Boot's Cellar) Exeter, 1975. Part 1: Roman military* Exeter Museums Archaeological Field Unit report 93.08 [ADS: https://doi.org/10.5284/1035198]

Bedford, J.B. and Salvatore, J.P. 1993c *Excavations at the Old Wool Market, Queen Street (Marks and Spencer) Exeter, 1978. Part 1: Roman military* Exeter Museums Archaeological Field Unit report 93.09 [ADS: https://doi.org/10.5284/1035205]

Bedford, J.B. and Salvatore, J.P. 1993d *Excavations at 196–97 High Street, Exeter, 1972–73. Part 1: Roman military* Exeter Museums Archaeological Field Unit report 93.15 [ADS: https://doi.org/10.5284/1035180]

Bedford, J.B. and Salvatore, J.P. 1993e *Excavations at 198 High Street, Exeter, 1975. Part 1: Roman military* Exeter Museums Archaeological Field Unit report 93.16 [ADS: https://doi.org/10.5284/1035192]

Bedford, J.B. and Salvatore, J.P. 1993f *Excavations at Upper Paul Street, Exeter, 1986* Exeter Museums Archaeological Field Unit report 93.22 [ADS: https://doi.org/10.5284/1035223]

Bedford, J.B. and Salvatore, J.P. 1993g *Excavations at Paul Street, Exeter, 1982–85. Part 1: Roman military* Exeter Museums Archaeological Field Unit report 93.23 [ADS: https://doi.org/10.5284/1035213]

Bedford, J.B. and Salvatore, J.P. 1994a *Excavations at Lucky Lane, Exeter, 1980. Part 1: Roman military* Exeter Museums Archaeological Field Unit report 94.08 [ADS: https://doi.org/10.5284/1035211]

Bedford, J.B. and Salvatore, J.P. 1994b *Excavations at Friars Walk, Exeter, 1973. Part 1: Roman military* Exeter Museums Archaeological Field Unit report 94.09 [ADS: https://doi.org/10.5284/1035183]

Bedford, J.B., Brown, S.W. and Salvatore, J.P 1994 *Excavations at the Valiant Soldier, Exeter, 1973–74. Part 1: Roman military* Exeter Museums Archaeological Field Unit report 94.11 [ADS: https://doi.org/10.5284/1035181]

Bell, M. and Bradshaw, R. 1983 'Roman lava querns from Exeter', *Proceedings of the Devon Archaeological Society* 41, 128–30

Beltrán de Heredia, J. 2012 'Les gerres de transport marítim: producció I comerç a Barcelona', *QUARHIS*, època II, 8, 81–109

Berardi, P. 1984 *L'antica maiolica di Pesaro dal XIV al XVII secolo* Florence, Sansoni

Berthault, F. 1999 'Les amphores de la place Camille-Jullian à Bordeaux', *Aquitania* 16, 159–66

Berthault, F. 2012 'Un site fondamental pour l'étude des amphores', in Maurin (ed.) 2012, 311–25

Berti, F. 1983 'Il bleu graffito di Montelupo', *Atti XVI convegno internazionale della ceramica* Albisola, Centro ligure per la storia della ceramica, 211–18

Berti, F. 1997 *Storia della ceramica di Montelupo: uomini e fornaci in un centro di produzione dal XIV al XVIII secolo*, 1. *Le ceramiche da mensa dalle origini alla fine del XV secolo* Montelupo Fiorentino, Aedo

Berti, F. 1998 *Storia della ceramica di Montelupo: uomini e fornaci in un centro di produzione dal XIV al XVIII secolo*, 2. *Le ceramiche da mensa dal 1480 alla fine del XVIII secolo* Montelupo Fiorentino, Aedo

Berti, F. (ed.) 2003 *Storia della ceramica di Montelupo: uomini e fornaci in un centro di produzione dal XIV al XVIII secolo, 5. Le botteghe: tecnologia, produzione, committenze* Montelupo Fiorentino, Aedo

Berti, F. 2008 *Il Museo della Ceramica di Montelupo: storia, tecnologia, collezioni* Florence, Polistampa

Besly, E. 2006 'The coins, post AD 250', in Fulford *et al.* 2006, 81–5

Besly, E. and Bland R. 1983 *The Cunetio Treasure* London, British Museum

Besombes, P.-A. 2004 *Trésors monétaires, XXI, Le dépôt de 22,438 monnaies du gué de Saint-Léonard (Mayenne)* Paris, Bibliothèque nationale de France

Besombes, P.-A. and Barrandon, J.-N. 2000 'Nouvelles propositions de classement du monnayage de bronze de Claude Ier', *Revue Numismatique* 155, 161–88

Best, J.E. 2005 *Archaeological recording and excavation at Bray Valley Quarries, Brayford, Devon* Exeter, Exeter Archaeology [ADS: https://doi.org/10.5284/1030439]

Bettencourt, J. and Carvalho, P. 2007 *Relatório dos trabalhos de escavaçao efectuados em 2005 no âmbito do projecto Ria de Aveiro A 2000 (FCT)*, Trabalhos do Centro Nacional de Arqueologia Náutica e Subaquática 42 Lisboa, Instituto Portugués de Arqueologia

Betts, I.M. 2016 'Tin-glazed tiles in Surrey', *Surrey Archaeological Collections* 99, 1–28

Betts, I.M. 2017 'The supply of tile to Roman London', in Bird 2017, 368–83

Betts, I.M. and Foot, R. 1994 'A newly identified late Roman tile group from southern England', *Britannia* 25, 21–34

Betts, I.M. and Weinstein, R.I. 2010 *Tin-glazed tiles from London* London, Museum of London Archaeology

BGS (British Geological Survey) 1975 *British regional geology: South-West England*, Keyworth, British Geological Survey

BGS (British Geological Society) 2001 *Solid geology map: UK south sheet 1:625,000*, 4th edition Keyworth, British Geological Survey

Biddle, M. and Barclay, K 1974 'Winchester ware', in Evison *et al.* (eds) 1974, 137–65

Bidwell, P.T 1979 *The legionary bath-house and basilica and forum at Exeter with a summary account of the legionary fortress* Exeter, Exeter City Council and the University of Exeter

Bidwell, P.T. 1980 *Roman Exeter: fortress and town* Exeter, Exeter Museums Service

Bidwell, P.T. 1982 'Roman occupation?', in Higham *et al.* 1982, 25–7

Bidwell, P.T. 1986 'Roman pottery and tiles', in Gaskell Brown (ed.) 1986, 13

Bidwell, P.T. 1999 'A survey of pottery production and supply at Colchester', in Symonds and Wade 1999, 488–99

Bidwell, P.T. 2002 (June) 'Great sites: Exeter Roman baths', *British Archaeology* 65, 12–15

Bidwell, P.T. 2014 'The coarse pottery', in Smart 2014, 49–55

Bidwell, P.T. 2016 'Fifth century pottery in Devon and north east Cornwall', in Gerrard (ed.) 2016 [IA: http://dx.doi.org/10.11141/ia.41.1]

Bidwell, P.T. forthcoming a 'The Roman pottery', in Steinmetzer, Stead, Pearce, Bidwell, and Allan forthcoming

Bidwell, P.T. forthcoming b 'The Roman pottery', in Salvatore *et al.* forthcoming

Bidwell, P.T. and Boon, G.C. 1976 'An antefix type of the Second Augustan Legion from Exeter', *Britannia* 7, 278–80

Bidwell, P.T. and Croom, A. 2015 'The Roman pottery', in Hughes 2015, 127–53

Bidwell, P.T. and Croom, A. 2020 'Smythen Street, Exeter ESS01. The Roman pottery' Unpublished report: [https://humanities.exeter.ac.uk/media/universityofexeter/collegeofhumanities/archaeology/ourresearch/exeteraplaceintime/Exeter_Smythen_Street_Roman_pottery_report_by_Bidwell_and_Croom.pdf]

Bidwell, P.T. and Croom, A. forthcoming a 'The coarse pottery', in *Excavations by AOC Archaeology at Glasgow Road, Camelon, Falkirk*

Bidwell, P.T. and Croom, A. forthcoming b 'The Roman pottery', in report on excavations at Okehampton Roman fort by AC Archaeology

Bidwell, P.T. and Croom, A. forthcoming c 'The Roman pottery', in report on excavations at Nelson Place, Bath

Bidwell, P., Croom, A. and McBride, R. 2011 'The pottery assemblage', in Reed *et al.* 2011, 93–117

Binford, L.R. 1984 *Faunal remains from Klasies River mouth* New York, Academic Press

Bird, D. (ed.) 2017 *Agriculture and industry in south-eastern Roman Britain* Oxford, Oxbow Books

Bird, J. (ed.) 1998 *Form and fabric. Studies in Rome's material past in honour of B.R. Hartley* Oxford, Oxbow Monograph 80

Bischoff, J.P. 1983 '"I cannot do't without counters": fleece weights and sheep breeds in late thirteenth- and early fourteenth-century England', *Agricultural History* 57 (2), 143–60

Bishop, M.C. 2012 *Handbook to Roman legionary fortresses* Barnsley, Pen and Sword Military

Black, E. 1985 'Hypocaust heating in domestic rooms in Roman Britain', *Oxford Journal of Archaeology* 4 (1), 77–92

Blair J. and Ramsay N. (eds) 1991 *English medieval industries: craftsmen, techniques, products* London, Hambledon Press

Blake, H. 1999 'De nomine Jhesu: an Italian export ware and the origin of maiolica pottery-making in the Low Countries', in Gaimster (ed.) 1999a, 23–56

Blake, H. 2000 'The formation of the second generation: a documented version of the origin and early history of the MRPG', *Medieval Ceramics* 24, 12–22

Blake, H. 2012 'Appendix 4: Italian wares', in Allan *et al.* 2012, 27–33

Blake, H. 2016 'Appendix F: Italian ceramics from Penhow', in Wrathmell 2016, 74–87

Blake, H. 2019 'Dopo il primato della maiolica: una riconversione industriale nel Valdarno', in Busti *et al.* (eds) 2019, 267–96, 355–6, 363–91

Blake, H. forthcoming a 'Archaic maiolicas in the North', in Sani and Mallet (eds) forthcoming

Blake, H. forthcoming b Blue-glazed Italo-Netherlandish Maiolica from George Street, Bridgwater, Somerset', in S. Hughes 'Excavations at George Street, Bridgwater', *Somerset Archaeology and Natural History*

Blake, H. forthcoming c 'From maiolica to terracotta: Montelupo and the Levant in the early modern period', *Proceedings of the 12th international congress on medieval & modern period Mediterranean ceramics* Athens

Blake, H. and Hughes, M.J. 2003 'The introduction of tin-glazed ceramics in north-western Europe: new data from the British Museum neutron activation analysis programme', in Bakirtzis (ed.) 2003, 447–54

Blake, H. and Hughes, M.J. 2015 'The provenance of Tuscan pottery found in Britain: the results of archaeometrical research', *Archeologia Postmedievale* 19, 137–84

Blake, H. and Hughes, M. 2016 'Archaeometrical research on the provenance of "Mediterranean Maiolica" and Italian pottery found in Great Britain', in Gonçalves and Gómez-Martínez (eds) 2016, 432–9

Blake, H. and Hughes, M.J. 2017 'The provenance of Tuscan pottery found in Britain: the results of archaeometrical research,' in Blake and Milanese (eds) 2017, 137–84

Blake, H. and Hughes, M.J. 2019 'An "early 14th–century" tin-glazed earthenware jar from Norwich and other archaic maiolicas excavated in the British Isles', in Edwards and Paynter (eds) 2019, 71–95

Blake, H. and Milanese, M. (eds) 2017 'Gran Bretagna e Italia tra Mediterraneo e Atlantico. Livorno – 'un porto inglese'', *Archeologia Postmedievale* 19, 137–84

Blake, H., Egan, G., Hurst, J.G. and New, E. 2003 'From popular devotion to resistance and revival in England: the cult of the holy name of Jesus and the Reformation', in Gaimster and Gilchrist (eds) 2003, 175–203

Blanchett, C. 2000 'The floor tiles at The Vyne, Hampshire, England', *Glazed Expressions* 41

Bland, R. and Loriot, X. 2010 *Roman and early Byzantine gold coins found in Britain and Ireland* London, Royal Numismatic Society Special Publication 46

Bland, R., Chadwick, A., Ghey, E, Haselgrove, C. and Mattingly, D. 2020 *Iron Age and Roman coin hoards in Britain* Oxford, Oxbow Books

Blaylock, S.R. 1990 'Exeter Guildhall', *Proceedings of the Devon Archaeological Society* 44, 123–78

Blaylock, S.R. 1991a *Bowhill, Exeter archive report II: the excavations of 1977–8* Exeter Museums Archaeological Field Unit report 91.06

Blaylock, S.R. 1991b Bowhill, *Exeter archive report III: building recording 1987–90* Exeter Museums Archaeological Field Unit report 91.07

Blaylock, S.R. 1991c *Excavation and fabric recording at the southern corner of Exeter Castle, 1990* Exeter Museums Archaeological Field Unit report 91.29

Blaylock, S.R. 1991d *St Katherine's Priory, Polsloe. Fabric survey of the west range 1979–80* Exeter Museums Archaeological Field Unit report 91.57

Blaylock, S.R. 1995 *Exeter city wall survey* Exeter, Exeter Archaeology

Blaylock, S.R. 1996 'Bell and cauldron founding in Exeter', *Historical Metallurgy* 30 (2), 72–82

Blaylock, S.R. 2000 'Excavation of an early post-medieval bronze foundry at Cowick Street, Exeter, 1999–2000', *Proceedings of the Devon Archaeological Society* 58, 1–92

Blaylock, S.R. 2004 *Bowhill: The archaeological study of a building under repair in Exeter, Devon, 1977–95* Swindon, English Heritage and Exeter, Exeter Archaeology

Blaylock, S.R. 2015 'The archaeology of West Country bronze foundries', in Allan *et al.* (eds) 2015, 271–308

Blaylock, S.R. and Norton, J. 1991 *Bowhill, Exeter, archive report IV, the screens passage excavation of 1989* Exeter Museums Archaeological Field Unit report 91.08

Blaylock, S. and Higham, R. forthcoming *Rougemont, Exeter: A Medieval Castle in its Urban Context: excavation and building recording at Exeter Castle, 1985–2016* Devon Archaeological Society monograph 2

Bochaca, M. 2012 'Sea travel at the end of the Middle Ages based on the account of the embassy to Spain and Portugal given by Roger Machado (1489)', *Mariner's Mirror* 98 (4), 436–47

Bocquet-Liénard, A. and Fajal, B. 2011 *À propo[t]s de l'usage, de la production et de la circulation des terres cuites dans l'Europe du Nord-Ouest autour des XIVe-XVIe siècles* Tables rondes du CRAHM 5, Caen, CRAHM

Boivin, A., Dufournier, D. and Lecler, *É. 1996* 'Nouvelles données sur la céramique très décorée rouennaise', in Piton (ed.) 1996, 61–84

Bojani, G.C. (ed.) 1997 *Per una storia della ceramica di Faenza: materiali dalle mura del Portello* Faenza, Edit Faenza

Bojani, G.C. (ed.) 2002 *I Della Rovere nell'Italia delle Corti*, 4. *Arte della maiolica* Urbino, QuattroVenti

Bond, J. and O'Connor, T. 1999 *Bones from medieval deposits at 16–22 Coppergate and other sites in York* York, Council for British Archaeology

Bonde, N., Tyers, I. and Wazny, T. 1997 'Where does the timber come from? Dendrochronological evidence of the timber trade in Northern Europe', in Sinclair *et al.* (eds) 1997, 201–4

Boon, G.C. 1974 *Silchester: the Roman town of Calleva* London, David and Charles

Booth, P., Dodd, A., Robinson, M. and Smith, A. 2007 *The Thames through time: the archaeology of the gravel terraces of the upper and middle Thames. The early historical period: AD 1–1000* Oxford Archaeology Thames Valley Landscapes Monograph 27

Borrego, M. and Saranova, R. 1994 'Envases cerámicos recuperados de las bóvedas de la iglesia de Santa María: Alicante, importante enclave comercial mediterráneo en el bajo medievo', LQNT 2, 181–98

Bowett, A. 2012 *Woods in British furniture-making 1400–1900: an illustrated historical dictionary* Wetherby, Oblong Creative

Bowsher, J. and Kenyon, R.F. forthcoming 'Claudian coinage', in *Bloomberg London excavation report* London, Museum of London Archaeology

Bradley, J., Gaimster, M., Haith, C. and Beaumont James, T. 1999 'Medieval Britain and Ireland in 1998', *Medieval Archaeology* 43, 226–302

Braithwaite, G. 2007 *Faces from the past: a study of Roman face pots from Italy and the western provinces of the Roman empire* Oxford, British Archaeology Reports International Series 1651

Brandão, J. 1990 [1552] *Grandeza e Abastança de Lisboa em 1552*, 2nd edition Lisbon, Livros Horizonte

Brice, A. (ed.) 1765 *The antique description and account of the city of Exeter in three parts, by John Vowell, alias Hoker* Exeter, North-gate Street

Brickley, M. and Ives, R. (eds) 2008 *The bioarchaeology of metabolic bone disease* Oxford, Elsevier

Brickley, M. and McKinley, J.I. (eds) 2004 *Guidelines to the standards for recording human remains, IFA paper No. 7* Southampton, BABAO

Bridge, M.C. 1986 'Tree-ring dates from Portsmouth Polytechnic: list 19', *Vernacular Architecture* 17, 53–4

Bridge, M.C. 2012 'Locating the origins of wood resources: a review of dendroprovenancing', *Journal of Archaeological Science* 39 (8), 2828–834

Bridge, M.C and Fowler, A.M. 2019 'A new way of looking at dendroprovenancing: spatial field correlations of residuals', *Dendrochronologia* 57 (for 2019)

Brindle, T. 2016 'The south-west', in Smith *et al.* 2016, 331–58

Brindle, T. and Brett, T. forthcoming *Dings Roman villa* Cotswold Archaeology report

Brindle, T., Holbrook, N. and Sausins, D. 2018 'A first-century A.D burial plot at Barnwood, Gloucestershire: excavations in 2013–14', *Britannia* 49, 147–77

Bristow, C.R., Edwards, R.A., Scrivener, R.C. and Williams, B.J. 1985 *Geology of Exeter and its environs* Exeter, British Geological Survey

Broady, P. 1979 'The pottery', in Fairclough 1979, 47–113

Brook, D. 1993 'Amphora stamps', in Manning 1993, 383–5

Brook, I. 2009 'Sinusitis', *Periodontology* 49, 126–39

Brooks, C. and Evans, D. 1988 *The great east window of Exeter Cathedral* Exeter, University of Exeter Press

Brooks, H. 2004 *Archaeological excavations at Head Street, Colchester, Essex, May–September 2000* Colchester, Colchester Archaeological Trust report 268

Brothwell, D. and Higgs, E. (eds) 1969 *Science in archaeology* London, Thames and Hudson

Brown, D.H. 2002 *Pottery in medieval Southampton c 1066–1510,* York, Council for British Archaeology

Brown, D.H. and Curnow, C. 2004 'A ceramic assemblage from the seabed near Kinlochbervie, Scotland, UK', *International Journal of Nautical Archaeology* 33 (1), 29–53

Brown, D.H. and Thomson, R. 1996 'La céramique fin XVè–début XVIè découverte dans les fouilles de Southampton (Angleterre)', *Bulletin du Groupe de Recherches et d'Etudes de la Céramique du Beauvaisis* 18, 37–59

Brown, D.H. and Vince, A.G. 1984 'Petrological aspects: the medieval pottery of Exeter under the microscope', in Allan 1984a, 32–4

Brown, D.H., Thomson, R. and Vince, A. 2006 'The pottery', in Saunders 2006, 269–95

Brown, S.W. 1988 'Excavations and building recording at Buckfast Abbey, Devon', *Proceedings of the Devon Archaeological Society* 46

Brown, S.W. 1991 *Excavations on the medieval Exe Bridge, St Edmund's Church and Frog Street tenements, Exeter, 1975–9* Exeter Museums Archaeological Field Unit report 91.52

Brown, S.W. 2005 *Exeter Cathedral archaeological recording: South Quire Aisle and St Gabriel's Chapel (external) 2005* Unpublished report to the Dean and Chapter of Exeter Cathedral

Brown, S.W. 2018 *Excavations and building recording at Buckfast Abbey, Devon, 1984–2017* Exeter, Devon Archaeological Society Occasional Paper 21

Brown, S.W. 2019 *The medieval Exe Bridge, St Edmund's Church, and excavation of waterfront houses, Exeter* Exeter, Devon Archaeological Society Monograph 1

Brown, S.W. and Holbrook, N. 1989 'A Roman site at Otterton Point', *Proceedings of the Devon Archaeological Society* 47, 29–42

Buckberry, J.C.A. 2007 'On sacred ground: social identity and churchyard burial in Lincolnshire and Yorkshire, *c.* 700–1100 AD', in *Anglo-Saxon Studies in Archaeology and History* 14, 117–29

Buckberry, J.C.A. (ed.) 2010 *Burial in later Anglo-Saxon England c. 650–1100 AD* Oxford, Oxbow Books

Buckland, P., Hey, D., O'Neill, R. and Tyers, I. 2013 *The Conisbrough estate and the southern boundary of Northumbria. Environmental and archaeological evidence from a late sixth/early seventh century structure and a later deer park boundary at Conisbrough, South Yorkshire* Unpublished report [https://www.academia.edu/16201756/Conisbrough_with_figures]

Buchsenschutz, O., Lepareux-Couturier, S. and Fronteau, G. 2017 *Les meules du Néolithique à l'époque médiévale: technique, culture, diffusion*, 43rd supplement, à la *Revue Archéologique de l'Est* Dijon, S.A.E.

Buckley, D. 2001 'Querns and millstones', in Anderson *et al.* 2001, 156–60

Bugalhão, J. and Coello, I.P. 2017 'Cerâmica moderna de Lisboa: proposta tipológica', *I Encontro de arqueologia de Lisboa: uma cidade em escavação*, Câmara Municipal de Lisboa, Lisbon, 107–45

Buikstra, J. and Beck, L. 2006 *Bioarchaeology: the contextual analysis of human remains* San Diego, Academic Press

Burnham, B.C., Keppie, L.J.F., Esmonde Cleary, A.S., Hassall, M.W.C. and Tomlin, R.S.O. 1994 'Roman Britain in 1993', *Britannia* 25, 245–315

Burnham, B.C., Keppie, L.J.F., Esmonde Cleary, A.S., Hassall, M.W.C. and Tomlin, R.S.O. 1995 'Roman Britain in 1994', *Britannia* 26, 325–90

Burnham, B.C., Keppie, L.J.F., Esmonde Cleary, A.S., Hassall, M.W.C. and Tomlin, R.S.O. 1996 'Roman Britain in 1995', *Britannia* 27, 389–457

Burnham, B.C., Keppie, L.J.F., Esmonde Cleary, A.S., Hassall, M.W.C. and Tomlin, R.S.O. 2000 'Roman Britain in 1999', *Britannia* 31, 371–449

Burnham, B.C., Hunter, F., Fitzpatrick, A.P., Hassall, M.W.C. and Tomlin, R.S.O. 2002 'Roman Britain in 2001', *Britannia* 38, 275–371

Burnham, B.C., Hunter, F., Fitzpatrick, Booth, P., Worrell, S., Tomlin, R.S.O. and Hassall, M.W.C. 2007 'Roman Britain in 2006', *Britannia* 33, 241–366

Burton, J. 1994 *Monastic and religious orders in Britain, 1000–1300* Cambridge, Cambridge University Press

Bush, H. and Zvelebil, M. 1991 *Health in past societies: bio-cultural interpretations of human skeletal remains in archaeological contexts* Oxford, Tempus Reparatum

Busti, G., Cesaretti, M. and Cocchi, F. (eds) 2019 *La maiolica italiana del Rinascimento: studi e ricerche* Turnhout, Brepols

Caessa, A., Nozes, C., Cameira, I. and Silva, R.B. da (eds) 2017 *I Encontro de Arqueologia de Lisboa: Uma Cidade em Escavação* Lisbon, Centro de Arqueologia de Lisbo

Carlyon, P.M. 1987 'Finds from the earthwork at Carvossa, Probus', *Cornish Archaeology* 26, 103–141

Carmona, R. and Santos, C. 2005 *Olaria da Mata da Machada: Cerâmicas dos séculos XV–XVI* Barreiro, Câmara Municipal do Barreiro

Carru, D. (ed.) 1995 *De l'Orient à la table du Pape: L'importation des céramiques dans la région d'Avignon au Moyen âge tardif, XIVe–XVIe siècles* Aix-en-Provence, Service d'archéologie de Vaucluse

Carswell, J. 1998 *Iznik pottery* London, British Museum

Carvalho, J.M.T. de, 1918 'A cerâmica Coimbrã: séculos XVI e XVII', *Revista da Universidade de Coimbra* 7 (5–6), 127–67

Carvalho, P. and Bettercourt, J. 2012 'De Aveiro para as margens do Atlântico: a carga do navio Ria de Aveiro A e a circulação de cerâmica na Época Moderna', in Teixeira and Bettencourt (eds) 2012, 733–48

Caselli, L. 2011 'Vittorio Cini collezionista: il corpus degli smalti', *Lettera da San Giorgio* 13, 15–19

Casimiro, T.M. 2011 *Portuguese faience in England and Ireland* Oxford, British Archaeological Reports International Series 2301

Casimiro, T.M. 2013 'Faiança portuguesa: datação e evolução crono-estilística', *Revista Portuguesa de Arqueologia* 16, 351–67

Castro, A., Paula, N.A., Torres, J.B., Curado, T. and Teixeira, A. 2017 'Evidências de produção oleira nos séculos XVI e XVII no Largo das Olarias, Mouraria (Lisboa)', *Arqueologia em Portugal 2017: estado da questão*, Associação dos Arqueologos Portugueses, Lisbon, 1731–49

Castro, F., Dórdio, P. and Teixeira, R. 1997 '200 anos de cerâmica na Casa do Infante (século XVI a meados do século XVIII): identificação visual e química dos fabricos', *3as Jornadas de Cerâmica Medieval e Pós-Medieval* Tondela, Câmara Municipal de Tondela, 223–30

Catarino, H. 1995 'Cerâmicas tardo-medievais/modernas do Alto Alentejo: a escavação de um silo na vila de Crato', *Actas das 1as Jornadas de Cerâmica Medieval e Pós-Medieval*, Tondela, 129–36

Chapelot, J. and Fossier, R. 1985 *The village and house in the middle ages* (translated by H. Cleere) Berkeley and Los Angeles, University of California Press

Chapman, E.M., Hunter, F., Booth, P., Wilson, P. Worrell, S., Tomlin, R.S.O. and Pearce, J. 2011 'Roman Britain in 2010', *Britannia* 42, 319–466

Chapman, S., Steinmetzer, M. and Bidwell, P. 2017 'St David's Church, Exeter', *Devon Archaeological Society Newsletter*, 4–5

Cherry, J. 1982 'Post-Medieval Britain in 1981', *Post-Medieval Archaeology* 16, 217–29

Cherry, J. 1991 'The medieval leather industry', in Blair and Ramsey (eds) 1991, 295–318

Childs, W. 1995 'Documentary evidence for the import of Spanish pottery to England in the Later Middle Ages (thirteenth to early sixteenth centuries)', in Gerrard *et al.* 1995, 25–31

Chilosi, C. (ed.) 2011 *Ceramiche della tradizione ligure: thesaurus di opere dal Medio Evo al primo Novecento* Cinisello Balsamo, Silvana

Ciaroni, A. 2004 *Maioliche del Quattrocento a Pesaro: frammenti di storia dell'arte ceramica dalla bottega dei Fedeli* Florence, Centro Di

Clapham, A.J. 1999 'Charred plant remains', in Fitzpatrick *et al.* 1999, 345–71

Clarke, H. 1992 'The Hanse and England: a survey of the evidence for contacts between England and the Baltic in the Middle Ages', *Archaeologia Elbingensis* 1, 135–8

Clarke, P. 2018 *St Sidwell's Point, Exeter Bus Station, Exeter* Cotswold Archaeology report 18554 [CA: https://reports.cotswoldarchaeology.co.uk/]

Clarke, P. 2019 *Project Sofia, phase 2, Belgrave Road, Exeter* Cotswold Archaeology report 880315_1

Clarke, T.H. 1974 'Lattimo – a group of Venetian glass enameled on an opaque-white ground', *Journal of Glass Studies* 16, 22–56

Clutterbuck, J. 2019 *The former Radmore & Tucker site, Frog Street, Exeter* Cotswold Archaeology report EX0031_1

Coelho, I.P. and Teixeira, A. 2018 'Glazed pottery production from Mata da Machada, Barreiro (Portugal)', in Yenisehirlioglu (ed.) 2018, 261–5

Coleman-Smith, R. and Pearson, T. 1988 *Excavations in the Donyatt potteries* Chichester, Phillimore

Coles, C. forthcoming a 'The animal bones of Roman Princesshay', in Steinmetzer, Stead *et al.* forthcoming

Coles, C. forthcoming b 'Medieval faunal bone from Princesshay Exeter', in Steinmetzer, Allan and Orme forthcoming

Coll Conesa, J. 1993 'Contenedores cerámicos medievales en las costas de Mallorca', *IV Congreso de Arqueología Medieval Española*, 1069–79

Coll Conesa, J. 2009 'Cobalt blue in medieval ceramic production in the Valencian workshops: Manises, Paterna and Valencia, Spain', *Medieval Ceramics* 31, 11–23

Collings, A.G. n.d. *Documentary references to the Turk's Head in St Pancras parish* Exeter Archaeology report

Collings, A.G. and Matthews, A.J. 1994 *Archaeological evaluation of 30/32 Longbrook Street, Exeter* Exeter Archaeology report 94.32

Collis, J. 1972 *Exeter excavations: the Guildhall Site* Exeter, University of Exeter

Cool, H.E.M. 2006 *Eating and drinking in Roman Britain* Cambridge, Cambridge University Press

Cooper, N.H. (ed.) 1990 *The Exeter area: proceedings of the 136th summer meeting of the Royal Archaeological Institute 1990* London, the Royal Archaeological Institute

Coppack, G. 1984 'Highly decorated pitcher', in Allan 1984a, 83, 87

Coque-Delhuille, B. and Gosselin-Vuilleumier, J. 1984 'L'évolution géomorphologique du massif de Devon-Cornwall (G.B.) au Crétacé et au Tertiaire: apport de la microscopie électronique a balayage', *Rev. features de Géologie Dynamique et de Géographie Physique* 25. fasc. 4, 245–56

Corfield, P. and Keene, D.J. (eds) 1990 *Work in towns, 850–1850* Leicester, University of Leicester Press

Correia, V. 1926 *Regimento dos Oficiais Mecânicos da mui nobre e sempre leal cidade de Lisboa* (1572) Coimbra, Imprenta da Universidade

Cosh, S.R. and Neal, D.S. 2005 *Roman mosaics of Britain. Volume 2: South-West Britain* London, Society of Antiquaries of London

Cotswold Archaeology 2015 *Archaeological monitoring and recording on Exeter gas main replacement scheme, West Street* Unpublished report in Exeter HER

Cotter J. 1997 *A twelfth-century pottery kiln at Pound Lane, Canterbury: evidence for an immigrant potter in the late Norman period* Canterbury, Canterbury Archaeological Trust Occasional Paper 1

Cotter, J.P. 1999 'Imported apothecary jars from Colchester, Essex', in Gaimster (ed.) 1999a, 167–9

Cowan, C. 1992 'A possible mansio in Roman Southwark: excavations at 15–23 Southwark Street, 1980–5', *Transactions of the London and Middlesex Archaeological Society* 43, 3–191

Cox, J. and Thorp, J.R.L. 2001 *Devon thatch: an illustrated history of thatching and thatched buildings in Devon* Tiverton, Devon Books

Cox, M. and Mays, S. (eds) 2000 *Human osteology in archaeology and forensic science* Cambridge, Cambridge University Press

Cox, P.W. and Hearne, C.M. 1991 *Redeemed from the heath: the archaeology of the Wytch Farm Oilfield (1987–90)* Dorchester, Dorset Natural History and Archaeological Society Monograph 9

Crabtree, P.J. 1990 'Zooarchaeology and complex societies: some uses of faunal analysis for the study of trade, social status, and ethnicity', *Archaeological Method and Theory* 2, 155–205

Craddock, P.T. 2009 'Mining and metallurgy', in Oleson (ed.) 2009, 93–120

Crawford, M.H. (ed.) 1996 *Roman statutes* London, Bulletin of the Institute of Classical Studies Supplement 64

Crawford, O.G.S. and Röder, J. 1955 'The quern quarries of Mayen in the Eifel', *Antiquity* 29, 68–77

Creighton, J. with Fry, R. 2016 *Silchester: changing visions of a Roman Town* London, The Society for the Promotion of Roman Studies Britannia Monograph 28

Cresswell, B.F. 1916 *The Edwardian inventories for the city and county of Exeter* London, Alcuin Club Collections 20

Crick, J. 2014 'The charter evidence for Exeter in the twelfth century, *Friends' News: the newsletter of The Friends of Exeter Cathedral Exeter*, 10–12.

Crocker, J. 2016a *Elizabethan inventories and wills of the Exeter Orphans' Court. Part 1* Exeter, Devon and Cornwall Records Society New Series 56

Crocker, J. 2016b *Elizabethan inventories and wills of the Exeter Orphans' Court. Part 2* Exeter, Devon and Cornwall Records Society New Series 57

Croom, A. and Bidwell, P. 2014 'The Roman pottery', in Morris 2014, 117–61

Crossley, D.W. (ed.) 1981 *Medieval industry* London, Council for British Archaeology Research Report 40

Crummy, N. (ed.) 1987 *The coins from excavations in Colchester 1971–9* Colchester, Colchester Archaeological Report 4

Crummy, P. 1987 'The coins as site dating evidence' in N. Crummy (ed.) 1987, 5–14

Cruse, J. and Heslop, D. 2015 *Querns and millstones at Heslington East* Unpublished report by University of York [to be published on the ADS]

Cunliffe, B. 1988 *Mount Batten, Plymouth: a prehistoric and Roman port* Oxford, Oxford University Committee for Archaeology Monograph 26

Cunliffe, B. 2013 *The Roman Villa at Brading, Isle of Wight: the excavations of 2008–10* Oxford, Oxford University School of Archaeology Monograph 77

Curnow, C. and Hughes, M. 2017 'A maiolica jar with grotesque decoration from New Street, Plymouth', in Blake and Milanese 2017, 231–8

Current Archaeology 1973 (July) 'Exeter', *Current Archaeology* 39, 102–10

Daly, A. 2007 *Timber, trade and tree-rings – a dendrochronological analysis of structural oak timber in north Europe, c. AD 1000 to c. AD 1650* Unpublished PhD thesis, University of Southern Denmark

Daniell, C. 1997 *Death and burial in medieval England* London, Routledge

Darling, M. 1985 'The other Roman pottery', in Pitts and St Joseph 1985, 323–38

Darling, M. 2002 'Pottery', in Webster 2002, 137–223

Darling, M. 2014 'Development of local pottery industries', in Darling and Precious 2014, 304–12

Darling, M. and Precious, B. 2014 *A corpus of Roman pottery from Lincoln* Lincoln Archaeological Studies No. 6, Oxford, Oxbow

Davey, P. and Hodges, R. (eds) 1983 *Ceramics and trade. The production and distribution of later medieval pottery in North-West Europe* Sheffield, University Press

Davies, B., Richardson, B. and Tomber, R. 1994 *The archaeology of Roman London. Volume 5: a dated corpus of early Roman pottery from the City of London* York, Council for British Archaeology Research Report 98

Davies, R.W. 1971 'The Roman military diet', *Britannia* 2, 122–42

Davison, B.K. 1972 'Castle Neroche: an abandoned Norman fortress in South Somerset', *Somerset Archaeology and Natural History* 116, 16–58

Davison, D.P. 1989 *The barracks of the Roman army from the 1st to 3rd centuries AD.* Oxford, British Archaeological Reports International Series 472

Dawes, J. and Magilton, J. 1980 *The cemetery of St Helen-on-the-Walls, Aldwark* York, York Archaeological Trust

Dawson, D. and Kent, O. 1999 'Reduction-fired low-temperature ceramics', *Post-Medieval Archaeology* 33, 164–78

Dawson, D. and Kent, O. 2008 'The development of the bottle kiln in pottery manufacture in Britain', *Post-Medieval Archaeology* 42 (1), 201–26

Dawson, D., Hall, T. and Iveson, L. 2015 'A group of late 13th/early 14th-century pottery from a garderobe pit excavated in the garden of Wells and Mendip Museum, 8 Cathedral Green, Wells, Somerset, 1996', *Somerset Archaeology and Natural History* 159, 109–39

De Groote, K., Tys, D. and Pieters, M. (eds) 2010 *Exchanging medieval material culture. Studies on archaeology and history presented to Frans Verhaeghe* Brussels, Relicta Monografieen 4

Degasperi, A. 2016 *Arte nell'arte: ceramiche medievali lette attraverso gli occhi dei grandi maestri toscani del Trecento e del Quattrocento* Florence, Firenze University Press

Degryse, P. and Braekmans, D. 2014 'Archaeology and anthropology: 14.14 elemental and isotopic analysis of ancient ceramics and glass', in Holland and Turekian (eds) 2014, 191–207

Delaine, J. and Johnston, D.E. (eds) 1999 *Roman baths and bathing. Proceedings of the First International Conference on Roman Baths held at Bath, England, 30 March–4 April 1992* Portsmouth (Rhode Island), Journal of Roman Archaeology Supplementary Series 37

Deroeux, D., Dufournier, D. and Hertig, A. 1994 'French medieval ceramics from the Bryggen excavations in Bergen', in *The Bryggen Papers* Bergen, University of Bergen Supplmentary Series 5, 161–208

Dessau, H. (ed.) 1892–1916 *Inscriptiones latinae selectae* Berlin, Beronlini apud Weidmannos

Devon Archaeological Society 1986 *Newsletter 1/1986* 33, 11–12

Dickinson, B.M. 1987 'Samian', in Carlyon 1987, 107–9

Dickinson, B.M. 1991 'Samian potters' stamps', in Holbrook and Bidwell 1991, 46–55

Dijkstra, J., Ostkamp, S. and Williams, G. (eds) 2006 *Archeologisch onderzoekop het terrein van de voormalige Berghuijskazerne te Middelburg* Amersfoort, ADC ArcheoProjecten

Diogo, A.M.D. and Trindade, L. 2000 'Cerâmicas de barro vermelho, encontradas em entulhos do terramoto de 1531, na intervenção arqueológica da Rua dos Correeiros, Lisboa', *Revista Portuguesa de Arqueologia* 3 (2), 201–35

Dobney, K and Rielly, K. 1988 'A method for recording archaeological animal bones: the use of diagnostic zones, *Circaea* 5 (2), 79–96

Dobney, K.M., Jaques, S.D. and Irving, B.G. 1995 *Of butchers and breeds: report on vertebrate remains from various sites in the city of Lincoln* Lincoln, City of Lincoln Archaeology Unit

Dollinger, P. 1970 *The German Hansa* Stanford, Stanford University Press

Dórdio, P., Teixeira, R. and Sá, A. 2001 'Faianças do Porto e Gaia: O recente contributo da arqueologia', *Itinerário da faiança Porto e Gaia* Lisbon, Museu Nacional Soares dos Reis, 119–64

Dore, J. 2007 'Coarseware', in Hanson 2007, 270–325

Douglas, A., Gerrard, J. and Sudds, B. 2011 *A Roman settlement and bath house at Shadwell: excavations at Tobacco Dock and Babe Ruth Restaurant, The Highway, London* London, Pre-Construct Archaeology Monograph 12

Down, A. 1989 *Chichester Excavations 6* Chichester, Phillimore

Drey, R.E.A. 1978 *Apothecary jars: pharmaceutical pottery and porcelain in Europe and the East, 1150–1850* London, Faber and Faber

Driesch, A. von den 1976 *A guide to the measurements of animal bones from archaeological sites,* Peabody Museum bulletin 1 Cambridge, MA, Harvard University

Driessen, M. 2009 'The early Flavian *castra* and the Flavian-Trajanic stone legionary fortress at Nijmegen (the Netherlands)', in Morillo *et al.* (eds) 2009, 1245–56

Drury, P. 2009 *Hill Hall, a singular house devised by a Tudor intellectual* London, Society of Antiquaries

Du Plat Taylor, J. and Cleere, H. (eds) 1978 *Roman shipping and trade: Britain and the Rhine provinces* York, Council for British Archaeology Research Report 24

Duggan, M. 2018 *Links to late antiquity. Ceramic exchange and contacts on the Atlantic seaboard in the 5th to 7th centuries* Oxford, British Archaeological Reports British Series 639

Dumortier, C. 1987 'Les faïenciers italiens à Anvers au XVIe siècle: aspects historiques', *Faenza* 73, 161–72

Dumortier, C. 2002 *Céramique de la Renaissance à Anvers: de Venise à Delft* Brussels, Racine

Dumortier, C. and Veeckman, J. 1994 'Un four de majoliques en activité à Anvers vers 1560', *Bulletin des Musées royaux d'Art et d'Histoire* 65, 163–217

Dungworth, D. 2000 'A note on the analysis of crucibles and moulds', *Historic Metallurgy* 34.2, 83–6

Dungworth, D. 2001 *Metal working evidence from Housesteads Roman Fort, Northumberland* Portsmouth, English Heritage Research Department Report Series 109/2001

Dungworth, D. and Starley, D. 2009 'The metalworking debris', in Rushworth (ed.) 2009, 579–88

Dufournier, D. 1981 'L'analyse des matières premieres argileuses dans la recherche de l'origine de fabrication des céramiques', *Revue d'Archeometrie,* supplement 3, 83–93

Dunning, G.C. 1961 'A group of English and imported medieval pottery from Lesnes Abbey, Kent and the trade in early Hispano-Moresque pottery to England', *Antiquaries Journal* 41, 1–12

Dunning, G.C. and Fox, A. 1951 'Twelfth-century pottery from Exeter', *Antiquaries Journal* 31, 180–7

Durrant, J. forthcoming 'Roman tile', in Steinmetzer *et al.* forthcoming, 79–83

Dyer, C. 1998 *Standards of living in the later Middle Ages: social change in England* c. *1200–1520* Cambridge, Cambridge University Press

Dyer, M. 2003 *Archaeological evaluation at the former Victoria Nurseries, Okehampton Street, Exeter* Exeter Archaeology report 03.29

Dyer, M. and Allan, J.P. 2004 'A newly-recorded length of Exeter's medieval and later water supply', *Proceedings of the Devon Archaeological Society* 62, 181–6

Dymond, R. 1882 'The history of the parish of St Petrock, Exeter, as shown by its churchwardens' accounts and other records', *Report and Transactions of the Devonshire Association* 14, 402–92

Earwood, C. and Salvatore, J.P. 1994 *Excavations at Holloway Street, Exeter, 1974. Part 1: Roman military* Exeter Museums Archaeological Field Unit report 94.10 [ADS: https://doi.org/10.5284/1035187]

Eckardt, H. (ed.) 2010 *Roman diasporas: archaeological approaches to mobility and diversity in the Roman world* Portsmouth (Rhode Island), Journal of Roman Archaeology Supplementary Series 78

Edwards, J. and Paynter, S. (eds) 2019 *Ceramics and glass: a tribute to Sarah Jennings* London, Medieval Pottery Research Group Paper 8

Egan, G. 1983 'Post-Medieval Britain in 1982', *Post-Medieval Archaeology* 17, 185–204

Egan, G. 1985 'Post-Medieval Britain in 1984', *Post-Medieval Archaeology* 19, 159–91

Egan, G. 1986 'Post-Medieval Britain in 1985', *Post-Medieval Archaeology* 20, 330–60

Egan, G. 1988 'Post-Medieval Britain in 1987', *Post-Medieval Archaeology* 22, 189–231

Egan, G. 1989 'Post-Medieval Britain in 1988', *Post-Medieval Archaeology* 23, 25–67

Egan, G. 1990 'Post-Medieval Britain in 1989', *Post-Medieval Archaeology* 24, 159–211

Ellis, P. (ed.) 2001 *Roman Wiltshire and after* Devizes, Wiltshire Archaeological and Natural History Society

English Heritage 1998 *Dendrochronology: guidelines on producing and interpreting dendrochronological dates* London, English Heritage

Erskine, A.M. 1981 *The accounts of the fabric of Exeter Cathedral, 1279–1353. Part 1: 1279–1326* Exeter, Devon and Cornwall Record Society, New Series, 24

Erskine, A.M. 1983 *The accounts of the fabric of Exeter Cathedral, 1279–1353. Part 2: 1328–1353* Exeter, Devon and Cornwall Record Society, New Series, 26

Erskine, A.M., Hope, V. and Lloyd, J. 1988 *Exeter Cathedral: a short history and description* Exeter, Dean and Chapter of Exeter

Evans, D.H. 2019 'Continental ceramic imports into Hull, *c.* 1260–1700', in Edwards and Paynter (eds) 2019, 97–128

Evans, D.R. and Hartley, K.F. 1997 'The mortaria', in Marvell and Owen John 1997, 315–25

Evans, J. and Elbeih, S.M. 1984 'Post-medieval food residues from Exeter', in Allan 1984a, 1–6

Evison, V.I., Hodges, H. and Hurst, J.G. (eds) 1974 *Medieval pottery from excavations* London, John Baker

Exeter Archaeology 1998 *Archaeological assessment and field evaluation of the Scot Hire site, Haven Road, Exeter* Exeter Archaeology report 98.45

Exeter Archaeology 2003 *Archaeological assessment and field evaluation of proposed redevelopment to the rear of the Royal Albert Memorial Museum, Bradninch Place, Exeter* Exeter Archaeology report 03.13

Exeter Archaeology 2005 *Archaeological assessment of land at Lower North Street, Exeter* Exeter Archaeology report 05.23 [ADS: https://doi.org/10.5284/1007833]

Exeter Archaeology 2007 *Archaeological monitoring of groundworks at Brunel Close, Exeter* draft HER entry in Exeter HER

Exeter Archaeology Archive Project (2015) *Exeter Archaeology Archive Project,* https://doi.org/10.5284/1035173

Exeter City Council 1971 *Archaeological advisory committee report* Exeter, Exeter City Council [ADS: https://doi.org/10.5284/1035173]

Exeter City Council 1972 *Archaeological advisory committee report* Exeter, Exeter City Council [ADS: https://doi.org/10.5284/1035173]

Exeter City Council 1973 *Archaeological Advisory Committee report* Exeter, Exeter City Council [ADS: https://doi.org/10.5284/1035173]

Exeter City Council 1974 *Archaeological Advisory Committee report* Exeter, Exeter City Council [ADS: https://doi.org/10.5284/1035173]

Exeter City Council 1975 *Archaeological advisory Committee report* Exeter, Exeter City Council [ADS: https://doi.org/10.5284/1035173]

Exeter City Council 1976 *Archaeological Advisory Committee report* Exeter, Exeter City Council [ADS: https://doi.org/10.5284/1035173]

Exeter City Council 1977 *Archaeological Advisory Committee report* Exeter, Exeter City Council [ADS: https://doi.org/10.5284/1035173]

Exeter City Council 1978 *Archaeological Advisory Committee report* Exeter, Exeter City Council [ADS: https://doi.org/10.5284/1035173]

Exeter City Council 1979 *Archaeological Advisory Committee report* Exeter, Exeter City Council [ADS: https://doi.org/10.5284/1035173]

Exeter City Council 1980 *Archaeological Advisory Committee report* Exeter, Exeter City Council [ADS: https://doi.org/10.5284/1035173]

Exeter City Council 1981 *Archaeological Advisory Committee report* Exeter, Exeter City Council [ADS: https://doi.org/10.5284/1035173]

Exeter City Council 1982 *Archaeological Advisory Committee report* Exeter, Exeter City Council [ADS: https://doi.org/10.5284/1035173]

Exeter City Council 1983 *Archaeological Advisory Committee report* Exeter, Exeter City Council [ADS: https://doi.org/10.5284/1035173]

Exeter City Council 1984 *Archaeological Advisory Committee report* Exeter, Exeter City Council [ADS: https://doi.org/10.5284/1035173]

Exeter City Council 1985 *Archaeological Advisory Committee report* Exeter, Exeter City Council [ADS: https://doi.org/10.5284/1035173]

Exeter City Council 1986 *Archaeological Advisory Committee report* Exeter, Exeter City Council [ADS: https://doi.org/10.5284/1035173]

Exeter City Council 1987 *Archaeological Advisory Committee report* Exeter, Exeter City Council [ADS: https://doi.org/10.5284/1035173]

Exeter City Council 1988 *Archaeological Advisory Committee report* Exeter, Exeter City Council [ADS: https://doi.org/10.5284/1035173]

Exeter City Council 1989 *Archaeological Advisory Committee report* Exeter, Exeter City Council [ADS: https://doi.org/10.5284/1035173]

Exeter City Council 1990 *Archaeological Advisory Committee report* Exeter, Exeter City Council [ADS: https://doi.org/10.5284/1035173]

Exeter City Council 1991 *Archaeological Advisory Committee report* Exeter, Exeter City Council [ADS: https://doi.org/10.5284/1035173]

Exeter City Council 1992 *Archaeological Advisory Committee report* Exeter, Exeter City Council [ADS: https://doi.org/10.5284/1035173]

Exeter City Council 1993 *Archaeological Advisory Committee report* Exeter, Exeter City Council [ADS: https://doi.org/10.5284/1035173]

Exeter City Council 1994 *Archaeological Advisory Committee report* Exeter, Exeter City Council [ADS: https://doi.org/10.5284/1035173]

Exeter City Council 1995 *Archaeological Advisory Committee report* Exeter, Exeter City Council [ADS: https://doi.org/10.5284/1035173]

Exeter City Council 1996 *Archaeological Advisory Committee report* Exeter, Exeter City Council [ADS: https://doi.org/10.5284/1035173]

Exeter City Council 1997 *Archaeological Advisory Committee report* Exeter, Exeter City Council [ADS: https://doi.org/10.5284/1035173]

Exeter Excavation Committee 1935 'Report of the Exeter Excavation Committee 1934–35', *Proceedings of the Devon Archaeological Exploration Society* 2 (3), 176–90

Fairclough, G.J. 1986 *Plymouth excavations: St Andrews Street 1976* Plymouth, Plymouth Museums Archaeological Series 2

Farnell, A.J. 2009 *Archaeological evaluation and recording at 48 Beacon Lane, Exeter* Exeter Archaeology report 09.92 [ADS: https://doi.org/10.5284/1022912]

Farnell, A.J. 2010a *Archaeological monitoring and recording at North Gate Court, Lower North Street, Exeter* Exeter Archaeology report 10.75 [ADS: https://doi.org/10.5284/1007831]

Farnell, A.J. 2010b 'A pit at Crosslands, Ipplepen: probable evidence for late Roman roof slate quarrying', *Proceedings of the Devon Archaeological Society* 68, 85–8

Farnell, A.J. 2015 'Multi-period settlement, burial, industry and agriculture: archaeological excavations 2007–2017 at Twinyeo Quarry, Chudleigh Knighton', *Proceedings of the Devon Archaeological Society* 73, 185–278

Farnell, A.J. 2018 *23–27 Mary Arches Street and Quintana Gate, Bartholomew Street West, Exeter, Devon* AC Archaeology report ACD1607/1/0

Farnell, A.J. and Passmore, A. 2017 *Land to the rear of nos 95–96 Fore Street, Exeter* AC Archaeology report ACD1562/2/0 [ADS: https://doi.org/10.5284/1046384]

Farnell, A.J. and Rainbird, P. 2018 *Land north of Wessex Close, Topsham, near Exeter, Devon* AC Archaeology report ACD 1360/3/1

Farnell, A.J. and Salvatore, J. 2010 *An archaeological trench evaluation of the Paris Street bus and coach station and adjacent land, Exeter* Exeter Archaeology report 10.21

Farnell, A.J., Cooke, P. and Hughes, S.A. 2016 *Land at Hill Barton Industrial Estate, Blackmore Road, Clyst St Mary, Devon* AC archaeology report ACD1115/1/1

Farris, G. and Ferrarese, V.A. 1969 'Contributo alla conoscenza della tipologia e della stilistica della maiolica ligure del XVI secolo', *Atti del secondo convegno (Albisola, 31 maggio – 2 giugno 1969)* Genoa, Centro ligure per la storia della ceramica, 11–45

Fedorowicz, J.K. 1980 *England's Baltic trade in the early seventeenth century* Cambridge, Cambridge University Press

Ferguson, R.S. 1893 'The Roman fort on Hardknott known as Hardknott Castle', *Transactions of the Cumberland and Westmorland Antiquarian & Archaeological Society* 12 (1), 376–90

Fernandes, I.M.G. 2012 *A loiça preta em Portugal: Estudo histórico, modos de fazer e de usar* Unpublished PhD thesis, Universidade do Minho

Filtzinger, P. 1972 *Novaesium V. Die römische keramik aus dem Militärbereich von Novaesium (etwa 25 bis 50 n. Chr.)*, Limesforschungen 11

Finlay, A.J., McComish, J.M., Ottley, C.J., Bates, C.R. and Selby, D. 2012 'Trace element fingerprinting of ceramic building material from Carpow and York Roman fortresses manufactured by the VI Legion', *Journal of Archaeological Science* 39 (7), 2385–91

Fitzpatrick, A.P. 2001 'Roman Britain in 2000. I. Sites explored. 8. South-western counties', *Britannia* 23, 294–7

Fitzpatrick, A.P. 2017 'The famous volcanic rock of the Eifel: was it imported to Britain in Prehistory?', in Shaffrey 2017b, 195–214

Fitzpatrick, A.P., Butterworth, C.A. and Grove, J. 1999 *Prehistoric and Roman sites in east Devon: the A30 Honiton to Exeter Improvement DBFO Scheme, 1996–9. Volume 2* Salisbury, Wessex Archaeology report 16 [ADS: https://doi.org/10.5284/1007940]

Fletcher, J.M. 1977 'Tree-ring chronologies for the 6th to 16th centuries for oaks of southern and eastern England', *Journal of Archaeological Science* 4, 335–52

Fletcher, J.M. (ed.) 1978 *Dendrochronology in Europe* Oxford, British Archaeological Reports International Series 51

Fletcher, J.M., Tapper, M., and Walker, F.S. 1974 'Dendrochronology – a reference curve for slow grown oaks, AD 1230 to 1546', *Archaeometry* 16 (1), 31–40

Formigo, F.A. 2014 *Estudo decorativo, morfológico e tecnológico da faiança de Coimbra* Dissertação de Mestrado, Instituto Politécnico de Tomar

Fornaciari, A. 2016 *La sostanza delle forme: morfologia e cronotipologia della maiolica di Montelupo Fiorentino* Florence, All'Insegna del Giglio

Forsyth, H. 1999 '16th century', in Johnstone (ed.) 1999, 12–27

Fox, A. 1951a 'Eighteenth report on the archaeology and early history of Devon', *Report and Transactions of the Devonshire Association.* 83, 36–42

Fox, A. 1951b 'The underground conduits in Exeter, exposed during reconstruction in 1950', *Report and Transactions of the Devonshire Association* 83, 172–8

Fox, A. 1952a *Roman Exeter (Isca Dumnoniorum): excavations in the war-damaged areas 1945–947* Manchester, Manchester University Press

Fox, A. 1952b 'Nineteenth report of the archaeology and early history of Devon', *Transactions of the Devonshire Association* 84, 242–8

Fox, A. 1953 'Excavations in Bear Street, Exeter, 1953', *Proceedings of the Devon Archaeological Exploration Society* 5 (1), 30–41

Fox, A. 1954 'Twenty-first report on the archaeology and early history of Devon', *Transactions of the Devonshire Association* 86, 274–8

Fox, A. 1956 'Twenty-third report on the archaeology and early history of Devon', *Transactions of the Devonshire Association* 88, 212–21

Fox, A. 1961 'Twenty-fifth report on the archaeology and early history of Devon', *Transactions of the Devonshire Association* 93, 61–80

Fox, A. 1963 '27th report on archaeology and early history', *Transactions of the Devonshire Association* 95, 74–86

Fox, A. 1966 'Roman Exeter (*Isca Dumnoniorum*), origins and early development', in Wacher (ed.) 1966, 46–51

Fox, A. 1968 'Excavations at the South Gate, Exeter, 1964–5', *Proceedings of the Devon Archaeological Society* 26, 1–20

Fox, A. and Dunning, G.C. 1957 'A medieval pottery kiln in Exeter', *Antiquaries Journal* 37, 43–53

Fox, A. and Ravenhill, W.L D. 1970 'Excavation of the Roman fort at Tregear, Nanstallon: fourth interim report', *Cornish Archaeology* 9, 99–101

Fox, A. and Ravenhill, W.L.D. 1972 'The Roman fort at Nanstallon, Cornwall', *Britannia* 3, 56–1 1

Fox, C. 1956 'The siting of the monastery of St Mary and St Peter in Exeter', in Harden (ed.) 1956, 202–17

Fox, C. and Radford, C.A.R. 1933 'Kidwelly Castle, Carmarthenshire: including a survey of the polychrome pottery found there and elsewhere in Britain', *Archaeologia* 83. 93–138

Fox, H. 1986 'Exeter, Devonshire', in Skelton and Harvey (eds) 1986, 164–9

Franklin, J. 2014 'The finds', in Masser *et al.* 2014, 28–42

Franklin, J. 2011 'Beer jugs, wine bottles and coffee pots – changing ceramic use in post-medieval Edinburgh', *Medieval Ceramics* 32, 23–34

Freestone, I. and Tite, M.S. 1986 'Refractories in the ancient and preindustrial world', in Kingery and Lense (eds) 1986, 35–63

Freestone, I., Johns, C. and Potter, T. (eds) 1982 *Current research in ceramics. Thin-section studies* London, British Museum Occasional Paper 32

Freeth, S.J. 1967 'A chemical study of some Bronze Age sherds', *Archaeometry* 10, 104–19

Frere, S.S. 1972 *Verulamium Excavations. Volume I* London, Reports of the Research Committee of the Society of Antiquaries of London 28

Frere, S.S. 1980 'Hyginus and the first cohort', *Britannia* 1 , 51–60

Frere, S.S. 1983 *Verulamium excavations. Volume 2* London, Reports of the Research Committee of the Society of Antiquaries of London 41

Frere, S.S. 2011 'The saga of Verulamium building XXVII 2', *Britannia* 42, 263–74

Frere, S.S. and Wilkes, J.J. 1989 *Strageath. Excavations within the Roman fort 1973–86* London, The Society for the Promotion of Roman Studies Britannia Monograph 9

Frere, S.S., Hassall, M.W.C. and Tomlin, R.S.O. 1977 'Roman Britain in 1976', *Britannia* 8, 356–449

Frere, S.S., Hassall, M.W.C. and Tomlin, R.S.O. 1983 'Roman Britain in 1982', *Britannia* 14, 280–35

Frere, S.S., Hassall, M.W.C. and Tomlin, R.S.O. 1985 'Roman Britain in 1984', *Britannia* 16, 252–332

Frere, S.S., Hassall, M.W.C. and Tomlin, R.S.O. 1987 'Roman Britain in 1986', *Britannia* 18, 301–77

Frere, S.S., Hassall, M.W.C. and Tomlin, R.S.O. 1988 'Roman Britain in 1987'. *Britannia* 19, 415–508

Frere, S.S., Hassall, M.W.C. and Tomlin, R.S.O. 1989 'Roman Britain in 1988', *Britannia* 20, 258–345

Frere, S.S., Hassall, M.W.C. and Tomlin, R.S.O. 1990 'Roman Britain in 1989', *Britannia* 21, 303–78

Friendship-Taylor, D. 1984 'The leather', in Allan 1984a, 323–33

Fulford, M.G. 1975 *New Forest Roman pottery: manufacture and distribution, with a corpus of pottery types* Oxford, British Archaeological Reports British Series 17

Fulford, M 2010 'Roman Britain: immigration and material culture', in Eckardt (ed.) 2010, 67–78

Fulford, M. (ed.) 2012 *Silchester and the study of Romano-British urbanism* Journal of Roman Archaeology Supplementary Series 90, 49–75

Fulford, M. and Allen, J.R.L. 1992 'Iron making at the Chesters Villa, Woolaston', *Britannia* 23, 159–217

Fulford, M. and Clarke, A. 2011 *Silchester: city in transition* London, The Society for the Promotion of Roman Studies Britannia Monograph 25

Fulford, M. and Holbrook, N. (eds) 2015 *The towns of Roman Britain: the contribution of commercial archaeology since 1990* London, The Society for the Promotion of Roman Studies Britannia Monograph 27

Fulford, M. and Timby, J. 2010 *Late Iron Age and Roman Silchester. Excavations on the site of the forum-basilica 1977, 1980–86* London, The Society for the Promotion of Roman Studies Britannia Monograph 15

Fulford, M., Clarke, A. and Eckardt, H. 2006 *Life and labour in late Roman Silchester. Excavations in Insula IX since 1997* London, The Society for the Promotion of Roman Studies Britannia Monograph 22

Fulford, M., Clarke, A., Durham, E. and Pankhurst, N. 2018 *Late Iron Age Calleva. The pre-conquest occupation at Silchester insula IX* London, The Society for the Promotion of Roman Studies Britannia Monograph 32

Funari, P.P.A. 1996 *Dressel 20 inscriptions from Britain and the consumption of Spanish olive oil* Oxford, British Archaeological Reports British Series 250

Gaimster, D.R.M. 1997 *German stoneware 1200–1900: archaeology and cultural history* London, British Museum

Gaimster, D.R.M. (ed.) 1999a *Maiolica in the north. The archaeology of tin-glazed earthenware in north-west Europe c.1500–1600* London, British Museum Occasional Paper 122

Gaimster, D.R.M. 1999b 'Imported maiolica vases bearing the royal coats of arms of England: a reconsideration', in Gaimster (ed.) 1999a, 141–5

Gaimster, D.R.M. 1999c 'Maiolica in the North: the shock of the new', in Gaimster (ed.) 1999a, 1–3

Gaimster, D.R.M. and Gilchrist, R. (eds) 2003 *The archaeology of Reformation 1480–1580* Leeds, Society of Post-Medieval Archaeology Monograph 1

Gaimster, D.R.M. and Hughes, M. 1999a 'The earliest maiolica stove in north-west Europe: re-analysis of the Dissolution finds from the Abbey of St Mary Graces London', in Gaimster 1999a, 185–8

Gaimster, D.R.M. and Hughes, M. 1999b 'South Netherlands maiolica floor tiles from the Broad Arrow tower, Tower of London', in Gaimster (ed.) 1999a, 175–9

Gaimster, D.R.M. and Nenk, B. 1997 'English households in transition c.1450–1550: the ceramic evidence', in D.R.M. Gaimster and P. Stamper (eds) 1997, 171–95

Gaimster, D.R.M. and Redknap, M. (eds) 1992 *Everyday and exotic pottery from Europe: studies in honour of John G. Hurst* Oxford, Oxbow Books

Gaimster, D.R.M. and Stamper, P. (eds) 1997 *The age of transition: the archaeology of English culture 1400–1600,* Oxford, Oxbow Books

Gaimster, M., Haith, C., Bradley, J. and Beaumont James, T., 1998 'Medieval Britain and Ireland in 1997', *Medieval Archaeology* 42, 107–90

Gallant, L. and Silvester, R.J. 1985 'An excavation on the Iron Age hillfort at Berry Down, Newton Abbot', *Proceedings of the Devon Archaeological Society* 43, 39–49

Gallois, R.W. 2004 'The stratigraphy of the Upper Greensand (Cretaceous) of south-west England', *Geoscience in south-west England* 11, 21–36

Galvan, L. and Sánchez, Á. 2005 'Intervención arqueológica preventiva: vigilancia arqueólogica de movimientos de tierras, C/Tetuán No 41, Lebrija, Sevilla', *Anuario de Arqueología Andaluza 2005*, 2883–8

Gardiner, J. (ed.) 2000 *Resurgam! Archaeology at Stonehouse, Mount Batten and Mount Wise Regeneration Areas, Plymouth* Plymouth, Plymouth Archaeology Occasional Paper 5

Gardner, C. 2009 *The Roman fort by Bainbridge: the examination of metalworking debris* Portsmouth, English Heritage (Research Department Report Series 16/2009)

Gardner, C. 2018 *Metalworking crucibles in Roman Britain* Unpublished PhD thesis, University College London [http://discovery.ucl.ac.uk/10056167/]

Gardner, C. and Marshall, M. forthcoming 'Crucibles', in Marshall and Wardle forthcoming

Garwood, P., Jennings, D., Skeates, R. and Toms, J. (eds) 1991 *Sacred and profane: proceedings of a conference on archaeology, ritual and religion, Oxford 1989* Oxford, Oxford Committee for Archaeology

Gaskell Brown, C. (ed.) 1986 *Plymouth excavations: the medieval waterfront, Woolster Street and Castle Street* Plymouth, Plymouth Museum Archaeological Series 3

Gaspar, A. and Gomes, A. 2012 'A cerâmica moderna do Castelo de S. Jorge: produção local de cerâmica comum, pintada a branco, moldada e vidrada e de faiança', in Teixeira and Bettencourt (eds) 2012, 719–32

Gaullieur, M.E. 1876 'Notes sur quelques artistes ou artisans bordelais oubliés ou peu connus', *Bulletin de la Société archéologique de Bordeaux* 3, 109–28.

Gent, T.H., Stead, P. and Woodgate, R. 2011 *Archaeological building survey, trench evaluation and watching brief at the former West of England Eye Infirmary, Magdalen Road, Exeter* Exeter Archaeology report 11.58 [ADS: https://doi.org/10.5284/1012251]

Gerrard, C.M. and Gutiérrez, A. 1991 'The thin-section analysis and macroscopic characterisation of some medieval and post-medieval pottery from northern Spain', in Middleton and Freestone (eds) 1991, 113–35

Gerrard, C.M., Gutiérrez, A. and Vince, A. (eds) 1995 *Spanish medieval ceramics in Spain and the British Isles* Oxford, British Archaeological Reports International Series 610

Gerrard, C.M., Gutiérrez, A., Hurst, J.G. and Vince, A.G. 1995 'A guide to Spanish medieval pottery', in Gerrard *et al.* (eds) 1995, 281–96

Gerrard, J. 2011 'Roman pottery', in Douglas *et al.* 2011, 61–86

Gerrard, J. (ed.) 2016 *Romano-British pottery in the fifth century*, Internet Archaeology Issue 41 [IA: https://intarch.ac.uk/journal/issue41/index.html]

Giertz, W. 1996 'Middle Meuse Valley ceramics of the Huy type: a preliminary analysis', *Medieval Ceramics* 20, 33–64

Gilchrist, R. and Green, C. 2015 *Glastonbury Abbey: archaeological investigations 1904–79* London, The Society of Antiquaries of London

Gilchrist, R. and Reynolds, A. (eds) 2009 *Reflections: 50 years of medieval archaeology 1957–2007* Leeds, Maney Publishing

Gilchrist, R. and Sloane, B. 2005 *Requiem: the medieval monastic cemetery in Britain* London, Museum of London Archaeological Service

Gluhak, T.L. and Hofmeister, W. 2011 'Geochemical provenance analyses of Roman lava millstones north of the Alps: a study of their distribution and implications for the beginning of Roman lava quarrying in the Eifel region (Germany)', *Journal of Archaeological Science* 38, 1603–20

Goggin, J.M. 1968 *Spanish maiolica in the New World: types of the sixteenth to eighteenth centuries* New Haven, Yale University Publications in Anthropology 72

Gonçalves, M.J. and Gómez-Martínez, S. (eds) 2016 *10th International conference on medieval pottery in the Mediterranean (X CICM2) Silves – Mértola, 22–27 October 2012* Mértola Campo Arqueológico de Mértola,

González Martí, M. 1944 *Cerámica del Levante Español siglos medievales: loza* 1 Barcelona, Editorial Labor

Good, G.L., Jones, R.H. and Ponsford, M.W. (eds) 1991 *Waterfront archaeology: proceedings of the third international conference, Bristol, 1988* York, Council for British Archaeology Research Report 74

Good, O. 2016 *Land at Tithe Barn Green, Monkerton, Exeter Devon* Cotswold Archaeology report 15853 [ADS: https://doi.org/10.5284/1040798]

Goodburn, D. 1995 'Beyond the post-hole: notes on stratigraphy and timber buildings from a London perspective', in Shepard (ed.) 1995, 43–52

Goodburn, R. 1976 'Roman Britain in 1975', *Britannia* 7, 290–392

Goodburn, R. 1978 'Roman Britain in 1977', *Britannia*, 9, 403–85

Goodburn, R. 1979 'Roman Britain in 1978', *Britannia*, 10, 267–364

Goodchild R.G. 1952 'Structural remains of the Roman period found in Exeter before 1942', in Fox 1952a, 98–104

Goodwin, N. 2007 *Archaeological monitoring and recording in Exeter Cathedral Yard* Exeter Archaeology report 07.72

Goodwin, N. and Gent, T.H. 2007 *Archaeological monitoring and recording at The Deanery, Exeter* Exeter Archaeology report 07.39

Gover, J.E.B., Mawer, A. and Stenton, F.M. 1932 *The place-names of Devon. Part 2* Cambridge, Cambridge University Press

Govier, L. 2017 *Bishop's Court Extension, Sidmouth, Exeter, Devon* AC Archaeology report ACD1455/2/1 [ADS: https://doi.org/10.5284/1052995]

Gowland, R. and Tompson, T. 2013 *Human identity and identification* Cambridge, Cambridge University Press

Gray, T. 2001 *Elizabethan Devon* Exeter, The Mint Press

Gray, T. 2005 *The chronicle of Exeter, 1205–1722* Exeter, The Mint Press

Green, C. 2017 'Querns and millstones in late Iron Age, and Roman London and south-east England', in Bird 2017, 156–179

Greene, J.P. and Greene, K.T. 1970 'A trial excavation on a Romano-British site at Clanacombe, Thurlestone, 1969', *Proceedings of the Devon Archaeological Society* 28, 130–136

Greene, K. 1978 'Roman trade between Britain and the Rhine provinces: the evidence of pottery to c AD 250', in du Plat Taylor and Cleere (eds) 1978, 52–8

Greene, K. 1979 *The Pre-Flavian fine wares, report on the excavations at Usk 1965–1976* Cardiff, University of Wales Press

Greene, K. 1991 'Pre-Flavian fine wares', in Holbrook and Bidwell 1991, 72–5

Greene, K.T. 1993 'The fortress coarseware', in Manning 1993, 3–124

Greenfield, E. 1964 'Excavation of a bombed site in Chapel St, Exeter', *Report and Transactions of the. Devonshire Association* 96, 339–79

Grew, F.O., Hassall, M.W.C. and Tomlin, R.S.O. 1980 'Roman Britain in 1979', *Britannia* 11, 346–417

Grew, F.O., Hassall, M.W.C. and Tomlin, R.S.O. 1981 'Roman Britain in 1980', *Britannia* 12, 313–96

Griffin, R.C. 2017 'Urbanization, economic change, and dental health in Roman and medieval Britain', *European Journal of Archaeology* 20, 346–67

Griffith, F.M. and Weddell, P. 1996 'Ironworking in the Blackdown Hills: results of recent survey', in Newman (ed.) 1996, 27–34

Griffiths, D.M. and Griffith, F.M. 1984 'An excavation at 39 Fore Street, Totnes', *Proceedings of the Devon Archaeological Society* 42, 77–100

Griffiths, M. 1974 'Recent Work by the Exeter Museums Archaeological Field Unit', *Proceedings of the Devon Archaeological Society* 32, 167–75

Grimes, W.F. 1930 *Holt, Denbighshire: The works-depot of the Twentieth Legion at Castle Lyons* Y Cymmrodor 41, London, Society of Cymmrodorion

Grinsell, L.V., Rahtz, P.A. and Warhurst, A. 1966 *The preparation of archaeological reports* London, John Baker

Grosso, O. and Morazzoni, G. 1939 *Mostra de l'antica maiolica ligure dal secolo XIV al secolo XVIII* Genoa, Ente provinciale per il turismo

Groves, C. 1992 *Dendrochronological analysis of timbers from New Baxtergate, Grimsby, Humberside 1986* English Heritage, Ancient Monuments Laboratory Report 8/92

Groves, C. 1998 'Appendix 7: dendrochronology', in S. Brown 1998, 90–9

Groves, C. 2004 'Dendrochronological analysis of timbers from Bowhill', in Blaylock 2004, 243–67

Groves, C. 2005 *Dendrochronological research in Devon: phase 1* English Heritage, Centre for Archaeology Report 56/2005

Groves, C. 2006 *Leigh Barton, Churchstow, Devon: scientific dating report – tree-ring analysis of timbers* English Heritage, Research Department Report Series 10/2006

Groves, C. and Hillam, J. 1993 *Tree-ring analysis of oak timbers from South Yarde, Rose Ash, Devon, 1992* English Heritage, Ancient Monuments Laboratory Report 36/93

Groves, J. 1999 'Pomeroy Wood', in Fitzpatrick *et al.* 1999, 224–384

Gual Camarena, M. 1976 *Vocabulario del comercio medieval* Barcelona, El Albir

Gutiérrez, A. 1999 'Some Italo-Netherlandish pottery from Winchester and Wickham, Hampshire', in Gaimster 1999a, 151–3

Gutiérrez, A. 2000 *Mediterranean pottery in Wessex households (13th to 17th centuries)* Oxford, British Archaeological Reports British Series 306

Gutiérrez, A. 2003 'A shipwreck cargo of Sevillian pottery from the Studland Bay wreck, Dorset, UK', *International Journal of Nautical Archaeology* 32 (1), 24–41

Gutiérrez, A. 2006 'Appendix 4: the sherd of Spanish pottery', in Parker *et al.* 2006, 193–240

Gutiérrez, A. 2007a 'Portuguese coarsewares in early modern England: reflections on an exceptional pottery assemblage from Southampton', *Post-Medieval Archaeology* 41 (1), 64–79

Gutiérrez, A. 2007b 'Post-Roman pottery', in Gerrard *et al.* 2007, 601–71

Gutiérrez, A. 2009 'The pottery', in Parham (ed.) 2009

Gutiérrez, A. 2012 'Of sundry colours and moulds: imports of early modern pottery along the Atlantic seaboard', in Teixeira and Bettencourt (eds) 2012, 37–50

Gutiérrez, A. forthcoming 'Material culture sealed by the 1522 landslide in Vila Franca do Campo, Azores'

Gutiérrez, A. and Brown, D.H. 1999 'Italo-Netherlandish Maiolica from Southampton', in Gaimster 1999a, 147–50

Haarer, F. (eds) 2014 *AD 410: The history and archaeology of late and post-Roman Britain* London, Society for the Promotion of Roman Studies

Hadley, D. 2001 *Death in medieval England* Stroud, Tempus Publishing Ltd

Haggarty, G.R. 2019 *French pottery in Scotland* c. *1250*–c. *1650: ceramic resource disk* Circulated privately

Haines, C. 2013 *Shepherd's Lane, Teignmouth, Devon* Cotswold Archaeology report 12373 [ADS: https://doi.org/10.5284/1028778]

Hall, D.W. (ed.) 2012 *Perth High Street: archaeological excavation 1975–77. Fascicule 2: the ceramics, the metalwork and the wood* Perth, Tayside and Fife Hall

Hall, D.W., Haggerty, G. and Vince, A. 2012 'The medieval pottery', in Hall (ed.) 2012, 37–73

Hall, J. 2005 'The shopkeepers and craft-workers of Roman London', in MacMahon and Price (eds) 2005, 125–44

Hall, J. and Wright, S.M. (eds) 2015 *Conservation and discovery – Peterborough Cathedral nave ceiling and related structures* London, Museum of London Archaeology

Hall, M.E.P. 1994 *Archaeological evaluation at Knapp's Site, Haven Road, Exeter* Exeter Museums Archaeological Field Unit report 94.86

Hall, M.E.P. 1995 *Archaeological recording at Exeter Quay, 1988–89* Exeter Archaeology report 95.41 [ADS: https://doi.org/10.5284/1035221]

Hall, M.E.P. and Blaylock, S.R. 1991 *Bowhill, Exeter, archive report I, the excavations of 1989* Exeter Museums Archaeological Field Unit report 91.05

Hall, M.E.P. and. Blaylock S.R. 1994 *Bowhill Exeter, archive report V, the excavations of 1993 in the south and west ranges* Exeter Museums Archaeological Field Unit report 94.106

Hall, M.E.P. and Sage, A.J. 1994 *Archaeological evaluation at Knapman's Yard, Friernhay Street, Exeter* Exeter Museums Archaeological Field Unit report 94.84

Hall, M.E.P., Henderson, C.G. and Watts, M.A. 1995 *Summary report on an archaeological evaluation of the former GPO sorting office and RSPCA site, Smythen Street/Market Street, Exeter* Exeter Archaeology report 95.50

Hanson, W.S. 2007 *Elginhaugh: a Flavian fort and its annexe* (2 vols) London, The Society for the Promotion of Roman Studies Britannia Monograph 23

Hanson, W.S., Daniels, C.M., Dore, J.N. and Gillam J.P. 1979 'The Agricolan supply base at Red House, Corbridge', *Archaeologia Aeliana*, 5th series 7, 1–98

Harden, D.B. (ed.) 1956 *Dark-age Britain, studies presented to E.T. Leeds* London, Methuen

Hartley, B.R. and Dickinson, B.M. 1993 'The samian stamps', in Manning 1993, 207–15

Hartley, K.F. 1991 'The mortaria', in Holbrook and Bidwell 1991, 189–215

Hartley, K.F. 1992 'Mortaria', in Holbrook and Bidwell 1992, 62–3

Hartley, K.F. 1993 'The mortaria', in Manning 1993, 389–437

Hartley, K.F. 2007 'Mortaria', in Hanson 2007, 326–78

Hartley, K.F. and Tomber, R. 2006 *A mortarium bibliography for Roman Britain* Journal of Roman Pottery Studies 13, Oxford, Oxbow Books

Harvey, B.F. 2006 'Monastic pittances in the Middle Ages', in Woolgar *et al.* (eds) 2006, 215–27

Harvey, H. 2011 *The story of Exeter* Stroud, Phillimore

Haslam, J. 1984 (ed.) *Anglo-Saxon towns in southern England* Chichester, Phillimore

Hassall, J. 1979 'North of the Golden Eagle Public House: lime kiln', in Baker *et al.* 1979, 46–51

Hassall, W.M.C., Wilson, D.R., Wright, R.P. and Rea, J. 1972 'Roman Britain in 1971', *Britannia* 3, 298–367

Hayfield, C. 1984 'Head of an aquamanile', in Allan 1984a, 76

Hein, A., Muller, N.S., Day, P.M., and Kilikoglou, V. 2008 'Thermal conductivity of archaeological ceramics: the effect of inclusions, porosity and firing temperature', *Thermochimica Acta* 480, 35–42

Henderson, C.G. 1981 'Exeter', in Milne and Hobley (eds) 1981, 119–22

Henderson, C.G. 1983 'A new bell-founding workshop [excavated in Paul Street, Exeter: late 17th–early 18th century]', *Historical Metallurgy* 17, 43

Henderson, C.G. 1984 'Paul Street excavations', *Archaeology in Exeter 1983/4* Exeter, Exeter Museums Archaeological Field Unit, 1–13

Henderson, C.G. 1985a 'Archaeological excavations at Alphington Street, St Thomas', *Exeter Archaeology 1984/5* Exeter, Exeter Museums Archaeological Field Unit, 1–15

Henderson, C.G. 1985b 'Paul Street excavations', *Exeter Archaeology 1984/5* Exeter, Exeter Museums Archaeological Field Unit, 24–9

Henderson, C.G. 1987 'Excavations at Hayes Barton, St Thomas', *Exeter Archaeology 1985/6* Exeter, Exeter Museums Archaeological Field Unit, 53–4

Henderson, C.G. 1988 'Exeter (*Isca Dumnoniorum*)', in Webster (ed.) 1988, 91–119

Henderson, C.G. 1990 'The Quay House and development of Exeter Quay' in Cooper (ed.) 1990, 52–5

Henderson, C.G. 1991a 'Aspects of the planning of the Neronian fortress of Legio II Augusta at Exeter' in Maxfield and Dobson (eds) 1991, 73–83

Henderson, C.G. 1991b 'The archaeology of Exeter Quay', *Devon Archaeology* 4, 1–15

Henderson, C.G. 1996 *Archaeological survey of Cricklepit Mill, Exeter. Part 1: the site* Exeter Archaeology report 96.36

Henderson, C.G. 1999 'The design of the Neronian fortress baths at Exeter', in Delaine and Johnston 1999, 164–83

Henderson, C.G. 2001 'The development of the south gate of Exeter and its role in the city's defences', *Proceedings of the Devon Archaeological Society* 59, 45–124

Henderson, C.G. and Bidwell, P.T. 1982 'The Saxon minster at Exeter', in Pearce (ed.) 1982, 145–75

Henderson, C.G. and Collings, A.G. 1997 *Archaeological assessment of the Guinness Trust Exeter Foyer site, Cricklepit Lower Mills, Exeter* Exeter Archaeology report 97.81

Henderson, C.G. and Holbrook, N. 1987 'The size of the Roman legionary fortress at Exeter', in *Exeter Archaeology 1985/6* Exeter, Exeter Museums Archaeological Field Unit, 51

Henderson, C.G., Dunkley, J.A. and Juddery, J.Z. 1987 'Archaeological investigations at Exeter Quay', *Exeter Archaeology 1985/6* Exeter, Exeter Museums Archaeological Field Unit, 1–19

Henderson, C.G., Salvatore, J.P. and Earwood, C. 1993a *Excavations at Goldsmith Street, Exeter, 1971–72. Part 1: Roman military* Exeter Museums Archaeological Field Unit report 93.34 [ADS: https://doi.org/10.5284/1035176]

Henderson, C.G., Salvatore, J.P. and Earwood, C. 1993b *Excavations at Trichay Street, Exeter, 1972–73. Part 1: Roman military* Exeter Museums Archaeological Field Unit report 93.35 [ADS: https://doi.org/10.5284/1035179]

Henderson, C.G., Bedford, J.B. and Colling, A.G. 1999 *Archaeological assessment and field evaluation of Princesshay Redevelopments Scheme* Exeter Archaeology report 99.15

Herz, N. and Garrison, E.G., 1998 *Geological methods for archaeology* New York and Oxford, Oxford University Press

Higgott, S. 2014 'Survey of Venetian and façon de venise enamelled and gilded glass made *c.* 1500–1550 and excavated from reliably dated contexts in Great Britain', in Barovier Mentasti and Tonini (eds) 2014, 69–90

Higham, R.A. and Henderson, C.G. 2011 'Danes Castle, Exeter: excavations 1992–3', *Proceedings of the Devon Archaeological Society* 69, 125–56

Higham, R.A., Allan, J.P. and Blaylock, S.R. 1982 'Excavations at Okehampton Castle, Devon: Part 2 – the bailey', *Proceedings of the Devon Archaeological Society* 40, 25–7

Hill, J. and Rowsome, P. 2011 *Roman London and the Walbrook stream crossing* London, Museum of London Archaeology Monograph 37

Hillam, J. 1978a *Tree-ring analysis of Trichay Street timbers, Exeter* English Heritage, Ancient Monuments Laboratory Report 2510

Hillam, J. 1978b *Exe Bridge: dendrochronological results* English Heritage, Ancient Monuments Laboratory Report 2729

Hillam, J. 1984a 'Tree-ring analysis of Trichay Street timber, Exeter', in Allan 1984a, 315–8

Hillam, J. 1984b 'Catalogue of Trichay Street timber', in Allan 1984b, 127–33

Hillam, J. 1984c *Tree-ring analysis of four oak timbers from Paul Street, Exeter (PS '82)* English Heritage, Ancient Monuments Laboratory Report 4164

Hillson, S. 1996 *Dental anthropology* Cambridge, Cambridge University Press

Hingley, R. 2018 *Londinium. A biography* London, Bloomsbury Academic

Historic England 2015 *Archaeometallurgy. Guidelines for best practice* London, Historic England

Hodge, A.T. 1992 *Roman aqueducts and water supply* London, Duckworth

Hodges, R. 1981 *The Hamwih pottery: the local and imported wares from 30 years' excavations at Middle Saxon Southampton and their European context* York, Council for British Archaeology Research Report 37

Hodges, R. and Mainman, A. 1984 'The Saxo-Norman imported pottery', in Allan 1984a, 13–18

Hodgson, N. 2003 *The Roman fort at Wallsend (*Segedunum*). Excavations in 1997–8* Newcastle upon Tyne, Tyne and Wear Museums Archaeological Monograph 2

Hodgson, N. and Bidwell, P. 2004 'Auxiliary barracks in a new light: recent discoveries on Hadrian's Wall', *Britannia* 35, 121–57

Hoffmann, B. 1995 'The quarters of legionary centurions of the principate', *Britannia* 26, 107–51

Holbrook, N. 1987 'Trial excavations at Honeyditches and the nature of the Roman occupation at Seaton', *Proceedings of the Devon Archaeological Society* 45, 59–74

Holbrook, N. 1989 'Roman lead sling-shot and an aureus from near Hawkesdown Hill hillfort, Axminster', *Proceedings of the Devon Archaeological Society* 47, 117–18

Holbrook, N. 1991 'The coarse pottery', in Maxfield 1991, 67–77

Holbrook, N. 1998 *Cirencester: the Roman town defences, public buildings and shops* Cirencester, Cirencester Excavations 5

Holbrook, N., 2001 'Coastal trade around the south-west peninsula of Britain in the later Roman period: a summary of the evidence', *Proceedings of the Devon Archaeological Society* 59, 149–158

Holbrook, N. 2015 'The towns of south-west England', in Fulford and Holbrook (eds) 2015, 90–116

Holbrook, N. 2018 'Discussion', in Brindle *et al.* 2018, 168–73

Holbrook, N. and Bidwell, P. 1991 *Roman finds from Exeter* Exeter City Council and the University of Exeter, Exeter Archaeological reports 4

Holbrook, N. and Bidwell, P.T. 1992 'Roman pottery from Exeter, 1980–1990', *Journal of Roman Pottery Studies* 5, 35–80

Holbrook, N. and Fox, A. 1987 'Excavations in the legionary fortress at Bartholomew Street East, Exeter, 1959', *Proceedings of the Devon Archaeological Society* 45, 23–57

Holbrook, N. and Salvatore, J.P. 1998 'The street system', in Holbrook 1998, 19–34

Holbrook, N. and Shiel, N. 2002 'A Claudian coin hoard from Roborough, Devon', *Proceedings of the Devon Archaeological Society* 60, 215–8

Holbrook, N., Johnson, P. and Thompson, L. 1989 'Roman mosaics from Catherine Street, Exeter', *Proceedings of the Devon Archaeological Society* 49, 43–52

Holbrook, N., Johnson, P. and Thompson, L. 1990 *Roman mosaics from Catherine Street* Exeter Museums Archaeological Field Unit report 90.39

Holdsworth, C. 1980 'Saint Boniface the monk', in Reuter (ed.) 1980, 47–68

Holland, H. and Turekian, K. (eds) 2014 *Treatise on geochemistry* Boston, Elsevier

Holloway, J. 2008 'Charcoal burial: a minority burial rite in early medieval Europe', in Murphy (ed.) 2008, 131–47

Holloway, J. 2010 'Material symbolism and death: charcoal burial in later Anglo-Saxon England', in Buckberry (ed.) 2010, 83–92

Hollstein, E. 1980 *Mitteleuropäische eichenchronologie* Mainz am Rhein, Phillip von Zabern

Holt, R. and Rosser, G. (eds) 1990 *The medieval town: a reader in English urban history 1200–1540* London, Longman

Honey, W.B. 1962 *English pottery and porcelain* London, A. & C. Black

Hook, D.R. and Gaimster, D.R.M. (eds) 1991 *Trade and discovery: the scientific study of artefacts from post-medieval Europe and beyond* London, British Museum Occasional Paper 109

Horner, L., Parry, S. and Lott, G. 2017 *Strategic stone study. A building stone atlas of Devon* Swindon, Historic England

Horsey, I.P. 1992 *Excavations in Poole 1973–1983* Dorchester, Dorset Natural History and Archaeological Society Monograph 10

Horsman, V., Milne, C. and Milne, G. 1988 *Aspects of Saxo-Norman London: I building and street development* London, London and Middlesex Archaeological Society

Hoskins, W.G. 1957 *Exeter in the seventeenth century: tax and rate assessments 1602–1699* Devon Cornwall Records Society New Series 2

Hoskins, W.G. (edited and updated by H. Harvey) 2004 *Two thousand years in Exeter: W.G. Hoskins* Chichester, Phillimore

Howard, M. 1998 *The Vyne: Hampshire* London, National Trust

Howard, R., Laxton, R.R. and Litton, C.D. 1999 *Tree-ring analysis of timbers from Exeter Guildhall, High Street, Exeter, Devon* English Heritage, Ancient Monuments Laboratory Report 56–1999

Howard, R., Laxton, R.R. and Litton, C.D. 2001a *Tree-ring analysis of timbers from Exeter Cathedral, Exeter, Devon* English Heritage, Centre for Archaeology Report 47–2001

Howard, R., Laxton, R.R. and Litton, C.D. 2001b *Tree-ring analysis of timbers from Exeter Cathedral, Exeter, Devon. Part 2, crossing and western roofs* English Heritage, Centre for Archaeology Report 54–2002

Howard, R., Laxton, R.R. and Litton, C.D. 2004 'Tree-ring analysis of timbers from four of the Exeter group of medieval roofs', in Blaylock 2004, 267–76

Hughes, M.J. 1991 'Provenance studies of Spanish medieval tin-glazed pottery by Neutron Activation Analysis', *Archaeological Sciences 1989*, 54–68

Hughes, M.J. 1995a 'Application of scientific analytical methods to Spanish medieval ceramics', in Gerrard *et al.* (eds) 2015, 359–69

Hughes, M.J. 1995b 'Neutron activation analysis of post-medieval European earthenware ceramics: a survey of current projects at the British Museum', in Hook and Gaimster (eds) 1995, 55–68

Hughes, M.J. 1998 'ICP-AES analysis of south Somerset pottery and south Netherlands tin-glazed maiolica from Cleeve Abbey', in Allan 1998, 59–75

Hughes, M.J. 2002 'Report on the analysis by Inductively-Coupled Plasma Atomic Emission Spectrometry (ICP-AES) of late 13th- to 14th-century pottery sherds from Haycroft Farm, Membury', in Allan and Langman 2002, 67–72

Hughes, M.J. 2002–3 'Analysis by Inductively-Coupled Plasma Atomic Emission Spectrometry (ICP-AES) of imported northern French pottery, including a sherd found at Althea Library, Padstow', in Manning and Stead 2003, 99–105

Hughes, M.J. 2003a 'Report on the analysis by Inductively-Coupled Plasma Atomic Emission Analysis (ICP–AES) of 13th-century pottery sherds from Sherborne Old Castle', in Allan 2003, 79–82

Hughes, M.J. 2003b 'Chemical analyses of Spanish ceramics from the Studland Bay wreck by ICP-AES and neutron activation', in Gutiérrez 2003, 37–41

Hughes, M.J. 2005 'The analysis by inductively coupled plasma -atomic emission analysis (ICP-AES) and -mass spectrometry (ICP-MS) of medieval pottery from Pigs Paradise, Lundy Island', in Allan and Blaylock 2005, 78–88

Hughes, M.J. 2008 'Inductively coupled plasma analysis of tin-glazed tiles and vessels produced at several centres in London', in Tyler *et al.* 2008, 120–31

Hughes, M.J. 2009a 'ICP-AES analysis of ceramic building material', in Drury 2009, 366–79

Hughes, M.J. 2009b 'Neutron activation analyses of selected maiolica from the British Museum collection', in Thornton and Wilson 1999, 719–21

Hughes, M.J. 2009–10 'Appendix 1: Inductively coupled plasma analysis of tin-glazed pottery and tiles from Godolphin House', in Allan 2009–10, 48–9, 287–92, colour pl. 13

Hughes, M.J. 2010a 'The analysis by Inductively Coupled Plasma-Atomic Emission Analysis (ICP-AES) and -Mass Spectrometry (ICP-MS) of Saxo-Norman pottery from Somerset', in Allan *et al.* 2010, 177–82

Hughes, M.J. 2010b 'Scientific analysis', in Betts and Weinstein 2010, 44–9

Hughes, M.J. 2013 *Chemical characterization by ICPS of tiles and pottery from Carew Manor* Unpublished report

Hughes, M.J. 2014a 'Appendix: Results of inductively-coupled plasma analysis of redware and maiolica', in Masser *et al.* 2014, 51–2

Hughes, M.J. 2014b, chapter 10 Appendix: Results of inductively coupled plasma analysis of redware and maiolica, in. Masser *et al,* 51-52

Hughes, M.J. 2014c 'Plasma spectrometry analysis (Atomic Emission ICP-AES) of post-Roman pottery from Calstock', in Allan 2014c, 70–7

Hughes, M.J. 2015a 'Inductively coupled plasma spectrometry (ICPS) analysis of tin-glazed pottery from Glastonbury Abbey', in Gilchrist and Green, 268–70

Hughes, M.J. 2015b 'Summary report on the ICP Plasma Spectrometry results on Saxon coarsewares and late medieval jugs from Glastonbury Abbey', in Allan *et al.* 2015a, 25–7

Hughes, M.J. 2015c *Plasma spectrometry analysis (ICP) of pottery from Marischal College, Aberdeen (site E93)* Unpublished report

Hughes, M.J., 2016 'Chemical analyses of Italian maiolica', in Wrathmell 2016, 69–73

Hughes, M.J. 2018 *Plasma Spectrometry analysis of three tiles from St Mary's church Kilkenny* Unpublished report

Hughes, M.J. 2019 'Plasma spectrometry analyses (ICPS) of French and English pottery from Tresco Channel', in Allan *et al.* 2019, 19–36

Hughes, M.J. and Gaimster, D. 1999 'Neutron activation analyses of maiolica from London, Norwich, the Low Countries and Italy, in Gaimster (ed.) 1999a, 57–89

Hughes, M.J. and Gaimster, D.R.M. 2002 'Neutron activation analyses of maiolica by the British Museum', in Veeckman (ed.) 2002, 215–41

Hughes, M.J. and Vince, A.G. 1986 'Neutron activation analysis and petrology of Hispano-Moresque pottery', in Olin and Blackman (eds) 1986, 353–67

Hughes, S. 2012 *Underground Passages, Exeter* AC Archaeology report ACD470/2/0 [ADS: https://doi.org/10.5284/1020069]

Hughes, S. 2015 'A prehistoric and Romano-British settlement at Aller Cross, Kingkerswell', *Proceedings of the Devon Archaeological Society* 73, 91–184

Hughes, S. 2016 *Land to the rear of 31 Cowick Street, Exeter, Devon* AC Archaeology report ACD1051/2/1 [ADS: https://doi.org/10.5284/1047654]

Hughes, S. 2019 *Renslade House, Bonhay Road, Exeter, Devon* AC Archaeology report ACD1659/1/0

Hurford, M., Howard, R., Arnold, A. and Tyers, C. 2009 *Exeter Cathedral, Exeter, Devon: tree-ring analysis of timbers from the Song School door* English Heritage, Research Department Report Series 35–2009

Hurst, H. 1985 *Kingsholm. Excavations at Kingsholm Close and other sites with a discussion of the archaeology of the area* Gloucester, Gloucester Archaeological Reports Volume 1

Hurst, J.G. 1970 'The Old Manor, Askett, appendix 1. South Netherlands Majolica', *Records of Buckinghamshire* 18, 362–4

Hurst, J.G. 1977a 'Spanish pottery imported into medieval Britain', *Medieval Archaeology* 21, 68–105

Hurst, J.G. 1977b 'Annotations on Anglo-Saxon pottery', *Medieval Ceramics* 1, 75–8

Hurst, J.G. 1987 'The imported wares', in Roebuck and Coppack 1987, 18–20

Hurst, J.G. 1991a 'Post-medieval pottery from Seville imported into north-west Europe', in Hook and Gaimster (eds) 1991, 45–54

Hurst, J.G. 1991b 'Italian pottery imported into Britain and Ireland', in Wilson (ed.) 1991, 212–31

Hurst, J.G. 1999 'Sixteenth-century south Netherlands Maiolica imported into Britain and Ireland', in Gaimster (ed.) 1999a, 91–106

Hurst, J.G. 2002 'Distribution and consumption of majolica in Britain', in Veeckman 2002, 313–31

Hurst, J.G. and Le Patourel, J. 1999 'Imported maiolica floor tiles from Whitehall Palace, London', in Gaimster (ed.) 1999a, 181–3

Hurst, J.G., Neal, D.S. and van Beuningen, H.J.E. 1986 *Pottery produced and traded in north-west Europe 1350–1650* Rotterdam Papers 6, Rotterdam, Museum Boymans-van Beuningen

Husi P. 2003 *La céramique médiévale et moderne du Centre-Ouest de la France (11e–17e siècle): Chrono-typologie de la céramique et approvisionnement de la vallée de la*

Loire moyenne (1Cédérom), 20e Supplément à la Revue Archéologique du Centre de la France Tours, FERAC

Irish, J.D. and Scott, G.R. (eds) 2016 *A companion to dental anthropology* Chichester, Wiley Blackwell

Isham, K. 2000 *Lime kilns and limeburners in Cornwall: an introduction* St Austell, Cornish Hillside Publications

Jackson, R. (ed.) 2006 *Excavations at St James's Priory, Bristol* Oxford, Regional Archaeological Services

James, S. 1988 'A reassessment of the chronological and typological framework of the Spanish Olive Jar', *Historical Archaeology* 22 (1), 43–66

Jarrett, C. and Blackmore, L. 2015 'Italian pottery in medieval and post-medieval London', *Archeologia Postmedievale* 19, 89–116

Jaspers, N.L. 2011 '"Clean, cheap & truly more enjoyable": Italian maiolica excavated in the Netherlands (1550–1700): the supremacy of Ligurian merchandise and rarities from other production regions', *Archeologia Postmedievale* 15, 11–39

Jenkins, A. 1806 *The history and description of the city of Exeter and its environs ancient and modern* Exeter, P. Hedgeland

Jenkins, D.T. (ed.) 2003 *The Cambridge history of western textiles. Part 1* Cambridge, Cambridge University Press

Johnson, E.V., Parmenter, P.C.R. and Outram, A.K. 2016 'A new approach to profiling taphonomic history through bone fracture analysis, with an example application to the Linearbandkeramik site of Ludwinowo 7', *Journal of Archaeological Science Report* 9, 623–9

Johnson, P. and Haynes, I. (eds) 1996 *Architecture in Roman Britain* York, Council for British Archaeology Research Report 94, 56–69

Johnstone, M. (ed.) 1999 *London eats out: 500 years of capital dining* London, Philip Wilson

Jones, M.J., Stocker, D. and Vince, A. 2003 *The city by the pool: assessing the archaeology of the city of Lincoln* Lincoln Archaeology Studies 10 Oxford, Oxbow Books

Jones, R. 1991 'Industry and environment in medieval Bristol', in Good *et al.* (eds) 1991, 19–26

Juddery, J.Z 1990a *Exebridge wardens' accounts, 1352–1450. Financial summaries and property rentals* Exeter Museums Archaeology Field Unit report 90.27

Juddery, J.Z 1990b *Exebridge wardens' accounts, 1450–1556. Financial summaries and property rentals* Exeter Museums Archaeology Field Unit report 90.30

Juddery, J.Z 1990c *Exebridge wardens' accounts, 1556–1630. Financial summaries and property rentals* Exeter Museums Archaeology Field Unit report 90.31

Juddery, J.Z. and Staniforth, P.R. 1986 *Timber supply for public works I, Exeter 1562–1766* Exeter Museums Archaeology Field Unit report

Juddery, J.Z. and Stoyle, M. 1995 *The aqueducts of medieval Exeter* Exeter Archaeology report 95.44

Katzenberg, M.A. 2000 'Stable isotope analysis: a tool for studying past diet, demography, and life history', in Katzenberg and Saunders (eds) 2008, 305–27

Katzenberg, M.A. and Saunders, S.R. (eds) 2008 *Biological anthropology of the human skeleton* 2nd edition Hoboken, Wiley-Liss

Kaye, J.M. (ed.) 1976 *The cartulary of God's House, Southampton* Southhampton, Southampton Records Series 20, 2 vols

Kearns, T. Martinón-Torres, M. and Rehren, T. 2010 'Metal to mould: alloy identification in experimental casting moulds', *Historical Metallurgy* 44.1, 48–58

Kelly, F.P. 1991 *Medieval art and architecture at Exeter Cathedral* Brit. Archaeol. Ass. Conference Trans. for 1985, London, Routledge

Kemmers, F. 2004 'Caligula on the Lower Rhine: coin finds from the Roman fort of Albaniana (The Netherlands)', *Revue Belge de Numismatique* 150, 15–49

Kendall, M. 2014 *Land north of Wessex Close, Topsham, Exeter, archaeological evaluation report* Wessex Archaeology report 103700.03 [ADS: https://doi.org/10.5284/1044378]

Kent, H.S.K. 1973 *War and trade in the northern seas: Anglo-Scandinavian economic relations in the mid-eighteenth century* Cambridge, Cambridge University Press

Kent, O. 2015 'Wares associated with specialist scientific and technical activities', in Allan *et al.* 2015, 276–8

Kenyon, R.F. 1987 'The Claudian coinage', in N. Crummy (ed.) 1987, 24–41

Kenyon, R.F. 1988 'Countermark PROB on coins of Claudius I', *Numismatic Chronicle* 148, 53–61

Kenyon, R.F. 1992 *The copying of bronze coins of Claudius I in Roman Britain* Unpublished PhD thesis, University College London [http://discovery.ucl.ac.uk/1546590/]

Keppie, L. 1984 *The making of the Roman army. From republic to empire* London, Batsford

Keppie, L.J.F., Esmonde Cleary, A.S., Hassall, M.W.C., Tomlin, R.S.O. and Burnham, B.C. 1999 'Roman Britain in 1998', *Britannia* 30, 319–86

Kerr-Peterson, K. 2015 'The ceramic building material', in Hughes 2015, 153–4

Kerr-Peterson, K. and Passmore, A. 2012 *1–11 Sidwell Street, Exeter, Devon* AC Archaeology report ACD368/2/1 [ADS: https://doi.org/10.5284/1012490]

King, A. 1999 'Diet in the Roman world: a regional inter-site comparison of the mammal bones', *Journal of Roman Archaeology* 12, 68–202

King, A.C. 1996 'The south-east façade of Meonstoke aisled building', in Johnson and Haynes (eds) 1996, 56–69

King, T., Humphery, L. and Hillson, S. 2005 'Linear enamel hypoplasias as indicators of systemic physiological stress: evidence from two known age-at-death and sex populations from post-medieval London', *American Journal of Physical Anthropology* 128, 547–59

Kingdom, M. 2019 *The past people of Exeter: health and status in the Middle Ages* Unpublished PhD thesis, University of Exeter, http://hdl.handle.net/10871/38166

Kingery, W.D. and Lense, E. (eds) 1986 *High technology ceramics: past, present, and future* Westerville (Ohio, The American Ceramic Society

Kirby, J., Nash, S. and Cannon, J. (eds) 2010 *Trade in artists materials, markets and commerce in Europe to 1700* London, Archetype

Kiss, C., Szilágyi, M., Paksy, A. and Poór, G. 2002 'Risk factors for diffuse idiopathic skeletal hyperostosis: a case-control study', *Rheumatology* 41, 27–30

Kjølbye-Biddle, B. 1992 'Dispersal or concentration: the disposal of the Winchester dead over 2000 years', in Bassett (ed.) 1992, 210–47

Kleineke, H. (ed.) 2013 *The chancery case between Nicholas Radford and Thomas Tremayne: the Exeter Depositions of 1439* Exeter, Devon and Cornwall Record Society new series 55

Knight, M. 1991 *Archaeological observations at St Sidwell's churchyard, Exeter* Exeter Museums Archaeological Field Unit report 91.50

Knowles, D. 1963 *The monastic order in England* Cambridge, Cambridge University Press

Knüsel, C. and Ogden, A., 2008 'Paleopathology', in Pearsal (ed.) 2008, 1795–1809

Koenen, C. 1904 'Beschreibung von Novaesium', *Bonner Jahrbücher* 111/112, 97–242

Kowaleski, M. 1990a 'Town and country in late medieval England: the hide and leather trade', in Corfield and Keene (eds) 1990, 57–73

Kowaleski, M. 1990b 'The commercial dominance of a medieval provincial oligarchy: Exeter in the late fourteenth century', in Holt and Rosser (eds) 1990, 184–215

Kowaleski, M. 1995 *Local markets and regional trade in medieval Exeter* Cambridge, Cambridge University Press

Kowaleski, M. 2019 *A guide to the records of medieval Exeter* Unpublished typescript, circulated privately

Krauskopf, K.B. and Bird, D.K. 1995 *Introduction to geochemistry* London, McGraw Hill

Laidlaw, M. 1999 'Ceramic building material', in Fitzpatrick *et al.* 1999, 327

Laidlaw, M. and Mepham, L. 1999 'Pottery', in Fitzpatrick *et al.* 1999, 178–84

Langman, G. and Allan, J.P. 1991 'Inventory of medieval and post-medieval pottery from sites excavated in Exeter 1986–90' Exeter Archaeology report 91.53

Langman, G. and Allan, J.P. 1999 'Inventory of medieval and post-medieval pottery from sites excavated in Exeter 1981–85' Exeter Archaeology report 99.50

Larsen, C.S. 1997 *Bioarchaeology: interpreting behaviour from the human skeleton* Cambridge, Cambridge University Press.

Larsen, C.S. 2002 'Bioarchaeology: the lives and lifestyles of past people', *Journal of Archaeological Research* 10, 119–66

Laubenheimer, F., and Marlière, E. 2010 Échanges et vie économie *dans le nord-ouest des Gaules (Nord/Pas-de-Calais, Picardie, Haute Normandie). Le Témoinage des Amphores du II*[e] *s. av. J.-C. au IV*[e] *s. ap. J.-C.* (2 vols) Franche-Comté, Presses Universitaires de Franche-Comté

Lauritsen, M.L. 2019 *Exeter from fort to city: a faunal perspective* Unpublished PhD thesis, University of Exeter

Lauritsen, M., Allen, R., Alves, J., Ameen, C., Fowler, T., Irving-Pease, E., Larson, G., Murphy, L., Outram, A., Pilgrim, E., Shaw, P. and Sykes, N. 2018 'Celebrating Easter, Christmas and their associated alien fauna', *World Archaeology,* 50 (2), 285–99

Lavagna, R. 1992 'Tipologie della maiolica del Cinquecento dagli scavi del Priamàr a Savona', *Atti XXV convegno internazionale della ceramica* Albisola, Centro ligure per la storia della ceramica, 135–47

Lavagna, R. 2011 'La maiolica ligure del XVI secolo', in Chilosi (ed.) 2011, 31–6

Lawson Jones, A. 2003 *Little Quoit Farm, St Columb Major, Cornwall. Excavation of a Romano-British smithing site* Cornwall Archaeological Unit report 2003R001 [ADS: https://doi.org/10.5284/1028735]

Le vert & le brun 1995 *Le vert & le brun de Kairouan à Avignon, céramiques du Xe au XVe siècle* Marseilles, Musées de Marseille

Leão, M. 1999 *A cerâmica em Vila Nova de Gaia* Vila Nova de Gaia, Fundação Manuel Leão

Leach, P. 1982 *Ilchester. Volume 1: excavations 1974–5* Western Archaeological Trust Monograph 3

Lega-Weekes, E. 1934 'The pre-Reformation history of St Katherine's priory', *Report and Transactions of the Devonshire Association* 66, 181–209

Leins, I. 2013 'Roman coins', in Passmore 2013, Appendix 3

Lemaître, S. 2000 'Les importations d'amphores de Méditerranée orientale à Lyon', *Rei Cretariae Romanae Fautorum Acta 36,* 467–76

Leonardi, C. 2002 'I maiolicari di Casteldurante a Venezia nei secoli XV–XVI', in Bojani 2002, 55–66

Lepine, D.N. and Orme, N. 2003 *Death and memory in medieval Exeter* Exeter, Devon and Cornwall Record Society

Leverett, M. and Valentin, J. 2005 *Archaeological evaluation at Dinham Road, St David's, Exeter* Exeter Archaeology report 05.53 [ADS: https://doi.org/10.5284/1028773]

Leverett, M., Manning, P. and Allan, J. 2011 *A guide to the archives of archaeological projects carried out in Exeter, 1970–90* Exeter Archaeology report 11.26 [http://humanities.exeter.ac.uk/archaeology/research/projects/place_in_time/]

Levitan, B. 1985 'Early 18th-century horncores from Shooting Marsh Stile', in *Exeter Archaeology 1984/5* Exeter, Exeter Museums Archaeological Field Unit, 15–18

Levitan, B. 1987 *Medieval animal husbandry in south west England: a selective review and suggested approach*, in Balaam *et al.* 1987, 51–80

Levitan, B. 1989 'Bone analysis and urban economy: examples of selectivity and a case for comparison', in Serjeantson and Waldron (eds) 1989, 161–88

Levitan, B. 2019 'The animal bones, with special emphasis on the horncore collection', in Brown 2019, 165–73

Lewis, E. (ed.) 1991 *Custom and ceramics: essays presented to Kenneth Barton* Wickham, APE

Light, T. and Ellis, P. 2009 *Bucknowle, a Romano-British villa and its antecedents: excavations 1976–1991* Dorchester, Dorset Natural History and Archaeological Society Monograph Series 18

Liss Archaeological Group 2016 'Roman villa at Liss, Hampshire, excavations 1992–2010', *Proceedings of the Hampshire Field Club and Archaeological Society* 71, 63–4

Litchenstein, L. and Hughes, S. 2020 *St Thomas Court, Cowick Street, Exeter, Devon* AC Archaeology report ACD1716/2/0

Lloyd Parry, H. 1936 *The history of Exeter Guildhall and the life within* Exeter, Townsend

Llubiá, L.M. 1967 *Cerámica medieval española* Barcelona, Colección Labor

Loader, E. 1999 'Worked stone', in Fitzpatrick *et al.* 1999, 281–2

Lockyear, K. (ed.) 2015 *Archaeology in Hertfordshire – recent research* Hatfield, Hertfordshire Publications

Lodwick, L. 2017 'Arable farming, plant foods and resources', in Allen *et al.* 2017 11–84

Loe, L. 1998a *Human remains from Friars Gate, Exeter, 1973* Exeter Archaeology report 98.68

Loe, L. 1998b *Human remains from St Katherine's Priory, Polsloe, Exeter, 1976–78* Exeter Archaeology report 98.69

Loe, L. 1998c *Human remains from Holloway Street, Exeter, 1974* Exeter Archaeology report 98.70

Loe, L., 2006 'Analysis of the human bone from sites 1 and 2', in Jackson (ed.) 2006, 105–20

López Elum, P. 1984 *Los orígenes de la cerámica de Manises y Paterna (1285–1335)* Valencia, F. Domenech

López Elum, P. 1986 'Origen y evolución de dos grandes centros alfareros', *III Congresso Internazionale La Ceramica Medievale nel Mediterraneo Occidentale*, Florence, 163–81

Lucy, S and Reynolds, A. (eds) 2002 *Burials in early medieval England and Wales* London, Society for Medieval Archaeology

Lysons, S. 1822 *Reliquiae Britannico-Romanae* VI

McAleer, J.P. 1984 'The façade of the Romanesque cathedral at Exeter', *Proceedings of the Devon Archaeological Society* 42, 71–6

McAleer, J.P. 1991 'The problem(s) of the St Edmund's Chapel at Exeter Cathedral', in Kelly (ed.) 1991, 157–61

McCutcheon, C. 2006 *Medieval pottery from Wood Quay, Dublin: the 1974–6 waterfront excavations* Dublin, Royal Irish Academy

McKinley, J.I. 2004 'Compiling a skeletal inventory: disarticulated and co-mingled remains', in Brickley and McKinley (eds) 2004, 20–4

MacMahon, A. 2003 *Taberna structures of Roman Britain* Oxford, British Archaeological Reports British Series 356

MacMahon, A. and Price, J. (eds) 2005 *Roman working lives and urban living* Oxford, Oxbow Books

McMillan, A.A., and Powell, J.H. 1999 *The classification of artificial (man made) ground and natural superfifical deposits* Nottingham, British Geological Survey Research Report 99–04

McWhirr, A. 1979a 'Roman tile kilns in Britain', in McWhirr (ed.) 1979, 97–191

McWhirr, A. (ed.) 1979b *Roman brick and tile: studies in the manufacture, distribution and use in the Western Empire* Oxford, British Archaeological Reports International Series 68

Machin, S.L. 2018 *Constructing Calleva: a multidisciplinary study of the production, distribution, and consumption of ceramic building materials at the Roman town of Silchester, Hampshire* Unbublished PhD thesis, University of Reading

Mainz Samian Research Project: www1.rgzm.de/Samian/Home

Mallet, J.V.G. 1972 'L'importazione della maiolica italiana in Inghilterra', *Atti V convegno internazionale della ceramica* Albisola, Centro ligure per la storia della ceramica, 251–64

Maltby, M. 1979 *The animal bones from Exeter, 1971–175* Sheffield, Exeter archaeological reports 2

Maltby, M. 2010 *Feeding a Roman town. Environmental evidence from excavations in Winchester, 1972–1985* Winchester, Winchester Museums

Maltby, M. 2014 'The exploitation of animals in Roman Britain', in Millett *et al.* (eds) 2016, 791–806

Maltby, M. 2015 'Commercial archaeology, zooarchaeology and Romano-British towns', in Fulford and Holbrook 2015, 175–93

Maniatis, Y. and Tite, M.S. 1981 'Technological examination of Neolithic-Bronze Age pottery from Central and Southeast Europe and from the Near East', *Journal of Archaeological Science* 8, 59–76

Manning, P. and Stead, P. 2002–3 'Excavation of an early Christian cemetery at Althea Library, Padstow', *Cornish Archaeology* 41–2, 97–104

Manning, W.H. 1981 *Report on the excavations at Usk 1965–1976. The fortress excavations 1968–1971* Cardiff, University of Wales Press

Manning, W.H. (ed.) 1993 *The Roman pottery. Report on the excavations at Usk, 1965–1976* Cardiff, University of Wales Press

Manning, W.H., and Scott, I.R. 1989 *Report on the excavations at Usk 1965–1976. The fortress excavations 1972–1974 and minor excavations on the fortress and Flavian fort* Cardiff, University of Wales Press

Mannoni, T. 1969 'Gli scarti di fornace e la cava del XVI secolo in via S. Vincenzo a Genova: dati geologici ed archeologici, analisi di materiali', *Atti del secondo convegno (Albisola, 31 maggio – 2 giugno 1969)* Genoa, Centro ligure per la storia della ceramica, 73–96

Marks, R. 1987 'The prophet Isaiah', in Alexander and Binski (eds) 1987, 532–4

Marques, A., Leitão, E. and Botelho, P. 2012 'Rua do Benformoso 168/186 (Lisboa-Mouraria/Intendente): entre a nova e a velha cidade, aspectos da sua evoluçao urbanistica', in Teixeira and Bettencourt (eds) 2012, 123–34

Marsden, P. 1987 *The Roman forum site in London* London, Her Majesty's Stationery Office

Marshall, M. and Wardle, A. forthcoming *Roman artefacts from the middle Walbrook valley: glass, small finds, coins and textiles from the Bloomberg excavations 2010–14* London, Museum of London Archaeology Monograph

Martin, C.J.M. 1979 'Spanish Armada pottery', *International Journal of Nautical Archaeology* 8 (4), 279–302

Martin, D.L., Harrod, R.P. and Ventura, R.P. 2013 *Bioarchaeology: an integrated approach to working with human remains* New York, Springer

Martín-Márquez, J, Rincón, J.Ma. and Romero, M. 2008 'Effect of firing temperature on sintering of porcelain stoneware tiles', *Ceramics International* 34, 1867–1873

Martinón-Torres, M. 2005 *Chemistry and crucibles in the Renaissance laboratory: an archaeometric and historical study* Unpublished PhD thesis, University College London

Martinón-Torres, M. and Rehren, T. 2009 'Post-medieval crucible production and distribution: a study of materials and materialities', *Archaeometry* 51.1, 49–74

Martinón-Torres, M. and Verrocchio, V. 2008 'Triangular crucibles from the Convent of San Domenico in L'Aquila', *Archeologia Postmedievale*, 12 (12), 97–113

Marvell, A.G. and Owen-John, H.S. 1997 Leucarum. *Excavations at the Roman auxiliary fort at Loughor, West Glamorgan 1982–84 and 1987–88* London, The Society for the Promotion of Roman Studies Britannia Monograph 12

Marzinot, F. 1979 *Ceramica e ceramisti in Liguria* Genoa, Sagep

Mason, D.J.P. 1985 *Excavations at Chester: 26–42 Lower Bridge Street 1974–6. The Dark Age and Saxon periods* Chester, Grosvenor Museum Archaeological Excavation and Survey Report 3

Mason, D.J.P. 2012 *Roman Chester. Fortress at the edge of the world,* 2nd edition Stroud, The History Press

Masser, P., Kimber, M, Franklin, J, Cross, M. and Tourunen, A. 2014, *Excavations at Jeffrey Street, Edinburgh: the development of closes and tenements north of the Royal Mile during the 16th-18th centuries,* Edinburgh, Society of Antiquaries of Scotland

Massing, A. (ed.) 2003 *The Thornham Parva Retable: technique, conservation and context of an English medieval painting*

London, Hamilton Kerr Institute University of Cambridge and Harvey Miller Publishers

Masson Phillips E.N. 1965 'Excavation of a Romano-British site at Lower Well Farm, Stoke Gabriel, Devon', *Proceedings of the Devon Archaeological Society* 23, 3–34

Matthews, A.J., Collings, A.G. and Allan, J.P. 2011 'The Ship Inn: a row of late medieval houses in St Martin's Lane, Exeter', *Proceedings of the Devon Archaeological Society* 69, 157–80

Mattingly, D. 2006 *An imperial possession: Britain in the Roman Empire, 54 BC–AD 409* London, Penguin Books

Maurin, L. (ed.) 2012 *Un quartier de Bordeaux du 1er au VIIIe siècle. Les fouilles de la place Camille-Jullian 1989–1990* Bordeaux, Documents archéologiques du Grand Sud-Ouest

Maxfield, V.A. 1991 'Tiverton Roman fort (Bolham): excavations 1981–1986', *Proceedings of the Devon Archaeological Society* 49, 25–98

Maxfield, V.A. and Dobson, M.J. (eds) 1991 *Roman frontier studies 1989* Exeter, University of Exeter Press

Mayes, A. and Hardy, A. 2004 'Excavations on the site of Bonhay Mills, Exeter, 2000–1', *Proceedings of the Devon Archaeological Society* 62, 153–69

Mays, S., Harding, C. and Heighway, C. 2007 *The churchyard, Wharram: a study of settlement on the Yorkshire Wolds 13* York, University of York

Meadow, R.H. 1999 'The use of size index scaling techniques for research on archaeological collections from the Middle East', in Becker *et al.* (eds) 1999, 285–300

Mendes, H., Pimenta, J. and Valongo, A. 2002 'Cerámicas medievais provenientes do escavação da Travessa da Lameira no. 21, centro histórico de Santarém', *Revista Portuguesa de Arqueologia* 5 (1), 259–76

Mepham, L. 2018 'Town and country: the production and distribution of Laverstock wares', *Medieval Ceramics* 39, 17–28

Mesquida, M. 2001 *Las ollerías de Paterna: tecnología y producción, vol. 1, siglos XII y XIII* Paterna, Ajuntament de Paterna

Michaelis, R.F. 1975 'The pewter saucer', in Platt and Coleman-Smith 1975, vol. 2, 250–1

Michelaki, K. and Hancock, R.G.V. 2011 'Chemistry versus data dispersion: is there a better way to interpret archaeometric data?', *Archaeometry* 53 (6), 1259–79

Middleton, A. and Freestone, I. (eds) 1991 *Recent developments in ceramic petrology* London, British Museum Occasional Paper 81

Milanese, M. 1980 'Il contributo del metodo archeologico stratigrafico alla conoscenza della maiolica ligure d'uso dei secoli XVI e XVII', *Faenza* 66, 337–41

Miles, D.W.H. 2002a *The tree-ring dating of the roof carpentry of the Eastern Chapels, North Nave Triforium, and North Porch, Salisbury Cathedral, Wiltshire* English Heritage, Centre for Archaeology Report 94/2002

Miles, D.W.H. 2002b *The tree-ring dating of the thirteenth-century nave doors at Salisbury Cathedral, Wiltshire* English Heritage, Centre for Archaeology Report 101/2002

Miles, D.W.H., Howard, R.E. and Simpson, G. 2004 *The tree-ring dating of the tower and spire at Salisbury Cathedral, Wiltshire* English Heritage, Centre for Archaeology Report 44/2004

Miles, H. 1977 'The Honeyditches Roman villa, Seaton, Devon', *Britannia* 8, 107–48

Miller, M.C.J. and DeVoto, J.G. 1994 *Polybius and pseudo-hyginus: the fortifications of the Roman camp* Chicago, Ares Publishers Inc.

Millett, M., Revell, L. and Moore, A., (eds) 2014 *The Oxford Handbook of Roman Britain* Oxford, Oxford University Press

Mills, C.M. 1988 *Dendrochronology of Exeter and its application* Unpublished PhD thesis, Sheffield University

Milne, G. 1992 *Timber building techniques in London* c.*900–1400: an archaeological study of waterfront installations and related material* London, London and Middlesex Archaeological Society

Milne, G. 1995 *Roman London* London, Seaby

Milne, G. and Hobley, B. (eds) 1981 *Waterfront archaeology in Britain and Europe* York, Council of British Archaeology Research Report 41

Miracle, P. and Milner, N. (eds) 2002 *Consuming passions and patterns of consumption* Cambridge, McDonald Institute for Archaeological Research

Molleson, T., Powers, R., Price, J. and Sheppard, P. 2016 'Anglo-Saxon and medieval populations from the Old and New Minster and cathedral cemeteries', in Stuckert (ed.) 2016, 261–390

Monaghan, J. 1993 *Roman pottery from the fortress: 9 Blake Street* York, The Archaeology of York 16, Facsimile 7

Monaghan, J. 1997 *Roman pottery from York* York, The Archaeology of York 16, Facsimile 8

Montague, L.A.D. 1935 'Report of the Exeter Excavation Committee', *Proceedings of the Devon Archaeological Exploration Society* 2 (3), 176–91

Montgomerie-Neilson, E. 1934 'Report of the Exeter Excavation Committee, I: introduction and conclusions', *Proceedings of the Devon Archaeological Exploration Society* 2 (2), 55–71

Montgomerie-Neilson, E. and Montague, L.A.D. 1931 'Exeter excavations, 1931', *Proceedings of the Devon Archaeological Exploration Society* 1 (3), 121–42

Montgomerie-Neilson, E. and Montague, L.A.D. 1933 'Report of the Exeter Excavation Committee. Part II: report on the excavations 1932–3', *Proceedings of the Devon Archaeological Exploration Society* 2 (1), 72–83

Moore Valeri, A. 1984a 'Florentine "zaffera a rilievo" maiolica: a new look at the "oriental influence"', *Archeologia Medievale* 11, 477–500

Moore Valeri, A. 1984b 'La mezzaluna dentata: le sue origini ed il suo sviluppo', *Faenza* 70, 375–80

Moorhead, S. 2001 'Roman coin finds from Wiltshire', in Ellis (ed.) 2001, 85–105

Moorhead, S. 2013 *A history of Roman coinage in Britain* Witham, Greenlight

Moorhead, S. 2015 'A survey of Roman coin finds from Hertfordshire', in Lockyear (ed.) 2015, 135–64

Moorhead, S. and Stuttard, D. 2012 *The Romans who shaped Britain* London, Thames and Hudson

Moorhead, S. and Walton, P. 2014 'Coinage at the end of Roman Britain', in Haarer (ed.) 2014, 99–116

Moorhead, S., Booth, A. and Bland, R. 2010 *The Frome Hoard* London, British Museum

Moorhouse, S. 1972 'Medieval distilling-apparatus of glass and pottery', *Medieval Archaeology* 16, 79–121

Moorhouse, S. 1981 'The medieval pottery industry and its markets', in Crossley (ed.) 1991, 96–125

Moorhouse, S. 1986 'Non-dating uses of medieval pottery', *Medieval Ceramics* 10, 85–123

Morazzoni, G. 1951 *La maiolica antica ligure* Milanc, Alfieri

Morazzoni, G. 1955 *La maiolica antica veneta*, 1, Milan, Alfieri

Morgado, P.J., da Silva, R.C. and Filipe, S.J. 2012 'A cerâmica do açúcar de Aveiro: recentes achados na área do antigo bairro das olarias', in Teixeira and Bettencourt (eds) 2012, 771–82

Morgan, R.A. 1976 *Tree-ring dating of the London Waterfronts* English Heritage, Ancient Monuments Laboratory Report 2118

Morgan, R.A. 1980 *Tree-ring dating at Goldsmith Street, Exeter* English Heritage, Ancient Monuments Laboratory Report 3026

Morgan, R.A. 1981 *Additional Goldsmith Street, Exeter, wood samples received for tree-ring analysis, 1981* English Heritage, Ancient Monuments Laboratory Report 3514

Morgan, R.A. 1984 'Tree-ring analysis of Goldsmith Street timber, Exeter', in Allan 1984a, 318–22

Morillo, A., Hanel, N. and Martín, E. (eds) 2009 *Limes XX. XX Congreso Internacional de Estudios sobre la Frontera Romana* (3 vols), Anejos de *Gladius* 13

Morris, B. 2014 *Land at Shortlands Lane Cullompton, Devon. Results of a desk-based assessment and archaeological excavation* SW Archaeology report 20140811, 201 [ADS: https://doi.org/10.5284/1035617]

Morris, E. 1978 'A seventeenth century pit deposit from Worcester', *Transactions of the Worcestershire Archaeological Society* 3 series 6, 83–7

Morris, M., Buckley, R. and Codd, M. 2011 *Visions of ancient Leicester. Reconstructing life in the Roman and medieval town from the archaeology of the Highcross Leicester excavations* Leicester, University of Leicester

Morris, P. and Montague, L.A.D. 1938 'A Romano-British building at Topsham', *Proceedings of the Devon Archaeological Exploration Society* 3 (2), 67–82

Morris, P., Montague, L.A.D. and Radford, C.A.R. 1946 'Report on the excavations in the Palace garden', *Proceedings of the. Devon Archaeological Exploration Society* 3 (3), 135–41

MPRG 1998 *A guide to the classification of medieval ceramic forms* London, Medieval Pottery Research Group

MPRG 2010 *Alan Vince archive: ceramic chemical composition database*, York, Archaeology Data Service

Mudd, A. 2017 *Land at Hill Barton, Exeter, Devon: post-excavation assessment and updated project design* Cotswold Archaeology report 16234

Mudd, A. and Joyce, S. 2014 *The archaeology of the South-West Reinforcement Gas Pipeline, Devon: investigations in 2005–2007* Cirencester, Cotswold Archaeology Monograph 6

Müldner, G., 2009 'Investigating medieval diet and society by stable isotope analysis on human bone', in Gilchrist and Reynolds (eds) 2009, 329–46

Munro, J.H. 2003 'Medieval woollens: textile technology and industrial organisation, *c.* 800–1500', in Jenkins (ed.) 2003, 181–227

Murphy, E. (ed.) 2008 *Deviant burial in the archaeological record* Oxford, Oxbow Books

Murray, H. 1983 *Viking and early medieval buildings in Dublin* Oxford, British Archaeological Reports British Series 119

Navarro Palazón, J. 1990 'Los materiales islámicos del Alfar Antiguo de San Nicolás de Murcia', *Fours de Poitiers et 'Testares' Medievaux en Méditerranée Occidentale: Méthodes et resultats* Madrid, Casa de Velázquez, 29–43

Navarro Palazón, J. and Jiménez, P. 1995 'La producción cerámica medieval de Murcia', in Gerrard *et al.* (eds) 1995, 183–212

Neal, D.S. and Cosh, S.R. 2009 *Roman mosaics of Britain. Volume 3: South-East Britain* London, Society Antiquaries of London

Neff, H., Bishop, R.L. and Sayre, E.V. 1988 'A simulation approach to the problem of tempering in compositional studies of archaeolgical ceramics', *Journal of Archaeological Science* 15 (2), 159–72

Nelson, G.C. 2016 'A host of other dental disorders', in Irish and Scott (eds) 2016, 471–83

Nenk, B. and Hughes, M.J., 2019 An Acceptable Science: Antwerp maiolica tiles from a Tudor manor house at Place Farm, Bletchingley, Surrey, in J. Edwards and S. Paynter, 129-144

Nenk, B.S. *et al.* 1991 'Medieval Britain and Ireland in 1990', *Medieval Archaeology* 35, 126–38

Nenk, B.S. *et al.* 1992 'Medieval Britain and Ireland in 1991', *Medieval Archaeology* 36, 184–308

Nenk, B.S. *et al.* 1993 'Medieval Britain and Ireland in 1992', *Medieval Archaeology* 37, 240–313

Nenk, B.S. *et al.* 1995 'Medieval Britain and Ireland in 1994', *Medieval Archaeology* 39, 180–293

Newman, P. (ed.) 1996 *The archaeology of mining and metallurgy in south west Britain* Peak District Matlock Mines Historical Society/Historical Mettalurgical Society

Newman, P, 2016 *The archaeology of mining and quarrying in England. Research Framework for the archaeology of the extractive industries in England. Resource Assessment and Research Agenda*, The National Association of Mining History Organisations (NAMHO)

Nicholson, R.A. and Hillam, J. 1987 'A dendrochronological analysis of oak timbers from the early medieval site at Dundas Wharf, Bristol', *Transactions of the Bristol and Gloucestershire Archaeological Society* 105, 133–45

Novak, M. 2015 'Dental health and diet in early medieval Ireland', *Archives of Oral Biology* 60, 1299–309

Nunes, T. and Filipe, I. 2012 'Quarteirão dos Lagares: contributo para a historia económica da Mouraria', in Teixeira and Bettencourt (eds) 2012, 141–50

Ogden, A. 2008 'Advances in the palaeopathology of teeth and jaws', in R. Pinhasi and S. Mays (eds) 2008 *Advances in human palaeopathology* Chichester, Whiley & Sons Ltd., 283–307

Oleson, J.P. (ed.) 2009 *The Oxford handbook of engineering and technology in the classical world* Oxford, Oxford University Press

Olin, J.S. and Blackman, M.J. (eds) 1986 *Proceedings of the 24th International Archaeometry Symposium* Washington DC, Smithsonian Institution Press

O'Mahoney, C. 1989 *The medieval pottery from Tintagel Castle* Redruth, Institute of Cornish Studies Special Report 8

Oost, T. and Veeckman, J., 2002 'Majolica in Antwerp: the archaeological evidence', in Veeckman (ed.) 2002, 51–68

Orellana, J. 2019 *St Sidwell's Point, Exeter Bus Station, Exeter. Archaeological excavation: fieldwork summary* Cotswold Archaeology report

Orme, N. 2009 *Exeter Cathedral: the first thousand years, 400–1550* Exeter, Impress Books

Orme, N. 2014 *The Churches of medieval Exeter* Exeter, Impress Books

Orme, N. 2015a 'St Nicholas Priory, Exeter', *Proceedings of the Devon Archaeological Society* 73, 315–35

Orme, N. 2015b 'Polsloe Priory, Exeter', *Transactions of the Devonshire Association* 147, 185–212

Orme, N. 2016 'The Franciscan friars of Exeter', *Proceedings of the Devon Archaeological Society* 74, 217–54

Orme, N. and Webster, M. 1995 *The English hospital 1070–1570* New Haven, Yale University Press

Ortner, D.J. 2003 *Identification of pathological conditions in human skeletal remains*, 2nd edition San Diego, Academic Press

Ortner, D.J. 2008a 'Differential diagnosis of skeletal lesions in infectious disease', in Pinhasi and Mays (eds) 2008, 191–214

Ortner, D.J. 2008b 'Forward', in Brickley and Ives (eds) 2008, xiii–xvi

Orton, C. and Hughes, M. 2013 *Pottery in archaeology* Cambridge, Cambridge University Press

Osborne, K. 2016 *Illuminating the chorus in the shadows: Elizabethan and Jacobean Exeter 1550–1610* Unpublished PhD thesis, University of Exeter [https://ore.exeter.ac.uk/repository/handle/10871/24298]

Osma, G.J. de 1906 *La loza dorada de Manises en el año 1454*, Textos y documentos valencianos I Madrid, Impr. de los hijos de M.G. Hernández

Osma, G.J. de 1911 *Adiciones a los textos y documentos valencianos: número II. Maestros alfareros de Manises, Paterna y Valencia* Madrid, Impr. de los hijos de M.G. Hernández

Osma, G.J. de 1912 *La loza dorada de Manises en el año 1454*, Textos y documentos valencianos 1, 2nd edition Madrid, Impr. de los hijos de M.G. Hernández

Osma, G.J. de 1923 *Los maestros alfareros de Manises, Paterna y Valencia*, 2nd edition Madrid, Editorial Reus

Ostkamp, S. 2006 'Het aardewerk uit de opgraving', in Dijkstra *et al.* (eds) 2006, 51–92

Ostkamp, S. and Kottman, J.F.P. 2006 'Bijlage 5.1 Catalogus met aardewerk- en glasvondsten', in Dijkstra *et al.* (eds) 2006, 271–378

Ostkamp, S., Roedema, R. and van Wilgen, R.P. 2002 'The introduction of majolica in Alkmaar', in Veeckman 2002, 449–64

Ottoway, P. 2017 *Winchester: Swithun's 'city of happiness and good fortune'* Oxford, Oxbow Books

Outram, A.K. 2001 'A new approach to identifying bone marrow and grease exploitation: why the "indeterminate" fragments should not be ignored', *Journal of Archaeological Science* 28, 401–10

Outram, A.K. 2002 'Bone fracture and within-bone nutrients: an experimentally based method for investigating levels of marrow exploitation', in Miracle and Milner (eds) 2002, 51–63

Palfreyman, A. and Ebbins, S. 2007 'A Romano-British quern manufacturing site at Blackbrook, Derbyshire', *Derbyshire Archaeological Journal* 127, 33–48

Papazian, C. and Campbell, E. 1992 'Medieval pottery and roof tiles in Wales AD 1100–1600', *Medieval and Later Pottery in Wales* 13, 1–107

Parham, D. (ed.) 2009 *Studland Bay wreck* Unpublished English Heritage report

Parker, R.W. 1996 *Archaeological survey of Cricklepit Mill, Exeter. Part 2: the buildings* Exeter Archaeology report 96.37

Parker, R.W. 1999 *Archaeological recording at no 18 North Street, Exeter* Exeter Archaeology report 99.78

Parker, R.W. and Allan, J.P. 2015 'The transformation of the building stock of Exeter, 1450–1700', in Allan *et al.* 2015, 35–67

Parker, R.W., and Collings, A. 2002 'St Catherine's Almshouses and the medieval canonry in Catherine Street, Exeter', *Proceedings of the Devon Archaeological Society* 60, 75–205

Parker, R., Allan, J., Fletcher, M., Higham, R. and Laithwaite, M. 2006 'The Bishop's palace at Chudleigh', *Proceedings of the Devon Archaeological Society* 64, 235–6

Parker, R.W., Bishop, P., Collings, A.G. and McNeilage, R. 2013 'No. 18 North Street, Exeter: a 17th-century merchant house with painted panelling', *Proceedings of the Devon Archaeological Society* 71, 123–86

Passmore, A.J. 2011a *195 High Street, Exeter: a town house and shop of* c. *1700* Exeter Archaeology report 11.19 [ADS: https://doi.org/10.5284/1008001]

Passmore, A.J. 2011b *Western Way (former Texaco garage site), Exeter, Devon* AC Archaeology report ACD362/2/0

Passmore, A.J. 2013 *Discovery Quarter, Mount Dinham, Exeter* AC Archaeology report ACD356/1/2 [ADS: https://doi.org/10.5284/1028784]

Passmore, A.J. forthcoming 'Excavations at Mount Dinham', Proceedings of the Devon Archaeological Society Occasional Paper

Passmore, A.J. and Coles, C. 2011 *Archaeological excavation at the Timepiece nightclub, Little Castle Street, Exeter* Exeter Archaeology report 11.01 [ADS: https://doi.org/10.5284/1008306]

Passmore, A.J. and Parker, R. 2012 *Magnolia House and Acacia Green, Friar's Green, Exeter (NGR SX 9210 9218)* AC Archaeology report ACD403/2/1 [ADS: https://doi.org/10.5284/1016102]

Passmore, A.J. and Rainbird, P. 2014 *Royal Albert Memorial Museum, Exeter, phase II landscaping* AC Archaeology report ACD354/2/1

Passmore, A.J. and Stead, P. 2012 *Nos 69–73 Sidwell Street, Exeter* AC Archaeology report ACD303/2/1 [ADS: https://doi.org/10.5284/1021110]

Passmore, A.J., Jones, P. and Allan, J.P. 2009 'Dyers, fullers and brewers: post-medieval housing and industries at Tudor Street, Exeter', *Proceedings of the Devon Archaeological Society* 67, 133–96

Payne, N. 2016 'Worked Stone', in Farnell *et al.* 2016, 12

Payne, N. 2017a *Exeter Road, Topsham, ceramic building material* AC Archaeology report ACD1123

Payne, N. 2017b 'The finds', in Govier 2017, 12–15

Payne, N. and Passmore, A. 2016 'The finds', in Valentin 2016, 3–4

Peacock, D.P.S. 1979a 'An ethnoarchaeological approach to the study of Roman bricks and tiles', in McWhirr (ed.) 1979, 5–10

Peacock, D.P.S. 1979b 'Amphorae identifications', in Bidwell 1979, table 10

Peacock, D.P.S. and Williams, D.F. 1986 *Amphorae and the Roman economy: an introductory guide* London, Longman

Pearce, J.E., Vince, A.G. and Jenner, M.A. 1985 *A dated type-series of London medieval pottery. Part 2: London-type ware* London, London and Middlesex Archaeological Society Special Paper 6

Pearce, P. 2007 *Archaeological excavations at Princesshay, Exeter, April 2005–March 2006: interim report* Exeter Archaeology report 07.40

Pearce, P. 2009 *Archaeological excavations at the Southgate Hotel, Southernhay, Exeter* Exeter Archaeology report 09.103 (6395) [ADS: https://doi.org/10.5284/1003297]

Pearce, P. and Parker, R.W. 2005 *Archaeological recording at George's Meeting, South Street, Exeter* Exeter Archaeology report 05.13

Pearce, S.M. (ed.) 1982 *The early church in western Britain and Ireland* Oxford, British Archaeological Reports British Series 102

Pears, B. and Smith, W. 2016 *Land at Penns Mount, Kingsteignton* AC Archaeology report 12/01737/MAJ

Pearsal, D. (ed.) 2008 *Encyclopedia of archceology* New York, Academic Press

Pearson, T. 1982 'The post-Roman pottery', in Leach 1982, 169–217

Pearson, T. and Oswald, A. 2000 'Quern manufacturing at Wharncliffe Rocks, Sheffield, South Yorkshire', EH Report

Pellant, J. 2007 *SPSS survival manual* Maidenhead, McGraw Hill/Open University Press

Pengelly, H. 1987 'The samian', in Sunter and Woodward 1987, 69–73

Perciuale, R. and Minsheu, J. 1599 *A dictionarie in Spanish and English* London, Bollifant

Pereira, F. and Dias, L.S. 2017 *Trabalhos Arqueológicos no âmbito da Obra de Reconstrução de habitação sita na Rua das Olarias 6, Tavira* Unpublished excavation report

Pérez Arantegui, J., Montull, B., Resano, M. and Ortega, J.M. 2009 'Materials and technological evolution of ancient cobalt-blue-decorated ceramics: pigments and work patterns in tin-glazed objects from Aragon (Spain) from the 15th to the 18th century AD', *Journal of the European Ceramics Society* 29, 2499–509

Perring, D. 2002 *The Roman house in Britain* Abingdon, Routledge

Pesante, L. and Satolli, A. (eds) 2019 *La maiolica e le altre arti: influssi, parallelismi, convergenze* Florence, Polistampa

Pessa, L. (ed.) 2014 *Turcherie: suggestioni dell'arte ottomana a Genova* Genoa, Sagep

Pessa, L. and Ramagli, P. (eds) 2010 *Ceramiche tra Oriente e Occidente: i reperti di epoca medievale e rinascimentale delle raccolte civiche genovesi* Genoa, De Ferrari

Petch, D.F. 1958 'Archaeological notes for the year, 1957', *Lincolnshire Architectural and Archaeological Society Reports and Papers* 7.2, 92–111

Phear, J.B. 1892 'Additional discoveries at the castle, Exeter', *Report and Transactions of the Devonshire Association* 24, 147–50

Piccolpasso, C. (1980) *The three books of the potter's art = I tre libri dell'arte del vasaio* London, Scolar

Pineda, G. 2004 'Informe de vigilancia arqueológica en C/ Ollerías esquina C/Cruz del Molinillo (Málaga)', *Anuario de Arqueología Andaluza 2004* vol. 3(1), 635–8

Pinhasi, R. and Mays, S. (eds) 2008 *Advances in human palaeo pathology* Chichester, Wiley & Sons Ltd

Pink, F. 2011 *Archaeological excavations at Verney Street, Exeter* Exeter Archaeology report 11.44

Piton, D. (ed.) 1996 *La céramique très decorée dans l'Europe du nord-ouest (X–XV siècle)*, numéro spécial de *Nord-Ouest Archéologie*, Musée de Berck 7

Pitts, L.F., and St Joseph, J.K. 1985 *Inchtuthil. The legionary fortress* London, The Society for the Promotion of Roman Studies Britannia Monograph 6

Pitts, M. 2014 'Reconsidering Britain's first urban communities', *Journal of Roman Archaeology* 27, 133–73

Platt, C.P.S. 1976 *The English medieval town* London, Secker and Warburg

Platt, C.P.S. and Coleman-Smith, R. 1975 *Excavations in medieval Southampton 1953–1969* Leicester, Leicester University Press

Pleguezuelo, A. and Lafuente, M.P. 1995 'Cerámicas de Andalucía Occidental (1200–1600)', in Gerrard *et al.* 1995, 217–44

Pollard, S. 1972 'The Honeyditches Roman villa, Seaton, Devon', *Proceedings of the Devon Archaeological Society* 30, 222–6

Pollard, S. 1974 'A Late Iron Age settlement and a Romano-British villa at Holcombe, near Uplyme, Devon', *Proceedings of the Devon Archaeological Society* 32, 59–162

Ponsford, C.N. 1978 *Time in Exeter* Exeter, Headwell Vale

Ponsford, M. 1991 'Dendrochronological dates from Dundas Wharf, Bristol, and the dating of Ham Green and other medieval pottery', in Lewis 1991, 81–103

Ponsford, M. 1992 'Post-Medieval Britain in 1991', *Post-Medieval Archaeology* 26, 95–156

Ponsford, M. 1993 'Post-Medieval Britain in 1992', *Post-Medieval Archaeology* 27, 205–96

Ponsford, M. and Jackson R. 1995 'Post-medieval Britain in 1994', *Post-Medieval Archaeology* 29, 113–93

Ponting, M. forthcoming 'Chemical analyses of Claudian coins', in *Bloomberg London excavation report* London, Museum of London Archaeology

Portman, D. 1966 *Exeter houses* Exeter, University of Exeter Press

Potts, P.J. 1987 *A handbook of silicate rock analysis* Glasgow, Blackie

Potts, P.J., Williams-Thorpe, O. and Webb, P.C. 1997 'The bulk analysis of silicate rocks by portable X-Ray fluorescence: effect of sample mineralogy in relation to the size of the excited volume', *Journal of Geostandards and Geoanalysis* 21 (1), 29–41

Preston, A. 1986 'Pottery: Summary table of forms and quantities', in Gaskell Brown 1986, 25–30

Puertas Tricas, R. 1992 'Málaga', *Mediterraneum: Cerámica medieval en España e Italia* Viterbo, Paul Edizioni Artistiche SRL, 121–51

Putnam, W.G. 1970 'Roman discoveries in Portland', *Proceedings of the Dorset Natural History and Archaeological Society* 92, 141–5

Quinn, P. 2013 *Ceramic petrography: the interpretation of archaeological pottery and related artefacts in thin section* Oxford, Archaeopress

Quinnell, H. 2003 'Roof tile from Little Quoit Farm with a comment on the tile from Magor villa' in Lawson Jones 2003, 47–8

Quinnell, H. 2015a 'The prehistoric pottery', in Hughes 2015, 117–21

Quinnell, H. 2015b 'The worked stone', in Hughes 2015, 158–61

Quinnell, H. 2017 'Prehistoric Exeter', *Proceedings of the Devon Archaeological Society* 75, 1–26

Quinnell, H. 2018a 'Stonework', in Farnell and Rainbird 2018, 45–6

Quinnell, H. 2018b 'Pottery', in Rainbird and Quinnell 2018, 128–32

Quinnell forthcoming, in Salvatore *et al* forthcoming

Quinnell, H. and Taylor, R. 2015 'Prehistoric and Romano-British pottery', in Farnell 2015, 225–35

Rackham, B. 1926 *Early Netherlands maiolica: with special reference to the tiles at the Vyne in Hampshire* London, Bless

Radford, C.A.R. 1937 'Report of the Exeter Excavation Committee: the Roman site at Topsham', *Proceedings of the Devon Archaeological Society* 3 (1), 4–23

Radford, C.A.R. and Morris, P. 1935 'Report of the Exeter Excavation Committee', *Proceedings of the Devon Archaeological Exploration Society* 2 (3), 176–90

Radford, C.A.R. and Morris, P. 1936 'Report of the Exeter Excavation Committee', *Proceedings of the Devon Archaeological Exploration Society* 2 (4), 224–40

Ragab, G., Elshahaly, M. and Bardin, T. 2017 'Gout: an old disease in new prespective – a review', *Journal of Advance Research* 8, 495–511

Raimbault, M. 1973 'La céramique gallo-romaine ditte "à l'éponge" dans l'ouest de la France', *Gallia* 31, 185–206

Rainbird, P. 2013 *Exeter Cathedral School, proposed new nursery, Cathedral Close, Exeter, Devon* AC Archaeology report ACD761/2/1 [ADS: https://doi.org/10.5284/1028523]

Rainbird, P. 2014 *Land to the east of Dean Clarke House, Southernhay, Exeter, Devon* AC Archaeology report ACD584/2/1 [ADS: https://doi.org/10.5284/1028447]

Rainbird, P. 2015 *Exeter Cathedral School, new nursery, Cathedral Close, Exeter, Devon* AC Archaeology report ACD909/2/1 [ADS: https://doi.org/10.5284/1046380]

Rainbird, P. 2017 *The former British Heart Foundation, 1 Cheeke Street, Exeter* AC Archaeology report ACD1619/1/0 [ADS: https://doi.org/10.5284/1047659]

Rainbird, P. and Farnell, A. 2019 'A hint of Exeter's hinterland and port: a new large aisled hall building at Wessex Close, Topsham, Devon', *Britannia* 50, 385–93

Rainbird, P. and Govier, L. 2017 *Land at Eagle Yard, Tudor Street, Exeter, Devon* AC Archaeology report ACD1352/2/1 [ADS: https://doi.org/10.5284/1047657]

Rainbird, P. and Quinnell, H. 2018 'The excavation of a late Iron Age and Romano-British enclosure at Tews Lane, Fremington, near Barnstaple', *Proceedings of the Devon Archaeological Society* 76, 115–39

Rainbird, P. and Valentin, J. 2016 *Land at Quay Hill and The Chapel, Exeter* AC Archaeology report ACD1339/1/5

Rainbird, P., de-Villiers, S. and Payne, N. 2014 *Eagle Yard, Tudor Street, Exeter* AC Archaeology report ACD817/2/1 [ADS: https://doi.org/10.5284/1034067]

Rankov, N.B., Hassall, M.W.C. and Tomlin, R.S.O. 1982 'Roman Britain in 1981', *Britannia* 13, 327–422

Ransom Pickard, Col. 1938 'The discovery of Roman remains at the corner of Fore Street – Market Street, Exeter', *Proceedings of the Devon Archaeological Exploration Society* 3 (2), 83–5

Ravanelli Guidotti, C. 1996 *Faenza-faïence: 'bianchi' di Faenza* Ferrara, Belriguardo

Ravanelli Guidotti, C. 1998 *Thesaurus di opere della tradizione di Faenza nelle raccolte del Museo internazionale delle ceramiche di Faenza* Faenza, Agenzia polo ceramico

Ravanelli Guidotti, C. 2004 *Ceramiche italiane datate dal XV al XIX secolo: per il 'Corpus della maiolica italiana' di Gaetano Ballardini* Faenza, Edit Faenza

Ravanelli Guidotti, C. 2019 'Rappresentazioni ceramiche in opere d'arte pittorica', in Pesante and Satolli (eds) 2019, 9–39

Ravenhill, M.R. and Rowe, M.M. 2000 *Devon maps and map-makers: manuscript maps before 1840. Volume 1* Exeter, Devon and Cornwall Records Society New Series 43

Rawlins, B., O'Donnell, K. and Imgham, M. 2003 *Geochemical survey of the Tamar catchment (south-west England)* Nottingham, British Geological Survey report CR/03/027

Reece, R. 1987 *Coinage in Roman Britain* London, Seaby

Reece, R. 1991a 'Roman coins from Exeter', in Holbrook and Bidwell 1991, 33–45

Reece, R. 1991b *Roman coins from 140 sites in Britain* Cirencester, Cotswold Studies IV

Reece, R. 1995 'Site-finds in Roman Britain', *Britannia* 26, 179–206

Reed, H. 1931 'Demolition of ancient buildings of Exeter during the last half-century', *Report and Transactions of the Devonshire Association* 63, 273–82

Reed, S.J. and Collings, A.G. 2000 *Archaeological desk-top assessment and evaluation of Everleight's Garage, Acland Road, Exeter* Exeter Archaeology report 00.49

Reed S.J., and Sage, S.A. 1996 *Archaeological evaluation at Guys Hilton Allotments, Okehampton Road, Exeter* Exeter Archaeology report 96.46

Reed, S.J., Bidwell, P.T. and Allan, J.P. 2011 'Excavations at Bantham, South Devon, and post-Roman trade in south-west England', *Medieval Archaeology* 55, 82–138

Reedy, C.L. 2008 *Thin section petrography of stone and ceramic cultural materials* London, Archetype Publications

Rees, S. 2011 'Agriculture', in Allason-Jones (ed.) 2011, 89–113

Rehren, T. and Kraus, K. 1999 'Cupel and crucible: the refining of debase silver in the Colonia Ulipa Traiana, Xanten', *Journal of Roman Archaeology* 12, 263–72

Resnick, D. 2002a 'Gouty arthritis', in Resnick (ed.) 2002b, 1519–59

Resnick, D. (ed.) 2002b *Diagnosis of bone and joint disorders*, 4th edition London, W.B. Saunders

Reuter, T. (ed.) 1980 *The greatest Englishman; essays on St Boniface and the church at Crediton* Exeter, Paternoster Press

Reynolds, P. 2010 *Hispania and the Roman Mediterranean, AD 100–70. Ceramics and trade* London, Duckworth

Rice, P. 1987 *Pottery analysis: a sourcebook* Chicago, University of Chicago

Richards, J. 2002 'The case of the missing Vikings: Scandinavian burial in the Danelaw', in Lucy and Reynolds (eds) 2002, 156–70

Ridgeway, V. and Watts, M. (eds) 2013 *Friars, quakers, industry and urbanisation: the archaeology of the Broadmead Expansion Project, Cabot Circus, Bristol, 2005–8* Cirencester and London, Cotswold Archaeology Monograph 5/Pre-Contruct Archaeology Monograph 16

Rigby, V. 2009 'Terra nigra and other imported fine wares', in Light and Ellis 2009, 139–40

Rigby, V. 1991 'Gaulish imports and related wares', in Holbrook and Bidwell 1991, 76–81

Rigold, S.E. 1954 'Totnes Castle. Recent excavations by the Ancient Monuments Department, Ministry of Works', *Report and Transactions of the Devonshire Association* 88, 228–56

Rippon, S. 2008 'Coastal trade in Roman Britain: the investigation of Crandon Bridge, Somerset, a Romano-British trans-shipment port beside the Severn Estuary', *Britannia* 39, 85–144

Rippon, S. 2012 *Making sense of an historic landscape* Oxford, Oxford University Press

Rippon, S. 2017 'Romano-British coarse ware industries and socio-economic interaction in eastern England', in Allen *et al.* 2017, 336–52

Rippon, S., Claughton, P. and Smart C. 2009 *Mining in a medieval landscape: the royal silver mines of the Tamar Valley* Exeter, University of Exeter Press.

Roberts, C. 2000 'Infectious disease in biocultural perspective: past, present and future in Britain', in Cox and Mays (eds) 2000, 145–62

Robertson, A.S. 2000 *An inventory of Romano-British coin hoards* London, Royal Numismatic Society Special Publication 20

Rodwell, K.A. 2003 'Nicholas Poyntz and Acton Court: a reformer's architecture', in Gaimster and Gilchrist (eds) 2003, 159–74

Roebuck, J. and Coppack, G. 1987 'A closely dated group of late medieval pottery from Mount Grace Priory', *Medieval Ceramics* 11, 15–24

Rogers, J. and Waldron, T. 1995 *A field guide to joint disease in archaeology* Chichester and New York, J. Wiley

Rollinson, H. 1993 *Using geochemical data: evaluation, presentation, interpretation* London, Routledge

Rowe, M.M. (ed.) 1977 *Tudor Exeter. Tax assessments 1489–1598 Including the military survey 1522* Exeter, Devon and Cornwall Records Society New Series 22

Rowe, M.M. and Cochlin, J.J. 1964 *Mayors of Exeter from the 13th century to the present day* Exeter, Exeter City Library

Rowe, M.M. and Jackson, A.M. 1973 *Exeter freemen 1266–1967* Exeter, Devon and Cornwall Records Society New Series 1

Rowe, M.M. and Ravenhill, M.R. 2002 *Devon maps and map-makers: manuscript maps before 1840. Volume I* Exeter, Devon and Cornwall Records Society New Series 43

Rushworth, A. (ed.) 2009 *Housesteads Roman Fort – the grandest station* London, English Heritage

Sabastro, M.A. 2011 *Intervención arqueológica preventiva: excavación arqueológica 'Proyecto básico de equipamiento multifuncional en calle Dos Aceras, 23, 25 y 27 (Málaga)'* Unpublished report Delegación Provincial de Cultura de Málaga, Junta de Andalucía, Málaga

Sage, A. and Allan, J. 2004 'The early Roman military defences, late Roman cemetery and later features at the Topsham School, Topsham', *Proceedings of the Devon Archaeological Society* 62, 1–39

Salvatore, J.P. 1993a *Observations and excavations at North Gate, Exeter, 1978. Part 1: Roman military* Exeter Museums Archaeological Field Unit report 93.28 [ADS: https://doi.org/10.5284/1035206]

Salvatore, J.P. 1993b *Excavations at 45–46 North Street, Exeter, 1974. Part 1: Roman military* Exeter Museums Archaeological Field Unit report 93.46 [ADS: https://doi.org/10.5284/1035188]

Salvatore, J.P. 1994a *Excavations at Southernhay Gardens, Exeter, 1974. Part 1: Roman military* Exeter Museums Archaeological Field Unit report 94.02 [ADS: https://doi.org/10.5284/1035186]

Salvatore, J.P. 2001 'Three Roman military cremation burials from Holloway Street, Exeter', *Proceedings of the Devon Archaeological Society* 59, 125–39

Salvatore, J.P. forthcoming 'Roman military activity beyond the *porta principalis sinistra* (southgate) of the legionary fortress of at Exeter', in *Roman Exeter*, Devon Archaeological Society Occasional Paper

Salvatore, J.P. and Simpson, S.J. 1992 *Excavations at Bartholomew St East, Exeter, 1980–81. Part 1: Roman military* Exeter Museums Archaeological Field Unit report 92.33 [ADS: https://doi.org/10.5284/1035210]

Salvatore, J.P. and Steinmetzer, M. 2018 'The recently discovered Roman military supply base at St Loye's College, Exeter, Devon, southwest Britain: interpretation and significance', in Sommer and Matešić (eds) 2018, 793–800

Salvatore, J.P., Steinmetzer, M. and Quinnell, H. forthcoming 'The Iron Age settlement, Roman military establishment, Roman civil occupation and mid-late Roman cemetery at the former St Loye's College, Topsham Road, Exeter', in *Roman Exeter*, Devon Archaeological Society Occasional Paper

Salzman, L.F. 1931 *English trade in the Middle Ages* London, Clarendon Press

Salzman, L.F. 1952 *Building in England down to 1540: a documentary history* Oxford, Oxford University Press

Sánchez-Cortegana, J.M. 1996 'La cerámica exportada a América en el siglo XVI a través de la documentación del Archivo General de Indias. I. Materiales arquitectónicos y contenedores de mercancías', *Laboratorio de Arte. Revista del Departamento de Historia del Arte* 9, 125–42

Sanford, R.F., Pierson, C.T. and Crovelli, R.A. 1993 'An objective replacement method for censored geochemical data', *Mathematical Geology* 25 (1), 59–80

Sani, E.P. 2012 *Italian Renaissance maiolica* London, V & A Publishing

Sani, E.P. and Mallet, J.V.G. (eds) forthcoming *Italian renaissance maiolica and its impact on Europe: papers in honour of professor Timothy Wilson* Oxford, Ashmolean Museum

Saranova, R. and Borrego, M. 1994 'El puerto de Alicante en los circuitos comerciales mediterráneos en la Baja Edad Media: contenedores cerámicos de transporte y anclaje', *IV Congreso de Arqueología Medieval Española* III, Alicante, 1059–68

Saunders, A. 2006 *Excavations at Launceston Castle, Cornwall* Leeds, Society for Medieval Archaeology Monograph 24

Schneider, N. 2003 *Still life: still life painting in the early modern period* Cologne, Taschen

Schofield, J. and Vince, A.G. 1998 *Medieval towns: the archaeology of British towns in their European setting* London and New York, Continuum

Schofield, J. and Vince, A.G. 2003 *Medieval towns: the archaeology of British towns in their European setting* 2nd edition London and New York, Continuum

Schroder, T. 2009 *British and continental gold and silver in the Ashmolean Museum* Oxford, Ashmolean Museum

Scott, E. 1991 'Animal and infant burials in Romano-British villas: a revitalization movement', in Garwood *et al.* (eds) 1991, 115–21

Scrivener, R.C. 1983 *Geology of sheet SX 99 NW (Brampford Speke, Devon). Geological report for DOE: land use planning* Exeter, Institute of Geological Services

Seager Smith, R., 1999 'Romano-British pottery', in Fitzpatrick *et al.* 1999, 286–327

Seager Smith, R., 2008 'Additional specialist report: finds, pottery', in *Suburban life in Roman* Durnovaria [https://www.wessexarch.co.uk/sites/default/files/projects/dorchester_county_hospital/09_Pottery.pdf]

Seager Smith, R. and Davies, S.M., 1993 'Roman pottery', in Woodward *et al.* 1993, 202–89

Sebastian, L. 2011 *A produção oleira de faiança em Portugal (séculos XVI–XVII)* Dissertação de Doutoramento, Universidade Nova de Lisboa

Sebastian, L. 2012 'Faiança portuguesa: centros produtores, matérias, técnicas de fabrico e critérios de distinção', in Teixeira and Bettencourt (eds) 2012, 937–50

Selwood, B. 1991 'Roofing slate', in Holbrook and Bidwell 1991, 282–4

Selwood, E.B., Edwards, R.A, Simpson, S., Chesher, J.A., Hamblin, R.J.O., Henson, M.R., Riddols, R.W. and Waters, R.A. 1984 *Geology of the country around Newton Abbot. Geological survey memoir for 1:50,000 geological sheet 339* Keyworth, British Geological Survey

Serjeantson, D. and Waldron, T. (eds) 1989 *Diet and craft in towns: the evidence of animal remains from the Roman to post-medieval periods* Oxford, British Archaeological Reports British Series 199

Serrano, M.L. 1994 'Transformación urbana: de cementerio islámico a centro alfarero en época cristiana (siglo XIV) en la ciudad de Valencia', *IV Congreso de Arqueología Medieval Española (Alicante 1993) II* Alicante, Diputación Provincial de Alicante, 193–203

Serrera, R.M. 2008 'La casa de contratación en el Alcázar de Sevilla (1503–1717)', *Boletín de la Real Academia Sevillana de Buenas Letras* 36, 141–76

Shaffrey, R. 2006 *Grinding and milling. Romano-British rotary querns made from Old Red Sandstone* Oxford, British Archaeological Reports British Series 409

Shaffrey, R. 2015 'Intensive milling practices in the Romano-British landscape of southern England. Using newly established criteria for distinguishing millstones from rotary querns', *Britannia* 46, 55–92

Shaffrey, R. 2016 'Appendix F Worked stone', in Good 2016, 62–63

Shaffrey, R. 2017a 'Worked and utilised stone', in Mudd 2017, 94–101

Shaffrey, R. (ed.) 2017b *Written in stone: papers on the function, form, and provenancing of prehistoric stone objects in memory of Fiona Roe* St Andrews, Highfield Press

Shaffrey, R. 2018 'Grain processing in and around Roman Cirencester. What can the querns and millstones tell us about supply to the Roman town?', *Transactions of the Bristol and Gloucestershire Archaeological Society* 136, 161–70

Shaffrey, R. in prep 'Supplying and feeding Roman Silchester: the querns and millstones'

Shaw, M. 1996 'The excavation of a late 15th- to 17th-century tanning complex at The Green, Northampton', *Post-Medieval Archaeology* 30, 63–127

Shennan, S. 1997 *Quantifying archaeology*, 2nd edition Edinburgh, Edinburgh University Press

Shepherd, E. (ed.) 1995 *Interpreting stratigraphy 5 – 1994 Norwich* York, University of York

Shiel, N. 1978 'Two recent coin hoards from Exeter', *Proceedings of the Devon Archaeological Society* 36, 256–8

Shiel, N. 1979 'Unpublished coins found in the area covered by the gazetteer prior to 1971', in Bidwell 1979, 165–7

Shiel, N. 1991 'Coin list', in Holbrook and Bidwell 1991, 24–33

Shiel, N. forthcoming 'Roman coins from Princesshay', in Steinmetzer, Stead, Pearce, Bidwell and Allan forthcoming

Sheil, N. and Reece, R. 1979 'The coins', in Bidwell 1979, 162–79

Shortt, W.T.P. 1840 *Sylva antiqua Iscana, numismatica, quinetiam figulina, or Roman and other antiquities of Exeter* Featherstone, Nichols and Sons

Siebenlist-Kerner, V. 1978 'The chronology, 1341–1636, for certain hillside oaks from Western England and Wales', in Fletcher (ed.) 1978, 157–61

Silva, F.G. da, 2012 'As formas de pão-de-açúcar da Mata da Machada, Barreiro', in Teixeira and Bettencourt (eds) 2012, 711–18

Silva, R.B. da, Miranda, P., Vieira, V.N., Vicente, A.M., Lopes, G.C. and Nozes, C. 2012 'Largo do Chafariz de dentro: alfama em época moderna', in Teixeira and Bettencourt (eds) 2012, 71–84

Silva, R.C. 2012 'Primeira abordagem a um depósito moderno no Antigo Paço Episcopal de Coimbra (Museu Nacional de Machado de Castro): a cerâmica desde meados do século XV à consolidação da Renascença', in Teixeira and Bettencourt (eds) 2012, 877–90

Silva, R.C. 2016 'The faience of the 2nd half of the 16th century at the Episcopal Palace of Coimbra (Portugal)' in Varela Gomes *et al.* (eds), 181–8

Silver, I. 1969 'The ageing of domestic animals', in Brothwell and Higgs (eds) 1969, 293–302

Silvester, R.J. 1981a 'An excavation at Dunkeswell', *Proceedings of the Devon Archaeological Society* 38, 57–62

Silvester, R.J. 1981b 'Excavations at Honeyditches Roman Villa, Seaton, in 1978', *Proceedings of the Devon Archaeological Society* 39, 37–87

Silvester, R.J. and Bidwell, P.T. 1984 'A Roman site at Woodbury, Axminster', *Proceedings of the Devon Archaeological Society* 42, 33–57

Simpson, H., Maloney, C., Wilkins, B. and Bethell, B. 2014 *Exeter Cathedral School, Exeter. Combined archaeological investigation works* AB Heritage report [ADS: https://doi.org/10.5284/1045904]

Simpson, S.J. 1987 'Excavation at Exe Street and Lower North Street', in *Exeter Archaeology 1985/6* Exeter, Exeter Museums Archaeological Field Unit

Simpson, S.J. 1993 *Exeter city walls: Westgate to Southgate, survey and excavation in the West Quarter* Exeter Museums Archaeological Field Unit report 93.73

Sims, R. and Kerr-Peterson, K. 2012 *Exe Bridges Retail Park, Cowick Street, Exeter* AC Archaeology report ACD259/2/1 [ADS: https://doi.org/10.5284/1016107]

Sinclair, A., Slater, E. and Gowlett, J. (eds) 1997 *Archaeological Sciences* Oxford, Oxbow Monograph 64

Sireix, C. 2005 'Bordeaux-*Burdigala* et la Bretagne romaine; quelques témoins archéologiques du commerce atlantique', *Aquitania* 21, 241–51

Sireix, C. (ed.) 2008 *La Cité Judiciaire. un quartier suburbain de Bordeaux antique* Bordeaux, Aquitania Supplement 15

Sireix, C. and Convertini, F. 1997 'La céramique à l'éponge de la région bordelaise: la céramique marbrée d'Aquitaine', SFECAG Actes du Congrès du Mans 1997, 321–33

Sireix, C. and Convertini, F. 2008 'Les céramiques à l'éponge', in Sireix (ed.) 2008, 437–46

Skelton, R.A. and Harvey, P.D.A. (eds) 1986 *Local maps and plans from medieval England* Oxford, Clarendon Press

Smart, C. 2014 *A Roman military complex and medieval settlement on Church Hill, Calstock, Cornwall: Survey and excavation 2007–2010* Oxford, British Archaeological Reports British Series 603

Smart, C. 2018 *Industry and the making of a rural landscape: iron and pottery production at Churchill's Farm, Hemyock, Devon* Oxford, British Archaeological Reports British Series 636

Smith, A., Allen, M., Brindle, T. and Fulford, M. 2016 *The rural settlement of Roman Britain* London, The Society for the Promotion of Roman Studies Britannia Monograph 29

Smith, N. 2011 *Introductions to heritage assets: pre-industrial lime kilns* Swindon, English Heritage

Smith, W. 2014 *The Quay Antiques Centre, Exeter, SWW new sewer* AC Archaeology report ACD846/2/1

Sommer, C.S. 1995 '"Where did they put the horses?", uberlegungen zu aufbau und stärke römischer auxiliartruppen und deren unterbringung in den kastellen', in *Provincialrömische Forschungen: Festschrift für Günter Ulbert zum 65. Geburtstag*, Espelkamp, 149–68

Sommer, C.S. and Matešić, S. (eds) 2018 *Limes XXIII. Proceedings of the 23rd International Congress of Roman Frontier Studies Ingolstadt 2015*, Beiträge zum Welterbe Limes, Sonderband 4/11, Mainz

Sousa, É., Silva, J. and Gomes, C. 2003 'Chemical and physical characterization of fragments from ceramics called "formas de açucar" exhumed in the town of Machico, Madeira island', *Proceedings of the EMAC '03 7th European Meeting on Ancient Ceramics* Lisbon, Instituto Tecnológico e Nuclear

Spoerry, P.S. 1990 'Ceramic production in medieval Dorset and the surrounding region', *Medieval Ceramics* 14, 3–17

Spriggs, A.I. 1964 'Oriental porcelain in Western paintings: 1450–1700', *Transactions of the Oriental Ceramic Society* 36, 73–87, pls 57–80

Staniforth, P.R. and Juddery, J.Z. 1991a *Exeter property deeds 1150–1450. Part 1* Exeter Museums Archaeological Field Unit report 91.45

Staniforth, P.R. and Juddery, J.Z. 1991b *Exeter property deeds 1150–1450. Part 2* Exeter Museums Archaeological Field Unit report 91.46

Staniforth, P.R. and Juddery, J.Z. 1991c *Exeter property deeds 1150–1450. Part 3* Exeter Museums Archaeological Field Unit report 91.47

Staniforth, P.R. and Juddery, J.Z. 1991d *Exeter property deeds 1150–1450. Part 4* Exeter Museums Archaeological Field Unit report 91.48

Stead, P.M. 1998–9 'Investigations at nos 4–6 Pydar Street, Truro', *Cornish Archaeology* 37–8, 178–89

Stead, P.M. 1999 *Archaeological evaluation of the former RSPCA site, Market Street, Exeter, 1998* Exeter Archaeology report 99.09

Stead, P.M. 2002 *Archaeological excavations at Market Street, Exeter: summary report* Exeter Archaeology report 02.90

Stead, P.M. 2003 'Excavation of the medieval waterfront at Dung Quay, Plymouth', *Proceedings of the Devon Archaeological Society* 61, 47–63

Stead, P.M. 2004 *Archaeological excavation of Southernhay East Car Park, Exeter* Exeter Archaeology report04.24 [ADS: https://doi.org/10.5284/1028780]

Stead, P.M. and Hall, M. 1991 *Lower Coombe Street, Exeter, report of excavations 1989–90* Exeter Museums Archaeological Field Unit report 91.09 [ADS: https://doi.org/10.5284/1035234]

Stead, P.M. and Parker, R.W. 1998 *Exeter Cathedral cloisters evaluation 1998* Exeter Archaeology report 98.66

Stead, P.M. and Dyer, M.J. 2003 *Archaeological excavation and building recording at the former Northcott Warehouse site, Haven Road, Exeter* Exeter Archaeology report 03.07

Stead, P.M., Manning, P. and Blaylock, S.R.1994 *Bowhill Exeter, archive report V, the excavation of the eastern courtyard, 1992* Exeter Museums Archaeological Field Unit report 94.107

Steinmetzer, M.F.R. 2007 *Archaeological excavation of land to the west of Cricklepit Mill, Exeter* Exeter Archaeology report 07.12

Steinmetzer, M.F.R. 2008 *Archaeological investigation and historic building recording at The Custom House, Exeter* Exeter Archaeology report 08.78 [ADS: https://doi.org/10.5284/1003558]

Steinmetzer, M.F.R. 2011 *Archaeological investigation and building recording at the Royal Albert Memorial Museum, Exeter* Exeter Archaeology report 11.06 [ADS: https://doi.org/10.5284/1007745]

Steinmetzer, M.F.R. 2016 *Archaeological monitoring and recording at 9 Verney Street, Exeter, Devon* Oakford Archaeology report 16.12 [ADS: https://doi.org/10.5284/1048070]

Steinmetzer, M.F.R. forthcoming 'Roman tile production site and post-medieval church at St David's, Queen's Terrace, Exeter', *Proceedings of the Devon Archaeological Society*

Steinmetzer, M.F.R., Allan, J.P. and Orme, N. forthcoming 'Excavations at Princesshay, Exeter, 1997–2006. Part 2: The archaeology and history of the Exeter Blackfriars and Bedford House', *Proceedings of the Devon Archaeological Society*

Steinmetzer, M.F.R., Stead, P., Pearce, P., Bidwell, P.T. and Allan, J.P. forthcoming 'Excavations at Princesshay, Exeter, 1997–2006. Part 1: Roman', in *Roman Exeter*, Devon Archaeological Society Occasional Paper

Stewart Brown Associates 2013 *St Stephen's Church, Exeter: archaeological fabric recording and excavation during reordering works 2011–2012* Stewart Brown Associates report [ADS: https://doi.org/10.5284/1016683]

Stoyle, M. 1995 *Exeter in the Civil War* Exeter, Devon Archaeological Society Monograph 6

Stoyle, M. 2014 *Water in the city: the aqueducts and underground passages of Exeter* Exeter, Exeter University Press

Straker, V., Robinson, M. and Robinson, E. 1984 'Biological investigations of waterlogged deposits in the Roman fortress ditch at Exeter', *Proceedings of the Devon Archaeological Society* 42, 59–69

Straube, B. 2017 'Jamestown, Virginia: Virginia Company period', *Ceramics in America 2017* [http://www.chipstone.org/article.php/782/Ceramics-in-America-2017/Jamestown,-Virginia:-Virginia-Company-Period]

Stroud, G. and Kemp, R.L. 1993 *Cemeteries of St Andrew, Fishergate* York, Council for British Archaeology

Stuckert, C.M. (ed.) *The people of early Winchester* Oxford, Clarendon Press

Sunter, N. and Woodward, P.J. 1987 *Romano-British industries in Purbeck* Dorchester, Dorset Natural History and Archaeological Society Monograph Series 6

Swan, V.G. 1984 *The pottery kilns of Roman Britain* London, Royal Commission on the Historical Monuments of England Supplementary Series 5

Swan, V.G., 2009 *Ethnicity, conquest and recruitment: two case studies from the northern military provinces* Journal of Roman Archaeology Supplementary Series 72

Swan, V.G. and Bidwell, P.T. 1998 'Camelon and Flavian troop-movements in southern Britain: some ceramic evidence', in Bird 1998, 21–30

Symonds, R.P. and Wade, S. (eds Bidwell, P. and Croom, A.) 1999 *Roman pottery from excavations in Colchester, 1971–86* Colchester, Colchester Archaeological Report 10

Tabachnick, B. and Fidell, L.S. 2007 *Using multivariate statistics*, 5th edition London, Pearson

Talbot, E.J. 1966 'The pottery', in Alcock 1966, 199–206

Tapley-Soper, H. 1924–5 'The Turk's Head, Exeter, 1569', *Devon Cornwall Notes Queries* 13, 118–19

Taylor, R.T. 2003a 'Petrological study of the temper of the pottery from Sherborne Old Castle', in Allan 2003, 77–8

Taylor, R.T. 2003b 'The petrology of some probable Breton pottery from Dung Quay, Plymouth', in Allan and Langman 2003, 62–3

Taylor, R.T. 2006 'Petrological study of Roman tiles from Hatherleigh Moor and other sites in mid and west Devon', in Wheeler and Laing-Trengrove 2006, 63–8

Taylor, R.T. 2010 'Petrological descriptions of sample sherds', in Allan *et al.* 2010, 173–7

Taylor, R.T. 2014a 'The petrology of the temper of post-Roman pottery', in Allan 2014a, 67–70

Taylor, R.T. 2014b 'Petrology of some pottery from the small medieval house at Edgewell Barton', in Allan 2014b, 153–4

Taylor, R.T. 2014c 'Petrological analysis: thin sections', in Smart 2014, 54

Taylor, R.T. and Wheeler, J. 2006 'Analysis of Roman tile from sites in Devon', in Wheeler and Laing-Trengrove 2006, 59–62

Tefler, A.A. 2009 *St Martin-in-the-Fields Church, St Martin's Place, London, WC2, City of Westminster: a post-excavation assessment and updated project design* Museum of London Archaeology report [ADS: https://doi.org/10.5284/1027304]

Teixeira, A. and Bettencourt, J.A. (eds) 2012 *Old and new worlds, International Congress of Early Modern Archaeology* Lisbon, Centro de História de Além-Mar

Temple, D.H. 2016 'Caries: the ancient scourge', in Irish and Scott (eds) 2016, 433–49

Thompson, M. and Walsh, J.N. 1989 *A handbook of inductively coupled plasma spectrometry*, 2nd edition Glasgow, Blackie

Thompson, V. 2004 *Dying and death in later Anglo-Saxon England* Woodbridge, The Boydell Press

Thomson, A., Haines, C., Havard, T. and Holt, R. 2014 *Wales and West Utilities gas main replacement programme 2012–14, Exeter* Cotswold Archaeology report 14280 [ADS: https://doi.org/10.5284/1046171]

Thorn, J. and Glascock, M. 2010 'New evidence for Apulian red-figure production centres', *Archaeometry* 52 (5), 777–95

Thornton, D. and Wilson, T. 2009 *Italian Renaissance ceramics: a catalogue of the British Museum collection*, London, British Museum

Thorp, J. undated [*c.* 1975–6] *198 High Street: Exeter Archaeology Building Record* Exeter Archaeology archive, Devon Heritage Centre

Thorp, J.R.L. 2012 'The construction, presentation, and development of a merchant's town house c.1500–1740: 38 North Street, Exeter', *Proceedings of the Devon Archaeological Society* 70, 134–47

Timby, J. 1987 'First century imports and native fine wares', in Sunter and Woodward 1987, 73–9

Timby, J. 2000 'The pottery', in Fulford and Timby 2000, 180–312

Timby, J. 2004 'The prehistoric and Roman pottery', in Brooks 2004, 50–75

Timby, J. 2006 'The pottery from the Late Roman deposits', in Fulford *et al.* 2006, 86–115

Timby, J. 2014 'The Gaulish imports', in Smart 2014, 45–7

Timby, J. 2018 'The pottery', in Fulford *et al.* 2018, 150–213

Timby, J. forthcoming 'The pottery', in report on excavations at Monty's Farm, Norton Fitzwarren, Somerset AC Archaeology report ACD1282

Timby, J. and Rigby, V. 2007 *Gallo-Belgic pottery database* [https://gallobelgic.thehumanjourney.net]

Tite, M.S. 2008 'Ceramic production, provenance and use – a review', *Archaeometry* 50, 216–31

Tizzard, A., Crooks, K., Priestley, S. and Bunce, A. 2017 *Archaeological investigation and recording: no 3 Well Street, Exeter, EX4 6QR* Border Archaeology report BA1212WSE [ADS: https://doi.org/10.5284/1046449]

Todd, M., 1993 'An Arretine vessel from Hembury', *Proceedings of the Devon Archaeological Society* 51, 208–9

Todd, M. 2002 'The Roman fort and later Roman site at Bury Barton', *Proceedings of the Devon Archaeological Society* 60, 37–58

Tomber, R. and Dore, J. 1998 *The national Roman fabric reference collection: a handbook* London, Museum of London Archaeology Service

Tomlin, R.S.O. 2016 *Roman London's first voices: writing tablets from the Bloomberg excavations, 2010–14* London, Museum of London Archaeology Monograph 72

Torres, J. 1990 'Um forno cerâmico dos seculos XV e XVI na cintura industrial de Lisboa', in Amigues and Bazzana (eds) 1990, 131–41

Torres, J. 2012 *Quotidianos no Convento de São Francisco de Lisboa: uma análise de cerâmica vidriada, faiança portuguesa e porcelana chinesa* Dissertação de Mestrado, Universidade Nova de Lisboa, Lisboa

Tyers, C. 2012 'Dendrochronology', in Thorp 2012, 228

Tyers, C. forthcoming *Re-evaluation of the dendrochronology of archaeological excavations in Exeter in the 1970s and 1980s and comparative material from Bristol* Historic England, Research Report Series

Tyers, C. and Tyers, I. 2015 'The date and origin of the medieval nave ceiling boards', in Hall and Wright (eds) 2015, 73–6

Tyers, C., Hurford, M., Arnold, A.J., Howard, R.E. and Thorp, J. forthcoming *Dendrochronological research in Devon: phase II* Historic England, Research Report Series

Tyers, I. 1998 *Tree-ring analysis and wood identification of timbers excavated on the Magistrates Court site, Kingston upon Hull, East Yorkshire* Archaeological Research and Consultancy at the University of Sheffield Report 410

Tyers, I. 2003 'Tree-ring analysis', in Massing (ed.) 2003, 113–21

Tyers, I. 2010 'Aspects of the European trade in oak boards to England 1200–1700', in Kirby *et al.* 2010, 42–9

Tyers, I. 2013 'Tree Ring Dating', in Ridgeway and Watts (eds) 2013, 93–5

Tyers, I. 2014 *Royal coat of arms for Edward VI from the Church of St Mary the Virgin, Westerham, Kent: scientific dating report – dendrochronological analysis of oak Boards* English Heritage, Research Report Series 30/2014

Tyler, K., Betts, I. and Stephenson, R. 2008 *London's delftware industry* London, Museum of London Monograph 40

Tyler, K.A. 2009 *Archaeological investigation of the Choakford to Langage gas pipeline, Sparkwell, South Hams, Exeter* Exeter Archaeology report 09.101

Uglow, J. 2000 'Three Romano-British sites in the lower Exe valley', *Proceedings of the Devon Archaeological Society* 58, 227–48

Unger, S. 2009 'Red or yellow? The changing colour of Roman London's roofline', *London Archaeologist* 12 (4), 107–13

Valentin, J. 2016 *Exeter Flood Defence Scheme (Zone 6), Exeter and Devon Crematorium, Topsham Road, Exeter* AC Archaeology report ACD1386/2/2

Valentine, L.N. 1965 *Ornament in medieval manuscripts: a glossary* London, Faber

Van der Veen, M. 1989 'Charred grain assemblages from Roman-period corn driers in Britain', *Archaeological Journal* 146, 302–19

Vannini, G. 1977 *La maiolica di Montelupo: scavo di uno scarico di fornace* Montelupo Fiorentino, Rinascita

Varela Gomes, R., Casimiro, T. and Varela Gomes, M. (eds) 2016 *Proceedings of the first international conference of Portuguese faience (16th–19th centuries)* Universidade Nova de Lisboa, Instituto de Arqueologia e Paleociências,

Veeckman, J. (ed.) 2002 *Majolica and glass: from Italy to Antwerp and beyond. The transfer of technology in the 16th–Early 17th Century* Antwerp, Stadt Antwerpen

Veeckman, J. 2010 'Sherds from a church. Maiolica production waste from the Augustinian friary in Antwerp', in De Groote *et al.* (eds) 2010, 177–88

Verhaeghe, F. and Janssen, H.L. 1984 'Early medieval Low Countries wares', in Allan 1984a, 18–20

Viana, M.A.C.R. 1973 *A margem sul do Estuario do Tejo: contribuiçao para um Projecto de Ordenamento do Terrirório, Tomo II* Montijo, Oficinas Gráficas da Gazeta do Sul

Vieira Ferreira, L.F., Ferreira Machado, I., Ferraria, A.M., Casimiro, T.M. and Colomban, Ph. 2013a 'Portuguese tin-glazed earthenware from the 16th century: a spectroscopic characterization of pigments, glazes and pastes', *Applied Surface Science* 285, 144–52

Vieira Ferreira, L.F., Casimiro, T.M. and Colomban, Ph. 2013b 'Portuguese tin-glazed earthenware from the 17th century. Part 1: Pigments and glazes characterization', *Spectrochimica Acta Part A: Molecular and Biomolecular Spectroscopy* 104, 437–44

Vieira Ferreira, L.F., Varela Gomes, M., Pereira, M.F.C., Santos, L.F. and Ferreira Machado, I. 2016 'A multi-technique study for the spectroscopic characterization of the ceramics from Santa Maria do Castelo church (Torres Novas, Portugal)', *Journal of Archaeological Science* 6, 182–9

Villanueva, O., Cabrera, B., Díaz, J. and Jiménez J. 2009 'La loza dorada en la corte de Arévalo (Ávila, España)', IX CICMMO, 495–7

Vilvorder, F., Symonds, R.P. and Rekk, S. 2000 'Les amphores orientales en Gaule Septentrionale et au sud-est de la Grande Bretagne', *Rei Cretariae Romanae Fautorum Acta 36*, 477–86

Vince, A.G. 1982 'Medieval and post-medieval Spanish pottery in the City of London', in Freestone *et al.* (eds) 1982, 135–44

Vince, A.G. 1984b 'The petrology of the products of the Bedford Garage kiln', in Allan 1984a, 32

Vince, A.G. 1984c 'A note on the petrology of the Spanish and Portuguese tin-glazed wares', in Allan 1984a, 146

Vince, A.G. 1985 'Saxon and medieval pottery in London: a review', *Medieval Archaeology* 29, 25–93

Vince, A.G. 2000 *Petrological and chemical analysis of pottery from the Millennium Bridge site, London* Lincoln, Assessment Report

Vince, A.G. 2005 *Characterisation of Carolingian pottery from La Londe, Normandy, using chemical analysis* [ADS: https://doi.org/10.5284/1000382]

Vince, A.G. 2010 Alan Vince archive (ICPS data): [ADS: https://doi.org/10.5284/1000382]

Vince, A.G. 2011 'Characterising French whiteware imports in Britain, Ireland and Northwest Europe', in Bocquet-Liénard and Fajal 2011, 97–208

Vince, A.G. and Brown, D.H. 2002 'Characterisation and identification of tin-glazed ceramics using inductively-coupled plasma spectroscopy', in Veeckman (ed.) 2002, 465–73

Vince, A.G. and Jones, R. 2005 'Normandy whitewares from Ronaldson's Wharf, Leith, Scotland', *Medieval Ceramics* 29, 24–9

Von Petrikovits, H. 1975 *Die Innenbauten römischer Legionslager während der Prinzipatszeit*, Abhandlungen der Rheinisch-Westfälischen Akademie der Wissenschaften, Bd 56

Wacher, J.S. (ed.) 1966 *The civitas capitals of Roman Britain* Leicester, University of Leicester

Waldron, T. 2007 *St Peter's, Barton-upon-Humber, Lincolnshire – a parish church and its community: the human remains* Oxford, Oxbow Books

Waldron, T. 2009 *Palaeopathology* Cambridge, Cambridge University Press

Walton, P. 2012 *Rethinking Roman Britain: coinage and archaeology* Wetteren, Moneta 137

Ward, C., McArthur, J. and Walsh, J.N. 1992 'Rare Earth element behaviour during evolution and alteration of the Dartmoor granite, SW England', *Journal of Petrology* 33, 785–815

Warry, P. 2006 *Tegulae: manufacture, typology and use in Roman Britain* Oxford, British Archaeological Reports British Series 417

Warry, P. 2010 'Legionary tile production in Britain', *Britannia* 41, 127–47

Warry, P. 2012 'The Silchester tile industry', in Fulford (ed) 2012, 49–75

Warry, P. 2013 'An assessment of the tegulae and imbrices and summary of the ceramic building materials from the 2008–10 excavation', in Cunliffe 2013, 148–54

Warry, P. 2015a 'A possible mid-fourth-century altar platform at Marcham/Frilford, Oxfordshire', *Britannia* 46, 273–79

Warry, P. 2015b *Ceramic building material from nine archaeological excavations in the city of Gloucester* Cotswold Archaeology report 15585

Warry, P. 2016 'Roofing material', in Liss Archaeological Group 2016, 63–4

Warry, P. 2017 'Production, distribution, use and curation: a study of stamped tile from Gloucestershire', *Britannia* 48, 77–115

Warry, P. forthcoming 'Ceramic building material', in Brindle and Brett, forthcoming

Watson, G.L. 2013 *Roger Machado: a life in objects* Unpublished PhD thesis, Southampton University

Watts, S. 2003 'The Longis querns uncovered', *The Alderney Society Bulletin* XXXVIII, 67–75

Watts, S. and Taylor, R. 2014 'The Romano-British quern fragment', in Morris 2014, 201

Wazny, T. 2002 'Baltic timber in western Europe – an exciting dendrochronological question', *Dendrochronologia* 20 (3), 313–20

Webster, G. (ed.) 1988 *Fortress into city. The consolidation of Roman Britain* London, B.T. Batsford

Webster, G. (Chadderton, J. (ed.)) 2002 *The legionary fortress at Wroxeter. Excavations by G. Webster, 1955–85* English Heritage Archaeological Report 19

Webster, L.E. and Cherry, J. 1972 'Medieval Britain in 1971', *Medieval Archaeology* 16, 147–211

Webster, L.E. and Cherry, J. 1974 'Medieval Britain in 1973', *Medieval Archaeology* 18, 174–223

Webster, L.E. and Cherry, J. 1979 'Medieval Britain in 1978', *Medieval Archaeology* 23, 234–78

Webster, P. 1992 'Roman pottery in south-east Wales: an introduction', *Journal of Roman Pottery Studies* 5, 111–21

Webster, P. 1993 'The post-fortress coarse wares', in Manning 1993, 227–361

Weddell, P.J. 1981 'Excavations at Southgate Cottages, Lydford', *Proceedings of the Devon Archaeological Society* 39, 119–40

Weddell, P.J. 1987a 'The outer ward of Exeter Castle', *Exeter Archaeology 1985/6* Exeter, Exeter Museums Archaeological Field Unit report, 51–2

Weddell, P.J. 1987b 'Excavations within the Anglo-Saxon enclosure at Berry Meadow, Kingsteignton, in 1985', *Proceedings of the Devon Archaeological Society* 45, 75–96

Weddell, P., Pink, F. and Valentin, J. 2016 *Land at Penns Mount, Vicarage Hill, Kingsteignton* AC Archaeology report ACD1479/4/2

Wessex Archaeology 2015 *Exeter flood defence scheme, Exeter, Devon* Wessex Archaeology report 105800.09

Westcote, T. 1630 *A view of Devonshire in 1630* (ed. Rev. G. Oliver and P. Jones, 1845)

Wheeler, J. and Laing-Trengrove, D 2006 'A Roman tile kiln on Hatherleigh Moor and the sources of some Roman tile in Devon', in *Proceedings of the Devon Archaeological Society* 64, 53–69

Wheeler, R.E.M. and Wheeler, T.V. 1936 *Verulamium. A Belgic and two Roman cities* Oxford, University Press, Reports of the Research Committee of the Society of Antiquaries of London 11

Wilke, D., Rauch, D. and Rauch, P. 2016 'Is non-destructive provenancing of pottery possible with just a few discriminative trace elements?', *Science & Technology of Archaeological Research* 2:2, 141–58

Wilkinson, B. 1931 *The medieval council of Exeter* History of Exeter Research Group Monograph 4 Manchester, University Press

Willan, T.S. 1959 *Studies in Elizabethan foreign trade* Manchester, University Press

Williams, D.F. 1979 *Petrology analysis of Spanish Armada pottery* Ancient Monuments Laboratory Report 2438

Williams, D.F. 1984a 'The petrology of the olive jars and Merida-type wares', in Allan 1984a, 145

Williams, D.F. 1984b 'The petrology of the possible Breton sherds', in Allan 1984a, 37

Williams, D.F. 1987 'A note on the petrology of the stamped tile of the Second Augustan Legion from Seaton', in Holbrook 1987, 72–3

Williams, D.F. 1991a 'Petrological examination of tiles from a number of Roman sites in Devon', in Holbrook and Bidwell 1991, Microfiche 21–3

Williams, D.F. 1991b 'Building materials', in Holbrook and Bidwell 1991, 281–2

Williams, D.F. 1992 'Amphorae', in Holbrook and Bidwell 1992, 56–62

Williams, D.F. 1993 'Amphorae', in Seager Smith and Davies 1993, 214–19

Williams, D.F. 2000 'The amphorae', in Fulford and Timby 2000, 219–25

Williams, D.F. 2011 'The amphorae', in Douglas *et al.* 2011, 78–81

Williams, D.F. and Carreras, C. 1995 'North African amphorae in Britain: a re-appraisal', *Britannia* 26, 231–52

Williams, R. 2004 *Limekilns and lime burning* Oxford, Shire Publications Ltd

Willis, S. 2005 *Samian pottery, a resource for the study of Roman Britain and beyond: the results of the English Heritage funded Samian Project. An e-monograph*, Internet Archaeology 17 [http://intarch.ac.uk/journal/issue17/1/toc.html]

Willmott, H. 2015 'Table glass in the West Country home, c. 1500–1700', in Allan *et al.* 2015, 321–38

Wilson, D.R., Wright, R.P. and Hassall, M.W.C. 1973 'Roman Britain in 1972', *Britannia* 4, 271–323

Wilson, D.R., Wright, R.P., Hassall, M.W.C., Bowman, A.K. and Thomas, J.D. 1974 'Roman Britain in 1973', *Britannia* 5, 396–480

Wilson, D.R., Wright, R.P., Hassall, M.W.C. and Tomlin, R.S.O. 1975 'Roman Britain in 1974', *Britannia* 6, 220–94

Wilson, T.H. 1987 'Maiolica in Renaissance Venice', *Apollo* 125, 184–9

Wilson, T.H. (ed.) 1991 *Italian renaissance pottery* London, British Museum

Wilson, T.H., Gaimster, D.R.M., Dawson, A. and Rudoe, J. 1988 'Recent acquisitions of post-medieval ceramics and glass in the British Museum's Department of Medieval and Later Antiquities (1982–88): supplement', *Burlington Magazine* 130, 399–404

Wilson, T.H. and Sani, E.P. (eds) 2007 *Le maioliche rinascimentali nelle collezioni della Fondazione Cassa di Risparmio di Perugia*, vol. 2 Città di Castello, Petruzzi

Wilthew, P. 1986 *Examination of slag from various Roman sites in Exeter* Ancient Monuments Laboratory Report 44/86

Wood, I. 2014 'Roman ceramic petrography', in Morris 2014, 162–9

Wood, J., Milner, G., Harpending, H. and Weiss, K.M. 1992 'The osteological paradox: problems of inferring prehistoric health from skeletal samples', *Current Anthropology* 33, 343–70

Wood, M. 1993 'A new form of céramique à l'éponge from Roman Britain', *Journal of Roman Pottery Studies* 6, 119–22

Woodward, P.J., Davies, S.M. and Graham, A.H. 1993 *Excavations at Greyhound Yard, Dorchester 1981–4* Dorchester, Dorset Natural History and Archaeological Society Monograph 12

Woolgar, C.M., Serjeantson, D. and Waldron, T. (eds) 2006 *Food in medieval England* Oxford, Oxford University Press

Woolner, Cmdr, Woolner, Mrs and Ledger, V. 1959 'North Tawton (Nemetostatio)', *Transactions of the Devonshire Association* 41, 174–5

Worth, R.N. 1891 'President's Address', *Report and Transactions of the Devonshire Association* 23, 82

Wrathmell, S. 2016 'Penhow Castle, Gwent: survey and excavation, 1976–9. Part 2: regional and imported pottery and other finds from the castle ditch', *Monmouthshire Antiquary* 32, 3–100

Wright, L. and Yoder, C., 2003 'Recent progress in bioarchaeology: approaches to the osteological paradox', *Journal of Archaeological Research* 11, 43–70

Wright, R.P. 1962 'Roman Britain in 1961: I. sites explored: II. Inscriptions', *Journal of Roman Studies* 52, 160–99

Yenisehirlioglu, F. (ed.) 2018 *XIth congress AIECM3 on medieval and modern period Mediterranean ceramics proceedings 1* Koç Universitesi VEKAM, Ankara

Yeomans, L.M. 2008 'Historical and zooarchaeological evidence of horn-working in post-medieval London', *Post-Medieval Archaeology* 42/1, 130–43

Youings, J. 1952 'The City of Exeter and the property of the dissolved monasteries', *Report and Transactions of the Devonshire Association* 84, 122–41

Youings, J. 1955 *Devon monastic lands: calendar of particulars for grants 1536–1558* Devon and Cornwall Record Society New Series 1

Youngs, S.M. and Clark, J. 1981 'Medieval Britain in 1980', *Medieval Archaeology* 25, 166–228

Youngs, S.M. and Clark, J. 1982 'Medieval Britain in 1981', *Medieval Archaeology* 26, 164–227

Youngs, S.M., Clark, J. and Barry, T.B 1984 'Medieval Britain and Ireland in 1983', *Medieval Archaeology* 28, 203–65

Youngs, S.M., Clark, J. and Barry, T.B. 1986 'Medieval Britain and Ireland in 1985', *Medieval Archaeology* 30, 114–98

Youngs, S.M., Clark, J. and Barry, T.B. 1987 'Medieval Britain and Ireland in 1986', *Medieval Archaeology* 31, 110–91

Youngs, S.M., Clark, J., Gaimster, D.R.M., Barry, T. and Margeson, S.M. 1988 'Medieval Britain and Ireland in 1987', *Medieval Archaeology* 32, 225–314

Zienkiewicz, J.D. 1993 'Excavations in the "Scamnum Tribunorum" at Caerleon: The Legionary Museum site 1983–5', *Britannia* 24, 27–140

Zozaya, J., Retuerce, M. and Aparicio, A. 1995 'Cerámica andalusí de reflejo dorado: 1195–1212', *Actes du 5ème Colloque sur la Céramique Médiévale* Rabat, Institut National des Sciences de l'Archéologie et du Patrimoine 121–4

Index

Numbers in *italic* denote pages with figures, those in **bold** denote pages with tables. Ceramic building material has been abbreviated to CBM.